2-13 *b* Cash to D, $6,200; *c* Net income to A, $26,400

2-14 *a* Lee, capital, $535,060; *b* Shares to Moss, 101,620; *d* Total stockholders' equity, $1,040,000

3-1 *a* Adjusted balances, $40,800

3-4 *a* Debit loss from fire, $27,040; *b* Debit loss from fire, $20,800

3-5 *a* Unadjusted balance, $33,895; *d* Adjusted balances, $41,695

3-6 *a* Combined net income, $83,400

3-7 *c* Combined net income, $46,920

3-8 *a* Adjusted balances, $138,890

3-9 *c* Combined net income, $95,500

3-10 Combined net income, $66,600

3-11 *a* Total assets: Dec. 31, Year 5, $540,000; Dec. 31, Year 4, $497,200; *b* Total financial resources provided, $118,300; *c* Total financial resources provided, $92,400

4-1 Debit goodwill, $350,000

4-2 *a* Credit retained earnings, $20,000; *b* Debit goodwill, $180,000

4-3 Credit paid-in capital in excess of par, $260,000

4-4 *a* Debit goodwill, $60,870; *b* Credit retained earnings, $150,000

4-5 Debit patent, $46,000

4-6 *a* Net credit to paid-in capital in excess of par, $1,700,000; *b* Debit goodwill, $4,355,000

4-7 Combined sales, $1,150,000

4-8 *a* Credit retained earnings, $16,000; *b* Credit retained earnings, $810,000

4-9 *a* Debit patent, $95,000

4-10 *a* Pooling earnings per share, $1.87; *b* Purchase earnings per share, $1.41; *c* Pro forma retained earnings: Pooling, $388,000; purchase, $200,000

4-11 *b* Credit paid-in capital in excess of par, $45,000

5-1 *b* Debit goodwill, $115,000, in elimination

5-2 *b* Consolidated plant assets, $3,510,000

5-3 *c* Minority interest in net assets, $140,000

5-4 *b* Consolidated goodwill, $35,000

5-5 Debit paid-in capital in excess of par, $120,000

5-6 Consolidated total assets, $7,684,870

5-7 Consolidated intangible assets, $215,000

5-8 *a* Credit cost of goods sold, $60,000; *b* Consolidated total assets, $1,854,000

5-9 *a* Total debits to investment account, $1,502,727; *b* Goodwill, $15,626

5-10 *a* Debit investment account, $70,000; *b* Minority interest in net assets, $62,000

6-1 *b* Balance of investment account, $501,000; *c* Debit goodwill, $39,000

6-2 Total credits to minority interest in net assets, $50,400

6-3 *b* Minori... $29,700

6-4 *b* Debit goodwill, $4...,000

6-5 *b* Credit to investment account, $345,425

6-6 *b* Total credits to minority interest in net assets: Sept. 30, Year 7, $170,250; Sept. 30, Year 8, $179,250

6-7 *b* Goodwill, $39,000

6-8 *b* Credit to investment account, $143,200

6-9 Consolidated total assets, $31,275,000

6-10 Consolidated net income, $120,000; consolidated retained earnings, $954,000; consolidated total assets, $3,930,000

7-1 Total stockholders' equity, $27,600,000

7-2 Intercompany interest, $417

7-3 *b* Debit retained earnings—Savoy, $17,550

7-4 *b* Debit retained earnings—Solis, $33,600

7-5 Intercompany interest, $225

7-6 *a* $7,200; *c* $68,850

7-7 *b* (2) Debit retained earnings—Semel, $9,000

7-8 *b* Debit retained earnings—Soule, $20,000

7-9 *c* Intercompany revenue (expenses), $6,911

7-10 *b* Consolidated total assets, $1,410,000

7-11 *b* Minority interest in net assets, $30,520

7-12 *b* Consolidated total assets, $889,750; consolidated retained earnings, $151,625

8-1 Gain on early extinguishment, $1,736

8-2 Debit minority interest in net assets, $1,875

8-3 Debit minority interest in net income, $11,803

8-4 *b* Gain on early extinguishment, $18,533

8-5 *b* Gain on early extinguishment, $31,227

8-6 *a* Consolidated net income; $3,194,576; consolidated retained earnings, $4,799,576

8-7 Minority interest in net income, $2,320; minority interest in net assets, $39,320

8-8 *b* Consolidated net income, $26,300; consolidated retained earnings, $115,400

8-9 Minority interest in net income, $10,636; minority interest in net assets, $93,836

8-10 Consolidated net income, $776,367; consolidated retained earnings, $2,943,867; consolidated total assets, $29,449,108

9-1 *b* Credit deferred income tax liability, $1,669

9-2 Debit goodwill, $82,250

9-4 Total financial resources provided, $358,000

9-6 *a* Credit other liabilities (deferred income tax liability), $2,592; *b* Consolidated net income, $105,711; consolidated retained earnings, $455,711; minority interest in net assets, $69,200

9-7 Consolidated net income, $63,731; consolidated retained earnings, $642,231; minority interest in net assets, $91,561

9-8 *a* Credit income taxes payable, $270; *b* Consolidated net income, $77,904;

Continued on inside back cover

MODERN ADVANCED
ACCOUNTING

MODERN ADVANCED ACCOUNTING

Third Edition

A. N. MOSICH, Ph.D., C.P.A.
Ernst & Whinney Professor of Accounting
University of Southern California

E. JOHN LARSEN, D.B.A., C.P.A.
Associate Professor of Accounting
University of Southern California

McGRAW-HILL BOOK COMPANY

New York | St. Louis | San Francisco | Auckland | Bogotá | Hamburg
Johannesburg | London | Madrid | Mexico | Montreal | New Delhi
Panama | Paris | São Paulo | Singapore | Sydney | Tokyo | Toronto

MODERN ADVANCED ACCOUNTING

7890   DOCDOC 8987

ISBN 0-07-040127-6

This book was set in Helvetica by Progressive Typographers.
The editor was Donald G. Mason;
the production supervisor was Phil Galea.
The cover was designed by Nicholas Krenitsky.
The cover photograph was taken by Demarco/Tomaccio Studio.
R. R. Donnelley & Sons Company was printer and binder.

Library of Congress Cataloging in Publication Data

Mosich, A. N.
    Modern advanced accounting.

    Rev. ed. of: Modern advanced accounting / Walter B.
Meigs, A. N. Mosich, E. John Larsen. c1979.
    Includes bibliographical references and index.
    1. Accounting. I. Larsen, E. John. II. Meigs,
Walter B. Modern advanced accounting. III. Title.
HF5635.M8756 1983   657'.046   82-18013
ISBN 0-07-040127-6

CONTENTS

V

accounting with goodwill. Illustration of purchase accounting with "negative goodwill." Pooling-of-interests accounting. Illustration of pooling-of-interests accounting. Popularity of pooling accounting. Abuses of pooling accounting. Abuses of purchase accounting. Action by the AICPA. Conditions requiring pooling accounting. Presentation of business combinations in financial statements. Disclosure of business combinations in notes to financial statements.

Criticism of purchase accounting. Criticism of pooling accounting. FASB study of accounting for business combinations.

Nature of consolidated financial statements. Should all subsidiaries be consolidated? The meaning of "controlling financial interest." Criticism of traditional concept of control. Unconsolidated subsidiaries in consolidated financial statements.

Nature of minority interest. Consolidated balance sheet for partially owned subsidiary. Alternative methods for valuing minority interest and goodwill. "Negative goodwill" in consolidated balance sheet. Footnote disclosure of consolidation policy. Advantages and shortcomings of consolidated financial statements.

Equity method. Cost method. Choosing between equity method and cost method. Illustration of equity method for wholly owned purchased subsidiary for first year after business

PART THREE ACCOUNTING FOR NONBUSINESS ORGANIZATIONS

PART FIVE ACCOUNTING FOR FIDUCIARIES

Accounting for a reorganization.   Footnote disclosure of
reorganization.   Evaluation of Bankruptcy Code.

PREFACE

The third edition of **Modern Advanced Accounting** represents a major revision. Although the number of chapters has been maintained at eighteen, extensive rearrangement of the subject matter has been made, and the emphasis given certain topics has been changed significantly.

This book may be used in a one-semester or two-quarter course, at either the undergraduate level or the graduate level. The emphasis throughout the book is on financial accounting concepts and on analysis of the problems that arise in the application of these underlying concepts to specialized accounting entities—partnerships, branches, affiliated companies, governmental units, nonprofit organizations, and estates and trusts—and on special topics such as installment sales, consignments, segments of business enterprises, interim reporting, accounting and reporting for the Securities and Exchange Commission, accounting for multinational enterprises, and bankruptcy.

The third edition reflects the continuing changes that have been occurring in the development of accounting principles and practices, with special attention to the official pronouncements and exposure drafts of the Financial Accounting Standards Board (FASB), the Securities and Exchange Commission (SEC), the American Institute of Certified Public Accountants (AICPA), and the National Council on Governmental Accounting (NCGA).

We have prepared the third edition of **Modern Advanced Accounting** as a companion volume for **Intermediate Accounting** (by the same author team), thus creating a coordinated series for the important intermediate-advanced financial accounting sequence of courses as a foundation for a professional education for accountants.

NEW FEATURES OF THIS EDITION

Every chapter has been updated to include recent changes in law and relevant pronouncements by accounting rule-making bodies. For example, the following have been fully incorporated in this edition: (1) FASB's "Objectives of Financial Reporting by Nonbusiness Organizations," (2) "Foreign Currency Translation" (*FASB Statement No. 52*), (3) NCGA's *Governmental Accounting and Financial Reporting Principles,* and (4) the *Bankruptcy Reform Act of 1978.*

The coverage of business combinations and consolidated financial statements has been expanded, although we again were able to deal with these topics in seven chapters. Pooling-type consolidations are presented in a single chapter (compared with two chapters in the second edition), and special topics are covered in two chapters (compared with one chapter in the earlier editions). Accounting for governmental units is presented in two chapters instead of one, the discussion of financial forecasts has been eliminated because the pressure for publication of financial forecasts has diminished in recent years, and a condensed presentation of accounting and reporting for the Securities and Exchange Commission is included in Chapter 15 of this edition.

Extensive efforts have been made to expand the number and variety of short exercises and problems. Many multiple-choice questions and problems relating to advanced accounting topics have been adapted from recent CPA examinations and included in the end-of-chapter learning materials (questions, exercises, cases, and problems).

We have divided the new edition into five sections to give clearer focus to the subject matter and to provide a psychological benefit for students by making the material appear more digestible.

ORGANIZATION OF SUBJECT MATTER

We anticipate that the organization of chapters into five cohesive and meaningful parts will be useful to instructors and students. This arrangement should facilitate the planning and presentation of the subject matter and, we hope, make it easier for students to learn and retain the concepts and procedures presented. A brief description of the contents of each of the five parts follows.

Part One: Accounting for partnerships and branches (Chapters 1 to 3)

The first part deals with the accounting principles and procedures for partnerships, joint ventures, and branch operations. Partnerships and joint ventures are covered in the first two chapters, which carry the student from the basic concepts often presented in the introductory accounting course to the CPA examination level, with its more complex problems of profit sharing, realignment of partners' equities, and liquidation. Chapter 3, which deals with home office–branch relationships and combined financial statements, provides a logical stepping-stone to the seven chapters dealing with business combinations and consolidated financial statements.

The general discussion of partnership operation and liquidation has been streamlined, and the accounting for the incorporation of a partnership has been relocated from *Intermediate Accounting* to Chapter 2. The Eliminations column in the working paper for combined financial statements of home office and branch is presented as a single column to parallel the form used in the working papers for consolidated financial statements in Chapters 5 to 10.

Part Two: Business combinations and consolidated financial statements (Chapters 4 to 10)

This important section of the book has been thoroughly revised and expanded in the third edition. By combining the two chapters on consolidated financial statements for pooling-type business combinations into a single chapter and splitting the special topics relating to consolidations into two chapters, we were able to present this section in seven chapters. This will permit students to absorb the key facets of purchase-type business combinations before being exposed to the consolidation techniques for pooling-type business combinations. Formal consolidated financial statements are illustrated in this edition, and the cost method of accounting for the investment in subsidiary is included in an appendix in order not to distract students from the more widely used and more appropriate equity method of accounting.

Among the new features in this section are (1) more extensive use of journal entries, ledger accounts, and illustrations to permit students to follow readily the changes in intercompany accounts and to understand the complex concepts presented; (2) expansion of the discussion relating to negative goodwill; (3) expanded discussion and illustrations of the equity method of accounting to cover two years subsequent to a business combination; and (4) illustration of accounting for the acquisition by the parent company of additional shares of common stock directly from the subsidiary. The use of a Retained Earnings of Subsidiary ledger account for a parent company under the equity method of accounting is extensively illustrated for both purchase-type and pooling-type business combinations.

Part Three: Accounting for nonbusiness organizations (Chapters 11 to 13)

The single chapter of the previous editions on accounting for governmental units is expanded to two chapters in this edition. The general fund is covered in Chapter 11, and the other funds and account groups are included in Chapter 12. This part of the book is concluded with a significantly updated Chapter 13, "Accounting for Nonprofit Organizations."

The objectives of financial reporting by nonbusiness organizations, as included in *FASB Statement of Financial Accounting Concepts No. 4,* are discussed in Chapter 11 to set the stage for the accounting principles illustrated in this section of the textbook. The discussion and illustrations relating to governmental units are based on *Governmental Accounting and Financial Reporting Principles,* issued in 1979 by the National Council on Governmental Accounting. With two chapters allocated to governmental units, we are able to present more complete illustrations of accounting procedures for capital projects funds, debt service funds, special assessment funds, agency and trust funds, and the general fixed assets and general long-term debt account groups.

Part Four: Special topics in financial accounting (Chapters 14 to 16)

We have relocated the coverage of installment sales and consignments to this section (Chapter 14) because of their specialized nature and because discussion of these topics in the front part of the book proved to be distracting. Industry segments, interim reports, and accounting and reporting for the SEC are covered in Chapter 15, including a description of the functions of the Chief Accountant, the Division of Corporation Finance, and the Division of Enforcement of the SEC. In Chapter 16, "Accounting for Multinational Enterprises," we have thoroughly incorporated the provisions of much-discussed **FASB Statement No. 52,** "Foreign Currency Translation," issued in 1981.

Part Five: Accounting for fiduciaries (Chapters 17 and 18)

The final section of the book includes chapters entitled "Bankruptcy: Liquidation and Reorganization" and "Accounting for Estates and Trusts." Although some instructors may not cover these two traditional topics in their courses, we feel that it is imperative to include them for those who wish to do so. Many accountants in today's practice environment must assist clients with problems of bankruptcy, liquidation, reorganization, and the accounting for estates and trusts.

We have incorporated the relevant provisions of the **Bankruptcy Reform Act of 1978** in Chapter 17. However, in our discussion of estates and trusts we focus on financial accounting matters rather than on the complex estate and inheritance tax provisions of federal and state statutes.

Carefully selected financial statements (or portions thereof) of publicly owned corporations and of a nonprofit organization (American Accounting Association) are presented in appendixes at the end of appropriate chapters. A complete *Form 10-K* of a publicly owned corporation is included in an appendix at the end of Chapter 15. Thus, students may trace many of the theoretical concepts in the text to real-world situations. As in prior editions, compound interest tables are included in an appendix at the end of the book.

The pronouncements of the FASB, the AICPA, the SEC, the now-defunct Accounting Principles Board, and other authoritative bodies are interwoven into the discussion and in problem material throughout the book. However, we believe that an accounting textbook should encourage students to participate in a critical evaluation of accounting principles and make them aware of the conflicts and shortcomings that exist within the traditional structure of accounting theory. Therefore, we have tried to provide students with a conceptual framework for making this evaluation.

REVIEW QUESTIONS, EXERCISES, CASES, AND PROBLEMS

An abundance of learning and assignment material is provided at the end of each chapter. This material is divided into four groups: review questions, exercises, cases, and problems. All end-of-chapter material has been tested in class by the authors.

The review questions are intended for use by students as a self-testing and review device to measure their comprehension of key points in each chapter. Many of the questions are provocative, which makes them suitable for class discussion and written assignments.

An exercise typically covers a specific point or topic and does not require extensive computations. Instructors may use the exercises to supplement problem assignments, for class discussion, and for examination purposes.

The cases require analytical reasoning but involve little or no quantitative data. Students are required to analyze business situations, to apply accounting principles, and to propose or evaluate a course of action. However, they are not required to prepare lengthy working papers or otherwise to manipulate accounting data on an extensive scale. The cases have proved to be an effective means of encouraging students to take positions in the argument of controversial accounting issues. Many of the cases have been adapted from actual business situations, court cases, or Uniform CPA Examinations. The review questions and cases are especially recommended if the instructor wishes to develop student skills in communicating accounting concepts and in evaluating the merits of opposing arguments.

Many of the problems are new, and those carried over from the second edition generally have been updated and revised. A feature of this edition is the inclusion of a large number of short problems closely correlated with the text material. The difficulty rating of problems is carefully tailored to help students achieve a smooth learning progression based on the "building-block approach." The book includes most of the problems in the Accounting Theory and Accounting Practice sections of recent Uniform CPA Examinations that are appropriate for advanced accounting, although many have been considerably modified to conform with the latest authoritative pronouncements. In addition, several problems have been designed especially to demonstrate the concepts presented in the theoretical discussion included in the chapter. Probably no more than a third of the cases and problems would be used in a given course; consequently, ample opportunity exists to vary homework assignments from semester to semester.

SUPPLEMENTS AVAILABLE WITH THIS EDITION

As was the case with previous editions, the third edition of **Modern Advanced Accounting** is accompanied by a comprehensive package of supplementary items for both students and instructors. For this edition, however, several innovations have been made:

For the student

1 A student **Study Guide,** prepared by the authors, is designed to help students measure their progress by providing immediate feedback. It contains an outline of the more important points for each chapter, plus a variety of objective questions and short exercises. Answers to the questions and exercises appear at the end of each Study Guide chapter to help students evaluate their understanding of the subject matter. The authors have found that use of the Study Guide by students considerably increases their learning.

2 **Accounting Work Sheets** (partially filled-in working papers) for the problems are available for purchase by students. On these work sheets the company names, problem numbers, numerous headings, and some preliminary data (such as trial balances) have been entered to save students' time and to facilitate rapid review by the instructor. Many adopters of previous editions have found that use of the partially filled-in working papers permits assignment of a wider variety of problems and eliminates much student frustration in deciding on a proper solution format.

3 A **Checklist of Key Figures** is provided for most problems. In this edition of **Modern Advanced Accounting** the checklist appears on the inside front and back covers of the textbook. The purpose of the checklist is to aid students in verifying intermediate figures in problem solutions and in discovering errors.

For the instructor

1 A comprehensive **Solutions Manual** is available from the publisher to adopters of the text. The Solutions Manual contains answers to all review questions, exercises, cases, and problems in the text. In addition, at the beginning of each chapter, there are short descriptions, time estimates, and difficulty ratings for each of the problems, to help instructors choose problems that best fit the needs of their individual classes and courses in terms of scope, level, and emphasis.

2 A booklet of **Examination Questions,** with test material arranged chapter by chapter, is available free of charge. It contains an abundant number of true-or-false and multiple-choice questions and short problems for each chapter. Instructors should find the booklet a most useful source of material when assembling their own examinations, since they can emphasize those topics or chapters that meet their course outline. Complete answers are provided for all questions and problems.

3 An **Instructor's Teaching Guide** is a new teaching aid available with this edition of the text. It is designed to assist instructors in preparing assignments and in covering the materials thoroughly in class. The authors' goals in providing this new supplement were to make the task of instructors easier and to enable them to use their time more efficiently, so that the students' learning process would be enhanced.

4 **Overhead Transparencies** of problem solutions are available for most of the problems in the text. For longer, more complex problems, the transparencies are considered by many instructors to be a highly effective means of showing desired organization and format of solutions.

CONTRIBUTIONS BY OTHERS

The many instructors and students who used the first two editions of this book have contributed to the improvements in this edition. Their suggestions for modification of certain problems and expansion or contraction of certain sections of the text material have been most useful. Especially helpful was the advice received from Robert W. Hill, California Polytechnic University at San Luis Obispo; Jerry Arnold, Alan A. Cherry, and John Lacey, of the University of Southern California; Joe J. Cramer, Howard University, Washington, D.C.

We would like to express our thanks for the many useful comments and suggestions provided by colleagues who reviewed this text during the course of its development, especially to Professor Irving M. Bonawitz, State University of New York at Albany; Professor Robert N. Freeman, University of California, Berkeley; Professor James E. Moon, The University of Tennessee at Chattanooga; Professor Corolyn Ofner, Saint Joseph's University; and Professor Maurice Stark, Kansas State University.

We are especially indebted to our former student, George W. Saunders, Jr., and to Professor Joseph F. Guy of Georgia State University for their review of the manuscript and problem material for accuracy and clarity.

Our sincere appreciation goes to our spouses, Dorothy Mosich and Kathleen Larsen, for their assistance in the preparation of this edition and for their patience during the writing and proofreading of the book.

We acknowledge the permission received from the American Institute of Certified Public Accountants to quote from many of its pronouncements and to adapt materials from the Uniform CPA Examinations. All quotations and material from the Uniform CPA Examinations are copyright by the American Institute of Certified Public Accountants.

We also are grateful to the Financial Accounting Standards Board, which granted us permission to quote from **FASB Statements, Discussion Memoranda, Interpretations,** and **Exposure Drafts.** All quotations used are copyrighted by the Financial Accounting Standards Board, High Ridge Park, Stamford, Connecticut 06905, U.S.A., and are reprinted with permission. Copies of the complete documents are available from the Financial Accounting Standards Board.

Our list of acknowledgments must include Walter B. Meigs, for his contributions and guidance in the preparation of the first two editions.

A. N. Mosich
E. John Larsen

ACCOUNTING
FOR PARTNERSHIPS
AND BRANCHES

1 PARTNERSHIP ORGANIZATION AND OPERATION

Nature of partnerships

Much of our discussion of partnerships is based on the Uniform Partnership Act, which has been adopted by many of the states. This Act defines a **partnership** (often referred to as a *firm*) as "an association of two or more persons to carry on, as co-owners, a business for profit." In this definition, the term **persons** includes individuals and other partnerships, and in some states corporations may become partners. The creation of a partnership requires no approval by the state; in fact, a partnership may be formed without a written contract, although a carefully formulated written contract is highly desirable.

Partnerships traditionally are associated with the practice of law, medicine, public accounting, and other professions, and also with small business enterprises. In some states the licensed professional person such as the CPA is forbidden to incorporate on grounds that the creation of a corporate entity might weaken the confidential relationship between the practitioner and the client. However, a number of states have approved legislation designed to permit **professional corporations.** A few large industrial and merchandising enterprises also operate as partnerships.

ORGANIZATION OF A PARTNERSHIP

Characteristics of a partnership

The basic characteristics of a partnership are summarized below:

Ease of Formation In contrast to a corporation, a partnership may be created by an oral or written contract between two or more persons, or may be implied by their conduct. This advantage of convenience and minimum expense in the formation of a partnership in some cases may be offset by certain difficulties inherent in such an informal organizational structure.

Limited Life A partnership may be ended by the death, retirement, bankruptcy, or incapacity of a partner. The admission of a new partner

3

to the partnership legally ends the former partnership and establishes a new one.

Mutual Agency   Each partner has the authority to act for the partnership and to enter into contracts on its behalf. However, acts beyond the normal scope of business operations, such as the borrowing of funds by a partner, generally do not bind the partnership unless specific authority has been given to the partner to enter into such transactions.

Unlimited Liability   The term *general partnership* refers to a firm in which all the partners are personally responsible for debts of the firm and all have authority to act for the firm. Each partner in a general partnership is personally responsible for the liabilities of the firm. Creditors having difficulty in collecting from the partnership will be likely to turn to those individual members of the firm who have other financial resources. In a *limited partnership* one or more of the partners has no personal liability for debts of the partnership. The activities of limited partners are somewhat restricted, and they must maintain an agreed investment in the partnership. Statutes providing for limited partnerships require that the firm identify itself publicly as a limited partnership and that at least one member of the firm be a general partner.

Co-ownership of Partnership Assets and Earnings   When individuals invest assets in a partnership, they retain no claim to those specific assets but simply acquire an ownership *equity in all assets* of the partnership. Every member of a partnership also has an ownership equity in earnings; in fact, participation in earnings and losses is one of the tests of the existence of a partnership.

Deciding between a partnership and a corporation

One of the most important considerations in choosing between a partnership and the corporate form of business organization is the income tax status of the enterprise and of its owners. A partnership pays no income tax but is required to file an annual *information return* showing its revenue and expenses, the amount of its net income, and the division of the net income among the partners. The partners include their respective shares of the *ordinary net income* from the partnership and such items as dividends, capital gains and losses, and charitable contributions on their individual income tax returns, regardless of whether they received more or less than this amount of cash from the partnership during the year.

The corporation is a separate legal entity subject to a corporate income tax. The net income, when and if distributed to stockholders in the form of dividends, also is taxable income to stockholders. Certain corporations with not more than 25 stockholders can elect not to be taxed as corporations, provided their income or loss is fully assumed by their stockholders. These "tax-option corporations" file information returns as do partnerships, and their stockholders report on individual tax returns their respective shares of the year's net income or loss. Thus, a partnership can incorporate as a **Subchapter S Corporation** to gain the advantages of limited liability but at the same time elect to be taxed as a partnership. Income tax rates and regulations are subject to frequent change, and new interpretations of the rules often arise. The tax status of the owners also is likely to change from year to year. For all these reasons, management should review the tax implications of the partnership and corporate forms of organization so that the business enterprise may adapt most successfully to the income tax environment.

The burden of taxation is not the only factor influencing a choice between the partnership and the corporate form of organization. Perhaps the factor that most often tips the scales in favor of incorporation is the opportunity for obtaining larger amounts of capital when ownership can be divided into shares of capital stock, readily transferable, and offering the advantages inherent in the separation of ownership and management.

Is the partnership a separate entity?

In accounting literature, the legal aspects of partnerships generally have received more emphasis than the managerial and financial issues. It has been common practice to distinguish a partnership from a corporation by saying that a partnership was an "association of persons" and a corporation was a separate entity. Such a distinction unfortunately stresses the legal form rather than the economic substance of the business organization. In terms of managerial policy and business objectives, many partnerships are as truly business and accounting entities as are corporations. Such partnerships typically are guided by long-range plans not likely to be affected by the admission or withdrawal of a single member. In these firms the accounting policies should reflect the fact that the partnership is an entity apart from its owners.

Viewing the partnership as a business and accounting entity often will aid in developing financial statements that provide the most meaningful picture of financial position and results of operations. Among the accounting policies to be stressed is continuity in asset valuation, despite changes in the income-sharing ratio and changes in personnel. Another helpful step may be recognition in expense accounts of the value of personal services rendered by partners who also hold managerial positions. In theoretical discussions, considerable support is found for viewing every business enterprise as an accounting entity, apart from its owners, regardless of the form of legal organization. A managing partner under this view is both an employee and an owner. The value of the personal services rendered by a partner is an expense of managing the partnership.

The inclusion of partners' salaries among expenses has been opposed by some accountants on grounds that partners' salaries may be set at unrealistic levels and that the partnership is an association of individuals who are owners and not employees of the partnership.

A partnership has the characteristics of a separate entity in that it may hold title to property in its own name, may enter into contracts, and in some states may sue or be sued as an entity. In practice, many accountants are accustomed to viewing partnerships as separate entities with continuity of accounting policies and asset valuations not broken by changes in partnership personnel.

The partnership contract

Although a partnership may exist on the basis of an oral agreement or be implied by the actions of its members, good business practice demands that the partnership contract be clearly stated in writing. Among the more important points to be covered by the partnership contract are:

1 The date of formation of the partnership, the duration of the contract, the names of the partners, and the name and business activities of the partnership.
2 The assets to be invested by each partner, the procedure for valuing noncash investments, and the penalties for failure to invest and maintain the agreed amount of capital.
3 The authority to be vested in each partner and the rights and duties of each.
4 The accounting period to be used, the nature of accounting records, financial statements, and audits by certified public accountants.
5 The plan for sharing net income or loss, including the frequency of income measurement and the distribution of the net income or loss to the partners.
6 The salaries and drawings allowed to partners and the penalties, if any, for excessive withdrawals.
7 Insurance on the lives of partners, with the partnership or surviving partners named as beneficiaries.
8 Provision for arbitration of disputes and liquidation of the partnership at the end of the specified term of the contract or at the death or withdrawal of a partner. Especially important in avoiding disputes is agreement on procedures for the valuation of the partnership and the method of settlement with the estate of a deceased partner.

One advantage of developing a partnership contract with the aid of attorneys and accountants is that the process of reaching agreement on specific issues will develop a better understanding among the partners on many issues that might be highly controversial if not settled at the outset. Of course, it is seldom possible to cover specifically in a partnership contract every issue that may later arise. Revision of the partnership contract generally requires the approval of all partners.

Disputes arising among partners that cannot be resolved by reference to the partnership contract may be settled by arbitration or in courts of law. The partner who is not satisfied with the handling of disputes always has the right to withdraw from the partnership.

Owners' equity accounts for partners

Accounting for a partnership differs from accounting for a single propri-etorship or a corporation with respect to the sharing of net income and losses and the maintenance of the owners' equity accounts. Although it would be possible to maintain partnership accounting records with only one equity account for each partner, the usual practice is to maintain three types of accounts. These equity accounts consist of (1) *capital* ac-counts, (2) *drawing* or *personal* accounts, and (3) accounts for *loans* to and from partners.

The original investment by each partner is recorded by debiting the assets invested, crediting any liabilities assumed by the firm, and cred-iting the partner's capital account with the current fair value of net assets invested. Subsequent to the original investment, the partner's eq-uity is *increased* by additional investments and by a share of net in-come; the partner's equity is *decreased* by withdrawal of assets and by a share of net losses.

Another possible source of increase or decrease in partners' equity arises from changes in ownership, as described in subsequent sections of this chapter.

The original investment of assets by partners is recorded by credits to the capital accounts; drawings by partners in anticipation of net income or drawings that are considered salary allowances are recorded by debits to the drawing accounts. However, a large withdrawal that is viewed as a permanent reduction in the ownership equity of a partner is debited directly to the partner's capital account.

At the end of the accounting period, the net income or net loss in the Income Summary account is transferred to the partners' capital ac-counts in accordance with the partnership contract. The debit balances in the drawing accounts at the end of the year also are closed to the partners' capital accounts. Because the accounting procedures for partners' equity accounts are not subject to state regulations as in the case of capital stock and other stockholders' equity accounts of a cor-poration, many deviations from the procedures described here are pos-sible.

Loans to and from partners

Occasionally, a partner may withdraw a substantial sum from the part-nership with the intention of repaying this amount. Such a transaction may be debited to the Loans Receivable from Partners account rather than to the partner's drawing account.

On the other hand, a partner may make an advance to the partnership that is viewed as a loan rather than an increase in the capital account. This type of transaction is recorded by a credit to Loans Payable to Part-ners and generally is accompanied by the issuance of a note payable. Amounts due from partners may be reflected as assets in the balance sheet and amounts owing to partners shown as liabilities. The classification of these items as current or long-term generally depends on the maturity date, although these **related party transactions** may result in noncurrent classification of the partners' loans, regardless of maturity dates.

If a substantial unsecured loan has been made by a partnership to one of the partners and repayment appears doubtful, the better financial statement presentation may be to offset the receivable against the partner's capital account. If this is not done, assets and the partners' equity may be inflated to the point of being misleading. In any event, adequate disclosure calls for separate listing of any receivables from partners.

Valuation of investments by partners

The investment by a partner in the firm often includes assets other than cash. It is imperative that the partners agree on the current fair value of assets at the time of their investment and that the assets be recorded at current fair values. Any gains or losses resulting from the disposal of such assets during the operation of the partnership, or at the time of liquidation, are divided according to the plan for sharing net income or losses. Equitable treatment of the individual partners, therefore, requires a starting point of current fair values recorded for all assets invested in the firm. It then will follow that partnership gains or losses from disposal of noncash assets invested by the partners will be limited to the difference between the disposal price and the current fair value of the assets when invested by the partners, adjusted for any depreciation or amortization to the date of disposal.

INCOME-SHARING PLANS

Partners' equity in assets versus share in earnings

The equity of a partner in the net assets of the partnership should be distinguished from a partner's share in earnings. Thus, to say that David Jones is a one-third partner is not a clear statement. Jones may have a one-third equity in the net assets but have a larger or smaller share in the earnings of the firm. Such a statement might also be interpreted to mean that Jones was entitled to one-third of the earnings, although his capital account represented much more or much less than one-third of the total partners' capital. To state the matter concisely, partners may agree on any type of **income-sharing plan** (or **profit and loss ratio**), regardless of the amount of their respective capital accounts. The Uniform Partnership Act states that if partners fail to specify a plan for sharing net income and net loss, **it shall be assumed that they intended to** *share equally.* Because income sharing is of such great importance, it is extremely rare to find a situation in which the partnership contract is silent on this point.

Division of net income or loss

The many possible plans for sharing of net income or loss among partners may be summarized into the following four categories:

1 Equally, or in some other ratio
2 In the ratio of partners' capital account balances on a particular date, or in the ratio of average capital account balances during the year
3 Allowing salaries to partners and dividing the remaining net income or loss in a specified ratio
4 Allowing salaries to partners, allowing interest on capital account balances, and dividing the remaining net income or loss in a specified ratio

These variations in income-sharing plans emphasize that the value of personal services rendered by individual partners may vary widely, as may the amounts of capital invested by each partner. The amount and quality of managerial services rendered and the amount of capital invested often are important factors in the success or failure of a partnership. Therefore, provisions may be made for salaries to partners and interest on their respective capital account balances as a preliminary step in the division of net income or loss. Any remaining net income or loss then may be divided in a specified ratio.

Another factor affecting the success of a partnership may be that one of the partners has large personal financial resources, thus giving the partnership a high credit rating. Similarly, partners who are well known in a profession or industry may contribute importantly to the success of the partnership even though they may not participate actively in the operations of the partnership. These two factors may be taken into account in the income-sharing plan by judicious selection of the ratio in which any remaining net income or loss is divided.

We now shall illustrate how each of the methods of dividing net income or loss may be applied. This series of illustrations is based on data for A & B Partnership, which earned a net income of $30,000 in Year 1, the first year of operations. The partnership contract provides that each partner may withdraw $500 on the last day of each month. The drawings are recorded by debits to the partners' drawing accounts and are not a factor in the division of net income or loss. All other withdrawals, investments, and net income or loss are entered in the partners' capital accounts.

Partner A originally invested $40,000 on January 1, Year 1, and invested an additional $10,000 on April 1. Partner B invested $80,000 on January 1 and withdrew $5,000 on July 1. These transactions are illustrated in the following capital, drawing, and Income Summary accounts:

General ledger accounts for Year 1

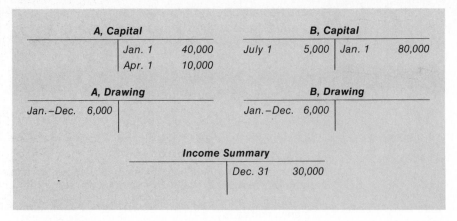

	A, Capital				B, Capital		
	Jan. 1	40,000	July 1	5,000	Jan. 1	80,000
	Apr. 1	10,000				

	A, Drawing			B, Drawing	
Jan.–Dec.	6,000		Jan.–Dec.	6,000	

	Income Summary	
	Dec. 31	30,000

Division of Earnings Equally or in Some Other Ratio Many partnership contracts provide that net income or loss is to be divided equally. Also, if the partners have made no specific agreement for sharing earnings, the Uniform Partnership Act provides that an intent of equal division will be assumed. The net income of $30,000 for the A & B Partnership is transferred at the end of Year 1 from the Income Summary account to the partners' capital accounts by the following journal entry:

Journal entry to close Income Summary account

Income Summary	30,000	
A, Capital		15,000
B, Capital		15,000

To record division of net income for Year 1 equally between A and B.

The drawing accounts are closed to the partners' capital accounts at the end of Year 1 as follows:

Journal entry to close drawing accounts

A, Capital	6,000	
B, Capital	6,000	
A, Drawing		6,000
B, Drawing		6,000

To close drawing accounts.

After the drawing accounts are closed, the capital accounts show the ownership equity of each partner.

If the A & B Partnership had reported a net loss of, say, $20,000 during the first year, the Income Summary account would show a debit balance of $20,000. This loss would be transferred to the partners' capital accounts by a debit to each capital account for $10,000 and a credit to the Income Summary account for $20,000.

Assuming that A and B share earnings in the ratio of 60% to A and 40% to B, and that net income amounted to $30,000, the net income would be divided $18,000 to A and $12,000 to B. The agreement that A should receive 60% of the net income (perhaps because of greater experience and personal contacts) would cause Partner A to absorb a larger share of the net loss if the business operated unprofitably. Some partnership contracts provide that a net income is to be divided in a certain ratio, such as 60% to A and 40% to B, but that a net loss is divided equally or in some other ratio. Another variation intended to compensate for unequal contributions by the partners provides that agreed ratio (60% and 40% in our example) shall be applicable to a given amount of income but that additional income shall be shared in some other ratio.

Division of Earnings in Ratio of Partners' Capital Account Balances Division of partnership earnings in proportion to the capital invested by each partner is most likely to be found in partnerships in which substantial investment is the principal ingredient for success. For example, a partnership engaged in the acquisition of land for investment might select this method of dividing net income. To avoid controversy, it is essential that the partnership contract specify whether the income-sharing ratio is based on the original capital investments, the capital account balances at the beginning of each year, the balances at the end of each year (before the distribution of net income or loss), or the average balances during each year.

Continuing our illustration for the A & B Partnership, assume that the partnership contract calls for division of net income in the ratio of *original capital investments.* The net income of $30,000 for Year 1 is divided as follows:

> **A: $30,000 × $40,000/$120,000 = $10,000**
>
> **B: $30,000 × $80,000/$120,000 = $20,000**

The journal entry to close the Income Summary account would be similar to the journal entry illustrated on page 10.

Assuming that the net income is divided in the ratio of capital account balances at the **end of the year** (before drawings and the distribution of net income), the net income of $30,000 for Year 1 is divided as follows:

> **A: $30,000 × $50,000/$125,000 = $12,000**
>
> **B: $30,000 × $75,000/$125,000 = $18,000**

Division of net income on the basis of (1) original capital investments, (2) yearly beginning capital account balances, or (3) yearly ending capital account balances may prove inequitable if there are material changes in capital accounts during the year. Use of average balances as a basis for sharing income is preferable because it reflects the capital actually available for use by the partnership during the year.

If the partnership contract provides for sharing net income in the ratio of average capital account balances during the year, it also should state the amount of drawings each partner may make without affecting the capital account. In our continuing example for the A & B Partnership, the partners are entitled to withdraw $500 monthly. Any additional withdrawals or investments are entered in the partners' capital accounts and therefore influence the computation of the average capital ratio. The partnership contract also should state whether capital account balances are to be computed to the nearest month or to the nearest day.

The computations of average capital account balances and the division of net income for the A & B Partnership for Year 1 follow:

A & B PARTNERSHIP
Computation of Average Capital Account Balances
For Year 1

Partner	Date	Increase (decrease) in capital	Capital account balance	Fraction of year unchanged	Average capital account balances
A	Jan. 1	$40,000	$40,000	1/4	$ 10,000
	Apr. 1	10,000	50,000	3/4	37,500
					$ 47,500
B	Jan. 1	80,000	80,000	1/2	$ 40,000
	July 1	(5,000)	75,000	1/2	37,500
					$ 77,500
Total average capitals for A and B					$125,000

Division of net income:

To A: $30,000 × $47,500/$125,000	$ 11,400
To B: $30,000 × $77,500/$125,000	18,600
Total net income	$ 30,000

Interest on Partners' Capital Account Balances with Remaining Net Income or Loss Divided in Specified Ratio In the preceding section, the plan for dividing the entire net income in the ratio of partners' capital account balances was based on the assumption that invested capital was the dominant factor in profitable operation of the partnership. However, in most cases the amount of invested capital is only one factor that contributes to the success of the partnership. Consequently, many partnerships choose to divide only a portion of net income in the capital ratio, and to divide the remainder equally or in some other ratio.

To allow interest on partners' capital account balances at 15%, for example, is the same as dividing a part of net income in the ratio of partners' capital balances. If the partners agree to allow interest on capital as a first step in the division of net income, they should specify the interest rate to be used and also state whether interest is to be computed on capital account balances on specific dates or on average balances during the year.

Let us again use our basic illustration for the A & B Partnership with a net income of $30,000 for Year 1, and capital account balances as shown on page 12. Assume that the partnership contract allows interest on partners' average capital account balances at 15%, with any remaining net income or loss to be divided equally. The net income of $30,000 for Year 1 is divided as follows:

<table>
<tr><td>Division of net income
with interest allowed on
average capital
balances</td><td></td><td>A</td><td>B</td><td>Combined</td></tr>
<tr><td></td><td>Interest on average capital balances:</td><td></td><td></td><td></td></tr>
<tr><td></td><td>A: $47,500 × 0.15 . . . .</td><td>$ 7,125</td><td></td><td>$ 7,125</td></tr>
<tr><td></td><td>B: $77,500 × 0.15 . . . .</td><td></td><td>$11,625</td><td>11,625</td></tr>
<tr><td></td><td>Subtotal . . . .</td><td></td><td></td><td>$18,750</td></tr>
<tr><td></td><td>Balance ($30,000 − $18,750) divided equally .</td><td>5,625</td><td>5,625</td><td>11,250</td></tr>
<tr><td></td><td>Totals . . . .</td><td>$12,750</td><td>$17,250</td><td>$30,000</td></tr>
</table>

The journal entry to close the Income Summary account at the end of Year 1 follows:

<table>
<tr><td>Closing the Income
Summary account</td><td>Income Summary . . . .</td><td>30,000</td><td></td></tr>
<tr><td></td><td>A, Capital . . . .</td><td></td><td>12,750</td></tr>
<tr><td></td><td>B, Capital . . . .</td><td></td><td>17,250</td></tr>
<tr><td></td><td>To record division of net income for Year 1.</td><td></td><td></td></tr>
</table>

As a separate case, assume that the A & B Partnership was unsuccessful in Year 1 and incurred a net loss of $1,000. If the partnership contract provides for allowing interest on capital accounts, this provision **must be enforced, regardless of whether operations are profitable or unprofitable.** The only justification for omitting the allowance of interest on partners' capital accounts during a loss year would be in the case of a partnership contract containing a specific provision requiring such omission. Note in the following analysis that the $1,000 debit balance in the Income Summary account resulting from the net loss is increased by the allowance of interest to $19,750 and is then divided equally between A and B:

	A	B	Combined
Interest on average capital balances:			
A: $47,500 × 0.15	$ 7,125		$ 7,125
B: $77,500 × 0.15		$11,625	11,625
Subtotal			$18,750
Resulting deficiency ($1,000 + $18,750) divided equally	(9,875)	(9,875)	(19,750)
Totals	$(2,750)	$ 1,750	$ (1,000)

The journal entry to close the Income Summary account at the end of Year 1 is shown below:

Closing the Income
Summary account with
a debit balance

A, Capital	2,750	
Income Summary		1,000
B, Capital		1,750
To record division of net loss for Year 1.		

At first thought, the idea of a net loss of $1,000 causing one partner's capital to increase and the other partner's capital to decrease may appear unreasonable, but there is sound logic to support this result. Partner B invested substantially more capital than did Partner A; this capital was used to carry on operations, and the fact that a net loss was incurred in the first year is no reason to ignore B's larger capital investment.

A significant contrast between two of the income-sharing plans we have discussed (the capital-ratio plan and the interest-on-capital-accounts plan) is apparent if we consider the case of a partnership operating at a loss. Under the capital-ratio plan, the partner who invested more capital is required to bear a larger share of the net loss. This result may be considered unreasonable, because the investment of capital presumably is not the cause of a net loss. Under the interest-on-capital-accounts plan of sharing earnings, the partner who invested more capital receives credit for this factor and is charged with a lesser share of the net loss, or may even end up with a net credit.

We have considered interest allowances on partners' capital accounts as a technique for sharing partnership earnings equitably but as having no effect on the determination of the net income or loss of the partnership. Interest on partners' capital accounts **is not an expense of the partnership,** but interest on loans from partners is regarded as expense and a factor in the determination of net income or loss. Similarly, interest earned on loans to partners represents an element of revenue. This treatment is consistent with the point made earlier that loans to and from partners are assets and liabilities of the partnership.

Another item of expense arising from dealings between a partnership and one of its partners is commonly encountered when the partnership leases property from a lessor who is also a partner. Rent expense and a liability for rent are recognized in such situations. The lessor, although a partner, also is a creditor of the partnership.

Salary Allowances with Remaining Net Income or Loss Divided in Specified Ratio In discussing salaries to partners, we must distinguish between salaries and drawings. Because the term *salaries* suggests weekly or monthly cash payments for personal services, accountants should be quite specific in suggesting and defining the terminology used in accounting for a partnership. We have used the term *drawings* in only one sense: a withdrawal of assets that reduces the partner's equity but plays no part in the division of net income. We shall limit the word *salaries* in partnership accounting to mean *a device for sharing net income.* When the term *salaries* is used with this meaning, the division of net income is the same, regardless of whether salaries have been paid.

A partnership contract that permits partners to make regular withdrawals of specific amounts should state whether such withdrawals are intended to be a factor in the division of net income or loss. Assume, for example, that the contract states that Partner A may make drawings of $300 monthly and Partner B $800. If the intent is not clearly stated to include or exclude these drawings as an element in the division of net income, controversy is probable, because one interpretation will favor Partner A and the opposing interpretation will favor Partner B.

Assuming that Partner A has more experience and ability than Partner B and also devotes more time to the partnership, it seems reasonable that the partners will want to recognize the more valuable contribution of personal services by A in choosing a plan for division of net income or loss. One approach to this objective would be to adopt an unequal ratio: for example, 70% of net income or loss to A and 30% to B. However, the use of such a ratio usually is not a satisfactory solution, for the same two reasons mentioned in criticizing the capital ratio as a profit-sharing plan. A ratio based only on personal services may not reflect the fact that other factors apart from personal services of partners are important in determining the profitability of the partnership. A second significant point is that if the partnership sustains a net loss, the partner rendering the most personal services will absorb a larger portion of the net loss.

A simple solution to the problem of recognizing unequal personal services by partners is to provide in the partnership contract for varying salary allowances to partners, with the remaining net income or loss divided equally or in some other ratio. Let us apply this reasoning to our continuing illustration for the A & B Partnership, and assume that the partnership contract provides for an annual salary of $10,000 to A and $6,000 to B, with any remaining net income or loss to be divided equally. The salaries are not actually paid during the year. The net income of $30,000 for Year 1 is divided as follows:

Division of net income with salary allowances

	A	B	Combined
Salaries	$10,000	$ 6,000	$16,000
Balance ($30,000 − $16,000) divided equally .	7,000	7,000	14,000
Totals	$17,000	$13,000	$30,000

If partners choose to take their monthly salaries in cash, these payments should be debited to the partners' drawing accounts.

Bonus to Managing Partner Based on Income A partnership contract may provide for a bonus to the managing partner equal to a given percentage of income. The contract should state whether the basis of the bonus is income before deduction of the bonus or income after the bonus. For example, assume that the A & B Partnership provides for a bonus to Partner A of 25% of income *before* deduction of the bonus, and that the remaining income is divided equally. As in the preceding examples, the income before the bonus is assumed to be $30,000. After the bonus of $7,500 to A, the remaining $22,500 of income is divided $11,250 to A and $11,250 to B. Thus, A's share of income is $18,750 and B's share is $11,250.

If the partnership contract provided for a bonus of 25% of income *after* the bonus to Partner A, the bonus is computed as follows:

Bonus based on income after bonus

Bonus + income after bonus = $30,000
>   **Let X = income after bonus**
>   **$0.25X$ = bonus**
> **Then $1.25X$ = $30,000 income before bonus**
>   **X = $30,000 ÷ 1.25**
>   **X = $24,000**
>   **$0.25X$ = $6,000 bonus to Partner A[1]**

Thus, the net income of $30,000 in this case is divided $18,000 to A and $12,000 to B.

[1] An alternative computation consists of converting the bonus percentage to a fraction. The bonus then can be computed by adding the numerator to the denominator and applying the resulting fraction to the income before the bonus. In the preceding example, 25% is converted to $\frac{1}{4}$, and by adding the numerator to the denominator, the $\frac{1}{4}$ becomes $\frac{1}{5}$ (4 + 1 = 5). One-fifth of $30,000 equals $6,000.

The concept of a bonus is not applicable to a net loss. When a partnership operates at a loss, the bonus provision is ignored. The partnership contract also may specify that extraordinary items or other unusual gains and losses are to be excluded from the basis for the computation of the bonus.

Salaries to Partners with Interest on Capital Accounts Many partnerships divide net income or loss by allowing salaries to partners and also interest on their capital account balances. Any remaining net income or loss is divided equally or in some other ratio. Such plans have the merit of recognizing that the value of personal services rendered by different partners may vary, and that differences in amounts invested also warrant recognition in an equitable plan for sharing net income or loss. The procedures for carrying out this type of plan are the same as those illustrated in earlier sections.

Financial statements for a partnership

Income Statement Explanations of the division of net income between partners may be included in the income statement or in a note to the financial statements. This information is sometimes referred to as the *distribution section* of the income statement. The following illustration for the A & B Partnership shows, in a highly condensed income statement for the year ended December 31, Year 1, the division of net income equally after a bonus to Partner A of 25% of income after the bonus:

A & B PARTNERSHIP
Income Statement
For Year Ended December 31, Year 1

Sales	$300,000
Cost of goods sold	180,000
Gross profit on sales	$120,000
Operating expenses	90,000
Net income	$ 30,000
Distribution of net income:	
Partner A (including bonus of $6,000)	$18,000
Partner B	12,000
Total	$30,000

If salaries paid to partners are included in operating expenses, the amount of such salaries should be disclosed. Internal reports used to appraise the performance of profit centers may call for different accounting concepts and classifications from those generally used for the financial statements prepared for outsiders. To develop meaningful cost data for internal use, accountants may treat partners' salaries as expenses rather than as a device for dividing net income. This approach is particularly appropriate if one profit center (for example, a branch) has a partner as active manager and another profit center is managed by a salaried employee.

Statement of Partners' Capital Partners generally want a complete explanation of the changes in their capital accounts each year. To meet this need, a *statement of partners' capital* generally is prepared. The following illustrative statement of partners' capital for the A & B Partnership is based on the capital accounts presented on page 10, and uses the division of net income for Year 1 illustrated in the income statement on page 17.

A & B PARTNERSHIP
Statement of Partners' Capital
For Year Ended December 31, Year 1

	A	B	Combined
Partners' capital, beginning of year	$40,000	$80,000	$120,000
Additional investment (or withdrawal) of capital	10,000	(5,000)	5,000
Balances before net income and drawings	$50,000	$75,000	$125,000
Add: Net income	18,000	12,000	30,000
Subtotal	$68,000	$87,000	$155,000
Less: Drawings	6,000	6,000	12,000
Partners' capital, end of year	$62,000	$81,000	$143,000

Partners' capital is reported as owners' equity in the balance sheet of the partnership, as illustrated on page 19.

Balance Sheet A condensed balance sheet for the A & B Partnership on December 31, Year 1, is presented on page 19.

Adjustment of net income of prior years

Any business enterprise, whether it be organized as a single proprietorship, partnership, or corporation, will from time to time discover errors made in the measurement of net income in prior accounting periods. Examples include errors in the computation of depreciation, errors in inventory valuation, and omission of accruals of revenue and expenses. When such errors come to light, the question arises as to whether the corrections should be treated as part of the determination of net income for the current period or as *prior period adjustments* and entered directly to partners' capital accounts.

A & B PARTNERSHIP
Balance Sheet
December 31, Year 1

Assets		Liabilities & Partners' Capital		
Current assets	$ 45,000	Current liabilities		$ 20,000
Other assets	155,000	Long-term debt		37,000
		Total liabilities		$ 57,000
		Partners' capital:		
		Partner A	$62,000	
		Partner B	81,000	143,000
		Total liabilities &		
Total assets	$200,000	partners' capital		$200,000

The correction of prior years' net income becomes particularly important when the profit-sharing plan has been changed. For example, assume that in Year 1 the net income for A & B Partnership was $30,000 and that the partners shared the net income equally, but in Year 2 they changed the income-sharing ratio to 60% for A and 40% for B. During Year 2, it was discovered that the inventories at the end of Year 1 were overstated by $10,000 because of clerical errors. The $10,000 reduction in the net income for Year 1 should be divided $5,000 to each partner, in accordance with the income-sharing ratio in effect for Year 1, the *year in which the error occurred.*

Somewhat related to the correction of errors of prior periods is the treatment of nonoperating gains and losses. When the income-sharing ratio of a partnership is changed, the partners should consider the differences that exist between the carrying amounts of assets and their current fair values. For example, assume that the A & B Partnership owns marketable securities acquired for $20,000 that have appreciated to $50,000 on the date when the income-sharing ratio is changed from 50% for each partner to 60% for A and 40% for B. If the securities were sold for $50,000 just prior to the change in the income-sharing ratio, the $30,000 gain would be divided $15,000 to A and $15,000 to B; if the securities were sold immediately after establishment of the 60:40 income-sharing ratio, the gain would be divided $18,000 to A and only $12,000 to B.

A solution sometimes suggested for such partnership problems is to revalue the assets to current fair value when the income-sharing ratio is changed or when a new partner is added or an old one retires. In most cases the revaluation of assets may be justified, but in general the continuity of historical cost valuations in a partnership is desirable, for the same reasons that support the use of the cost principle in a corporation. A secondary objection to revaluation of assets is that, with a few exceptions such as marketable securities, satisfactory evidence of current fair value is seldom available. The best solution to the problem of a change in the ratio of income sharing usually may be achieved by making appropriate adjustments among partners' capitals rather than by a restatement of carrying amounts.

When accountants act in the role of management consultants to a partnership, they should bring to the attention of the partners any significant differences between carrying amounts and current fair values of assets, and make the partners aware of the implications of a change in the income-sharing ratio.

CHANGES IN OWNERSHIP

Accounting for changes in partners

Most changes in the ownership of a partnership are accomplished without interruption of its operations. For example, when a large and well-established partnership promotes one of its employees to partner there is usually no significant change in the financial condition or the operating routines of the partnership. However, from a legal viewpoint a partnership is dissolved by the retirement or death of a partner or by the admission of a new partner.

Dissolution of a partnership also may result from the bankruptcy of the firm or of any partner, the expiration of a time period stated in the partnership contract, or the mutual agreement of the partners to end their association.[2] Thus, the term *dissolution* may be used to describe events ranging from a minor change of ownership interest not affecting operations of the partnership to a decision by the partners to terminate their business relationship.

Accountants are concerned with the economic substance of a transaction rather than with its legal form. Therefore, they must evaluate all the circumstances of the individual case to determine how a change in partners should be recorded. In the remaining pages of this chapter, we describe and illustrate the principal kinds of changes in the ownership of a partnership.

Accounting and managerial issues

Although a partnership is ended in a legal sense when a partner withdraws or a new partner is added, the partnership often continues with little outward evidence of change. In current accounting practice, a partner's interest often is viewed as a share in a continuing business enterprise that may be transferred, much as shares of capital stock are transferred between stockholders, without disturbing the continuity of

---

[2] The *dissolution* of a partnership is defined by the Uniform Partnership Act as "the change in the relation of the partners caused by any partner ceasing to be associated in the carrying on as distinguished from the winding up of the business."

the enterprise. For example, if a partner of a CPA firm wishes to retire or a new partner enters the firm, the contract for the change in ownership should be planned carefully to avoid disturbing client relationships. In a large CPA firm with hundreds of partners, the decision to promote an employee to the rank of partner often may be made by a committee rather than by action of all partners.

Changes in the ownership of a partnership raise a number of accounting and managerial issues on which the professional accountant can serve as consultant. Among these issues are the setting of terms for admission of a new partner, the possible revaluation of assets, the development of a new plan for the division of net income or loss, and the determination of the amount to be paid to a retiring partner.

Admission of a new partner

When a new partner is admitted to a firm of perhaps two or three partners, it is particularly appropriate to consider the fairness and adequacy of past accounting policies and the need for correction of errors in prior years' accounting data. The terms of admission of a new partner often are influenced by the level and trend of past earnings, because they may be indicative of future earnings. Sometimes specific accounting policies, such as the use of the completed-contract method of accounting for long-term construction contracts, may cause the accounting records to convey a misleading impression of earnings in the years preceding the admission of a new partner.

Adjustments of the accounting records may be necessary to restate the carrying amounts of assets and liabilities to current fair values before a new partner is admitted.

As an alternative to revaluation of the assets, it may be preferable to evaluate any discrepancies between the carrying amounts and current fair values of assets and adjust the terms for admission of the new partner. In other words, the amounts invested by the incoming partner can be set at a level that reflects the current fair value of the partnership, even though the carrying amounts of assets remain unchanged in the accounting records. If assets have appreciated in value but such appreciation is ignored, the disposal of the assets after admission of a new partner will cause the new partner to share in net income that accrued before the new partner joined the firm.

The admission of a new partner to a partnership may be effected by an *acquisition* of all or part of the interest of one or more of the existing partners, or by an *investment* of assets by the new partner, with a resultant increase in the net assets of the partnership.

Acquisition of an interest by direct payment to one or more partners

If a new partner acquires an interest from one or more of the existing partners, the transaction is recorded by opening a capital account for the new partner and decreasing the capital accounts of the selling partners by the same amount. No assets are received by the partnership; the transfer of assets is a private transaction between two or more partners.

As an illustration of this situation, assume that L and M share earnings equally and that each has a capital account balance of $60,000. Partner N (with the consent of M) acquires one-half of L's interest in the partnership. The journal entry to record this change in ownership follows:

N acquires one-half of L's interest in partnership

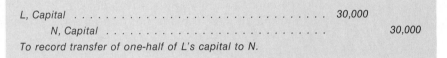

L, Capital	30,000	
N, Capital		30,000
To record transfer of one-half of L's capital to N.		

The price paid by N for half of L's interest may have been the carrying amount of $30,000 or it may have been more or less than the carrying amount. Possibly no price was established; L may have made a gift to N of the equity in the partnership, or perhaps N won it in a poker game. Regardless of the terms of the transaction between L and N, the journal entry illustrated above is all that is required in the partnership's accounting records. No change has occurred in the assets, liabilities, or total partners' capital of the partnership.

To explore further some of the implications involved in the acquisition of an interest by an incoming partner, assume that N paid $40,000 to L for one-half of L's $60,000 equity in the partnership. Some accountants have suggested that the willingness of the new partner to pay $10,000 in excess of carrying amount for a one-fourth interest in the total capital of the partnership indicates that the total capital is worth $40,000 ($10,000 ÷ 0.25 = $40,000) more than is shown in the accounting records. They reason that the assets should be written up by $40,000, or goodwill of $40,000 should be recorded with offsetting credits of $20,000 each to the capital accounts of the existing partners, L and M. However, most accountants take the position that the payment by N to L is a personal transaction between them and that the partnership, which has neither received nor distributed any assets, should make no journal entry, other than to transfer one-half of L's capital to N.

What are the arguments for these two opposing views? Those who advocate a write-up of assets stress the legal concept of dissolution of the former partnership and formation of a new partnership. This change in identity of owners, it is argued, justifies departure from the going-concern principle and the revaluation of assets to current fair values to achieve an accurate measurement of the capital invested by each member of the new partnership.

The opposing argument, that the acquisition of an interest by a new partner requires only a transfer from the capital account of the selling partner to the capital account of the new partner, is based on several points. First, the partnership did not participate in negotiating the price paid by N to L. Many factors other than the valuation of assets may have been involved in the negotiations between the two individuals. Perhaps N paid more than carrying amount because N was allowed very generous credit terms or received more than a one-fourth share in earnings. Perhaps the new partner was anxious to join the firm because of the personal abilities of L and M, or because of the anticipated growth in the particular industry. Based on these and other similar reasons, we may conclude that the price paid for a partnership interest by a new partner to an existing partner does not provide sufficient evidence to support extensive changes in the carrying amounts of the partnership's assets.

Investment in partnership by new partner

A new partner may gain admission by investing assets directly in the partnership, thus increasing the total assets and partners' capital of the partnership. For example, assume that X and Y share earnings equally and that each has a capital account balance of $60,000. Assume also that the carrying amounts of the partnership assets are approximately equal to current fair values and that Z owns a tract of land that could be used for expansion of operations. X and Y agree to admit Z to the partnership by investment of the land; earnings of the new firm are to be shared equally. The land had cost Z $50,000, but has a current fair value of $80,000. The admission of Z is recorded as follows:

New partner invests land	Land 80,000	
	Z, Capital	80,000
	To record admission of Z to partnership.	

Z has a capital account $20,000 larger than the capital accounts of X and Y. In other words, Z owns a 40% ($80,000 ÷ $200,000 = 0.40) interest in the firm. The fact that the three partners share earnings equally does not require that their capital accounts be equal.

Bonus or goodwill allowed to existing partners

In a profitable, well-established firm, the partners may insist that a portion of the investment by a new partner be allowed to them as a bonus or that goodwill be recorded and credited to the existing partners. The new partner may agree to such terms because of the benefits to be gained by becoming a member of a firm with high earning power.

Bonus to Existing Partners Assume that, in the A & B Partnership, A and B share earnings equally and have capital account balances of $45,000 each. The carrying amounts of the partnership net assets are assumed to approximate current fair values. The partners agree to admit C to a one-third interest in capital and a one-third share in earnings for an investment of $60,000. The total assets of the new firm amount to $150,000 ($45,000 + $45,000 + $60,000 = $150,000). The following journal entry gives C a one-third interest in capital, and credits the $10,000 bonus equally between A and B in accordance with their prior contract to share earnings equally:

<table>
<tr><td>Recording bonus to existing partners</td><td>Cash . . . .</td><td>60,000</td><td></td></tr>
<tr><td></td><td>A, Capital . . . .</td><td></td><td>5,000</td></tr>
<tr><td></td><td>B, Capital . . . .</td><td></td><td>5,000</td></tr>
<tr><td></td><td>C, Capital . . . .</td><td></td><td>50,000</td></tr>
</table>

To record investment by C for a one-third interest in capital, with bonus of $10,000 divided equally between A and B.

Goodwill to Existing Partners In the preceding illustration, C invested $60,000 but received a capital account of only $50,000, representing a one-third interest in the firm. C might prefer that the full amount invested, $60,000, be credited to C's capital account. This could be done while still allotting C a one-third interest if goodwill is recorded in the accounting records, with the offsetting credit divided equally between the two existing partners. If C is to be given a one-third interest represented by a capital account of $60,000, the total indicated capital of the partnership is $180,000, and the total capital of A and B must equal $120,000 ($180,000 × $\frac{2}{3}$ = $120,000). Because their present combined capital accounts amount to $90,000, a write-up of $30,000 in the net assets is recorded as follows:

<table>
<tr><td>Recording implied goodwill</td><td>Cash . . . .</td><td>60,000</td><td></td></tr>
<tr><td></td><td>Goodwill . . . .</td><td>30,000</td><td></td></tr>
<tr><td></td><td>A, Capital . . . .</td><td></td><td>15,000</td></tr>
<tr><td></td><td>B, Capital . . . .</td><td></td><td>15,000</td></tr>
<tr><td></td><td>C, Capital . . . .</td><td></td><td>60,000</td></tr>
</table>

To record investment by C for a one-third interest in capital, with goodwill of $30,000 divided equally between A and B.

Evaluation of Bonus and Goodwill Methods When a new partner invests an amount larger than the carrying amount of the interest acquired, the transaction usually should be recorded by allowing a bonus to the existing partners. The bonus method has the advantage of adhering to the cost principle and views the partnership as a continuing accounting entity. The alternative method of recording the goodwill implied by the amount invested by the new partner is not considered acceptable by the authors. Use of the goodwill method signifies the substitution of estimated current fair value of an asset rather than valuation on a cost basis. The goodwill of $30,000 recorded in the preceding example was not paid for by the partnership. Its existence is implied by the amount invested by the new partner for a one-third interest in the firm. The amount invested by the new partner may have been influenced by many factors, some of which may be personal rather than economic in nature.

Apart from the questionable theoretical basis for such recognition of goodwill, there are other practical difficulties. The presence of goodwill created in this manner is likely to evoke criticism of the partnership's financial statements, and such criticism may lead the partnership to amortize or to write off the goodwill.[3] Also, if the partnership should be liquidated, the goodwill probably would have to be written off as a loss. Will the recording of goodwill and its subsequent write-off injure one partner and benefit another? The net results to the individual partners will be the same under the bonus and goodwill methods only if two specific conditions are met: (1) the new partner's share of earnings must be equal to the percentage equity in net assets the new partner receives at the time of admission, and (2) the existing partners must continue to share earnings between themselves in the same ratio as in the original partnership. Both these conditions were met in our example; that is, the new partner received a one-third interest in the net assets and earnings, and the existing partners shared earnings equally both before and after the admission of C to the partnership.

Assume, however, that A, B, and C agreed to share earnings 40%, 40%, and 20%, respectively. The goodwill method would benefit C and injure A and B as compared with the bonus method. This is illustrated on page 26. The first of the two necessary conditions for equivalent results from the bonus method and goodwill method is no longer met. Partner C's share of earnings is not equal to C's share of assets. C is now assumed to have a 20% share of earnings, although as in the preceding example C has a one-third share of assets. The use of the goodwill method for the admission of C and the subsequent write-off of the goodwill would cause a $4,000 ($54,000 − $50,000 = $4,000) shift of capital from Partners A and B to Partner C. The preceding discussion may be summarized as follows: ***When the new partner's share of earnings exceeds the new partner's share of assets, the new partner will benefit from the use of the bonus method.***

---

[3] According to *APB Opinion No. 17,* "Intangible Assets," only purchased goodwill should be recorded in the accounting records, and it must be amortized over a period of 40 years or less.

Comparison of bonus and goodwill methods

	A	B	C	Combined
Capital balances if bonus method is used.	$50,000	$50,000	$50,000	$150,000
Capital balances if goodwill method is used.	$60,000	$60,000	$60,000	$180,000
Write-off of goodwill (40%, 40%, 20%).	(12,000)	(12,000)	(6,000)	(30,000)
Capital balances after write-off of goodwill	$48,000	$48,000	$54,000	$150,000

Fairness of Asset Valuation   In the preceding examples of bonus or goodwill allowed to the existing partners, it was assumed that the carrying amounts of assets in the accounting records of the original partnership approximated current fair values. However, if land and buildings, for example, have been owned by the partnership for many years, their carrying amounts and current fair values may be quite far apart.

To bring this problem into focus, let us assume that the net assets of the A & B Partnership, carried at $90,000, were estimated to have a current fair value of $120,000 at the time of admission of C as a partner. Our previous example called for C to receive a one-third interest for an investment of $60,000. Why not write up the assets from $90,000 to $120,000, with a corresponding increase in the capital accounts of the existing partners? Neither a bonus nor the recognition of goodwill then would be necessary to record the admission of C to a one-third interest for an investment of $60,000 because this investment is equal to one-third of the total capital of $180,000 ($120,000 + $60,000 = $180,000).

Such restatement of asset values would not be acceptable practice in a corporation simply because the market price of the corporation's capital stock had risen. If we assume the existence of certain conditions in a partnership, adherence to cost as a basis for asset valuation is as appropriate a policy as for a corporation. These specific conditions are that the income-sharing ratio should correspond to the share of equity held by each partner, and that the income-sharing ratio should continue unchanged. When these conditions do not exist, a restatement of assets from carrying amount to current fair value may be the most convenient method of achieving equity among the partners.

Bonus or goodwill allowed to new partner

An existing partnership may be anxious to admit a new partner to the firm, because the partnership needs cash or because the new partner has valuable skills and business contacts. To ensure the admission of the new partner, the present firm may offer the new partner a larger capital account balance than the amount invested by the new partner.

Bonus to New Partner Assume that F and G, who share earnings equally and have capital account balances of $35,000 each, offer H a one-third interest in assets and a one-third share of earnings for an investment of $20,000 cash. Their offer is based on a need for more cash and on the conviction that H's personal skills and business contacts will be of great value to the partnership. The investment of $20,000 by H, when added to the existing capital of $70,000, gives a total capital of $90,000, of which H is entitled to one-third, or $30,000. The excess of H's capital account balance over the amount invested represents a $10,000 bonus allowed to H by F and G. Because F and G share earnings equally, the $10,000 bonus is debited to their capital accounts in equal amounts, as shown by the following journal entry to record the admission of H to the partnership:

Recording bonus to new partner

Cash	20,000	
F, Capital	5,000	
G, Capital	5,000	
H, Capital		30,000
To record admission of H, with bonus of $10,000 from F and G.		

In outlining this method of accounting for the admission of H, we have assumed that the net assets of the partnership were valued properly. If the admission of the new partner to a one-third interest for an investment of $20,000 was based on recognition that the net assets of the partnership were worth only $40,000, consideration should be given to writing down net assets by $30,000. Such write-downs would be proper if, for example, accounts receivable included doubtful accounts or if inventories were obsolete.

Goodwill to New Partner Assume that the new partner H is the owner of a successful business enterprise that H invests in the partnership rather than making an investment in cash. Using the same data as in the preceding example, assume that F and G with capital account balances of $35,000 each give H a one-third interest in assets and earnings. The identifiable tangible and intangible net assets comprising the enterprise owned by H are worth $20,000, but, because of its superior earnings record, a current fair value for this enterprise is agreed to be $35,000. The admission of H to the partnership is recorded as shown on page 28.

The point to be stressed here is that generally goodwill is recognized as part of the investment of a new partner *only when the new partner invests a going business enterprise of superior earning power.* If H is admitted by reason of a cash investment and is credited with a capital account larger than the cash invested, the difference should be recorded as a bonus to H from the existing partners, or undervalued tangi-

New partner invests goodwill

Identifiable Tangible and Intangible Net Assets 20,000	
Goodwill 15,000	
H, Capital	35,000
To record admission of H; goodwill is assigned to business	
enterprise invested by H.	

ble assets should be written up to current fair value. Goodwill should be recorded only when substantiated by objective evidence.

Retirement of a partner

A partner retiring from a partnership usually receives cash or other assets directly from the partnership. It is also possible that a retiring partner might arrange for the sale of a partnership interest to one or more of the continuing partners or to an outsider. Because we have already considered the accounting principles applicable to the latter situation, our discussion of the retirement of a partner is limited to the situation in which the partner receives settlement from the assets of the partnership.

An assumption underlying this discussion is that the partner has a right to withdraw under the terms of the partnership contract. A partner always has the ***power*** to withdraw, as distinguished from the ***right*** to withdraw. A partner who withdraws in violation of the terms of the partnership contract, and without the consent of the other partners, may be liable for damages.

Computation of the Settlement Price   What is a fair measurement of the equity of a retiring partner? A first indication is the amount of the retiring partner's capital account balance, but this amount may need to be adjusted before it represents an equitable settlement price. Adjustments may include the correction of errors in accounting data or the recognition of differences between carrying amounts of net assets and their current fair values. Before making any adjustments, the accountant should refer to the partnership contract, which may contain specific provisions for computing the amount to be paid a retiring partner. For example, these provisions might require an appraisal of assets, an audit by certified public accountants, or a valuation of the partnership as a going concern according to a prescribed formula. If the partnership has not maintained accurate accounting records or has not been audited, it is possible that the capital account balances are misstated because of incorrect depreciation expense, failure to provide for doubtful accounts expense, and other accounting deficiencies.

If the partnership contract does not contain provisions for the computation of the retiring partner's equity, the accountant may be able to obtain authorization from the partners to follow a specific approach to determine an equitable settlement price.

In most cases, the equity of the retiring partner is computed on the basis of current fair values of partnership net assets. The gain or loss indicated by the difference between the carrying amounts of assets and their current fair values is divided in the income-sharing ratio. After the equity of the retiring partner has been computed in terms of current fair values for assets, the partners may agree to settle by payment of this amount, or they may agree on a different amount. The computation of an estimated current fair value for the partner's equity is a necessary step in reaching a settlement. An independent decision is made whether to record the current fair values and the related changes in partners' capital in the accounting records.

Payment of Bonus to Retiring Partner   The partnership contract may provide for recognition of goodwill at the time of a partner's retirement and may specify the methods for computing the goodwill. Usually the amount of the computed goodwill is allocated to the partners' capital accounts in the income-sharing ratio. For example, assume that C is to retire from the A, B & C Partnership. Each partner has a capital account balance of $60,000, and earnings are shared equally. The partnership contract states that a retiring partner is to receive the balance in the retiring partner's capital account plus a share of any goodwill. At the time of C's retirement, goodwill in the amount of $30,000 is computed to the mutual satisfaction of the partners. In the opinion of the authors, this goodwill should not be entered in the accounting records of the partnership.

Serious objections exist to recording goodwill as determined in this fashion. Because only $10,000 of the goodwill is included in the payment for C's equity, the remaining $20,000 of goodwill **has not** been paid for by the partnership. Its inclusion in the balance sheet of the partnership is not supported by either the cost principle or objective evidence. The fact that the partners "voted" for $30,000 of goodwill does not meet the need for objective evidence of asset values. As an alternative, it would be possible to record only $10,000 of goodwill and credit C's capital for the same amount, because this amount was paid for by the partnership as a condition of C's retirement. This method is perhaps more justifiable, but objective evidence that goodwill exists still is lacking. The most satisfactory method of accounting for the retirement of partner C is to treat the amount paid to C for goodwill as a $10,000 bonus. Because the settlement with C is for the balance of C's capital account of $60,000, plus estimated goodwill of $10,000, the journal entry on page 30 to record the amount paid to C is recommended.

The bonus method illustrated here is appropriate whenever the settlement with the retiring partner exceeds the carrying amount of that partner's capital. The agreement for settlement may or may not use the

Bonus paid to a retiring partner

C, Capital	60,000	
A, Capital	5,000	
B, Capital	5,000	
Cash		70,000

To record payment to retiring partner C, including a bonus of $10,000.

term *goodwill;* the essence of the matter is the determination of the amount to be paid to the retiring partner.

Settlement with Retiring Partner for Less than Carrying Amount A partner anxious to escape from an unsatisfactory business situation may accept less than his or her equity on retirement. In other cases, willingness by a retiring partner to accept a settlement below carrying amount may reflect personal problems. Another possible explanation is that the retiring partner considers the net assets of the partnership to be overvalued, or anticipates lower earnings in future years.

In brief, there are many factors that may induce a partner to accept less than the carrying amount of his or her capital account balance on withdrawal from a partnership. Because a settlement below carrying amount seldom is supported by objective evidence of overvaluation of assets, the preferred accounting treatment is to leave net asset valuations undisturbed unless a large amount of goodwill is carried in the accounting records. The difference between the retiring partner's capital account balance and the amount paid in settlement should be credited as a bonus to the continuing partners.

For example, assume that A, B, and C share earnings equally and that each has a capital account balance of $60,000. B retires from the partnership and receives $50,000. The journal entry to record B's retirement follows:

Bonus to continuing partners

B, Capital	60,000	
Cash		50,000
A, Capital		5,000
C, Capital		5,000

To record retirement of partner B for an amount less than carrying amount of B's equity.

The final settlement with a retiring partner often is deferred for some time after the partner's withdrawal to permit the accumulation of cash, the determination of net income to date of withdrawal, the obtaining of bank loans, or other steps needed to complete the transaction. The retirement of a partner does not terminate the retiring partner's personal responsibility for partnership debts existing on the date of retirement.

Death of a Partner A partnership contract often provides that partners shall acquire life insurance policies on each others' lives so that funds will be available for settlement with the estate of a deceased partner. A **buy-sell agreement** may be formed by the partners, whereby the partners commit their estates to sell their equities in the partnership and the surviving partners to acquire such equities. Another form of such an agreement gives the surviving partners an **option to buy,** or "right of first refusal," rather than imposing an obligation to buy.

REVIEW QUESTIONS

1 In the formation of a partnership, partners often invest such assets as land, buildings, and machinery as well as cash. Should these noncash assets be recorded by the partnership at current fair value, at cost to the partners, or at some other amount? Give reasons for your answer.

2 Some CPA firms have thousands of staff members, and hundreds of partners, and operate on a national or international basis. Would the corporate form of organization be more appropriate than the partnership form for such large organizations? Explain.

3 Explain the proper presentation in the balance sheet of loans to and from partners, and the accounting treatment of interest on such loans.

4 Explain how partners' salaries should be shown in the income statement of a partnership, if at all.

5 List at least five items that should be included in a partnership contract.

6 List at least five methods by which earnings may be divided among partners.

 *7* Ainsley & Burton admitted Paul Craig to a one-third interest in the firm for his investment of $50,000. Does this offer mean that Craig would be entitled to one-third of the partnership earnings?

8 Duncan and Eastwick are negotiating a partnership contract, with Duncan investing $60,000 and Eastwick $20,000. Duncan suggests that interest be allowed on average capital account balances at 8% and that any remaining earnings be divided in the ratio of average capital account balances. Eastwick prefers that the entire earnings be divided in the ratio of average capital account balances. Comment on these proposals.

9 The partnership contract of Peel and Quay is very brief on the subject of sharing earnings. It states: "Earnings are to be divided 80% to Peel and 20% to Quay, and each partner is entitled to draw $2,000 a month." What difficulties do you see in implementing this contract? Illustrate possible difficulties under the assumption that the partnership had net income of $100,000 in the first year.

10 Muir and Miller operated a partnership for several years, sharing net income and losses equally. On January 1, Year 6, they agreed to revise the income-sharing ratio to 70% for Muir and 30% for Miller, because of Miller's desire for semiretirement. On March 1 the partnership received $10,000 in settlement of a disputed error on a contract completed in Year 5. Because the outcome of the dispute had been considered highly uncertain, no receivable had been recognized. Explain the accounting treatment you would recommend for the $10,000 cash receipt.

11 Should the carrying amounts of partnership assets be restated to correspond with current fair values whenever a partner withdraws or a new partner is admitted to the firm? Explain fully and give specific examples.

12 A new partner admitted to an established firm often is required to invest an amount of cash larger than the carrying amount of the interest in net assets the new partner acquires. In what ways may such a transaction be recorded? What is the principal argument for each method?

13 Bono, Claire, and Drummond have operated a partnership for many years and have shared net income and losses equally. The partners now agree that Gray, a key employee of the firm who is an able manager but has limited financial resources, should become a partner with a one-sixth interest in capital. It is further agreed that the four partners will share net income and losses equally in the future. Bono suggests that the net assets in the accounting records of the partnership should be restated to current fair values at the time Gray is admitted, but Claire and Drummond advocate that the accounting records be left undisturbed. What is the argument for restating net assets at the time of Gray's admission? What alternative, if any, would you suggest for such restatement of net assets?

14 The partnership of Ed Loeser, Peter Wylie, and Herman Martin has operated successfully for many years, but Martin now plans to retire. In discussions of the settlement to be made with Martin, the point was made that inventories had been valued on a lifo basis for many years. Martin suggested that the current replacement cost of the inventories be determined and the excess of this amount over the carrying amount be regarded as a gain to be shared equally. Loeser objected to this suggestion on grounds that any method of inventory valuation would give reasonably accurate results provided it were followed consistently and that a departure from the long-established method of inventory valuation used by the partnership would produce an erroneous earnings picture over the life of the partnership. Evaluate the objections raised by Loeser.

15 George Lewis and Anna Marlin are partners who share net income and losses equally. They offer to admit Betty Naylor to a one-third interest in assets and in earnings for an investment of $50,000 cash. The total capital of the partnership prior to Naylor's admission was $110,000. Naylor makes a counteroffer of $40,000, explaining that her investigation of the partnership indicates that many receivables are past due and that a significant amount of obsolescence exists in the inventories. Lewis and Marlin deny both these points. They contend that inventories are valued in accordance with generally accepted accounting principles and that the receivables are fully collectible. However, after prolonged negotiation, the admission price of $40,000 proposed by Naylor is agreed upon. Explain two ways in which the admission of Naylor could be recorded and indicate which method is preferable. Comment on the possibility of recording goodwill.

16 Two partners invested $200 each to form a partnership for the construction of a shopping center. The partnership obtained a loan of $800,000 to finance construction, but no payment on this loan was due for two years. Each partner withdrew cash of $50,000 from the partnership from the proceeds of the loan. How should the investment of $400 and the withdrawal of $100,000 be presented in the balance sheet of the partnership?

17 An auditor was asked to give an opinion on the financial statements of a limited partnership in which a corporation is the general partner. Should the financial statements of the limited partnership and the auditor's report thereon include the financial statements of the general partner?

EXERCISES

Ex. 1-1 Select the best answer for each of the following multiple-choice questions:

1 On March 1, Year 1, Sally Smith and Diane Dale formed a partnership, each investing assets (at current fair values) as follows:

	Smith	Dale
Cash	$30,000	$ 70,000
Equipment	35,000	75,000
Building		225,000

The building is subject to a mortgage note payable of $180,000, which is to be assumed by the partnership. The partnership contract provides that Smith and Dale share net income and losses 30% and 70%, respectively. On March 1, Year 1, the balance in Dale's capital account should be:
a $190,000 **b** $205,000 **c** $214,000 **d** $270,000

2 The capital account balances of the partnership of Newton, Sharman, and Jackson on June 1, Year 1, are presented below, along with their respective income-sharing percentages:

Paul Newton (50%)	$139,200
Gene Sharman ($33\frac{1}{3}$%)	208,800
John Jackson ($16\frac{2}{3}$%)	96,000
Total	$444,000

On June 1, Year 1, Edward Sidney was admitted to the partnership when he acquired, for $132,000, a proportionate interest from Newton and Sharman in the net assets and income of the partnership. As a result of this transaction, Sidney acquired a one-fifth interest in the net assets and income of the partnership. Assuming that implied goodwill is not to be recorded, what is the combined gain realized by Newton and Sharman on the sale of a portion of their interests in the partnership to Sidney?
a $0 **b** $43,200 **c** $62,400 **d** $82,000

3 Adonis and Brutus share net income and losses in the ratio of 7:3, respectively. On November 5, Year 4, their capital account balances were as follows:

Adonis	$70,000
Brutus	60,000

Adonis and Brutus agreed to admit Cato as a partner with a one-third interest in the partnership capital and net income or losses for an investment of $50,000. The new partnership will begin with total capital of $180,000. Immediately after Cato's admission to the partnership, what are the capital account balances of Adonis, Brutus, and Cato, respectively?

a $60,000, $60,000, $60,000
b $63,000, $57,000, $60,000
c $63,333, $56,667, $60,000
d $70,000, $60,000, $50,000

Questions *4* and *5* are based on the following information:

Presented below is the condensed balance sheet of the partnership of Kane, Clark, and Lane, who share income and losses in the ratio of 6:3:1, respectively:

Assets

Cash	$ 85,000
Other assets	415,000
Total assets	$500,000

Liabilities & Partners' Capital

Liabilities	$ 80,000
Kane, capital	252,000
Clark, capital	126,000
Lane, capital	42,000
Total liabilities & partners' capital	$500,000

4 The assets and liabilities in the above balance sheet are fairly valued, and the partnership wishes to admit Bayer with a 25% interest in the capital and income without recording goodwill or bonus. How much should Bayer invest in cash or other assets?

a $70,000   *b* $105,000   *c* $125,000   *d* $140,000

5 Assume that the partners agree instead to sell Bayer 20% of their respective interests in capital and income for a total payment of $90,000. The payment by Bayer is to be made directly to the individual partners. The partners agree that implied goodwill is to be recorded prior to the acquisition by Bayer. What are the capital account balances of Kane, Clark, and Lane, respectively, after the acquisition by Bayer?

a $198,000, $99,000, $33,000
b $201,600, $100,800, $33,600
c $216,000, $108,000, $36,000
d $255,600, $127,800, $42,600

Ex. 1-2   Monte Whipple, a partner in the Deep Venture Partnership, has a 30% participation in net income or losses. Whipple's capital account had a net decrease of $60,000 during Year 4. During Year 4, Whipple withdrew $130,000 (debited to his capital account) and invested assets with a current fair value of $25,000.

Compute the net income of the Deep Venture Partnership for Year 4.

Ex. 1-3   The partnership contract of the Dunin, Lum & Beers Partnership provided that Dunin as managing partner should receive a bonus equal to 20% of earnings and that the remaining earnings should be divided 40% each to Dunin and Lum and 20% to Beers. Earnings for the first year (before the bonus) amounted to $63,600.

Explain two alternative ways in which the bonus provision could be interpreted. Compute the division of the year's earnings under each alternative.

Ex. 1-4   Emma Neal and Sally Drew are partners sharing net income or losses equally; each has a capital account balance of $100,000. Drew (with the consent of Neal) sold one-fifth of her interest to her daughter Paula for $25,000, with payment to be made in five annual installments without any interest charge.

Prepare a journal entry to record the change in ownership, and explain why you would or would not recommend a change in the valuation of net assets in the accounting records of the partnership.

Ex. 1-5 L and M are partners with capital account balances of $70,000 each who share net income or losses equally. The partners agree to admit N to a one-third interest in net assets and a one-third share in net income or losses for N's investment of $100,000 in the firm. Assume that the net assets are fairly valued and that N's admission is recorded by allowing a bonus to L and M.

Prepare a journal entry to record the admission of N to the partnership.

Ex. 1-6 Assume that A and B share earnings and losses in a 60:40 ratio. Their capital account balances are A, $60,000 and B, $40,000. They agree to admit C to a 30% interest in net assets and a 20% interest in earnings for C's investment of $51,000. The new income-sharing ratio is to be 48:32:20 for A, B, and C, respectively. The partners are discussing whether to record the admission of C by a bonus to A and B or by recording goodwill.

What would be the amount of the bonus to A and B, respectively? What would be the total goodwill implied by C's investment? Would the goodwill method be more advantageous to C if the goodwill were written off in full two years later? What would be the dollar amount of the advantage or disadvantage to C from use of the goodwill method?

Ex. 1-7 The partnership of Timish and Hamilton was formed on March 1. The current fair values of the assets invested by each partner are as follows:

	Timish	Hamilton
Cash	$ 25,000	$35,000
Inventories		55,000
Land		25,000
Building		75,000
Equipment	115,000	

The building is subject to a mortgage loan of $30,000, which is to be assumed by the partnership. The partnership contract provides that Timish and Hamilton share net income and losses 40% and 60%, respectively.

a Compute the balance of Hamilton's capital account on March 1, assuming that each partner is credited for the full amount of net assets invested.

b If the partnership contract provides that the partners initially should have an equal interest in partnership capital with no recognition of intangible assets, what would be the balance in Timish's capital account on March 1?

Ex. 1-8 Lewis and Mason have capital account balances at the beginning of the year of $40,000 and $45,000, respectively. They share net income and losses as follows: (1) 8% interest on beginning capital balances, (2) salary allowance of $15,000 to Lewis and $7,500 to Mason, and (3) remainder in 3:2 ratio. The partnership reported net income of $10,000 for the current year, before interest and salary allowances to partners.

a Show how the net income of $10,000 should be divided between Lewis and Mason.

b Assuming that Lewis and Mason simply agree to share earnings in a 3:2 ratio with a minimum of $15,000 guaranteed to Mason, show how the net income of $10,000 should be divided between Lewis and Mason.

Ex. 1-9 Activity in the capital accounts for Hare and Ida for Year 10 follows:

	Hare	Ida
Balances, Jan. 1	$20,000	$40,000
Investment, July 1	10,000	
Withdrawal, Oct. 1		20,000

Net income for the year amounted to $24,000 before interest or salary allowances.

Determine the division of the net income under each of the following assumptions:

a The partnership contract is silent as to sharing of net income and losses.

b Net income and losses are divided on the basis of average capital account balances (not including the net income or loss for the current year).

c Net income and losses are divided on the basis of beginning capital account balances.

d Net income and losses are divided on the basis of ending capital account balances (not including the net income for the current year).

Ex. 1-10 Floyd Austin and Samuel Bradford are partners who share net income and losses equally and have equal capital account balances. The net assets of the partnership have a carrying amount of $40,000. Jason Crade is admitted to the partnership with a one-third interest in earnings and net assets. To acquire this interest, Crade invests $17,000 cash in the partnership.

Prepare journal entries to show two methods of recording the admission of Crade in the accounting records of the partnership. State the conditions (if any) under which each method would be appropriate.

Ex. 1-11 A and B have capital account balances of $15,000 and $10,000, respectively. They share net income and losses in a 3 : 1 ratio. What journal entries would be made to record the admission of C to the partnership under each of the following conditions?

a C invests $15,000 for a one-fourth interest in net assets; the total partnership capital after C's admission is to be $40,000.

b C invests $15,000, of which $5,000 is considered a bonus to A and B. In conjunction with the admission of C, the carrying amount of the inventories is increased by $8,000. C's capital account is recorded at $10,000.

Ex. 1-12 Paul and Quinn formed a partnership on January 2, Year 4, and agreed to share net income and losses 90% and 10%, respectively. Paul invested cash of $25,000. Quinn invested no assets but had a specialized expertise and managed the firm full time. There were no withdrawals during the year. The partnership contract provided for the following:

(1) Partners' capital accounts are to be credited annually with interest at 5% of beginning capital account balances.

(2) Quinn is to be paid a salary of $1,000 a month.

(3) Quinn is to receive a bonus of 20% of income before deduction of salary, bonus, and interest on partners' capital account balances.

(4) Bonus, interest, and Quinn's salary are to be considered expenses.

The Year 4 income statement for the partnership includes the following:

Revenue	$96,450
Expenses (including salary, interest, and bonus to Quinn)	49,700
Net income	$46,750

Compute Quinn's bonus for Year 4.

Ex. 1-13 On June 30, Year 2, the balance sheet for the partnership of Tanabe, Usui, and Seashore and their respective income-sharing percentages were as follows:

Assets

Current assets	$185,000
Plant assets (net)	200,000
Total assets	$385,000

Liabilities & Partners' Capital

Accounts payable	$ 85,000
Tanabe, loan	15,000
Tanabe, capital (20%)	70,000
Usui, capital (20%)	65,000
Seashore, capital (60%)	150,000
Total liabilities & partners' capital	$385,000

Tanabe decided to retire from the partnership, and by mutual agreement the plant assets were adjusted to their current fair value of $260,000. The partnership paid $92,000 cash for Tanabe's equity in the partnership, exclusive of the loan, which was repaid in full. No goodwill was recorded in this transaction.

Prepare journal entries to record the adjustment of assets to current fair value and Tanabe's retirement from the partnership.

Ex. 1-14 The accountant for the Fox, Gee & Hay Partnership prepared the following journal entries during the year ended August 31, Year 10:

Year 9

Sept. 1

Cash	50,000	
Goodwill	150,000	
Fox, Capital ($150,000 × 0.25)		37,500
Gee, Capital ($150,000 × 0.75)		112,500
Hay, Capital		50,000

To record admission of Hay for a 20% interest in net assets, with goodwill credited to Fox and Gee in their former income-sharing ratio. Goodwill is computed as follows:

Implied total capital, based on Hay's investment ($50,000 × 5)	$250,000
Less: Net assets prior to Hay's admission	100,000
Goodwill	$150,000

Year 10

Aug. 31

Income Summary	30,000	
Fox, Capital ($30,000 × 0.20)		6,000
Gee, Capital ($30,000 × 0.60)		18,000
Hay, Capital ($30,000 × 0.20)		6,000

To divide net income for the year in the residual income-sharing ratio of Fox, 20%; Gee, 60%; Hay, 20%. Provision in partnership contract requiring $40,000 annual salary allowance to Hay is disregarded because net income is only $30,000.

Prepare journal entries on August 31, Year 10, to correct the accounting records, which have not been closed for the year ended August 31, Year 10. Assume that Hay's admission to the partnership should have been recorded by the bonus method.

CASES

Case 1-1 When asked how the organizers of a business enterprise might choose between a partnership and a corporation in order to minimize the burden of taxation, an accounting student replied as follows:

"The choice is very simple. Organization as a partnership will result in only one income tax, that is, the tax on individual income. If the enterprise is incorporated, it must pay income taxes, and in addition the stockholders must pay income taxes when the net income of the corporation is distributed to them. Consequently, the partnership form of organization always provides a lesser burden of taxation."

Instructions Do you agree with the student? Explain.

Case 1-2 X, Y, and Z, partners who share net income and losses equally, reported operating income of $30,000 for the first year of operations. However, near the end of the year, they learned of two unfavorable developments: (a) the bankruptcy of Sasha, maker of a two-year promissory note for $20,000 payable to Partner X that had been indorsed to the partnership by Partner X at face amount as X's original investment; and (b) the appearance on the market of new competing patented devices that rendered worthless a patent transferred to the partnership by Partner Y at a value of $10,000 as part of Y's original investment.

The partnership had retained the promissory note with the expectation of discounting it when cash was needed. Quarterly interest payments had been received regularly prior to the bankruptcy of Sasha, but present prospects were for no further collections of interest or principal.

Partner Z states that the $30,000 operating income should be divided $10,000 to each partner, with the $20,000 loss on the note debited to the capital account of Partner X and the $10,000 loss on the patent debited to the capital account of Partner Y.

Instructions Do you agree with Partner Z? Explain.

Case 1-3 Sally Decker and Jane Evanson have been partners for many years and have shared net income and losses equally. They own and operate a resort hotel that includes a golf course and other recreational facilities. Decker has maintained a larger capital investment than Evanson, but Evanson has devoted much more time to the management of the hotel.

The hotel is located in one of the fastest-growing areas in the country and has been expanding rapidly. To help meet the problems of expansion, the partners admit Laura Fane as a partner with a one-third interest in net assets and earnings. Fane is known as an excellent administrator and has ample cash to invest for her share in the partnership. You are retained by the partnership to give advice on any accounting issues created by the admission of Fane as a partner.

Instructions List the accounting issues that deserve consideration. Prepare a set of recommendations to guide the partners in dealing with them.

Case 1-4 Mark Granich and Mike Pickett formed a partnership on January 2. Granich invested cash of $50,000 and Pickett invested cash of $20,000 and marketable securities (short-term investments) with a current fair value of $80,000. A portion of the securities was sold at carrying amount in January to provide funds for operations.

The partnership contract stated that net income and losses were to be divided in the capital ratio and that each partner was entitled to withdraw $1,000 monthly. Granich withdrew $1,000 on the last day of each month, but Pickett made no withdrawals until July 1, when he withdrew all the securities that had not been sold by the partnership. The securities that Pickett withdrew had a current fair value of $41,000 when invested in the partnership on January 2 and a current fair value of $62,000 on July 1 when withdrawn. Pickett instructed the accountant for the partnership to record the transaction by reducing his capital account by $41,000, which was done. Income from operations for the first year amounted to $24,000. Income tax issues may be ignored.

Instructions You are asked to determine the proper division of net income for the first year. If the income-sharing provision of the partnership contract is at all unsatisfactory, state the assumptions you would make to arrive at an equitable interpretation of the partners' intentions. What adjustments, if any, do you believe should be made in the accounting records of the partnership?

PROBLEMS

1-1 The Leeds & Mayes Partnership was organized and began operations on March 1, Year 1. On that date, Leeann Leeds invested $150,000, and Marilyn Mayes invested land and building with current fair values of $80,000 and $100,000, respectively. Mayes also invested $60,000 in the partnership on November 1, Year 1, because of a shortage of working capital. The partnership contract includes the following income-sharing plan:

	Leeds	Mayes
Annual salary	$18,000	$24,000
Annual interest on average capital account balances	10%	10%
Remainder	50%	50%

The annual salary may be withdrawn by each partner in 12 monthly installments.

During the year ended February 28, Year 2, the Leeds & Mayes Partnership had net sales of $500,000, cost of goods sold of $280,000, and operating expenses of $100,000 (excluding partners' salaries and interest on partners' average capital account balances). Each partner had monthly cash drawings in accordance with the partnership contract.

Instructions

a Prepare a condensed income statement for the Leeds & Mayes Partnership for the year ended February 28, Year 2. Show the division of net income in a supporting exhibit.

b Prepare a statement of partners' capital for the Leeds & Mayes Partnership for the year ended February 28, Year 2.

1-2 Grove and Hayes share net income or losses 40% and 60%, respectively. On January 2, Year 6, Lisa Ivan was admitted to the new Grove, Hayes & Ivan Partnership by the investment of the net assets of her highly profitable single proprietorship. The partners agreed to the following current fair values of the identifiable net assets of Ivan's single proprietorship:

Current assets	$ 70,000
Plant assets	230,000
Total assets	$300,000
Less: Liabilities	200,000
Net assets	$100,000

The balance sheet of the Grove & Hayes Partnership on December 31, Year 5, follows:

GROVE & HAYES PARTNERSHIP
Condensed Balance Sheet
December 31, Year 5

Assets		Liabilities & Partners' Capital	
Current assets	$100,000	Liabilities	$300,000
Plant assets (net)	500,000	Louis Grove, capital	200,000
		Ray Hayes, capital	100,000
Total	$600,000	Total	$600,000

Ivan's capital account was credited for $120,000. The partners agreed further that the carrying amounts of the net assets of the Grove & Hayes Partnership were equal to their current fair values, and that the accounting records of the old partnership should be used for the new partnership. The following income-sharing plan was adopted for the new partnership:

(1) A bonus of 10% of net income after deduction of the bonus to Ivan as managing partner
(2) Remaining net income or loss as follows: 30% to Grove, 40% to Hayes, and 30% to Ivan

For the year ended December 31, Year 6, the Grove, Hayes & Ivan Partnership had net income of $55,000 before the bonus to Ivan.

Instructions Prepare journal entries for the Grove, Hayes & Ivan Partnership to record the following (include supporting computations in the explanations for the entries):
a The admission of Ivan to the partnership on January 2, Year 6.
b The division of net income for the year ended December 31, Year 6.

1-3 Donald and Erika formed a partnership at the beginning of Year 1. Their capital accounts show the following changes during Year 1:

	Donald	Erika
Original investment, Jan. 3, Year 1	$120,000	$180,000
Investments: May 1	15,000	
July 1		15,000
Withdrawals: Nov. 1	(30,000)	(75,000)
Capital account balances, Dec. 31, Year 1	$105,000	$120,000

The net income for Year 1, before allowances for salaries or interest, was $69,600. The net income included an extraordinary gain of $12,000.

Instructions Determine each partner's share of net income to the nearest dollar, assuming the following alternative income-sharing plans:
a The partnership contract is silent as to division of net income or loss.
b Income before extraordinary items is shared equally after allowance of 10% interest on average capital account balances (computed to the nearest month) and after allowance of $20,000 to Donald and $30,000 to Erika as salaries. Extraordinary items are shared in the ratio of original investments.
c Income before extraordinary items is shared on the basis of average capital account balances, and extraordinary items are shared on the basis of original investments.

d Income before extraordinary items is shared equally between Donald and Erika, after allowance of a 25% bonus to Erika based on income before extraordinary items after the bonus. Extraordinary items are shared on the basis of original investments.

1-4 The Alex, Baron & Crane Partnership was formed on January 2, Year 1. The original cash investments were as follows:

Alex	$ 96,000
Baron	144,000
Crane	216,000

According to the partnership contract, net income or loss is to be divided among the partners as follows:

(1) Salaries of $14,400 for Alex, $12,000 for Baron, and $13,600 for Crane
(2) Interest at 12% on the average capital account balances during the year
(3) Remainder divided equally

Net income for the year ended December 31, Year 1, was $92,080. Alex invested an additional $24,000 in the partnership on July 1; Crane withdrew $36,000 from the partnership on October 1; and Alex, Baron, and Crane withdrew $15,000 each against their shares of net income for the year.

Instructions
a Prepare a working paper to divide the net income among the partners. Show supporting computations.
b Prepare a statement of partners' capital for the year ended December 31, Year 1.

1-5 C and D wish to acquire the partnership interest of their partner E on July 10, Year 3. Partnership assets are to be used to acquire E's partnership interest. The balance sheet for the CDE Partnership on that date shows the following:

CDE PARTNERSHIP
Balance Sheet
July 10, Year 3

Assets		Liabilities & Partners' Capital	
Cash	$ 74,000	Liabilities	$ 45,000
Receivables (net)	36,000	C, capital	120,000
Equipment (net)	135,000	D, capital	60,000
Goodwill	30,000	E, capital	50,000
Total	$275,000	Total	$275,000

C, D, and E share earnings in the ratio of 3:2:1, respectively.

Instructions Records E's withdrawal under each of the following assumptions:
a E is paid $54,000, and the excess paid over the balance of E's capital account balance is recorded as a bonus to E from C and D.
b E is paid $45,000, and the difference is recorded as a bonus to C and D from E.
c E is paid $45,000, and goodwill currently in the accounting records of the partnership is reduced by the total amount implicit in the transaction.
d E accepts cash of $40,500 and equipment with a current fair value of $9,000. The equipment cost $30,000 and was 60% depreciated, with no residual value.

Record any gain or loss on the disposal of the equipment directly in the partners' capital accounts.

1-6 Linz and Ohno started a partnership in Year 1. Each partner invested $12,000 cash and was entitled to receive 50% of net income and losses. At the beginning of Year 3, Ruiz was admitted to the partnership for an investment of $14,500. Ruiz's admission to the partnership was recorded by a debit to Cash and a credit to Ruiz, Capital for $14,500. The income-sharing ratio for the new partnership was set at 3:2:1 for Linz, Ohno, and Ruiz, respectively.

Additional information is given below for each of the first four years ending on December 31:

	Year 1	Year 2	Year 3	Year 4	Total
Net income as reported	$18,000	$27,500	$36,000	$44,700	$126,200
Drawings (equal amounts for each partner)	15,000	22,000	27,000	15,600	79,600
Accounts receivable not recorded at year-end	5,000	8,000	15,000	18,000	46,000
Merchandise erroneously omitted from inventories at year-end	3,000	4,500	6,600	11,300	25,400
Accounts payable not recorded at year-end	6,000	4,000	10,000	17,500	37,500
Capital account balances at end of year:					
Linz	13,500	16,250	25,250	42,400	
Ohno	13,500	16,250	19,250	28,950	
Ruiz			11,500	13,750	

Each year the income statement was prepared on the cash basis of accounting; that is, accounts receivable were not recorded and payments for merchandise were treated as cost of goods sold. All accounts receivable are considered collectible.

Instructions

a Prepare a statement of partners' capital covering the four-year period based on the accrual basis of accounting. Combine net income and drawings for Years 1 and 2 and for Years 3 and 4. Prepare an exhibit to restate net income from the cash to the accrual basis of accounting for the first two-year period (Years 1 and 2) and for the second two-year period (Years 3 and 4).

b Prepare a balance sheet for the partnership on December 31, Year 4. Prepare an exhibit to compute cash (assuming that the only assets and liabilities are cash, accounts receivable, inventories, and accounts payable).

c Using the information given in the problem and the partners' capital account balances on December 31, Year 4, determined in part **a**, prepare a journal entry to restate the accounting records of the partnership from the cash basis of accounting to the accrual basis of accounting.

1-7 Allen, Bates, and Cray share net income and losses in a 3:2:1 ratio, respectively. The partnership has been successful, as indicated by the data (at the top of page 43) concerning the partners' capital accounts.

At this time, Cray became ill and retired from the partnership, receiving $30,000 cash. Allen and Bates decided to continue the partnership and to share net income and losses equally. However, as a condition of this change in the income-sharing ratio, Bates agreed to invest an additional $12,000 cash in the firm. The investment was made, but the partners had difficulty in agreeing on the

	Original investments	Retained earnings	Present balances
Allen, capital	$38,000	$42,000	$ 80,000
Bates, capital	21,300	28,000	49,300
Cray, capital	11,500	12,500	24,000
Totals	$70,800	$82,500	$153,300

method to be used in recording Cray's withdrawal from the firm. Allen wanted to record the entire amount of goodwill of the partnership implied by the amount paid for Cray's interest. Bates argued that the amount of goodwill to be recorded should not be larger than the amount paid for Cray's share of the partnership goodwill. The accountant for the firm pointed out that the income-sharing ratio was being changed and suggested that this was a reason for recognizing the goodwill of the partnership prior to Cray's withdrawal. Cray suggested that the entire controversy over goodwill could be avoided by recording any amount paid to a withdrawing partner in excess of that partner's capital account balance as a bonus from the other partners.

Instructions

a Prepare journal entries in the accounting records of the partnership required by the recommendation of each of the three partners (three independent sets of journal entries).

b Assume that the partnership is sold to Western Company for $171,300 cash shortly after the withdrawal of Cray, with Western assuming the partnership liabilities. Prepare analyses showing how the cash would be divided between Allen and Bates under each of the three alternative methods for handling the withdrawal of Cray as previously described.

c For this portion of the problem, assume the same data as to original investments and retained earnings by Allen, Bates, and Cray. However, rather than having Cray withdraw from the partnership, assume that the three partners agree to admit Dale as a fourth partner for an investment of $45,100 cash in the firm. Dale is given a 25% interest in the net assets and a 25% share in net income and losses. Allen, Bates, and Cray will share the remaining 75% of net income and losses in the same original ratio existing among them prior to admission of Dale to the firm. Allen, Bates, and Cray each withdraw $10,000 cash from the partnership. Prepare the journal entries needed to record the withdrawals of cash and the admission of Dale to the partnership under (1) the goodwill method, and (2) the bonus method.

d Assume the same facts presented in *c* above, and further that the partnership net assets are sold for $176,400 shortly after the admission of Dale to the firm. The purchaser assumes the partnership liabilities. Prepare an analysis showing how the cash would be distributed among the four partners if the admission of Dale had been recorded by use of (1) the goodwill method, and (2) the bonus method.

1-8 A paint store operated as a partnership by D, E, and F was completely destroyed by fire on December 31, Year 12. The only assets remaining were the bank account with a balance of $26,765 and a claim against an insurance company that was settled for $220,000 early in Year 13. All accounting records were destroyed in the fire. All creditors of the partnership have presented their claims, which amounted in total to $32,000 on December 31, Year 12.

The present partnership was formed on January 2, Year 11. Prior to that time D and E had been partners for several years and had shared net income and losses equally. No written partnership contract was prepared for the new firm, and a dispute has arisen as to the terms of the partners' oral contract for sharing net income and losses. The new firm has not used the services of certified public accountants, except for assistance with the information return required for income tax purposes on December 31, Year 11.

You are retained by the partnership to determine the income-sharing plan that was followed for Year 11 and to apply this same plan to the events of Year 12, thus determining the present equity of each partner in the partnership. The partners agree in writing that the income-sharing plan used in Year 11 was correct and should be applied in an identical manner to the net income or loss for Year 12. The information available to you consists of a copy of the information tax return of the partnership for Year 11, and a statement of the withdrawals made by the partners during Year 12. This latter statement has been agreed to in writing by the partners and appears as follows:

	D	E	F	Combined
Merchandise	$ 1,500	$850	$2,300	$ 4,650
Salaries	8,000		6,000	14,000
Other cash withdrawals	750			750
Total withdrawals	$10,250	$850	$8,300	$19,400

Partner D explained to you that the $750 in "other cash withdrawals" resulted from the partnership's accidental payment of a personal debt of D when the invoice was sent to the partnership address.

From the partnership information tax return for Year 11, you obtain the following information:

	D	E	F	Combined
Capital balances, Jan. 1, Year 11	$40,000	$50,000	$92,500	$182,500
Capital balances, Dec. 31, Year 11	$51,000	$61,000	$85,300	$197,300
Division of net income for Year 11:				
Salaries	$12,000	$15,000	$ 6,000	$ 33,000
Interest on capital balances .	2,000	2,500	4,625	9,125
Remainder (15:30:55 ratio) .	6,821	13,643	25,011	45,475
Totals	$20,821	$31,143	$35,636	$ 87,600

Instructions

a Prepare a statement of partners' capital for the D, E & F Partnership for Year 12, supported by a summary showing the computation of net income or loss for Year 12 and the division of the net income or loss among the partners in accordance with the income-sharing plan followed in Year 11. Round computations to the nearest dollar.

b How much cash will each partner receive if the D, E & F Partnership is terminated early in Year 13?

1-9 The Beran & Curb Partnership has maintained its accounting records on the accrual basis of accounting, except for the method of handling credit losses. Doubtful accounts expense has been recognized by a direct write-off to expense at the time specific accounts receivable were determined to be uncollectible.

The partners are anticipating the admission of a third member, Franco Meglio, to the firm, and they retain you to review the accounting records before this action is taken. You suggest that the firm change retroactively to the allowance method of accounting for doubtful accounts receivable so that the planning for admission of Meglio can be based on the accrual basis of accounting. The following information is available:

Year accounts receivable originated	Accounts receivable written off			Additional estimated uncollectible accounts
	Year 2	Year 3	Year 4	
1	$1,200	$ 200		
2	1,500	1,300	$ 600	$ 450
3		1,800	1,400	1,250
4			2,200	4,800
Totals . . .	$2,700	$3,300	$4,200	$6,500

The partners shared earnings equally until Year 4. In Year 4 the income-sharing plan was changed as follows: salaries of $8,000 and $6,000 to be allowed Beran and Curb, respectively; the remainder to be divided 60% to Beran and 40% to Curb. Net income of the partnership for Year 4 was $42,000.

Instructions

a Prepare a journal entry giving effect to the change in accounting method for doubtful accounts expense. Support the entry with a summary showing changes in net income for the year.

b Assume that after you prepared the journal entry in **a** above, Beran's capital is reported at $48,000 and Curb's capital is reported at $22,000. If Franco Meglio invested $30,000 for a 20% interest in net assets of the partnership and a 25% share in net income, illustrate by journal entries two methods that may be used to record Meglio's admission to the partnership. Any increase in the capital of Beran and Curb is to be divided 60% and 40%. What method would be more advantageous to Meglio if the goodwill is later substantiated through a sale of the partnership at a gain? What method would be more advantageous to Meglio if we assume that the goodwill is written off in the year following his admission to the firm?

1-10 The law firm of L, M, and N was organized on January 3, Year 1, when the three attorneys decided to combine their individual law practices. The partners reached agreement on the following matters:

(1) All partners would invest in the firm the assets and liabilities of their single proprietorships and would be credited with capital accounts equal to the carrying amounts of the net assets taken over by the partnership. The partners personally guaranteed that the accounts receivable invested were collectible. The assets and liabilities acquired by the partnership in this manner were as follows:

	L	M	N
Cash	$10,000	$10,000	$10,000
Accounts receivable	28,000	12,000	32,000
Law library and furniture	8,600	5,000	12,400
Accumulated depreciation	(4,800)	(3,000)	(9,400)
Total assets	$41,800	$24,000	$45,000
Less: Accounts payable	1,600	3,800	4,400
Net assets (capital invested)	$40,200	$20,200	$40,600

(2) The partners decided to occupy N's office space until the lease expired on June 30, Year 1. The monthly rental was $1,200, but the partners agreed that this was an excessive rate for the space provided and that $900 monthly would be reasonable. They agreed that the excess rent would be charged to N at the end of the year. When the lease expired on June 30, Year 1, the partners moved to a new office with a monthly rental of $1,000.

(3) The income-sharing agreement did not provide for salaries to the partners but specified that individual partners should receive 20% of the gross fees billed to their respective clients during the first year of the partnership. The balance of the fees after deduction of operating expenses was to be credited to the partners' capital accounts as follows: L, 40%; M, 40%; N, 20%.

A new partner, Z, was admitted to the partnership on April 1, Year 1; Z was to receive 20% of the fees from new clients after April 1 after deduction of expenses applicable to these fees. Expenses were to be apportioned to the new clients' fees in the same ratio that total expenses, other than doubtful accounts expense, bore to total gross fees.

(4) Fees were billed during Year 1 as follows:

L's clients	$ 44,000
M's clients	24,000
N's clients	22,000
New clients acquired after Jan. 3, Year 1:	
Prior to Apr. 1	6,000
After Apr. 1	24,000
Total revenue from fees	$120,000

(5) Total expenses for Year 1 were $38,700, excluding depreciation and doubtful accounts expense but including the total amount paid for rent. The partnership uses the direct write-off method for doubtful accounts expense. Depreciation was to be computed at the rate of 10% on original cost to individual partners of depreciable assets invested by them. Depreciable assets were acquired during Year 1 for $10,000, on which one-half year's depreciation was to be taken.

(6) Cash withdrawals debited to the partners' drawing accounts during Year 1 were as follows:

L	$10,400
M	8,800
N	11,600
Z	5,000
Total	$35,800

(7) Accounts receivable invested by L in the amount of $2,400 and by M in the amount of $900 proved to be uncollectible. Also, a new client billed in March for $3,000 had received a discharge in bankruptcy, in which a settlement of 40 cents on the dollar was made.

Instructions Prepare a statement of partners' capital for the year ended December 31, Year 1. Show supporting computations and disregard income taxes.

1-11 The Ebony Partnership engaged you to adjust its accounting records and convert them to the accrual basis of accounting in anticipation of the admission of Orr as a new partner. Some ledger accounts were on the accrual basis and others were on the cash basis. The accounting records were closed on December 31, Year 5, by the accountant for the partnership, who prepared the following general ledger trial balance:

EBONY PARTNERSHIP
Trial Balance
December 31, Year 5

Cash	$ 18,250	
Accounts receivable	40,000	
Inventories	26,000	
Land	79,000	
Buildings	50,000	
Accumulated depreciation of buildings		$ 2,000
Equipment	56,000	
Accumulated depreciation of equipment		8,250
Goodwill	5,000	
Accounts payable		64,000
Reserve for future inventory losses		10,000
Lui, capital		60,000
Mason, capital		80,000
Neary, capital		50,000
Totals	$274,250	$274,250

Your inquiries disclosed the following:

(1) The partnership was organized on January 2, Year 4, with no provision in the partnership contract for the sharing of net income and losses. During Year 4, net income was distributed equally among the partners. The partnership contract was amended effective January 1, Year 5, to provide for the following income-sharing ratio: Lui, 50%; Mason, 30%; and Neary, 20%. The amended partnership contract also stated that the accounting records were to be maintained on the accrual basis of accounting and that any adjustments necessary for Year 5 should be allocated according to the Year 5 distribution of earnings.

(2) The following amounts were not recorded as prepayments or accruals:

	December 31,	
	Year 5	Year 4
Unexpired insurance	$1,450	$ 650
Advances from customers	200	1,100
Accrued interest payable		300

The advances from customers were recorded as sales in the year the cash was received.

(3) In Year 5, a provision of $10,000 was recorded (by a debit to expense) for anticipated declines in inventory prices. You convinced the partners that the provision was unnecessary and should be removed from the accounting records.

(4) Equipment acquired for $4,400 on January 3, Year 5, was debited to expense. This equipment has an estimated economic life of 10 years and an estimated residual value of $400. The partnership depreciates its equipment by the declining-balance method at twice the straight-line rate.

(5) The partners agreed to establish an allowance for doubtful accounts at 2% of current accounts receivable and 5% of past-due accounts. On December 31, Year 4, the partnership had $54,000 of accounts receivable, of which only $4,000 was past due. On December 31, Year 5, 15% of accounts receivable

was past due, of which $4,000 represented sales made in Year 4, and was considered collectible. The partnership had written off uncollectible accounts receivable in the year the accounts became worthless as follows:

	Year 5	Year 4
Year 5 accounts receivable	*$ 800*	
Year 4 accounts receivable	*1,000*	*$250*

(6) Goodwill was recorded improperly in Year 5 and credited to the partners' capital accounts in the income-sharing ratio in recognition of an increase in the value of the partnership resulting from improved sales volume. The partners agreed to write off the goodwill before Orr was admitted to the partnership.

Instructions

a Prepare an adjusted trial balance for the partnership on December 31, Year 5, on the accrual basis of accounting. All adjustments affecting net income should be made directly to partners' capital accounts. Number and explain the adjustments in the working paper. Show supporting computations. (Do not prepare formal financial statements or formal journal entries. The working paper should have pairs of columns for Unadjusted Trial Balance, Adjustments, and Adjusted Trial Balance.)

b Without prejudice to your solution to part *a* above, assume that the net assets of the partnership were properly valued, that the adjusted total of the partners' capital on December 31, Year 5, was $196,000, and that Orr invested $75,000 in the partnership. Compute the amount of goodwill that might be recorded in the partnership accounting records under each of the following alternative assumptions, and allocate the goodwill to the partners:

(1) Orr is to be granted a one-fourth interest in the partnership. The other partners will retain their 50:30:20 income-sharing ratio for the remaining three-fourths interest in earnings.

(2) The partnership has been earning, and expects to continue to earn, an annual return of 22% on invested capital. The normal rate of return for comparable partnerships is 20%. The superior earnings (expected earnings of the new partnership in excess of the normal rate of return) are to be capitalized as goodwill at 25%. The partners are to share earnings (including any goodwill) in the following ratio: Lui, 40%; Mason, 30%; Neary, 10%; Orr, 20%.

2 PARTNERSHIP LIQUIDATION; JOINT VENTURES

LIQUIDATION OF A PARTNERSHIP

The meaning of liquidation

The liquidation of a partnership means winding up its activities, usually by selling assets, paying liabilities, and distributing any remaining cash to the partners. In some cases, the partnership net assets may be sold as a unit; in other cases, the assets may be sold in installments, and most or all of the cash received must be used to pay creditors. A business enterprise that has ended normal operations and is in the process of converting its assets to cash and making settlement with its creditors is said to be *in liquidation,* or in the process of being liquidated. This process of liquidation may be completed quickly, or it may require several months or even years.

The term *liquidation* also is used in a narrower sense to mean the payment of liabilities; however, in this chapter we use it only in the broader sense of bringing to a close the activities of a partnership. Another term commonly used in liquidation is *realization,* which means the conversion of assets to cash.

When the decision is made to liquidate a partnership, the accounting records should be adjusted and closed, and the net income or loss for the final period of operations entered in the capital accounts of the partners.

The liquidation process usually begins with the sale of noncash assets. The losses or gains from realization of assets should be divided among the partners in the income-sharing ratio and entered in their capital accounts. The amounts shown as their respective equities at this point are the basis for settlement. However, before any payment to partners, all outside creditors must be paid in full. If the cash obtained from the sale of assets is insufficient to pay liabilities in full, any unpaid creditor may act to enforce collection from the personal assets of any partner, regardless of whether that partner has a positive or negative capital account balance. As pointed out in Chapter 1, a partnership is viewed as an entity for many purposes such as changes in partners, but it cannot use the shield of a separate entity to protect partners personally against the claims of partnership creditors.

Division of losses and gains during liquidation

The underlying theme in accounting for the liquidation of a partnership may be stated as follows: *Distribute the loss or gain from the realization of assets before distributing the cash.* As assets are sold, any loss or gain is allocated to the partners' capital accounts in the income-sharing ratio. The income-sharing ratio used during the operation of the partnership also is applicable to the losses and gains during liquidation, unless the partners have a different agreement.

When the net loss or gain from liquidation is divided among the partners, the final balances in the partners' capital and loan accounts will be equal to the cash available for distribution to them. *Payments are then made in the amounts of the partners' respective equities in the partnership.*

Distribution of cash or other assets to partners

The amount of cash, if any, that a partner is entitled to receive in a liquidation cannot be determined until partners' capital accounts have been adjusted for any loss or gain on the realization of the assets. Strictly interpreted, this reasoning might indicate that no cash can be distributed to a partner until after all the assets have been sold, because the net loss or gain will not be known until the sale of all assets has been completed. In this chapter we illustrate a series of liquidations in which the realization of assets is completed before any payments are made to partners. Also, we consider liquidation in installments; that is, payments to partners after a portion of the assets has been sold and all liabilities paid, but with the final loss or gain from sale of the remaining assets not known. The installment payments to partners are computed by a method that provides a safeguard against overpayment.

An important service by accountants to a partnership in liquidation is to determine proper distribution of cash or other assets to individual partners after the liabilities have been paid. The partners may choose to receive certain assets, such as automobiles or furniture, *in kind* rather than to convert such property to cash. Regardless of whether cash or other assets are distributed to partners, it is imperative to follow the basic rule that no distribution of assets may be made to partners until after all possible losses and liquidation expenses have been considered. Failure to follow this basic rule may result in overpayments to one or more partners and underpayments to others. If a partner who receives the overpayment is unable to return the excess payment, the person who authorized such payments may become personally liable for any losses sustained by the other partners.

The Uniform Partnership Act lists the order for distribution of cash by a liquidating partnership as (1) payment of creditors in full, (2) payment of partners' loan accounts, and (3) payment of partners' capital accounts. The indicated priority of partners' loans over partners' capital appears to be a legal fiction. This rule is nullified for all practical purposes by an established legal doctrine called the **right of offset.** If a partner's capital account has a debit balance (or even a potential debit balance depending on possible future losses), any credit balance in that partner's loan account must be offset against the deficiency (or potential deficiency) in the capital account. However, if a partner with a loan account receives any cash, the payment is recorded by a debit to the loan account.

Because of the right of offset, the total amount of cash received by a partner during liquidation always will be the same as if loans to the partnership had been recorded in the partner's capital account. Furthermore, the existence of a partner's loan account will not advance the time of payment to any partner during the liquidation. Consequently, in the preparation of a **statement of realization and liquidation** (see page 53) the number of columns may be reduced by combining the amount of a partner's loan with the amount shown in the partner's capital account. The statement of realization and liquidation then will include only one column for each partner; the first amount in the column will be the total equity (including any loans) of the partner at the beginning of liquidation.

Combining the capital and loan accounts of a partner in the statement of realization and liquidation does not imply combining these accounts in the ledger. Separate ledger accounts for capital and for loans should be maintained to provide a clear record of the terms under which assets were invested by the partners.

Final settlement with partners

The amount that each partner receives from the liquidation of a partnership will be equal to (1) the capital invested, whether recorded in a capital account or in a loan account; (2) a share of operating net income or loss minus drawings; and (3) a share of loss or gain from the realization of assets in the course of liquidation. In other words, each partner will receive in the settlement the amount of his or her equity in the partnership. The amount of a partner's equity is increased by the positive factors of investing capital and sharing in net income; it is decreased by the negative factors of drawings and sharing in net losses. If the negative factors are larger, the partner will have a capital deficiency (a debit balance in a capital account), and the partner must pay to the partnership the amount of such deficiency. Failure to make good a capital deficiency by payment to the partnership would mean that the partner had not lived up to the partnership contract for sharing net income or loss.

This would cause the other partners to bear more than their contractual share of losses, and thus to receive less in settlement than their equities in the partnership.

Equity of each partner is sufficient to absorb loss from liquidation

Assume that A and B, who share net income and losses equally, decide to liquidate their partnership. A balance sheet on June 30, Year 5, just prior to liquidation, follows:

Balance sheet prior to liquidation

A & B PARTNERSHIP
Balance Sheet
June 30, Year 5

Assets		Liabilities & Partners' Capital	
Cash	$10,000	Liabilities	$20,000
Other assets	75,000	B, loan	20,000
		A, capital	40,000
		B, capital	5,000
Total	$85,000	Total	$85,000

As a first step in the liquidation, the noncash assets with a carrying amount of $75,000 are sold for cash of $35,000, with a resultant loss of $40,000 absorbed equally by A and B. Because B's capital account is only $5,000, it is necessary for the accountant to exercise the right of offset by transferring $15,000 from B's loan account to B's capital account. The statement of realization and liquidation on page 53, covering the period July 1–15, Year 5, shows the division of the loss between the partners, the payment of creditors, and the distribution of the remaining cash to the partners. (The income-sharing ratio appears next to each partner's name.)

In the statement of realization and liquidation, B's loan account of $20,000 and capital account of $5,000 may be combined to obtain an equity of $25,000 for B. As stated earlier, such a procedure would be appropriate because the legal priority of a partner's loan account has no significance in determining either the total amount of cash paid to a partner or the timing of cash payments to partners during liquidation.

In the preceding illustration, partner A received cash of $20,000 and partner B received $5,000. Neither partner received payment until after creditors had been paid in full. Because assets consist entirely of $25,000 cash at this point, it is reasonable to assume that checks to A and B for $20,000 and $5,000, respectively, were written and delivered to the partners at the same time. It is apparent that a partner's loan account has no special significance in the liquidation process. Therefore, in succeeding illustrations we do not show a partner's loan account in a

A & B PARTNERSHIP
Statement of Realization and Liquidation
July 1–15, Year 5

	Assets				Partners' capital	
	Cash	Other	Liabilities	B, loan	A(50%)	B(50%)
Balances before liquidation	$10,000	$75,000	$20,000	$20,000	$40,000	$ 5,000
Sale of assets at a loss of $40,000	35,000	(75,000)			(20,000)	(20,000)
Balances	$45,000		$20,000	$20,000	$20,000	$(15,000)
Payment to creditors	(20,000)		(20,000)			
Balances	$25,000			$20,000	$20,000	$(15,000)
Offset B's capital deficit against loan account				(15,000)		15,000
Balances	$25,000			$ 5,000	$20,000	$ -0-
Payments to partners	(25,000)			(5,000)	(20,000)	-0-

separate column of the statement of realization and liquidation. Whenever a partner's loan account is encountered, it may be combined with the partner's capital account balance in the statement of realization and liquidation.

Equity of one partner is not sufficient to absorb that partner's share of loss from liquidation

In this case, the loss on realization of assets when distributed in the income-sharing ratio results in a debit balance in the capital account of one of the partners. It may be assumed that the partner with a debit balance has no loan account, or that the total of the partner's capital account and loan account combined is less than the partner's share of the loss on realization. To fulfill an agreement to share a given percentage of partnership earnings, the partner must pay to the partnership sufficient cash to eliminate any capital deficiency. If the partner is unable to do so, the deficiency must be absorbed by the other partners as an additional loss to be shared in the same proportion as they have previously shared earnings among themselves. To illustrate, assume the balance sheet at the top of page 54 for the D, E & F Partnership just prior to liquidation.

The income-sharing ratio is D, 20%; E, 40%; and F, 40%. The other assets with a carrying amount of $80,000 are sold for $50,000 cash, resulting in a loss of $30,000. Partner F is charged with 40% of this loss, or $12,000, which creates a deficiency of $3,000 in F's capital account. In the statement of realization and liquidation on page 54, it is assumed that F pays the $3,000 to the partnership.

Balance sheet for
partnership to be
liquidated

D, E & F PARTNERSHIP

Balance Sheet

May 20, Year 10

Assets		Liabilities & Partners' Capital	
Cash	$ 20,000	Liabilities.	$ 30,000
Other assets	80,000	D, capital.	40,000
		E, capital	21,000
		F, capital	9,000
Total	$100,000	Total	$100,000

Illustration
of
completed
liquidation

D, E & F PARTNERSHIP

Statement of Realization and Liquidation

May 21–31, Year 10

	Assets			Partners' capital		
	Cash	Other	Liabilities	D(20%)	E(40%)	F(40%)
Balances before liquidation	$20,000	$80,000	$30,000	$40,000	$21,000	$ 9,000
Sale of assets at a loss of $30,000	50,000	(80,000)		(6,000)	(12,000)	(12,000)
Balances	$70,000		$30,000	$34,000	$ 9,000	$ (3,000)
Payment to creditors. . . .	(30,000)		(30,000)			
Balances	$40,000			$34,000	$ 9,000	$ (3,000)
Cash received from F . . .	3,000					3,000
Balances	$43,000			$34,000	$ 9,000	$ -0-
Payments to partners . . .	(43,000)			(34,000)	(9,000)	-0-

Next, let us change one condition of the preceding illustration by assuming that partner F was not able to pay the $3,000 debt to the partnership. If the cash on hand after payment of creditors is to be distributed to D and E without a delay to determine the collectibility of the $3,000 claim against F, the statement of realization and liquidation would appear as illustrated at the top of page 55.

The cash payments of $33,000 to D and $7,000 to E leave each of them with a sufficient credit balance to absorb their share of the additional loss if F is unable to pay the $3,000 debt to the partnership. The income-sharing ratio is 20% for D and 40% for E; consequently, the possible additional loss of $3,000 would be charged to them in the proportion of $2/6$ or $1,000 to D, and $4/6$ or $2,000 to E. The payment of the $40,000 cash available to partners is divided between them in a manner

Illustration of incomplete liquidation

D, E & F PARTNERSHIP
Statement of Realization and Liquidation
May 21–31, Year 10

	Assets			Partners' capital		
	Cash	Other	Liabilities	D(20%)	E(40%)	F(40%)
Balances before liquidation	$20,000	$80,000	$30,000	$40,000	$21,000	$ 9,000
Sale of assets at a loss of $30,000	50,000	(80,000)		(6,000)	(12,000)	(12,000)
Balances	$70,000		$30,000	$34,000	$ 9,000	$ (3,000)
Payment to creditors	(30,000)		(30,000)			
Balances	$40,000			$34,000	$ 9,000	$ (3,000)
Payments to partners . . .	(40,000)			(33,000)	(7,000)	
Balances				$ 1,000	$ 2,000	$ (3,000)

that reduces D's capital account balance to $1,000 and E's balance to $2,000.

If the $3,000 is later collected from F, this amount will be divided $1,000 to D and $2,000 to E. The preceding statement of realization and liquidation then may be completed as follows:

Completion of liquidation: deficiency paid by Partner F

	Cash	D(20%)	E(40%)	F(40%)
Balance from top of page		$1,000	$2,000	$(3,000)
Cash received from F	$3,000			3,000
Payments to partners	(3,000)	(1,000)	(2,000)	

However, if the $3,000 due from F is determined to be uncollectible, the statement of realization and liquidation would be completed with the write-off of F's deficit shown as an additional loss absorbed by D and E as follows:

Completion of liquidation: Partner F unable to pay deficiency

	Cash	D(20%)	E(40%)	F(40%)
Balances from top of page		$1,000	$2,000	$(3,000)
Additional loss from inability to collect deficiency from F		(1,000)	(2,000)	3,000

Equities of two partners are not sufficient to absorb their shares of loss from liquidation

We already have observed that inability of a partner to make good a deficiency in a capital account causes an additional loss to the other partners. A partner may have sufficient capital, or combination of capital and loan accounts, to absorb any direct share of loss on the realization of assets, but not a sufficient equity to absorb additional actual or potential losses caused by inability of the partnership to collect the deficiency in another partner's capital account. In brief, one capital deficiency, if not collectible, may cause a second capital deficiency that may or may not be collectible.

Assume that J, K, L, and M, partners, share net income and losses 10%, 20%, 30%, and 40%, respectively. Their capital account balances for the period August 1–15, Year 4, are as shown in the statement of realization and liquidation on page 57. The assets are realized at a loss of $80,000, and creditors are paid in full. Cash of $20,000 is available for distribution to the partners. In this distribution, the guiding principle is to pay each partner an amount equal to the excess of a partner's capital account balance over any additional possible losses that may be charged to each partner. In other words, a partner's capital account balance is reduced to an amount necessary to absorb any additional losses that may be charged against that partner because of the uncollectibility of deficiencies owed by other partners.

Exhibit 1 below, prepared in support of the statement of realization and liquidation on page 57, shows that the $20,000 of available cash can

Exhibit 1

J, K, L & M PARTNERSHIP
Computation of Cash Payments to Partners
August 15, Year 4

	Partners' capital			
	J(10%)	K(20%)	L(30%)	M(40%)
Capital account balances before distribution of cash to partners	$22,000	$16,000	$ 6,000	$(24,000)
Additional loss to J, K, and L if M's deficiency is uncollectible (ratio of 10:20:30).	(4,000)	(8,000)	(12,000)	24,000
Balances.	$18,000	$ 8,000	$ (6,000)	
Additional loss to J and K if L's deficiency is uncollectible (ratio of 10:20).	(2,000)	(4,000)	6,000	
Amounts that may be paid to partners.	$16,000	$ 4,000		

J, K, L & M PARTNERSHIP
Statement of Realization and Liquidation
August 1–15, Year 4

| | Assets | | | Partners' capital | | | |
	Cash	Other	Liabilities	J(10%)	K(20%)	L(30%)	M(40%)
Balances before liquidation	$ 20,000	$200,000	$120,000	$30,000	$32,000	$30,000	$ 8,000
Sales of assets at a loss of $80,000 . . .	120,000	(200,000)		(8,000)	(16,000)	(24,000)	(32,000)
Balances	$140,000		$120,000	$22,000	$16,000	$ 6,000	$(24,000)
Payment to creditors	(120,000)		(120,000)				
Balances	$ 20,000			$22,000	$16,000	$ 6,000	$(24,000)
Payments to partners (**Exhibit 1** on page 56). . . .	(20,000)			(16,000)	(4,000)		
Balances				$ 6,000	$12,000	$ 6,000	$(24,000)

be distributed $16,000 to J and $4,000 to K. If the $24,000 deficiency in M's capital proves uncollectible, the additional loss to be divided among the other three partners will cause L's capital account to change from a $6,000 credit balance to a $6,000 debit balance (deficiency). L, therefore, is not eligible to receive a cash payment. If this deficiency in L's capital account proves uncollectible, the balances remaining in the capital accounts of J and K, after the cash payment indicated above, will be equal to the amounts ($2,000 and $4,000, respectively) needed to absorb the additional loss shifted from L's capital account.

The statement of realization and liquidation for the period August 1–15, Year 4, illustrated on page 57.

Partnership is insolvent but partners are personally solvent

If a partnership is **insolvent,** at least one and perhaps all of the partners will have debit balances in their capital accounts. In any event, the total of the debit balances will exceed the total of the credit balances. If the partner or partners with a capital deficiency pay the required amount, the partnership will have cash to pay its liabilities in full. However, the creditors may demand payment from **any** partner individually, regardless of whether a partner's capital account shows a deficiency or a credit balance. In terms of relationships with creditors, the partnership is not a separate entity. A partner who makes payments to partnership creditors receives a credit to the capital account. As an illustration of an insolvent partnership whose partners are personally solvent (have assets in excess of liabilities) assume that N, O, and P, who share net income and losses equally, present the following balance sheet just prior to liquidation on May 10, Year 8:

N, O & P PARTNERSHIP
Balance Sheet
May 10, Year 8

Assets		Liabilities & Partners' Capital	
Cash	$ 15,000	Liabilities	$ 65,000
Other assets	85,000	N, capital	18,000
		O, capital	10,000
		P, capital	7,000
Total	$100,000	Total	$100,000

On May 12, Year 8, the other assets with a carrying amount of $85,000 are sold for $40,000 cash, which causes a loss of $45,000 to be divided equally among the partners. The total cash of $55,000 is paid to the creditors, which leaves unpaid liabilities of $10,000. Partner N has a credit balance of $3,000 after absorbing one-third of the loss. Partners O and P owe the partnership $5,000 and $8,000, respectively. Assuming that on May 30, Year 8, O and P pay in the amounts of their deficiencies, the partnership will use $10,000 of the $13,000 available cash to pay the remaining liabilities and will distribute $3,000 to N. These events are portrayed in the statement of realization and liquidation below:

N, O & P PARTNERSHIP
Statement of Realization and Liquidation
May 10–30, Year 8

	Assets		Liabilities	Partners' capital		
	Cash	Other		N($\frac{1}{3}$)	O($\frac{1}{3}$)	P($\frac{1}{3}$)
Balance before liquidation . .	$15,000	$85,000	$65,000	$18,000	$10,000	$ 7,000
Sale of assets at a loss of						
$45,000	40,000	(85,000)		(15,000)	(15,000)	(15,000)
Balances	$55,000		$65,000	$ 3,000	$ (5,000)	$ (8,000)
Partial payment to creditors .	(55,000)		(55,000)			
Balances	$ -0-		$10,000	$ 3,000	$ (5,000)	$ (8,000)
Cash received from O and P .	13,000				5,000	8,000
Balances	$13,000		$10,000	$ 3,000		
Final payment to creditors . .	(10,000)		(10,000)			
Balances	$ 3,000			$ 3,000		
Payment to N	(3,000)			(3,000)		

Assume that there was some delay in collecting the $13,000 in deficiencies from O and P, and during this period the creditors demanded and received payment of their $10,000 in claims from partner N. This payment by N would cause N's equity to increase from $3,000 to $13,000. When the $13,000 is received from O and P by the partnership, it would be paid to N.

Another alternative is that creditors might collect the final $10,000 due them directly from O or P. Payments by these partners to creditors would be credited to their capital accounts and thus would eliminate or reduce their debts to the firm. As long as we assume that the partners with deficiencies make payment to the partnership or directly to partnership creditors, the results are the same. Creditors will be paid in full and partners will share losses on liquidation as provided in the partnership contract.

Partnership is insolvent and partners are personally insolvent

In the preceding illustration of an insolvent partnership, we assumed that the partners were personally solvent and therefore able to pay their capital deficiencies. We shall now consider an insolvent partnership in which one or more of the partners are personally insolvent. This situation raises a question as to the relative rights of two groups of creditors: (1) those persons who extended credit to the partnership, and (2) those persons who extended credit to the partners as individuals. The relative rights of these two groups of creditors are governed by the provisions of the Uniform Partnership Act relating to the **marshaling of assets.** These rules provide that assets of the partnership are first available to creditors of the partnership, and that assets owned individually by the partners are first available to their personal creditors. After the debts of the partnership have been paid in full, the creditors of an individual partner have a claim against the assets (if any) of the partnership to the extent of that partner's equity in the partnership.

After the personal creditors of a partner have been paid in full from the personal assets of the partner, any remaining personal assets are available to partnership creditors, regardless of whether the partner's capital account shows a credit or a debit balance. Such claims by creditors of the partnership are permitted only when these creditors are unable to obtain payment from the partnership.

To illustrate the relative rights of creditors of an insolvent partnership and personal creditors of an insolvent partner, assume that R, S, and T, who share net income and losses equally, have the following balance sheet just prior to liquidation on November 30, Year 10:

R, S & T PARTNERSHIP
Balance Sheet
November 30, Year 10

Assets		Liabilities & Partners' Capital	
Cash	$ 10,000	Liabilities	$ 60,000
Other assets	100,000	R, capital	5,000
		S, capital	15,000
		T, capital	30,000
Total	$110,000	Total	$110,000

Assume also that on November 30, Year 10, the partners have the following personal assets and liabilities apart from the equities they have in the partnership:

List of personal assets and liabilities

Partner	Personal assets	Personal liabilities
R	$100,000	$25,000
S	50,000	50,000
T	5,000	60,000

The realization of partnership assets results in a loss of $60,000, as shown in the statement of realization and liquidation below for the period December 1–12, Year 10:

Liquidation not completed

R, S & T PARTNERSHIP
Statement of Realization and Liquidation
December 1–12, Year 10

| | Assets | | | Partners' capital | | |
	Cash	Other	Liabilities	R($\frac{1}{3}$)	S($\frac{1}{3}$)	T($\frac{1}{3}$)
Balances before liquidation	$10,000	$100,000	$60,000	$ 5,000	$15,000	$30,000
Sale of assets at a loss of $60,000	40,000	(100,000)		(20,000)	(20,000)	(20,000)
Balances	$50,000		$60,000	$(15,000)	$ (5,000)	$10,000
Payment to creditors	(50,000)		(50,000)			
Balances			$10,000	$(15,000)	$ (5,000)	$10,000

The creditors of the partnership have received all the assets of the partnership and still have unpaid claims of $10,000. They cannot collect from S or T personally because the personal assets of these two partners are just sufficient or are insufficient to meet their personal liabilities. However, the partnership creditors can collect the $10,000 in full from R, who is personally solvent. By chance, R has a capital deficiency of $15,000, but this is of no concern to creditors of the partnership, who can collect in full from any partner who has sufficient personal assets, regardless of whether that partner's capital account has a debit or a credit balance. The statement of realization and liquidation is now continued (see below) to show the payment by R personally of the final

Continuation of statement of realization and liquidation

| | | | Partners' capital | | |
	Cash	Liabilities	R($\frac{1}{3}$)	S($\frac{1}{3}$)	T($\frac{1}{3}$)
Balances carried forward . .		$10,000	$(15,000)	$(5,000)	$10,000
Payment by R to partnership creditors		(10,000)	10,000		
Balances			$ (5,000)	$(5,000)	$10,000
Additional investment by R .	$5,000		5,000		
Balances	$5,000			$(5,000)	$10,000
Payment to T (or T's creditors)	(5,000)				(5,000)
Balances				$(5,000)	$ 5,000

$10,000 due to partnership creditors. Because our assumptions about R's personal finances showed that R had $100,000 of assets and only $25,000 in liabilities, R is able to invest the additional $5,000 needed to offset the capital deficiency. This $5,000 cash is paid to partner T, the only partner with a positive capital account balance.

The continued statement of realization and liquidation now shows that S owes $5,000 to the firm; however, S's personal assets of $50,000 are exactly equal to S's personal liabilities of $50,000. Under the Uniform Partnership Act, all the personal assets of S will go to personal creditors; therefore, the $5,000 deficiency in S's capital account represents an additional loss to be shared equally by R and T. To conclude the liquidation, R, who is personally solvent, will be required to pay $2,500 to the partnership, and the amount will go to T or to T's personal creditors, because T is insolvent. These payments are shown below to complete the statement of realization and liquidation for the R, S & T Partnership:

Completion of liquidation

	Cash	Partners' capital		
		R ($\frac{1}{3}$)	S ($\frac{1}{3}$)	T ($\frac{1}{3}$)
Balances carried forward			$(5,000)	$5,000
Write off S's deficiency as uncollectible . . .		$(2,500)	5,000	(2,500)
Balances		$(2,500)		$2,500
Cash invested by R	$2,500	2,500		
Balances	$2,500			$2,500
Payment to T (or T's creditors).	(2,500)			(2,500)

The final results of the liquidation show that the partnership creditors received payment in full because of the personal financial status of partner R. Because R was personally solvent, the personal creditors of R also were paid in full. The personal creditors of S were paid in full, thereby exhausting S's personal assets; however, because S failed to make good the $5,000 capital deficiency, an additional loss of $5,000 was shifted to R and T. The personal creditors of T received all of T's personal assets of $5,000 and also $7,500 from the partnership, representing T's equity in the firm. However, T's personal creditors were able to collect only $12,500 ($5,000 + $7,500 = $12,500) on their total claims of $60,000.

INSTALLMENT PAYMENTS TO PARTNERS

In the illustrations of partnership liquidation in the preceding sections, all the assets were sold and the total loss from liquidation was divided

... e to them. However, ... over many months or ... artners usually will want t... ner than waiting until all asse... ...ment payments to partners are prop... ...e used to ensure that all creditors are pa... ...s are paid more than the amount to which they ... all losses on realization of assets have become kn...

Liquidation in ins... ..ay be regarded as a process of selling some assets, paying cre... , paying the remaining available cash to partners, selling additional assets, and making further payments to partners. The liquidation continues until all assets have been sold and all cash has been distributed to creditors and partners.

The circumstances of installment liquidation are likely to vary; consequently, our approach is to emphasize the general principles guiding liquidation in installments rather than to provide illustrative models of all possible liquidation situations. Among the variables that cause partnership liquidations to differ are the sufficiency of each partner's capital to absorb that partner's share of the possible losses remaining after each installment, the shifting of losses from one partner to another because of inability to collect a capital deficiency, the offsetting of loan accounts against capital deficiencies, and the possible need for setting aside cash to meet future liquidation expenses or unpaid liabilities.

General principles guiding installment payment procedures

The critical element in installment liquidations is that the liquidator authorizes cash payments to partners before losses that may be incurred on the liquidation are known. If payments are made to partners and later losses cause deficiencies to develop in the capital accounts, the liquidator will have to ask for the return of the payments. If the payments cannot be recovered, the liquidator may be personally liable to the other partners for the loss caused them by the improper distribution of cash. Because of this danger, the only safe policy for determining installment cash payments to partners follows:

1 Assume a total loss on all remaining assets and provide for all possible losses, including potential liquidation expenses.
2 Assume that any partner with a potential capital deficiency will be unable to pay anything to the firm; in other words, distribute each installment of cash as if no more cash would be forthcoming, either from sale of assets or from collection of deficiencies from partners.

Under these assumptions the liquidator will authorize a payment to a partner only if that partner has a credit balance in the capital account (or in the capital and loan accounts combined) in excess of the amount required to absorb a portion of the maximum possible loss that may be incurred on liquidation. A partner's "share of the maximum possible loss" would include any loss that may result from the inability of partners to make good any potential capital deficiencies.

When installment payments are made according to these rules, the effect will be to bring the equities of the partners to the income-sharing ratio as quickly as possible. *When installment payments have proceeded to the point that the partners' capital account balances (equities) correspond to the income-sharing ratio, all subsequent payments may be made in that ratio,* because each partner's equity will be sufficient to absorb an appropriate share of the maximum possible remaining loss.

Advance planning for installment payments to partners

The amounts of cash that could be distributed safely to the partners each month (or at any other point in time) may be determined by computing the impact on partners' equities (capital and loan balances) of the maximum possible remaining loss. Although this method is sound, it is somewhat cumbersome. Furthermore, it does not show at the beginning of the liquidation how cash will be divided among the partners as it becomes available. For these reasons, it is more efficient to prepare a complete *cash distribution program* in advance to show how cash will be divided during liquidation. If such a program is prepared, any amounts of cash received from the sale of partnership assets can be paid immediately to the partners as specified in this program.

Assume that X, Y, and Z, who share net income and losses in a 4:3:2 ratio, decide to liquidate and want a complete cash distribution program prepared in advance. The balance sheet for the X, Y & Z Partnership just prior to liquidation on July 5, Year 1, is as follows:

X, Y & Z PARTNERSHIP
Balance Sheet
July 5, Year 1

Assets		Liabilities & Partners' Capital	
Cash	$ 8,000	Liabilities	$ 61,000
Other assets	192,000	X, capital	40,000
		Y, capital	45,000
		Z, capital	54,000
Total	$200,000	Total	$200,000

The first $61,000 of available cash must, of course, be paid to creditors; any additional amount can be paid to partners. The amount of cash to be paid to partners during liquidation may be developed as illustrated on page 65. The steps used to prepare this cash distribution program are explained on page 66.

X, Y & Z PARTNERSHIP

Cash Distributions to Partners during Liquidation

July 5, Year 1

	X	Y	Z
Capital account balances before liquidation . .	$40,000	$45,000	$54,000
Income-sharing ratio	4	3	2
Divide capital account balances before liquidation by income-sharing ratio to obtain capital per unit of income sharing for each partner . .	$10,000	$15,000	$27,000
Required reduction in capital per unit of income sharing for Z to bring Z's balance down to the next highest balance (for partner Y). This is the amount of the first cash distribution to a partner **per unit** of the partner's income sharing. Because Z has 2 units of income sharing, Z will receive the first $24,000 ($12,000 × 2 = $24,000)			(12,000)
Capital per unit of income sharing	$10,000	$15,000	$15,000
Required reduction in capital per unit of income sharing for Y and Z to bring their balances down to X's balance, which is the lowest capital per unit of income sharing. The required reduction is multiplied by each partner's income-sharing ratio to determine the amount of cash to be paid. Thus Y receives $15,000 ($5,000 × 3 = $15,000), and Z receives $10,000 ($5,000 × 2 = $10,000)		(5,000)	(5,000)
Capital per unit of income sharing after payment of $15,000 to Y and $34,000 to Z. **Remaining cash now may be distributed in the income-sharing ratio**	$10,000	$10,000	$10,000

Summary of cash distribution program:

			X	Y	Z
To creditors before partners receive anything	$ 61,000				
To partners:					
(1) First distribution of $24,000 to Z: $12,000 × 2		24,000			$24,000
(2) Second distribution of $25,000 to Y and Z in 3:2 ratio:					
Y—$5,000 × 3	$15,000				
Z—$5,000 × 2	10,000	25,000		$15,000	10,000
		$110,000			
(3) Any amount in excess of $110,000 to X, Y, and Z in income-sharing ratio			4/9	3/9	2/9

1 The "capital account balances before liquidation" represent the **equities** of the partners in the partnership, that is, the balance in a partner's capital account, plus or minus the balance (if any) of a loan made by a partner to the partnership or a loan made by the partnership to a partner.

2 The capital account balance before liquidation for each partner is divided by each partner's income-sharing ratio to determine the amount of capital per unit of income sharing for each partner. This step is critical because it (**a**) identifies the partner with the largest capital per unit of income sharing who, therefore, will be the first to receive cash, (**b**) facilitates the ranking of partners in the order in which they are entitled to receive cash, and (**c**) provides the basis for determining the amount of cash each partner receives at various stages of liquidation. Because Z's capital per unit of income sharing is largest ($27,000), Z will be the first to receive cash, followed by Y, and finally by X.

3 Z receives enough cash to bring Z's capital of $27,000 per unit of income sharing down to $15,000 so that it will be equal to the balance for Y, the second ranking partner. To accomplish this, Z's capital per unit of income sharing must be reduced by $12,000, and because Z has two units of income sharing, Z must receive $24,000 ($12,000 × 2 = $24,000) before Y receives any cash.

4 At this point, the capital per unit of income sharing for Y and for Z is $15,000, indicating that they are entitled to receive cash until their capital per unit of income sharing is reduced by $5,000 to bring them down to the $10,000 balance for X, the lowest ranking partner. Because Y has three units and Z has two units of income sharing, Y receives $15,000 ($5,000 × 3 = $15,000) and Z receives an additional $10,000 ($5,000 × 2 = $10,000) before X receives any cash. After Z receives $24,000, Y and Z would share any amount of cash available up to a maximum amount of $25,000 in a 3:2 ratio.

5 After Y has received $15,000 and Z has received $34,000 ($24,000 + $10,000 = $34,000), the capital per unit of income sharing is $10,000 for each partner, and any additional cash is paid to the partners in the income-sharing ratio (4:3:2), because their capital account balances have been reduced to the income-sharing ratio. This is illustrated below:

	X($\frac{4}{9}$)	Y($\frac{3}{9}$)	Z($\frac{2}{9}$)
Capital account balances before liquidation . .	$40,000	$45,000	$54,000
First payment of cash to Z			(24,000)
Second payment of cash to Y and Z in 3:2 ratio		(15,000)	(10,000)
Capital account balances (in income-sharing ratio of 4:3:2) after payment of $49,000 to Y and Z	$40,000	$30,000	$20,000

Only when installment payments reach the point at which partners' capital account balances correspond to the income-sharing ratio can subsequent payments be made in that ratio.[1]

[1] The procedure for preparing a cash distribution program illustrated above can be used regardless of the number of partners involved and the complexity of the income-sharing ratio. For example, assume that partners share earnings as follows: A 41.2%, B 32.3%, C 26.5%. We may view the income-sharing ratio as 412 for A, 323 for B, and 265 for C and apply the same technique illustrated in this section.

We should point out that a cash distribution program, such as the one on page 65, also may be used to ascertain an equitable distribution of noncash assets to partners. The current fair value of noncash assets such as marketable securities, inventories, or equipment distributed to partners should be treated as equivalent to cash payments. If a distribution of noncash assets departs from the cash distribution program by giving one of the partners a larger distribution than that partner is entitled to receive, subsequent distributions should be adjusted to allow the remaining partners to "make up" the distribution prematurely made to one of the partners. In such cases, a **revised cash distribution program must be prepared,** because the original relationship among the partners' capital account balances has been disrupted.

Any losses or gains on the sale of assets during liquidation are allocated to the partners in the income-sharing ratio. Thus, the degree to which the capital account balances do not correspond with the income-sharing ratio is not altered by such losses or gains. Consequently, losses or gains from the realization of assets in the course of partnership liquidation do not affect the cash distribution program prepared prior to the start of liquidation.

To illustrate how the cash distribution program can be used, assume that the realization of assets by the X, Y & Z Partnership from July 5 to September 30, Year 1, is as follows:

	X, Y & Z PARTNERSHIP		
	Realization of Assets		
	July 5–September 30, Year 1		
Date	**Carrying amount of assets sold**	**Loss on sale**	**Cash received by partnership**
July 31	$ 62,000	$13,500	$ 48,500
August 31	66,000	36,000	30,000
September 30	64,000	31,500	32,500
Totals	$192,000	$81,000	$111,000

The cash available each month should be paid to creditors and partners according to the summary of cash distribution program on page 65. The distributions of cash appear at the top of page 68.

The entire cash balance of $56,500 available on July 31 is paid to creditors, leaving $4,500 in unpaid liabilities. When $30,000 becomes available on August 31, $4,500 should be paid to creditors, leaving $25,500 to be paid to the partners according to the cash distribution program developed earlier. The program calls for Z to receive the first $24,000 available for distribution to partners, and for Y and Z to share the next $25,000 in a 3:2 ratio. On August 31 only $1,500 ($30,000 −

X, Y & Z PARTNERSHIP
Distributions of Cash to Creditors and Partners
July 5–September 30, Year 1

Date	Cash	Liabilities	Partners' capital		
			$X(\frac{4}{9})$	$Y(\frac{3}{9})$	$Z(\frac{2}{9})$
July 31 (includes $8,000 on hand on July 5)	$ 56,500	$56,500			
August 31	30,000	4,500			$24,000 ⎫ 600 ⎭
				$ 900	
September 30	32,500			14,100	9,400 ⎫ 2,000 ⎭
			$4,000	3,000	
Totals	$119,000	$61,000	$4,000	$18,000	$36,000

$4,500 − $24,000 = $1,500) is available for payment to Y and Z; thus Y and Z receive $900 and $600, respectively. Of the $32,500 available on September 30, the first $23,500 is paid to Y and Z in a 3:2 ratio, or $14,100 and $9,400, respectively, in order to complete the distribution of $25,000 to Y and Z before X participates; this leaves $9,000 ($32,500 − $23,500 = $9,000) to be distributed to X, Y, and Z in the 4:3:2 income-sharing ratio.

A complete statement of realization and liquidation for X, Y & Z Partnership is presented on page 69.

The summary journal entries required to record the realization of assets and to complete the liquidation of the X, Y & Z Partnership appear on page 70.

Withholding of cash for unpaid liabilities and liquidation expenses

As previously emphasized, creditors are entitled to payment in full before anything is paid to partners. However, in some cases the liquidator may find it more convenient to set aside in a separate fund the cash required to pay certain liabilities, and to distribute the remaining cash to the partners. The withholding of cash for payment of recorded liabilities is appropriate when for any reason it is not practicable or advisable (as when the amount of the claim is in dispute) to pay an obligation before cash is distributed to partners. An amount of cash set aside, and equal to recorded unpaid liabilities, is not a factor in computing possible future losses; the possible future loss is measured by the amount of non-cash assets, any *unrecorded* liabilities, and any potential liquidation expenses that may be incurred.

Any expenses incurred during the liquidation should be deducted to determine the cash available for distribution to partners. Expenses of liquidation thereby are treated as part of the total loss from liquidation.

X, Y & Z PARTNERSHIP
Statement of Realization and Liquidation
July 5–September 30, Year 1

	Assets			Partners' capital		
	Cash	Other	Liabilities	X($\frac{4}{9}$)	Y($\frac{3}{9}$)	Z($\frac{2}{9}$)
Balances before liquidation	$ 8,000	$192,000	$61,000	$40,000	$45,000	$54,000
July 31 installment:						
Sale of assets at a loss of $13,500	48,500	(62,000)		(6,000)	(4,500)	(3,000)
Balances.	$56,500	$130,000	$61,000	$34,000	$40,500	$51,000
Payment to creditors . . .	(56,500)		(56,500)			
Balances.	$ -0-	$130,000	$ 4,500	$34,000	$40,500	$51,000
Aug. 31 installment:						
Sale of assets at a loss of $36,000	30,000	(66,000)		(16,000)	(12,000)	(8,000)
Balances.	$30,000	$ 64,000	$ 4,500	$18,000	$28,500	$43,000
Payment to creditors . . .	(4,500)		(4,500)			
Balances before any payments to partners	$25,500	$ 64,000		$18,000	$28,500	$43,000
Payments to partners . . .	(25,500)				(900)	(24,600)
Balances.	$ -0-	$ 64,000		$18,000	$27,600	$18,400
Sept. 30 installment:						
Sale of assets at a loss of $31,500	32,500	(64,000)		(14,000)	(10,500)	(7,000)
Balances.	$32,500			$ 4,000	$17,100	$11,400
Payments to partners . . .	(32,500)			(4,000)	(17,100)	(11,400)

However, in some cases, the liquidator may wish to withhold cash in anticipation of future liquidation expenses. The amount of cash withheld or set aside for future liquidation expenses or for payment of liabilities not recorded in the accounting records should be combined with the noncash assets in the computation of the maximum possible loss that may be incurred to complete the liquidation of the partnership.

INCORPORATION OF A PARTNERSHIP

Most partnerships should evaluate the possible advantages to be gained by incorporating. Among such advantages are limited liability, ease of attracting outside capital, and possible income tax savings.

To assure that each partner receives an equitable portion of the capital stock issued by the new corporation, the assets of the partnership

**Journal entries to
record liquidation**

July 31	Cash	48,500	
	X, Capital	6,000	
	Y, Capital	4,500	
	Z, Capital	3,000	
	Other Assets		62,000

To record sale of assets and division of $13,500 loss
among partners in 4:3:2 ratio.

	Liabilities	56,500	
	Cash		56,500

To record partial payment to creditors.

Aug. 31	Cash	30,000	
	X, Capital	16,000	
	Y, Capital	12,000	
	Z, Capital	8,000	
	Other Assets		66,000

To record sale of assets and division of $36,000 loss
among partners in 4:3:2 ratio.

	Liabilities	4,500	
	Y, Capital	900	
	Z, Capital	24,600	
	Cash		30,000

To record payment of balance due to creditors and
first installment to partners.

Sept. 30	Cash	32,500	
	X, Capital	14,000	
	Y, Capital	10,500	
	Z, Capital	7,000	
	Other Assets		64,000

To record sale of remaining assets and division of
$31,500 loss among partners in 4:3:2 ratio.

	X, Capital	4,000	
	Y, Capital	17,100	
	Z, Capital	11,400	
	Cash		32,500

To record final installment to partners to complete
the liquidation of the partnership.

must be adjusted to current fair value before being transferred to the corporation. Any identifiable intangible asset or goodwill developed by the partnership is included among the assets transferred to the corporation.

To illustrate the incorporation of a partnership, assume that Blair and Benson, partners who share net income and losses in a 4:1 ratio, organize B & B Corporation to take over the net assets of the partnership. The balance sheet of the partnership on June 30, Year 10, the date of incorporation, is as follows:

BLAIR & BENSON PARTNERSHIP
Balance Sheet
June 30, Year 10

Assets

Cash		$12,000
Accounts receivable	$28,100	
Less: Allowance for doubtful accounts	600	27,500
Inventories		25,500
Equipment	$60,000	
Less: Accumulated depreciation of equipment	26,000	34,000
Total assets		$99,000

Liabilities & Partners' Capital

Liabilities:		
Accounts payable		$35,000
Partners' capital:		
Blair, capital	$47,990	
Benson, capital	16,010	64,000
Total liabilities & partners' capital		$99,000

After an appraisal of the equipment and an audit of the financial statements, it is agreed that the following adjustments are required to restate the net assets of the partnership to current fair value:

(1) Increase the allowance for doubtful accounts to $1,000.
(2) Increase the inventories to current replacement cost of $30,000.
(3) Increase the equipment to reproduction cost new of $70,000, less accumulated depreciation on this basis of $30,500, that is, to a current fair value of $39,500.
(4) Record accrued liabilities of $1,100.
(5) Record goodwill of $10,000.

B & B Corporation is authorized to issue 10,000 shares of $10 par common stock. It issues 5,500 shares of common stock valued at $15 a share to the partnership, in exchange for the net assets of the partnership. The 5,500 shares received by the partnership are divided between the partners on the basis of the adjusted balances in their capital accounts. Partners may withdraw small amounts of cash to round their capital account balances to even amounts, thus avoiding the issuance of fractional shares. This step completes the dissolution and liquidation of the partnership.

Although the accounting records of the partnership may be modified to serve as the records of the new corporation, it is customary to open a new set of records for the corporation. If this alternative is followed, the procedures required are:

In accounting records of partnership:

1 Prepare journal entries for revaluation of assets, including recognition of goodwill, if any.
2 Record any cash withdrawals necessary to adjust partners' capital account balances to round amounts. (In some instances the contract may call for transfer to the corporation of all assets except cash.)
3 Record the transfer of assets and liabilities to the corporation, the receipt of the common stock by the partnership, and the distribution of the common stock to the partners in settlement of the balances in their capital accounts.

The journal entries to adjust and eliminate the accounting records of the Blair & Benson Partnership are illustrated on page 73.

In accounting records of new corporation:

1 Record the acquisition of assets and liabilities (including obligation to pay for the net assets) from the partnership at current fair values.
2 Record the issuance of common stock at current fair value in payment of the obligation to the partnership.

The journal entries to open the accounting records of B & B Corporation on June 30, Year 10, are illustrated at the top of page 74.

Note that the allowance for doubtful accounts is recorded in the accounting records of B & B Corporation because the specific accounts receivable that may not be collected are not known. In contrast, the depreciation recorded by the Blair & Benson Partnership is ignored because the "cost" of the equipment to the new corporation is $39,500. The opening balance sheet for B & B Corporation appears at the bottom of page 74.

Income tax aspects concerning incorporation of a partnership

For income tax purposes, no gain or loss is recognized on the incorporation of a partnership if the former partners hold control of the corporation immediately after the transfer. As a result of this rule, the income tax basis of the assets transferred is the same for the corporation as it was for the partnership. The depreciation program is continued for income tax purposes on the basis of the original cost to the partnership. *Control* of the corporation is defined for income tax purposes as owner-

Journal entries for Blair & Benson Partnership

Inventories ($30,000 − $25,500)	4,500	
Equipment ($70,000 − $60,000)	10,000	
Goodwill	10,000	
Allowance for Doubtful Accounts ($1,000 − $600)		400
Accumulated Depreciation of Equipment		
($30,500 − $26,000).		4,500
Accrued Liabilities		1,100
Blair, Capital ($18,500 × 0.80)		14,800
Benson, Capital ($18,500 × 0.20).		3,700

To adjust assets and liabilities to agreed amounts and to divide net gain of $18,500 between partners in 4:1 ratio.

Receivable from B & B Corporation ($64,000 + $18,500)	82,500	
Accounts Payable	35,000	
Accrued Liabilities	1,100	
Allowance for Doubtful Accounts	1,000	
Accumulated Depreciation of Equipment	30,500	
Cash		12,000
Accounts Receivable.		28,100
Inventories.		30,000
Equipment		70,000
Goodwill		10,000

To record transfer of assets and liabilities to B & B Corporation.

Common Stock of B & B Corporation	82,500	
Receivable from B & B Corporation		82,500

To record receipt of 5,500 shares of $10 par common stock valued at $15 a share in payment for net assets transferred to B & B Corporation.

Blair, Capital ($47,990 + $14,800)	62,790	
Benson, Capital ($16,010 + $3,700)	19,710	
Common Stock of B & B Corporation		82,500

To record distribution of common stock of B & B Corporation to partners: 4,186 shares to Blair and 1,314 shares to Benson.

ship of 80% or more of the voting capital stock and also at least 80% of any other classes of capital stock outstanding.

Thus, a conflict exists between the action required for income tax purposes and that indicated by accounting theory. From the viewpoint of accounting theory, the assets appropriately are recorded in the accounting records of the corporation at the new cost basis established by the transfer of ownership and substantiated by the market (or current

Journal entries for B & B Corporation

Cash	12,000	
Accounts Receivable	28,100	
Inventories	30,000	
Equipment	39,500	
Goodwill	10,000	
Allowance for Doubtful Accounts		1,000
Accounts Payable		35,000
Accrued Liabilities		1,100
Payable to Blair & Benson Partnership		82,500

To record acquisition of assets and liabilities from Blair & Benson Partnership.

Payable to Blair & Benson Partnership	82,500	
Common Stock, $10 par		55,000
Paid-in Capital in Excess of Par		27,500

To record issuance of 5,500 shares of common stock valued at $15 a share in payment for net assets of Blair & Benson Partnership.

B & B CORPORATION
Balance Sheet
June 30, Year 10

Assets

Cash		$ 12,000
Accounts receivable	$28,100	
Less: Allowance for doubtful accounts	1,000	27,100
Inventories		30,000
Equipment		39,500
Goodwill		10,000
Total assets		$118,600

Liabilities & Stockholders' Equity

Liabilities:		
Accounts payable		$ 35,000
Accrued liabilities		1,100
Total liabilities		$ 36,100
Stockholders' equity:		
Common stock, $10 par, authorized 10,000 shares, issued		
and outstanding 5,500 shares	$55,000	
Paid-in capital in excess of par	27,500	82,500
Total liabilities & stockholders' equity		$118,600

fair) value of the shares of capital stock issued for these assets. As a practical solution to this conflict between income tax requirements and theoretical considerations, the corporation may wish to maintain a separate set of supplementary records for depreciable assets to facilitate the computation of depreciation expense allowable for income tax purposes.

JOINT VENTURES

A *joint venture* differs from a partnership in that it is limited to carrying out a single project, such as the sale of a lot of merchandise or construction of a building. Historically, joint ventures were used to finance the sale or exchange of a cargo of merchandise in a foreign country. In an era when marine transportation and foreign trade involved many hazards, individuals (*venturers*) would band together to undertake a venture of this type. The capital required usually was larger than one person could provide, and the risks were too great to be borne alone. Because of the risks involved and the relatively short duration of the project, no net income was recognized until the venture was completed. At the end of the voyage, the net income was divided among the participants and their association was ended.

In its traditional form, the accounting for a joint venture did not follow the accrual basis of accounting. The assumption of continuity was not appropriate; instead of the determination of net income at regular intervals, the measurement and reporting of net income or loss awaited the completion of the venture.

Present-day ventures

In today's business community, joint ventures are less common but still are employed for many projects such as (1) the purchase, development, and sale of a specific tract of real estate; (2) exploration for oil and gas; and (3) the construction of a bridge, building, or dam.

The term **corporate joint venture** also is used at present by many large American corporations to describe overseas operations by a corporation whose ownership is divided between an American company and a foreign company. Many examples of jointly owned companies also are found in some domestic industries. A corporate joint venture and the accounting for such a venture are described in *APB Opinion No. 18* as follows:

> "Corporate joint venture" refers to a corporation owned and operated by a small group of businesses (the "joint venturers") as a separate and specific business or project for the mutual benefit of the members of the group. A government may also be a member of the group. The purpose of a corporate joint venture frequently is to share risks and rewards in developing a new market, product or technology; to combine complementary technological knowledge;

or to pool resources in developing production or other facilities. A corporate joint venture also usually provides an arrangement under which each joint venturer may participate, directly or indirectly, in the overall management of the joint venture. Joint venturers thus have an interest or relationship other than as passive investors. An entity which is a subsidiary of one of the "joint venturers" is not a corporate joint venture. The ownership of a corporate joint venture seldom changes, and its stock is usually not traded publicly. A minority public ownership, however, does not preclude a corporation from being a corporate joint venture.[2]

. . . .

The Board concludes that the equity method best enables investors in corporate joint ventures to reflect the underlying nature of their investment in those ventures. Therefore, investors should account for investments in common stock of corporate joint ventures by the equity method, both in consolidated financial statements and in parent-company financial statements prepared for issuance to stockholders as the financial statements of the primary reporting entity.[3]

. . . .

When investments in common stock of corporate joint ventures or other investments of 50% or less accounted for under the equity method are, in the aggregate, material in relation to the financial position or results of operations of an investor, it may be necessary for summarized information as to assets, liabilities, and results of operations of the investees to be presented in the notes or in separate statements, either individually or in groups, as appropriate.[4]

Our use of the term *joint venture* in this chapter is in the traditional meaning of a partnership limited to carrying out a single project.

Accounting for a joint venture

The key issue in accounting for a joint venture is whether to establish a separate set of accounting records for the venture. If a separate set of accounting records is not established, two alternative methods may be used. One method is to record all transactions of the venture in the accounting records of each venturer. Each venturer opens a Joint Venture account and also a receivable or payable for every other venturer. The other method is to record in the accounting records of each venturer only those venture transactions in which each venturer is involved directly.

Separate Set of Accounting Records The complexity of modern business, the emphasis on good organization and strong internal control, the importance of income taxes, the extent of government regulation, and the need for preparation and retention of adequate accounting records are strong arguments for establishing a complete separate set of accounting records for every joint venture of large size and long duration. This

[2] *APB Opinion No. 18,* "The Equity Method of Accounting for Investments in Common Stock," AICPA (New York: 1971), pp. 348–349.
[3] Ibid., p. 355.
[4] Ibid., p. 361.

approach views the joint venture as an accounting entity. Each venturer is credited for the amount of cash or noncash assets invested by each. The fiscal year of the joint venture may or may not coincide with the fiscal years of the venturers, but the use of the accrual basis of accounting and periodic financial statements for the venture permit regular reporting of the share of net income or loss allocable to each venturer.

The accounting records of such a joint venture will include the usual accounts for assets, liabilities, owners' equity, revenue, and expenses. The entire accounting process will conform to generally accepted accounting principles, from the recording of transactions to the preparation of financial statements.

Each venturer opens an Investment in Joint Venture account. This account is debited for assets invested in the venture, for any services performed for the venture, and for the proper share of any venture net income. The Investment in Joint Venture account is credited for any amounts received from the venture and for a proper share of any venture net loss. The Investment in Joint Venture account normally will have a debit balance, representing the venturer's net investment in the venture. A participant does not record any journal entries for transactions between the venture and the other venturers. The Investment in Joint Venture account will appear in the balance sheet of each venturer as an asset, either current or noncurrent, depending upon the expected completion date for the venture.

No Separate Set of Accounting Records If a separate set of accounting records is not maintained by the venture, each venturer may record all transactions entered into by the venture, or each venturer may record only those transactions in which that venturer is involved directly. Let us assume the first method is in use. Thus, if Paula Nance invests merchandise in a venture, she debits Joint Venture and credits Inventories. Each of the other venturers prepares a journal entry debiting Joint Venture and crediting an account with Nance. When a sale is made, the venturer handling the transaction debits Cash or Accounts Receivable and credits Joint Venture. The other venturers debit the venturer who made the sale and credit Joint Venture. In brief, each venturer maintains a complete record of all transactions by the joint venture and of the equities of the other venturers.

Upon completion of the joint venture, the net income or loss is shown by the balance in the Joint Venture account. Assuming that a net income has been realized, the journal entry for each venturer to divide the net income and to close the Joint Venture account will be to debit Joint Venture for the balance, credit every other venturer for an appropriate share of the net income, and credit Income Summary for the venturer's own share. Each venturer will then have an account balance with each of the other venturers; the final step is to make payment or collection of these balances.

If a joint venture has not been completed on the date one of the venturers prepares a balance sheet, only the equity of that venturer should be presented as an asset. Because the ledger account Joint Venture shows the total investment by all venturers, the balance of this account less the equities of the other venturers should be listed as an asset in the balance sheet.

The operation of a joint venture without a separate set of accounting records is appropriate only when the venture is expected to be of short duration and does not involve complex or numerous transactions. If prompt communication among venturers is not practicable, convenience may dictate that individual venturers record only transactions of the venture in which each is directly involved.

REVIEW QUESTIONS

1 Agasse and Bowman, partners, have capital accounts of $60,000 and $80,000, respectively. In addition, Agasse has made a noninterest-bearing loan of $20,000 to the firm. Agasse and Bowman now decide to liquidate their partnership. What priority or advantage, if any, will Agasse enjoy in the liquidation with respect to the loan account?

2 State briefly the procedure to be followed in a partnership liquidation when a debit balance arises in the capital account of one of the partners.

3 In the liquidation of the partnership of Camm, Dehn, and Ellerman, the sale of the assets resulted in a loss that produced the following balances in the capital accounts: Camm, $25,000 credit; Dehn, $12,500 credit; and Ellerman, $5,000 debit. The partners shared net income and losses in a 5:3:2 ratio. All liabilities have been paid, and $32,500 of cash is available for distribution to partners. However, it is not possible to determine at present whether Ellerman will be able to make good the $5,000 capital deficiency. May the cash on hand be distributed without a delay to determine the collectibility of the amount due from Ellerman? Explain.

4 After disposing of all assets and distributing all available cash to creditors, the A, B & C Partnership still had accounts payable of $12,000. The capital account of Partner A showed a credit balance of $16,000 and that of B a credit balance of $2,000. Creditors of the partnership demanded payment from A, who replied that the three partners shared earnings equally and had begun operations with equal capital investments. A, therefore, offered to pay the creditors one-third of their claims and no more. What is your opinion of the position taken by A? What is the balance in C's capital account? What journal entry, if any, should be made in the partnership accounting records for a payment by A personally to the partnership creditors?

5 In the Avery, Blum & Chee Partnership, Avery serves as managing partner. The partnership contract provides that Avery is entitled to an annual salary of $12,000, payable in 12 equal monthly installments, and that remaining net income or loss shall be divided equally. On June 30, the partnership suspended operations and began liquidation. Because of a shortage of working capital, Avery had not drawn any salary for the last two months of operations. How should Avery's claim for $2,000 of "unpaid wages" be handled in the liquidation of the partnership?

6 M and N are partners and have agreed to share earnings equally. State your reasons in support of dividing losses incurred in liquidation equally or in the ratio of capital account balances.

7 State briefly the basic principle to be observed in the distribution of cash to partners when the liquidation of a partnership extends over several months.

8 During the installment liquidation of a partnership, it is necessary to determine the possible future loss from sale of the remaining assets. What journal entries, if any, should be made to reflect in the partners' capital accounts their respective shares of the maximum possible loss that may be incurred during the remaining stages of liquidation?

9 The X, Y & Z Partnership is liquidated over a period of 11 months, with several distributions of cash to the partners. Will the total amount of cash received by each partner under these circumstances be more, less, or the same amount as if the liquidator had retained all cash until all assets had been sold and had then made a single payment to the partners?

10 Under what circumstances, if any, is it sound practice for a partnership undergoing installment liquidation to distribute cash to partners in the income-sharing ratio?

11 Judd, Klein, and Lund, partners who share earnings equally, have capital account balances of $30,000, $25,000, and $21,000, respectively, when the partnership begins liquidation. Among the assets is a note receivable from Klein in the amount of $7,000. All liabilities have been paid. The first assets sold during the liquidation are marketable securities with a carrying amount of $15,000, for which cash of $18,000 is received. How should this $18,000 be divided among the partners?

12 When the R, S & T Partnership began the process of liquidation, the capital account balances were R, $38,000; S, $35,000; and T, $32,000. When the liquidation was complete, R had received less cash than either of the other two partners. List several factors that might explain why the partner with the largest capital account balance might receive the smallest amount of cash in liquidation.

13 A partnership operated by Mann and Field decided to incorporate as Manfield Corporation. The entire capital stock of the new corporation was divided equally between Mann and Field because they had been equal partners. An appraisal report obtained on the date of incorporation indicated that the land and buildings had increased in value by 50% while owned by the partnership. Should the assets be increased to appraisal value or maintained at original cost to the partnership when transferred to the corporation's accounting records? If the assets are revalued, will the corporation be permitted to take depreciation on the increased valuations for income tax purposes? Explain.

14 Explain how a *joint venture* differs from a partnership.

15 When the concept of the joint venture is considered from a historical viewpoint, how has the process of net income determination differed from that of a partnership or corporation? Does this difference prevail in present practice?

16 What are *corporate joint ventures?* What accounting procedures for such ventures were recommended in *APB Opinion No. 18?*

EXERCISES

Ex. 2-1 Select the best answer for each of the following multiple-choice questions:

1 Which of the following will not result in a dissolution of a partnership?
  a The bankruptcy of a partner, as long as the partnership itself remains solvent
  b The death of a partner, as long as the deceased partner's will provides that the executor shall become a partner in the deceased partner's place
  c The wrongful withdrawal of a partner in contravention of the partnership contract
  d The assignment by a partner of his or her entire partnership interest to another party

2 An insolvent partner's obligation to pay any deficiency in his or her capital account ranks:
  a Ahead of claims of unpaid creditors of the partnership
  b Second to claims of individual creditors of the insolvent partner
  c Before claims of the individual creditors of the partner and claims of unpaid creditors of the partnership
  d In some other order

3 During the liquidation of the Wayne, Forbes, Cable & Towne Partnership, Forbes paid a partnership account payable in the amount of $3,600. The appropriate journal entry in the partnership accounting records is:
  a No entry
  b Accounts Payable 3,600
        Forbes, Capital 3,600
  c Cash 3,600
        Forbes, Capital 3,600
  d Accounts Payable 3,600
        Forbes, Drawing 3,600

4 Q, R, S, and T are partners sharing net income and losses equally. The partnership is insolvent and is to be liquidated. The status of the partnership and each partner is as follows:

	Partnership capital account balance	Personal assets (exclusive of partnership interest)	Personal liabilities (exclusive of partnership interest)
Q	$15,000 cr	$100,000	$40,000
R	10,000 cr	30,000	60,000
S	20,000 dr	80,000	5,000
T	30,000 dr	1,000	28,000

  Assuming that the Uniform Partnership Act applies, the creditors of the partnership:
  a Must first seek recovery against S, because S is solvent personally and has a negative capital balance
  b Will not be paid in full regardless of how they proceed legally, because the partnership assets are less than the partnership liabilities
  c Will have to share R's interest in the partnership on a pro rata basis with R's personal creditors
  d Have first claim to the partnership assets before any partner's personal creditors have rights to the partnership assets

5 Jenson, Smith, and Hart, partners, share net income and losses in the ratio of 5:3:2, respectively. The partners decided to liquidate the partnership when its assets consisted of cash, $40,000, and other assets, $210,000; the liabilities and partners' capital were as follows:

Liabilities	$60,000
Jenson, capital	48,000
Smith, capital	72,000
Hart, capital	70,000

The partnership will be liquidated over a prolonged period of time. As cash is available it will be distributed to the partners. The first sale of noncash assets with a carrying amount of $120,000 realized $90,000. How much cash should be distributed to each partner after this sale?

	Jenson	Smith	Hart
a	$45,000	$27,000	$18,000
b	$35,000	$21,000	$14,000
c	$ –0–	$30,000	$40,000
d	$ –0–	$28,800	$41,200

Ex. 2-2 Pullias and Mautner are partners who share net income and losses in a 60:40 ratio. They have decided to liquidate their partnership. A portion of the assets has been sold, but other assets with a carrying amount of $42,000 still must be realized. All liabilities have been paid, and cash of $20,000 is available for distribution to partners. The capital accounts show balances of $40,000 for Pullias and $22,000 for Mautner.

How should the cash be divided?

Ex. 2-3 Nicosia and Odmark started a partnership some years ago and managed to operate profitably for several years. Recently, however, they lost a substantial legal suit and incurred unexpected losses on accounts receivable and inventories. As a result, they decided to liquidate. They sold all assets, and only $18,000 was available to pay liabilities, which amounted to $33,000. Their capital account balances before the start of liquidation and their income-sharing ratios are shown below:

	Capital account balances	Income-sharing ratios
Nicosia	$23,000	60%
Odmark	13,500	40%

a Compute the total loss incurred on the liquidation of the partnership.
b Show how the final settlement should be made between the partners, after Nicosia pays $15,000 to creditors. Nicosia is personally insolvent after paying the creditors, but Odmark has personal net assets in excess of $100,000.

Ex. 2-4 After sale of a portion of the assets of the X, Y & Z Partnership, which is being liquidated, the capital accounts are X, $33,000; Y, $40,000; and Z, $42,000. Cash of $42,000 and other assets with a carrying amount of $78,000 are on hand. Creditors' claims total $5,000. X, Y, and Z share net income and losses equally.

Compute the cash payments that can be made to the partners at this time.

Ex. 2-5 When Kane and Lobo, partners who shared earnings equally, were incapacitated in an airplane accident, a liquidator was appointed to wind up their partnership. The accounting records showed cash, $35,000; other assets, $110,000; liabilities, $20,000; Kane's capital, $71,000; and Lobo's capital, $54,000. Because of the highly specialized nature of the noncash assets, the liquidator anticipated that considerable time would be required to dispose of them. The expenses of liquidating the partnership (advertising, rent, travel, etc.) are estimated at $10,000.

Compute the amount of cash that can be distributed safely to each partner at this time.

Ex. 2-6   The following balance sheet was prepared for the Pardee, Quon & Ramsey Partnership on March 31, Year 8. (Each partner's income-sharing ratio is given in parentheses):

Assets		Liabilities & Partners' Capital	
Cash	$ 25,000	Liabilities	$ 52,000
Other assets	180,000	Pardee, capital (40%) . . .	40,000
		Quon, capital (40%)	65,000
		Ramsey, capital (20%) . . .	48,000
Total	$205,000	Total	$205,000

  a The partnership is being liquidated by the sale of assets in installments. The first sale of noncash assets having a carrying amount of $90,000 realizes $50,000, and all cash available after settlement with creditors is distributed to partners. Compute the amount of cash each partner should receive in the first installment.
  b If the facts are as in **a** above, except that $3,000 cash is withheld for possible liquidation expenses, how much cash should each partner receive?
  c As a separate case, assume that each partner properly received some cash in the distribution after the second sale of assets. The cash to be distributed amounts to $14,000 from the third sale of assets, and unsold assets with a $6,000 carrying amount remain. How should the $14,000 be distributed to partners?

Ex. 2-7   On November 10, Year 3, D, E, and F, partners, have capital account balances of $20,000, $25,000, and $9,000, respectively, and share net income and losses in 4 : 2 : 1 ratio.

  a Prepare a cash distribution program for liquidation of the partnership in installments.
  b How much will be paid to all partners if D receives only $4,000 on liquidation?
  c If D received a $13,000 share of the cash paid pursuant to liquidation, how much did F receive?
  d If E received only $11,000 as a result of the liquidation, what was the loss to the partnership on the sale of assets? (No partner invested any additional assets in the partnership.)

Ex. 2-8   The balance sheet for P & Q Partnership on June 1 of Year 10 follows:

Assets		Liabilities & Partners' Capital	
Cash	$ 5,000	Liabilities	$20,000
Other assets	55,000	P, capital	22,500
		Q, capital	17,500
Total	$60,000	Total	$60,000

Partners share net income and losses as follows: P, 60%; Q, 40%. In June, assets with a carrying amount of $22,000 are sold for $18,000, creditors are paid in full, and $2,000 is paid to partners in a manner to reduce their capital account balances closer to the income-sharing ratio. In July, assets with a carrying amount of $10,000 are sold for $12,000, liquidation expenses of $500 are paid, and cash of $12,500 is distributed to partners. In August, the remaining assets are sold for $22,500, and final settlement is made between the partners.
Compute the amount of cash each partner should receive in June, July, and August.

Ex. 2-9 The net equities and income-sharing ratios for E, F, G, and H, partners, before liquidation on May 5, Year 5, are as follows:

	E	F	G	H
Net equity in partnership	$36,000	$32,400	$8,000	$(100)
Income-sharing ratio	6	4	2	1

Assets will be sold for cash significantly in excess of carrying amounts.

Prepare a program showing how cash should be distributed to the partners as it becomes available in the course of liquidation.

Ex. 2-10 McKee and Nelson enter into a contract to speculate on the stock market, each using approximately $5,000 of personal cash. The net income and losses are to be divided equally, and settlement is to be made at the end of the year after all securities have been sold. A summary of the monthly brokerage statements for the year follows:

	McKee	Nelson
Total of all purchase confirmations	$45,000	$18,000
Total of all sales confirmations	48,700	16,800
Interest charged on margin accounts	80	50
Dividends credited to accounts	40	100

How should settlement be made between McKee and Nelson at the end of the year?

Ex. 2-11 The balance sheet for the Conner & Wayland Partnership, immediately before the partnership was incorporated as Conway Corporation, follows:

CONNER & WAYLAND PARTNERSHIP
Balance Sheet
September 30, Year 5

Assets		Liabilities & Partners' Capital	
Cash	$ 10,500	Accounts payable	$ 16,400
Accounts receivable	15,900		
Inventories	42,000	Conner, capital	60,000
Equipment (net of $18,000		Wayland, capital	52,000
accumulated depreciation)	60,000		
Total	$128,400	Total	$128,400

The following adjustments to the balance sheet of the partnership are recommended by a CPA before new accounting records for Conway Corporation are opened:

(1) An allowance for doubtful accounts is established in the amount of $1,200.
(2) Short-term prepayments of $800 are recorded.
(3) The current fair value of inventories is $48,000, and the current fair value of equipment is $72,000.
(4) Accrued liabilities are estimated at $750.

Prepare an opening balance sheet for Conway Corporation on October 1, Year 5, assuming that 10,000 shares of $5 par common stock are issued to the partners in exchange for their equities in the partnership. Equipment is recorded at current fair value; 50,000 shares of common stock are authorized to be issued.

CASES

Case 2-1   The Hodgkins, Olafson & Stevens Partnership is insolvent and in the process of liquidation under the Uniform Partnership Act. After the assets were converted to cash and the resultant liquidation loss was distributed equally among the partners, their financial positions were as follows:

	Equity in partnership	Personal financial position other than equity in partnership	
		Assets	Liabilities
Scott Hodgkins	$30,000	$110,000	$45,000
Greg Olafson	(21,000)	20,000	40,000
Brent Stevens	(55,000)	55,000	45,000

Instructions Explain the prospects for collection by:
a The creditors of the partnership.
b The personal creditors of each partner.
c Hodgkins from the other partners. Compute the total loss that Hodgkins will absorb on the liquidation of the partnership.

Case 2-2   On November 15, Year 1, in beginning the liquidation of the X, Y & Z Partnership, the liquidator found that an 8% note payable for $100,000 issued by the partnership had six months remaining until maturity on May 15, Year 2. Interest had been paid to November 15. Terms of the note provided that interest at 8% to the maturity date must be paid in full in the event the note is paid prior to maturity. The liquidator had paid all other liabilities and had on hand cash of $150,000. The remain. ig noncash assets had a carrying amount of $200,000. The liquidator believed that six months would be required to dispose of them and that the realization of the noncash assets over this period would produce cash at least 25% in excess of the carrying amount of the assets.

Partner X made the following statement to the liquidator: "I realize you can't pay the partners until creditors have been paid in full, but I need cash for another venture. So I'd like for you to pay the note and interest to May 15, Year 2, immediately and to distribute the remaining cash to the partners." Partner Y objected to this proposal for immediate cash payments because it would entail a loss of $4,000. Y argued that if such action were taken, the total interest cost of $4,000 should be debited to X's capital account. Partner Z had no particular concern in the matter, but as a convenience agreed to assume the note liability in return for $102,000 cash payment from the liquidator. To protect the noteholder against loss, Z offered to deposit collateral of $104,000 in U.S. government bonds. The noteholder expressed willingness to accept this arrangement. Partner Z specified that the proposed payment of $102,000 would be in Z's new role as a creditor and that it would not affect Z's right to receive any cash distributions in the course of liquidation.

Instructions Evaluate the proposal by each partner. What action should be taken by the liquidator? Would your answer differ if the assumptions were changed to indicate a probable loss on the realization of the remaining noncash assets?

Case 2-3   Lois Allen and Barbara Brett formed a partnership and share net income and losses equally. Although the partners began business with equal capitals, Allen made more frequent withdrawals than Brett, with the result that her capital account became the smaller of the two. The partners have now decided to liquidate the partnership on June 30; on that date the accounting records were closed and financial statements were prepared. The balance sheet showed a capital account for Allen of $40,000 and Brett's capital as $60,000. In addition, the balance sheet showed that Brett had made a $10,000 loan to the partnership.

The liquidation of the partnership was managed by Allen, because Brett was hospitalized by an auto accident on July 1, the day after regular operations were suspended. The procedures followed by Allen were as follows: First, to sell all the assets at the best prices obtainable; second, to pay the creditors in full; third to pay Brett's loan account; and fourth, to divide all remaining cash between Brett and herself in the 40:60 ratio represented by their capital account balances.

When Brett was released from the hospital on July 5, Allen informed her that through good luck and hard work, she had been able to sell the assets and complete the liquidation during the five days of Brett's hospitalization. As the first step in the liquidation, Allen delivered two cashier's checks to Brett. One check was for $10,000 in payment of the loan account; the other was in settlement of Brett's capital account balance.

Instructions

a Do you approve the procedures followed in the liquidation? Explain fully.

b Assume that the liquidation procedures followed resulted in the payment of $24,000 to Brett in addition to the payment of her loan account in full. What was the amount of gain or loss on the liquidation? If you believe that other methods should have been followed in the liquidation, explain how much more or less Brett would have received under the procedure you recommend.

Case 2-4 In reply to a question as to how settlement with partners should be made during liquidation of a partnership, Student J made the following statement:

"Accounting records usually are based on cost and reflect the going-concern principle. When a partnership is liquidated, it is often necessary to sell the assets for a fraction of their carrying amount. Consequently, a partner usually receives in liquidation a settlement far below the amount of his or her equity in the partnership."

Student K offered the following comment:

"I agree fully with what J has said, but she might have gone further and added that no payment should ever be made to any partner until all the assets of the partnership have been sold and all creditors have been paid in full. Until these steps have been completed, the residual amount available for distribution to partners is unknown, and therefore any earlier payment to a partner might have to be returned. If partners were unable to return such amount, the person who authorized the payments might be held personally responsible."

Student L made the following statement:

"In the liquidation of a partnership, each partner receives the amount of his or her equity—no more and no less. As to timing of payments, it is often helpful to a partner to receive a partial payment before the assets are sold and creditors are paid in full. If proper precautions are taken, such early partial payments are quite satisfactory."

Instructions Evaluate the statement made by each student.

PROBLEMS

2-1 Carson and Worden decided to dissolve and liquidate their partnership on September 23, Year 10. On that date, the balance sheet of the partnership was as shown at the top of page 86 (partners' income-sharing percentages are indicated parenthetically).

On September 23, Year 10, other assets with a carrying amount of $70,000 were sold for $60,000, and $64,000 cash was distributed to creditors and part-

CARSON & WORDEN PARTNERSHIP

Balance Sheet

September 23, Year 10

Assets		Liabilities & Partners' Capital	
Cash	$ 5,000	Accounts payable	$ 15,000
Other assets	100,000	Loan payable to Worden .	10,000
		Carson, capital (40%) . . .	60,000
		Worden, capital (60%) . . .	20,000
Total	$105,000	Total	$105,000

ners. On October 1, Year 10, the remaining other assets were sold for $18,000 and all available cash was distributed to partners.

Instructions

a Prepare a cash distribution program on September 23, Year 10, to determine the proper distribution of cash to partners as it becomes available.

b Prepare journal entries on September 23, Year 10, and October 1, Year 10, to record the sales of assets and distributions of cash to creditors and partners.

2-2 On December 31, Year 5, the accounting records of the X, Y & Z Partnership included the following information:

X, drawing (debit balance)	$(24,000)
Z, drawing (debit balance)	(9,000)
Y, loan	30,000
X, capital	123,000
Y, capital	100,500
Z, capital	108,000

Total assets amounted to $478,500, including $52,500 cash, and liabilities totaled $150,000. The partnership was liquidated on December 31, Year 5, and Z received $83,250 cash pursuant to the liquidation. X, Y, and Z share net income and losses in a 5:3:2 ratio, respectively.

Instructions

a Compute the total loss from the liquidation of the partnership.

b Prepare a statement of realization and liquidation.

c Prepare journal entries for the accounting records of the partnership to complete the liquidation.

2-3 The following balance sheet was prepared for Cody's, a partnership, immediately prior to liquidation:

CODY'S

Balance Sheet

March 31, Year 5

Assets		Liabilities & Partners' Capital	
Cash	$ 10,000	Liabilities	$ 27,000
Investments in common		John Coe, capital	72,000
stocks	20,000	Karen Dee, capital	31,000
Other assets	100,000		
Total	$130,000	Total	$130,000

Coe and Dee share operating income in a 2:1 ratio and capital gains and losses in a 3:1 ratio. The transactions to complete the liquidation are as follows:

Apr. 1 Coe takes over the portfolio of investments in common stocks at an agreed current fair value of $44,000.

Apr. 3 Other assets and the trade name, Cody's, are sold to Wong Products for $200,000 face amount of 12% bonds with a current fair value of $180,000. The gain on this transaction is a capital gain.

Apr. 7 Wong Products 12% bonds with a face amount of $40,000 are sold for $35,600 cash. The loss on this transaction is a capital loss.

Apr. 8 Liabilities are paid.

Apr. 10 Coe withdraws $100,000 face amount and Dee withdraws $60,000 face amount of Wong Products 12% bonds at carrying amounts.

Apr. 15 Any available cash is paid to Coe and Dee.

Instructions Prepare journal entries for Cody's to record the foregoing transactions.

2-4 Following is the balance sheet for the Adams, Barna & Coleman Partnership on June 4, Year 5:

ADAMS, BARNA & COLEMAN PARTNERSHIP
Balance Sheet
June 4, Year 5

Assets		Liabilities & Partners' Capital	
Cash	$ 6,000	Liabilities	$ 20,000
Other assets	94,000	Barna, loan	4,000
		Adams, capital	27,000
		Barna, capital	39,000
		Coleman, capital	10,000
Total	$100,000	Total	$100,000

The partners share net income and losses as follows: Adams, 40%; Barna, 40%; and Coleman, 20%. On June 4, Year 5, other assets were sold for $30,700, and $20,500 had to be paid to liquidate the liabilities because of unrecorded claims amounting to $500. Adams and Barna are personally solvent, but Coleman's personal liabilities exceed personal assets by $6,000.

Instructions

a Prepare a statement of realization and liquidation. Combine Barna's loan and capital account balances.

b Prepare journal entries to record the liquidation.

c How much cash would other assets have to realize on liquidation in order that Coleman would take enough cash out of the partnership to pay personal creditors in full? Assume that $20,500 is required to liquidate the partnership liabilities.

2-5 The accountant for the Horizon Partnership prepared the balance sheet at the top of page 88 immediately prior to liquidation of the partnership.

During May, Year 3, assets with a carrying amount of $105,000 were sold for $75,000 cash, and all liabilities were paid. During June, assets with a carrying amount of $61,000 were sold for $25,000 cash, and in July the remaining assets with a carrying amount of $114,000 were sold for $81,000 cash. The cash available at the end of each month was distributed promptly. The partners shared net income and losses equally.

HORIZON PARTNERSHIP
Balance Sheet
April 30, Year 3

Assets		Liabilities & Partners' Capital	
Cash	$ 20,000	Liabilities	$ 80,000
Other assets	280,000	Holman, capital	60,000
		Rizzo, capital	70,000
		Onegin, capital	90,000
Total	$300,000	Total	$300,000

Instructions

a Prepare a statement of realization and liquidation covering the entire period of liquidation, and a supporting working paper showing the computation of installment payments to partners as cash becomes available.

b At what point in liquidation did the partners' capital accounts have balances corresponding to the income-sharing ratio? Of what significance is this relationship with respect to subsequent cash distributions to partners?

2-6 Love, Mears, and Newman decided to form a partnership on January 10, Year 6. Their capital investments and income-sharing ratios are listed below:

Love: $45,000—50%

Mears: $30,000—30%, with a salary allowance of $18,000 a year, or a proportionate amount for a period less than a year

Newman: $24,000—20%

During the first six months of Year 6, the partners were not particularly concerned over the poor volume of business and the net loss of $42,000 reported by their accountant, because they had been told that it would take at least six months to establish their business and to achieve profitable operations. Business during the second half of the year did not improve, and the partners decided to go out of business before additional losses were incurred. The decision to liquidate was hastened when two major customers filed bankruptcy petitions.

The sale of assets was completed in October, Year 6, and all available cash was paid to creditors. Suppliers' invoices of $5,400 remained unpaid at this time. The personal financial status of each partner on October 31, Year 6, was as follows:

	Personal assets	Personal liabilities
Love	$30,000	$25,500
Mears	60,000	15,000
Newman	75,000	42,000

The partners had made no cash withdrawals during Year 6; however, in August Newman had withdrawn merchandise with a cost of $1,200 and Mears had taken title to equipment at a current fair value of $750, which was equal to the carrying amount of the equipment.

The partners have decided to end the partnership immediately and to arrive at a settlement in accordance with the provisions of the Uniform Partnership Act.

Instructions Prepare a four-column statement of partners' capital (including liquidation) for the period January 10, Year 6, to October 31, Year 6. You need not show the changes in liabilities, cash, or noncash assets; however, the changes in the combined capital and individual capital accounts of the three partners should be shown.

2-7 Partners Denson, Eastin, and Feller share net income and losses in a 5:3:2 ratio, respectively. At the end of a very unprofitable year, they decided to liquidate the firm. The partners' capital account balances on this date were as follows: Denson, $22,000; Eastin, $24,900; Feller, $15,000. The liabilities in the balance sheet amounted to $30,000, including a loan of $10,000 from Denson. The cash balance was $6,000.

The partners plan to sell the noncash assets on a piecemeal basis and to distribute cash as rapidly as it becomes available. All three partners are personally solvent.

Instructions Answer each of the following questions and show how you reached your conclusions. (Each question is independent of the others. An advance program for cash distributions to partners would be helpful.)

a If Eastin received $2,000 from the first distribution of cash, how much did Denson and Feller each receive at that time?

b If Denson received a total of $20,000 as a result of the liquidation, what was the total amount realized by the partnership on the sale of the noncash assets?

c If Feller received $6,200 on the first distribution of cash, how much did Denson receive at that time?

2-8 Adderly and Boggs were attorneys who became acquainted because of their interest in auto racing. They decided to form a partnership, and persuaded a third attorney, Cobb, to join with them. The partnership had limited accounting records, but an employee maintained a careful daily record of cash receipts, which were almost entirely checks received through the mail. The only other record was the checkbook used for all payments by the partnership. Some working papers were on file relating to income tax information returns of prior years.

Early in Year 5, the partners quarreled over the use of partnership funds; this quarrel led to a decision to liquidate the firm as of June 30, Year 5. You were retained to assemble the financial data needed for an equitable distribution of assets. You learn that the partnership was formed in Year 1, with equal capital investments and agreement to share net income and losses equally. By inspection of the income tax return for the year ended December 31, Year 4, you determine that the amounts of depreciable assets and accumulated depreciation on December 31, Year 4, were as follows:

	Depreciable assets (cost)	Accumulated depreciation, Dec. 31, Year 4
Office equipment	$ 7,500	$ 2,250
Library of reference books	4,500	900
Automobiles:		
Bentley—assigned to Adderly	20,000	6,000
Buick—assigned to Boggs	5,000	1,000
Cadillac—assigned to Cobb	15,000	3,000
Totals	$52,000	$13,150

By reference to the cash records, you find that fees received from clients for the first six months of Year 5 amounted to $310,000. Cash payments are summarized at the top of page 90.

The automobiles were depreciated on a straight-line basis over a five-year economic life with no residual value, and depreciation was treated as an expense of the partnership. A 10-year economic life was used for depreciation of office equipment and the library. As a step in the liquidation, the partners agreed that the automobiles acquired from partnership funds should be retained by the partners to whom assigned. They also agreed on equal distribution of the office equipment among them in kind. The entire library will be distributed to Adderly.

Automobile and miscellaneous expenses	$ 9,490
Entertainment expense	30,000
Wages and salaries expense	80,510
Rent expense	9,000
Drawings: Adderly	45,000
Drawings: Boggs	50,000
Drawings: Cobb	60,000
Total cash payments	$284,000

All assets distributed were assigned current fair values equal to carrying amounts.

Cash on hand and in bank on June 30, Year 5, amounted to $70,010. **The capital account balances of the partners were equal on December 31, Year 4.** Assume that the partnership had no other assets or liabilities, either at the beginning or at the end of the six-month period ended June 30, Year 5.

Instructions Prepare a statement of partners' capital for the period January 1 to June 30, Year 5, including the final distribution of cash and other assets to partners. To support this statement, prepare an income statement for the six months ended June 30, Year 5.

2-9 On August 10, Year 4, Alison Ho, Jodie Thompson, and George Cole agreed to acquire a speculative second mortgage note on undeveloped real estate. They invested $110,800, $66,100, and $25,000, respectively, and agreed on an income-sharing ratio of 4:2:1, respectively.

On September 1, Year 4, the partnership acquired for $201,000 a second mortgage note with an unpaid principal balance of $245,000. The amount paid included interest accrued from June 30, Year 4, and legal fees of $1,000. The note principal matures at the rate of $5,000 each quarter. Interest at the annual rate of 12% on the unpaid principal balance also is due quarterly.

Regular interest and principal payments were received on September 30 and December 31, Year 4. A petty cash fund of $100 was established, and collection expenses of $260 were paid in December.

In addition to the regular payment on September 30, the mortgagor made an early payment of $20,000 principal plus a penalty of 2% (on $20,000) for early payment.

Because of the speculative nature of the second mortgage note, the partners agreed to defer recognition of the discount as revenue until their investment of $201,000 had been fully recovered.

Instructions
a Assuming that no cash distributions were made to the partners, prepare a working paper to compute the amount of cash available for distribution to the partners on December 31, Year 4.
b After payment of collection expenses, the partners wish to distribute the cash as soon as possible so that they individually can reinvest it. Prepare a working paper showing how any available cash should be distributed to the partners by installments as it becomes available.
c Show how the cash on hand on December 31, Year 4, as computed in **a**, should be distributed to the partners.

2-10 After several years of successful operation of a partnership, Luis and Anna decided to incorporate and sell stock to public investors.

On January 2, Year 5, Luisanna, Inc., was organized with authorization to issue 150,000 shares of $10 par common stock. It issued 20,000 shares for cash to public investors at $16 a share. Luis and Anna agreed to accept shares at the same price in amounts equal to their respective capital account balances, after making the adjustments indicated below and after making cash withdrawals sufficient to avoid the need for issuing less than a multiple of 100 shares to either of the two partners. In payment for such shares, the partnership's net assets were transferred to the corporation and common stock certificates were issued. A new set of accounting records was opened for the corporation.

The after-closing trial balance of the Luis & Anna Partnership on December 31, Year 4, follows:

LUIS & ANNA PARTNERSHIP
After-Closing Trial Balance
December 31, Year 4

Cash	$ 37,000	
Accounts receivable	30,000	
Inventories	56,000	
Land	28,000	
Buildings	50,000	
Accumulated depreciation of buildings		$ 17,000
Accounts payable		10,000
Luis, capital		63,000
Anna, capital		111,000
Totals	$201,000	$201,000

The partnership contract provided that Luis is to receive 40% of net income or loss and Anna 60%. The partners approved the following adjustments to the accounting records of the partnership on December 31, Year 4:

(1) Record short-term prepayments of $1,500 and accrued liabilities of $750.
(2) Provide an allowance for doubtful accounts of $12,000.
(3) Increase the carrying amount of land to a current fair value of $45,000.
(4) Increase inventories to present replacement cost of $75,000.

Instructions
a Prepare a single journal entry to adjust the accounting records of the Luis & Anna Partnership to current fair value. Also prepare all other entries needed to record the foregoing transactions.
b Prepare the journal entries necessary to record the foregoing transactions in the accounting records of Luisanna, Inc., on January 2, Year 5.
c Prepare the opening balance sheet for Luisanna, Inc., after the foregoing transactions have been recorded.

2-11 Independence Day Venture was formed by Bob, Cid, and Don to sell hot dogs on July 4, Year 1. Bob agreed to construct a stand on Don's front lawn and charge the construction costs to operations as an expense. Don agreed, but asked $25 for the cost of sod replacement and cleaning the lawn after July 4. The venturers decided that net income would be distributed first by the $25 payment to Don for lawn rental and then by a 40% commission on sales made by each venturer. The balance of net income would be distributed 75% to Bob and 25% to Cid. They also agreed that a cash box would only complicate matters and that all purchases and sales transactions would be out-of-pocket and the responsibility of each venturer. All sales were made at a 100% markup on cost, and the ending inventory of supplies might be purchased from the joint venture by any of the venturers at 50% of cost.

The activity of the joint venture for the period July 2 to 5, Year 1, is summarized at the top of page 92.

July 2   Bob constructed a stand on Don's front lawn at a cost of $100.
July 3   Bob paid $1,000 for supplies (rolls, weiners, mustard, etc.), and Don paid
         $50 for a city permit to operate the concession.
July 4   Bob purchased additional supplies for $1,500. Sales of hot dogs were as
         follows: Bob, $1,700; Cid, $2,600; and Don, $500.
July 5   Don paid $90 for three fire extinguishers; these were distributed to the
         venturers for their personal use. Don agreed to pay $45 for the stand.
         The balance of the inventory of supplies was taken by Bob at 50% of
         cost.

Instructions   Prepare a working paper analysis that will give the venturers the
following information: (**a**) net income or loss from operation of the joint venture,
(**b**) distribution of net income or loss to the venturers, and (**c**) the final settlement
among the venturers.

The following headings are suggested for the working paper: Transactions;
Inventory Reconciliation (at cost); Net Income or Loss; Bob, Capital; Cid, Capital; Don, Capital.

2-12   D, E & F Partnership has called on you to assist in winding up the affairs of the
partnership. You are able to gather the following information:

(1) The trial balance of the partnership on March 1, Year 3, is as follows:

D, E & F PARTNERSHIP
Trial Balance
March 1, Year 3

Cash	$ 10,000	
Accounts receivable (net)	22,000	
Inventories	14,000	
Plant assets (net)	99,000	
D, loan receivable	12,000	
F, loan receivable	7,500	
Accounts payable		$ 21,000
D, capital		67,000
E, capital		45,000
F, capital		31,500
Totals	$164,500	$164,500

(2) The partners share net income and losses as follows: D, 40%; E, 40%; and F,
20%.
(3) The partners are considering an offer of $104,000 for the accounts receiv-
able, inventories, and plant assets on March 1, Year 3.

Instructions

a Prepare a cash distribution program as of March 1, Year 3, and show how the
total available cash of $114,000 ($10,000 + $104,000 = $114,000) would be
distributed if the accounts receivable, inventories, and plant assets are sold
for $104,000.
b Assume the same facts as in **a**, except that the partners have decided to liquidate the partnership instead of accepting the offer of $104,000. Cash is distrib-
uted to the partners at the end of each month. A summary of the liquidation
transactions follows:

March: $16,500 collected on accounts receivable, balance is uncollectible.

$10,000 received for all inventories.

$1,000 liquidation expenses paid.

$8,000 cash retained for possible liquidation expenses.

April: $1,500 liquidation expenses paid. As part payment of F's capital account balance, F accepted equipment that had a carrying amount of $4,000. The partners agreed that a current fair value of $10,000 was appropriate for the equipment for liquidation purposes.

$3,500 cash retained for possible liquidation expenses.

May: $92,000 received on sale of remaining plant assets.

$1,000 liquidation expenses paid. No cash was retained.

Prepare a summary of cash distributions for the three months ended May 31, Year 3, that shows how the cash was distributed each month.

2-13 A, B, C, and D decided to liquidate their partnership. They plan to sell the assets gradually in order to minimize losses. They share net income and losses as follows: A 40%; B 35%; C 15%; and D 10%. Presented below is the partnership's trial balance on October 1, Year 8, the date on which liquidation began:

A, B, C & D PARTNERSHIP

Trial Balance

October 1, Year 8

Cash	$ 23,400	
Accounts receivable (net)	51,800	
Inventories, Oct. 1, Year 8	85,200	
Equipment (net)	39,600	
Accounts payable		$ 29,000
A, loan		12,000
B, loan		20,000
A, capital		40,000
B, capital		43,000
C, capital		36,000
D, capital		20,000
Totals	$200,000	$200,000

Instructions

a Prepare a working paper on October 1, Year 8, showing how cash will be distributed among partners in installments as it becomes available. To simplify computations, restate the income-sharing ratio to 8:7:3:2.

b On October 31, Year 8, cash of $65,200 was available for creditors and partners. How should the $65,200 be distributed?

c If, instead of being liquidated, the partnership continued operations and earned $69,300 for the year ended September 30, Year 9, how should this income be divided if, in addition to the aforementioned income-sharing arrangement, it was provided that D receive a bonus of 5% of the income after treating the bonus as an expense? The income of $69,300 is before deduction of the bonus to D.

2-14 John Lee and Fred Moss started separate manufacturing enterprises and operated as single proprietorships for many years. In Year 8, they agreed to form a partnership, each transferring the assets and liabilities of his proprietorship to the new partnership.

Their income-sharing plan has been altered several times since Year 8, in order to recognize the changing contribution of each partner to the success of the partnership. The current plan calls for the partnership net income (before interest on capital account balances and partners' salaries) to be distributed as follows:

(1) Interest of 10% a year on beginning capital account balances.
(2) Salary allowances: Lee, $25,000; Moss, $20,000.
(3) Balance of net income, 60% to Lee and 40% to Moss.
(4) Interest and salary allowances are to be allocated to partners, regardless of the amount of net income. Any excess of such allowances over the amount of net income available is to be absorbed by Lee and Moss in the residual income-sharing ratio.

On December 31, Year 16, the accountant for the partnership prepared the following preliminary balance sheet:

LEE & MOSS PARTNERSHIP
Preliminary Balance Sheet
December 31, Year 16

Assets			Liabilities & Partners' Capital		
Cash		$ 180,000	Notes payable		$ 154,500
Notes receivable		60,000	Accounts payable		135,000
Accounts receivable		250,000	Accrued liabilities		20,000
Less: Allowance for doubtful			Mortgage note payable		310,000
accounts		(15,000)	Lee, capital,		
Inventories		225,000	Jan. 1, Year 16	$521,900	
Land		150,000	Lee, drawings	(40,000)	481,900
Buildings (net of accumulated			Moss, capital, Jan.		
depreciation of $200,000)		500,000	1, Year 16	$428,600	
Machinery (net of accum-			Moss, drawings	(30,000)	398,600
ulated depreciation of			Net income for Year 16		100,000
$120,000)		250,000			
Total		$1,600,000	Total		$1,600,000

Incorporation of partnership

The net income of $100,000 for Year 16 was distributed according to the partnership contract, and the partners decided to incorporate as the L & M Corporation, effective December 31, Year 16, as follows:

(1) Each partner is to receive 25,000 shares of 10% cumulative, $10 par preferred stock. A total of 100,000 shares of preferred stock is authorized to be issued. The current fair value of the preferred stock is equal to its par value.
(2) A total of 250,000 shares of common stock with a stated value of $0.10 a share will be issued to the partners in proportion to their adjusted capital account balances [item (3) below] after issuance of the preferred stock. A total of 500,000 shares of common stock is authorized to be issued.
(3) The accounting records of the partnership will be retained by the corporation; however, the following adjustments are required:

(a) Short-term prepayments of $10,000 (consisting of rents, supplies, insurance, etc.) have been recorded as expenses by the partnership. The partners wish to report these assets in the opening balance sheet of the corporation.

(b) Costs of organizing the corporation, $12,500, have been inadvertently recorded as expenses by the partnership during Year 16.

(c) The accrued liabilities in the partnership's balance sheet on December 31, Year 16, do not include $3,000 of interest that has accrued on notes payable.

The activities of the L & M Corporation for the year ended December 31, Year 17, are summarized below:

(4) Net income (after income taxes) amounted to $120,000.

(5) Dividends of $1 a share were declared and paid on the preferred stock, and cash dividends of $0.12 a share were declared and paid on the common stock.

Instructions

a Allocate the net income of $100,000 for Year 16 to the partners pursuant to the income-sharing plan, and compute the capital account balance for each partner on December 31, Year 16.

b Starting with the capital account balances on December 31, Year 16, as determined in part *a*, prepare a working paper to adjust the partners' capital accounts in accordance with the incorporation plan and determine the number of shares of common stock to be issued to each partner. (Round shares to be issued to the nearest whole share.)

c Prepare journal entries on December 31, Year 16, to adjust the accounting records of the partnership, and to change the partnership to a corporation. Assume that the preferred stock and common stock are issued directly to Lee and Moss instead of first being transferred to the partnership.

d Prepare the stockholders' equity section of the balance sheet for the L & M Corporation on December 31, Year 17.

3 ACCOUNTING FOR BRANCHES; COMBINED FINANCIAL STATEMENTS

Branches and divisions

As a business enterprise grows it often establishes branches to market its products over a larger territory. The term **branch** has been used to describe a business unit located at some distance from the home office that carries merchandise, makes sales, approves customers' credit, and makes collections from its customers.

A branch may obtain merchandise solely from the home office, or a portion may be purchased from outside suppliers. The cash receipts of the branch often are deposited in a bank account belonging to the home office; the branch expenses then are paid from an imprest cash fund or a bank account provided by the home office. As the imprest fund is depleted, the branch submits a list of cash payments supported by vouchers and receives a check from the home office to replenish the fund.

The use of an imprest fund gives the home office strong control over the cash transactions of the branch. However, it is common practice for a large branch to maintain its own bank accounts; that is, to deposit its cash receipts and issue its own checks. The extent of autonomy and responsibility given to a branch varies even among different branches of the same business enterprise.

A segment of a business enterprise also may be operated as a **division.** The accounting procedures for a division not organized as a separate corporation (**subsidiary company**) are similar to those used for branches. When a segment of a business enterprise is operated as a separate corporation, consolidated financial statements generally would be required. Consolidated financial statements are described in Chapters 5 through 10; accounting and reporting problems for segments of business enterprises are included in Chapter 15.

Accounting system for a sales agency

The term *sales agency* sometimes is applied to a business unit that performs only a small portion of the functions traditionally associated with a branch. For example, a sales agency usually carries samples of products but does not have an inventory of merchandise. Orders are taken from customers and transmitted to the home office, which approves the customers' credit and ships the merchandise directly to customers. The agency's accounts receivable are maintained at the home office, which also performs the collection function. An imprest cash fund generally is maintained at the sales agency for the payment of operating expenses.

A sales agency that does not carry an inventory of merchandise, maintain receivables, or make collections has no need for a complete set of accounting records. All that is needed is a record of sales to customers and a summary of cash payments supported by vouchers.

If the home office wants to measure the profitability of each sales agency separately, it will establish in the general ledger separate revenue and expense accounts in the name of the agency, for example, Sales: Lakeview Agency; Rent Expense: Lakeview Agency. The cost of goods sold by each agency also must be determined. When a perpetual inventory system is in use, shipments to customers of the Lakeview Agency are debited to Cost of Goods Sold: Lakeview Agency and credited to Inventories.

When a periodic inventory system is used, a shipment of goods sold by an agency may be recorded by a debit to Cost of Goods Sold: Lakeview Agency and a credit to Shipments to Agencies. This journal entry is recorded only at the end of the accounting period if a memorandum record is maintained during the period listing the cost of goods shipped to fill sales orders received from agencies. At the end of the period the Shipments to Agencies account is offset against the total of beginning inventories and purchases to determine the cost of goods available for sale for the home office in its own operations.

Office furniture or other assets located at a sales agency may be carried in a separate account in the general ledger of the home office, or control over such assets may be achieved by use of a subsidiary ledger with a detail record for each item showing cost, location, and other data.

Illustrative Journal Entries for a Sales Agency The journal entries required for the home office in connection with the operation of a sales agency are illustrated on page 98, assuming that the perpetual inventory system is used.

Accounting system for a branch

The extent of the accounting activity at a branch depends on company policy. The policies of one company may provide for a complete set of

Journal entries for home
office to record agency
activities

HOME OFFICE
General Journal

Inventory of Samples: Lakeview Agency	*1,500*	
Inventories		*1,500*
To record merchandise shipped to agency for use as samples.		
Imprest Cash Fund: Lakeview Agency	*1,000*	
Cash		*1,000*
To establish agency imprest cash fund.		
Accounts Receivable	*50,000*	
Sales: Lakeview Agency		*50,000*
To record sales made through Lakeview Agency.		
Cost of Goods Sold: Lakeview Agency	*35,000*	
Inventories		*35,000*
To record cost of goods sold through Lakeview Agency.		
Various Expense Accounts: Lakeview Agency	*10,000*	
Cash		*10,000*
To replenish imprest cash fund. (This entry represents several checks sent to the agency during the accounting period.)		
Sales: Lakeview Agency	*50,000*	
Cost of Goods Sold: Lakeview Agency		*35,000*
Various Expense Accounts: Lakeview Agency		*10,000*
Income Summary: Lakeview Agency		*5,000*
To close revenue and expense accounts to a separate Income Summary account for sales agency.		
Income Summary: Lakeview Agency	*5,000*	
Income Summary		*5,000*
To close agency net income to Income Summary account.		

accounting records at each branch; policies of another company may concentrate all accounting records in the home office. In some of the drug and grocery chain stores, for example, the branches submit daily reports and documents to the home office, which enters all transactions by branches in computerized accounting records kept in a central location. The home office may not even conduct operations of its own but merely serve as an accounting and control center for the branches.

In many fields of business, a branch maintains a complete set of accounting records consisting of journals, ledgers, and a chart of accounts similar to those of an independent business enterprise. Financial statements are prepared at regular intervals by the branch and forwarded to the home office. The number and types of accounts, the internal control system, the form and content of financial statements, and the accounting policies generally are prescribed by the home office.

In the remainder of this chapter we are concerned with a branch operation that maintains a complete set of accounting records. Transactions recorded by branches ordinarily should include all controllable expenses and revenue for which branch managers are responsible. If branch managers have responsibility over all branch assets and all expenditures, then the branch accounting records should reflect this responsibility. Expenses such as depreciation are not subject to control by branch managers; therefore, both the plant assets and the related depreciation accounts generally are maintained by the home office.

Reciprocal accounts

The accounting records maintained by a branch include a Home Office account that is credited for all merchandise, cash, or other resources provided by the home office; it is debited for all cash, merchandise, or other assets sent by the branch to the home office or to other branches. The Home Office account is an ownership equity account that shows the net investment by the home office in the branch. At the end of the accounting period when the branch closes its accounting records, the Income Summary account is closed to the Home Office account. A net income increases the credit balance in the Home Office account; a net loss decreases this balance.

In the home office accounting records, a *reciprocal account* with a title such as Investment in Branch is maintained. This asset account is debited for cash, merchandise, and services provided to the branch by the home office, and for net income reported by the branch. It is credited for the cash or other assets received from the branch, and for any net loss reported by the branch. Thus, the Investment in Branch account reflects the *equity method* of accounting. A separate investment account generally is maintained by the home office for each branch. If there is only one branch, the account title is likely to be Investment in Branch; if there are numerous branches, each account title includes a name or number to identify the individual branch.

Expenses incurred by home office and charged to branches

Some business enterprises follow a policy of notifying branches of expenses incurred by the home office on the branches' behalf. As previously mentioned, plant assets located at branches generally are carried in the home office accounting records. If a plant asset is acquired by the home office for the branch, the journal entry for the acquisition is a debit to an asset account and credit to Cash or Accounts Payable. If the branch acquires a plant asset, it debits the Home Office account and credits Cash or Accounts Payable. The home office debits an asset account, such as Equipment: Elba Branch, and credits the reciprocal account Investment in Elba Branch.

The home office also usually acquires insurance, pays property and other taxes, and arranges for advertising that benefits all branches. Clearly, such expenses as depreciation, property taxes, insurance, and advertising must be considered in determining the profitability of a branch. A policy decision must be made as to whether these expense data are to be retained at the home office or are to be reported to the branches so that the income statement prepared by each branch will give a complete picture of its operations.

If the home office does not make sales itself but functions only as an accounting and control center, most or all of its expenses may be allocated to the branches. To facilitate comparison of the operating results of the various branches, the home office may charge each branch interest on the capital invested in that branch. Such interest expense recorded by the branches would be offset by interest revenue recorded by the home office and would not appear in the *combined* income statement of the business enterprise as a whole.

Alternative methods of billing merchandise shipments to branch

Three alternative methods are available to the home office for billing merchandise shipped to a branch. The shipments may be billed (1) at cost, (2) at cost plus an appropriate percentage, or (3) at retail selling price.[1] Of course, the shipment of merchandise to a branch does not constitute a sale, because ownership of the merchandise does not change.

Billing *at cost* is the simplest procedure and is widely used. It avoids the complication of unrealized gross profit in inventories and permits the financial statements of branches to give a meaningful picture of operations. However, billing merchandise to branches at cost attributes all gross profits of the enterprise to the branches, even though some of the merchandise may be manufactured by the home office. Under these circumstances, cost may not be the most realistic basis for billing shipments to branches.

Billing shipments to a branch *at a percentage above cost* (such as 110% of cost) may be intended to allocate a reasonable gross profit to home office operations. When merchandise is billed to a branch at a price above cost, the net income reported by the branch will be understated and the ending inventories will be overstated for the enterprise as a whole. Adjustments must be made by the home office to eliminate the excess of billed prices over cost in the preparation of combined financial statements for the home office and the branch.

---

[1] Billing of merchandise to branches at a price above cost is illustrated on pages 107 to 110.

Billing shipments to a branch **at retail selling price** may be based on a desire to strengthen internal control over inventories. The Inventories account of the branch shows the merchandise received and sold at retail selling prices. Consequently, the account will show the ending inventories that should be on hand priced at retail. The home office record of shipments to a branch, when considered along with sales reported by the branch, provides a perpetual inventory stated at selling price. If the physical inventories taken periodically at the branch do not agree with the amounts thus determined, an error or theft is indicated and should be investigated promptly.

Separate financial statements for branch and home office

A separate income statement and balance sheet should be prepared for the branch so that management of the enterprise may review the operating results and financial position of the branch. The income statement has no unusual features if merchandise is billed to the branch at cost. However, if merchandise is billed to the branch at retail selling price, the income statement will show a net loss approximating the amount of operating expenses. The only unusual aspect of the balance sheet for a branch is the use of the Home Office account in lieu of the ownership equity accounts for a separate business enterprise. The separate financial statements prepared for a branch may be revised at the home office to include expenses incurred by the home office allocable to the branch, and to show branch operations after elimination of any intracompany profits on merchandise shipments.

Separate financial statements also may be prepared for the home office so that management will be able to appraise the results of its operations and its financial position. However, it is important to emphasize that separate financial statements of the home office and of the branch are prepared for internal use only; they do not meet the needs of investors, or other external users of financial statements.

Combined financial statements for home office and branch

A balance sheet for distribution to creditors, stockholders, and government agencies must show the financial position of the business enterprise as a **single entity.** A convenient starting point in the preparation of a combined balance sheet consists of the adjusted trial balances of the home office and of the branch. A working paper for the combination of these trial balances is illustrated on page 106.

The assets and liabilities of the branch are substituted for the Investment in Branch account included in the home office trial balance. Similar accounts are combined to produce one amount for the total cash, accounts receivable, and other assets and liabilities of the enterprise as a whole.

In the preparation of a combined balance sheet, reciprocal accounts are eliminated because they lose all significance when the branch and home office are viewed as a single entity. The Home Office account is offset against the Investment in Branch account; also any receivables and payables between branches or between the home office and a branch are eliminated.

The operating results of the enterprise (the home office and all branches) are shown by an income statement in which the revenue and expenses of the branches are combined with corresponding revenue and expenses for the home office. Any intracompany profits or losses must be eliminated.

Illustrative Journal Entries of Operation of a Branch Assume that Smaldino Company bills merchandise to Branch X at cost, and that the branch maintains complete accounting records and prepares financial statements. ***Both the home office and the branch use the perpetual inventory system.*** Equipment used at the branch is carried in the home office accounting records. Certain expenses, such as advertising and insurance, are incurred by the home office on behalf of the branch and are billed to the branch. Transactions during the first year (Year 1) of operations of the branch are summarized below:

Transactions for Year 1:

(1) Cash of $1,000 was sent to the branch
(2) Merchandise with a cost of $60,000 was shipped to the branch
(3) Equipment was acquired by the branch for $500, to be carried in home office accounting records (Other assets for the branch normally are acquired by the home office)
(4) Credit sales by the branch amounted to $80,000; the cost of the merchandise sold was $45,000
(5) Collections of accounts receivable by the branch amounted to $62,000
(6) Payments for operating expenses by the branch totaled $20,000
(7) Cash of $37,500 was remitted by the branch to the home office
(8) Operating expenses incurred by the home office and charged to the branch totaled $3,000

These transactions are recorded by the home office and by the branch as illustrated on page 103.

When the branch obtains merchandise from outsiders as well as from the home office, the merchandise acquired from the home office should be recorded in a separate Inventories from Home Office account.

In the home office accounting records, the Investment in Branch X account has a debit balance of $26,000 (before the accounting records are closed and the branch net income of $12,000 is transferred to the Investment in Branch X account), as illustrated on page 104.

In the branch accounting records, the Home Office account has a

Typical home office and branch transactions (perpetual inventory system)

Home Office Accounting Records			Branch Accounting Records		
(1) Investment in			Cash	1,000	
Branch X	1,000		Home Office . .		1,000
Cash		1,000			
(2) Investment in			Inventories	60,000	
Branch X	60,000		Home Office . .		60,000
Inventories . .		60,000			
(3) Equipment:			Home Office	500	
Branch X	500		Cash		500
Investment in					
Branch X . . .		500			
(4) None			Accounts		
			Receivable.	80,000	
			Cost of Goods Sold . .	45,000	
			Sales		80,000
			Inventories . . .		45,000
(5) None			Cash	62,000	
			Accounts		
			Receivable . . .		62,000
(6) None			Operating Expenses .	20,000	
			Cash		20,000
(7) Cash	37,500		Home Office	37,500	
Investment in			Cash		37,500
Branch X		37,500			
(8) Investment in			Operating Expenses .	3,000	
Branch X	3,000		Home Office . .		3,000
Operating					
Expenses . . .		3,000			

credit balance of $26,000 (before the accounting records are closed and the net income of $12,000 is transferred to the Home Office account), as shown on page 104.

Assume that the perpetual inventories of $15,000 ($60,000 − $45,000 = $15,000) at the end of Year 1 for Branch X had been verified by a physical count. The adjusting and closing entries relating to the branch are given at the bottom of page 104.

Reciprocal account in home office general ledger

Investment in Branch X

Date	Explanation	Debit	Credit	Balance
	Cash sent to branch	1,000		1,000 dr
	Merchandise billed to branch at cost	60,000		61,000 dr
	Equipment acquired by branch, carried in home office account-ing records		500	60,500 dr
	Cash received from branch		37,500	23,000 dr
	Operating expenses billed to branch	3,000		26,000 dr

Reciprocal account in branch general ledger

Home Office

Date	Explanation	Debit	Credit	Balance
	Cash received from home office		1,000	1,000 cr
	Merchandise received from home office		60,000	61,000 cr
	Equipment acquired by branch	500		60,500 cr
	Cash sent to home office	37,500		23,000 cr
	Operating expenses billed by home office		3,000	26,000 cr

Adjusting and closing entries (perpetual inventory system)

Home Office Accounting Records	Branch Accounting Records
None	Sales 80,000
	Cost of Goods Sold 45,000
	Operating Expenses . . . 23,000
	Income Summary 12,000
Investment in Branch X 12,000	Income Summary . . . 12,000
Income: Branch X 12,000	Home Office . . 12,000
Income: Branch X . . . 12,000	None
Income Summary 12,000	

Working paper for combined financial statements

A working paper for combined financial statements has three purposes: (1) to combine ledger account balances for like assets and liabilities, (2) to eliminate any intracompany profits or losses, and (3) to eliminate the reciprocal accounts. The working paper illustrated on page 106 for Smaldino Company is based on the branch transactions illustrated on pages 102 and 103 and additional assumed data for the home office trial balance. All the routine year-end adjusting entries are assumed to have been made, and the working paper is begun with the adjusted trial balances of the home office and the branch. Income taxes are ignored in this illustration.

Note that the $26,000 debit balance in the Investment in Branch X account and the $26,000 credit balance in the Home Office account are the balances before the respective accounting records are closed, that is, before the $12,000 net income of the branch is entered in these two reciprocal accounts. In the Elimination column, elimination (a) offsets the Investment in Branch X account against the Home Office account. **This elimination appears in the working paper only;** it is not recorded in the accounting records of either the home office or the branch, because its only purpose is to facilitate the preparation of combined financial statements.

Combined Financial Statements Illustrated The working paper on page 106 provides the information for the combined financial statements of Smaldino Company below and on page 107.

SMALDINO COMPANY
Income Statement
For Year Ended December 31, Year 1

Sales	$480,000
Cost of goods sold	280,000
Gross profit on sales	$200,000
Operating expenses	113,000
Net income	$ 87,000
Earnings per share	$ 5.80

SMALDINO COMPANY
Statement of Retained Earnings
For Year Ended December 31, Year 1

Retained earnings, beginning of year	$ 70,000
Add: Net income	87,000
Subtotal	$157,000
Less: Dividends	40,000
Retained earnings, end of year	$117,000

SMALDINO COMPANY
Working Paper for Combined Financial Statements of Home Office and Branch X
For Year Ended December 31, Year 1
(Perpetual Inventory System: Billings at Cost)

| | Adjusted trial balances | | | | Elimination | Combined | |
| | Home office | | Branch | | | | |
	Debit	Credit	Debit	Credit	Debit (Credit)	Debit	Credit
Income statement							
Sales		400,000		80,000			480,000
Cost of goods sold .	235,000		45,000			280,000	
Operating expenses	90,000		23,000			113,000	
Subtotals	325,000	400,000	68,000	80,000		393,000	480,000
Net income (to							
statement of re-							
tained earnings							
below).	75,000		12,000			87,000	
Totals	400,000	400,000	80,000	80,000		480,000	480,000
Statement of retained							
earnings							
Retained earnings,							
Jan. 1, Year 1 . . .		70,000					70,000
Net income (from							
above).		75,000		12,000			87,000
Dividends	40,000					40,000	
Retained earnings,							
Dec. 31, Year 1 (to							
balance sheet							
below).						117,000	
Totals						157,000	157,000
Balance sheet							
Cash	24,000		5,000			29,000	
Accounts receivable							
(net)	40,000		18,000			58,000	
Inventories	45,000		15,000			60,000	
Investment in							
Branch X	26,000				(a) (26,000)		
Equipment.	150,000					150,000	
Accumulated							
depreciation		10,000					10,000
Accounts payable. .		20,000					20,000
Home office				26,000	(a) 26,000		
Common stock,							
$10 par		150,000					150,000
Retained earnings							
(from above)							117,000
Totals	325,000	325,000	38,000	38,000	-0-	297,000	297,000

(a) To eliminate reciprocal accounts.

SMALDINO COMPANY
Balance Sheet
December 31, Year 1

Assets

Cash		$ 29,000
Accounts receivable (net)		58,000
Inventories		60,000
Equipment	$150,000	
Less: Accumulated depreciation	10,000	140,000
Total assets		$287,000

Liabilities & Stockholders' Equity

Liabilities:		
Accounts payable		$ 20,000
Stockholders' equity:		
Common stock, $10 par	$150,000	
Retained earnings	117,000	267,000
Total liabilities & stockholders' equity		$287,000

Billing of merchandise to branches at price above cost

As explained earlier, some business enterprises bill merchandise to branches at cost plus a markup percentage, or at retail selling price. Because both these methods involve similar modifications of accounting procedures, a single example illustrates the key points involved. We shall now repeat the illustration for Smaldino Company, with one changed assumption: the home office bills merchandise to the branch at 50% above cost.

Under this assumption the journal entries for the first year's transactions by the home office and the branch are the same as those previously presented on page 103, except for the journal entries showing shipments from the home office to the branch. These shipments ($60,000 + 50% markup = $90,000) are recorded under a perpetual inventory system as follows:

Shipment to branch at a price above cost (perpetual inventory system)	Home Office Accounting Records	Branch Accounting Records
	(2) Investment in	Inventories 90,000
	Branch X. 90,000	Home Office . . 90,000
	Inventories . . . 60,000	
	Allowance for	
	Overvaluation	
	of Inventories:	
	Branch X 30,000	

In the home office accounting records the Investment in Branch X account now has a debit balance of $56,000 before the accounting records are closed and the branch net income or loss is entered in the Investment in Branch X account. This amount is $30,000 larger than the $26,000 balance in the prior illustration; the increase represents the 50% markup over cost of the merchandise shipped to Branch X. The Investment in Branch X account is illustrated below:

<table>
<tr><td rowspan="2" style="text-align:left">Reciprocal account in
home office ledger</td><td colspan="6" style="text-align:center">Investment in Branch X</td></tr>
<tr><td>Date</td><td>Explanation</td><td>Debit</td><td>Credit</td><td>Balance</td></tr>
<tr><td></td><td>Cash sent to branch</td><td>1,000</td><td></td><td>1,000 dr</td></tr>
<tr><td></td><td>Merchandise billed to branch at
  50% above cost</td><td>90,000</td><td></td><td>91,000 dr</td></tr>
<tr><td></td><td>Equipment acquired by branch,
  carried in home office account-
  ing records</td><td></td><td>500</td><td>90,500 dr</td></tr>
<tr><td></td><td>Cash received from branch</td><td></td><td>37,500</td><td>53,000 dr</td></tr>
<tr><td></td><td>Operating expenses billed to
  branch</td><td>3,000</td><td></td><td>56,000 dr</td></tr>
</table>

In the branch accounting records the Home Office account now has a credit balance of $56,000, before the accounting records are closed and the branch net income or loss is entered in the Home Office account:

<table>
<tr><td rowspan="2" style="text-align:left">Reciprocal account in
branch ledger</td><td colspan="6" style="text-align:center">Home Office</td></tr>
<tr><td>Date</td><td>Explanation</td><td>Debit</td><td>Credit</td><td>Balance</td></tr>
<tr><td></td><td>Cash received from home office</td><td></td><td>1,000</td><td>1,000 cr</td></tr>
<tr><td></td><td>Merchandise received from home
  office</td><td></td><td>90,000</td><td>91,000 cr</td></tr>
<tr><td></td><td>Equipment acquired by branch</td><td>500</td><td></td><td>90,500 cr</td></tr>
<tr><td></td><td>Cash sent to home office</td><td>37,500</td><td></td><td>53,000 cr</td></tr>
<tr><td></td><td>Operating expenses billed by
  home office</td><td></td><td>3,000</td><td>56,000 cr</td></tr>
</table>

The branch recorded the merchandise received from the home office at the billed price of $90,000; the home office recorded the shipment by credits of $60,000 to Inventories and $30,000 to the Allowance for Overvaluation of Inventories: Branch X account. Use of the allowance account enables the home office to maintain a record of the cost of merchandise shipped to the branch, as well as the amount of the unrealized gross profit on the shipments.

At the end of the accounting period, the branch will report its inventories (based on billed prices) at $22,500. The cost of these inventories is $15,000 (computed as follows: $22,500 ÷ 1.50 = $15,000). In the home office accounting records, the required balance in the Allowance for Overvaluation of Inventories: Branch X account is $7,500; thus, this account must be reduced from its present balance of $30,000 to $7,500. The reason for this reduction is that the 50% markup of billed prices over cost has become realized gross profit with respect to the merchandise sold by the branch. Consequently, at the end of the year the home office should reduce its allowance for overvaluation of the branch inventories to the $7,500 excess valuation contained in the ending inventories. The adjustment of $22,500 in the allowance account is transferred as a credit to the Income: Branch X account, because it represents additional gross profit on branch operations over that reported by the branch. Thus, the actual net income for the branch is $12,000, the same as in the prior illustration in which merchandise was billed to the branch at cost. Under the present assumption, however, the branch reports a net loss of $10,500. This amount is recorded by the home office and adjusted to a net income of $12,000, as shown by the following journal entries at the end of Year 1:

End-of-period journal entries	*Home Office Accounting Records*		
	Income: Branch X	*10,500*	
	Investment in Branch X		*10,500*
	To record net loss reported by branch.		
	Allowance for Overvaluation of Inventories: Branch X	*22,500*	
	Income: Branch X		*22,500*
	To reduce allowance to amount by which ending inventories of branch exceed cost.		
	Income: Branch X	*12,000*	
	Income Summary		*12,000*
	To close branch net income (as adjusted) to Income Summary.		

After these journal entries have been posted, the accounts in the home office general ledger used to portray branch operations appear as shown on page 110.

In a separate balance sheet for the home office, the $7,500 credit balance in the Allowance for Overvaluation of Inventories: Branch X account is deducted from the $45,500 debit balance in the Investment in Branch X account.

End-of-period balances in home office accounting records

Investment in Branch X

Date	Explanation	Debit	Credit	Balance
	Cash sent to branch	1,000		1,000 dr
	Merchandise billed to branch at 50% above cost	90,000		91,000 dr
	Equipment acquired by branch, carried in home office accounting records		500	90,500 dr
	Cash received from branch		37,500	53,000 dr
	Operating expenses billed to branch	3,000		56,000 dr
	Net loss for Year 1 reported by branch		10,500	45,500 dr

Allowance for Overvaluation of Inventories: Branch X

Date	Explanation	Debit	Credit	Balance
	Markup of merchandise shipped to branch during Year 1 (50% of cost)		30,000	30,000 cr
	Realization of 50% markup on merchandise sold by branch during Year 1	22,500		7,500 cr

Income: Branch X

Date	Explanation	Debit	Credit	Balance
	Net loss reported by branch for Year 1	10,500		10,500 dr
	Realization of 50% markup on merchandise sold by branch		22,500	12,000 cr
	Net income of branch (as adjusted) closed to Income Summary account	12,000		-0-

The closing entries for the branch at the end of Year 1 are on page 111. After these closing entries have been posted by the branch, the Home Office account in the branch accounting records (on page 111) will have a credit balance of $45,500, the same as the debit balance in the Investment in Branch X account in the accounting records of the home office.

Working paper when billings to branches are at prices above cost

The working paper for combined financial statements when billings to the branch are made at prices above cost is shown on pages 112 and

Closing entries for
branch (perpetual
inventory system)

Branch Accounting Records

Sales	80,000	
Income Summary	10,500	
Cost of Goods Sold		67,500
Operating Expenses		23,000
To close revenue and expense accounts.		
Home Office	10,500	
Income Summary		10,500
To close the net loss in the Income Summary account to the		
Home Office account.		

Compare this account
with Investment in
Branch X account on
page 110

Home Office

Date	Explanation	Debit	Credit	Balance
	Cash received from home office		1,000	1,000 cr
	Merchandise received from home office		90,000	91,000 cr
	Equipment acquired by branch	500		90,500 cr
	Cash sent to home office	37,500		53,000 cr
	Operating expenses billed by home office		3,000	56,000 cr
	Net loss for Year 1	10,500		45,500 cr

113. It differs from the previously illustrated working paper by the inclusion of an elimination to restate the ending inventories of the branch to cost. Also, the net loss reported by the branch is adjusted by the $22,500 of merchandise markup that was realized as a result of sales by the branch. As stated earlier, the amounts in the Eliminations column appear only in the working paper. The amounts represent a mechanical step to aid in the preparation of combined financial statements and are not entered in the accounting records of either the home office or the branch.

Note that the amounts in the Combined columns of this working paper are exactly the same as in the working paper prepared when the merchandise shipments to the branch were billed at cost. Consequently, the combined financial statements would be identical with those presented on pages 105 and 107.

Treatment of beginning inventories priced above cost

The working paper on pages 112 and 113 shows how the ending inventories and the related allowance for overvaluation of inventories were

SMALDINO COMPANY

Working Paper for Combined Financial Statements of Home Office and Branch X

For Year Ended December 31, Year 1

(Perpetual Inventory System: Billings above Cost)

	Adjusted trial balances				Eliminations	Combined	
	Home office		Branch				
	Debit	Credit	Debit	Credit	Debit (Credit)	Debit	Credit
Income statement							
Sales		400,000		80,000			480,000
Cost of goods sold	235,000		67,500		(a) (22,500)	280,000	
Operating expenses	90,000		23,000			113,000	
Subtotals	325,000	400,000	90,500	80,000		393,000	480,000
Net income (to statement of retained earnings below)	75,000		10,500		(b) 22,500	87,000	
Totals	400,000	400,000	90,500	90,500		480,000	480,000
Statement of retained earnings							
Retained earnings, Jan. 1, Year 1		70,000					70,000
Net income (from above)		75,000		10,500	(b) (22,500)		87,000
Dividends	40,000					40,000	

	Home Office	Branch X	Eliminations Dr	Eliminations Cr	Combined (Dr)	Combined (Cr)
Retained earnings, Dec. 31, Year 1 (to balance sheet below)	117,000					157,000
Totals						157,000
Balance sheet						
Cash	24,000	5,000			29,000	
Accounts receivable (net)	40,000	18,000			58,000	
Inventories, Dec. 31, Year 1	45,000	22,500		(a) (7,500)	60,000	
Allowance for overvaluation of inventories: Branch X	30,000		(a) 30,000			
Investment in Branch X	56,000			(c) (56,000)		
Equipment	150,000				150,000	
Accumulated depreciation	10,000					10,000
Accounts payable	20,000					20,000
Home office		56,000	(c) 56,000			
Common stock, $10 par	150,000					150,000
Retained earnings (from above)	117,000					117,000
Totals	355,000	355,000	56,000	56,000	56,000	56,000	-0-	297,000	297,000

(a) To reduce ending inventories and cost of goods sold of branch to cost, and to eliminate balance in Allowance for Overvaluation of Inventories: Branch X account.

(b) To increase net income of branch by portion of merchandise markup that was realized.

(c) To eliminate reciprocal accounts.

handled. However, because this was the first year of operations for the branch, no beginning inventories were involved.

Perpetual Inventory System   Under the perpetual inventory system, no special problems arise when the beginning inventories of the branch include an element of unrealized gross profit. The working paper eliminations would be similar to those illustrated on pages 112 and 113.

Periodic Inventory System   We shall continue the illustration for Smaldino Company for a second year of operations (Year 2) to demonstrate the handling of beginning inventories carried by the branch at an amount above cost. However, we shall assume that both the home office and Branch X adopted the periodic inventory system in Year 2. When the periodic inventory system is used, the home office credits Shipments to Branch (a contra account to Purchases) for the cost of merchandise shipped and Allowance for Overvaluation of Inventories for the markup over cost. The branch debits Shipments from Home Office (analogous to Purchases account) for the billed price of merchandise received.

The beginning inventories for Year 2 were carried by Branch X at $22,500, or 150% of the cost of $15,000. Assume that during Year 2 the home office shipped to Branch X merchandise that cost $80,000 and was billed at $120,000, and that Branch X sold merchandise that was billed at $112,500 for $150,000. The journal entries to record the shipments and sales under a periodic inventory system are illustrated below:

	Home Office Accounting Records		Branch Accounting Records	
Shipments to branch at a price above cost (periodic inventory system)	Investment in		Shipments from	
	Branch X 120,000		Home Office 120,000	
	Shipments to		Home	
	Branch X . . .	80,000	Office	120,000
	Allowance for			
	Overvalua-			
	tion of			
	Inventories:			
	Branch X . . .	40,000		
	None		Cash (or Accounts	
			Receivable) 150,000	
			Sales	150,000

The branch inventories at the end of Year 2 amounted to $30,000 at billed price, representing cost of $20,000 plus a 50% markup. The flow of merchandise for Branch X during Year 2 is summarized at the top of page 115.

SMALDINO COMPANY
Flow of Merchandise for Branch X
During Year 2

	Cost	Markup	Billed price
Beginning inventories	$15,000	$ 7,500	$ 22,500
Add: Shipments from home office	80,000	40,000	120,000
Available for sale	$95,000	$47,500	$142,500
Less: Ending inventories	(20,000)	(10,000)	(30,000)
Merchandise sold	$75,000	$37,500	$112,500

The activities of the branch for Year 2 are reflected in the three home office ledger accounts below and at the top of page 116.

End-of-period balances in home office accounting records

Investment in Branch X

Date	Explanation	Debit	Credit	Balance
	Balance, Dec. 31, Year 1			45,500 dr
	Merchandise billed to branch at 50% above cost	120,000		165,500 dr
	Cash received from branch		113,000	52,500 dr
	Operating expenses billed to branch	4,500		57,000 dr
	Net income for Year 2 reported by branch	10,000		67,000 dr

Allowance for Overvaluation of Inventories: Branch X

Date	Explanation	Debit	Credit	Balance
	Balance, Dec. 31, Year 1 (see page 110)			7,500 cr
	Markup of merchandise shipped to branch during Year 2 (50% of cost)		40,000	47,500 cr
	Realization of 50% markup on merchandise sold by branch during Year 2	37,500		10,000 cr

In the home office accounting records at the end of Year 2, the balance required in the Allowance for Overvaluation of Inventories: Branch X account is $10,000, that is, the billed price of $30,000 less cost of $20,000 for merchandise in the ending inventories. The allowance account, therefore, is reduced from its present balance of $47,500 to $10,000. This reduction of $37,500 represents the 50% markup of mer-

Income: Branch X

Date	Explanation	Debit	Credit	Balance
	Net income reported for Year 2 by branch		10,000	10,000 cr
	Realization of 50% markup on merchandise sold by branch during Year 2		37,500	47,500 cr
	Net income of branch (as adjusted) closed to Income Summary account	47,500		-0-

chandise above cost that was realized by the branch during Year 2 and is credited to the Income: Branch X account.

The Home Office account in the branch general ledger shows the following activity for Year 2:

Reciprocal account in branch ledger

Home Office

Date	Explanation	Debit	Credit	Balance
	Balance, Dec. 31, Year 1			45,500 cr
	Merchandise received from home office		120,000	165,500 cr
	Cash sent to home office	113,000		52,500 cr
	Operating expenses billed by home office		4,500	57,000 cr
	Net income for Year 2		10,000	67,000 cr

The working paper for combined financial statements under the periodic inventory system appears on pages 118 and 119.

Closing Entries The closing entries for the branch and the adjusting and closing entries for the home office at the end of Year 2 are illustrated on page 117.

Reconciliation of reciprocal ledger accounts

At the end of an accounting period, the balance of the Investment in Branch account in the home office accounting records may not agree with the balance of the Home Office account in the branch accounting records, because certain transactions may have been recorded by one office but not by the other. The situation is comparable to that of recon-

Branch Accounting Records

Inventories, Dec. 31, Year 2	30,000	
Sales	150,000	
Inventories, Dec. 31, Year 1		22,500
Shipments from Home Office		120,000
Operating Expenses		27,500
Income Summary		10,000

To record ending inventories and to close beginning inventories, revenue, and expense accounts.

Income Summary	10,000	
Home Office		10,000

To close Income Summary account.

Adjusting and closing
entries for home office
(periodic inventory
system)

Home Office Accounting Records

Investment in Branch X	10,000	
Income: Branch X		10,000

To record net income reported by branch.

Allowance for Overvaluation of Inventories: Branch X	37,500	
Income: Branch X		37,500

To recognize as realized income the markup of merchandise applicable to goods sold by branch during Year 2.

Income: Branch X	47,500	
Income Summary		47,500

To close branch income to Income Summary account.

Inventories, Dec. 31, Year 2	70,000	
Sales	500,000	
Shipments to Branch X	80,000	
Inventories, Dec. 31, Year 1		45,000
Purchases		400,000
Operating Expenses		120,000
Income Summary		85,000

To record ending inventories and to close beginning inventories, revenue, and expense accounts.

Income Summary	132,500	
Retained Earnings		132,500

To close Income Summary account.

Retained Earnings	60,000	
Dividends		60,000

To close Dividends account.

SMALDINO COMPANY

Working Paper for Combined Financial Statements of Home Office and Branch X

For Year Ended December 31, Year 2

(Periodic Inventory System: Billings above Cost)

| | Adjusted trial balances | | | | Eliminations | Combined | |
| | Home office | | Branch | | | | |
	Debit	Credit	Debit	Credit	Debit (Credit)	Debit	Credit
Income statement							
Sales		500,000		150,000			650,000
Inventories, Dec. 31, Year 1	45,000		22,500		(b) (7,500)	60,000	
Purchases	400,000					400,000	
Shipments to Branch X		80,000			(a) 80,000		
Shipments from Home Office			120,000		(a) (120,000)		
Inventories, Dec. 31, Year 2		70,000		30,000	(c) 10,000		90,000
Operating expenses	120,000		27,500			147,500	
Subtotal	565,000	650,000	170,000	180,000		607,500	740,000
Net income (to statement of retained earnings below)	85,000		10,000		(d) 37,500	132,500	
Totals	650,000	650,000	180,000	180,000	(d) -0-	740,000	740,000
Statement of retained earnings							
Retained earnings, Dec. 31, Year 1		117,000					117,000
Net income (from above)		85,000		10,000	(d) (37,500)		132,500

					Eliminations		
Dividends	60,000					60,000	
Retained earnings, Dec. 31, Year 2 (to balance sheet below)						189,500	
Totals						249,500	249,500

Balance sheet

					Eliminations		
Cash	30,000		9,000			39,000	
Accounts receivable (net)	64,000		28,000			92,000	
Inventories, Dec. 31, Year 2	70,000		30,000		(c) (10,000)	90,000	
Allowance for overvaluation of inventories: Branch X		47,500			(a) 40,000 (b) 7,500		
Investment in Branch X	57,000				(e) (57,000)		
Equipment	158,000					158,000	
Accumulated depreciation		15,000					15,000
Accounts payable		24,500					24,500
Home office				57,000	(e) 57,000		
Common stock, $10 par		150,000					150,000
Retained earnings (from above)		150,000					189,500
Totals	439,000	439,000	67,000	67,000	-0-	379,000	379,000

(a) To eliminate reciprocal accounts for merchandise shipments.
(b) To reduce beginning inventories of branch to cost.
(c) To reduce ending inventories of branch to cost.
(d) To increase net income of branch by portion of merchandise markup that was realized.
(e) To eliminate reciprocal accounts.

ciling the ledger account for Cash in Bank with the balance in the monthly bank statement. The lack of agreement between the reciprocal account balances causes no difficulty during an accounting period, but at the end of the period the reciprocal account balances must be brought into agreement before combined financial statements are prepared.

As an illustration of the procedure for reconciling reciprocal account balances at the year-end, assume that the home office and branch accounting records of Mercer Company contain the following data on December 31, Year 10:

Reciprocal accounts before adjustments

Investment in Branch A (in accounting records of Home Office)

Date	Explanation	Debit	Credit	Balance
Year 10				
Nov. 30	Balance			62,500 dr
Dec. 10	Cash received from branch		20,000	42,500 dr
Dec. 27	Collection of branch accounts receivable		1,000	41,500 dr
Dec. 29	Merchandise shipped to branch	8,000		49,500 dr

Home Office (in accounting records of Branch A)

Date	Explanation	Debit	Credit	Balance
Year 10				
Nov. 30	Balance			62,500 cr
Dec. 7	Cash sent to home office	20,000		42,500 cr
Dec. 28	Acquired equipment	3,000		39,500 cr
Dec. 30	Collection of home office accounts receivable		2,000	41,500 cr

Comparison of the two reciprocal accounts discloses the four reconciling items described below:

(1) *A debit of $8,000 in the Investment in Branch A account without a related credit in the Home Office account.*

On December 29, the home office shipped merchandise costing $8,000 to the branch. The home office debits its account with the branch on the date merchandise is shipped, but the branch credits its account with the home office when the merchandise is received, perhaps a few days later. The required journal entry on December 31, Year 10, in the **branch accounting records,** assuming use of the perpetual inventory system, appears at the top of page 121.

In determining its ending inventories, the branch must add to the inventories on hand the $8,000 of merchandise in transit. This merchandise will appear in the branch balance sheet and also as part of the total inventories in the combined financial statements.

Inventories	*8,000*	
Home Office		*8,000*
To record shipment of merchandise in transit from home office.		

(2) **_A credit of $1,000 in the Investment in Branch A account without a related debit in the Home Office account._**

On December 27, accounts receivable of the branch were collected by the home office. The collection was recorded by the home office by a debit to Cash and a credit to Investment in Branch A. No journal entry was made by the branch; therefore, the following journal entry is required **_in the branch accounting records_** on December 31, Year 10:

Home Office	*1,000*	
Accounts Receivable		*1,000*
To record collection of accounts receivable by home office.		

(3) **_A debit of $3,000 in the Home Office account without a related credit in the Investment in Branch A account._**

On December 28, the branch acquired equipment for $3,000. Because the equipment used by the branch is carried in the home office accounting records, the journal entry made by the branch was a debit to Home Office and a credit to Cash. No journal entry was made by the home office; therefore, the following journal entry is required on December 31, Year 10, **_in the home office accounting records:_**

Equipment: Branch A	*3,000*	
Investment in Branch A		*3,000*
To record equipment acquired by branch.		

(4) **_A credit of $2,000 in the Home Office account without a related debit in the Investment in Branch A account._**

On December 30, accounts receivable of the home office were collected by the branch. The collection was recorded by the branch by a debit to Cash and a credit to Home Office. No journal entry was made by the home office; therefore, the following journal entry is required **_in the home office accounting records on_** December 31, Year 10:

Investment in Branch A	*2,000*	
Accounts Receivable		*2,000*
To record collection of accounts receivable by branch.		

The effect of the foregoing end-of-period journal entries is to update the reciprocal accounts, as shown by the reconciliation below:

MERCER COMPANY—HOME OFFICE AND BRANCH A
Reconciliation of Reciprocal Accounts
December 31, Year 10

	Investment in Branch A account (in home office accounting records)	Home Office account (in branch accounting records)
Balances before adjustments . .	$49,500 dr	$41,500 cr
Add: (1) Merchandise shipped to branch by home office		8,000
(4) Home office accounts receivable collected by branch	2,000	
Less: (2) Branch accounts receivable collected by home office		(1,000)
(3) Equipment acquired by branch	(3,000)	
Balances after adjustments	$48,500 dr	$48,500 cr

Transactions between branches

Efficient operations may on occasion require that assets be transferred from one branch to another. Normally a branch does not carry a reciprocal account with another branch but records the transfer in the Home Office account. For example, if Branch A ships merchandise to Branch B, Branch A debits Home Office and credits Inventories (assuming that the perpetual inventory system is used). Upon receipt of the merchandise, Branch B debits Inventories and credits Home Office. The home office records the transfer between branches by a debit to Investment in Branch B and a credit to Investment in Branch A.

The transfer of merchandise from one branch to another does not justify increasing the carrying amount of inventories by the freight costs incurred because of the indirect routing. The amount of freight costs properly included in inventories at a branch is limited to the cost of shipping the merchandise directly from the home office to its present location. Excess freight costs should be recorded as expenses of the home office.

To illustrate the accounting for excess freight costs on interbranch transfers of merchandise, assume the following data. The home office shipped merchandise costing $6,000 to Branch D and paid freight costs of $400. Subsequently, the home office instructed Branch D to transfer this merchandise to Branch E. Freight costs of $300 were paid by Branch D to carry out this order. If the merchandise had been shipped directly from the home office to Branch E, the freight costs would have been $500. The journal entries required in the three sets of accounting records (assuming that the perpetual inventory system is used) are as follows:

In Home Office accounting records:

```
Investment in Branch D . . . . . . . . . . . . . . . . . . . . . . . . . .   6,400
    Inventories . . . . . . . . . . . . . . . . . . . . . . . . . . . . .          6,000
    Cash . . . . . . . . . . . . . . . . . . . . . . . . . . . . . . . . .            400
To record shipment of merchandise and payment of freight costs.


Investment in Branch E . . . . . . . . . . . . . . . . . . . . . . . . .   6,500
Excess Freight Expense—Interbranch Transfers . . . . . . . . . .    200
    Investment in Branch D . . . . . . . . . . . . . . . . . . . . . .          6,700
To record transfer of merchandise from Branch D to Branch E.
Interbranch freight of $300 paid by Branch D caused total freight
costs on this merchandise to exceed direct shipment costs by
$200 ($400 + $300 − $500 = $200).
```

In Branch D accounting records:

```
Inventories . . . . . . . . . . . . . . . . . . . . . . . . . . . . . . . .   6,000
Freight In . . . . . . . . . . . . . . . . . . . . . . . . . . . . . . . . .     400
    Home Office . . . . . . . . . . . . . . . . . . . . . . . . . . . . .          6,400
To record receipt of merchandise from home office with freight
costs paid in advance by home office.


Home Office . . . . . . . . . . . . . . . . . . . . . . . . . . . . . . . .   6,700
    Inventories . . . . . . . . . . . . . . . . . . . . . . . . . . . . .          6,000
    Freight In . . . . . . . . . . . . . . . . . . . . . . . . . . . . . .            400
    Cash . . . . . . . . . . . . . . . . . . . . . . . . . . . . . . . . .            300
To record transfer of merchandise to Branch E by order of home
office and payment of freight costs of $300.
```

In Branch E accounting records:

Inventories	6,000	
Freight In	500	
Home Office		6,500

To record receipt of merchandise from Branch D transferred by
order of home office and normal freight costs billed by home
office.

Recording excess freight costs on merchandise transferred from one
branch to another as an expense is an example of the accounting principle that "losses" should be given prompt recognition. The excess
freight costs from such shipments generally result from inefficient planning of original shipments and should not be included in inventories.

In treating excess freight costs of interbranch transfers as expenses
attributable to the home office, we have assumed that the home office
makes the decisions directing all shipments. If branch managers are
given authority to order transfers of merchandise between branches,
the excess freight costs should be recorded as expenses attributable to
the branches.

Start-up costs of opening new branches

The establishment of a new branch often requires the incurring of considerable cost before a significant flow of revenue can be generated.
Operating losses in the first few months are very likely. Some business
enterprises would prefer to capitalize these start-up losses on the
grounds that such losses are necessary to successful operation at a new
location. However, most enterprises recognize start-up costs in connection with the opening of a new branch as an expense of the accounting
period in which the costs are incurred.

The decision should be based on the principle that net income is
measured by matching expired costs against realized revenue. If costs
can be shown to benefit future accounting periods, they should be deferred and allocated to those periods. Seldom is there positive assurance that a new branch will achieve a profitable level of operations in
later years.

REVIEW QUESTIONS

1 Explain the usual distinctions between a **sales agency** and a **branch.**

2 Palmer Company has several sales agencies and wishes to determine the
profitability of each. Describe the principal accounting procedures that you
would recommend be performed by the home office and by the individual
sales agencies to achieve this goal.

3 Some branches maintain complete accounting records and prepare financial statements in much the same way as an autonomous business enterprise. Other branches perform only limited accounting functions, with most accounting activity concentrated in the home office. Assuming that a branch has a fairly complete set of accounting records, what criterion or principle would you suggest be used in deciding whether various types of expenses applicable to the branch should be recorded by the home office or by the branch?

4 Explain the use of **reciprocal accounts** in home office and branch accounting systems in conjunction with a periodic inventory system.

5 The branch and home office reciprocal accounts of Meadow Company are not in balance at the year-end by a substantial amount. What factors might have caused this?

6 Canyon Company operates a number of branches but centralizes its accounting records in the home office and maintains rigorous control of branch operations. The home office finds that Branch D has ample inventories of a certain item of merchandise but that Branch E is almost out of this item. The home office therefore instructs Branch D to ship merchandise with a cost of $5,000 to Branch E. What journal entry should Branch D make, and what principle should guide the treatment of freight costs? (Assume that Branch D uses the perpetual inventory system.)

7 The president of Valley Company informs you that a branch store is being opened and requests your advice as follows: "I have been told that we may bill merchandise shipped to the branch at cost, at selling price, or anywhere in between. Do certified public accountants really have that much latitude in the application of generally accepted accounting principles?"

8 The policies of Hillmart Company provide that equipment in use by its branches shall be carried in the accounting records of the home office. Acquisitions of new equipment may be made either by the home office or by a branch with the approval of the home office. Slauson Branch, with the approval of the home office, acquired new equipment at a cost of $8,000. Prepare journal entries for the Slauson Branch and the home office to record the acquisition of this equipment.

9 Groves Company operates ten branches in addition to its main store, and bills merchandise shipped to the branches at 10% above cost. All plant assets are carried in the home office accounting records. The home office also conducts a regular advertising program that benefits all branches. Each branch maintains its own acounting records and prepares separate financial statements. In the home office, the accounting department prepares (**a**) financial statements for the main store; (**b**) revised financial statements for each branch; and (**c**) combined financial statements for the enterprise as a whole.

Explain the purpose of the financial statements prepared by the branches, the home office financial statements, the revised financial statements for the branches, and the combined financial statements.

EXERCISES

Ex. 3-1 Select the best answer for each of the following multiple-choice questions:

1 If the home office of Lacey Company maintains the accounting records for the plant assets of the Northern Branch, and the branch acquired equipment for $5,000 cash, the appropriate journal entry for the branch is:

    a Debit the Home Office account and credit a plant asset account for $5,000
    b Debit the Home Office account and credit Cash for $5,000
    c Debit a plant asset account and credit the Home Office account for $5,000
    d Debit Cash and credit the Home Office account for $5,000

2 The home office of Lauro Company, which bills merchandise shipped to the Southern Branch at an amount in excess of cost, prepared the following journal entry at the end of the fiscal year:

Income: Southern Branch 82,000
    Investment in Southern Branch   82,000

The most probable explanation for the journal entry is:
    a To record net income reported by branch
    b To close branch net loss (as adjusted)
    c To record net loss reported by branch
    d To close branch net income (as adjusted)

3 A possible shortcoming of billing at cost the merchandise shipped from a home office to a branch is:
    a All gross profit on the sale of merchandise is attributed to the home office
    b The branch has difficulty in applying the retail method of inventory
    c Gross profit information is concealed from branch personnel
    d Gross profit of the home office is understated
    e None of the foregoing

4 The fiscal year of Robards Company, located in New Orleans, ends September 30. On September 30, Year 1, the Home Office of Robards shipped merchandise costing $18,000 to the Baton Rouge Branch at a billed price of $24,000 and prepared an appropriate journal entry for the shipment. The Baton Rouge Branch had not received the merchandise on September 30, Year 1. Both the Home Office and the Baton Rouge Branch use the perpetual inventory system. The end-of-period adjustments for Robards Company on September 30, Year 1, should include:
    a A debit to Inventories and a credit to Home Office in the branch accounting records
    b A debit to Investment in Baton Rouge Branch and a credit to Inventories in the home office accounting records
    c A debit to Home Office and a credit to Inventories in the branch accounting records
    d Some other journal entry

Ex. 3-2 Prepare journal entries in the home office and Branch P accounting records for each of the following transactions (omit explanations):

    a Home office transferred cash of $5,000 and merchandise (at cost) of $10,000 to Branch P. Both the home office and the branch use the perpetual inventory system.
    b Home office allocated operating expenses of $1,500 to Branch P.
    c Branch P informed the home office that it had collected $416 on a note payable to the home office. Principal amount of the note was $400.
    d Branch P made sales of $12,500, terms 2/10, n/30, and incurred operating expenses of $2,500. The cost of goods sold was $8,000, and the operating expenses were paid in cash.
    e Branch P reported a net income of $500. (Debit Income Summary in branch accounting records.)

Ex. 3-3 Tillman Textile Company has a single branch in Toledo. On March 1, Year 1, the accounting records of the company include an Allowance for Overvaluation of Inventories: Toledo Branch account with a balance of $32,000. During March, merchandise costing $36,000 was shipped to the Toledo Branch and billed at a price representing a 40% markup on the billed price. On March 31, the branch prepared an income statement indicating a net loss of $11,500 for March, with ending inventories at billed price of $25,000.

a What was the cost of the branch inventories on March 1, assuming a uniform markup on all shipments to the branch?

b Prepare the journal entry to adjust the Allowance for Overvaluation of Inventories: Toledo Branch account on March 31 in the accounting records of the home office.

c What was the correct net income or net loss for the Toledo Branch for the month of March as indicated by the foregoing information?

Ex. 3-4 The home office bills its only branch at 25% above cost for all merchandise shipped to the branch. Both the home office and the branch use the periodic inventory system. During Year 5, the home office shipped merchandise to the branch at a billed price of $30,000. Branch inventories for Year 5 were as follows:

	Jan. 1	Dec. 31
Purchased from home office (at billed price)	$15,000	$19,500
Purchased from outsiders	6,800	8,670

a Prepare the journal entries (including adjusting entries) that should appear in the accounting records of the home office for Year 5 to reflect the foregoing information.

b Assuming that the home office holds merchandise costing $29,500, including $2,500 held on consignment, show how the inventories should be reported in a combined balance sheet for the home office and the branch at the end of Year 5.

Ex. 3-5 Gustafson Company bills its only branch for merchandise at 30% above cost. The branch sells the merchandise at 10% above billed price. Shortly after the close of business on January 28, some of the branch merchandise was destroyed by fire. The following additional information is available:

Inventories, Jan. 1 (at billed price from home office)	$15,600
Inventories, Jan. 28 of merchandise not destroyed (at selling price) . . .	7,150
Shipments from home office from Jan. 1 to Jan. 28 (at billed price) . . .	71,500
Sales from Jan. 1 to Jan. 28	51,840
Sales returns from Jan. 1 to Jan. 28 (merchandise actually returned) . .	3,220
Sales allowances from Jan. 1 to Jan. 28 (price adjustments)	300

a Compute the estimated cost (to the home office) of the merchandise destroyed by fire.

b Prepare the journal entry in the accounting records of the branch to recognize the uninsured fire loss. Both the home office and the branch use the perpetual inventory system.

Ex. 3-6 The ledger accounts at the top of page 128 appear in the accounting records of the Corman Branch on December 31. The branch collects noninterest-bearing notes receivable as an accommodation to the home office and deposits the proceeds in a home office bank account.

a Reproduce the Investment in Corman Branch account in the home office accounting records, assuming that all intracompany transactions are recorded in a single reciprocal account by the home office.

b Prepare the journal entries required to bring the branch accounting records up to date, assuming that the branch should use a single reciprocal account to record intracompany transactions.

Home Office

Date	Explanation	Debit	Credit	Balance
Jan. 1	Balance			22,180 cr
	Merchandise received from home office		18,300	40,480 cr
	Supplies received from home office		610	41,090 cr
	Cash remitted to home office	8,100		32,990 cr
	Merchandise returned to home office	630		32,360 cr
	Acquisition of fixtures	3,000		29,360 cr

Home Office Notes Collected

Date	Explanation	Debit	Credit	Balance
Jan. 1	Balance			1,350 cr
	Notes collected		800	2,150 cr
	Cash deposited in home office bank account	1,550		600 cr

Income Summary

Date	Explanation	Debit	Credit	Balance
	Revenue		21,900	21,900 cr
	Expenses	19,040		2,860 cr

CASES

Case 3-1   You are engaged in the audit of Deloitte Corporation, which opened its first branch office in Year 10. During the audit the president, George Deloitte, raises the question of the accounting treatment of the branch office operating loss for its first year, which is material in amount.

Deloitte proposes to capitalize the operating loss as a start-up cost to be amortized over a five-year period, stating that branch offices of other companies engaged in the same industry generally suffer a first-year operating loss that is invariably capitalized, and you are aware of this practice. Therefore, according to Deloitte, the loss should be capitalized so that the accounting will be conservative and consistent with established industry practices.

Instructions
a Discuss Deloitte's use of the terms **conservative** and **consistent** from the standpoint of accounting terminology. Discuss the accounting treatment you would recommend.
b What disclosure, if any, would be required in the financial statements of Deloitte Corporation?

Case 3-2   Santana Company operates a number of branches as well as a main store. Each branch stocks a complete line of merchandise obtained almost entirely from the home office. The branches also handle their own billing, approve customer credit, and make cash collections. Each branch has its own bank account, and each maintains complete accounting records. All noncurrent assets at the branches, consisting chiefly of furniture and office equipment, are carried in the home office accounting records and are depreciated by the straight-line method at 10% a year.

On July 1, Year 1, the Denver Branch acquired office equipment on the orders of the newly appointed branch manager. The equipment had a list price of $2,400, but was acquired on the installment plan with no cash down payment and 24 monthly payments of $110 beginning August 1, Year 1. No journal entry was made for this transaction by the branch until August 1, when the first monthly payment was recorded by a debit to Miscellaneous Expenses. The same journal entry was made for the next four monthly payments made during Year 1. On December 2 the branch manager became aware, during a meeting at the home office, that equipment could be acquired by the branches only with prior approval by the home office. Regardless of whether the home office or the branches acquired plant assets, such assets were to be carried in the home office accounting records. To avoid criticism, the Denver Branch manager immediately disposed of the office equipment acquired July 1 by sale for $1,500 cash to an independent store. The manager then paid the balance due on the installment contract using a personal check and the $1,500 check received from sale of the equipment. In consideration of the advance payment of the remaining installments on December 3, the equipment dealer agreed to a $100 reduction in the total balance of the contract. No journal entry was made for the disposal of the equipment or the settlement of the liability.

Assume that you are a CPA engaged to audit the financial statements of Santana Company. During your visit to the Denver Branch you analyze the Miscellaneous Expenses account and investigate the five monthly debits of $110. This investigation discloses the acquisition and subsequent disposal of the office equipment. After some hesitation, the branch manager gives you a full explanation of the events.

Instructions
a Would you, as an independent auditor, take any action on this matter? Indicate the major issues involved rather than the accounting details. Give reasons for your answer.
b Prepare the journal entries that should have been made for the entire series of events in the accounting records of the Denver Branch. Assume that Santana Company accepts responsibility for the branch manager's actions.
c Prepare the journal entries that should have been made in the home office accounting records for the entire series of events, assuming that the home office was informed of each event and accepts responsibility for all actions by the branch manager.
d As an independent situation from **b** and **c**, prepare journal entries to correct the accounting records with a minimum of work. One compound journal entry in each set of accounting records is suggested. Assume that interest expense belongs in the branch accounting records. Also assume that Santana wishes to show in the branch accounting records a liability to the branch manager for personal "loans," if any, and will consider later any disciplinary action to be taken. The accounting records have not been closed for Year 1.

PROBLEMS

3-1 Included in the accounting records of the home office and West Branch, respectively, of Simms Company were the following ledger accounts for the month of January:

Investment in West Branch (in Home Office accounting records)

Date		Explanation	Debit	Credit	Balance
Jan.	1	Balance			39,200 dr
	9	Shipment of merchandise	4,000		43,200 dr
	21	Receipt of cash		1,600	41,600 dr
	27	Collection of branch accounts re-ceivable		800	40,800 dr
	31	Shipment of merchandise	3,200		44,000 dr

Home Office (in West Branch accounting records)

Date		Explanation	Debit	Credit	Balance
Jan.	1	Balance			39,200 cr
	10	Receipt of merchandise		4,000	43,200 cr
	19	Remittance of cash	1,600		41,600 cr
	28	Acquisition of furniture	1,200		40,400 cr
	30	Return of excess merchandise	1,500		38,900 cr
	31	Remittance of cash	500		38,400 cr

Instructions

a Prepare a working paper to reconcile the reciprocal accounts to the corrected balances on January 31.

b Prepare journal entries on January 31, for the (1) home office, and (2) West Branch of Simms Company to bring the accounting records up to date. Both the home office and the branch use the perpetual inventory system.

3-2 Harvey's Hobby Shop established the Rodeo Drive Branch on January 2, Year 3, During the first year of operations, Harvey's Hobby Shop shipped to the branch merchandise that cost $200,000. Billings were made at prices 20% above cost. Freight costs of $10,000 were paid by the home office. Sales by the branch were $300,000 and operating expenses were $64,000, all for cash. On December 31, Year 3, the branch took a physical inventory that showed merchandise on hand of $48,000 at billed prices. Both the home office and the branch use the periodic inventory system.

Instructions   Prepare journal entries for the branch and the home office to record the foregoing transactions, ending inventories, and other related adjusting and closing entries on December 31, Year 3. (Allocate a proportional amount of freight costs to the ending inventories of the branch.)

3-3 Digi's Designs bills shipments of merchandise to its Camden Branch at 140% of cost. During the first year after the branch was established, the following were among the transactions completed:

(1) The home office shipped merchandise with a cost of $100,000 to the Camden Branch.
(2) The Camden Branch sold for $80,000 cash merchandise that was billed by the home office at $70,000, and incurred operating expenses of $20,000 (all paid in cash).
(3) The physical inventories taken by the Camden Branch at the end of the first year were $68,600 at billed prices.

Instructions

a Assuming that the perpetual inventory system is used both by the home office and by the Camden Branch, prepare for the first year:

(1) All journal entries, including closing entries, in the accounting records of the Camden Branch.

(2) All journal entries, including the adjustment of the inventories overvaluation account, in the accounting records of the home office.

b Assuming that the periodic inventory system is used both by the home office and by the Camden Branch, prepare for the first year:

(1) All journal entries, including the closing entry, in the accounting records of the Camden Branch.

(2) All journal entries, including the adjustment of the inventories overvaluation account, in the accounting records of the home office.

3-4 Summerland Corporation operates a branch in Dallas to which it bills merchandise at prices 30% above cost. The branch obtains merchandise only from the home office and sells the merchandise at prices averaging 15% above the prices billed by the home office. Both the home office and the branch maintain perpetual inventory records and both close their accounting records on December 31.

On March 10, Year 9, a fire at the branch destroyed a part of the inventories. Immediately after the fire, a physical inventory taken of the merchandise on hand and not damaged showed it to have a selling price of $11,960. On January 1, Year 9, the inventories of the branch at billed price had been $15,600. Shipments from the home office during the period January 1 to March 10 were billed to the Dallas Branch in the amount of $57,200. The branch accounting records show that sales during this period were $41,472, before sales returns of $808.

Instructions Prepare the journal entries necessary to record the uninsured loss from fire in the (*a*) branch accounting records, and (*b*) home office accounting records. Show supporting computations for all amounts. Assume that the loss was reported by the branch to the home office and that it was recorded in the intracompany reciprocal accounts.

3-5 On December 31, Year 5, the Investment in Soto Branch account in the general ledger of the home office of Isotope Company shows a debit balance of $40,000. You ascertain the following facts in analyzing this account:

(1) On December 31, merchandise billed at $5,800 was in transit from the home office to the branch. The periodic inventory system is used by both the home office and the branch.

(2) The branch collected home office accounts receivable of $275; the home office was not notified.

(3) On December 29, the home office mailed a check for $2,000 to the branch, but the accountant for the home office recorded the check as a debit to the Charitable Contributions account; the branch had not received the check as of December 31.

(4) Branch net income for December was recorded erroneously by the home office at $840 instead of $480. The credit was recorded by the home office in the Income: Soto Branch account.

(5) The branch returned supplies costing $220 to the home office; the home office had not recorded the receipt of the supplies. The home office records acquisitions of supplies in the Inventory of Supplies account.

Instructions

a Assuming that all other transactions have been recorded properly, prepare a working paper to determine the unadjusted balance of the Home office account in the general ledger of the branch on December 31, Year 5.

b Prepare the journal entries for the home office to bring its accounting records up to date. Closing entries have not been made.

c Prepare the journal entries for the Soto Branch to bring its accounting records up to date.

d Prepare a reconciliation on December 31, Year 5, of the Investment in Soto Branch account in the accounting records of the home office and the Home Office account in the accounting records of the Soto Branch. Use a single column for each account and start with the unadjusted balances.

3-6 On January 4, Year 5, Hong Kong Toy Company opened its first branch with instructions to Sylvia Cho, the branch manager, to perform the functions of granting credit, billing customers, accounting for receivables, and making cash collections. The branch paid its operating expenses by checks drawn on its bank account. The branch obtained merchandise solely from the home office; billings for these shipments were at cost to the home office. The adjusted trial balances for the home office and the branch on December 31, Year 5, were as follows:

HONG KONG TOY COMPANY
Adjusted Trial Balances
December 31, Year 5

	Home office		Branch	
	Debit	**Credit**	**Debit**	**Credit**
Cash	$ 42,000		$ 14,600	
Notes receivable	7,000			
Accounts receivable (net)	80,400		37,300	
Inventories.	95,800		24,200	
Furniture and equipment (net) .	48,100			
Investment in branch	82,700			
Accounts payable		$ 41,000		
Common stock, $2 par		200,000		
Home office				$ 82,700
Retained earnings, Dec. 31, Year 4		25,000		
Sales		360,000		101,100
Cost of goods sold	200,500		85,800	
Operating expenses	69,500		21,900	
Totals	$626,000	$626,000	$183,800	$183,800

The physical inventories on December 31, Year 5, were in agreement with the perpetual records of the home office and the branch.

Instructions
a Prepare a seven-column working paper for combined financial statements of the home office and branch.
b Prepare the closing journal entries on December 31, Year 5, in the accounting records of the branch.
c Prepare the adjusting and closing journal entries pertaining to branch operations in the accounting records of the home office.

3-7 You are engaged to make an audit for the year ended December 31, Year 1, of Sierra Company, which carries on merchandising operations at both a home office and a branch. The unadjusted trial balances of the home office and the branch are given on page 133.

SIERRA COMPANY
Unadjusted Trial Balances
December 31, Year 1

	Home office Dr (Cr)	Branch Dr (Cr)
Cash	$ 20,000	$ 7,975
Inventories, Jan. 1, Year 1	23,000	11,550
Miscellaneous assets (net)	200,000	48,450
Investment in branch	60,000	
Allowance for overvaluation of branch inventories,		
Jan. 1, Year 1	(1,000)	
Purchases	190,000	
Shipments from home office		104,500
Freight in from home office		5,225
Operating expenses	42,000	24,300
Current liabilities	(35,000)	(8,500)
Home office		(51,000)
Sales	(155,000)	(142,500)
Shipments to branch	(110,000)	
Common stock, $2.50 par	(200,000)	
Retained earnings, Jan. 1, Year 1	(34,000)	
Totals	$ –0–	$ –0–

The audit on December 31, Year 1, disclosed the following:

(1) The branch office deposits all cash receipts in a local bank for the account of the home office. The audit working papers for the cash cutoff include the following:

Amount	Date deposited by branch	Date recorded by home office
$1,050	Dec. 27, Year 1	Dec. 31, Year 1
1,100	Dec. 30, Year 1	Not recorded
600	Dec. 31, Year 1	Not recorded
300	Jan. 2, Year 2	Not recorded

(2) The branch pays operating expenses incurred locally from an imprest bank account that is maintained with a balance of $2,000. Checks are drawn once a week on this imprest account, and the home office is notified of the amount needed to replenish the account. On December 31, Year 1, an $1,800 reimbursement check was in transit from the home office to the branch office.

(3) The branch receives all its merchandise from the home office. The home office bills the merchandise at 10% above cost. On December 31, Year 1, a shipment with a billed price of $5,500 was in transit to the branch. Freight costs typically are 5% of billed price. Freight costs are considered to be inventoriable costs. Both the home office and the branch use the periodic inventory system.

(4) Beginning inventories in the trial balance are shown at the respective costs to the home office and to the branch. The inventories on December 31, Year 1, were as follows:

Home office, at cost $30,000

Branch, at billed price (excluding shipment in transit and freight) .   9,900

Instructions

a Prepare journal entries to adjust the accounting records of the home office on December 31, Year 1.

b Prepare journal entries to adjust the accounting records of the branch on December 31, Year 1.

c Prepare a working paper for combined financial statements of the home office and the branch (use the form on pages 118 and 119). Determine the amounts for the adjusted trial balances for the home office and the branch by incorporating the journal entries in **a** and **b** with the amounts in the unadjusted trial balances.

3-8 The reciprocal ledger accounts below and at the top of page 135 are included in the accounting records of the home office and the Pico Branch of Elsinore Company on April 30, Year 2.

Investment in Pico Branch

Date	Explanation	Debit	Credit	Balance
Year 2				
Feb. 1	Balance			124,630 dr
6	Shipment of merchandise, 160 cases @ $49	7,840		132,470 dr
17	Note receivable collected by branch	2,500		134,970 dr
Mar. 31	Cash deposited by branch		2,000	132,970 dr
Apr. 2	Merchandise returned by branch		450	132,520 dr
26	Loss on disposal of branch equipment	780		133,300 dr
28	Operating expenses charged to branch	1,200		134,500 dr
29	Corrected loss on disposal of branch equipment from $780 to $250		530	133,970 dr

You have been retained by the company to assist it with some accounting work preliminary to the preparation of financial statements for the quarter ended April 30, Year 2. Additional information available to you follows:

(1) Branch equipment is carried in the accounting records of the home office; the home office notifies the branch periodically as to the amount of depreciation applicable to equipment used by the branch. Gains or losses on disposal of branch equipment are reported to the branch and included in the branch income statement.

(2) Because of the error in recording the shipment from the home office on February 8, Year 2, the sale of the 160 cases has been debited improperly to cost of goods sold at $46.75 a case.

(3) The branch frequently makes collections of home office accounts receivable, and the home office also collects receivables belonging to the branch. On April 30, Year 2, the branch collected accounts receivable of $350 belonging to the home office, but the branch employee who recorded the collection mistakenly treated the accounts receivable as belonging to the branch.

Home Office

Date	Explanation	Debit	Credit	Balance
Year 2				
Feb. 1	Balance			124,630 cr
8	Merchandise from home office, 160 cases @ $49		7,480	132,110 cr
14	Received shipment directly from supplier, invoice to be paid by home office		2,750	134,860 cr
15	Note receivable collected for home office		2,500	137,360 cr
Mar. 30	Deposited cash in account of home office	2,000		135,360 cr
31	Returned merchandise to home office	450		134,910 cr
Apr. 29	Paid repair bill for home office	375		134,535 cr
30	Excess merchandise returned to home office (billed at cost)	5,205		129,330 cr
30	Net income for quarter (preliminary)		9,210	138,540 cr

(4) The branch recorded the preliminary net income of $9,210 by a debit to Income Summary and a credit to Home Office, although the revenue and expense accounts had not been closed.

Instructions

a Reconcile the reciprocal accounts to the correct balances on April 30, Year 2. Use a four-column working paper (debit and credit columns for the Investment in Pico Branch account in the home office accounting records and debit and credit columns for the Home Office account in the branch accounting records). Start with the unadjusted balances on April 30, Year 2, and work to corrected balances, inserting full explanations of all adjusting or correcting items.

b Prepare individual journal entries for the branch to bring its accounting records up to date, assuming that corrections still can be made to revenue and expense accounts. The branch uses the perpetual inventory system. Do not prepare closing entries.

c Prepare individual journal entries for the home office to bring its accounting records up to date. Assume that the home office uses the perpetual inventory system and has not prepared closing entries. Do not prepare closing entries.

3-9 The unadjusted general ledger trial balances on December 31, Year 3, for California Fruits, Inc., and its Bear Valley Branch are shown at the top of page 136. Your audit disclosed the following:

(1) On December 23, Year 3, the branch manager acquired equipment for $4,000, but failed to notify the home office. The branch accountant, knowing that equipment is carried in the home office general ledger, recorded the proper journal entry in the branch accounting records. It is the company's policy not to record any depreciation on equipment acquired in the last half of a year.

(2) On December 27, Year 3, Mojave Company, a customer of the Bear Valley Branch, erroneously paid its account of $2,000 to the home office. The ac-

CALIFORNIA FRUITS, INC.
Unadjusted Trial Balances
December 31, Year 3

	Home office Dr (Cr)	Bear Valley Branch Dr (Cr)
Cash	$ 18,000	$ 18,000
Accounts receivable (net)	35,000	12,000
Inventories, Jan. 1, Year 3 (at cost to home office) . .	70,000	15,000
Equipment (net)	90,000	
Investment in Bear Valley Branch	30,000	
Accounts payable	(36,000)	(13,500)
Accrued liabilities	(14,000)	(2,500)
Home office		(19,000)
Common stock, $10 par	(50,000)	
Retained earnings, Jan. 1, Year 3	(48,000)	
Sales	(429,000)	(95,000)
Purchases	290,000	24,000
Shipments from home office		45,000
Operating expenses	44,000	16,000
Totals	$ –0–	$ –0–

countant made the correct journal entry in the home office general ledger but did not notify the branch.

(3) On December 30, Year 3, the branch remitted cash of $5,000, which was not received by the home office as of December 31, Year 3.

(4) On December 31, Year 3, the branch erroneously recorded the December allocated expenses from the home office as $500 instead of $1,500.

(5) On December 31, Year 3, the home office shipped merchandise billed at $3,000 to the branch; the shipment was not received by the branch as of December 31, Year 3.

(6) The inventories on December 31, Year 3, excluding the shipment in transit, are: home office—$60,000 (at cost); branch—$20,000 (consisting of $18,000 from home office at billed price and $2,000 from suppliers). Both the home office and the branch use the periodic inventory system.

(7) The home office billed shipments to the branch at 20% above cost, although the billing should have been at cost. The Sales account was credited for the invoice price by the home office.

Instructions

a Prepare journal entries to bring the accounting records of the home office up to date and to correct any errors on December 31, Year 3. Record ending inventories by an offsetting credit to the Income Summary account.

b Prepare journal entries to bring the accounting records of the branch up to date and to correct any errors on December 31, Year 3. Record ending inventories at cost to the home office by an offsetting credit to the Income Summary account.

c Prepare a working paper to summarize the operations of California Fruits, Inc., for the year ended December 31, Year 3. Disregard income taxes and use the following column headings:

Revenue and expenses	Home office	Branch	Combined

3-10 Franco Meglio's, a single proprietorship, sells merchandise at its home office location and also through a branch in Moreno Springs. The home office bills merchandise shipped to the branch at 125% of cost, and is the only supplier for the branch. Shipments of merchandise to the branch have been recorded improperly by credits to Sales for the billed price. Both the home office and the branch use the perpetual inventory system.

Meglio engages you to audit its financial statements for the year ended December 31, Year 5. This is the first time the proprietorship has utilized the services of an independent accountant. You are provided with the following unadjusted trial balances:

FRANCO MEGLIO'S
Unadjusted Trial Balances
December 31, Year 5

	Home office Dr (Cr)	Moreno Springs Branch Dr (Cr)
Cash	$ 39,000	$ 3,000
Accounts receivable (net)	20,000	22,000
Inventories	30,000	8,000
Investment in Moreno Springs Branch	45,000	
Equipment (net)	150,000	
Accounts payable	(23,000)	
Accrued liabilities		(2,000)
Long-term note payable	(51,000)	
Franco Meglio, capital, Jan. 1, Year 5	(192,000)	
Franco Meglio, drawing	42,000	
Home office		(10,000)
Sales	(350,000)	(150,000)
Cost of goods sold	220,000	93,000
Operating expenses	70,000	36,000
Totals	$ –0–	$ –0–

Additional information disclosed by your examination includes the following:

(1) On January 1, Year 5, inventories of the home office amounted to $25,000 and inventories of the branch amounted to $6,000. During Year 5, the branch was billed for $105,000 for shipments from the home office.
(2) On December 31, Year 5, the home office billed the branch for $12,000, representing the branch's share of operating expenses paid by the home office. This billing has not been recorded by the branch.
(3) All cash collections made by the branch are deposited in a local bank to the account of the home office. Deposits of this nature included the following:

Amount	Date deposited by branch	Date recorded by home office
$5,000	Dec. 28, Year 5	Dec. 31, Year 5
3,000	Dec. 30, Year 5	Not recorded
7,000	Dec. 31, Year 5	Not recorded
2,000	Jan. 2, Year 6	Not recorded

(4) Operating expenses incurred locally by the branch are paid from an imprest bank account that is reimbursed periodically by the home office. Just prior to the end of Year 5, the home office forwarded a reimbursement check in the amount of $3,000, which was not received by the branch as of December 31, Year 5.

(5) A shipment of merchandise from the home office to the branch is in transit on December 31, Year 5.

Instructions

a Prepare journal entries to adjust the accounting records of the home office on December 31, Year 5. Establish an allowance for overvaluation of branch inventories.

b Prepare journal entries to adjust the accounting records of the branch on December 31, Year 5.

c Prepare a working paper for combined financial statements of the home office and the branch (use the form illustrated on pages 112 and 113). Determine the amounts for the adjusted trial balances for the home office and the branch by incorporating the journal entries in **a** and **b** with the amounts in the unadjusted trial balances.

d After the working paper in **c** is completed, prepare all required adjusting and closing entries in the accounting records of the home office.

3-11 Comparative balance sheets for the home office of Rancho Corporation follow:

RANCHO CORPORATION—HOME OFFICE
Balance Sheets

Assets	Dec. 31, Year 5	Dec. 31, Year 4
Cash	$ 23,000	$ 25,600
Accounts receivable	95,000	80,000
Allowance for doubtful accounts	(3,000)	(2,400)
Inventories	100,000	112,000
Equipment (net)	200,000	180,000
Investment in Villa Branch	110,000	
Investment in Villa, Inc. (100%)		80,000
Total assets	$525,000	$475,200

Liabilities & Stockholders' Equity

	Dec. 31, Year 5	Dec. 31, Year 4
Accounts payable	$ 88,000	$ 95,300
Accrued liabilities	3,500	2,700
Common stock, $5 par	200,000	200,000
Retained earnings	233,500	177,200
Total liabilities & stockholders' equity	$525,000	$475,200

The home office acquired equipment for $50,000 cash in Year 5, and equipment with a carrying amount of $10,000 was sold at a loss of $3,000. The loss was debited to the Retained Earnings account by mistake. Dividends of $32,000 were declared and paid during Year 5, and net income for Year 5 was $91,300, including $40,000 earned by the branch. The branch remitted $10,000 to the home office at the end of Year 5. Comparative balance sheets for Villa Branch and Villa, Inc., are as follows:

VILLA BRANCH AND VILLA, INC.
Balance Sheets

	Dec. 31, Year 5	Dec. 31, Year 4
Assets		
Cash	$ 28,000	$ 15,000
Accounts receivable (no allowance)	25,000	20,000
Inventories	70,500	65,000
Short-term prepayments	1,500	2,000
Total assets	$125,000	$102,000
Liabilities & Stockholders' Equity		
Accounts payable	$ 15,000	$ 22,000
Common stock, no par		10,000
Retained earnings		70,000
Home office	110,000	
Total liabilities & stockholders' equity	$125,000	$102,000

The branch was operated as a wholly owned subsidiary corporation (Villa, Inc.) until January 1, Year 5, at which time the corporation was liquidated and reorganized as a branch.

Instructions

a Prepare comparative combined (or consolidated) balance sheets for Rancho Corporation on December 31, Year 4, and on December 31, Year 5. In the consolidation of the financial statements of the two corporations, the Investment in Villa, Inc., (in Rancho's accounting records) is eliminated against the stockholders' equity accounts of Villa, Inc.

b Prepare a statement of changes in financial position for Rancho Corporation on the working capital concept for Year 5, assuming that the accounts of Villa, Inc., were consolidated with the accounts of Rancho Corporation on December 31, Year 4. Do not include the composition of working capital in the statement of changes in financial position.

c Prepare a statement of changes in financial position for Rancho Corporation on the cash concept for Year 5, assuming that the accounts of Villa, Inc., were consolidated with the accounts of Rancho Corporation on December 31, Year 4. Do not include the composition of working capital in the statement of changes in financial position.

BUSINESS COMBINATIONS AND CONSOLIDATED FINANCIAL STATEMENTS

4 BUSINESS COMBINATIONS

Business combinations are events or transactions in which two or more business enterprises, or their net assets, are brought under common control into a single accounting entity. Other terms frequently applied to business combinations are **mergers** and **acquisitions.**

Business combinations have been frequent and numerous in the United States. Statistics issued by W. T. Grimm & Co., a financial consulting firm that compiles data on business combinations, show that as many as 4,000 or more business combinations have been completed in some recent years.

The Financial Accounting Standards Board has suggested the following definitions for terms commonly used in discussions of business combinations:[1]

1 **Combined enterprise.** The accounting entity that results from a business combination

2 **Constituent companies.** The business enterprises that enter into a combination

3 **Combinor.** A constituent company entering into a combination whose owners as a group end up with control of the ownership interests in the combined enterprise

4 **Combinee.** A constituent company other than the combinor in a business combination

In the first section of this chapter we discuss reasons for the popularity of business combinations and techniques for arranging them. Then, the two methods of accounting for business combinations, that is, **purchase** and **pooling of interests,** are explained and illustrated. In the final section we evaluate the theory of purchase accounting and pooling-of-interests accounting.

BUSINESS COMBINATIONS: WHY AND HOW?

Why do business enterprises enter into a business combination? Although a number of reasons have been cited, probably the overriding one for **combinors** in recent years has been **growth.** Business enterprises have major operating objectives other than growth, but that goal increasingly has motivated combinor managements to undertake business combinations. Advocates of this **external** method of achieving growth point out that it is much more rapid than growth through **inter-**

---

[1] *FASB Discussion Memorandum,* "An Analysis of Issues Related to Accounting for Business Combinations and Purchased Intangibles," FASB (Stamford: 1976), p. 3.

nal means. There is no question that expansion and diversification of product lines, or enlarging the market share for current products, is achieved readily through a business combination with another enterprise. However, the disappointing experiences of many combinors engaging in business combinations suggest that much can be said in favor of more gradual and reasoned growth through internal means, using available management and financial resources.

Other reasons often advanced in support of business combinations are obtaining new management strength or better use of existing management, and achieving manufacturing or other operating economies. In addition, a business combination may be undertaken for the income tax advantages available to one or more parties to the combination.

Antitrust considerations

One danger faced by large corporations that undertake business combinations is the possibility of antitrust litigation. The U.S. government often has expressed opposition to unwarranted concentration of economic power in large business enterprises. Consequently, business combinations frequently have been attacked by the Federal Trade Commission or the Antitrust Division of the Department of Justice, under the provisions of Section 7 of the Clayton Act, which reads in part as follows:

> . . . no corporation engaged in commerce shall acquire, directly or indirectly, the whole or any part of the stock or other share capital and no corporation subject to the jurisdiction of the Federal Trade Commission shall acquire the whole or any part of the assets of another corporation engaged also in commerce, where in any line of commerce in any section of the country the effect of such acquisition may be substantially to lessen competition or to tend to create a monopoly.

The breadth of the preceding legislation has led to federal antitrust action against all types of business combinations: *horizontal* (combinations involving enterprises in the same industry), *vertical* (combinations between an enterprise and its customers or suppliers), and *conglomerate* (combinations between enterprises in unrelated industries or markets).

Methods for arranging business combinations

The four common methods for carrying out a business combination are statutory merger, statutory consolidation, acquisition of capital stock, and acquisition of assets.

Statutory Merger As its name implies, a statutory merger is executed under provisions of applicable state laws. In a statutory merger, the boards of directors of the two or more corporations involved approve a plan for the exchange of voting common stock (and perhaps some preferred stock, cash, or long-term debt) of one of the corporations (the *survivor*) for all the voting common stock of the other corporations. Shareholders of all constituent corporations must approve the terms of the merger; some states require approval of a two-thirds majority of shareholders. The surviving corporation issues its capital stock to the shareholders of the other corporations in exchange for their holdings, thus acquiring those companies' net assets (assets less liabilities). The other corporations then cease to exist as separate legal entities, and their activities often are continued as *divisions* of the survivor.

Statutory Consolidation A statutory consolidation also is consummated in accordance with applicable state laws. However, in a consolidation a *new* corporation is formed to issue its capital stock for the capital stock of two or more existing corporations, which then go out of existence. The new corporation thus acquires the net assets of the defunct corporations, whose activities may be continued as divisions of the new corporation.

Acquisition of Capital Stock One corporation (the *investor*) may issue capital stock, cash, debt, or a combination thereof to acquire all or part of the voting capital stock of another corporation (the *investee*). This stock acquisition program may function through direct acquisition in the stock market, through negotiations with the principal shareholders of a closely held corporation, or through a tender offer. A *tender offer* is a publicly announced intention to acquire, for a stated amount of cash or shares of capital stock, a maximum number of shares of the combinee's capital stock "tendered" by holders thereof to an agent, such as a commercial bank. The price per share stated in the tender offer usually is well above the prevailing market price of the combinee's capital stock. If more than 50% of the combinee's voting capital stock is acquired, that corporation becomes *affiliated* with the combinor as a *subsidiary* but is not liquidated and remains a separate legal entity. Business combinations arranged through capital stock acquisitions require authorization by the combinor's board of directors, and may require ratification by the combinee's shareholders.

Acquisition of Assets A business enterprise may acquire all or most of the assets of another enterprise for cash, debt, capital stock, or a combination thereof. The transaction must be approved by the boards of directors and stockholders of the constituent companies. The selling enterprise may continue its existence as a separate entity or it may be liquidated; it does not become an *affiliate* of the combinor.

Establishing the price for a business combination

An important early step in planning a combination is deciding on an appropriate price to pay. The amount of cash or debt securities, or the number of shares of capital stock, to be issued in a business combination usually is determined by variations of the following methods:

1 Capitalization of expected average annual earnings of the combinee at a desired rate of return

2 Determination of current fair value of the combinee's net assets (including goodwill)

The price for a business combination consummated for cash or debt is usually expressed in terms of the total dollar amount of the consideration issued. When capital stock is issued in a business combination, the price is expressed as a ratio of the number of shares of the combinor's capital stock to be exchanged for each share of the combinee's capital stock.

Illustration of Exchange Ratio   The negotiating officers of Palmer Corporation have agreed with the shareholders of Simpson Company to acquire all 20,000 outstanding shares of Simpson common stock for a total price of $1,800,000. Palmer's common stock presently is trading on the open market at $65 a share. Stockholders of Simpson agree to accept 30,000 shares of Palmer's common stock at a value of $60 a share in exchange for their stock holdings in Simpson. The exchange ratio is expressed as 1.5 shares of Palmer's common stock for each share of Simpson's common stock, in accordance with the following computation:

Computation of exchange ratio in business combination	*Number of shares of Palmer Corporation common stock to be issued* . . 30,000
	Number of shares of Simpson Company common stock to be exchanged 20,000
	Exchange ratio: 30,000 ÷ 20,000 . . . . 1.5 : 1

METHODS OF ACCOUNTING FOR BUSINESS COMBINATIONS

Purchase accounting

Because the majority of business combinations involve an identified combinor and one or more combinees, many accountants consider it logical to account for business combinations, regardless of how consummated, as the acquisition of assets. Thus, assets (including goodwill) acquired in a business combination for cash would be recorded at the amount of cash paid, and assets acquired in a business combination involving the issuance of capital stock would be recorded at the current fair value of the assets or of the capital stock, whichever was more clearly evident. This approach is known as *purchase accounting* for business combinations, and was widely used prior to the increase in popularity of pooling-of-interests accounting.

APB Opinion No. 16, "Business Combinations," set forth the concept of purchase accounting as follows:[2]

> Accounting for a business combination by the purchase method follows principles normally applicable under historical-cost accounting to record acquisitions of assets and issuances of stock and to accounting for assets and liabilities after acquisition.

Determination of cost of a combinee

The cost of a combinee in a business combination accounted for by the purchase method is the total of the consideration paid by the combinor, the combinor's **direct** "out-of-pocket" costs of the combination, and any **contingent consideration** that is determinable on the date of the business combination.

Amount of Consideration This is the total amount of cash paid, the current fair value of other assets distributed, the discounted present value of debt securities issued, and the current fair value of equity securities issued by the combinor.

Out-of-Pocket Costs Included in this category are legal fees and finder's fees. A **finder's fee** is paid to the investment banking firm or other organizations or individuals that investigated the combinee, assisted in determining the price of the business combination, and otherwise rendered services to bring about the combination.

Costs of registering and issuing debt securities in a business combination are debited to Bond Issue Costs; they are not part of the cost of the combinee. Costs of registering and issuing equity securities are not direct costs of the business combination, but are offset against the proceeds from the issuance of the securities. Indirect out-of-pocket costs of the combination are expensed as incurred by the constituent companies.

Contingent Consideration Contingent consideration is additional cash, other assets, or securities that may be issuable in the future contingent upon future events, such as a specified level of earnings or a designated market price for a security issued to complete the business combination. Contingent consideration that is **determinable** on the consummation date of a combination is recorded as part of the cost of the combination; contingent consideration **not determinable** on the date of the combination is recorded as an additional cost of the combination when the contingency is resolved and the additional consideration is paid or issued (or becomes payable or issuable).

Illustration of Contingent Consideration The contract for Norton Company's acquisition of the net assets of Robinson Company provided that

[2] *APB Opinion No. 16,* "Business Combinations," AICPA (New York: 1970), p. 311.

Norton would pay $800,000 cash for Robinson's net assets (including goodwill), which would be set up in the Robb Division of Norton Company. The following contingent consideration also was included in the contract:

1 Norton was to pay Robinson $100 a unit for all sales by Robb Division of a slow-moving product that had been written down to scrap value by Robinson prior to the business combination. No portion of the $800,000 price for Robinson's net assets involved the slow-moving product.

2 Norton was to pay Robinson 25% of any pre-tax accounting income of Robb Division for each of the four years subsequent to the business combination.

On January 2, Year 1, the date of completion of the business combination, Robinson Company had firm, noncancelable sales orders for 500 units of the slow-moving product. The sales orders and all the slow-moving product were transferred to Norton by Robinson.

Norton's cost of the net assets acquired from Robinson should include $50,000 ($100 × 500 = $50,000) for the **determinable** contingent consideration attributable to the backlog of sales orders for the slow-moving product. However, because any pre-tax accounting income of Robb Division for the next four years cannot be determined on January 2, Year 1, no provision for the 25% contingent consideration is included in Norton's cost on January 2, Year 1.

Allocation of cost of a combinee

APB Opinion No. 16 provided the following principles for allocating cost of a combinee in a purchase-type business combination:[3]

> First, all identifiable assets acquired . . . and liabilities assumed in a business combination . . . should be assigned a portion of the cost of the acquired company, normally equal to their fair values at date of acquisition.

> Second, the excess of the cost of the acquired company over the sum of the amounts assigned to identifiable assets acquired less liabilities assumed should be recorded as goodwill.

Identifiable Assets and Liabilities   **APB Opinion No. 16** provided guidelines for assigning values to a purchased combinee's identifiable assets and liabilities.[4] Among these were: present values for receivables and liabilities; net realizable values for marketable securities, finished goods and goods in process inventories, and plant assets held for sale or for temporary use; appraised values for intangible assets, land, natural resources, and nonmarketable securities; and replacement cost for material inventories and plant assets held for long-term use.

In addition, the FASB has provided the following guidelines for matters not dealt with in **APB Opinion No. 16:**

---

[3] Ibid., p. 318.
[4] Ibid., pp. 318–320.

1 A part of the cost of a purchased combinee should be allocated to identifiable tangible and intangible assets that resulted from research and development activities of the combinee or are to be used in research and development activities of the combined enterprise. Subsequently, such assets are to be expensed, as required by *FASB Statement No. 2,* "Accounting for Research and Development Costs," unless they can be used for other than research and development activities in the future.[5]

2 In a purchase-type business combination, leases of the combinee are classified by the combined enterprise as they were by the combinee unless the provisions of a lease are modified to the extent it must be considered a new lease.[6] Thus, unmodified capital leases of the combinee are treated as capital leases by the combined enterprise, and the leased property and related obligation are capitalized in accordance with the guidelines of *APB Opinion No. 16.*

3 Because an unused investment tax credit may not be recognized as an asset under the provisions of *APB Opinion No. 2,* "Accounting for the 'Investment Credit'," any unused investment tax credit of a purchased combinee is not recognized in the accounting records of the combined enterprise until the credit is used to offset the federal income taxes payable of the combined enterprise. At that time, goodwill recorded in the business combination is decreased (or "negative goodwill" is increased) by the amount of the investment tax credit used, and the revised goodwill or "negative goodwill" is amortized over its remaining economic life.[7] (Goodwill and "negative goodwill" are discussed further in subsequent sections of this chapter.)

4 A combinee in a purchase-type business combination may have *preacquisition contingencies,* defined as contingent assets (other than potential income tax benefits of a loss carryforward), contingent liabilities, or contingent impairments of assets, that existed prior to completion of the business combination. If so, an *allocation period,* generally not longer than one year from the date the combination is completed, may be used to determine the current fair value of a preacquisition contingency. A portion of the cost of a purchased combinee is allocated to a preacquisition contingency whose fair value is determined during the allocation period. Otherwise, an estimated amount is assigned to a preacquisition contingency if it appears probable that an asset existed, a liability had been incurred, or an asset had been impaired at the completion of the combination. Any adjustment of the carrying amount of a preacquisition contingency subsequent to the end of the allocation period is included in the determination of net income for the accounting period of the adjustment.[8]

Goodwill Goodwill frequently is recorded in business combinations, because the total cost of the combinee exceeds the current fair value of identifiable net assets of the combinee. The amount of goodwill recorded on the date of a purchase-type business combination may be revised subsequently for utilization of unused investment tax credits of the combinee, as described in the preceding section. Goodwill also may be revised if an operating loss carryforward of the combinee is realized

[5] *FASB Interpretation No. 4,* "Applicability of *FASB Statement No. 2* to Business Combinations Accounted for by the Purchase Method," FASB (Stamford: 1975), pp. 1–3.

[6] *FASB Interpretation No. 21,* "Accounting for Leases in a Business Combination," FASB (Stamford: 1978), pp. 6–7.

[7] *FASB Interpretation No. 25,* "Accounting for an Unused Investment Tax Credit," FASB (Stamford: 1978), p. 6.

[8] *FASB Statement No. 38,* "Accounting for Preacquisition Contingencies of Purchased Enterprises," FASB (Stamford: 1980), pp. 2–4.

by the combined enterprise subsequent to the date of a business combination.[9] In such a case, the debit to Goodwill is offset by a credit to a Prior Period Adjustment account.[10]

"Negative Goodwill"   In some business combinations (known as *bargain purchases*), the current fair values assigned to the net assets acquired exceed the total cost of the combinee. A bargain purchase is most likely to occur for a combinee with a history of losses or when stock prices are extremely low. The excess of the current fair values over total cost is applied pro rata to reduce (but not below zero) the amounts initially assigned to noncurrent assets other than long-term investments in marketable securities.[11] If the foregoing proration does not extinguish the *bargain-purchase excess,* a deferred credit, sometimes termed *negative goodwill,* is established. Negative goodwill means an excess of current fair value of the combinee's identifiable net assets over their cost to the combinor. It is amortized over the period benefited, not to exceed 40 years.[12]

Illustration of purchase accounting with goodwill

On December 31, Year 1, Mason Company (the combinee) was merged into Saxon Corporation (the combinor or surviving company). Both companies used the same accounting principles for assets, liabilities, revenue, and expenses and both have a December 31 fiscal year. Saxon exchanged 150,000 shares of its $10 par common stock (current fair value $25 a share) for all 100,000 issued and outstanding shares of Mason's no par, $10 stated value common stock. In addition, Saxon paid the following out-of-pocket costs associated with the business combination:

Combinor's out-of-pocket costs of business combination	
CPA audit fees for SEC registration statement	$ 60,000
Legal fees:	
For the business combination	10,000
For SEC registration statement	50,000
Finder's fee	56,250
Printer's charges for printing securities and SEC registration statement	23,000
SEC registration statement fee	750
Total out-of-pocket costs of business combination.	$200,000

There was no contingent consideration in the merger contract.

[9] *APB Opinion No. 16,* p. 320.
[10] *FASB Statement No. 16,* "Prior Period Adjustments," FASB (Stamford: 1977), p. 5.
[11] *APB Opinion No. 16,* p. 318.
[12] Ibid., p. 321.

Immediately prior to the merger, Mason Company's condensed balance sheet was as follows:

MASON COMPANY (Combinee)
Balance Sheet (prior to business combination)
December 31, Year 1

Assets

Current assets	$1,000,000
Plant assets (net)	3,000,000
Other assets	600,000
Total assets	$4,600,000

Liabilities & Stockholders' Equity

Current liabilities	$ 500,000
Long-term debt	1,000,000
Common stock, $10 stated value.	1,000,000
Paid-in capital in excess of stated value	700,000
Retained earnings.	1,400,000
Total liabilities & stockholders' equity	$4,600,000

Using the guidelines in **APB Opinion No. 16,** "Business Combinations," the board of directors of Saxon Corporation determined the current fair values of Mason Company's identifiable assets and liabilities (identifiable net assets) as follows:

Current assets	$1,150,000
Plant assets (net).	3,400,000
Other assets.	600,000
Current liabilities.	(500,000)
Long-term debt (discounted present value)	(950,000)
Identifiable net assets of combinee	$3,700,000

The condensed journal entries on page 152 are required for Saxon Corporation (the combinor) to record the merger with Mason Company on December 31, Year 1, as a purchase-type business combination.

Accounting for the income tax effects of business combinations is considered in Chapter 9.

Mason Company (the combinee) prepares the condensed journal entry at the top of page 153 to record the liquidation of the company on December 31, Year 1.

Combinor's journal
entries for a
purchase-type business
combination

SAXON CORPORATION (Combinor)
Journal Entries
December 31, Year 1

Investment in Mason Company Common Stock (150,000 shares × $25).	3,750,000	
Common Stock.		1,500,000
Paid-in Capital in Excess of Par.		2,250,000

To record merger with Mason Company as a purchase.

Investment in Mason Company Common Stock ($10,000 + $56,250)	66,250	
Paid-in Capital in Excess of Par ($200,000 − $66,250) . .	133,750	
Cash		200,000

To record payment of costs incurred in merger with Mason Company. Legal and finder's fees in connection with the merger are recorded as an investment cost; other out-of-pocket costs are recorded as a reduction in the proceeds received from issuance of common stock.

Current Assets	1,150,000	
Plant Assets (net)	3,400,000	
Other Assets	600,000	
Discount on Long-Term Debt	50,000	
Goodwill	116,250	
Current Liabilities		500,000
Long-Term Debt		1,000,000
Investment in Mason Company Common Stock . .		3,816,250

To allocate cost of Mason Company investment to identifiable assets and liabilities, with the remainder to goodwill. (Income tax effects are disregarded.) Amount of goodwill is computed as follows:

Total cost of investment ($3,750,000 + $66,250)		$3,816,250
Less: Carrying amount of identifiable net assets ($4,600,000 − $1,500,000)	$3,100,000	
Excess (deficiency) of current fair values of identifiable net assets over carrying amounts:		
Current assets	150,000	
Plant assets (net). . .	400,000	
Long-term debt. . . .	50,000	3,700,000
Amount of goodwill		$ 116,250

Recording the
liquidation of combinee

MASON COMPANY (Combinee)
Journal Entry
December 31, Year 1

Current Liabilities	500,000	
Long-Term Debt	1,000,000	
Common Stock	1,000,000	
Paid-in Capital in Excess of Stated Value	700,000	
Retained Earnings	1,400,000	
Current Assets		1,000,000
Plant Assets (net)		3,000,000
Other Assets		600,000

To record liquidation of company in conjunction with
merger with Saxon Corporation.

Illustration of purchase accounting with "negative goodwill"

On December 31, Year 1, Davis Corporation acquired the net assets of
Fairmont Corporation for $400,000 cash, in a purchase-type business
combination. Davis paid legal fees of $40,000 in connection with the
combination. The condensed balance sheet of Fairmont Corporation
prior to the business combination, with related current fair value data, is
presented below:

Balance sheet of
combinee on date of
business combination

FAIRMONT CORPORATION
Balance Sheet
December 31, Year 1

	Carrying amount	Current fair value
Assets		
Current assets	$ 190,000	$ 200,000
Investment in marketable securities	50,000	60,000
Plant assets (net)	870,000	900,000
Intangible assets (net)	90,000	100,000
Total assets	$1,200,000	$1,260,000
Liabilities & Stockholders' Equity		
Current liabilities	$ 240,000	$ 240,000
Long-term debt	500,000	520,000
Total liabilities	$ 740,000	$ 760,000
Common stock, $1 par	$ 600,000	
Deficit	(140,000)	
Total stockholders' equity	$ 460,000	
Total liabilities & stockholders' equity	$1,200,000	

Thus, Davis Corporation acquired identifiable net assets with a current fair value of $500,000 ($1,260,000 − $760,000 = $500,000) for a total cost of $440,000 ($400,000 + $40,000 = $440,000). The $60,000 excess of current fair value of the net assets over their cost to Davis ($500,000 − $440,000 = $60,000) is prorated to the plant assets and intangible assets in the ratio of their respective current fair values, as follows:

Allocation of excess of current fair value over cost of identifiable net assets

$$\text{To plant assets: } \$60,000 \times \frac{\$900,000}{\$900,000 + \$100,000} \quad \cdots \cdots \cdots \cdots \quad \$54,000$$

$$\text{To intangible assets: } \$60,000 \times \frac{\$100,000}{\$900,000 + \$100,000} \quad \cdots \cdots \cdots \quad 6,000$$

Total excess of current fair value of identifiable net assets over combinor's cost. $60,000

No part of the $60,000 excess is allocated to current assets or to investments in marketable securities.

The journal entries at the top of page 155 record Davis Corporation's acquisition of the net assets of Fairmont Corporation and payment of the legal fees of $40,000.

Pooling-of-interests accounting

The major premise of the pooling-of-interests method was that certain business combinations *involving the issuance of capital stock* were more in the nature of a *combining of stockholder interests* than an *acquisition of assets* or *raising of capital.* Combining of stockholder interests was evidenced by combinations involving common stock exchanges between corporations of approximately equal size. The shareholders and managements of these corporations continued their relative interests and activities in the combined enterprise as they previously did in the separate corporations. Because neither of the like-size constituent companies could be considered the *combinor,* the pooling-of-interests method of accounting provided for carrying forward the combined assets, liabilities, and retained earnings of the constituent companies at their *carrying amounts* in the accounting records of the constituent companies. The current fair value of the capital stock issued to effect the business combination and the current fair value of the combinee's net assets are disregarded in a pooling of interests.

Illustration of pooling-of-interests accounting

The Saxon Corporation–Mason Company business combination described on page 150 would be accounted for as a pooling of interests by

Combinor's journal
entries for a
purchase-type business
combination

DAVIS CORPORATION (Combinor)
Journal Entries
December 31, Year 1

Investment in Net Assets of Fairmont Corporation.	400,000	
Cash		400,000
To record acquisition of net assets of Fairmont Corporation.		
Investment in Net Assets of Fairmont Corporation.	40,000	
Cash		40,000
To record payment of legal fees incurred in acquisition of net assets of Fairmont Corporation.		
Current Assets	200,000	
Investments in Marketable Securities.	60,000	
Plant Assets ($900,000 − $54,000)	846,000	
Intangible Assets ($100,000 − $6,000)	94,000	
Current Liabilities		240,000
Long-Term Debt		500,000
Premium on Long-Term Debt ($520,000 − $500,000) .		20,000
Investment in Net Assets of Fairmont Corporation . . .		440,000
To allocate cost of net assets acquired to identifiable net assets, with excess of current fair value of the net assets over their cost prorated to noncurrent assets other than investments in marketable securities. (Income tax effects are disregarded.)		

the journal entries at the top of page 156, in Saxon Corporation's accounting records.

Because a pooling-type business combination is a combining of stockholder interests rather than an acquisition of assets, an Investment in Mason Company Common Stock account is not used in the journal entries on page 156. Instead, in the first journal entry, Mason's assets, liabilities, and retained earnings are assigned their carrying amounts in Mason's premerger balance sheet (see page 151). Because the common stock issued by Saxon Corporation must be recorded at *par* (150,000 shares × $10 = $1,500,000), the $200,000 credit to paid-in capital in excess of par is a **balancing amount** for the journal entry. It is verified in the middle of page 156.

If the par value of common stock issued by Saxon Corporation had **exceeded** the total paid-in capital of Mason Company, Saxon's Paid-in Capital in Excess of Par account would have been **debited** in the illustrated journal entry. If the balance of Saxon's Paid-in Capital in Excess

Combinor's
journal entries
for a pooling-type
business combination

SAXON CORPORATION (Combinor)
Journal Entries
December 31, Year 1

Current Assets	1,000,000	
Plant Assets (net)	3,000,000	
Other Assets	600,000	
Current Liabilities		500,000
Long-Term Debt		1,000,000
Common Stock		1,500,000
Paid-in Capital in Excess of Par		200,000
Retained Earnings		1,400,000

To record merger with Mason Company as a pooling of interests.

Expenses of Business Combination	200,000	
Cash		200,000

To record payment of out-of-pocket costs incurred in merger with Mason Company.

Computation of credit to
paid-in capital in excess
of par

Total paid-in capital of Mason Company prior to merger	$1,700,000
Par value of Saxon Corporation common stock issued in merger	1,500,000
Amount credited to Saxon Corporation's paid-in capital in excess of par	$ 200,000

of Par account were insufficient to absorb the debit, the Retained Earnings account would be reduced.

The expenses of business combination recorded in the second journal entry are not deductible for income tax purposes; thus Saxon Corporation should not adjust its income taxes expense and liability accounts.

Mason Company's journal entry to record the liquidation of the company would be identical to the journal entry previously illustrated on page 153.

Popularity of pooling accounting

The pooling method of accounting for business combinations was sanctioned initially by the AICPA in *Accounting Research Bulletin No. 40,* "Business Combinations," issued in 1950. However, *ARB No. 40* provided few criteria for identifying the business combinations that qualified for pooling accounting, and was therefore unsatisfactory as a guide for this accounting method. Consequently, in 1957 *ARB No. 48,* "Business Combinations," superseded the previous pronouncement with an expanded discussion of the pooling method. ***ARB No. 48*** continued to permit pooling accounting for most business combinations involving an exchange of equity securities. However, ***ARB No. 48*** also failed to provide definitive guidelines for identifying the business combinations that qualified for pooling accounting. As a result, a substantial number of business combinations arranged during the 1950s and 1960s were accounted for as poolings, despite the fact that the "combining of stockholder interests" aspect was absent.

Why had pooling accounting become so popular? Some of the reasons are apparent from the following comparison of the combined Saxon Corporation journal entries illustrated previously for the merger with Mason Company:

Comparison of combinor's journal entries—purchase and pooling

	Purchase accounting	Pooling accounting
Current Assets	1,150,000	1,000,000
Plant Assets (net)	3,400,000	3,000,000
Other Assets	600,000	600,000
Discount on Long-Term Debt . . .	50,000	
Goodwill	116,250	
Expenses of Business Combination		200,000
Current Liabilities	500,000	500,000
Long-Term Debt	1,000,000	1,000,000
Common Stock	1,500,000	1,500,000
Paid-in Capital in Excess of Par	2,116,250	200,000
Retained Earnings		1,400,000
Cash	200,000	200,000

To record merger with Mason Company.

Differences in Net Assets The first difference to consider in comparing the foregoing journal entries is that the net assets recorded under the purchase method ($3,616,250) exceed the pooling-method net assets ($2,900,000) by $716,250. The composition of the $716,250 is summarized at the top of page 158.

If we assume that the $400,000 difference in plant assets is attributable to depreciable assets, total expenses of Saxon Corporation for years subsequent to December 31, Year 1, will be $716,250 larger under purchase accounting than under pooling accounting. Assume, for example, that the $150,000 difference in current assets is attributable to inventories that will be allocated to cost of goods sold on a fifo basis;

Composition of difference in net assets—purchase versus pooling

Excess of purchase asset values over pooling asset values:	
Current assets	*$150,000*
Plant assets	*400,000*
Goodwill	*116,250*
Excess of pooling liability values over purchase liability values:	
Long-term debt	*50,000*
Excess of purchase net assets values over pooling net assets values . .	*$716,250*

the average economic life of plant assets is 10 years; the goodwill is to be amortized over a 40-year period; and the long-term debt has a remaining five-year term to maturity.[13] Saxon Corporation's **pre-tax income** for the year ending December 31, Year 2, would be nearly $203,000 less under purchase accounting than under pooling accounting, attributable to the following larger expenses under purchase accounting:

Difference in pre-tax income—purchase versus pooling

Cost of goods sold	*$150,000*
Depreciation ($400,000 $\times \frac{1}{10}$)	*40,000*
Amortization of goodwill ($116,250 $\times \frac{1}{40}$)	*2,906*
Interest expense ($50,000 $\times \frac{1}{5}$)	*10,000*
Excess of Year 2 pre-tax income under pooling accounting rather than	
under purchase accounting	*$202,906*

It is true that pre-tax income for the year ended December 31, Year 1 (the year of the merger), is reduced $200,000 in pooling accounting, because the pooling method included the immediate **expensing** of the out-of-pocket costs of the business combination. However, this situation tends to be obscured by the fact that the income statements of Saxon Corporation and Mason Company would be combined in pooling accounting for the **entire** year ended December 31, Year 1 (as described in a subsequent section of this chapter).

In summary, the favorable effect of pooling accounting on post-combination earnings has been the main reason for the popularity of this accounting method.

---

[13] For simplicity, the discount on long-term debt is amortized by the straight-line method. Theoretically, and in actual practice, the *effective interest* method described in *Intermediate Accounting* of this series should be used when the difference between the two methods is material in amount.

Differences in Total Paid-in Capital The increase in Saxon Corporation's total paid-in capital is $1,916,250 less ($3,616,250 − $1,700,000 = $1,916,250) under pooling accounting than under purchase accounting. Of this difference, $1,200,000 ($1,400,000 − $200,000 = $1,200,000) is attributable to a net increase in Saxon Corporation's retained earnings under the pooling accounting method. If state laws make this $1,200,000 available as a basis for dividend declaration, another advantage of the pooling method of accounting is readily apparent.

Impact of Divergent Price-Earnings Ratios Even more dramatic than the preceding advantages inherent in the pooling-of-interests method of accounting is the potential impact on the market price of Saxon Corporation's common stock if the price-earnings ratios for Saxon's and Mason's common stock differed significantly prior to the merger. Suppose, for example, that Saxon Corporation and Mason Company had the following financial measurements prior to the business combination:

	Saxon Corporation	Mason Company
Selected financial measurements prior to business combination		
Year ended Dec. 31, Year 1:		
Net income	$500,000*	$375,000
Earnings per share	$0.50	$3.75
On Dec. 31, Year 1:		
Number of shares of common stock outstanding . .	1,000,000†	100,000†
Market price per share	$25	$30
Price-earnings ratio	50	8

* Net of $200,000 expenses of business combination.
† Outstanding during entire year.

After consummation of the business combination as a pooling, Saxon Corporation's income statement for the year ended December 31, Year 1, reports the combined enterprise's net income as $875,000—the total of the separate net incomes of the constituent companies. "Pooled" earnings per share for Saxon thus is increased to approximately $0.76. This increased amount of earnings per share is computed by dividing combined earnings of $875,000 by 1,150,000 (1,000,000 + 150,000 = 1,150,000), the **effective** number of shares of Saxon's common stock outstanding during the year ended December 31, Year 1. If the price-earnings ratio for Saxon's common stock continued unchanged, the stock's market price would increase after the merger to

$38 a share ($0.76 × 50 = $38), a 52% increase. Saxon Corporation probably would attain the reputation of an "exciting growth company," and Saxon's directors likely would seek out other prospects for pooling-type business combinations.

Less spectacular advantages attributed to the pooling method of accounting for business combinations result from the fact that the carrying amounts of assets and liabilities of the combinee are not restated. Pooling accounting thus parallels income tax accounting if the business combination qualifies as a "tax-free corporate reorganization." Further, goodwill amortization (not deductible in the computation of taxable income) is not required in the pooling method.

Abuses of pooling accounting

The attractive features of pooling accounting described in the preceding section, together with the absence of firm guidelines for poolings in **ARB No. 48,** led to a number of serious abuses of the method. Among these abuses were retroactive poolings; retrospective poolings; part-pooling, part-purchase accounting; treasury stock issuances; issuances of unusual securities; creation of "instant earnings"; contingent payouts; and "burying" the costs of pooling-type business combinations.

Retroactive Poolings   After **ARB No. 48** was issued, some accountants interpreted its provisions as permitting pooling accounting for many business combinations that already had been accounted for as purchases under **ARB No. 40.** Accordingly, a significant number of business combinations recorded as purchases in the late 1950s and early 1960s were **restated retroactively** as poolings in subsequent years. Such restatements raised questions in the minds of users of financial statements as to the integrity of both the initial and the revised accounting for the business combinations.

Retrospective Poolings   The theory that the constituent companies in a pooling business combination were **effectively combined** in accounting periods preceding the actual business combination led to the practice of **retrospective poolings.** This technique involved the consummation of pooling business combinations after the close of a combinor's fiscal year but prior to the issuance of its annual financial statements. The income statement that ultimately was issued included the operating results of the subsequently pooled combinee on a retrospective basis. Thus, a desired earnings per share amount might have been attained simply by a working paper adjustment.

Part-Pooling, Part-Purchase Accounting   Some business combinations involving the issuance of common stock as well as cash and debt were accounted for as *poolings* to the extent of the stock issuance, and as *purchases* for the remainder of the consideration. This hybrid method was inconsistent with any orderly structure of accounting theory.

Treasury Stock Issuances Pooling accounting required the exchange of common stock between the constituent companies. One method devised to avoid the potential dilution of earnings per share resulting from common stock issuances was the cash acquisition of treasury stock, and its subsequent reissuance in a pooling-type business combination. If substance is emphasized over form, such a combination is effected for *cash,* not for *previously unissued stock.*

Issuances of Unusual Securities As another means of minimizing the dilutive effects of common stock issuances in poolings, many unusual securities were devised to consummate business combinations. These securities, usually in the form of either preferred stock or a special class of common stock, were in most cases convertible to the combinor's voting common stock. In substance, these unusual securities were not equivalent to voting common stock, yet the business combinations involving these securities frequently were treated as poolings.

Creation of "Instant Earnings" The discussion on pages 157 to 160, comparing the purchase and pooling journal entries for Saxon Corporation, pointed out how pooling accounting could *instantly increase earnings per share* for the year of a business combination. Another technique for creating instant earnings was the sale of a combinee's assets shortly after the pooling combination. Because the selling price generally exceeded the carrying amounts of the assets, a one-time gain was created. The selling price usually paralleled the current fair value of the combinor's capital stock issued in the pooling combination. Thus, the instant earnings were fictitious because the gain in effect represented proceeds from the capital stock issued to effect the combination.

Contingent Payouts If the "combining of stockholder interests" feature of a pooling combination were genuine, there would be no unresolved contingencies with respect to the number of shares of common stock to be issued in the combination. Nevertheless, a large number of business combinations involving contingent issuances of additional shares of common stock were accounted for as poolings.

"Burying" the Costs of Pooling-Type Business Combinations The out-of-pocket costs of most pooling-type business combinations effected before 1970 were debited to paid-in capital in excess of par rather than to expenses of the combined enterprise. This accounting method violated the basic assumption that a pooling is not in substance an *acquisition* of one business enterprise by another or an *obtaining of new capital.*

Abuses of purchase accounting

Purchase accounting was not free of abuses during the 1950s and 1960s. The principal abuse of purchase accounting was the failure to allocate the cost of a combinee to the identifiable net assets acquired and to goodwill. Instead, an "Excess of Cost over Net Assets Acquired" account was created and presented in the post-combination balance sheet as an intangible asset—usually not subject to amortization. Consequently, reported earnings subsequent to these purchase-type combinations were the same as though pooling accounting had been used. Also, as in pooling-type business combinations, "instant earnings" often were created by the sale of understated identifiable assets shortly after the purchase-type combination.

Action by the AICPA

In 1970 the AICPA's Accounting Principles Board reacted to the abuses of pooling accounting and purchase accounting by tightening the rules permitting pooling to be used and by limiting drastically the range of situations in which pooling would be allowed. The Board's action is summarized in the following paragraph of *APB Opinion No. 16,* "Business Combinations":[14]

> The Board concludes that the purchase method and the pooling of interests method are both acceptable in accounting for business combinations, although *not as alternatives* in accounting for the same business combination. A business combination which meets specified conditions requires accounting by the pooling of interests method. A new basis of accounting is not permitted for a combination that meets the specified conditions, and the assets and liabilities of the combining companies are combined at their recorded amounts. All other business combinations should be accounted for as an acquisition of one or more companies by a corporation. The cost to an acquiring corporation of an entire acquired company should be determined by the principles of accounting for the acquisition of an asset. That cost should then be allocated to the identifiable individual assets acquired and liabilities assumed based on their fair values; the unallocated cost should be recorded as goodwill. [Emphasis added.]

By this action the Accounting Principles Board eliminated many of the abuses of pooling accounting and purchase accounting described on pages 160 to 162. Retrospective poolings and part-pooling, part-purchase accounting were expressly prohibited. Substantial restrictions were placed on the use of treasury stock and hybrid securities to consummate pooling-type combinations. Pooling accounting was forbidden for a combination containing any contingent payout provisions or plans to dispose of assets acquired in the combination. Out-of-pocket costs of pooling-type combinations were required to be expensed, even though these costs were not deductible for income tax purposes.

[14] *APB Opinion No. 16,* p. 283.

Conditions requiring pooling accounting

The APB provided 12 conditions for business combinations that were to be accounted for as poolings. The conditions, ***all of which were to be satisfied for pooling to be appropriate,*** were divided into three groups as follows:

1 *Attributes of the combining companies.* The conditions in this group were designed to assure that the pooling-type business combination was truly a combining of two or more enterprises whose common stockholder interests were previously independent of each other.

2 *Manner of combining ownership interests.* The conditions in this group supported the requirement for pooling accounting that an exchange of stock to combine existing voting common stock interests actually took place, in substance as well as in form.

3 *Absence of planned transactions.* The planned transactions prohibited by this group of conditions were those that would be inconsistent with the combining of entire existing interests of common stockholders.

A business combination that meets the APB's 12 conditions is accounted for as a pooling, regardless of the legal form of the combination (statutory merger, statutory consolidation, acquisition of capital stock, acquisition of assets). An acquisition of assets may be construed as an "exchange of voting common stock interests" if all the specified conditions for a pooling are met.

The appendix on pages 170 and 171 includes the 12 conditions established by the Accounting Principles Board for pooling accounting. Many of the conditions are self-explanatory. However, four of them warrant brief explanation.

Independence of Constituent Companies On the dates of initiation and consummation of a business combination, no constituent company may have more than a 10% ownership of the outstanding voting common stock of another constituent company. Otherwise, the companies could not be considered independent of each other, because ownership of more than 10% of an investee's common stock often enables the investor to have some degree of influence over the investee.

Substantially All Voting Common Stock This condition requires that at least 90% of the combinee's outstanding voting common stock be exchanged for the combinor's majority voting common stock. The following are ***excluded*** from the computation of the number of shares exchanged:

1 Shares acquired before the date the business combination is initiated and held by the combinor or its subsidiaries on that date

2 Shares acquired by the combinor or its subsidiaries after the combination is initiated, other than in exchange for the combinor's voting common stock

3 Shares of the combinee still outstanding on the date the combination is consummated

In addition, any voting common stock of the combinor owned or acquired by the combinee before the business combination must be considered. These combinor shares are converted to equivalent shares of the combinee for the 90% test.

To illustrate the application of the "independence" and "90% of voting common stock" tests, assume that on March 13, Year 2, Patton Corporation and Sherman Company initiated a plan of business combination. Under the plan, $1\frac{1}{2}$ shares of Patton's voting common stock (1,000,000 shares issued prior to March 13, Year 2) were to be exchanged for each outstanding share of Sherman's common stock (100,000 shares issued prior to March 13, Year 2).

At this time, Patton owned 7,500 shares of Sherman's common stock, and Sherman owned 6,000 shares of Patton's voting common stock; in addition, 500 shares of Sherman's common stock were in Sherman's treasury. Neither Patton's ownership of 7.54% of Sherman's outstanding common stock (7,500 ÷ 99,500 = 7.54%) nor Sherman's ownership of 0.6% of Patton's outstanding common stock (6,000 ÷ 1,000,000 = 0.6%) exceeds the 10% limitation of the **independence of constituent companies requirement.** On March 26, Year 2, Patton acquired in the open market for cash 1,000 shares (1.005%) of Sherman's common stock; and on June 30, Year 2, Patton issued 136,500 shares of its voting common stock in exchange for 91,000 outstanding shares of Sherman's common stock to complete the business combination.

Computation of the 90% requirement follows:

Computation of "substantially all voting common stock" pooling requirement

Total Sherman Company shares issued, June 30, Year 2		*100,000*
Less: Shares in Sherman's treasury		*500*
Total Sherman shares outstanding, June 30, Year 2		*99,500*
Less:		
Sherman shares owned by Patton Corporation, Mar. 13, Year 2	*7,500*	
Sherman shares acquired by Patton for cash, Mar. 26, Year 2	*1,000*	
Equivalent number of Sherman shares represented by Patton's common stock owned by Sherman, Mar. 13, Year 2 (6,000 ÷ 1½)	*4,000*	*12,500*
Effective number of Sherman shares acquired June 30, Year 2, in exchange for Patton's common stock		*87,000*
Application of 90% requirement (99,500 × 90%)		*89,550*

Thus, the 91,000 shares of Sherman Company common stock actually exchanged on June 30, Year 2, are in effect restated to 87,000 shares. Because the restated amount is less than 90% of Sherman's 99,500 shares outstanding, the business combination does not qualify for pooling accounting.

Restrictions on Treasury Stock To preclude the treasury stock abuses described on page 161, *APB Opinion No. 16* provided that any treasury stock issued by the combinor in a business combination qualifying for pooling accounting must have been acquired in accordance with a systematic plan of treasury stock acquisitions. The systematic plan of acquisitions must have been established *for at least two years prior to the initiation of a combination;* and the treasury stock acquisitions must be required for stock option and stock purchase plans, or for other recurring stock distributions. Treasury stock meeting the foregoing restrictions is said to be *untainted.* Any untainted treasury stock issued to effect a pooling-type business combination is accounted for as though it had been retired and then issued as previously unissued stock.

No Pending Provisions For pooling accounting to be appropriate for a business combination, no additional capital stock must be contingently issuable to former shareholders of a combinee after a combination has been initiated. In addition, no capital stock must have been issued to an escrow agent pending the resolution of a contingency.

Presentation of business combinations in financial statements

Under both purchase accounting and pooling accounting, the balance sheet for a combined enterprise issued as of the date of a business combination accomplished through a statutory merger, statutory consolidation, or acquisition of assets includes all the assets and liabilities of the constituent companies. (The *consolidated* balance sheet issued following a combination that results in a parent-subsidiary relationship is described in Chapters 5 and 7.) The form of the combined enterprise's income statement for the accounting period in which a combination is carried out depends on whether purchase or pooling accounting is used to record the combination.

Purchase The income statement of the combined enterprise for the accounting period in which a purchase-type business combination occurred includes the operating results of the combinee *after the date of the combination only.* For example, under purchase accounting, Saxon Corporation's postmerger income statement for the year ended December 31, Year 1, would be identical to Saxon's premerger income statement shown in the pooling accounting illustration on page 166, except that net income would be $700,000 and operating expenses would be $1,100,000. (The $200,000 out-of-pocket costs of the business combination are not recorded as expenses in purchase accounting; $66,250 is part of the cost to Saxon of Mason's net assets, and $133,750 is a reduction in Saxon's paid-in capital in excess of par.)

Pooling The income statement of the combined enterprise for the accounting period in which a pooling-type business combination took place includes the results of operations of the constituent companies *as though the combination had been completed at the beginning of the period.* According to *APB Opinion No. 20* "Accounting Changes," a business combination accounted for by the pooling method results in a *change in the reporting entity.*[15] Comparative financial statements for preceding periods must be restated in order to show financial information for the new reporting entity for all periods.[16] Intercompany transactions prior to the combination must be eliminated from the combined income statements in a manner comparable to that described in Chapter 3 for branches.

This presentation stems from the concept that a business combination accounted for as a pooling is a *combining of stockholder interests* rather than an *acquisition of assets.* Because stockholder interests are combined, previous financial statements showing changes in those interests also are combined.

To illustrate, assume that the income statements of Saxon Corporation and Mason Company for the year ended December 31, Year 1, (prior to completion of their merger described earlier in this chapter), were as follows:

Income statements of constituent companies prior to business combination

SAXON CORPORATION AND MASON COMPANY
Income Statements
For Year Ended December 31, Year 1

	Saxon Corporation	Mason Company
Sales	$10,000,000	$5,000,000
Costs and expenses:		
Cost of goods sold	$ 7,000,000	$3,000,000
Operating expenses	1,300,000*	962,000
Interest expense	150,000	100,500
Income taxes expense	1,050,000	562,500
Total costs and expenses	$ 9,500,000	$4,625,000
Net income	$ 500,000	$ 375,000

* Includes $200,000 expenses of business combination.

Assume also that Mason's interest expense includes $25,000 paid to Saxon on a loan that was repaid prior to December 31, Year 1, and that Saxon's sales revenue includes $25,000 (an immaterial amount) interest revenue received from Mason.

[15] *APB Opinion No. 20*, "Accounting Changes," AICPA (New York: 1971), p. 388.
[16] Ibid., p. 398.

The working paper for the postmerger income statement of Saxon Corporation under pooling accounting is illustrated below. The amounts in the Combined column are reported in Saxon's published postmerger income statement for the year ended December 31, Year 1.

SAXON CORPORATION
Working Paper for Combined Income Statement (Pooling of Interests)
For Year Ended December 31, Year 1

	Saxon Corporation	Mason Company	Eliminations	Combined
Sales	10,000,000	5,000,000	(a) (25,000)	14,975,000
Costs and expenses:				
Cost of goods sold	7,000,000	3,000,000		10,000,000
Operating expenses.	1,300,000	962,000		2,262,000
Interest expense.	150,000	100,500	(a) (25,000)	225,500
Income taxes expense . . .	1,050,000	562,500		1,612,500
Total costs and expenses	9,500,000	4,625,000	(25,000)	14,100,000
Net income	500,000	375,000	-0-	875,000

Explanation of combination elimination:
(a) To eliminate intercompany interest received by Saxon Corporation from Mason Company.

Disclosure of business combinations in notes to financial statements

Because of the complex nature of business combinations and their effects on the financial position and operating results of the combined enterprise, extensive disclosure is required for the periods in which they occur. The following notes, from recent annual reports of two publicly owned companies, illustrate the required disclosures for a purchase and a pooling of interests:

Purchase   On April 2, Year 2, the Company acquired substantially all the assets, including inventory, of Combinee Company for $8,400,000 cash and an agreement to make future payments through July, Year 5, contingent on sales of one of the acquired brands.

The acquisition has been accounted for as a purchase, and the excess ($399,000) of the consideration paid upon acquisition over the current fair value of the identifiable tangible and intangible net assets acquired is being amortized over 15 years. Contingent payments are also being recorded as intangible assets and amortized over the then remaining economic life. The results of operations of Combinee are included in the consolidated statement of income since the date of acquisition. Had the acquisition taken place on January 1, Year 1, unaudited pro forma sales for the years ended December 31, Year 2 and Year 1, would be $793,627,000 and $777,715,000, respectively, with unaudited pro forma net income of $9,879,000 and $12,015,000, respectively, and unaudited pro forma earnings per share of $1.17 and $1.40, respectively. Such pro forma data reflect adjustments for amortization of intangible assets and imputed interest.*

Pooling of Interests In November, Year 2, the Company merged with Combinee Company in exchange for 6,477,000 shares of the Company's common stock. This merger has been accounted for as a pooling of interests, and, accordingly, all financial data for accounting periods prior to the merger have been restated to combine the operations of the Company and Combinee.

Net revenue and net income of the separate companies for the 39 weeks ended November 3, Year 2 (interim period nearest the combination date), and fiscal Year 1 are as follows:

	Net revenue (millions)	Net income (millions)
39 weeks ended Nov. 3, Year 2 (unaudited):		
Combinor, as previously reported	$1,848.7	$ 43.2
Combinee	137.2	10.4
Combined	$1,985.9	$ 53.6
Fiscal year ended Feb. 3, Year 1:		
Combinor, as previously reported	$2,582.6	$ 90.0
Combinee	150.1	11.4
Combined	$2,732.7	$101.4

* Although the disclosure of pro forma earnings data is sanctioned by *APB Opinion No. 16,* the SEC reportedly opposes such disclosure in filings with the Commission.

APPRAISAL OF ACCOUNTING STANDARDS FOR BUSINESS COMBINATIONS

The accounting standards for business combinations described and illustrated in the preceding pages of this chapter may be criticized on grounds that they are not consistent with the conceptual framework of accounting.

Criticism of purchase accounting

The principal criticisms of purchase accounting center on the recognition of goodwill. Many accountants take exception to the **residual** basis for valuing goodwill established in **APB Opinion No. 16.** These critics contend that part of the amounts thus assigned to goodwill probably apply to other **identifiable** intangible assets. Accordingly, goodwill in a business combination should be valued **directly** by use of methods described in **Intermediate Accounting** of this series. Any remaining cost not directly allocated to all identifiable tangible and intangible assets and to goodwill would be apportioned to those assets based on the amounts assigned in the first valuation process.

The mandatory amortization of goodwill, prescribed in **APB Opinion No. 17,** is considered by some accountants to be inappropriate for goodwill attributable to a business combination. These accountants recommend treating the amount assigned to goodwill in a business combination as a reduction of stockholders' equity of the combined enterprise.

The accounting described on page 150 for the excess of current fair values over total cost in a bargain-purchase business combination also has been challenged. Critics maintain there is no theoretical support for the arbitrary reduction of previously determined current fair values of assets by an apportioned amount of the bargain-purchase excess. They suggest the amortization treatment described on page 150 for the **entire** bargain purchase excess.

Other accountants question whether current fair values of the **combinor's** net assets—especially goodwill—should be ignored in accounting for a purchase-type business combination. They maintain it is inconsistent to reflect current fair values for net assets of the **combinee only,** in view of the significance of many combinations involving large constituent companies.

Criticism of pooling accounting

The principal objections raised to pooling accounting are summarized below:

1 Despite the elaborate framework for pooling accounting established in **APB Opinion No. 16,** this accounting method is founded upon a delicate assumption. This assumption—that some business combinations involving exchanges of voting common stock result in a combining of stockholder interests rather than an acquisition of assets—is difficult to support in accounting theory. Two **Accounting Research Studies** recommended abolishing the pooling accounting method for business combinations between independent constituent companies.[17]

2 There is no explicit disclosure of the current fair value of the combinor's common stock exchanged in a business combination accounted for as a pooling. The disclosure required by **APB Opinion No. 16** is limited to stating the number of shares of common stock issued in a pooling-type business combination. Thus, there is no way of ascertaining the current fair value of the consideration issued in the combination.

3 The assets of the combinee in a pooling-type business combination are not accounted for at their cost to the combinor. In the illustrated pooling accounting for the merger of Saxon Corporation and Mason Company (pages 156 to 157), the net assets of Mason were recorded in Saxon's accounting records at $3,100,000, the carrying amounts in Mason's accounting records. This amount is $716,250 less than the **cost** of Mason's net assets of $3,816,250 as reflected in the purchase accounting illustration.

---

[17] Arthur R. Wyatt, *Accounting Research Study No. 5,* "A Critical Study of Accounting for Business Combinations," AICPA (New York: 1963), p. 105; George R. Catlett and Norman O. Olson, *Accounting Research Study No. 10,* "Accounting for Goodwill," AICPA (New York: 1968), pp. 106, 109.

4 A consequence of the misstatement of asset values is that net income for each accounting period subsequent to a pooling-type business combination is misstated.

The foregoing are powerful criticisms, and are difficult to refute. Despite its alleged flaws, purchase accounting for business combinations appears conceptually superior in every respect to pooling-of-interests accounting.

FASB study of accounting for business combinations

In recognition of the unsatisfactory state of accounting for business combinations, the Financial Accounting Standards Board initiated a study of the subject shortly after the Board's inception. A lengthy *FASB Discussion Memorandum,* "An Analysis of Issues Related to Accounting for Business Combinations and Purchased Intangibles," was issued in 1976. However, the FASB deferred further efforts on the study, pending completion of the project to develop a conceptual framework for financial accounting and reporting (described in *Intermediate Accounting* of this series). In 1981, the FASB removed the business combinations and purchased intangibles project from its agenda "because of (its) low priority in relation to other existing and potential projects."[18] The action of the Board may be questioned, in light of the criticisms of current accounting standards for business combinations described in the foregoing section.

APPENDIX: SPECIFIED CONDITIONS FOR POOLING-OF-INTERESTS ACCOUNTING

1 *Attributes of the constituent companies*
   a Each of the constituent companies is autonomous and has not been a subsidiary or division of another corporation within two years before the plan of combination is initiated.
   b Each of the constituent companies is independent of the other companies.

2 *Manner of combining ownership interests*
   a The combination is effected in a single transaction or is completed in accordance with a specific plan within one year after the plan is initiated.
   b A corporation offers and issues only common stock with rights identical to those of the majority of its outstanding voting common stock in exchange for substantially all the voting common stock interest of another company at the date the plan of combination is consummated.
   c None of the constituent companies changes the equity interest of the voting common stock in contemplation of effecting the combination either within two years before the plan of combination is initiated or between the dates the combination is initiated and consummated; changes in contemplation of effecting the combination may include distributions to stockholders and additional issuances, exchanges, and retirements of securities.
   d Each of the constituent companies reacquires shares of voting common stock only for purposes other than business combinations, and no company

---

[18] *Status Report,* FASB (Stamford: Apr. 10, 1981), p. 3.

reacquires more than a normal number of shares between the dates the plan of combination is initiated and consummated.
   e The ratio of the interest of an individual common stockholder to those of other common stockholders in a constituent company remains the same as a result of the exchange of common stock to effect the combination.
   f The voting rights to which the common stock ownership interests in the resulting combined enterprise are entitled are exercisable by the stockholders; the stockholders are neither deprived of nor restricted in exercising those rights for a period.
   g The combination is resolved at the date the plan is consummated and no provisions of the plan relating to the issue of securities or other consideration are pending.

3 *Absence of planned transactions*
   a The combined enterprise does not agree directly or indirectly to retire or reacquire all or part of the common stock issued to effect the combination.
   b The combined enterprise does not enter into other financial arrangements for the benefit of the former stockholders of a constituent company, such as a guaranty of loans secured by stock issued in the combination, which in effect negates the exchange of equity securities.
   c The combined enterprise does not intend or plan to dispose of a significant part of the assets of the constituent companies within two years after the combination other than disposals in the ordinary course of business of the former separate companies and to eliminate duplicate facilities or excess capacity.

SOURCE: Adapted from *APB Opinion No. 16,* "Business Combinations," AICPA (New York: 1970), pp. 295–304.

REVIEW QUESTIONS

1 Define a *business combination.*

2 Differentiate between a *statutory merger* and a *statutory consolidation.*

3 Identify two methods that may be used, individually or jointly, to determine an appropriate price to pay for a combinee in a business combination.

4 State how each of the following out-of-pocket costs of a merger purchase-type business combination should be accounted for:
   a Printing costs for proxy statement mailed to combinor's shareholders in advance of special meeting to ratify terms of the merger
   b Legal fees for negotiating the merger
   c CPA firm's fees for auditing SEC registration statement covering shares of common stock issued in the merger
   d Printing costs for securities issued in the merger
   e Legal fees for SEC registration statement covering shares of common stock issued in the merger
   f CPA firm's fees for advice on income tax aspects of the merger

5 The word "goodwill" often appears in connection with business combinations. Explain the meaning of *goodwill* and *negative goodwill.*

6 a Define *contingent consideration* in a business combination.
   b If a plan for a business combination includes a provision for contingent consideration, is pooling accounting appropriate for the combination? Explain.

7 How is the cost of a combinee allocated in a purchase-type business combination?

8 Is any portion of the costs of a combinee in a purchase-type business combination allocated to an unused investment tax credit of the combinee? Explain.

9 Define the term **preacquisition contingencies.**

10 Distinguish between a **purchase** and a **pooling of interests** in terms of the entity relationships between the constituent companies and the combined enterprise. (Do not discuss accounting differences.)

11 If a business combination meets the 12 conditions requiring treatment as a pooling, what is the accounting effect as compared with a purchase interpretation?

12 Comment on the following quotation:

> It is our judgment that the weight of logic and consistency supports the conclusion that business combinations between independent entities are exchange transactions involving a transfer of assets and that the accounting action to account for exchange transactions is necessary to reflect properly the results of business combinations.

13 Discuss some of the reasons for the popularity of pooling accounting for business combinations.

14 Identify five abuses of pooling accounting during the 1960s.

15 How do the journal entries to the Paid-in Capital in Excess of Par account differ in purchase accounting and pooling accounting?

16 Differentiate **retrospective poolings** from **retroactive poolings.**

17 Critics have charged that pooling accounting creates **instant earnings.** How is this accomplished?

18 What information is disclosed in notes to the financial statements of a combined enterprise following a pooling-type business combination?

19 How has purchase accounting for business combinations been criticized?

EXERCISES

Ex. 4-1   Select the best answer for each of the following multiple-choice questions:

    1 Which of the following is the appropriate basis for valuing plant assets acquired in a purchase-type business combination carried out by an exchange of cash for common stock?
       a Current fair value
       b Carrying amount
       c Original cost plus any excess of purchase price over carrying amount of the plant assets acquired
       d Original cost

2 In order for a business combination to be accounted for as a pooling of interests, the minimum amount of the combinee's common stock that must be exchanged for the combinor's common stock is:
a 100%   **b** 90%   **c** 80%   **d** 51%

3 How should long-term debt assumed in a business combination be valued under each of the following methods?

Purchase	Pooling of interests
a Carrying amount	Carrying amount
b Carrying amount	Current fair value
c Current fair value	Current fair value
d Current fair value	Carrying amount

4 Combinor Corporation issued nonvoting preferred stock with a current fair value of $4,000,000 in exchange for all the outstanding common stock of Combinee Company. On the date of the exchange, Combinee had identifiable net assets with a carrying amount of $2,000,000 and a current fair value of $2,500,000. In addition, Combinor issued preferred stock valued at $400,000 to an individual as a finder's fee in arranging the merger business combination. As a result of this transaction, Combinor should record an increase in net assets of:
a $2,000,000   **b** $2,500,000   **c** $2,900,000   **d** $4,400,000
e Some other amount

5 Goodwill from a business combination:
a Should be expensed in the year of the combination
b Is an asset that is not subject to amortization
c Is an intangible asset
d Occurs in a pooling of interests

6 Which of the following is a potential abuse that can arise when a business combination is accounted for as a pooling of interests?
a Assets of the combinee may be overvalued when the price paid by the combinor is allocated among specific assets
b Liabilities of the combinee may be undervalued when the price paid by the combinor is allocated among specific liabilities
c An undue amount of cost may be assigned to goodwill, thus potentially allowing for an overstatement of pooled earnings
d Earnings of the combined enterprise may be increased because of the combination only, and not as a result of efficient operations

Ex. 4-2 Gamma Corporation was organized in a statutory consolidation to combine the resources of Alpha Company and Beta, Inc., in a business combination accounted for by the pooling method. On January 2, Year 1, Gamma issued 65,000 shares of its $10 par common stock in exchange for all the outstanding common stock of Alpha and Beta. The stockholders' equity of Alpha and Beta on January 2, Year 1, were as follows:

	Alpha Company	Beta, Inc.	Totals
Common stock, $1 par	$150,000	$450,000	$600,000
Paid-in capital in excess of par	20,000	55,000	75,000
Retained earnings	110,000	210,000	320,000
Total stockholders' equity	$280,000	$715,000	$995,000

Compute the balance of Gamma's Paid-in Capital in Excess of Par account immediately after the business combination. Disregard out-of-pocket costs of the business combination.

Ex. 4-3 On March 31, Year 3, Combinor Corporation acquired the identifiable net assets of Combinee Company for $800,000 cash. On the date of the business combination, Combinee had no long-term investments in marketable securities and had $100,000 of liabilities. The current fair values of Combinee's assets on March 31, Year 3, were as follows:

Current assets	$ 400,000
Noncurrent assets	600,000
Total current fair value	$1,000,000

Out-of-pocket costs of the business combination may be disregarded.

Prepare journal entries for Combinor on March 1, Year 3, to record its business combination with Combinee.

Ex. 4-4 Synde Corporation (the survivor) issued its preferred stock with a current fair value of $1,000,000 in exchange for all the outstanding common stock of Moro Company, which had identifiable net assets with a carrying amount of $500,000 and a current fair value of $600,000. In addition, Synde issued preferred stock valued at $120,000 to an investment banker as a finder's fee for arranging the merger business combination.

Compute the total increase in Synde's net assets resulting from the business combination with Moro.

Ex. 4-5 Webb Corporation paid $100,000 cash for the net assets of Lorne Company, which consisted of the following:

	Carrying amount	Current fair value
Current assets	$20,000	$ 28,000
Plant assets (net)	80,000	110,000
Liabilities	(20,000)	(18,000)
Net assets	$80,000	$120,000

Compute the amount at which Webb should record the plant assets acquired from Lorne.

Ex. 4-6 Loo Corporation offered to exchange two shares of its common stock for each share of Nash Company common stock. On the date of the offer, Loo held 3,000 shares (3%) of Nash common stock and Nash held 500 shares (0.05%) of Loo common stock. In later cash transactions, Loo acquired 2,000 shares (2%) of Nash common stock and Nash acquired 2,500 shares (0.25%) of Loo common stock. At all times the number of shares of common stock outstanding was 1,000,000 for Loo and 100,000 for Nash. After consummation of the business combination, Loo held 100,000 shares of Nash common stock.

Compute the number of shares of Nash Company common stock considered exchanged in determining whether this business combination should be accounted for as a pooling of interests.

Ex. 4-7 The condensed balance sheet of Leno Company on March 31, Year 8, is given at the top of page 175.

On March 31, Year 8, Kinder Corporation paid $700,000 cash for all the net assets of Leno (except cash) in a business combination qualifying for purchase accounting. The carrying amounts of Leno's other current assets and current liabilities were the same as their current fair values. However, current fair values of

LENO COMPANY
Condensed Balance Sheet
March 31, Year 8

Assets

Cash	$ 20,000
Other current assets	140,000
Plant assets (net)	740,000
Total assets	$900,000

Liabilities & Stockholders' Equity

Current liabilities	$ 80,000
Long-term debt	200,000
Common stock, $2 par	180,000
Paid-in capital in excess of par	120,000
Retained earnings	320,000
Total liabilities & stockholders' equity	$900,000

Leno's plant assets and long-term debt were $920,000 and $190,000, respectively.

Also on March 31, Kinder paid the following out-of-pocket costs for the business combination with Leno:

Legal fees	$ 10,000
Finder's fee	70,000
CPA firm's fee for audit of Leno Company's March 31, Year 8, financial statements	20,000
Total out-of-pocket costs of business combination	$100,000

Compute the amount of goodwill or "negative goodwill" in the business combination of Kinder Corporation and Leno Company.

Ex. 4-8   The condensed balance sheet of Munoz Company on February 28, Year 7, with related current fair values of assets and liabilities, appears on page 176.

On February 28, Year 7, Seville Corporation issued 600,000 shares of its $1 par common stock (current fair value $25 a share) to Maria Munoz, sole stockholder of Munoz Company, for all 500,000 shares of Munoz Company common stock owned by her, in a merger business combination qualifying for pooling accounting. Because the merger was negotiated privately and Maria Munoz signed a "letter agreement" not to dispose of the Seville common stock she received, the Seville stock was not subject to SEC registration requirements. Thus, only $5,000 in legal fees was incurred to effect the merger; these fees were paid in cash by Seville on February 28, Year 7.

Prepare journal entries to record the business combination in the accounting records of Seville Corporation.

Ex. 4-9   On November 1, Year 4, Sullivan Corporation issued 50,000 shares of its common stock in exchange for all the common stock of Mears Company in a statutory merger. Out-of-pocket costs of the business combination may be disregarded. Sullivan tentatively recorded the shares of common stock issued at par and debited Investment in Mears Company Common Stock for $500,000. Mears Company was liquidated and became Mears Division of Sullivan.

MUNOZ COMPANY
Balance Sheet
February 28, Year 7

	Carrying amount	Current fair value
Assets		
Current assets	$ 500,000	$ 580,000
Plant assets (net)	1,000,000	1,150,000
Other assets	300,000	350,000
Total assets	$1,800,000	
Liabilities & Stockholders' Equity		
Current liabilities	$ 300,000	300,000
Long-term debt	400,000	380,000
Common stock, $1 par	500,000	
Paid-in capital in excess of par	200,000	
Retained earnings	400,000	
Total liabilities & stockholders' equity	$1,800,000	

The net income of Sullivan and Mears Company or Mears Division during Year 4 was as follows:

	Jan. 1–Oct. 31	Nov. 1–Dec. 31
Sullivan Corporation	$420,000	$80,000*
Mears Company	350,000	
Mears Division of Sullivan Corporation		50,000

* Excludes any portion of Mears Division net income.

Condensed balance sheet and other data for Year 4 follow:

	Sullivan Corporation		Mears Company Oct. 31	Mears Division of Sullivan Corporation Dec. 31
	Oct. 31	Dec. 31		
Assets	$3,500,000	$4,080,000	$4,000,000	$4,150,000
Liabilities	500,000	500,000	1,000,000	1,100,000
Common stock, $10 par	2,000,000	2,500,000	2,000,000	
Retained earnings . . .	1,000,000	1,080,000*	1,000,000	
Market price per share of common stock	100	130	20	

* Excludes any portion of Mears Division net income.

Neither company paid dividends during Year 4. In recent months, Sullivan's common stock has been selling at about 40 times earnings; prior to November 1, Year 4, Mears Company common stock had been selling at 10 times earnings.

Answer the following questions, **assuming that the differences between current fair values and carrying amounts of Mears Company's identifiable net assets apply to land.** Show supporting computations.

a Assuming that the merger is accounted for as a pooling, what is Sullivan's net income for Year 4?

b What is the amount of the Year 4 earnings per share for Sullivan on a pooling basis?

c If the merger had been accounted for as a purchase, what would Sullivan's net income have been for Year 4?

d What is Sullivan's earnings per share for Year 4 on a purchase basis?

e What is the amount of retained earnings on a pooling basis at the end of Year 4?

f What is the amount of retained earnings on a purchase basis at the end of Year 4?

CASES

Case 4-1 When a business combination is effected by an exchange of common stock, the transaction is accounted for either as a purchase or as a pooling of interests. The methods are not optional, and may yield significantly different results as to financial position and results of operations of the combined enterprise.

Instructions Discuss the supportive arguments for each of the following methods of accounting for business combinations:

a Purchase method

b Pooling-of-interests method

Do not discuss the rules for distinguishing between a purchase and a pooling of interests.

Case 4-2 The boards of directors of Carter Corporation, Fulton Company, Russell, Inc., and Towne Corporation are meeting jointly to discuss plans for a statutory merger. Each of the corporations has one class of common stock outstanding; Fulton also has one class of preferred stock outstanding. Although terms have not as yet been settled, Carter will be the surviving corporation. Because the directors want to conform to generally accepted accounting principles, they have asked you to attend the meeting as an advisor.

Instructions Consider each of the following questions independently of the others and answer each in accordance with generally accepted accounting principles. Explain your answers.

a Assume that the merger will be consummated August 31, Year 5. Explain the philosophy underlying the accounting and how the balance sheet accounts of each of the four corporations will appear in Carter's balance sheet on September 1, Year 5, if the merger is accounted for as a:

(1) Pooling

(2) Purchase

b Assume that the merger will be consummated August 31, Year 5. Explain how the income statement accounts of each of the four corporations will be accounted for in Carter's income statement for the year ended December 31, Year 5, if the merger is accounted for as a:

(1) Pooling

(2) Purchase

c Some of the directors believe that the terms of the merger should be agreed on immediately and that the method of accounting to be used may be chosen at some later date. Others believe that the terms of the merger and the accounting method to be used are closely related. Which position is correct? Explain.

d Carter and Towne are comparable in size; Russell and Fulton are much smaller. How do these facts affect the choice of accounting method for the merger?

e Fulton was formerly a subsidiary of Garson Corporation, which has no other relationship to any of the four companies discussing the business combination. Garson voluntarily spun off Fulton 18 months ago. What effect, if any, do these facts have on the choice of accounting method for the merger?

f Carter holds 2,000 of Fulton's 10,000 outstanding shares of preferred stock and 15,000 of Russell's 100,000 outstanding shares of common stock. All of Carter's holdings were acquired during the first three months of Year 5. What effect, if any, do these facts have on the choice of accounting method?

g Because the directors feel that one of Towne's major divisions will not be compatible with the operations of the combined enterprise, they anticipate that it will be sold as soon as possible after the business combination is consummated. They expect to have no trouble in finding a buyer. What effect, if any, do these facts have on the choice of accounting method?

Case 4-3   You have been engaged to examine the financial statements of Solamente Corporation for the fiscal year ended May 31, Year 6. You discover that on June 1, Year 5, Mika Company was merged into Solamente in a business combination qualifying for purchase accounting. You also find that both Solamente and Mika (prior to its liquidation) incurred legal fees, accounting fees, and printing costs for the business combination; both companies debited those costs to an intangible asset ledger account entitled "Cost of Business Combination." In its journal entry to record the business combination with Mika, Solamente increased its Cost of Business Combination account by an amount equal to the balance in Mika's comparable ledger account.

Instructions   Evaluate Solamente's accounting for the out-of-pocket costs of the business combination with Mika.

Case 4-4   Satchell Corporation and Mobley Company, both of which have only voting common stock outstanding, are considering a statutory merger whereby Satchell would be the survivor. The terms of the business combination provide that the transaction would be carried out by Satchell exchanging one share of its unissued common stock for each two shares of Mobley's outstanding common stock. Prior to the date of the contemplated exchange, Satchell had acquired 5% of Mobley's outstanding common stock, which it holds as an investment. Mobley, on the same date, owns 2% of Satchell's outstanding common stock. All the remaining outstanding common stock of Mobley will be acquired by Satchell in the contemplated exchange. Neither of the two companies has ever had any affiliation as a subsidiary or division of any other company.

Instructions

a How is a determination made as to whether a business combination is accounted for as a pooling or as a purchase? (Do not enumerate specific criteria.)

b Based only on the facts above, discuss the specific criteria that would qualify or disqualify the Satchell–Mobley business combination for pooling accounting.

c What additional requirements (other than those discussed in **b** above) must be met in order for this business combination to be accounted for as a pooling?

Case 4-5   After extended negotiations, Combinor Corporation acquired from Combinee Company most of the latter's assets on June 30, Year 3. At the time of the acquisition, Combinee's accounting records (adjusted to June 30, Year 3) reflected the descriptions and amounts that appear at the top of page 179 for the assets acquired.

You ascertain that the valuation accounts were Allowance for Doubtful Accounts, Allowance for Price Decline in Inventories, and Accumulated Depreciation.

	Cost	Valuation accounts	Carrying amounts
Accounts receivable	$ 83,600	$ 3,000	$ 80,600
Inventories	107,000	5,200	101,800
Land	20,000		20,000
Buildings	207,500	73,000	134,500
Machinery and equipment	205,000	41,700	163,300
Goodwill	50,000		50,000
Totals	$673,100	$122,900	$550,200

During the extended negotiations, Combinee held out for a consideration of approximately $600,000 (depending upon the level of accounts receivable and inventories). However, on June 30, Year 3, Combinee agreed to accept Combinor's offer of $450,000 cash plus 1% of Combinor's net sales (as defined in the contract) of the next five years, with payments at the end of each year. Combinee expects that Combinor's total net sales during this five-year period will exceed $15,000,000.

Instructions

a How should Combinor Corporation account for the business combination? Explain.

b Discuss the propriety of recording goodwill in the accounting records of Combinor Corporation for the business combination.

Case 4-6 On February 15, Year 6, negotiating officers of Shane Corporation agreed with George Merlo, sole shareholder of Merlo Company and Merlo Industries, Inc., to acquire all his common stock ownership in the two companies as follows:

(1) 10,000 shares of Shane's $1 par common stock (current fair value $25 a share) would be issued to George Merlo on February 28, Year 6, for his 1,000 shares of $10 par common stock of Merlo Company. In addition, 10,000 shares of Shane common stock would be issued to George Merlo on February 28, Year 11, if aggregate net income of Merlo Company for the five-year period then ended exceeded $300,000.

(2) $250,000 cash would be paid to George Merlo on February 28, Year 6, for his 10,000 shares of $1 par common stock of Merlo Industries, Inc. In addition $250,000 in cash would be paid to George Merlo on February 28, Year 11, if aggregate net income of Merlo Industries, Inc., for the five-year period then ended exceeded $300,000.

Both Merlo Company and Merlo Industries, Inc., are to be merged into Shane on February 28, Year 6, and are to continue operations after that date as divisions of Shane. George Merlo also agreed not to compete with Shane for the period March 1, Year 6, through February 28, Year 11. Because the merger was negotiated privately and George Merlo signed a "letter agreement" not to dispose of the Shane common stock he received, the business combination was not subject to the jurisdiction of the SEC. Out-of-pocket costs of the business combination were negligible.

Selected financial statement data of the three constituent companies as of February 28, Year 6 (prior to the merger), were as follows:

	Shane Corporation	Merlo Company	Merlo Industries, Inc.
Total assets	$25,000,000	$ 500,000	$ 600,000
Stockholders' equity	10,000,000	200,000	300,000
Net sales	50,000,000	1,500,000	2,500,000
Earnings per share	5	30	3

The controller of Shane prepared the following condensed journal entries to record the merger on February 28, Year 6:

Assets	500,000	
Liabilities		300,000
Common Stock		10,000
Common Stock to Be Issued		10,000
Paid-in Capital in Excess of Par		180,000

To record merger with Merlo Company as a pooling.

Assets	650,000	
Goodwill	150,000	
Liabilities		300,000
Payable to George Merlo		250,000
Cash		250,000

To record merger with Merlo Industries, Inc., as a purchase, with assets and liabilities of Merlo Industries, Inc., recorded at current fair values and goodwill to be amortized over a 40-year economic life.

Instructions Do you concur with the controller's journal entries? Discuss.

PROBLEMS

4-1 The balance sheet of Combinee Company on October 31, Year 5, was as follows:

COMBINEE COMPANY
Balance Sheet
October 31, Year 5

Assets

Cash	$ 60,000
Other current assets	420,000
Plant assets (net)	920,000
Total assets	$1,400,000

Liabilities & Stockholders' Equity

Current liabilities	$ 180,000
Long-term debt	250,000
Common stock, $5 par	200,000
Paid-in capital in excess of par	320,000
Retained earnings	450,000
Total liabilities & stockholders' equity	$1,400,000

After a thorough study, Combinor Corporation's board of directors established the following current fair values for Combinee's identifiable net assets other than cash:

Other current assets	$ 500,000
Plant assets (net).	1,000,000
Current liabilities	180,000
Long-term debt	250,000

Accordingly, on October 31, Year 5, Combinor issued 100,000 shares of its $10 par (current fair value $13) common stock for all the net assets of Combinee in a business combination qualifying for purchase accounting. Also on October 31, Year 5, Combinor paid the following out-of-pocket costs in connection with the combination:

Finder's fee and legal fees	$180,000
Costs associated with SEC registration statement	120,000
Total out-of-pocket costs of business combination	$300,000

Instructions Prepare journal entries in the accounting records of Combinor Corporation on October 31, Year 5, to record the business combination with Combinee Company. Disregard income taxes.

4-2 Condensed balance sheets of Conner Company and Capsol Company on July 31, Year 9, were as follows:

	Conner Company	Capsol Company
Total assets	$700,000	$670,000
Total liabilities	$300,000	$300,000
Common stock, $25 par	200,000	250,000
Paid-in capital in excess of par	80,000	130,000
Retained earnings (deficit)	120,000	(10,000)
Total liabilities & stockholders' equity	$700,000	$670,000

On July 31, Year 9, Conner and Capsol entered into a statutory consolidation. The new company, Consol Corporation, issued 75,000 shares of $10 par common stock for all the outstanding common stock of Conner and Capsol. Out-of-pocket costs of the business combination may be disregarded.

Instructions

a Prepare a journal entry to record the business combination in the accounting records of Consol as a pooling.
b Prepare a journal entry to record the business combination in the accounting records of Consol as a purchase. Assume that Capsol is the combinor; that current fair values of identifiable assets are $800,000 for Conner and $700,000 for Capsol; that each company's liabilities are fairly stated at $300,000; and that the current fair value of Consol's common stock is $14 a share. Disregard income taxes.

4-3 The condensed balance sheets of Stole Corporation, the combinor, prior to and subsequent to its March 1, Year 4, merger with Moore Company, appear at the top of page 182.
Prior to the business combination, Moore had total assets of $1,200,000 and total liabilities of $300,000. Out-of-pocket costs of the business combination were paid by Stole on March 1, Year 4.

Instructions Reconstruct the journal entries that Stole prepared on March 1, Year 4, to record the business combination with Moore. Disregard income taxes.

STOLE CORPORATION

Balance Sheets Prior to and Subsequent to Business Combination

March 1, Year 4

	Prior to business combination	Subsequent to business combination
Assets		
Current assets	$ 500,000	$ 850,000
Plant assets (net)	1,000,000	1,800,000
Total assets	$1,500,000	$2,650,000
Liabilities & Stockholders' Equity		
Current Liabilities	$ 350,000	$ 600,000
Long-term debt	100,000	150,000
Common stock, $1 par	400,000	700,000
Paid-in capital in excess of par	310,000	570,000
Retained earnings	340,000	630,000
Total liabilities & stockholders' equity	$1,500,000	$2,650,000

4-4 On October 31, Year 9, Stevens Corporation issued 20,000 shares of its $1 par (current fair value $20) common stock for all the outstanding common stock of Morgan Company in a statutory merger. Out-of-pocket costs of the business combination paid by Stevens on October 31, Year 9, were as follows:

Direct costs of the business combination	$20,870
Costs of registering and issuing common stock	31,130
Total out-of-pocket costs of business combination	$52,000

Morgan's balance sheet on October 31, Year 9, follows:

MORGAN COMPANY

Balance Sheet

October 31, Year 9

Assets

Inventories	$140,000
Other current assets	80,000
Plant assets (net)	380,000
Total assets	$600,000

Liabilities & Stockholders' Equity

Payable to Stevens Corporation	$ 75,000
Other liabilities	225,000
Common stock, $3 par	30,000
Paid-in capital in excess of par	120,000
Retained earnings	150,000
Total liabilities & stockholders' equity	$600,000

Other information:

(1) The current fair values of Morgan's other current assets and all its liabilities equaled the carrying amounts on October 31, Year 9.

(2) Current fair values of Morgan's inventories and plant assets were $160,000 and $420,000, respectively, on October 31, Year 9.

(3) Stevens's October 31, Year 9, balance sheet included an asset entitled Receivable from Morgan Company in the amount of $75,000.

Instructions Prepare Stevens Corporation's journal entries on October 31, Year 9, to record the business combination with Morgan Company:

a As a purchase (Disregard income taxes.)

b As a pooling of interests

4-5 The balance sheet on March 31, Year 7, and the related current fair value data for Ambrose Company are as follows:

AMBROSE COMPANY

Balance Sheet

March 31, Year 7

	Carrying amount	Current fair value
Assets		
Current assets	$ 500,000	$ 575,000
Plant assets (net)	1,000,000	1,200,000
Patent (net)	100,000	50,000
Total assets	$1,600,000	
Liabilities & Stockholders' Equity		
Current liabilities	$ 300,000	$ 300,000
Long-term debt	400,000	450,000
Common stock, $10 par	100,000	
Retained earnings	800,000	
Total liabilities & stockholders' equity	$1,600,000	

On April 1, Year 7, Baxter Corporation issued 50,000 shares of its $5 par common stock (current fair value $14 a share) and $225,000 cash for the net assets of Ambrose Company, in a business combination qualifying for purchase accounting. Of the $125,000 out-of-pocket costs paid by Baxter on April 1, Year 7, $50,000 were legal fees and finders' fees related to the business combination.

Instructions Prepare journal entries to record the business combination in the accounting records of Baxter Corporation. Disregard income tax considerations.

4-6 Molo Company merged into Stave Corporation in a business combination completed April 30, Year 5. Out-of-pocket costs paid by Stave on April 30, Year 5, in connection with the combination were as follows:

Finder's fee and legal fees relating to the business combination	$15,000
Cost associated with SEC registration statement for securities issued to complete the business combination	10,000
Total out-of-pocket costs of business combination	$25,000

The individual balance sheets of the constituent companies immediately prior to the merger were as follows:

STAVE CORPORATION AND MOLO COMPANY
Balance Sheets
April 30, Year 5

	Stave Corporation	Molo Company
Assets		
Current assets	$ 4,350,000	$ 3,000,000
Plant assets (net)	18,500,000	11,300,000
Patents	450,000	200,000
Deferred charges	150,000	
Total assets	$23,450,000	$14,500,000
Liabilities & Stockholders' Equity		
Liabilities	$ 2,650,000	$ 2,100,000
Common stock, $10 par	12,000,000	
Common stock, $5 par		3,750,000
Paid-in capital in excess of par	4,200,000	3,200,000
Retained earnings	5,850,000	5,450,000
Less: Treasury stock, at cost, 100,000 shares . . .	(1,250,000)	
Total liabilities & stockholders' equity	$23,450,000	$14,500,000

You have obtained the following additional information:

(1) The current fair values of the identifiable assets and liabilities of Stave Corporation and Molo Company were as follows on April 30, Year 5:

STAVE CORPORATION AND MOLO COMPANY
Current Fair Values of Identifiable Net Assets
April 30, Year 5

	Stave Corporation	Molo Company
Current assets	$ 4,950,000	$ 3,400,000
Plant assets (net)	22,000,000	14,000,000
Patents	570,000	360,000
Deferred charges	150,000	
Liabilities	(2,650,000)	(2,100,000)
Identifiable net assets	$25,020,000	$15,660,000

(2) There were no intercompany transactions prior to the business combination.

(3) Before the business combination, Stave had 3,000,000 shares of common stock authorized, 1,200,000 shares issued, and 1,100,000 shares outstanding. Molo had 750,000 shares of common stock authorized, issued, and outstanding. The treasury stock of Stave was "untainted."

(4) Molo Company was liquidated on completion of the merger.

Instructions Prepare journal entries in the accounting records of Stave Corporation to record the business combination with Molo Company under each of the following independent assumptions:

a Stave exchanged 400,000 shares of previously unissued common stock and 100,000 shares of treasury stock for all the outstanding common stock of Molo. All the conditions for pooling accounting enumerated in *APB Opinion No. 16,* "Business Combinations," were met.

b Stave paid $3,100,000 cash and issued 16% debentures at face amount of $16,900,000 for all the outstanding common stock of Molo. The current fair value of the debentures is equal to their face amount. (Disregard income taxes.)

4-7 As of the close of business August 31, Year 2, Mullin Company merged into Samos Corporation in a business combination meeting the 12 conditions for pooling accounting listed in *APB Opinion No. 16,* "Business Combinations." Premerger income statements of the constituent companies for the year ended August 31, Year 2, were as follows:

SAMOS CORPORATION AND MULLIN COMPANY
Income Statements
For Year Ended August 31, Year 2

	Samos Corporation	Mullin Company
Revenue:		
Net sales	$800,000	$550,000
Interest	20,000	
Rent		50,000
Total revenue	$820,000	$600,000
Costs and expenses:		
Cost of goods sold	$480,000	$300,000
Operating expenses	75,000	50,000
Interest expense	15,000	10,000
Income taxes expense	150,000	144,000
Total costs and expenses	$720,000	$504,000
Net income	$100,000	$ 96,000

During the year prior to the merger, Mullin had obtained from and repaid to Samos a $100,000, 15%, 90-day loan; Samos had rented for the entire year a sales office owned by Mullin with a monthly rent of $500 plus 1% of net sales; and Samos had sold to Mullin at Samos's regular markup, goods costing $120,000, all of which Mullin sold during the year ended August 31, Year 2, to outside customers at Mullin's regular markup.

Instructions

a Prepare the working paper eliminations (in journal entry form) for Samos Corporation's postmerger income statement for the year ended August 31, Year 2. Disregard income taxes.

b Prepare a working paper for the postmerger combined income statement of Samos Corporation for the year ended August 31, Year 2.

4-8 On June 30, Year 2, Capsule Company and Compari Company entered into a statutory consolidation. A new company, Cap-Com Corporation, issued 100,000 shares of its 500,000 authorized shares of no-par, $5 stated value common stock as follows:

(1) 60,000 shares for all 10,000 outstanding shares of Capsule's $2 par common stock

(2) 40,000 shares for all 15,000 outstanding shares of Compari's $1 par common stock

Costs of $50,000 associated with the statutory consolidation (legal and audit fees, printing charges, SEC fees) were paid in cash on June 30, Year 2 (prior to the consolidation), by Capsule on behalf of Cap-Com. There were no other intercompany transactions.

Following are condensed financial statements of Capsule and Compari for the year ended June 30, Year 2, prior to the consolidation:

CAPSULE COMPANY AND COMPARI COMPANY
Balance Sheets
June 30, Year 2

	Capsule Company	Compari Company
Assets		
Current assets	$ 200,000	$300,000
Receivable from Cap-Com Corporation	50,000	
Plant assets (net)	700,000	500,000
Other assets	60,000	10,000
Total assets	$1,010,000	$810,000
Liabilities & Stockholders' Equity		
Current liabilities	$ 160,000	$ 80,000
Long-term debt	200,000	90,000
Common stock	20,000	15,000
Paid-in capital in excess of par	80,000	150,000
Retained earnings	550,000	475,000
Total liabilities & stockholders' equity	$1,010,000	$810,000

CAPSULE COMPANY AND COMPARI COMPANY
Statements of Income and Retained Earnings
For Year Ended June 30, Year 2

Net sales	$2,000,000	$3,000,000
Costs and expenses:		
Cost of goods sold	$1,200,000	$2,000,000
Operating expenses	400,000	500,000
Interest expense	15,000	10,000
Income taxes expense	231,000	294,000
Total costs and expenses	$1,846,000	$2,804,000
Net income	$ 154,000	$ 196,000
Retained earnings, beginning of year	396,000	279,000
Retained earnings, end of year	$ 550,000	$ 475,000

Capsule costs its inventories on the fifo basis; Compari uses lifo cost for inventories. As part of the consolidation contract, Compari agreed to change its inventories valuation method from lifo to fifo. Relevant data for Compari are as follows:

	Lifo cost	Fifo cost
Inventories, June 30, Year 2	$100,000	$150,000
Inventories, June 30, Year 1	90,000	130,000

Instructions

a Prepare the adjusting journal entry on June 30, Year 2, to change Compari Company's inventories from lifo cost to fifo cost. Compari's combined federal and state income tax rate is 60%. (**Note:** In accordance with **APB Opinion No. 20,** "Accounting Changes," a change from lifo to another inventory costing method requires the retroactive adjustment of retained earnings.)

b Prepare the June 30, Year 2, journal entry of Cap-Com Corporation to record the statutory consolidation as a pooling. Do not include revenue and expenses in the journal entry.

c Compute the pooled net income of Cap-Com Corporation for the year ended June 30, Year 2.

4-9 Coolidge Corporation agreed to pay $850,000 cash and issue 50,000 shares of its $10 par ($20 market value a share) common stock on September 30, Year 4, to Hoover Company for all the net assets of Hoover except cash. In addition, Coolidge agreed that if the market value of its common stock was not $20 a share or more on September 30, Year 5, a sufficient number of additional shares of common stock would be issued to Hoover to make the aggregate market value of its Coolidge common shareholdings equal to $1,000,000 on that date.

The balance sheet of Hoover on September 30, Year 4, with related current fair values of assets and liabilities, is presented below:

HOOVER COMPANY
Balance Sheet
September 30, Year 4

	Carrying amount	Current fair value
Assets		
Cash	$ 100,000	$ 100,000
Accounts receivable (net)	300,000	300,000
Inventories	600,000	680,000
Short-term prepayments	20,000	20,000
10% investment in Truman Company common stock		
(long-term, marketable)	100,000	180,000
Land	500,000	650,000
Other plant assets (net)	1,000,000	1,250,000
Patent (net)	80,000	100,000
Total assets	$2,700,000	

Liabilities & Stockholders' Equity		
Current liabilities	$ 700,000	$ 700,000
Long-term debt	500,000	480,000
Common stock, $5 par	600,000	
Paid-in capital in excess of par	400,000	
Retained earnings	500,000	
Total liabilities & stockholders' equity	$2,700,000	

Out-of-pocket costs of the business combination paid by Coolidge on September 30, Year 4, were as follows:

Audit fees—SEC registration statement	$ 30,000
Finder's fee (2% of aggregate consideration)	35,000
Legal fees—business combination	15,000
Legal fees—SEC registration statement	20,000
Printing costs—securities and SEC registration statement	25,000
SEC registration fee	350
Total out-of-pocket costs of business combination	$125,350

Instructions

a Prepare the September 30, Year 4, journal entries in the accounting records of Coolidge Corporation to reflect the foregoing transactions. Disregard income taxes.

b Assume that on September 30, Year 5, the market value of Coolidge Corporation's common stock was $16 a share. Prepare a journal entry to record the issuance of additional shares of Coolidge common stock to Hoover Company on that date and the payment of cash in lieu of fractional shares, if any.

4-10 The board of directors of Simeon Corporation is considering a merger with Masha Company. The most recent financial statements and other financial data for the two companies, both of which use the same accounting principles and practices, are shown below and at the top of page 189.

SIMEON CORPORATION AND MASHA COMPANY
Balance Sheets
October 31, Year 8

	Simeon Corporation	Masha Company
Assets		
Current assets	$ 500,000	$200,000
Plant assets (net)	1,000,000	500,000
Other assets	300,000	100,000
Total assets	$1,800,000	$800,000
Liabilities & Stockholders' Equity		
Current liabilities	$ 400,000	$100,000
Long-term debt	500,000	300,000
Common stock, $10 par	600,000	100,000
Paid-in capital in excess of par	100,000	100,000
Retained earnings	200,000	200,000
Total liabilities & stockholders' equity	$1,800,000	$800,000

Simeon's directors estimate that the out-of-pocket costs of the merger will be as follows:

Finder's fee and legal fees for the merger	$ 5,000
Costs associated with SEC registration statement	7,000
Total out-of-pocket costs of merger	$12,000

SIMEON CORPORATION AND MASHA COMPANY
Statements of Income and Retained Earnings
For Year Ended October 31, Year 8

	Simeon Corporation	Masha Company
Net sales	$5,000,000	$1,000,000
Costs and expenses:		
Costs of goods sold	$3,500,000	$ 600,000
Operating expenses	1,000,000	200,000
Interest expense	200,000	50,000
Income taxes expense	180,000	90,000
Total costs and expenses	$4,880,000	$ 940,000
Net income	$ 120,000	$ 60,000
Retained earnings, beginning of year	80,000	140,000
Retained earnings, end of year	$ 200,000	$ 200,000
Earnings per share	$2.00	$6.00
Price-earnings ratio	10	5

The discounted present values of Masha's liabilities on October 31, Year 8, are equal to their carrying amounts. Current fair values of Masha's assets on that date are as follows:

Current assets (*difference from balance sheet amount of $200,000 attributable to inventories carried at fifo cost that were sold during year ended Oct. 31, Year 9*) $230,000

Plant assets (*difference from balance sheet amount of $500,000 attributable to land—$60,000 and to depreciable assets with a five-year remaining economic life—$40,000*) 600,000

Other assets (*difference from balance sheet amount of $100,000 attributable to leasehold with a remaining term of four years*) 120,000

Simeon's board of directors is considering two alternative plans for effecting the merger, as follows:

Plan 1 Issue 30,000 shares of common stock for all the outstanding common stock of Masha in a business combination meeting the 12 conditions for pooling accounting enumerated in *APB Opinion No. 16,* "Business Combinations."

Plan 2 Issue 15,000 shares of common stock with a current fair value of $20 a share, $100,000 cash, and a 15%, three-year note for $200,000 for all the outstanding common stock of Masha. The current fair value of the note is equal to its face amount.

Under either plan, Masha would be liquidated but would continue operations as a division of Simeon.

Instructions To assist Simeon Corporation's board of directors in their evaluation of the two plans, compute or prepare the following for each plan as though the merger had been effected on October 31, Year 8 (disregard income taxes):

a Net income and earnings per share (rounded to the nearest cent) of Simeon for the year ended October 31, Year 8.

b Net income and earnings per share (rounded to the nearest cent) of Simeon for the year ending October 31, Year 9, assuming the same sales and cost patterns for the year ended October 31, Year 8. Goodwill, if any, is to be amortized over 40 years.

c Pro forma balance sheets following the business combination on October 31, Year 8.

4-11 Financial statements of Segal Corporation and Maynard Company for the six months ended June 30, Year 7, appear below and at the top of page 191.

SEGAL CORPORATION AND MAYNARD COMPANY
Balance Sheets
June 30, Year 7

	Segal Corporation	Maynard Company
Assets		
Cash	$ 25,500	$ 1,500
Notes and accounts receivable (net)	24,500	7,500
Inventories, at fifo cost	42,000	8,800
Receivable from Maynard Company	7,600	
Plant assets (net)	59,500	35,800
Other assets	4,500	200
Total assets	$163,600	$53,800
Liabilities & Stockholders' Equity		
Notes and accounts payable	$ 20,700	$39,920
Payable to Segal Corporation		7,600
Income taxes payable	11,400	
Other liabilities	1,500	2,200
Common stock, $10 par	50,000	
Common stock, $100 par		25,000
Paid-in capital in excess of par	30,000	32,000
Retained earnings (deficit)	50,000	(52,920)
Total liabilities & stockholders' equity	$163,600	$53,800

The pre-tax accounting income (loss) of Segal and Maynard for the last six years is as follows (pre-tax accounting income and taxable income are the same):

	Segal Corporation	Maynard Company
Year 1 (Year in which Maynard Company was organized)	$18,000	$(4,000)
Year 2	(7,500)	4,000
Year 3	12,600	(15,000)
Year 4	14,900	(6,000)
Year 5	31,200	(7,000)
Year 6	28,900	(11,100)

On July 1, Year 7, Maynard's stockholders transferred to Segal their shares of Maynard $100 par common stock in exchange for unissued Segal $10 par com-

SEGAL CORPORATION AND MAYNARD COMPANY
Statements of Income and Retained Earnings (Deficit)
For Six Months Ended June 30, Year 7

	Segal Corporation	Maynard Company
Revenue:		
Net sales	$150,000	$ 60,000
Other revenue	5,000	
Total revenue	$155,000	$ 60,000
Costs and expenses:		
Cost of goods sold	$105,000	$ 54,000
Operating expenses	31,000	12,100
Income taxes expense	11,400	
Total costs and expenses	$147,400	$ 66,100
Net income (loss)	$ 7,600	$ (6,100)
Add: Retained earnings (deficit), beginning of period	44,900	(46,820)
Subtotal	$ 52,500	$(52,920)
Less: Dividends	2,500	
Retained earnings (deficit), end of period	$ 50,000	$(52,920)

mon stock. The terms of the merger provided that the current fair value of the common stock of each corporation is to be its carrying amount, except that *an allowance is to be made for the value of any net operating loss carryforward.* Obtaining the benefit of the loss carryforward deduction was not the principal purpose of the merger. (Assume a combined federal and state income tax rate of 60% and that the state net operating loss carryover rules are the same as the federal rules, which provide that an operating loss of the current year may be carried back three years and then forward 15 years. Disregard out-of-pocket costs of the merger.)

Instructions
a Compute (1) the total number of shares of Segal Corporation common stock to be distributed to shareholders of Maynard Company and (2) the exchange ratio of Segal common stock for Maynard common stock.
b Prepare a journal entry for Segal Corporation to record the merger with Maynard Company as a pooling.
c Prepare a journal entry for Maynard Company to record the merger with Segal Corporation. Assume that Maynard did not record in its accounting records the potential income tax benefit of its operating loss carryforward.

5 CONSOLIDATED FINANCIAL STATEMENTS: ON DATE OF PURCHASE BUSINESS COMBINATION

In Chapter 4 we used the terms *investor* and *investee* in our discussion of business combinations involving a combinor's acquisition of common stock of a combinee corporation. If the investor acquires more than 50% of the voting common stock of the investee, *a parent-subsidiary relationship* is established. The investee becomes a *subsidiary* of the acquiring *parent company* (investor) but remains a separate legal entity.

Strict adherence to the legal aspects of such a business combination would require the issuance of separate financial statements for the parent company and the subsidiary on the date of the combination, and also for all subsequent accounting periods of the affiliation. However, such strict adherence to legal form would ignore the substance of most parent-subsidiary relationships. A parent company and its subsidiary usually are a single *economic entity.* In recognition of this fact, *consolidated financial statements* are issued to report the financial position and operating results of a parent company and its subsidiaries as though they comprised a single accounting entity.

Nature of consolidated financial statements

Consolidated financial statements are similar to the combined financial statements described in Chapter 3 for a home office and its branches. Assets, liabilities, revenue, and expenses of the parent company and its subsidiaries are totaled; intercompany transactions and balances are eliminated; and the final consolidated amounts are reported in the consolidated balance sheet, statements of income and retained earnings, and statement of changes in financial position.

However, the separate legal entity status of the parent and subsidiary corporations necessitates consolidation eliminations that generally are more complex than the combination eliminations described in Chapter 3 for a home office and its branches. Before illustrating consolidation eliminations, we shall examine some basic principles of consolidation.

Should all subsidiaries be consolidated?

A wide range of consolidation practices exists among major corporations in the United States.[1] For example, the 35th edition of **Accounting Trends & Techniques** (published in 1981), the AICPA's annual survey of accounting practices in the published financial statements of 600 companies, reported the following:[2]

1 A total of 422 companies consolidated all significant subsidiaries, but 170 companies excluded some significant subsidiaries from the consolidated financial statements. (The remaining 8 companies surveyed did not issue consolidated financial statements.)

2 The principal types of subsidiaries excluded from consolidation were foreign subsidiaries, finance-related subsidiaries, and real estate subsidiaries. "Finance-related subsidiaries" include finance companies, insurance companies, banks, and leasing companies.

In the authors' opinion, such wide variations in consolidation policy are undesirable and difficult to justify from a theoretical point of view. The purpose of consolidated financial statements is to present for a single accounting entity the combined resources, obligations, and operating results of a family of related corporations; consequently, there is no theoretical reason for excluding from consolidation any subsidiary that is *controlled.* The argument that finance-related subsidiaries should not be consolidated with parent manufacturing or retailing enterprises because of their unique features is difficult to justify when one considers the wide variety of production, marketing, and service enterprises that are consolidated in a **conglomerate** or highly diversified family of corporations.

The meaning of "controlling financial interest"

Traditionally, an investor's direct or indirect ownership of more than 50% of an investee's voting common stock has been required to evidence the controlling financial interest underlying a parent-subsidiary

---

[1] Adequate guidelines for consolidation policies have not been provided by the FASB or the AICPA; a limited step in this direction was contained in the following excerpt from *Accounting Research Bulletin No. 51;* "There is a presumption that consolidated statements are more meaningful than separate statements and that they are usually necessary for a fair presentation when one of the companies in the group directly or indirectly has a controlling financial interest in the other companies." *ARB No. 51,* "Consolidated Financial Statements," AICPA (New York: 1959), p. 41.

[2] *Accounting Trends & Techniques,* 35th ed., AICPA (New York: 1981), p. 56.

relationship. However, even though such a common stock ownership exists, other circumstances may negate the parent company's **actual** control of the subsidiary. For example, a subsidiary that is in liquidation or reorganization in bankruptcy is not controlled by its parent company. Also, a foreign subsidiary in a country having severe production, monetary, or income tax restrictions may be subject to the authority of the foreign country rather than of the parent company.

It is important to recognize that a parent company's control of a subsidiary may be achieved **indirectly.** For example, if Plymouth Corporation owns 85% of the outstanding voting common stock of Selwyn Company and 45% of Talbot Company's common stock, and Selwyn also owns 45% of Talbot's common stock, both Selwyn and Talbot are controlled by Plymouth, because it effectively controls 90% of Talbot. This effective control consists of 45% owned directly and 45% indirectly.

Criticism of traditional concept of control

Some accountants have challenged the traditional definition of **control** described in the preceding section, which emphasizes **legal form.** These accountants maintain that an investor owning less than 50% of an investee's voting common stock **in substance** may control the affiliate, especially if the remaining common stock is scattered among a large number of shareholders who do not attend shareholder meetings or give proxies. Effective control of an investee also is possible if the individuals comprising management of the investor corporation own a substantial number of shares of common stock of the investee or successfully solicit proxies from the investee's other shareholders. These arguments merit further study in the search for a less arbitrary definition of **control** than the one described in the preceding section.

Unconsolidated subsidiaries in consolidated financial statements

Generally accepted accounting principles[3] require the use of the **equity method** of accounting for most unconsolidated subsidiaries in consolidated financial statements. The equity method of accounting, which is discussed in depth in Chapters 6 and 7, reflects the parent company's share of the earnings or losses of an unconsolidated subsidiary on a single line in the consolidated income statement. Use of the equity method of accounting results in an amount for consolidated net income identical to the amount that would have resulted from consolidating the subsidiary.

---

[3] *APB Opinion No. 18,* "The Equity Method of Accounting for Investments in Common Stock," AICPA (New York: 1971), pp. 353–354.

CONSOLIDATION OF WHOLLY OWNED SUBSIDIARY ON DATE OF PURCHASE-TYPE BUSINESS COMBINATION

To illustrate consolidated financial statements for a parent company and a wholly owned purchased subsidiary, assume that on December 31, Year 1, Palm Corporation issued 10,000 shares of its common stock (current fair value $45 a share) to shareholders of Starr Company for all the outstanding common stock of Starr. There was no contingent consideration. Out-of-pocket costs of the business combination paid by Palm on December 31, Year 1, consisted of the following:

Combinor's out-of-pocket costs of business combination

Finder's and legal fees relating to business combination	$50,000
Costs associated with SEC registration statement	35,000
Total out-of-pocket costs of business combination	$85,000

The business combination qualifies for purchase accounting; Starr Company is to continue its corporate existence as a wholly owned subsidiary of Palm Corporation. Both business enterprises have a December 31 fiscal year and use the same accounting principles and procedures; thus, no adjusting entries are required for either enterprise prior to the combination. The combined federal and state income tax rate for each enterprise is 60%.

Financial statements of Palm Corporation and Starr Company for their fiscal year ended December 31, Year 1, prior to consummation of the business combination, are shown on page 196.

The December 31, Year 1, current fair values of Starr Company's identifiable assets and liabilities were the same as their carrying amounts, except for the three assets listed below:

Current fair values of selected assets of combinee

	Current fair values, Dec. 31, Year 1
Inventories	$135,000
Plant assets (net)	365,000
Patent	25,000

Because Starr is continuing as a separate corporation and generally accepted accounting principles do not sanction write-ups of assets of a going concern, Starr does not prepare journal entries for the business combination. Palm Corporation records the combination as a purchase on December 31, Year 1, with the journal entries on page 197.

PALM CORPORATION AND STARR COMPANY
Separate Financial Statements
For Year Ended December 31, Year 1

	Palm Corporation	Starr Company
Income Statements		
Revenue		
Net sales	$ 990,000	$600,000
Interest revenue	10,000	
Total revenue	$1,000,000	$600,000
Costs and expenses		
Cost of goods sold	$ 635,000	$410,000
Operating expenses	80,000	30,000
Interest expense	50,000	30,000
Income taxes expense	141,000	78,000
Total costs and expenses	$ 906,000	$548,000
Net income	$ 94,000	$ 52,000
Statements of Retained Earnings		
Retained earnings, beginning of year	$ 65,000	$100,000
Add: Net income	94,000	52,000
Subtotal	$ 159,000	$152,000
Less: Dividends	25,000	20,000
Retained earnings, end of year	$ 134,000	$132,000
Balance Sheets		
Assets		
Cash	$ 100,000	$ 40,000
Inventories	150,000	110,000
Other current assets	110,000	70,000
Receivable from Starr Company	25,000	
Plant assets (net)	450,000	300,000
Patent		20,000
Total assets	$ 835,000	$540,000
Liabilities & Stockholders' Equity		
Payable to Palm Corporation		$ 25,000
Income taxes payable	$ 66,000	10,000
Other liabilities	285,000	115,000
Common stock, $10 par	300,000	
Common stock, $5 par		200,000
Paid-in capital in excess of par	50,000	58,000
Retained earnings	134,000	132,000
Total liabilities & stockholders' equity	$ 835,000	$540,000

Combinor's journal
entries for
purchase-type business
combination on
December 31, Year 1

PALM CORPORATION (Combinor)
Journal Entries
December 31, Year 1

Investment in Starr Company Common Stock (10,000 × $45)	450,000	
Common Stock (10,000 × $10)		100,000
Paid-in Capital in Excess of Par		350,000

To record issuance of 10,000 shares of common stock for all the outstanding common stock of Starr Company in a purchase-type business combination.

Investment in Starr Company Common Stock	50,000	
Paid-in Capital in Excess of Par	35,000	
Cash		85,000

To record payment of out-of-pocket costs of business combination with Starr Company. Finder's and legal fees relating to the combination are recorded as additional costs of the investment; costs associated with the SEC registration statement are recorded as an offset to the previously recorded proceeds from the issuance of common stock.

The first journal entry above is similar to the entry illustrated in Chapter 4 (page 152) for a merger accounted for as a purchase. An Investment in Common Stock account is debited with the current fair value of the combinor's common stock issued to effect the business combination, and the paid-in capital accounts are credited in the usual manner for any common stock issuance. In the second journal entry, the **direct** out-of-pocket costs of the business combination are debited to the Investment in Common Stock account, and the costs that are associated with the SEC registration statement, being costs of issuing the common stock, are applied to reduce the proceeds of the common stock issuance.

Unlike the journal entries for a merger accounted for as a purchase illustrated in Chapter 4, the foregoing journal entries do not include any debits or credits to record individual assets and liabilities of Starr Company in the accounting records of Palm Corporation. The reason is that Starr was not **liquidated** as in a merger; it maintains its status as a separate legal entity.

After the foregoing journal entries have been posted, the affected ledger accounts of Palm Corporation (the combinor) appear as shown on page 198.

Ledger accounts of combinor affected by business combination

Cash

Date	Explanation	Debit	Credit	Balance
12/31/1	Balance forward			100,000 dr
12/31/1	Out-of-pocket costs of business combination		85,000	15,000 dr

Investment in Starr Company Common Stock

Date	Explanation	Debit	Credit	Balance
12/31/1	Issuance of common stock in business combination	450,000		450,000 dr
12/31/1	Direct out-of-pocket costs of business combination	50,000		500,000 dr

Common Stock, $10 Par

Date	Explanation	Debit	Credit	Balance
12/31/1	Balance forward			300,000 cr
12/31/1	Issuance of common stock in business combination		100,000	400,000 cr

Paid-in Capital in Excess of Par

Date	Explanation	Debit	Credit	Balance
12/31/1	Balance forward			50,000 cr
12/31/1	Issuance of common stock in business combination		350,000	400,000 cr
12/31/1	Out-of-pocket costs of business combination	35,000		365,000 cr

Working Paper for Consolidated Balance Sheet Purchase accounting for the business combination of Palm Corporation and Starr Company requires a fresh start for the consolidated entity. This reflects the theory that a business combination that meets the requirements for purchase accounting is an *acquisition* of the combinee's net assets (assets less liabilities) by the combinor. The operating results of Palm and Starr prior to the date of their business combination are those of two separate *economic*—as well as *legal*—entities. Accordingly, a consolidated balance sheet is the only *consolidated* financial statement issued by Palm on December 31, Year 1, the date of the purchase-type business combination of Palm and Starr.

Preparation of a consolidated balance sheet usually requires the use of a *working paper for consolidated balance sheet.* The form of the working paper, with the individual balance sheet amounts included for both Palm Corporation and Starr Company, is presented on page 199.

Form of working paper for consolidated balance sheet

Wholly owned subsidiary on date of purchase-type business combination

PALM CORPORATION AND SUBSIDIARY
Working Paper for Consolidated Balance Sheet
December 31, Year 1

	Palm Corporation	Starr Company	Eliminations increase (decrease)	Consolidated
Assets				
Cash.	15,000	40,000		
Inventories	150,000	110,000		
Other current assets . . .	110,000	70,000		
Intercompany receivable (payable)	25,000	(25,000)		
Investment in Starr Company common stock. . .	500,000			
Plant assets (net)	450,000	300,000		
Patent.		20,000		
Goodwill				
Total assets	1,250,000	515,000		
Liabilities & Stockholders' Equity				
Income taxes payable . .	66,000	10,000		
Other liabilities	285,000	115,000		
Common stock, $10 par .	400,000			
Common stock, $5 par. .		200,000		
Paid-in capital in excess of par	365,000	58,000		
Retained earnings.	134,000	132,000		
Total liabilities & stockholders' equity .	1,250,000	515,000		

Developing the Elimination Palm Corporation's Investment in Starr Company Common Stock account in the working paper for consolidated balance sheet is similar to a home office's Investment in Branch account, as described in Chapter 3. However, Starr Company is a **separate corporation**, not a **branch;** therefore, Starr has the three conventional stockholders' equity accounts rather than the Home Office reciprocal account used by a branch. Accordingly, the elimination for the **intercompany** accounts of Palm and Starr must **decrease to zero** the Investment in Starr Company Common Stock account of Palm and the three stockholders' equity accounts of Starr. Decreases in assets are effected by **credits,** and decreases in stockholders' equity accounts are effected by **debits;** therefore, the elimination for Palm Corporation and subsidiary on December 31, Year 1 (the date of the purchase-type business combination), is begun as follows (a journal entry format is used to facilitate review of the elimination):

Common Stock—Starr	200,000
Paid-in Capital in Excess of Par—Starr	58,000
Retained Earnings—Starr	132,000
	(390,000)
Investment in Starr Company Common Stock—Palm .	500,000

The footing of $390,000 of the debit items of the foregoing partial elimination represents the carrying amount of the net assets of Starr Company and is $110,000 less than the credit item of $500,000, which represents the cost of Palm Corporation's investment in Starr. As indicated on page 195, part of the $110,000 difference is attributable to the excess of current fair values over carrying amounts of certain **identifiable** assets of Starr. This excess is summarized below (the current fair values of all other assets and liabilities are equal to their carrying amounts):

	Current fair values	Carrying amounts	Excess of current fair values over carrying amounts
Inventories.	$135,000	$110,000	$25,000
Plant assets (net).	365,000	300,000	65,000
Patent	25,000	20,000	5,000
Totals	$525,000	$430,000	$95,000

We already have indicated that generally accepted accounting principles preclude the write-up of a going concern's assets. Thus, to conform to the requirements of purchase accounting for business combinations, the foregoing excess of current fair values over carrying amounts must be incorporated in the consolidated balance sheet of Palm Corporation and subsidiary by means of the elimination. **Increases** in assets are recorded by **debits;** thus, the elimination for Palm Corporation and subsidiary begun above is **continued** at the top of page 201 (in journal entry format).

The revised footing of $485,000 of the debit items of the foregoing partial elimination is equal to the current fair value of the **identifiable** tangible and intangible net assets of Starr Company. Thus, the $15,000 difference ($500,000 − $485,000 = $15,000) between the cost of Palm Corporation's investment in Starr and the current fair value of Starr's identifiable net assets represents **goodwill** of Starr, in accordance with

Use of elimination to reflect current fair values of combinee's identifiable assets	Common Stock—Starr	200,000
	Paid-in Capital in Excess of Par—Starr	58,000
	Retained Earnings—Starr	132,000
	Inventories—Starr ($135,000 − $110,000).	25,000
	Plant Assets (net)—Starr ($365,000 − $300,000).	65,000
	Patent—Starr ($25,000 − $20,000)	5,000
		⟨485,000⟩
	Investment in Starr Company Common Stock—Palm	500,000

purchase accounting theory for business combinations, described in Chapter 4 (pages 146 to 154). Consequently, the December 31, Year 1, elimination for Palm Corporation and subsidiary is completed with a $15,000 **debit** to Goodwill—Starr.

Completed Elimination and Working Paper for Consolidated Balance Sheet
The completed elimination for Palm Corporation and subsidiary (in journal entry format) appears below, and the related working paper for consolidated balance sheet appears on page 202.

Completed working paper elimination for wholly owned purchased subsidiary on date of business combination	**PALM CORPORATION AND SUBSIDIARY** **Working Paper Elimination** **December 31, Year 1**	
	(a) Common Stock—Starr.	200,000
	Paid-in Capital in Excess of Par—Starr	58,000
	Retained Earnings—Starr	132,000
	Inventories—Starr ($135,000 − $110,000).	25,000
	Plant Assets (net)—Starr ($365,000 − $300,000).	65,000
	Patent—Starr ($25,000 − $20,000)	5,000
	Goodwill—Starr ($500,000 − $485,000)	15,000
	Investment in Starr Company Common Stock—Palm	500,000
	To eliminate intercompany investment and equity accounts of subsidiary on date of business combination; and to allocate excess of cost over carrying amount of identifiable assets acquired, with remainder to goodwill. (Income tax effects are disregarded.)	

The following features of the working paper for consolidated balance sheet on the date of the purchase-type business combination should be emphasized:

1 The elimination is not entered in either the parent company's or the subsidiary's accounting records; it simply is a part of the working paper for preparation of a consolidated balance sheet.

Wholly owned subsidiary on date of purchase-type business combination

PALM CORPORATION AND SUBSIDIARY
Working Paper for Consolidated Balance Sheet
December 31, Year 1

	Palm Corporation	Starr Company	Eliminations increase (decrease)		Consolidated
Assets					
Cash.	15,000	40,000			55,000
Inventories	150,000	110,000	(a)	25,000	285,000
Other current assets . . .	110,000	70,000			180,000
Intercompany receivable (payable)	25,000	(25,000)			
Investment in Starr Company common stock. . .	500,000		(a)	(500,000)	
Plant assets (net)	450,000	300,000	(a)	65,000	815,000
Patent.		20,000	(a)	5,000	25,000
Goodwill			(a)	15,000	15,000
Total assets	1,250,000	515,000		(390,000)	1,375,000
Liabilities & Stockholders' Equity					
Income taxes payable . .	66,000	10,000			76,000
Other liabilities	285,000	115,000			400,000
Common stock, $10 par .	400,000				400,000
Common stock, $5 par. .		200,000	(a)	(200,000)	
Paid-in capital in excess of par	365,000	58,000	(a)	(58,000)	365,000
Retained earnings.	134,000	132,000	(a)	(132,000)	134,000
Total liabilities & stockholders' equity.	1,250,000	515,000		(390,000)	1,375,000

2 The elimination is used to reflect differences between current fair values and carrying amounts of the subsidiary's identifiable net assets because the subsidiary did not write up its assets to current fair values on the date of the business combination.

3 The Eliminations column in the working paper for consolidated balance sheet reflects *increases* and *decreases,* rather than *debits* and *credits.* Debits and credits are not appropriate in a working paper dealing with *financial statements* rather than *trial balances.*

4 *Intercompany receivables* and *payables* are placed on the same line of the working paper for consolidated balance sheet and are combined to produce consolidated amounts of zero.

5 The respective corporations are identified in the components of the elimination. The reason for precise identification is explained in Chapter 8 dealing with the eliminations of intercompany profits.

6 The consolidated paid-in capital accounts are those of the parent company only. Subsidiaries' paid-in capital accounts **always** are eliminated in the process of consolidation.

7 Consolidated retained earnings on the date of the purchase-type business combination includes only the retained earnings of the parent company. This treatment is consistent with the theory that purchase accounting reflects a fresh start in an acquisition of net assets (assets less liabilities), not a combining of existing stockholder interests.

8 The amounts in the Consolidated column of the working paper for consolidated balance sheet reflect the financial position of a **single economic entity** comprising **two legal entities,** with all **intercompany** balances of the two entities eliminated.

Consolidated Balance Sheet The amounts in the Consolidated column of the working paper for consolidated balance sheet are presented in the customary fashion in the following **consolidated balance sheet** of Palm Corporation and subsidiary. In the interest of brevity, notes to financial statements and other required disclosures are omitted.

PALM CORPORATION AND SUBSIDIARY
Consolidated Balance Sheet
December 31, Year 1

Assets

Current assets:		
Cash		$ 55,000
Inventories.		285,000
Other		180,000
Total current assets		$ 520,000
Plant assets (net)		815,000
Intangible assets:		
Goodwill	$15,000	
Patent	25,000	40,000
Total assets		$1,375,000

Liabilities & Stockholders' Equity

Liabilities:		
Income taxes payable		$ 76,000
Other		400,000
Total liabilities		$ 476,000
Stockholders' equity:		
Common stock, $10 par	$400,000	
Paid-in capital in excess of par.	365,000	
Retained earnings	134,000	899,000
Total liabilities & stockholders' equity		$1,375,000

In addition to the foregoing **consolidated** balance sheet on December 31, Year 1, Palm Corporation's published financial statements for the year ended December 31, Year 1, include the **unconsolidated** income statement and statement of retained earnings illustrated on page 196.

CONSOLIDATION OF PARTIALLY OWNED SUBSIDIARY ON DATE OF PURCHASE-TYPE BUSINESS COMBINATION

The consolidation of a parent company and its **partially owned** subsidiary differs from the consolidation of a wholly owned subsidiary in one major respect—the recognition of minority interest. **Minority interest** is a term applied to the claims of shareholders other than the parent company against the net income or losses and net assets of the subsidiary. The minority interest in the subsidiary's net income or losses is reported in the consolidated income statement, and the minority interest in the subsidiary's net assets is reported in the consolidated balance sheet.

To illustrate the consolidation techniques for a purchase-type business combination involving a partially owned subsidiary, assume the following facts. On December 31, Year 1, Post Corporation issued 57,000 shares of its common stock (current fair value $20 a share) to shareholders of Sage Company in exchange for 38,000 of the 40,000 outstanding shares of Sage's common stock in a purchase-type business combination. Thus, Post acquired a 95% interest (38,000 ÷ 40,000 = 0.95) in Sage, which became Post's subsidiary. There was no contingent consideration. Out-of-pocket costs of the combination, paid in cash by Post on December 31, Year 1, were as follows:

Combinor's out-of-pocket costs of business combination	
Finder's and legal fees relating to business combination	$ 52,250
Costs associated with SEC registration statement	72,750
Total out-of-pocket costs of business combination	$125,000

Financial statements of Post Corporation and Sage Company for their fiscal year ended December 31, Year 1, prior to the business combination, are presented on page 205. There were no intercompany transactions prior to the combination.

The December 31, Year 1, current fair values of Sage Company's identifiable assets and liabilities were the same as their carrying amounts, except for the assets listed at the bottom of page 205.

Sage Company does not prepare journal entries related to the business combination, because Sage is continuing as a separate corporation, and generally accepted accounting principles do not permit the write-up of assets of a going concern. Post records the combination

POST CORPORATION AND SAGE COMPANY
Separate Financial Statements
For Year Ended December 31, Year 1

	Post Corporation	Sage Company
Income Statements		
Net sales	$5,500,000	$1,000,000
Costs and expenses		
Cost of goods sold.	$3,850,000	$ 650,000
Operating expenses	600,000	100,000
Interest expense	75,000	40,000
Income taxes expense.	585,000	126,000
Total costs and expenses	$5,110,000	$ 916,000
Net income	$ 390,000	$ 84,000
Statements of Retained Earnings		
Retained earnings, beginning of year	$ 810,000	$ 290,000
Add: Net income	390,000	84,000
Subtotal	$1,200,000	$ 374,000
Less: Dividends	150,000	40,000
Retained earnings, end of year	$1,050,000	$ 334,000
Balance Sheets		
Assets		
Cash	$ 200,000	$ 100,000
Inventories	800,000	500,000
Other current assets	550,000	215,000
Plant assets (net)	3,500,000	1,100,000
Goodwill	100,000	
Total assets	$5,150,000	$1,915,000
Liabilities & Stockholders' Equity		
Income taxes payable	$ 100,000	$ 76,000
Other liabilities	2,450,000	870,000
Common stock, $1 par	1,000,000	
Common stock, $10 par		400,000
Paid-in capital in excess of par	550,000	235,000
Retained earnings	1,050,000	334,000
Total liabilities & stockholders' equity	$5,150,000	$1,915,000

Current fair values of selected assets of combinee

	Current fair values, Dec. 31, Year 1
Inventories	$ 526,000
Plant assets (net)	1,290,000
Leasehold	30,000

with Sage as a purchase by means of the following journal entries on December 31, Year 1:

POST CORPORATION (Combinor)
Journal Entries
December 31, Year 1

Investment in Sage Company Common Stock (57,000 × $20).	1,140,000	
Common Stock (57,000 × $1)		57,000
Paid-in Capital in Excess of Par.		1,083,000

To record issuance of 57,000 shares of common stock for 38,000 of the 40,000 outstanding shares of Sage Company common stock in a purchase-type business combination.

Investment in Sage Company Common Stock	52,250	
Paid-in Capital in Excess of Par.	72,750	
Cash		125,000

To record payment of out-of-pocket costs of business combination with Sage Company. Finder's and legal fees relating to the combination are recorded as additional costs of the investment; costs associated with the SEC registration statement are recorded as an offset to the previously recorded proceeds from the issuance of common stock.

After the foregoing journal entries have been posted, the affected ledger accounts of Post Corporation are as illustrated on page 207.

Developing the Elimination   The preparation of the elimination for a parent company and a partially owned purchased subsidiary parallels that for a wholly owned purchased subsidiary described earlier in this chapter. First, the ***intercompany*** accounts are reduced to zero, as follows (in journal entry format):

Common Stock —Sage	400,000	
Paid-in Capital in Excess of Par —Sage	235,000	
Retained Earnings —Sage	334,000	
	(969,000)	
Investment in Sage Company Common Stock —		
Post		1,192,250

The footing of $969,000 of the debit items of the above partial elimination represents total stockholders' equity of Sage Company and is $223,250 less than the credit item of $1,192,250. Part of this $223,250

Ledger accounts of combinor affected by business combination

Cash

Date	Explanation	Debit	Credit	Balance
12/31/1	Balance forward			200,000 dr
12/31/1	Out-of-pocket costs of business combination		125,000	75,000 dr

Investment in Sage Company Common Stock

Date	Explanation	Debit	Credit	Balance
12/31/1	Issuance of common stock in business combination	1,140,000		1,140,000 dr
12/31/1	Direct out-of-pocket costs of business combination	52,250		1,192,250 dr

Common Stock, $1 Par

Date	Explanation	Debit	Credit	Balance
12/31/1	Balance forward			1,000,000 cr
12/31/1	Issuance of common stock in business combination		57,000	1,057,000 cr

Paid-in Capital in Excess of Par

Date	Explanation	Debit	Credit	Balance
12/31/1	Balance forward			550,000 cr
12/31/1	Issuance of common stock in business combination		1,083,000	1,633,000 cr
12/31/1	Out-of-pocket costs of business combination	72,750		1,560,250 cr

difference is the excess of the total of the cost of Post Corporation's investment in Sage Company and the **minority interest** in Sage Company's net assets over the carrying amounts of Sage's identifiable net assets. This excess may be computed as follows, from the data provided on page 205 (the current fair values of all other assets and liabilities are equal to their carrying amounts):

Difference between current fair values and carrying amounts of combinee's identifiable assets

	Current fair value	Carrying amount	Excess of current fair values over carrying amounts
Inventories.	$ 526,000	$ 500,000	$ 26,000
Plant assets (net).	1,290,000	1,100,000	190,000
Leasehold	30,000		30,000
Totals	$1,846,000	$1,600,000	$246,000

Under generally accepted accounting principles, the foregoing differences are not entered in Sage Company's accounting records. Thus, to conform to the requirements of purchase accounting, the differences must be reflected in the consolidated balance sheet of Post Corporation and subsidiary by means of the elimination, which is continued below:

Use of elimination to reflect current fair values of identifiable assets of purchased subsidiary on date of business combination

Common Stock—Sage	400,000
Paid-in Capital in Excess of Par—Sage	235,000
Retained Earnings—Sage	334,000
Inventories—Sage ($526,000 − $500,000)	26,000
Plant Assets (net)—Sage ($1,290,000 − $1,100,000)	190,000
Leasehold—Sage	30,000
	1,215,000
Investment in Sage Company Common Stock— Post	1,192,250

The revised footing of $1,215,000 of the debit items of the above partial elimination represents the current fair value of Sage Company's *identifiable* net assets on December 31, Year 1.

Two items now must be recognized to complete the elimination for Post Corporation and subsidiary. First, the **minority interest** in the identifiable net assets (at current fair values) of Sage company is recognized by a **credit.** The minority interest is computed below:

Computation of minority interest in combinee's identifiable net assets

Current fair value of Sage Company's identifiable net assets	$1,215,000
Minority interest ownership in Sage Company's identifiable net assets	
(100% minus Post Corporation's 95% interest)	0.05
Minority interest in Sage Company's identifiable net assets	
($1,215,000 × 0.05)	$ 60,750

Second, the goodwill acquired by Post Corporation in the business combination with Sage Company is recognized by a **debit.** The goodwill is computed below:

Computation of goodwill acquired by combinor

Cost of Post Corporation's 95% interest in Sage Company	$1,192,250
Less: Current fair value of Sage Company's identifiable net assets acquired by Post ($1,215,000 × 0.95)	1,154,250
Goodwill acquired by Post Corporation.	$ 38,000

The working paper elimination for Post Corporation and subsidiary may now be completed as follows:

Completed working
paper elimination for
partially owned
purchased subsidiary on
date of business
combination

POST CORPORATION AND SUBSIDIARY
Working Paper Elimination
December 31, Year 1

(a) *Common Stock—Sage.* 400,000
    Paid-in Capital in Excess of Par—Sage. 235,000
    Retained Earnings—Sage. 334,000
    Inventories—Sage ($526,000 − $500,000) 26,000
    Plant Assets (net)—Sage ($1,290,000 − $1,100,000) . . 190,000
    Leasehold—Sage. 30,000
    Goodwill—Post ($1,192,250 − $1,154,250) 38,000
    Investment in Sage Company Common Stock—
        Post. 1,192,250
    Minority Interest in Net Assets of Subsidiary 60,750
*To eliminate intercompany investment and equity ac-
counts of subsidiary on date of business combination;
to allocate excess of cost over carrying amount of
identifiable assets acquired, with remainder to goodwill;
and to establish minority interest in net assets of subsidiary on date of business combination ($1,215,000 ×
0.05 = $60,750). (Income tax effects are disregarded.)*

Working Paper for Consolidated Balance Sheet   The working paper for the consolidated balance sheet on December 31, Year 1, for Post Corporation and subsidiary is shown on page 210.

Nature of minority interest

The appropriate classification and presentation of minority interest in consolidated financial statements has been a perplexing problem for accountants. Over the years, two theories for consolidated financial statements have been developed to account for minority interest—the **parent company theory** and the **entity theory.** One authority has described these two theories as follows:[4]

> The "parent company" concept views consolidated statements as an exten-
> sion of parent company statements, in which the investment account of the
> parent is replaced by the individual assets and liabilities underlying the par-
> ent's investment, and subsidiaries are viewed as almost the equivalent of
> branches. When subsidiary ownership is not complete, the consolidation pro-

[4] *Consolidated Financial Statements,* Accountants International Study Group (Plaistow, England: 1973), p. 7.

Partially owned subsidiary on date of purchase-type business combination

POST CORPORATION AND SUBSIDIARY

Working Paper for Consolidated Balance Sheet

December 31, Year 1

	Post Corporation	Sage Company	Eliminations increase (decrease)		Consolidated
Assets					
Cash.	75,000	100,000			175,000
Inventories	800,000	500,000	(a)	26,000	1,326,000
Other current assets . . .	550,000	215,000			765,000
Investment in Sage Company common stock. . .	1,192,250		(a)	(1,192,250)	
Plant assets (net)	3,500,000	1,100,000	(a)	190,000	4,790,000
Leasehold			(a)	30,000	30,000
Goodwill	100,000		(a)	38,000	138,000
Total assets	6,217,250	1,915,000		(908,250)	7,224,000
Liabilities & Stockholders' Equity					
Income taxes payable . .	100,000	76,000			176,000
Other liabilities	2,450,000	870,000			3,320,000
Minority interest in net assets of subsidiary . . .			(a)	60,750	60,750
Common stock, $1 par. .	1,057,000				1,057,000
Common stock, $10 par .		400,000	(a)	(400,000)	
Paid-in capital in excess of par	1,560,250	235,000	(a)	(235,000)	1,560,250
Retained earnings.	1,050,000	334,000	(a)	(334,000)	1,050,000
Total liabilities & stockholders' equity .	6,217,250	1,915,000		(908,250)	7,224,000

cess segregates the minority interest in the partially owned subsidiary. *The minority interest is considered to be an outside group and a liability as far as the parent shareholder is concerned.*

. . . .

In contrast to the parent company concept, the "entity" concept views consolidated statements as those of an economic entity with *two classes of proprietary interest*—the major or dominant interest and the minority interest. It holds that in consolidation these interests should be treated consistently. The consolidated statements are not viewed as an extension of parent company statements; rather, they are viewed as an expression of the financial position and operating results of a distinct "consolidated entity" consisting of a number of related companies whose relationship arises from common control (based on powers conferred by share ownership). When related companies are viewed as parts of such an entity, the minority interest, instead of representing an accountability to an outside group by the parent, represents *"a part of capital."*

As indicated in the foregoing quotation, the *parent company theory* of consolidated financial statements views the minority interest in net assets of a subsidiary as a *liability.* This liability is increased each accounting period subsequent to the date of a purchase-type business combination by an *expense* representing the minority's share of the subsidiary's net income (or decreased by the minority's share of the subsidiary's net loss). Dividends declared by the subsidiary to minority shareholders decrease the liability to them. Consolidated net income is reported *net* of the minority's share of the subsidiary's net income, as illustrated in Chapter 6.

In the *entity theory,* the minority interest in the subsidiary's net assets is included in the stockholders' equity section of the consolidated balance sheet. The consolidated income statement presents the minority interest in the subsidiary's net income as a *subdivision of total consolidated net income,* similar to the distribution of net income of a partnership (see page 17).

In the authors' opinion, the entity theory of reporting minority interest overemphasizes the *legal aspects* of the separate corporate organizations comprising a parent–subsidiary relationship. In substance, minority shareholders are a special class of creditors of the consolidated entity, because in the usual case they exercise *no ownership control whatsoever* over the operations of either the parent company or the subsidiary. If consolidated financial statements are to present fairly the operating results and financial position of a single economic entity, the niceties of minority shareholders' ownership of a part of the subsidiary should be ignored. Consequently, the parent company theory of accounting for minority interest in subsidiary is stressed throughout this book.

Consolidated balance sheet for partially owned subsidiary

The consolidated balance sheet of Post Corporation and its partially owned subsidiary, Sage Company, is shown on page 212. The consolidated amounts are taken from the working paper for consolidated balance sheet on page 210.

The inclusion of minority interest in net assets of subsidiary in the liabilities section of the consolidated balance sheet of Post Corporation and subsidiary is consistent with the *parent company theory* of consolidated financial statements. It should be noted that there is no ledger account for minority interest in net assets of subsidiary, in either the parent company's or the subsidiary's accounting records.

Alternative methods for valuing minority interest and goodwill

The computation of minority interest in subsidiary and goodwill on page 208 is based on two premises. First, the *identifiable net assets* of a partially owned purchased subsidiary should be valued on a single basis—

POST CORPORATION AND SUBSIDIARY
Consolidated Balance Sheet
December 31, Year 1

Assets

Current assets:

Cash		$ 175,000
Inventories		1,326,000
Other		765,000
Total current assets		$2,266,000
Plant assets (net)		4,790,000

Intangible assets:

Goodwill	$138,000	
Leasehold	30,000	168,000
Total assets		$7,224,000

Liabilities & Stockholders' Equity

Liabilities:

Income taxes payable		$ 176,000
Other		3,320,000
Minority interest in net assets of subsidiary		60,750
Total liabilities		$3,556,750

Stockholders' equity:

Common stock, $1 par	$1,057,000	
Paid-in capital in excess of par	1,560,250	
Retained earnings	1,050,000	3,667,250
Total liabilities & stockholders' equity		$7,224,000

current fair value. Second, only the subsidiary goodwill **acquired** by the parent company should be recognized, in accordance with the cost principle for valuing assets. This computational method is consistent with the **parent company theory** of consolidated financial statements.

Two alternatives to the procedure described above have been suggested. The first alternative would assign current fair values to a partially owned purchased subsidiary's identifiable net assets **only to the extent of the parent company's ownership interest therein.** Under this alternative, $233,700 ($246,000 × 0.95 = $233,700) of the total difference between current fair values and carrying amounts of Sage Company's identifiable net assets summarized on page 207 would be reflected in the aggregate debits to inventories, plant assets, and leasehold in the working paper elimination for Post Corporation and subsidiary on December 31, Year 1. The minority interest in net assets of subsidiary would be based on the **carrying amounts** of Sage Company's identifiable net assets, rather than on their **current fair values,** and would be computed as follows: $969,000 × 0.05 = $48,450. Goodwill would be $38,000, as in the preceding illustration. Supporters of this alternative, which also is consistent with the **parent company theory** of consolidated financial statements, argue that current fair values of a combinee's identifiable net assets should be reflected in consolidated financial statements only to the extent (percentage) that they have been **acquired** by the **combinor.** The balance of the combinee's net assets, and the related minority interest in the net assets, should be reflected in consolidated financial statements at the carrying amounts as reflected in the subsidiary's accounting records.

The other alternative for valuing minority interest in net assets of subsidiary and goodwill is to obtain a current fair value for **100%** of a partially owned purchased subsidiary's **total** net assets, either through independent measurement of the minority interest or by **inference** from the cost of the parent company's investment in the subsidiary. Independent measurement of the minority interest might be accomplished by reference to quoted market prices of publicly traded common stock owned by minority shareholders of the subsidiary. The computation of minority interest and goodwill of Sage Company by inference from the cost of Post Corporation's investment in Sage is illustrated below:

Computation of minority interest and goodwill of partially owned purchased subsidiary based on implied total current fair value of subsidiary	*Total cost of Post Corporation's investment in Sage Company* $1,192,250
	Post's percentage ownership of Sage 95%
	Implied current fair value of 100% of Sage's total net assets
	($1,192,250 ÷ 0.95) $1,255,000
	Minority interest ($1,255,000 × 0.05). . . . . $ 62,750
	Goodwill ($1,255,000 − $1,215,000, the current fair value of Sage's
	identifiable net assets) . . . . $ 40,000

Supporters of this approach, which is consistent with the **entity theory** of consolidated financial statements, contend that a **single valuation method** should be used for all net assets of a purchased subsidiary—including goodwill—regardless of the existence of a minority interest in the subsidiary. They further maintain that the goodwill should be attributed to the **subsidiary,** rather than to the **parent company,** as is done for a wholly owned purchased subsidiary, in accordance with the theory of purchase accounting for business combinations.

A summary of the three methods for valuing minority interest and goodwill of a partially owned purchased subsidiary (derived from the December 31, Year 1, business combination of Post Corporation and Sage Company) appears on page 214.

The authors have chosen to reflect, in subsequent chapters of this book, the method illustrated in the elimination on page 209 (method 1

Comparison of three methods for valuing minority interest and goodwill of partially owned purchased subsidiary

	Total identifiable net assets	Minority interest in net assets of subsidiary	Goodwill
1 Identifiable net assets recognized at current fair value; minority interest in net assets of subsidiary based on identifiable net assets (a)	$1,215,000	$60,750	$38,000
2 Identifiable net assets recognized at current fair value only to extent of parent company's interest; balance of net assets and minority interest in net assets of subsidiary reflected at carrying amounts (a)	1,202,700*	48,450	38,000
3 Current fair value, through independent measurement or inference, assigned to total net assets of subsidiary, including goodwill (b).	1,215,000	62,750	40,000

* $969,000 + ($246,000 × 0.95) = $1,202,700
(a) Consistent with **parent company theory** of consolidated financial statements.
(b) Consistent with **entity theory** of consolidated financial statements.

above), not for its conceptual superiority, but because it has substantial usage in current accounting practice.[5]

"Negative goodwill" in consolidated balance sheet

A purchase-type business combination that results in a parent company –subsidiary relationship may involve an excess of current fair values of the subsidiary's identifiable net assets over the cost of the parent company's investment in the subsidiary's common stock. If so, the accounting principles described in Chapter 4 (page 150) are applied. The excess of current fair values over cost is applied pro rata to reduce the amounts initially assigned to noncurrent assets other than long-term investments in marketable securities. Any remaining excess is established as a deferred credit and amortized over a maximum period of 40 years.

Illustration of "Negative Goodwill": Wholly Owned Subsidiary On December 31, Year 1, Plowman Corporation acquired all the outstanding common stock of Silbert Company for $850,000 cash, including direct out-of-pocket costs of the purchase-type business combination. Stockholders' equity of Silbert totaled $800,000, consisting of common stock, $100,000; paid-in capital in excess of par, $300,000; and retained earn-

[5] *FASB Discussion Memorandum,* "An Analysis of Issues Related to Accounting for Business Combinations and Purchased Intangibles," (Stamford: 1976), p. 107.

ings, $400,000. The current fair values of Silbert's identifiable net assets were the same as their carrying amounts, except for the following:

<table>
<tr><td rowspan="2">Current fair values of
selected assets
of combinee</td><td></td><td>*Current
fair values*</td><td>*Carrying
amounts*</td></tr>
<tr><td>Inventories. . . . .</td><td>$339,000</td><td>$320,000</td></tr>
<tr><td></td><td>Long-term investments in marketable securities . . . . .</td><td>61,000</td><td>50,000</td></tr>
<tr><td></td><td>Plant assets (net) . . . .</td><td>1,026,000</td><td>984,000</td></tr>
<tr><td></td><td>Intangible assets (net) . . . .</td><td>54,000</td><td>36,000</td></tr>
</table>

Thus, the current fair values of Silbert's identifiable net assets exceeded the amount paid by Plowman by $40,000 [($800,000 + $19,000 + $11,000 + $42,000 + $18,000) − $850,000 = $40,000]. The December 31, Year 1, working paper elimination for Plowman Corporation and subsidiary is shown below:

<table>
<tr><td rowspan="10">Working paper
elimination for wholly
owned purchased
subsidiary with
"negative goodwill" on
date of business
combination</td><td colspan="2" align="center">*PLOWMAN CORPORATION AND SUBSIDIARY*
Working Paper Elimination
December 31, Year 1</td></tr>
<tr><td>(a) Common Stock—Silbert . . . .</td><td>100,000</td><td></td></tr>
<tr><td>Paid-in Capital in Excess of Par—Silbert . . . .</td><td>300,000</td><td></td></tr>
<tr><td>Retained Earnings—Silbert . . . .</td><td>400,000</td><td></td></tr>
<tr><td>Inventories—Silbert ($339,000 − $320,000). . . . .</td><td>19,000</td><td></td></tr>
<tr><td>Long-Term Investments in Marketable Securities—Silbert
($61,000 − $50,000) . . . .</td><td>11,000</td><td></td></tr>
<tr><td>Plant Assets (net)—Silbert ($1,026,000 − $984,000) −
($40,000 × 0.95)] . . . .</td><td>4,000</td><td></td></tr>
<tr><td>Intangible Assets (net)—Silbert [($54,000 − $36,000) −
($40,000 × 0.05)] . . . .</td><td>16,000</td><td></td></tr>
<tr><td>Investment in Silbert Company Common Stock—
Plowman . . . .</td><td></td><td>850,000</td></tr>
<tr><td>To eliminate intercompany investment and equity ac-
counts of subsidiary on date of business combination;
and to allocate $40,000 excess of current fair values of
subsidiary's identifiable net assets over cost to subsid-
iary's plant assets and intangible assets in ratio of
$1,026,000:$54,000, or 95:5. (Income tax effects are dis-
regarded.)</td><td></td><td></td></tr>
</table>

Illustration of "Negative Goodwill": Partially Owned Subsidiary Let us change the Plowman Corporation–Silbert Company business combination described in the foregoing section by assuming that Plowman acquired **98%,** rather than **100%,** of Silbert's common stock for $833,000 ($850,000 × 0.98 = $833,000) on December 31, Year 1, with all other facts remaining unchanged. The excess of current fair values of Silbert's identifiable net assets over Plowman's cost is $39,200 [($890,000 × 0.98) − $833,000 = $39,200]. Under these circumstances, the working paper elimination for Plowman Corporation and subsidiary on December 31, Year 1, is as shown below:

Working paper elimination for partially owned purchased subsidiary with "negative goodwill" on date of business combination

PLOWMAN CORPORATION AND SUBSIDIARY
Working Paper Elimination
December 31, Year 1

(a) *Common Stock—Silbert*	*100,000*	
Paid-in Capital in Excess of Par—Silbert	*300,000*	
Retained Earnings—Silbert	*400,000*	
Inventories—Silbert ($339,000 − $320,000)	*19,000*	
Long-Term Investments in Marketable Securities—Silbert ($61,000 − $50,000)	*11,000*	
Plants Assets (net)—Silbert {$42,000 − ([($890,000 × 0.98) − $833,000] × 0.95)}	*4,760*	
Intangible Assets (net)—Silbert [$18,000 − ($39,200 × 0.05)]	*16,040*	
Investment in Silbert Company Common Stock— Plowman		*833,000*
Minority Interest in Net Assets of Subsidiary ($890,000 × 0.02)		*17,800*

To eliminate intercompany investment and equity accounts of subsidiary on date of business combination; to allocate parent company's share of excess ($39,200) of current fair values of subsidiary's identifiable net assets over cost to subsidiary's plant assets and intangible assets in ratio of 95%:5%; and to establish minority interest in net assets of subsidiary on date of business combination. (Income tax effects are disregarded.)

Footnote disclosure of consolidation policy

The "Summary of Significant Accounting Policies" footnote required by **APB Opinion No. 22,** "Disclosure of Accounting Policies," should include a description of consolidation policy reflected in consolidated financial statements. The following excerpt from an annual report of a publicly owned corporation is typical:

Principles of Consolidation—The consolidated financial statements include the accounts of the Company and its subsidiaries, all of which are wholly owned. All significant intercompany accounts are eliminated in consolidation.

The excess of net assets of acquired subsidiaries over cost is being amortized over ten-year periods from their respective dates of acquisition.

Another example of disclosure of consolidation policy is shown in Chapter 15.

Advantages and shortcomings of consolidated financial statements

Consolidated financial statements are useful principally to stockholders and prospective investors of the parent company. These users of consolidated financial statements are provided with comprehensive financial information for the economic unit represented by the parent company and its subsidiaries, without regard for legal separateness of the constituent companies.

Creditors of each consolidated company and minority shareholders of subsidiaries find only limited use for consolidated financial statements, because such statements do not show the financial position or operating results of the individual companies comprising the consolidated group. In addition, creditors of the constituent companies cannot ascertain the asset coverages for their respective claims. But perhaps the most telling criticism of consolidated financial statements in recent years has come from financial analysts. These critics have pointed out that consolidated financial statements of diversified companies (conglomerates) are impossible to classify into a single industry. Thus, say the financial analysts, consolidated financial statements of a conglomerate cannot be used for comparative purposes. The problem of financial reporting by diversified companies is considered in Chapter 15.

REVIEW QUESTIONS

1 The use of consolidated financial statements for reporting to stockholders is common. Under some conditions, however, it is the practice to exclude certain subsidiaries from consolidation. List the conditions under which subsidiaries often are excluded from consolidated financial statements.

2 The principal limitation of consolidated financial statements is their lack of separate information about the assets, liabilities, revenue, and expenses of the individual companies included in the consolidation. List the problems that users of consolidated financial statements encounter as a result of this limitation.

3 What criteria could influence a parent company in its decision to include a subsidiary in consolidated financial statements, or to exclude the subsidiary? Explain.

4 Discuss the similarities and dissimilarities between consolidated financial statements for parent company and subsidiaries, and combined financial statements for segments (branches) of a single legal entity.

5 Are eliminations for the preparation of consolidated financial statements recorded in the accounting records of the parent company or of the subsidiary? Explain.

6 If a business combination resulting in a parent-subsidiary relationship is accounted for as a purchase, the identifiable net assets of the subsidiary must be reflected at their current fair values in the consolidated balance sheet on the date of the business combination. Does this require the subsidiary to record the current fair values of the identifiable net assets in its accounting records? Explain.

7 The controller of Pastor Corporation, which has just become the parent of Sexton Company in a purchase-type business combination, inquires if a consolidated income statement is required for the year ended on the date of the combination. What is your reply? Explain.

8 Differentiate between a **working paper for consolidated balance sheet** and a **consolidated balance sheet.**

9 Describe three methods that have been proposed for valuing minority interest and related goodwill in the consolidated balance sheet of a parent company and its partially owned purchased subsidiary.

10 Compare the **parent company theory** and the **entity theory** of consolidated financial statements as they relate to the classification of minority interest in net assets of subsidiary in the consolidated balance sheet.

EXERCISES

Ex. 5-1 Select the best answer for each of the following multiple-choice questions:

1 On the date of a purchase-type business combination resulting in a parent company–subsidiary relationship, consolidated paid-in capital in excess of par includes the paid-in capital in excess of par of:
a Both the parent company and the subsidiary
b The parent company only
c The subsidiary only
d Both the parent company and the subsidiary, plus an amount to balance the journal entry to record the business combination

2 On November 4, Year 4, Pegler Corporation paid $500,000 cash and issued 100,000 shares of $1 par common stock with a current fair value of $10 a share for all 50,000 outstanding shares of $5 par common stock (carrying amount $20 a share) of Stadler Company, which became a subsidiary of Pegler. Also on November 4, Year 4, Pegler paid $50,000 for finder's and legal fees related to the business combination and $80,000 for costs associated with the SEC registration statement for the common stock issued in the combination. The net result of Pegler's journal entries to record the combination is to:
a Debit Investment in Stadler Company Common stock for $1,000,000
b Credit Paid-in Capital in Excess of Par for $900,000
c Debit Expenses of Business Combination for $130,000
d Credit Cash for $630,000

3 Under the parent company theory of determining minority interest in the net assets of a partially owned purchased subsidiary on the date of the business combination, the minority interest percentage is applied to the:
a Carrying amount of subsidiary's total net assets
b Current fair value of subsidiary's identifiable net assets

       c Carrying amount of subsidiary's identifiable net assets
       d Current fair value of subsidiary's total net assets

4 Consolidated financial statements *always should exclude* from consolidation any subsidiaries:
       a In foreign countries
       b In bankruptcy proceedings
       c That are finance companies
       d That are controlled indirectly

5 On June 30, Year 8, Porus Corporation acquired for cash at $10 a share all 100,000 shares of the outstanding common stock of Sorus Company. The total current fair value of identifiable assets of Sorus was $1,400,000 on June 30, Year 8, including the appraised value of Sorus Company's plant assets (its only noncurrent assets) of $250,000. The consolidated balance sheet of Porus Corporation and subsidiary on June 30, Year 8, should include:
       a A deferred credit (negative goodwill) of $150,000
       b Goodwill of $150,000
       c A deferred credit (negative goodwill) of $400,000
       d Goodwill of $400,000
       e None of the foregoing

Ex. 5-2 Painter Corporation acquired 80% of the outstanding common stock of Santiago Company on October, 31, Year 6, for $800,000, including out-of-pocket costs of the business combination. The working paper elimination (in journal entry form) on that date was as follows (explanation omitted):

PAINTER CORPORATION AND SUBSIDIARY

Working Paper Elimination

October 31, Year 6

Common Stock—Santiago	50,000
Paid-in Capital in Excess of Par—Santiago	60,000
Retained Earnings—Santiago	490,000
Inventories—Santiago	50,000
Plant Assets (net)—Santiago	100,000
Goodwill—Painter [$800,000 − ($750,000 × 0.80)]	200,000
Investment in Santiago Company Common Stock—	
Painter	800,000
Minority Interest in Net Assets of Subsidiary	
($750,000 × 0.20)	150,000

    Assuming that a value is to be imputed for 100% of Santiago's net assets (including goodwill) from Painter's $800,000 cost, compute the debit to Goodwill and the credit to Minority Interest in Net Assets of Subsidiary in the foregoing working paper elimination.

Ex. 5-3 On March 31, Year 2, Port Corporation acquired for $8,000,000 cash all the outstanding common stock of Starboard Company when Starboard's balance sheet showed net assets of $6,400,000. Out-of-pocket costs of the business combination may be disregarded. Starboard's identifiable net assets had current fair values different from carrying amounts as follows:

	Carrying amounts	Current fair values
Plant assets (net)	$10,000,000	$11,500,000
Other assets	1,000,000	700,000
Long-term debt	6,000,000	5,600,000

Compute the amount of goodwill, if any, to be included in the consolidated balance sheet of Port Corporation and subsidiary on March 31, Year 2.

Ex. 5-4 Paige Corporation acquired 70% of the outstanding common stock of Stone Company on July 31, Year 8. The unconsolidated balance sheet of Paige immediately after the purchase-type business combination and the consolidated balance sheet of Paige Corporation and subsidiary are as follows:

PAIGE CORPORATION AND SUBSIDIARY
Unconsolidated and Consolidated Balance Sheets
July 31, Year 8

	Unconsolidated	Consolidated
Assets		
Current assets	$106,000	$146,000
Investment in Stone Company common stock	100,000	
Plant assets (net)	270,000	370,000
Goodwill		11,100
Total assets	$476,000	$527,100
Liabilities & Stockholders' Equity		
Current liabilities	$ 15,000	$ 28,000
Minority interest in net assets of subsidiary . .		38,100
Common stock	350,000	350,000
Retained earnings	111,000	111,000
Total liabilities & stockholders' equity	$476,000	$527,100

Of the excess payment for the investment in Stone Company common stock, $10,000 was ascribed to undervaluation of Stone's plant assets and the balance was ascribed to goodwill. Current assets of Stone include a $2,000 receivable from Paige that arose before the business combination.

a Compute the total current assets in Stone Company's separate balance sheet on July 31, Year 8.

b Compute the total stockholders' equity in Stone Company's separate balance sheet on July 31, Year 8.

c Show how the goodwill of $11,100 included in the consolidated balance sheet was computed.

Ex. 5-5 Combinor Corporation and Combinee Company have been operating separately for five years. Each company has a minimal amount of liabilities and a simple capital structure consisting solely of common stock. Combinor, in exchange for its unissued common stock, acquired 80% of the outstanding common stock of Combinee. This was a "tax-free" stock-for-stock exchange for federal income tax purposes. Combinee's identifiable net assets had a current fair value of $800,000 and a carrying amount of $600,000. The current fair value of the Combinor common stock issued in the business combination was $700,000.

Compute the minority interest in net assets of subsidiary and the goodwill that would appear in the consolidated balance sheet of Combinor Corporation and subsidiary, under three alternative methods of computation as illustrated on page 214.

Ex. 5-6 Shown on page 221 are the December 31, Year 3, balance sheets of two companies prior to their business combination.

POCO CORPORATION AND SMALL COMPANY
Separate Balance Sheets
December 31, Year 3

	Poco Corporation	Small Company
Assets		
Cash	$ 3,000	$ 100
Inventories (at fifo cost, which approximates current		
fair value)	2,000	200
Plant assets *(net)*	5,000	700*
Total assets	$10,000	$1,000
Liabilities & Stockholders' Equity		
Current liabilities	$ 600	$ 100
Common stock, $1 par	1,000	100
Paid-in capital in excess of par	3,000	200
Retained earnings	5,400	600
Total liabilities & stockholders' equity	$10,000	$1,000

* *Current fair value on Dec. 31, Year 3, is $1,500.*

a On December 31, Year 3, Poco Corporation acquired all the outstanding common stock of Small Company for $2,000 cash. Compute the amount of goodwill that should appear in the consolidated balance sheet of Poco Corporation and subsidiary on December 31, Year 3.

b On December 31, Year 3, Poco Corporation acquired all the outstanding common stock of Small Company for $1,600 cash. Compute the amount of plant assets that should appear in the consolidated balance sheet of Poco Corporation and subsidiary on December 31, Year 3.

Ex. 5-7 On November 1, Year 4, Parker Corporation issued 10,000 shares of its $10 par ($30 current fair value) common stock for 85 of the 100 outstanding shares of Sacco Company's $100 par common stock, in a purchase-type business combination. Out-of-pocket costs of the business combination were as follows:

Legal and finder's fees associated with the business combination	$36,800
Costs incurred for SEC registration statement for Parker's common stock	20,000
Total out-of-pocket costs of business combination	$56,800

On November 1, Year 4, the current fair values of Sacco's identifiable net assets were equal to their carrying amounts. On that date, Sacco's stockholders' equity consisted of the following:

Common stock, $100 par	$ 10,000
Paid-in capital in excess of par	140,000
Retained earnings	70,000
Total stockholders' equity	$220,000

Prepare the journal entries in Parker Corporation's accounting records to record the business combination with Sacco Company.

Ex. 5-8 The condensed individual and consolidated balance sheets of Perth Corporation and its subsidiary, Sykes Company, on the date of their business combination appear on page 222.

PERTH CORPORATION AND SUBSIDIARY
Individual and Consolidated Balance Sheets
June 30, Year 3

	Perth Corporation	Sykes Company	Consolidated
Assets			
Cash	$ 100,000	$ 40,000	$ 140,000
Inventories	500,000	90,000	610,000
Other current assets	250,000	60,000	310,000
Investment in Sykes Company common stock	440,000		
Plant assets (net)	1,000,000	360,000	1,440,000
Goodwill	100,000		120,000
Total assets	$2,390,000	$550,000	$2,620,000
Liabilities & Stockholders' Equity			
Income taxes payable	$ 40,000	$ 35,000	$ 75,000
Other liabilities	580,600	195,000	775,600
Common stock	1,020,000	200,000	1,020,000
Paid-in capital in excess of par . . .	429,400	210,000	429,400
Retained earnings (deficit)	320,000	(90,000)	320,000
Total liabilities & stockholders' equity	$2,390,000	$550,000	$2,620,000

Reconstruct the working paper elimination (in journal entry form) indicated by the above data. Disregard income taxes.

Ex. 5-9 Simplex Company's balance sheet on December 31, Year 6, was as follows:

SIMPLEX COMPANY
Balance Sheet
December 31, Year 6

Assets

Cash	$ 100,000
Accounts receivable (net)	200,000
Inventories	510,000
Plant assets (net)	900,000
Total assets	$1,710,000

Liabilities & Stockholders' Equity

Current liabilities	$ 310,000
Long-term debt	500,000
Common stock, $1 par	100,000
Paid-in capital in excess of par	200,000
Retained earnings	600,000
Total liabilities & stockholders' equity	$1,710,000

On December 31, Year 6, Protex Corporation acquired all the outstanding common stock of Simplex for $1,500,000 cash, including direct out-of-pocket costs. On that date, the current fair value of Simplex's inventories was $450,000 and the current fair value of Simplex's plant assets was $1,000,000. The current fair values of all other assets and liabilities of Simplex were equal to their carrying amounts.

a Compute the amount of goodwill that should appear in the December 31, Year 6, consolidated balance sheet of Protex Corporation and subsidiary.

b Compute the amount of consolidated retained earnings that should appear in the December 31, Year 6, consolidated balance sheet of Protex Corporation and subsidiary, assuming that Protex's unconsolidated balance sheet on that date included retained earnings of $2,500,000.

Ex. 5-10   The working paper elimination on August 31, Year 5, for the consolidated balance sheet of Payton Corporation and subsidiary is shown below. On that date, Payton acquired most of the outstanding common stock of Sutton Company for cash.

PAYTON CORPORATION AND SUBSIDIARY

Working Paper Elimination

August 31, Year 5

Common Stock—Sutton	60,000	
Paid-in Capital in Excess of Par—Sutton	35,250	
Retained Earnings—Sutton	50,100	
Inventories—Sutton	3,900	
Plant Assets (net)—Sutton	28,500	
Patent—Sutton	4,500	
Goodwill—Payton	5,280	
Investment in Sutton Company Common Stock—Payton		165,660
Minority Interest in Net Assets of Subsidiary		21,870

To eliminate intercompany investment and equity accounts of subsidiary on date of business combination; to allocate excess of cost over current fair values of identifiable net assets acquired to goodwill; and to establish minority interest in net assets of subsidiary on date of purchase-type business combination. (Income tax effects are disregarded.)

Answer the following questions (show supporting computations):

a What percentage of the outstanding common stock of the subsidiary was acquired by the parent company?

b What was the aggregate current fair value of the subsidiary's identifiable net assets on August 31, Year 5?

c What amount would be assigned to goodwill under the method that infers a total current fair value for the subsidiary's total net assets, based on the parent company's investment?

d What amount would be assigned to minority interest in subsidiary under the method described in **c**?

CASES

Case 5-1   The minority interest in a subsidiary might be presented several ways in a consolidated balance sheet.

Instructions Discuss the propriety of reporting the minority interest in the consolidated balance sheet:

a As a liability

b As a part of stockholders' equity

c In a separate classification between liabilities and stockholders' equity

Case 5-2 On January 2, Year 2, the board of directors of Photo Corporation assigned to a voting trust 15,000 shares of the 60,000 shares of Soto Company common stock owned by Photo. The trustee of the voting trust controls 40,000 of Soto's 105,000 shares of issued common stock, of which 5,000 shares are in Soto's treasury. The term of the voting trust is three years.

Instructions Are consolidated financial statements appropriate for Photo Corporation and Soto Company for the three years ending December 31, Year 4? Explain.

Case 5-3 On July 31, Year 5, Paley Corporation transferred all right, title, and interest in several of its current research and development projects to Carla Saye, sole shareholder of Saye Company, in exchange for 55 of the 100 shares of Saye Company common stock owned by Carla Saye. On the same date, Martin Morgan, who is not related to Paley Corporation, Saye Company, or Carla Saye, acquired for $45,000 cash the remaining 45 shares of Saye Company common stock owned by Carla Saye. Carla Saye notified the directors of Paley Corporation of the sale of the stock to Morgan.

Because Paley had expensed the costs related to the research and development when the costs were incurred, Paley's controller prepared the following journal entry to record the business combination with Saye Company:

Investment in Saye Company Common Stock (55 × $1,000) . .   55,000

    Gain on Disposal of Intangible Assets   55,000

To record transfer of research and development projects to Carla Saye in exchange for 55 shares of Saye Company common stock. Valuation of the investment is based on an unrelated cash sale of Saye Company common stock on this date.

Instructions

a Do you concur with the foregoing journal entry? Explain.

b Should the $55,000 gain appear in consolidated financial statements of Paley Corporation and subsidiary on July 31, Year 5? Explain.

Case 5-4 On May 31, Year 6, Patrick Corporation acquired at 100, $500,000 face amount of Stear Company's 10-year, 12%, convertible debentures due May 31, Year 11. The debentures were convertible to 50,000 shares of Stear's voting common stock ($1 par), of which 40,000 shares were issued and outstanding on May 31, Year 6. The controller of Patrick, who also is one of three Patrick officers who serve on the five-member board of directors of Stear, proposes to issue consolidated financial statements for Patrick Corporation and Stear Company on May 31, Year 6.

Instructions Do you agree with the Patrick controller's proposal? Explain, including in your discussion appropriate financial statement disclosure of the "related party" status of Patrick Corporation and Stear Company.

Case 5-5 In Year 6, Pinch Corporation, a chain of discount stores, began a program of business combinations with its suppliers. On May 31, Year 6, the close of its fiscal year, Pinch paid $8,500,000 cash and issued 100,000 shares of its common stock (current fair value $20 a share) for all 10,000 outstanding shares of common stock of Silver Company. Silver was a furniture manufacturer whose products were sold in Pinch's stores. Total stockholders' equity of Silver on May 31, Year 6, was $9,000,000. Out-of-pocket costs attributable to the business combination itself (as opposed to the SEC registration statement for the 100,000 shares of Pinch's common stock) paid by Pinch on May 31, Year 6, totaled $100,000.

In the consolidated balance sheet of Pinch Corporation and subsidiary on May 31, Year 6, the $1,600,000 difference between the parent company's cost and the carrying amounts of the subsidiary's identifiable net assets was allocated in accordance with purchase accounting as follows:

Inventories	$ 250,000
Plant assets	850,000
Patents	300,000
Goodwill	200,000
Total excess of cost over carrying amounts of subsidiary's net assets	$1,600,000

Under terms of the indenture for a $1,000,000 debenture bond liability of Silver, Pinch is obligated to maintain Silver as a separate corporation and to issue a separate balance sheet for Silver each May 31. Pinch's controller contends that Silver's balance sheet on May 31, Year 6, should show net assets of $10,600,000 —their cost to Pinch. Silver's controller disputes this valuation, claiming that generally accepted accounting principles require issuance of a historical cost balance sheet for Silver on May 31, Year 6.

Instructions
a Present arguments in favor of the Pinch controller's position.
b Present arguments in favor of the Silver controller's position.
c Which position do you approve? Explain.

PROBLEMS

5-1 On September 30, Year 1, Planck Corporation issued 100,000 shares of its $5 par common stock (current fair value $12 a share) for 18,800 shares of the outstanding $20 par common stock of Soper Company. The $150,000 out-of-pocket costs of the business combination paid by Planck on September 30, Year 1, were allocable as follows: 60% to legal fees and finder's fee directly related to the business combination, and 40% to the SEC registration statement for Planck's common stock issued in the business combination. There was no contingent consideration.

Immediately prior to the business combination, balance sheets of the constituent companies were as follows:

PLANCK CORPORATION AND SOPER COMPANY
Separate Balance Sheets
September 30, Year 1

	Planck Corporation	Soper Company
Assets		
Cash	$ 200,000	$ 100,000
Accounts receivable (*net*)	400,000	200,000
Inventories (*net*)	600,000	300,000
Plant assets (*net*)	1,300,000	1,000,000
Total assets	$2,500,000	$1,600,000

(Continued)

Liabilities & Stockholders' Equity

Current liabilities	$ 800,000	$ 400,000
Long-term debt		100,000
Common stock, $5 par	1,000,000	
Common stock, $20 par		400,000
Paid-in capital in excess of par	200,000	
Retained earnings	500,000	700,000
Total liabilities & stockholders' equity	$2,500,000	$1,600,000

Current fair values of Soper's identifiable net assets differed from their carrying amounts as follows:

	Current fair values, Sept. 30, Year 1
Inventories	$ 340,000
Plant assets (net)	1,100,000
Long-term debt	90,000

Instructions

a Prepare journal entries for Planck Corporation on September 30, Year 1, to record the business combination with Soper Company as a purchase.

b Prepare a working paper for consolidated balance sheet and related working paper elimination (in journal entry form) for Planck Corporation and subsidiary on September 30, Year 1. Balances in the working papers should reflect the journal entries in **a**. Disregard income taxes.

5-2 Balance sheets of Pageant Corporation and Symbol Company on May 31, Year 4, together with current fair values of Symbol's identifiable net assets, are shown below:

PAGEANT CORPORATION AND SYMBOL COMPANY
Separate Balance Sheets
May 31, Year 4

	Pageant Corporation	Symbol Company Carrying amounts	Symbol Company Current fair values
Assets			
Cash	$ 550,000	$ 10,000	$ 10,000
Accounts receivable (net)	700,000	60,000	60,000
Inventories	1,400,000	120,000	140,000
Plant assets (net)	2,850,000	610,000	690,000
Total assets	$5,500,000	$800,000	
Liabilities & Stockholders' Equity			
Current liabilities	$ 500,000	$ 80,000	$ 80,000
Long-term debt	1,000,000	400,000	440,000
Common stock, $10 par	1,500,000	100,000	
Paid-in capital in excess of par	1,200,000	40,000	
Retained earnings	1,300,000	180,000	
Total liabilities & stockholders' equity	$5,500,000	$800,000	

On May 31, Year 4, Pageant acquired all 10,000 shares of Symbol's outstanding common stock by paying $300,000 cash to Symbol's shareholders and $50,000 cash for finder's and legal fees relating to the business combination. There was no contingent consideration, and Symbol became a subsidiary of Pageant.

Instructions

a Prepare journal entries to record the business combination of Pageant Corporation and Symbol Company on May 31, Year 4.

b Prepare a working paper for consolidated balance sheet of Pageant Corporation and subsidiary on May 31, Year 4, and the related working paper elimination (in journal entry form). Balances in the working papers should reflect the journal entries in **a**. Disregard income taxes.

5-3 On April 30, Year 6, Powell Corporation issued 30,000 shares of its no-par common stock with a stated value of $5 a share and a current fair value of $20 a share for 8,000 shares of Seaver Company's $10 par common stock. There was no contingent consideration; out-of-pocket costs of the business combination, paid by Seaver on behalf of Powell on April 30, Year 6, were as follows:

Finder's and legal fees relating to business combination	$40,000
Costs associated with SEC registration statement	30,000
Total out-of-pocket costs of business combination	$70,000

Balance sheets of the constituent companies on April 30, Year 6, prior to the business combination, are shown below:

POWELL CORPORATION AND SEAVER COMPANY
Separate Balance Sheets
April 30, Year 6

	Powell Corporation	Seaver Company
Assets		
Cash	$ 50,000	$ 150,000
Accounts receivable (net)	230,000	200,000
Inventories	400,000	350,000
Plant assets (net)	1,300,000	560,000
Total assets	$1,980,000	$1,260,000
Liabilities & Stockholders' Equity		
Current liabilities	$ 310,000	$ 250,000
Long-term debt	800,000	600,000
Common stock, no-par, $5 stated value	400,000	
Common stock, $10 par		100,000
Paid-in capital in excess of par or stated value . . .	100,000	360,000
Retained earnings (deficit)	370,000	(50,000)
Total liabilities & stockholders' equity	$1,980,000	$1,260,000

Current fair values of Seaver's identifiable net assets were the same as their carrying amounts, except for the following:

	Current fair values, *Apr. 30, Year 6*
Inventories	$440,000
Plant assets (net)	780,000
Long-term debt	620,000

Instructions

a Prepare a journal entry for Seaver Company on April 30, Year 6, to record its payment of out-of-pocket costs of the business combination on behalf of Powell Corporation.

b Prepare journal entries for Powell Corporation to record the purchase-type business combination with Seaver Company on April 30, Year 6.

c Prepare a working paper for consolidated balance sheet of Powell Corporation and subsidiary on April 30, Year 6, and the related working paper elimination (in journal entry form). Balances in the working papers should reflect the journal entries in **a** and **b**. Disregard income taxes.

5-4 On July 31, Year 10, Pell Corporation issued 20,000 shares of its $2 par common stock (current fair value $10 a share) for all 5,000 shares of outstanding $5 par common stock of Swift Company, which is to remain a separate corporation. Out-of-pocket costs of the business combination, paid by Pell on July 31, Year 10, are shown below:

Finder's and legal fees related to business combination	$20,000
Costs associated with SEC registration statement for Pell common stock	10,000
Total out-of-pocket costs of business combination	$30,000

The constituent companies' balance sheets on July 31, Year 10, prior to the business combination, follow:

PELL CORPORATION AND SWIFT COMPANY
Separate Balance Sheets
July 31, Year 10

	Pell Corporation	Swift Company
Assets		
Current assets	$ 800,000	$150,000
Plant assets (net)	2,400,000	300,000
Goodwill		20,000
Total assets	$3,200,000	$470,000
Liabilities & Stockholders' Equity		
Current liabilities	$ 400,000	$120,000
Long-term debt	1,000,000	200,000
Common stock, $2 par	800,000	
Common stock, $5 par		25,000
Paid-in capital in excess of par	400,000	50,000
Retained earnings	600,000	75,000
Total liabilities & stockholders' equity	$3,200,000	$470,000

Swift's goodwill resulted from its July 31, Year 4, acquisition of the net assets of Solo Company.

Swift's assets and liabilities having July 31, Year 10, current fair values different from their carrying amounts were as follows:

	Carrying amounts	Current fair values
Inventories	$ 60,000	$ 65,000
Plant assets (net)	300,000	340,000
Long-term debt	200,000	190,000

There were no intercompany transactions prior to the business combination, and there was no contingent consideration in connection with the combination.

Instructions

a Prepare Pell Corporation's journal entries on July 31, Year 10, to record the business combination with Swift Company as a purchase.

b Prepare the working paper elimination (in journal entry form) and the related working paper for consolidated balance sheet of Pell Corporation and subsidiary on July 31, Year 10. Balances in the working papers should reflect the journal entries in **a**. Disregard income taxes.

5-5 The unconsolidated and consolidated balance sheets of Prosper Corporation and subsidiary on August 31, Year 6, the date of Prosper's business combination with Santee Company, are shown below:

PROSPER CORPORATION
Unconsolidated and Consolidated Balance Sheets
August 31, Year 6

	Unconsolidated	Consolidated
Assets		
Cash	$ 120,000	$ 160,000
Accounts receivable (net)	380,000	540,000
Inventories	470,000	730,000
Investment in Santee Company common stock	380,000	
Plant assets (net)	850,000	1,470,000
Goodwill		8,000
Total assets	$2,200,000	$2,908,000
Liabilities & Stockholders' Equity		
Current liabilities	$ 430,000	$ 690,000
Long-term debt	550,000	730,000
Premium on long-term debt		20,000
Minority interest in net assets of subsidiary . .		248,000
Common stock, $1 par	500,000	500,000
Paid-in capital in excess of par	440,000	440,000
Retained earnings	280,000	280,000
Total liabilities & stockholders' equity	$2,200,000	$2,908,000

On August 31, Year 6, Prosper had paid cash of $3 a share for 60% of the outstanding shares of Santee's $1 par common stock, and $20,000 cash for legal fees in connection with the business combination. There was no contingent consideration. The equity (book value) of Santee's common stock on August 31, Year 6, was $2.80 a share, and the amount of Santee's retained earnings was twice as large as the amount of its paid-in capital in excess of par. The excess of current fair value of Santee's plant assets over their carrying amount on August 31, Year 6, was $1\frac{2}{3}$ times as large as the comparable excess for Santee's inventories on that date. The current fair values of Santee's cash, accounts receivable (net), and current liabilities were equal to their carrying amounts on August 31, Year 6.

Instructions Reconstruct the working paper elimination (in journal entry form) for the working paper for consolidated balance sheet of Prosper Corporation and subsidiary on August 31, Year 6. Disregard income taxes and show supporting computations.

5-6 On October 31, Year 4, Pagel Corporation acquired 83% of the outstanding common stock of Sayre Company in exchange for 50,000 shares of Pagel's $2 par ($10 current fair value a share) common stock. There was no contingent consideration. Out-of-pocket costs of the business combination paid by Pagel on October 31, Year 4, were as follows:

Legal and finder's fees related to business combination	$34,750
Costs associated with SEC registration statement for Pagel's common stock	55,250
Total out-of-pocket costs of business combination	$90,000

There were no intercompany transactions between the constituent companies prior to the business combination. Sayre is to be a subsidiary of Pagel. The separate balance sheets of the constituent companies prior to the business combination follow:

PAGEL CORPORATION AND SAYRE COMPANY
Separate Balance Sheets
October 31, Year 4

	Pagel Corporation	Sayre Company
Assets		
Cash	$ 250,000	$ 150,000
Inventories	860,000	600,000
Other current assets	500,000	260,000
Plant assets (net)	3,400,000	1,500,000
Patents (net)		80,000
Total assets	$5,010,000	$2,590,000
Liabilities & Stockholders' Equity		
Income taxes payable	$ 40,000	$ 60,000
Other current liabilities	390,000	854,000
Long-term debt	950,000	1,240,000
Common stock, $2	1,500,000	
Common stock, $10 par		100,000
Paid-in capital in excess of par	1,500,000	
Retained earnings	630,000	336,000
Total liabilities & stockholders' equity	$5,010,000	$2,590,000

Current fair values of Sayre's identifiable net assets were the same as their carrying amounts on October 31, Year 4, except for the following:

Inventories	$ 620,000
Plant assets (net)	1,550,000
Patents (net)	95,000
Long-term debt	1,225,000

Instructions

a Prepare Pagel Corporation's journal entries on October 31, Year 4, to record the business combination with Sayre Company as a purchase.

b Prepare the working paper eliminations (in journal entry form) on October 31, Year 4, and the related working paper for the consolidated balance sheet of Pagel Corporation and subsidiary. Balances in the working papers should reflect the journal entries in **a**. Disregard income taxes.

5-7 On January 31, Year 3, Porcino Corporation issued $50,000 cash, 6,000 shares of $2 par common stock (current fair value $15 a share), and a 5-year, 14%, $50,000 promissory note payable for all 10,000 shares of Secor Company's outstanding common stock, which were owned by Lawrence Secor. The only out-of-pocket costs paid by Porcino to complete the business combination were legal fees of $10,000, because Porcino's common stock issued in the combination was not subject to the registration requirements of the SEC. There was no contingent consideration, and 14% was a fair rate of interest for the promissory note issued by Porcino in connection with the business combination.

Balance sheets of Porcino and Secor on January 31, Year 3, prior to the business combination, were as follows:

PORCINO CORPORATION AND SECOR COMPANY
Separate Balance Sheets
January 31, Year 3

	Porcino Corporation	Secor Company
Assets		
Inventories	$ 380,000	$ 60,000
Other current assets	640,000	130,000
Plant assets (net)	1,520,000	470,000
Intangible assets (net)	160,000	40,000
Total assets	$2,700,000	$700,000
Liabilities & Stockholders' Equity		
Current liabilities	$ 420,000	$200,000
Long-term debt	650,000	300,000
Common stock, $2 par	800,000	
Common stock, $15 par		150,000
Paid-in capital in excess of par	220,000	160,000
Retained earnings (deficit)	610,000	(110,000)
Total liabilities & stockholders' equity	$2,700,000	$700,000

Current fair values of Secor's identifiable net assets that differed from their carrying amounts on January 31, Year 3, were as follows:

	Current fair values
Inventories	$ 70,000
Plant assets (net)	540,000
Intangible assets (net)	60,000
Long-term debt	350,000

Instructions

a Prepare journal entries for Porcino Corporation on January 31, Year 3, to record its business combination with Secor Company.

b Prepare a working paper for consolidated balance sheet of Porcino Corporation and subsidiary on January 31, Year 3, and the related working paper elimination (in journal entry form). Balances in the working papers should reflect the journal entries in **a**. Disregard income taxes.

5-8　On June 30, Year 7, Pandit Corporation issued a $300,000 note payable, due $60,000 a year with interest at 15% beginning June 30, Year 8, for 8,500 of the 10,000 outstanding shares of $10 par common stock of Singh Company. Legal fees of $20,000 incurred by Pandit in connection with the business combination were paid on June 30, Year 7.

　　Balance sheets of the constituent companies, immediately following the business combination, are shown below:

PANDIT CORPORATION AND SINGH COMPANY
Separate Balance Sheets
June 30, Year 7

	Pandit Corporation	Singh Company
Assets		
Cash	$　80,000	$ 60,000
Accounts receivable (net)	170,000	90,000
Inventories	370,000	120,000
Investment in Singh Company common stock	320,000	
Plant assets (net)	570,000	240,000
Goodwill	50,000	
Total assets	$1,560,000	$510,000
Liabilities & Stockholders' Equity		
Accounts payable	$　220,000	$120,000
Income taxes payable	100,000	40,000
15% note payable, due $60,000 annually	300,000	
Common stock, $10 par	250,000	100,000
Paid-in capital in excess of par	400,000	130,000
Retained earnings	290,000	120,000
Total liabilities & stockholders' equity	$1,560,000	$510,000

Other information

(1) An independent audit of Singh Company's financial statements for the year ended June 30, Year 7, disclosed that Singh's July 1, Year 6, inventories had been overstated $60,000 due to double counting; and that Singh had omitted from its June 30, Year 7, inventories merchandise shipped FOB shipping point by a vendor on June 30, Year 7, at an invoiced amount of $35,000. Cor-

rections of Singh's inventories errors are not reflected in Singh's balance sheet on page 232.

(2) Both Pandit and Singh had combined federal and state income tax rates of 60%.

(3) Current fair values of Singh's net assets reflected in Singh's balance sheet on June 30, Year 7, differed from carrying amounts as follows:

	Current fair values
Inventories	$150,000
Plant assets (net)	280,000

Instructions

a Prepare a journal entry or entries to correct the inventories misstatements in Singh Company's financial statements for the year ended June 30, Year 7. Singh's accounting records have not been closed for the year ended June 30, Year 7.

b Prepare a working paper elimination (in journal entry form) and a working paper for the consolidated balance sheet of Pandit Corporation and subsidiary on June 30, Year 7. The amounts for Singh Company should reflect the adjusting journal entry or entries prepared in **a**.

5-9   Shown below are the balance sheets of Pliny Corporation and Sylla Company on December 31, Year 6, prior to their business combination:

PLINY CORPORATION AND SYLLA COMPANY
Separate Balance Sheets
December 31, Year 6

	Pliny Corporation	Sylla Company
Assets		
Inventories	$ 800,000	$ 300,000
Other current assets	1,200,000	500,000
Long-term investments in marketable securities . . .		200,000
Plant assets (net)	2,500,000	900,000
Intangible assets (net)	100,000	200,000
Total assets	$4,600,000	$2,100,000
Liabilities & Stockholders' Equity		
Current liabilities	$1,400,000	$ 300,000
10% note payable, due June 30, Year 16	2,000,000	
12% bonds payable, due Dec. 31, Year 11		500,000
Common stock, $1 par	600,000	200,000
Paid-in capital in excess of par	200,000	400,000
Retained earnings	400,000	700,000
Total liabilities & stockholders' equity	$4,600,000	$2,100,000

On December 31, Year 6, Pliny paid $100,000 cash and issued $1,500,000 face amount of 14%, 10-year bonds for all the outstanding common stock of Sylla, which became a subsidiary of Pliny. On the date of the business combination, 16% was a fair rate of interest for the bonds of both Pliny and Sylla, which paid interest on June 30 and December 31. There was no contingent consideration involved in the business combination, but Pliny paid the following out-of-pocket costs on December 31, Year 6:

Finder's and legal fees relating to business combination $50,000

Costs associated with SEC registration statement for Pliny's bonds . . .   40,000

Total out-of-pocket costs of business combination $90,000

In addition to the 12% bonds payable, Sylla had identifiable net assets with current fair values that differed from carrying amounts on December 31, Year 6, as follows:

	Current fair values
Inventories	$330,000
Long-term investments in marketable securities	230,000
Plant assets (net)	940,000
Intangible assets (net)	220,000

Instructions

a Prepare journal entries for Pliny Corporation to record the business combination with Sylla Company on December 31, Year 6. Use the appendix in back of the book to compute present value, rounded to nearest dollar, of the 14% bonds issued by Pliny.

b Prepare a working paper for consolidated balance sheet for Pliny Corporation and subsidiary on December 31, Year 6, and the related working paper elimination (in journal entry form). Use the appendix in back of the book to compute present value, rounded to nearest dollar, of the 12% bonds payable of Sylla. Amounts in the working papers should reflect the journal entries in **a**. Disregard income taxes.

5-10 You have been engaged to examine the financial statements of Parthenia Corporation and subsidiary for the year ended June 30, Year 6. The working paper for consolidated balance sheet of Parthenia and subsidiary on June 30, Year 6, prepared by Parthenia's inexperienced accountant, is on page 235.

In the course of your examination, you review the following June 30, Year 6, journal entries in the accounting records of Parthenia Corporation:

Investment in Storey Company Common Stock	220,000	
Goodwill	60,000	
Cash		280,000

To record acquisition of 4,000 shares of Storey Company's outstanding common stock in a purchase-type business combination, and to record acquired goodwill as follows:

Cash paid for Storey common stock $280,000

Less: Stockholders' equity of Storey, June 30,

Year 6   220,000

Goodwill acquired . . . . $ 60,000

Expenses of Business Combination	10,000	
Cash		10,000

To record payment of legal fees in connection with business combination with Storey Company.

PARTHENIA CORPORATION AND SUBSIDIARY
Working Paper for Consolidated Balance Sheet
June 30, Year 6

	Parthenia Corporation	Storey Company	Eliminations increase (decrease)	Consolidated
Assets				
Cash.	60,000	50,000		110,000
Accounts receivable (net) .	120,000	90,000		210,000
Inventories	250,000	160,000		410,000
Investment in Storey Company common stock.	220,000		(a) (220,000)	
Plant assets (net)	590,000	500,000		1,090,000
Goodwill	60,000			60,000
Total assets	1,300,000	800,000	(220,000)	1,880,000
Liabilities & Stockholders' Equity				
Current liabilities	200,000	280,000		480,000
Long-term debt	500,000	300,000		800,000
Common stock, $5 par. . .	100,000			100,000
Common stock, $10 par . .		50,000	(a) (50,000)	
Paid-in capital in excess of par	200,000	70,000	(a) (70,000)	200,000
Retained earnings	300,000	100,000	(a) (100,000)	300,000
Total liabilities & stockholders' equity . .	1,300,000	800,000	(220,000)	1,880,000

Your inquiries of directors and officers of Parthenia and your review of supporting documents disclosed the following current fair values for Storey's identifiable net assets that differ from carrying amounts on June 30, Year 6:

	Current fair values
Inventories	$180,000
Plant assets (net)	530,000
Long-term debt	260,000

Instructions
a Prepare a journal entry or entries to correct Parthenia Corporation's accounting for its June 30, Year 6, business combination with Storey Company. Parthenia's accounting records have not been closed.

b Prepare a corrected working paper for consolidated balance sheet of Parthenia Corporation and subsidiary on June 30, Year 6, and related working paper elimination (in journal entry form). Amounts in the working papers should reflect the journal entries in *a*. Disregard income taxes.

6 CONSOLIDATED FINANCIAL STATEMENTS: SUBSEQUENT TO DATE OF PURCHASE BUSINESS COMBINATION

Subsequent to the date of a business combination, the parent company must account for the operating results of the subsidiary: the subsidiary's net income or net loss, and dividends declared and paid by the subsidiary. In addition, a number of intercompany transactions that frequently occur in a parent company–subsidiary relationship must be accounted for.

In this chapter, we describe and illustrate the accounting for operating results of purchased subsidiaries. Accounting for operating results of pooled subsidiaries and for intercompany transactions not involving a profit or a loss is illustrated in Chapter 7; Chapter 8 includes a discussion of accounting for intercompany transactions involving a profit or a loss.

ACCOUNTING FOR OPERATING RESULTS OF WHOLLY OWNED PURCHASED SUBSIDIARIES

In accounting for the operating results of consolidated purchased subsidiaries, a parent company may choose the *equity method* or the *cost method* of accounting.

Equity method

In the equity method of accounting, the parent company records its share of the subsidiary's net income or net loss, adjusted for amortization of differences between current fair values and carrying amounts of a purchased subsidiary's net assets on the date of the business combination, as well as its share of dividends declared by the subsidiary. Thus, the equity method of accounting for a subsidiary's operating results is similar to home office accounting for a branch's operations, as described in Chapter 3.

Proponents of the equity method of accounting maintain that the method is consistent with the accrual basis of accounting, because it recognizes increases or decreases in the carrying amount of the parent company's investment in the subsidiary when they are ***realized*** by the subsidiary as net income or net loss, not when they are ***paid*** by the subsidiary as dividends. Thus, proponents claim, the equity method stresses the ***economic substance*** of the parent company–subsidiary relationship because the two companies constitute a single economic entity for accounting purposes. Proponents of the equity method also claim that dividends declared by a subsidiary cannot constitute ***revenue*** to the parent company, as maintained by advocates of the cost method; instead, dividends are a liquidation of a portion of the parent company's investment in the subsidiary.

Cost method

In the cost method of accounting, the parent company accounts for the operations of a subsidiary only to the extent that dividends are declared by the subsidiary. Dividends declared by the subsidiary from net income subsequent to the business combination are ***revenue*** to the parent company; dividends declared by the subsidiary in excess of post-combination net income constitute a reduction of the parent company's investment in the subsidiary. Net income or net loss of the subsidiary is ***not recorded*** by the parent company when the cost method of accounting is used.

Supporters of the cost method contend that the method appropriately recognizes the ***legal form*** of the parent company–subsidiary relationship. Parent company and subsidiary are separate legal entities; accounting for a subsidiary's operations should recognize the separateness, according to proponents of the cost method. Thus, a parent company realizes revenue from an investment in a subsidiary when the subsidiary declares a dividend, not when the subsidiary reports net income. The cost method of accounting is illustrated in the appendix on pages 270 to 276.

Choosing between equity method and cost method

Consolidated financial statement amounts are the same, regardless of whether a parent company uses the equity method or the cost method to account for a subsidiary's operations. However, the working paper eliminations used in the two methods are different, as illustrated in subsequent sections of this chapter.

The equity method of accounting is appropriate for *pooled* subsidiaries as well as *purchased* subsidiaries. The cost method, on the other hand, is compatible with *purchase accounting* only. In purchase accounting, the parent company's original investment in the subsidiary is recorded at *cost.* Hence, accounting for operating results of purchased subsidiaries by the cost method may be considered a logical extension of purchase accounting. However, in pooling accounting the parent company's investment on the date of the business combination is recorded at the carrying amount of the subsidiary's net assets. As a result, the parent company's Investment in Subsidiary Common Stock account reflects the parent's equity in the subsidiary's net assets on the date of the business combination; *there is no cost of a pooled subsidiary.* The equity method of accounting for a pooled subsidiary's operations thus is consistent with pooling accounting, as illustrated in Chapter 7, and is stressed in this book.

Illustration of equity method for wholly owned purchased subsidiary for first year after business combination

Assume that Palm Corporation appropriately had used purchase accounting for the December 31, Year 1, business combination with its wholly owned subsidiary, Starr Company (see pages 195 and 196 for a description of the purchase-type business combination), and that Starr reported net income of $60,000 (income statement is on page 244) for the year ended December 31, Year 2. Assume further that on December 20, Year 2, Starr's board of directors declared a cash dividend of $0.60 a share on the 40,000 outstanding shares of common stock owned by Palm. The dividend was payable January 8, Year 3, to stockholders of record December 29, Year 2.

Starr's December 20, Year 2, journal entry to record the dividend declaration is as follows:

Wholly owned subsidiary's journal entry for declaration of dividend	*Year 2*		
	Dec. 20 Dividends (40,000 × $0.60) 24,000	
	Intercompany Dividends Payable	24,000
	To record declaration of dividend payable Jan. 8, Year 3, to stockholders of record Dec. 29, Year 2.	

Starr's credit to the Intercompany Dividends Payable account indicates that the liability for dividends payable to the parent company *must be eliminated* in the preparation of consolidated financial statements for the year ended December 31, Year 2.

Under the equity method of accounting, Palm Corporation prepares the following journal entries to record the dividend and net income of Starr for the year ended December 31, Year 2:

Parent company's equity-method journal entries to record operating results of wholly owned purchased subsidiary

> **PALM CORPORATION**
> *General Journal*
>
> *Year 2*
> *Dec. 20 Intercompany Dividends Receivable. 24,000*
> *   Investment in Starr Company Common Stock .   24,000*
> *   To record dividend declared by Starr Company, pay-*
> *   able Jan. 8, Year 3, to stockholders of record Dec. 29,*
> *   Year 2.*
>
> *Dec. 31 Investment in Starr Company Common Stock. 60,000*
> *   Intercompany Investment Income 60,000*
> *   To record 100% of Starr Company's net income for*
> *   the year ended Dec. 31, Year 2. (Income tax effects*
> *   are disregarded.)*

The first journal entry records the dividend declared by the subsidiary in the Intercompany Dividends Receivable account, and is the counterpart of the subsidiary's journal entry to record the declaration of the dividend. The credit to the Investment in Starr Company Common Stock account in the first journal entry reflects an underlying premise of the equity method of accounting: dividends declared by a subsidiary represent a return of a portion of the parent company's investment in the subsidiary.

The second journal entry records the parent company's 100% share of the subsidiary's net income for Year 2. The subsidiary's net income *accrues* to the parent company under the equity method of accounting, similar to the accrual of interest on a note receivable.

The income tax effects of Palm Corporation's accrual of its share of Starr Company's reported net income are disregarded at this time. Income tax allocation problems associated with all aspects of parent company and subsidiary accounting are considered in Chapter 9.

Adjustment of Purchased Subsidiary's Net Income   Because we have assumed in this chapter that Palm Corporation's business combination with Starr Company was accounted for as a *purchase,* Palm must prepare a third equity-method journal entry on December 31, Year 2, to adjust Starr's net income for depreciation and amortization attributable to the differences between the current fair values and carrying amounts of Starr's net assets on the date of the Palm-Starr business combination.

Because such differences are not recorded by the subsidiary, the subsidiary's **net income is overstated** from the point of view of the consolidated entity.

Let us assume that the December 31, Year 1, differences between the current fair values and carrying amounts of Starr Company's net assets were as follows:

<table>
<tr><td colspan="4"></td></tr>
<tr><td>Inventories . . . .</td><td></td><td></td><td>$ 25,000</td></tr>
<tr><td>Plant assets (net):</td><td></td><td></td><td></td></tr>
<tr><td> Land . . . .</td><td></td><td>$15,000</td><td></td></tr>
<tr><td> Building (economic life 15 years) . . . .</td><td></td><td>30,000</td><td></td></tr>
<tr><td> Machinery (economic life 10 years) . . . .</td><td></td><td>20,000</td><td>65,000</td></tr>
<tr><td>Patent (economic life 5 years) . . . .</td><td></td><td></td><td>5,000</td></tr>
<tr><td>Goodwill (economic life 30 years) . . . .</td><td></td><td></td><td>15,000</td></tr>
<tr><td>   Total . . . .</td><td></td><td></td><td>$110,000</td></tr>
</table>

Differences between current fair values and carrying amounts of wholly owned purchased subsidiary's assets on date of business combination

Palm Corporation prepares the following additional journal entry to reflect the effects of amortization of the differences between the current fair values and carrying amounts of Starr Company's net assets on Starr's net income for the year ended December 31, Year 2:

Parent company's equity-method journal entry to record operating results of wholly owned purchased subsidiary attributable to amortization of subsidiary's net assets

PALM CORPORATION
General Journal

Year 2

Dec. 31 Intercompany Investment Income 30,500

           Investment in Starr Company Common Stock .   30,500

    To amortize differences between current fair values
    and carrying amounts of Starr Company's net assets
    on Dec. 31, Year 1, as follows:

Inventories—to cost of goods sold	$25,000
Building—depreciation ($30,000 ÷ 15). .	2,000
Machinery—depreciation ($20,000 ÷ 10)	2,000
Patent—amortization ($5,000 ÷ 5)	1,000
Goodwill—amortization ($15,000 ÷ 30) .	500
Total amortization applicable to Year 2	$30,500

    (Income tax effects are disregarded.)

After the three foregoing journal entries are posted, Palm Corporation's Investment in Starr Company Common Stock and Intercompany Investment Income ledger accounts appear on page 241.

Developing the Elimination Palm Corporation's use of the equity method of accounting for its investment in Starr Company resulted in a balance

Ledger accounts of parent company using equity method of accounting for wholly owned purchased subsidiary

Investment in Starr Company Common Stock

Date	Explanation	Debit	Credit	Balance
12/31/1	Issuance of common stock in business combination	450,000		450,000 dr
12/31/1	Direct out-of-pocket costs of business combination	50,000		500,000 dr
12/20/2	Dividend declared by Starr		24,000	476,000 dr
12/31/2	Net income of Starr	60,000		536,000 dr
12/31/2	Amortization of differences between current fair values and carrying amounts of Starr's net assets		30,500	505,500 dr

Intercompany Investment Income

Date	Explanation	Debit	Credit	Balance
12/31/2	Net income of Starr		60,000	60,000 cr
12/31/2	Amortization of differences between current fair values and carrying amounts of Starr's net assets	30,500		29,500 cr

in the investment account that is a mixture of two components: (1) the carrying amount of Starr's identifiable net assets, and (2) the date-of-business combination excess of the current fair values of the subsidiary's net assets (including goodwill) over their carrying amounts, net of amortization ("current fair value excess"). These components are analyzed as follows:

PALM CORPORATION
Analysis of Investment in Starr Company Common Stock Account
For Year Ended December 31, Year 2

	Carrying amount	Current fair value excess	Total	
Beginning balances	$390,000	$110,000	$500,000	
Net income of Starr	60,000		60,000	Intercompany investment income, $29,500
Amortization of differences between current fair values and carrying amounts of Starr's net assets		(30,500)	(30,500)	
Dividend declared by Starr .	(24,000)		(24,000)	
Ending balances	$426,000	$ 79,500	$505,500	

The $426,000 ending balance of the Carrying Amount column agrees with the total stockholders' equity of Starr Company on December 31, Year 2 (see Balance Sheet section of working paper for consolidated financial statements on page 244), as follows:

Subsidiary's stockholder's equity at end of Year 2

Common stock, $5 par.	$200,000
Paid-in capital in excess of par.	58,000
Retained earnings	168,000
Total stockholders' equity.	$426,000

The $79,500 ending balance of the Current Fair Value Excess column agrees with the December 31, Year 2, total of the unamortized balances for each of the respective assets of Starr Company, as shown below:

Unamortized differences between current fair values and carrying amounts of wholly owned purchased subsidiary's assets one year subsequent to business combination

	Balance, Dec. 31, Year 1 (p. 240)	Amortization for Year 2 (p. 240)	Balance, Dec. 31, Year 2
Inventories	$ 25,000	$(25,000)	
Plant assets (net):			
Land	$ 15,000		$15,000
Building	30,000	$ (2,000)	28,000
Machinery	20,000	(2,000)	18,000
Total plant assets	$ 65,000	$ (4,000)	$61,000
Patent.	$ 5,000	$ (1,000)	$ 4,000
Goodwill	15,000	(500)	14,500
Totals.	$110,000	$(30,500)	$79,500

It is evident from the analysis on page 241 that the working paper elimination subsequent to the date of a purchase-type business combination must include accounts that appear in the constituent companies' income statements and statements of retained earnings, as well as in their balance sheets, because **all three basic financial statements must be consolidated for accounting periods subsequent to the date of a purchase-type business combination.** (A consolidated statement of changes in financial position is prepared from the three basic **consolidated** financial statements and other information, as explained in Chapter 9.) The accounts that must be included in the elimination are the subsidiary's stockholders' equity, certain assets, costs and expenses, and dividends; and the investment and intercompany investment income of the parent company. Assuming that Starr Company allocates machinery depreciation and patent amortization entirely to cost of goods sold, goodwill amortization entirely to operating expenses, and building depreciation 50% each to cost of goods sold and operating expenses, the working paper elimination for Palm Corporation and subsidiary on December 31, Year 2, is as follows:

<table>
<tr><td style="text-align:right; vertical-align:top; width:25%">Working paper
elimination for wholly
owned purchased
subsidiary subsequent
to date of business
combination</td>
<td style="border:1px solid #000; padding:15px">

PALM CORPORATION AND SUBSIDIARY
Working Paper Elimination
December 31, Year 2

</td></tr>
</table>

(a) Common Stock—Starr. 200,000

    Paid-in Capital in Excess of Par—Starr 58,000

    Retained Earnings—Starr 132,000

    Intercompany Investment Income—Palm. 29,500

    Plant Assets (net)—Starr ($65,000 − $4,000) 61,000

    Patent—Starr ($5,000 − $1,000) 4,000

    Goodwill—Starr ($15,000 − $500) 14,500

    Cost of Goods Sold—Starr 29,000

    Operating Expenses—Starr 1,500

        Investment in Starr Company Common Stock—

        Palm 505,500

        Dividends—Starr 24,000

To carry out the following:

(1) Eliminate intercompany investment and equity accounts of subsidiary **at beginning of year,** and subsidiary dividend.

(2) Provide for Year 2 depreciation and amortization on differences between current fair values and carrying amounts of Starr's net assets as follows:

	Cost of goods sold	Operating expenses
Inventories sold	$25,000	
Building depreciation	1,000	$1,000
Machinery depreciation . . .	2,000	
Patent amortization	1,000	
Goodwill amortization. . . .		500
Totals	$29,000	$1,500

(3) Allocate unamortized differences between combination date current fair values and carrying amounts of Starr's net assets to appropriate assets.

(Income tax effects are disregarded.)

Working Paper for Consolidated Financial Statements The working paper for consolidated financial statements for Palm Corporation and subsidiary for the year ended December 31, Year 2, is on page 244. The intercompany receivable and payable is the $24,000 dividend payable by

Equity method: Wholly owned subsidiary subsequent to date of purchase-type business combination

PALM CORPORATION AND SUBSIDIARY
Working Paper for Consolidated Financial Statements
For Year Ended December 31, Year 2

	Palm Corporation	Starr Company	Eliminations increase (decrease)		Consolidated
Income Statement					
Revenue					
Net sales.	1,100,000	680,000			1,780,000
Intercompany investment income	29,500		(a)	(29,500)	
Total revenue.	1,129,500	680,000		(29,500)	1,780,000
Costs and expenses					
Cost of goods sold	700,000	450,000	(a)	29,000	1,179,000
Operating expenses	151,000	80,000	(a)	1,500	232,500
Interest expense	49,000				49,000
Income taxes expense.	120,000	90,000			210,000
Total costs and expenses.	1,020,000	620,000		30,500*	1,670,500
Net income.	109,500	60,000		(60,000)	109,500
Statement of Retained Earnings					
Retained earnings, beginning of year . . .	134,000	132,000	(a)	(132,000)	134,000
Net income.	109,500	60,000		(60,000)	109,500
Subtotal	243,500	192,000		(192,000)	243,500
Dividends.	30,000	24,000	(a)	(24,000)	30,000
Retained earnings, end of year.	213,500	168,000		(168,000)	213,500
Balance Sheet					
Assets					
Cash.	15,900	72,100			88,000
Intercompany receivable (payable)	24,000	(24,000)			
Inventories.	136,000	115,000			251,000
Other current assets	88,000	131,000			219,000
Investment in Starr Company common stock	505,500		(a)	(505,500)	
Plant assets (net)	440,000	340,000	(a)	61,000	841,000
Patent.		16,000	(a)	4,000	20,000
Goodwill			(a)	14,500	14,500
Total assets	1,209,400	650,100		(426,000)	1,433,500
Liabilities & Stockholders' Equity					
Income taxes payable	40,000	20,000			60,000
Other liabilities	190,900	204,100			395,000
Common stock, $10 par	400,000				400,000
Common stock, $5 par.		200,000	(a)	(200,000)	
Paid-in capital in excess of par.	365,000	58,000	(a)	(58,000)	365,000
Retained earnings	213,500	168,000		(168,000)	213,500
Total liabilities & stockholders' equity .	1,209,400	650,100		(426,000)	1,433,500

* An increase in total costs and expenses and a decrease in net income.

Starr to Palm on December 31, Year 2. (The advances by Palm to Starr that were outstanding on December 31, Year 1, were repaid by Starr January 2, Year 2.)

The following aspects of the working paper for consolidated financial statements of Palm Corporation and subsidiary should be emphasized:

1 The intercompany receivable and payable, placed in adjacent columns on the same line, are offset without a formal elimination.

2 The elimination cancels all intercompany transactions and balances not dealt with by the offset technique described in **1** above.

3 The elimination cancels the subsidiary's retained earnings balance **at the beginning of the year** (the date of the business combination), so that the three basic financial statements of the two companies each may be consolidated in turn. (All financial statements of a parent company and a purchased subsidiary are consolidated subsequent to the business combination.)

4 It assumed that the fifo method is used by Starr Company to account for inventories; thus, the $25,000 difference attributable to Starr's beginning inventories is allocated to cost of goods sold.

5 Income tax effects of the elimination's increase in Starr Company's expenses are not included in the elimination. Accounting for income taxes in consolidated financial statements is considered in Chapter 9.

6 One of the effects of the elimination is to reduce the differences between the current fair values and the carrying amounts of the subsidiary's net assets, excepting land, on the business combination date. The effect of the reduction is as follows:

Aggregate difference on date of business combination (Dec. 31, Year 1)	$110,000
Less: Reduction in elimination (a) ($29,000 + $1,500)	30,500
Unamortized difference, Dec. 31, Year 2	$ 79,500

The joint effect of Palm Corporation's use of the equity method of accounting and the annual elimination will be to extinguish $64,500 of the $79,500 difference above through Palm's Investment in Starr Company Common Stock account. The $15,000 balance applicable to Starr's land will not be extinguished.

7 The parent company's use of the equity method of accounting results in the following equalities:

Parent company net income = consolidated net income
Parent company retained earnings = consolidated retained earnings

These equalities exist when the equity method of accounting is used **if there are no intercompany profits accounted for in the determination of consolidated net assets.** Intercompany profits are discussed in Chapter 8.

8 Despite the equalities indicated above, **consolidated financial statements** are superior to **parent company financial statements** for the presentation of financial position and operating results of parent and subsidiary companies. The effect of the consolidation process for Palm Corporation and subsidiary is to reclassify Palm's $29,500 share of its subsidiary's adjusted net income to the revenue and expense components of that net income. Similarly, Palm's

$505,500 investment in the subsidiary is replaced by the assets and liabilities comprising the subsidiary's net assets.

9 Purchase accounting theory requires the exclusion from consolidated retained earnings of a subsidiary's retained earnings on date of a purchase-type business combination. Palm Corporation's use of the equity method of accounting meets this requirement. Palm's ending retained earnings balance in the working paper, which is equal to consolidated retained earnings, includes Palm's $29,500 share of the subsidiary's adjusted net income for the year ended December 31, Year 2, the first year of the parent-subsidiary relationship.

Consolidated Financial Statements The consolidated income statement, statement of retained earnings, and balance sheet of Palm Corporation and subsidiary for the year ended December 31, Year 2, appear on page 247. The amounts in the consolidated financial statements are taken from the Consolidated column in the working paper on page 244.

Closing Entries After consolidated financial statements have been completed, both the parent company and its subsidiaries prepare and post closing entries, to complete the accounting cycle for the fiscal year. The subsidiary's closing entries are prepared in the usual fashion. However, the parent company's use of the equity method of accounting necessitates specialized closing entries.

The equity method of accounting ignores legal form in favor of the economic substance of the relationship between a parent company and its subsidiaries. However, state corporation laws require a careful accounting for retained earnings available for dividends. Accordingly, Palm Corporation should prepare the following closing entries on December 31, Year 2, after the consolidated financial statements have been completed:

Parent company's closing entries under the equity method of accounting for purchased subsidiary

PALM CORPORATION
General Journal

Net Sales	1,100,000	
Intercompany Investment Income	29,500	
Costs and Expenses.		1,020,000
Retained Earnings of Subsidiary		
($29,500 − $24,000)		5,500
Retained Earnings ($109,500 − $5,500)		104,000
To close revenue and expense accounts; to transfer net income legally available for dividends to retained earnings; and to segregate 100% share of adjusted net income of subsidiary not distributed as dividends by the subsidiary.		
Retained Earnings.	30,000	
Dividends		30,000
To close Dividends account.		

PALM CORPORATION AND SUBSIDIARY
Consolidated Income Statement
For Year Ended December 31, Year 2

Net sales		$1,780,000
Costs and expenses:		
Cost of goods sold	$1,179,000	
Operating expenses	232,500	
Interest expense.	49,000	
Income taxes expense	210,000	
Total costs and expenses.		1,670,500
Net income.		$ 109,500
Earnings per share of common stock (40,000 shares outstanding). . .		$2.74

PALM CORPORATION AND SUBSIDIARY
Consolidated Statement of Retained Earnings
For Year Ended December 31, Year 2

Retained earnings, beginning of year	$134,000
Add: Net income	109,500
Subtotal	$243,500
Less: Dividends ($0.75 a share)	30,000
Retained earnings, end of year	$213,500

PALM CORPORATION AND SUBSIDIARY
Consolidated Balance Sheet
December 31, Year 2

Assets

Current assets:		
Cash		$ 88,000
Inventories.		251,000
Other		219,000
Total current assets		$ 558,000
Plant assets (net)		841,000
Intangible assets:		
Goodwill	$14,500	
Patent	20,000	34,500
Total assets		$1,433,500

Liabilities & Stockholders' Equity

Liabilities:		
Income taxes payable		$ 60,000
Other		395,000
Total liabilities		$ 455,000
Stockholders' equity:		
Common stock, $10 par	$400,000	
Paid-in capital in excess of par.	365,000	
Retained earnings	213,500	978,500
Total liabilities & stockholders' equity		$1,433,500

After the foregoing closing entries have been posted, Palm Corporation's Retained Earnings and Retained Earnings of Subsidiary ledger accounts appear as follows:

Parent company's ledger accounts for retained earnings

Retained Earnings

Date	Explanation	Debit	Credit	Balance
12/31/1	Balance			134,000 cr
12/31/2	Close net income available for dividends		104,000	238,000 cr
12/31/2	Close Dividends account	30,000		208,000 cr

Retained Earnings of Subsidiary

Date	Explanation	Debit	Credit	Balance
12/31/2	Close net income not available for dividends		5,500	5,500 cr

The first closing entry excludes from Palm Corporation's retained earnings the amount of Palm's net income not available for dividends to Palm's shareholders—$5,500. This amount is computed as follows:

Adjusted net income of Starr Company recorded by Palm Corporation in Intercompany Investment Income account	$29,500
Less: Dividends declared by Starr to Palm.	24,000
Amount of Starr's adjusted net income not distributed as a dividend to Palm.	$ 5,500

Palm's Retained Earnings of Subsidiary account thus contains the amount of the purchased subsidiary's adjusted net income (less net losses) *since the date of the business combination* that has not been distributed by the subsidiary to the parent company as dividends. This amount is termed the *undistributed earnings of the subsidiary,* and is equal to the net increase in the balance of Palm's Investment in Starr Company Common Stock account (page 241) since the date of the business combination ($505,500 − $500,000 = $5,500). In addition, the total of the ending balances of Palm's Retained Earnings and Retained Earnings of Subsidiary ledger accounts is equal to consolidated retained earnings, as shown below:

Total of parent company's two account balances equals consolidated retained earnings

Balances, Dec. 31, Year 2:	
Retained earnings	$208,000
Retained earnings of subsidiary	5,500
Total (equal to consolidated retained earnings, Dec. 31, Year 2—see page 244)	$213,500

Illustration of equity method for wholly owned purchased subsidiary for second year after business combination

In this section, we continue the Palm Corporation–Starr Company example to demonstrate application of the equity method of accounting for a wholly owned purchased subsidiary for the second year following the business combination. On December 17, Year 3, Starr Company de-

Ledger accounts of parent company under the equity method of accounting for wholly owned purchased subsidiary

Investment in Starr Company Common Stock

Date	Explanation	Debit	Credit	Balance
12/31/1	Issuance of common stock in business combination	450,000		450,000 dr
12/31/1	Direct out-of-pocket costs of business combination	50,000		500,000 dr
12/20/2	Dividend declared by Starr		24,000	476,000 dr
12/31/2	Net income of Starr	60,000		536,000 dr
12/31/2	Amortization of differences between current fair values and carrying amounts of Starr's net assets		30,500	505,500 dr
12/17/3	Dividend declared by Starr		40,000	465,500 dr
12/31/3	Net income of Starr	90,000		555,500 dr
12/31/3	Amortization of differences between current fair values and carrying amounts of Starr's net assets		5,500*	550,000 dr

Intercompany Investment Income

Date	Explanation	Debit	Credit	Balance
12/31/2	Net income of Starr		60,000	60,000 cr
12/31/2	Amortization of differences between current fair values and carrying amounts of Starr's net assets	30,500		29,500 cr
12/31/2	Closing entry	29,500		-0-
12/31/3	Net income of Starr		90,000	90,000 cr
12/31/3	Amortization of differences between current fair values and carrying amounts of Starr's net assets	5,500*		84,500 cr

* Building depreciation ($30,000 ÷ 15) $2,000
  Machinery depreciation ($20,000 ÷ 10) 2,000
  Patent amortization ($5,000 ÷ 5) 1,000
  Goodwill amortization ($15,000 ÷ 30) 500
    Total amortization applicable to Year 3 . . . . $5,500

clared a dividend of $40,000, payable January 6, Year 4, to Palm Corporation, the stockholder of record December 28, Year 3. For the year ended December 31, Year 3, Starr reported net income of $90,000.

After the posting of appropriate Year 3 journal entries under the equity method of accounting, selected ledger accounts for Palm Corporation appear as shown on page 249.

Developing the Elimination The working paper elimination for December 31, Year 3, is developed in much the same way as the elimination for December 31, Year 2, as follows:

Working paper
elimination for wholly
owned purchased
subsidiary subsequent
to date of business
combination

PALM CORPORATION AND SUBSIDIARY
Working Paper Elimination
December 31, Year 3

(a) Common Stock—Starr 200,000
 Paid-in Capital in Excess of Par—Starr 58,000
 Retained Earnings—Starr ($168,000 − $5,500) 162,500
 Retained Earnings of Subsidiary—Palm 5,500
 Intercompany Investment Income—Palm 84,500
 Plant Assets (net)—Starr ($61,000 − $4,000) 57,000
 Patent—Starr ($4,000 − $1,000) 3,000
 Goodwill—Starr ($14,500 − $500) 14,000
 Cost of Goods Sold—Starr 4,000
 Operating Expenses—Starr 1,500
   Investment in Starr Company Common Stock—
    Palm 550,000
    Dividends—Starr 40,000

To carry out the following:

(1) Eliminate intercompany investment and equity accounts of subsidiary **at beginning of year,** and subsidiary dividend.

(2) Provide for Year 3 depreciation and amortization on differences between current fair values and carrying amounts of Starr's net assets as follows:

	Cost of goods sold	Operating expenses
Building depreciation	$1,000	$1,000
Machinery depreciation	2,000	
Patent amortization	1,000	
Goodwill amortization		500
Totals	$4,000	$1,500

(3) Allocate unamortized differences between combination date current fair values and carrying amounts of Starr's net assets to appropriate assets.

(Income tax effects are disregarded.)

The principal new feature of the foregoing elimination is the treatment of the Retained Earnings account of the subsidiary, Starr Company. Because consolidated retained earnings of Palm Corporation and subsidiary on December 31, Year 2, included the amount of $5,500, representing the undistributed earnings of the subsidiary for the year ended December 31, Year 2, only $162,500 ($168,000 − $5,500 = $162,500) is eliminated from the subsidiary's retained earnings on January 1, Year 3. In addition, the $5,500 balance (before the closing entry for Year 3) in the parent company's Retained Earnings of Subsidiary account is eliminated, to avoid "double counting" of the undistributed earnings of the subsidiary as of January 1, Year 3, in the consolidated financial statements of Palm Corporation and subsidiary for the year ended December 31, Year 3.

Working Paper for Consolidated Financial Statements The features of the December 31, Year 3, elimination for Palm Corporation and subsidiary described in the foregoing paragraph are illustrated in the following partial working paper for consolidated financial statements. The amounts presented for Palm Corporation are assumed for illustrative purposes.

Equity method: Wholly owned subsidiary subsequent to date of purchase-type business combination

PALM CORPORATION AND SUBSIDIARY
Partial Working Paper for Consolidated Financial Statements
For Year Ended December 31, Year 3

	Palm Corporation	Starr Company	Eliminations increase (decrease)	Consolidated
Statement of Retained Earnings				
Retained earnings beginning of year .	208,000	168,000	(a) (162,500)	213,500
Net income.	244,500	90,000	(90,000)*	244,500
Subtotal	452,500	258,000	(252,500)	458,000
Dividends.	60,000	40,000	(a) (40,000)	60,000
Retained earnings, end of year	392,500	218,000	(212,500)	398,000
Balance Sheet				
Common stock, $10 par	400,000			400,000
Common stock, $5 par.		200,000	(a) (200,000)	
Paid-in capital in excess of par.	365,000	58,000	(a) (58,000)	365,000
Retained earnings	392,500	218,000	(212,500)	398,000
Retained earnings of subsidiary	5,500		(a) (5,500)	
Total stockholders' equity.	1,163,000	476,000	(476,000)	1,163,000
Total liabilities & stockholders' equity .	x,xxx,xxx	xxx,xxx	(476,000)	x,xxx,xxx

*Decrease in intercompany investment income ($84,500), plus total increase in costs and expenses ($4,000 + $1,500), equals $90,000.

The elimination of only $162,500 of the balance of the subsidiary's beginning-of-year retained earnings results in consolidated retained earnings of $213,500 at the beginning of the year (January 1, Year 3). This amount is equal to consolidated retained earnings on December 31, Year 2 (see page 244). In addition, the total of the parent company's two retained earnings–type accounts in the working paper for consolidated financial statements ($392,500 + $5,500 = $398,000) is identical to the amount of consolidated retained earnings on December 31, Year 3.

Closing Entries The amount of the undistributed earnings of Starr Company for Year 3 is $44,500, computed as follows:

Adjusted net income of Starr Company recorded by Palm Corporation in Intercompany Investment Income account	$84,500
Less: Dividends declared by Starr to Palm.	40,000
Amount of Starr's adjusted net income not distributed as a dividend to Palm.	$44,500

In the December 31, Year 3, closing entries for Palm Corporation, $44,500 of Palm's $244,500 net income for Year 3 is closed to the Retained Earnings of Subsidiary account. The remaining $200,000 ($244,500 − $44,500 = $200,000) is closed to the Retained Earnings account, because it is available for dividends to the shareholders of Palm. Following the posting of the closing entries, the two accounts appear as follows:

Parent company's ledger accounts for retained earnings

Retained Earnings

Date	Explanation	Debit	Credit	Balance
12/31/1	Balance			134,000 cr
12/31/2	Close net income available for dividends		104,000	238,000 cr
12/31/2	Close Dividends account	30,000		208,000 cr
12/31/3	Close net income available for dividends		200,000	408,000 cr
12/31/3	Close Dividends account	60,000		348,000 cr

Retained Earnings of Subsidiary

Date	Explanation	Debit	Credit	Balance
12/31/2	Close net income not available for dividends		5,500	5,500 cr
12/31/3	Close net income not available for dividends		44,500	50,000 cr

Once again, the balance of Palm's Retained Earnings of Subsidiary account, $50,000, is equal to the net increase in the balance of Palm's Investment in Starr Company Common Stock account (page 249) since the date of the business combination ($550,000 − $500,000 = $50,000). Further, the total of the ending balances of the foregoing retained earnings accounts, $398,000 ($348,000 + $50,000 = $398,000) is equal to consolidated retained earnings of $398,000 on December 31, Year 3 (see page 251).

ACCOUNTING FOR OPERATING RESULTS OF PARTIALLY OWNED PURCHASED SUBSIDIARIES

Accounting for the operating results of a partially owned purchased subsidiary requires the computation of the minority interest in net income or net losses of the subsidiary. Thus, under the parent company theory of consolidated financial statements, the consolidated income statement of a parent company and its partially owned purchased subsidiary includes an expense, minority interest in net income (or loss) of subsidiary. The minority interest in net assets of the subsidiary is included among liabilities in the consolidated balance sheet.

Illustration of equity method for partially owned purchased subsidiary for first year after business combination

The Post Corporation–Sage Company consolidated entity described in Chapter 5 (pages 204 and 205) is used in this section to illustrate the equity method of accounting for the operating results of a partially owned purchased subsidiary. Post owns 95% of the outstanding common stock of Sage.

Assume that Sage Company on November 24, Year 2, declared a $1 a share dividend, payable December 16, Year 2, to shareholders of record December 1, Year 2, and that Sage reported net income of $90,000 for the year ended December 31, Year 2.

The journal entries at the top of page 254 record the above dividend in Sage's accounting records. The journal entries in the middle of page 254 are required in the accounting records of Post Corporation.

As pointed out on page 239, a purchase-type business combination involves a restatement of net asset values of the subsidiary. Sage Company's reported net income of $90,000 does not reflect cost expirations attributable to Sage's restated net asset values, **because the restatements were not recorded in Sage's accounting records.** Consequently, the amortization of the $246,000 difference between the current fair values of Sage's identifiable net assets on the date of the business combination and the carrying amounts of those net assets must be accounted for by Post Corporation. Assume, as in Chapter 5 (page 207), that the difference was allocable to Sage's identifiable assets as shown at the bottom of page 254.

Partially owned subsidiary's journal entries for declaration and payment of dividend

Year 2

Nov. 24 Dividends (40,000 × $1).   40,000
                    Dividends Payable ($40,000 × 0.05)   2,000
                    Intercompany Dividends Payable
                       ($40,000 × 0.95)   38,000
              To record declaration of dividend payable Dec. 16,
              Year 2, to stockholders of record Dec. 1, Year 2.

Dec. 16 Dividends Payable   2,000
              Intercompany Dividends Payable   38,000
                    Cash.   40,000
              To record payment of dividend declared Nov. 24,
              Year 2, to stockholders of record Dec. 1, Year 2.

Parent company's equity-method journal entries to record operating results of partially owned purchased subsidiary

POST CORPORATION
General Journal

Year 2

Nov. 24 Intercompany Dividends Receivable.   38,000
                    Investment in Sage Company Common Stock .   38,000
              To record dividend declared by Sage Company, pay-
              able Dec. 16, Year 2, to stockholders of record Dec. 1,
              Year 2.

Dec. 16 Cash   38,000
                    Intercompany Dividends Receivable.   38,000
              To record receipt of dividend from Sage Company.

       31 Investment in Sage Company Common Stock
              ($90,000 × 0.95)   85,500
                    Intercompany Investment Income   85,500
              To record 95% of net income of Sage Company for the
              year ended Dec. 31, Year 2. (Income tax effects are
              disregarded.)

Differences between current fair value and carrying amounts of partially owned purchased subsidiary's identifiable net assets on date of business combination

Inventories.		$ 26,000
Plant assets (net):		
Land	$60,000	
Building (economic life 20 years)	80,000	
Machinery (economic life 5 years).	50,000	190,000
Leasehold (economic life 6 years)		30,000
Total		$246,000

In addition, Post acquired in the business combination goodwill (to be amortized over 40 years) attributable to Sage in the amount of $38,000, computed as follows:

<table>
<tr><td style="width:20%">**Computation of goodwill acquired by combinor**</td><td>Cost of Post Corporation's 95% interest in Sage Company . . . .</td><td>$1,192,250</td></tr>
<tr><td></td><td>Less: 95% of $1,215,000 aggregate current fair values of Sage's identifiable net assets. . . . .</td><td>1,154,250</td></tr>
<tr><td></td><td>Goodwill acquired by Post (to be amortized over 40 years) . . . .</td><td>$ 38,000</td></tr>
</table>

Post Corporation prepares the following additional journal entry on December 31, Year 2, under the equity method of accounting to reflect the effects of the differences between current fair values and carrying amounts of the partially owned subsidiary's identifiable net assets:

<table>
<tr><td style="width:20%">**Parent company's equity-method journal entry to record amortization of partially owned purchased subsidiary's identifiable net assets**</td><td colspan="2">Intercompany Investment Income . . . . 42,750</td></tr>
<tr><td></td><td colspan="2">   Investment in Sage Company Common Stock. . . . . . .   42,750</td></tr>
<tr><td></td><td colspan="2">To amortize differences between current fair values and carrying amounts of Sage Company's identifiable net assets on December 31, Year 1, as follows:</td></tr>
<tr><td></td><td>Inventories—to cost of good sold . . . .</td><td>$26,000</td></tr>
<tr><td></td><td>Building—depreciation ($80,000 ÷ 20). . . . .</td><td>4,000</td></tr>
<tr><td></td><td>Machinery—depreciation ($50,000 ÷ 5) . . . .</td><td>10,000</td></tr>
<tr><td></td><td>Leasehold—amortization ($30,000 ÷ 6) . . . .</td><td>5,000</td></tr>
<tr><td></td><td>Total difference applicable to Year 7 . . . .</td><td>$45,000</td></tr>
<tr><td></td><td>Amortization for Year 7: $45,000 × 0.95 . . . .</td><td>$42,750</td></tr>
<tr><td></td><td colspan="2">(Income tax effects are disregarded.)</td></tr>
</table>

Next, Post prepares the following journal entry on December 31, Year 2, to record the amortization of goodwill acquired by Post in the business combination with Sage:

<table>
<tr><td style="width:20%">**Parent company's equity-method journal entry to record amortization of goodwill**</td><td colspan="2">Amortization Expense ($38,000 ÷ 40) . . . . 950</td></tr>
<tr><td></td><td colspan="2">   Investment in Sage Company Common Stock . . . .   950</td></tr>
<tr><td></td><td colspan="2">To amortize goodwill acquired in business combination with partially owned purchased subsidiary over an economic life of 40 years.</td></tr>
</table>

Note that the amortization of the goodwill is debited to Amortization Expense, not to Intercompany Investment Income. The reason for this treatment is explained on page 256.

After the preceding journal entries are posted, Post Corporation's Investment in Sage Company Common Stock and Intercompany Investment Income ledger accounts appear as follows:

Ledger accounts of parent company under equity method of accounting for partially owned purchased subsidiary

Investment in Sage Company Common Stock

Date	Explanation	Debit	Credit	Balance
12/31/1	Issuance of common stock in business combination	1,140,000		1,140,000 dr
12/31/1	Out-of-pocket costs of business combination	52,250		1,192,250 dr
11/24/2	Dividend declared by Sage		38,000	1,154,250 dr
12/31/2	Net income of Sage	85,500		1,239,750 dr
12/31/2	Amortization of differences between current fair values and carrying amounts of Sage's identifiable net assets		42,750	1,197,000 dr
12/31/2	Amortization of goodwill		950	1,196,050 dr

Intercompany Investment Income

Date	Explanation	Debit	Credit	Balance
12/31/2	Net income of Sage		85,500	85,500 cr
12/31/2	Amortization of differences between current fair values and carrying amounts of Sage's identifiable net assets	42,750		42,750 cr

The $42,750 balance in Post Corporation's Intercompany Investment Income account represents 95% of the $45,000 adjusted net income ($90,000 − $45,000 = $45,000) of Sage Company for the year ended December 31, Year 2.

Amortization of Goodwill Attributable to Partially Owned Subsidiary As explained in Chapter 5 (page 208), goodwill in a business combination involving a partially owned subsidiary is attributed to the *parent company* rather than the *subsidiary* under the widely used accounting practice illustrated in this text. Consequently, amortization of the goodwill is debited to the Amortization Expense account of the parent company, with an offsetting credit to the investment account. Thus, this treatment differs from the amortization of goodwill attributable to a wholly owned subsidiary. As illustrated on page 240, amortization of a wholly owned subsidiary's goodwill is debited to the parent company's Intercompany Investment Income account.

Developing the Eliminations Post Corporation's use of the equity method of accounting for its investment in Sage Company resulted in a balance in the investment account that is a mixture of three components: (1) the carrying amount of Sage's identifiable net assets, (2) the "current fair value excess," which is attributable to Sage's **identifiable** net assets, and (3) the goodwill acquired by Post in the business combination with Sage. These components are analyzed below:

POST CORPORATION
Analysis of Investment in Sage Company Common Stock Account
For Year Ended December 31, Year 2

	Carrying amount	Current fair value excess	Goodwill	Total	
Beginning balances. .	$920,550	$233,700	$38,000	$1,192,250	
Net income of Sage. .	85,500			85,500	⎫
Amortization of differences between current fair values and carrying amounts of Sage's identifiable net assets		(42,750)		(42,750)	Intercompany investment income, $42,750
Amortization of goodwill			(950)	(950)	
Dividend declared by Sage	(38,000)			(38,000)	
Ending balances. . . .	$968,050	$190,950	$37,050	$1,196,050	

The minority interest in Sage's net assets may be analyzed similarly, except there is no goodwill attributable to the minority interest.

POST CORPORATION
Analysis of Minority Interest in Net Assets of Sage Company
For Year Ended December 31, Year 2

	Carrying amount	Current fair value excess	Total	
Beginning balances	$48,450	$12,300	$60,750	
Net income of Sage	4,500		4,500	⎫ Minority interest in net income of subsidiary, $2,250
Amortization of differences between current fair values and carrying amounts of Sage's identifiable net assets		(2,250)	(2,250)	
Dividend declared by Sage	(2,000)		(2,000)	
Ending balances	$50,950	$10,050	$61,000	

The $1,019,000 ($968,050 + $50,950 = $1,019,000) total of the ending balances of the Carrying Amount columns of the two foregoing analyses agrees with the total stockholders' equity of Sage Company on December 31, Year 2 (see Balance Sheet section of working paper for consolidated financial statements on page 260), as follows:

Subsidiary's stockholders' equity at end of Year 2

Common stock, $10 par	$ 400,000
Paid-in capital in excess of par.	235,000
Retained earnings.	384,000
Total stockholders' equity.	$1,019,000

The $201,000 ($190,950 + $10,050 = $201,000) total of the ending balances of the Current Fair Value Excess columns of the two analyses agrees with the December 31, Year 2, total of the unamortized balances for each of the respective identifiable assets of Sage Company, as shown below:

Unamortized differences between current fair values and carrying amounts of partially owned purchased subsidiary's identifiable assets one year subsequent to business combination

	Balances, Dec. 31, Year 1 (page 254)	Amortization for Year 2 (page 255)	Balances, Dec. 31, Year 2
Inventories.	$ 26,000	$(26,000)	
Plant assets (net):			
Land	$ 60,000		$ 60,000
Building	80,000	$ (4,000)	76,000
Machinery	50,000	(10,000)	40,000
Total plant assets	$190,000	$(14,000)	$176,000
Leasehold	$ 30,000	$ (5,000)	$ 25,000
Totals	$246,000	$(45,000)	$201,000

Assuming that Sage Company allocates machinery depreciation and leasehold amortization entirely to cost of goods sold, and building depreciation 50% each to cost of goods sold and operating expenses, the working paper eliminations for Post Corporation and subsidiary on December 31, Year 2, are as shown on page 259.

Working Paper for Consolidated Financial Statements The working paper for consolidated financial statements for Post Corporation and subsidiary for the year ended December 31, Year 2, is shown on page 260.

The following aspects of the working paper for consolidated financial statements of Post Corporation and subsidiary should be emphasized:

1 Income tax effects of the increase in Sage Company's costs and expenses are not included in elimination (a). Income tax accounting in consolidated financial statements is considered in Chapter 9.

POST CORPORATION AND SUBSIDIARY
Working Paper Eliminations
December 31, Year 2

(a) Common Stock—Sage.	400,000	
Paid-in Capital in Excess of Par—Sage.	235,000	
Retained Earnings—Sage.	334,000	
Intercompany Investment Income—Post	42,750	
Plant Assets (net)—Sage ($190,000 − $14,000)	176,000	
Leasehold—Sage ($30,000 − $5,000)	25,000	
Goodwill—Post ($38,000 − $950)	37,050	
Cost of Goods Sold—Sage	43,000	
Operating Expenses—Sage	2,000	
Investment in Sage Company Common Stock—		
Post.		1,196,050
Dividends—Sage		40,000
Minority Interest in Net Assets of Subsidiary		
($60,750 − $2,000)		58,750

To carry out the following:

(1) Eliminate intercompany investment and equity accounts of subsidiary **at beginning of year,** and subsidiary dividends.

(2) Provide for Year 2 depreciation and amortization on differences between current fair values and carrying amounts of Sage's identifiable net assets as follows:

	Cost of goods sold	Operating expenses
Inventories sold	$26,000	
Building depreciation. . . .	2,000	$2,000
Machinery depreciation . .	10,000	
Leasehold amortization . .	5,000	
Totals	$43,000	$2,000

(3) Allocate unamortized differences between combination date current fair values and carrying amounts to appropriate assets.

(4) Establish minority interest in net assets of subsidiary at beginning of year ($60,750), less minority share of dividends declared by subsidiary during year ($40,000 × 0.05 = $2,000).

(Income tax effects are disregarded.)

(b) Minority Interest in Net Income of Subsidiary	2,250	
Minority Interest in Net Assets of Subsidiary . . .		2,250

To establish minority interest in subsidiary's adjusted net income for Year 2 as follows:

Net income of subsidiary	$90,000
Net reduction in elimination (a)	(45,000)
Adjusted net income of subsidiary	$45,000
Minority share: $45,000 × 0.05	$ 2,250

Equity method: Partially owned subsidiary subsequent to date of purchase-type business combination

POST CORPORATION AND SUBSIDIARY
Working Paper for Consolidated Financial Statements
For Year Ended December 31, Year 2

	Post Corporation	Sage Company	Eliminations increase (decrease)		Consolidated
Income Statement					
Revenue					
Net sales	5,611,000	1,089,000			6,700,000
Intercompany investment income	42,750		(a)	(42,750)	
Total revenue	5,653,750	1,089,000		(42,750)	6,700,000
Costs and expenses					
Cost of goods sold	3,925,000	700,000	(a)	43,000	4,668,000
Operating expenses	556,950*	129,000	(a)	2,000	687,950
Interest and income taxes expense	710,000	170,000			880,000
Minority interest in net income of subsidiary			(b)	2,250	2,250
Total costs and expenses	5,191,950	999,000		47,250†	6,238,200
Net Income	461,800	90,000		(90,000)	461,800
Statement of Retained Earnings					
Retained earnings, beginning of year	1,050,000	334,000	(a)	(334,000)	1,050,000
Net income	461,800	90,000		(90,000)	461,800
Subtotal	1,511,800	424,000		(424,000)	1,511,800
Dividends	158,550	40,000	(a)	(40,000)	158,550
Retained earnings, end of year	1,353,250	384,000		(384,000)	1,353,250
Balance Sheet					
Assets					
Inventories	861,000	439,000			1,300,000
Other current assets	639,000	371,000			1,010,000
Investment in Sage Company common stock .	1,196,050		(a)	(1,196,050)	
Plant assets (net)	3,600,000	1,150,000	(a)	176,000	4,926,000
Leasehold			(a)	25,000	25,000
Goodwill	95,000		(a)	37,050	132,050
Total assets	6,391,050	1,960,000		(958,000)	7,393,050
Liabilities & Stockholders' Equity					
Liabilities	2,420,550	941,000			3,361,550
Minority interest in net assets of			(a)	58,750	
subsidiary			(b)	2,250	61,000
Common stock, $1 par	1,057,000				1,057,000
Common stock, $10 par		400,000	(a)	(400,000)	
Paid-in capital in excess of par	1,560,250	235,000	(a)	(235,000)	1,560,250
Retained earnings	1,353,250	384,000		(384,000)	1,353,250
Total liabilities & stockholders' equity	6,391,050	1,960,000		(958,000)	7,393,050

* Includes $950 amortization of goodwill.
† An increase in total costs and expenses and a decrease in net income.

2 Elimination (a) cancels Sage's retained earnings *at the beginning of the year.* This step is essential for the preparation of all three basic consolidating financial statements.

3 The parent company's use of the equity method of accounting results in the following equalities:

> **Parent company net income = consolidated net income**
> **Parent company retained earnings = consolidated retained earnings**

These equalities exist in the equity method of accounting if there are no intercompany profits eliminated for the determination of consolidated net assets. Intercompany profits are discussed in Chapter 8.

4 One of the effects of elimination (a) is to reduce the differences between the current fair values of the subsidiary's identifiable net assets on the business combination date and their carrying amounts on that date. The effect of the reduction is as follows:

> *Aggregate difference on date of business combination*
> *(Dec 31, Year 1). . . . .* $246,000
> *Less: Reduction in elimination (a) ($43,000 + $2,000) . . . .* 45,000
> *Unamortized difference, Dec. 31, Year 2 . . . .* $201,000

The joint effect of Post's use of the equity method of accounting and the annual eliminations will be to extinguish $141,000 of the remaining $201,000 difference through Post's Investment in Sage Company Common Stock account. The $60,000 balance applicable to Sage's land will not be extinguished.

5 The minority interest in net assets of subsidiary on December 31, Year 2, may be verified as follows:

> *Sage Company's total stockholders' equity, Dec. 31, Year 2 . . . .* $1,019,000
> *Add: Unamortized difference computed in 4, above . . . .* 201,000
> *Sage's adjusted stockholders' equity, Dec. 31, Year 2 . . . .* $1,220,000
> *Minority interest in net assets of subsidiary ($1,220,000 × 0.05) . . . . .* $ 61,000

6 The minority interest in net income of subsidiary is recognized in elimination (b) in the amount of $2,250 (5% of the adjusted net income of Sage Company) as an increase in minority interest in net assets of subsidiary and a decrease in the amount of consolidated net income.

Consolidated Financial Statements The consolidated income statement, statement of retained earnings, and balance sheet of Post Corporation and subsidiary for the year ended December 31, Year 2, appear on page 262. The amounts in the consolidated financial statements are taken from the Consolidated column in the working paper on page 260.

POST CORPORATION AND SUBSIDIARY
Consolidated Income Statement
For Year Ended December 31, Year 2

Net sales		$6,700,000
Costs and expenses:		
Cost of goods sold	$4,668,000	
Operating expenses	687,950	
Interest and income taxes expense	880,000	
Minority interest in net income of subsidiary.	2,250	
Total costs and expenses.		6,238,200
Net income.		$ 461,800
Earnings per share of common stock (1,057,000 shares outstanding).		$0.44

POST CORPORATION AND SUBSIDIARY
Consolidated Statement of Retained Earnings
For Year Ended December 31, Year 2

Retained earnings, beginning of year	$1,050,000
Add: Net income	461,800
Subtotal	$1,511,800
Less: Dividends ($0.15 a share).	158,550
Retained earnings, end of year	$1,353,250

POST CORPORATION AND SUBSIDIARY
Consolidated Balance Sheet
December 31, Year 2

Assets

Current assets:		
Inventories.		$1,300,000
Other		1,010,000
Total current assets		$2,310,000
Plant assets (net)		4,926,000
Intangible assets:		
Goodwill	$132,050	
Leasehold	25,000	157,050
Total assets		$7,393,050

Liabilities & Stockholders' Equity

Liabilities:		
Other than minority interest		$3,361,550
Minority interest in net assets of subsidiary		61,000
Total liabilities		$3,422,550
Stockholders' equity:		
Common stock, $1 par	$1,057,000	
Paid-in capital in excess of par.	1,560,250	
Retained earnings.	1,353,250	3,970,500
Total liabilities & stockholders' equity		$7,393,050

Closing Entries As indicated in a previous section of this chapter, legal considerations necessitate the following closing entries for Post Corporation on December 31, Year 2:

Parent company's closing entries under the equity method of accounting for purchased subsidiary

POST CORPORATION General Journal		
Net Sales	5,611,000	
Intercompany Investment Income	42,750	
Costs and Expenses.		5,191,950
Retained Earnings of Subsidiary [($45,000 −		
$40,000) × 0.95)]		4,750
Retained Earnings ($461,800 − $4,750)		457,050
To close revenue and expense accounts; to transfer net income legally available for dividends to retained earnings; and to segregate 95% share of adjusted net income of subsidiary not distributed as dividends.		
Retained Earnings.	158,550	
Dividends		158,550
To close Dividends account.		

After the foregoing closing entries have been posted, Post's Retained Earnings and Retained Earnings of Subsidiary ledger accounts appear as follows:

Parent company's ledger accounts for retained earnings

Retained Earnings

Date	Explanation	Debit	Credit	Balance
12/31/1	Balance			1,050,000 cr
12/31/2	Close net income available for dividends		457,050	1,507,050 cr
12/31/2	Close Dividends account	158,550		1,348,500 cr

Retained Earnings of Subsidiary

Date	Explanation	Debit	Credit	Balance
12/31/2	Close net income not available for dividends		4,750	4,750 cr

The $4,750 balance of Post's Retained Earnings of Subsidiary ledger account represents Post's share of the undistributed earnings of Sage Company for the year ended December 31, Year 2. The undistributed earnings of the subsidiary may be reconciled to the increase in Post's investment account balance as follows:

Undistributed earnings of subsidiary, year ended December 31, Year 2 . . $4,750
Less: Amortization of goodwill acquired in business combination (page 255)   950
Increase in balance of Investment in Sage Company Common Stock
    account during Year 2 ($1,196,050 − $1,192,250) $3,800

In addition, the total of the ending balances of Post's Retained Earnings and Retained Earnings of Subsidiary ledger accounts is equal to consolidated retained earnings, as shown below:

Total of parent
company's two account
balances equals
consolidated retained
earnings

Balances, Dec. 31, Year 2:
    Retained earnings $1,348,500
    Retained earnings of subsidiary   4,750
        Total (equal to consolidated retained earnings, Dec. 31, Year 2—
        see page 260) $1,353,250

Illustration of equity method for partially owned purchased subsidiary for second year after business combination

In this section, we continue the Post Corporation–Sage Company example to demonstrate application of the equity method of accounting for a partially owned purchased subsidiary for the second year following the business combination. On November 22, Year 3, Sage Company declared a dividend of $50,000, payable December 17, Year 3, to stockholders of record December 1, Year 3. For the year ended December 31, Year 3, Sage reported net income of $105,000. Post's share of the dividend was $47,500 ($50,000 × 0.95 = $47,500), and Post's share of Sage's reported net income was $99,750 ($105,000 × 0.95 = $99,750).

After the posting of appropriate Year 3 journal entries under the equity method of accounting, selected ledger accounts for Post Corporation appear as shown on page 265.

Developing the Eliminations   The working paper eliminations for December 31, Year 3, are developed in much the same way as for the eliminations for December 31, Year 2, as illustrated on page 266.

Because consolidated retained earnings of Post Corporation and subsidiary on December 31, Year 2, included the amount of $4,750, representing the parent company's share of the undistributed earnings of the subsidiary for the year ended December 31, Year 2, only $379,250 ($384,000 − $4,750 = $379,250) is eliminated from the subsidiary's retained earnings on January 1, Year 3. In addition, the $4,750 balance

Ledger accounts of parent company under equity method of accounting for partially owned purchased subsidiary

Investment in Sage Company Common Stock

Date	Explanation	Debit	Credit	Balance
12/31/1	Issuance of common stock in business combination	1,140,000		1,140,000 dr
12/31/1	Direct out-of-pocket costs of business combination	52,250		1,192,250 dr
11/24/2	Dividend declared by Sage		38,000	1,154,250 dr
12/31/2	Net income of Sage	85,500		1,239,750 dr
12/31/2	Amortization of differences between current fair values and carrying amounts of Sage's identifiable net assets		42,750	1,197,000 dr
12/31/2	Amortization of goodwill		950	1,196,050 dr
11/22/3	Dividend declared by Sage		47,500	1,148,550 dr
12/31/3	Net income of Sage	99,750		1,248,300 dr
12/31/3	Amortization of differences between current fair values and carrying amounts of Sage's identifiable net assets		18,050*	1,230,250 dr
12/31/3	Amortization of goodwill		950	1,229,300 dr

Intercompany Investment Income

Date	Explanation	Debit	Credit	Balance
12/31/2	Net income of Sage		85,500	85,500 cr
12/31/2	Amortization of differences between current fair values and carrying amounts of Sage's identifiable net assets	42,750		42,750 cr
12/31/2	Closing entry	42,750		-0-
12/31/3	Net income of Sage		99,750	99,750 cr
12/31/3	Amortization of differences between current fair values and carrying amounts of Sage's identifiable net assets	18,050*		81,700 cr

```
* Building depreciation ($80,000 ÷ 20) . . . . . . . . . . . . . . .   $ 4,000
  Machinery depreciation ($50,000 ÷ 5) . . . . . . . . . . . . . .      10,000
  Leasehold amortization (30,000 ÷ 6) . . . . . . . . . . . . . . .      5,000
  Total amortization applicable to Year 3 . . . . . . . . . . . . .    $19,000
  Post Corporation's share ($19,000 × 0.95) . . . . . . . . . . . .    $18,050
```

(before the closing entry for Year 3) in the parent company's Retained Earnings of Subsidiary account is eliminated, to avoid "double counting" of the undistributed earnings of the subsidiary as of January 1, Year 3, in the consolidated financial statements of Post Corporation and subsidiary for the year ended December 31, Year 3.

**Working paper
eliminations for partially
owned purchased
subsidiary subsequent
to date of business
combination**

POST CORPORATION AND SUBSIDIARY
Working Paper Eliminations
December 31, Year 3

(a)	Common Stock—Sage.	400,000
	Paid-in Capital in Excess of Par—Sage.	235,000
	Retained Earnings—Sage ($384,000 − $4,750)	379,250
	Retained Earnings of Subsidiary—Post.	4,750
	Intercompany Investment Income—Post	81,700
	Plant Assets (net)—Sage ($176,000 − $14,000)	162,000
	Leasehold—Sage ($25,000 − $5,000)	20,000
	Goodwill—Post ($37,050 − $950)	36,100
	Cost of Goods Sold—Sage	17,000
	Operating Expenses—Sage.	2,000

	Investment in Sage Company Common Stock—	
	Post	1,229,300
	Dividends—Sage	50,000
	Minority Interest in Net Assets of Subsidiary	
	($61,000 − $2,500).	58,500

To carry out the following:

(1) Eliminate intercompany investment and equity accounts of subsidiary **at beginning of year,** and subsidiary dividend.

(2) Provide for Year 3 depreciation and amortization on differences between current fair values and carrying amounts of Sage's identifiable net assets as follows:

	Cost of goods sold	Operating expenses
Building depreciation	$ 2,000	$2,000
Machinery depreciation . . .	10,000	
Leasehold amortization . . .	5,000	
Totals.	$17,000	$2,000

(3) Allocate unamortized differences between combination date current fair values and carrying amounts to appropriate assets.

(4) Establish minority interest in net assets of subsidiary at beginning of year ($61,000), less minority share of dividends declared by subsidiary during year ($50,000 × 0.05 = $2,500).

(Income tax effects are disregarded.)

(b)	Minority Interest in Net Income of Subsidiary	4,300	
	Minority Interest in Net Assets of Subsidiary . . .		4,300

To establish minority interest in subsidiary's adjusted net income for Year 3 as follows:

Net income of subsidiary	$105,000
Net reduction in elimination (a)	(19,000)
Adjusted net income of subsidiary	$ 86,000
Minority share: $86,000 × 0.05.	$ 4,300

Working Paper for Consolidated Financial Statements The aspects of the December 31, Year 3, eliminations for Post Corporation and subsidiary described in the foregoing paragraph are illustrated in the following partial working paper for consolidated financial statements. The amounts presented for Post Corporation are assumed.

Equity method: Partially owned subsidiary subsequent to date of purchase-type business combination

POST CORPORATION AND SUBSIDIARY
Partial Working Paper for Consolidated Financial Statements
For Year Ended December 31, Year 3

	Post Corporation	Sage Company	Eliminations increase (decrease)		Consolidated
Statement of Retained Earnings					
Retained earnings, beginning of year . .	1,348,500	384,000	(a)	(379,250)	1,353,250
Net income	352,600	105,000		(105,000)*	352,600
Subtotal	1,701,100	489,000		(484,250)	1,705,850
Dividends	158,550	50,000	(a)	(50,000)	158,550
Retained earnings, end of year	1,542,550	439,000		(434,250)	1,547,300
Balance Sheet					
Minority interest in net assets of			(a)	58,500	
subsidiary			(b)	4,300	62,800
Total liabilities	x,xxx,xxx	xxx,xxx		62,800	xxx,xxx
Common stock, $1 par	1,057,000				1,057,000
Common stock, $10 par.		400,000	(a)	(400,000)	
Paid-in capital in excess of par	1,560,250	235,000	(a)	(235,000)	1,560,250
Retained earnings	1,542,550	439,000		(434,250)	1,547,300
Retained earnings of subsidiary	4,750		(a)	(4,750)	
Total stockholders' equity	4,164,550	1,074,000		(1,074,000)	4,164,550
Total liabilities & stockholders' equity .	x,xxx,xxx	x,xxx,xxx		(1,011,200)	x,xxx,xxx

* Decrease in intercompany investment income ($81,700), plus total increase in costs and expenses ($17,000 + $2,000 + $4,300), equals $105,000.

The December 31, Year 3, balance of the minority interest in net assets of subsidiary may be verified as follows:

Proof of minority interest in net assets of subsidiary	Sage Company's total stockholders' equity, Dec. 31, Year 3 . . . . . . $1,074,000
	Add: Unamortized difference between combination date current fair values and carrying amounts of Sage's identifiable net assets ($162,000 + $20,000) 182,000
	Sage's adjusted stockholders' equity, Dec. 31, Year 3 . . . . $1,256,000
	Minority interest in net assets of subsidiary ($1,256,000 × 0.05) . . . . $ 62,800

Closing Entries Post Corporation's share of the undistributed earnings of Sage Company for Year 3 is $34,200, computed as follows:

<table>
<tr><td rowspan="4" align="left">Parent company's share
of undistributed
earnings of subsidiary</td><td>Adjusted net income of Sage Company recorded by Post Corporation in</td><td></td></tr>
<tr><td>Intercompany Investment Income account . . . .</td><td>$81,700</td></tr>
<tr><td>Less: Post's share of dividends declared by Sage ($50,000 × 0.95) . . . .</td><td>47,500</td></tr>
<tr><td>Post's share of amount of Sage's adjusted net income not distributed as
dividends . . . .</td><td>$34,200</td></tr>
</table>

In the December 31, Year 3, closing entries for Post Corporation, $34,200 of Post's net income for Year 3 is closed to the Retained Earnings of Subsidiary account. The remaining $318,400 ($352,600 − $34,200 = $318,400) is closed to the Retained Earnings account, because it is available for dividends to the shareholders of Post. Following the posting of the closing entries, the two ledger accounts appear as follows:

Parent company's ledger accounts for retained earnings

Retained Earnings

Date	Explanation	Debit	Credit	Balance
12/31/1	Balance			1,050,000 cr
12/31/2	Close net income available for dividends		457,050	1,507,050 cr
12/31/2	Close Dividends account	158,550		1,348,500 cr
12/31/3	Close net income available for dividends		318,400	1,666,900 cr
12/31/3	Close Dividends account	158,550		1,508,350 cr

Retained Earnings of Subsidiary

Date	Explanation	Debit	Credit	Balance
12/31/2	Close net income not available for dividends		4,750	4,750 cr
12/31/3	Close net income not available for dividends		34,200	38,950 cr

The $38,950 balance of Post's Retained Earnings of Subsidiary account represents Post's share of the undistributed earnings of Sage Company since the date of the business combination. The undistributed earnings of the subsidiary may be reconciled to the increase in Post's investment account balance as follows:

Reconciliation of undistributed earnings of subsidiary

Undistributed earnings of subsidiary	*$38,950*
Less: Amortization of goodwill acquired in business combination	
($950 × 2)	*1,900*
Increase in balance of Investment in Sage Company Common Stock account since date of business combination ($1,229,300 − $1,192,250) . .	*$37,050*

In addition, the total of the ending balances of Post's Retained Earnings and Retained Earnings of Subsidiary ledger accounts is equal to consolidated retained earnings, as shown below:

Total of parent company's two account balances equals consolidated retained earnings

Balances, Dec. 31, Year 3:	
Retained earnings	*$1,508,350*
Retained earnings of subsidiary	*38,950*
Total (equal to consolidated retained earnings, Dec. 31, Year 3— see page 267)	*$1,547,300*

Concluding comments on equity method of accounting

In today's accounting environment, the equity method of accounting for a subsidiary's operations is preferable to the cost method (illustrated in the Appendix on pages 270 to 276) for the following reasons:

1 The equity method emphasizes **economic substance** of the parent company–subsidiary relationship, while the cost method emphasizes **legal form.** More and more, modern accounting stresses substance over form.

2 The equity method permits the use of **parent company journal entries** to reflect many items that must be included in **working paper eliminations** in the cost method (see pages 272 and 273). Formal journal entries in the accounting records provide a better record than do working paper eliminations.

3 The equity method facilitates issuance of separate financial statements for the parent company, if required by Securities and Exchange Commission regulations or other considerations. Generally accepted accounting principles require the equity method of accounting for unconsolidated subsidiaries in separate parent-company financial statements.[1]

4 Except when intercompany profits (discussed in Chapter 8) exist in assets or liabilities to be consolidated, the parent company's net income and combined retained earnings account balances are identical in the equity method to the related consolidated amounts. Thus, the equity method provides a useful self-checking technique.

5 As demonstrated in Chapter 7, the cost method is not considered appropriate for accounting for a pooled subsidiary's operations.

For these reasons, the equity method of accounting for a subsidiary's operations is emphasized in the following chapters.

---

[1] *APB Opinion No. 18,* "The Equity Method of Accounting for Investments in Common Stock," AICPA (New York: 1971), pp. 353–354.

APPENDIX: COST METHOD FOR
PARTIALLY OWNED PURCHASED SUBSIDIARY

To illustrate the cost method of accounting for the operating results of a purchased subsidiary, we return to the Post Corporation–Sage Company business combination, which involves a partially owned subsidiary. Post acquired 95% of Sage's outstanding common stock at a total cost (including out-of-pocket costs) of $1,192,250 on December 31, Year 1. Sage's operations for the first two years following the business combination included the following:

Year ended Dec. 31,	Net income	Dividends declared
Year 2	$ 90,000	$40,000
Year 3	105,000	50,000

Illustration of cost method for partially owned
purchased subsidiary for first year after business combination

If Post Corporation used the cost method, rather than the equity method, of accounting for Sage Company's operating results for the year ended December 31, Year 2, Post would not prepare journal entries to reflect Sage's net income for the year. Post would record Sage's dividend declaration as follows on November 24, Year 2:

<table>
<tr><td>Parent company's cost-method journal entry to record dividend declared by partially owned purchased subsidiary</td><td>Intercompany Dividends Receivable 38,000
Intercompany Dividends Revenue 38,000
To record dividend declared by Sage Company, payable Dec. 16, Year 2, to stockholders of record Dec. 1, Year 2. (Income tax effects are disregarded.)</td></tr>
</table>

Post's journal entry for receipt of the dividend from Sage would be the same under the cost method as under the equity method of accounting illustrated previously in this chapter.

Working Paper for Consolidated Financial Statements The working paper for consolidated financial statements and the related working paper eliminations for Post Corporation and subsidiary for the year ended December 31, Year 2, appear on pages 271 to 273.

Cost method: Partially owned subsidiary subsequent to date of purchase-type business combination

POST CORPORATION AND SUBSIDIARY
Working Paper for Consolidated Financial Statements
For Year Ended December 31, Year 2

	Post Corporation	Sage Company	Eliminations increase (decrease)		Consolidated
Income Statement					
Revenue					
Net sales.	5,611,000	1,089,000			6,700,000
Intercompany dividends revenue	38,000		(c)	(38,000)	
Total revenue.	5,649,000	1,089,000		(38,000)	6,700,000
Costs and expenses					
Cost of goods sold.	3,925,000	700,000	(b)	43,000	4,668,000
Operating expenses	556,000	129,000	(b)	2,950	687,950
Interest and income taxes expense	710,000	170,000			880,000
Minority interest in net income of subsidiary .			(d)	2,250	2,250
Total costs and expenses.	5,191,000	999,000		48,200*	6,238,200
Net income.	458,000	90,000		(86,200)	461,800
Statement of Retained Earnings					
Retained earnings, beginning of year	1,050,000	334,000	(a)	(334,000)	1,050,000
Net income.	458,000	90,000		(86,200)	461,800
Subtotal	1,508,000	424,000		(420,200)	1,511,800
Dividends.	158,550	40,000	(c)	(40,000)	158,550
Retained earnings, end of year	1,349,450	384,000		(380,200)	1,353,250
Balance Sheet					
Assets					
Inventories	861,000	439,000	(a)	26,000	1,300,000
			(b)	(26,000)	
Other current assets	639,000	371,000			1,010,000
Investment in Sage Company common stock . .	1,192,250		(a)	(1,192,250)	
Plant assets (net)	3,600,000	1,150,000	(a)	190,000	4,926,000
			(b)	(14,000)	
Leasehold			(a)	30,000	25,000
			(b)	(5,000)	
Goodwill	95,000		(a)	38,000	132,050
			(b)	(950)	
Total assets	6,387,250	1,960,000		(954,200)	7,393,050
Liabilities & Stockholders' Equity					
Liabilities.	2,420,550	941,000			3,361,550
Minority interest in net assets of subsidiary . . .			(a)	60,750	61,000
			(c)	(2,000)	
			(d)	2,250	
Common stock, $1 par.	1,057,000				1,057,000
Common stock, $10 par		400,000	(a)	(400,000)	1,560,250
Paid-in capital in excess of par.	1,560,250	235,000	(a)	(235,000)	1,353,250
Retained earnings.	1,349,450	384,000		(380,200)	
Total liabilities & stockholders' equity	6,387,250	1,960,000		(954,200)	7,393,050

* An increase in total costs and expenses and a decrease in net income.

Working paper eliminations for partially owned purchased subsidiary subsequent to date of business combination

POST CORPORATION AND SUBSIDIARY
Working Paper Eliminations
December 31, Year 2

(a) Common Stock—Sage.   400,000

Paid-in Capital in Excess of Par—Sage.   235,000

Retained Earnings—Sage.   334,000

Inventories—Sage   26,000

Plant Assets (net)—Sage   190,000

Leasehold—Sage.   30,000

Goodwill—Post   38,000

    Investment in Sage Company Common Stock—

    Post   1,192,250

    Minority Interest in Net Assets of Subsidiary. . . .   60,750

To eliminate intercompany investment and equity accounts of subsidiary **on date of business combination;** to allocate excess of cost over carrying amounts of identifiable assets acquired, with remainder to goodwill; and to establish minority interest in net assets of subsidiary on date of business combination ($1,215,000 × 0.05 = $60,750).

(b) Cost of Goods Sold—Sage   43,000

Operating Expenses—Sage.   2,000

Operating Expenses—Post   950

    Inventories—Sage   26,000

    Plant Assets (net)—Sage   14,000

    Leasehold—Sage.   5,000

    Goodwill—Post   950

(1) To provide for Year 2 depreciation and amortization on differences between business combination date current fair values and carrying amounts of Sage's identifiable assets as follows:

	Cost of goods sold	Operating expenses
Inventories sold	$26,000	
Building depreciation . . .	2,000	$2,000
Machinery depreciation . .	10,000	
Leasehold amortization . .	5,000	
Totals.	$43,000	$2,000

(2) To amortize goodwill acquired in business combination ($38,000 ÷ 40 = $950).

(Income tax effects are disregarded.)

(Continued)

POST CORPORATION AND SUBSIDIARY
Working Paper Eliminations (concluded)
December 31, Year 2

(c) Intercompany Dividends Revenue—Post 38,000
    Minority Interest in Net Assets of Subsidiary 2,000
        Dividends—Sage   40,000
    To eliminate intercompany dividends and minority share
    thereof ($40,000 × 0.05 = $2,000).

(d) Minority Interest in Net Income of Subsidiary 2,250
        Minority Interest in Net Assets of Subsidiary . . .   2,250
    To establish minority interest in subsidiary's adjusted net
    income for Year 2 as follows:
        Net income of subsidiary $90,000
        Net reduction in elimination (b) . . . . (45,000)
        Adjusted net income of subsidiary $45,000
        Minority share: $45,000 × 0.05 . . . . $ 2,250

The following points relative to the cost-method working papers for Post Corporation and subsidiary should be noted:

1 The consolidated amounts in the cost-method working paper for consolidated financial statements are identical to the consolidated amounts in the equity-method working paper (page 260). This outcome results from the differing eliminations used in the two methods.

2 Three cost-method eliminations, (a), (b), and (c), are required to accomplish what a single equity-method elimination, (a) on page 259, does. The reason is that the parent company's accounting records are used in the equity method to reflect the parent's share of the subsidiary's adjusted net income or net loss.

3 Elimination (a) deals with the intercompany investment and subsidiary equity accounts **on the date of the business combination.** This elimination is identical to the one on page 209 of Chapter 5. This accounting technique is necessary because the parent's Investment in Sage Company Common Stock account is maintained at the **cost of the original investment** in the cost method.

4 The parent company's cost-method net income and retained earnings are not the same as the consolidated amounts. Thus, the consolidated amounts on December 31, Year 2, may be proved as shown on page 274, to assure their accuracy.

Closing Entries There are no unusual features of closing entries for a parent company that uses the cost method of accounting for a subsidiary's operating results. The Intercompany Dividends Revenue account is closed with other revenue accounts to retained earnings. Because the parent company does not record the undistributed earnings of subsidiaries under the cost method, a Retained Earnings of Subsidiary ledger account is unnecessary in the cost method.

Consolidated net income:

Net income of Post Corporation	$ 458,000
Less: Amortization of business combination goodwill	(950)
Add: Post's share of Sage Company's adjusted net income not distributed as dividends [($45,000 − $40,000) × 0.95)]	4,750
Consolidated net income.	$ 461,800

Consolidated retained earnings:

Retained earnings of Post Corporation	$1,349,450
Less: Amortization of business combination goodwill	(950)
Add: Post's share of adjusted net increase in Sage Company's retained earnings [($50,000 − $45,000) × 0.95].	4,750
Consolidated retained earnings.	$1,353,250

Illustration of cost method for partially owned purchased subsidiary for second year after business combination

The only journal entry prepared by Post Corporation for the Year 3 operating results of Sage Company under the cost method of accounting is to accrue $47,500 of intercompany dividends revenue ($50,000 × 0.95 = $47,500) on November 22, Year 3. The eliminations working paper follows:

Working paper eliminations for partially owned purchased subsidiary subsequent to date of business combination

POST CORPORATION AND SUBSIDIARY
Working Paper Eliminations
December 31, Year 3

(a) Common Stock—Sage.	400,000	
Paid-in Capital in Excess of Par—Sage.	235,000	
Retained Earnings—Sage.	334,000	
Inventories—Sage	26,000	
Plant Assets (net)—Sage	190,000	
Leasehold—Sage.	30,000	
Goodwill—Post	38,000	
Investment in Sage Company Common Stock—Post		1,192,250
Minority Interest in Net Assets of Subsidiary. . .		60,750

To eliminate intercompany investment and equity accounts of subsidiary **on date of business combination;** to allocate excess of cost over carrying amounts of identifiable assets acquired, with remainder to goodwill, and to establish minority interest in net assets of subsidiary on date of business combination.

(Continued)

POST CORPORATION AND SUBSIDIARY
Working Paper Eliminations (concluded)
December 31, Year 3

(b) Retained Earnings—Sage.   45,000

     Retained Earnings—Post   950

     Cost of Goods Sold—Sage   17,000

     Operating Expenses—Sage.   2,000

     Operating Expenses—Post   950

          Inventories—Sage   26,000

          Plant Assets (net)—Sage   28,000

          Leasehold—Sage.   10,000

          Goodwill—Post   1,900

     To provide for Years 2 and 3 depreciation and amortiza-
     tion on differences between business combination date
     current fair values and carrying amounts of Sage's
     identifiable assets and of Post's goodwill. Year 2
     amounts are debited to the respective retained earnings
     accounts; Year 3 amounts are debited to appropriate
     expense accounts.

(c) Retained Earnings—Sage ($61,000 − $60,750)   250

          Minority Interest in Net Assets of Subsidiary. . .   250

     To provide for net increase in minority interest from date
     of business combination to **beginning of year.**

(d) Intercompany Dividends Revenue—Post.   47,500

     Minority Interest in Net Income of Subsidiary   2,500

          Dividends—Sage   50,000

     To eliminate intercompany dividends and minority share
     thereof ($50,000 × 0.05 = $2,500).

(e) Minority Interest in Net Income of Subsidary   4,300

          Minority Interest in Net Assets of Subsidiary. . .   4,300

     To establish minority interest in subsidiary's adjusted
     net income for Year 3 as follows:

          Net income of subsidiary $105,000

          Net reduction in elimination (b) . . . . . .   (19,000)

          Adjusted net income of subsidiary . . . . $ 86,000

          Minority share: $86,000 × 0.05. . . . . . . $ 4,300

Because the parent company does not record depreciation and amortization applicable to the differences between the current fair values and carrying amounts of the subsidiary's identifiable net assets, elimination (b) must provide for total depreciation and amortization for

both years since the business combination. In addition, elimination (c) must account for the net increase in the minority interest in net assets of the subsidiary from the business combination date to the beginning of the current year.

Working Paper for Consolidated Financial Statements The following partial working paper for consolidated financial statements illustrates the retained earnings changes for Post Corporation and subsidiary during Year 3. The consolidated amounts are identical to those under the equity method of accounting (see page 267).

Cost method: Partially owned subsidiary subsequent to date of purchase-type business combination

POST CORPORATION AND SUBSIDIARY
Partial Working Paper for Consolidated Financial Statements
For Year Ended December 31, Year 3

	Post Corporation	Sage Company	Eliminations increase (decrease)		Consolidated
Statement of Retained Earnings					
Retained earnings, beginning			(a)	(334,000)	
of year	1,349,450	384,000	(b)	(45,950)	1,353,250
			(c)	(250)	
Net income	319,350	105,000		(71,750)*	352,600
Subtotal	1,668,800	489,000		(451,950)	1,705,850
Dividends	158,550	50,000	(d)	(50,000)	158,550
Retained earnings, end of year	1,510,250	439,000		(401,950)	1,547,300

* Decrease in intercompany dividends revenue ($47,500), plus total increase in costs and expenses ($17,000 + $2,000 + $950 + $4,300), equals $71,750.

REVIEW QUESTIONS

1 "Consolidated financial statement balances will be the same, regardless of whether a parent company uses the equity method or the cost method to account for a subsidiary's operations." Why is this quotation true?

2 Both Parnell Corporation and Plankton Company have wholly owned subsidiaries. Parnell Corporation's general ledger has an Intercompany Dividend Revenue account, and an Intercompany Investment Income account appears in Plankton Company's ledger. Do both companies use the same method of accounting for their subsidiaries' operating results? Explain.

3 When there are no intercompany profits or losses in consolidated assets or liabilities, the equity method of accounting produces parent company net income that equals consolidated net income. The equity method also results in parent company retained earnings of the same amount as consolidated retained earnings. Why, then, are consolidated financial statements considered superior to the separate financial statements of the parent company when the parent company uses the equity method? Explain.

4 Describe the special features of closing entries for a parent company that accounts for its subsidiary's operating results by the equity method.

5 Plumstead Corporation's 92%-owned subsidiary declared a dividend of $3 a share on its 50,000 outstanding shares of common stock. How would Plumstead record this dividend under
a The equity method of accounting?
b The cost method of accounting?

6 Discuss some of the advantages that result from the use of the equity method, rather than the cost method, of accounting for a subsidiary's operating results.

7 Strake Company, a 90%-owned subsidiary of Peale Corporation, reported net income of $50,000 for the first fiscal year following the business combination. However, the working paper elimination for the minority interest in the subsidiary's net income was in the amount of $3,500 rather than $5,000. Can this difference be justified? Explain. YES

8 Is a Retained Earnings of Subsidiary ledger account required for a parent company that uses the cost method of accounting for the subsidiary's operations? Explain.

EXERCISES

Ex. 6-1 Select the best answer for each of the following multiple-choice questions:

1 Which of the following ledger accounts is used in both the equity method and the cost method of accounting for the operating results of a subsidiary?
a Intercompany Investment Income
b Intercompany Dividends Receivable
c Intercompany Dividends Revenue
d Minority Interest in Net Income of Subsidiary

2 The end-of-period closing entries for a parent company that uses the equity method of accounting for the subsidiary's operating results credits the parent's share of the undistributed earnings of the subsidiary to the following ledger account:
a Intercompany Investment Income
b Retained Earnings
c Investment in Subsidiary Common Stock
d Retained Earnings of Subsidiary

3 The Amortization Expense account of a parent company usually is debited in the equity method of accounting for the operating results of:
a A wholly owned purchased subsidiary
b A partially owned purchased subsidiary
c Either a wholly owned or a partially owned purchased subsidiary
d Neither a wholly owned nor a partially owned purchased subsidiary

4 Dividends declared by a subsidiary that are payable to minority shareholders of the subsidiary are credited by the subsidiary to:
a Minority interest in net income of subsidiary
b Minority interest in net assets of subsidiary
c Dividends payable
d Intercompany dividends payable

5 Plover Corporation accounts for its 80%-owned purchased subsidiary, Swallow Company, under the equity method of accounting. For the fiscal year ended March 31, Year 5, Swallow reported net income of $100,000, but declared no dividends. Amortization of differences between current fair values and carrying amounts of Swallow's identifiable net assets for the year ended March 31, Year 5, totaled $40,000. Plover's closing entry for the year ended March 31, Year 5, should include:

a A credit of $48,000 to Intercompany Investment Income
b A credit of $60,000 to Retained Earnings of Subsidiary
c A debit of $60,000 to Intercompany Investment Income
d A credit of $48,000 to Retained Earnings of Subsidiary

Ex. 6-2 The working paper elimination (in journal entry form) for Purling Corporation and Subsidiary on October 31, Year 6, the date of the business combination, was:

PURLING CORPORATION AND SUBSIDIARY
Working Paper Elimination
October 31, Year 6

(a) Common Stock—Stagg 100,000
Paid-in Capital in Excess of Par—Stagg 150,000
Retained Earnings—Stagg 200,000
Plant Assets—Stagg (depreciable) 250,000
Goodwill—Stagg   60,000
    Investment in Stagg Company Common Stock—
    Purling   760,000

To eliminate intercompany investment and equity accounts of subsidiary on date of business combination; and to allocate excess of cost over carrying amount of identifiable assets acquired, with remainder to goodwill.

During the year ended October 31, Year 7, Stagg Company reported net income of $50,000, and on October 31, Year 7, Stagg declared dividends of $20,000, payable November 16, Year 7. Stagg depreciates plant assets by the straight-line method at a 10% rate and amortizes intangible assets by the straight-line method over a 40-year life. Stagg includes plant assets depreciation in cost of goods sold and goodwill amortization in operating expenses.

a Prepare Purling Corporation's October 31, Year 7, journal entries to record the operating results and dividend of Stagg Company under the equity method of accounting. Disregard income taxes. Omit explanations.
b Prepare the October 31, Year 7, working paper elimination for Purling Corporation and subsidiary, in journal entry form. Disregard income taxes. Omit explanation.

Ex. 6-3 Pilchard Corporation's general ledger included the Investment in Shad Company Common Stock ledger account (at the top of page 279) on December 31, Year 3.
Prepare a three-column Retained Earnings of Subsidiary ledger account for Pilchard Corporation and post appropriate closing entries for December 31, Year 2, and December 31, Year 3, to this account.

Ex. 6-4 The retained earnings accounts of Putter Corporation and its 80%-owned purchased subsidiary, Simmer Company, appear on pages 279 and 280 for the two fiscal years following their business combination on May 31, Year 6. There were no intercompany profits or losses in transactions between the two enterprises during the two years ended May 31, Year 8.

Investment in Shad Company Common Stock

Date	Explanation	Debit	Credit	Balance
12/31/1	Issuance of common stock in business combination	840,000		840,000 dr
12/31/1	Direct out-of-pocket costs of business combination	40,000		880,000 dr
10/14/2	Dividend declared by Shad		20,000	860,000 dr
12/31/2	Net income of Shad	60,000		920,000 dr
12/31/2	Amortization of differences between current fair values and carrying amounts of Shad's net assets		14,500	905,500 dr
10/18/3	Dividends declared by Shad		50,000	855,500 dr
12/31/3	Net income of Shad	90,000		945,500 dr
12/31/3	Amortization of differences between current fair values and carrying amounts of Shad's net assets		4,500	941,000 dr

Putter Corporation:

Retained Earnings

Date	Explanation	Debit	Credit	Balance
5/31/6	Balance			640,000 cr
5/31/7	Close net income available for dividends ($140,000 − $28,000)		112,000	752,000 cr
5/31/7	Close Dividends account	60,000		692,000 cr
5/31/8	Close net income available for dividends ($180,000 − $52,000)		128,000	820,000 cr
5/31/8	Close Dividends account	80,000		740,000 cr

Retained Earnings of Subsidiary

Date	Explanation	Debit	Credit	Balance
5/31/7	Close net income not available for dividends {[($80,000 − $15,000) − $30,000] × 0.80}		28,000	28,000 cr
5/31/8	Close net income not available for dividends {[($120,000 − $5,000) − $50,000] × 0.80}		52,000	80,000 cr

(Continued)

Simmer Company:

Retained Earnings

Date	Explanation	Debit	Credit	Balance
5/31/6	Balance			100,000 cr
5/31/7	Close net income		80,000	180,000 cr
5/31/7	Close Dividends account	30,000		150,000 cr
5/31/8	Close net income		120,000	270,000 cr
5/31/8	Close Dividends account	50,000		220,000 cr

Prepare the statement of retained earnings section of the working paper for consolidated financial statements of Putter Corporation and subsidiary for the fiscal year ended May 31, Year 8.

Ex. 6-5 Pinson Corporation owns a 90% interest in a purchased subsidiary, Solomon Company, which is accounted for by the equity method. During Year 5, Pinson had income, exclusive of intercompany investment income, of $145,000, and Solomon had net income of $120,000. Solomon declared and paid a $40,000 dividend during Year 5. There were no differences between the current fair values and carrying amounts of Solomon's identifiable net assets on the date of the business combination.

Compute the consolidated net income of Pinson Corporation and subsidiary for Year 5.

Ex. 6-6 On March 31, Year 1, Pitt Corporation acquired for cash 90% of the outstanding common stock of Scow Company. The $100,000 excess of Pitt's investment over 90% of the current fair value (and carrying amount) of Scow's identifiable net assets was allocable to goodwill having an estimated economic life of 25 years on March 31, Year 1. For the fiscal year ended March 31, Year 2, Scow reported a net loss of $130,000 and declared no dividends.

What amount, disregarding income taxes, should Pitt Corporation record in its Intercompany Investment Income account under the equity method of accounting for the fiscal year ended March 31, Year 2? Show computations.

Ex. 6-7 Following are all details of three ledger accounts of a parent company that uses the equity method of accounting for its subsidiary's operating results:

Intercompany Dividends Receivable

Aug. 16, Year 8	36,000	Aug. 27, Year 8	36,000

Investment in Subsidiary Common Stock

Sept. 1, Year 7	630,000	Aug. 16, Year 8	36,000
Aug. 31, Year 8	72,000	Aug. 31, Year 8	5,000

Intercompany Investment Income

Aug. 31, Year 8	5,000	Aug. 31, Year 8	72,000

What is the most logical explanation for each of the transactions recorded in the above ledger accounts?

Ex. 6-8 On January 2, Year 6, Parr Corporation acquired 75% of the outstanding common stock of Spade Company for $345,000 cash, including out-of-pocket costs. The investment is accounted for by the equity method. On that date, Spade's identifiable net assets (carrying amount and current fair value) were $300,000. Parr has determined that the excess of the cost of its investment in Spade's identifiable net assets has an indeterminant economic life.

Spade's net income for the year ended December 31, Year 6, was $160,000. During Year 6, Parr received $60,000 cash dividends from Spade. There were no other transactions between the two enterprises.

Compute the balance of Parr Corporation's Investment in Spade Company Common Stock account (after adjustment) on December 31, Year 6, disregarding income taxes.

Ex. 6-9 Seal Company, wholly owned purchased subsidiary of Presto Corporation, reported net income of $90,000 and paid dividends of $35,000 for the first year following the business combination. Goodwill computed in accordance with purchase accounting amounted to $64,000 on the date of the business combination, and had an estimated economic life of 20 years. Exclusive of Seal's operations, Presto had net income of $180,000 for the first year following the business combination.

Disregarding income taxes, compute the net income of Presto Corporation under (**a**) the equity method, and (**b**) the cost method of accounting for the operating results of Seal Company.

Ex. 6-10 The balance of Putnam Corporation's Investment in Salisbury Company Common Stock ledger account on September 30, Year 6, was $265,000. The 20% minority interest in net assets of subsidiary in the consolidated balance sheet of Putnam Corporation and subsidiary on September 30, Year 6, was $60,000. For the fiscal year ended September 30, Year 7, Salisbury reported net income of $50,000 and declared and paid dividends of $18,750. Amortization for the fiscal year ended September 30, Year 7, was as follows:

Differences between current fair values and carrying amounts of Salisbury's identifiable net assets on date of business combination $4,500

Goodwill acquired by Putnam in business combination 1,000

Compute the following:

a Balance of Putnam's Investment in Salisbury Company Common Stock ledger account on September 30, Year 7

b Balance of Putnam's Intercompany Investment Income ledger account on September 30, Year 7, before closing entries

c Amount of closing entry credit to Putnam's Retained Earnings of Subsidiary ledger account on September 30, Year 7

d Minority interest in net income of subsidiary in consolidated income statement of Putnam Corporation and subsidiary for year ended September 30, Year 7

e Minority interest in net assets of subsidiary in consolidated balance sheet of Putnam Corporation and subsidiary on September 30, Year 7

CASES

Case 6-1 The most common method of accounting for the operating results of subsidiaries is the equity method.

Instructions Answer the questions shown below with respect to the equity method of accounting:

a Under what circumstances should the equity method of accounting be applied?

b At what amount should the initial investment be recorded, and what events subsequent to the initial investment (if any) would change this amount?

c How is investment income recognized under the equity method of accounting, and how is the amount determined?

Case 6-2 Financial accounting usually emphasizes the economic substance of events, even though the legal form may differ and suggest different treatment. For example, under the accrual basis of accounting, expenses are recognized when incurred (substance) rather than when cash is paid (form).

Although the feature of substance over form exists in most generally accepted accounting principles and practices, there are times when form prevails over substance.

Instructions For each of the following topics, discuss the underlying theory in terms of both substance and form, that is, substance over form and possibly form over substance. Each topic should be discussed independently.

a Consolidated financial statements

b Equity method of accounting for investments in common stock of subsidiaries and influenced investees

Case 6-3 You have recently been hired for the position of controller of Precision Corporation, a manufacturing enterprise that has begun a program of expansion through business combinations. On February 1, Year 4, two weeks prior to your controllership appointment, Precision completed the acquisition of 85% of the outstanding common stock of Sloan Company for $255,000 cash, including out-of-pocket costs. You are engaged in a discussion with Precision's chief accountant concerning the appropriate accounting method for Precision's interest in Sloan Company's operating results. The chief accountant strongly supports the cost method of accounting, offering the following arguments:

(1) The cost method recognizes that Precision and Sloan are separate legal entities.

(2) The existence of a minority interest in Sloan requires emphasis on the legal separateness of the two companies.

(3) A parent company recognizes revenue under the cost method only when the subsidiary declares dividends. Such dividend revenue is consistent with the revenue realization principle of financial accounting. The Intercompany Investment Income account recorded in the equity method of accounting does not fit the definition of realized revenue.

(4) Use of the equity method of accounting might result in Precision's declaring dividends to its shareholders out of "paper" retained earnings that belong to Sloan.

(5) The cost method is consistent with other aspects of historical-cost accounting, because working paper eliminations, rather than journal entries in ledger accounts, are used to recognize amortization of differences between current fair values and carrying amounts of Sloan's identifiable net assets.

Instructions Prepare a rebuttal to each of the chief accountant's arguments.

PROBLEMS

6-1 The working paper elimination for Pakistan Corporation and subsidiary on March 31, Year 7, the date of the purchase-type business combination, was as follows:

PAKISTAN CORPORATION AND SUBSIDIARY
Working Paper Elimination
March 31, Year 7

(a) Common Stock, $1 par—Sikkim 50,000
  Paid-in Capital in Excess of Par—Sikkim 100,000
  Retained Earnings—Sikkim 150,000
  Inventories—Sikkim (fifo cost) 20,000
  Land—Sikkim 50,000
  Other Plant Assets—Sikkim (economic life 10 years) . . 80,000
  Goodwill—Sikkim (economic life 40 years) 40,000
    Investment in Sikkim Company Common Stock—
    Pakistan   490,000

To eliminate intercompany investment and equity accounts of subsidiary on date of business combination;
and to allocate excess of cost over carrying amounts
of identifiable assets acquired, with remainder to goodwill. (Income tax effects are disregarded.)

For the fiscal year ended March 31, Year 8, Sikkim Company reported net income of $60,000. Sikkim declared a cash dividend of $0.40 a share on March 1,
Year 8, and paid the dividend on March 15, Year 8. (Sikkim had not declared or
paid dividends during the year ended March 31, Year 7.) Sikkim uses the
straight-line method for depreciation expense and amortization expense, both of
which are included in operating expenses.

Instructions
a Prepare journal entries in the accounting records of Pakistan Corporation to
 record the operating results of Sikkim Company for the year ended March 31,
 Year 8, under the equity method of accounting. Disregard income taxes.
b Prepare three-column ledger accounts for Pakistan Corporation's Investment
 in Sikkim Company Common Stock and Intercompany Investment Income accounts, and post the journal entries in *a*.
c Prepare a working paper elimination for Pakistan Corporation and subsidiary
 on March 31, Year 8, in journal entry form. Disregard income taxes.

6-2   Placer Corporation's October 31, Year 4, journal entries to record the operations
  of its 80%-owned purchased subsidiary, Sybarite Company, during the first fiscal
  year following the business combination, were as follows:

PLACER CORPORATION
Journal Entries
October 31, Year 4

Intercompany Dividends Receivable 16,000
  Investment in Sybarite Company Common Stock . . .   16,000
To record $1 a share dividend declared by Sybarite Company,
payable Nov. 7, Year 4, to stockholders of record Oct. 31,
Year 4.

Investment in Sybarite Company Common Stock 40,000
  Intercompany Investment Income   40,000

(Continued)

To record 80% of Sybarite Company's reported net income for the year ended Oct. 31, Year 4. (Income tax effects are disregarded).

Intercompany Investment Income	22,400	
Investment in Sybarite Company Common Stock . . .		22,400

To amortize differences between current fair values and carrying amounts of Sybarite Company's identifiable net assets on Oct. 31, Year 3:

Inventories—to cost of goods sold	$20,000
Plant assets—depreciation ($80,000 ÷ 10)	8,000
Total difference	$28,000
Amortization: $28,000 × 0.80	$22,400

(Income tax effects are disregarded.)

Amortization Expense ($40,000 ÷ 40 years)	1,000	
Investment in Sybarite Company Common Stock . . .		1,000

To amortize goodwill acquired in business combination with partially owned purchased subsidiary over an economic life of 40 years.

Other information:

(1) Placer acquired 16,000 shares of Sybarite's $1 par common stock on October 31, Year 3, at a total cost, including out-of-pocket costs, of $240,000. The minority interest in net assets of subsidiary on that date was $50,000.

(2) On October 31, Year 4, the balances of Sybarite's Common Stock, Paid-in Capital in Excess of Par, and Retained Earnings ledger accounts were in the ratio of 1:3:5, respectively.

(3) Sybarite allocates depreciation expense 75% to cost of goods sold and 25% to operating expenses.

Instructions Prepare working paper eliminations for Placer Corporation and subsidiary on October 31, Year 4. (Suggestion: Use T accounts to determine balances in key accounts of the parent company and subsidiary.) Disregard income taxes.

6-3 On January 2, Year 6, Pilot Corporation made the following investments:

(1) Acquired for cash 80% of the outstanding common stock of Stewart Company at $70 a share. The stockholders' equity of Stewart on January 2, Year 6, consisted of the following:

Common stock, $50 par	$50,000
Retained earnings	20,000
Total stockholders' equity	$70,000

(2) Acquired for cash 70% of the outstanding common stock of Skate Company at $40 a share. The stockholders' equity of Skate on January 2, Year 6, consisted of the following:

Common stock, $20 par	$ 60,000
Paid-in capital in excess of par	20,000
Retained earnings	40,000
Total stockholders' equity	$120,000

Out-of-pocket costs of the two business combinations may be disregarded. An
analysis of the retained earnings of each company for Year 6 follows:

	Pilot Corporation	Stewart Company	Skate Company
Balances, beginning of year.	$240,000	$20,000	$40,000
Net income (loss)	104,600*	36,000	(12,000)
Cash dividends declared and paid, Dec. 31, Year 6	(40,000)	(16,000)	(9,000)
Balances, end of year	$304,600*	$40,000	$19,000

* Before giving effect to journal entries in **a**(2), below.

Instructions
a Prepare journal entries for Pilot Corporation to record the following for Year 6:
   (1) Investments in subsidiaries' common stock
   (2) Parent company's share of subsidiaries' net income or net loss (disregarding income taxes)
   (3) Parent company's share of subsidiaries' dividends declared (Do not prepare journal entries for receipt of cash.)
b Compute the amount of minority interest in each subsidiary's net assets on December 31, Year 6.
c Compute the amount that should be reported as consolidated retained earnings of Pilot Corporation and subsidiaries on December 31, Year 6. Show supporting computations. Disregard income taxes.

6-4   Analyses of the Investment in State Company Common Stock ledger account of Pablo Corporation (State's parent company), the minority interest in net assets of State Company, and the differences between current fair values and carrying amounts of State Company's identifiable net assets on May 31, Year 3, the date of the Pablo–State business combination, are as follows for the fiscal year ended May 31, Year 4:

PABLO CORPORATION
Analysis of Investment in State Company Common Stock Account
For Year Ended May 31, Year 4

	Carrying amount	Current fair value excess	Goodwill	Total	
Beginning balances. .	$400,000	$80,000	$50,000	$530,000	
Net income of State	80,000			80,000	⎫
Amortization of differences between current fair values and carrying amounts of State's identifiable net assets		(7,200)		(7,200)	⎬ Intercompany investment income, $72,800
Amortization of goodwill			(2,000)	(2,000)	
Dividends declared by State	(30,000)			(30,000)	
Ending balances. . . .	$450,000	$72,800	$48,000	$570,800	

(Continued)

PABLO CORPORATION

Analysis of Minority Interest in Net Assets of State Company

For Year Ended May 31, Year 4

	Carrying amount	Current fair value excess	Total	
Beginning balances	$100,000	$20,000	$120,000	
Net income of State	20,000		20,000	*Minority interest in net income of subsidiary, $18,200*
Amortization of differences between current fair values and carrying amounts of State's identifiable net assets		(1,800)	(1,800)	
Dividends declared by State	(7,500)		(7,500)	
Ending balances	$112,500	$18,200	$130,700	

PABLO CORPORATION

Analysis of Differences between Current Fair Values and Carrying Amounts of State Company's Identifiable Net Assets

For Year Ended May 31, Year 4

	Balances, May 31, Year 3	Amortization for Year 4	Balances, May 31, Year 4
Plant assets (net):			
Land	$ 39,000		$39,000
Buildings.	36,000	$4,000	32,000
Machinery	25,000	5,000	20,000
Total plant assets	$100,000	$9,000	$91,000

State Company had 10,000 shares of $1 par common stock outstanding on May 31, Year 4, that had been issued for $5 a share when State was organized. There has been no change in State's paid-in capital since State's organization. State includes depreciation expense on plant assets in cost of goods sold. Dividends were declared by State on May 31, Year 4.

Instructions

a Reconstruct Pablo Corporation's journal entries for the year ended May 31, Year 4, to record the operating results of State Company under the equity method of accounting. Disregard income taxes.

b Prepare working paper eliminations for Pablo Corporation and subsidiary, in journal entry form, on May 31, Year 4. Disregard income taxes.

6-5 Parch Corporation acquired 82% of Steppe Company's outstanding common stock for $328,000 cash on March 31, Year 8. Out-of-pocket costs of the business combination may be ignored. Steppe's stockholders' equity accounts on March 31, Year 8, were as follows:

Common stock, $2 par	$ 50,000
Paid-in capital in excess of par	75,000
Retained earnings	135,000
Total stockholders' equity	$260,000

All of Steppe's identifiable net assets were fairly valued at their March 31, Year 8, carrying amounts except for the following:

	Carrying amounts	Current fair values
Land	$100,000	$120,000
Building (net) (10-year economic life)	200,000	250,000
Patent (net) (8-year economic life)	60,000	80,000

Any goodwill resulting from the business combination is amortized over the maximum period of 40 years. Steppe uses the straight-line method for depreciation and amortization. Steppe includes depreciation expense in cost of goods sold and amortization expense in operating expenses.

During the year ended March 31, Year 9, Steppe reported net income of $1.20 a share and declared and paid no dividends. There were no intercompany transactions between Parch and Steppe.

Instructions

a Prepare Parch Corporation's journal entries to record Steppe Company's operating results for the fiscal year ended March 31, Year 9, under the equity method of accounting. Disregard income taxes.

b Prepare the working paper eliminations for Parch Corporation and subsidiary on March 31, Year 9. Disregard income taxes.

6-6 Pavich Corporation acquired 75% of the outstanding common stock of Sisler Company on October 1, Year 6, for $547,500, including direct out-of-pocket costs. Sisler's stockholders' equity on October 1, Year 6, was as follows:

Common stock, $5 par	$250,000
Paid-in capital in excess of par	100,000
Retained earnings	200,000
Total stockholders' equity	$550,000

Current fair values of Sisler's identifiable net assets exceeded their carrying amounts as follows:

	Excess of current fair values over carrying amounts
Inventories	$30,000
Plant assets (net) (economic life 10 years)	50,000
Patents (net) (economic life 5 years)	20,000

Pavich amortizes goodwill over a 40-year economic life, and both Pavich and Sisler include depreciation expense in cost of goods sold and amortization expense in operating expenses. Both companies use the straight-line method for depreciation and amortization.

For the two fiscal years ended September 30, Year 8, Sisler reported net income and declared and paid dividends as follows:

Year ended Sept. 30,	Net income	Dividends
Year 7	$ 80,000	$10,000
Year 8	120,000	75,000

Instructions

a Prepare journal entries for Pavich Corporation on September 30, Year 7, and September 30, Year 8, to record under the equity method of accounting the operating results of Sisler Company for the two fiscal years ended on those dates. Do not prepare entries for the declaration of Sisler's dividends; assume the dividends were received by Pavich on September 30 of each year. Disregard income taxes.

b Prepare working paper eliminations for Pavich Corporation and subsidiary on September 30, Year 7, and September 30, Year 8. Disregard income taxes.

c Prepare a three-column ledger account for Pavich Corporation's Retained Earnings of Subsidiary account, showing the closing entries posted to that account on September 30, Year 7, and September 30, Year 8.

6-7 The working paper elimination for Plumm Corporation and its wholly owned purchased subsidiary, Stamm Company, on the date of the business combination was as follows:

PLUMM CORPORATION AND SUBSIDIARY

Working Paper Elimination

November 30, Year 1

Common Stock—Stamm	80,000
Paid-in Capital in Excess of Par—Stamm	200,000
Retained Earnings—Stamm	220,000
Inventories—Stamm	20,000
Goodwill—Stamm	40,000
Investment in Stamm Company Common Stock—Plumm	560,000

To eliminate intercompany investment and equity accounts of subsidiary on date of business combination, and to allocate excess of cost over carrying amounts of identifiable assets acquired, with remainder to goodwill having an economic life of 40 years. (Income tax effects are disregarded.)

Financial statements of Plumm and Stamm for the fiscal year ended November 30, Year 2, were as follows:

PLUMM CORPORATION AND STAMM COMPANY

Financial Statements

For Year Ended November 30, Year 2

	Plumm Corporation	Stamm Company
Income Statements		
Revenue:		
Net sales	$800,000	$415,000
Intercompany investment income	69,000	
Total revenue	$869,000	$415,000

(Continued)

Costs and expenses:		
Cost of goods sold	$500,000	$110,000
Operating expenses	200,000	80,000
Income taxes expense	60,000	135,000
Total costs and expenses	$760,000	$325,000
Net income	$109,000	$ 90,000

Statements of Retained Earnings

Retained earnings, beginning of year	$640,000	$220,000
Net income	109,000	90,000
Subtotal	$749,000	$310,000
Dividends	60,000	30,000
Retained earnings, end of year	$689,000	$280,000

Balance Sheets
Assets

Investment in Stamm Company common stock	$ 599,000	
Other	1,840,000	$960,000
Total assets	$2,439,000	$960,000

Liabilities & Stockholders' Equity

Liabilities	$ 650,000	$400,000
Common stock, $1 par	500,000	80,000
Paid-in capital in excess of par	600,000	200,000
Retained earnings	689,000	280,000
Total liabilities & stockholders' equity	$2,439,000	$960,000

Instructions

a Reconstruct the journal entries for Plumm Corporation on November 30, Year 2, under the equity method of accounting, to record the operating results of Stamm Company for the fiscal year ended November 30, Year 2, including Stamm's dividend declared and paid on that date. (Do not prepare a journal entry for the declaration of the dividend.) Disregard income taxes.

b Prepare a working paper for consolidated financial statements of Plumm Corporation and subsidiary for the fiscal year ended November 30, Year 2, and the related working paper elimination. Include goodwill amortization in operating expenses. Disregard income taxes.

6-8 Ping Corporation acquired 80% of the outstanding common stock of Stang Company on December 31, Year 2, for $120,000. On that date, Stang had one class of common stock outstanding at a par value of $100,000 and retained earnings of $30,000. Ping had a $50,000 deficit in retained earnings.

Ping acquired the Stang common stock from Stang's major stockholder primarily to acquire control of signboard leases owned by Stang. The leases will expire on December 31, Year 7, and Ping's executives estimated that the leases, which cannot be renewed, were worth at least $20,000 more than their carrying amount when the Stang common stock was acquired. Stang includes signboard leases amortization in other expenses.

The financial statements for both companies for the year ended December 31, Year 6, are as follows:

PING CORPORATION AND SUBSIDIARY
Financial Statements
For Year Ended December 31, Year 6

	Ping Corporation	Stang Company
Income Statements		
Net sales	$420,000	$300,000
Costs and expenses:		
Cost of goods sold	$315,000	$240,000
Other expenses	65,000	35,000
Total costs and expenses	$380,000	$275,000
Net income	$ 40,000	$ 25,000
Statements of Retained Earnings		
Retained earnings, beginning of year	$ 15,000	$ 59,000
Net income	40,000	25,000
Subtotal	$ 55,000	$ 84,000
Dividends		9,000
Retained earnings, end of year	$ 55,000	$ 75,000
Balance Sheets		
Assets		
Current assets	$172,000	$199,100
Investment in Stang Company common stock	120,000	
Land	25,000	10,500
Building and equipment	200,000	40,000
Accumulated depreciation	(102,000)	(7,000)
Signboard leases (net)		8,400
Total assets	$415,000	$251,000
Liabilities & Stockholders' Equity		
Dividends payable		$ 9,000
Other current liabilities	$ 60,000	67,000
Common stock, $1 par	300,000	100,000
Retained earnings	55,000	75,000
Total liabilities & stockholders' equity	$415,000	$251,000

Stang declared a 9% cash dividend on December 20, Year 6, payable January 16, Year 7, to stockholders of record December 31, Year 6. Ping carries its investment at cost and had not recorded Stang's dividend on December 31, Year 6. Neither company paid dividends during Year 6.

Instructions
a Prepare adjusting entries for Ping Corporation on December 31, Year 6, to convert its accounting for Stang Company's operating results to the equity method of accounting. Disregard income taxes.

b Prepare the working paper for consolidated financial statements of Ping Corporation and subsidiary on December 31, Year 6, and the related working paper eliminations. Balances for Ping Corporation should reflect the adjusting entries in **a**. Disregard income taxes.

6-9   On June 30, Year 6, Petal Corporation acquired for cash of $19 a share, including out-of-pocket costs, all the outstanding common stock of Sepal Company. Both companies continued to operate as separate entities and both companies have calendar years. Petal adopted the equity method of accounting for Sepal's operating results.

(1) On June 30, Year 6, Sepal's balance sheet was as follows:

SEPAL COMPANY

Balance Sheet

June 30, Year 6

Assets

Cash	$ 700,000
Accounts receivable (net)	600,000
Inventories	1,400,000
Plant assets (net)	3,300,000
Other assets	500,000
Total assets	$6,500,000

Liabilities & Stockholders' Equity

Accounts payable and other current liabilities	$ 700,000
Long-term debt	2,600,000
Other liabilities	200,000
Common stock, $1 par	1,000,000
Paid-in capital in excess of par	400,000
Retained earnings	1,600,000
Total liabilities & stockholders' equity	$6,500,000

(2) On June 30, Sepal's assets and liabilities having current fair values that were different from carrying amounts were as follows:

	Current fair values
Plant assets (net)	$16,400,000
Other assets	200,000
Long-term debt	2,200,000

The differences between current fair values and carrying amounts resulted in a debit or credit to depreciation or amortization for the consolidated financial statements for the six-month period ended December 31, Year 6, as follows:

Plant assets (net)	$500,000 debit
Other assets	10,000 credit
Long-term debt	5,000 debit
Total	$495,000 debit

(3) The amount paid by Petal in excess of the current fair value of the identifiable net assets of Sepal is attributable to expected future earnings of Sepal and will be amortized over the maximum allowable period.

(4) The Year 6 net income or net loss for each company was as follows:

	Petal Corporation	Sepal Company
Jan. 1 to June 30	$ 250,000	$ (750,000)
July 1 to Dec. 31	1,070,000	1,250,000

The $1,070,000 net income of Petal includes Petal's equity in the adjusted net income of Sepal for the six months ended December 31, Year 6.

(5) On December 31, Year 6, the balance sheets for both companies were as follows:

PETAL CORPORATION AND SUBSIDIARY
Balance Sheets
December 31, Year 6

	Petal Corporation	Sepal Company
Assets		
Cash	$ 3,500,000	$ 625,000
Accounts receivable (net)	1,400,000	1,500,000
Inventories	1,000,000	2,500,000
Investment in Sepal Company common stock	19,720,000	
Plant assets (net)	2,000,000	3,100,000
Other assets	100,000	475,000
Total assets	$27,720,000	$8,200,000
Liabilities & Stockholders' Equity		
Accounts payable and other current liabilities	$ 1,500,000	$1,100,000
Long-term debt	4,000,000	2,600,000
Other liabilities	750,000	250,000
Common stock, $1 par	10,000,000	1,000,000
Paid-in capital in excess of par	5,000,000	400,000
Retained earnings	6,470,000	2,850,000
Total liabilities & stockholders' equity	$27,720,000	$8,200,000

Instructions Prepare the consolidated balance sheet of Petal Corporation and its wholly owned subsidiary, Sepal Company, on December 31, Year 6. Do not use a working paper, but show supporting computations. Disregard income taxes.

6-10 The financial statements of Princeton Corporation and Stonier Company, Princeton's wholly owned subsidiary, were as follows for the year ended December 31, Year 6:

PRINCETON CORPORATION AND STONIER COMPANY
Financial Statements
For Year Ended December 31, Year 6

	Princeton Corporation	Stonier Company
Income Statements		
Revenue:		
Net sales	$1,000,000	$ 880,000
Intercompany investment income	76,000	
Total revenue	$1,076,000	$ 880,000
Costs and expenses:		
Cost of goods sold	$ 800,000	$ 600,000
Operating expenses	90,000	80,000
Income taxes expense	66,000	120,000
Total costs and expenses	$ 956,000	$ 800,000
Net income	$ 120,000	$ 80,000
Statements of Retained Earnings		
Retained earnings, beginning of year	$ 842,000	$ 230,000
Net income	120,000	80,000
Subtotal	$ 962,000	$ 310,000
Dividends	50,000	50,000
Retained earnings, end of year	$ 912,000	$ 260,000
Balance Sheet		
Assets		
Current assets	$ 840,000	$ 450,000
Investment in Stonier Company common stock ...	438,000	
Plant assets (net)......................	1,622,000	830,000
Intangible assets (net)..................	100,000	60,000
Total assets	$3,000,000	$1,340,000
Liabilities & Stockholders' Equity		
Liabilities	$ 946,000	$ 930,000
Common stock, $1 par	600,000	50,000
Paid-in capital in excess of par	500,000	100,000
Retained earnings	912,000	260,000
Retained earnings of subsidiary	42,000	
Total liabilities & stockholders' equity	$3,000,000	$1,340,000

There were no changes in the paid-in capital accounts of Stonier since December 31, Year 3, the date of the Princeton–Stonier business combination. Stonier's Retained Earnings account since the business combination date but prior to closing entries of December 31, Year 6, is shown at the top of page 294.

Retained Earnings

Date	Explanation	Debit	Credit	Balance
12/31/3	Balance			150,000 cr
12/31/4	Close net income		80,000	230,000 cr
12/31/4	Close Dividends account	40,000		190,000 cr
12/31/5	Close net income		100,000	290,000 cr
12/31/5	Close Dividends account	60,000		230,000 cr

Princeton Corporation's Investment in Stonier Company Common Stock and Retained Earnings of Subsidiary accounts appeared as shown below, prior to closing entries of December 31, Year 6.

Investment in Stonier Company Common Stock

Date	Explanation	Debit	Credit	Balance
12/31/3	Total costs of business combination	370,000		370,000 dr
12/20/4	Dividend declared by Stonier		40,000	330,000 dr
12/31/4	Net income of Stonier	80,000		410,000 dr
12/31/4	Amortization of differences between current fair values and carrying amounts of Stonier's identifiable net assets		34,000(1)	376,000 dr
12/20/5	Dividend declared by Stonier		60,000	316,000 dr
12/31/5	Net income of Stonier	100,000		416,000 dr
12/31/5	Amortization of differences between current fair values and carrying amounts of Stonier's identifiable net assets		4,000(2)	412,000 dr
12/20/6	Dividend declared by Stonier		50,000	362,000 dr
12/31/6	Net income of Stonier	80,000		442,000 dr
12/31/6	Amortization of differences between current fair values and carrying amounts of Stonier's identifiable net assets		4,000(2)	438,000 dr

(1) Cost of goods sold, $30,000; depreciation of plant assets, $4,000
(2) Depreciation of plant assets, $4,000

Retained Earnings of Subsidiary

Date	Explanation	Debit	Credit	Balance
12/31/4	Close net income not available for dividends		6,000	6,000 cr
12/31/5	Close net income not available for dividends		36,000	42,000 cr

On December 31, Year 3, the date of the Princeton-Stonier purchase-type business combination, a $20,000 excess of current fair values of Stonier's identifiable net assets over the total cost of Princeton's investment was applied to reduce the current fair value excess attributable to Stonier's plant assets from $60,000 to $40,000. This amount was being amortized by the straight-line method in Princeton's equity-method journal entries over the ten-year economic life of Stonier's plant assets. Stonier includes depreciation expense in operating expenses.

Instructions Prepare a working paper for consolidated financial statements of Princeton Corporation and subsidiary on December 31, Year 6, and the related working paper elimination, disregarding income taxes.

7 CONSOLIDATED FINANCIAL STATEMENTS: POOLING BUSINESS COMBINATION

In this chapter, we discuss consolidated financial statements of parent corporations and pooled subsidiaries, both on, and subsequent to, the date of the pooling-type business combination. We conclude the chapter with illustrations of intercompany transactions that do not involve a profit or a loss.

Consolidated financial statements on the date of a pooling-type business combination differ in several respects from consolidated financial statements on the date of a purchase-type business combination. Among these differences are the following:

1 All four financial statements of the parent company and pooled subsidiary are consolidated on the date of a pooling-type combination, in accordance with the theory that a pooling is a combining of past and present shareholder interests. In contrast, only a consolidated balance sheet is appropriate on the date of a purchase-type combination.

2 Current fair values of the subsidiary's net assets are not reflected in the consolidated balance sheet for a pooled subsidiary as they are for a purchased subsidiary.

3 Consolidated retained earnings on the date of a pooling-type combination include the parent company's share of the subsidiary's retained earnings on that date. In contrast, only the amount of the parent company's retained earnings is included in consolidated retained earnings on the date of a purchase-type combination.

In the two sections that follow, we describe and illustrate (1) the consolidation of a wholly owned pooled subsidiary, and (2) the consolidation of a partially owned pooled subsidiary.

CONSOLIDATION OF WHOLLY OWNED POOLED SUBSIDIARY ON DATE OF BUSINESS COMBINATION

To illustrate the consolidated financial statements for a wholly owned pooled subsidiary on the date of the business combination, we return to the Palm Corporation–Starr Company business combination described in Chapter 5 (page 195) and assume that the combination qualified for pooling accounting rather than for purchase accounting. As indicated in Chapter 5, on December 31, Year 1, the end of a fiscal year, Palm issued 10,000 shares of its $10 par common stock for all the outstanding common stock of Starr and paid out-of-pocket costs of $85,000 in connection with the combination. Separate financial statements of the two constituent companies prior to the combination appear on page 298; these statements are identical to those on page 196 of Chapter 5.

The following journal entries are prepared by Palm on December 31, Year 1, to record the combination as a pooling:

Combinor's journal entries for pooling-type business combination

PALM CORPORATION (Combinor)
General Journal
December 31, Year 1

Investment in Starr Company Common Stock ($200,000 + $58,000 + $132,000)	390,000	
Common Stock (10,000 × $10)		100,000
Paid-in Capital in Excess of Par ($258,000 − $100,000)		158,000
Retained Earnings of Subsidiary		132,000
To record issuance of 10,000 shares of common stock for all the outstanding common stock of Starr Company in a pooling-type business combination.		
Expenses of Business Combination	85,000	
Cash		85,000
To record payment of out-of-pocket costs of business combination with Starr Company.		

The first of the foregoing journal entries records Palm's investment in Starr's common stock at the **carrying amount** of Starr's stockholders' equity on December 31, Year 1 ($200,000 + $58,000 + $132,000 = $390,000). In addition, a Retained Earnings of Subsidiary account is established to record the amount of Starr's retained earnings on December 31, Year 1. This separate account emphasizes that Starr's retained earnings are not a source of dividends to Palm's shareholders, as is often true in a statutory merger. The first journal entry thus reflects the underlying theory of pooling accounting—the **combining of stock-**

PALM CORPORATION AND STARR COMPANY
Separate Financial Statements
For Year Ended December 31, Year 1

	Palm Corporation	Starr Company
Income Statements		
Revenue		
Net sales	$ 990,000	$600,000
Interest revenue	10,000	
Total revenue	$1,000,000	$600,000
Costs and expenses		
Cost of goods sold	$ 635,000	$410,000
Operating expenses	80,000	30,000
Interest expense	50,000	30,000
Income taxes expense	141,000	78,000
Total costs and expenses	$ 906,000	$548,000
Net income	$ 94,000	$ 52,000
Statements of Retained Earnings		
Retained earnings, beginning of year	$ 65,000	$100,000
Add: Net income	94,000	52,000
Subtotal	$ 159,000	$152,000
Less: Dividends	25,000	20,000
Retained earnings, end of year	$ 134,000	$132,000
Balance Sheets		
Assets		
Cash	$ 100,000	$ 40,000
Inventories	150,000	110,000
Other current assets	110,000	70,000
Receivable from Starr Company	25,000	
Plant assets (net)	450,000	300,000
Patent		20,000
Total assets	$ 835,000	$540,000
Liabilities & Stockholders' Equity		
Payable to Palm Corporation		$ 25,000
Income taxes payable	$ 66,000	10,000
Other liabilities	285,000	115,000
Common stock, $10 par	300,000	
Common stock, $5 par		200,000
Paid-in capital in excess of par	50,000	58,000
Retained earnings	134,000	132,000
Total liabilities & stockholders' equity	$ 835,000	$540,000

holder interests concept—while recognizing the separate corporate identity (in a legal sense) of the pooled subsidiary.

In the second journal entry, all out-of-pocket costs of the business combination are recorded as expenses. As explained in Chapter 4, this procedure is required in a pooling-type combination.

Although Palm's expenses are increased in the second journal entry, there is no adjustment of Palm's income taxes expense or liability accounts. Costs of a pooling-type combination expensed for financial accounting are not deductible for income tax purposes. The U.S. Treasury Department considers such costs to be capital expenditures, rather than expenditures that may be either deducted when incurred or amortized over a period of years.[1]

After the foregoing journal entries have been posted, the affected financial statement items for Palm Corporation have the following balances:

<table>
<tr><td rowspan="8">**Balances of financial statement items of combinor affected by business combination**</td><td>* Operating expenses ($80,000 + $85,000) . . . .</td><td>$165,000</td></tr>
<tr><td>Net income ($94,000 − $85,000) . . . .</td><td>9,000</td></tr>
<tr><td>Cash ($100,000 − $85,000) . . . .</td><td>15,000</td></tr>
<tr><td>Investment in Starr Company common stock . . . .</td><td>390,000</td></tr>
<tr><td>Common stock, $10 par ($300,000 + $100,000) . . . .</td><td>400,000</td></tr>
<tr><td>Paid-in capital in excess of par ($50,000 + $158,000) . . . .</td><td>208,000</td></tr>
<tr><td>Retained earnings ($134,000 − $85,000) . . . .</td><td>49,000</td></tr>
<tr><td>Retained earnings of subsidiary . . . .</td><td>132,000</td></tr>
</table>

* Controlling account for Expenses of Business Combination ledger account.

In a pooling-type business combination involving a wholly owned subsidiary, the Investment in Subsidiary Common Stock account is similar to the Investment in Branch account illustrated in Chapter 3 for a home office. However, the subsidiary's three stockholders' equity accounts (which total $390,000), rather than a single Home Office (or Parent Company) account, offset Palm Corporation's Investment in Starr Company Common Stock account.

Working Paper for Consolidated Financial Statements When a business combination qualifies for pooling accounting, all four financial statements are consolidated for the accounting period ended on the date of the combination. This is consistent with the assumption that a pooling is a combining of stockholder interests, rather than an acquisition of assets.

The working paper for consolidated financial statements for Palm Corporation and subsidiary for the year ended December 31, Year 1, is presented on page 300. The working paper elimination appears at the top of page 301. All intercompany transactions and balances, includ-

[1] U.S. Treasury Regulations, Section 1.248-1 (b) (3) (i).

Wholly owned subsidiary on date of pooling-type business combination

PALM CORPORATION AND SUBSIDIARY
Working Paper for Consolidated Financial Statements
For Year Ended December 31, Year 1

	Palm Corporation	Starr Company	Eliminations increase (decrease)	Consolidated
Income Statement				
Revenue				
Net sales	990,000	600,000		1,590,000
Intercompany revenue (expense) . .	10,000	(10,000)		
Total revenue.	1,000,000	590,000		1,590,000
Costs and expenses				
Cost of goods sold	635,000	410,000		1,045,000
Operating expenses	165,000	30,000		195,000
Interest expense	50,000	20,000		70,000
Income taxes expense	141,000	78,000		219,000
Total costs and expenses	991,000	538,000		1,529,000
Net income	9,000	52,000		61,000
Statement of				
Retained Earnings				
Retained earnings, beginning of year .	65,000	100,000		165,000
Net income	9,000	52,000		61,000
Subtotal	74,000	152,000		226,000
Dividends	25,000	20,000		45,000
Retained earnings, end of year.	49,000	132,000		181,000
Balance Sheet				
Assets				
Cash	15,000	40,000		55,000
Inventories.	150,000	110,000		260,000
Other current assets	110,000	70,000		180,000
Intercompany receivable (payable) . .	25,000	(25,000)		
Investment in Starr Company common				
stock	390,000		(a) (390,000)	
Plant assets (net).	450,000	300,000		750,000
Patent		20,000		20,000
Total assets	1,140,000	515,000	(390,000)	1,265,000
Liabilities &				
Stockholders' Equity				
Income taxes payable	66,000	10,000		76,000
Other liabilities	285,000	115,000		400,000
Common stock, $10 par.	400,000			400,000
Common stock, $5 par		200,000	(a) (200,000)	
Paid-in capital in excess of par	208,000	58,000	(a) (58,000)	208,000
Retained earnings	49,000	132,000		181,000
Retained earnings of subsidiary	132,000		(a) (132,000)	
Total liabilities & stockholders'				
equity.	1,140,000	515,000	(390,000)	1,265,000

> **PALM CORPORATION AND SUBSIDIARY**
> **Working Paper Elimination**
> **December 31, Year 1**
>
> (a) Common Stock—Starr   200,000
>   Paid-in Capital in Excess of Par—Starr   58,000
>   Retained Earnings of Subsidiary—Palm   132,000
>   Investment in Starr Company Common Stock—
>   Palm   390,000
>   To eliminate intercompany investment and related ac-
>   counts for stockholders' equity of subsidiary on date of
>   business combination.

ing $10,000 interest received during Year 1 by Palm on its cash advances to Starr, are eliminated in the process of consolidation.

In reviewing the working paper for consolidated financial statements for a pooling-type business combination, you should note the following points:

1 A separate consolidated statement of changes in financial position is not illustrated at this point in order to focus attention on more fundamental issues. Once the consolidated balance sheet, consolidated income statement, and consolidated statement of retained earnings are available, a consolidated statement of changes in financial position can be prepared from comparative consolidated statements and supplementary data relating to depreciation, amortization, and comparable items. A consolidated statement of changes in financial position is illustrated in Chapter 9.

2 Intercompany revenue and expenses are placed on the same line in adjacent columns of the income statement section of the working paper, so that they are offset without a formal elimination. There are no other intercompany items that require use of the Eliminations column in the income statement section of the working paper.

3 Each pair of financial statements is consolidated in turn, in the sequence of the conventional accounting cycle. Thus, consolidated net income is carried forward to the consolidated statement of retained earnings, and the amount of consolidated retained earnings is carried forward to the consolidated balance sheet.

4 Dividends declared by Starr Company *are not eliminated* in the statement of retained earnings section of the working paper because the dividends were paid prior to the pooling-type business combination to the former shareholders of Starr, not to Palm Corporation.

5 Consolidated retained earnings includes the retained earnings of both Palm and Starr, in accordance with the pooling theory of accounting for a business combination. Thus, the separate Retained Earnings of Subsidiary account of Palm is eliminated, so that the individual Retained Earnings accounts of the parent company and subsidiary may be combined.

Consolidated Financial Statements   The consolidated financial statements of Palm Corporation and subsidiary (page 302) include the amounts in the Consolidated column of the working paper for consolidated finan-

PALM CORPORATION AND SUBSIDIARY
Consolidated Income Statement
For Year Ended December 31, Year 1

Net sales		$1,590,000
Costs and expenses:		
Cost of goods sold	$1,045,000	
Operating expenses	195,000	
Interest expense.	70,000	
Income taxes expense	219,000	1,529,000
Net income.		$ 61,000
Earnings per share of common stock (40,000 shares outstanding). . .		$1.53

PALM CORPORATION AND SUBSIDIARY
Consolidated Statement of Retained Earnings
For Year Ended December 31, Year 1

Retained earnings, beginning of year, as previously reported.		$ 65,000
Add: Adjustment to reflect pooling of interests with Starr Company. .		100,000
Retained earnings, beginning of year, as restated		$ 165,000
Add: Net income		61,000
Subtotal		$ 226,000
Less: Dividends:		
Palm Corporation ($0.83⅓ a share).	$25,000	
Starr Company, prior to business combination	20,000	45,000
Retained earnings, end of year		$ 181,000

PALM CORPORATION AND SUBSIDIARY
Consolidated Balance Sheet
December 31, Year 1

Assets

Current assets:		
Cash		$ 55,000
Inventories.		260,000
Other		180,000
Total current assets		$ 495,000
Plant assets (net)		750,000
Patent.		20,000
Total assets		$1,265,000

Liabilities & Stockholders' Equity

Liabilities:		
Income taxes payable		$ 76,000
Other		400,000
Total liabilities		$ 476,000
Stockholders' equity:		
Common stock, $10 par	$400,000	
Paid-in capital in excess of par.	208,000	
Retained earnings	181,000	789,000
Total liabilities & stockholders' equity		$1,265,000

cial statements on page 300. Because all intercompany transactions and balances have been eliminated in the computation of the consolidated amounts, these balances reflect only the transactions of Palm and Starr with **outside parties.**

There are no unusual features of a consolidated income statement or a consolidated balance sheet in a pooling-type business combination involving a wholly owned subsidiary. However, because a pooling represents an accounting change of the type classified as a **change in the reporting entity,**[2] the consolidated statement of retained earnings of Palm Corporation and subsidiary for the year ended December 31, Year 10, shown on page 302, includes an "adjustment to reflect pooling of interests with Starr Company." This item represents the retroactive application of the pooling accounting method to include Starr's beginning-of-year retained earnings of $100,000 with Palm's beginning-of-year retained earnings of $65,000.

CONSOLIDATION OF PARTIALLY OWNED POOLED SUBSIDIARY ON DATE OF BUSINESS COMBINATION

Under the assumption that the Post Corporation–Sage Company business combination described in Chapter 5 (page 204) qualified for pooling accounting rather than for purchase accounting, it is used in this section to illustrate consolidated financial statements for a partially owned pooled subsidiary on the date of the business combination. As indicated in Chapter 5, on December 31, Year 1, the end of a fiscal year, Post issued 57,000 shares of its common stock in exchange for 38,000 of the 40,000 outstanding shares of Sage's common stock, and paid $125,000 out-of-pocket costs of the business combination. Separate financial statements of the two constituent companies prior to the combination appear on page 304; these statements are identical to those on page 205.

Post's December 31, Year 1, journal entries to record the business combination with Sage as a pooling are at the top of page 305. Note that the first of the journal entries on page 305 records Post Corporation's **95% share** of the net assets (carrying amount $969,000) and retained earnings of Sage Company.

As pointed out on page 299, out-of-pocket costs of a pooling-type business combination expensed for financial accounting are not deductible or amortizable for income tax purposes. Thus, although the second of the foregoing journal entries increases Post Corporation's expenses, its income taxes expense and liability accounts are not adjusted. The costs of the business combination represent a **permanent difference,** rather than a **timing difference,** between Post's pre-tax accounting income and taxable income. There is no income tax advantage

[2] *APB Opinion No. 20,* "Accounting Changes," AICPA (New York: 1971), p. 388.

POST CORPORATION AND SAGE COMPANY
Separate Financial Statements
For Year Ended December 31, Year 1

	Post Corporation	Sage Company
Income Statements		
Net sales	$5,500,000	$1,000,000
Costs and expenses		
Costs of goods sold	$3,850,000	$ 650,000
Operating expenses	600,000	100,000
Interest expense	75,000	40,000
Income taxes expense.	585,000	126,000
Total costs and expenses	$5,110,000	$ 916,000
Net income	$ 390,000	$ 84,000
Statements of Retained Earnings		
Retained earnings, beginning of year	$ 810,000	$ 290,000
Add: Net income	390,000	84,000
Subtotal	$1,200,000	$ 374,000
Less: Dividends	150,000	40,000
Retained earnings, end of year.	$1,050,000	$ 334,000
Balance Sheets		
Assets		
Cash	$ 200,000	$ 100,000
Inventories.	800,000	500,000
Other current assets	550,000	215,000
Plant assets (net).	3,500,000	1,100,000
Goodwill	100,000	
Total assets	$5,150,000	$1,915,000
Liabilities & Stockholders' Equity		
Income taxes payable	$ 100,000	$ 76,000
Other liabilities	2,450,000	870,000
Common stock, $1 par.	1,000,000	
Common stock, $10 par		400,000
Paid-in capital in excess of par.	550,000	235,000
Retained earnings	1,050,000	334,000
Total liabilities & stockholders' equity	$5,150,000	$1,915,000

Combinor's journal entries for pooling-type business combination

POST CORPORATION (Combinor)
General Journal
December 31, Year 1

Investment in Sage Company Common Stock [($400,000 + $235,000 + $334,000) × 0.95]	920,550	
Common Stock (57,000 × $1)		57,000
Paid-in Capital in Excess of Par [($635,000 × 0.95) − $57,000]		546,250
Retained Earnings of Subsidiary ($334,000 × 0.95) . .		317,300

To record issuance of 57,000 shares of common stock for 38,000 of the 40,000 shares of outstanding common stock of Sage Company in a pooling-type business combination.

Expenses of Business Combination	125,000	
Cash		125,000

To record payment of out-of-pocket costs of business combination with Sage Company.

to a pooling corporation for out-of-pocket costs of the business combination, just as an acquiring corporation receives no income tax benefits from the amortization of purchased goodwill.

After the preceding journal entries have been posted in the ledger, Post Corporation's relevant financial statement items have the following balances:

Balances of financial statement items of combinor affected by business combination

* Operating expenses ($600,000 + $125,000).	$ 725,000
Net income ($390,000 − $125,000).	265,000
Cash ($200,000 − $125,000).	75,000
Investment in Sage Company common stock	920,550
Common stock ($1,000,000 + $57,000)	1,057,000
Paid-in capital in excess of par ($550,000 + $546,250).	1,096,250
Retained earnings ($1,050,000 − $125,000).	925,000
Retained earnings of subsidiary	317,300

* Controlling account for Expenses of Business Combination ledger account.

Working Paper for Consolidated Financial Statements The working paper for consolidated financial statements for Post Corporation and subsidiary is presented on page 306; the working paper eliminations appear at the top of page 307.

Partially owned subsidiary on date of pooling-type business combination

POST CORPORATION AND SUBSIDIARY
Working Paper for Consolidated Financial Statements
For Year Ended December 31, Year 1

	Post Corporation	Sage Company	Eliminations increase (decrease)		Consolidated
Income Statement					
Net sales.	5,500,000	1,000,000			6,500,000
Costs and expenses					
Cost of goods sold	3,850,000	650,000			4,500,000
Operating expenses	725,000	100,000			825,000
Interest expense	75,000	40,000			115,000
Income taxes expense	585,000	126,000			711,000
Minority interest in net income of subsidiary			(b)	4,200	4,200
Total costs and expenses.	5,235,000	916,000		4,200	6,155,200
Net income	265,000	84,000		(4,200)	344,800
Statement of Retained Earnings					
Retained earnings, beginning of year .	810,000	290,000	(a)	(14,500)	1,085,500
Net income	265,000	84,000		(4,200)	344,800
Subtotal	1,075,000	374,000		(18,700)	1,430,300
Dividends	150,000	40,000	(a)	(2,000)	188,000
Retained earnings, end of year.	925,000	334,000		(16,700)	1,242,300
Balance Sheet **Assets**					
Cash	75,000	100,000			175,000
Inventories.	800,000	500,000			1,300,000
Other current assets	550,000	215,000			765,000
Investment in Sage Company common stock.	920,550		(a)	(920,550)	
Plant assets (net).	3,500,000	1,100,000			4,600,000
Goodwill	100,000				100,000
Total assets	5,945,550	1,915,000		(920,550)	6,940,000
Liabilities & Stockholders' Equity					
Income taxes payable	100,000	76,000			176,000
Other liabilities	2,450,000	870,000			3,320,000
Minority interest in net assets of subsidiary.			(a) (b)	44,250 4,200	48,450
Common stock, $1 par	1,057,000				1,057,000
Common stock, $10 par.		400,000	(a)	(400,000)	
Paid-in capital in excess of par	1,096,250	235,000	(a)	(235,000)	1,096,250
Retained earnings	925,000	334,000		(16,700)	1,242,300
Retained earnings of subsidiary	317,300		(a)	(317,300)	
Total liabilities & stockholders' equity.	5,945,550	1,915,000		(920,550)	6,940,000

POST CORPORATION AND SUBSIDIARY
Working Paper Eliminations
December 31, Year 1

(a) Common Stock—Sage. 400,000
 Paid-in Capital in Excess of Par—Sage. 235,000
 Retained Earnings—Sage ($290,000 × 0.05) 14,500
 Retained Earnings of Subsidiary—Post. 317,300
  Investment in Sage Company Common Stock—
  Post. 920,550
  Dividends—Sage ($40,000 × 0.05) 2,000
  Minority Interest in Net Assets of Subsidiary
  ($46,250 − $2,000) 44,250
 To eliminate intercompany investment and establish
 minority interest in net assets of subsidiary at beginning
 of year [($400,000 + $235,000 + $290,000) × 0.05 =
 $46,250], less minority interest in dividends ($40,000 ×
 0.05 = $2,000).

(b) Minority Interest in Net Income of Subsidiary 4,200
  Minority Interest in Net Assets of Subsidiary 4,200
 To establish minority interest in net income of subsidiary
 for year ended Dec. 31, Year 1 ($84,000 × 0.05 = $4,200).

The following should be stressed in a review of the working paper for consolidated financial statements of Post Corporation and subsidiary under the pooling theory:

1 In elimination (a), the minority shareholders' 5% interest in the subsidiary's beginning-of-year retained earnings balance and dividends declared by the subsidiary are eliminated, so that these amounts will be excluded from the consolidated statement of retained earnings.

2 The $4,200 debit to Minority Interest in Net Income of Subsidiary in elimination (b) is posted to the income statement section of the working paper for consolidated financial statements; the $14,500 debit to the Retained Earnings account of Sage Company in elimination (a) is posted to the **beginning-of-year** line in the statement of retained earnings section of the working paper. All eliminations that affect consolidated statements other than the consolidated balance sheet are posted directly to the appropriate consolidated statements sections.

3 As in the previously illustrated working paper for consolidated financial statements in this chapter, the net income totals of the income statement section are brought forward to the statement of retained earnings section, and the end-of-year retained earnings balances in the latter section are forwarded to the consolidated balance sheet section.

4 The combined effect of the $14,500 and $4,200 debit items of eliminations (a) and (b) is to include in end-of-year consolidated retained earnings only Post Corporation's 95% interest in the end-of-year retained earnings of Sage Company. Thus, total consolidated retained earnings on December 31, Year 1, is composed of the following:

Composition of consolidated retained earnings at end of year

Retained earnings of Post Corporation	$ 925,000
95% of Retained earnings of Sage Company ($334,000 × 0.95)	317,300
Consolidated retained earnings, end of year	$1,242,300

5 The combined effect of the $44,250 and $4,200 credit items of eliminations (a) and (b) is to reflect the minority interest in the net assets of the subsidiary on December 31, Year 1 ($48,450), at its correct amount of 5% of Sage Company's total stockholders' equity ($400,000 + $235,000 + $334,000 = $969,000; $969,000 × 0.05 = $48,450) on that date.

Consolidated Financial Statements The consolidated financial statements for Post Corporation and subsidiary incorporate the amounts in the Consolidated column of the working paper for consolidated financial statements, as shown on page 309.

The consolidated financial statements of a parent company and its partially owned subsidiary on page 309 are similar in format to those for a parent company and its wholly owned subsidiary illustrated on page 302. The principal difference is the presence of minority interest in net income of the subsidiary in the consolidated income statement and minority interest in net assets of the subsidiary in the consolidated balance sheet. In addition, the amounts attributable to the subsidiary in the consolidated statement of retained earnings are the **parent company's 95% share only,** as the following computations demonstrate:

Computation of amounts in consolidated statement of retained earnings

Adjustment to beginning-of-year retained earnings to reflect pooling of interests ($290,000 × 0.95)	$275,500
Dividends of subsidiary prior to business combination ($40,000 × 0.95)	$ 38,000

CONSOLIDATION OF WHOLLY OWNED POOLED SUBSIDIARY SUBSEQUENT TO DATE OF BUSINESS COMBINATION

In the following two sections, we continue the Palm Corporation–Starr Company and the Post Corporation–Sage Company examples to illustrate the preparation of consolidated financial statements subsequent to the date of a pooling-type business combination.

The equity method of accounting for pooled subsidiaries

A parent company's investment account for a subsidiary acquired in a pooling-type business combination originally reflects the parent's share of the **carrying amount** of the subsidiary's net assets. Thus, there is no

POST CORPORATION AND SUBSIDIARY
Consolidated Income Statement
For Year Ended December 31, Year 1

Net sales		$6,500,000
Costs and expenses:		
Cost of goods sold	$4,500,000	
Operating expenses	825,000	
Interest expense.	115,000	
Income taxes expense	711,000	
Minority interest in net income of subsidiary.	4,200	6,155,200
Net income.		$ 344,800
Earnings per share of common stock (1,057,000 shares outstanding).		$0.33

POST CORPORATION AND SUBSIDIARY
Consolidated Statement of Retained Earnings
For Year Ended December 31, Year 1

Retained earnings, beginning of year, as previously reported.		$ 810,000
Add: Adjustment to reflect pooling of interests with Sage Company. .		275,500
Retained earnings, beginning of year, as restated		$1,085,500
Add: Net income		344,800
Subtotal		$1,430,300
Less: Dividends:		
Post Corporation ($0.15 a share).	$150,000	
Sage Company, prior to business combination	38,000	188,000
Retained earnings, end of year.		$1,242,300

POST CORPORATION AND SUBSIDIARY
Consolidated Balance Sheet
December 31, Year 1
Assets

Current assets:		
Cash		$ 175,000
Inventories.		1,300,000
Other		765,000
Total current assets		$2,240,000
Plant assets (net)		4,600,000
Goodwill		100,000
Total assets		$6,940,000

Liabilities & Stockholders' Equity

Liabilities:		
Income taxes payable		$ 176,000
Other		3,320,000
Minority interest in net assets of subsidiary		48,450
Total liabilities		$3,544,450
Stockholders' equity:		
Common stock, $1 par.	$1,057,000	
Paid-in capital in excess of par.	1,096,250	
Retained earnings.	1,242,300	3,395,550
Total liabilities & stockholders' equity		$6,940,000

cost of the investment in a pooled subsidiary; the investment is recorded at the *parent's equity in the subsidiary's net assets.* It follows that the *equity method of accounting* is appropriate for the operating results of a pooled subsidiary subsequent to the business combination, and that the *cost method of accounting* is not appropriate for a pooled subsidiary.

To illustrate the equity method of accounting for a wholly owned pooled subsidiary, we return to the December 31, Year 1, business combination of Palm Corporation and Starr Company, and assume that it has been accounted for as a pooling, as described on page 297.

For the year ended December 31, Year 2, Starr had net income of $60,000. Starr's board of directors on December 20, Year 2, declared a cash dividend of $0.60 a share on the 40,000 outstanding shares of Starr common stock. The dividend was payable January 8, Year 3, to stockholders of record December 29, Year 2.

Under the equity method of accounting, Palm prepares the following journal entries to record the operating results of Starr for the year ended December 31, Year 2:

<table>
<tr><td style="vertical-align:top; width:25%">Parent company's equity-method journal entries to record operating results of wholly owned pooled subsidiary</td><td>

PALM CORPORATION
General Journal

Year 2

Dec. 20   Intercompany   Dividends   Receivable   (40,000 × $0.60).   24,000

         Investment in Starr Company Common Stock .   24,000
         To record dividend declared by Starr Company, payable Jan. 8, Year 3, to stockholders of record Dec. 29, Year 2.

     31   Investment in Starr Company Common Stock.   60,000

         Intercompany Investment Income   60,000
         To record 100% of Starr Company's net income for the year ended Dec. 31, Year 2. (Income tax effects are disregarded.)

</td></tr>
</table>

After the foregoing journal entries are posted, Palm's Investment in Starr Company Common Stock ledger account appears at the top of page 311.

The $426,000 balance of Palm's Investment in Starr Company Common Stock account on December 31, Year 2, exactly offsets the stockholder's equity accounts of Starr on that date (see Starr's December 31, Year 2, balance sheet on page 312) as shown in the second illustration on page 311.

Ledger account of parent company using equity method of accounting for wholly owned pooled subsidiary

Investment in Starr Company Common Stock				
Date	Explanation	Debit	Credit	Balance
12/31/1	Issuance of common stock in business com- bination			390,000 dr
12/20/2	Dividend declared by Starr		24,000	366,000 dr
12/31/2	Net income of Starr	60,000		426,000 dr

Stockholders' equity of wholly owned pooled subsidiary equals balance of parent company's investment account

Starr Company's stockholders' equity accounts:
Common stock, $5 par $200,000
Paid-in capital in excess of par 58,000
Retained earnings 168,000
    Total stockholders' equity of Starr Company $426,000

The Investment in Starr Company Common Stock ledger account thus reflects Palm's 100% equity in the net assets of Starr at carrying amount.

Working Paper for Consolidated Financial Statements The working paper for consolidated financial statements for Palm Corporation and subsidiary for the year ended December 31, Year 2, is presented on page 312; the working paper elimination appears at the top of page 313. The intercompany receivable and payable is the $24,000 dividend payable by Starr to Palm on December 31, Year 2. (The advances by Palm Corporation to Starr Company that were outstanding on December 31, Year 1, were repaid by Starr on January 2, Year 2.)

The following aspects of the working paper for consolidated financial statements for Palm Corporation and subsidiary should be emphasized:

1 The intercompany receivable and payable, placed in adjacent columns on the same line, are offset without a formal elimination.

2 The elimination cancels all intercompany transactions and balances not dealt with by the offset described in 1 above.

3 **Consolidated net income** is the same as the **parent company's net income.** Also, **consolidated retained earnings** is equal to the total of the parent company's two retained earnings amounts in the working paper, as shown below.

Total of parent company's two retained earnings amounts in working paper equals consolidated retained earnings

Palm Corporation's retained earnings amounts:
Retained earnings $159,000
Retained earnings of subsidiary 132,000
    Total (equal to consolidated retained earnings) $291,000

Equity method: Wholly owned subsidiary subsequent to date of pooling-type business combination

PALM CORPORATION AND SUBSIDIARY
Working Paper for Consolidated Financial Statements
For Year Ended December 31, Year 2

	Palm Corporation	Starr Company	Eliminations increase (decrease)	Consolidated
Income Statement				
Revenue				
Net sales	1,100,000	680,000		1,780,000
Intercompany investment income. .	60,000		(a) (60,000)	
Total revenue.	1,160,000	680,000	(60,000)	1,780,000
Costs and expenses				
Costs of goods sold.	700,000	450,000		1,150,000
Operating expenses	151,000	80,000		231,000
Interest expense	49,000			49,000
Income taxes expense	120,000	90,000		210,000
Total costs and expenses	1,020,000	620,000		1,640,000
Net income	140,000	60,000	(60,000)	140,000
Statement of				
Retained Earnings				
Retained earnings, beginning of year .	49,000	132,000		181,000
Net income	140,000	60,000	(60,000)	140,000
Subtotal.	189,000	192,000	(60,000)	321,000
Dividends	30,000	24,000	(a) (24,000)	30,000
Retained earnings, end of year.	159,000	168,000	(36,000)	291,000
Balance Sheet				
Assets				
Intercompany receivables (payables).	24,000	(24,000)		
Investment in Starr Company				
common stock.	426,000		(a) (426,000)	
Other assets.	679,900	674,100		1,354,000
Total assets	1,129,900	650,100	(426,000)	1,354,000
Liabilities &				
Stockholders' Equity				
Liabilities.	230,900	224,100		455,000
Common stock, $10 par.	400,000			400,000
Common stock, $5 par		200,000	(a) (200,000)	
Paid-in capital in excess of par	208,000	58,000	(a) (58,000)	208,000
Retained earnings	159,000	168,000	(36,000)	291,000
Retained earnings of subsidiary	132,000		(a) (132,000)	
Total liabilities & stockholders' equity.	1,129,900	650,100	(426,000)	1,354,000

PALM CORPORATION AND SUBSIDIARY
Working Paper Elimination
December 31, Year 2

(a) Common Stock—Starr	200,000	
Paid-in Capital in Excess of Par—Starr	58,000	
Retained Earnings of Subsidiary—Palm	132,000	
Intercompany Investment Income—Palm	60,000	
Investment in Starr Company Common Stock— Palm		426,000
Dividends—Starr		24,000

To eliminate intercompany investment, related accounts for stockholder's equity of subsidiary, and investment income from subsidiary.

This equality results from Palm's use of the equity method of accounting for its investment in Starr.

4 The elimination cancels the parent company's Retained Earnings of Subsidiary account, because it carries a balance equal to the subsidiary's retained earnings **at the beginning of Year 2.** In this manner, each of the three financial statements (income statement, statement of retained earnings, and balance sheet) can be consolidated accurately.

Consolidated Financial Statements   The consolidated financial statements of Palm Corporation and subsidiary on page 314 are prepared from the amounts in the Consolidated column of the working paper for consolidated financial statements (page 312). The consolidated statement of retained earnings is prepared in the customary manner, because the business combination was completed in the prior accounting period.

Closing Entries   The equity method of accounting ignores legal form in favor of the economic substance of the relationship between a parent company and its subsidiary. However, state corporation laws necessitate a careful accounting for retained earnings available for dividends. Accordingly, Palm Corporation prepares the closing entries at the top of page 315, on December 31, Year 2, after the consolidated financial statements have been completed.

PALM CORPORATION AND SUBSIDIARY
Consolidated Income Statement
For Year Ended December 31, Year 2

Net sales		$1,780,000
Costs and expenses:		
Cost of goods sold	$1,150,000	
Operating expenses	231,000	
Interest expense.	49,000	
Income taxes expense	210,000	1,640,000
Net income.		$ 140,000
Earnings per share of common stock (40,000 shares outstanding). . .		$3.50

PALM CORPORATION AND SUBSIDIARY
Consolidated Statement of Retained Earnings
For Year Ended December 31, Year 2

Retained earnings, beginning of year	$ 181,000
Add: Net income	140,000
Subtotal	$ 321,000
Less: Dividends ($0.75 a share).	30,000
Retained earnings, end of year	$ 291,000

PALM CORPORATION AND SUBSIDIARY
Consolidated Balance Sheet
December 31, Year 2

Assets

Other assets	$1,354,000

Liabilities & Stockholders' Equity

Liabilities.		$ 455,000
Stockholders' equity:		
Common stock, $10 par	$400,000	
Paid-in capital in excess of par.	208,000	
Retained earnings	291,000	899,000
Total liabilities & stockholders' equity		$1,354,000

The first closing entry excludes from Palm Corporation's retained earnings the amount of Palm's net income not available for dividends to Palm's shareholders—$36,000. This amount is computed in the second illustration on page 315.

Parent company's closing entries under equity method of accounting for pooled subsidiary

PALM CORPORATION
General Journal
December 31, Year 2

Net Sales	1,100,000	
Intercompany Investment Income	60,000	
Costs and Expenses.		1,020,000
Retained Earnings of Subsidiary ($60,000 −		
$24,000)		36,000
Retained Earnings ($140,000 − $36,000).		104,000

To close revenue and expense accounts; to transfer net income legally available for dividends to retained earnings; and to segregate 100% share of net income of subsidiary not distributed as dividends by subsidiary.

Retained Earnings.	30,000	
Dividends		30,000

To close Dividends account.

Computation of undistributed earnings of subsidiary

Net income of Starr recorded by Palm Corporation	$60,000
Less: Dividends declared by Starr to Palm.	24,000
Amount of Starr's net income not distributed as a dividend to Palm (undistributed earnings of subsidiary).	$36,000

After the foregoing closing entries have been posted, Palm's Retained Earnings and Retained Earnings of Subsidiary accounts appear as follows:

Parent company's ledger accounts for retained earnings

Retained Earnings

Date	Explanation	Debit	Credit	Balance
12/31/1	Balance			49,000 cr
12/31/2	Close net income available for dividends		104,000	153,000 cr
12/31/2	Close Dividends account	30,000		123,000 cr

Retained Earnings of Subsidiary

Date	Explanation	Debit	Credit	Balance
12/31/1	Pooling-type business combination		132,000	132,000 cr
12/31/2	Close net income not available for dividends		36,000	168,000 cr

The $168,000 after-closing balance of Palm's Retained Earnings of Subsidiary ledger account is equal to the after-closing balance of Starr's Retained Earnings ledger account (see Starr's balance sheet on page 312) In addition, the $291,000 total ($123,000 + $168,000 = $291,000) of Palm's two ledger accounts for retained earnings is equal to consolidated retained earnings of Palm Corporation and subsidiary on December 31, Year 2.

In the December 31, Year 3, working paper elimination for Palm Corporation and subsidiary, the December 31, Year 2, balance of Palm's Retained Earnings of Subsidiary ledger account would be eliminated. For example, if Starr Company declared a dividend of $50,000 and had net income of $100,000 for the year ended December 31, Year 3, the working paper elimination for Palm Corporation and subsidiary on that date would be as follows:

PALM CORPORATION AND SUBSIDIARY
Working Paper Elimination
December 31, Year 3

(a) Common Stock—Starr	200,000	
Paid-in Capital in Excess of Par—Starr	58,000	
Retained Earnings of Subsidiary—Palm	168,000	
Intercompany Investment Income—Palm	100,000	
Investment in Starr Company Common Stock—		
Palm ($426,000 + $100,000 − $50,000)		476,000
Dividends—Starr		50,000

To eliminate intercompany investment, related accounts for stockholders' equity of subsidiary, and investment income from subsidiary.

CONSOLIDATION OF PARTIALLY OWNED POOLED SUBSIDIARY SUBSEQUENT TO DATE OF BUSINESS COMBINATION

The Post Corporation–Sage Company pooling-type business combination described on page 303 is used in this section to illustrate the preparation of consolidated financial statements for a parent company and its partially owned pooled subsidiary for the year following the business combination.

Assume that on November 24, Year 2, Sage Company declared a $1 a share dividend payable December 16, Year 2, to shareholders of record December 1, Year 2, and that Sage had net income of $90,000 for the year ended December 31, Year 2. The following journal entries recognize the dividend in the accounting records of Sage:

Partially owned subsidiary's journal entries for declaration and payment of dividend

SAGE COMPANY
General Journal

Year 2

Nov. 24	Dividends (40,000 × $1)	40,000	
	Dividends Payable ($40,000 × 0.05)		2,000
	Intercompany Dividends Payable ($40,000 × 0.95)		38,000
	To record declaration of dividend payable Dec. 16, Year 2, to stockholders of record Dec. 1, Year 2.		
Dec. 16	Dividends Payable	2,000	
	Intercompany Dividends Payable	38,000	
	Cash.		40,000
	To record payment of dividend declared Nov. 24, Year 2, to stockholders of record Dec. 1, Year 2.		

The following journal entries are required in the accounting records of Post under the equity method of accounting:

Parent company's equity-method journal entries to record operating results of partially owned pooled subsidiary

POST CORPORATION
General Journal

Year 2

Nov. 24	Intercompany Dividends Receivable.	38,000	
	Investment in Sage Company Common Stock .		38,000
	To record dividend declared by Sage Company, payable Dec. 16, Year 2, to stockholders of record Dec. 1, Year 2.		
Dec. 16	Cash	38,000	
	Intercompany Dividends Receivable.		38,000
	To record receipt of dividend from Sage Company.		
31	Investment in Sage Company Common Stock ($90,000 × 0.95)	85,500	
	Intercompany Investment Income		85,500
	To record 95% of net income of Sage Company for year ended Dec. 31, Year 2, (Income tax effects are disregarded.)		

After these journal entries are posted, Post Corporation's Investment in Sage Company Common Stock account is as shown on page 318.

The $968,050 balance of Post Corporation's Investment in Sage Company Common Stock account on December 31, Year 2, is equal to 95% of the total of Sage's stockholders' equity accounts on that date, as computed in the second illustration on page 318.

Ledger account of
parent company under
equity method of
accounting for partially
owned pooled
subsidiary

Investment in Sage Company Common Stock

Date	Explanation	Debit	Credit	Balance
12/31/1	Issuance of common stock in business combination			920,550 dr
11/24/2	Dividend declared by Sage		38,000	882,550 dr
12/31/2	Net income of Sage	85,500		968,050 dr

95% of total
stockholders' equity of
partially owned pooled
subsidiary equals
balance of parent
company's investment
account

Sage Company's stockholders' equity accounts:

Common stock, $10 par	$ 400,000
Paid-in capital in excess of par	235,000
Retained earnings	384,000
Total stockholders' equity of Sage Company	$1,019,000
95% of Sage's stockholders' equity ($1,019,000 × 0.95)	$ 968,050

Thus, the Investment in Sage Company Common Stock ledger account reflects Post's 95% equity in the net assets of Sage at Sage's carrying amount.

Working Paper for Consolidated Financial Statements The working paper for consolidated financial statements for Post Corporation and subsidiary for the year ended December 31, Year 2, is given on page 319; the working paper eliminations are given at the top of page 320.

The following aspects of the working paper for consolidated financial statements for Post Corporation and subsidiary are worthy of emphasis:

1 Consolidated net income is the same as the parent company's net income. Also, the amount of consolidated retained earnings is equal to the total of the parent company's two retained earnings amounts in the working paper, as follows:

Total of parent
company's two retained
earnings amounts
equals consolidated
retained earnings

Post Corporation's retained earnings amounts:

Retained earnings	$1,271,950
Retained earnings of subsidiary	317,300
Total (equal to consolidated retained earnings)	$1,589,250

2 The combined effect of the $46,450 and $4,500 credit amounts in eliminations (a) and (b) is to present the minority interest in net assets of subsidiary on December 31, Year 2, at the correct amount of 5% of Sage Company's total stockholders' equity on that date ($400,000 + $235,000 + $384,000 = $1,019,000; $1,019,000 × 0.05 = $50,950).

Equity method: Partially owned subsidiary subsequent to date of pooling-type business combination

POST CORPORATION AND SUBSIDIARY
Working Paper for Consolidated Financial Statements
For Year Ended December 31, Year 2

	Post Corporation	Sage Company	Eliminations increase (decrease)		Consolidated
Income Statement					
Revenue					
Net sales	5,611,000	1,089,000			6,700,000
Intercompany investment income. .	85,500		(a)	(85,500)	
Total revenue.	5,696,500	1,089,000		(85,500)	6,700,000
Costs and expenses					
Cost of goods sold	3,925,000	700,000			4,625,000
Operating expenses	556,000	129,000			685,000
Interest and income taxes expense .	710,000	170,000			880,000
Minority interest in net income of					
subsidiary			(b)	4,500	4,500
Total costs and expenses	5,191,000	999,000		4,500	6,194,500
Net income	505,500	90,000		(90,000)	505,500
Statement of					
Retained Earnings					
Retained earnings, beginning of year.	925,000	334,000	(a)	(16,700)	1,242,300
Net income	505.500	90,000		(90,000)	505,500
Subtotal	1,430,500	424,000		(106,700)	1,747,800
Dividends	158,550	40,000	(a)	(40,000)	158,550
Retained earnings, end of year.	1,271,950	384,000		(66,700)	1,589,250
Balance Sheet					
Assets					
Investment in Sage Company					
common stock.	968,050		(a)	(968,050)	
Other assets.	5,195,000	1,960,000			7,155,000
Total assets	6,163,050	1,960,000		(968,050)	7,155,000
Liabilities &					
Stockholders' Equity					
Liabilities.	2,420,550	941,000			3,361,550
Minority interest in net assets of					
subsidiary.			(a)	46,450	50,950
			(b)	4,500	
Common stock, $1 par	1,057,000				1,057,000
Common stock, $10 par.		400,000	(a)	(400,000)	
Paid-in capital in excess of par	1,096,250	235,000	(a)	(235,000)	1,096,250
Retained earnings	1,271,950	384,000		(66,700)	1,589,250
Retained earnings of subsidiary	317,300		(a)	(317,300)	
Total liabilities & stockholders'					
equity.	6,163,050	1,960,000		(968,050)	7,155,000

POST CORPORATION AND SUBSIDIARY
Working Paper Eliminations
December 31, Year 2

(a) Common Stock—Sage 400,000
    Paid-in Capital in Excess of Par—Sage 235,000
    Retained Earnings—Sage ($334,000 × 0.05) 16,700
    Retained Earnings of Subsidiary—Post 317,300
    Intercompany Investment Income—Post 85,500
        Investment in Sage Company Common Stock—
        Post. 968,050
        Dividends—Sage 40,000
        Minority Interest in Net Assets of Subsidiary
        ($48,450 − $2,000) 46,450
    To eliminate intercompany investment and related ac-
    counts for stockholders' equity of subsidiary at beginning
    of Year 2, and investment income from subsidiary; and to
    establish minority interest in net assets of subsidiary at
    beginning of year ($48,450) less minority dividends
    ($40,000 × 0.05 = $2,000).

(b) Minority Interest in Net Income of Subsidiary 4,500
        Minority Interest in Net Assets of Subsidiary 4,500
    To establish minority interest in net income of subsidiary
    for year ended Dec. 31, Year 2 ($90,000 × 0.05 = $4,500).

Consolidated Financial Statements The consolidated financial statements of Post Corporation and subsidiary on page 321 are prepared from the Consolidated column of the working paper for consolidated financial statements on page 319.

Closing Entries Post Corporation prepares the closing entries on page 322 on December 31, Year 2, after the consolidated financial statements have been completed. After the posting of the two closing entries, Post's Retained Earnings and Retained Earnings of Subsidiary ledger accounts are as illustrated on page 322.

The $364,800 after-closing balance of Post's Retained Earnings of Subsidiary ledger account is equal to 95% of the after-closing balance of Sage's Retained Earnings ledger account ($384,000 × 0.95 = $364,800). In addition, the $1,589,250 total ($1,224,450 + $364,800 = $1,589,250) of Post's two ledger accounts for retained earnings is equal to consolidated retained earnings of Post Corporation and subsidiary on December 31, Year 2.

POST CORPORATION AND SUBSIDIARY
Consolidated Income Statement
For Year Ended December 31, Year 2

Net sales		$6,700,000
Costs and expenses:		
Cost of goods sold	$4,625,000	
Operating expenses	685,000	
Interest and income taxes expense	880,000	
Minority interest in net income of subsidiary.	4,500	6,194,500
Net income.		$ 505,500

Earnings per share of common stock (1,057,000 shares outstanding) .	$0.48

POST CORPORATION AND SUBSIDIARY
Consolidated Statement of Retained Earnings
For Year Ended December 31, Year 2

Retained earnings, beginning of year	$1,242,300
Add: Net income	505,500
Subtotal	$1,747,800
Less: Dividends ($0.15 a share).	158,550
Retained earnings, end of year	$1,589,250

POST CORPORATION AND SUBSIDIARY
Consolidated Balance Sheet
December 31, Year 2

Assets

Other assets	$7,155,000

Liabilities & Stockholders' Equity

Liabilities:		
Other liabilities		$3,361,550
Minority interest in net assets of subsidiary		50,950
Total liabilities		$3,412,500
Stockholders' equity:		
Common stock, $1 par.	$1,057,000	
Paid-in capital in excess of par.	1,096,250	
Retained earnings.	1,589,250	3,742,500
Total liabilities & stockholders' equity		$7,155,000

Parent company's
closing entries under
equity method of
accounting for pooled
subsidiary

POST CORPORATION
General Journal
December 31, Year 2

Net Sales	5,611,000	
Intercompany Investment Income	85,500	
Costs and Expenses.		5,191,000
Retained Earnings of Subsidiary [($90,000 − $40,000) × 0.95]		47,500
Retained Earnings ($505,500 − $47,500).		458,000

To close revenue and expense accounts; to transfer net
income legally available for dividends to retained earnings; and to segregate 95% share of net income of subsidiary not distributed as dividends by subsidiary.

Retained Earnings.	158,550	
Dividends		158,550

To close Dividends account.

Parent company's
ledger accounts for
retained earnings

Retained Earnings

Date	Explanation	Debit	Credit	Balance
12/31/1	Balance			925,000 cr
12/31/2	Close net income available for dividends		458,000	1,383,000 cr
12/31/2	Close Dividends account	158,550		1,224,450 cr

Retained Earnings of Subsidiary

Date	Explanation	Debit	Credit	Balance
12/31/1	Pooling-type business combination		317,300	317,300 cr
12/31/2	Close net income not available for dividends		47,500	364,800 cr

In the December 31, Year 3, working paper eliminations for Post Corporation and Subsidiary, the December 31, Year 2, balance of Post's Retained Earnings of Subsidiary ledger account would be eliminated. For
example, if Sage Company declared dividends of $50,000 ($47,500 to
Post and $2,500 to minority shareholders) and had net income of
$105,000 ($99,750 to Post and $5,250 to minority shareholders) for the
year ended December 31, Year 3, the working paper eliminations for
Post Corporation and subsidiary on that date would be as follows:

POST CORPORATION AND SUBSIDIARY
Working Paper Eliminations
December 31, Year 3

(a) Common Stock—Sage.	400,000	
Paid-in Capital in Excess of Par—Sage.	235,000	
Retained Earnings—Sage ($384,000 × 0.05).	19,200	
Retained Earnings of Subsidiary—Post.	364,800	
Intercompany Investment Income—Post	99,750	
Investment in Sage Company Common Stock—		
Post ($968,050 + $99,750 − $47,500).		1,020,300
Dividends—Sage		50,000
Minority Interest in Net Assets of Subsidiary		
($50,950 − $2,500).		48,450

To eliminate intercompany investment and related accounts for stockholders' equity of subsidiary at beginning of Year 3, and investment income from subsidiary; and to establish minority interest in net assets of subsidiary at beginning of Year 3 ($50,950) less minority dividends ($2,500).

(b) Minority Interest in Net Income of Subsidiary	5,250	
Minority Interest in Net Assets of Subsidiary. . .		5,250

To establish minority interest in net income of subsidiary for year ended Dec. 31, Year 3.

ACCOUNTING FOR INTERCOMPANY TRANSACTIONS NOT INVOLVING PROFIT OR LOSS

Subsequent to the date of a business combination, a parent company and its subsidiaries may enter into a number of business transactions with each other. Both the parent and the subsidiary companies should account for these intercompany transactions in a manner that facilitates the consolidation process. To this end, separate ledger accounts should be established for all intercompany assets, liabilities, revenue, and expenses. These separate accounts clearly identify those intercompany items that must be eliminated in the preparation of consolidated financial statements. The accounting techniques described above are designed to assure that consolidated financial statements include only those balances and transactions resulting from the *consolidated group's dealings with outsiders.*

Among the numerous types of transactions (other than dividends) consummated between a parent company and its subsidiaries are the following:

Sales of merchandise
Sales of land or depreciable assets
Sales of intangible assets
Loans on promissory notes or open account
Leases of assets
Rendering of services

The first three types of transactions listed above usually involve an element of profit or loss, which complicates the preparation of consolidated financial statements. Discussion of these intercompany transactions is deferred until Chapter 8.

Loans on notes or open account

Parent companies generally have more extensive financial resources or bank lines of credit than do their subsidiaries. Also, it may be more economical in terms of favorable interest rates for the parent company to carry out all the affiliated group's borrowings from financial institutions. Under these circumstances, the parent company will make loans to its subsidiaries for their working capital or other needs. Generally, the rate of interest on such loans exceeds the parent company's borrowing rate.

To illustrate, assume that during the year ended December 31, Year 3, Palm Corporation made the following cash loans to its wholly owned subsidiary, Starr Company, on promissory notes:

Loans by parent company to wholly owned subsidiary

Date of note	Term of note, months	Interest rate, %	Amount
Feb. 1, Year 3	6	10	$10,000
Apr. 1, Year 3	6	10	15,000
Sept. 1, Year 3	6	10	21,000
Nov. 1, Year 3	6	10	24,000

To differentiate properly between intercompany loans and loans with outsiders, Palm Corporation and Starr Company would use the ledger accounts shown on page 325 to record the foregoing transactions (assuming all promissory notes were paid when due). In the working paper for consolidated financial statements for Palm Corporation and subsidiary for the year ended December 31, Year 3, the accounts appear as shown on page 325.

It is apparent from the illustration on page 325 that careful identification of intercompany ledger account balances in the accounting rec-

Ledger accounts of parent company and subsidiary for intercompany loan transactions

PALM CORPORATION LEDGER				STARR COMPANY LEDGER			
Intercompany Notes Receivable				**Intercompany Notes Payable**			
Feb. 1	10,000	Aug. 1	10,000	Aug. 1	10,000	Feb. 1	10,000
Apr. 1	15,000	Oct. 1	15,000	Oct. 1	15,000	Apr. 1	15,000
Sept. 1	21,000					Sept. 1	21,000
Nov. 1	24,000					Nov. 1	24,000

PALM CORPORATION LEDGER			STARR COMPANY LEDGER		
Intercompany Interest Receivable			**Intercompany Interest Payable**		
Dec. 31	1,100			Dec. 31	1,100

PALM CORPORATION LEDGER			STARR COMPANY LEDGER		
Intercompany Interest Revenue			**Intercompany Interest Expense**		
	Aug. 1	500	Aug. 1	500	
	Oct. 1	750	Oct. 1	750	
	Dec. 31	1,100	Dec. 31	1,100	

PALM CORPORATION AND SUBSIDIARY
Partial Working Paper for Consolidated Financial Statements
For Year Ended December 31, Year 3

	Palm Corporation	Starr Company	Eliminations increase (decrease)	Consolidated
Income Statement				
Intercompany revenue (expenses)	2,350	(2,350)		
Balance Sheet				
Intercompany receivables (payables)	46,100	(46,100)		

ords of the affiliated companies is essential for correct elimination of the intercompany items in the working paper for consolidated financial statements.

Discounting of Intercompany Notes If an intercompany note receivable is discounted by the holder, the note in effect is payable to an *outsider*—the discounting bank. Consequently, discounted intercompany notes are *not eliminated* in the working paper for consolidated financial statements.

Suppose, for example, that on December 1, Year 3, Palm Corporation had discounted the $24,000 note receivable from Starr Company at a 12% discount rate. Palm would prepare the following journal entry:

Parent company's
journal entry for
discounting of note
receivable from
subsidiary

PALM CORPORATION
General Journal

Cash ($25,200 − $1,260)   23,940
Interest Expense ($1,260 discount − $1,000*)   260
    Intercompany Notes Receivable   24,000
    Intercompany Interest Revenue ($24,000 × 0.10 × $\frac{1}{12}$) .   200
To record discounting of 10%, six-month note receivable from
Starr Company dated Nov. 1, Year 3, at a discount rate of 12%.
Cash proceeds are computed as follows:
  Maturity value of note [$24,000 + ($24,000 × 0.10 × $\frac{6}{12}$)] . . . $25,200
  Discount ($25,200 × 0.12 × $\frac{5}{12}$)   1,260
  Proceeds $23,940

* Interest that accrues to discounting bank during discount period.

The foregoing journal entry recognizes intercompany interest revenue for the one month the note was held by Palm. This approach is required because Starr will reflect in its accounting records one month of intercompany interest expense on the note.

To assure proper accountability for the $24,000 note, Palm should notify Starr of the discounting. Starr would then prepare the following journal entry on December 1, Year 3:

Subsidiary journal entry
for parent company's
discounting of note
payable by subsidiary to
parent company

STARR COMPANY
General Journal

Intercompany Notes Payable   24,000
Intercompany Interest Expense   200
    Notes Payable   24,000
    Interest Payable   200
To transfer 10%, six-month note payable to Palm Corporation
dated Nov. 1, Year 3, from intercompany notes to outsider
notes. Action is necessary because Palm Corporation discounted the note on this date.

In the foregoing journal entry, Starr credited Interest Payable rather than Intercompany Interest Payable for the $200 accrued interest on the note. This approach is required because the discounting bank, not Palm, is now the payee for the total maturity value of the note.

Under the note discounting assumption, the ledger accounts related to intercompany notes would appear in the December 31, Year 3, working paper for consolidated financial statements as follows:

PALM CORPORATION AND SUBSIDIARY
Partial Working Paper for Consolidated Financial Statements
For Year Ended December 31, Year 3

	Palm Corporation	Starr Company	Eliminations increase (decrease)	Consolidated
Income Statement				
Intercompany revenue				
(expenses)	2,150*	(2,150)*		
Balance Sheet				
Intercompany receiv-				
ables (payables)	21,700†	(21,700)†		

* $200 less than in illustration on page 325 because $24,000 discounted note earned interest for one month rather than two months.
† $21,000 note dated Sept. 1, Year 3, plus $700 accrued interest.

Leases of assets

If a parent company leases assets to a subsidiary, or vice versa, it is essential that both affiliates use the same accounting principles for the lease. If the lease is an **operating lease,**[3] the lessor affiliate should account for rental payments as intercompany rent revenue, and the lessee affiliate should record the payments as intercompany rent expense. For a **capital lease,**[3] the lessor affiliate should record a sale of the asset, and the lessee affiliate should account for the lease as a "purchase" of the asset. Accounting for a capital lease often involves intercompany profits or losses, which are discussed in Chapter 8.

To illustrate consolidation techniques for an intercompany **operating lease,** assume that Palm Corporation leases space for a sales office to Starr Company under a 10-year lease dated February 1, Year 3. The lease requires monthly rentals of $2,500 payable in advance the first day of each month beginning February 1, Year 3.

In the income statement section of the working paper for consolidated financial statements for the year ended December 31, Year 3, Palm's $27,500 intercompany rent revenue would be offset against Starr's intercompany rent expense in a manner similar to the offset of intercompany interest revenue and expense illustrated previously. There would be no intercompany assets or liabilities to be offset in an operating lease for which rent is payable in advance at the beginning of each month.

[3] The accounting for operating leases and capital leases is included in the *Intermediate Accounting* book of this series.

Rendering of services

One affiliate may render services to another, with resultant intercompany fee revenue and expenses. A common example is the ***management fee*** charged by a parent company to its subsidiaries.

Management fees often are billed monthly by the parent company, computed as a percentage of the subsidiary's net sales, number of employees, total assets, or some other measure. No new consolidation problems are introduced by intercompany fee revenue and expenses. However, care must be taken to make certain that both the parent company and the subsidiary record the fee billings in the same accounting period.

Income taxes applicable to intercompany transactions

The intercompany revenue and expense transactions illustrated in this chapter do not include an element of intercompany profit or loss for the consolidated entity. This is true because the revenue of one affiliate exactly offsets the expense of the other affiliate in the income statement section of the working paper for consolidated financial statements. Consequently, there are no income tax effects associated with the elimination of the intercompany revenue and expenses, whether the parent company and its subsidiaries file separate income tax returns or a consolidated income tax return.

Summary: Intercompany transactions and balances

The preceding sections have emphasized the necessity of clearly identifying intercompany ledger account balances in the accounting records of both the parent company and the subsidiary. This careful identification facilitates the elimination of intercompany items in the preparation of consolidated financial statements. Sometimes, the separate financial statements of a parent company and a subsidiary include differing balances for intercompany items that should offset. Before preparation of the working paper for consolidated financial statements, any necessary journal entries to correct intercompany balances or to bring such balances up to date should be prepared.

REVIEW QUESTIONS

1 Depending on circumstances, a busines combination may be accounted for as a purchase or as a pooling of interests. Discuss the differences between (1) a consolidated balance sheet prepared on the date of a purchase-type business combination, and (2) a consolidated balance sheet prepared on the date of a pooling-type business combination.

2 Explain the purpose of the Retained Earnings of Subsidiary ledger account used for a pooled subsidiary.

3 How does the balance in a parent company's Retained Earnings of Subsidiary ledger account for a pooled subsidiary differ from the balance of the same account for a purchased subsidiary?

4 For the year ended October 31, Year 2, Staley Company had net income of $60,000. As of the close of business that date, Pryor Corporation acquired most of the outstanding common stock of Staley Company in exchange for Pryor's unissued common stock.

The working paper eliminations for Pryor Corporation and subsidiary for the year ended October 31, Year 2, included the following (explanation omitted):

Minority Interest in Net Income of Subsidiary *1,200*

    Minority Interest in Net Assets of Subsidiary *1,200*

a Was the business combination of Pryor Corporation and Staley Company accounted for as a purchase or as a pooling of interests? Explain.
b What percentage of Staley's outstanding common stock was exchanged for Pryor's common stock? Explain.

5 The retained earnings balances of Pelham Corporation and Skeene Company on September 30, Year 5, were $2,000,000 and $800,000, respectively. At the close of business that date, Skeene became a subsidiary of Pelham when Pelham acquired 95% of Skeene's outstanding common stock.

What is the amount of consolidated retained earnings in the consolidated balance sheet of Pelham Corporation and subsidiary on September 30, Year 5, if the business combination is accounted for as:
a A purchase? Explain.
b A pooling of interests? Explain.

6 Why is the equity method of accounting for a subsidiary's operating results consistent with the pooling theory of accounting for a business combination?

7 How should a parent company and subsidiary account for intercompany transactions and balances to assure their correct elimination in the preparation of consolidated financial statements? Explain.

8 What are five common intercompany transactions between a parent company and its subsidiary?

9 Primak Corporation rents a sales office to its wholly owned subsidiary under an operating lease requiring rent of $2,000 a month. What are the income tax effects of the elimination of Primak's $24,000 rent revenue and the subsidiary's $24,000 rent expense in the preparation of a consolidated income statement? Explain.

10 Is an intercompany note receivable that has been discounted at a bank eliminated in the preparation of a consolidated balance sheet? Explain.

11 Describe the special features of the closing entry for a parent company that uses the equity method of accounting for the operating results of a pooled subsidiary.

EXERCISES

Ex. 7-1   Select the best answer for each of the following multiple-choice questions:

1 The balance of the parent company's Investment in Subsidiary Common Stock ledger account for a 98%-owned pooled subsidiary should always equal:

a The total of the subsidiary's stockholders' equity accounts

b The total of the subsidiary's asset accounts

c The total of the subsidiary's stockholders' equity accounts plus the unamortized date-of-business-combination differences between the current fair values and carrying amounts of the subsidiary's identifiable net assets

d Some other amount

2 A ledger account that is not affected by a subsidiary's journal entry to record the parent company's discounting of a note receivable from the subsidiary during the accounting period in which the note was received is:

a Notes Payable

b Intercompany Notes Payable

c Interest Payable

d Intercompany Interest Payable

e None of the foregoing

3 The stockholders' equity section of the March 31, Year 7, balance sheet of Silver Company was as follows:

Common stock, $1 par	$ 50,000
Paid-in capital in excess of par	100,000
Retained earnings	150,000
Total stockholders' equity	$300,000

On March 31, Year 7, Pearl Corporation issued 25,000 shares of its $2 par common stock for all the outstanding common stock of Silver in a pooling-type business combination. Silver became a subsidiary of Pearl. Pearl's March 31, Year 7, journal entry to record the business combination should include a credit to the Retained Earnings account in the amount of:

a $0   **b** $150,000   **c** $200,000   **d** $350,000

e None of the foregoing

4 In the consolidated statement of retained earnings for the fiscal year in which a pooling-type business combination occurred, dividends declared by the pooled subsidiary during that fiscal year but prior to the business combination are:

a Presented separately

b Combined with dividends declared by the parent company

c Eliminated

d Treated in some other manner

5 On October 31, Year 2, the end of a fiscal year, Perch Corporation acquired 94% of the outstanding common stock of Salmon Company in a pooling-type business combination. To effect the combination, Perch issued 47,000 shares of its $10 par common stock having a current fair value of $20 a share. On the date of the combination, the stockholders' equity of Salmon was as follows:

Common stock, $50 stated value	$ 50,000
Paid-in capital in excess of stated value	150,000
Retained earnings	400,000
Total stockholders' equity	$600,000

In its journal entry (disregarding out-of-pocket costs) to record the business combination, Perch should:

a Debit the Investment in Salmon Company Common Stock account $940,000
b Credit the Retained Earnings of Subsidiary account $400,000
c Debit the Paid-in Capital in Excess of Par account (which had a balance of $1,840,000) $282,000
d Credit the Common Stock account $47,000

6 Refer to the facts in **5**. The October 31, Year 2, working paper eliminations for Perch Corporation and subsidiary should include a:

a $376,000 debit to Retained Earnings of Subsidiary—Perch
b $600,000 credit to Investment in Salmon Company Common Stock—Perch
c $47,000 debit to Common Stock—Salmon
d $400,000 debit to Retained Earnings—Salmon

7 At the beginning of Year 1, Primero Corporation exchanged its voting common stock for 99% of Secundo Company's outstanding common stock in a pooling-type business combination. Primero adopted the equity method of accounting for its investment in Secundo. There were no transactions involving intercompany profits between the two companies during Year 1. The Year 1 separate income statements for Primero and Secundo showed net income of $46,180 and $9,000, respectively, disregarding income tax effects resulting from Primero's use of the equity method. Consolidated net income of Primero Corporation and subsidiary for Year 1 is:

a $46,180   b $55,180   c $55,090   d $54,628
e None of the foregoing or not determinable from the information given

Ex. 7-2   On March 31, Year 4, Spirea Company, the wholly owned subsidiary of Peony Corporation, prepared the following journal entry at the instruction of Peony:

Intercompany Notes Payable	18,000	
Intercompany Interest Expense	270	
Notes Payable		18,000
Interest Payable		270

To transfer 18%, 60-day note payable to Peony Corporation dated March 1, Year 4, from intercompany notes to outsider notes. Action is necessary because Peony discounted the note at 20% on this date.

Prepare a journal entry for Peony Corporation on March 31, Year 4, to record the discounting of the Spirea Company note at First National Bank. Use a 360-day year.

Ex. 7-3   On page 332 is the statement of retained earnings section of the working paper for consolidated financial statements for Pierce Corporation and subsidiary for the year ended March 31, Year 7, the date Pierce exchanged 10,000 shares of its common stock for 92% of the outstanding common stock of Sill Company in a pooling-type business combination.

	Pierce Corporation	Sill Company	Eliminations increase (decrease)		Consolidated
Retained earnings, beginning of year	100,000	50,000	(a)	(4,000)	146,000
Net income.	60,000	40,000		(3,200)	96,800
Subtotal	160,000	90,000		(7,200)	242,800
Dividends.	20,000				20,000
Retained earnings, end of year.	140,000	90,000		(7,200)	222,800

Prior to the business combination, Pierce had 100,000 shares of common stock outstanding for many years.

Prepare a consolidated statement of retained earnings for Pierce Corporation and subsidiary for the year ended March 31, Year 7.

Ex. 7-4   Pross Corporation owns 90% of the outstanding common stock of Stump Company, acquired in a pooling-type business combination January 31, Year 1. For the year ended January 31, Year 2, Pross Corporation's unconsolidated income statement was as follows:

PROSS CORPORATION

Income Statement

For Year Ended January 31, Year 2

Revenue	
Net sales	$500,000
Intercompany investment income	27,000
Intercompany revenue	23,000
Total revenue	$550,000
Costs and expenses	510,000
Net income	$ 40,000

During the year ended January 31, Year 2, both Pross and Stump declared and paid dividends of $10,000.

Prepare closing entries for Pross Corporation on January 31, Year 2.

Ex. 7-5   Ponce Corporation completed a pooling-type business combination with Skaggs Company on December 31, Year 6. 48,000 of Skaggs's 50,000 shares of outstanding common stock were exchanged in the combination.

Skaggs reported net income of $0.80 a share for Year 7 and declared dividends of $0.35 a share on December 13, Year 7, payable January 6, Year 8, to stockholders of record December 23, Year 7. There were no other intercompany transactions during Year 7.

Prepare journal entries to record:

a Skaggs Company's dividend declaration in its accounting records.

b Skaggs Company's operating results for Year 7 in Ponce Corporation's accounting records under the equity method of accounting.

Ex. 7-6   On November 1, Year 4, Pollitt Corporation issued 10,000 shares of its $10 par ($30 current fair value) common stock for 99 of the 100 outstanding shares of Simon Company's $100 par common stock, in a pooling-type business combination. Out-of-pocket costs of the business combination were as follows:

Legal fees and finder's fee associated with business combination *$15,000*

Costs incurred for SEC registration statement for Pollitt's common

stock *20,000*

Total out-of-pocket costs of business combination *$35,000*

On November 1, Year 4, Simon Company's stockholders' equity was as follows:

Common stock, $100 par . . . . *$ 10,000*

Paid-in capital in excess of par *140,000*

Retained earnings *70,000*

Total stockholders' equity *$220,000*

Prepare journal entries in Pollitt Corporation's accounting records to record the business combination with Simon Company.

Ex. 7-7 On March 13, Year 7, Parker Corporation loaned $100,000 to its subsidiary, Sark Company, on a 90-day, 16% promissory note. On April 12, Year 7, Parker discounted the Sark note at First National Bank at a 20% discount rate.

Compute the debit to the Cash account in Parker Corporation's journal entry to record the discounting of the Sark Company note. Round to the nearest dollar.

Ex. 7-8 The January 2, Year 3, balance sheets of two companies prior to their business combination follow:

	Poult Corporation	Saki Company
	(in thousands of dollars)	
Assets		
Cash	$ 6,000	$ 200
Inventories	4,000	400
Plant assets (net)	10,000	1,400
Total assets.	$20,000	$2,000
Liabilities & Stockholders' Equity		
Current liabilities.	$ 1,200	$ 200
Common stock, $1 par	2,000	200
Paid-in capital in excess of par	6,000	400
Retained earnings	10,800	1,200
Total liabilities & stockholders' equity	$20,000	$2,000

On January 2, Year 3, Poult Corporation acquired all the outstanding common stock of Saki Company by issuing 200,000 shares of common stock (current fair value $20 a share) in a pooling-type business combination.

Compute the consolidated paid-in capital in excess of par in the January 2, Year 3, consolidated balance sheet of Poult Corporation and subsidiary.

Ex. 7-9 On March 1, Year 2, Payton Corporation loaned $10,000 to its subsidiary, Slagle Company, on a 90-day, 14% promissory note. On March 31, Year 2, Payton discounted the Slagle note at the bank at an 18% discount rate.

Prepare Payton Corporation's journal entry to record the discounting of the note. Round all amounts to the nearest dollar.

Ex. 7-10 On September 30, Year 7, Prosit Corporation combined with Skoal Company in a purchase-type business combination. Skoal's net income for the fiscal year ended September 30, Year 7, was $10,000, and Skoal neither declared nor paid dividends during the year. There were no intercompany transactions between the two companies prior to the business combination.

The working paper elimination for Prosit Corporation and subsidiary on September 30, Year 7, was as follows:

PROSIT CORPORATION AND SUBSIDIARY
Working Paper Elimination
September 30, Year 7

(a) *Common Stock—Skoal*	*50,000*	
Paid-in Capital in Excess of Par—Skoal	*60,000*	
Retained Earnings—Skoal	*70,000*	
Inventories—Skoal	*20,000*	
Plant Assets (net)—Skoal	*40,000*	
Goodwill—Prosit	*18,000*	
Investment in Skoal Company Common Stock— Prosit		*234,000*
Minority Interest in Net Assets of Subsidiary		*24,000*

To eliminate intercompany investment and equity accounts of subsidiary on date of business combination; to allocate excess of cost over carrying amounts of identifiable assets acquired, with remainder to goodwill; and to establish minority interest in net assets of subsidiary on date of business combination ($240,000 × 0.10 = $24,000).

Prepare working paper eliminations for Prosit Corporation and subsidiary under the assumption that the business combination of Prosit and Skoal had been accounted for as a pooling rather than as a purchase.

Ex. 7-11 Pender Corporation uses the equity method of accounting for the operating results of its 97%-owned pooled subsidiary, Sebo Company. For Year 6, Pender had net sales of $2,000,000 and total costs and expenses of $1,700,000. Sebo reported net income of $150,000 and declared dividends of $70,000.

Prepare Pender Corporation's journal entries to record its share of Sebo Company's dividends and net income for Year 6.

Ex. 7-12 The working paper eliminations for Pillar Corporation and its 99%-owned pooled subsidiary on March 31, Year 2, the date of the business combination, follow:

PILLAR CORPORATION AND SUBSIDIARY
Working Paper Eliminations
March 31, Year 2

(a) Common Stock—Scanlon   200,000

      Paid-in Capital in Excess of Par—Scanlon   300,000

      Retained Earnings of Subsidiary—Pillar   396,000

      Retained Earnings—Scanlon   3,500

           Investment in Scanlon Company Common

             Stock —Pillar   891,000

             Dividends—Scanlon   300

             Minority Interest in Net Assets of Subsidiary . . .   8,200

      To eliminate intercompany investment and establish minority interest in net assets of subsidiary at beginning of year, less minority dividends.

(b) Minority Interest in Net Income of Subsidiary   800

        Minority Interest in Net Assets of Subsidiary . . .   800

      To establish minority interest in net income of subsidiary for year ended March 31, Year 2.

Prior to the business combination with Pillar, Scanlon declared and paid dividends of $30,000 during the year ended March 31, Year 2.

Prepare a separate statement of retained earnings for Scanlon Company for the year ended March 31, Year 2, prior to the business combination with Pillar Corporation.

Ex. 7-13   Paley Corporation erroneously used the cost method of accounting for the operating results of its 94%-owned pooled subsidiary, Selma Company, with which Paley combined on May 31, Year 3. Details of Selma's Retained Earnings ledger account for the three years since that date follow.

Retained Earnings

May 26, Year 4 Dividends	30,000	May 31, Year 3 Balance	470,000
May 31, Year 5 Net loss	20,000	May 31, Year 4 Net income	60,000
May 24, Year 6 Dividends	30,000	May 31, Year 6 Net income	80,000

Prepare an adjusting entry for Paley Corporation on May 31, Year 6, to convert its accounting for its subsidiary's operating results to the equity method. The entry should include the account or accounts necessary for Paley's income statement for the year ended May 31, Year 6.

Ex. 7-14   Saticoy Company, a wholly owned pooled subsidiary of Porterville Corporation, reported net income of $70,000 and declared dividends of $20,000 for the year ended December 31, Year 6. Porterville had total revenue of $2,000,000, exclusive of intercompany investment income, and total costs and expenses of $1,200,000 for the year ended December 31, Year 6. Porterville declared dividends of $180,000 during Year 6.

Prepare Porterville Corporation's closing entries on December 31, Year 6.

Ex. 7-15   During the year ended October 31, Year 5, Strickland Company, 96%-owned pooled subsidiary of Prykop Corporation, had net income of $50,000 and declared dividends of $20,000 on October 20, Year 5, payable November 10, Year 5, to stockholders of record October 31, Year 5.

a Prepare journal entries for Prykop Corporation to record Strickland Company's operating results and dividend declaration for the year ended October 31, Year 5. Disregard income taxes.

b Prepare the working paper elimination for the minority interest in Strickland Company's net income for the year ended October 31, Year 5. Disregard income taxes.

CASES

Case 7-1   On March 1, Year 6, Perlmuth Corporation signed a preliminary agreement to consummate a business combination with Stabler Company that met the prerequisites for pooling accounting. A condition of the combination was that the Perlmuth Corporation common stock issued to Ralph Stabler, sole shareholder of Stabler Company, would be registered with the SEC. However, Perlmuth Corporation withdrew its registration statement for the common stock because of adverse stock market conditions. Accordingly, the business combination was never completed.

On April 30, Year 7, Progress Corporation issued its common stock, which was registered with the SEC, for all the outstanding common stock of Stabler Company. All the requirements of pooling accounting appeared to be met in the Progress–Stabler business combination. However on learning of Perlmuth's aborted combination with Stabler Company, the auditors for Progress Corporation, questioned whether the following provision for pooling accounting, set forth in **APB Opinion No. 16,** "Business Combinations," applied:

Each of the combining companies is autonomous and has not been a subsidiary or division of another corporation within two years before the plan of combination is initiated.

Instructions   Does the Progress Corporation–Stabler Company business combination qualify for pooling accounting? Explain.

Case 7-2   As independent auditor of a new client, Aqua Water Corporation, you are reviewing the working paper for consolidated financial statements prepared by Arthur Brady, Aqua Water's accountant. Aqua Water distributes water to homeowners in a suburb of a large city. Aqua Water purchases the water from its subsidiary, Aqua Well Company. Aqua Water organized Aqua Well five years ago and acquired all its common stock for cash on that date.

During the course of your audit, you have learned the following:

(1) Both Aqua Water and Aqua Well are public utilities subject to the jurisdiction of the state's Public Utilities Commission.
(2) Aqua Well charges Aqua Water for the transmission of water from wells to consumers. The transmission charge, at the customary utility rate, was approved by the state's Public Utilities Commission.
(3) Aqua Well charges Aqua Water separately for the volume of water delivered to Aqua Water's customers.
(4) Your audit working papers show the following audited amounts for the two companies' separate financial statements:

	Aqua Water Corporation	Aqua Well Company
Total revenue	$3,500,000	$ 300,000
Net income	300,000	50,000
Total assets	5,700,000	1,000,000
Stockholders' equity	2,500,000	600,000

The working paper for consolidated financial statements prepared by Aqua Water Corporation's accountant appears in order, except that Aqua Well's Transmission Revenue account of $60,000 is not offset against Aqua Water's Transmission Expense account of the same amount. The accountant explained that, because the transmission charge by Aqua Well is at the customary utility rate approved by the state's Public Utilities Commission, the charge should not be treated as intercompany revenue and expense. Furthermore, Brady points out, the working paper for consolidated financial statements does offset Aqua Well's Water Sales account of $200,000 against Aqua Water's Water Purchases account of the same amount.

Instructions Do you concur with the accountant's (Brady's) position? Explain.

Case 7-3 On January 2, Year 5, Preston Corporation paid $1,000,000 cash, including direct out-of-pocket costs, for all of Storey Company's outstanding common stock. The carrying amount of Storey's identifiable net assets on January 2, Year 5, was $880,000. Both Preston and Storey have operated profitably for many years, both have December 31 fiscal years, and each has only common stock outstanding. The business combination should be accounted for by the purchase method, in which Preston should follow certain principles in allocating its investment cost to the assets acquired and liabilities assumed.

Instructions
a Describe the principles that Preston Corporation should follow in allocating its investment cost to the assets acquired and liabilities assumed, for a January 2, Year 5, consolidated balance sheet.
b Independent of your answer to *a,* assume that on January 2, Year 5, Preston Corporation acquired all of Storey Company's outstanding common stock in exchange for Preston common stock, and that all conditions for pooling accounting were met. Describe the principles that Preston should follow in applying the pooling accounting method to the business combination with Storey, in the preparation of a consolidated balance sheet on January 2, Year 5.

PROBLEMS

7-1 On January 2, Year 6, Petro Corporation issued 200,000 shares of its common stock in exchange for 100,000 shares of Swiss Company's outstanding common stock in a pooling-type business combination. The current fair value of Petro's common stock was $40 a share on the date of the combination. The balance sheets of Petro and Swiss immediately before the combination contained the following information:

Petro Corporation

Common stock, $5 par; authorized 1,000,000 shares; issued and outstanding 600,000 shares	$ 3,000,000
Paid-in capital in excess of par	6,000,000
Retained earnings	11,000,000
Total stockholders' equity	$20,000,000

(Continued)

Swiss Company

Common stock, $10 par; authorized 250,000 shares; issued and out-
standing 100,000 shares $1,000,000
Paid-in capital in excess of par   2,000,000
Retained earnings   4,000,000
  Total stockholders' equity $7,000,000

Additional information is as follows:

(1) Net income for the year ended December 31, Year 6, was $1,150,000 for Petro and $350,000 for Swiss. The net income for Petro does not include its share of Swiss Company's net income.
(2) During Year 6, Petro declared and paid $900,000 in dividends to its stockholders and Swiss declared and paid $220,000 in dividends to Petro.

Instructions Prepare the stockholders' equity section of the consolidated balance sheet of Petro Corporation and subsidiary on December 31, Year 6. Prepare a supporting analysis for consolidated retained earnings. Disregard income tax considerations.

7-2 On October 21, Year 9, Prentiss Corporation loaned to its 92%-owned pooled subsidiary, Scopes Company, $100,000 on a 90-day, 15% (a year) promissory note. On October 31, Year 9, Prentiss discounted the Scopes note at City Bank, at a discount rate of 18% a year.

Instructions Prepare journal entries for the foregoing transactions:
a In the accounting records of Prentiss Corporation
b In the accounting records of Scopes Company

Round all amounts to the nearest dollar.

7-3 On July 31, Year 7, Pinto Corporation issued 15,000 shares of its $100 par common stock for 9,700 shares of Savoy Company's 10,000 outstanding shares of $50 par common stock. Out-of-pocket costs of $150,000 were paid by Pinto on July 31, Year 7. The business combination qualified for pooling accounting, and Savoy Company became a subsidiary of Pinto Corporation. Immediately following the combination, Pinto's general ledger included the following account balances:

Investment in Savoy Company Common Stock . . . . $1,789,650 dr
Retained Earnings of Subsidiary (Savoy Company) . . . .   625,650 cr

Savoy reported net income of $60,000 and paid no dividends for the fiscal year ended July 31, Year 7.

Instructions
a Reconstruct Pinto Corporation's journal entries to record the pooling-type business combination with Savoy Company on July 31, Year 7.
b Prepare working paper eliminations for Pinto Corporation and subsidiary on July 31, Year 7.

7-4 On September 30, Year 1, the end of a fiscal year, Pirtle Corporation issued 100,000 shares of its $5 par common stock (current fair value $12 a share) for 18,800 shares of the outstanding $20 par common stock of Solis Company. The $150,000 out-of-pocket costs of the business combination paid by Pirtle on September 30, Year 1, were allocable as follows: 60% to legal fees and finder's fee directly related to the business combination, and 40% to the SEC registration statement for Pirtle common stock issued in the business combination.

Immediately prior to the business combination, stockholders' equity accounts of the two companies were as follows:

	Pirtle Corporation	Solis Company
Common stock	$4,000,000	$ 400,000
Paid-in capital in excess of par	1,500,000	
Retained earnings	3,000,000	700,000*
Total stockholders' equity	$8,500,000	$1,100,000

* Net income $260,000, dividends $120,000, for fiscal year ended Sept. 30, Year 1

Instructions

a Prepare Pirtle Corporation's journal entries on September 30, Year 1, to record the business combination with Solis Company as a pooling.

b Prepare working paper eliminations for Pirtle Corporation and subsidiary on September 30, Year 1.

7-5 Pillsbury Corporation has begun making working capital loans to its wholly owned subsidiary, Sarpy Company, on 15% promissory notes. The following 120-day loans were made prior to June 30, Year 3, the close of the fiscal year:

May 1, Year 3	$15,000
May 31, Year 3	20,000

On June 6, Year 3, Pillsbury discounted the May 1 note at a bank, at an 18% discount rate.

Instructions Prepare journal entries to record the note transactions and related June 30, Year 3, adjustments:

a In the accounting records of Pillsbury Corporation

b In the accounting records of Sarpy Company

Round all amounts to the nearest dollar.

7-6 Separate statements of retained earnings for Pedro Corporation and Santo Company for the fiscal year ended May 31, Year 2 (prior to their business combination), follow:

PEDRO CORPORATION AND SANTO COMPANY

Separate Statements of Retained Earnings

For Year Ended May 31, Year 2

	Pedro Corporation	Santo Company
Retained earnings, beginning of year	$500,000	$290,000
Net income	100,000	80,000
Subtotals	$600,000	$370,000
Dividends	40,000	25,000
Retained earnings, end of year	$560,000	$345,000

On May 31, Year 2, Pedro issued 50,000 shares of its $1 par common stock for 54,600 of the 60,000 outstanding shares of $3 par common stock of Santo. Total paid-in capital attributable to Santo's common stock was $7 a share. The

$30,000 out-of-pocket costs of the pooling-type business combination were paid by Pedro on May 31, Year 2. There were no intercompany transactions prior to the date of the combination.

Instructions   Prepare a working paper to compute the following:
a Minority interest in net income of Santo company for the year ended May 31, Year 2.
b Consolidated net income for Pedro Corporation and subsidiary for the year ended May 31, Year 2.
c Minority interest in net assets of Santo Company on May 31, Year 2.
d Consolidated retained earnings for Pedro Corporation and subsidiary on May 31, Year 2.

7-7   The accountant of Purvis Corporation prepared the following journal entries on March 1, Year 8:

Investment in Semel Company Common Stock	783,000	
Minority Interest in Net Assets of Subsidiary	16,000	
Common Stock		49,000
Paid-in Capital in Excess of Par of Subsidiary		300,000
Retained Earnings of Subsidiary		450,000

To record issuance of 4,900 shares of $10 par common stock for 9,800 of 10,000 outstanding shares of Semel Company $5 par common stock in pooling-type business combination; to bring forward Semel's Paid-in Capital in Excess of Par and Retained Earnings accounts at their carrying amounts in Semel's accounting records; and to provide for minority interest in Semel's net assets ($800,000) on March 1, Year 8.

Investment in Semel Company Common Stock	80,000	
Paid-in Capital in Excess of Par	70,000	
Cash		150,000

To record payment of out-of-pocket costs of business combination with Semel Company as follows:

Finder's fee and legal fees relating to business combination	$ 80,000
Costs associated with SEC registration statement	70,000
Total out-of-pocket costs of business combination	$150,000

Instructions
a Prepare journal entries to correct Purvis Corporation's accounting for its business combination with Semel Company on March 1, Year 8.
b Assuming that Semel Company had net income of $100,000 and declared no dividends for the fiscal year ended February 28, Year 9, prepare (1) a journal entry to record Semel's net income in the accounting records of Purvis Corporation on February 28, Year 9, and (2) working paper eliminations required for the preparation of consolidated financial statements for Purvis Corporation and subsidiary for the year ended February 28, Year 9. (Disregard income taxes.)

7-8 The working paper eliminations for Poole Corporation and subsidiary on October 31, Year 4, the date of the pooling-type business combination, were as follows (in journal entry form):

POOLE CORPORATION AND SUBSIDIARY

Working Paper Eliminations

October 31, Year 4

(a) Common Stock—Soule 100,000
Paid-in Capital in Excess of Par—Soule 150,000
Retained Earnings—Soule ($160,000 × 0.10) 16,000
Retained Earnings of Subsidiary—Poole ($200,000 ×
  0.90) 180,000
      Investment in Soule Company Common Stock—
        Poole ($450,000 × 0.90) 405,000
      Minority Interest in Net Assets of Subsidiary
        ($410,000 × 0.10) 41,000
To eliminate intercompany investment and establish minority interest in net assets of subsidiary at beginning of year (Nov. 1, Year 3).

(b) Minority Interest in Net Income of Subsidiary ($40,000 ×
  0.10) 4,000
      Minority Interest in Net Assets of Subsidiary 4,000
To establish minority interest in net income of subsidiary for year ended Oct. 31, Year 4.

During the fiscal year ended October 31, Year 5, Soule reported net income of $50,000, and on October 31, Year 5, Soule declared dividends of $20,000.

Instructions

a Prepare Poole Corporation's October 31, Year 5, journal entries to record the operating results and dividends of Soule Company under the equity method of accounting. Disregard income taxes.

b Prepare the October 31, Year 5, working paper eliminations for Poole Corporation and subsidiary.

7-9 Pittsburgh Corporation completed a business combination with Syracuse Company on April 30, Year 7. Immediately thereafter, Pittsburgh began making cash advances on open account to Syracuse at a 10% annual interest rate. In addition, Syracuse agreed to pay a monthly management fee to Pittsburgh of 2% of monthly net sales. Payment was to be made no later than the tenth day of the month following Syracuse's accrual of the fee.

During your examination of the financial statements of Pittsburgh Corporation and Syracuse Company on July 31, Year 7, the end of the fiscal year, you discover that each company has set up only one account—entitled Intercompany Account—to record all intercompany transactions. Details of the two accounts on July 31, Year 7, are given on page 342.

PITTSBURGH CORPORATION LEDGER

Intercompany Account—Syracuse Company

Date	Explanation	Debit	Credit	Balance
May 2	Cash advance paid	4,500		4,500 dr
May 27	Cash advance paid	9,000		13,500 dr
June 11	Management fee received		2,000	11,500 dr
June 12	Repayment of May 2 advance and interest		4,550	6,950 dr
June 21	Cash advance paid	10,000		16,950 dr
July 11	Management fee received		2,200	14,750 dr
July 27	Repayment of May 27 advance and interest		9,150	5,600 dr
July 31	Cash advance paid	5,000		10,600 dr

SYRACUSE COMPANY LEDGER

Intercompany Account—Pittsburgh Corporation

Date	Explanation	Debit	Credit	Balance
May 3	Cash advance received		4,500	4,500 cr
May 28	Cash advance received		9,000	13,500 cr
June 10	Management fee paid ($100,000 × 0.02)	2,000		11,500 cr
June 11	Repayment of May 2 advance and interest	4,550		6,950 cr
June 22	Cash advance received		10,000	16,950 cr
July 10	Management fee paid ($110,000 × 0.02)	2,200		14,750 cr
July 26	Repayment of May 27 advance and interest	9,150		5,600 cr

Your audit working papers show audited net sales of $330,000 for Syracuse Company for the three months ended July 31, Year 7. You agree to the companies' use of a 360-day year for computing interest.

Instructions

a Prepare adjusting journal entries for Pittsburgh Corporation on July 31, Year 7. Establish appropriate separate intercompany accounts in the journal entries.

b Prepare adjusting journal entries for Syracuse Company on July 31, Year 7. Establish appropriate separate intercompany accounts in the journal entries.

c Prepare a partial working paper for consolidated financial statements to include the intercompany accounts established in *a* and *b*.

7-10 On July 31, Year 10, Prill Corporation issued 20,000 shares of its $2 par common stock (current fair value $10 a share) for all 5,000 shares of outstanding $5 par common stock of Stewart Company, which is to remain a separate corporation. Out-of-pocket costs of the pooling-type business combination, paid by Prill on July 31, Year 10, were as follows:

Finder's fee and legal fees relating to business combination $20,000

Costs associated with SEC registration statement for Prill's common
   stock issued in combination   10,000

     Total out-of-pocket costs of business combination $30,000

    Separate balance sheets of the constituent companies on July 31, Year 10, prior to the business combination, follow:

PRILL CORPORATION AND STEWART COMPANY
Separate Balance Sheets
July 31, Year 10

	Prill Corporation	Stewart Company
Assets		
Current assets	$450,000	$150,000
Plant assets (net)	520,000	300,000
Goodwill		20,000
Total assets	$970,000	$470,000
Liabilities & Stockholders' Equity		
Current liabilities	$300,000	$120,000
Long-term debt	100,000	200,000
Common stock, $2 par	200,000	
Common stock, $5 par		25,000
Paid-in capital in excess of par	250,000	50,000
Retained earnings	120,000	75,000
Total liabilities & stockholders' equity	$970,000	$470,000

    Stewart's goodwill resulted from the July 31, Year 4, acquisition of the net assets of Townsend Company in a purchase-type business combination. Stewart's identifiable assets and liabilities having July 31, Year 10, current fair values different from their carrying amounts were as follows:

	Current fair values	Carrying amounts
Inventories	$ 65,000	$ 60,000
Plant assets (net)	340,000	300,000
Long-term debt	190,000	200,000

    There were no intercompany transactions prior to the business combination.

Instructions

a Prepare Prill Corporation's journal entries on July 31, Year 10, to record the business combination with Stewart Company as a pooling.

b Prepare working paper eliminations and a working paper for a consolidated balance sheet of Prill Corporation and subsidiary on July 31, Year 10. Balances for Prill Corporation should reflect the journal entries in **a**.

7-11   On October 31, Year 4, Prouty Corporation acquired 93% of the outstanding common stock of Stovall Company in exchange for 50,000 shares of Prouty's $2 par ($10 current fair value) common stock. Out-of-pocket costs of the pooling-type business combination paid by Prouty Corporation on October 31, Year 4, were as shown at the top of page 345. There were no intercompany transactions between the two companies prior to the business combination. Stovall is to be a subsidiary of Prouty.

Separate financial statements of the two companies prior to the business combination are presented below:

PROUTY CORPORATION AND STOVALL COMPANY
Separate Financial Statements
For Year Ended October 31, Year 4

	Prouty Corporation	Stovall Company
Income Statements		
Net sales	$1,500,000	$ 800,000
Costs and expenses		
Cost of goods sold	$1,000,000	$ 480,000
Operating expenses	150,000	80,000
Interest expense	50,000	25,000
Income taxes expense	180,000	129,000
Total costs and expenses	$1,380,000	$ 714,000
Net income	$ 120,000	$ 86,000
Statements of Retained Earnings		
Retained earnings, beginning of year	$ 560,000	$ 250,000
Add: Net income	120,000	86,000
Subtotals	$ 680,000	$ 336,000
Less: Dividends	50,000	
Retained earnings, end of year	$ 630,000	$ 336,000
Balance Sheets		
Assets		
Cash	$ 250,000	$ 150,000
Inventories	860,000	600,000
Other current assets	500,000	260,000
Plant assets (net)	3,400,000	1,500,000
Patents		80,000
Total assets	$5,010,000	$2,590,000
Liabilities & Stockholders' Equity		
Income taxes payable	$ 40,000	$ 60,000
Other current liabilities	390,000	854,000
Long-term debt	950,000	1,240,000
Common stock, $2 par	1,500,000	
Common stock, $10 par		100,000
Paid-in capital in excess of par	1,500,000	
Retained earnings	630,000	336,000
Total liabilities & stockholders' equity	$5,010,000	$2,590,000

Legal fees and finder's fee relating to business combination $34,750
Costs associated with SEC registration statement for Prouty's common
  stock issued in combination   55,250
    Total out-of-pocket costs of business combination $90,000

Instructions

a Prepare Prouty Corporation's journal entries on October 31, Year 4, to record the business combination with Stovall Company as a pooling.

b Prepare the working paper eliminations (in journal entry form) and the working paper for consolidated financial statements on October 31, Year 4, of Prouty Corporation and subsidiary. Balances for Prouty Corporation should reflect the journal entries in **a.**

7-12   On January 2, Year 3, Poland Corporation exchanged its common stock for 100% of Serbia Company's common stock on a 1 for 4 basis. Poland's common stock was selling on the market for $7 a share at the time, and the investment was recorded on this basis. The common stock exchanged was treasury stock that had been acquired for $4.50 a share three years prior to the business combination. The business combination qualified for pooling accounting. Out-of-pocket costs of the business combination may be ignored.

There was no market price available for Serbia's common stock on the date of the business combination. The stockholders' equity per share of Serbia's common stock was $1.60. Poland's board of directors justified the exchange ratio for the Serbia common stock on the grounds that the value of plant assets was understated.

Separate balance sheets of the two companies on December 31, Year 3, were as follows:

POLAND CORPORATION AND SERBIA COMPANY
Separate Balance Sheets
December 31, Year 3

	Poland Corporation	Serbia Company
Assets		
Cash	$ 50,000	$ (1,800)
Notes receivable	42,000	
Notes receivable discounted	(15,000)	
Accrued interest receivable	1,450	
Accounts receivable	68,000	68,800
Receivable from Serbia Company	25,000	
Inventories	177,000	22,500
Investment in Serbia Company common stock	70,000	
Plant assets	290,000	240,000
Accumulated depreciation	(40,000)	(60,000)
Other assets	42,000	3,000
Total assets	$710,450	$272,500

(Continued)

POLAND CORPORATION AND SERBIA COMPANY
Separate Balance Sheets (concluded)
December 31, Year 3

	Poland Corporation	Serbia Company
Liabilities & Stockholders' Equity		
Notes payable	$ 45,000	$ 25,000
Accrued interest payable	300	4,750
Accounts payable	85,400	33,800
Payable to Poland Corporation		25,000
Other accrued liabilities	13,000	9,075
16% bonds payable, due Apr. 1, Year 13		100,000
Common stock, $5 par	300,000	
Common stock, $1 par		40,000
Paid-in capital in excess of par	150,000	
Retained earnings	116,750	34,875
Total liabilities & stockholders' equity	$710,450	$272,500

The following additional information is available:

(1) The income statement data for the two companies for the year ended December 31, Year 3, were as follows:

	Poland Corporation	Serbia Company
Net sales	$600,000	$200,000
Costs and expenses	550,000	189,125
Net income	$ 50,000	$ 10,875

(2) Poland wired $13,000 to Serbia's bank on January 2, Year 4, to cover the cash overdraft and to provide cash for working capital. The $13,000 was considered an additional advance to Serbia.

(3) Serbia's notes payable include a $10,000, 15% demand note payable to the president of Poland, who is not an officer of Serbia. The note is dated July 1, Year 2, and interest is payable on July 1 and January 1. The remaining Serbia notes payable, on which interest had been paid to December 31, Year 3, are payable to Poland, which discounted them at a bank.

Instructions
a Prepare adjusting entries for Poland Corporation on December 31, Year 3.

b Prepare a working paper for consolidated balance sheet on December 31, Year 3, and related working paper eliminations for Poland Corporation and subsidiary. Balances for Poland Corporation should reflect the adjusting entries in **a**.

Disregard income taxes.

8 CONSOLIDATED FINANCIAL STATEMENTS: INTERCOMPANY PROFITS AND LOSSES

Many transactions between a parent company and its subsidiaries may involve a profit or loss. Among these transactions are intercompany sales of merchandise, intercompany sales of plant assets, and intercompany sales of intangible assets. Until intercompany profits or losses in such transactions are *realized* through the sale of the asset to an *outsider,* the profits or losses must be eliminated in the preparation of consolidated financial statements.

In addition, a parent or subsidiary company's acquisition of its affiliate's bonds *in the open market* may result in a *realized gain or loss to the consolidated entity.* Such a realized gain or loss is not included in the income statement of either the parent company or the subsidiary, but it must be included in the consolidated income statement.

In this chapter we discuss the working paper eliminations for intercompany transactions of the types described above. We illustrate intercompany transactions involving *profits,* although such transactions also may involve losses.

Importance of eliminating or including intercompany profits and losses

At the outset, we must stress the importance of eliminating *unrealized* intercompany profits and losses and including *realized* gains or losses in the preparation of consolidated income statements. Failure to eliminate *unrealized* profits and losses would result in consolidated income statements reflecting not only results of transactions with those outside the consolidated entity, but also the result of *related-party* activities within the affiliated group. Similarly, nonrecognition of *realized* gains and losses would misstate consolidated net income. The parent com-

347

pany's management would have free rein to manipulate net income if intercompany profits and losses were not eliminated in the preparation of consolidated income statements.

INTERCOMPANY SALES OF MERCHANDISE

Intercompany sales of merchandise are a natural outgrowth of **vertical** business combinations, which involve a combinor and one or more of its customers or suppliers as combinees. **Downstream** intercompany sales of merchandise are those from a parent company to its subsidiaries. **Upstream** intercompany sales are those from subsidiaries to the parent company. **Lateral** intercompany sales are between two subsidiaries of the same parent company.

The intercompany sales of merchandise between a parent company and its subsidiary are similar to the intracompany shipments by a home office to a branch, described in Chapter 3.

Intercompany sales of merchandise at cost

Intercompany sales of merchandise may be made at a price equal to the selling company's cost. If so, the working paper elimination is the same whether all the goods were sold by the purchasing affiliate or whether some of the goods remained in the purchaser's inventories on the date of the consolidated financial statements. For example, assume that Palm Corporation (the parent company) during the year ended December 31, Year 3, sold merchandise costing $150,000 to Starr Company (the subsidiary) at a selling price equal to the cost of the merchandise. Assume further that Starr's December 31, Year 3, inventories included $25,000 of merchandise obtained from Palm and that Starr still owed Palm $15,000 for merchandise purchases on December 31, Year 3. (Starr also purchased merchandise from other suppliers during Year 3.)

The two companies would prepare the aggregate journal entries illustrated on page 349 for the foregoing transactions, assuming that both companies used the perpetual inventory system.

The working paper for consolidated financial statements for Palm Corporation and subsidiary for the year ended December 31, Year 3, would include the data on page 350 with regard to intercompany sales of merchandise only.

Note that Starr Company's cost of goods sold for Year 3 and inventories on December 31, Year 3, are not affected by working paper eliminations. From a consolidated entity viewpoint, both Starr's cost of goods sold and Starr's inventories are stated at **cost;** no element of intercompany profit or loss is involved. In effect, Starr served as a conduit to outside customers for Palm's merchandise.

Journal entries for parent company's downstream sales of merchandise to subsidiary at cost

Explanations	Palm Corporation General Journal	Starr Company General Journal

(1) Palm Corporation sold merchandise to Starr Company	Intercompany Accounts Receivable 150,000
	   Intercompany Sales . . . 150,000
	
	Intercompany Cost of Goods Sold 150,000
	   Inventories 150,000
		Inventories 150,000
		   Intercompany Accounts Payable 150,000

(2) Starr paid cash to Palm for merchandise purchased	Cash 135,000
	   Intercompany Accounts Receivable 135,000
		Intercompany Accounts Payable 135,000
		   Cash 135,000

(3) Starr sold merchandise purchased from Palm (Starr's selling prices are assumed)		Accounts Receivable 160,000
		   Sales 160,000
		
		Cost of Goods Sold 125,000
		   Inventories 125,000

PALM CORPORATION AND SUBSIDIARY
Partial Working Paper for Consolidated Financial Statements
For Year Ended December 31, Year 3

	Palm Corporation	Starr Company	Eliminations increase (decrease)	Consolidated
Income Statement				
Intercompany revenue (expenses)	*			
Balance Sheet				
Intercompany receivable (payable)	15,000	(15,000)		

* Palm Corporation's $150,000 intercompany sales and intercompany cost of goods sold are offset in Palm's separate income statement.

Unrealized intercompany profit in ending inventories

More typical than the intercompany sales of merchandise at cost described in the preceding section are intercompany sales involving a gross profit. The gross profit margin may be equal to, more than, or less than the margin on sales to outsiders. The selling affiliate's intercompany gross profit is *realized* through the purchasing affiliate's sales to outsiders. Consequently, any merchandise purchased from an affiliated company that remains unsold on the date of a consolidated balance sheet results in the *overstatement* (from a *consolidated* point of view) of the purchaser's ending inventories. The overstatement is equal to the amount of the selling affiliate's *unrealized* intercompany gross profit included in the ending inventories. This overstatement is canceled through an appropriate working paper elimination in the preparation of consolidated financial statements.

Suppose, for example, that Sage Company (the partially owned subsidiary) during the year ended December 31, Year 3, began selling merchandise to Post Corporation (the parent company) at a gross profit margin of 20%. Sales by Sage to Post for the year totaled $120,000, of which $40,000 remained unsold by Post on December 31, Year 3. On that date, Post owed $30,000 to Sage for merchandise. Both companies used the perpetual inventory system.

The transactions described in the foregoing paragraph are recorded in summary form by the two companies as illustrated on page 351.

The intercompany gross profit in Sage's sales to Post during the year ended December 31, Year 3, is analyzed at the top of page 352. This analysis shows that the intercompany gross profit on sales by Sage to Post totaled $24,000, and that $16,000 of this intercompany profit was realized through Post's sales to outside customers. The remaining

Journal entries for partially owned subsidiary's upstream sales of merchandise to parent company at a gross profit

Explanations	Post Corporation General Journal	Sage Company General Journal

(1) Sage Company sold merchandise to Post Corporation	Inventories 120,000
	  Intercompany Accounts
	    Payable 120,000
		Intercompany Accounts
		  Receivable 120,000
		    Intercompany Sales. . . 120,000
		
		Intercompany Cost of Goods
		  Sold 96,000
		    Inventories 96,000

(2) Post paid cash to Sage for merchandise purchased	Intercompany Accounts
	  Payable 90,000
	    Cash. 90,000
		Cash 90,000
		  Intercompany Accounts
		    Receivable 90,000

(3) Post sold merchandise purchased from Sage (Post's selling prices are assumed)	Accounts Receivable. 100,000
	  Sales 100,000
	
	Cost of Goods Sold 80,000
	  Inventories 80,000	

Analysis of gross profit in partially owned subsidiary's upstream sales of merchandise to parent company

	Selling price	Cost	Gross profit (20%)
Beginning inventories			
Add: Sales	$120,000	$96,000	$24,000
Subtotal	$120,000	$96,000	$24,000
Less: Ending inventories	40,000	32,000	8,000
Cost of goods sold	$ 80,000	$64,000	$16,000

$8,000 of intercompany profit remains **unrealized** in Post's inventories on December 31, Year 3.

The following working paper elimination is required for Sage's intercompany sales of merchandise to Post for the year ended December 31, Year 3:

POST CORPORATION AND SUBSIDIARY
Partial Working Paper Eliminations
December 31, Year 3

(b) Intercompany Sales—Sage.	120,000	
Intercompany Cost of Goods Sold—Sage		96,000
Cost of Goods Sold—Post		16,000
Inventories—Post		8,000

To eliminate intercompany sales, cost of goods sold, and unrealized intercompany profit in inventories. (Income tax effects are disregarded.)

The effects of the elimination are threefold. First, it eliminates Sage's intercompany sales to Post and the related intercompany cost of goods sold; this avoids the overstatement of the **consolidated** amounts for sales and cost of goods sold, which should represent merchandise transactions with customers outside the consolidated entity. Second, the elimination removes the intercompany profit from Post's cost of goods sold, thus restating it to the cost of the **consolidated entity.** Finally, the elimination reduces the consolidated inventories to **actual cost** for the consolidated entity.

Entering the preceding elimination in the working paper for consolidated financial statements results in the balances shown at the top of page 353 (amounts for total sales to outsiders and cost of goods sold are assumed).

Note that the $120,000 elimination of intercompany sales, less the $112,000 total ($16,000 + $96,000 = $112,000) of the cost of goods sold eliminations, equals $8,000—the amount of the intercompany profit eliminated from inventories. This $8,000 unrealized intercompany profit

POST CORPORATION AND SUBSIDIARY Partial Working Paper for Consolidated Financial Statements For Year Ended December 31, Year 3				
	Post Corporation	Sage Company	Eliminations increase (decrease)	Consolidated
Income Statement				
Revenue				
Sales	5,800,000	1,200,000		7,000,000
Intercompany sales		120,000	(b) (120,000)	
Costs and expenses				
Cost of goods sold .	4,100,000	760,000	(b) (16,000)	4,844,000
Intercompany cost				
of goods sold . . .		96,000	(b) (96,000)	
Balance Sheet				
Assets				
Intercompany receiv-				
able (payable)	(30,000)	30,000		
Inventories	900,000	475,000	(b) (8,000)	1,367,000

is attributable to Sage Company—the **seller** of the merchandise—and **must be taken into account in the determination of the minority interest in Sage's net income** for the year ended December 31, Year 3. The $8,000 also enters into the computation of Sage's retained earnings on December 31, Year 3. These procedures are illustrated in the following sections.

If the intercompany sales of merchandise are made by a parent company or by a wholly owned subsidiary, there is no effect on any minority interest in net income or loss, **because the selling affiliate does not have minority shareholders.** Thus, it is important to identify, by company name, the ledger accounts that are affected by working paper eliminations for intercompany sales of merchandise, so that the minority interest in net income or loss of a partially owned subsidiary that makes upstream or lateral sales of merchandise at a gross profit may be computed correctly.

Intercompany profit in beginning and ending inventories

The working paper elimination for intercompany sales of merchandise is complicated by intercompany profits in the **beginning** inventories of the purchaser. It is generally assumed that, on a first-in, first-out basis, the intercompany profit in the purchaser's **beginning** inventories is realized through sales to outsiders during the ensuing accounting period.

Only the intercompany profit in **ending** inventories remains unrealized at the end of the period.

Continuing the illustration from the preceding section, assume that Sage Company's intercompany sales of merchandise to Post Corporation during the year ended December 31, Year 4, are analyzed as follows:

**Analysis of gross profit
in partially owned
subsidiary's upstream
sales of merchandise to
parent company**

	Selling price	Cost	Gross profit (20%)
Beginning inventories	$ 40,000	$ 32,000	$ 8,000
Add: Sales	150,000	120,000	30,000
Subtotal	$190,000	$152,000	$38,000
Less: Ending inventories	60,000	48,000	12,000
Cost of goods sold	$130,000	$104,000	$26,000

Sage's intercompany sales and intercompany cost of goods sold for the year ended December 31, Year 3, had been closed to Sage's Retained Earnings account. Consequently, Sage's December 31, Year 3, retained earnings was overstated by $7,600 (95% of the $8,000 unrealized intercompany profit in Post's inventories on December 31, Year 3). The remaining $400 of unrealized profit on December 31, Year 3, is attributable to the minority interest in net assets of Sage Company, the **seller** of the merchandise. The following working paper elimination on December 31, Year 4, reflects these facts:

POST CORPORATION AND SUBSIDIARY

Partial Working Paper Eliminations

December 31, Year 4

(b) Retained Earnings—Sage ($8,000 × 0.95)	7,600	
Minority Interest in Net Assets of Subsidiary ($8,000 × 0.05)	400	
Intercompany Sales—Sage	150,000	
Intercompany Cost of Goods Sold—Sage		120,000
Cost of Goods Sold—Post		26,000
Inventories—Post		12,000
To eliminate intercompany sales, cost of goods sold, and unrealized intercompany profit in inventories. (Income tax effects are disregarded.)		

Intercompany profit in inventories and amount of minority interest

Accountants have given considerable thought to intercompany profits in purchases and sales transactions of partially owned subsidiaries. There is general agreement that all the unrealized intercompany profit in a partially owned subsidiary's ending inventories should be eliminated for consolidated financial statements. *This holds true whether the sales to the subsidiary are downstream from the parent company or are made by a wholly owned subsidiary of the same parent.*

There has been no such agreement on the treatment of intercompany profit in the parent company's or a subsidiary's inventories from upstream or lateral sales by a partially owned subsidiary. Two alternative approaches have been suggested:

1 The first approach is elimination of intercompany profit only to the extent of the parent company's ownership interest in the selling subsidiary's common stock. This approach is based on the "parent company theory" of consolidated financial statements (see Chapter 5, pages 209 to 211), in which the minority interest is considered to be a *liability* of the consolidated entity. If the minority shareholders are considered **outside creditors,** intercompany profit in the parent company's ending inventories has been *realized* to the extent of the minority shareholders' interest in the selling subsidiary's common stock.

2 The second approach is elimination of all the intercompany profit. The "entity theory" of consolidated financial statements (see Chapter 5, page 210), in which the minority interest is considered to be a *part of consolidated stockholders' equity,* underlies this approach. If minority shareholders are *part owners* of consolidated assets, their share of intercompany profits in inventories has not been realized.

The AICPA sanctioned the second approach, in the following passage from *Accounting Research Bulletin No. 51:*[1]

The amount of intercompany profit or loss to be eliminated . . . is not affected by the existence of a minority interest. The complete elimination of the intercompany profit or loss is consistent with the underlying assumption that the consolidated statements represent the financial position and operating results of a single business enterprise. The elimination of the intercompany profit or loss may be allocated proportionately between the majority and minority interests.

Consequently, intercompany profits or losses in inventories resulting from *upstream or lateral sales of merchandise by a partially owned subsidiary* must be considered in the determination of minority interest in net income of the subsidiary, and in the computation of retained earnings of the subsidiary. The subsidiary's net income must be *increased* by the *realized* intercompany profit in the purchasing affiliate's *beginning* inventories and *decreased* by the *unrealized* intercompany profit in the purchasing affiliate's *ending* inventories. Failure to do so would attribute the entire intercompany profit effects to the *consolidated* net income. See page 374 for an illustration of the computation of minority interest in net income of a partially owned subsidiary that makes intercompany sales of merchandise.

Should net profit or gross profit be eliminated?

Some accountants have discussed the propriety of eliminating intercompany **net profit,** rather than **gross profit,** in inventories of the con-

[1] *ARB No. 51,* "Consolidated Financial Statements," AICPA (New York: 1959), p. 45.

solidated entity. There is little theoretical support for such a proposal. First, elimination of intercompany net profit would in effect capitalize operating (selling and administrative) expenses in consolidated inventories. Selling expenses are always period costs, and only in unusual circumstances are some administrative expenses capitalized in inventories as product costs. Second, determination of net profit for particular merchandise requires many assumptions as to allocations of common costs.

INTERCOMPANY SALES OF PLANT ASSETS AND INTANGIBLE ASSETS

Intercompany sales of plant assets and intangible assets differ from intercompany sales of merchandise in two significant respects. First, intercompany sales of plant and intangible assets between affiliated companies are rare transactions. In contrast intercompany sales of merchandise recur frequently, once a program of such sales has been established. Second, the relatively long economic lives of plant assets and intangible assets require the passage of many accounting periods before intercompany gains or losses on sales of these assets are realized in transactions with outsiders. Conversely, intercompany profits in consolidated inventories at the end of one accounting period usually are realized in sales to outsiders during the ensuing period.

These differences have their counterparts in the working paper eliminations for intercompany profits or losses on sales of plant assets or intangible assets described in the following sections.

Intercompany gain on sale of land

Suppose that, during the year ended December 31, Year 3, Post Corporation (the parent company) sold to Sage Company (the partially owned subsidiary) for $175,000 a parcel of land that had cost Post $125,000. Sage acquired the land for a new building site. The two companies would record the transaction as follows (disregarding income tax effects to Post Corporation):

Journal entries for parent company's downstream sale of land to partially owned subsidiary

Post Corporation General Journal		Sage Company General Journal	
Cash 175,000		Land 175,000	
Land	125,000	Cash	175,000
Intercompany		To record acquisition	
Gain on Sale		of land from Post	
of Land	50,000	Corporation.	
To record sale of land			
to Sage Company.			

In consolidated financial statements for the year ended December 31, Year 3, the land must be presented at its historical cost to the consolidated entity. Also, the $50,000 intercompany gain must be eliminated, because it has not been **realized** in a transaction with an outsider. Accordingly, the following working paper elimination is required on December 31, Year 3:

POST CORPORATION AND SUBSIDIARY

Partial Working Paper Eliminations

December 31, Year 3

(c) *Intercompany Gain on Sale of Land—Post* 50,000

         Land—Sage. 50,000

    To eliminate unrealized intercompany gain on sale of land.

    (Income tax effects are disregarded.)

The working paper elimination appears as follows in the working paper for consolidated financial statements for the year ended December 31, Year 3:

POST CORPORATION AND SUBSIDIARY

Partial Working Paper for Consolidated Financial Statements

For Year Ended December 31, Year 3

	Post Corporation	Sage Company	Eliminations increase (decrease)	Consolidated
Income Statement				
Intercompany gain on sale of land . .	50,000		(c) (50,000)	
Balance Sheet				
Land		175,000	(c) (50,000)	125,000

Because land is not a depreciable asset, in subsequent years no journal entries affecting the land would be made by Sage unless the land were resold to an outsider (or back to Post). Nevertheless, in ensuing years, as long as Sage owns the land, its $175,000 cost to Sage is overstated $50,000 for consolidated financial purposes. Because the gain of $50,000 on the sale of land was closed to Post's Retained Earnings account on December 31, Year 3, the working paper elimination at the top of page 358 is required for Year 4 and subsequent years.

The working paper elimination has no effect on the minority interest in the net income or net assets of the subsidiary, because **the unrealized gain was attributable entirely to the parent company, the seller.**

POST CORPORATION AND SUBSIDIARY
Partial Working Paper Eliminations
December 31, Year 4

(c) Retained Earnings—Post.	50,000	
Land—Sage.		50,000
To eliminate unrealized intercompany gain in land. (Income tax effects are disregarded.)		

Suppose that, instead of constructing a building on the land, Sage sold the land to an outsider for $200,000 during the year ended December 31, Year 5. Sage would prepare the following journal entry to record the sale:

Subsidiary's journal entry for sale of land to an outsider

Cash	200,000	
Land		175,000
Gain on Sale of Land		25,000
To record sale of land to an outsider.		

The consolidated income statement for the year ended December 31, Year 5, must show that, for **consolidated** purposes, a **$75,000 gain was realized** on Sage's sale of the land. This $75,000 gain consists of the $25,000 gain recorded by Sage, and the $50,000 intercompany gain on Post's sale of the land to Sage two years earlier. The following working paper elimination is required on December 31, Year 5:

POST CORPORATION AND SUBSIDIARY
Partial Working Paper Eliminations
December 31, Year 5

(c) Retained Earnings—Post.	50,000	
Gain on Sale of Land—Sage.		50,000
To transfer $50,000 unrealized gain on Post Corporation's sale of land to Sage Company to the gain on sale of land by Sage to an outsider. (Income tax effects are disregarded.)		

Note that in the foregoing elimination the $50,000 intercompany gain that originally was unrealized by Post, the **intercompany** seller of the land, is attributed to Sage, the **seller of the land to an outsider.** This treatment, which differs from the accounting for the realization of intercompany gross profit on sales of merchandise (see page 350), is justified because land is not a product that is sold by a company other than a land development company. Thus, the affiliate selling the land to an out-sider should receive the *total* benefit from the gain realized by the con-solidated entity. In contrast, the intercompany purchaser of merchan-dise acts as *agent* for the intercompany seller in realizing, on that seller's behalf, the intercompany profit through sales of the merchan-dise to outsiders.

The $50,000 gain attributed to Sage in the working paper elimination on December 31, Year 5, enters into the computation of the minority in-terest in Sage's net income for Year 5. No further eliminations would be required subsequent to Year 5.

Intercompany gain on sale of depreciable plant asset

Annual depreciation provisions cause a significant difference in the working paper eliminations for an unrealized intercompany gain on the sale of a depreciable plant asset, compared with the eliminations de-scribed in the preceding section. Because the unrealized intercompany gain must be eliminated from the valuation of the depreciable asset for a consolidated balance sheet, the appropriate gain element also must be eliminated from the related depreciation expense in the consolidated in-come statement. This is illustrated in the following pages.

Intercompany Gain on Date of Sale of Depreciable Plant Asset The date-of-sale working paper eliminations for the intercompany sale of a depreci-able plant asset is identical to the comparable elimination for land. On the date of sale, no depreciation has been recognized by the affiliate that acquired the plant asset.

To illustrate, assume that on December 31, Year 3, Sage Company (the partially owned subsidiary) sold machinery to Post Corporation (the parent company). Details of the sale and of the machinery follow:

Selling price of machinery to Post Corporation	$60,000
Cost of machinery to Sage Company when acquired Jan. 2, Year 1 . . .	50,000
Estimated residual value:	
To Sage Company, Jan. 2, Year 1	$ 4,000
To Post Corporation, Dec. 31, Year 3	4,000
Economic life:	
To Sage Company, Jan. 2, Year 1	10 years
To Post Corporation, Dec. 31, Year 3	5 years
Annual depreciation expense (straight-line method):	
To Sage Company—$46,000 × 0.10	$ 4,600
To Post Corporation—$56,000 × 0.20	11,200

Details of machinery sold upstream to parent company by partially owned subsidiary

The two companies would account for the sale on December 31, Year 3, as follows (disregarding income tax effects to Sage):

Journal entries for partially owned subsidiary's upstream sale of machinery to parent company

Post Corporation General Journal	Sage Company General Journal
Machinery 60,000	Cash. 60,000
Cash. 60,000	Accumulated Deprecia-
To record acquisition of	tion ($4,600 × 3). . . . 13,800
machinery from Sage	Machinery 50,000
Company.	Intercompany
	Gain on Sale of
	Machinery 23,800
	To record sale of ma-
	chinery to Post Corpora-
	tion.

The following working paper elimination is required for consolidated financial statements on December 31, Year 3, the date of intercompany sale of the machinery:

POST CORPORATION AND SUBSIDIARY
Partial Working Paper Eliminations
December 31, Year 3

(d) Intercompany Gain on Sale of Machinery—Sage 23,800
           Machinery—Post.   23,800
    To eliminate unrealized intercompany gain on sale of ma-
    chinery. (Income tax effects are disregarded.)

The elimination results in the machinery being included in the consolidated balance sheet at its carrying amount to Sage Company—the seller—as follows:

Effect of elimination of unrealized intercompany profit on upstream sale of machinery

Cost of machinery to Post Corporation (acquirer parent company). . . .	$60,000
Less: Amount of elimination—intercompany gain	23,800
Difference—equal to cost ($50,000), less accumulated depreciation ($13,800) of machinery to Sage Company (seller subsidiary)	$36,200

Elimination of the $23,800 intercompany gain on the sale of machinery *is taken into account in the determination of the minority interest in the net income of the partially owned subsidiary—the seller—* for Year 3. The $23,800 elimination also enters into the computation of Sage's retained earnings, for consolidation purposes, on December 31, Year 3. These matters are illustrated on page 374.

Intercompany Gain Subsequent to Date of Sale of Depreciable Plant Asset
An appropriate intercompany gain element must be eliminated from depreciation expense for a plant asset sold by one affiliate to another at a gain. The following working paper elimination for Post Corporation and subsidiary on December 31, Year 4 (one year after the intercompany sale of machinery), illustrates this point:

> **POST CORPORATION AND SUBSIDIARY**
> **Partial Working Paper Eliminations**
> **December 31, Year 4**
>
> (d) Retained Earnings—Sage ($23,800 × 0.95) 22,610
>   Minority Interest in Net Assets of Subsidiary ($23,800 ×
>   0.05) 1,190
>   Accumulated Depreciation—Post 4,760
>   Machinery—Post. 23,800
>   Depreciation Expense—Post 4,760
> To eliminate unrealized intercompany gain in machinery
> and in related depreciation. (Income tax effects are disregarded.) Gain element in depreciation computed as
> $23,800 × 0.20 = $4,760, based on five-year economic life.

Because Sage Company's intercompany gain on sale of the machinery was closed to Sage's Retained Earnings account, the working paper elimination on December 31, Year 4, corrects the overstatement of Sage's beginning-of-year retained earnings from the viewpoint of the consolidated entity. In addition, the minority interest's share of the overstatement in the beginning retained earnings of Sage is recognized.

The intercompany gain eliminated from Post Corporation's depreciation expense may be verified as follows:

Verification of intercompany gain element in depreciation expense of parent company

Post's annual depreciation expense [($60,000 − $4,000) × 0.20] $11,200
Less: Depreciation expense for a five-year economic life, based on Sage's
  carrying amount on date of sale [($36,200 − $4,000) × 0.20] 6,440
Difference—equal to intercompany gain element in Post's annual depreciation expense . . . . $ 4,760

Intercompany Gain in Depreciation and Minority Interest From the point of view of the consolidated entity, the intercompany gain element of the acquiring affiliate's annual depreciation expense represents a **realization** of a portion of the intercompany gain by the selling affiliate. Depreciation, in this view, is in effect an **indirect sale** of a portion of the machinery to the customers of Post Corporation—the acquirer of the machinery. The selling prices of Post's products produced by the machinery are established at amounts adequate to cover all costs of producing the products, including depreciation expense.

Thus, the $4,760 credit to Post's depreciation expense in the December 31, Year 4, working paper elimination illustrated on page 361 in effect *increases* Sage's net income for consolidated purposes. *This increase must be considered in the computation of the minority interest in the subsidiary's net income* for the year ended December 31, Year 4, *and of the subsidiary's retained earnings on that date,* as illustrated on page 381.

Intercompany Gain in Later Years Working paper eliminations for later years in the economic life of the machinery sold at an intercompany gain must reflect the fact that the intercompany gain element in the *acquiring affiliate's* annual depreciation expense in effect represents a *realization* of the intercompany gain by the *selling affiliate.* For example, the working paper elimination for Post Corporation and subsidiary on December 31, Year 5 (two years following the intercompany sale of the machinery), is as follows:

POST CORPORATION AND SUBSIDIARY
Partial Working Paper Eliminations
December 31, Year 5

(d) Retained Earnings—Sage [($23,800 − $4,760) × 0.95] . . .	18,088	
Minority Interest in Net Assets of Subsidiary [($23,800 − $4,760) × 0.05]	952	
Accumulated Depreciation—Post ($4,760 × 2)	9,520	
Machinery—Post		23,800
Depreciation Expense—Post		4,760

To eliminate unrealized intercompany gain in machinery and related depreciation. (Income tax effects are disregarded.)

The credit amounts of the preceding consolidation elimination for Year 5 are the same as those for Year 4. The credit amounts will remain unchanged for all consolidation eliminations during the remaining economic life of the machinery, because of the parent company's use of the straight-line method of depreciation. The $19,040 total ($18,088 + $952 = $19,040) of the debits to Sage's Retained Earnings account and to the minority interest in net assets of subsidiary represents the *unrealized* portion of the intercompany gain at the beginning of Year 5. Each succeeding year, the unrealized portion of the intercompany gain *decreases,* as indicated by the following summary of the working paper elimination *debits* for those years:

POST CORPORATION AND SUBSIDIARY
Partial Working Paper Eliminations—Debits Only
December 31, Year 6 through Year 8

	Year ended Dec. 31,		
	Year 6	Year 7	Year 8
Debits			
(d) Retained earnings—Sage.	$13,566	$ 9,044	$ 4,522
Minority interest in net assets of sub-			
sidiary.	714	476	238
Accumulated depreciation—Post	14,280	19,040	23,800

At the end of Year 8, the entire $23,800 of intercompany gain has been realized through Post Corporation's annual depreciation charges. Thereafter, the following working paper elimination is required for the machinery until it is sold or scrapped:

POST CORPORATION AND SUBSIDIARY
Partial Working Paper Eliminations
December 31, Year 9

Accumulated Depreciation—Post	23,800	
Machinery—Post		23,800

To eliminate intercompany gain in machinery and related ac-
cumulated depreciation. (Income tax effects are disregarded.)

Intercompany gain on sale of intangible asset

The working paper eliminations for intercompany gains on sales of intangible assets are similar to those for intercompany gains in depreciable plant assets, except that no accumulated amortization account may be involved. The unrealized intercompany gain of the selling affiliate is realized through periodic amortization expense recorded by the acquiring affiliate.

ACQUISITION OF AFFILIATE'S BONDS

The intercompany profits (gains) or losses on intercompany sales of merchandise, plant assets, and intangible assets are, on the date of sale, *unrealized* gains or losses resulting from transactions between two affiliated corporations. Intercompany gains and losses may be *realized by the consolidated entity* when one affiliate acquires in the open market bonds issued by another affiliate. The gain or loss on such a transaction is **imputed,** because the transaction is not consummated between the two affiliates. No realized or unrealized intercompany gain or loss would result from the **direct** acquisition of one affiliate's bonds by another affiliate, because the cost of the investment to the acquirer would be **exactly offset** by the issuance price of the debt.

Illustration of acquisition of affiliate's bonds

Assume that on January 1, Year 3, Sage Company (the partially owned subsidiary) issued to the public $500,000 face amount of 10% bonds due January 1, Year 8. The bonds were issued at a price to yield a 12% return to investors. Interest was payable annually on January 1. Bond issue costs are disregarded in this example.

The net proceeds of the bond issue to Sage were $463,952, computed as follows:[2]

<table>
<tr><td style="width:25%">Computation of proceeds of bonds issued by partially owned subsidiary</td><td>Present value of $500,000 in five years @ 12%, with interest paid annually
($500,000 × 0.567427) . . . .</td><td>$283,713</td></tr>
<tr><td></td><td>Add: Present value of $50,000 each year for five years @ 12% ($50,000 × 3.604776) . . . .</td><td>180,239</td></tr>
<tr><td></td><td>Proceeds of bond issue . . . .</td><td>$463,952</td></tr>
</table>

During the year ended December 31, Year 3, Sage prepares the following journal entries for the bonds, including the amortization of bond discount by the **interest method:**

<table>
<tr><td style="width:25%">Partially owned subsidiary's journal entries for bonds</td><td colspan="3" style="text-align:center">**SAGE COMPANY**
General Journal</td></tr>
<tr><td></td><td colspan="3">Year 3</td></tr>
<tr><td></td><td>Jan. 1</td><td>Cash . . . .   463,952</td><td></td></tr>
<tr><td></td><td></td><td>   Discount on Bonds Payable . . . .   36,048</td><td></td></tr>
<tr><td></td><td></td><td>   Bonds Payable . . . .</td><td>500,000</td></tr>
<tr><td></td><td></td><td colspan="2">   To record issuance of 10% bonds due Jan. 1, Year
    8, at a discount to yield 12%.</td></tr>
<tr><td></td><td>Dec. 31</td><td>Interest Expense ($463,952 × 0.12) . . . .</td><td>55,674</td></tr>
<tr><td></td><td></td><td>   Interest Payable ($500,000 × 0.10) . . . . . .</td><td>50,000</td></tr>
<tr><td></td><td></td><td>   Discount on Bonds Payable . . . .</td><td>5,674</td></tr>
<tr><td></td><td></td><td colspan="2">   To record accrual of annual interest on 10%
    bonds.</td></tr>
</table>

---

[2] *Intermediate Accounting* of this series contains comprehensive discussion of computations of bond issuance proceeds. The Appendix in the back of this book contains compound interest tables.

On December 31, Year 3, the balance of Sage's Discount on Bonds Payable ledger account was $30,374 ($36,048 − $5,674 = $30,374).

Assume that on December 31, Year 3, Post Corporation (the parent company) had cash available for investment. With a market yield rate of 15% on that date, Sage Company's 10% bonds could be acquired at a substantial discount. Consequently, Post acquired in the open market on December 31, Year 3, $300,000 face amount (or 60% of the total issue of $500,000) of the bonds for $257,175 plus $30,000 accrued interest for one year ($300,000 × 0.10 = $30,000). The $257,175 acquisition cost is computed as follows:

Present value of $300,000 in four years @ 15%, with interest paid annually ($300,000 × 0.571753)	$171,526
Add: Present value of $30,000 each year for four years @ 15% ($30,000 × 2.854978)	85,649
Cost to Post Corporation of $300,000 face amount of bonds	$257,175

Post prepares the following journal entry on December 31, Year 3, to record the acquisition of Sage's bonds:

POST CORPORATION
General Journal

Investment in Sage Company Bonds	257,175	
Intercompany Interest Receivable	30,000	
Cash		287,175

To record acquisition of $300,000 face amount of Sage Company's 10% bonds due Jan. 1, Year 8, and accrued interest for one year.

On receiving notification of the parent company's acquisition of the bonds, Sage Company prepares the following journal entry on December 31, Year 3, to record the **intercompany** status of a portion of its bonds payable:

SAGE COMPANY
General Journal

Bonds Payable	300,000	
Discount on Intercompany Bonds Payable ($30,374 × 0.60)	18,224	
Interest Payable ($50,000 × 0.60)	30,000	
Intercompany Bonds Payable		300,000
Discount on Bonds Payable		18,224
Intercompany Interest Payable		30,000

To transfer to intercompany accounts all amounts attributable to bonds acquired by parent company in open market.

From the standpoint of the consolidated entity, Post Corporation's acquisition of Sage Company's bonds is equivalent to the **early extinguishment** of the bonds at a **realized** gain of $24,601, computed:

Computation of realized
gain on parent
company's open-market
acquisition of
subsidiary's bonds

Carrying amount of Sage Company's bonds acquired by Post Corporation on Dec. 31, Year 3 ($300,000 − $18,224)	$281,776
Less: Cost of Post Corporation's investment	257,175
Realized gain on early extinguishment of bonds	$ 24,601

The $24,601 realized gain **is not recorded** in the accounting records of either the parent company or the subsidiary. Instead, it is recognized in the following working paper elimination on December 31, Year 3:

POST CORPORATION AND SUBSIDIARY
Partial Working Paper Eliminations
December 31, Year 3

(e) Intercompany Bonds Payable—Sage	300,000	
Discount on Intercompany Bonds Payable—Sage		18,224
Investment in Sage Company Bonds—Post		257,175
Gain on Early Extinguishment of Bonds—Sage . .		24,601

To eliminate subsidiary's bonds acquired by parent and to recognize gain on the retirement of the bonds. (Income tax effects are disregarded.)

Disposition of Gain on Acquisition of Bonds The working paper elimination illustrated above attributes the gain on Post Corporation's acquisition of its subsidiary's bonds to Sage Company—the subsidiary. This treatment of the gain follows from the assumption that the parent company's open-market acquisition of the subsidiary's bonds was, in substance, the early extinguishment of the bonds by the subsidiary. The parent company acted as **agent** for the subsidiary in the open-market transaction; thus, the gain is attributed to the subsidiary. Under this consolidated approach, the accounting for the gain on the acquisition of the subsidiary's bonds is the same as if the **subsidiary itself** had reacquired and retired the bonds.

The entire realized gain of $24,601 is reported in the consolidated income statement of Post Corporation and subsidiary for the year ended December 31, Year 3.[3] If the gain is **material,** it is reported as an **extraordinary item,** net of income taxes.[4]

[3] APB Opinion No. 26, "Early Extinguishment of Debt," AICPA (New York: 1973), pp. 501–502.
[4] FASB Statement No. 4, "Reporting Gains and Losses from Extinguishment of Debt," FASB (Stamford: 1975), p. 3.

Minority Interest in Gain on Acquisition of Bonds   As discussed in the preceding section, the gain on Post Corporation's acquisition of its subsidiary's bonds is attributed to the partially owned subsidiary. It follows that *the gain should be considered in the computation of the minority interest in the subsidiary's net income* for the year ended December 31, Year 3. Also, the gain is included in the computation of the subsidiary's retained earnings on December 31, Year 3, for consolidated purposes. These matters are illustrated on page 374.

Accounting for gain in subsequent years

In the four years following Post Corporation's acquisition of Sage Company's bonds, the gain *realized but unrecorded* on the date of acquisition is in effect *recorded* by the consolidated entity through the differences in the two affiliates' amortization and accumulation of bond discount. (It is essential that the affiliate that acquired the bonds undertake an accumulation program consistent with that of the affiliate that issued the bonds; thus, Post Corporation should adopt the interest method of amortization used by Sage.) To illustrate this concept, the accounting for the bond interest by the two companies for the year ended December 31, Year 4, is presented on page 368, and the relevant ledger accounts of both companies relative to the intercompany bonds are illustrated below and on pages 368 and 369 for the four years the bonds remain outstanding.

Parent company's ledger accounts for intercompany bonds

POST CORPORATION LEDGER
Investment in Sage Company Bonds

Date	Explanation	Debit	Credit	Balance
12/31/3	Acquisition of $300,000 face amount of bonds	257,175		257,175 dr
12/31/4	Accumulation of discount ($38,576 − $30,000)	8,576		265,751 dr
12/31/5	Accumulation of discount ($39,863 − $30,000)	9,863		275,614 dr
12/31/6	Accumulation of discount ($41,342 − $30,000)	11,342		286,956 dr
12/31/7	Accumulation of discount ($43,044 − $30,000)	13,044		300,000 dr

Intercompany Interest Revenue

Date	Explanation	Debit	Credit	Balance
12/31/4	($257,175 × 0.15)		38,576	38,576 cr
12/31/4	Closing entry	38,576		-0-
12/31/5	($265,751 × 0.15)		39,863	39,863 cr
12/31/5	Closing entry	39,863		-0-
12/31/6	($275,614 × 0.15)		41,342	41,342 cr
12/31/6	Closing entry	41,342		-0-
12/31/7	($286,956 × 0.15)		43,044*	43,044 cr
12/31/7	Closing entry	43,044		-0-

* Adjusted $1 for rounding.

Affiliated companies' journal entries for bonds for year ended December 31, Year 4

	Post Corporation General Journal		Sage Company General Journal	
Year 4				
Jan. 1	Cash 30,000		Intercompany Interest	
	Intercompany		Payable 30,000	
	Interest Receivable	30,000	Interest Payable 20,000	
	To record receipt of accrued interest purchased on Sage Company's 10% bonds.		Cash	50,000
			To record payment of accrued interest on 10% bonds.	
Dec. 31	Intercompany Interest		Intercompany Interest	
	Receivable 30,000		Expense 33,813	
	Investment in Sage Company Bonds 8,576		Interest Expense 22,542	
	Intercompany		Intercompany	
	Interest Revenue .	38,576	Interest Payable .	30,000
	To accrue annual interest on Sage Company's 10% bonds ($257,175 × 0.15 = $38,576).		Interest Payable . .	20,000
			Discount on Intercompany Bonds	
			Payable	3,813
			Discount on Bonds	
			Payable	2,542
			To accrue annual interest on 10% bonds. Interest is computed as follows: Intercompany ($300,000 − $18,224) × 0.12 = $33,813 Other ($200,000 − $12,150) × 0.12 = $22,542	

Subsidiary's ledger accounts for intercompany bonds

SAGE COMPANY LEDGER
Intercompany Bonds Payable

Date	Explanation	Debit	Credit	Balance
12/31/3	Bonds acquired by parent company		300,000	300,000 cr

Discount on Intercompany Bonds Payable

Date	Explanation	Debit	Credit	Balance
12/31/3	Bonds acquired by parent company	18,224		18,224 dr
12/31/4	Amortization ($33,813 − $30,000)		3,813	14,411 dr
12/31/5	Amortization ($34,271 − $30,000)		4,271	10,140 dr
12/31/6	Amortization ($34,783 − $30,000)		4,783	5,357 dr
12/31/7	Amortization ($35,357 − $30,000)		5,357	-0-

Intercompany Interest Expense

Date	Explanation	Debit	Credit	Balance
12/31/4	($300,000 − $18,224) × 0.12	33,813		33,813 dr
12/31/4	Closing entry		33,813	-0-
12/31/5	($300,000 − $14,411) × 0.12	34,271		34,271 dr
12/31/5	Closing entry		34,271	-0-
12/31/6	($300,000 − $10,140) × 0.12	34,783		34,783 dr
12/31/6	Closing entry		34,783	-0-
12/31/7	($300,000 − $5,357) × 0.12	35,357		35,357 dr
12/31/7	Closing entry		35,357	-0-

A comparison of the yearly journal entries to Post Corporation's Intercompany Interest Revenue account and Sage Company's Intercompany Interest Expense account demonstrates that the difference between the annual entries in the two accounts represents the **recording,** in the separate companies' accounting records, of the $24,601 gain **realized but unrecorded** when the parent company acquired the subsidiary's bonds in the open market. A summary of the differences between the two intercompany interest accounts appears at the top of page 370.

Differences between
parent's Intercompany
Interest Revenue
account and
subsidiary's
Intercompany Interest
Expense account are
equal to realized gain
on parent's acquisition
of subsidiary's bonds

Year ended Dec. 31,	Post Corporation's intercompany interest revenue	Sage Company's intercompany interest expense	Difference—representing recording of realized gain
Year 4	$ 38,576	$ 33,813	$ 4,763
Year 5	39,863	34,271	5,592
Year 6	41,342	34,783	6,559
Year 7	43,044	35,357	7,687
Totals	$162,825	$138,224	$24,601

Working Paper Elimination on December 31, Year 4 The working paper elimination for the bonds and interest on December 31, Year 4, is as shown below:

POST CORPORATION AND SUBSIDIARY
Partial Working Paper Eliminations
December 31, Year 4

(e) Intercompany Interest Revenue—Post   38,576

Intercompany Bonds Payable—Sage   300,000

Discount on Intercompany Bonds Payable—
Sage   14,411

Investment in Sage Company Bonds—Post   265,751

Intercompany Interest Expense—Sage   33,813

Retained Earnings—Sage ($24,601 × 0.95).   23,371

Minority Interest in Net Assets of Subsidiary
($24,601 × 0.05)   1,230

To eliminate subsidiary's bonds owned by parent company, and related interest revenue and expense; and to increase subsidiary's beginning retained earnings by amount of unamortized realized gain on the retirement of the bonds. (Income tax effects are disregarded.)

The working paper elimination effectively reduces consolidated income before minority interest by $4,763 ($38,576 − $33,813 = $4,763). As indicated above, the $4,763 is the difference between the eliminated intercompany interest revenue of the parent company and the eliminated intercompany interest expense of the subsidiary. Failure to eliminate intercompany interest in this manner would result in a $4,763 overstatement of pre-minority interest consolidated income for Year 4, because the *entire* $24,601 realized gain on the parent company's acquisition of the subsidiary's bonds was recognized in the consolidated income statement for Year 3—the year the bonds were acquired, as evidenced by the $24,601 credited to Retained Earnings—Sage and to Minority Interest in Net Assets of Subsidiary in the elimination.

The $4,763 reduction of consolidated income before minority interest is attributable to the subsidiary, because the original imputed gain to which the $4,763 relates was allocated to the subsidiary. Consequently, **the $4,763 must be considered in the computation of minority interest in net income of the subsidiary** for the year ended December 31, Year 4. The $4,763 also enters into the computation of the subsidiary's retained earnings on December 31, Year 4, for consolidation purposes. These amounts associated with Sage Company's bonds are reflected in the working paper for consolidated financial statements for the year ended December 31, Year 4, as illustrated on pages 378 and 379.

Working Paper Elimination on December 31, Year 5 The working paper elimination on December 31, Year 5, is as follows:

POST CORPORATION AND SUBSIDIARY *Partial Working Paper Eliminations* *December 31, Year 5*		
(e) *Intercompany Interest Revenue—Post*	39,863	
Intercompany Bonds Payable—Sage	300,000	
Discount on Intercompany Bonds Payable— Sage		10,140
Investment in Sage Company Bonds—Post		275,614
Intercompany Interest Expense—Sage		34,271
Retained Earnings—Sage [($24,601 − $4,763) × 0.95]		18,846
Minority Interest in Net Assets of Subsidiary [($24,601 − $4,763) × 0.05]		992
To eliminate subsidiary's bonds owned by parent company, and related interest revenue and expense; and to increase subsidiary's beginning retained earnings by amount of unamortized realized gain on the retirement of the bonds. (Income tax effects are disregarded.)		

Comparable working paper eliminations would be appropriate for Years 6 and 7. After Sage Company paid the bonds in full on maturity, no further working paper eliminations for the bonds would be required.

Reissuance of intercompany bonds

The orderly amortization of a realized gain on the acquisition of an affiliate's bonds is disrupted if the acquiring affiliate sells the bonds to outsiders before they mature. A **transaction** gain or loss on such a sale is not *realized* by the consolidated entity. Logic requires that a working paper elimination must be prepared to treat the transaction gain or loss as premium or discount on the reissued bonds, as appropriate. These complex issues are rarely encountered; thus, they are not illustrated here.

ILLUSTRATION OF EFFECT OF INTERCOMPANY PROFITS (GAINS) ON MINORITY INTEREST

To illustrate the effect of intercompany profits (gains) on the computation of minority interest in the net income of a partially owned subsidiary, we return to the example of Post Corporation and its 95%-owned purchased subsidiary, Sage Company. The working paper eliminations for Post Corporation and subsidiary on pages 373 and 374 are taken from page 266 of Chapter 6, and from pages 352, 357, 360, and 366 of this chapter. These eliminations are followed by a *revised* elimination (which differs from the one on page 266 of Chapter 6) for minority interest in net income of subsidiary.

In elimination (*f*), the effects of the other eliminations on the subsidiary's net income are applied to compute an adjusted net income of the subsidiary, for consolidation purposes. The minority percentage then is applied to determine the minority interest in net income of the subsidiary. The rationale for these procedures follows:

> *Elimination*(a) increases costs and expenses of the subsidiary, thus decreasing the subsidiary's net income, a total of $19,000.
>
> *Elimination* (b) reduces the subsidiary's gross profit on sales by $24,000 ($120,000 − $96,000 = $24,000); however, $16,000 of the gross profit was realized by the parent company in its sales to outsiders. The net effect on the subsidiary's net income is a decrease of $8,000 ($24,000 − $16,000 = $8,000).
>
> *Elimination* (c) removes a gain account of the parent company; it does not affect the subsidiary's net income.
>
> *Elimination* (d) removes a gain account of the subsidiary and reduces the subsidiary's net income by $23,800.
>
> *Elimination* (e) attributes a gain on early extinguishment of bonds to the subsidiary, thus increasing the subsidiary's net income by $24,601.

Working Paper for Consolidated Financial Statements A partial working paper for consolidated financial statements for Post Corporation and subsidiary for the year ended December 31, Year 3, is given on page 375. The amounts for Post Corporation and Sage Company are the same as in the illustration on page 267 of Chapter 6. The illustration demonstrates that, when intercompany profits exist, consolidated net income is not the same as the parent company's net income under the equity method of accounting for the subsidiary's operations; nor is consolidated retained earnings the same as the total of the parent company's two retained earnings accounts. ($1,542,550 + $4,750 = $1,547,300; consolidated retained earnings is $1,490,461.) In the comprehensive

POST CORPORATION AND SUBSIDIARY
Working Paper Eliminations
December 31, Year 3

(a) *Common Stock—Sage*.   400,000
    Paid-in Capital in Excess of Par—Sage.   235,000
    Retained Earnings—Sage ($384,000 − $4,750)   379,250
    Retained Earnings of Subsidiary—Post.   4,750
    Intercompany Investment Income—Post.   81,700
    Plant Assets (net)—Sage ($176,000 − $14,000)   162,000
    Leasehold—Sage ($25,000 − $5,000)   20,000
    Goodwill—Post ($37,050 − $950)   36,100
    Cost of Goods Sold—Sage.   17,000
    Operating Expenses—Sage.   2,000
        Investment in Sage Company Common Stock—
          Post   1,229,300
        Dividends—Sage   50,000
        Minority Interest in Net Assets of Subsidiary
        ($61,000 − $2,500).   58,500

To carry out the following:

(1) *Eliminate intercompany investment and equity accounts of subsidiary* **at beginning of year,** *and subsidiary dividend.*

(2) *Provide for Year 3 depreciation and amortization on differences between current fair values and carrying amounts of Sage's identifiable net assets as follows:*

	Cost of goods sold	Operating expenses
Building depreciation . .	$ 2,000	$2,000
Machinery depreciation .	10,000	
Leasehold amortization .	5,000	
Totals.	$17,000	$2,000

(3) *Allocate unamortized differences between combination-date current fair values and carrying amounts to appropriate assets.*

(4) *Establish minority interest in net assets of subsidiary at beginning of year ($61,000), less minority share of dividends declared by subsidiary during year ($50,000 × 0.05 = $2,500).*

(Income tax effects are disregarded.)

POST CORPORATION AND SUBSIDIARY
Working Paper Eliminations (concluded)
December 31, Year 3

(b) *Intercompany Sales—Sage*	120,000	
Intercompany Cost of Goods Sold—Sage		96,000
Cost of Goods Sold—Post		16,000
Inventories—Post		8,000

To eliminate intercompany sales, cost of goods sold, and unrealized profit in inventories. (Income tax effects are disregarded.)

(c) *Intercompany Gain on Sale of Land—Post*	50,000	
Land—Sage		50,000

To eliminate unrealized intercompany gain on sale of land. (Income tax effects are disregarded.)

(d) *Intercompany Gain on Sale of Machinery—Sage*	23,800	
Machinery—Post		23,800

To eliminate unrealized intercompany gain on sale of machinery. (Income tax effects are disregarded.)

(e) *Intercompany Bonds Payable—Sage*	300,000	
Discount on Intercompany Bonds Payable—Sage		18,224
Investment in Sage Company Bonds—Post		257,175
Gain on Early Extinguishment of Bonds—Sage		24,601

To eliminate subsidiary's bonds acquired by parent, and to recognize gain on the retirement of the bonds. (Income tax effects are disregarded.)

(f) *Minority Interest in Net Income of Subsidiary*	3,940	
Minority Interest in Net Assets of Subsidiary		3,940

To establish minority interest in subsidiary's adjusted net income for Year 3 as follows:

Net income of subsidiary		$105,000
Adjustments for working paper eliminations:		
(a) ($17,000 + $2,000)	(19,000)	
(b)	(8,000)	
(d)	(23,800)	
(e)	24,601	
Adjusted net income of subsidiary		$ 78,801
Minority share ($78,801 × 0.05)		$ 3,940

Equity method: Partially owned subsidiary subsequent to date of purchase-type business combination

POST CORPORATION AND SUBSIDIARY
Partial Working Paper for Consolidated Financial Statements
For Year Ended December 31, Year 3

	Post Corporation	Sage Company	Eliminations increase (decrease)		Consolidated
Statement of Retained Earnings					
Retained earnings, beginning of year	1,348,500	384,000	(a)	(379,250)	1,353,250
Net income	352,600	105,000		(161,839)*	295,761
Subtotal	1,701,100	489,000		(541,089)	1,649,011
Dividends	158,550	50,000	(a)	(50,000)	158,550
Retained earnings, end of year	1,542,550	439,000		(491,089)	1,490,461
Balance Sheet Liabilities & Stockholders' Equity					
Minority interest in net assets of subsidiary. . . .			(a)	58,500	
			(f)	3,940	62,440
Total liabilities	x,xxx,xxx	xxx,xxx		62,440	x,xxx,xxx
Common stock, $1 par . .	1,057,000				1,057,000
Common stock, $10 par. .		400,000	(a)	(400,000)	
Paid-in capital in excess of par	1,560,250	235,000	(a)	(235,000)	1,560,250
Retained earnings	1,542,550	439,000		(491,089)	1,490,461
Retained earnings of subsidiary	4,750		(a)	(4,750)	
Total stockholders' equity.	4,164,550	1,074,000		(1,130,839)	4,107,711
Total liabilities & stockholders' equity	x,xxx,xxx	x,xxx,xxx		(1,068,399)	x,xxx,xxx

* Net decrease in revenue (and gains): $81,700 + $120,000 + $50,000 + $23,800 − $24,601 . . . . $250,899
   Less: Net decrease in costs and expenses: $96,000 + $16,000 − $19,000 − $3,940 89,060
   Decrease in combined net incomes to compute consolidated net income $161,839

illustration that follows, we demonstrate how consolidated net income and consolidated retained earnings may be verified when intercompany profits are involved in the consolidation process.

COMPREHENSIVE ILLUSTRATION OF WORKING PAPER FOR CONSOLIDATED FINANCIAL STATEMENTS

In Chapters 5 through 8 we have explained and illustrated a number of aspects of working papers for consolidated financial statements. The comprehensive illustration that follows incorporates most of these aspects. The illustration is for Post Corporation and its partially owned purchased subsidiary, Sage Company, for the year ended December 31, Year 4.

The ledger accounts for Post Corporation's Investment in Sage Company Common Stock, Retained Earnings, and Retained Earnings of Subsidiary, and for Sage Company's Retained Earnings, are presented on page 377. Closing entries for Year 4 are not reflected in the retained earnings accounts. Review of these accounts should aid in understanding the illustrative working paper for consolidated financial statements on pages 378 and 379 and the related working paper eliminations on pages 380 and 381.

Following are important features of the working paper for consolidated financial statements and related working paper eliminations for Post Corporation and subsidiary for the year ended December 31, Year 4:

1 Intercompany investment income of Post Corporation for Year 4 is computed as follows:

Computation of intercompany investment income	$115,000 (Sage Company's net income for Year 4) × 0.95. . . . . $109,250
	Less: $19,000 (Year 4 amortization of differences between current fair values and carrying amounts of Sage Company's identifiable net assets on date of business combination) × 0.95 18,050
	Intercompany investment income of Post Corporation for Year 4 . . . . $ 91,200

2 Post Corporation's intercompany revenue of $14,000 is a management fee from Sage Company, computed as 1% of Sage's $1,400,000 net sales for Year 4 ($1,400,000 × 0.01 = $14,000).

3 The income tax effects of Post Corporation's use of the equity method of accounting for its subsidiary's operations are not reflected in Post's income taxes expense for Year 4. Income tax effects associated with the equity method of accounting are considered in Chapter 9.

4 Consolidated retained earnings of Post Corporation and subsidiary at the beginning of Year 4 ($1,490,461) is identical to consolidated retained earnings at the end of Year 3 (see page 375).

5 The net intercompany payable of Post Corporation on December 31, Year 4, is computed at the top of page 382.

POST CORPORATION LEDGER
Investment in Sage Company Common Stock

Date	Explanation	Debit	Credit	Balance
12/31/1	Total cost of business combination	1,192,250		1,192,250 dr
11/24/2	Dividend declared by Sage Company		38,000	1,154,250 dr
12/31/2	Net income of Sage	85,500		1,239,750 dr
12/31/2	Amortization of differences		42,750	1,197,000 dr
12/31/2	Amortization of goodwill		950	1,196,050 dr
11/22/3	Dividend declared by Sage		47,500	1,148,550 dr
12/31/3	Net income of Sage	99,750		1,248,300 dr
12/31/3	Amortization of differences		18,050	1,230,250 dr
12/31/3	Amortization of goodwill		950	1,229,300 dr
11/25/4	Dividends declared by Sage		57,000	1,172,300 dr
12/31/4	Net income of Sage	109,250		1,281,550 dr
12/31/4	Amortization of differences		18,050	1,263,500 dr
12/31/4	Amortization of goodwill		950	1,262,550 dr

Retained Earnings

Date	Explanation	Debit	Credit	Balance
12/31/1	Balance			1,050,000 cr
12/31/2	Close net income available for dividends		457,050	1,507,050 cr
12/31/2	Close Dividends account	158,550		1,348,500 cr
12/31/3	Close net income available for dividends		318,400	1,666,900 cr
12/31/3	Close Dividends account	158,550		1,508,350 cr

Retained Earnings of Subsidiary

Date	Explanation	Debit	Credit	Balance
12/31/2	Close net income not available for dividends		4,750	4,750 cr
12/31/3	Close net income not available for dividends		34,200	38,950 cr

SAGE COMPANY LEDGER
Retained Earnings

Date	Explanation	Debit	Credit	Balance
12/31/1	Balance		334,000	334,000 cr
12/31/2	Close net income		90,000	424,000 cr
12/31/2	Close Dividends account	40,000		384,000 cr
12/31/3	Close net income		105,000	489,000 cr
12/31/3	Close Dividends account	50,000		439,000 cr

POST CORPORATION AND SUBSIDIARY
Working Paper for Consolidated Financial Statements
For Year Ended December 31, Year 4

	Post Corporation	Sage Company	Eliminations increase (decrease)		Consolidated
Income Statement					
Revenue					
Net sales	5,900,000	1,400,000			7,300,000
Intercompany sales . . .		150,000	(b)	(150,000)	
Intercompany interest revenue.	38,576		(e)	(38,576)	
Intercompany investment income	91,200		(a)	(91,200)	
Intercompany revenue (expenses).	14,000	(14,000)			
Total revenue	6,043,776	1,536,000		(279,776)	7,300,000
Costs and expenses			(a)	17,000	
			(b)	(26,000)	
Cost of goods sold . . .	4,300,000	950,000	(d)	(4,760)	5,236,240
Intercompany cost of goods sold.		120,000	(b)	(120,000)	
Operating expenses. . .	677,133	122,145	(a)	2,000	801,278
Intercompany interest expense		33,813	(e)	(33,813)	
Interest expense	51,518	22,542			74,060
Income taxes expense .	554,925	172,500			727,425
Minority interest in net income of subsidiary. .			(f)	4,600	4,600
Total costs and expenses	5,583,576	1,421,000		(160,973)*	6,843,603
Net income	460,200	115,000		(118,803)	456,397
Statement of Retained Earnings			(a)	(400,050)	
			(b)	(7,600)	
Retained earnings, beginning of year	1,508,350	439,000	(c)	(50,000)	1,490,461
			(d)	(22,610)	
			(e)	23,371	
Net income	460,200	115,000		(118,803)	456,397
Subtotal	1,968,550	554,000		(575,692)	1,946,858
Dividends	158,550	60,000	(a)	(60,000)	158,550
Retained earnings, end of year	1,810,000	494,000		(515,692)	1,788,308

* A **decrease** in total costs and expenses and an **increase** in net income.

POST CORPORATION AND SUBSIDIARY
Working Paper for Consolidated Financial Statements (continued)
For Year Ended December 31, Year 4

	Post Corporation	Sage Company	Eliminations increase (decrease)		Consolidated
Balance Sheet					
Assets					
Intercompany receivables (payables)	(3,500)	3,500			
Inventories.	950,000	500,000	(b)	(12,000)	1,438,000
Other current assets	760,000	428,992			1,188,992
Investment in Sage Company common stock	1,262,550		(a)	(1,262,550)	
Investment in Sage Company bonds.	265,751		(e)	(265,751)	
Plant assets (net).	3,700,000	1,300,000	(a)	148,000	5,128,960
			(d)	(19,040)	
Land (for building site) . .		175,000	(c)	(50,000)	125,000
Leasehold			(a)	15,000	15,000
Goodwill	85,000		(a)	35,150	120,150
Total assets	7,019,801	2,407,492		(1,411,191)	8,016,102
Liabilities & Stockholders' Equity					
Bonds payable		200,000			200,000
Intercompany bonds payable		300,000	(e)	(300,000)	
Discount on bonds payable		(9,608)			(9,608)
Discount on intercompany bonds payable.		(14,411)	(e)	(14,411)*	
Other liabilities	2,553,601	802,511			3,356,112
Minority interest in net assets of subsidiary. . . .			(a)	59,800	64,040
			(b)	(400)	
			(d)	(1,190)	
			(e)	1,230	
			(f)	4,600	
Common stock, $1 par . .	1,057,000				1,057,000
Common stock, $10 par. .		400,000	(a)	(400,000)	
Paid-in capital in excess of par	1,560,250	235,000	(a)	(235,000)	1,560,250
Retained earnings	1,810,000	494,000		(515,692)	1,788,308
Retained earnings of subsidiary	38,950		(a)	(38,950)	
Total liabilities & stockholders' equity	7,019,801	2,407,492		(1,411,191)	8,016,102

* A **decrease** in discount on intercompany bonds payable and an **increase** in total liabilities and stockholders' equity.

POST CORPORATION AND SUBSIDIARY
Working Paper Eliminations
December 31, Year 4

(a) Common Stock—Sage.	400,000	
Paid-in Capital in Excess of Par—Sage.	235,000	
Retained Earnings—Sage ($439,000 − $38,950).	400,050	
Retained Earnings of Subsidiary—Post.	38,950	
Intercompany Investment Income—Post.	91,200	
Plant Assets (net)—Sage ($162,000 − $14,000)	148,000	
Leasehold—Sage ($20,000 − $5,000)	15,000	
Goodwill—Post ($36,100 − $950)	35,150	
Cost of Goods Sold—Sage	17,000	
Operating Expenses—Sage.	2,000	
Investment in Sage Company Common Stock—		
Post		1,262,550
Dividends—Sage		60,000
Minority Interest in Net Assets of Subsidiary . . .		59,800

To carry out the following:

(1) Eliminate intercompany investment and equity accounts of subsidiary at beginning of year, and subsidiary dividend.

(2) Provide for Year 4 depreciation and amortization on differences between current fair values and carrying amount of Sage's identifiable net assets as follows:

	Cost of goods sold	Operating expenses
Building depreciation . . .	$ 2,000	$2,000
Machinery depreciation . . . . tion	10,000	
Leasehold amortization . . . . tion	5,000	
Totals.	$17,000	$2,000

(3) Allocate unamortized differences between combination-date current fair values and carrying amounts to appropriate assets.

(4) Establish minority interest in net assets of subsidiary at beginning of year, excluding intercompany profits effects ($62,800), less minority share of dividends declared by subsidiary during year ($60,000 × 0.05 = $3,000).

(Income tax effects are disregarded.)

(Continued)

(b) Retained Earnings—Sage...............	7,600	
Minority Interest in Net Assets of Subsidiary.......	400	
Intercompany Sales—Sage...............	150,000	
Intercompany Cost of Goods Sold—Sage		120,000
Cost of Goods Sold—Post		26,000
Inventories—Post..............		12,000

To eliminate intercompany sales, cost of goods sold, and unrealized profits in inventories. (Income tax effects are disregarded.)

(c) Retained Earnings—Post	50,000	
Land—Sage		50,000

To eliminate unrealized intercompany gain in land. (Income tax effects are disregarded.)

(d) Retained Earnings—Sage.................	22,610	
Minority Interest in Net Assets of Subsidiary.......	1,190	
Accumulated Depreciation—Post	4,760	
Machinery—Post		23,800
Depreciation Expense—Post		4,760

To eliminate unrealized intercompany gain in machinery and in related depreciation. (Income tax effects are disregarded.)

(e) Intercompany Interest Revenue—Post	38,576	
Intercompany Bonds Payable—Sage	300,000	
Discount on Intercompany Bonds Payable—Sage		14,411
Investment in Sage Company Bonds—Post ...		265,751
Intercompany Interest Expense—Sage		33,813
Retained Earnings—Sage..............		23,371
Minority Interest in Net Assets of Subsidiary...		1,230

To eliminate subsidiary's bonds owned by parent company, and related interest revenue and expense; and to increase subsidiary's beginning retained earnings by amount of unamortized realized gain on the retirement of the bonds. (Income tax effects are disregarded.)

(f) Minority Interest in Net Income of Subsidiary.......	4,600	
Minority Interest in Net Assets of Subsidiary...		4,600

To establish minority interest in subsidiary's adjusted net income for Year 4, as follows:

Net income of subsidiary	$115,000	
Adjustments for working paper eliminations:		
(a) ($17,000 + $2,000)...........	(19,000)	
(b) [($150,000 − $120,000) − $26,000] .	(4,000)	
(d)	4,760	
(e) ($38,576 − $33,813)..........	(4,763)	
Adjusted net income of subsidiary	$ 91,997	
Minority share ($91,997 × 0.05)	$ 4,600	

Computation of net intercompany payable of parent company

Accounts payable to Sage Company for merchandise purchases		$47,500
Less: Interest receivable from Sage Company (page 368) . .	$30,000	
Management fee receivable from Sage Company. . . .	14,000	44,000
Net intercompany payable		$ 3,500

6 Elimination (a) continues the amortization of differences between current fair values and carrying amounts of the subsidiary's net assets on the date of the business combination of Post Corporation and Sage Company (see Chapter 6, page 261).

7 The $62,800 minority interest at beginning of year, excluding intercompany profits effects, as set forth in the explanation for elimination (a)(4), is computed as follows:

Computation of minority interest at beginning of year

Stockholders' equity of Sage Company, Dec. 31, Year 3:		
Common stock, $10 par		$ 400,000
Paid-in capital in excess of par		235,000
Retained earnings		439,000
Total stockholders' equity		$1,074,000
Add: Unamortized differences between current fair values and carrying amounts of Sage's identifiable net assets, Dec. 31, Year 3 (see page 373):		
Plant assets	$162,000	
Leasehold	20,000	182,000
Total adjusted net assets of Sage, Dec. 31, Year 3		$1,256,000
Minority interest therein ($1,256,000 × 0.05)		$ 62,800

8 Eliminations (b), (c), (d), and (e) are identical to the eliminations illustrated in this chapter on pages 354, 358, 361, and 370, respectively. For posting to the working paper for consolidated financial statements, elimination (d) was condensed. The credit to Depreciation Expense in elimination (d) is posted to Cost of Goods Sold in the income statement section of the working paper.

9 The effects of eliminations (a) through (e) on the computation of minority interest in net income of the subsidiary, in elimination (f), are analyzed as follows:

Elimination (a) increases costs and expenses of the subsidiary, thus decreasing the subsidiary's net income, a total of $19,000.

Elimination (b) reduces the subsidiary's gross profit on sales by $30,000 ($150,000 − $120,000 = $30,000); however, $26,000 of gross profit was realized by the parent company in its sales to outsiders. The net effect on the subsidiary's net income is a decrease of $4,000 ($30,000 − $26,000 = $4,000).

Elimination (c) does not affect the net income of the subsidiary.

Elimination (d) includes a $4,760 credit to the parent company's depreciation expense, which in effect is a realization of a portion of the intercompany profit on the subsidiary's sale of machinery to the parent company (see page 361). Thus, the subsidiary's net income is increased by $4,760.

Elimination (e) decreases intercompany interest revenue by $38,576 and decreases intercompany interest expense by $33,813. The difference, $4,763 ($38,576 − $33,813 = $4,763), is a reduction of the subsidiary's net income, to avoid double counting of the realized but unrecorded gain on the retirement of the subsidiary's bonds in the previous year (see page 371).

10 Because of the elimination of intercompany profits (gains), consolidated net income for the year ended December 31, Year 4, does not equal the parent company's equity-method net income. Consolidated net income may be verified as follows:

Verification of consolidated net income

Net income of Post Corporation		*$460,200*
Less: Post's share of adjustments to subsidiary's net income for intercompany profits (gains):		
Elimination (b) [($150,000 − $120,000) − $26,000]	*$(4,000)*	
Elimination (d)	*4,760*	
Elimination (e) ($38,576 − $33,813)	*(4,763)*	
Total	*$(4,003)*	
Post's share [$(4,003) × 0.95]		*(3,803)*
Consolidated net income		*$456,397*

11 Similarly, consolidated retained earnings on December 31, Year 4, does not equal the total of the two parent company retained earnings accounts in the working paper for consolidated financial statements. Consolidated retained earnings may be verified as follows:

Verification of consolidated retained earnings

Total of Post Corporation's two retained earnings accounts ($1,810,000 + $38,950)		*$1,848,950*
Adjustments:		
*Post's share of adjustments to subsidiary's net income (see **10**, above)*		*(3,803)*
Intercompany gain in Post's retained earnings—elimination (c)		*(50,000)*
Post's share of adjustments to subsidiary's beginning retained earnings for intercompany profits (gains):		
Elimination (b)	*$ (7,600)*	
Elimination (d)	*(22,610)*	
Elimination (e)	*23,371*	*(6,839)*
Consolidated retained earnings		*$1,788,308*

12 The consolidated amounts in the working paper for consolidated financial statements represent the financial position and operating results of Post Corporation and subsidiary resulting from the consolidated entity's transactions with **outsiders.** All intercompany transactions, profits (gains), and balances have been eliminated in the computation of the consolidated amounts.

REVIEW QUESTIONS

1 How are consolidated financial statements affected if unrealized intercompany profits resulting from transactions between a parent company and its subsidiaries are not eliminated? Explain.

2 What consolidated financial statement categories are affected by intercompany sales of merchandise at a profit? Explain.

3 Some accountants advocate the elimination of intercompany profit in the parent company's ending inventories only to the extent of the parent's ownership interest in the selling subsidiary's common stock. What argument can be advanced in opposition to this treatment of intercompany profit in the parent company's ending inventories?

4 How do intercompany sales of plant assets and intangible assets differ from intercompany sales of merchandise?

5 Is intercompany gain on the sale of land ever *realized?* Explain.

6 Sayles Company, a 90%-owned subsidiary of Partin Corporation, sold to Partin for $10,000 a machine with a carrying amount of $8,000, no residual value, and an economic life of four years. Explain how the intercompany gain element of Partin Corporation's annual depreciation expense for the machine is accounted for in the working paper for consolidated financial statements.

7 "No intercompany gain or loss should be recognized when a parent company acquires in the open market outstanding bonds of its subsidiary, because the transaction is not an *intercompany* transaction." Do you agree with this statement? Explain.

8 What accounting problems result from the reissuance by a subsidiary of parent company bonds acquired in the open market by the subsidiary? Explain.

9 Intercompany profits (gains) or losses in inventories, plant assets, or bonds result in consolidated net income that differs from the parent company's equity-method net income. Why is this true? Explain.

10 How is the intercompany profit in a subsidiary's *beginning* inventories resulting from the parent company's sales of merchandise to the subsidiary accounted for in a working paper elimination? Explain.

11 How is minority interest in net income of a partially owned subsidiary affected by working paper eliminations for intercompany profits? Explain.

EXERCISES

Ex. 8-1 Select the best answer for each of the following multiple-choice questions:

1 During the fiscal year ended October 31, Year 3, Phipp Corporation sold merchandise costing $600,000 to its 80%-owned subsidiary, Smythe Company, at a gross profit rate of 40%. At billed prices, Smythe's beginning and ending inventories included merchandise purchased from Phipp in the amount of $72,000 and $90,000, respectively. Disregarding income taxes, the October 31, Year 3, working paper elimination for Phipp Corporation and subsidiary should include a:

a Debit of $38,400 to Retained Earnings—Smythe

b Credit of $392,800 to Cost of Goods Sold—Smythe

    c Debit of $1,000,000 to Sales—Phipp

    d Debit of $400,000 to Gross Profit on Sales—Phipp

2 The minority interest in net income of a partially owned subsidiary for the year ended December 31, Year 7, is affected by:

    a The parent company's sale of machinery to the subsidiary at a gain during Year 7

    b The subsidiary's open-market acquisition of the parent company's bonds at a discount during Year 7

    c The parent company's sale to outside customers during Year 7 of merchandise obtained from the subsidiary for more than the subsidiary's cost during Year 7

    d None of the foregoing

3 When a parent company acquires outstanding bonds of its subsidiary at a cost less than the subsidiary's carrying amount, the resulting gain is:

    a Realized and recorded in the subsidiary's accounting records

    b Realized, but not recorded in the subsidiary's accounting records

    c Unrealized, but recorded in the subsidiary's accounting records

    d Unrealized and not recorded in the subsidiary's accounting records

4 A debit to minority interest in net assets of subsidiary in a working paper elimination for intercompany sales of merchandise indicates that:

    a The parent company sold merchandise to a partially owned subsidiary during a prior accounting period

    b A partially owned subsidiary sold merchandise to a wholly owned subsidiary during a prior accounting period

    c Either the parent company or a wholly owned subsidiary sold merchandise to a partially owned subsidiary during the current accounting period

    d Any one of the foregoing transactions occurred

5 On November 1, Year 4, the beginning of a fiscal year, Sync Company, the 70%-owned subsidiary of Pike Corporation, sold to Pike for $180,000 a machine with a carrying amount to Sync of $140,000. Pike established an 8-year economic life with no residual value for the machine and adopted the straight-line method of depreciation. The appropriate working paper elimination for Pike Corporation and subsidiary on October 31, Year 7, the end of a fiscal year, should include a debit to Retained Earnings—Sync of:

    a $21,000   **b** $25,000   **c** $30,000   **d** $40,000   **e** Some other amount

6 On December 31, Year 6, Passey Corporation prepared the following working paper elimination (Scully Company is an 80%-owned subsidiary):

Intercompany 9% Bonds Payable—Scully	500,000	
Discount on Intercompany 9% Bonds Payable—		
Scully		28,796
Investment in Scully Company 9% Bonds—		
Passey		420,076
Gain on Early Retirement of Bonds—Scully		51,128

To eliminate subsidiary's 9% bonds (interest payable each December 31), due December 31, Year 15, acquired by parent at a 12% yield rate (bonds were issued at a 10% yield rate), and to recognize gain on the retirement of the bonds (Income tax effects are disregarded.)

If both Passey and Scully use the interest method of amortization of bond discount, the appropriate working paper elimination for Passey Corporation and subsidiary for the year ended December 31, Year 7, will include a credit to Intercompany Interest Expense—Scully in the amount of:

> **a** $45,000 ($500,000 × 0.09)
> **b** $47,120 ($471,204 × 0.10)
> **c** $50,409 ($420,076 × 0.12)
> **d** $42,408 ($471,204 × 0.09)
> **e** None of the foregoing

Ex. 8-2   Among the working paper eliminations of Parke Corporation and Subsidiary on December 31, Year 5, was the following (explanation omitted):

Retained Earnings—Selma ($18,750 × 0.90)	16,875	
Minority Interest in Net Assets of Subsidiary ($18,750 × 0.10) .	1,875	
Accumulated Depreciation—Parke	12,500	
Machinery—Parke		25,000
Depreciation Expense—Parke ($25,000 ÷ 4)		6,250

Answer the following questions:

a What is the probable explanation of the foregoing elimination?

b How many years have elapsed since the underlying intercompany transaction? Explain.

c How does the credit to Depreciation Expense—Parke enter into the determination of consolidated net income for Parke Corporation and subsidiary for the year ended December 31, Year 5? Explain.

Ex. 8-3   Peggy Corporation supplies all the merchandise sold by its wholly owned subsidiary, Sally Company. Both Peggy and Sally use perpetual inventory systems. Peggy bills merchandise to Sally at a price 25% in excess of Peggy's cost. For the fiscal year ended November 30, Year 8, Peggy's sales to Sally were $120,000 at billed prices. At billed prices, Sally's December 1, Year 7, inventories were $18,000, and its November 30, Year 8, inventories were $24,000.

Prepare an analysis of intercompany sales, cost of goods sold, and gross profit in inventories for the year ended November 30, Year 8. Your analysis should show selling price, cost, and gross profit for each of the three intercompany items.

Ex. 8-4   On October 1, Year 4, the beginning of a fiscal year, Patria Corporation acquired new equipment for $14,500 from its 90%-owned subsidiary, Selena Company. The equipment cost Selena $9,000 and had an economic life of 10 years on October 1, Year 4. Patria uses the sum-of-the-years'-digits depreciation method.

Prepare a working paper elimination for Patria Corporation and subsidiary on September 30, Year 6, the end of a fiscal year. Disregard income taxes.

Ex. 8-5   Solaw Company, the wholly owned subsidiary of Polka Corporation, issued 10%, five-year bonds on May 1, Year 1, at their face amount of $100,000. Interest is payable annually. On April 30, Year 2, the end of a fiscal year, Polka acquired in the open market 40% of Solaw outstanding bonds at a 12% yield, plus accrued interest for one year.

Compute the amount of cash paid by Polka and the gain on the early extinguishment of the bonds. Round all computations to the nearest dollar. Disregard income taxes.

Ex. 8-6   Palimino Corporation acquired a 70% interest in Sokal Company in Year 2. For the years ended December 31, Year 3 and Year 4, Sokal had net income of $80,000 and $90,000, respectively. During Year 3, Sokal sold merchandise to Palimino for $10,000 at a gross profit of $2,000. The merchandise was resold during Year 4 by Palimino to outsiders for $15,000.

Compute the minority interest in Sokal's net income for Year 3 and Year 4. Disregard income taxes.

Ex. 8-7   On November 1, Year 5, the beginning of a fiscal year, Sinn Company, the 90%-owned subsidiary of Parr Corporation, issued to the public $100,000 face amount of 5-year, 9% bonds, interest payable each November 1, for $103,993—an 8% yield. Bond issue costs may be disregarded.

On October 31, Year 6, the end of a fiscal year, Parr acquired in the open market $60,000 face amount of Sinn's 9% bonds for $58,098—a 10% yield. The realized gain on the transaction reported in the October 31, Year 6, consolidated income statement of Parr Corporation and subsidiary was $3,889. Sinn and Parr use the interest method of amortization of bond premium and accumulation of bond discount.

Compute the missing amounts in the working paper elimination below. Round all amounts to the nearest dollar. Disregard income taxes.

PARR CORPORATION AND SUBSIDIARY
Partial Working Paper Eliminations
October 31, Year 7

Intercompany Interest Revenue—Parr	(1) 5810
Intercompany Bonds Payable—Sinn	60,000
Premium on Intercompany Bonds Payable—Sinn 58098+3889 - 690 (2) 1546	
Investment in Sinn Company Bonds—Parr . 58098 - 5400	(3) 58508
Intercompany Interest Expense—Sinn	(4) 4959
Retained Earnings—Sinn	(5) 3500
Minority Interest in Net Assets of Subsidiary	389

To eliminate subsidiary's bonds owned by a parent company, and related interest revenue and expense; and to increase subsidiary's beginning retained earnings by amount of unamortized realized gain on the retirement of the bonds. (Income tax effects are disregarded.)

Ex. 8-8   Pele Corporation acquired 70% of the outstanding common stock of Shad Company on August 1, Year 2. During the fiscal year ended July 31, Year 3, Pele sold merchandise to Shad in the amount of $120,000; the merchandise was priced at 20% above Pele's cost. Shad had 30% of this merchandise in inventories on July 31, Year 3.

Prepare a working paper elimination for Pele Corporation and subsidiary on July 31, Year 3. Disregard income taxes.

Ex. 8-9   On January 2, Year 1, Steve Company, an 80%-owned subsidiary of Paulo Corporation, sold to its parent company for $20,000 cash a machine with a carrying amount of $16,000, a five-year economic life, and no residual value. Both Paulo and Steve use the straight-line method of depreciation for all machinery.

Compute the missing amounts in the working paper eliminations below. Use the identifying numbers for the missing amounts in your solution.

	December 31, Year 2	December 31, Year 4
Minority Interest in Net Assets of Subsidiary . .	(1) 640	(4) 320
Retained Earnings—Steve	(2) 2560	(5) 1280
Accumulated Depreciation—Paulo	(3) 1600	(6) 3200
Machinery—Paulo	4,000	4,000
Depreciation Expense—Paulo	800	800

To eliminate unrealized intercompany gain in machinery and in related depreciation. (Income tax effects are disregarded.)

CASES

Case 8-1 Powell Corporation has begun selling idle machinery from a discontinued product line to a wholly owned subsidiary, Seeley Company, which requires the machinery in its operations. Powell had transferred the machinery from the Machinery account to an Idle Machinery account and had written down the machinery to net realizable value based on quotations from used machinery dealers. Depreciation of the idle machinery was terminated when the product line was discontinued.

During Year 3, Powell's sales of idle machinery to Seeley totaled $50,000 and were accounted for by Powell and Seeley in the following aggregate journal entries:

Powell Corporation Journal Entries

Cash	50,000	
Sales of Idle Machinery		50,000

To record sales of idle machinery to Seeley Company.

Cost of Idle Machinery Sold	40,000	
Idle Machinery		40,000

To write off net realizable value of idle machinery sold to Seeley Company.

Seeley Company Journal Entries

Machinery	50,000	
Cash		50,000

To record acquisition of used machinery from Powell Corporation.

Depreciation Expense	5,000	
Accumulated Depreciation of Machinery		5,000

To provide, in accordance with regular policy, depreciation for one-half year in year of acquisition of machinery, based on economic life of five years and no residual value.

On December 31, Year 3, the accountant for Powell Corporation prepared the following working paper elimination:

Retained Earnings—Powell	10,000	
Machinery—Seeley		10,000

To eliminate unrealized intercompany gain in machinery.

Instructions Evaluate the journal entries and working paper elimination shown above.

Case 8-2 The existence of intercompany profits in consolidated inventories as a result of sales of merchandise by a partially owned subsidiary to its parent company has given rise to the following three viewpoints as to how such profits should be treated for consolidated financial statements:

  a Only the parent company's share of intercompany profits in inventories should be eliminated.

  b The entire amount of intercompany profits in inventories should be eliminated against the equities of the controlling and minority groups in proportion to their interests.

c The entire amount of intercompany profits in inventories should be eliminated against consolidated retained earnings.

Instructions Present arguments to support each viewpoint.

Case 8-3 Sawhill Company, one of two wholly owned subsidiaries of Peasley Corporation, is in liquidation. On October 31, Year 8, the close of a fiscal year, Sawhill sold accounts receivable with a carrying amount of $50,000 to Shelton Company, the other wholly owned subsidiary of Peasley Corporation, for a gain of $10,000. Shelton debited the $10,000 to a deferred charge account, which is to be amortized to expense in proportion to the amounts collected on the receivables Shelton acquired from Sawhill. The $10,000 gain appeared in the consolidated income statement of Peasley Corporation and Shelton Company for the year ended October 31, Year 8; Sawhill Company was not included in the consolidated financial statements on that date because it was in liquidation. Peasley uses the equity method of accounting for its investments in both Shelton and Sawhill.

Instructions Evaluate the accounting described above.

PROBLEMS

8-1 Parley Corporation owns 90% of the outstanding common stock of Silton Company. Both Parley and Silton have a February 28 (or 29) fiscal year-end. On March 1, Year 4, Silton sold to Parley for $100,000 a warehouse recorded in Silton's Leasehold Improvements account on that date at a carrying amount (net) of $80,000. Parley is amortizing the warehouse on the straight-line basis over the remaining term of the operating lease, which expires February 28, Year 14.

On March 1, Year 5, Parley acquired in the open market for $48,264 cash (a 10% yield) one-half of Silton's $100,000 face amount 8% bonds due February 28, Year 7. The bonds had been issued at their face amount on March 1, Year 2, with interest payable annually on February 28. Silton and Parley use the interest method of amortization and accumulation of bond discount.

Instructions Prepare working paper eliminations on February 28, Year 6, for Parley Corporation and subsidiary. Disregard income taxes.

8-2 Peke Corporation sells merchandise to its 75%-owned subsidiary, Stoke Company, at a markup of 25% on cost. Stoke sells merchandise to Peke at a markup of 25% on selling price. Merchandise transactions between the two companies for the fiscal year ended June 30, Year 2, were as follows, at selling prices:

	Peke sales to Stoke	Stoke sales to Peke
July 1, Year 1, inventories of purchaser	$ 48,000	$ 30,000
Sales during year	600,000	800,000
Subtotals	$648,000	$830,000
Less: June 30, Year 2, inventories of purchaser	60,000	40,000
Cost of goods sold during year	$588,000	$790,000

Instructions Prepare working paper eliminations on June 30, Year 2, for Peke Corporation and subsidiary. Disregard income taxes.

8-3 For the fiscal year ended April 30, Year 7, Scala Company, a 90%-owned pooled subsidiary of Padua Corporation, had net income of $120,000. During the year ended April 30, Year 7, the following transactions occurred:

(1) Padua sold merchandise to Scala for $180,000, at a markup of 20% on Padua's cost. Merchandise acquired from Padua in Scala's inventories totaled $54,000 on May 1, Year 6, and $84,000 on April 30, Year 7, at billed prices.

(2) On May 1, Year 6, Scala sold to Padua for $80,000 a machine with a carrying amount to Scala of $56,000. Padua established a remaining economic life of eight years, no residual value, and the straight-line method of depreciation for the machine.

(3) On April 30, Year 7, Padua acquired in the open market $200,000 face amount of Scala's 10%, ten-year bonds for $158,658, a yield rate of 14%. Scala had issued $400,000 face amount of the bonds on October 31, Year 6, for $354,120, a yield rate of 12%. The bonds pay interest each April 30 and October 31; Padua acquired its bond investment after the interest for April 30, Year 7, had been paid to the previous bondholders. Scala and Padua use the interest method of amortization or accumulation of bond discount.

Instructions Prepare working paper eliminations for Padua Corporation and subsidiary on April 30, Year 7, including minority interest in net income of subsidiary. Disregard the elimination for the intercompany investment; also disregard income taxes.

8-4 On July 1, Year 8, the beginning of a fiscal year, Pacific Corporation and its wholly owned subsidiary, Sommer Company, entered into the following transactions:

(1) Pacific sold to Sommer for $16,000 a machine with a carrying amount of $12,000 ($30,000 cost less $18,000 accumulated depreciation). Sommer estimated an economic life of eight years and no residual value for the machine. Sommer uses the straight-line method of depreciation for all plant assets.

(2) Pacific acquired in the open market for $361,571 (a 12% yield) four-fifths of Sommer's outstanding 8% bonds due June 30, Year 11, after interest had been paid on the bonds. Sommer's accounting records on July 1, Year 8, included the following balances:

8% bonds payable, due June 30, Year 11	$500,000
Discount on 8% bonds payable	24,870

The 8% bonds (interest payable each June 30) had been issued by Sommer July 1, Year 6, to yield 10%. Bond issue costs may be disregarded. Interest expense recorded by Sommer through Year 8 was as follows:

Year ended June 30, Year 7	$46,209
Year ended June 30, Year 8	46,830

Sommer and Pacific use the interest method of amortization or accumulation of bond discount.

Instructions

a Prepare journal entries for Pacific Corporation to record the two transactions with Sommer Company on July 1, Year 8, and interest revenue for the year ended June 30, Year 9. Disregard income taxes.

b Prepare working paper eliminations for Pacific Corporation and subsidiary on June 30, Year 9. Disregard income taxes.

8-5 On August 31, Year 4, the end of a fiscal year, Silver Company, a wholly owned subsidiary of Pollard Corporation, issued to the public, at a yield rate of 11%, $800,000 face amount of 10%, 10-year bonds, with interest payable each February 28 and August 31. Bond issue costs may be disregarded. On August 31, Year 5, Pollard acquired $600,000 face amount of Silver's 10% bonds at a yield rate of 12%. On that date, Silver's Discount on Bonds Payable account had a debit balance of $44,985. Both companies use the interest method of amortization or accumulation of bond discount, and both companies close their accounting records only at the end of the fiscal year.

Instructions

a Set up three-column ledger accounts for Pollard Corporation's Investment in Silver Company Bonds and Intercompany Interest Revenue, and for Silver Company's Intercompany Bonds Payable, Discount on Intercompany Bonds Payable, and Intercompany Interest Expense. Record in the ledger accounts all transactions involving Silver's 10% bonds from August 31, Year 5, through August 31, Year 6. Round all amounts to the nearest dollar. Disregard income taxes, and do not prepare closing entries.

b Prepare working paper eliminations for Pollard Corporation and subsidiary on August 31, Year 5, and August 31, Year 6. Disregard income taxes.

8-6 Patrick Corporation issued 100,000 shares of its $10 par common stock to acquire all the outstanding $10 par common stock of Shannon Company on December 31, Year 9, the end of a fiscal year, in a pooling-type business combination. In addition, Patrick acquired for $220,424, at a 12% yield rate, $250,000 face amount of Shannon's 9%, ten-year bonds due June 30, Year 15, with interest payable each December 31 and June 30. After completion of the business combination and journal entries to transfer merchandise transactions between Patrick and Shannon to appropriate intercompany accounts, the separate financial statements of the two companies appear on page 392.

On December 31, Year 9, one-half of the merchandise acquired by Patrick from Shannon prior to the pooling-type business combination remained unsold.

Instructions

a Prepare a working paper for consolidated financial statements and related working paper eliminations for Patrick Corporation and subsidiary on December 31, Year 9. Disregard income taxes.

b Prepare a consolidated statement of retained earnings for Patrick Corporation and subsidiary for the year ended December 31, Year 9.

8-7 Power Corporation acquired 80% of Snyder Company's 1,250 shares of $100 par common stock outstanding on July 1, Year 6, for $158,600, including out-of-pocket costs of the purchase-type business combination. The excess of the current fair value of Snyder's identifiable net assets over their carrying amounts on July 1, Year 6, was attributable as follows:

To inventories	$3,000
To equipment (five-year economic life on July 1, Year 6)	4,000
To goodwill (five-year economic life on July 1, Year 6)	Remainder
	of excess

In addition, on July 1, Year 6, Power acquired in the open market at face amount $40,000 of Snyder Company's 6% bonds payable. Interest is payable by Snyder each July 1 and January 1.

Financial statements for Power Corporation and Snyder Company for the period ended December 31, Year 6, are on page 393.

The following information also is available:

(1) Intercompany sales data for the six months ended December 31, Year 6, are shown at the top of page 394.

PATRICK CORPORATION AND SHANNON COMPANY
Separate Financial Statements
For Year Ended December 31, Year 9

	Patrick Corporation	Shannon Company
Income Statements		
Revenue		
Net sales	$15,000,000	$10,000,000
Intercompany sales		600,000
Total revenue	$15,000,000	$10,600,000
Costs and expenses		
Cost of goods sold	$ 6,000,000	$ 6,000,000
Intercompany cost of goods sold		480,000
Operating expenses	3,600,000	1,199,500
Interest expense	150,000	108,000
Income taxes expense	3,150,000	1,687,500
Total costs and expenses	$12,900,000	$ 9,475,000
Net income	$ 2,100,000	$ 1,125,000
Statements of Retained Earnings		
Retained earnings, beginning of year	$ 2,400,000	$ 275,000
Add: Net income	2,100,000	1,125,000
Subtotal	$ 4,500,000	$ 1,400,000
Less: Dividends	800,000	270,000
Retained earnings, end of year	$ 3,700,000	$ 1,130,000
Balance Sheets		
Assets		
Cash	$ 750,000	$ 300,000
Accounts receivable (net)	1,950,000	450,000
Intercompany accounts receivable		300,000
Inventories	2,100,000	950,000
Investment in Shannon Company common stock . .	2,205,000	
Investment in Shannon Company bonds	220,424	
Plant assets (net)	4,660,000	2,000,000
Other assets	564,576	350,000
Total assets	$12,450,000	$ 4,350,000
Liabilities & Stockholders' Equity		
Intercompany accounts payable	$ 300,000	
Other current liabilities	1,450,000	$ 945,000
Bonds payable	1,500,000	950,000
Intercompany bonds payable		250,000
Common stock, $10 par	3,000,000	900,000
Paid-in capital in excess of par	1,370,000	175,000
Retained earnings	3,700,000	1,130,000
Retained earnings of subsidiary	1,130,000	
Total liabilities & stockholders' equity	$12,450,000	$ 4,350,000

POWER CORPORATION AND SNYDER COMPANY
Separate Financial Statements
For Periods Ended December 31, Year 6

	Power Corporation (year ended 12-31-6)	Snyder Company (six months ended 12-31-6)
Income Statements		
Revenue		
Net sales	$ 902,000	$400,000
Intercompany sales	60,000	105,000
Intercompany interest revenue (expense) . . .	1,200	(1,200)
Intercompany investment income	13,280	
Intercompany loss on sale of equipment . . .	(2,000)	
Total revenue	$ 974,480	$503,800
Costs and expenses		
Cost of goods sold	$ 720,000	$300,000
Intercompany cost of goods sold	50,000	84,000
Operating expenses	124,480	99,800
Total costs and expenses	$ 894,480	$483,800
Net income	$ 80,000	$ 20,000
Statements of Retained Earnings		
Retained earnings, beginning of period	$ 220,000	$ 50,000
Add: Net income	80,000	20,000
Subtotal	$ 300,000	$ 70,000
Less: Dividends	36,000	9,000
Retained earnings, end of period	$ 264,000	$ 61,000
Balance Sheets		
Assets		
Intercompany receivables (payables)	$ 100	$ (100)
Inventories, at fifo cost	300,000	75,000
Investment in Snyder Company common stock	164,340	
Investment in Snyder Company bonds	40,000	
Plant assets	794,000	280,600
Accumulated depreciation	(260,000)	(30,000)
Other assets	610,900	73,400
Total assets	$1,649,340	$398,900
Liabilities & Stockholders' Equity		
Dividends payable		$ 1,600
Bonds payable	$ 600,000	45,000
Intercompany bonds payable		40,000
Other liabilities	376,340	114,300
Common stock, $100 par	360,000	125,000
Paid-in capital in excess of par	49,000	12,000
Retained earnings	264,000	61,000
Total liabilities & stockholders' equity	$1,649,340	$398,900

	Power Corporation	Snyder Company
Intercompany accounts payable at end of year	$13,000	$ 5,500
Intercompany purchases in inventories at		
end of year	25,000	18,000

(2) On October 1, Year 6, Power sold to Snyder for $12,000 equipment having a carrying amount of $14,000 on that date. Snyder established a five-year economic life, no residual value, and the straight-line method of depreciation for the equipment. Snyder includes depreciation in operating expenses.

(3) Dividends were declared by Snyder as follows:

Sept. 30, Year 6	$1,000
Dec. 31, Year 6	8,000
Total dividends declared	$9,000

Instructions Prepare a working paper for consolidated financial statements and related working paper eliminations for Power Corporation and subsidiary for the year ended December 31, Year 6. Disregard income taxes.

8-8   On January 2, Year 1, Pritchard Corporation issued 5,000 shares of its $10 par common stock in exchange for all 3,000 shares of Spangler Company's $20 par common stock outstanding on that date. Out-of-pocket costs of the pooling-type business combination were negligible.

Financial statements of the two companies for the year ended December 31, Year 1, are presented on page 395.

The following additional information is available:

(1) On December 31, Year 1, Spangler owed Pritchard $16,000 on open account and $8,000 on 12% demand notes dated July 1, Year 1 (interest payable at maturity). Pritchard discounted $3,000 of the notes received from Spangler with the bank on July 1, Year 1, without notifying Spangler of this action.

(2) During Year 1, Pritchard sold to Spangler for $40,000 merchandise that cost $30,000. Spangler's December 31, Year 1, inventories included $10,000 of this merchandise priced at Spangler's cost.

(3) On July 1, Year 1, Spangler sold equipment with a carrying amount of $15,000 to Pritchard for $17,000. Pritchard recorded depreciation on the equipment in the amount of $850 for Year 1. The economic life of the equipment on the date of sale was 10 years. Pritchard includes depreciation in operating expenses.

(4) Spangler shipped merchandise to Pritchard on December 31, Year 1, and recorded an intercompany account receivable of $6,000 for the sale. Spangler's cost for the merchandise was $4,800. Because the merchandise was in transit, Pritchard did not record the transaction. The terms of the sale were FOB shipping point.

(5) Spangler declared a dividend of $1.50 a share on December 31, Year 1, payable on January 10, Year 2. Pritchard made no journal entry for the dividend declaration.

Instructions

a Prepare adjusting journal entries for Pritchard Corporation and Spangler Company on December 31, Year 1.

b Prepare a working paper for consolidated financial statements and related working paper eliminations for Pritchard Corporation and subsidiary on December 31, Year 1. Disregard income taxes.

8-9   The separate financial statements on page 396 were prepared after completion of the December 31, Year 4, audit of Pye Corporation and its subsidiaries, Sidey

PRITCHARD CORPORATION AND SPANGLER COMPANY
Separate Financial Statements
For Year Ended December 31, Year 1

	Pritchard Corporation	Spangler Company
Income Statements		
Revenue		
Net sales	$499,850	$298,240
Intercompany sales	40,000	6,000
Intercompany interest revenue (expense)	300	(480)
Intercompany investment income	10,200	
Intercompany gain on sale of equipment		2,000
Total revenue	$550,350	$305,760
Costs and expenses		
Cost of goods sold	$400,000	$225,000
Intercompany cost of goods sold	30,000	4,800
Operating expenses	88,450	65,760
Total costs and expenses	$518,450	$295,560
Net income	$ 31,900	$ 10,200
Statements of Retained Earnings		
Retained earnings, beginning of year	$ 67,000	$ 22,100
Add: Net income	31,900	10,200
Subtotals	$ 98,900	$ 32,300
Less: Dividends		4,500
Retained earnings, end of year	$ 98,900	$ 27,800
Balance Sheets		
Assets		
Intercompany receivables (payables)	$ 21,300	$ (22,980)
Inventories	81,050	49,840
Investment in Spangler Company common stock . . .	112,300	
Plant assets	83,200	43,500
Accumulated depreciation	(12,800)	(9,300)
Other assets	71,150	56,200
Total assets	$356,200	$117,260
Liabilities & Stockholders' Equity		
Liabilities	$ 56,700	$ 9,460
Common stock, $10 par	120,000	
Common stock, $20 par		60,000
Paid-in capital in excess of par	58,500	20,000
Retained earnings	98,900	27,800
Retained earnings of subsidiary	22,100	
Total liabilities & stockholders' equity	$356,200	$117,260

PYE CORPORATION, SIDEY COMPANY, AND SHORER COMPANY
Separate Financial Statements
For Periods Ended December 31, Year 4

	Pye Corporation (year ended 12-31-4)	Sidey Company (year ended 12-31-4)	Shorer Company (six months ended 12-31-4)
Income Statements			
Revenue			
Net sales	$ 920,000	$245,000	$310,000
Intercompany sales.	40,000	30,000	60,000
Dividend revenue	6,800		
Gain on sale of plant assets	5,000		
Intercompany gain on sale of plant assets	4,000		
Intercompany revenue (expenses)	12,000	(6,000)	(6,000)
Intercompany investment loss of Sidey Company. . . .	(45,000)		
Intercompany investment income of Shorer Company .	108,800		
Total revenue	$1,051,600	$269,000	$364,000
Costs and expenses			
Cost of goods sold	$ 788,000	$273,000	$168,000
Intercompany cost of goods sold	32,000	27,000	42,000
Operating expenses	73,200	29,000	18,000
Total costs and expenses	$ 893,200	$329,000	$228,000
Net income (loss)	$ 158,400	$ (60,000)	$136,000
Statements of Retained Earnings			
Retained earnings, beginning of period	$ 611,000		$ 80,000
Add: Net income (loss)	158,400	$ (60,000)	136,000
Subtotals	$ 769,400	$ (60,000)	$216,000
Less: Dividends	48,000		14,000
Retained earnings (deficit), end of year	$ 721,400	$ (60,000)	$202,000
Balance Sheets			
Assets			
Intercompany receivables (payables)	$ 12,000	$ (6,000)	$ (6,000)
Inventories	242,900	70,000	78,000
Investment in Sidey Company common stock	105,000		
Investment in Shorer Company common stock	269,500		
Other investments	185,000		
Plant assets (net)	279,000	51,000	78,000
Other assets	174,000	52,000	170,000
Total assets	$1,267,400	$167,000	$320,000
Liabilities & Stockholders' Equity			
Accounts payable	$ 46,000	$ 27,000	$ 18,000
Common stock, $20 par	500,000	200,000	100,000
Retained earnings (deficit)	721,400	(60,000)	202,000
Total liabilities & stockholders' equity	$1,267,400	$167,000	$320,000

Company and Shorer Company. The subsidiary investments are accounted for by the equity method of accounting.

The following additional information is available:

(1) Sidey was formed by Pye on January 2, Year 4. To secure additional capital, 25% of Sidey's authorized common stock was sold at par to outsiders. Pye acquired for cash the remaining authorized common stock at par.

(2) On July 1, Year 4, Pye acquired from stockholders 4,000 shares of Shorer's common stock for $175,000, including out-of-pocket costs. The balance sheet for Shorer on July 1, Year 4, follows:

SHORER COMPANY

Balance Sheet

July 1, Year 4

Assets

Current assets	$165,000
Plant assets (net)	60,000
Total assets	$225,000

Liabilities & Stockholders' Equity

Current liabilities	$ 45,000
Common stock, $20 par	100,000
Retained earnings	80,000
Total liabilities & stockholders' equity	$225,000

The current fair values of Shorer's identifiable net assets on July 1, Year 4, were the same as their carrying amounts. Pye's board of directors determined that Shorer's goodwill had an economic life of five years.

(3) The following intercompany sales were made during Year 4:

	Sales	Included in pur-chaser's Dec. 31, Year 4, inventories
Pye to Shorer	$ 40,000	$15,000
Sidey to Shorer	30,000	10,000
Shorer to Pye	60,000	21,900
Totals	$130,000	$46,900

(4) On January 2, Year 4, Pye sold a punch press to Sidey. The punch press had been acquired by Pye on January 2, Year 2, and was being depreciated by the straight-line method over a ten-year economic life. Sidey computed depreciation by the same method based on the remaining economic life, and included the depreciation in cost of goods sold. Details of the sale were as follows:

Cost of punch press	$25,000
Less: Accumulated depreciation	5,000
Carrying amount of punch press	$20,000
Sales price	24,000
Gain on sale of punch press	$ 4,000

(5) Cash dividends were declared and paid on the following dates in Year 4:

	Pye Corporation	*Shorer Company*
June 30	*$22,000*	*$ 6,000*
Dec. 31	*26,000*	*14,000*
Total cash dividends declared and paid	*$48,000*	*$20,000*

(6) Pye billed each subsidiary $6,000 at year-end for management fees in Year 4. The invoices were paid in January, Year 5.

Instructions Prepare a working paper for consolidated financial statements and related working paper eliminations for Pye Corporation and subsidiaries on December 31, Year 4. Disregard income taxes.

8-10 On June 30, Year 2, Pasini Corporation acquired all the outstanding common stock of Seymour Company for $3,605,000 cash and Pasini's common stock having a current fair value of $4,100,000. Out-of-pocket costs of the business combination were negligible. On the date of the combination, the carrying amounts and current fair values of Seymour's identifiable assets and liabilities were as follows:

	Carrying amounts	*Current fair values*
Cash	*$ 160,000*	*$ 160,000*
Accounts receivable (net)	*910,000*	*910,000*
Inventories	*860,000*	*1,025,186*
Building	*9,000,000*	*7,250,000*
Furniture	*3,000,000*	*2,550,000*
Accumulated depreciation	*(5,450,000)*	
Intangible assets (net)	*150,000*	*220,000*
Total assets	*$8,630,000*	*$12,115,186*
Notes payable	*$ 500,000*	*$ 500,000*
Accounts payable	*580,000*	*580,000*
5% mortgage note payable	*4,000,000*	*3,710,186*
Total liabilities	*$5,080,000*	*$ 4,790,186*

Financial statements of the two companies on December 31, Year 2, appear on page 399.

By the year-end, December 31, Year 2, the net balance of Seymour's accounts receivable on June 30, Year 2, had been collected; the inventories on June 30, Year 2, had been debited to cost of goods sold; the $500,000 note had been paid (on July 1, Year 2); and the accounts payable on June 30, Year 2, had been paid.

As of June 30, Year 2, Seymour Company's building and furniture had estimated economic lives of ten years and eight years, respectively. All intangible assets had an estimated economic life of 20 years. All depreciation and amortization is computed by the straight-line method.

As of June 30, Year 2, the 5% mortgage note payable had eight equal annual payments remaining, with the next payment due June 30, Year 3. The current fair value of the note was based on a 7% interest rate.

Prior to June 30, Year 2, there were no intercompany transactions between Pasini and Seymour; however, during the last six months of Year 2 the following intercompany transactions occurred:

(1) Pasini sold $400,000 of merchandise to Seymour. The cost of the merchandise to Pasini was $360,000. Of this merchandise, $75,000 remained on hand on December 31, Year 2.

PASINI CORPORATION AND SEYMOUR COMPANY
Separate Financial Statements
For Periods Ended December 31, Year 2

	Pasini Corporation (year ended 12-31-2)	Seymour Company (six months ended 12-31-2)
Income Statements		
Revenue		
Net sales	$25,600,000	$6,000,000
Intercompany sales	400,000	
Intercompany revenue (expenses)	180,000	(180,000)
Intercompany investment income	82,082	
Total revenue	$26,262,082	$5,820,000
Cost and expenses		
Cost of goods sold	$17,640,000	$3,950,000
Intercompany cost of goods sold	360,000	
Depreciation expense	3,701,000	600,000
Amortization expense		3,750
Other operating expenses	3,130,000	956,000
Interest expense	662,000	100,000
Total costs and expenses	$25,493,000	$5,609,750
Net income	$ 769,082	$ 210,250
Statements of Retained Earnings		
Retained earnings, beginning of period	$ 2,167,500	$ 650,000
Net income	769,082	210,250
Retained earnings, end of period	$ 2,936,582	$ 860,250
Balance Sheets		
Assets		
Intercompany receivables (payables)	$ 55,500	$ (55,500)
Inventories	2,031,000	1,009,500
Other current assets	2,326,457	1,026,526
Investment in Seymour Company common stock . .	7,787,082	
Investment in Pasini Corporation bonds		281,349
Buildings	17,000,000	9,000,000
Furniture	4,200,000	3,000,000
Accumulated depreciation	(8,000,000)	(6,050,000)
Intangible assets (net)		146,250
Total assets	$25,400,039	$8,358,125
Liabilities & Stockholders' Equity		
Current liabilities	$ 2,017,343	$ 597,875
Mortgage notes payable	6,786,500	4,000,000
$7\frac{1}{2}$% bonds payable	700,000	
Intercompany $7\frac{1}{2}$% bonds payable	300,000	
Discount on $7\frac{1}{2}$% bonds payable	(9,020)	
Discount on intercompany $7\frac{1}{2}$% bonds payable	(3,866)	
$8\frac{1}{4}$% bonds payable	3,900,000	
Common stock	8,772,500	2,900,000
Retained earnings	2,936,582	860,250
Total liabilities & stockholders' equity	$25,400,039	$8,358,125

(2) On December 31, Year 2, Seymour acquired in the open market $300,000 of Pasini's $7\frac{1}{2}$% bonds payable for $303,849, including $22,500 interest receivable. Pasini had issued $1,000,000 of these five-year, $7\frac{1}{2}$% bonds on January 1, Year 1, for $980,036 to yield 8%.

(3) Many of the management functions of the two companies have been combined since the business combination. Pasini charges Seymour a $30,000 monthly management fee.

(4) On December 31, Year 2, Seymour owed Pasini two months' management fees and $18,000 for merchandise purchases.

Instructions Prepare a working paper for consolidated financial statements and related working paper eliminations for Pasini Corporation and subsidiary on December 31, Year 2. Round all computations to the nearest dollar. Disregard income taxes.

9 CONSOLIDATED FINANCIAL STATEMENTS: INCOME TAXES, CHANGES IN FINANCIAL POSITION, AND INSTALLMENT ACQUISITIONS

In this chapter, we consider two topics that have relevance for every parent company–subsidiary relationship: (1) income taxes, and (2) the consolidated statement of changes in financial position. In addition, we deal with accounting for installment acquisitions of a subsidiary in a purchase-type business combination.

INCOME TAXES IN BUSINESS COMBINATIONS AND CONSOLIDATIONS

Accounting for income taxes for a consolidated entity has received considerable attention from accountants in recent years, primarily because of the growing emphasis on income tax allocation and disclosure in financial statements. Accounting for income taxes in business combinations and consolidated financial statements may be subdivided into three sections: (1) income taxes attributable to current fair values of a purchased subsidiary's identifiable net assets; (2) income taxes attributable to undistributed earnings of subsidiaries; and (3) income taxes attributable to unrealized intercompany profits (gains).

401

Income taxes attributable to current fair values of purchased subsidiary's identifiable net assets

Income tax accounting requirements for business combinations often differ from financial accounting requirements. A purchase-type business combination, which requires a revaluation of the combinee's identifiable net assets, may meet the requirements for a "tax-free corporate reorganization" under the Internal Revenue Code, in which a new income tax basis may not be required for the combinee's net assets. Similarly, a pooling-type business combination, in which there is no revaluation of the combinee's net assets, may not be a "tax-free corporate reorganization," and the income tax basis of the combinee's net assets may be changed. In such situations, a **permanent difference** may result between provisions for depreciation and amortization in the combinee company's financial statements and income tax returns.

In recognition of this problem, **APB Opinion No. 16,** "Business Combinations," included the following provision for income tax considerations in the valuation of a purchased combinee's net assets:[1]

> The market or appraisal values of specific assets and liabilities determined . . . (for a purchased combinee) may differ from the income tax bases of those items. Estimated future tax effects of differences between the tax bases and amounts otherwise appropriate to assign to an asset or liability are one of the variables in estimating fair value. Amounts assigned to identifiable assets and liabilities should, for example, recognize that the fair value of an asset to an acquirer is less than its market or appraisal value if all or a portion of the market or appraisal value is not deductible for income taxes. The impact of tax effects on amounts assigned to individual assets and liabilities depends on numerous factors, including imminence or delay of realization of the asset value and the possible timing of tax consequences. Since differences between amounts assigned and tax bases are not timing differences . . ., the acquiring corporation should not record deferred tax accounts at the date of acquisition.

To illustrate the application of the above, assume that the purchase-type business combination of Principia Corporation and its subsidiary, Sandusky Company, completed on June 1, Year 7, met the requirements for a "tax-free corporate reorganization" for income tax purposes. Sandusky's building, which had a remaining economic life of ten years with no residual value on June 1, Year 7, had an appraised value of $100,000 and a carrying amount of $80,000 on that date. Assuming a combined federal and state income tax rate of 60%, Sandusky's building should be valued in the June 1, Year 7, consolidated balance sheet of Principia Corporation and subsidiary at $88,000, computed as follows:

Valuation of building for consolidation purposes

Appraised value of building, June 1, Year 7	$100,000
Less: Income taxes effect of nondeductible depreciation [($100,000 − $80,000) × 0.60]	12,000
Current fair value of building, June 1, Year 7	$ 88,000

[1] *APB Opinion No. 16,* pp. 320–321.

Straight-line method depreciation in the consolidated income statements of Principia Corporation and subsidiary for the ten years subsequent to the purchase-type business combination would include depreciation expense of $8,800 a year ($88,000 ÷ 10 = $8,800) attributable to Sandusky's building. The $8,800 amount for annual depreciation is composed of the following:

Depreciation expense

Depreciation for income tax purposes ($80,000 ÷ 10 years)	*$8,000*
Add: Depreciation, net of income taxes effect, on $20,000 difference between appraised value and carrying amount on date of business combination {[$20,000 × (1.00 − 0.60)] ÷ 10 years}	*800*
Total depreciation expense for consolidated income statement ($88,000 ÷ 10 years)	*$8,800*

Income taxes attributable to undistributed earnings of subsidiaries

Generally accepted accounting principles for income taxes associated with the undistributed earnings of subsidiaries are contained in **APB Opinion No. 23,** "Accounting for Income Taxes—Special Areas." The principal provisions of **APB Opinion No. 23** are as follows:[2]

The Board concludes that including undistributed earnings of a subsidiary in the pretax accounting income of a parent company, either through consolidation or accounting for the investment by the equity method, may result in a timing difference, in a difference that may not reverse until indefinite future periods, or in a combination of both types of differences, depending on the intent and actions of the parent company.

Timing difference. The Board believes it should be presumed that all undistributed earnings of a subsidiary will be transferred to the parent company. Accordingly, the undistributed earnings of a subsidiary included in consolidated income (or in income of the parent company) should be accounted for as a timing difference, except to the extent that some or all of the undistributed earnings meet the criteria in [the paragraph entitled "Indefinite reversal criteria"].

Indefinite reversal criteria. The presumption that all undistributed earnings will be transferred to the parent company may be overcome, and no income taxes should be accrued by the parent company, if sufficient evidence shows that the subsidiary has invested or will invest the undistributed earnings indefinitely or that the earnings will be remitted in a tax-free liquidation.

Thus, income tax allocation accounting generally is appropriate for undistributed earnings of a subsidiary. Measurement problems involved in the computation of the income taxes are no excuse for ignoring the required allocation, according to **APB Opinion No. 23:**[3]

Income taxes of the parent company applicable to a timing difference in undistributed earnings of a subsidiary are necessarily based on estimates and assumptions. For example, the tax effect may be determined by assuming

---

[2] *APB Opinion No. 23,* "Accounting for Income Taxes—Special Areas," AICPA (New York: 1972), pp. 446–447.

[3] Ibid., p. 446.

that unremitted earnings were distributed in the current period and that the parent company received the benefit of all available tax-planning alternatives and available tax credits and deductions. The income tax expense of the parent company should also include taxes that would have been withheld if the undistributed earnings had been remitted as dividends.

Illustration of Income Tax Allocation for Undistributed Earnings of Subsidiaries Pinkley Corporation owns 75% of the outstanding common stock of Seabright Company, which it acquired for cash on April 1, Year 2. Goodwill acquired by Pinkley in the purchase-type business combination was $30,000; Seabright's identifiable net assets were fairly valued at their carrying amounts. For the fiscal year ended March 31, Year 3, Pinkley had pre-tax accounting income, exclusive of goodwill amortization and intercompany investment income under the equity method of accounting, of $100,000. Seabright's pre-tax accounting income was $50,000, and dividends paid by Seabright during Year 3 totaled $10,000. The combined federal and state income tax rate for both companies is 60%. Both federal and state income tax laws provide for a dividend received deduction rate of 85% on dividends from domestic corporations. Neither Pinkley nor Seabright had any other timing differences; neither had any income subject to capital gains or preference income tax rates; and there were no intercompany profits resulting from transactions between Pinkley and Seabright.

Seabright's journal entry to accrue income taxes on March 31, Year 3, is as follows:

Subsidiary's journal entry for accrual of income taxes

Income Taxes Expense	30,000	
Income Taxes Payable		30,000

To provide for income taxes for Year 3 as follows: $50,000 × 0.60 = $30,000.

On March 31, Year 3, Pinkley prepares the journal entries on page 405 for income taxes payable, the subsidiary's operating results, and deferred income taxes.

Income taxes attributable to unrealized intercompany profits (gains)

Federal income tax laws permit an affiliated group of corporations to file a consolidated income tax return rather than separate returns. Intercompany profits (gains) and losses are eliminated in a consolidated income tax return just as they are in consolidated financial statements. An "affiliated group" for federal income tax purposes is defined at the top of page 406.[4]

---

[4] United States, *Internal Revenue Code of 1954,* sec. 1504(a).

PINKLEY CORPORATION
Journal Entries
March 31, Year 3

Amortization Expense	750	
Investment in Seabright Company Common Stock		750

To record amortization of goodwill for Year 3: $30,000 ÷ 40 = $750.

Income Taxes Expense	60,000	
Income Taxes Payable		60,000

To provide for income taxes for Year 3 on income exclusive of goodwill amortization (not deductible) and intercompany investment income as follows: $100,000 × 0.60 = $60,000.

Cash	7,500	
Investment in Seabright Company Common Stock		7,500

To record dividend received from subsidiary: $10,000 × 0.75 = $7,500.

Investment in Seabright Company Common Stock	15,000	
Intercompany Investment Income		15,000

To accrue share of subisidary's net income for Year 3: $20,000* × 0.75 = $15,000.

Income Taxes Expense	1,350	
Income Taxes Payable		675
Deferred Income Tax Liability		675

To provide for income taxes on intercompany investment income from subsidiary as follows:

Net income of subsidiary	$20,000
Less: Depreciation and amortization attributable to differences between current fair values and carrying amounts of subsidiary's net assets	-0-
Income of subsidiary subject to income taxes . . .	$20,000
Parent company's share ($20,000 × 0.75)	$15,000
Less: Dividend received deduction ($15,000 × 0.85)	12,750
Amount subject to income taxes	$ 2,250
Income taxes expense ($2,250 × 0.60)	$ 1,350
Taxes currently payable based on dividend received [($7,500 × 0.15) × 0.60)]	$ 675
Taxes deferred until earnings remitted by subsidiary	675
Income taxes expense	$ 1,350

* $50,000 − $30,000 = $20,000

. . . the term "affiliated group" means one or more chains of includible corporations connected through stock ownership with a common parent corporation which is an includible corporation if—

(1) Stock possessing at least 80 percent of the voting power of all classes of stock and at least 80 percent of each class of the nonvoting stock of each of the includible corporations (except the common parent corporation) is owned directly by one or more of the other includible corporations; and

(2) The common parent corporation owns directly stock possessing at least 80 percent of the voting power of all classes of stock and at least 80 percent of each class of the nonvoting stock of at least one of the other includible corporations

As used in this subsection, the term "stock" does not include nonvoting stock which is limited and preferred as to dividends, . . .

If a parent company and its subsidiaries do not qualify for the "affiliated group" status, or if they otherwise elect to file separate income tax returns, the following accounting principle governs the treatment of income taxes attributable to unrealized intercompany profits:[5]

If income taxes have been paid on intercompany profits remaining within the group, such taxes should be deferred.

The deferral of income taxes accrued or paid on unrealized intercompany profits is best illustrated by returning to the intercompany profits examples in Chapter 8.

Income Taxes Attributable to Unrealized Intercompany Profits in Inventories
For unrealized intercompany profits in inventories at the end of the first year of an affiliated group's operations, we return to the working paper elimination on page 352 for Post Corporation and Sage Company on December 31, Year 3, which is as follows:

Elimination of unrealized intercompany profit in ending inventories

Intercompany Sales—Sage	120,000	
Intercompany Cost of Goods Sold—Sage		96,000
Cost of Goods Sold—Post.		16,000
Inventories—Post		8,000

To eliminate intercompany sales, cost of goods sold, and unrealized intercompany profit in inventories.

If Post and Sage file separate income tax returns for Year 3, and the combined federal and state income tax rate is 60%, the following additional elimination is required on December 31, Year 3:

Elimination for income taxes attributable to unrealized intercompany profit in ending inventories

Prepaid Income Taxes—Sage	4,800	
Income Taxes Expense—Sage		4,800

To defer income taxes provided on separate income tax returns of subsidiary applicable to unrealized intercompany profits in parent company's inventories on Dec. 31, Year 3: $8,000 \times 0.60 = \$4,800$.

[5] ARB No. 51, "Consolidated Financial Statements," AICPA (New York: 1959), p. 46.

The $4,800 reduction in the income taxes expense of Sage Company (the partially owned subsidiary) enters into the computation of the minority interest in the net income of the subsidiary for the year ended December 31, Year 3.

With regard to unrealized intercompany profits in beginning and ending inventories, we refer to the working paper elimination (on page 354), for the year ended December 31, Year 4, which follows:

Elimination of intercompany profits in beginning and ending inventories

Retained Earnings—Sage ($8,000 × 0.95).	7,600	
Minority Interest in Net Assets of Subsidiary ($8,000 × 0.05)	400	
Intercompany Sales—Sage	150,000	
Intercompany Cost of Goods Sold—Sage. . . . . . . `.` . .		120,000
Cost of Goods Sold—Post		26,000
Inventories—Post		12,000
To eliminate intercompany sales, cost of goods sold, and unrealized intercompany profit in inventories.		

Assuming separate income tax returns for Post Corporation and Sage Company for Year 4 and an income tax rate of 60%, the following additional eliminations are appropriate on December 31, Year 4:

Eliminations for income taxes attributable to intercompany profits in ending and beginning inventories

Prepaid Income Taxes—Sage.	7,200	
Income Taxes Expense—Sage		7,200
To defer income taxes provided on separate income tax returns of subsidiary applicable to unrealized intercompany profits in parent company's inventories on Dec. 31, Year 4: $12,000 × 0.60 = $7,200.		
Income Taxes Expense—Sage	4,800	
Retained Earnings—Sage ($4,800 × 0.95; or $7,600 ×		
0.60)		4,560
Minority Interest in Net Assets of Subsidiary ($4,800 × 0.05;		
or $400 × 0.60)		240
To provide for income taxes attributable to realized intercompany profits in parent company's inventories on Dec. 31, Year 3: $8,000 × 0.60 = $4,800.		

The second elimination reflects the income tax effects of the *realization* by the consolidated group, on a first-in, first-out basis, of the intercompany profits in the parent company's *beginning* inventories.

Income Taxes Attributable to Unrealized Intercompany Gain in Land Under generally accepted accounting principles, gains and losses from sales of plant assets are not reported as extraordinary items.[6] Thus, intra-period income tax allocation is not appropriate for such gains and losses.

The intercompany gain on Post Corporation's sale of land to Sage Company during Year 3 is eliminated by the following, December 31, Year 3, working paper elimination (from page 357):

Elimination of unrealized intercompany gain in land

Intercompany Gain on Sale of Land—Post	*50,000*	
Land—Sage		*50,000*
To eliminate unrealized intercompany gain on sale of land.		

If Post and Sage filed separate income tax returns for Year 3, the following elimination accompanies the one illustrated above, assuming a combined federal and state "capital gains" income tax rate of 35%:

Elimination for income taxes attributable to unrealized intercompany gain in land—for accounting period of sale

Prepaid Income Taxes—Post.	*17,500*	
Income Taxes Expense—Post		*17,500*
To defer income taxes provided on separate income tax returns of parent company applicable to unrealized intercompany gain in subsidiary's land on Dec. 31, Year 3: $50,000 × 0.35 = $17,500.		

In years subsequent to Year 3, as long as the subsidiary owned the land, the following elimination accompanies the elimination that debits Retained Earnings—Post $50,000 and credits Land—Sage $50,000:

Elimination for income taxes attributable to unrealized intercompany gain in land—for accounting periods subsequent to sale

Prepaid Income Taxes—Post.	*17,500*	
Retained Earnings—Post		*17,500*
To defer income taxes attributable to unrealized intercompany gain in subsidiary's land.		

In a period in which the subsidiary resold the land to an outsider, the appropriate elimination would be a debit to Income Taxes Expense—Sage and a credit to Retained Earnings—Post, in the amount of $17,500, because the $50,000 gain that previously was unrealized would be allocated to Sage.

Income Taxes Attributable to Unrealized Intercompany Gain in a Depreciable Plant Asset As pointed out in Chapter 8, the intercompany gain in the

---

[6] *APB Opinion No. 30,* pp. 566 and 568.

sale of a depreciable plant asset is realized through the periodic depreciation of the asset. Therefore, the related deferred income taxes "turn around" as depreciation expense is taken on the asset.

To illustrate, we refer to the illustration in Chapter 8, page 360, of the December 31, Year 3, working paper elimination for the unrealized intercompany gain in Post Corporation's machinery, which is reproduced below:

Elimination of unrealized intercompany gain in machinery	*Intercompany Gain on Sale of Machinery—Sage.* 23,800	
	Machinery—Post	*23,800*
	To eliminate unrealized intercompany gain on sale of machinery.	

Assuming separate income tax returns and a combined federal and state income tax rate of 60%, the tax-deferral elimination on December 31, Year 3 (date of the intercompany sale of machinery), is as follows:

Elimination for income taxes atrributable to unrealized intercompany gain in machinery—for accounting period of sale	*Prepaid Income Taxes—Sage* 14,280	
	Income Taxes Expense—Sage.	*14,280*
	To defer income taxes provided on separate income tax returns of subsidiary applicable to unrealized intercompany gain in parent company's machinery on Dec. 31, Year 3: $23,800 × 0.60 = $14,280.	

The $14,280 increase in the subsidiary's net income is included in the computation of the minority interest in the subsidiary's net income for Year 3. For the year ended December 31, Year 4, the elimination of the intercompany gain (see page 361) is as follows:

Elimination of intercompany gain in machinery and in related depreciation	*Retained Earnings—Sage ($23,800 × 0.95)* 22,610	
	Minority Interest in Net Assets of Subsidiary ($23,800 × 0.05) . 1,190	
	Accumulated Depreciation—Post 4,760	
	Machinery—Post	*23,800*
	Depreciation Expense—Post.	*4,760*
	To eliminate unrealized intercompany gain in machinery and in related depreciation. Gain element in depreciation computed as $23,800 ÷ 5 = $4,760, based on five-year economic life of machinery.	

For the year ended December 31, Year 4, the elimination for income taxes attributable to the intercompany gain is as follows:

Elimination for income taxes attributable to intercompany gain in machinery—for first year subsequent to sale

Income Taxes Expense—Sage	*2,856*	
Prepaid Income Taxes—Sage ($14,280 − $2,856)	*11,424*	
Retained Earnings—Sage ($14,280 × 0.95; or $22,610 × 0.60)		*13,566*
Minority Interest in Net Assets of Subsidiary ($14,280 × 0.05; or $1,190 × 0.60)		*714*

To provide for income taxes expense on intercompany gain realized through parent company's depreciation: $4,760 × 0.60 = $2,856; and to defer income taxes attributable to remainder of unrealized gain.

Comparable consolidation eliminations would be necessary on December 31, Years 5, 6, 7, and 8.

Income Taxes Attributable to Intercompany Gain on Retirement of Bonds As pointed out in Chapter 8, a gain or loss is recognized in consolidated financial statements for one affiliate's open-market acquisition of another affiliate's bonds. Thus, income taxes attributable to the gain or loss should be provided for in a working paper elimination.

Referring to Post Corporation's December 31, Year 3, open-market acquisition of Sage Company's bonds (see page 366), we have the following working paper elimination on December 31, Year 3:

Elimination for realized gain on retirement of affiliate's bonds

Intercompany Bonds Payable—Sage	*300,000*	
Discount on Intercompany Bonds Payable—Sage		*18,224*
Investment in Sage Company Bonds—Post		*257,175*
Gain on Early Extinguishment of Bonds—Sage		*24,601*

To eliminate subsidiary's bonds acquired by parent, and to recognize gain on the retirement of the bonds.

The appropriate elimination to accompany the one above is as follows, assuming that (1) the combined income tax rate is 60%, (2) separate income tax returns are filed, and (3) the gain on early extinguishment of bonds is not material and thus is not reported as an extraordinary item in the consolidated income statement of Post Corporation and subsidiary for Year 3:

Elimination for income taxes attributable to realized gain on retirement of affiliate's bonds—for accounting period of retirement

Income Taxes Expense—Sage	*14,760*	
Deferred Income Tax Liability—Sage		*14,760*

To provide for income taxes attributable to subsidiary's realized gain on parent company's acquisition of the subsidiary's bonds: $24,601 × 0.60 = $14,760.

The additional expense of the subsidiary recorded in the preceding elimination enters into the computation of the minority interest in net income of the subsidiary for Year 3.

In periods subsequent to the date of the acquisition of the bonds, the **actual** income taxes expense of both the parent company and the subsidiary reflect the effects of the intercompany interest revenue and expense. The income tax effects of the difference between intercompany interest revenue and expense represents the "turnaround" of the $14,760 deferred income tax liability in the foregoing elimination. For example, the working paper elimination for intercompany bonds of Post Corporation and subsidiary on December 31, Year 4 (see page 370), is repeated here:

Elimination for intercompany bonds one year after acquisition

Intercompany Interest Revenue—Post.	38,576	
Intercompany Bonds Payable—Sage.	300,000	
Discount on Intercompany Bonds Payable—Sage. . .		14,411
Investment in Sage Company Bonds—Post.		265,751
Intercompany Interest Expense—Sage.		33,813
Retained Earnings—Sage ($24,601 × 0.95)		23,371
Minority Interest in Net Assets of Subsidiary ($24,601 × 0.05).		1,230

To eliminate subsidiary's bonds owned by parent company, and related interest revenue and expense; and to increase subsidiary's beginning retained earnings by amount of un-amortized realized gain on the retirement of the bonds.

The foregoing elimination is accompanied by the following additional elimination on December 31, Year 4:

Elimination for income taxes attributable to gain on acquisition of affiliate's bonds—for first year subsequent to acquisition

Retained Earnings—Sage ($14,760 × 0.95; or $23,371 × 0.60)	14,022	
Minority Interest in Net Assets of Subsidiary ($14,760 × 0.05; or $1,230 × 0.60)	738	
Income Taxes Expense—Sage [($38,576 − $33,813) × 0.60].		2,858
Deferred Income Tax Liability—Sage ($14,760 − $2,858).		11,902

To reduce the subsidiary's income taxes expense for amount attributable to **recorded** intercompany gain (for consolidation purposes) on subsidiary's bonds; and to provide for remaining deferred income taxes on unrecorded portion of gain.

Summary: Income Taxes Attributable to Intercompany Profits (Gains) In this section we have illustrated the interperiod allocation of income taxes attributable to intercompany profits (gains) of affiliated companies that file separate income tax returns. The elimination of unrealized intercompany profits (gains) results in timing difference in which taxable income exceeds pre-tax accounting income in the accounting period of the intercompany gain; thus, prepaid income taxes must be accounted for in working paper eliminations that accompany the profit (gain) eliminations. In the case of intercompany bonds, pre-tax accounting income exceeds taxable income in the accounting period of the realized gain; thus, a deferred income tax liability must be provided in a working paper elimination.

The illustrative working paper eliminations for Post Corporation and subsidiary for the year ended December 31, Year 4, outlined in the preceding pages, are summarized below and on pages 413 and 414.

All the foregoing eliminations, excepting (d) and (e), affect the net income of Sage Company, the partially owned subsidiary. The appropriate amounts in those eliminations are included in the computation of minority interest in net income of subsidiary for Year 4.

POST CORPORATION AND SUBSIDIARY
Partial Working Paper Eliminations
December 31, Year 4

(b) Retained Earnings—Sage ($8,000 × 0.95)	7,600	
Minority Interest in Net Assets of Subsidiary ($8,000 × 0.05)	400	
Intercompany Sales—Sage	150,000	
Intercompany Cost of Goods Sold—Sage		120,000
Cost of Goods Sold—Post		26,000
Inventories—Post		12,000

To eliminate intercompany sales, cost of goods sold, and unrealized intercompany profit in inventories.

(c) Prepaid Income Taxes—Sage	7,200	
Income Taxes Expense—Sage		7,200

To defer income taxes provided on separate income tax returns of subsidiary applicable to unrealized intercompany profits in parent company's inventories on Dec. 31, Year 4: $12,000 × 0.60 = $7,200.

Income Taxes Expense—Sage	4,800	
Retained Earnings—Sage ($4,800 × 0.95; or $7,600 × 0.60)		4,560
Minority Interest in Net Assets of Subsidiary ($4,800 × 0.05; or $400 × 0.60)		240

To provide for income taxes attributable to realized intercompany profits in parent company's inventories on Dec. 31, Year 3: $8,000 × 0.60 = $4,800.

(Continued)

(d) *Retained Earnings—Post* *50,000*
        Land—Sage *50,000*
      To eliminate unrealized intercompany gain in land.

(e) *Prepaid Income Taxes—Post* *17,500*
        Retained Earnings—Post *17,500*
      To defer income taxes attributable to unrealized inter-
      company gain in subsidiary's land.

(f) *Retained Earnings—Sage ($23,800 × 0.95)* *22,610*
     Minority Interest in Net Assets of Subsidiary ($23,800 ×
        0.05) *1,190*
     Accumulated Depreciation—Post *4,760*
        Machinery—Post *23,800*
        Depreciation Expense—Post *4,760*
      To eliminate unrealized intercompany gain in machinery
      and in related depreciation. Profit element in deprecia-
      tion computed as $23,800 × 0.20 = $4,760, based on
      five-year economic life of machinery.

(g) *Income Taxes Expense—Sage* *2,856*
     Prepaid Income Taxes—Sage ($14,280 − $2,856). *11,424*
        Retained Earnings—Sage ($14,280 × 0.95; or
        $22,610 × 0.60). *13,566*
        Minority Interest in Net Assets of Subsidiary
        ($14,280 × 0.05; or $1,190 × 0.60) *714*
      To provide for income taxes expense on intercompany
      gain realized through parent company's depreciation:
      $4,760 × 0.60 = $2,856; and to defer income taxes attri-
      butable to remainder of unrealized gain.

(h) *Intercompany Interest Revenue—Post* *38,576*
     Intercompany Bonds Payable—Sage *300,000*
        Discount on Intercompany Bonds Payable—
        Sage *14,411*
        Investment in Sage Company Bonds—Post *265,751*
        Intercompany Interest Expense—Sage *33,813*
        Retained Earnings—Sage ($24,601 × 0.95). *23,371*
        Minority Interest in Net Assets of Subsidiary
        ($24,601 × 0.05) *1,230*
      To eliminate subsidiary's bonds owned by parent com-
      pany, and related interest revenue and expense; and to
      increase subsidiary's beginning retained earnings by
      amount of unamortized realized gain on the retirement of
      the bonds.

(Continued)

(i) Retained Earnings —Sage ($14,760 × 0.95; or $23,371 × 0.60) 14,022

Minority Interest in Net Assets of Subsidiary ($14,760 × 0.05; or $1,230 × 0.60) 738

Income Taxes Expense—Sage [($38,576 − $33,813) × 0.60] 2,858

Deferred Income Tax Liability—Sage ($14,760 − $2,858) 11,902

To reduce the subsidiary's income taxes expense for amount attributable to **recorded** intercompany gain (for consolidation purposes) on subsidiary's bonds; and to provide for remaining deferred income taxes on unrecorded portion of gain.

CONSOLIDATED STATEMENT OF CHANGES IN FINANCIAL POSITION

The consolidated financial statements issued by publicly owned companies include a statement of changes in financial position, generally prepared on a working capital concept. Such a statement may be prepared as described in the **Intermediate Accounting** text of this series; however, when the statement is prepared on a consolidated basis, a number of special problems arise. Some of these are described below:

1 Depreciation and amortization expense, as reported in the consolidated income statement, is added to combined net income, **including the minority interest in net income of subsidiary,** in the consolidated statement of changes in financial position. The depreciation and amortization expense in a purchase-type business combination is based on the current fair values of the assets, including any goodwill, of subsidiaries on the dates of the business combinations. Net income applicable to minority interests is included in the computation of working capital provided from operations, because 100% of working capital of all subsidiaries is included in a consolidated balance sheet.

2 Only cash dividends declared by the parent company and the cash dividends declared by partially owned subsidiary companies **to minority shareholders** are reported as applications of working capital. Cash dividends declared by subsidiaries to the parent company have no effect on consolidated working capital, because cash is transferred entirely **within the affiliated group** of companies. Dividends declared to minority stockholders that are material in amount should be listed separately or disclosed parenthetically in the consolidated statement of changes in financial position.

3 An acquisition by the parent company of additional shares of common stock directly from a subsidiary does not change the amount of consolidated working capital and thus is not reported in a consolidated statement of changes in financial position.

4 An acquisition by the parent company of additional shares of common stock from minority shareholders reduces consolidated working capital. Consequently, such an acquisition is reported in the consolidated statement of

changes in financial position as a financial resource (working capital or cash) applied.

5 A sale of part of the investment in a subsidiary company increases consolidated working capital (and the amount of minority interest) and thus is reported as a financial resource provided in the consolidated statement of changes in financial position. A gain or loss from such a sale represents an adjustment to combined net income of the parent company and its subsidiaries in the measurement of working capital provided from operations.

Illustration of consolidated statement of changes in financial position

Parent Corporation has owned 100% of the common stock of Sub Company for several years. The business combination of Parent and Sub was a pooling-type combination. Sub has outstanding only one class of common stock, and its total stockholders' equity at the end of Year 10 was $500,000. At the beginning of Year 11, Parent sold 30% of its investment in Sub's common stock to outsiders for $205,000, which was $55,000 more than the carrying amount of the stock in Parent's accounting records. Sub had net income of $100,000 in Year 11 and declared cash dividends of $60,000 near the end of Year 11. During Year 11, Parent issued additional common stock and cash of $290,000 in exchange for plant assets with a current fair value of $490,000.

The consolidated income statement for Year 11, the consolidated statement of retained earnings for Year 11, and the comparative consolidated balance sheets on December 31, Year 10 and Year 11, are presented on page 416.

A working paper for a consolidated statement of changes in financial position on a working capital concept for Year 11 is shown on page 417. The consolidated statement of changes in financial position for Parent Corporation and subsidiary for Year 11 is on page 418.

The following items in the consolidated statement of changes in financial position warrant special emphasis:

1 The working capital provided from operations **includes** the minority interest in net income of Sub Company.

2 The working capital provided from operations **excludes** the gain of $55,000 from sale of the investment in Sub Company common stock; thus, the entire proceeds of $205,000 are reported as a provision of consolidated working capital.

3 Only the dividends declared to stockholders of Parent Corporation ($160,000) and to minority stockholders of Sub Company ($18,000) are reported as applications of consolidated working capital.

4 The issuance of common stock by Parent Corporation to acquire plant assets is an **exchange transaction** (as defined in **APB Opinion No. 19**) and is reported as both a provision and an application of consolidated working capital, even though no working capital accounts were affected directly by the exchange transaction.

PARENT CORPORATION AND SUBSIDIARY
Consolidated Income Statement
For Year Ended December 31, Year 11

Sales and other revenue (including gain of $55,000 on sale of investment in Sub Company common stock)		$2,450,000
Costs and expenses:		
Cost of goods sold	$1,500,000	
Depreciation and amortization expense.	210,000	
Other operating expenses.	190,000	1,900,000
Income before income taxes		$ 550,000
Income taxes expense.		250,000
Combined net income		$ 300,000
Less: Minority interest in net income of subsidiary		30,000
Consolidated net income		$ 270,000
Earnings per share		$5.14

PARENT CORPORATION AND SUBSIDIARY
Consolidated Statement of Retained Earnings
For Year Ended December 31, Year 11

Retained earnings, beginning of year.	$670,000
Add: Net income	270,000
Subtotal	$940,000
Less: Dividends ($2.91 a share)	160,000
Retained earnings, end of year.	$780,000

PARENT CORPORATION AND SUBSIDIARY
Consolidated Balance Sheets
December 31,

	Year 11	Year 10
Assets		
Current assets.	$1,200,000	$ 900,000
Plant assets	3,000,000	2,510,000
Less: Accumulated depreciation	(1,300,000)	(1,100,000)
Intangible assets (net)	240,000	250,000
Total assets	$3,140,000	$2,560,000
Liabilities & Stockholders' Equity		
Current liabilities	$ 505,000	$ 490,000
Long-term debt	693,000	600,000
Minority interest in net assets of subsidiary	162,000	
Common stock, $10 par	550,000	500,000
Paid-in capital in excess of par.	450,000	300,000
Retained earnings.	780,000	670,000
Total liabilities & stockholders' equity	$3,140,000	$2,560,000

PARENT CORPORATION AND SUBSIDIARY
Working Paper for Consolidated Statement of Changes in Financial Position
(Working Capital Concept)
For Year Ended December 31, Year 11

	Account balances, Dec. 31, Year 10	Analysis of transactions for Year 11		Account balances, Dec. 31, Year 11
		Debit	Credit	
Working capital.	410,000	(x) 285,000		695,000
Plant assets	2,510,000	(7) 290,000		3,000,000
		(8) 200,000		
Intangible assets (net)	250,000		(2) 10,000	240,000
Totals	3,170,000			3,935,000
Accumulated depreciation	1,100,000		(2) 200,000	1,300,000
Long-term debt.	600,000		(5) 93,000	693,000
Minority interest in net assets of subsidiary.		(9) 18,000	(3) 150,000	
			(4) 30,000	162,000
Common stock, $10 par	500,000		(6) 50,000	550,000
Pain-in capital in excess of par	300,000		(6) 150,000	450,000
Retained earnings	670,000	(9) 160,000	(1) 270,000	780,000
Totals	3,170,000	953,000	953,000	3,935,000

Financial resources provided:			
Operations—net income.	(1) 270,000		
Add: Depreciation and amortization expense	(2) 210,000		From operations, $455,000
Minority interest in net income of subsidiary.	(4) 30,000		
Less: Gain on sale of investment in Sub Company common stock		(3) 55,000	
Sale of investment in Sub Company common stock	(3) 205,000		
Increase in long-term debt.	(5) 93,000		
Issuance of common stock in exchange for plant assets	(6) 200,000		
Financial resources applied:			
Acquisition of plant assets for cash		(7) 290,000	
Acquisition of plant assets in exchange for common stock		(8) 200,000	
Declaration of dividends, including $18,000 to minority shareholders of Sub Company		(9) 178,000	
Total financial resources provided and applied.	1,008,000	723,000	
Increase in working capital		(x) 285,000	
Totals.	1,008,000	1,008,000	

PARENT CORPORATION AND SUBSIDIARY
Consolidated Statement of Changes in Financial Position
(Working Capital Concept)
For Year Ended December 31, Year 11

Financial resources provided

Working capital provided from operations:

Operations—Net income, including minority interest of $30,000 . .	$300,000
Add: Depreciation and amortization expense	210,000
Less: Gain on sale of investment in Sub Company common stock	(55,000)
Working capital provided from operations	$455,000
Sale of investment in Sub Company common stock.	205,000
Long-term borrowing	93,000
Issuance of common stock in exchange for plant assets.	200,000
Total financial resources provided.	$953,000

Financial resources applied

Acquisition of plant assets for cash	$290,000	
Acquisition of plant assets in exchange for common stock	200,000	
Declaration of cash dividends, including $18,000 to minority shareholders of Sub Company	178,000	
Total financial resources applied.		668,000
Increase in financial resources: working capital		$285,000

Composition of working capital

	End of Year 11	End of Year 10	Increase (decrease) in working capital
Current assets.	$1,200,000	$900,000	$300,000
Less: Current liabilities	505,000	490,000	(15,000)
Working capital	$ 695,000	$410,000	
Increase in working capital			$285,000

INSTALLMENT ACQUISITION OF SUBSIDIARY

A parent company may obtain control of a subsidiary in a series of acquisitions of the subsidiary's common stock, rather than in a single transaction constituting a business combination. Such a combination is a **purchase,** because a **pooling cannot be effected in installments.**

In accounting for installment acquisitions of common stock of the eventual subsidiary, accountants are faced with a difficult question: At what point in the installment acquisition sequence should current fair values be determined for the subsidiary's identifiable net assets, in accordance with purchase accounting for business combinations?[7] A practical answer is: Current fair values for the subsidiary's net assets should be ascertained on the date when the parent company attains control of the subsidiary. On that date, the purchase-type business combination is completed.

However, this answer is not completely satisfactory, because generally accepted accounting principles require use of the equity method of accounting for investments in common stock sufficient to enable the investor to influence significantly the operating and financial policies of the investee.[8] A 20% common stock investment is presumed, in the absence of contrary evidence, to be the minimum ownership interest for exercising significant operating and financial influence over the investee. Furthermore, **APB Opinion No. 18** requires retroactive application of the equity method of accounting when an investor's ownership interest reaches 20%. The following example illustrates these points.

Illustration of installment acquisition of parent company's controlling interest

Prinz Corporation, which has a February 28 fiscal year, acquired 9,500 shares of Scarp Company's 10,000 shares of outstanding $5 par common stock as follows (out-of-pocket costs are disregarded):

Parent company's installment acquisition of controlling interest in subsidiary

Date	Number of shares of Scarp Company common stock acquired	Method of payment by Prinz Corporation	Carrying amount of Scarp Company's identifiable net assets
Mar. 1, Year 2	1,000	$ 10,000 cash	$80,000
Mar. 1, Year 3	2,000	22,000 cash	85,000
Mar. 1, Year 4	6,500	28,000 cash 50,000, 15% 5-year promissory note	90,000
Totals.	9,500	$110,000	

The above analysis indicates that Prinz made investments at a cost of $10, $11, and $12 a share in Scarp's common stock on dates when the net assets (book value) per share of Scarp's common stock was $8, $8.50, and $9, respectively. The practicality of ascertaining current fair

[7] As indicated in Chapter 4, pooling accounting is appropriate only for business combinations involving the exchange of 90% or more of the combinee's common stock in a single transaction or in accordance with a specific plan.

[8] *APB Opinion No. 18,* "The Equity Method of Accounting for Investments in Common Stock," AICPA (New York: 1971), pp. 355–356.

values for Scarp's net assets on March 1, Year 4, the date Prinz attained control of Scarp, is apparent.

In addition to the Common Stock account with a balance of $50,000 (10,000 × $5 = $50,000) and a Paid-in Capital in Excess of Par account with a balance of $10,000, Scarp had a Retained Earnings account that showed the following changes:

Retained Earnings account of investee

	Retained Earnings			
Date	Explanation	Debit	Credit	Balance
Mar. 1, Year 2	Balance			20,000 cr
Feb. 10, Year 3	Dividends: $1, a share	10,000		10,000 cr
Feb. 28, Year 3	Net income		15,000	25,000 cr
Feb. 17, Year 4	Dividends: $1 a share	10,000		15,000 cr
Feb. 28, Year 4	Net income		15,000	30,000 cr

Parent company's journal entries for installment acquisition

Prinz prepares the journal entries on pages 421 and 422 (in addition to the usual end-of-period adjusting and closing entries) to record its investment in Scarp's common stock. (All dividends declared by Scarp are assumed to have been paid in cash on the declaration date, and income tax effects are disregarded.)

Prinz's acquisition of 6,500 shares of Scarp's outstanding common stock on March 1, Year 4, is a purchase-type business combination. Accordingly, Prinz should apply the principles of purchase accounting described in Chapters 4 and 5, including the valuation of Scarp's identifiable net assets at their current fair values. Any excess of the $78,000 cost of Prinz's investment over Prinz's 65% share of the current fair value of Scarp's identifiable net assets should be assigned to goodwill and amortized over a period of 40 years or less.

Criticism of Foregoing Approach The foregoing illustration of accounting for the installment acquisition of an eventual subsidiary's common stock may be criticized for its handling of goodwill. On three separate dates spanning two years, goodwill was recognized in Prinz's three acquisitions of outstanding common stock of Scarp. Furthermore, the three goodwill amounts are amortized over three different 40-year (or shorter) periods.

It might be argued that the current fair values of Scarp's identifiable net assets should be determined on each of the three dates Prinz acquired Scarp common stock. However, such a theoretically precise application of accounting principles for long-term investments in common

PRINZ CORPORATION
Journal Entries

Year 2

Mar. 1 Investment in Scarp Company Common Stock   10,000
        Cash   10,000
        To record acquisition of 1,000 shares of Scarp Company's outstanding common stock.

Year 3

Feb. 10 Cash   1,000
        Dividend Revenue   1,000
        To record receipt of $1 a share cash dividend on 1,000 shares of Scarp Company common stock.

Mar. 1 Investment in Scarp Company Common Stock   22,000
        Cash   22,000
        To record acquisition of 2,000 shares of Scarp Company's outstanding common stock.

Mar. 1 Investment in Scarp Company Common Stock   450
        Retained Earnings of Investee   450
        To change retroactively accounting for investment in Scarp Company to equity method from cost method, and to record retroactively 10% share of Scarp Company's net income for year ended Feb. 28, Year 3, as follows:

    Share of Scarp's net income, Year 3 ($15,000 × 0.10) $1,500
    Less: Amortization of goodwill acquired Mar. 1, Year 2: $10,000 cost, minus ($80,000 × 0.10) = $2,000 goodwill; $2,000 ÷ 40 years = amortization for Year 3 . . 50
    Subtotal $1,450
    Less: Dividend revenue recorded in Year 3. 1,000
    Prior period adjustment to Retained Earnings of Investee ledger account. . . . . . . $ 450

(Continued)

Year 4

Feb. 17 Cash *3,000*

           Investment in Scarp Company Common Stock .   *3,000*

           To record receipt of $1 a share cash dividend on 3,000

           shares of Scarp Company's common stock.

Feb. 28 Investment in Scarp Company Common Stock *4,500*

                   Investment Income. *4,500*

           To record share of Scarp Company's net income for

           year ended Feb. 28, Year 4 ($15,000 $\times$ 0.30 = $4,500).

Feb. 28 Investment Income. *175*

                 Investment in Scarp Company Common Stock .   *175*

           To record amortization of goodwill for Year 4 as

           follows:

               Acquisition of Mar. 1, Year 2: $2,000 $\div$ 40 . . *$ 50*

               Acquisition of Mar. 1, Year 3: $22,000 cost,

               minus ($85,000 $\times$ 0.20) = $5,000 goodwill;

               $5,000 $\div$ 40 = amortization for Year 4 . . . . *125*

               Total amortization *$175*

Mar. 1 Investment in Scarp Company Common Stock *78,000*

                 Cash *28,000*

                 Notes Payable.   *50,000*

           To record acquisition of 6,500 shares of Scarp Com-

           pany's outstanding common stock for cash and a 15%,

           five-year promissory note.

stock appears unwarranted in terms of cost-benefit analysis. Until Prinz attained control of Scarp, the amortization elements of Prinz's investment income presumably would not be material. Thus, the goodwill approach illustrated in the preceding section of this chapter appears to be practical and consistent with the following passage from **APB Opinion No. 18:**[9]

> The carrying amount of an investment in common stock of an investee that qualifies for the equity method of accounting . . . may differ from the underlying equity in net assets of the investee . . . if the investor is unable to relate the difference to specific accounts of the investee, the difference should be considered to be goodwill and amortized over a period not to exceed forty years, . . .

[9] Ibid., p. 360.

Working paper for consolidated financial statements

The working paper for consolidated financial statements and related working paper eliminations for Prinz Corporation and subsidiary on March 1, Year 4, and for subsequent accounting periods are prepared in accordance with the procedures for purchased subsidiaries outlined in prior chapters. Prinz's retroactive application of the equity method of accounting for its investment in Scarp's common stock results in the Investment in Scarp Company Common Stock and Retained Earnings of Subsidiary (Investee) ledger accounts on March 1, Year 4, as follows:

Selected ledger accounts of parent company

Investment in Scarp Company Common Stock

Date	Explanation	Debit	Credit	Balance
3/1/2	Acquisition of 1,000 shares	10,000		10,000 dr
3/1/3	Acquisition of 2,000 shares	22,000		32,000 dr
3/1/3	Retroactive application of equity method of accounting	450		32,450 dr
2/17/4	Dividends: $1 a share		3,000	29,450 dr
2/28/4	Share of net income	4,500		33,950 dr
2/28/4	Amortization of goodwill		175	33,775 dr
3/1/4	Acquisition of 6,500 shares	78,000		111,775 dr

Retained Earnings of Subsidiary (Investee)

Date	Explanation	Debit	Credit	Balance
3/1/3	Retroactive application of equity method of accounting		450	450 cr
2/28/4	Closing entry—share of Scarp Company adjusted net income not declared as a dividend [($4,500 − $175) − $3,000]		1,325	1,775 cr

If the current fair value of Scarp's identifiable net assets on March 1, Year 4, was $90,000, the same as the carrying amount of the net assets on that date, the working paper elimination for Prinz and subsidiary on March 1, Year 4, is as illustrated on page 424.

On March 1, Year 4, the date the purchase-type business combination of Prinz Corporation and Scarp Company was completed, only a consol-

PRINZ CORPORATION AND SUBSIDIARY
Working Paper Elimination
March 1, Year 4

(a) Common Stock, $5 par—Scarp   50,000

     Paid-in Capital in Excess of Par—Scarp   10,000

     Retained Earnings—Scarp ($30,000 − $1,775)   28,225

     Retained Earnings of Subsidiary (Investee)—Prinz   1,775

     Goodwill—Prinz {$1,900 + $4,875 + [$78,000 −

       ($90,000 × 0.65)]} . . . . •.   26,275

         Investment in Scarp Company Common Stock—

           Prinz   111,775

         Minority Interest in Net Assets of Subsidiary.   4,500

     To eliminate intercompany investment and equity accounts of subsidiary on date of purchase-type business combination; to allocate excess of cost over current fair value (equal to carrying amounts) of identifiable net assets acquired to goodwill; and to establish minority interest in subsidiary on date of business combination ($90,000 × 0.05 = $4,500).

idated balance sheet is appropriate, for reasons discussed in Chapter 5. On page 425 is a working paper for consolidated balance sheet of Prinz and Scarp on March 1, Year 4, that reflects the foregoing working paper elimination. Amounts for Prinz and Scarp, other than those illustrated in the elimination, have been assumed. Also, there were no intercompany transactions between the two companies prior to March 1, Year 4.

The $1,775 portion of Scarp's retained earnings attributable to Prinz's 30% ownership of Scarp common stock prior to the business combination is not eliminated. Thus, consolidated retained earnings on March 1, Year 4, the date of the purchase-type business combination, includes the $1,775 amount plus Prinz's own retained earnings of $210,000, for a total of $211,775.

For fiscal years subsequent to March 1, Year 4, Prinz reflects in its accounting records 95% of the operating results of Scarp. In addition, Prinz debits the Amortization Expense ledger account for each period's amortization of the three goodwill amounts acquired by Prinz in the installment investments in Scarp's common stock.

PRINZ CORPORATION AND SUBSIDIARY
Working Paper for Consolidated Balance Sheet
March 1, Year 4

	Prinz Corporation	Scarp Company	Eliminations increase (decrease)		Consolidated
Assets					
Current assets	400,000	140,000			540,000
Investment in Scarp Company common stock	111,775		(a)	(111,775)	
Plant assets (net)	1,200,000	160,000			1,360,000
Goodwill			(a)	26,275	26,275
Total assets	1,711,775	300,000		(85,500)	1,926,275
Liabilities & Stockholders' Equity					
Current liabilities	200,000	60,000			260,000
Long-term debt	800,000	150,000			950,000
Minority interest in net assets of subsidiary . . .			(a)	4,500	4,500
Common stock, $1 par . .	150,000				150,000
Common stock, $5 par . .		50,000	(a)	(50,000)	
Paid-in capital in excess of par	350,000	10,000	(a)	(10,000)	350,000
Retained earnings.	210,000	30,000	(a)	(28,225)	211,775
Retained earnings of subsidiary.	1,775		(a)	(1,775)	
Total liabilities & stockholders' equity	1,711,775	300,000		(85,500)	1,926,275

REVIEW QUESTIONS

1 Under what circumstances do income tax considerations enter into the determination of current fair values of a combinee's identifiable assets in a purchase-type business combination?

2 Discuss the following quotation:

> The "indefinite reversal criteria" provisions of **APB Opinion No. 23** allow the decision to remit cash from a subsidiary to a parent to affect the income of the parent. This occurs because the full tax expense associated with the earnings of the subsidiary has not been recorded.

3 A parent company and its subsidiary file separate income tax returns. How do the consolidated deferred income taxes associated with the intercompany gain on the parent company's sale of a depreciable plant asset to its subsidiary "turn around"? Explain.

4 Are cash dividends declared to minority shareholders included in the consolidated statement of changes in financial position? Explain.

5 How is the equity method of accounting applied when a parent company attains control of a subsidiary in a series of common stock acquisitions? Explain.

6 At what stage in the installment acquisition of an eventual subsidiary's outstanding common stock should the parent company ascertain the current fair values of the subsidiary's identifiable net assets? Explain.

7 Are income tax allocation procedures necessary in working paper eliminations for a parent company and subsidiaries that file consolidated income tax returns? Explain.

8 What amounts comprise consolidated retained earnings on the date of a purchase-type business combination that involves installment acquisitions of the subsidiary's outstanding common stock?

EXERCISES

Ex. 9-1 Select the best answer for each of the following multiple-choice questions:

1 On the date of a purchase-type business combination, the elimination included a debit to Retained Earnings of Subsidiary—Parent. This debit indicates that:
  a The parent company acquired the controlling interest in the subsidiary in installments
  b The subsidiary was partially owned
  c The subsidiary declared dividends in excess of net income
  d There was an error in the working paper elimination

2 A debit to Prepaid Income Taxes—Subsidiary and a credit to Income Taxes Expense—Subsidiary in a working paper elimination for a parent company and subsidiary that file separate income tax returns indicates that:
  a The parent company had an unrealized intercompany profit (gain) on a transaction with the subsidiary
  b The subsidiary had a realized gain on the parent company's open-market acquisition of the subsidiary's bonds payable
  c The subsidiary had an unrealized intercompany profit (gain) on a transaction with the parent company
  d The parent company had a realized loss on the subsidiary's open-market acquisition of the parent company's bonds payable

3 Parle Corporation and its 80% owned subsidiary, Sabe Company, file separate income tax returns, and each has a combined federal and state income tax rate of 60%. The working paper eliminations of Parle Corporation and Subsidiary on April 30, Year 5, included the following:

Income Taxes Expense—Sabe 11,415
    Deferred Income Tax Liability—Sabe   11,415
To provide for income taxes attributable to subsidiary's realized gain on parent company's acquisition of the subsidiary's bonds payable.

If the working paper eliminations on October 31, Year 5, for the subsidiary's bonds owned by the parent company included a debit to Intercompany Interest Revenue—Parle of $11,106 and a credit to Intercompany Interest Expense—Sabe of $10,661, an accompanying elimination should include:

a A debit to Income Taxes Expense—Sabe of $267 ($445 × 0.60)
b A credit to Income Taxes Expense—Sabe of $267 ($445 × 0.60)
c A credit to Income Taxes Expense—Sabe of $6,664 ($11,106 × 0.60)
d A debit to Income Taxes Expense—Sabe of $6,397 ($10,661 × 0.60)
e None of the foregoing

4 How should the parent company's acquisition of additional shares of previously unissued common stock directly from the subsidiary be reported in the consolidated statement of changes in financial position on the working capital concept?

a As working capital applied
b As working capital provided
c As working capital provided and applied (an exchange transaction)
d It is not reported

5 On April 30, Year 2, the end of a fiscal year, Pasha Corporation's Retained Earnings of Investee (Sahib Company) ledger account had a credit balance of $10,000. On May 1, Year 2, Pasha acquired 45% of Sahib's outstanding common stock, which completed the acquisition of a controlling interest of 85% in Sahib. Sahib had a Retained Earnings account credit balance of $180,000 on April 30, Year 2. The working paper elimination for consolidated financial statements of Pasha Corporation and subsidiary on May 1, Year 2, should include a debit to Retained Earnings—Sahib in the amount of:

a $0   b $10,000   c $170,000   d $180,000   e Some other amount

6 If a parent company acquires a controlling interest in a subsidiary through a series of acquisitions of the subsidiary's outstanding common stock, the investor parent company should begin applying the equity method of accounting for its investment in the subsidiary's common stock:

a Retroactively when at least 20% of the outstanding common stock has been acquired
b Prospectively when at least 20% of the outstanding common stock has been acquired
c Retroactively when more than 50% of the outstanding common stock has been acquired
d Prospectively when more than 50% of the outstanding common stock has been acquired

Ex. 9-2   Salvo Company merged with Mango Company in a purchase-type business combination. As a result, goodwill was recorded. For income tax purposes, the business combination was considered to be a tax-free corporate reorganization.

One of Mango's assets was a building with an appraised value of $150,000 on the date of the business combination. The building had a carrying amount of $90,000, net of accumulated depreciation based on the double-declining-balance method of depreciation, for financial accounting purposes.

Assuming a 60% income tax rate, compute the amount at which Salvo should record the building in its accounting records as a result of the merger.

Ex. 9-3   On October 31, Year 2, P Corporation acquired in the open market $500,000 face amount of the 10%, ten-year bonds due October 31, Year 11, of its wholly owned subsidiary, S Company. The bonds had been issued by S on October 31, Year 1, to yield 12%. P's investment was at a 15% yield rate. Both P and S file separate federal and state income tax returns. Both companies are subject to a combined federal and state income tax rate of 60%, and neither company has any items requiring interperiod or intraperiod income tax allocation other than the S Company bonds, on which interest is payable Oct. 31. Working paper eliminations related to the bonds on October 31, Year 2, and October 31, Year 3, with certain amounts omitted, are as follows:

P CORPORATION AND SUBSIDIARY
Partial Working Paper Eliminations
October 31, Year 2

Intercompany Bonds Payable—S	500,000	
Discount on Intercompany Bonds Payable—S		53,283
Investment in S Company Bonds—P		380,710
Gain on Early Extinguishment of Bonds—S		66,007*

To eliminate subsidiary's bonds acquired by parent company and to recognize realized gain on the retirement of the bonds.

Income Taxes Expense—S	(1)	
Deferred Income Tax Liability—S		(2)

To provide for income taxes attributable to subsidiary's realized gain on parent company's acquisition of the subsidiary's bonds.

* Not material

P CORPORATION AND SUBSIDIARY
Partial Working Paper Eliminations
October 31, Year 3

Intercompany Interest Revenue—P	57,107	
Intercompany Bonds Payable—S	500,000	
Discount on Intercompany Bonds Payable—S		49,725
Investment in S Company Bonds—P		387,817
Intercompany Interest Expense—S		53,558
Retained Earnings—S		66,007

To eliminate subsidiary's bonds owned by parent company, and related interest revenue and expense; and to increase subsidiary's beginning retained earnings by amount of unamortized realized gain on the retirement of the bonds.

Retained Earnings—S	(3)	
Income Taxes Expense—S		(4)
Deferred Income Tax Liability—S		(5)

To reduce the subsidiary's income taxes expense for amount attributable to recorded intercompany gain (for consolidation purposes) on subsidiary's bonds; and to provide for remaining deferred income taxes on unrecorded portion of gain.

Compute the five missing amounts in the foregoing working paper eliminations.

Ex. 9-4   During the fiscal year ended November 30, Year 9, Pederson Corporation sold merchandise costing $100,000 to its 80%-owned subsidiary, Solomon Company, at a gross profit rate of 20%. On November 30, Year 9, Solomon's inventories included merchandise acquired from Pederson at a billed price of $30,000—a $10,000 increase over the comparable amount in Solomon's November 30, Year 8, inventories. Both Pederson and Solomon file separate income tax returns, and both are subject to a combined federal and state income tax rate of 60%.

Prepare working paper eliminations for merchandise and related income taxes, in journal entry form, for Pederson Corporation and subsidiary on November 30, Year 9.

Ex. 9-5   In Year 5, Pryor Corporation formed a wholly owned foreign subsidiary. Year 5 pre-tax accounting income for the subsidiary was $500,000. The income tax rate of the country in which the foreign subsidiary was domiciled was 40%. None of the foreign subsidiary's earnings in Year 5 was paid as a dividend to Pryor; however, there is nothing to indicate that these earnings will not be remitted to Pryor in the future.

The country in which the foreign subsidiary is domiciled does not impose an income tax on remittances to the United States. An income tax credit is allowed in the United States for income taxes payable in the country in which the foreign subsidiary is domiciled.

Assuming that the income tax rate in the United States is 48%, compute the total amount of income taxes expense relating to the foreign subsidiary that should be included in the consolidated income statement of Pryor Corporation and subsidiary for Year 5.

Ex. 9-6   On October 31, Year 5, Salvador Company, 80%-owned subsidiary of Panama Corporation, sold to its parent company for $20,000 a patent with a carrying amount of $15,000 to Salvador on that date. Remaining legal life of the patent on October 31, Year 5, was five years; the patent was expected to produce revenue for Panama during the entire five-year period. Panama and Salvador file separate income tax returns; their combined federal and state income tax rate is 60%. Panama uses an Accumulated Amortization of Patent ledger account.

Prepare the working paper eliminations, including income tax allocation, for Panama Corporation and subsidiary with respect to the patent: **(a)** on October 31, Year 5; and **(b)** on October 31, Year 6.

Ex. 9-7   Prieto Corporation declared and paid cash dividends of $250,000 and distributed a 5% stock dividend in Year 5. The market value of the shares distributed pursuant to the 5% stock dividend was $600,000. Prieto owns 100% of the common stock of S Company and 75% of the common stock of SS Company. In Year 5, S declared and paid a cash dividend of $100,000 on the common stock and $25,000 on its $5 cumulative preferred stock. None of the preferred stock is owned by Prieto. In Year 5, SS declared and paid cash dividends of $44,000 on its common stock, the only class of capital stock issued.

Compute the amount that should be reported as working capital applied to payment of dividends in the Year 5 consolidated statement of changes in financial position for Prieto Corporation and subsidiaries.

Ex. 9-8   The consolidated statement of changes in financial position for Paradise Corporation and its partially owned subsidiaries for Year 2 will be prepared on a working capital concept. Using the following letters, indicate how each of the 13 items listed on page 430 should be reported in the statement. A given item may be reported more than one way.

A–O = Add to combined net income in the determination of consolidated working capital provided from operations

D–O = Deduct from combined net income in the determination of consolidated working capital provided from operations

FP = A financial resource provided

FA = A financial resource applied
N   = Not included or separately disclosed in the consolidated statement of changes in financial position

1 The minority interest in net income of subsidiaries is $37,500.

2 Paradise issued a bond payable to a subsidiary company in exchange for plant assets with a current fair value of $180,000.

3 Paradise distributed a 10% stock dividend; the additional shares of common stock issued had a current fair value of $675,000.

4 Paradise declared and paid a cash dividend of $200,000.

5 Long-term debt of Paradise in the amount of $2 million was converted to common stock.

6 A subsidiary sold plant assets to outsiders at the carrying amount of $80,000.

7 Paradise's share of the net income of an unconsolidated subsidiary totaled $28,000. The subsidiary did not declare or pay cash dividends in Year 2.

8 Consolidated depreciation and amortization expense totaled $285,000.

9 A subsidiary company amortized $3,000 of premium on bonds payable owned by outsiders.

10 Paradise sold its entire holdings in an 80%-owned subsidiary for $3 million.

11 Paradise merged with Sun Company in a pooling-type business combination; 150,000 shares of common stock with a current fair value of $4.5 million were issued by Paradise for 98% of Sun's common stock.

12 Paradise received cash dividends of $117,000 from its consolidated subsidiaries.

13 The consolidated subsidiaries of Paradise declared and paid cash dividends of $21,500 to minority stockholders.

Ex. 9-9 On August 1, Year 6, Packard Corporation acquired 1,000 of the 10,000 outstanding shares of Stenn Company's $1 par common stock for $5,000. Stenn's identifiable net assets had a current fair value and carrying amount of $40,000 on that date. Stenn had net income of $3,000 and declared and paid dividends of the same amount for the year ended July 31, Year 7. On August 1, Year 7, Packard acquired 4,500 more shares of Stenn's outstanding common stock for $22,500. The current fair values and carrying amounts of Stenn's identifiable net assets were still $40,000 on that date. Stenn had net income of $7,500 and declared no dividends for the year ended July 31, Year 8.

Prepare journal entries in Packard Corporation's accounting records for the above facts for the two years ended July 31, Year 8. Omit explanations and disregard income tax effects.

Ex. 9-10 Select the best answer for each of the following multiple-choice questions:

1 With respect to the difference between taxable income and pre-tax accounting income, the tax effect of the undistributed earnings of a subsidiary included in consolidated net income normally should be:

a Accounted for as a timing difference

b Accounted for as a permanent difference

c Ignored because it must be based on estimates and assumptions

d Ignored because it cannot be presumed that all undistributed earnings of a subsidiary will be transferred to the parent company

2 Under the equity method of accounting for a subsidiary's operating results, the effect on the investor of dividends received from the investee usually is:

a A reduction of deferred income taxes and a reduction of investment

b A reduction of deferred income taxes and no effect on investment

c No effect on deferred income taxes and a reduction of investment

d No effect on deferred income taxes and no effect on investment

3 Sorter Company, a subsidiary of Polley Corporation, did not declare dividends from its Year 5 net income in Year 5. Polley should recognize income taxes on its share of Sorter's net income in its Year 5 financial statements only if:

    a Sorter Company is a domestic corporation

    b The net income will be remitted in a tax-free transaction within the foreseeable future

    c The net income will be remitted in a taxable transaction on or before March 15, Year 6

    d Remittance of the net income in a taxable transaction will not be postponed indefinitely

4 Accounting for the income tax effect of a difference between taxable income and pre-tax accounting income with respect to undistributed earnings of a subsidiary is similar to a situation involving:

    a Profits (gains) on assets within the consolidated group that are eliminated in consolidated financial statements

    b Profits (gains) on intercompany transactions that are taxed when reported in separate income tax returns

    c Rents and royalties that are taxed when collected and deferred in financial statements until earned

    d Profits on installment sales that are recognized in financial statements on the date of sale and reported in income tax returns when the installment receivables are collected

5 A Deferred Income Tax Liability account is credited in a working paper elimination for the income tax effects of:

    a Intercompany profits in inventories

    b Intercompany gain in land

    c Intercompany gain in a depreciable plant asset or an intangible asset

    d All of the above

    e None of the above

CASES

Case 9-1 On January 2, Year 1, Preble Corporation acquired 15% of the outstanding common stock of Searle Company for cash. On January 2, Year 2, Preble acquired an additional 25% of Searle's outstanding common stock in exchange for Preble's common stock. On January 2, Year 3, Preble acquired the remaining 60% of Searle's outstanding common stock for cash. Both Preble and Searle have December 31 fiscal years.

    Instructions Describe how Preble Corporation should apply the equity method of accounting for the operating results of Searle Company.

Case 9-2 On April 1, Year 4, the beginning of a fiscal year, Paddock Corporation acquired 98% of the outstanding common stock of Serge Company in a pooling-type business combination. In your examination of the consolidated financial statements of Paddock Corporation and subsidiary for the year ended March 31, Year 5, you discover that Serge had net income of $50,000 for the year, but did not declare or pay any cash dividends. Nonetheless, Paddock did not accrue deferred income taxes applicable to Serge's undistributed earnings, despite Paddock's having adopted the equity method of accounting for Serge's operating results.

    In response to your inquiries, the controller of Paddock pointed out that Serge's severe cash shortage made the declaration and payment of cash dividends by Serge doubtful for the next several years. Therefore, stated the controller, a provision for deferred income taxes on Serge's undistributed earnings for the year ended March 31, Year 5, is inappropriate under generally accepted accounting principles.

    Instructions Do you agree with the Paddock Corporation controller's interpretation of generally accepted accounting principles for the undistributed earnings of Serge Company? Explain.

PROBLEMS

9-1 The working paper eliminations for intercompany bonds of Pullet Corporation and its wholly owned subsidiary on November 30, Year 3, the end of a fiscal year, follow. The bonds, which had been issued by Sagehen Company for a five-year term on November 30, Year 2, to yield 10%, were acquired in the open market by Pullet on November 30, Year 3, to yield 12%. Interest on the bonds is payable at the rate of 8% each November 30, Year 3 through Year 7. Both companies use the interest method of amortization or accumulation of bond premium or discount.

PULLET CORPORATION AND SUBSIDIARY

Partial Working Paper Eliminations

November 30, Year 3

Intercompany Bonds Payable—Sagehen	60,000	
Discount on Intercompany Bonds Payable—Sagehen .		3,804
Investment in Sagehen Company Bonds—Pullet		52,710
Gain on Early Extinguishment of Bonds—Sagehen . .		3,486*

To eliminate subsidiary's bonds payable acquired by parent, and to recognize gain on the retirement of the bonds.

Income Taxes Expense—Sagehen	2,092	
Deferred Income Tax Liability—Sagehen		2,092

To provide for income taxes attributable to subsidiary's realized gain on parent company's acquisition of the subsidiary's bonds payable: $3,486 \times 0.60 = \$2,092$.

* Not material

Instructions

a Prepare journal entries in the accounting records of Pullet Corporation and Sagehen Company to record intercompany interest revenue and expense, respectively, on November 30, Year 4. Disregard Sagehen's bonds owned by outsiders.

b Prepare working paper eliminations for Pullet Corporation and subsidiary on November 30, Year 4, including allocation of income taxes.

9-2 On January 2, Year 1, Presto Corporation issued 10,000 shares of its $1 par (current fair value $40) common stock for all 50,000 shares of Shuey Company' outstanding common stock in a statutory merger that qualified as a purchase-type business combination. Out-of-pocket costs in connection with the combination, paid by Presto on January 2, Year 1, were as follows:

Finder's fee and legal fees relating to the business combination	$60,000
Costs associated with SEC registration statement for securities issued to complete the business combination	30,000
Total out-of-pocket costs of business combination	$90,000

For income tax purposes, the business combination qualified as a ''Type A tax-free corporate reorganization.'' The balance sheet of Shuey Company on January 2, Year 1, with associated appraised or market values of assets and liabilities, was as follows:

SHUEY COMPANY
Balance Sheet
January 2, Year 1

	Carrying amount	Appraised or market value
Assets		
Cash	$ 20,000	$ 20,000
Short-term investments	30,000	45,000
Accounts receivable (net)	80,000	80,000
Inventories	120,000	160,000
Short-term prepayments	10,000	10,000
Plant assets (net)	430,000	490,000
Intangible assets (net)	110,000	130,000
Total assets	$800,000	$935,000
Liabilities & Stockholders' Equity		
Liabilities:		
Notes payable	$ 60,000	$ 60,000
Accounts payable	90,000	90,000
Income taxes payable	30,000	30,000
Long-term debt	300,000	300,000
Total liabilities	$480,000	$480,000
Stockholders' equity:		
Common stock, $2 par	$100,000	
Paid-in capital in excess of par	100,000	
Retained earnings	120,000	
Total stockholders' equity	$320,000	
Total liabilities & stockholders' equity	$800,000	

The combined federal and state income tax rates for both Presto and Shuey are 60% for ordinary income and 35% for capital gains.

Instructions Prepare journal entries to record the purchase-type business combination of Presto Corporation and Shuey Company on January 2, Year 1, in the accounting records of Presto. Current fair values assigned to Shuey's identifiable assets must include appropriate income tax effects. (The capital gains tax rate is applicable to the short-term investments only.)

9-3   Condensed balance sheets of Pellerin Corporation and its subsidiary, Sigmund Company, on the dates indicated, appear on page 434. Both companies have a December 31 fiscal year.

Pellerin acquired 30,000 shares of Sigmund's outstanding common stock on January 2, Year 3, at a cost of $480,000; and 60,000 shares on September 30, Year 3, at a cost of $1,760,000. Pellerin obtained control over Sigmund for the valuable patents owned by Sigmund.

Sigmund amortizes the cost of patents on a straight-line basis. Any amount allocated to patents as a result of the business combination is to be amortized over the five-year remaining economic life of the patents from January 2, Year 3.

Sigmund declared and paid a cash dividend of $300,000 on December 31, Year 3. Pellerin has not recorded the declaration or the receipt of the dividend.

Instructions Prepare journal entries for Pellerin Corporation on December 31, Year 3, to account for its investments in Sigmund Company under the equity

PELLERIN CORPORATION AND SIGMUND COMPANY
Separate Balance Sheets
Various Dates, Year 3

	Pellerin Corporation	Sigmund Company		
	Dec. 31, Year 3	Jan. 2, Year 3	Sept. 30, Year 3	Dec. 31, Year 3
Assets				
Cash.	$ 400,000	$ 550,000	$ 650,000	$ 425,000
Fees and royalties receivable		250,000	450,000	500,000
Investment in Sigmund Company common stock	2,240,000			
Patents		1,000,000	850,000	800,000
Other assets	4,360,000			200,000
Total assets	$7,000,000	$1,800,000	$1,950,000	$1,925,000
Liabilities & Stockholders' Equity				
Liabilities	$ 400,000	$ 200,000	$ 150,000	$ 275,000
Common stock, $10 par .	5,000,000	1,000,000	1,000,000	1,000,000
Retained earnings.	1,600,000	600,000	800,000	650,000
Total liabilities & stockholders' equity.	$7,000,000	$1,800,000	$1,950,000	$1,925,000

method of accounting. Disregard income taxes, and do not prepare journal entries for Pellerin's **acquisition** of the investments in Sigmund.

9-4 Consolidated financial statements of Porcelain Corporation and its 80%-owned subsidiary for the year ended December 31, Year 8, including a comparative consolidated balance sheet on December 31, Year 7, are shown on page 435.

Additional information
(1) On December 31, Year 8, Porcelain issued 40,000 shares of common stock to the public at $1.75 a share.
(2) The affiliated companies acquired plant assets for $220,000 cash during the year ended December 31, Year 8. Also during the year, Skinner Company, the 80%-owned subsidiary of Porcelain, sold equipment with a carrying amount of $100,000 for $150,000 cash.
(3) Skinner declared and paid dividends totaling $25,000 during the year ended December 31, Year 8.

Instructions Prepare a consolidated statement of changes in financial position, under the working capital concept, for Porcelain Corporation and subsidiary for the year ended December 31, Year 8, without using a working paper.

9-5 The following transactions took place between Parkhurst Corporation and its wholly owned subsidiary, Sandland Company, during the fiscal year ended March 31, Year 6:

PORCELAIN CORPORATION AND SUBSIDIARY
Consolidated Income Statement
For Year Ended December 31, Year 8

Revenue		
Net sales		$1,200,000
Gain on sale of plant assets		50,000
Total revenue		$1,250,000
Costs and expenses		
Cost of goods sold	$700,000	
Depreciation expense	40,000	
Amortization expense	20,000	
Other operating expenses	120,000	
Interest expense	50,000	
Income taxes expense	192,000	
Minority interest in net income of subsidiary	10,000	1,132,000
Net income		$ 118,000
Earnings per share		$1.97

PORCELAIN CORPORATION AND SUBSIDIARY
Consolidated Statement of Retained Earnings
For Year Ended December 31, Year 8

Retained earnings, beginning of year	$180,000
Add: Net income	118,000
Subtotal	$298,000
Less: Dividends ($1 a share)	60,000
Retained earnings, end of year	$238,000

PORCELAIN CORPORATION AND SUBSIDIARY
Consolidated Balance Sheets
December 31,

	Year 8	Year 7
Assets		
Current assets	$ 300,000	$200,000
Plant assets (net)	680,000	600,000
Goodwill (net)	140,000	160,000
Total assets	$1,120,000	$960,000
Liabilities & Stockholders' Equity		
Liabilities		
Current liabilities	$ 187,000	$110,000
Note payable, due $50,000 each Dec. 31, plus interest at 10%	450,000	500,000
Minority interest in net assets of subsidiary	85,000	80,000
Total liabilities	$ 722,000	$690,000
Stockholders' equity		
Common stock, $1 par	$ 100,000	$ 60,000
Paid-in capital in excess of par	60,000	30,000
Retained earnings	238,000	180,000
Total stockholders' equity	$ 398,000	$270,000
Total liabilities & stockholders' equity	$1,120,000	$960,000

(1) Parkhurst sold to Sandland at a 30% gross profit rate merchandise with a total sale price of $200,000. Sandland's March 31, Year 6, inventories included $40,000 (billed prices) of the merchandise obtained from Parkhurst—a $20,000 increase from the related April 1, Year 5, inventories amount. Both Parkhurst and Sandland use the perpetual inventory system.

(2) On April 1, Year 5, Sandland sold to Parkhurst for $50,000 a machine with a carrying amount of $30,000 on that date. The estimated economic life of the machine to Parkhurst was five years, with no residual value. Parkhurst uses the straight-line method of depreciation for all plant assets.

(3) On February 28, Year 6, Parkhurst sold land for a plant site to Sandland for $480,000. The land had a carrying amount to Parkhurst of $360,000.

(4) On March 31, Year 6, following Sandland's payment of interest to bondholders, Parkhurst acquired in the open market for $487,537, a 16% yield, 60% of Sandland's 12%, 10-year bonds dated March 31, Year 5. The bonds had been issued to the public by Sandland on March 31, Year 5, to yield 14%. On March 31, Year 6, following the payment of interest, Sandland's accounting records included the following ledger account balances relative to the bonds:

12% bonds payable.	$1,000,000 cr
Discount on 12% bonds payable.	100,590 dr

Both Parkhurst and Sandland use the interest method of amortization or accumulation of bond discount.

Combined federal and state income tax rates for the two affiliated companies are 60% for ordinary income and 35% for capital gains.

Instructions Prepare working paper eliminations, including income taxes allocation, for Parkhurst Corporation and subsidiary on March 31, Year 6. Round all amounts to the nearest dollar.

9-6 Paine Corporation owns 99% of the outstanding common stock of Spilberg Company, acquired July 1, Year 5, in a pooling-type business combination, and 90% of the outstanding common stock of Sykes Company, acquired July 1, Year 5, in a purchase-type business combination that reflected goodwill of $52,200. All identifiable net assets of Sykes were fairly valued at their carrying amounts on July 1, Year 5. Goodwill is amortized over 40 years.

Separate financial statements of Paine, Spilberg, and Sykes for the fiscal year ended June 30, Year 6, prior to income tax provisions and equity-method accruals in the accounting records of Paine, appear on page 437.

Intercompany profits in June 30, Year 6, inventories resulting from Paine's sales to its subsidiaries during the fiscal year ended June 30, Year 6, are as follows:

In Spilberg Company's inventories—$6,000

In Sykes Company's inventories—$7,500

Instructions

a Prepare Paine Corporation's June 30, Year 6, journal entries for income taxes and equity-method accruals. The combined federal and state income tax rate is 60%. All three companies declared dividends on June 30, Year 6.

b Prepare a working paper for consolidated financial statements and related working paper eliminations, including income taxes allocation, for Paine Corporation and subsidiaries for the year ended June 30, Year 6. The three affiliated companies file separate income tax returns. Amounts for Paine Corporation should reflect the journal entries in **a**.

PAINE CORPORATION AND SUBSIDIARIES
Separate Financial Statements
For Year Ended June 30, Year 6

	Paine Corporation	Spilberg Company	Sykes Company
Income Statements			
Revenue			
Net sales	$1,000,000	$ 550,000	$ 220,000
Intercompany sales	100,000		
Total revenue	$1,100,000	$ 550,000	$ 220,000
Costs and expenses			
Cost of goods sold	$ 700,000	$ 357,500	$ 143,000
Intercompany cost of goods sold . . .	70,000		
Operating expenses	130,000	92,500	27,000
Interest expense	50,000		
Income taxes expense		60,000	30,000
Total costs and expenses	$ 950,000	$ 510,000	$ 200,000
Net income	$ 150,000	$ 40,000	$ 20,000
Statements of Retained Earnings			
Retained earnings, beginning of year. .	$ 103,000	$ 300,000	$ 150,000
Add: Net income	150,000	40,000	20,000
Subtotals	$ 253,000	$ 340,000	$ 170,000
Less: Dividends.	50,000	20,000	10,000
Retained earnings, end of year	$ 203,000	$ 320,000	$ 160,000
Balance Sheets			
Assets			
Inventories.	$1,000,000	$ 800,000	$ 700,000
Investment in Spilberg Company common stock.	990,000		
Investment in Sykes Company common stock.	574,200		
Other assets.	1,501,300	1,260,000	790,000
Total assets	$4,065,500	$2,060,000	$1,490,000
Liabilities & Stockholders' Equity			
Intercompany dividends payable		$ 19,800	$ 9,000
Other liabilities	$1,965,500	1,020,200	891,000
Common stock, $1 par	1,000,000	500,000	300,000
Paid-in capital in excess of par	600,000	200,000	130,000
Retained earnings	203,000	320,000	160,000
Retained earnings of subsidiaries	297,000		
Total liabilities & stockholders' equity.	$4,065,500	$2,060,000	$1,490,000

9-7   Pickens Corporation acquired 10% of the 100,000 outstanding shares of $2.50 par common stock of Skiffen Company on December 31, Year 6, for $38,000. An additional 70,000 shares were acquired for $315,700 on January 2, Year 8 (at which time there was no material difference between the current fair values and carrying amounts of Skiffen's identifiable net assets). Out-of-pocket costs of the business combination were negligible.

The separate financial statements of Pickens Corporation and subsidiary for the year ended December 31, Year 8, appear on page 439.

Additional information
(1) Pickens Corporation's ledger accounts for Investment in Skiffen Company Common Stock, Deferred Income Tax Liability, Retained Earnings, and Retained Earnings of Subsidiary appear as follows (before December 31, Year 8, closing entries).

Investment in Skiffen Company Common Stock

Date	Explanation	Debit	Credit	Balance
12/31/6	Acquisition of 10,000 shares	38,000		38,000 dr
1/2/8	Acquisition of 70,000 shares	315,700		353,700 dr
1/2/8	Retroactive application of equity method of accounting [($40,000 − $5,000) × 0.10]	3,500		357,200 dr
12/15/8	Dividend declared by Skiffen ($11,000 × 0.80)		8,800	348,400 dr
12/31/8	Net income of Skiffen ($56,000 × 0.80)	44,800		393,200 dr
12/31/8	Amortization of goodwill ($25,200 ÷ 40)		630	392,570 dr

Deferred Income Tax Liability

Date	Explanation	Debit	Credit	Balance
1/2/8	Income taxes applicable to undistributed earnings of subsidiary ($3,500 × 0.60)		2,100	2,100 cr
12/31/8	Income taxes applicable to undistributed earnings of subsidiary [($56,000 − $11,000) × 0.60]		27,000	29,100 cr

Retained Earnings

Date	Explanation	Debit	Credit	Balance
12/31/6	Balance			540,000 cr
12/31/7	Close net income		55,000	595,000 cr

Retained Earnings of Subsidiary

Date	Explanation	Debit	Credit	Balance
1/2/8	Retroactive application of equity method of accounting		3,500	3,500 cr

PICKENS CORPORATION AND SUBSIDIARY
Separate Financial Statements
For Year Ended December 31, Year 8

Income Statements	Pickens Corporation	Skiffen Company
Revenue		
Net sales	$ 840,000	$360,000
Intercompany sales	80,600	65,000
Intercompany gain on sale of equipment	9,500	
Intercompany interest revenue	2,702	
Intercompany investment income	44,800	
Total revenue	$ 977,602	$425,000
Costs and expenses		
Cost of goods sold	$ 546,000	$252,000
Intercompany cost of goods sold	56,420	48,750
Interest expense	32,000	9,106
Intercompany interest expense		2,276
Other operating expenses	271,382	56,868
Total costs and expenses	$ 905,802	$369,000
Net income	$ 71,800	$ 56,000

Statements of Retained Earnings

	Pickens Corporation	Skiffen Company
Retained earnings, beginning of year	$ 595,000	$136,000
Add: Net income	71,800	56,000
Subtotals	$ 666,800	$192,000
Less: Dividends	20,000	11,000
Retained earnings, end of year	$ 646,800	$181,000

Balance Sheets
Assets

	Pickens Corporation	Skiffen Company
Intercompany receivables (payables)	$ 35,800	$ (35,800)
Inventories	180,000	96,000
Investment in Skiffen Company common stock	392,570	
Investment in Skiffen Company bonds	27,918	
Plant assets (net)	781,500	510,000
Accumulated depreciation	(87,000)	(85,000)
Other assets	333,782	146,500
Total assets	$1,664,570	$631,700

Liabilities & Stockholders' Equity

	Pickens Corporation	Skiffen Company
Dividends payable	$ 20,000	$ 2,200
Bonds payable	400,000	120,000
Intercompany bonds payable		30,000
Discount on bonds payable		(4,281)
Discount on intercompany bonds payable		(1,070)
Deferred income tax liability	29,100	
Other liabilities	151,170	24,851
Common stock, $2.50 par	400,000	250,000
Paid-in capital in excess of par	14,000	29,000
Retained earnings	646,800	181,000
Retained earnings of subsidiary	3,500	
Total liabilities & stockholders' equity	$1,664,570	$631,700

(2) Skiffen Company's Retained Earnings ledger account appears as follows:

Retained Earnings

Date	Explanation	Debit	Credit	Balance
12/31/6	Balance			101,000 cr
12/31/7	Close net income		40,000	141,000 cr
12/31/7	Close Dividends account	5,000		136,000 cr

(3) Information relating to intercompany sales for Year 8:

	Pickens Corporation	Skiffen Company
Dec. 31, Year 8, inventory of intercompany merchandise purchases, on first-in, first-out basis . .	$26,000	$22,000
Intercompany payables, Dec. 31, Year 8.	12,000	7,000

(4) Pickens acquired $30,000 face amount of Skiffen's 6% bonds in the open market on January 2, Year 8, for $27,016—a 10% yield. Skiffen had issued the bonds on January 2, Year 6, to yield 8% and has been paying the interest each December 31. Any gain or loss on early extinguishment of the bonds is immaterial.

(5) On September 1, Year 8, Pickens sold equipment with a cost of $40,000 and accumulated depreciation of $9,300 to Skiffen for $40,200. On September 1, Year 8, the equipment had an estimated economic life of 10 years and no residual value. Skiffen includes depreciation in other operating expenses.

(6) Skiffen owed Pickens $32,000 on December 31, Year 8, for noninterest-bearing cash advances.

(7) Pickens and Skiffen file separate income tax returns. The combined federal and state income tax rate is 60%.

Instructions Prepare a working paper for consolidated financial statements and related working paper eliminations for Pickens Corporation and subsidiary on December 31, Year 8, including income taxes allocation. Round all amounts to nearest dollar.

9-8 On January 2, Year 6, Plummer Corporation acquired a controlling interest of 75% in the outstanding common stock of Sinclair Company for $96,000, including direct out-of-pocket costs of the business combination. Separate financial statements for the two companies for the year ended December 31, Year 6, are presented on page 441.

Additional information

(1) Sinclair sold machinery with a carrying amount of $4,000, no residual value, and a remaining economic life of five years to Plummer for $4,800 on December 31, Year 6.

(2) Sinclair's depreciable plant assets had a composite estimated remaining economic life of five years on January 2, Year 6.

PLUMMER CORPORATION AND SINCLAIR COMPANY
Separate Financial Statements
For Year Ended December 31, Year 6

	Plummer Corporation	Sinclair Company
Income Statements		
Revenue		
Net sales	$772,000	$426,000
Intercompany sales	78,000	104,000
Dividend revenue		750
Intercompany gain on sale of machinery		800
Intercompany investment income	31,163	
Other revenue	9,000	2,900
Total revenue	$890,163	$534,450
Costs and expenses		
Cost of goods sold	$445,000	$301,200
Intercompany cost of goods sold	65,000	72,800
Depreciation expense	65,600	11,200
Other operating expenses	150,463	52,375
Income taxes expense	80,100	58,125
Total costs and expenses	$806,163	$495,700
Net income	$ 84,000	$ 38,750
Statements of Retained Earnings		
Retained earnings, beginning of year	$378,000	$112,000
Add: Net income	84,000	38,750
Subtotals	$462,000	$150,750
Less: Dividends	7,500	4,000
Retained earnings, end of year	$454,500	$146,750
Balance Sheets		
Assets		
Short-term investments		$ 18,000
Intercompany receivables (payables)	$ 16,000	(16,000)
Inventories	275,000	135,000
Other current assets	309,100	106,750
Investment in Sinclair Company common stock	124,163	
Plant assets	518,000	279,000
Accumulated depreciation	(298,200)	(196,700)
Total assets	$944,063	$326,050
Liabilities & Stockholders' Equity		
Dividends payable	$ 7,500	
Income taxes payable	80,100	$ 58,125
Other current liabilities	215,963	91,175
Common stock, $10 par	150,000	
Common stock, $5 par		20,000
Paid-in capital in excess of par	36,000	10,000
Retained earnings	454,500	146,750
Total liabilities & stockholders' equity	$944,063	$326,050

(3) Data on intercompany sales of merchandise follow:

	In purchaser's inventory, Dec. 31, Year 6	Amount payable by purchaser, Dec. 31, Year 6
Plummer Corporation to Sinclair Company	$24,300	$24,000
Sinclair Company to Plummer Corporation	18,000	8,000

(4) Both companies are subject to a combined federal and state income tax rate of 60%. Plummer is entitled to a dividend received deduction of 85%. Each company will file separate income tax returns for Year 6. Except for Plummer's Intercompany Investment Income account, there are no timing differences for either company.

(5) Plummer's ledger accounts for Investment in Sinclair Company Common Stock and Intercompany Investment Income appear as follows (before December 31, Year 6, closing entries):

Investment in Sinclair Company Common Stock

Date	Explanation	Debit	Credit	Balance
1/2/6	Acquisition of 3,000 shares	96,000		96,000 dr
12/31/6	Net income of Sinclair ($38,750 × 0.75)	29,063		125,063 dr
12/31/6	Amortization of "negative goodwill" {[($142,000 × 0.75) − $96,000] ÷ 5}	2,100		127,163 dr
12/31/6	Dividend declared by Sinclair ($4,000 × 0.75)		3,000	124,163 dr

Intercompany Investment Income

Date	Explanation	Debit	Credit	Balance
12/31/6	Net income of Sinclair		29,063	29,063 cr
12/31/6	Amortization of "negative goodwill"		2,100	31,163 cr

Instructions

a Prepare December 31, Year 6, adjusting journal entries to provide for income tax allocation in the accounting records of Plummer Corporation due to Plummer's use of the equity method of accounting for the subsidiary's operating results. Round all amounts to the nearest dollar.

b Prepare a working paper for consolidated financial statements and related working paper eliminations, including those for income tax allocation, for Plummer Corporation and subsidiary on December 31, Year 6. Amounts for Plummer should reflect the journal entries in **a**.

9-9 The separate financial statements of Potash Corporation and its 90%-owned subsidiary, Silicone Company, for the period ended December 31, Year 4, appear on page 443.

POTASH CORPORATION AND SILICONE COMPANY
Separate Financial Statements
For Period Ended December 31, Year 4

	Potash Corporation (year ended 12/31/4)	Silicone Company (four months ended 12/31/4)
Income Statements		
Revenue		
Net sales	$ 600,000	$300,000
Intercompany sales	85,000	81,000
Intercompany gain on sale of equipment ..	6,000	
Investment income	19,200	
Intercompany investment income	28,800	
Total revenue	$ 739,000	$381,000
Costs and expenses		
Cost of goods sold	$ 400,000	$150,000
Intercompany cost of goods sold	68,000	60,000
Operating expenses	121,000	91,000
Income taxes expense:		
Current	82,800	48,000
Deferred	7,200	
Total costs and expenses	$ 679,000	$349,000
Net income	$ 60,000	$ 32,000
Statements of Retained Earnings		
Retained earnings, beginning of period	$ 561,000	$160,000
Add: Net income	60,000	32,000
Subtotals....................	$ 621,000	$192,000
Less: Dividends..................	120,000	40,000
Retained earnings, end of period	$ 501,000	$152,000
Balance Sheets		
Assets		
Current assets	$ 555,000	$269,000
Intercompany dividends receivable (payable) .	36,000	(36,000)
Investment in Silicone Company common		
stock......................	254,567	
Plant assets (net).................	370,000	188,000
Total assets	$1,215,567	$421,000
Liabilities & Stockholders' Equity		
Accounts payable	$ 201,127	$117,000
Dividends payable		4,000
Income taxes payable	49,600	48,000
Deferred income tax liability	21,240	
Common stock, $10 par	400,000	100,000
Retained earnings	501,000	152,000
Retained earnings of subsidiary	42,600	
Total liabilities & stockholders' equity	$1,215,567	$421,000

Additional information

(1) Potash Corporation initially acquired 30% of the outstanding common stock of Silicone Company on December 31, Year 2. On December 31, Year 4, the percentage ownership is 90%.

(2) Potash's Investment in Silicone Company Common Stock, Deferred Income Tax Liability, and Retained Earnings of Subsidiary (Investee) ledger accounts prior to December 31, Year 4, closing entries appear as follows:

Investment in Silicone Company Common Stock

Date	Explanation	Debit	Credit	Balance
12/31/2	Acquisition of 3,000 shares	35,400		35,400 dr
12/31/3	Net income of Silicone ($78,000 × 0.30)	23,400		58,800 dr
8/31/4	Net income of Silicone ($64,000 × 0.30)	19,200		78,000 dr
9/1/4	Acquisition of 6,000 shares	184,000		262,000 dr
12/15/4	Dividend declared by Silicone ($40,000 × 0.90)		36,000	226,000 dr
12/31/4	Net income of Silicone ($32,000 × 0.90)	28,800		254,800 dr
12/31/4	Amortization of goodwill [($28,000 ÷ 40) × $\frac{4}{12}$]		233	254,567 dr

Deferred Income Tax Liability

Date	Explanation	Debit	Credit	Balance
12/31/3	($23,400 × 0.60)		14,040	14,040 cr
12/31/4	[($19,200 + $28,800 − $36,000) × 0.60]		7,200	21,240 cr

Retained Earnings of Subsidiary (Investee)

Date	Explanation	Debit	Credit	Balance
12/31/3	Closing entry—share of Silicone Company net income not paid as a dividend ($78,000 × 0.30)		23,400	23,400 cr
8/31/4	Closing entry—share of Silicone Company net income not paid as a dividend ($64,000 × 0.30)		19,200	42,600 cr

(3) Silicone's Retained Earnings account (prior to December 31, Year 4, closing entries) is shown on page 445.

(4) On October 1, Year 4, Potash sold equipment with a carrying amount of $36,000 to Silicone for $42,000. Silicone adopted the straight-line method of depreciation, a 10-year economic life, and no residual value for the equipment. Silicone includes depreciation in operating expenses.

(5) Intercompany profits in ending inventories are as follows: Potash, $7,000; Silicone, $8,000.

Retained Earnings

Date	Explanation	Debit	Credit	Balance
12/31/2	Balance			18,000 cr
12/31/3	Close net income		78,000	96,000 cr
8/31/4	Close net income		64,000	160,000 cr

(6) On December 15, Year 4, Silicone declared a cash dividend of $4 a share, payable on January 7, Year 5, to stockholders of record December 31, Year 4.

(7) Both Potash and Silicone are subject to a combined federal and state income tax rate of 60%, and the two companies will file separate income tax returns for Year 4. There are no timing differences for the individual companies other than the timing difference resulting from Potash's use of the equity method of accounting for Silicone's operating results.

Instructions Prepare a working paper for consolidated financial statements of Potash Corporation and subsidiary for the four months ended December 31, Year 4, and related working paper eliminations, including income tax allocation.

10 CONSOLIDATED FINANCIAL STATEMENTS: SPECIAL PROBLEMS

In this chapter we consider the following special problems that might arise in the preparation of consolidated financial statements:

Changes in parent company's ownership interest in a subsidiary
Subsidiary with preferred stock outstanding
Stock dividends distributed by a subsidiary
Treasury stock transactions of a subsidiary
Indirect shareholdings and parent company's common stock owned by a subsidiary

CHANGES IN PARENT COMPANY OWNERSHIP INTEREST IN A SUBSIDIARY

Subsequent to the date of a business combination, a parent company might acquire stockholdings of the subsidiary's minority shareholders; or the parent company might sell some of its shares of subsidiary common stock to outsiders. Also, the subsidiary itself might issue additional shares of common stock to the public, or to the parent company. We consider the accounting treatment for each of these situations in the following sections.

Parent company acquisition of minority interest

Purchase accounting should be applied to the parent company's acquisition of all or part of the minority interest in net assets of the subsidiary, even though the business combination had been accounted for as a pooling.[1] Any other approach would be inconsistent with the basic premises of pooling accounting.

To illustrate the acquisition of a subsidiary's minority interest, we re-

---

[1] *APB Opinion No. 16,* "Business Combinations," AICPA (New York: 1970), p. 294.

turn to the Prinz Corporation–Scarp Company illustration in Chapter 9 (pages 419 to 425) and assume that Scarp had net income of $25,000 for the fiscal year ended February 28, Year 5, and declared dividends totaling $15,000 on February 14, Year 5. Under the equity method of accounting, Prinz Corporation's Investment in Scarp Company Common Stock and Retained Earnings of Subsidiary ledger accounts appear as follows (before February 28, Year 5, closing entries):

Selected ledger accounts of parent company

PRINZ CORPORATION LEDGER
Investment in Scarp Company Common Stock

Date	Explanation	Debit	Credit	Balance
3/1/2	Acquisition of 1,000 shares	10,000		10,000 dr
3/1/3	Acquisition of 2,000 shares	22,000		32,000 dr
3/1/3	Retroactive application of equity method of accounting	450		32,450 dr
2/17/4	Dividends: $1 a share		3,000	29,450 dr
2/28/4	Share of net income ($15,000 × 0.30)	4,500		33,950 dr
2/28/4	Amortization of goodwill		175	33,775 dr
3/1/4	Acquisition of 6,500 shares	78,000		111,775 dr
2/14/5	Dividends: $1.50 a share (9,500 × $1.50)		14,250	97,525 dr
2/28/5	Share of net income ($25,000 × 0.95)	23,750		121,275 dr
2/28/5	Amortization of goodwill [$175 + ($19,500 ÷ 40)]		663	120,612 dr

Retained Earnings of Subsidiary

Date	Explanation	Debit	Credit	Balance
3/1/3	Retroactive application of equity method of accounting		450	450 cr
2/28/4	Closing entry—share of subsidiary's adjusted net income not declared as a dividend [($4,500 − $175) − $3,000]		1,325	1,775 cr

The working paper eliminations for the fiscal year ended February 28, Year 5, are given on page 448 (disregarding income taxes).

Assume further that on March 1, Year 5, Prinz acquired for $6,000 the 500 shares of Scarp's common stock owned by minority shareholders. Because the minority interest in net assets of subsidiary in the consolidated balance sheet of Prinz and subsidiary on February 28, Year 5, to-

PRINZ CORPORATION AND SUBSIDIARY
Working Paper Eliminations
February 28, Year 5

(a) Common Stock, $5 par—Scarp	50,000	
Paid-in Capital in Excess of Par—Scarp	10,000	
Retained Earnings—Scarp ($30,000 − $1,775)	28,225	
Retained Earnings of Subsidiary—Prinz	1,775	
Intercompany Investment Income—Prinz	23,750	
Goodwill—Prinz [($1,900 − $50) + ($4,875 − $125) +		
($19,500 − $488)]	25,612	
Investment in Scarp Company Common Stock—		
Prinz		120,612
Dividends—Scarp		15,000
Minority Interest in Net Assets of Subsidiary		
($4,500 − $750)		3,750

To eliminate intercompany investment and equity accounts of subsidiary at beginning of year; to allocate excess of cost over current fair values (equal to carrying amounts) of identifiable net assets acquired to goodwill; and to establish minority interest in net assets of subsidiary at beginning of year ($4,500), less minority share of dividends ($15,000 × 0.05 = $750).

(b) Minority Interest in Net Income of Subsidiary ($25,000 ×		
0.05)	1,250	
Minority Interest in Net Assets of Subsidiary		1,250

To establish minority interest in net income of subsidiary for year ended February 28, Year 5.

taled $5,000 ($3,750 + $1,250 = $5,000), an additional $1,000 of goodwill must be amortized by Prinz over a maximum period of 40 years, beginning March 1, Year 5. Under the equity method of accounting, Prinz accrues 100% of Scarp's net income subsequent to March 1, Year 5, and there is no minority interest to be accounted for in consolidation.

If Prinz paid *less* than the carrying amount of the minority interest acquired, the appropriate accounting treatment of the difference is not clear. Presumably, the excess of minority interest carrying amount over Prinz's cost should be allocated pro rata to the carrying amounts of Scarp's noncurrent assets other than long-term investments in marketable securities. This approach would be consistent with the theory of purchase accounting set forth in Chapter 4 (pages 146 to 150). However, assuming that the difference between carrying amount and cost is immaterial, it may be treated as an offset to goodwill implicit in earlier acquisitions of Scarp's common stock and amortized over the remaining economic life of that goodwill.

Parent company sale of a portion of its subsidiary common stockholdings

A parent company with a substantial ownership interest in a subsidiary may sell a portion of that interest for several reasons. Perhaps the parent company is short of cash, or the earnings of the subsidiary are unsatisfactory. The parent company may recognize that a subsidiary may be controlled effectively with just over 50% ownership of its outstanding common stock, and that an 80% or 90% ownership of a subsidiary may tie up excessive amounts of capital. Some corporations in recent years have sold a portion of a newly acquired subsidiary's common stock in order to generate cash for additional business combinations.

Sale of all of an ownership interest in a subsidiary involves accounting for and presentation of the disposal of a segment of a business enterprise. This topic is considered in Chapter 15.

Accounting for a parent company's sale of a part of its investment in a subsidiary is similar to the accounting for disposal of any noncurrent asset. The carrying amount of the subsidiary common stock sold is removed from the parent company's Investment in Subsidiary Common Stock account, and the difference between that carrying amount and the cash or current fair value of other consideration received is recorded as a gain or loss on disposal of the stock. Under generally accepted accounting principles, the gain or loss *is not an extraordinary item* for consolidated income statement presentation.[2]

Unless the business combination had resulted from an installment acquisition of the subsidiary's common stock, there is no significant change in the working paper eliminations after the parent's sale of part of its ownership interest in the subsidiary. However, the minority interest in the subsidiary's net income and net assets increases. The parent company's equity-method journal entries for the subsidiary's operations are changed only for the decrease in the percentage of the parent's ownership interest in the subsidiary.

When control was acquired by installment purchases of the subsidiary's common stock, *specific identification* should be used to account for the carrying amount of the subsidiary stock sold. There must be an accompanying adjustment in the parent company's application of the equity method of accounting for the subsidiary's operating results. For example, purchased goodwill may no longer be accounted for in the working paper for consolidated financial statements if the block of subsidiary common stock to which it applies was sold by the parent company.

Illustration of Parent Company Sale of Subsidiary Stockholding Returning to the Prinz Corporation–Scarp Company affiliation, assume that Scarp declared a $15,000 dividend to Prinz on February 12, Year 6, and had net

[2] *APB Opinion No. 30,* "Reporting the Results of Operations," AICPA (New York: 1973), p. 566.

income of $35,000 for the year ended February 28, Year 6. Under these circumstances Prinz's investment account and Retained Earnings of Subsidiary account (before February 28, Year 6, closing entries) appear as follows:

Investment in Scarp Company Common Stock

Date	Explanation	Debit	Credit	Balance
3/1/2	Acquisition of 1,000 shares	10,000		10,000 dr
3/1/3	Acquisition of 2,000 shares	22,000		32,000 dr
3/1/3	Retroactive application of equity method of accounting	450		32,450 dr
2/17/4	Dividends: $1 a share		3,000	29,450 dr
2/28/4	Share of net income ($15,000 × 0.30)	4,500		33,950 dr
2/28/4	Amortization of goodwill		175	33,775 dr
3/1/4	Acquisition of 6,500 shares	78,000		111,775 dr
2/14/5	Dividends: $1.50 a share (9,500 × $1.50)		14,250	97,525 dr
2/28/5	Share of net income ($25,000 × 0.95)	23,750		121,275 dr
2/28/5	Amortization of goodwill		663	120,612 dr
3/1/5	Acquisition of 500 shares	6,000		126,612 dr
2/12/6	Dividends: $1.50 a share (10,000 × $1.50)		15,000	111,612 dr
2/28/6	Share of net income ($35,000 × 1.00)	35,000		146,612 dr
2/28/6	Amortization of goodwill [$663 + ($1,000 ÷ 40)]		688	145,924 dr

Retained Earnings of Subsidiary

Date	Explanation	Debit	Credit	Balance
3/1/3	Retroactive application of equity method of accounting		450	450 cr
2/28/4	Closing entry—share of Scarp Company adjusted net income not paid as a dividend [($4,500 − $175) − $3,000]		1,325	1,775 cr
2/28/5	Closing entry—share of subsidiary's net income not declared as a dividend ($23,750 − $14,250)		9,500	11,275 cr

Under these circumstances, the working paper elimination for Prinz Corporation and its owned subsidiary on February 28, Year 6, is as follows (disregarding income taxes):

PRINZ CORPORATION AND SUBSIDIARY
Working Paper Elimination
February 28, Year 6

(a) Common Stock, $5 par—Scarp   50,000

    Paid-in Capital in Excess of Par—Scarp   10,000

    Retained Earnings—Scarp [($30,000 + $25,000 −

      $15,000) − $11,275]   28,725

    Retained Earnings of Subsidiary—Prinz   11,275

    Intercompany Investment Income—Prinz   35,000

    Goodwill—Prinz [($25,612 + $1,000) − $688]   25,924

      Investment in Scarp Company Common Stock—

        Prinz   145,924

      Dividends—Scarp   15,000

    To eliminate intercompany investment and equity accounts of subsidiary at beginning of year, and to allocate excess of cost over current fair values (equal to carrying amount) of identifiable net assets acquired to goodwill.

Continuing the illustration, assume that, in order to raise cash for additional business combinations, Prinz on March 1, Year 6, sold in the open market the 1,000 and 2,000 shares of Scarp common stock acquired March 1, Year 2, and March 1, Year 3, respectively, for $55,000. The sale resulted in a gain of $12,575, computed as follows:

Computation of gain on parent company's sale of portion of subsidiary stockholdings

Proceeds of sale		$55,000
Less: Carrying amount of 1,000 shares of Scarp common stock		
acquired Mar. 1, Year 2:		
Cost	$10,000	
Add: Share of Scarp's net income, Years 3–6		
($90,000 × 0.10)	9,000	
Less: Share of Scarp's dividends, Years 3–6		
($50,000 × 0.10)	(5,000)	
Amortization of goodwill ($50 × 4)	(200)	(13,800)
Carrying amount of 2,000 shares of Scarp common stock		
acquired Mar. 1, Year 3:		
Cost	$22,000	
Add: Share of Scarp's net income, Years 4–6		
($75,000 × 0.20)	15,000	
Less: Share of Scarp's dividends, Years 4–6		
($40,000 × 0.20)	(8,000)	
Amortization of goodwill ($125 × 3)	(375)	(28,625)
Gain on sale of portion of subsidiary stockholdings		$12,575

The following journal entry is prepared by Prinz Corporation on March 1, Year 6, to record the sale of its investment in Scarp Company common stock:

<table>
<tr><td></td><td></td><td></td></tr>
</table>

Parent company's journal entry to record sale of portion of investment in subsidiary

Cash	55,000	
Investment in Scarp Company Common Stock ($13,800 +		
$28,625)		42,425
Realized Gain on Sale of Investment in Subsidiary		12,575
To record sale of 3,000 shares of Scarp Company common stock at a gain.		

For a consolidated balance sheet of Prinz Corporation and subsidiary on March 1, Year 6, following Prinz's sale of Scarp common stock, the following working paper elimination is required:

PRINZ CORPORATION AND SUBSIDIARY
Working Paper Elimination
March 1, Year 6

(a) Common Stock, $5 par—Scarp	50,000	
Paid-in Capital in Excess of Par—Scarp	10,000	
Retained Earnings—Scarp [($40,000 + $35,000 −		
$15,000) − $31,275]	28,725	
Retained Earnings of Subsidiary—Prinz ($11,275 +		
$35,000 − $15,000)	31,275	
Goodwill—Prinz [$25,924 − ($1,800 + $4,625)]	19,499	
Investment in Scarp Company Common Stock		
($145,924 − $42,425)		103,499
Minority Interest in Net Assets of Subsidiary		
[($50,000 + $10,000 + $60,000) × 0.30]		36,000
To eliminate intercompany investment and equity accounts of subsidiary; to allocate excess of cost over current fair values (equal to carrying amount) of identifiable net assets acquired to goodwill; and to establish minority interest in net assets of subsidiary.		

The foregoing elimination recognizes only the goodwill applicable to Prinz Corporation's March 1, Year 4, and March 1, Year 5, acquisitions of Scarp Company common stock. The total goodwill of $19,499 is comprised of the following:

Computation of goodwill on March 1, Year 6

Mar. 1, Year 4, acquisition [$19,500 − ($488 × 2)]	$18,524
Mar. 1, Year 5, acquisition ($1,000 − $25)	975
Total goodwill, Mar. 1, Year 6	$19,499

Also reflected in the foregoing elimination is the minority interest in net assets of subsidiary that resulted from Prinz's disposal of 30% of its investment in Scarp's common stock. The amount of the minority interest is developed from the carrying amounts of Scarp's identifiable net assets of $120,000 on March 1, Year 6.

Subsidiary's issuance of additional shares of common stock to the public

Instead of obtaining funds by selling a portion of its ownership interest in a subsidiary, the parent company may instruct the subsidiary to issue additional shares of common stock to the public. The cash obtained would be available to the consolidated group through intercompany transactions. Unless the parent company acquires shares of common stock on a pro rata basis along with present minority shareholders in the subsidiary's stock issuance, as in a stock rights offering, the parent's percentage ownership interest in the subsidiary changes. In addition, unless the subsidiary issues additional common stock to the public at a price per share equal to the per-share carrying amount of the subsidiary's outstanding common stock, there is a realized gain or loss to the parent company. These two points are illustrated in the following section.

Illustration of Subsidiary's Issuance of Additional Common Stock to the Public On January 2, Year 1, Paulson Corporation acquired 80% of the outstanding common stock of Spaulding Company for $240,000. Out-of-pocket costs of the business combinations are disregarded in this illustration. Spaulding's stockholders' equity accounts on January 2, Year 1, were as follows:

Stockholders' equity of subsidiary on date of purchase-type business combination	Common stock, $5 par . . . . $ 50,000
	Paid-in capital in excess of par 75,000
	Retained earnings 100,000
	Total stockholders' equity $225,000

The current fair values of Spaulding's identifiable net assets on January 2, Year 1, were equal to their carrying amounts. Thus, the $60,000 excess of the cost of Paulson's investment ($240,000) over 80% of the $225,000 current fair value of Spaulding's identifiable net assets ($225,000 × 0.80 = $180,000) was attributable to goodwill, which is amortized over 40 years.

For the year ended December 31, Year 1, Spaulding had net income of $20,000 and declared and paid cash dividends of $10,000 ($1 a share). On December 31, Year 1, Spaulding issued 2,000 shares of common stock in a public offering at $33 a share, net of costs of issuing the stock, for a total of $66,000. Thus, after the closing process, Spaulding's stockholders' equity on December 31, Year 1, amounted to $301,000 ($225,000 + $20,000 − $10,000 + $66,000 = $301,000), and consisted of the following ledger account balances:

<table>
<tr><td rowspan="5">**Stockholders' equity of purchased subsidiary after issuance of common stock to public**</td><td>Common stock, $5 par ($50,000 + $10,000) . . . .</td><td>$ 60,000</td></tr>
<tr><td>Paid-in capital in excess of par ($75,000 + $56,000) . . . .</td><td>131,000</td></tr>
<tr><td>Retained earnings ($100,000 + $20,000 − $10,000). . . . .</td><td>110,000</td></tr>
<tr><td>Total stockholders' equity. . . . .</td><td>$301,000</td></tr>
</table>

Paulson's investment account under the equity method of accounting appears below:

Investment in Spaulding Company Common Stock

<table>
<tr><td rowspan="11">**Parent company's investment account**</td><td>Date</td><td>Explanation</td><td>Debit</td><td>Credit</td><td>Balance</td></tr>
<tr><td>1/2/1</td><td>Acquisition of 8,000 shares in business combination</td><td>240,000</td><td></td><td>240,000 dr</td></tr>
<tr><td>12/31/1</td><td>Dividend ($10,000 × 0.80)</td><td></td><td>8,000</td><td>232,000 dr</td></tr>
<tr><td>12/31/1</td><td>Share of net income ($20,000 × 0.80)</td><td>16,000</td><td></td><td>248,000 dr</td></tr>
<tr><td>12/31/1</td><td>Amortization of goodwill ($60,000 ÷ 40)</td><td></td><td>1,500</td><td>246,500 dr</td></tr>
<tr><td>12/31/1</td><td>Gain on subsidiary's issuance of common stock to public</td><td>12,667</td><td></td><td>259,167 dr</td></tr>
</table>

The December 31, Year 1, increase of $12,667 in Paulson's investment account is offset by a credit to a nonoperating gain account. The $12,667 is Paulson's share of the increase in Spaulding's net assets resulting from Spaulding's issuance of common stock to the public at $33 a share. The $33 a share issuance price exceeds the $30.81 carrying amount ($246,500 ÷ 8,000 shares = $30.81) a share of Paulson's investment account prior to Spaulding's common stock issuance. The $12,667 debit to Paulson's investment account is computed on page 455.

The analysis on page 455 reflects the effect of the decrease of Paulson's percentage interest in Spaulding's outstanding common stock from 80% before the public stock issuance to $66\frac{2}{3}$% after the issuance. Nevertheless, the issuance price of $33 a share exceeded the $30.81

Computation of gain to parent company resulting from subsidiary's issuance of common stock to public

	Total	Paulson's share	Minority's share
Carrying amount of Spaulding Company's identifiable net assets after common stock issuance to public	$301,000	(66⅔%)† $200,667	(33⅓%) $100,333
Carrying amount of Spaulding Company's identifiable net assets before common stock issuance to public	235,000*	(80%) 188,000‡	(20%) 47,000
Difference	$ 66,000	$ 12,667	$ 53,333

* $225,000 + $20,000 − $10,000 = $235,000

† 8,000 ÷ (10,000 + 2,000) = 66⅔%

‡ Paulson's share of Spaulding's identifiable net assets [($225,000 + $20,000 − $10,000) × 0.80] $188,000

Add: Unamortized goodwill ($60,000 − $1,500) 58,500

Balance of Paulson's Investment in Spaulding Company Common Stock account $246,500

carrying amount per share of Paulson's original investment in Spaulding, thus resulting in the $12,667 nonoperating gain to Paulson.

The working paper eliminations on page 456 are appropriate for Paulson Corporation and subsidiary following Spaulding's common stock issuance on December 31, Year 1, assuming that there were no other intercompany transactions or profits for Year 1.

The **nonoperating gain** treatment accorded to the $12,667 increase in Paulson's interest in Spaulding is not accepted universally. As one authority has stated.[3]

> . . . the SEC has adopted the position that the issue of shares by a subsidiary company to the public at an amount per share in excess of book value does not give rise to a gain to the parent interest in the consolidated income statement. In such circumstances, the SEC has generally required the gain to be credited direct to paid-in capital in consolidated financial statements. However, many accountants hold the view that consolidated paid-in capital should arise solely from transactions with stockholders of the parent company, and accordingly that subsidiary capital changes which affect the parent's share of stockholders' equity of the subsidiary should generally result in recognition of gain or loss or adjustment of goodwill on consolidation.

[3] *Consolidated Financial Statements*, Accountants International Study Group (Plaistow, England: 1973), p. 13.

PAULSON CORPORATION AND SUBSIDIARY
Working Paper Eliminations
December 31, Year 1

(a) Common Stock—Spaulding	60,000	
Paid-in Capital in Excess of Par—Spaulding.	131,000	
Retained Earnings—Spaulding.	100,000	
Goodwill—Paulson ($60,000 − $1,500)	58,500	
Intercompany Investment Income—Paulson ($20,000 ×		
0.80)	16,000	
Investment in Spaulding Company Common		
Stock—Paulson		259,167
Dividends—Spaulding		10,000
Minority Interest in Net Assets of Subsidiary		
($45,000 − $2,000 + $53,333)		96,333

To eliminate intercompany investment and related equity accounts of subsidiary (retained earnings of subsidiary is at the beginning of year); to eliminate subsidiary's dividends declared; to record unamortized balance of goodwill on Dec. 31, Year 1; and to provide for minority interest in net assets of subsidiary at beginning of year ($225,000 × 0.20 = $45,000), less dividends to minority shareholders ($10,000 × 0.20 = $2,000), plus minority interest's share of proceeds of public stock issuance ($66,000 − $12,667 = $53,333).

(b) Minority Interest in Net Income of Subsidiary	4,000	
Minority Interest in Net Assets of Subsidiary		4,000

To provide for minority interest in subsidiary's Year 1 net income as follows: $20,000 × 0.20 = $4,000.

Subsidiary's issuance of additional shares of common stock to parent company

Instead of issuing additional common stock to the public, a subsidiary might issue the additional stock to the parent company. This eventuality might occur if the parent company desired to increase its total investment in the subsidiary, or if the parent wished to reduce the influence of minority shareholders of the subsidiary.

To illustrate, we return to the Paulson Corporation–Spaulding Company illustration and assume that on December 31, Year 1, Spaulding issued 2,000 shares of common stock to Paulson at $33 a share, for a total of $66,000. Under these circumstances, Paulson's investment account increases to a balance of $309,333 ($246,500 + $66,000 cost of common stock acquired − $3,167 nonoperating loss = $309,333). The nonoperating loss of $3,167 is computed as follows:

Computation of loss to parent company resulting from subsidiary's issuance of common stock to parent

	Total	Paulson's share	Minority's share
Carrying amount of Spaulding Company's identifiable net assets after common stock issuance to parent . .	$301,000	(83⅓%)* $250,833	(16⅔%) $50,167
Carrying amount of Spaulding Company's identifiable net assets before common stock issuance to parent . .	235,000	(80%) 188,000†	(20%) 47,000
Difference	$ 66,000	$ 62,833	$ 3,167‡

* (8,000 + 2,000) ÷ (10,000 + 2,000) = 83⅓%
† Paulson's share of Spaulding's identifiable net assets $188,000
  Add: Unamortized goodwill ($60,000 − $1,500) 58,500
     Balance of Paulson's Investment in Spaulding Company Common Stock $246,500
‡ Nonoperating loss to parent company

The working paper eliminations for Paulson Corporation and subsidiary following Spaulding's common stock issuance on December 31, Year 1, are presented below and on page 458.

PAULSON CORPORATION AND SUBSIDIARY
Working Paper Eliminations
December 31, Year 1

(a) Common Stock—Spaulding	60,000	
Paid-in Capital in Excess of Par—Spaulding.	131,000	
Retained Earnings—Spaulding.	100,000	
Goodwill—Paulson ($60,000 − $1,500)	58,500	
Intercompany Investment Income—Paulson ($20,000 × 0.80)	16,000	
Investment in Spaulding Company Common Stock—Paulson		309,333
Dividends—Spaulding		10,000
Minority Interest in Net Assets of Subsidiary ($45,000 − $2,000 + $3,167)		46,167

To eliminate intercompany investment and related equity accounts of subsidiary (retained earnings of subsidiary is at the beginning of year); to eliminate subsidiary's dividends declared; to record unamortized balance of the goodwill on Dec. 31, Year 1; and to provide for minority interest in subsidiary at beginning of year ($225,000 × 0.20 = $45,000), less dividends to minority shareholders ($10,000 × 0.20 = $2,000), plus minority interest's share of proceeds of common stock issuance to parent company ($3,167).

(Continued)

(b) Minority Interest in Net Income of Subsidiary *4,000*
         Minority Interest in Net Assets of Subsidiary *4,000*
      To provide for minority interest in subsidiary's Year 1 net
      income as follows: $20,000 × 0.20 = $4,000.

SUBSIDIARY WITH PREFERRED STOCK OUTSTANDING

Some combinees in a business combination have outstanding preferred stock. If a parent company acquires all of a subsidiary's preferred stock, together with all or a majority of its voting common stock, the working paper for consolidated financial statements and working paper eliminations are similar to those illustrated in Chapters 5 through 9. If less than 100% of the subsidiary's preferred stock is acquired by the parent company, the preferences associated with the preferred stock must be considered in the determination of the minority interest in the net assets and net income of the subsidiary.

Illustration of minority interest in subsidiary with preferred stock

Suppose, for example, that on July 1, Year 4, Praeger Corporation paid $200,000 (including direct out-of-pocket costs of the business combination) for 60% of Simmon Company's 10,000 shares of outstanding $1 par, 6% cumulative preferred stock and 80% of Simmon's 50,000 shares of outstanding $2 par common stock. The preferred stock has a liquidation preference of $1.10 a share and is callable at $1.20 a share plus cumulative preferred dividends in arrears. The stockholders' equity of Simmon on July 1, Year 4, was as follows:

Stockholders' equity of subsidiary on date of purchase-type business combination

6% preferred stock, $1 par	*$ 10,000*
Common stock, $2 par	*100,000*
Paid-in capital in excess of par.	*30,000*
Retained earnings	*50,000*
Total stockholders' equity.	*$190,000*

There were no cumulative preferred dividends in arrears on July 1, Year 4. The current fair values of Simmon's identifiable net assets on July 1, Year 4, were equal to their carrying amounts on that date.

The presence of the preferred stock raises two questions:

1 What part if any, does the preferred stock play in the determination of the goodwill acquired in the business combination?

2 Which per-share amount—$1 par, $1.10 liquidation preference, or $1.20 call price—should be used to measure the minority interest in Simmon's net assets on July 1, Year 4?

In the opinion of the authors, the following are logical answers to the two questions:

1 The preferred stock does not enter into the determination of the goodwill acquired in the business combination. Typically, preferred stockholders have no voting rights; thus, in a business combination, preferred stock may in substance be considered **debt** rather than **owners' equity.** Accordingly, the amount paid by the combinor for the subsidiary's common stock should be the measure of the goodwill.

2 The call price should be used to measure the minority interest of the preferred shareholders in Simmon's net assets on July 1, Year 4. The call price generally is the maximum claim on net assets imposed by the preferred stock contract. Furthermore, the call price is the amount that Simmon would pay, on a going-concern basis, to liquidate the preferred stock. Use of the preferred stock's liquidation value in the determination of the minority shareholders' interest in the subsidiary's net assets would stress a **quitting-concern** approach, rather than a going-concern principle. Finally, the par of the preferred stock has no real significance as a measure of value for the preferred stock.

In accordance with the foregoing discussion, Praeger prepares the following journal entry to record the business combination with Simmon on July 1, Year 4. (Out-of-pocket costs of the combination are not accounted for separately in this illustration.)

Parent company's journal entry for purchase-type business combination involving subsidiary's preferred stock	*Investment in Simmon Company Preferred Stock (6,000*	
	× $1.20)	*7,200*
	Investment in Simmon Company Common Stock ($200,000 −	
	$7,200) 192,800	
	Cash	*200,000*
	To record business combination with Simmon Company.	

The working paper elimination for Praeger and subsidiary on July 1, Year 4, is illustrated on page 460.

PRAEGER CORPORATION AND SUBSIDIARY
Working Paper Elimination
July 1, Year 4

Preferred Stock—Simmon	10,000	
Common Stock—Simmon	100,000	
Paid-in Capital in Excess of Par—Simmon	30,000	
Retained Earnings—Simmon	50,000	
Goodwill—Praeger {$192,800 − [($190,000 − $12,000 call price of preferred stock) × 0.80]}	50,400	
Investment in Simmon Company Preferred Stock—Praeger.		7,200
Investment in Simmon Company Common Stock—Praeger.		192,800
Minority Interest in Net Assets of Subsidiary—Preferred (4,000 × $1.20).		4,800
Minority Interest in Net Assets of Subsidiary—Common ($178,000 × 0.20)		35,600

To eliminate intercompany investment and related equity accounts of subsidiary on date of business combination; to record excess of cost attributable to common stock over 80% share of current fair value of subsidiary's identifiable net assets as goodwill; and to provide for minority interest in subsidiary's preferred stock and in net assets applicable to common stock on date of business combination.

The following aspects of this elimination should be emphasized:

1 Simmon's goodwill is measured by the difference between the cost assigned to Praeger's investment in Simmon's common stock over Praeger's share of the current fair value of Simmon's net assets applicable to common stock; Simmon's preferred stock does not enter the computation of the goodwill.

2 The minority interest in the subsidiary's preferred stock is measured by the 4,000 shares of preferred stock owned by minority shareholders multiplied by the $1.20 call price per share.

3 The minority interest in the subsidiary's common stock is computed as 20% of the $178,000 ($190,000 − $12,000 = $178,000) net asset value of Simmon's common stock.

Preferred stock considerations subsequent to date of business combination

Regardless of whether Simmon's preferred dividend is paid or omitted in years subsequent to July 1, Year 4, the preferred dividend affects the computation of the minority interest of common shareholders in the net income of Simmon. For example, assume that Simmon had net income of $50,000 for the fiscal year ended June 30, Year 5, and declared and paid the preferred dividend of $0.06 a share and a common dividend of

$0.50 a share on June 30, Year 5. Praeger records these elements of Simmon's operating results as follows on June 30, Year 5, under the equity method of accounting:

PRAEGER CORPORATION

Journal Entries

June 30, Year 5

Cash	20,360	
Investment in Simmon Company Common Stock		20,000
Intercompany Dividend Revenue		360

To record receipt of dividends declared and paid by Simmon Company as follows:

Preferred stock: 6,000 × $0.06	$ 360	
Common stock: 40,000 × $0.50	20,000	
Total cash received	$20,360	

Investment in Simmon Company Common Stock	39,520	
Intercompany Investment Income		39,520

To record share of Simmon Company's net income applicable to common stock as follows:

Simmon Company's net income	$50,000	
Less: Preferred dividend (10,000 × $0.06)	600	
Net income attributable to common stock	$49,400	
Parent company's share ($49,400 × 0.80)	$39,520	

(Income tax effects are disregarded.)

Amortization Expense	1,260	
Investment in Simmon Company Common Stock		1,260

To provide for Year 5 amortization of Simmon Company's goodwill acquired on date of business combination as follows:

Simmon's goodwill acquired on date of business combination	$50,400	
Amortization ($50,400 ÷ 40)	$ 1,260	

After the foregoing journal entries are posted, Praeger's Investment in Simmon Company Common Stock ledger account appears as follows:

Investment account of parent company

Investment in Simmon Company Common Stock

Date	Explanation	Debit	Credit	Balance
7/1/4	Acquisition of 40,000 shares	192,800		192,800 dr
6/30/5	Dividends: $0.50 a share		20,000	172,800 dr
6/30/5	Share of net income	39,520		212,320 dr
6/30/5	Amortization of goodwill		1,260	211,060 dr

If there are no other intercompany transactions or profits, the June 30, Year 5, working paper eliminations for Praeger Corporation and subsidiary are as shown below:

PRAEGER CORPORATION AND SUBSIDIARY
Working Paper Eliminations
June 30, Year 5

(a) *Preferred Stock—Simmon*	10,000	
Common Stock—Simmon	100,000	
Paid-in Capital in Excess of Par—Simmon	30,000	
Retained Earnings—Simmon	50,000	
Intercompany Dividend Revenue—Praeger	360	
Intercompany Investment Income—Praeger	39,520	
Goodwill—Praeger ($50,400 − $1,260)	49,140	
Investment in Simmon Company Preferred Stock—Praeger		7,200
Investment in Simmon Company Common Stock—Praeger		211,060
Minority Interest in Net Assets of Subsidiary—Preferred ($4,800 − $240)		4,560
Minority Interest in Net Assets of Subsidiary—Common [$35,600 − ($25,000 × 0.20)]		30,600
Dividends—Simmon [(10,000 × $0.06) + (50,000 × $0.50)]		25,600

To eliminate intercompany investment and related equity accounts of subsidiary at beginning of year; to eliminate subsidiary's dividends declared; to record unamortized balance of goodwill on June 30, Year 5; and to provide for minority interest in subsidiary's preferred stock and common stock at beginning of year, less dividends to minority shareholders.

(b) *Minority Interest in Net Income of Subsidiary*	10,120	
Minority Interest in Net Assets of Subsidiary—Preferred		240
Minority Interest in Net Assets of Subsidiary—Common [($50,000 − $600) × 0.20]		9,880

To provide for minority interest in net income of subsidiary for Year 5.

In the review of the June 30, Year 5, journal entries of Praeger and the working paper eliminations on that date, the following points should be noted:

1 Praeger Corporation's accounting for its investment in the subsidiary's preferred stock essentially is the cost method. This method is appropriate as long as the subsidiary declares and pays the cumulative preferred dividend annually. If the subsidiary had **passed** the preferred dividend of $600 for the year ended June 30, Year 5, Praeger would have recorded the passed preferred dividend under the equity method of accounting as follows:

<table>
<tr>
<td>**Parent company's journal entry for passed preferred dividend of subsidiary**</td>
<td>*Investment in Simmon Company Preferred Stock* *360*
      Intercompany Investment Income. *360*
To accrue cumulative preferred dividend passed by subsidiary's board
of directors ($600 × 0.60 = $360).</td>
</tr>
</table>

The working paper eliminations in the year of a passed cumulative preferred dividend would be the same as those illustrated on page 462, except that the minority interest in the subsidiary's preferred stock would be $240 ($600 × 0.40 = $240) larger because of the effect of the passed dividend. (Of course, no common dividend could be declared if the cumulative preferred dividend were passed.)

2 The net result of the foregoing journal entries and working paper eliminations is that the subsidiary's net income of $50,000 is allocated as follows:

<table>
<tr>
<td rowspan="2">**Allocation of subsidiary's net income to preferred and common shareholders**</td>
<td></td>
<td>**Total**</td>
<td>**Consolidated net income**</td>
<td>**Minority interest**</td>
</tr>
<tr>
<td>*To preferred shareholders:*
  10,000 shares × $0.06, in
  ratio of 60% and 40% . . . . .</td>
<td>*$ 600*</td>
<td>*$ 360*</td>
<td>*$ 240*</td>
</tr>
<tr>
<td></td>
<td>*To common shareholders in*
  80:20 ratio . . . .</td>
<td>*49,400*</td>
<td>*39,520*</td>
<td>*9,880*</td>
</tr>
<tr>
<td></td>
<td>*Net income of subsidiary.* . . .</td>
<td>*$50,000*</td>
<td>*$39,880*</td>
<td>*$10,120*</td>
</tr>
</table>

Other Types of Preferred Stock   Treatment similar to that illustrated in the foregoing section is appropriate for the minority interest in a subsidiary having other types of outstanding preferred stock. If the preferred stock were **noncumulative,** there would be no parent company accrual of passed dividends. If the preferred stock were **participating** (which seldom is the case), the subsidiary's retained earnings would be allocated to the minority interests in preferred stock and common stock according to the terms of the **participation clause.**

STOCK DIVIDENDS DISTRIBUTED BY A SUBSIDIARY

If a parent company uses the equity method of accounting for the operating results of a subsidiary, the subsidiary's declaration and issuance of a common stock dividend has no effect on the parent's Investment in Subsidiary Common Stock account. As emphasized in **Intermediate Accounting** of this series, receipt of a stock dividend does not represent dividend revenue to the investor.

After the declaration of a common stock dividend not exceeding 20 to 25%, the subsidiary's retained earnings is reduced by an amount equal to the current fair value of the stock issued as a dividend. This reduction and the offsetting increase in the subsidiary's paid-in capital accounts must be incorporated in the working paper eliminations subsequent to the issuance of the stock dividend. Thus, the amount of consolidated retained earnings is not affected by a subsdiary's stock dividend. As emphasized by the AICPA:[4]

> . . . the retained earnings in the consolidated financial statements should reflect the accumulated earnings of the consolidated group not distributed to the shareholders of, or capitalized by, the parent company.

Illustration of subsidiary stock dividend

On June 30, Year 5, the date of the pooling-type business combination of Pasco Corporation and Salvo Company, the working paper elimination was as follows:

PASCO CORPORATION AND SUBSIDIARY
Working Paper Elimination
June 30, Year 5

(a) Common Stock, $1 par—Salvo	150,000	
Paid-in Capital in Excess of Par—Salvo	200,000	
Retained Earnings of Subsidiary—Pasco	250,000	
Investment in Salvo Company Common Stock—Pasco		600,000

To eliminate intercompany investment and related accounts for stockholders' equity of subsidiary on date of pooling-type business combination.

On June 18, Year 6, Salvo distributed 15,000 shares of its $1 par common stock to Pasco as a 10% stock dividend. Salvo debited the Dividends ledger account for $75,000, the current fair value of the common stock distributed as a dividend (15,000 × $5 = $75,000). Pasco prepared no journal entry for the stock dividend, but it did record the subsidiary's net income for the fiscal year ended June 30, Year 6, under the equity method of accounting as follows:

Parent company's equity-method journal entry to record operating results of wholly owned pooled subsidiary

Investment in Salvo Company Common Stock	180,000	
Intercompany Investment Income		180,000

To record 100% of Salvo Company's net income for the year ended June 30, Year 6. (Income tax effects are disregarded.)

---

[4] *ARB No. 51*, "Consolidated Financial Statements," AICPA (New York: 1959), p. 46.

On June 30, Year 6, the working paper elimination for Pasco Corporation and Subsidiary is as follows:

PASCO CORPORATION AND SUBSIDIARY
Working Paper Elimination
June 30, Year 6

(a) Common Stock, $1 par—Salvo ($150,000 + $15,000) . .   165,000

Paid-in Capital in Excess of Par—Salvo ($200,000 +
$60,000)   260,000

Retained Earnings of Subsidiary—Pasco   250,000

Intercompany Investment Income—Pasco   180,000

    Investment in Salvo Company Common Stock—

      Pasco ($600,000 + $180,000)   780,000

      Dividends—Salvo   75,000

To eliminate intercompany investment, related accounts
for stockholder's equity of subsidiary, and investment
income from subsidiary.

In its closing entries on June 30, Year 6, Pasco credits its Retained Earnings of Subsidiary ledger account for $105,000, the amount of the undistributed earnings of the subsidiary ($180,000 − $75,000 = $105,000). This closing entry brings the balance of the account to $355,000 ($250,000 + $105,000 = $355,000), which is the same as the balance of Salvo's Retained Earnings ledger account ($250,000 + $180,000 − $75,000 = $355,000).

TREASURY STOCK TRANSACTIONS OF A SUBSIDIARY

Treasury stock owned by a subsidiary on the date of a business combination is treated as **retired stock** in the preparation of consolidated financial statements. A working paper elimination should be prepared to account for the "retirement" of the treasury stock by the **par** or **stated value method.**

Illustration of treasury stock owned by subsidiary on combination date

Palance Corporation acquired all 49,000 shares of the outstanding common stock of Sizemore Company on March 1, Year 6, for $147,000, including direct out-of-pocket costs. Sizemore's stockholders' equity on that date was as follows:

Stockholders' equity of subsidiary with treasury stock on date of purchase-type business combination

Common stock, $1 par.	$ 50,000
Paid-in capital in excess of par.	25,000
Retained earnings	50,000
Total paid-in capital and retained earnings	$125,000
Less: 1,000 shares of treasury stock, at cost.	2,000
Total stockholders' equity.	$123,000

On the date of the combination, the current fair values of Sizemore's identifiable net assets equaled their carrying amounts.

The working paper eliminations for Palance Corporation and subsidiary on March 1, Year 6, are as follows:

PALANCE CORPORATION AND SUBSIDIARY
Working Paper Eliminations
March 1, Year 6

(a) Common Stock—Sizemore.	1,000	
Paid-in Capital in Excess of Par—Sizemore.	500	
Retained Earnings—Sizemore.	500	
Treasury Stock—Sizemore		2,000

To account for subsidiary's treasury stock as though it had been retired.

(b) Common Stock—Sizemore ($50,000 − $1,000).	49,000	
Paid-in Capital in Excess of Par—Sizemore ($25,000 − $500)	24,500	
Retained Earnings—Sizemore ($50,000 − $500)	49,500	
Goodwill—Sizemore ($147,000 − $123,000).	24,000	
Investment in Sizemore Company Common Stock—Palance		147,000

To eliminate intercompany investment and equity accounts of subsidiary on date of business combination; and to allocate excess of cost over current fair values (and carrying amounts) of identifiable net assets acquired to goodwill.

In the first elimination, paid-in capital in excess of par of the subsidiary is reduced by the pro rata portion ($25,000 ÷ 50,000 shares = $0.50 a share) applicable to the treasury stock. The remainder of the cost of the treasury stock is allocated to the subsidiary's retained earnings.

If, subsequent to the date of a business combination, a subsidiary acquires for its treasury some or all of the shares of its common stock owned by minority shareholders, an elimination similar to the first one is appropriate. In addition, a gain or loss to the parent company is recognized in a manner similar to that illustrated in the section of this chapter for subsidiary issuances of common stock to the public (pages 453 to 456).

Illustration of treasury stock acquired by subsidiary subsequent to combination

On December 31, Year 1, Portola Corporation acquired 80% of the outstanding common stock of Stanley Company for $44,000, including direct out-of-pocket costs of the business combination. Stanley's stockholders' equity on December 31, Year 1, was as follows, with current fair values of identifiable net assets equal to carrying amounts:

Stockholders' equity of subsidiary on date of purchase-type business combination

Common stock, $10 par	$10,000
Paid-in capital in excess of par	15,000
Retained earnings	25,000
Total stockholders' equity	$50,000

For the year ended December 31, Year 2, Stanley declared dividends of $4,000 and had net income of $10,000. Portola's investment account appeared as follows on December 31, Year 2:

Investment account of parent company

Investment in Stanley Company Common Stock

Date	Explanation	Debit	Credit	Balance
12/31/1	Acquisition of 800 shares	44,000		44,000 dr
12/28/2	Dividends: $4 a share			
	($4,000 × 0.80)		3,200	40,800 dr
12/31/2	Share of net income			
	($10,000 × 0.80)	8,000		48,800 dr
12/31/2	Amortization of goodwill			
	($4,000* ÷ 40)		100	48,700 dr

* $44,000 − ($50,000 × 0.80) = $4,000 goodwill

The working paper eliminations for Portola Corporation and subsidiary on December 31, Year 2, are as follows:

PORTOLA CORPORATION AND SUBSIDIARY
Working Paper Eliminations
December 31, Year 2

(a) Common Stock—Stanley	10,000	
Paid-in Capital in Excess of Par—Stanley.	15,000	
Retained Earnings—Stanley.	25,000	
Intercompany Investment Income—Portola	8,000	
Goodwill—Portola ($4,000 − $100).	3,900	
Investment in Stanley Company Common Stock—		
Portola		48,700
Dividends—Stanley		4,000
Minority Interest in Net Assets of Subsidiary		
($10,000 − $800)		9,200

To eliminate intercompany investment and equity accounts
of subsidiary at beginning of year; to allocate excess of cost
over current fair values (and carrying amounts) of identifiable net assets acquired to goodwill; and to establish
minority interest in net assets of subsidiary at beginning
of year ($50,000 × 0.20 = $10,000), less minority share of
dividends declared by subsidiary during year ($4,000 ×
0.20 = $800).

(b) Minority Interest in Net Income of Subsidiary ($10,000 ×		
0.20)	2,000	
Minority Interest in Net Assets of Subsidiary		2,000

To establish minority interest in subsidiary's net income for
Year 2.

On January 2, Year 3, Stanley paid $7,400 to acquire 100 shares of its common stock from a dissident minority shareholder. Stanley's journal entry to record the acquisition of treasury stock was as follows:

Subsidiary's journal entry for acquisition of treasury stock

Treasury Stock (100 × $74)	7,400	
Cash		7,400

To record acquisition of common stock from a dissident minority shareholder.

The $74 a share acquisition cost of the treasury stock exceeds the $60.88 a share ($48,700 ÷ 800 = $60.88) of Portola's investment in Stanley's common stock. Thus, Portola incurred a nonoperating loss of $1,600, computed as follows (the $1,600 loss is credited to Portola's investment account):

Computation of loss to parent company resulting from subsidiary's acquisition of treasury stock from minority shareholder

	Total	Portola's share	Minority's share
Carrying amount of Stanley's net assets before acquisition of treasury stock	$56,000*	($\frac{8}{10}$) $44,800†	($\frac{2}{10}$) $11,200‡
Carrying amount of Stanley's net assets after acquisition of treasury stock	48,600	($\frac{8}{9}$) 43,200	($\frac{1}{9}$) 5,400
Difference—equal to cost of treasury stock	$ 7,400	$ 1,600	$ 5,800

* $50,000 + $10,000 − $4,000 = $56,000
† Portola's share of Stanley's net assets $44,800
  Unamortized goodwill   3,900
  Balance of Portola's investment account $48,700
‡ $9,200 + $2,000 = $11,200

If a consolidated balance sheet of Portola Corporation and subsidiary were prepared on January 2, Year 3, the working paper eliminations would be as follows:

PORTOLA CORPORATION AND SUBSIDIARY
Working Paper Eliminations
January 2, Year 3

(a) Common Stock—Stanley (100 × $10)   1,000
    Paid-in Capital in Excess of Par—Stanley (100 × $15) . . .   1,500
    Retained Earnings—Stanley [100 × ($74 − $10 − $15)] . .   4,900
        Treasury Stock—Stanley   7,400
    To account for subsidiary's treasury stock as though it had been retired.

(b) Common Stock—Stanley ($10,000 − $1,000)   9,000
    Paid-in Capital in Excess of Par—Stanley ($15,000 − $1,500) 13,500
    Retained Earnings—Stanley [($25,000 + $10,000 − $4,000) − ($4,900 + $4,800)] 21,300
    Retained Earnings of Subsidiary—Portola ($8,000 − $3,200)   4,800
    Goodwill—Portola   3,900
        Investment in Stanley Company Common Stock—Portola ($48,700 − $1,600)   47,100
        Minority Interest in Net Assets of Subsidiary   5,400
    To eliminate intercompany investment and equity accounts of subsidiary; to allocate excess of cost over current fair values of identifiable net assets acquired to goodwill; and to establish minority interest in net assets of subsidiary.

INDIRECT SHAREHOLDINGS AND PARENT COMPANY'S COMMON STOCK OWNED BY A SUBSIDIARY

In the early history of business combinations resulting in parent company–subsidiary relationships, complex indirect or reciprocal shareholdings frequently were encountered. **Indirect shareholdings** are those involving such relationships as one subsidiary and the parent company jointly owning a controlling interest in another subsidiary, or a subsidiary company being itself the parent company of its own subsidiary. **Reciprocal shareholdings** involve subsidiary ownership of shares of the parent company's common stock.

Indirect shareholdings

Business combinations in recent years generally have been far less complex than those described above. There usually has been a single parent company and one or more subsidiaries, and indirect shareholdings have been the exception rather than the rule. Accountants, faced with the problems of preparing a working paper for consolidated financial statements for parent company–subsidiary relationships involving indirect shareholdings, must follow carefully the common stock ownership percentages and apply the equity method of accounting for the various subsidiaries' operating results.

Illustration of Indirect Shareholdings On December 31, Year 2, Placer Corporation acquired 160,000 shares (80%) of the outstanding common stock of Shabot Company for $476,240, and 36,000 shares (45%) of Sur Company's outstanding common stock for $182,000. Both amounts included direct out-of-pocket costs of the common stock acquisitions. On December 31, Year 2, Shabot owned 20,000 shares (25%) of Sur's outstanding common stock; accordingly, Placer acquired indirect control of Sur as well as direct control of Shabot in the business combination.

Separate balance sheets of Shabot and Sur on December 31, Year 2, prior to the business combination, follow:

SHABOT COMPANY AND SUR COMPANY
Separate Balance Sheets
December 31, Year 2

	Shabot Company	Sur Company
Assets		
Current assets	$ 360,400	$190,600
Investment in Sur Company common stock	91,950	
Plant assets (net)	640,650	639,400
Total assets	$1,093,000	$830,000

(Continued)

Liabilities & Stockholders' Equity		
Current liabilities.	$ 210,200	$ 80,500
Long-term debt.	300,000	389,500
Common stock, $1 par	200,000	80,000
Paid-in capital in excess of par	150,000	120,000
Retained earnings	222,850	160,000
Retained earnings of investee	9,950	
Total liabilities & stockholders' equity	$1,093,000	$830,000

Shabot's Investment in Sur Company Common Stock and Retained Earnings of Investee ledger accounts appeared as follows on December 31, Year 2:

Selected ledger accounts of subsidiary investor

Investment in Sur Company Common Stock				
Date	*Explanation*	*Debit*	*Credit*	*Balance*
12/31/1	Acquisition of 20,000 shares	82,000		82,000 dr
12/6/2	Dividends: $0.25 a share		5,000	77,000 dr
12/31/2	Share of net income			
	($60,000 × 0.25)	15,000		92,000 dr
12/31/2	Amortization of goodwill			
	($2,000 ÷ 40)		50	91,950 dr

Retained Earnings of Investee				
Date	*Explanation*	*Debit*	*Credit*	*Balance*
12/31/2	Closing entry—share of Sur Company adjusted net income not paid as a dividend [($15,000 − $50) − $5,000]		9,950	9,950 cr

The ledger accounts of Shabot indicate that Shabot had applied the equity method of accounting for its investment in the influenced investee, Sur, and that the $2,000 excess of the cost of Shabot's investment over the underlying equity of Sur's identifiable net assets was allocated to goodwill having an economic life of 40 years.

The current fair values of the identifiable net assets of both Shabot and Sur equaled their carrying amounts on December 31, Year 2. Accordingly, goodwill acquired by Placer in the business combination with Shabot and Sur was computed as follows:

	Shabot Company	Sur Company
Cost of investment	$476,240	$182,000
Less: Current fair value of identifiable net assets acquired:		
Shabot ($582,800 × 0.80)	466,240	
Sur ($360,000 × 0.45)		162,000
Goodwill (economic life 40 years)	$ 10,000	$ 20,000

PLACER CORPORATION AND SUBSIDIARIES
Working Paper for Consolidated Balance Sheet
December 31, Year 2

	Placer Corporation	Shabot Company	Sur Company	Eliminations increase (decrease)		Consolidated
Assets						
Current assets	1,400,000	360,400	190,600			1,951,000
Investment in Shabot Company common stock	476,240			(a)	(476,240)	
Investment in Sur Company common stock	182,000	91,950		(b) (b)	(91,950) (182,000)	
Plant assets (net)	3,800,000	640,650	639,400			5,080,050
Goodwill				(a) (b)	10,000 21,950	31,950
Total assets	5,858,240	1,093,000	830,000		(718,240)	7,063,000
Liabilities & Stockholders' Equity						
Current liabilities	600,000	210,200	80,500			890,700
Long-term debt	3,000,000	300,000	389,500			3,689,500
Minority interest in net assets of subsidiaries				(a) (b)	116,560 108,000	224,560
Common stock, $1 par	1,200,000	200,000	80,000	(a) (b)	(200,000) (80,000)	1,200,000
Paid-in capital in excess of par	500,000	150,000	120,000	(a) (b)	(150,000) (120,000)	500,000
Retained earnings.	558,240	222,850	160,000	(a) (b)	(222,850) (160,000)	558,240
Retained earnings of investee		9,950		(a)	(9,950)	
Total liabilities & stockholders' equity	5,858,240	1,093,000	830,000		(718,240)	7,063,000

Working Paper for Consolidated Balance Sheet on Date of Business Combination The working paper for consolidated balance sheet of Placer Corporation and subsidiaries on December 31, Year 2, the date of the purchase-type business combination, appears on page 472, and the related working paper eliminations are as follows:

PLACER CORPORATION AND SUBSIDIARIES
Working Paper Eliminations
December 31, Year 2

(a) Common Stock—Shabot 200,000

Paid-in Capital in Excess of Par—Shabot 150,000

Retained Earnings—Shabot. 222,850

Retained Earnings of Investee—Shabot 9,950

Goodwill—Placer 10,000

　　　Investment in Shabot Company Common Stock—

　　　Placer 476,240

　　　Minority Interest in Net Assets of Subsidiaries

　　　($582,800 × 0.20). 116,560

To eliminate intercompany investment and equity accounts of Shabot Company on date of business combination; to allocate excess of cost over current fair values (and carrying amounts) of identifiable net assets acquired to goodwill; and to establish minority interest in net assets of Shabot on date of business combination.

(b) Common Stock—Sur. 80,000

Paid-in Capital in Excess of Par—Sur. 120,000

Retained Earnings—Sur. 160,000

Goodwill—Placer ($1,950 + $20,000) 21,950

　　　Investment in Sur Company Common Stock—Placer ... 182,000

　　　Investment in Sur Company Common Stock—Shabot ... 91,950

　　　Minority Interest in Net Assets of Subsidiaries

　　　($360,000 × 0.30). 108,000

To eliminate intercompany investments and equity accounts of Sur Company on date of business combination; to allocate excess of cost over current fair values (and carrying amounts) of identifiable net assets acquired to goodwill; and to establish minority interest in net assets of Sur on date of business combination.

The following two aspects of the working paper eliminations deserve special emphasis:

1 In elimination (*a*), Shabot Company's Retained Earnings of Investee account balance on the date of the business combination is reduced to zero. Because

Placer Corporation is the parent company in the Placer–Shabot–Sur business combination, Shabot's ownership of 20,000 shares of Sur's outstanding common stock on the date of the combination is not construed as an installment acquisition by Placer; thus consolidated retained earnings on the date of combination does not include Shabot's share of Sur's retained earnings.

2 In elimination (*b*), both the $20,000 goodwill acquired by Placer (see page 472) and the goodwill implicit in Shabot's investment in Sur ($2,000 − $50 = $1,950) are included in consolidated goodwill, because the current fair values of Sur's identifiable net assets equaled their carrying amounts on the date of combination. The entire goodwill is attributable to Placer because of the existence of minority interests in both Shabot and Sur.

Working Paper Eliminations Subsequent to Business Combination For the year ended December 31, Year 3, Shabot Company had income of $150,000 (exclusive of investment income from Sur) and declared dividends of $60,000; Sur Company had net income of $80,000 and declared dividends of $20,000. These operating results are recorded in the investment accounts of Placer and Shabot on page 475, under the equity method of accounting. The working paper eliminations for Placer Corporation and subsidiaries on December 31, Year 3, are on page 476.

Parent company's common stock owned by a subsidiary

The traditional approach by accountants to problems of *reciprocal shareholdings* involved complex mathematical allocations of the individual affiliated companies' net income or loss to consolidated net income or loss and to minority interest. These allocations typically involved matrices or simultaneous equations.

Accountants have come to question the traditional approach to reciprocal shareholdings. The principal criticism is that strict application of mathematical allocations for reciprocal shareholdings violates the *going-concern* aspect of consolidated financial statements in favor of a *liquidation* approach. A related criticism is the emphasis of the traditional approach on *legal form* of the reciprocal shareholdings, rather than upon *economic substance.* When a subsidiary acquires outstanding common stock of the parent company, it has been argued, the shares of parent company common stock owned by the subsidiary are in essence *treasury stock* to the consolidated entity. The treasury stock treatment for reciprocal shareholdings was sanctioned by the American Accounting Association and by the AICPA as follows:

> Shares of the controlling company's capital stock owned by a subsidiary before the date of acquisition of control should be treated in consolidation as treasury stock. Any subsequent acquisition or sale by a subsidiary should likewise be treated in the consolidated statements as though it had been the act of the controlling company.[5]

> Shares of the parent held by a subsidiary should not be treated as outstanding stock in the consolidated balance sheet.[6]

---

[5] *Accounting and Reporting Standards for Corporate Financial Statements,* "Consolidated Financial Statements," AAA (Madison: 1957), p. 44.
[6] *ARB No. 51,* p. 45.

Investment accounts of
parent company and
subsidiary

PLACER CORPORATION LEDGER
Investment in Shabot Company Common Stock

Date	Explanation	Debit	Credit	Balance
12/31/2	Acquisition of 160,000 shares	476,240		476,240 dr
12/6/3	Dividends: $0.30 a share		48,000	428,240 dr
12/31/3	Share of net income ($150,000 × 0.80)	120,000		548,240 dr
12/31/3	Amortization of goodwill ($10,000 ÷ 40)		250	547,990 dr

Investment in Sur Company Common Stock

Date	Explanation	Debit	Credit	Balance
12/31/2	Acquisition of 36,000 shares	182,000		182,000 dr
12/6/3	Dividends: $0.25 a share		9,000	173,000 dr
12/31/3	Share of net income ($80,000 × 0.45)	36,000		209,000 dr
12/31/3	Amortization of goodwill ($20,000 ÷ 40)		500	208,500 dr

SHABOT COMPANY LEDGER
Investment in Sur Company Common Stock

Date	Explanation	Debit	Credit	Balance
12/31/1	Acquisition of 20,000 shares	82,000		82,000 dr
12/6/2	Dividends: $0.25 a share		5,000	77,000 dr
12/31/2	Share of net income ($60,000 × 0.25)	15,000		92,000 dr
12/31/2	Amortization of goodwill ($2,000 ÷ 40)		50	91,950 dr
12/6/3	Dividends: $0.25 a share		5,000	86,950 dr
12/31/3	Share of net income ($80,000 × 0.25)	20,000		106,950 dr
12/31/3	Amortization of goodwill ($2,000 ÷ 40)		50	106,900 dr

The authors concur with the view that a subsidiary's shareholdings of parent company voting common stock in essence are treasury stock to the consolidated entity. This position is analogous to that set forth in Chapter 9 for intercompany bondholdings. There, the point was made that a subsidiary acquiring parent company bonds payable in the open market is acting on behalf of the parent in the reacquisition of the bonds for the consolidated entity's treasury.

PLACER CORPORATION AND SUBSIDIARIES
Working Paper Eliminations
December 31, Year 3

(a) Common Stock—Shabot 200,000

Paid-in Capital in Excess of Par—Shabot 150,000

Retained Earnings—Shabot. 222,850

Retained Earnings of Investee—Shabot 9,950

Intercompany Investment Income—Placer.......... 120,000

Goodwill—Placer ($10,000 − $250) 9,750

    Investment in Shabot Company Common Stock—

    Placer 547,990

    Dividends—Shabot.................... 60,000

    Minority Interest in Net Assets of Subsidiaries

    ($116,560 − $12,000) 104,560

To eliminate intercompany investment and equity accounts of Shabot Company at beginning of year, and subsidiary dividends; to allocate unamortized excess of cost over current fair values of identifiable net assets to goodwill; and to establish minority interest in net assets of Shabot at beginning of year ($116,560), less dividends to minority shareholders ($60,000 × 0.20 = $12,000).

(b) Common Stock—Sur. 80,000

Paid-in Capital in Excess of Par—Sur. 120,000

Retained Earnings—Sur. 160,000

Intercompany Investment Income—Placer.......... 36,000

Intercompany Investment Income—Shabot 20,000

Goodwill—Placer [($1,950 − $50) + ($20,000 − $500)] . 21,400

    Investment in Sur Company Common Stock—

    Placer 208,500

    Investment in Sur Company Common Stock—

    Shabot....................................... 106,900

    Dividends—Sur 20,000

    Minority Interest in Net Assets of Subsidiaries

    ($108,000 − $6,000) 102,000

To eliminate intercompany investment and equity accounts of Sur Company at beginning of year, and subsidiary dividends; to allocate unamortized excess of cost over current fair values of identifiable net assets to goodwill; and to establish minority interest in net assets of Sur at beginning of year ($108,000), less dividends to minority shareholders ($20,000 × 0.30 = $6,000).

(c) Minority Interest in Net Income of Subsidiaries

    [($150,000 × 0.20) + ($80,000 × 0.30)]. 54,000

    Minority Interest in Net Assets of Subsidiaries... 54,000

To establish minority interest in subsidiaries' net income for Year 3.

To illustrate the accounting and working eliminations for parent company's common stock owned by a subsidiary, assume that on May 1, Year 7, the beginning of a fiscal year, Springer Company acquired for $50,000 in the open market 5,000 shares, or 5%, of the outstanding $1 par common stock of its parent company, Prospect Corporation. On April 30, Year 8, Prospect declared and paid a cash dividend of $1.20 a share.

Springer prepares the following journal entries for its investment in Prospect's common stock, under the appropriate cost method of accounting:

Subsidiary's journal entries for investment in parent company's common stock

SPRINGER COMPANY
Journal Entries

Year 7
May 1 Investment in Prospect Corporation Common Stock . 50,000
            Cash.   50,000
            To record acquisition of 5,000 shares of parent company's outstanding common stock at $10 a share.

Year 8
Apr. 30 Cash. 6,000
            Intercompany Dividend Revenue   6,000
            To record dividend of $1.20 a share on 5,000 shares of parent company's common stock.

The working paper eliminations for Prospect Corporation and subsidiary on April 30, Year 8, are the following:

PROSPECT CORPORATION AND SUBSIDIARY
Partial Working Paper Eliminations
April 30, Year 8

(b) Treasury Stock—Prospect 50,000
       Investment in Prospect Corporation Common Stock
       —Springer   50,000
       To transfer subsidiary's investment in parent company's common stock to treasury stock category.

(c) Intercompany Dividend Revenue—Springer 6,000
       Dividends—Prospect   6,000
       To eliminate parent company dividends received by subsidiary.

The effect of the second elimination is to remove the parent company dividends applicable to the consolidated treasury stock. The result is that, in the consolidated statement of retained earnings, dividends are in the amount of $114,000 ($120,000 − $6,000 = $114,000), representing the $1.20 a share dividend on 95,000 shares of parent company common stock that are outstanding from the viewpoint of the consolidated entity.

Concluding comments on special problems

In this chapter we have discussed a number of special problems that might arise in the preparation of consolidated financial statements. We have purposely not discussed earnings per share computations for a consolidated entity, because in most circumstances the standards for earnings per share computations set forth in *Intermediate Accounting* of this series apply to the computation of consolidated earnings per share. The problems that arise in earnings per share computations when a subsidiary has securities that are common stock equivalents or are otherwise *dilutive* are highly technical and too specialized to warrant inclusion in our discussion of the basic concepts relating to consolidated financial statements.

Unresolved problems in accounting principles for consolidated financial statements

Generally accepted accounting principles for consolidated financial statements, described and illustrated in Chapters 5 through 10, are considered to be unsatisfactory in several respects by many accountants. Perhaps the most comprehensive critique of accounting principles for consolidations was provided by a major CPA firm as follows:[7]

(1) **Criteria for Inclusion or Exclusion**—Problems continue to exist as to the appropriateness or inappropriateness of consolidating certain units. There seems to be a wide range of practice in regard to leaving companies out of consolidation; the reasons vary from too small a proportion of ownership (even though more than 50%) to the assertion that the unconsolidated subsidiary is in a business completely unrelated to the main function of the entity. Also, although a consensus may have been reached on Western European countries, there is still some confusion about whether or not foreign subsidiaries are to be consolidated.

(2) **Combined Statements**—Not enough emphasis has been given to situations where combined statements—such as those of complementary companies owned by the same individual—would be the proper economic representation. A reevaluation of situations under which combined statements may be appropriate would also help answer the component reporting question. For example, it might be determined, based on the entity theory, that a separate presentation of the financial statements of certain kinds of components would not be a fair presentation in conformity with generally accepted accounting principles, because the entity as a whole is not reflected in the financial statements.

(3) **Related Parties**—Although not directly brought up by *ARB 51,* the question of related parties, or at least that part of it relating to components, is

---

[7] Touche Ross & Co., *Open Line: A Letter to Accounting Educators,* February 1979. See also Benjamin S. Neuhausen, "Consolidation and the Equity Method—Time for an Overhaul," *Journal of Accountancy,* (February 1982), pp. 54–66.

exceedingly difficult. Questions are turning up on a daily basis, probably because of a very real predisposition on the part of investors and the SEC that transactions between or among related parties are "tainted" and in a majority of circumstances probably result in an accounting effect which is incorrect—at least if a profit has been recognized by the reporting component. . . .

(4) **Change in Ownership**—When the parent company sells some of its investment in an investee, the result is a gain or loss. When the investee sells some of its stock (resulting in the same proportionate change in ownership of the investor) the result is a capital transaction.* In effect, the result is the same, but the accounting is different. This must be made consistent.

(5) **Parent Company Only Statements**—Clarification is needed as to the usefulness of parent company only statements. Rarely should they be the primary presentation for shareholders. Their presentation as supplementary data should be carefully defined; . . .

In addition, the equity method of accounting for investments in subsidiaries should be required in parent company financial statements, even where the parent statements are not the primary presentation.

(6) **Stock Dividends of Subsidiaries**—. . . Capitalization of retained earnings by subsidiaries should be reflected in consolidated statements.

(7) **Elimination of Intercompany Profit**—Elimination based on proportion of ownership is economically indefensible. Resolving the related party question [(3) on page 478] will possibly bear this out.

(8) **Retained Earnings Available for Dividends**—The widespread use of equity accounting occasioned by *APB 18* has raised a potential conflict between the legal determination of retained earnings available for dividends and the accounting definition of retained earnings to be reported in consolidated financial statements. Some state laws do not recognize the equity accounting principle and, therefore, a company incorporated in those states may not pay dividends out of retained earnings recognized on the equity method.

This has been a long-standing conflict, but it was not significant prior to the adoption of *APB Opinion 18.* However, with equity accounting being applied to the earnings of a nonsubsidiary investee, there may be a substantial time lag between the accrual of current earnings and the remission of those earnings. . . .

(9) **Parent Cost "Push Down"**—Where separate financial statements of a subsidiary are presented, it seems appropriate that the parent's cost be "pushed down" into the financial statements of the subsidiary (so that current fair values of the subsidiary's net assets on the date of combination are reflected).

(10) **Minority Interest Represented by Preferred Stock**—Where all or substantially all of the minority interest in a subsidiary company is represented by outstanding nonconvertible preferred stock of the subsidiary, the preferred dividend requirement should probably be reflected in the consolidated accounts as interest expense and the preferred stock minority interest reflected as subordinated debt. This would also be the appropriate accounting for all preferred stocks with mandatory redemption features.

It is evident from the foregoing that considerable reform is needed in the accounting principles and practices for consolidated financial statements. In 1982, the FASB added to its agenda a project entitled "Consolidations and the Equity Method" to meet this need.

---

* See discussion on page 455 regarding the SEC's position.

REVIEW QUESTIONS

1 ***APB Opinion No. 16,*** "Business Combinations," requires use of the purchase method of accounting for a parent company's acquisition of all or part of the minority interest in net assets of a subsidiary, even though the business combination was a pooling-type combination. Discuss the reasoning in support of this requirement.

2 If a parent company acquires the minority interest in net assets of a subsidiary at less than carrying amount, what accounting treatment is appropriate for the difference? Explain.

3 Why does a parent company realize a gain or a loss when a subsidiary issues common stock to the public at a price per share that differs from the carrying amount per share of the parent company's investment in the subsidiary's common stock? Explain.

4 Explain how the minority interest in net assets of a subsidiary is affected by the parent company's ownership of 70% of the subsidiary's outstanding common stock and 60% of the subsidiary's outstanding 7%, cumulative, fully participating preferred stock.

5 Describe how the parent company's accounting records are affected when a subsidiary acquires for its treasury all or part of its outstanding common stock owned by minority shareholders.

6 "The treasury stock treatment for shares of parent company voting common stock owned by a subsidiary overstates consolidated net income and understates the minority interest in net income of the subsidiary." Do you agree? Explain.

7 Shares of its own common stock held by a corporation in its treasury are not entitled to dividends. However, a subsidiary receives dividends on shares of its parent company's common stock owned by the subsidiary. For consolidated financial statements, these parent company shares are considered equivalent to treasury stock of the consolidated entity. Is there an inconsistency in this treatment? Explain.

8 Does the declaration of a stock dividend by a subsidiary necessitate any special treatment in working paper eliminations? Explain.

9 Is a gain or a loss realized by a parent company on the sale of part of its investment in common stock of a subsidiary eliminated in the preparation of consolidated financial statements? Explain.

EXERCISES

Ex. 10-1 Select the best answer for each of the following multiple-choice questions:

1 A subsidiary's issuance of voting common stock to the public for net proceeds of $26 a share results in:
  a A nonoperating gain if the per-share carrying amount of the parent company's investment in the subsidiary is more than $26 a share
  b An extraordinary gain if the per-share carrying amount of the parent company's investment in the subsidiary is less than $26 a share

    c An extraordinary loss if the per-share carrying amount of the parent company's investment in the subsidiary is more than $26 a share

    d A nonoperating loss if the per-share carrying amount of the parent company's investment in the subsidiary is more than $26 a share

2 In consolidated financial statements, shares of the parent company's common stock that are owned by the subsidiary should be treated as:

    a Outstanding common stock

    b Retired common stock

    c Treasury stock—common

    d Some other item

3 The minority interest of a subsidiary's preferred shareholders in the subsidiary's net assets should be computed by multiplying the number of shares of preferred stock owned by minority shareholders by the:

    a Call price per share of the preferred stock

    b Liquidation value per share of the preferred stock

    c Stated value per share of the preferred stock

    d Current fair value per share of the preferred stock

4 Treasury stock of a subsidiary should be treated in consolidation as:

    a Retired

    b Treasury stock of the consolidated entity

    c An offset to consolidated retained earnings

    d Treasury stock of the parent company

5 A parent company should use the equity method of accounting for an investment in the preferred stock of a subsidiary:

    a In all cases

    b If the subsidiary declares a dividend on the preferred stock

    c If the preferred stock is participating

    d If the subsidiary passes a dividend and the preferred stock is cumulative

6 When a parent company acquires both preferred stock and common stock of the subsidiary in a business combination, goodwill arising from the combination should be computed based on:

    a Cost allocated to preferred stock only

    b Cost allocated to common stock only

    c Cost allocated to both preferred stock and common stock

    d Some other measure

Ex. 10-2 On August 1, Year 4, the beginning of a fiscal year, Pressman Corporation acquired 95% of the outstanding common stock of Sycamore Company in a pooling-type business combination. Among the intercompany transactions between Pressman and Sycamore subsequent to August 1, Year 4, were the following:

    (1) On May 31, Year 5, Sycamore declared a 10% stock dividend on its 10,000 outstanding shares of $10 par common stock having a current fair value of $18 a share. The 1,000 shares of the stock dividend were issued June 18, Year 5.

    (2) On July 28, Year 5, Sycamore acquired in the open market, for $15,000, 1,000 of the 100,000 outstanding shares of Pressman's $1 par common stock. Pressman declared no dividends during the year ended July 31, Year 5.

    Prepare working paper eliminations on July 31, Year 5, for Pressman Corporation and subsidiary, for the foregoing intercompany transactions.

Ex. 10-3 The stockholders' equity section of Stegg Company's August 31, Year 2, balance sheet was as follows:

8% cumulative preferred stock, $1 par, dividends in arrears two years, authorized, issued, and outstanding 100,000 shares, callable at $1.10 a share plus dividends in arrears	$ 100,000
Common stock, $2 par, authorized, issued, and outstanding 100,000 shares	200,000
Paid-in capital in excess of par—common stock	150,000
Retained earnings	750,000
Total stockholders' equity	$1,200,000

On August 31, Year 2, Panay Corporation acquired 50,000 shares of Stegg's outstanding preferred stock and 75,000 shares of Stegg's outstanding common stock for a total cost—including out-of-pocket costs—of $1,030,500. The current fair values of Stegg's identifiable net assets were equal to their carrying amounts on August 31, Year 2.

Answer the following questions (show supporting computations):

a What amount of the $1,030,500 total cost is assignable to Stegg's preferred stock?
b What is the minority interest of preferred shareholders in Stegg's net assets on August 31, Year 2?
c What is the amount of goodwill acquired by Panay August 31, Year 2?
d What is the minority interest of common shareholders in Stegg's net assets on August 31, Year 2?

Ex. 10-4 On March 31, Year 4, the consolidated balance sheet of Polberg Corporation and its 85%-owned subsidiary, Serrano Company, showed goodwill of $65,400 and minority interest in net assets of subsidiary of $22,800. On April 1, Year 4, Polberg paid $10,000 to minority shareholders who owned 500 of Serrano's 10,000 shares of issued common stock.

Compute goodwill and minority interest in net assets of subsidiary for inclusion in the consolidated balance sheet of Polberg Corporation and subsidiary on April 1, Year 4.

Ex. 10-5 On January 2, Year 3, Prester Corporation organized Shire Company, paying $40,000 for 10,000 shares of Shire's $1 par common stock. On January 3, Year 3, before beginning operations, Shire issued 2,000 shares of its $1 par common stock to the public for net proceeds of $11,000.

Compute the nonoperating gain or loss to Prester that resulted from Shire's issuance of common stock to the public.

Ex. 10-6 On September 30, Year 6, prior to the declaration of a 15% stock dividend by its subsidiary, Sabro Company, on that date, Placard Corporation's accountant prepared the following tentative working paper elimination:

(a) Common Stock, $2 par—Sabro	80,000	
Paid-in Capital in Excess of Par—Sabro	40,000	
Retained Earnings—Sabro ($130,000 − $10,000)	120,000	
Retained Earnings of Subsidiary—Placard	10,000	
Intercompany Investment Income—Placard	70,000	
Goodwill—Sabro	20,000	
Investment in Sabro Company Common Stock—Placard		340,000

To eliminate intercompany investment and equity accounts of subsidiary at beginning of year, and investment income from subsidiary; and to allocate excess of cost over current fair values (and carrying amounts) of identifiable net assets acquired to goodwill.

The current fair value of the dividend shares issued by Sabro was $5 a share. Placard had net sales of $840,200 and total costs and expenses of $668,500 for the year ended September 30, Year 6.

a Prepare a revised working paper elimination for Placard Corporation and subsidiary on September 30, Year 6, to reflect the effects of Sabro's stock dividend. Omit explanation, but show supporting computations.

b Prepare a closing entry for Placard Corporation on September 30, Year 6. Omit explanation, but show supporting computations.

Ex. 10-7 On December 31, Year 4, the date of a purchase-type business combination between Portland Corporation and Salem Company, Salem had 50,000 shares of $5 par common stock authorized, 20,000 shares issued (total net issue proceeds were $160,000), and 500 shares in the treasury, with a total cost of $5,500. The balance of Salem's Retained Earnings account was $240,000 on December 31, Year 4.

Prepare a working paper elimination for Portland Corporation and subsidiary on December 31, Year 4, to account for the subsidiary's treasury stock as though it had been retired.

Ex. 10-8 Simplex Company, the partially owned subsidiary of Polyglot Corporation, had net income of $342,800 for the year ended May 31, Year 6. Simplex declared a dividend of $12 a share on its 10,000 shares of outstanding 12%, $100 par, cumulative preferred stock, and a dividend of $8 a share on its 80,000 shares of outstanding $1 par common stock. Polyglot owns 7,000 shares of preferred stock and 60,000 shares of common stock of Simplex. There were no dividends in arrears on the preferred stock.

Prepare a working paper as on page 463 to show the allocation of Simplex Company's $342,800 net income for the year ended May 31, Year 6, to consolidated net income and to the minority interest in net income of subsidiary.

Ex. 10-9 On January 2, Year 7, Prince Corporation organized Sabine Company with authorized common stock of 10,000 shares, $5 par. Prince acquired 4,000 shares of Sabine's common stock at $8 a share, and Samnite Company, a wholly owned subsidiary of Prince, acquired the 6,000 remaining authorized shares of Sabine's common stock at $8 a share. For the year ended December 31, Year 7, Sabine had net income of $80,000 and declared dividends of $2 a share on December 28, Year 7, payable on January 25, Year 8.

Prepare journal entries under the equity method of accounting to record the operating results of Sabine Company for Year 7 in the accounting records of **a** Prince Corporation, and **b** Samnite Company. Omit explanations.

Case 10-1 **CASES**

Scarbo Company, a wholly owned subsidiary of Poller Corporation, is in need of additional long-term financing. Under instructions from Poller, Scarbo offers 5,000 shares of its previously unissued $2 par common stock to shareholders of Poller at a price of $10 a share. The offer is fully subscribed by Poller's shareholders, and the common stock is issued for $50,000 cash on June 30, Year 6.

After the common stock issuance, Poller owns 45,000 shares, or 90%, of the 50,000 outstanding shares of Scarbo common stock, and shareholders of Poller own 5,000 shares, or 10%, of Scarbo's outstanding common stock. By comparing Poller's 90% interest in Scarbo's net assets after the common stock issuance with the parent company's 100% interest in the subsidiary's net assets before the stock issuance, Poller's accountant computed a $4,000 nonoperating gain for entry in Poller's accounting records. The controller of Poller objected to the accountant's entry. The controller pointed out that the 5,000 shares of Scarbo common stock were issued to Poller's shareholders, not to outsiders, and that it is a basic accounting principle that a corporation cannot profit from common stock issuances to its shareholders.

Instructions Evaluate the objections of Poller Corporation's controller.

Case 10-2 On January 2, Year 3, Phoenix Corporation acquired for cash all the outstanding common stock of Scottsdale Company and 70% of the outstanding common stock of Sonoma Company. Included among the assets of Scottsdale are investments in 80% of the outstanding common stock of Spokane Company and 30% of the outstanding common stock of Sonoma Company.

Instructions Discuss the accounting principles that Phoenix Corporation should use for its investment in Scottsdale Company and in its financial statements issued subsequent to the business combination with Scottsdale.

Case 10-3 On March 1, Year 1, Paton Corporation, a manufacturer, organized a wholly owned subsidiary finance company, Sterling Company, to acquire Paton's installment contracts for sales of its products. Paton acquired all 10,000 shares of Sterling's $5 par common stock on March 1, Year 1.

By February 28, Year 4, Sterling had accumulated a retained earnings balance of $120,000, which also was reflected in Paton Corporation's Retained Earnings of Subsidiary account, under the equity method of accounting. As of the close of business February 28, Year 4, Sterling declared and issued a 100% stock dividend. In connection with the dividend, Sterling transferred $50,000 from its Retained Earnings ledger account to its Common Stock account.

The bank that provides Sterling's line of credit has requested separate financial statements for both Paton and Sterling, as well as consolidated financial statements, for the year ended February 28, Year 4. Paton's controller is concerned about the inconsistency resulting from the fact that Paton's Retained Earnings of Subsidiary ledger account has a balance of $120,000 on February 28, Year 4, but Sterling's Retained Earnings account balance is $70,000 on that date. The controller asks your opinion of the propriety of transferring $50,000 from Paton's Retained Earnings of Subsidiary ledger account to its Paid-in Capital in Excess of Par account.

Instructions What is your opinion of the controller's proposal? Explain.

PROBLEMS

10-1 Scrip Company, the 80%-owned subsidiary of Pinch Corporation, had 10,000 shares of $5 par common stock outstanding on March 31, Year 5, the date of the Pinch–Scrip business combination, with total stockholders' equity of $300,000 and total paid-in capital equal in amount to retained earnings on that date. Goodwill in the amount of $40,000 (remaining economic life of 40 years) and minority interest in net assets of subsidiary of $60,000 appeared in the consolidated balance sheet of Pinch Corporation and subsidiary on March 31, Year 5. The current fair values of Scrip's identifiable net assets equaled their carrying amounts on March 31, Year 5.

On April 1, Year 5, Pinch paid $44,000 to a minority shareholder for 1,000 shares of Scrip common stock. For the year ended March 31, Year 6, Scrip had net income of $90,000 and declared and paid dividends of $3 a share (during March, Year 6).

Instructions Prepare working paper eliminations for Pinch Corporation and subsidiary on March 31, Year 6. Pinch amortizes goodwill over a 40-year economic life. Disregard income taxes.

10-2 On January 2, Year 6, Prime Corporation issued 50,000 shares of $10 par (current fair value $25 a share) common stock and paid $140,000 out-of-pocket costs for all the outstanding common stock of Showboat Company in a pooling-type business combination. On the date of the combination, Showboat's stockholders' equity consisted of the following:

Common stock, $1 par	$400,000
Paid-in capital in excess of par	300,000
Retained earnings	250,000
Total paid-in capital and retained earnings	$950,000
Less: 20,000 shares of treasury stock, at cost	50,000
Total stockholders' equity	$900,000

On December 29, Year 6, Showboat declared a dividend of $0.10 a share, payable in Year 7. For the year ended December 31, Year 6, Showboat had net income of $90,000.

Instructions

a Prepare journal entries in the accounting records of Prime Corporation to record the operating results of Showboat Company for Year 6, under the equity method of accounting. Disregard income taxes.

b Prepare working paper eliminations for Prime Corporation and subsidiary on December 31, Year 6. Disregard income taxes.

10-3 The working paper eliminations for Pumble Corporation and its pooled subsidiary on October 31, Year 9, were as follows:

PUMBLE CORPORATION AND SUBSIDIARY
Working Paper Eliminations
October 31, Year 9

(a) Common Stock—Salton	10,000	
Paid-in Capital in Excess of Par—Salton	60,000	
Retained Earnings—Salton ($80,000 × 0.02)	1,600	
Retained Earnings of Subsidiary—Pumble ($80,000 × 0.98)	78,400	
Intercompany Investment Income—Pumble ($40,000 × 0.98)	39,200	
Investment in Salton Company Common Stock—Pumble ($180,000 × 0.98)		176,400
Dividends—Salton		10,000
Minority Interest in Net Assets of Subsidiary ($3,000 − $200)		2,800

To eliminate intercompany investment and related accounts for stockholders' equity of subsidiary at beginning of year, and investment income from subsidiary; and to establish minority interest in net assets of subsidiary at beginning of year ($150,000 × 0.02 = $3,000), less minority dividends ($10,000 × 0.02 = $200).

(b) Minority Interest in Net Income of Subsidiary ($40,000 × 0.02)	800	
Minority Interest in Net Assets of Subsidiary		800

To establish minority interest in net income of subsidiary for year ended October 31, Year 9.

On November 1, Year 9, Salton issued 1,000 additional shares of $1 par common stock to Pumble for $20 a share. (Out-of-pocket costs of the stock issuance may be disregarded.) On October 31, Year 10, Salton declared a dividend of $2 a share, and for the year ended October 31, Year 10, Salton had net income of $35,000.

Instructions

a Prepare journal entries in the accounting records of Pumble Corporation to record the operating results of Salton Company for the year ended October 31, Year 10, under the equity method of accounting. Round Pumble's new percentage interest in Salton to two decimal places, and all dollar amounts to the nearest dollar. Disregard income taxes.

b Prepare working paper eliminations for Pumble Corporation and subsidiary on October 31, Year 10. Round all amounts to the nearest dollar. Disregard income taxes.

10-4 Separate and consolidated financial statements of Peterson Corporation and its wholly owned subsidiary, Swanson Company, for the year ended May 31, Year 4, appear on page 487. The two companies use intercompany accounts only for receivables and payables.

Additional information

(1) All of Swanson's identifiable net assets were fairly valued at their carrying amounts on May 31, Year 2—the date of the Peterson–Swanson business combination. Thus, the $50,000 excess of Peterson's investment in Swanson over the carrying amounts of Swanson's identifiable net assets was attributable to goodwill with an economic life of 40 years.

(2) Peterson sells merchandise to Swanson at Peterson's regular markup.

(3) Swanson acquired 1,000 shares of Peterson's common stock on June 10, Year 3, and Peterson acquired its treasury stock on May 26, Year 4.

Instructions Reconstruct the working paper eliminations for Peterson Corporation and subsidiary on May 31, Year 4. Disregard income taxes, and omit explanations for the eliminations.

10-5 Financial statements of Pomerania Corporation and its two subsidiaries for the year ended December 31, Year 8, are shown on page 488.

Additional information

(1) Pomerania Corporation's Investment in Slovakia Company Common Stock ledger account appears as follows:

Investment in Slovakia Company Common Stock

Date	Explanation	Debit	Credit	Balance
Year 8				
Jan. 2	Cost of 5,000 shares	71,400		71,400 dr
June 30	20% of dividend declared		9,000	62,400 dr
June 30	20% of net income for			
	Jan. 2–June 30	12,000		74,400 dr
July 1	Cost of 15,000 shares	223,200		297,600 dr
Dec. 31	80% of dividend declared		24,000	273,600 dr
Dec. 31	80% of net income for			
	July 1–Dec. 31	32,000		305,600 dr

PETERSON CORPORATION AND SUBSIDIARY
Separate and Consolidated Financial Statements
For Year Ended May 31, Year 4

	Peterson Corporation	Swanson Company	Consolidated
Income Statements			
Revenue			
Net sales	$10,000,000	$4,600,000	$12,900,000
Other revenue	270,000	20,000	38,250
Total revenue	$10,270,000	$4,620,000	$12,938,250
Costs and expenses			
Cost of goods sold	$ 6,700,000	$3,082,000	$ 8,085,300
Other operating expenses . .	2,920,000	1,288,000	4,209,250
Total costs and ex-			
penses	$ 9,620,000	$4,370,000	$12,294,550
Net income	$ 650,000	$ 250,000	$ 643,700
Statements of			
Retained Earnings			
Retained earnings, beginning			
of year	$ 2,420,000	$ 825,000	$ 2,529,300
Add: Net income.	650,000	250,000	643,700
Subtotals	$ 3,070,000	$1,075,000	$ 3,173,000
Less: Dividends	300,000	175,000	297,000
Retained earnings, end of			
year.	$ 2,770,000	$ 900,000	$ 2,876,000
Balance Sheets			
Assets			
Intercompany receivables			
(payables)	$ 520,000	$ (520,000)	
Short-term investments.	400,000	150,000	$ 530,000
Inventories	1,100,000	610,000	1,693,500
Investment in Swanson Com-			
pany common stock	1,097,500		
Other assets	2,800,000	1,370,000	4,170,000
Goodwill			47,500
Total assets	$ 5,917,500	$1,610,000	$ 6,441,000
Liabilities &			
Stockholders' Equity			
Liabilities	$ 2,075,000	$ 560,000	$ 2,635,000
Common stock, $10 par	1,000,000	150,000	1,000,000
Retained earnings.	2,770,000	900,000	2,876,000
Retained earnings of sub-			
sidiary	122,500		
Treasury stock	(50,000)		(70,000)
Total liabilities & stock-			
holders' equity	$ 5,917,500	$1,610,000	$ 6,441,000

POMERANIA CORPORATION AND SUBSIDIARIES
Separate Financial Statements
For Year Ended December 31, Year 8

	Pomerania Corporation	Slovakia Company	Sylvania Company
Income Statements			
Revenue			
Net sales	$1,120,000	$900,000	$700,000
Intercompany sales	140,000		
Intercompany investment income	44,000		
Total revenue	$1,304,000	$900,000	$700,000
Costs and expenses			
Cost of goods sold	$ 800,000	$650,000	$550,000
Intercompany cost of goods sold.	100,000		
Operating expenses.	300,000	150,000	130,000
Total costs and expenses	$1,200,000	$800,000	$680,000
Net income	$ 104,000	$100,000	$ 20,000
Statements of Retained Earnings			
Retained earnings, beginning of year	$ 126,200	$107,000	$100,000
Add: New income	104,000	100,000	20,000
Subtotals	$ 230,200	$207,000	$120,000
Less: Dividends	22,000	75,000	
Retained earnings, end of year	$ 208,200	$132,000	$120,000
Balance Sheets			
Assets			
Intercompany receivables (payables).	$ 63,400	$ (41,000)	$ (22,400)
Inventories	290,000	90,000	115,000
Investment in Slovakia Company common stock	305,600		
Investment in Slovakia Company bonds	20,800		
Investment in Sylvania Company preferred stock	7,000		
Investment in Sylvania Company common stock	196,000		
Other assets.	836,400	555,000	510,000
Total assets.	$1,719,200	$604,000	$602,600
Liabilities and Stockholders' Equity			
Dividends payable	$ 22,000	$ 6,000	
Bonds payable	285,000	125,000	$125,000
Intercompany bonds payable		25,000	
Discount on bonds payable	(8,000)	(10,000)	
Discount on intercompany bonds payable. . . .		(2,000)	
Other liabilities	212,000	78,000	107,600
Preferred stock, $20 par	400,000		50,000
Common stock, $10 par.	600,000	250,000	200,000
Retained earnings	208,200	132,000	120,000
Total liabilities & stockholders' equity	$1,719,200	$604,000	$602,600

(2) The accountant for Pomerania made no equity-method journal entries for Pomerania's investments in Sylvania's preferred stock and common stock. Pomerania acquired 250 shares of Sylvania's fully participating noncumulative preferred stock for $7,000 and 14,000 shares of Sylvania's common stock for $196,000 on January 2, Year 8. Out-of-pocket costs of the business combination were negligible.

(3) Sylvania's December 31, Year 8, inventories included $22,400 of merchandise purchased from Pomerania for which no payment had been made.

(4) Pomerania acquired in the open market twenty-five $1,000 face amount 6% bonds of Slovakia for $20,800 on December 31, Year 8. The bonds have a December 31 interest payment date, and a maturity date of December 31, Year 10.

(5) Slovakia owed Pomerania $17,000 on December 31, Year 8, for a noninterest-bearing cash advance.

Instructions

a Prepare adjusting journal entries for Pomerania Corporation on December 31, Year 8, to account for investments in Sylvania Company preferred stock and common stock by the equity method. Disregard income taxes.

b Prepare a working paper for consolidated financial statements and related working paper eliminations for Pomerania Corporation and subsidiaries on December 31, Year 8. Disregard income taxes.

10-6 Plover Corporation acquired for $151,000, including direct out-of-pocket costs of the business combination, 100% of the common stock and 20% of the preferred stock of Starling Company on June 30, Year 1. On that date, Starling's retained earnings balance was $41,000. The current fair values of Starling's identifiable assets and liabilities and preferred stock did not differ materially from their carrying amounts on June 30, Year 1.

The separate financial statements of Plover and Starling for Year 2 are shown below and on page 490.

PLOVER CORPORATION AND SUBSIDIARY
Separate Financial Statements
For Year Ended December 31, Year 2

	Plover Corporation	Starling Company
Income Statements		
Revenue		
Net sales	$1,562,000	
Intercompany sales	238,000	
Earned revenue on contracts		$1,210,000
Intercompany earned revenue on contracts		79,000
Interest revenue	19,149	
Intercompany investment income	42,500	
Intercompany dividend revenue	500	
Intercompany gain on sale of land	4,000	
Intercompany interest revenue (expense)	851	(851)
Total revenue	$1,867,000	$1,288,149
Costs and expenses		
Cost of goods sold	$ 942,500	
Intercompany cost of goods sold	212,500	
Cost of earned revenue on contracts		$ 789,500

(*Continued*)

PLOVER CORPORATION AND SUBSIDIARY
Separate Financial Statements (concluded)
For Year Ended December 31, Year 2

	Plover Corporation	Starling Company
Income Statements		
Intercompany cost of earned revenue on contracts		62,500
Operating expenses	497,000	360,000
Interest expense	49,000	31,149
Total costs and expenses	$1,701,000	$1,243,149
Net income	$ 166,000	$ 45,000
Statements of Retained Earnings		
Retained earnings, beginning of year	$ 139,311	$ 49,500
Add: Net income	166,000	45,000
Subtotals.	$ 305,311	$ 94,500
Less: Dividends		2,500
Retained earnings, end of year	$ 305,311	$ 92,000
Balance Sheets		
Assets		
Intercompany receivables (payables)	$ 35,811	$ 21,189
Costs and estimated earnings in excess of billings on uncompleted contracts		30,100
Inventories	217,000	117,500
Investment in Starling Company common stock . .	202,000	
Land	34,000	42,000
Other plant assets (net)	717,000	408,000
Other assets	153,000	84,211
Total assets	$1,358,811	$ 703,000
Liabilities & Stockholders' Equity		
Dividends payable		$ 2,000
Mortgage notes payable	$ 592,000	389,000
Other liabilities	203,000	70,000
5% noncumulative, nonparticipating preferred stock, $1 par		50,000
Common stock, $10 par	250,000	100,000
Retained earnings	305,311	92,000
Retained earnings of subsidiary	8,500	
Total liabilities & stockholders' equity	$1,358,811	$ 703,000

Transactions between Plover and Starling during the year ended December 31, Year 2, follow:

(1) On January 2, Year 2, Plover sold land with an $11,000 carrying amount to Starling for $15,000. Starling made a $3,000 down payment and signed an 8% mortgage note payable in 12 equal quarterly payments of $1,135, including interest, beginning March 31, Year 2.

(2) Starling produced equipment for Plover under two separate contracts. The first contract, which was for office equipment, was begun and completed

during Year 2 at a cost to Starling of $17,500. Plover paid $22,000 cash for the equipment on April 17, Year 2. The second contract was begun on February 15, Year 2, but will not be completed until May of Year 3. Starling has incurred $45,000 costs under the second contract as of December 31, Year 2, and anticipates additional costs of $30,000 to complete the $95,000 contract. Starling accounts for all contracts under the percentage-of-completion method of accounting. Plover has made no journal entry in its accounting records for the uncompleted contract as of December 31, Year 2. Plover depreciates all its equipment by the straight-line method over a 10-year estimated economic life with no residual value. Plover takes a half year's depreciation in the year of acquisition of plant assets and includes depreciation in operating expenses.

(3) On December 1, Year 2, Starling declared a 5% cash dividend on its preferred stock, payable January 15, Year 3, to stockholders of record December 14, Year 2.

(4) Plover sells merchandise to Starling at an average markup of 12% of cost. During the year, Plover billed Starling $238,000 for merchandise shipped, for which Starling paid $211,000 by December 31, Year 2. Starling has $11,200 of this merchandise on hand on December 31, Year 2.

Instructions

a Reconstruct the Intercompany Receivables (Payables) accounts of the affiliates on December 31, Year 2.

b Prepare adjusting journal entries for December 31, Year 2, based on your analysis in *a* above.

c Prepare a working paper for consolidated financial statements and related working paper eliminations for Plover Corporation and subsidiary for Year 2. Round all computations to the nearest dollar. Disregard income taxes.

10-7 On February 1, Year 5, Pullard Corporation acquired all the outstanding common stock of Staley Company for $5,850,000, including direct out-of-pocket costs of the business combination, and 20% of Staley's preferred stock for $150,000. On the date of the combination, the carrying amounts and current fair values of Staley's identifiable assets and liabilities were as follows:

	Carrying amounts	Current fair values
Cash	$ 200,000	$ 200,000
Notes receivable	85,000	85,000
Accounts receivable (net)	980,000	980,000
Inventories	828,000	700,000
Land	1,560,000	2,100,000
Other plant assets	7,850,000	10,600,000
Accumulated depreciation	(3,250,000)	(4,000,000)
Other assets	140,000	50,000
Total assets	$8,393,000	$10,715,000
Notes payable	$ 115,000	$ 115,000
Accounts payable	400,000	400,000
7% bonds payable	5,000,000	5,000,000
Total liabilities	$5,515,000	$ 5,515,000

Preferred stock, noncumulative, nonparticipating; $5 par and call price per share; authorized, issued, and outstanding 150,000 shares . . . . $ 750,000

(Continued)

Common stock; $10 par; authorized, issued, and out-	
standing 100,000 shares	*1,000,000*
Paid-in capital in excess of par (common stock) . .	*122,000*
Retained earnings	*1,006,000*
Total stockholders' equity	*$2,878,000*
Total liabilities & stockholders' equity	*$8,393,000*

Separate financial statements of Pullard and Staley for the period ended October 31, Year 5, are shown below and on page 493.

PULLARD CORPORATION AND STALEY COMPANY
Separate Financial Statements
For Period Ended October 31, Year 5

	Pullard Corporation (year ended 10/31/5)	Staley Company (9 mos. ended 10/31/5)
Income Statements		
Revenue		
Net sales	$18,042,000	$5,530,000
Intercompany sales	158,000	230,000
Intercompany investment income	505,150	
Interest revenue	26,250	1,700
Intercompany interest revenue	78,750	
Total revenue	$18,810,150	$5,761,700
Costs and expenses		
Cost of goods sold	$10,442,000	$3,010,500
Intercompany cost of goods sold	158,000	149,500
Depreciation expense	1,103,000	588,750
Operating expenses	3,448,500	1,063,900
Interest expense	806,000	190,650
Intercompany interest expense		78,750
Total costs and expenses	$15,957,500	$5,082,050
Net income	$ 2,852,650	$ 679,650
Statements of Retained Earnings		
Retained earnings, beginning of period	$12,683,500	$1,006,000
Add: Net income	2,852,650	679,650
Retained earnings, end of period	$15,536,150	$1,685,650
Balance Sheets		
Assets		
Cash	$ 822,000	$ 530,000
Notes receivable		85,000
Accounts receivable (net)	2,723,700	1,346,400
Intercompany receivables	12,300	
Inventories	3,204,000	1,182,000
Investment in Staley Company common stock .	6,355,150	

(Continued)

PULLARD CORPORATION AND STALEY COMPANY
Separate Financial Statements (concluded)
For Period Ended October 31, Year 5

	Pullard Corporation (year ended 10/31/5)	Staley Company (9 mos. ended 10/31/5)
Investment in Staley Company preferred stock.	150,000	
Investment in Staley Company bonds	1,500,000	
Land	4,000,000	1,560,000
Other plant assets	17,161,000	7,850,000
Accumulated depreciation	(6,673,000)	(3,838,750)
Other assets	263,000	140,000
Total assets	$29,518,150	$8,854,650

Liabilities & Stockholders' Equity

Notes payable		$ 115,000
Accounts payable	$ 1,342,000	169,700
Intercompany payables		12,300
7% bonds payable		3,500,000
Intercompany 7% bonds payable		1,500,000
Long-term debt	10,000,000	
Preferred stock, $5 par		750,000
Common stock, $10 par	2,400,000	1,000,000
Paid-in capital in excess of par	240,000	122,000
Retained earnings	15,536,150	1,685,650
Total liabilities & stockholders' equity	$29,518,150	$8,854,650

By the fiscal year-end, October 31, Year 5, the following transactions had taken place:

(1) The balance of Staley's net accounts receivable on February 1, Year 5, had been collected.
(2) Staley's inventories on February 1, Year 5, had been debited to cost of goods sold. Staley uses the perpetual inventory system.
(3) Prior to February 1, Year 5, Pullard had acquired, at face amount, $1,500,000 of Staley's 7% bonds payable. The bonds mature on August 31, Year 11, with interest payable annually each August 31.
(4) As of February 1, Year 5, Staley's other plant assets had a composite remaining economic life of six years. Staley used the straight-line method of depreciation, with no residual value. Staley's depreciation expense for the nine months ended October 31, Year 5, was based on the former depreciation rates in effect prior to the business combination.
(5) The other assets consist entirely of long-term investments made by Staley and do not include any investment in Pullard.
(6) During the nine months ended October 31, Year 5, the following intercompany sales occurred:

	Pullard to Staley	Staley to Pullard
Net sales	$158,000	$230,000
Included in purchaser's inventories, Oct. 31, Year 5 .	36,000	12,000
Balance unpaid, Oct. 31, Year 5	16,800	22,000

Pullard sells to Staley at cost. Staley sells to Pullard at selling prices that include a gross profit margin of 35%. There were no intercompany sales prior to February 1, Year 5.

(7) Neither company declared dividends during the period covered by their separate financial statements.

(8) Staley's goodwill recognized in the business combination was $1,400,000. The companies' policy is to amortize intangible assets over a 20-year economic life, and to include the amortization among operating expenses.

(9) The $505,150 balance in Pullard's Intercompany Investment Income account is computed as follows:

Net income of Staley for nine months ended Oct. 31, Year 5 . . . . $679,650

Less: Amortization of differences between current fair values and
  carrying amounts of Staley's identifiable net assets on Feb. 1, Year
  5:

    Inventories—to cost of goods sold . . . . $(128,000)

    Other plant assets—depreciation [($6,600,000 −

    $4,600,000) ÷ 6] × $\frac{3}{4}$ 250,000

    Goodwill—amortization ($1,400,000 ÷ 20) × $\frac{3}{4}$ . .   52,500   174,500

    Balance, Oct. 31, Year 5 . . . . $505,150

Instructions Prepare a working paper for consolidated financial statements and related working paper eliminations for Pullard Corporation and subsidiary on October 31, Year 5. Round all computations to the nearest dollar. Disregard income taxes.

10-8 The separate financial statements of Pennington Corporation and its subsidiary, Singleton Company, for the year ended December 31, Year 5, are on page 495.

Additional information

(1) On January 2, Year 3, Pennington acquired from John Singleton, the sole shareholder of Singleton Company, for $440,000 cash, both a patent with a current fair value of $40,000 and 80% of the outstanding common stock of Singleton Company. Out-of-pocket costs of the business combination were negligible. The total stockholder's equity of Singleton Company on January 2, Year 3, was $500,000, and the current fair values of Singleton's identifiable assets and liabilities were equal to their carrying amounts on that date. Pennington debited the entire $440,000 to the Investment in Singleton Company Common Stock ledger account. The patent, for which no amortization has been provided by Pennington, had a remaining economic life of four years on January 2, Year 3.

(2) On July 1, Year 5, Pennington reduced its investment in Singleton Company to 75% by selling Singleton common stock for $70,000 to an unaffiliated company. Pennington recorded the $70,000 as a credit to the Investment in Singleton Company Common Stock ledger account.

(3) For the six months ended June 30, Year 5, Singleton had net income of $140,000. Pennington recorded 80% of this amount in its accounting records prior to the sale of Singleton common stock.

(4) During Year 4, Singleton sold merchandise to Pennington for $130,000, at a markup of 30% on Singleton's cost. On January 1, Year 5, $52,000 of this merchandise remained in Pennington's inventories. The merchandise was sold in February, Year 5, at a gross profit of $8,000.

(5) In November, Year 5, Pennington sold merchandise to Singleton for the first time. Pennington's cost for this merchandise was $80,000, and the sale was made at 120% of cost. Singleton's inventories on December 31, Year 5, included merchandise purchased from Pennington in the amount of $24,000.

PENNINGTON CORPORATION AND SINGLETON COMPANY
Separate Financial Statements
For Year Ended December 31, Year 5

	Pennington Corporation	Singleton Company
Income Statements		
Revenue		
Net sales	$3,904,000	$1,700,000
Intercompany sales	96,000	
Intercompany investment income	232,000	
Intercompany dividend revenue	75,000	
Total revenue	$4,307,000	$1,700,000
Costs and expenses		
Cost of goods sold	$2,902,000	$1,015,000
Intercompany cost of goods sold	80,000	
Interest expense		7,800
Operating expenses	400,000	377,200
Total costs and expenses	$3,382,000	$1,400,000
Net income	$ 925,000	$ 300,000
Statements of Retained Earnings		
Retained earnings, beginning of year	$1,748,000	$ 640,000
Add: Net income	925,000	300,000
Subtotals.	$2,673,000	$ 940,000
Less: Dividends	170,000	100,000
Retained earnings, end of year	$2,503,000	$ 840,000
Balance Sheets		
Assets		
Cash	$ 486,000	$ 249,600
Accounts receivable (net)	190,000	185,000
Intercompany receivables	45,000	
Inventories	475,000	355,000
Investment in Singleton Company common stock .	954,000	
Investment in Singleton Company bonds	58,000	
Plant assets (net)	2,231,000	530,000
Total assets	$4,439,000	$1,319,600
Liabilities & Stockholders' Equity		
Accounts payable	$ 384,000	$ 62,000
Bonds payable		60,000
Intercompany bonds payable		60,000
Discount on bonds payable		(1,200)
Discount on intercompany bonds payable		(1,200)
Common stock, $10 par	1,200,000	250,000
Paid-in capital in excess of par		50,000
Retained earnings	2,503,000	840,000
Retained earnings of subsidiary	352,000	
Total liabilities & stockholders' equity	$4,439,000	$1,319,600

(6) On December 31, Year 5, a $45,000 cash payment was in transit from Singleton to Pennington.

(7) In December, Year 5, Singleton declared and paid cash dividends of $100,000.

(8) On December 31, Year 5, Pennington acquired for $58,000, 50% of Singleton's outstanding bonds. The management of Pennington intends to keep the Singleton bonds until their maturity on December 31, Year 9.

Instructions

a Prepare journal entries to correct the accounting records of Pennington Corporation on December 31, Year 5. Disregard income taxes.

b Prepare a working paper for consolidated financial statements and related working paper eliminations for Pennington Corporation and subsidiary for the year ended December 31, Year 5. Amounts for Pennington Corporation should reflect the journal entries in *a.* Disregard income taxes.

10-9 Pastore Corporation acquired an 80% interest in Seville Company on December 31, Year 5, for a total consideration of $1 million. The acquisition cost consisted of $850,000 cash and $150,000 current fair value of securities of Redeker, Inc., which had been owned by Pastore as a long-term investment. The investment in Seville is accounted for by Pastore under the equity method of accounting. The consolidated balance sheet for the two companies on December 31, Year 5, follows:

PASTORE CORPORATION AND SUBSIDIARY
Consolidated Balance Sheet
December 31, Year 5

Assets		Liabilities & Stockholders' Equity	
Cash	$ 750,000	Notes payable (current). .	$1,500,000
Accounts receivable		Accounts payable	1,000,000
(net).	1,300,000	Minority interest in net	
Inventories	2,250,000	assets of subsidiary . . .	250,000
Plant assets.	3,850,000	Common stock	1,000,000
Less: Accumulated		Paid-in capital in excess	
depreciation.	(1,400,000)	of par	800,000
		Retained earnings	2,200,000
		Total liabilities & stock-	
Total assets	$6,750,000	holders' equity	$6,750,000

The excess of the carrying amount of Seville common stock over the cost of Pastore's investment was $250,000, which included the amount imputed to the minority interest. The excess was deducted from Seville's plant assets and pre-business combination net income in the accounting records of Seville.

On July 2, Year 6, Pastore sold a 10% interest in Seville for $150,000. The net income, cash dividends, and depreciation expense for each company for Year 6 are summarized at the top of page 497. The net income of Pastore includes intercompany investment income from Seville and the gain or loss on the sale of Seville's common stock.

	Pastore Corporation	Seville Company
Net income for first half of Year 6	$260,000	$72,500
Net income for second half of Year 6	273,500	82,500
Cash dividends declared and paid in December, Year 6	100,000	30,000
Depreciation expense for Year 6	225,000	55,000

The separate unclassified balance sheets for Pastore Corporation and Seville Company on December 31, Year 6, are given below:

PASTORE CORPORATION AND SEVILLE COMPANY
Separate Balance Sheets
December 31, Year 6

Assets	Pastore Corporation	Seville Company	Liabilities & Stockholders' Equity	Pastore Corporation	Seville Company
Cash	$ 695,000	$ 260,000	Notes payable . .	$1,100,000	$ 310,000
Accounts receivable (net).	900,000	500,000	Accounts payable	569,000	450,000
Inventories	1,600,000	750,000	Bonds payable . .	500,000	
Investment in Seville Company common stock	962,500		Common stock . .	1,000,000	500,000
			Paid-in capital in excess of par . .	800,000	
Plant assets. . . .	3,500,000	1,250,000	Retained earnings	2,633,500	875,000
Less: Accumulated depreciation	(1,055,000)	(625,000)	Total liabilities & stockholders'		
Total assets . .	$6,602,500	$2,135,000	equity.	$6,602,500	$2,135,000

Instructions (Disregard income taxes)
a Compute the consolidated net income for Year 6.
b Prepare a consolidated balance sheet on December 31, Year 6, without using a working paper.
c Prepare a consolidated statement of changes in financial position on a working capital concept for Year 6. A working paper is not required.
d Reconcile the amount of minority interest on December 31, Year 5, with the amount of minority interest on December 31, Year 6.

10-10 Separate balance sheets of Parker Corporation, Siegel Company, and Spurgeon Company on December 31, Year 3, are shown on page 498.
On January 2, Year 4, Parker acquired 70% of the outstanding common stock of Siegel for $680,000 and 40% of the outstanding common stock of Spurgeon for $330,000. On the same date, Siegel also acquired 40% of the outstanding common stock of Spurgeon for $330,000. (Out-of-pocket costs of the business combination may be disregarded.) Both Parker and Siegel had borrowed cash from banks on December 31, Year 3, to finance the common stock acquisitions.
The current fair values of both Siegel's and Spurgeon's identifiable net assets were the same as their carrying amounts on January 2, Year 4. Both Parker and Siegel use a 30-year economic life for goodwill.

PARKER CORPORATION, SIEGEL COMPANY, AND SPURGEON COMPANY
Separate Balance Sheets
December 31, Year 3

	Parker Corporation	Siegel Company	Spurgeon Company
Assets			
Current assets	$1,820,800	$ 920,000	$ 650,000
Plant assets (net).	3,260,700	740,000	1,260,000
Total assets	$5,081,500	$1,660,000	$1,910,000
Liabilities & Stockholders' Equity			
Current liabilities	$1,020,200	$ 400,600	$ 240,300
Long-term debt	1,240,700	380,500	930,200
Common stock, $1 par	820,000	200,000	400,000
Paid-in capital in excess of par . .	300,000	400,000	200,000
Retained earnings	1,700,600	278,900	139,500
Total liabilities & stockholders' equity.	$5,081,500	$1,660,000	$1,910,000

Instructions

a Prepare journal entries in the accounting records of Parker Corporation and Siegel Company on January 2, Year 4, to record the business combination of Parker, Siegel, and Spurgeon Company. Disregard income taxes.

b Prepare a working paper for consolidated balance sheet and working paper eliminations for Parker Corporation and subsidiaries on January 2, Year 4. Amounts for Parker and Siegel should reflect the journal entries in *a.* Disregard income taxes.

3

ACCOUNTING
FOR NONBUSINESS
ORGANIZATIONS

11 GOVERNMENTAL UNITS: GENERAL FUND

Collectively, governmental units and nonprofit organizations are known as **nonbusiness organizations.** The two types of nonbusiness organizations have several characteristics in common as well as some differentiating features. Thus, it is convenient to discuss accounting principles for the two types of nonbusiness organizations in a separate section of this book. In this chapter we discuss the objectives of financial reporting for nonbusiness organizations, the nature of governmental units, accounting principles for governmental units, and the accounting for a governmental unit's general fund. Chapter 12 deals with accounting for other funds and account groups of a governmental unit. Accounting for nonprofit organizations is covered in Chapter 13.

OBJECTIVES OF FINANCIAL REPORTING FOR NONBUSINESS ORGANIZATIONS

For many years, neither the AICPA nor the FASB gave attention to the accounting problems of nonbusiness organizations. Thus, the development of accounting principles for those organizations was left to other authorities, or to individual accountants. During the 1970s, a number of factors caused both the AICPA and the FASB to consider the need for a comprehensive body of accounting principles for nonbusiness organizations. Among these factors were the desperate financial condition of many United States cities and other governmental units, and scandals associated with the fund-raising activities of a few nonprofit organizations.

As a result of the factors described in the foregoing paragraph, the FASB added financial reporting by nonbusiness organizations to the scope of its conceptual framework for financial accounting and reporting project, which is described in **Intermediate Accounting** of this series. In **Statement of Financial Accounting Concepts No. 4,** "Objectives of Financial Reporting by Nonbusiness Organizations," the FASB developed the following objectives:[1]

1 Financial reporting by nonbusiness organizations should provide information that is useful to present and potential resource providers and other

[1] *Statement of Financial Accounting Concepts No. 4,* "Objectives of Financial Reporting by Nonbusiness Organizations," FASB (Stamford: 1980), pp. xiii–xiv.

users in making rational decisions about the allocation of resources to those organizations.

2 Financial reporting should provide information to help present and potential resource providers and other users in assessing the services that a nonbusiness organization provides and its ability to continue to provide those services.

3 Financial reporting should provide information that is useful to present and potential resource providers and other users in assessing how managers of a nonbusiness organization have discharged their stewardship responsibilities and about other aspects of their performance.

4 Financial reporting should provide information about the economic resources, obligations, and net resources of an organization, and the effects of transactions, events, and circumstances that change resources and interests in those resources.

5 Financial reporting should provide information about the performance of an organization during a period. Periodic measurement of the changes in the amount and nature of the net resources of a nonbusiness organization and information about the service efforts and accomplishments of an organization together represent the information most useful in assessing its performance.

6 Financial reporting should provide information about how an organization obtains and spends cash or other liquid resources, about its borrowing and repayment of borrowing, and about other factors that may affect an organization's liquidity.

7 Financial reporting should include explanations and interpretations to help users understand financial information provided.

The FASB stated that it was aware of no persuasive evidence that the seven objectives outlined in the foregoing section were inappropriate for general-purpose external financial reports of state and local governmental units. However, the FASB deferred a final decision on the matter, pending resolution of the question of how accounting standards for state and local governmental units should be established. The FASB explicitly recognized that accounting and reporting standards for the federal government were not addressed in *Statement of Financial Accounting Concepts No. 4.*[2] Furthermore, that Statement did not establish standards prescribing accounting procedures or disclosure practices for particular items or events, because such prescriptions are made by *Statements of Financial Accounting Standards.*[3]

NATURE OF GOVERNMENTAL UNITS

Students beginning the study of accounting for governmental units temporarily must set aside many of the familiar accounting principles for business enterprises. Such fundamental concepts of accounting theory for business enterprises as the nature of the accounting entity, the primacy of the income statement, and the pervasiveness of the ac-

---

[2] Ibid., p. 2
[3] Ibid., p. ii.

crual basis of accounting have limited relevance in accounting for governmental units. Consequently, we begin our discussion with the features of governmental units that give rise to unique accounting concepts.

When thinking of governmental units of the United States, one tends to focus on the federal government, or on the governments of the 50 states. However, in addition to those major governmental units and the governments of the several U.S. territories, there are the following governmental units in the United States:[4]

More than 3,000 counties
Nearly 17,000 townships
Nearly 19,000 municipalities
More than 15,000 school districts
Nearly 26,000 special districts (port authorities, airports, public buildings, libraries, and others)

Despite the wide range in size and scope of governance, the governmental units listed above have a number of characteristics in common. Among these characteristics are the following:

1 *Organization to serve the citizenry.* A basic tenet of governmental philosophy in the United States is that governmental units exist to serve the citizens subject to their jurisdiction. Thus, the citizens as a whole establish governmental units through the constitutional and charter process. In contrast, business enterprises are created by only a limited number of individuals.

2 *General absence of the profit motive.* With few exceptions, governmental units render services to the citizenry without the objective of profiting from those services. Business enterprises are motivated to earn profits.

3 *Taxation as the principal source of revenue.* The citizens subject to a governmental unit's jurisdiction provide resources to the governmental unit principally through taxation. Many of these taxes are paid on a self-assessment basis. There is no comparable revenue source for business enterprises.

4 *Impact of the legislative process.* Operations of governmental units are for the most part initiated by various legislative enactments, such as operating budgets, borrowing authorizations, and tax levies. Business enterprises are also affected by federal, state, and local laws and regulations, but not to such a direct extent.

5 *Stewardship for resources.* A primary responsibility of governmental units in financial reporting is to demonstrate adequate stewardship for resources provided by their citizenry. Business enterprises have a comparable responsibility to their owners, but not to the same extent as governmental units.

The five foregoing characteristics of governmental units are major determinants of accounting principles for such units.

ACCOUNTING PRINCIPLES FOR GOVERNMENTAL UNITS

For many years, accounting principles for governmental units have been established by the National Council on Governmental Accounting

---

[4] "How Government Affects Our Lives," *U.S. News & World Report,* May 11, 1981, p. 46.

(NCGA), a 21-member organization composed primarily of local, state, and national finance officers, including two Canadian finance officers. Until 1979, the source of accounting principles for governmental units was a 1968 publication, **Governmental Accounting, Auditing, and Financial Reporting.** In 1979, the NCGA issued **Statement 1, Governmental Accounting and Financial Reporting Principles,** which included the following 12 principles of accounting for state and local governmental units:[5]

Accounting and reporting capabilities

1 A governmental accounting system must make it possible both: (a) to present fairly and with full disclosure the financial position and results of financial operations of the funds and account groups of the governmental unit in conformity with generally accepted accounting principles; and (b) to determine and demonstrate compliance with finance-related legal and contractual provisions.

Fund accounting systems

2 Governmental accounting systems should be organized and operated on a fund basis. A **fund** is defined as a fiscal and accounting entity with a self-balancing set of accounts recording cash and other financial resources, together with all related liabilities and residual equities or balances, and changes therein, which are segregated for the purpose of carrying on specific activities or attaining certain objectives in accordance with special regulations, restrictions, or limitations.

Types of funds

3 The following types of funds should be used by state and local governments:

Governmental Funds

(1) *The General Fund*—to account for all financial resources except those required to be accounted for in another fund.

(2) *Special Revenue Funds*—to account for the proceeds of specific revenue sources (other than special assessments, expendable trusts, or for major capital projects) that are legally restricted to expenditure for specified purposes.

(3) *Capital Projects Funds*—to account for financial resources to be used for the acquisition or construction of major capital facilities (other than those financed by proprietary funds, Special Assessment Funds, and Trust Funds).

(4) *Debt Service Funds*—to account for the accumulation of resources for, and the payment of, general long-term debt principal and interest.

(5) *Special Assessment Funds*—to account for the financing of public improvements or services deemed to benefit the properties against which special assessments are levied.

Proprietary Funds

(6) *Enterprise Funds*—to account for operations (a) that are financed and operated in a manner similar to private business enterprises—where the intent of the governing body is that the costs (expenses, including depreciation) of providing goods or services to the general public on a continuing basis be financed or recovered primarily through user charges; or (b) where the governing body has decided that periodic determination of revenues earned, expenses incurred, and/or net income is appropriate for capital maintenance, public policy, management control, accountability, or other purposes.

(7) *Internal Service Funds*—to account for the financing of goods or services provided by one department or agency to other departments or

[5] National Council on Governmental Accounting, *Governmental Accounting and Financial Reporting Principles,* Municipal Finance Officers Association of the United States and Canada (Chicago: 1979), pp. 2–4.

agencies of the governmental unit, or to other governmental units, on a cost-reimbursement basis.

Fiduciary Funds

(8) *Trust and Agency Funds*—to account for assets held by a governmental unit in a trustee capacity or as an agent for individuals, private organizations, other governmental units, and/or other funds. These include (a) Expendable Trust Funds, (b) Nonexpendable Trust Funds, (c) Pension Trust Funds, and (d) Agency Funds.

Number of funds

4 Governmental units should establish and maintain those funds required by law and sound financial administration. Only the minimum number of funds consistent with legal and operating requirements should be established, however, since unnecessary funds result in inflexibility, undue complexity, and inefficient financial administration.

Accounting for fixed assets and long-term liabilities

5 A clear distinction should be made between (a) fund fixed assets and general fixed assets and (b) fund long-term liabilities and general long-term debt.

   a Fixed assets related to specific proprietary funds or Trust Funds should be accounted for through those funds. All other fixed assets of a governmental unit should be accounted for through the General Fixed Assets Account Group.

   b Long-term liabilities of proprietary funds, Special Assessment Funds, and Trust Funds should be accounted for through those funds. All other unmatured general long-term liabilities of the governmental unit should be accounted for through the General Long-Term Debt Account Group.

Valuation of fixed assets

6 Fixed assets should be accounted for at cost or, if the cost is not practicably determinable, at estimated cost. Donated fixed assets should be recorded at their estimated fair value at the time received.

Depreciation of fixed assets

7 *a* Depreciation of general fixed assets should not be recorded in the accounts of governmental funds. Depreciation of general fixed assets may be recorded in cost accounting systems or calculated for cost finding analyses; and accumulated depreciation may be recorded in the General Fixed Assets Account Group.

   b Depreciation of fixed assets accounted for in a proprietary fund should be recorded in the accounts of that fund. Depreciation is also recognized in those Trust Funds where expenses, net income, and/or capital maintenance are measured.

Accrual basis in governmental accounting

8 The modified accrual or accrual basis of accounting, as appropriate, should be utilized in measuring financial position and operating results.

   a *Governmental fund* revenues and expenditures should be recognized on the modified accrual basis. Revenues should be recognized in the accounting period in which they become available and measurable. Expenditures should be recognized in the accounting period in which the fund liability is incurred, if measurable, except for unmatured interest on general long-term debt and on special assessment indebtedness secured by interest-bearing special assessment levies, which should be recognized when due.

   b *Proprietary fund* revenues and expenses should be recognized on the accrual basis. Revenues should be recognized in the accounting period in which they are earned and become measurable; expenses should be recognized in the period incurred, if measurable.

   c *Fiduciary fund* revenues and expenses or expenditures (as appropriate) should be recognized on the basis consistent with the fund's accounting measurement objective. Nonexpendable Trust and Pension Trust Funds should be accounted for on the accrual basis; Expendable Trust Funds should be accounted for on the modified accrual basis. Agency Fund assets and liabilities should be accounted for on the modified accrual basis.

Budgeting, budgetary control, and budgetary reporting

    d *Transfers* should be recognized in the accounting period in which the interfund receivable and payable arise.

9 *a* An annual budget(s) should be adopted by every governmental unit.

    b The accounting system should provide the basis for appropriate budgetary control.

    c Budgetary comparisons should be included in the appropriate financial statements and schedules for governmental funds for which an annual budget has been adopted.

Transfer, revenue, expenditure, and expense account classification

10 *a* Interfund transfers and proceeds of general long-term debt issues should be classified separately from fund revenues and expenditures or expenses.

    b Governmental fund revenues should be classified by fund and source. Expenditures should be classified by fund, function (or program), organization unit, activity, character, and principal classes of objects.

    c Proprietary fund revenues and expenses should be classified in essentially the same manner as those of similar business organizations, functions, or activities.

Common terminology and classification

11 A common terminology and classification should be used consistently throughout the budget, the accounts, and the financial reports of each fund.

Interim and annual financial reports

12 *a* Appropriate interim financial statements and reports of financial position, operating results, and other pertinent information should be prepared to facilitate management control of financial operations, legislative oversight, and, where necessary or desired, for external reporting purposes.

    b A comprehensive annual financial report covering all funds and account groups of the governmental unit—including appropriate combined, combining, and individual fund statements; notes to the financial statements; schedules; narrative explanations; and statistical tables—should be prepared and published.

    c General-purpose financial statements may be issued separately from the comprehensive annual financial report. Such statements should include the basic financial statements and notes to the financial statements that are essential to fair presentation of financial position and operating results (and changes in financial position of proprietary funds and similar trust funds).

Principles 2 and 3, and 8 to 11, are discussed in the following sections of this chapter. Chapter 12 covers principles 4 to 7 and 12, and funds other than the general fund identified in principle 3.

Funds: The accounting entities for governmental units (principles 2 and 3)

In accounting for business enterprises, **economic substance** of financial transactions is emphasized over their **legal form.** Thus, capital leases that are in substance installment acquisitions of personal property are accounted for as such in the financial statements of business enterprises. Similarly, minority interest in a consolidated subsidiary, although theoretically a part of consolidated stockholders' equity, generally is reported as a liability under the "parent company theory" of consolidated financial statements.

In contrast, accounting for governmental units emphasizes **legal** *form* over *economic substance.* This emphasis is necessitated by the characteristics of governmental units discussed in a preceding section of this chapter—especially the impact of the legislative process and the stewardship for resources. Emphasis on legal form for governmental units is manifested in several aspects of accounting for such units.

Accounting for business enterprises emphasizes the economic entity as an accounting unit. Thus, a partnership is considered to be an accounting entity separate from partners; and consolidated financial statements are issued for a group of affiliated—but legally separate— corporations that comprise a single economic entity under common control.

There is generally no single accounting entity for a specific governmental unit, such as a city or a county. Instead, the accounting entity for governmental units is the fund. As defined in principle 2, a *fund* is an accounting entity that includes *cash* and *other financial resources,* liabilities, and residual equities or balances. These elements are accounted for as a unit in accordance with laws or regulations established by the governmental unit involved.

Principle 3 identifies eight types of funds used in accounting for governmental units, grouped into three categories. The *governmental funds* account for financial resources of a governmental unit that are used in day-to-day operations. The *proprietary funds* carry out governmental unit activities that closely resemble the operations of a business enterprise. *Fiduciary funds* account for resources not *owned* by a governmental unit, but administered by the unit as a *custodian* or *fiduciary.*

Every governmental unit has a general fund. As indicated by principle 4, any additional funds should be established as required by legislative action and the maintenance of adequate custodianship for financial resources of the governmental unit. Accounting for the general fund is discussed in subsequent sections of this chapter; accounting for other funds is explained in Chapter 12. At this point, we must emphasize that a governmental unit *does not have a single accounting entity* to account for its financial resources, obligations, revenues, and expenditures.

The modified accrual basis of accounting (principle 8)

Except for enterprise funds and internal service funds, which record sales of goods or services, governmental accounting does not emphasize the results of the governmental unit's operations for a fiscal year. Financial reporting for governments instead focuses on the stewardship provided for the governmental unit's assets. One consequence is that a *modified accrual basis of accounting* is appropriate for the five governmental funds and for expendable trust funds, as indicated by principle 8. The conventional accrual basis of accounting is used for the two proprietary funds, nonexpendable trust funds, and pension trust funds.

The National Council on Governmental Accounting has defined the modified accrual basis of accounting as follows:[6]

> **Revenue Recognition**   Revenues and other governmental fund financial resource increments (e.g., bond issue proceeds) are recognized in the accounting period in which they become susceptible to accrual—that is, when they become both **measurable** and **available** to finance expenditures of the fiscal period. **Available** means collectible within the current period or soon enough thereafter to be used to pay liabilities of the current period. . . .
>
> **Expenditure Recognition**   . . . the measurement focus of governmental fund accounting is upon **expenditures**—decreases in net financial resources —rather than expenses. Most expenditures and transfers out are measurable and should be recorded when the related liability is incurred . . . .
>
> . . . alternative expenditure recognition methods in governmental fund accounting, usually of a relatively minor nature, include: . . .
> (1) Inventory items (e.g., materials and supplies) may be considered expenditures either when purchased (purchases method) or when used (consumption method), but significant amounts of inventory should be reported in the balance sheet.
> (2) Expenditures for insurance and similar services extending over more than one accounting period need not be allocated between or among accounting periods, but may be accounted for as expenditures of the period of acquisition.

Revenues   Few revenues of the five governmental funds and expendable trust funds are susceptible to accrual. For example, there generally is no basis for the accrual of self-assessed taxes such as income taxes, sales taxes, and taxes on gross business receipts. Similarly, fees for business licenses, marriage licenses, and comparable permits generally are recorded when received in cash, because these fees are not billable in advance of the service or granting of a permit.

Perhaps the most commonly accrued revenue of a governmental unit is property taxes. These taxes customarily are billed by the governmental unit to the property owner and generally are payable in the fiscal year for which billed.

In summary, the cash basis of accounting is appropriate for many revenues of the five governmental funds (general, special revenue, capital projects, debt service, and special assessment) and expendable trust funds.

Expenditures   Because of the lack of emphasis on operating results, funds other than the two proprietary funds (enterprise and internal service) account for authorized **expenditures** of the government's resources, rather than accounting for **expenses** of operations. There is no attempt to match **cost expirations** against **realized revenues** in funds other than enterprise funds and internal service funds. As a result, depreciation is recorded only in enterprise funds and internal service funds, and, if appropriate, in certain trust funds. Similarly, there is no doubtful taxes expense in the general fund or in special revenue funds,

---

[6] Ibid., pp. 11–12.

because tax revenues susceptible to accrual are recorded in an amount *net* of the estimated uncollectible portion of the related receivables, as illustrated on page 514.

Recording the budget (principle 9)

Budgets are key elements of legislative control over governmental units. The executive branch of a governmental unit proposes the budgets, the legislative branch reviews, modifies, and enacts the budgets, and finally the executive branch approves the budgets and carries out their provisions.

The two basic classifications of budgets for governmental units are the same as those for business enterprises—annual budgets and long-term or capital budgets. *Annual budgets* include the *estimated revenues* and *appropriations* for expenditures for a specific fiscal year of the governmental unit. Annual budgets are appropriate for the general fund and special revenue funds; they sometimes are used for debt service funds. An expendable trust fund also may have an annual budget, depending upon the terms of the *trust indenture. Capital budgets,* which are used to control the expenditures for construction projects or other plant asset acquisitions, may be appropriate for capital projects funds and special assessment funds. The annual or capital budgets often are recorded in all these funds, to aid in accounting for compliance with legislative authorizations.

The operations of the two proprietary funds (enterprise and internal service) are similar to those of business enterprises. Consequently, annual budgets are used by these funds as a managerial planning and control device *rather than as a legislative control tool.* Thus, annual budgets of enterprise funds and internal service funds generally *are not recorded in ledger accounts by these funds.*

Types of Annual Budgets One or more of four types of annual budgets may be used by a governmental unit. A *traditional budget* emphasizes, by department, the *object* of each authorized expenditure. For example, under the legislative activity of the general government function, the traditional budget may include authorized expenditures for personal services, supplies, and capital outlays.

A *program budget* stresses measurement of total cost of a specific governmental unit *program,* regardless of how many departments of the governmental unit are involved in the program. Object of expenditure information is of secondary importance in a program budget.

In a *performance budget,* there is an attempt to relate the input of governmental resources to the output of governmental services. For example, the total estimated expenditures of the enforcement section of the taxation department might be compared to the aggregate collections of additional tax assessments budgeted for the fiscal year.

The fourth type of annual budget for a governmental unit is the *plan-*

ning, programming, budgeting system (*PPBS*). This budgeting technique has been described as follows:[7]

> PPBS attempts to apply concepts of program and performance budgeting to the tasks of identifying the fundamental objectives of a government; selections are made from among alternative ways of attaining these objectives, on the basis of the full analysis of respective cost implications and expected benefit results of the alternatives.

Regardless of which types of annual budgets are used by a governmental unit, the final budget adopted by the governmental unit's legislative body will include *estimated revenues* for the fiscal year and the *appropriations* for expenditures authorized for that year. If the estimated revenues of the budget exceed appropriations (as required by law for many governmental units), there will be a *budgetary surplus;* if appropriations exceed estimated revenues in the budget, there will be a *budgetary deficit.*

Journal Entry for a General Fund Budget   To illustrate the recording of an annual budget in the accounting records of a general fund, assume that the Town of Verdant Glen in June, Year 5, adopted the following condensed annual budget for its General Fund for the fiscal year ending June 30, Year 6:

Budget of general fund		
Estimated revenues:		
General property taxes		*$700,000*
Other		*100,000*
Total estimated revenues		*$800,000*
Estimated other financing sources		*50,000*
Subtotal		*$850,000*
Less: Appropriations:		
General government	*$420,000*	
Other	*340,000*	
Total appropriations	*$760,000*	
Estimated other financing uses	*60,000*	*820,000*
Excess of estimated revenues and other financing sources over appropriations and other financing uses (budgetary surplus)		*$ 30,000*

The journal entry to record the annual budget on July 1, Year 5, is on page 511. An analysis of each of the accounts in the foregoing journal entry follows:

1 The Estimated Revenues and Estimated Other Financing Sources accounts may be considered *pseudo asset* accounts because they reflect resources ex-

---

[7] *Audits of State and Local Governmental Units,* AICPA (New York: 1974), pp. 27–28.

511

Journal entry for budget of general fund

Estimated Revenues.	800,000	
Estimated Other Financing Sources	50,000	
Appropriations		760,000
Estimated Other Financing Uses.		60,000
Budgetary Fund Balance		30,000

To record annual budget adopted for fiscal year ending June 30, Year 6.

pected to be received by the General Fund during the fiscal year. These accounts are not actual assets, because they do not fit the accounting definition of an asset as a probable economic benefit obtained or controlled by a particular entity as a result of past transactions or events.[8] Thus, the two accounts in substance are **memorandum accounts,** useful for control purposes only, that will be closed after the issuance of financial statements for the General Fund for the fiscal year ending June 30, Year 6.

2 The Estimated Other Financing Sources account includes the budgeted amounts of such nonrevenues items as proceeds from the disposal of plant assets and transfers in from other funds. (See principle **10a,** page 506.)

3 The Appropriations and Estimated Other Financing Uses accounts may be considered **pseudo liability** accounts because they reflect the legislative body's commitments to expend General Fund resources as authorized in the annual budget. These accounts are not genuine liabilities because they do not fit the definition of a liability as a probable future sacrifice of economic benefits arising from present obligations of a particular entity to transfer assets or provide services to other entities in the future as a result of past transactions or events.[9] The Appropriations and Estimated Other Financing Uses accounts are **memorandum accounts,** useful for control purposes only, that will be closed after issuance of year-end financial statements for the General Fund.

4 The Estimated Other Financing Uses account includes budgeted amounts of transfers out to other funds, which are not expenditures. (See principle **10a,** page 506.)

5 The Budgetary Fund Balance account, as its title implies, is an account that balances the debit and credit entries to accounts of a budget journal entry. Although similar to the owners' equity accounts of a business enterprise in this balancing feature, the Budgetary Fund Balance account does not purport to show an ownership interest in a general fund's assets. At the end of the fiscal year, the Budgetary Fund Balance account is closed by a journal entry that reverses the original entry for the budget.

The journal entry to record the Town of Verdant Glen General Fund's annual budget for the year ending June 30, Year 6, is accompanied by detailed entries to subsidiary ledgers for both estimated revenues and appropriations. The budget of the Town of Verdant Glen General Fund purposely was condensed; in practice, the general fund's estimated revenues and appropriations would be detained by source and function, re-

[8] *Statement of Financial Accounting Concepts No. 3,* "Elements of Financial Statements of Business Enterprises," FASB (Stamford: 1980), p. xi.
[9] Ibid.

spectively, into one or more of the following widely used subsidiary ledger categories (see principle *10b,* page 506):[10]

Estimated revenues:
  Taxes
  Licenses and permits
  Intergovernmental revenues
  Charges for services
  Fines and forfeits
  Miscellaneous

Appropriations:
  General government
  Public safety
  Public works
  Health and welfare
  Culture—recreation
  Conservation of natural resources
  Debt service
  Intergovernmental expenditures
  Miscellaneous

In summary, budgets of a governmental unit often are recorded in the accounting records of the five governmental funds. An expendable trust fund also may record a budget if required to do so by the trust indenture. The recording of the budget initiates the accounting cycle for each of the funds listed above. Recording the budget also facilitates the preparation of financial statements that compare budgeted and actual amounts of revenues and expenditures.

Encumbrances and Budgetary Control Because of the need for the expenditures of governmental units to be in accordance with appropriations of governing legislative bodies, an *encumbrance* accounting technique is used for the general fund, special revenue funds, capital projects funds, and special assessment funds. When a purchase order for goods or services is issued to a supplier by one of those funds, a journal entry similar to the following is made in the accounting records of the fund:

Journal entry for encumbrances

Encumbrances   18,413
*   Fund Balance Reserved for Encumbrances. 18,413*
To record encumbrance for purchase order No. 1685 issued to
Wilson Company.

When the supplier's invoice for the ordered merchandise or services is received by the governmental unit, it is recorded and the related encumbrance is reversed as illustrated at the top of page 513.

As indicated by the example on page 513, the invoice amount may differ from the amount of the governmental unit's purchase order because of such items as shipping charges, sales taxes, and price changes.

The encumbrance technique is a memorandum method for assuring that total expenditures for a fiscal year do not exceed appropriations. Encumbrance journal entries *are not necessary for normal recurring expenditures such as salaries and wages, utilities, and rent.* The encumbrance technique used in accounting for governmental units has no counterpart in accounting for business enterprises.

---

[10] *Governmental Accounting, Auditing, and Financial Reporting,* Municipal Finance Officers Association of the United States and Canada (Chicago: 1980), pp. 84–97.

Expenditures	18,507	
Vouchers Payable.		18,507

To record invoice received from Wilson Company under purchase order No. 1685.

Fund Balance Reserved for Encumbrances	18,413	
Encumbrances		18,413

To reverse encumbrance for purchase order No. 1685 issued to Wilson Company.

ACCOUNTING FOR A GOVERNMENTAL UNIT'S GENERAL FUND

As indicated on page 504, a general fund is used to account for all transactions of a governmental unit not accounted for in one of the other seven types of funds. Thus, the general fund as an accounting entity serves the same *residual* purpose that the general journal provides as an accounting record. Although the general fund is residual, it usually accounts for the largest aggregate dollar amounts of the governmental unit's revenues and expenditures.

In illustrating the accounting for a general fund, we expand the example of the Town of Verdant Glen used in the preceding section.

Illustration of accounting for a general fund

Assume that the balance sheet of the Town of Verdant Glen General Fund on June 30, Year 5 (**prior to the journal entry for the Fiscal Year 6 budget** illustrated on page 511), was as follows:

TOWN OF VERDANT GLEN GENERAL FUND
Balance Sheet
June 30, Year 5

Assets

Cash		$160,000
Inventory of supplies		40,000
Total assets.		$200,000

Liabilities & Fund Balance

Vouchers payable		$ 80,000
Fund balance:		
Reserved for inventory of supplies	$40,000	
Unreserved	80,000	120,000
Total liabilities & fund balance		$200,000

The fund balance reserved for inventory of supplies is analogous to an appropriation of retained earnings in a business enterprise. It represents a reservation of the General Fund's fund balance, so that the $40,000 nonexpendable portion of the General Fund's total assets will not be appropriated for expenditures in the legislative body's adoption of the annual budget for the General Fund for the year ending June 30, Year 6.

Assume that, in addition to the budget illustrated on page 510, the Town of Verdant Glen General Fund had the following summarized transactions for the fiscal year ended June 30, Year 6:

1 Property taxes were billed in the amount of $720,000, of which $14,000 was of doubtful collectibility.

2 Property taxes collected in cash totaled $650,000; other revenues collected totaled $102,000.

3 Property taxes in the amount of $13,000 were uncollectible.

4 Purchase orders were issued to outside suppliers in the total amount of $360,000.

5 Expenditures for the year totaled $760,000, of which $90,000 applied to additions to inventory of supplies, and $350,000 applied to $355,000 of the purchase orders in the total amount of $360,000 issued during the year.

6 Billings for services and supplies from the Enterprise Fund and the Internal Service Fund totaled $30,000 and $20,000, respectively.

7 Cash payments on vouchers payable totaled $770,000. Cash payments to the Enterprise Fund and the Internal Service Fund were $25,000 and $14,000, respectively.

8 Transfers of cash to the Debt Service Fund for maturing principal and interest on general obligation serial bonds totaled $11,000.

9 A payment of $50,000 in lieu of property taxes was received from the Enterprise Fund.

10 Supplies with a cost of $80,000 were used during the year.

11 All uncollected property taxes on June 30, Year 6, were delinquent.

After the journal entry for the budget is recorded, as illustrated on page 511, the following journal entries, numbered to correspond to the transactions listed above, are entered in the accounting records of the Town of Verdant Glen General Fund during the year ended June 30, Year 6:

TOWN OF VERDANT GLEN GENERAL FUND
General Journal

1 Taxes Receivable—Current	720,000	
Allowance for Uncollectible Current Taxes		14,000
Revenues		706,000
To accrue property taxes billed and to provide for estimated uncollectible portion.		

As indicated earlier, the modified accrual basis of accounting for a general fund permits the accrual of property taxes, because they are *billed* to the property owners by the Town of Verdant Glen. The estimated uncollectible property taxes are *offset* against the total taxes billed; the net amount represents *actual revenues* from property taxes for the year.

2 Cash.	752,000	
Taxes Receivable—Current		650,000
Revenues		102,000
To record collections of property taxes and other revenues		
for the year.		

Under the modified accrual basis of accounting, revenues not susceptible to accrual are recorded on the cash basis. However, any taxes or other revenues collected in advance of the fiscal year to which they apply are credited to a liability account.

If a governmental unit's general fund has a cash shortage prior to collection of property taxes, it may issue short-term *tax anticipation notes* to borrow cash. Typically, tax anticipation notes are repaid from proceeds of the subsequent tax collections.

3 Allowance for Uncollectible Current Taxes	13,000	
Taxes Receivable—Current		13,000
To write off receivables for property taxes that are uncol-		
lectible.		

The foregoing journal entry represents a shortcut approach. In an actual situation, uncollectible property taxes first would be transferred, together with estimated uncollectible amounts, to the Taxes Receivable—Delinquent account from the Taxes Receivable—Current account. Any amounts collected on these delinquent taxes would include revenues for interest and penalties required by law. Any uncollected delinquent taxes would be transferred, together with estimated uncollectible amounts, to the Tax Liens Receivable account. After the passage of an appropriate statutory period, the governmental unit might satisfy its tax lien by selling the property on which the taxes were levied.

4 Encumbrances.	360,000	
Fund Balance Reserved for Encumbrances.		360,000
To record purchase orders issued during the year.		

Encumbrance journal entries are designed to prevent the overexpending of an appropriated amount in the budget. The journal entry to the Encumbrances account is posted in detail to reduce the unexpended balances of each applicable appropriation in the subsidiary ledger for appropriations. The unexpended balance of each appropriation thus is reduced for the amount committed by the issuance of purchase orders.

---

5 a *Expenditures* 670,000
 Inventory of Supplies 90,000
  Vouchers Payable 760,000
To record expenditures for the year.

The Expenditures account is debited with all expenditures, regardless of purpose, except for additions to the inventory of supplies. Principal and interest payments on debt, additions to the governmental unit's plant assets, payments for goods or services to be received in the future —all are debited to Expenditures rather than to asset or liability accounts. (Expenditures for debt principal and interest and plant asset additions also are recorded **on a memorandum basis** in the general long-term debt and general fixed assets account groups, respectively, as explained in Chapter 12.)

The accounting for general fund expenditures described above emphasizes once again the importance of the annual budget in the accounting for a general fund. Expenditures are chargeable to amounts appropriated by the legislative body of the governmental unit. The detailed items making up the $670,000 total debit to the Expenditures account in the foregoing journal entry are posted to the appropriations subsidiary ledger as reductions of unexpended balances of each appropriation.

---

5 b *Fund Balance Reserved for Encumbrances* 355,000
 Encumbrances 355,000
To reverse encumbrances applicable to vouchered expenditures totaling $350,000.

Recording actual expenditures of $350,000 (included in the $670,000 total in entry **5a** above) relevant to purchase orders totaling $355,000 makes this amount of the previously recorded encumbrances no longer necessary. Accordingly, $355,000 of encumbrances is reversed; the reversal is posted to the detailed appropriations subsidiary ledger as well as to the general ledger. Encumbrances of $5,000 remain outstanding.

6 Other Financing Uses.	50,000	
Payable to Enterprise Fund		30,000
Payable to Internal Service Fund		20,000
To record billings for services and supplies received from other funds.		

Billings from other funds of the governmental unit are not vouchered for payment, as are billings from outside suppliers. Instead, billings from other funds are recorded in separate liability accounts. The related debit is to the Other Financing Uses account rather than to the Expenditures account.

7 Vouchers Payable.	770,000	
Payable to Enterprise Fund	25,000	
Payable to Internal Service Fund.	14,000	
Cash.		809,000
To record payment of liabilities during the year.		
8 Other Financing Uses.	11,000	
Cash		11,000
To record transfer to Debt Service Fund for maturing principal and interest on general obligation serial bonds.		
9 Cash.	50,000	
Other Financing Sources.		50,000
To record payment in lieu of property taxes received from Enterprise Fund.		

Amounts transferred in to the General Fund from other funds do not represent revenues. They are recorded in the Other Financing Sources account.

10 Expenditures	80,000	
Inventory of Supplies		80,000
To record cost of supplies used during the year.		
Unreserved Fund Balance.	10,000	
Fund Balance Reserved for Inventory of Supplies . .		10,000
To increase inventory of supplies reserve to agree with balance of Inventory of Supplies account at end of year ($50,000 − $40,000 = $10,000).		

The immediately preceding journal entry represents a reservation of a portion of the Fund Balance account to prevent its being appropriated improperly to finance a deficit annual budget for the General Fund for the year ending June 30, Year 7. Only cash and other monetary assets of a general fund are available for appropriation to finance authorized expenditures of the succeeding fiscal year.

11 *Taxes Receivable—Delinquent.*	*57,000*	
Allowance for Uncollectible Current Taxes.	*1,000*	
Taxes Receivable—Current.		*57,000*
Allowance for Uncollectible Delinquent Taxes.		*1,000*
To transfer delinquent taxes and related estimated uncollectible amounts from the current classification.		

The foregoing journal entry clears the Taxes Receivable—Current account and the related contra account for uncollectible amounts so that they will be available for accrual of property taxes for the fiscal year ending June 30, Year 7.

Trial balance at end of fiscal year for a general fund

After all the foregoing journal entries (including the budget entry on page 511) have been posted to the general ledger of the Town of Verdant Glen General Fund, the trial balance on June 30, Year 6, is as illustrated at the top of page 519.

Financial statements for a general fund

The results of operations (that is, net income or net loss) are not significant for a general fund. Instead, two financial statements—a statement of revenues, expenditures, and changes in fund balance and a balance sheet—are appropriate. These two financial statements are shown on pages 519 and 520 for the Town of Verdant Glen's General Fund for the year ended June 30, Year 6. The following aspects of the Town of Verdant Glen General Fund financial statements should be emphasized:

1 The statement of revenues, expenditures, and changes in fund balance compares budgeted with actual amounts. This comparison aids in the appraisal of the stewardship for the General Fund's resources and the compliance with legislative appropriations. (Expenditures in excess of appropriated amounts generally are not permitted unless a supplementary appropriation is made by the legislative body of the governmental unit.)

2 The amounts received from and paid to other funds of the Town of Verdant Glen are termed **operating transfers in** and **operating transfers out** respectively, to distinguish them from other types of financing sources and uses that might have been received or paid by the General Fund.

TOWN OF VERDANT GLEN GENERAL FUND
Trial Balance
June 30, Year 6

	Debit	Credit
Cash.	$ 142,000	
Taxes receivable—delinquent	57,000	
Allowance for uncollectible delinquent taxes		$ 1,000
Inventory of supplies.	50,000	
Vouchers payable.		70,000
Payable to Enterprise Fund.		5,000
Payable to Internal Service Fund.		6,000
Fund balance reserved for encumbrances		5,000
Fund balance reserved for inventory of supplies		50,000
Unreserved fund balance		70,000
Budgetary fund balance.		30,000
Estimated revenues.	800,000	
Estimated other financing sources.	50,000	
Appropriations.		760,000
Estimated other financing uses.		60,000
Revenues.		808,000
Other financing sources		50,000
Expenditures.	750,000	
Other financing uses	61,000	
Encumbrances.	5,000	
Totals.	$1,915,000	$1,915,000

TOWN OF VERDANT GLEN GENERAL FUND
Statement of Revenues, Expenditures, and Changes in Fund Balance
For Year Ended June 30, Year 6

	Budget	Actual	Variance favorable (unfavorable)
Revenues:			
Taxes	$700,000	$706,000	$ 6,000
Other.	100,000	102,000	2,000
Total revenues.	$800,000	$808,000	$ 8,000
Expenditures:*			
General government	$420,000	$409,000	$11,000
Other.	340,000	341,000	(1,000)
Total expenditures	$760,000	$750,000	$10,000
Excess of revenues over expenditures . . .	$ 40,000	$ 58,000	$18,000
Other financing sources (uses):			
Operating transfers in	50,000	50,000	
Operating transfers out	(60,000)	(61,000)	(1,000)
Excess of revenues and other sources over expenditures and other uses	$ 30,000	$ 47,000	$17,000
Fund balance, beginning of year	120,000	120,000	
Fund balance, end of year	$150,000	$167,000	$17,000

* Breakdown of actual amounts between general government and other categories is assumed.

TOWN OF VERDANT GLEN GENERAL FUND
Balance Sheet
June 30, Year 6

Assets

Cash.	$142,000
Taxes receivable, net of allowance for estimated uncollectible amounts,	
$1,000	56,000
Inventory of supplies.	50,000
Total assets	$248,000

Liabilities & Fund Balance

Liabilities:		
Vouchers payable . . . . .'.		$ 70,000
Payable to other funds		11,000
Total liabilities		$ 81,000
Fund balance:		
Reserved for encumbrances	$ 5,000	
Reserved for inventory of supplies.	50,000	
Unreserved.	112,000	167,000
Total liabilities & fund balance		$248,000

3 The assets of the General Fund include only monetary assets and inventory. Expenditures for prepayments other than supplies and for plant assets are not recorded as assets in the General Fund.

4 The unreserved fund balance in the balance sheet, $112,000, is a balancing amount to make the total of the reserved and unreserved fund balance equal to $167,000, the final amount in the statement of revenues, expenditures, and changes in fund balance. After the posting of the closing entries illustrated in the next section, the ending balance of the Unreserved Fund Balance ledger account is $112,000 (see page 522).

Closing entries for a general fund

After financial statements have been prepared for the Town of Verdant Glen General Fund, the budgetary and actual revenues, expenditures, and encumbrances accounts must be closed, to clear them for the next fiscal year's activities. The closing entries at the top of page 521 are appropriate for the Town of Verdant Glen General Fund on June 30, Year 6. The journal entries on page 521 do not close the Fund Balance Reserved for Encumbrances account. Thus, the reserve represents a restriction on the fund balance on June 30, Year 6, because the Town of Verdant Glen General Fund is committed in Fiscal Year 7 to make estimated expenditures of $5,000 attributable to budgetary appropriations carried over from Fiscal Year 6. If the Fund Balance Reserved for Encumbrances account had been closed, the Unreserved Fund Balance account would have been overstated by $5,000. The Unreserved Fund

Closing entries for general fund

Unreserved Fund Balance	*5,000*	
Encumbrances		*5,000*
To close Encumbrances account.		
Appropriations	*760,000*	
Estimated Other Financing Uses	*60,000*	
Budgetary Fund Balance	*30,000*	
Estimated Revenues		*800,000*
Estimated Other Financing Sources		*50,000*
To close budgetary accounts. (See page 511.)		
Revenues	*808,000*	
Other Financing Sources	*50,000*	
Expenditures		*750,000*
Other Financing Uses		*61,000*
Unreserved Fund Balance		*47,000*
To close revenues, expenditures, and other financing sources and uses.		

Balance account must represent the amount of the General Fund's assets that is available for appropriation for a ***deficit budget*** in Fiscal Year 7. When expenditures applicable to the $5,000 outstanding encumbrances on June 30, Year 6, are vouchered for payment in the succeeding fiscal year, the Fund Balance Reserved for Encumbrances account is debited for $5,000, the Vouchers Payable is credited for the amount to be paid, and the balancing debit or credit is entered in the Unreserved Fund Balance account.

The budgetary accounts are closed at the end of the fiscal year because they are no longer required for control over revenues, expenditures, and other financing sources and uses. The amounts in the journal entry that closed the budgetary accounts were taken from the original journal entry to record the budget (page 511).

After the June 30, Year 6, closing entries for the Town of Verdant Glen General Fund are posted, the Unreserved Fund Balance ledger account appears as shown at the top of page 522.

Unreserved Fund
Balance ledger account
of general fund

Unreserved Fund Balance				
Date	Explanation	Debit	Credit	Balance
6/30/5	Balance			80,000 cr
6/30/6	Increase in amount reserved for inventory of supplies (page 517)	10,000		70,000 cr
6/30/6	Close Encumbrances account (page 521)	5,000		65,000 cr
6/30/6	Close excess of revenues and other financing sources over expenditures and other financing uses (page 521)		47,000	112,000 cr

REVIEW QUESTIONS

1 What are **nonbusiness organizations?**

2 Does the FASB currently establish accounting principles for governmental units? Explain.

3 Did the FASB recommend objectives of financial reporting by the federal government?

4 What characteristics of governmental units have a significant influence on the accounting for governmental units? Explain.

5 What is a **fund** in accounting for governmental units?

6 What is the support for each of the following accounting principles for governmental units?
  a The modified accrual basis of accounting
  b The encumbrance accounting technique
  c Recording the budget in the accounting records

7 Differentiate between a **program budget** and a **performance budget.**

8 The Estimated Revenues account of a governmental unit's general fund may be viewed as a **pseudo asset,** and the Appropriations account may be viewed as a **pseudo liability.** Why is this true?

9 What does the reference to a general fund as **residual** mean? Explain.

10 a What are the basic financial statements for a governmental unit's general fund?
  b What are the principal differences between the financial statements of a governmental unit's general fund and the financial statements of a business enterprise?

11 What revenues of a general fund usually are accrued? Explain.

12 Distinguish between the Expenditures ledger account of a governmental unit's general fund and the expense accounts of a business enterprise.

13 The accounting records for the City of Worthington General Fund include a ledger account titled Fund Balance Reserved for Inventory of Supplies. Explain the purpose of this account.

14 Explain the use of the Other Financing Sources and Other Financing Uses ledger accounts of a governmental unit's general fund.

15 What is the function of the Budgetary Fund Balance account of a general fund?

EXERCISES

Ex. 11-1 Select the best answer for each of the following multiple-choice questions:

1 Repairs that have been made for a governmental unit, and for which an invoice has been received, should be recorded in the General Fund as an:
   a Appropriation   **b** Encumbrance   **c** Expenditure   **d** Expense

2 Under the modified accrual basis of accounting, which of the following taxes usually is recorded in the accounting records of a governmental unit's general fund before it is collected?
   a Property   **b** Income   **c** Gross receipts   **d** Gift
   e None of the foregoing

3 One of the differences between accounting for a governmental unit and accounting for a business enterprise is that a governmental unit should:
   a Not record depreciation expense in any of its funds
   b Always establish and maintain complete self-balancing accounts for each fund
   c Use only the cash basis of accounting
   d Use only the modified accrual basis of accounting

4 Which of the following general fund ledger accounts is closed at the end of the fiscal year?
   a Unreserved fund balance
   b Expenditures
   c Vouchers payable
   d Fund balance reserved for encumbrances
   e None of the foregoing

5 The offset for a general fund journal entry crediting the Allowance for Uncollectible Current Taxes ledger account is a debit to the:
   a Uncollectible Current Taxes Expense account
   b Unreserved Fund Balance account
   c Allowance for Uncollectible Delinquent Taxes account
   d Revenues account

6 The purpose of a governmental unit general fund's Fund Balance Reserved for Inventory of Supplies ledger account is to:
   a Earmark resources for replacement of supplies
   b Provide for outstanding purchase orders for supplies
   c Prevent improper appropriation of the fund balance to finance a deficit budget
   d Accomplish none of the above

7 The Town of Newbold General Fund issued purchase orders totaling $630,000 to vendors and suppliers. Which of the following journal entries (explanation omitted) is prepared to record this transaction?

(a) Encumbrances   630,000
    Fund Balance Reserved for Encumbrances   630,000
  b Expenditures   630,000
    Vouchers Payable   630,000
  c Expenses   630,000
    Accounts Payable   630,000
  d Fund Balance Reserved for Encumbrances   630,000
    Encumbrances   630,000
  e None of the foregoing

Ex. 11-2   On July 25, Year 3, office supplies estimated to cost $2,390 were ordered from a vendor for delivery to the office of the city manager of Gaskill. The City of Gaskill maintains a perpetual inventory system for such supplies. The supplies ordered July 25 were received on August 9, Year 3, accompanied by an invoice for $2,500.

    Prepare journal entries to record the foregoing transactions in the City of Gaskill General Fund.

Ex. 11-3   The after-closing trial balance of the Winton County General Fund included the following ledger account balances on June 30, Year 2:

Taxes receivable—delinquent . . . . $30,200 dr
Allowance for uncollectible delinquent taxes . . . . 1,300 cr

The property taxes assessments for the year ending June 30, Year 3, totaled $640,000; 4% of Winston County's property tax assessments have been uncollectible in past fiscal years.

    Prepare a journal entry for the property taxes of Winston County's General Fund on July 1, Year 2, the date on which the property taxes for the year ending June 30, Year 3, were billed to taxpayers.

Ex. 11-4   The Glengarry School District General Fund had an inventory of supplies (and related reserve) of $60,200 on July 1, Year 8. For the year ended June 30, Year 9, supplies costing $170,900 were acquired; related purchase orders totaled $168,400. The physical inventory of unused supplies on June 30, Year 9, totaled $78,300.

    Prepare journal entries for the foregoing facts for the year ended June 30, Year 9. Omit explanations.

Ex. 11-5   Among the journal entries of Rainbow County General Fund for the year ended June 30, Year 7, were the following:

7/1/6   Accounts Receivable   800,000
    Cash   800,000
    To record nonreturnable transfer of cash to Internal
    Service Fund to provide working capital to establish
    that fund.

9/1/6   Equipment   120,000
    Vouchers Payable   120,000
    To record acquisition of equipment having a 10-year
    economic life and no residual value.

2/1/7 *Cash* 608,200

    Income Taxes Receivable   608,200

    To record January, Year 7, collection of income taxes

    for Calendar Year 6 that were accrued on January 2,

    Year 7, in the total amount of $1,940,800.

  Prepare journal entries on June 30, Year 7, in the accounting records of Rainbow County General Fund to correct the records, assuming that the remaining income taxes collections for Year 7 were accounted for on the cash basis of accounting.

Ex. 11-6 The Unreserved Fund Balance of the Town of Oldberry appeared as follows on June 30, Year 4:

Unreserved Fund Balance

Date	Explanation	Debit	Credit	Balance
6/30/3	Balance			62,400 *cr*
6/30/4	Decrease in amount reserved for inventory of supplies		3,700	66,100 *cr*
6/30/4	Close Encumbrances account	6,200		59,900 *cr*
6/30/4	Close excess of revenues ($840,200) over expenditures ($764,800)		75,400	135,300 *cr*

  The Town of Oldberry did not have any other financing sources or uses during the year ended June 30, Year 4.

  Reconstruct the journal entries indicated by the foregoing information.

Ex. 11-7 Following is the statement of revenues, expenditures, and changes in fund balance for the Village of Mortimer General Fund for the year ended June 30, Year 8. The village did not have any other financing sources or uses for the year. Unfilled purchase orders on June 30, Year 8, totaled $11,400.

VILLAGE OF MORTIMER GENERAL FUND

Statement of Revenues, Expenditures, and Changes in Fund Balance

For Year Ended June 30, Year 8

	Budget	Actual	Variance favorable (unfavorable)
Revenues:			
Taxes.	$820,000	$814,200	$(5,800)
Other.	160,000	162,500	2,500
Total revenues	$980,000	$976,700	$(3,300)
Expenditures:			
General government.	$615,000	$618,800	$(3,800)
Other.	275,000	277,400	(2,400)
Total expenditures.	$890,000	$896,200	$(6,200)
Excess of revenues over expenditures	$ 90,000	$ 80,500	$(9,500)
Fund balance, beginning of year.	280,400	280,400	
Fund balance, end of year	$370,400	$360,900	$(9,500)

Prepare closing entries for the Village of Mortimer General Fund on June 30, Year 8.

Ex. 11-8 On July 1, Year 9, the general ledger of the City of Winkle had the following fund balance accounts:

Reserved for inventory of supplies	$ 80,600
Reserved for encumbrances	18,100
Unreserved	214,700

The budget for the year ending June 30, Year 10, showed a budgetary surplus of $20,400. Revenues for the year ended June 30, Year 10, exceeded expenditures by $37,600. There were no other financing sources or uses for the year. The physical inventory of supplies on June 30, Year 10, was $88,200, and outstanding encumbrances on June 30, Year 10, totaled $14,800.

Compute the balance of the Unreserved Fund Balance ledger account (after posting of closing entries) for the City of Winkle on June 30, Year 10.

CASES

Case 11-1 The inexperienced accountant of Corbin City prepared the following financial statements for the city's general fund:

CORBIN CITY GENERAL FUND
Income Statement
For Year Ended June 30, Year 9

Revenues:		
Taxes		$640,000
Other		180,000
Total revenues		$820,000
Expenses:		
General government	$600,000	
Depreciation	60,000	
Other	120,000	780,000
Net income		$ 40,000

CORBIN CITY GENERAL FUND
Statement of Changes in Fund Balance
For Year Ended June 30, Year 9

Fund balance, beginning of year	$4,850,000
Add: Net income	40,000
Fund balance, end of year	$4,890,000

CORBIN CITY GENERAL FUND
Balance Sheet
June 30, Year 9

Assets

Cash	$ 260,000
Property taxes receivable—delinquent	80,000
Inventory of supplies	110,000
Plant assets (net)	4,620,000
Total assets	$5,070,000

Liabilities, Reserves & Fund Balance

Vouchers payable	$ 160,000
Reserve for delinquent property taxes	20,000
Fund balance	4,890,000
Total liabilities, reserves & fund balance	$5,070,000

Instructions Identify the deficiencies of the foregoing financial statements of Corbin City General Fund. There are no arithmetic errors in the statements. Disregard notes to financial statements.

Case 11-2 Bertram Kent, an officer of a publicly owned corporation, has been elected to the city council of Independence City. Kent has asked you to explain the principal differences in the accounting and financial reporting of a city as compared with a business enterprise.

Instructions
a Describe the principal differences in the accounting and financial reporting of a city as compared with a business enterprise.
b The general funds of some governmental units do not reflect inventories of supplies in the accounting records or financial statements. Is this omission justifiable?
c Should depreciation be recorded in the general fund of a governmental unit? Explain.

PROBLEMS

11-1 The information at the top of page 528 was taken from the accounting records of the General Fund of the City of Lory after the records had been closed for the fiscal year ended June 30, Year 3. The budget for the fiscal year ended June 30, Year 3, included estimated revenues of $2,000,000 and appropriations of $1,940,000. There were no other financing sources or uses.

Instructions Prepare journal entries to record the budgeted and actual transactions of the City of Lory General Fund for the fiscal year ended June 30, Year 3. Also prepare closing entries. Do not differentiate between current and delinquent taxes receivable.

11-2 At the start of your examination of the financial statements of the City of Riverdale, you discovered that the City's accountant failed to maintain separate funds. The trial balance on page 528 of the City of Riverdale General Fund for the year ended December 31, Year 11, was available.

CITY OF LORY GENERAL FUND

	After-closing trial balance, June 30, Year 2	Transactions July 1, Year 2, to June 30, Year 3		After-closing trial balance, June 30, Year 3
		Debit	Credit	
Debits				
Cash.	$700,000	$1,820,000	$1,852,000	$668,000
Taxes receivable. . .	40,000	1,870,000	1,828,000	82,000
Total debits . . .	$740,000			$750,000
Credits				
Allowance for uncol-				
lectible taxes	$ 8,000	8,000	10,000	$ 10,000
Vouchers payable . .	132,000	1,852,000	1,840,000	120,000
Fund balance:				
Reserved for en-				
cumbrances . . .		1,000,000	1,070,000	70,000
Unreserved.	600,000	70,000	20,000	550,000
Total credits. . .	$740,000	$6,620,000	$6,620,000	$750,000

CITY OF RIVERDALE GENERAL FUND
Trial Balance
December 31, Year 11

	Debit	Credit
Cash	$ 207,500	
Taxes receivable—current	148,500	
Allowance for uncollectible current taxes		$ 6,000
Revenues		992,500
Expenditures	760,000	
Donated land	190,000	
Construction in process—River Bridge	130,000	
River Bridge bonds payable		100,000
Contracts payable—River Bridge		30,000
Vouchers payable		7,500
Unreserved fund balance		300,000
Totals	$1,436,000	$1,436,000

Additional information

(1) The budget for Year 11, not recorded in the accounting records, was as follows: Estimated revenues, $815,000; appropriations, $775,000. There were no other financing sources or uses.

(2) Outstanding purchase orders on December 31, Year 11, for operating expenditures not recorded in the accounting records, totaled $2,500.

(3) Included in the Revenues account is a credit of $190,000 representing the current fair value of land donated by the state as a site for construction of the River Bridge.

(4) The taxes receivable became delinquent on December 31, Year 11.

Instructions Prepare adjusting journal entries on December 31, Year 11, to correct the accounting records of the City of Riverdale General Fund. Adjusting entries for other funds and closing entries are not required.

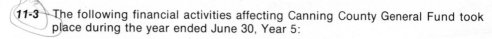

11-3 The following financial activities affecting Canning County General Fund took place during the year ended June 30, Year 5:

(1) The following budget was adopted:

Estimated revenues:	
Property taxes	*$4,500,000*
Licenses and permits	*300,000*
Fines	*200,000*
Total estimated revenues	*$5,000,000*
Appropriations:	
General government	*$1,500,000*
Police services	*1,200,000*
Fire department services	*900,000*
Public works services	*800,000*
Acquisition of fire engines	*400,000*
Total appropriations	*$4,800,000*

There were no other financing sources or uses budgeted.

(2) Property tax bills totaling $4,650,000 were mailed. It was estimated that $150,000 of this amount will be uncollectible.

(3) Property taxes totaling $3,900,000 were collected. The $150,000 previously estimated to be uncollectible remained unchanged, but $630,000 was reclassified as delinquent. It is estimated that delinquent taxes will be collected soon enough after June 30, Year 5, to make these taxes available to finance obligations incurred during the year ended June 30, Year 5. There was no balance of uncollected taxes on July 1, Year 4.

(4) Other cash collections were as follows:

Licenses and permits	*$270,000*
Fines	*200,000*
Sale of public works equipment (original cost, $75,000)	*15,000*
Total other cash collections	*$485,000*

(5) No encumbrances were outstanding on June 30, Year 4. The following purchase orders were executed:

	Total amount	Outstanding, June 30, Year 5
General government	*$1,050,000*	*$ 60,000*
Police services	*300,000*	*30,000*
Fire department services	*150,000*	*15,000*
Public works services	*250,000*	*10,000*
Fire engines	*400,000*	
Totals	*$2,150,000*	*$115,000*

(6) The following vouchers were approved:

General government	$1,440,000
Police services	1,155,000
Fire department services	870,000
Public works services	700,000
Fire engines	400,000
Total vouchers approved	$4,565,000

(7) Vouchers totaling $4,600,000 were paid.

Instructions Prepare journal entries to record the foregoing financial activities in the Canning County General Fund for the year ended June 30, Year 5. Disregard interest accruals and closing entries.

11-4 The trial balance of Arden School District General Fund is presented below:

ARDEN SCHOOL DISTRICT GENERAL FUND
Trial Balance
December 31, Year 5

	Debit	Credit
Cash	$ 47,250	
Short-term investments	11,300	
Taxes receivable—delinquent	30,000	
Inventory of supplies	11,450	
Vouchers payable		$ 20,200
Payable to Internal Service Fund		950
Fund balance reserved for encumbrances		2,800
Fund balance reserved for inventory of supplies		11,450
Unreserved fund balance		59,400
Budgetary fund balance		7,000
Estimated revenues	1,007,000	
Appropriations		985,000
Estimated other financing uses		15,000
Revenues		1,008,200
Expenditures	990,200	
Other financing uses	10,000	
Encumbrances	2,800	
Totals	$2,110,000	$2,110,000

The balance of the Fund Balance Reserved for Inventory of Supplies ledger account on December 31, Year 4, was $9,500.

Instructions
a Prepare the following financial statements for Arden School District General Fund for the year ended December 31, Year 5:
(1) Statement of revenues, expenditures, and changes in fund balance
(2) Balance sheet
b Prepare closing entries for Arden School District General Fund on December 31, Year 5.

11-5 The following summary of transactions was taken from the accounting records of Melton School District General Fund before the accounting records had been closed for the year ended June 30, Year 5:

MELTON SCHOOL DISTRICT GENERAL FUND
Summary of Transactions
For Year Ended June 30, Year 5

	After-closing balances, June 30, Year 4	Before-closing balances, June 30, Year 5
Ledger accounts with debit balances:		
Cash	$400,000	$ 700,000
Taxes receivable	150,000	170,000
Estimated revenues		3,000,000
Expenditures		2,700,000
Other financing uses		142,000
Encumbrances		91,000
Totals	$550,000	$6,803,000
Ledger accounts with credit balances:		
Allowance for uncollectible taxes	$ 40,000	$ 70,000
Vouchers payable	80,000	408,000
Payable to other funds	210,000	142,000
Fund balance reserved for encumbrances	60,000	91,000
Unreserved fund balance	160,000	162,000
Revenues from taxes		2,800,000
Other revenues		130,000
Budgetary fund balance		20,000
Appropriations		2,810,000
Estimated other financing uses		170,000
Totals	$550,000	$6,803,000

Additional information

(1) The estimated taxes receivable for the year ended June 30, Year 5, were $2,870,000, and taxes collected during the year totaled $2,810,000.

(2) An analysis of the transactions in the Vouchers Payable ledger account for the year ended June 30, Year 5, follows:

	Debit (credit)
Current year expenditures (all subject to encumbrances)	$(2,700,000)
Expenditures applicable to June 30, Year 4, outstanding encumbrances	(58,000)
Vouchers for payments to other funds	(210,000)
Cash payments	2,640,000
Net change	$ (328,000)

(3) During Year 5 the General Fund was billed $142,000 for services furnished by other funds of Melton School District.

(4) On May 2, Year 5, purchase orders were issued for new textbooks at an esti-mated cost of $91,000. The books were to be delivered in August, Year 5.

Instructions

a Based on the foregoing data, reconstruct the original journal entries to record all transactions of Melton School District General Fund for the year ended June 30, Year 5, including the recording of the budget for the year. Disregard current and delinquent taxes receivable. (Hint: The $2,000 difference between the $60,000 fund balance reserved for encumbrances on June 30, Year 4, and the $58,000 amount vouchered for the related expenditures is credited to the Unreserved Fund Balance account.)

b Prepare closing entries on June 30, Year 5.

c Prepare an after-closing trial balance for Melton School District General Fund on June 30, Year 5.

11-6 Because the controller of the City of Romaine resigned, the assistant controller attempted to compute the cash required to be derived from property taxes for the General Fund for the year ending June 30, Year 7. The computation was made as of January 1, Year 6, to serve as a basis for establishing the property tax rate for the fiscal year ending June 30, Year 7. The mayor of Romaine has re-quested you to review the assistant controller's computations and obtain other necessary information to prepare for the City of Romaine General Fund a formal estimate of the cash required to be derived from property taxes for the fiscal year ending June 30, Year 7. Following are the computations prepared by the assistant controller:

City resources other than proposed property tax levy:

Estimated General Fund cash balance, Jan. 1, Year 6	$ 352,000
Estimated cash receipts from property taxes, Jan. 1 to June 30, Year 6	2,222,000
Estimated cash revenues from investments, Jan. 1, Year 6, to June 30, Year 7	442,000
Estimated proceeds from issuance of general obligation bonds in August, Year 6	3,000,000
Total City resources	$6,016,000
General Fund requirements:	
Estimated expenditures, Jan. 1 to June 30, Year 6	$1,900,000
Proposed appropriations, July 1, Year 6, to June 30, Year 7	4,300,000
Total General Fund requirements	$6,200,000

Additional information

(1) The General Fund cash balance required for July 1, Year 7, is $175,000.

(2) Property tax collections are due in March and September of each year. You note that during February, Year 6, estimated expenditures will exceed avail-able cash by $200,000. Pending collection of property taxes in March, Year 6, this deficiency will have to be met by the issuance of 30-day tax-anticipation notes of $200,000 at an estimated interest rate of 12% a year.

(3) The proposed general obligation bonds will be issued by the City of Romaine Enterprise Fund to finance the construction of a new water pumping station.

Instructions Prepare a working paper as of January 1, Year 6, to compute the property tax levy required for the City of Romaine General Fund for the fiscal year ending June 30, Year 7.

11-7 The following data were taken from the accounting records of the Town of Tosca General Fund after the records had been closed for the fiscal year ended June 30, Year 3:

TOWN OF TOSCA GENERAL FUND

Data from Accounting Records

For Year Ended June 30, Year 3

	Balances July 1, Year 2	Fiscal Year 3 changes		Balances June 30, Year 3
		Debit	Credit	
Assets				
Cash	$180,000	$ 955,000	$ 880,000	$255,000
Taxes receivable	20,000	809,000	781,000	48,000
Allowance for uncollectible				
taxes	(4,000)	6,000	9,000	(7,000)
Total assets	$196,000			$296,000
Liabilities & Fund Balance				
Vouchers payable	$ 44,000	880,000	889,000	$ 53,000
Payable to Internal Service				
Fund	2,000	7,000	10,000	5,000
Payable to Debt Service				
Fund	10,000	60,000	100,000	50,000
Fund balance reserved				
for encumbrances	40,000	40,000	47,000	47,000
Unreserved fund balance. .	100,000	47,000	88,000	141,000
Total liabilities & fund				
balance	$196,000	$2,804,000	$2,804,000	$296,000

Additional data

(1) The budget for Fiscal Year 3 provided for estimated revenues of $1,000,000 and appropriations of $965,000. There were no other financing sources or uses budgeted.

(2) Expenditures totaling $895,000, in addition to those chargeable against the Fund Balance Reserved for Encumbrances ledger account, were made.

(3) The actual expenditure chargeable against the July 1, Year 2, Fund Balance Reserved for Encumbrances ledger account was $37,000.

Instructions Reconstruct the journal entries, including closing entries, for the Town of Tosca General Fund indicated by the foregoing data for the year ended June 30, Year 3. Do not attempt to differentiate between current and delinquent taxes receivable.

12 GOVERNMENTAL UNITS: OTHER FUNDS AND ACCOUNT GROUPS

In this chapter we discuss and illustrate accounting for a governmental unit's funds other than the general fund, and for the general fixed assets and general long-term debt account groups. Also covered in this chapter are the form and content of annual reports of governmental units and an appraisal of accounting principles for governmental units.

GOVERNMENTAL FUNDS

Accounting for the four governmental funds (special revenue funds, capital projects funds, debt service funds, special assessment funds) other than the general fund generally incorporates many of the accounting principles discussed in Chapter 11. For example, the modified accrual basis of accounting is appropriate for all governmental funds, and recording the budget (together with encumbrance accounting) is mandatory for special revenue funds and often useful for debt service funds, capital projects funds, and special assessment funds.

Accounting for special revenue funds

As indicated in principle 3 on page 504, special revenue funds are established by governmental units to account for the collections and expenditures associated with specialized revenue sources that are earmarked by law or regulation to finance specified governmental operations. Fees for rubbish collection, state gasoline taxes, and traffic violation fines are examples of governmental unit revenues accounted for in separate special revenue funds.

Account titles, budgetary processes, and financial statements for special revenue funds are similar to those for general funds; therefore, they are not illustrated in this section.

Accounting for capital projects funds

Capital projects funds of a governmental unit record the receipt and payment of cash for the construction or acquisition of the governmental unit's plant assets, other than those financed by special assessment funds, proprietary funds, or trust funds. The resources for a capital projects fund usually are derived from proceeds of general obligation bonds, but the resources may also come from current tax revenues or from grants or shared revenues of other governmental units.

A capital budget, rather than an annual budget, is the **control device** appropriate for a capital projects fund. The capital budget should deal with both the authorized expenditures for the project and the bonds or other sources of revenues for the project.

Journal Entries for Capital Projects Fund On July 1, Year 5, the Town of Verdant Glen authorized a $500,000, 20-year, 15% general obligation bond issue to finance an addition to the town's high school. A capital budget was approved for the amount of the bonds, but it was not to be integrated in the accounting records of the capital projects fund authorized for the project. The journal entries on page 536 illustrate the issuance of the bonds and other activities of the Town of Verdant Glen Capital Projects Fund for the year ended June 30, Year 6. The following features of the journal entries should be noted:

1 The capital budget for the high school addition is not entered in the accounting records of the Capital Projects Fund. The indenture for the 20-year, 15% general obligation bonds provides adequate control.

2 Neither the liability nor the discount applicable to the 20-year general obligation bonds is recorded in the Capital Projects Fund. The liability for the bonds is recorded at face amount in the general long-term debt account group (see page 556).

3 The proceeds of the general obligation bonds represent other financing sources to the Capital Projects Fund. The interest earned on the short-term investment in U.S. Treasury bills represents revenues to the Capital Projects Fund.

4 The encumbrances and expenditures accounting for the Capital Projects Fund is similar to that for the General Fund illustrated in Chapter 11. Also, closing entries for the two types of governmental funds are similar.

Expenditures for construction recorded in the Town of Verdant Glen Capital Projects Fund are accompanied in the General Fixed Assets Account Group by a journal entry at the end of the fiscal year with a debit to Construction in Progress and a credit to Investment in Fixed Assets from Capital Projects Fund. The accounting for the general fixed assets account group is illustrated in a subsequent section of this chapter.

At the end of each fiscal year prior to completion of a capital project, the Revenues, Other Financing Sources, Expenditures, and Encumbrances accounts of the Capital Projects Fund are closed to the Unreserved Fund Balance account. Upon completion of the project, the entire Capital Projects Fund is closed by a transfer of any unused cash to the Debt Service Fund or the General Fund, as appropriate; the Other

TOWN OF VERDANT GLEN CAPITAL PROJECTS FUND
General Journal

Cash	470,188	
Other Financing Sources		470,188

To record issuance of 20-year, 15% general obligation bonds due July 1, Year 25, interest payable Jan. 1 and July 1, to yield 16%, face amount $500,000.

Investments	325,000	
Cash		325,000

To record acquisition of $350,000 face amount of U.S. Treasury bills, maturity 26 weeks.

Encumbrances	482,000	
Fund Balance Reserved for Encumbrances		482,000

To record contracts with architect and construction contractor and issuance of purchase orders.

Cash	350,000	
Investments		325,000
Revenues		25,000

To record receipt of cash for matured U.S. Treasury bills.

Expenditures	378,000	
Vouchers Payable		378,000

To record expenditures for the year.

Fund Balance Reserved for Encumbrances	368,200	
Encumbrances		368,200

To reverse encumbrances applicable to vouchered expenditures.

Vouchers Payable	327,500	
Cash		327,500

To record payment of vouchers during the year.

Unreserved Fund Balance ($482,000 − $368,200)	113,800	
Encumbrances		113,800

To close Encumbrances account.

Revenues	25,000	
Other Financing Sources	470,188	
Expenditures		378,000
Unreserved Fund Balance		117,188

To close revenues, expenditures, and other financing sources.

Financing Sources account of the receiving fund would be credited. Any cash deficiency in the Capital Projects Fund probably would be made up by the General Fund; this financing would be credited to the Other Financing Sources account of the Capital Projects Fund and debited to the Other Financing Uses account of the General Fund.

Financial Statements for Capital Projects Fund A capital projects fund issues the same financial statements as a general fund—a statement of revenues, expenditures, and changes in fund balance, and a balance sheet. For the Town of Verdant Glen Capital Projects Fund, these financial statements are as follows for the year ended June 30, Year 6:

TOWN OF VERDANT GLEN CAPITAL PROJECTS FUND
Statement of Revenues, Expenditures, and Changes in Fund Balance
For Year Ended June 30, Year 6

Revenues:	
Miscellaneous	$ 25,000
*Expenditures:**	
Construction contracts	$ 287,600
Engineering and other	90,400
Total expenditures	$ 378,000
Excess (deficiency) of revenues over expenditures	$(353,000)
Other financing sources:	
Proceeds of general obligation bonds	470,188
Excess of revenues and other financing sources over expenditures	$ 117,188
Fund balance, beginning of year	-0-
Fund balance, end of year	$ 117,188

* Breakdown of expenditures is assumed.

TOWN OF VERDANT GLEN CAPITAL PROJECTS FUND
Balance Sheet
June 30, Year 6

Assets

Cash		$167,688

Liabilities & Fund Balance

Liabilities:		
Vouchers payable		$ 50,500
Fund balance:		
Reserved for encumbrances	$113,800	
Unreserved	3,388	117,188
Total liabilities & fund balance		$167,688

To reiterate, the assets constructed with resources of the Capital Projects Fund do not appear in that fund's balance sheet. Constructed plant assets appear in the governmental unit's general fixed assets account group. Furthermore, the general obligation bonds issued to finance the Capital Projects Fund are not a liability of that fund. Prior to the maturity date or dates of the bonds, the liability is carried in the general long-term debt account group (see page 556). On the date the bonds mature, the related liability is transferred to the debt service fund or to the general fund from the general long-term debt account group.

Accounting for debt service funds

Payments of principal and interest on long-term bonds of a governmental unit, other than special assessment bonds, revenue bonds, and general obligation bonds serviced by an enterprise fund, are accounted for either in the general fund or in debt service funds. *Special assessment bonds* are repaid from the proceeds of special assessment levies against specific properties receiving benefits from the special assessment improvements; accordingly, these bonds are accounted for in special assessment funds. *Revenue bonds* are payable from the earnings of a governmental unit enterprise and are accounted for in the appropriate enterprise fund. In some cases, *general obligation bonds,* which are backed by the full faith and credit of the issuing governmental unit, will be repaid from the resources of a governmental unit enterprise. These general obligation bonds are reported as liabilities of the appropriate enterprise fund.

We must stress that the liability for bonds payable from resources of the general fund or a debt service fund is not recorded in that fund until the debt matures. Prior to maturity date, the bond liability is carried in the general long-term debt account group.

The two customary types of general obligation bonds whose servicing is recorded in debt service funds are the following:

Serial bonds, with principal payable in annual installments over the term of the bond issue

Term bonds, with principal payable in total on a fixed maturity date, generally from proceeds of an accumulated sinking fund

Generally, legal requirements govern the establishment of debt service funds. In the absence of legal requirements or of a formal plan for accumulation of a sinking fund for repayment of a general obligation term bond, there is no need for a debt service fund to be created.

Journal Entries for Debt Service Fund   To illustrate the journal entries that are typical for a debt service fund, let us assume that the Town of Verdant Glen had only two general obligation bond issues outstanding during the year ended June 30, Year 6: A $100,000, 10% serial bond issue whose final annual installment of $10,000 was payable on January 1,

Year 6, and a $500,000, 15% term bond issue due July 1, Year 25 (see page 535). The Town Council had authorized establishment of a debt service fund for the serial bonds. However, sinking fund accumulations on the term bonds were not required to begin until July 1, Year 8; therefore, a debt service fund for those bonds was unnecessary during the year ended June 30, Year 6.

Interest on both general obligation bond issues was payable each January 1 and July 1. Interest payments on the term bonds were recorded in the General Fund during the year ended June 30, Year 6, and were included in expenditures of that fund, as illustrated on page 516. Interest payments on the serial bonds were made from the Debt Service Fund to a fiscal agent, for remission to the bondholders.

The June 30, Year 5, balance sheet of the Town of Verdant Glen Debt Service Fund for the serial bonds was as follows:

TOWN OF VERDANT GLEN DEBT SERVICE FUND
Balance Sheet
June 30, Year 5

Assets

Cash $342

Liabilities & Fund Balance

Fund balance reserved for debt service $342

The journal entries for the Debt Service Fund for the year ended June 30, Year 6, are presented on page 540. Following are significant aspects of the illustrated journal entries for the Debt Service Fund:

1 There was no journal entry to record an annual budget. Generally, indentures for general obligation bonds provide sufficient safeguards (such as restricting the fund balance of the debt service fund solely for the payment of debt and related servicing costs), so that recording the budget in the Debt Service Fund is unnecessary. (Note, however, on page 517 of Chapter 11 that the General Fund's other financing use for payment of $11,000 to the Debt Service Fund had been included in the General Fund's annual budget.)

2 Expenditures for principal and interest payments of the Debt Service Fund are recorded only on the maturity dates of the obligations. Prior to the maturity dates, the liabilities are carried in the general long-term debt account group (see page 556). Because a debt service fund does not issue purchase orders, encumbrance accounting is not required.

3 The closing entry extinguishes all remaining ledger account balances of the Debt Service Fund, because the final serial principal payment had been made.

The modified accrual basis of accounting is appropriate for a debt service fund. Thus, any property taxes specifically earmarked for servicing of a governmental unit's general obligation bonds may be accrued as revenues in the debt service fund. The accounting for such a tax accrual is the same as that for the general fund.

TOWN OF VERDANT GLEN DEBT SERVICE FUND
General Journal

Cash	11,000	
Other Financing Sources		11,000

To record receipt of cash from General Fund for payment of
serial bond principal ($10,000) and interest ($1,000) maturing
on July 1, Year 5, and Jan. 1, Year 6.

Cash with Fiscal Agent	11,000	
Cash.		11,000

To record payment of cash to bank trust department acting as
fiscal agent for payment of serial bond principal and interest.

Expenditures	11,000	
Matured Bonds Payable		10,000
Matured Interest Payable		1,000

To record expenditures for interest due July 1, Year 5, and
principal and interest due Jan. 1, Year 6.

Matured Bonds Payable	10,000	
Matured Interest Payable	1,000	
Cash with Fiscal Agent.		11,000

To record fiscal agent's payments of bond principal and
interest.

Expenditures	342	
Cash.		342

To record payment of fiscal agent for services during year ended
June 30, Year 6.

Other Financing Sources	11,000	
Fund Balance Reserved for Debt Service	342	
Expenditures		11,342

To close fund on extinguishment of related serial bonds.

For a term bond, which requires the accumulation of a sinking fund,
the journal entries for a debt service fund include the investment of cash
in interest-bearing securities and the collection of interest. Under the
modified accrual basis of accounting, interest revenue accrued on sinking fund investments at the end of the governmental unit's fiscal year is
recorded in the accounting records of the debt service fund.

Financial Statements for Debt Service Fund We already have illustrated a
balance sheet for a debt service fund on page 539. There is no balance
sheet for the Town of Verdant Glen Debt Service Fund on June 30, Year

6, because the fund was completely closed. The statement of revenues, expenditures, and changes in fund balance for the Town of Verdant Glen Debt Service Fund is as follows for the year ended June 30, Year 6:

TOWN OF VERDANT GLEN DEBT SERVICE FUND

Statement of Revenues, Expenditures, and Changes in Fund Balance

For Year Ended June 30, Year 6

Expenditures:	
Principal retirement	$ 10,000
Interest and charges by fiscal agent	1,342
Total expenditures.	$ 11,342
Excess (deficiency) of revenues over expenditures.	$(11,342)
Other financing sources:	
Operating transfers in.	11,000
Excess (deficiency) of revenues and other financing sources over expenditures	$ (342)
Fund balance, beginning of year.	342
Fund balance, end of year	$ -0-

Accounting for special assessment funds

A special assessment fund accounts for the assets, liabilities, revenues, and expenditures attributable to special tax assessments, payable in installments, that are levied on property owners in the governmental unit's jurisdiction. These tax assessments finance construction projects primarily for the benefit of the assessed property owners.

Accounting for a special assessment fund is in many respects a composite of the accounting for a debt service fund and a capital projects fund. The accounting records of a special assessment fund include both the proceeds and the servicing of the *special assessment bonds* that are issued to finance the construction project prior to the collection of special assessments receivable.

Journal Entries for Special Assessment Fund The town council of the Town of Verdant Glen enacted a special assessment for paving streets and installing sidewalks in a section of the town. The total assessment was $250,000, payable in five annual installments, beginning July 1, Year 5. Interest on unpaid balances at 16% a year was payable annually, beginning July 1, Year 6. To finance the cost of the construction project, the Town Council authorized the issuance of $200,000 face amount, 14%, four-year special assessment bonds, payable $50,000 a year plus interest payable annually, beginning July 1, Year 6. The Town Council approved contracts with a firm of contractors for the paving work.

Following are journal entries for the Town of Verdant Glen Special Assessment Fund for the year ended June 30, Year 6:

TOWN OF VERDANT GLEN SPECIAL ASSESSMENT FUND
General Journal

Special Assessments Receivable—Current	50,000	
Special Assessments Receivable—Deferred	200,000	
Revenues		50,000
Deferred Revenues.		200,000

To record special assessment levied on property owners benefited by paving and sidewalk project.

Cash	50,000	
Special Assessments Receivable—Current		50,000

To record receipt of current special assessment payments.

Cash	196,183	
Discount on Bonds Payable	3,817	
Bonds Payable		200,000

To record issuance of $200,000 face amount of 14%, four-year special assessment bonds to yield 15%.

Encumbrances	238,000	
Fund Balance Reserved for Encumbrances		238,000

To record contract with contractor and issuance of various purchase orders.

Expenditures	126,000	
Vouchers Payable		126,000

To record expenditures for construction for the year.

Fund Balance Reserved for Encumbrances	129,000	
Encumbrances		129,000

To reverse encumbrances applicable to vouchered expenditures.

Vouchers Payable	109,600	
Cash		109,600

To record payment of vouchers during the year.

Interest Receivable	32,000	
Revenues		32,000

To accrue interest on deferred special assessments on June 30, Year 6: $200,000 \times 0.16 = $32,000.

Expenditures	29,427	
Discount on Bonds Payable		1,427
Interest Payable		28,000

To accrue interest on special assessment bonds on June 30, Year 6: $200,000 \times 0.14 = $28,000; and to provide for expenditures represented by effective interest on bonds: $196,183 \times 0.15 = $29,427.

(Continued)

TOWN OF VERDANT GLEN SPECIAL ASSESSMENT FUND
General Journal (concluded)

Deferred Revenues	50,000	
Revenues		50,000

To transfer revenues represented by special assessment installment receivable in year ending June 30, Year 7, to current category.

Special Assessments Receivable—Current	50,000	
Special Assessments Receivable—Deferred.		50,000

To transfer special assessment installment receivable on July 1, Year 6, to current category.

Unreserved Fund Balance ($238,000 − $129,000)	109,000	
Encumbrances		109,000

To close Encumbrances account.

Revenues ($50,000 + $32,000 + $50,000)	132,000	
Unreserved Fund Balance	23,427	
Expenditures ($126,000 + $29,427)		155,427

To close revenues and expenditures.

Significant features of the foregoing journal entries are as follows:

1 The capital budget for the paving and sidewalks project is not entered in the accounting records of the Special Assessment Fund. The Town Council's approval of the special assessment and the related bonds provides adequate control.

2 A **current** and **deferred** breakdown is provided for both the special assessments receivable and the related revenues. It is inappropriate to consider the total of the special assessments as revenues of the fiscal year in which the special assessment fund was established, because the collection of the related receivables is spread over a five-year period.

3 The special assessment bonds are repayable serially over a four-year period, from proceeds of the annual collections of special assessments and related interest receivable. Accordingly, the present value of the 14% bonds at the 15% yield rate is computed as illustrated at the top of page 544.

4 The encumbrances and expenditures accounting for the Special Assessment Fund is similar to that for the Capital Projects Fund illustrated on page 536. Also, closing entries are similar to those for the other governmental funds (General Fund, Special Assessment Fund, Capital Projects Fund, and Debt Service Fund) illustrated in this chapter and in Chapter 11.

5 Both interest receivable and interest payable are accrued by the Special Assessment Fund at the end of the year, in accordance with the modified accrual basis of accounting. If differences between the two types of interest are not material, the accruals may be omitted.[1]

[1] National Council on Governmental Accounting, *Governmental Accounting and Financial Reporting Principles,* Municipal Finance Officers Association of the United States and Canada (Chicago: 1979), p. 12.

Principal and interest due July 1, Year 6:
  ($50,000 + $28,000) × 0.869565* . . . . $ 67,826
Principal and interest due July 1, Year 7:
  ($50,000 + $21,000) × 0.756144*   53,686
Principal and interest due July 1, Year 8:
  ($50,000 + $14,000) × 0.657516*   42,081
Principal and interest due July 1, Year 9:
  ($50,000 + $7,000) × 0.571753*   32,590
  Present value (proceeds) of special assessment bonds at 15%
    yield basis $196,183

* From Table 2 of the Appendix in back of the book.

6 At the end of the fiscal year, the special assessments receivable that are to be collected in the following fiscal year, and the related revenue, are transferred from the **deferred** to the **current** classification. However, a comparable transfer is not required for the current portion of the special assessment bonds payable.

Trial Balance at End of Fiscal Year for Special Assessment Fund Following is the trial balance of the Town of Verdant Glen Special Assessment Fund on June 30, Year 6, prior to the closing entry for revenues and expenditures:

TOWN OF VERDANT GLEN SPECIAL ASSESSMENT FUND
Trial Balance
June 30, Year 6

	Debit	Credit
Cash.	$136,583	
Special assessments receivable—current	50,000	
Special assessments receivable—deferred.	150,000	
Interest receivable	32,000	
Vouchers payable.		$ 16,400
Interest payable.		28,000
Deferred revenues		150,000
Bonds payable.		200,000
Discount on bonds payable.	2,390	
Fund balance reserved for encumbrances		109,000
Unreserved fund balance	109,000	
Revenues.		132,000
Expenditures.	155,427	
Totals.	$635,400	$635,400

the public (and in some cases to other activities of the governmental unit) at a profit. Consequently, the accounting for enterprise funds is more akin to business enterprise accounting than the accounting for any other governmental unit fund. For example, the accrual basis of accounting is used for an enterprise fund, with short-term prepayments, depreciation expense, and doubtful accounts expense recorded in the fund's accounting records. The enterprise fund's accounting records also include the plant assets owned by the fund, as well as the liabilities for revenue bonds and any general obligation bonds payable by the fund. Encumbrance accounting is not used for enterprise funds, and their annual budgets generally are not recorded in the accounting records. Retained earnings of an enterprise fund may be debited with cash remittances to the general fund, similar to dividends declared and paid by a business enterprise.

However, there are a number of differences between accounting for an enterprise fund and accounting for a business enterprise. Among these differences are the following:

1 Enterprise funds are not subject to federal and state income taxes. However, an enterprise fund may be required to make payments in lieu of property or franchise taxes to the general fund. (See page 517 of Chapter 11.)

2 There is no capital stock in an enterprise fund's balance sheet. Instead, Contributions accounts set forth, in a **fund equity** section of the balance sheet, the assets contributed to the enterprise fund by the governmental unit, by customers of the enterprise fund, or by other public agencies.

3 An enterprise fund has many restricted assets, which are segregated from current assets in the balance sheet. Cash deposits made by customers of a utility enterprise fund, which are to assure the customers' payment for utility services, are restricted for cash or interest-bearing investments to offset the enterprise fund's liability for the customers' deposits. Cash received from proceeds of revenue bonds issued by the enterprise fund is restricted to payments for construction of plant assets financed by issuance of the bonds. Part of the cash generated by the enterprise fund's operations must be set aside and invested for payment of interest and principal of the revenue bonds issued by the enterprise fund.

4 Current liabilities payable from restricted assets are segregated from other current liabilities of an enterprise fund in a section that precedes long-term liabilities.

5 A number of retained earnings reserves appear in the accounting records of an enterprise fund. These reserves are equal to the cash and investments restricted to payment of revenue bond interest and principal.

Accounting for internal service funds

An internal service fund is established to sell goods and services to other funds of the governmental unit, but not to the public. This type of fund is created to assure uniformity and economies in the procurement of goods and services for the governmental unit as a whole, such as stationery supplies and the maintenance and repairs of motor vehicles.

The operations of internal service funds resemble those of a business enterprise, except that internal service funds are not profit-motivated.

The revenues of internal service funds should be sufficient to cover all their operating costs and expenses, with perhaps a modest profit margin. In this way, the resources of internal service funds are "revolving"; the original contribution from the governmental unit to establish an internal service fund is expended for supplies, operating equipment, and employees' salaries or wages, and the amounts expended then are recouped through billings to other funds of the governmental unit.

Although an internal service fund should use an annual budget for managerial planning and control purposes, the budget need not be recorded in the accounting records of the fund. The accrual basis of accounting, including the perpetual inventory system and depreciation of plant assets, is required for an internal service fund. Encumbrance accounting is not required but may be useful in controlling nonrecurring purchase orders of an internal service fund.

Because internal service funds do not issue revenue bonds and do not receive contributions or deposits from customers, the financial statements of internal service funds are nearly identical in form and content to those of business enterprises. However, similar to enterprise funds, internal service funds do not have owners' equity in their balance sheets. A Contribution from Government ledger account accompanies the Retained Earnings account in the *fund equity* section of the balance sheet for an internal service fund.

FIDUCIARY FUNDS

Expendable trust funds, nonexpendable trust funds, pension trust funds, and agency funds constitute the fiduciary funds of a governmental unit. The position of the governmental unit with respect to such funds is one of a *custodian* or a *trustee,* rather than an *owner.*

In explaining the accounting principles for state and local governmental units, the National Council on Governmental Accounting described accounting for trust funds as follows:[2]

> Each trust fund is classified for accounting measurement purposes as either a governmental fund or a proprietary fund. Expendable trust funds are accounted for in essentially the same manner as governmental funds. Nonexpendable trust funds and pension trust funds are accounted for in essentially the same manner as proprietary funds. Agency funds are purely custodial (assets equal liabilities) and thus do not involve measurement of results of operations.

Accounting for agency funds

Agency funds are of short duration. Typically, agency funds are used to account for sales taxes collected by a state government on behalf of the municipalities and townships of the state, and for payroll taxes and

[2] Ibid., p. 6.

other deductions withheld from salaries and wages payable to employees of a governmental unit. The amounts withheld subsequently are paid to a federal or state collection unit.

Agency funds do not have operations during a fiscal year; thus, the only financial statement for an agency fund is a balance sheet showing the cash or receivables of the fund and the amounts payable to other funds or governmental units or to outsiders.

Accounting for expendable and nonexpendable trust funds

Trust funds of a governmental unit are longer-lived than agency funds. An **expendable trust fund** is one whose principal and income both may be expended to achieve the objectives of the trust. A **nonexpendable trust fund** is one whose revenues are expended to carry out the objectives of the trust; the principal remains intact. For example, an **endowment** established by the grantor of a trust may specify that the revenues from the endowment are to be expended by the governmental unit for student scholarships, but the endowment principal is not to be expended. A nonexpendable trust fund requires two separate trust fund accounting entities—one for principal and one for revenues. Accounting for the two separate trust funds requires a careful distinction between transactions affecting the principal—such as changes in the investment portfolio—and transactions affecting revenues—such as cash dividends and interest on the investment portfolio. The **trust indenture,** which is the legal document establishing the trust, should specify distinctions between principal and revenues. If the trust indenture is silent with respect to such distinctions, the trust law of the governmental unit governs separation of principal trust fund and revenues trust fund transactions.

Because the governmental unit serves as a custodian for a trust fund, accounting for a trust fund should comply with the trust indenture under which the fund was established. Among the provisions that might affect the accounting for a trust fund are requirements that the annual budget for the trust fund be recorded in its accounting records and that depreciation be recorded for an endowment principal trust fund that includes depreciable assets.

To illustrate accounting for expendable and nonexpendable trust funds, assume that Karl and Mabel Root, residents of the Town of Verdant Glen, contributed marketable securities with a market value of $100,000 on July 1, Year 5, to a trust to be administered by the Town of Verdant Glen as trustee. Principal of the gift was to be maintained in an Endowment Principal Nonexpendable Trust Fund. Revenues from the marketable securities were to be used for scholarships for qualified students to attend Verdant Glen College; the revenues and expenditures for scholarships were to be accounted for in an Endowment Revenues Expendable Trust Fund. The Bank of Verdant Glen trust department was

Explanation of transactions	Account titles	Endowment Principal Nonexpendable Trust Fund		Endowment Revenues Expendable Trust Fund	
Receipt of marketable securities in trust.	Investments	100,000			
	Revenues		100,000		
Accrual of revenues on marketable securities	Interest Receivable	5,000			
	Dividends Receivable	8,000			
	Revenues		13,000		
Receipt of interest and dividends	Cash	13,000			
	Interest Receivable		5,000		
	Dividends Receivable.		8,000		
Recognition of liability to Revenues Trust Fund for interest and dividends	Operating Transfers Out	13,000			
	Payable to Revenues Trust Fund		13,000		
	Receivable from Principal Trust Fund. . . .			13,000	
	Other Financing Sources				13,000
Transfer of cash from Principal Trust Fund to Revenues Trust Fund.	Payable to Revenues Trust Fund	13,000			
	Cash		13,000		
	Cash			13,000	
	Receivable from Principal Trust Fund				13,000
Payment of scholarships to students James Rich and Janet Wells.	Expenditures			12,000	
	Cash.				12,000
Payment of trustee's fee	Expenditures			500	
	Cash.				500
Closing entries	Revenues.	113,000			
	Operating Transfers Out		13,000		
	Fund Balance Reserved for Endowment		100,000		
	Other Financing Sources			13,000	
	Expenditures.				12,500
	Fund Balance Reserved for Scholarships				500

to receive an annual trustee's fee of $500 for administering the two trust funds on behalf of the Town of Verdant Glen.

Journal entries for the two trust funds for the year ended June 30, Year 6, are summarized on page 550.

Financial Statements of Nonexpendable Trust Fund   Because accounting for nonexpendable trust funds parallels accounting for proprietary funds, the financial statements for a nonexpendable trust fund are a statement of revenues, expenses, and changes in fund balance; a balance sheet; and a statement of changes in financial position. Financial statements of the Town of Verdant Glen Endowment Principal Nonexpendable Trust Fund are shown below and at the top of page 552 for the year ended June 30, Year 6.

TOWN OF VERDANT GLEN ENDOWMENT PRINCIPAL
NONEXPENDABLE TRUST FUND
Statement of Revenues, Expenses, and Changes in Fund Balance
For Year Ended June 30, Year 6

Operating revenues:	
Interest	$ 5,000
Dividends	8,000
Gifts	100,000
Total operating revenues	$113,000
Operating transfers out	13,000
Net income	$100,000
Fund balance, beginning of year	-0-
Fund balance, end of year	$100,000

TOWN OF VERDANT GLEN ENDOWMENT PRINCIPAL
NONEXPENDABLE TRUST FUND
Balance Sheet
June 30, Year 6

Assets

Investments	$100,000

Liabilities & Fund Balance

Fund balance reserved for endowment	$100,000

(Continued)

Financial Statements of Expendable Trust Fund   Accounting for expendable trust funds is comparable to accounting for governmental funds; therefore, financial statements for expendable trust funds are a statement of revenues, expenditures, and changes in fund balance, and a

TOWN OF VERDANT GLEN ENDOWMENT PRINCIPAL
NONEXPENDABLE TRUST FUND
Statement of Changes in Financial Position
For Year Ended June 30, Year 6

Financial resources provided

Operations—net income $100,000

Financial resources applied   -0-

Increase in financial resources: working capital. $100,000

	Increase in working capital
Investments	$100,000

balance sheet. For the Town of Verdant Glen Endowment Revenues Expendable Trust Fund, financial statements for the year ended June 30, Year 6, are as follows:

TOWN OF VERDANT GLEN ENDOWMENT REVENUES
EXPENDABLE TRUST FUND
Statement of Revenues, Expenditures, and Changes in Fund Balance
For Year Ended June 30, Year 6

Revenues. . . . . $ -0-

Expenditures:

Education . . . . $ 12,000

Administration   500

Total expenditures. . . . . $ 12,500

Excess (deficiency) of revenues over expenditures. . . . . $(12,500)

Operating transfers in   13,000

Excess of revenues and other financing sources over expenditures. . . $ 500

Fund balance, beginning of year. . . . .   -0-

Fund balance, end of year . . . . $ 500

TOWN OF VERDANT GLEN ENDOWMENT REVENUES
EXPENDABLE TRUST FUND
Balance Sheet
June 30, Year 6

Assets

Cash $500

Liabilities & Fund Balance

Fund balance reserved for scholarships $500

There is no unreserved fund balance for either of the Town of Verdant Glen Trust Funds, because the trust indenture required the reservation of the entire fund balance of each fund to achieve the purpose of the trust.

Accounting for pension trust funds

Pension trust funds are perhaps the most complex of all the funds of a governmental unit, because they involve accounting for liabilities and fund balance reserves that are computed on the basis of actuarial assumptions. These actuarial assumptions include life expectancies of employees covered by the governmental unit's pension plans and rates of earnings on pension trust fund assets.

Pension trust funds are accounted for in essentially the same manner as proprietary funds, although pension trust funds do not have plant assets or depreciation expense. Thus, the accounting records of pension trust funds are maintained under the accrual basis of accounting and include all assets, liabilities, revenues, and expenses of the fund. The costs of administering some pension trust funds may be borne by the general fund of the governmental unit.

Because of the complexities of pension trust funds, illustrative journal entries for a pension trust fund are beyond the scope of this discussion. The financial statements on page 554 for the Town of Verdant Glen Employees' Retirement System Pension Trust Fund for the year ended June 30, Year 6, illustrate some of the accounting concepts involved.

Following is a discussion of important features of the financial statements for the Town of Verdant Glen Employees' Retirement System Pension Trust Fund:

1 Interest revenues and interest receivable of a pension trust fund include revenues such as dividends and rent, as well as interest itself, on the investments of the trust fund.

2 Contributions revenues represent amounts received from both the governmental unit and its employees under the **contributory pension plan** of the Town of Verdant Glen. (In a **noncontributory pension plan,** only the governmental unit would provide contributions to the pension trust fund.) From the point of view of the governmental unit, contributions to a pension trust fund are expenditures of the general fund.

3 Benefit payments are pension payments to retired employees of the Town of Verdant Glen. Refunds are amounts repaid to resigned employees or to estates of deceased employees for amounts contributed by them to the pension trust fund.

4 Annuities payable represent the unpaid current installments of pensions payable to retired employees.

5 The fund balance reserved for employees' retirement system is the total of several ledger accounts of the pension trust fund that are established to record the actuarially determined present values of the pensions ultimately to be paid to retired employees of the governmental unit.

6 The deficit in the unreserved fund balance in effect is the unfunded prior service cost of the pension trust fund. (**Prior service cost** of a pension plan is the

TOWN OF VERDANT GLEN EMPLOYEES' RETIREMENT SYSTEM
PENSION TRUST FUND
Statement of Revenues, Expenses, and Changes in Fund Balance
For Year Ended June 30, Year 6

Operating revenues:

Interest	$ 14,300
Contributions	82,400
Total operating revenues	$ 96,700

Operating expenses:

Benefit payments	$ 23,400
Refunds	12,200
Total operating expenses	$ 35,600
Net income	$ 61,100
Fund balance, beginning of year	483,200
Fund balance, end of year	$544,300

TOWN OF VERDANT GLEN EMPLOYEES' RETIREMENT SYSTEM
PENSION TRUST FUND
Balance Sheet
June 30, Year 6

Assets

Cash	$ 12,300
Investments, at cost (market value $583,800)	552,100
Interest receivable	8,600
Total assets	$573,000

Liabilities & Fund Balance

Liabilities:

Annuities payable		$ 28,700
Fund balance:		
Reserved for employees' retirement system	$727,800	
Unreserved (deficiency)	(183,500)	544,300
Total liabilities & fund balance		$573,000

TOWN OF VERDANT GLEN EMPLOYEES' RETIREMENT SYSTEM
PENSION TRUST FUND
Statement of Changes in Financial Position
For Year Ended June 30, Year 6

Financial resources provided

Operations—net income	$61,100
Sale or maturity of investments	22,800
Total financial resources provided	$83,900

Financial resources applied

Acquisition of investments	68,200
Increase in financial resources: working capital	$15,700

Increase (decrease) in working capital

Cash	$18,400
Interest receivable	4,200
Annuities payable	(6,900)
Increase in working capital	$15,700

estimated cost of employee services for years prior to the date of an actuarial valuation of the pension plan.)

7 In the statement of changes in financial position, working capital does not include the investments of the pension trust fund.

GENERAL FIXED ASSETS AND GENERAL LONG-TERM DEBT ACCOUNT GROUPS

Principle 5 of the accounting principles for state and local governmental units described in Chapter 11 (page 505) requires governmental units to use **account groups** to record plant assets and long-term debt of the governmental unit not recorded in a fund. A governmental unit's general fixed assets and general long-term debt account groups are not **funds;** they are **memorandum accounts.** Their purpose is to provide in one record the governmental unit's plant assets and long-term liabilities that are not recorded in one of the governmental unit's funds. Plant assets are recorded in enterprise, trust, and internal service funds; bond liabilities are recorded in debt service, enterprise, and special assessment funds.

Accounting for general fixed assets account groups

Assets in the general fixed assets account group are recorded at their cost to the governmental unit or at their current fair value if donated to the governmental unit. The offsetting credit is to a memorandum account such as Investment in General Fixed Assets from (the source of the asset).

In accordance with principle 7 (page 505), depreciation may be recorded in the general fixed assets account group, with a debit to the appropriate Investment in General Fixed Assets account and a credit to an Accumulated Depreciation account. When a plant asset is sold or retired by the governmental unit, the carrying amount of the asset is removed from memorandum accounts in the general fixed assets account group; the sales proceeds are recorded as other financing sources in the general fund.

The journal entries on page 556 are typical of those for a governmental unit's general fixed assets account group. The first entry incorporates the assumption that equipment acquisitions were included in the expenditures of the Town of Verdant Glen General Fund for the year ended June 30, Year 6 (see page 516); the other two journal entries are made on June 30, Year 6, to record construction projects of the Town of Verdant Glen Capital Projects Fund (page 536) and Special Assessment Fund (page 542), respectively.

Accounting for general long-term debt account groups

General obligation bonds of a governmental unit, both serial and term, that are not recorded in an enterprise fund are recorded as memoran-

TOWN OF VERDANT GLEN GENERAL FIXED ASSETS ACCOUNT GROUP
General Journal

Machinery and Equipment   26,400
    Investment in General Fixed Assets from General Fund
      Revenues   26,400
To record acquisition of equipment by General Fund.

Construction in Progress   378,000
    Investment in General Fixed Assets from Capital Proj-
      ects Fund   378,000
To record construction work in progress on high school
addition.

Construction in Progress   126,000
    Investment in General Fixed Assets from Special As-
      sessment Fund   126,000
To record construction work in progress on street paving and
sidewalk installation.

dum credits in the general long-term debt account group. The offsetting
memorandum debit entry is to an account such as Amount to Be Provided. When cash and other assets for the ultimate payment of a bond
issue have been accumulated in a debt service fund, an Amount Available in Debt Service Fund account is debited and the Amount to Be Provided account is credited. When the bonds are paid by the debt service
fund, the memorandum accounts are reversed in the general long-term
debt account group in a closing entry at the end of the fiscal year.

The following journal entries for the Town of Verdant Glen General
Long-Term Debt Account Group parallel the corresponding journal entries in the Debt Service Fund (page 540) and the Capital Projects Fund
(page 536), respectively:

TOWN OF VERDANT GLEN GENERAL LONG-TERM DEBT ACCOUNT GROUP
General Journal

Amount Available in Debt Service Fund   10,000
    Amount to Be Provided   10,000
To record amount acquired by Debt Service Fund from Gen-
eral Fund for retirement of principal of general obligation
serial bonds.

Amount to Be Provided   500,000
    Bonds Payable   500,000
To record issuance of general obligation term bonds for con-
struction of addition to high school.

ANNUAL REPORTS OF GOVERNMENTAL UNITS

Principle *12b* of accounting for state and local governmental units (page 506 of Chapter 11) required governmental units to issue annual financial reports. The following general outline and minimum contents were specified:[3]

> **1** *Introductory Section*
> (Table of contents, letter(s) of transmittal, and other material deemed appropriate by management)
> **2** *Financial Section*
>   **a** *Auditor's Report*
>   **b** *General-Purpose Financial Statements (Combined Statements—Overview)*
>   (1) Combined Balance Sheet—All Fund Types and Account Groups
>   (2) Combined Statement of Revenues, Expenditures, and Changes in Fund Balances—All Governmental Fund Types
>   (3) Combined Statement of Revenues, Expenditures, and Changes in Fund Balances—General and Special Revenue Fund Types (and similar governmental fund types for which annual budgets have been legally adopted)
>   (4) Combined Statement of Revenues, Expenses, and Changes in Retained Earnings (or Equity)—All Proprietary Fund Types
>   (5) Combined Statement of Changes in Financial Position—All Proprietary Fund Types
>   (6) Notes to the financial statements (Trust Fund operations may be reported in (2), (4), and (5) above, as appropriate, or separately.)
>   **c** *Combining and Individual Fund and Account Group Statements and Schedules*
>   (1) Combining Statements—By Fund Type—where a governmental unit has more than one fund of a given fund type
>   (2) Individual fund and account group statements—where a governmental unit has only one fund of a given type and for account groups and/or where necessary to present prior year and budgetary comparisons
>   (3) Schedules
>   (a) Schedules necessary to demonstrate compliance with finance-related legal and contractual provisions
>   (b) Schedules to present information spread throughout the statements that can be brought together and shown in greater detail (e.g., taxes receivable, including delinquent taxes; long-term debt; investments; and cash receipts, disbursements, and balances)
>   (c) Schedules to present greater detail for information reported in the statements (e.g., additional revenue sources detail and object of expenditure data by departments). . . .
> **3** *Statistical Tables*

It is evident from the foregoing listing that financial reports of governmental units may be voluminous, and perhaps even overwhelming, in content. For example, the **combined financial statements** included in the financial section of the financial report do not show single combined amounts; the statements include columns for each of the eight fund types and two account groups, together with **memorandum only**

---

[3] Ibid., pp. 19–20.

total columns for both the current year and the prior year. Comparable multicolumn presentations constitute the **combining** statements and schedules. Thus, the principal financial statements included in the annual financial reports are far more complex than the **consolidated** financial statements of business enterprises making up a parent company–subsidiaries group.

Appraisal of accounting principles for governmental units

The 12 accounting principles for state and local governmental units established by the National Council of Governmental Accounting (see pages 504 to 506) brought about significant improvements in governmental accounting. However, considerable dissatisfaction still exists. Much of this dissatisfaction centers on fund accounting and the voluminous financial statements included in annual reports of governmental units.

In recognition of the need for further improvements in accounting for governmental units, the Financial Accounting Foundation, which oversees and raises cash for the Financial Accounting Standards Board, has approved the formation of a Governmental Accounting Standards Board (GASB) of five members to establish accounting standards for governmental unit accounting and financial reporting. When GASB is organized, the National Council on Governmental Accounting will transfer its activities to the new board.

REVIEW QUESTIONS

1 Describe the taxes or fees of governmental units that often are accounted for in special revenue funds.

2 How are proceeds of general obligation bonds issued to finance a construction project accounted for in a capital projects fund? Explain.

3 Is a separate debt service fund established for every issue of general obligation bonds of a governmental unit? Explain.

4 The following journal entry appeared in the Debt Service Fund of Charter County:

Cash with Fiscal Agent	*83,000*	
Cash		*83,000*

What is the probable explanation for this journal entry?

5 Why does a governmental unit's enterprise fund have a number of restricted assets in its balance sheet? Explain.

6 How is the Contribution from Government ledger account presented in the financial statements of a governmental unit's internal service fund? Explain.

7 Explain the nature of the **contributions revenues** appearing in the statement of revenues, expenses, and changes in fund balance of a governmental unit's pension trust fund.

8 Under what circumstances are general obligation bonds of a governmental unit recorded in the governmental unit's enterprise fund? Explain.

9 Discuss the similarities and differences between a governmental unit's capital projects fund and special assessment fund.

10 The accounting for a governmental unit's enterprise fund is in many respects similar to the accounting for a business enterprise, yet there are a number of differences between the two types of accounting. Identify at least three of the differences.

11 Accounting for nonexpendable trusts for which a governmental unit acts as custodian requires the establishment of two separate trust funds. Why is this true?

12 Is a consolidated balance sheet appropriate for all funds and account groups of a governmental unit? Explain.

EXERCISES

Ex. 12-1 Select the best answer for each of the following multiple-choice questions:

1 The liability for a governmental unit's revenue bonds appears in:
a An enterprise fund
b A debt service fund
c The general long-term debt account group
d A special assessment fund

2 Which of the following funds does not use the encumbrance technique?
a General fund
b Capital projects fund
c Internal service fund
d None of the foregoing funds

3 Which of the following ledger accounts would be included in the general long-term debt account group?
a Amount to Be Provided
b Unreserved Fund Balance
c Fund Balance Reserved for Encumbrances
d Cash

4 Customers' meter deposits that cannot be spent for normal operating purposes are classified as restricted cash in the balance sheet of which fund?
a Internal service fund
b Trust fund
c Agency fund
d Enterprise fund

5 The general fixed assets account group is used for the plant assets of the:
a Special assessment fund
b Enterprise fund
c Trust fund
d Internal service fund

6 A city should record depreciation as an expense in its:
a General fund and enterprise fund

b Internal service fund and general fixed assets account group
c Enterprise fund and internal service fund
d Enterprise fund and capital projects fund

Ex. 12-2 The ledger accounts listed below frequently appear in the accounting records of governmental units:

Account	*Fund or account group*
1 *Bonds Payable*	*a* *General fund*
2 *Fund Balance Reserved for*	*b* *Special revenue fund*
Encumbrances	*c* *Capital projects fund*
3 *Contribution from Government*	*d* *Special assessment fund*
4 *Equipment*	*e* *Debt service fund*
5 *Appropriations*	*f* *Internal service fund*
6 *Estimated Revenues*	*g* *Trust or agency fund*
7 *Taxes Receivable—Current*	*h* *Enterprise fund*
	i *General fixed assets account group*
	j *General long-term debt account group*

Select the appropriate identifying letter to indicate the governmental unit fund or account group in which those ledger accounts might properly appear. An account might appear in more than one fund or account group.

Ex. 12-3 A citizen of Hays City donated ten acres of undeveloped land to the city for a future school site. The donor's cost of the land was $555,000. The current fair value of the land was $850,000 on the date of the gift.

Prepare a journal entry in the appropriate fund or account group to record the foregoing gift. Identify the fund or account group.

Ex. 12-4 The Enterprise Fund of Orchard City billed the General Fund $16,400 for utility services on May 31, Year 5.

Prepare journal entries for the foregoing billing in the Orchard City General Fund and Enterprise Fund.

Ex. 12-5 On July 1, property taxes totaling $480,000, of which $1\frac{1}{2}$% was estimated to be uncollectible, were levied by the County of Larchmont Special Revenue Fund. Property taxes collected by the Special Revenue Fund during July totaled $142,700.

Prepare journal entries in the County of Larchmont Special Revenue Fund for the foregoing transactions.

Ex. 12-6 On July 1, Year 4, the City of Varro paid $860,000 from the General Fund for a central garage to service its vehicles, with $467,500 being applicable to the building, which has an economic life of 25 years, $232,600 to land, and $109,900 to machinery that has an economic life of 15 years. A $50,000 cash contribution was received by the garage from the General Fund on the same date.

Prepare the journal entry or entries to record the foregoing transactions in the appropriate fund established for the central garage. Identify the fund.

Ex. 12-7 On June 30, Year 1, the Town of Warren issued $800,000 face amount of 16% special assessment bonds at 100 to finance in part a street improvement project estimated to cost $860,000. The project is to be paid by a $60,000 contribution from the Town of Warren General Fund and by an $800,000 special assessment against property owners (payable in five equal annual installments beginning July 1, Year 1).

Prepare the journal entry or entries to record the foregoing transactions in the appropriate fund established for the street improvement project. Identify the fund.

Ex. 12-8 On July 1, Year 7, the County of Pinecrest issued $1,200,000 of 30-year, 16% general obligation term bonds of the same date at 100 to finance the construction of a public health center.

Prepare the journal entry or entries to record the foregoing transaction in all funds or account groups affected. Identify the funds or account groups.

Ex. 12-9 Agatha Morris, a citizen of Roark City, donated common stock valued at $220,000 to the city under a trust indenture dated July 1, Year 6. Under the terms of the indenture, the principal amount is to be kept intact; use of dividends revenues from the common stock is restricted to financing academic scholarships for college students. On December 14, Year 6, dividends of $42,000 were received on the common stock donated by Morris.

Prepare the journal entries to record the foregoing transactions in the appropriate funds. Identify the funds. Disregard entries for accrual of dividends. Omit explanations.

Ex. 12-10 On April 30, Year 5, the fiscal agent for the Town of Wallen Debt Service Fund paid the final serial payment of $50,000 on the Town's 16% general obligation bonds, together with semiannual interest. The Debt Service Fund had provided sufficient cash to the fiscal agent a few days earlier.

Prepare a journal entry for the Town of Wallen Debt Service Fund to record the fiscal agent's payment of bond principal and interest on April 30, Year 5.

CASES

Case 12-1 The controller of the City of Darby has asked your advice on the accounting for an installment contract payable by the city. The contract covers the costs of installing automatic gates, coin receptacles, and ticket dispensers for the 20 city-owned parking lots in the downtown district. Installation of the self-parking equipment resulted in a decrease in the required number of parking attendants for the city-owned parking lots and a reduction in the salaries and related expenditures of the City of Darby General Fund.

The contract is payable monthly in amounts equal to 40% of the month's total parking revenue for the 20 lots. Because no legal or contractual provisions require the City of Darby to establish an enterprise fund for the parking lots, both parking revenue and parking-lot maintenance and repairs expenditures are recorded in the City of Darby General Fund. The parking-lot sites are carried at cost in the City of Darby General Fixed Assets Account Group.

The city controller describes the plans for accounting for payments on the contract as follows: Monthly payments under the contract are to be debited to the Expenditures account of the General Fund and to the Debt Service section of the expenditures subsidiary ledger. The payments also will be recorded in the General Fixed Assets Account Group as additions to the Improvements Other than Buildings ledger account. A footnote to the General Fund balance sheet will disclose the unpaid balance of the installment contract at the end of each fiscal year. The unpaid balance of the contract will not be included in the General Long-Term Debt Account Group because the contract does not represent a liability for borrowing of cash, as do the bond and other long-term debt liabilities of the City of Darby.

Instructions What is your advice to the controller of the City of Darby? Explain.

Case 12-2   You have been requested to examine the financial statements of the funds and account groups of Ashburn City for the fiscal year ended June 30, Year 7. During the course of your examination you learn that on July 1, Year 6, the city issued at face amount $1,000,000 20-year, 16% general obligation serial bonds to finance additional power-generating facilities for the Ashburn City electric utility. Principal and interest on the bonds are repayable by the Ashburn City Electric Utility Enterprise Fund. However, for the first five years of the serial maturities of the bonds—July 1, Year 7, through July 1, Year 11—a special tax levy accounted for in the Ashburn City Special Revenue Fund is to contribute to the payment of 80% of the interest and principal of the general obligation bonds. At the end of the five-year period, it is anticipated that revenue from the electric utility's new power-generating facilities will create cash flow for the Ashburn City Electric Utility Enterprise Fund sufficient to pay all the serial maturities and interest of the general obligation bonds during the period July 1, Year 12, through July 1, Year 26.

You find that the accounting records of the Ashburn City Electric Utility Enterprise Fund include the following ledger account balances relative to the general obligation bonds on June 30, Year 7:

16% general obligation serial bonds payable ($50,000 due July 1,	
Year 7)	$1,000,000 cr
Interest payable (interest on the bonds is payable annually each	
July 1)	160,000 cr
Interest expense	160,000 dr

The statement of revenues, expenditures, and changes in fund balance for the year ended June 30, Year 7, prepared by the accountant for the Ashburn City Electric Utility Enterprise Fund shows a net loss of $40,000. You also learn that on July 1, Year 7, the Ashburn City Special Revenue Fund paid $168,000 ($210,000 × 0.80 = $168,000) and the Ashburn City Electric Utility Enterprise Fund paid the remaining $42,000 ($210,000 × 0.20 = $42,000) to the fiscal agent for the 16% general obligation serial bonds. The $210,000 was the total of the $50,000 principal and $160,000 interest due on the bonds July 1, Year 7. In the Enterprise Fund's journal entry to record payment of the bond principal and interest, the amount of $168,000 was credited to the Contribution from Government ledger account.

Instructions   Do you concur with the Ashburn City Electric Utility Enterprise Fund's accounting and reporting treatment for the 16% general obligation serial bonds? Discuss.

Case 12-3   Wallace and Brenda Stuart, residents of Colby City, have donated their historic mansion, "Greystone," in trust to Colby City to serve as a tourist attraction. For a nominal charge, tourists will be guided through Greystone to observe the paintings, sculptures, antiques, and other art objects collected by the Stuarts, as well as the mansion's unique architecture.

The trust indenture executed by the Stuarts provides that the admissions charges to Greystone (which was appraised at $5,000,000 on the date of the trust indenture) are to cover the operating expenditures associated with the tours, as well as maintenance and repairs costs for Greystone. Any excess of admissions revenues over the foregoing expenditures and costs is to be donated to Colby University for scholarships to art and architecture students.

Instructions   Discuss the fund accounting issues, and related accounting matters such as depreciation, that should be considered by officials of Colby City with respect to the Stuart Trust.

PROBLEMS

12-1 On July 1, Year 6, the Town of Logan began two construction projects: (1) an addition to the town hall accounted for in a capital projects fund, and (2) a curbing construction project accounted for in a special assessment fund. The special assessment totaled $400,000, payable by the assessed citizens in five annual installments beginning July 1, Year 6, together with interest at 16% a year on the unpaid assessments. Other details for the year ended June 30, Year 7, were as follows:

	Capital Projects Fund	Special Assessment Fund
Bonds issued July 1, Year 6, at face amount	$600,000 face amount, 14%, 20-year general obligation bonds, interest payable Jan. 1 and July 1	$320,000 face amount 15%, 4-year special assessment bonds, interest payable July 1
Total encumbrances	$530,200	$384,600
Total expenditures	$380,600	$360,300
Encumbrances applicable to expenditures	$382,100	$354,700
Total cash paid on vouchers	$322,700	$347,600

Instructions Prepare journal entries, including year-end accruals but excluding closing entries, for (**a**) the Town of Logan Capital Projects Fund, and (**b**) the Town of Logan Special Assessment Fund.

12-2 In compliance with a newly enacted state law, Diggs County assumed the responsibility of collecting all property taxes levied within its boundaries as of July 1, Year 5. A composite property tax rate per $100 of net assessed valuation was developed for the fiscal year ending June 30, Year 6, and is presented below:

Diggs County General Fund	$ 6.00
Evans City General Fund	3.00
Hickman Township General Fund	1.00
Total	$10.00

All property taxes are due in quarterly installments. After collection, taxes are distributed to the governmental units represented in the composite rate.

In order to administer collection and distribution of such taxes, the County has established a Tax Agency Fund.

Additional information

(1) In order to reimburse the County for estimated administrative expenses of operating the Tax Agency Fund, the Tax Agency Fund is to deduct 2% from the tax collections each quarter for Evans City and Hickman Township. The total amount deducted is to be remitted to the Diggs County General Fund.

(2) Current year tax levies to be collected by the Tax Agency Fund are as follows:

	Gross levy	Estimated amount to be collected
Diggs County	$3,600,000	$3,500,000
Evans City	1,800,000	1,740,000
Hickman Township	600,000	560,000
Totals	$6,000,000	$5,800,000

(3) As of September 30, Year 5, the Tax Agency Fund had received $1,440,000 in first-quarter payments. On October 1, Year 5, this fund made a distribution to the three governmental units.

Instructions
For the period July 1, Year 5, through October 1, Year 5, prepare journal entries (explanations omitted) to record the transactions described above for the following funds:
Diggs County Tax Agency Fund
Diggs County General Fund
Evans City General Fund
Hickman Township General Fund
Your working paper should be organized as follows:

Account title	Diggs County Tax Agency Fund Dr(Cr)	Diggs County General Fund Dr(Cr)	Evans City General Fund Dr(Cr)	Hickman Township General Fund Dr(Cr)

12-3   The City of Ordway's fiscal year ends on June 30. During the fiscal year ended June 30, Year 2, the City authorized the construction of a new library and the issuance of general obligation term bonds to finance the construction of the library. The authorization imposed the following restrictions:

(1) Construction cost was not to exceed $5,000,000
(2) Annual interest rate was not to exceed 15%

The City does not record project authorizations, but other appropriate accounts are maintained. The following transactions relating to the financing and constructing of the library occurred during the fiscal year ended June 30, Year 3:

(1) On July 1, Year 2, the City issued $5,000,000 of 30 year, 14% general obligation bonds for $5,100,000. The semiannual interest dates are December 31 and June 30.
(2) On July 3, Year 2, the Library Capital Projects Fund invested $4,900,000 in short-term notes. This investment was at face value, with no accrued interest. Interest on cash invested by the Library Capital Projects Fund must be transferred to the Library Debt Service Fund. During the fiscal year ending June 30, Year 3, estimated interest to be earned is $140,000.
(3) On July 5, Year 2, the City signed a contract with Premier Construction Company to build the library for $4,980,000
(4) On January 15, Year 3, the Library Capital Projects Fund received $3,040,000, from the maturity of short-term notes acquired on July 3, Year 2. The cost of these notes was $3,000,000. The interest of $40,000 was transferred to the Library Debt Service Fund.
(5) On January 20, Year 3, Premier Construction Company billed the City $3,000,000 for work performed on the new library. The contract calls for 10% retention until final inspection and acceptance of the building. The Library Capital Projects Fund paid Premier $2,700,000.

(6) On June 30, Year 3, the Library Capital Projects Fund prepared closing entries.

Instructions

a Prepare journal entries to record the six preceding sets of facts in the City of Ordway Library Capital Projects Fund. Omit journal entry explanations. Use the following account titles:
Cash
Encumbrances·
Expenditures
Fund Balance Reserved for Encumbrances
Interest Receivable
Investments
Other Financing Sources
Payable to Library Debt Service Fund
Unreserved Fund Balance
Vouchers Payable
Do not record journal entries in any other fund or account group.

b Prepare a balance sheet for the City of Ordway Library Capital Projects Fund on June 30, Year 3.

12-4   The Town of Northville was incorporated and began operations on July 1, Year 1. The following transactions occurred during the first fiscal year, July 1, Year 1, to June 30, Year 2:

(1) The Town Council adopted a budget for general operations during the fiscal year ending June 30, Year 2. Revenues were estimated at $400,000. Legal authorizations for budgeted expenditures were $394,000. There were no other financing sources or uses.

(2) Property taxes were levied in the amount of $390,000; it was estimated that 2% of this amount would be uncollectible. These taxes are available on the date of levy to finance current expenditures.

(3) During the year a resident of the town donated marketable securities valued at $50,000 to the town under a trust. The terms of the trust indenture stipulated that the principal amount is to be kept intact; use of revenues generated by the securities is restricted to financing college scholarships for needy students. Revenue earned and received on these marketable securities amounted to $5,500 through June 30, Year 2.

(4) A General Fund transfer of $55,000 was made to establish an Internal Service Fund to provide for a permanent investment in inventory of supplies.

(5) The Town Council decided to install lighting in the town park, and a special assessment project was authorized to install the lighting at a cost of $75,000. The assessments were levied for $72,000, with the town contributing $3,000 from the General Fund. All assessments were collected during the year, including the General Fund contribution.

(6) A contract for $75,000 was approved for the installation of the lighting. On June 30, Year 2, the contract was completed but not approved. The contractor was paid all but 5%, which was retained to ensure compliance with the terms of the contract. Encumbrances accounts are maintained.

(7) During the year, the Internal Service Fund purchased various supplies at a cost of $41,900.

(8) Cash collections recorded by the General Fund during the year were as follows:

Property taxes	$386,000
Licenses and permits	7,000

(9) The Town Council decided to build a hall at an estimated cost of $500,000 to replace space occupied in rented facilities. The town does not record

project authorizations. It was decided that general obligation bonds bearing interest at 12% would be issued. On June 30, Year 2, the bonds were issued at their face amount of $500,000, payable June 30, Year 22. No contracts have been signed for this project and no expenditures have been made.

(10) A fire truck was acquired for $15,000, and the voucher was approved and paid by the General Fund. This expenditure previously had been encumbered for $15,000.

Instructions Prepare journal entries to record each of the foregoing transactions in the appropriate fund or account group. Omit explanations for the journal entries. Do not prepare closing entries for any fund. Organize your working paper as follows:

Transaction No.	Fund or account group	Account titles	Debit	Credit

Number each journal entry to correspond with the transactions described above. Use the funds (show fund symbol in working paper) and account titles below:

Capital Projects Fund (CPF)
  Cash
  Other Financing Sources

Endowment Principal Trust Fund (EPF)
  Cash
  Investments
  Operating Transfers Out
  Payable to Endowment Revenues Trust Fund
  Revenues

Endowment Revenues Trust Fund (ERF)
  Cash
  Other Financing Sources
  Receivable from Endowment Principal Trust Fund

General Fixed Assets Account Group (GFA)
  Improvements Other than Buildings
  Investment in General Fixed Assets
  Machinery and Equipment

General Fund (GF)
  Allowance for Uncollectible Current Taxes
  Appropriations
  Budgetary Fund Balance
  Cash
  Encumbrances
  Estimated Revenues
  Expenditures
  Fund Balance Reserved for Encumbrances
  Other Financing Uses
  Payable to Special Assessment Fund
  Revenues
  Taxes Receivable—Current
  Vouchers Payable

General Long-Term Debt Account Group (GLTD)
  Amount to Be Provided
  Bonds Payable

Internal Service Fund (ISF)
  Cash
  Contribution from Government
  Inventory of Supplies

Special Assessment Fund (SAF)
Cash
Encumbrances
Expenditures
Fund Balance Reserved for Encumbrances
Other Financing Sources
Receivable from General Fund
Revenues
Special Assessments Receivable—Current
Vouchers Payable

12-5 The City of Cavendish operates a central garage in an Internal Service Fund to provide garage space and repairs for all city-owned and operated vehicles. The Internal Service Fund was established by a contribution of $200,000 from the General Fund on July 1, Year 1, at which time the building was acquired. The after-closing trial balance on June 30, Year 3, was as follows:

CITY OF CAVENDISH INTERNAL SERVICE FUND
After-Closing Trial Balance
June 30, Year 3

	Debit	*Credit*
Cash	$150,000	
Receivable from General Fund	20,000	
Inventory of material and supplies	80,000	
Land	60,000	
Building	200,000	
Accumulated depreciation of building		$ 10,000
Machinery and equipment	56,000	
Accumulated depreciation of machinery and equipment		12,000
Vouchers payable		38,000
Contribution from government		200,000
Unreserved retained earnings		306,000
Totals	$566,000	$566,000

The following information applies to the fiscal year ended June 30, Year 4:

(1) Material and supplies were purchased on account for $74,000.
(2) The perpetual inventory balance of material and supplies on June 30, Year 4, was $58,000, which agreed with the physical count on that date.
(3) Salaries and wages paid to employees totaled $230,000, including related fringe benefits.
(4) A billing was received from the Enterprise Fund for utility charges totaling $30,000, and was paid.
(5) Depreciation of the building was recorded in the amount of $5,000. Depreciation of the machinery and equipment amounted to $8,000.
(6) Billings to other funds for services rendered to them were as follows:

General Fund	$262,000
Enterprise Fund	84,000
Special Revenue Fund	32,000

(7) Unpaid interfund receivable balances on June 30, Year 4, were as follows:

General Fund . . . . $ 6,000

Special Revenue Fund 16,000

(8) Vouchers payable on June 30, Year 4, were $14,000.

Instructions For the period July 1, Year 3, through June 30, Year 4, prepare journal entries to record all the transactions in the Internal Service Fund accounting records. Omit explanations for the entries. Use the following account titles, in addition to those included in the June 30, Year 3, after-closing trial balance:

Operating Expenses
Payable to Enterprise Fund
Receivable from Enterprise Fund
Receivable from Special Revenue Fund
Revenues

12-6 In a special election held on May 1, Year 3, the citizens of the City of Wilmont approved a $10,000,000 issue of 16% general obligation bonds maturing in Year 23. The proceeds of the bonds will be used to help finance the construction of a new civic center. The total cost of the project was estimated at $15,000,000. The remaining $5,000,000 will be financed by an irrevocable state grant, which has been awarded. A capital projects fund was established to account for this project and was designated the Civic Center Capital Projects Fund.

The following transactions occurred during the fiscal year beginning July 1, Year 3, and ending June 30, Year 4:

(1) On July 1, the General Fund loaned $500,000 to the Civic Center Construction Fund for defraying engineering and other costs.
(2) Preliminary engineering and planning costs of $320,000 were paid to Akron Company. There had been no encumbrance for this cost.
(3) On December 1, the bonds were issued at 101.
(4) On March 15, a contract for $12,000,000 was entered into with Carlson Construction Company for the major part of the project.
(5) Purchase orders were placed for material estimated to cost $55,000.
(6) On April 1, a partial payment of $2,500,000 was received from the state government.
(7) The material that was ordered previously was received at a cost of $51,000 and paid for.
(8) On June 15, a progress billing of $2,000,000 was received from Carlson Construction Company for work done on the project. In accordance with the contract, the city will withhold 6% of any billing until the project is completed.
(9) The General Fund was repaid the $500,000 previously loaned.

Instructions Prepare general journal entries to record the transactions in the Civic Center Capital Projects Fund for the period July 1, Year 3, through June 30, Year 4, and the closing entries on June 30, Year 4. Omit explanations for the journal entries. Use the following account titles in the journal entries:

Cash
Encumbrances
Expenditures
Fund Balance Reserved for
  Encumbrances
Other Financing Sources

Payable to General Fund
Receivable from State Government
Revenues
Unreserved Fund Balance
Vouchers Payable

12-7 Your examination of the financial statements of the Town of Novis for the year ended June 30, Year 6, disclosed that the Town's inexperienced accountant was uninformed regarding governmental accounting and recorded all transactions in the General Fund. The following Town of Novis General Fund trial balance was prepared by the accountant:

TOWN OF NOVIS GENERAL FUND
Trial Balance
June 30, Year 6

	Debit	Credit
Cash	$ 12,900	
Accounts receivable	1,200	
Taxes receivable—current	8,000	
Vouchers payable		$ 15,000
Appropriations		350,000
Expenditures	332,000	
Estimated revenues	290,000	
Revenues		320,000
Town property	16,100	
Bonds payable	48,000	
Unreserved fund balance		23,200
Totals	$708,200	$708,200

Your audit disclosed the following:

(1) The accounts receivable balance was due from the Town's water utility for the sale of obsolete equipment on behalf of the General Fund. Accounts for the water utility operated by the Town are maintained in an enterprise fund.

(2) The total tax levy for the year was $270,000. The Town's tax collection experience in recent years indicates an average loss of 3% of the total tax levy for uncollectible taxes.

(3) On June 30, Year 6, the Town retired at face amount 12% general obligation serial bonds totaling $30,000. The bonds had been issued on July 1, Year 5, in the total amount of $150,000. Interest paid during the year also was recorded in the Bonds Payable account. There is no debt service fund for the serial bonds.

(4) On July 1, Year 5, to service various departments the Town Council authorized a supply room with an inventory not to exceed $10,000. During the year supplies totaling $12,300 were purchased and debited to Expenditures. The physical inventory taken on June 30, Year 6, disclosed that supplies totaling $8,400 had been used. No internal service fund was authorized by the Town Council.

(5) Expenditures for Year 6 included $2,600 applicable to purchase orders issued in the prior year. Outstanding purchase orders on June 30, Year 6, not entered in the accounting records, amounted to $4,100.

(6) The amount of $8,200, receivable from the state during Fiscal Year 6 for the Town's share of state gasoline taxes, had not been entered in the accounting records, because the state was late in remitting the $8,200.

(7) Equipment costing $7,500, which had been acquired by the General Fund, was removed from service and sold for $900 during the year, and new equipment costing $17,000 was acquired. These transactions were recorded in the Town Property ledger account. The Town does not record depreciation in the General Fixed Assets Account Group.

Instructions

a Prepare adjusting and closing entries for the Town of Novis General Fund on June 30, Year 6.

b Prepare an after-closing trial balance for the Town of Novis General Fund for the year ended June 30, Year 6.

c Prepare adjusting entries for any other funds or account groups. (The Town's accountant had recorded all the foregoing transactions in the General Fund, and had prepared no journal entries for other funds or account groups.)

12-8   You were engaged as independent auditor of the City of Engle for the year ended June 30, Year 2. You found the following ledger accounts, among others, in the accounting records of the General Fund for the year ended June 30, Year 2:

Special Cash

Date	Explanation	Ref.	Debit	Credit	Balance
Year 1					
Aug. 1		CR 58	301,000		301,000 dr
Sept. 1		CR 60	80,000		381,000 dr
Dec. 1		CD 41		185,000	196,000 dr
Year 2					
Feb. 1		CD 45		24,000	172,000 dr
June 1		CR 64	52,667		224,667 dr
June 30		CD 65		167,000	57,667 dr

Construction in Progress—Main Street Sewer

Date	Explanation	Ref.	Debit	Credit	Balance
Year 1					
Dec. 1		CD 41	185,000		185,000 dr
Year 2					
June 30		CD 65	167,000		352,000 dr

Bonds Payable

Date	Explanation	Ref.	Debit	Credit	Balance
Year 1					
Aug. 1		CR 58		300,000	300,000 cr
Year 2					
June 1		CR 64		50,000	350,000 cr

Premium on Bonds Payable

Date	Explanation	Ref.	Debit	Credit	Balance
Year 1					
Aug. 1		CR 58		1,000	1,000 cr

Assessments Revenues

Date	Explanation	Ref.	Debit	Credit	Balance
Year 1					
Sept. 1		CR 60		80,000	80,000 cr

Interest Expense

Date	Explanation	Ref.	Debit	Credit	Balance
Year 2					
Feb. 1		CD 45	24,000		24,000 dr
June 1		CR 64		2,667	21,333 dr

The ledger accounts resulted from the project described below:

The city council authorized the Main Street Sewer Project and a five-year, 16% bond issue of $350,000 dated August 1, Year 1, to permit deferral of assessment payments. According to the terms of the authorization, the property owners were to be assessed 80% of the estimated cost of construction; the balance was to be made available by the City of Engle General Fund on October 1, Year 1. On September 1, Year 1, the first of five equal annual assessment installments was collected from the property owners, and a contract for construction of the sewer was signed. The deferred assessments were to bear interest at 18% from September 1, Year 1. The project was expected to be completed by October 31, Year 2.

Instructions

a Prepare journal entries that should have been made in the City of Engle Special Assessment Fund for the year ended June 30, Year 2. Amortize the bond premium by the straight-line method. Do not prepare closing entries.

b Prepare journal entries on June 30, Year 2, for City of Engle funds and account groups, other than the Special Assessment Fund, to record properly the results of transactions of the Main Street Sewer Project.

12-9 The following deficit budget was proposed for Year 3 for the Angelus School District General Fund:

ANGELUS SCHOOL DISTRICT GENERAL FUND

Budget

For Year Ending December 31, Year 3

Fund balance, Jan. 1, Year 3	$128,000
Revenues:	
Property taxes	112,000
Investment interest	4,000
Total	$244,000
Expenditures:	
Operating	$120,000
County treasurer's fees	1,120
Bond interest	50,000
Fund balance, Dec. 31, Year 3	72,880
Total	$244,000

A general obligation bond issue of the School District was proposed in Year 2. The proceeds were to be used for a new school. There are no other outstanding bond issues. Information about the bond issue follows:

Principal amount	$1,000,000
Interest rate	15%
Bonds dated	Jan. 1, Year 3
Coupons mature	Jan. 1 and July 1, beginning July 1, Year 3
Bonds mature serially at the rate of $100,000 a year, starting Jan. 1, Year 5.	

The School District uses a separate bank account for each fund. The General Fund trial balance on December 31, Year 2, follows:

ANGELUS SCHOOL DISTRICT GENERAL FUND
Trial Balance
December 31, Year 2

	Debit	Credit
Cash	$ 28,000	
Temporary investments—U.S. Treasury 12% bonds, interest payable on May 1 and Nov. 1	100,000	
Unreserved fund balance		$128,000
Totals	$128,000	$128,000

The county treasurer collects the property taxes and withholds a fee of 1% on all collections. The transactions for Year 3 were as follows:

Jan. 1   The proposed budget was adopted, the general obligation bond issue was authorized, and the property taxes were levied.

Feb. 28   Net property tax receipts from county treasurer, $49,500, were deposited.

Apr. 1   General obligation bonds were issued at 101 plus accrued interest. It was directed that the premium be used for payment of interest by the General Fund.

Apr. 2   The School District paid $147,000 for the new school site.

Apr. 3   A contract for $850,000 for the new school was approved.

May 1   Interest was received on temporary investments.

July 1   Interest was paid on bonds.

Aug. 31   Net property tax receipts from county treasurer, $59,400, were deposited.

Nov. 1   Payment on new school construction contract, $200,000, was made.

Nov. 1   Interest was received on temporary investments.

Dec. 31   Operating expenditures during the year were $115,000. (Disregard vouchering.)

Instructions   Prepare journal entres to record the foregoing Year 3 transactions in the following funds or account groups. (Closing entries are not required.)
a General Fund
b Capital Projects Fund
c General Fixed Assets Account Group
d General Long-Term Debt Account Group

Angelus School District does not use a Debt Service Fund.

12-10   The City of Rowland City Hall Capital Projects Fund was established on July 1, Year 2, to account for the construction of a new city hall. The building was to be constructed on a site owned by the City, and the building construction was financed by the issuance on July 1, Year 2, of $1,000,000 face amount of 14%, 10-year term bonds.

The only funds in which the transactions pertaining to the new city hall were recorded were the Capital Projects Fund and the General Fund. The Capital Projects Fund's trial balance on June 30, Year 3, follows:

CITY OF ROWLAND CITY HALL CAPITAL PROJECTS FUND
Trial Balance
June 30, Year 3

	Debit	Credit
Cash	$ 793,000	
Vouchers payable		$ 11,000
Fund balance reserved for encumbrances		723,000
Appropriations		1,015,000
Expenditures	240,500	
Encumbrances	715,500	
Totals	$1,749,000	$1,749,000

An analysis of the Fund Balance Reserved for Encumbrances ledger account follows:

	Debit (Credit)
Contract with General Construction Company	$(750,000)
Purchase orders placed for material and supplies	(55,000)
Receipt of and payment for material and supplies	14,500
Payment of General Construction Company invoice, less 10%	
retention	67,500
Balance of Fund Balance Reserved for Encumbrances account, June 30, Year 3	$(723,000)

An analysis of the Appropriations account follows:

	Debit (Credit)
Face amount of bonds	$(1,000,000)
Premium on bonds	(15,000)
Balance of Appropriations account, June 30, Year 3	$(1,015,000)

An analysis of the Expenditures account follows:

	Debit (Credit)
Progress billing invoice from General Construction Company (with which the City contracted for the construction of the new city hall for $750,000; other contracts will be let for heating, air conditioning, etc.) showing 10% of the work completed	$ 75,000
Charge from General Fund for clearing the building site	11,000
Payments to suppliers for building material and supplies	14,500
Payment of interest on bonds outstanding	140,000
Balance of Expenditures account, June 30, Year 3	$240,500

Instructions

a Prepare a working paper for the City of Rowland City Hall Capital Projects Fund on June 30, Year 3, showing:

(1) Preliminary trial balance.

(2) Adjustments. (Formal adjusting entries are not required; however, explain adjustments at bottom of working paper.)

(3) Adjusted trial balance.

b Prepare the required adjusting or closing entries on June 30, Year 3, for the following:

(1) Debt Service Fund

(2) General Fixed Assets Account Group

(3) General Long-Term Debt Account Group

13 ACCOUNTING FOR NONPROFIT ORGANIZATIONS

A *nonprofit organization* is a legal and accounting entity that is operated for the benefit of society as a whole, rather than for the benefit of an individual proprietor or a group of partners or shareholders. Thus, the concept of net income is not meaningful for a nonprofit organization. Instead, as the internal service fund described in Chapter 12, a nonprofit organization strives only to obtain revenue and support sufficient to cover its expenses.

Nonprofit organizations comprise a significant segment of the United States economy. Colleges and universities, voluntary health and welfare organizations such as United Way, some hospitals, philanthropic foundations such as the Ford Foundation and the Rockefeller Foundation, professional societies such as the AICPA, and civic organizations such as Kiwanis are familiar examples of nonprofit organizations.

For many years, the accounting standards and practices that constitute generally accepted accounting principles were not considered to be entirely applicable to nonprofit organizations. The following quotation, which formerly appeared in various auditing publications of the AICPA, outlines this situation:[1]

> . . . the statements . . . of a not-for-profit organization . . . may reflect accounting practices differing in some respects from those followed by enterprises organized for profit. In some cases generally accepted accounting principles applicable to not-for-profit organizations have not been clearly defined. In those areas where the independent auditor believes generally accepted accounting principles have been clearly defined, he may state his opinion as to the conformity of the financial statements either with *generally accepted accounting principles* or (less desirably) with *accounting practices* for not-for-profit organizations in the particular field, and in such circumstances he may refer to financial position and results of operations. In those areas where he believes generally accepted accounting principles have not been clearly defined, the provisions covering special reports as discussed under cash basis and modified accrual basis statements are applicable.

In the period 1972 to 1974, the unsettled state of accounting for nonprofit organizations was improved by the AICPA's issuance of three *Industry Audit Guides:* "Hospital Audit Guide," "Audits of Colleges and Universities," and "Audits of Voluntary Health and Welfare Organiza-

---

[1] *Statement on Auditing Standards No. 1,* "Codification of Auditing Standards and Procedures," AICPA (New York: 1973), p. 136.

tions."[2] The status of an *Industry Audit Guide* is set forth in each Guide; the following language in the "Hospital Audit Guide" is typical:[3]

> This audit guide is published for the guidance of members of the Institute in examining and reporting on financial statements of hospitals. It represents the considered opinion of the Committee on Health Care Institutions and as such contains the best thought of the profession as to the best practices in this area of reporting. Members should be aware that they may be called upon to justify departures from the Committee's recommendations.

The accounting concepts included in an *Industry Audit Guide* have the *substantial authoritative support* required for all generally accepted accounting principles.

The three *Industry Audit Guides* on page 575 list only three types of nonprofit organizations. Thus, in 1978, the AICPA issued *Statement of Position 78-10,* "Accounting Principles and Reporting Practices for Certain Nonprofit Organizations," which applies to at least 18 types of nonprofit organizations, ranging from cemetery societies to zoological and botanical societies.[4]

The existence of four sources of authoritative support for generally accepted accounting principles for nonprofit organizations has led to some inconsistencies among the accounting standards for such organizations. In time, the FASB may resolve these inconsistencies as part of its work on accounting concepts for nonbusiness organizations, described in Chapter 11 (pages 501 and 502).

Characteristics of nonprofit organizations

Nonprofit organizations are in certain respects hybrid because they have some characteristics comparable to those of governmental units and other characteristics similar to those of business enterprises.

Among the features of nonprofit organizations that resemble characteristics of governmental units are the following:

1 *Service to society.* Nonprofit organizations render services to society as a whole. The members of this society may range from a limited number of citizens of a community to almost the entire population of a city, state, or nation. Similar to the services rendered by governmental units, the services of nonprofit organizations are of benefit to the many rather than the few.

2 *No profit motivation.* Nonprofit organizations do not operate with the objective of earning a profit. Consequently, nonprofit organizations usually are exempt from federal and state income taxes. Governmental units, except for enterprise funds, have the same characteristics. (As pointed out in Chapter 12, enterprise funds sometimes are assessed an amount in lieu of property taxes by the legislative branch of the government.)

---

[2] Audits of Colleges and Universities" was amended in 1974 by the AICPA in *Statement of Position 74-8,* "Financial Accounting and Reporting by Colleges and Universities." "Hospital Audit Guide" was amended in 1978 by the AICPA in *Statement of Position 78-1,* "Accounting by Hospitals for Certain Marketable Equity Securities."

[3] "Hospital Audit Guide," AICPA (New York: 1972).

[4] *Statement of Position 78-10,* "Accounting Principles and Reporting Practices for Certain Nonprofit Organizations," AICPA (New York: 1978), p. 8.

3 *Financing by the citizenry.* As with governmental units, most nonprofit organizations depend on the general population for a substantial portion of their support, because revenue from charges for their services is not intended to cover all their operating costs. Exceptions are professional societies and the philanthropic foundations established by wealthy individuals or families. Whereas the citizenry's contributions to government revenue are mostly **involuntary** taxes, their contributions to nonprofit organizations are **voluntary** donations.

4 *Stewardship for resources.* Because a substantial portion of the resources of a nonprofit organization are donated, the organization must account for the resources on a stewardship basis similar to that of governmental units. The stewardship requirement makes **fund accounting** appropriate for most nonprofit organizations as well as for governmental units.

5 *Importance of budget.* The four preceding characteristics of nonprofit organizations cause their **annual budget** to be as important as for governmental units. Nonprofit organizations may employ a **traditional budget,** a **program budget,** a **performance budget,** or a **planning, programming, budgeting system.** These types of operating budgets are described in Chapter 11.

Among the characteristics of nonprofit organizations that resemble those of business enterprises are the following:

1 *Governance by board of directors.* As with a business corporation, a nonprofit corporation is governed by elected or appointed directors, trustees, or governors. In contrast, the legislative and executive branches of a governmental unit share the responsibilities of its governance.

2 *Measurement of cost expirations.* Governance by a board of directors means that a nonprofit organization does not answer to a lawmaking body as does a governmental unit. One consequence is that **cost expirations,** or **expenses,** rather than **expenditures,** usually are reported in the **statement of activity** (explained on page 590) of a nonprofit organization. Allocation of expenses (including depreciation) and revenue to the appropriate accounting period thus is a common characteristic of nonprofit organizations and business enterprises.

3 *Use of accrual basis of accounting.* Nonprofit organizations employ the same accrual basis of accounting used by business enterprises. The modified accrual basis of accounting used by some governmental unit funds is inappropriate for nonprofit organizations.

ACCOUNTING FOR NONPROFIT ORGANIZATIONS

The accounting entity for most nonprofit organizations is the **fund,** which is defined in Chapter 11 (page 504). Separate funds are necessary to distinguish between assets that may be used as authorized by the board of directors and assets whose use is restricted by donors. Funds commonly used by nonprofit organizations include the following:

Unrestricted fund (sometimes called **unrestricted current fund** or **current unrestricted fund**)

Restricted fund (sometimes called **restricted current fund** or **current restricted fund**)

Endowment fund

Agency fund (sometimes called **custodian fund**)

Annuity and life income funds

Loan fund

Plant fund (sometimes called *land, building, and equipment fund*)

Revenue, support, and capital additions of nonprofit organizations

Nonprofit organizations obtain revenue from the sale of goods and services, and from sources such as membership dues and interest and dividends on investments. Typically, such revenue is inadequate to cover the expenses of the organizations; thus, they solicit support and capital additions from various donors. **Support** consists primarily of contributions from individuals, other nonprofit organizations, and governmental units to be used for current operations. **Capital additions** were defined by the AICPA as follows:[5]

> Capital additions include nonexpendable gifts, grants, and bequests restricted by donors to endowment, plant, or loan funds either permanently or for extended periods of time. Capital additions also include legally restricted investment income and gains or losses on investments held in such funds that must be added to the principal.

Unrestricted fund

In many respects, the **unrestricted fund** of a nonprofit organization is similar to the **general fund** of a governmental unit. The unrestricted fund includes all the assets of a nonprofit organization that are available for use as authorized by the board of directors and are not restricted for specific purposes. Thus, comparable to the general fund of a governmental unit, the unrestricted fund of a nonprofit organization is residual in nature.

Designated Fund Balance of Unrestricted Fund The board of directors of a nonprofit organization may designate a portion of an unrestricted fund's assets for a specific purpose. The earmarked portion should be accounted for as a segregation of the unrestricted fund balance, rather than as a separate restricted fund. For example, if the board of directors of Civic Welfare, Inc., earmarks $25,000 of the unrestricted fund's assets for the acquisition of office equipment, the following journal entry is prepared for Civic Welfare, Inc., Unrestricted Fund:

Journal entry for designation of portion of fund balance of unrestricted fund

Undesignated Fund Balance	25,000	
Designated Fund Balance—Office Equipment		25,000
To record designation of portion of fund balance for acquisition of office equipment.		

[5] Ibid., p. 19.

The Designated Fund Balance—Office Equipment account is similar to a retained earnings appropriation account of a corporation and is reported in the balance sheet of Civic Welfare, Inc., as a portion of the fund balance of the Unrestricted Fund.

Revenue and Support of Unrestricted Fund The revenue and support of the unrestricted fund of a nonprofit organization are derived from a number of sources. For example, a hospital derives unrestricted fund revenue and support from patient services, educational programs, research and other grants, unrestricted gifts, unrestricted income from endowment funds, and miscellaneous sources such as donated material and services. A university's sources of unrestricted fund revenue and support include student tuition and fees; governmental grants and contracts; gifts and private grants; unrestricted income from endowment funds; and revenue from auxiliary activities such as student residences, food services, and intercollegiate athletics. The principal support sources of voluntary health and welfare organizations' unrestricted funds (and all other funds) are cash donations and pledges. Revenue may include membership dues, interest, dividends, and gains on the sale of investments.

Revenue for Services A hospital's patient service revenue and a university's tuition and fees revenue are accrued at full rates, *even though part or all of the revenue is to be waived or otherwise adjusted.* Suppose, for example, that Community Hospital's patient service revenue records for June, Year 3, include the following amounts:

Patient service revenue components of a hospital

Gross patient service revenue (before recognition of charity allowances and contractual adjustments)	$100,000
Charity allowances for indigent patients	8,000
Amount to be received from Civic Welfare, Inc., for services to indigent patients	3,000
Contractual adjustment allowed to Blue Cross	16,000

The journal entries at the top of page 580 are appropriate for the Community Hospital Unrestricted Fund on June 30, Year 3. The contractual adjustments recorded in the third journal entry on page 580 illustrate a unique feature of a hospital's operations. Many hospital receivables are collectible from a *third-party payer,* rather than from the patient receiving services. Among third-party payers are the U.S. government (Medicare and Medicaid programs), state programs such as Medical in California, Blue Cross, and private medical insurance carriers. The hospital's contractual agreements with third-party payers usually provide for payments by the third parties at less than full billing rates.

Accounts Receivable	100,000	
Patient Service Revenue		100,000

To record gross patient service revenue for month of June at full rates.

Accounts Receivable	3,000	
Charity Allowances	5,000	
Allowances and Doubtful Accounts		8,000

To record gross charity allowances for June ($8,000), less amount receivable from Civic Welfare, Inc. ($3,000).

Contractual Adjustments	16,000	
Allowances and Doubtful Accounts		16,000

To record contractual adjustments allowed to Blue Cross for June.

Provision for Doubtful Accounts	12,000	
Allowances and Doubtful Accounts		12,000

To provide for doubtful accounts for June.

In the statement of activity of Community Hospital for June, Year 3, the Charity Allowances, Contractual Adjustments, and Provision for Doubtful Accounts ledger accounts for the month are deducted from the Patient Service Revenue account to compute net patient service revenue for the month. The Allowances and Doubtful Accounts ledger account is offset against the Accounts Receivable account in the balance sheet, and the write-off of an account receivable is recorded in the customary fashion. For example, the uncollectible accounts receivable of indigent patients would be written off by Community Hospital by the following journal entry in the Unrestricted Fund on June 30, Year 3:

Allowances and Doubtful Accounts	5,100	
Accounts Receivable		5,100

To write off uncollectible accounts receivable of indigent patients as follows:

J. R. English	$1,500
R. L. Knight	1,100
S. O. Newman	2,500
Total	$5,100

Donated Material and Services In addition to cash contributions, nonprofit organizations receive donations of material and services. For example, a hospital may receive free drugs, or a "thrift store" may receive articles of clothing. The donated material should be recorded in the Inventories account at its current fair value, with a credit to a support account in the unrestricted fund, as illustrated in the following journal entry for Community Hospital:

Journal entry for donated material

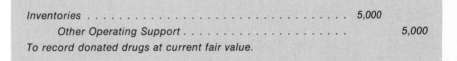

Inventories 5,000
      Other Operating Support 5,000
To record donated drugs at current fair value.

Donated services are recorded in the unrestricted fund as salaries expense, with an offset to a support account, if the services are rendered to the nonprofit organization in an employee-employer relationship. The value assigned to the services is the going salary rate for comparable salaried employees of the entity, less any meals or other living costs absorbed for the donor of the services by the nonprofit organization. The AICPA established the following requirements for recording donated services in the accounting records of a nonprofit organization:[6]

(1) The services performed are significant and form an integral part of the efforts of the organization as it is presently constituted; the services would be performed by salaried personnel if donated or contributed services were not available for the organization to accomplish its purpose; and the organization would continue this program or activity.

(2) The organization controls the employment and duties of the service donors. The organization is able to influence their activities in a way comparable to the control it would exercise over employees with similar responsibilities. This includes control over time, location, nature, and performance of donated or contributed services.

(3) The organization has a clearly measurable basis for the amount to be recorded.

(4) The services of the reporting organization are not principally intended for the benefit of its members. Accordingly, donated and contributed services would not normally be recorded by organizations such as religious communities, professional and trade associations, labor unions, political parties, fraternal organizations, and social and country clubs.

To illustrate the accounting for donated services that meet the foregoing criteria, assume that the services of volunteer nurses' aides were valued at $26,400 for the month of June, Year 3, by Community Hospital, and that the value of meals provided at no cost to the volunteers during the month was $2,100. The journal entry at the top of page 582 is appropriate for Community Hospital on June 30, Year 3.

Pledges A *pledge* is a commitment by a prospective donor to contribute a specific amount of cash to a nonprofit organization on a future date or in installments. Because the pledge is in writing and signed by the *pled-*

[6] Ibid., pp. 23–24.

Journal entry for donated services

Salaries Expense	24,300	
Other Operating Support		24,300

To record donated services at current fair value of $26,400 less $2,100 value of meals provided to donors. (Income tax effects are disregarded.)

gor, it resembles in form the ***promissory note*** used in business. However, pledges generally are not enforceable contracts.

Under the accrual basis of accounting, unrestricted pledges are recorded as receivables and support (in the accounting period specified by the pledgor) in the unrestricted fund of a nonprofit organization, with appropriate provision for doubtful accounts. Recording of support from pledges in this fashion is required by "Hospital Audit Guide," "Audits of Voluntary Health and Welfare Organizations," and by ***Statement of Position 78-10.***[7] However, the "Audits of Colleges and Universities" ***Industry Audit Guide*** makes the recording of pledges optional, as indicated below:[8]

> Pledges of gifts . . . should be disclosed in the notes unless they are reported in the financial statements. The notes to the financial statements should disclose the gross amounts by time periods over which the pledges are to be collected. . . .
> If the pledges are reported in the financial statements, they should be accounted for at their estimated net realizable value in the same manner as gifts received. . . .

The reason for the inconsistent treatment of pledges in the four accounting guides is not apparent. "Audits of Colleges and Universities" apparently sanctions use of notes to financial statements to correct an error in the application of accounting principles—the omission of receivables and support—in the financial statements themselves. The authors believe this to be an improper use of notes to financial statements.

To illustrate the accounting for pledges, assume that Civic Welfare, Inc., a nonprofit organization, received pledges totaling $200,000 in a fund-raising drive. Based on past experience, 15% of the pledges are considered to be doubtful of collection. The journal entries at the top of page 583 are appropriate.

Contributions support is shown in the statement of activity net of the provision for doubtful pledges. Pledges receivable are presented in the balance sheet net of the allowance for doubtful pledges. The write-off of uncollectible pledges is recorded by a debit to the Allowance for Doubtful Pledges account and a credit to the Pledges Receivable account.

[7] "Hospital Audit Guide," p. 10; "Audits of Voluntary Health and Welfare Organizations." AICPA (New York: 1974), p. 14; "Accounting Principles and Reporting Practices for Certain Nonprofit Organizations," pp. 22–23.
[8] "Audits of Colleges and Universities," AICPA (New York: 1973), p. 8.

Journal entries to record receivable for pledges and doubtful pledges

Pledges Receivable	200,000	
Contributions Support.		200,000
To record receivable for pledges.		
Provision for Doubtful Pledges	30,000	
Allowance for Doubtful Pledges		30,000
To record provision for doubtful pledges ($200,000 × 0.15 = $30,000).		

Revenue from Pooled Investments Many of the funds of nonprofit organizations have cash available for investments in securities and other money-market instruments. To provide greater efficiency and flexibility in investment programs, the investment resources of all funds of a nonprofit organization may be pooled for investment by a single portfolio manager. The pooling technique requires a careful allocation of investment revenue, including gains and losses, to each participating fund.

To illustrate the pooling of investments, assume that on January 2, Year 5, four funds of Civic Welfare, Inc., a nonprofit organization, pooled their individual investments as follows:

Pooling of investments by nonprofit organization on Jan. 2, Year 5

	Cost	Current fair value	Original equity,%
Unrestricted Fund	$ 20,000	$ 18,000	15
Restricted Fund	15,000	21,600	18
Plant Fund.	10,000	20,400	17
Wilson Endowment Fund	55,000	60,000	50
Totals	$100,000	$120,000	100

The original equity percentages in the above tabulation are based on *current fair value,* not on *cost.* The current fair values of the pooled investments on January 2, Year 5, represent a common "measuring rod" not available in the cost amounts, which represent current fair values on various dates the investments were acquired.

Realized gains (or losses) and interest and dividend revenue of the pooled investments during Year 5 are allocated to the four funds in the ratio of the original equity percentages. For example, if $18,000 realized gains of the investment pool during Year 5 are reinvested, and if interest and dividend revenue of $9,000 is realized and distributed by the pool during Year 5, these amounts are allocated as shown at the top of page 584.

Each of the funds participating in the investment pool debits Investments and credits Gains on Sale of Investments for its share of the $18,000. Each fund also debits Cash and credits Interest and Dividends

Allocation of Year 5
revenue from pooled
investments to
respective funds

	Original equity, %	Realized gains	Interest and dividends revenue
Unrestricted Fund	15	$ 2,700	$1,350
Restricted Fund	18	3,240	1,620
Plant Fund.	17	3,060	1,530
Wilson Endowment Fund	50	9,000	4,500
Totals	100	$18,000	$9,000

Revenue or Fund Balance for its share of the $9,000 received from interest and dividends.

If another fund of Civic Welfare, Inc., entered the investment pool on December 31, Year 5, the original equity percentages would have to be revised, based on the December 31, Year 5, current fair values of the investment portfolio. For example, if the Harris Endowment Fund entered the Civic Welfare, Inc., investment pool (with a current fair value of $144,000) on December 31, Year 5, with investments having a cost of $32,000 and a current fair value of $36,000 on that date, the equity percentages would be revised as illustrated below:

Revision of fund
equities in pooled
investments on Dec. 31,
Year 5

	Cost*	Current fair value†	Revised equity, %
Unrestricted Fund	$ 22,700	$ 21,600	12.0
Restricted Fund	18,240	25,920	14.4
Plant Fund.	13,060	24,480	13.6
Wilson Endowment Fund	64,000	72,000	40.0
Subtotals	$118,000	$144,000	
Harris Endowment Fund	32,000	36,000	20.0
Totals	$150,000	$180,000	100.0

* Cost for four original pool member funds includes $18,000 realized gains of Year 5.
† Current fair value of original pooled investments totaling $144,000 on December 31, Year 5, allocated to original pool member funds based on original equity percentages computed on page 583.

Realized gains (or losses) and interest and dividend revenue for accounting periods subsequent to December 31, Year 5, are allocated in the revised equity percentages. The revised equity percentages are maintained until the membership of the investment pool changes again.

Expenses of Unrestricted Fund   The expenses of unrestricted funds are similar in many respects to those of a business enterprise—salaries and wages, supplies, maintenance, research, and the like. The question of whether depreciation should be recorded as an expense by a nonprofit organization has not been answered uniformly by the AICPA. The "Hospital Audit Guide," "Audits of Voluntary Health and Welfare Organizations," and **Statement of Position 78-10** specify that depreciation generally should be recorded as an expense of each accounting period.[9] However, "Audits of Colleges and Universities" takes a contrary position:[10]

> Current funds expenditures . . . comprise . . . all expenses incurred, determined in accordance with the generally accepted accrual method of accounting, except for the omission of depreciation. . . .
> Depreciation expense related to depreciable assets comprising the physical plant is reported neither in the statement of current funds revenues, expenditures, and other changes nor in the statement of changes in unrestricted current funds balance. The reason for this treatment is that these statements present expenditures and transfers of current funds rather than operating expenses in conformity with the reporting objectives of accounting for resources received and used rather than the determination of net income. Depreciation allowances, however, may be reported in the balance sheet and the provision for depreciation reported in the statement of changes in the balance of the investment-in-plant fund subsection of the plant funds group.

In the opinion of the authors, the activities of colleges and universities are not so different from those of other nonprofit organizations that the recognition of depreciation expense is inappropriate for colleges and universities.

However, **Statement of Position 78-10** does not require depreciation of assets that are **not exhaustible,** such as landmarks, cathedrals, historical treasures, and structures used primarily as houses of worship.[11]

Assets and Liabilities of Unrestricted Fund Most assets and liabilities of a nonprofit organization's unrestricted fund are similar to the current assets and liabilities of a business enterprise. Cash, investments, accounts receivable, receivables from other funds, inventories, and short-term prepayments are typical assets of an unrestricted fund.

"Audits of Colleges and Universities" and "Audits of Voluntary Health and Welfare Organizations" segregate plant assets into a separate fund. In contrast, "Hospital Audit Guide" takes the following position:[12]

> Property, plant and equipment and related liabilities should be accounted for as a part of unrestricted funds, since segregation in a separate fund would imply the existence of restrictions on asset use.

In the opinion of the authors, segregation of plant assets in a separate fund is logical accounting practice for any nonprofit organization that uses fund accounting. Plant assets, with their extended economic

[9] "Hospital Audit Guide," p. 4; "Audits of Voluntary Health and Welfare Organizations," p. 12; "Accounting Principles and Reporting Practices for Certain Nonprofit Organizations," pp. 35–36.
[10] "Audits of Colleges and Universities," pp. 26, 9–10.
[11] "Accounting Principles and Reporting Practices for Certain Nonprofit Organizations," p. 36.
[12] "Hospital Audit Guide," p. 4.

life, should not be included in the same fund as liquid assets that are used in current operations of a nonprofit organization.

The liabilities of an unrestricted fund include payables, accruals, and deferred revenue comparable to those of a business enterprise, as well as amounts payable to other funds.

Restricted fund

Nonprofit organizations establish **restricted funds** to account for assets available for current use but expendable only as authorized by the donor of the assets. Thus, a restricted fund of a nonprofit organization resembles the special revenue fund of a governmental unit, because the assets of both types of funds may be expended only for specified purposes.

The AICPA's "Hospital Audit Guide" includes in the restricted funds category a broad spectrum of restricted resources:[13]

Funds for specific operating purposes
Funds for additions to property, plant, and equipment
Endowment funds

In contrast, "Audits of Colleges and Universities" and "Audits of Voluntary Health and Welfare Organizations" limit the restricted fund category to resources for specific operating purposes.[14]

The assets of restricted funds are not derived from the operations of the nonprofit organization. Instead, the assets are obtained from (1) restricted gifts or grants from individuals or governmental units, (2) revenue from restricted fund investments, (3) gains on sales of investments of the restricted fund, and (4) restricted income from endowment funds. These assets are transferred to the unrestricted fund at the time the designated expenditure is made, with a credit to the Other Operating Support account if the expenditure is for current operating purposes, or to the Fund Balance account if the expenditure is for plant assets.

To illustrate, assume that on July 1, Year 4, Robert King donated $50,000 to Community Hospital, a nonprofit organization, for the acquisition of beds for a new wing of the hospital. On August 1, Year 4, Community Hospital paid $51,250 for the beds. These transactions are recorded by Community Hospital as shown on page 587.

Endowment fund

An **endowment fund** of a nonprofit organization is comparable with a **nonexpendable trust fund** of a governmental unit, described in Chapter 12. A **pure endowment fund** is one for which the principal must be held indefinitely in revenue-producing investments. Only the reve-

---

[13] Ibid., p. 9.
[14] "Audits of Colleges and Universities," p. 16; "Audits of Voluntary Health and Welfare Organizations," p. 2.

Journal entries for restricted donation

In Robert King Restricted Fund:

Year 4

July 1 Cash   50,000
                    Fund Balance   50,000
                To record receipt of gift from Robert King for acquisi-
                tion of beds for new wing.

Aug. 1 Fund Balance   50,000
                    Payable to Unrestricted Fund   50,000
                To record obligation to Unrestricted Fund for cost of
                beds for new wing in accordance with Robert King's
                gift.

In Unrestricted Fund:

Year 4

Aug. 1 Plant Assets   51,250
                    Cash   51,250
                To record acquisition of beds for new wing.

          1 Receivable from Robert King Restricted Fund   50,000
                    Fund Balance   50,000
                To record receivable from Robert King Restricted Fund
                for beds acquired.

nue from the pure endowment fund's investments may be expended by the nonprofit organization. In contrast, the principal of a **term endowment fund** may be expended after the passage of a period of time or the occurrence of an event stipulated by the donor of the endowment principal. A **quasi-endowment fund** is established by the board of directors of a nonprofit organization, rather than by an outside donor. At the option of the board, the principal of a quasi-endowment fund later may be expended by the entity that established the fund.

The revenue of endowment funds is handled in accordance with the instructions of the donor or the board of directors. If there are no restrictions on the use of endowment fund income, it is transferred to the nonprofit organization's unrestricted fund. Otherwise, the endowment fund revenue is transferred to an appropriate restricted fund.

Agency fund

An **agency fund** of a nonprofit organization is identical to its counterpart in a governmental unit. An agency fund is used to account for assets held by a nonprofit organization as a custodian. The assets are disbursed only as instructed by their owner.

For example, a university may act as custodian of cash of a student organization. The university disburses the cash as directed by the appropriate officers of the student organization. The undistributed cash of the student organization is reported as a *liability* of the university's agency fund, rather than as a *fund balance,* because the university has no equity in the fund.

Annuity and life income funds

Annuity Fund Assets may be contributed to a nonprofit organization with the stipulation that the organization pay specified amounts periodically to designated recipients, for a specified time period. An *annuity fund* is established by the nonprofit organization to account for this arrangement. At the end of the specified time period for the periodic payments, the unexpended assets of the annuity fund are transferred to the unrestricted fund, or to a restricted fund or endowment fund specified by the donor.

The journal entries on page 589 illustrate the accounting for the Ruth Collins Annuity Fund of Ridgedale College, a nonprofit organization, for the fund's first fiscal year ending June 30, Year 2. Note on page 589 that, in the first journal entry on June 30, Year 2, the revenue and gains on the annuity fund's share of the investment pool are credited to the Annuity Payable ledger account. This is necessary because the actuarial computation of the annuity on the date of establishment of the annuity fund valued the annuity liability at its then present value.

Life Income Fund A *life income fund* is used to account for stipulated payments to a named beneficiary (or beneficiaries) during the beneficiary's lifetime. In a life income fund, only the *income* is paid to the beneficiary. Thus, payments to a life income fund's beneficiary vary from one accounting period to the next, but payments from an annuity fund are fixed in amount.

Loan fund

A *loan fund* may be established by any nonprofit organization, but loan funds most frequently are included in the accounting records of colleges and universities. Student loan funds usually are *revolving;* that is, as old loans are repaid, new loans are made from the receipts. Loans receivable are carried in the loan fund at estimated realizable value; provisions for doubtful loans are debited directly to the Fund Balance account, not to an expense account. Interest on loans is credited to the Fund Balance account, ordinarily on the cash basis of accounting.

Plant fund

We have already noted (page 585) the inconsistent accounting treatment for plant assets of hospitals as compared with colleges and univer-

Journal entries for annuity fund

Year 1

July 1   Cash   50,000
           Annuity Payable.   35,000
           Fund Balance   15,000

        To record receipt of cash from Andrea Collins for an annuity of $6,000 a year each June 30 to Ruth Collins for her lifetime. Liability is recorded at the actuarially determined present value of the annuity, based on life expectancy of Ruth Collins.

1   Investments   45,000
           Cash   45,000

        To record acquisition of interest in Ridgedale College's investment pool.

Year 2

June 30 Cash   1,500
      Investments   2,000
           Annuity Payable.   3,500

        To record share of revenue and gains of Ridgedale College investment pool.

30 Annuity Payable.   6,000
           Cash   6,000

        To record payment of current year's annuity to Ruth Collins.

30 Fund Balance   1,000
           Annuity Payable.   1,000

        To record actuarial loss based on revised life expectancy actuarial valuation of Ruth Collins annuity.

sities and voluntary health and welfare organizations. There are also inconsistencies in the contents of the **plant funds** of the three types of nonprofit organizations, as follows:

1 A **plant replacement and expansion fund** is a subdivision of the **restricted fund** category of a hospital. In the hospital's plant replacement and expansion fund are recorded the cash, investments, and receivables earmarked by donors for expenditure for plant assets.[15]

2 The following excerpt describes the accounting for the plant fund of a voluntary health and welfare organization:[16]

    Land, building and equipment fund (often referred to as plant fund) is often used to accumulate the net investment in fixed assets and to account

[15] "Hospital Audit Guide," pp. 9, 41.
[16] "Audits of Voluntary Health and Welfare Organizations," pp. 2–3.

for the unexpended resources contributed specifically for the purpose of acquiring or replacing land, buildings, or equipment for use in the operations of the organization. Mortgages or other liabilities relating to these assets are also included in this fund. When additions to land, buildings, or equipment used in carrying out the organization's program and supporting services are acquired with unrestricted fund resources, the amount expended for such assets should be transferred from the unrestricted fund to the plant fund and should be accounted for as a direct addition to the plant fund balance. Gains or losses on the sale of fixed assets should be reflected as income items in the plant fund accounts. The proceeds from the sale of fixed assets should be transferred to the unrestricted fund; such transfers should be reflected as direct reductions and additions to the respective fund balances.

3 In contrast to the two preceding types of plant funds, "Audits of Colleges and Universities" provides for the following:[17]

> The plant funds group consists of (1) funds to be used for the acquisition of physical properties for institutional purposes but unexpended at the date of reporting; (2) funds set aside for the renewal and replacement of institutional properties; (3) funds set aside for debt service charges and for the retirement of indebtedness on institutional properties; and (4) funds expended for and thus invested in institutional properties.
>
> Some institutions combine the assets and liabilities of the four subfund groups for reporting purposes; however, separate fund balances should be maintained. Resources restricted by donors or outside agencies for additions to plant should be recorded directly in the particular fund subgroup, generally unexpended plant funds.

Thus, in the three AICPA *Industry Audit Guides* for nonprofit organizations, we find wide variations in the composition and accounting for plant funds. The differences in the plant funds of the three types of nonprofit organizations are not supported by any theoretical differences in their accounting objectives.

Financial statements for nonprofit organizations

All nonprofit organizations issue a balance sheet incorporating all funds of the organization. The assets, liabilities, and fund balances for each fund are listed in horizontal or vertical sequence in the balance sheet. This type of balance sheet presentation emphasizes the unitary nature of the nonprofit organization, despite its use of separate funds for accountability purposes.

Because a nonprofit organization does not operate for gain, an income statement is inappropriate. Instead, a *statement of activity,* with a title such as "statement of revenue, expenses, support, and capital additions," is issued, with the final amount labeled "Excess of revenue and support over expenses" or a similar caption. Changes in fund balances may be summarized in a separate statement or may be annexed to the statement of activity.

[17] "Audits of Colleges and Universities," p. 44.

The AICPA's "Hospital Audit Guide" recommends a statement of changes in financial position for the unrestricted fund.[18] However, "Audits of Voluntary Health and Welfare Organizations" and "Audits of Colleges and Universities" waive a statement of changes in financial position, because the information is available in the other financial statements.[19] **Statement of Position 78-10** requires nonprofit organizations that it covers to present a statement of changes in financial position.[20]

Many of the matters discussed in this chapter are illustrated in the financial statements and notes to financial statements of the American Accounting Association, a nonprofit organization, in the Appendix of this chapter beginning on page 592.

Appraisal of accounting standards for nonprofit organizations

The accounting principles recommended by the AICPA for colleges and universities, hospitals, voluntary health and welfare organizations, and other nonprofit organizations collectively disclose many inconsistencies. More coordination in the efforts of the various committees that developed the separate sets of accounting principles probably would have eliminated most of these inconsistencies. It is to be hoped that the FASB soon will address the accounting for nonprofit organizations and, drawing on the objectives of financial reporting by nonbusiness organizations discussed in **Statement of Financial Accounting Concepts No. 4** (see pages 501 and 502), will develop uniform accounting standards for all nonprofit organizations.

APPENDIX: FINANCIAL STATEMENTS AND NOTES OF AMERICAN ACCOUNTING ASSOCIATION (starts on page 592)

---

[18] "Hospital Audit Guide," p. 38.

[19] "Audits of Voluntary Health and Welfare Organizations," pp. 33; "Audits of Colleges and Universities," p. 55.

[20] Accounting Principles and Reporting Practices for Certain Nonprofit Organizations," p. 11.

AMERICAN ACCOUNTING ASSOCIATION

REPORT OF INDEPENDENT CERTIFIED PUBLIC ACCOUNTANTS

To the Executive Committee,

American Accounting Association:

We have examined the balance sheet of AMERICAN ACCOUNTING ASSOCIATION as of August 31, 1981, and the related statements of support, revenue and expenses and changes in fund balances and changes in financial position for the year then ended. Our examination was made in accordance with generally accepted auditing standards and, accordingly, included such tests of the accounting records and such other auditing procedures as we considered necessary in the circumstances.

In our opinion, the financial statements referred to above present fairly the financial position of American Accounting Association as of August 31, 1981, and the results of its operations and the changes in its fund balances and changes in its financial position for the year then ended, in conformity with generally accepted accounting principles applied on a basis consistent with that of the preceding year.

Our examination was made for the purpose of forming an opinion on the basic financial statements taken as a whole. The statement of contributions earned for the year ended August 31, 1981, (Exhibit I) is presented for purposes of additional analysis and is not a required part of the basic financial statements. Such information has been subjected to the auditing procedures applied in the examination of the basic financial statements and, in our opinion, is fairly stated in all material respects in relation to the basic financial statements taken as a whole.

COOPERS & LYBRAND

Tampa, Florida
October 21, 1981

AMERICAN ACCOUNTING ASSOCIATION
BALANCE SHEET, August 31, 1981

	UNRESTRICTED		RESTRICTED			
	General Fund	Publications Fund	Sections Fund	Fellowship Fund	Educational Research Fund	Total All Funds
ASSETS						
Current assets:						
Cash, including invested cash of $11,525	$ 12,970	–	–	–	–	$ 12,970
Certificates of deposit	200,780	–	–	–	–	200,780
Marketable securities, at cost which approximates market (Note 1)	338,953	–	–	–	–	338,953
Current portion of pledges receivable (Note 1)	50,000	–	–	$ 5,000	$43,380	98,380
Accounts and interest receivable	31,877	$ 5,187	–	–	–	37,064
Publications inventory (Notes 1 and 3)	–	110,531	–	–	–	110,531
Prepaids and other assets	3,808	–	–	–	–	3,808
Due from (to) other funds	(90,628)	(21,071)	$56,254	28,878	26,567	–
Total current assets	547,760	94,647	56,254	33,878	69,947	802,486
Pledges receivable, less current portion (Note 1)	95,547	–	–	10,000	–	105,547
Property and equipment, at cost less accumulated depreciation of $28,872 (Notes 1 and 2)	160,148	–	–	–	–	160,148
	$803,455	$ 94,647	$56,254	$43,878	$69,947	$1,068,181
LIABILITIES AND FUND BALANCES						
Current liabilities:						
Accounts payable and accrued liabilities	$ 66,600	–	–	$11,800	–	$ 78,400
Accounts payable – research projects (Note 1)	45,174	–	–	–	$27,120	72,294
Current portion of deferred revenue (Note 1):						
Membership dues	71,277	–	–	–	–	71,277
Subscriptions	22,944	–	–	–	–	22,944
Current portion of deferred support (Note 1)	60,000	–	–	5,000	42,827	107,827
Total current liabilities	265,995	–	–	16,800	69,947	352,742
Deferred revenue, less current portion (Note 1):						
Membership dues	613	–	–	–	–	613
Subscriptions	1,395	–	–	–	–	1,395
Deferred support, less current portion (Note 1)	67,678	–	–	5,000	–	72,678
	69,686	–	–	5,000	–	74,686
Commitment (Note 4)						
Fund balances (Note 3)						
Unrestricted:						
Designated for fund purposes	–	$ 94,647	–	–	–	94,647
Undesignated, available for general purposes	455,774	–	–	–	–	455,774
Total unrestricted	455,774	94,647	–	–	–	550,421
Restricted	12,000	–	$56,254	22,078	–	90,332
Total fund balances	467,774	94,647	56,254	22,078	–	640,753
	$803,455	$ 94,647	$56,254	$43,878	$69,947	$1,068,181

See accompanying notes.

ANNUAL REPORT

STATEMENT OF SUPPORT, REVENUE AND EXPENSES AND CHANGES IN FUND BALANCES
for the year ended August 31, 1981

| | UNRESTRICTED | | RESTRICTED | | | |
	General Fund	Publications Fund	Sections Fund	Fellowship Fund	Educational Research Fund	Total All Funds
REVENUE AND SUPPORT (Note 1)						
Membership dues	$266,861	–	$55,068	–	–	$321,929
Subscriptions	69,911	–	–	–	–	69,911
Advertising	65,187	–	–	–	–	65,187
Publication sales	7,986	$67,611	2,353	–	–	77,950
Contributions (Exhibit I)	118,513	–	–	$26,410	$36,620	181,543
Interest and dividend income	63,438	–	–	–	–	63,438
Income from annual convention net of direct costs of $152,000	9,222	–	–	–	–	9,222
Other revenue, primarily programs and seminars	82,074	–	400	–	–	82,474
	683,192	67,611	57,821	26,410	36,620	871,654
EXPENSES (Note 1)						
Cost of publications:						
The Accounting Review and Committee Reports Supplement	175,569	–	–	–	–	175,569
Other	24,920	27,069	22,910	–	–	74,899
Programs and seminars	158,350	–	–	–	–	158,350
Research and education	28,413	–	–	–	36,620	65,033
Committees	39,005	–	–	–	–	39,005
Officers' meetings	32,493	–	–	–	–	32,493
Administration	189,232	–	24,496	–	–	213,728
Financial Accounting Foundation contribution	9,658	–	–	–	–	9,658
American Assembly of Collegiate Schools of Business contribution	5,000	–	–	–	–	5,000
Fellowship grants	–	–	–	24,500	–	24,500
Other expenses	16,840	–	–	–	–	16,840
	679,480	27,069	47,406	24,500	36,620	815,075
Excess of support and revenue over expenses	3,712	40,542	10,415	1,910	–	56,579
Fund balances, beginning of year	464,062	54,105	45,839	20,168	–	584,174
Fund balances, end of year	$467,774	$94,647	$56,254	$22,078	$ –	$640,753

See accompanying notes.

STATEMENT OF CHANGES IN FINANCIAL POSITION
for the year ended August 31, 1981

| | UNRESTRICTED | | RESTRICTED | | | |
	General Fund	Publications Fund	Sections Fund	Fellowship Fund	Educational Research Fund	Total All Funds
SOURCES OF FUNDS						
From operations:						
Revenue and support in excess of expenses	$ 3,712	$40,542	$10,415	$ 1,910	–	$ 56,579
Add depreciation, which does not require funds	10,386	–	–	–	–	10,386
Funds provided from operations	14,098	40,542	10,415	1,910	–	66,965
Decrease (increase) in:						
Pledges receivable, current and long-term	(14,547)	–	–	–	$36,620	22,073
Marketable securities	42,732	–	–	–	–	42,732
Increase (decrease) in:						
Deferred revenue, current and long-term	2,705	–	–	–	–	2,705
Accounts payable – research projects	10,124	–	–	–	15,120	25,244
Interfund borrowings	(8,641)	18,476	(7,505)	12,790	(15,120)	–
Total sources of funds	46,471	59,018	2,910	14,700	36,620	159,719
USES OF FUNDS						
Increase (decrease) in:						
Inventory	–	56,426	–	–	–	56,426
Accounts and interest receivable	5,993	(350)	–	–	–	5,643
Prepaids and other assets	196	–	–	–	–	196
Decrease (increase) in:						
Accounts payable and accrued liabilities	(8,286)	2,942	2,910	9,700	–	7,266
Deferred support, current and long-term	(15,730)	–	–	5,000	36,620	25,890
Purchase of property and equipment	32,473	–	–	–	–	32,473
Total uses of funds	14,646	59,018	2,910	14,700	36,620	127,894
Net sources of funds	31,825	–	–	–	–	31,825
Cash and certificates of deposit, beginning of year	181,925	–	–	–	–	181,925
Cash and certificates of deposit, end of year	$213,750	$ –	$ –	$ –	$ –	$213,750

See accompanying notes.

NOTES TO FINANCIAL STATEMENTS AUGUST 31, 1981

1. SUMMARY OF SIGNIFICANT ACCOUNTING POLICIES:

Accounting Method –

The financial statements of American Accounting Association (the Association) are prepared in accordance with the Statement of Position entitled "Accounting Principles and Reporting Practices for Certain Nonprofit Organizations" prepared by the American Institute of Certified Public Accountants.

Pledges –

Pledges are recorded as receivables in the year made. Pledges for support of future periods are recorded as deferred amounts in the respective funds to which they apply. Support restricted by the donor for use in specified programs is recognized when the related program expenses are incurred.

Marketable Securities –

Marketable securities are recorded at cost.

Inventory –

Publications inventory is stated at the lower of cost (first-in, first-out) or market.

Depreciation –

Depreciation is provided using the straight-line method over the estimated useful lives of the assets. Depreciation expense of $10,386 is included in administrative expense.

Dues and Subscriptions –

General membership dues and subscriptions are recognized in the applicable membership and subscription period.

Publication Revenue –

Publication revenue is recognized when the related publications are issued.

Fellowship Grants –

Fellowship grants are expensed at the time the grant is approved by the Association.

Research Projects –

Research project expenses related to projects authorized by the Director of Research and Director of Education are accrued in the year the projects are authorized.

Income Taxes –

Pursuant to a determination letter received from the Internal Revenue Service, the Association is exempt from Federal income tax under Section 501(c)(3) of the Internal Revenue Code.

2. PROPERTY AND EQUIPMENT:

Property and equipment at August 31, 1981, consisted of the following:

Land	$ 29,748
Land improvements	13,246
Building	77,172
Furniture and equipment	40,062
Construction in progress	28,792
	189,020
Less accumulated depreciation	28,872
	$160,148

3. FUNDS:

The assets, liabilities and fund balances of the Association are reported in five self-balancing funds, as follows:

General Fund –

The General Fund is used to account for the operations of the Association, as well as those operations and activities not accounted for in other established funds. At August 31, 1981, $12,000 of the General Fund has been restricted for use in minority programs.

Publications Fund –

This fund was established to record the sale of publications of the Association other than *The Accounting Review* (which is provided to members in connection with payment of membership dues) and publications funded specifically by other funds.

Sections Fund –

This fund was established to account for the activities of the Association's special-interest membership groups, such as the auditing section, public sector section, etc.

Fellowship Fund –

This fund was established to record the operations of the fellowship program. Fellowships are awarded using funds generated by contributions to this fund.

Educational Research Fund –

This fund was established to record research projects which are directly funded by the related pledges received.

4. EMPLOYEE BENEFIT PLAN:

The Association has a contributory money purchase plan which covers substantially all employees. The Association's policy is to fund all related costs, which approximated $6,800 in 1981.

5. COMMITMENT:

In June 1981 the Association entered into a construction contract for expansion of its existing facilities. The remaining commitment at August 31, 1981, was approximately $63,000.

EXHIBIT I
STATEMENT OF CONTRIBUTIONS EARNED
FOR THE YEAR ENDED AUGUST 31, 1981

GENERAL FUND:

The Touche Ross Foundation	$ 82,444
Deloitte Haskins & Sells Foundation:	
1981 contribution	1,200
Recognition in 1981 of	
previously deferred support	31,369
Exxon Corporation	3,500
	$118,513

FELLOWSHIP FUND:

The Arthur Young Foundation	$ 5,000
Coopers & Lybrand Foundation	5,000
Ernst & Whinney Foundation	5,000
American Accounting Association	
members and others	4,910
The Touche Ross Foundation	3,000
Price Waterhouse Foundation	2,000
South-Western Publishing Company	1,000
International Business Machine Corporation	500
	$ 26,410

EDUCATIONAL RESEARCH FUND:

Coopers & Lybrand – recognition in	
1981 of previously deferred support	$ 36,620

REVIEW QUESTIONS

1 What is a **nonprofit organization?**

2 List four types of nonprofit organizations in the United States.

3 What role do the AICPA's **Industry Audit Guides** play in the establishment of accounting principles for nonprofit organizations? Explain.

4 What are the three characteristics of nonprofit organizations that resemble those of governmental units?

5 What characteristics of nonprofit organizations resemble those of business enterprises?

6 Define the following terms applicable to nonprofit organizations:
a **Designated Fund Balance.**
b **Third-party payer**
c **Pledge**
d **Pooled investments**
e **Term endowment fund**

7 Differentiate between an **annuity fund** and a **life income fund** of a nonprofit organization.

8 There are several inconsistencies in the accounting principles for like items in the AICPA's **Industry Audit Guides** for nonprofit organizations. Identify three of these inconsistencies.

9 Hospitals and universities often "abate" or otherwise reduce their basic revenue charges to patients and students, respectively. How are these reductions reflected in the revenue accounting for the two types of nonprofit organizations? Explain.

10 a Should a nonprofit organization record donated material in its accounting records? Explain.
b Should a nonprofit organization record donated services in its accounting records? Explain.

11 Identify the financial statements that are issued by a hospital.

12 How do **support** and **capital additions** differ from **revenue** of a nonprofit organization? Explain.

13 What plant assets of nonprofit organizations need not be depreciated, according to **Statement of Position 78-10** "Accounting Principles and Reporting Practices for Certain Nonprofit Organizations"?

EXERCISES

Ex. 13-1 Select the best answer for each of the following multiple-choice questions:

1 The basis of accounting used by nonprofit organizations is the:
a Cash basis
b Modified accrual basis
c Accrual basis
d Modified cash basis

2 Interest is accounted for in a university's student loan fund on:
- **a** The modified accrual basis of accounting
- **b** The accrual basis of accounting
- **c** The cash basis of accounting
- **d** Some other basis of accounting

3 Which of the following receipts is recorded in a restricted fund in the accounting records of a university?
- **a** Tuition
- **b** Student laboratory fees
- **c** Housing fees
- **d** None of the foregoing

4 Which of the following funds of a voluntary health and welfare organization does not have a counterpart fund in governmental accounting?
- **a** Current unrestricted fund
- **b** Land, building, and equipment fund
- **c** Agency fund
- **d** Endowment fund

5 A voluntary health and welfare organization received a pledge in Year 1 from a donor specifying that the amount pledged be used in Year 3. The donor paid the pledge in cash in Year 2. The pledge should be accounted for as:
- **a** A deferred credit in the balance sheet at the end of Year 1 and as support in Year 2
- **b** A deferred credit in the balance sheet at the end of Year 1 and Year 2 and as support in Year 3
- **c** Support in Year 1
- **d** Support in Year 2 and no deferred credit in the balance sheet at the end of Year 1

6 The Charity Allowances ledger account of a nonprofit hospital is a/an:
- **a** Contra-asset account
- **b** Expense account
- **c** Contra-revenue account
- **d** Loss account

Ex. 13-2 In your examination of the financial statements of Cordova Hospital, a nonprofit organization, for the year ended March 31, Year 6, you note the following journal entry in the Unrestricted Fund:

Inventories	200	
Cash		200

To record purchase of medicine and drugs from manufacturer at nominal cost. Current fair value of the items totals $6,400.

Prepare a journal entry to correct the accounting records of the Unrestricted Fund of Cordova Hospital.

Ex. 13-3 During the month of October, Year 4, volunteer teachers' aides rendered services at no cost to Warner School, a nonprofit private elementary school. Salary rates for comparable employees of Warner School applied to the services gave a total value of $3,400. Complimentary meals given to the volunteers at the Warner School cafeteria during October, Year 4, cost $180. The volunteer teachers' aides' services met the specifications for donated services in **Statement of Position 78-10,** "Accounting Principles and Reporting Practices for Certain Nonprofit Organizations."

Prepare a journal entry in the Warner School Unrestricted Fund to record the services donated to Warner School during the month of October, Year 4. Disregard income taxes.

Ex. 13-4 For the month of September, Year 6, Redwood Hospital's patient service revenue records included the following:

Amount to be received from United Way for indigent patients	$ 16,500
Charity allowances for indigent patients	32,000
Contractual adjustment allowed for Medicare patients	18,500
Gross patient service revenue (before recognition of charity allowances and contractual adjustments)	225,000

Prepare the September 30, Year 6, journal entries to record the foregoing in the accounting records of Redwood Hospital.

Ex. 13-5 On July 1, Year 5, three funds of Wilmington College pooled their individual investments, as follows:

	Cost	Current fair value
Restricted Fund	$ 80,000	$ 90,000
Quasi-Endowment Fund	120,000	126,000
Annuity Fund	150,000	144,000
Totals	$350,000	$360,000

During the year ended June 30, Year 6, the Wilmington College investment pool, managed by the Unrestricted Fund, reinvested realized gains of $10,000 and received dividends and interest totaling $18,000.

Prepare journal entries on June 30, Year 6, for each of the three Wilmington College funds to reflect the results of the investment pool's operations during Fiscal Year 6. Do not use Receivable from Unrestricted Fund ledger accounts.

Ex. 13-6 In your examination of the financial statements of Local Health Center, a nonprofit organization, you find the following journal entries in the Restricted Fund:

Receivable from Unrestricted Fund	10,000	
Fund Balance		10,000
To record board of directors' authorization of resources to be expended for clinic equipment.		

Clinic Equipment	9,500	
Accounts Payable		9,500
To record receipt of invoice for clinic equipment.		

No related journal entries had been made in any other fund.

Prepare adjusting journal entries on December 31, Year 1, for all affected funds of Local Health Center.

Ex. 13-7 The "Summary of Significant Accounting Policies" note to the financial statements prepared by the controller of Wabash Hospital for the year ended June 30, Year 3, includes the following sentence: "Pledges for contributions are recorded when the cash is received." Another note reads as follows:

Pledges Unrestricted pledges receivable, received and collected during the year ended June 30, Year 3, were as follows:

Pledges receivable, July 1, Year 2 (10% doubtful)	$ 50,000
New pledges received during year ended June 30, Year 3	300,000
Pledges receivable, July 1, Year 2, determined to be uncollectible during year	(15,000)
Pledges collected in cash during year ended June 30, Year 3	(275,000)
Pledges receivable, June 30, Year 3 (12% doubtful)	$ 60,000

All pledges are due six months from the date of the pledge. Pledge support is recorded in the Unrestricted Fund.

Assume that you are engaged in the examination of the financial statements of Wabash Hospital for the year ended June 30, Year 3, and are satisfied with the propriety of the amounts recorded in the hospital's "Pledges" note. Prepare the necessary adjusting entry for the Unrestricted Fund of Wabash Hospital on June 30, Year 3.

CASES

Case 13-1 During the June 20, Year 10, meeting of the board of directors of Roakdale Nursing Home, a nonprofit organization, the following discussion transpired:

Chair. "We shall now hear the report from the controller."

Controller. "Our unrestricted contributions are at an all-time high. I projected an Unrestricted Fund excess of revenue over expenses of $100,000 for the year ending June 30."

Chair. "That's too large an amount for us to have a successful fund-raising drive next year. I'll entertain a motion that $80,000 of unrestricted contributions be transferred to the Restricted Fund."

Director Walker. "So moved."

Director Hastings. "Second."

Chair. "All those in favor say 'aye'."

All Directors. "Aye."

Chair. "The chair directs the controller to prepare the necessary journal entries for the Unrestricted Fund and the Restricted Fund."

Instructions Do you concur with the action taken by the board of directors of Roakdale Nursing Home? Explain.

Case 13-2 The controller of Lakeland Hospital, a nonprofit organization, proposes to present the Provision for Doubtful Accounts Receivable account as an expense in the statement of activity of Lakeland Hospital Unrestricted Fund. As the hospital's independent auditor you oppose this treatment. You point out that the AICPA's "Hospital Audit Guide" requires the provision for doubtful accounts to be offset against gross patient service revenue in the statement of activity of a hospital's unrestricted fund. The controller's rejoinder is that there are so many contradictions among the AICPA's **Industry Audit Guides** for nonprofit organizations that there should be some latitude for managers of nonprofit organizations to report operating results on the same basis as a business enterprise.

Instructions How would you respond to the controller of Lakeland Hospital? Support your reply by sound accounting theory for nonprofit organizations.

Case 13-3 The characteristics of voluntary health and welfare organizations differ in certain respects from the characteristics of governmental units. As an example, voluntary health and welfare organizations derive their support primarily from voluntary contributions, but governmental units derive their revenues from taxes and services.

Instructions

a Describe **fund accounting** and discuss whether its use is consistent with the concept that an accounting entity is an economic unit that has control over resources, accepts responsibilities for making and carrying out commitments, and conducts economic activity.

b Distinguish between the accrual basis of accounting and the modified accrual basis of accounting and indicate which method should be used for a voluntary health and welfare organization.

c Discuss how methods used to account for plant assets differ between voluntary health and welfare organizations and governmental units.

Case 13-4 The board of trustees of Toledo Day Care Center, a nonprofit organization, has asked you, as independent auditor for the Center, to attend a meeting of the board of trustees and participate in the discussion of a proposal to create one or more endowment funds. At the meeting, the board members ask you numerous questions regarding the operations and the accounting treatment of endowment funds. Among the questions posed by trustees were the following:

(1) Is only the revenue of an endowment fund expendable for current operations?

(2) Under what circumstances, if any, may endowment fund principal be expended at the discretion of the board?

(3) Must a separate set of accounting records be established for each endowment fund, or may all endowment fund operations be accounted for in the restricted fund?

Instructions Prepare a reply for each of the trustees' questions. Number your replies to correspond with the question numbers.

PROBLEMS

13-1 On July 1, Year 6, the four funds of Suburban Welfare Services, a nonprofit organization, formed an investment pool. On that date, cost and current fair value of the investment pool were as follows:

	Cost	Current fair value
Unrestricted Fund	$ 50,000	$ 59,400
Restricted Fund	20,000	16,200
Plant Fund	80,000	89,100
Arnold Life Income Fund	100,000	105,300
Totals	$250,000	$270,000

During the six months ended December 31, Year 6, the investment pool, managed by the Unrestricted Fund, reinvested realized gains totaling $15,000 and received dividends and interest totaling $25,000, which was distributed to the participating funds. On December 31, Year 6, the Restricted Fund withdrew from the pool and was awarded securities in the amount of its share of the pool's aggregate December 31, Year 6, current fair value of $300,000. On January 2, Year 7, the Edwards Endowment Fund entered the Suburban Welfare Services investment pool with investments having a cost of $70,000 and a current fair value of $78,000. During the six months ended June 30, Year 7, the investment pool reinvested realized gains totaling $40,000 and received dividends and interest totaling $60,000, which was distributed to the participating funds.

Instructions

a Prepare a working paper for the Suburban Welfare Services investment pool, computing the following (round all percentages to two decimal places):

(1) Original equity percentages, July 1, Year 6
(2) Revised equity percentages, January 2, Year 7

b Prepare journal entries to record the operations of the Suburban Welfare Services investment pool in the accounting records of the Unrestricted Fund. Use Payable to Restricted Fund, Payable to Plant Fund, and Payable to Arnold Life Income Fund ledger accounts for amounts payable to other funds.

13-2   Among the transactions of the Unrestricted Fund of Harbor Hospital, a nonprofit organization, for the month of October, Year 8, were the following:

(1) Gross patient service revenue of $80,000 was billed to patients. Provision was made for indigent patient charity allowances of $4,000, of which amount $2,500 was receivable from Bovard Welfare Organization; contractual adjustments allowed to Medicaid of $6,000; and doubtful accounts of $8,000.
(2) Donated services approximating $10,000 at going salary rates were received from volunteer nurses. Meals costing $200 were served to the volunteer nurses at no charge by the Harbor Hospital cafeteria.
(3) New pledges, due in three months, totaling $5,000 were received from various donors. Collections on pledges amounted to $3,500, and the provision for doubtful pledges for October, Year 8, was $800.
(4) Paid the $500 monthly annuity established for Arline E. Walters by a contribution by Walters to Harbor Hospital three years ago.
(5) Received and expended $3,000 from Charles Watson Restricted Fund for new surgical equipment, as authorized by the donor.

Instructions
a Prepare the journal entries for the October, Year 8, transactions of the Harbor Hospital Unrestricted Fund. Number each group of entries to correspond to the number of each transactions group.
b Prepare journal entries required for other funds of Harbor Hospital as indicated by the transactions of the Unrestricted Fund.

13-3   Presented below is the current funds balance sheet of State University at the end of the fiscal year ended June 30, Year 8:

STATE UNIVERSITY

Current Funds Balance Sheet

June 30, Year 8

Assets			Liabilities & Fund Balances		
Unrestricted Fund			**Unrestricted Fund**		
Cash	$210,000		Accounts payable . .	$ 45,000	
Accounts receivable			Deferred revenue . .	66,000	
for student tuition			Fund balance	515,000	$626,000
and fees, less allowance for doubtful					
accounts, $9,000 . .	341,000				
State appropriation					
receivable	75,000	$626,000			
Restricted Fund			**Restricted Fund**		
Cash	$ 7,000		Fund balance		67,000
Investments	60,000	67,000			
Total		$693,000	Total		$693,000

The following transactions occurred during the fiscal year ended June 30, Year 9:

(1) On July 7, Year 8, a gift of $100,000 was received from an alumnus. The alumnus requested that one half of the gift be used for the acquisition of books for the university library and that the remainder be used for the establishment of a scholarship. The alumnus further requested that the revenue generated by the scholarship fund be used annually to award a scholarship to a qualified disadvantaged student, with the principal remaining intact. On July 20, Year 8, the board of trustees resolved that the cash of the newly established scholarship (endowment) fund would be invested in bank certificates of deposit. On July 21, Year 8, the certificates of deposit were acquired.

(2) Revenue from student tuition and fees applicable to the year ended June 30, Year 9, amounted to $1,900,000. Of this amount, $66,000 was collected in the prior year and $1,686,000 was collected during the year ended June 30, Year 9. In addition, on June 30, Year 9, the university had received cash of $158,000, representing tuition and fees for the session beginning July 1, Year 9.

(3) During the year ended June 30, Year 9, the university had collected $349,000 of the outstanding accounts receivable at the beginning of the year. The balance was determined to be uncollectible and was written off against the allowance account. On June 30, Year 9, the allowance account was increased by $3,000.

(4) During the year interest charges of $6,000 were earned and collected on late student fee payments.

(5) During the year the state appropriation was received. An additional unrestricted appropriation of $50,000 was made by the state, but had not been paid to the university as of June 30, Year 9.

(6) Unrestricted cash gifts totaling $25,000 were received from alumni of the university.

(7) During the year restricted fund investments of $21,000 were sold for $26,000. Investment earnings amounting to $1,900 were received. (Credit Fund Balance.)

(8) During the year unrestricted operating expenses of $1,777,000 were recorded. On June 30, Year 9, $59,000 of these expenses remained unpaid.

(9) Restricted cash of $13,000 was spent for authorized purposes during the year. An equal amount was transferred from fund balance to revenue of the restricted fund.

(10) The accounts payable on June 30, Year 8, were paid during the year.

(11) During the year, $7,000 interest was earned and received on the certificate of deposit acquired in accordance with the board of trustees resolution discussed in item (1). (Credit Fund Balance.)

Instructions Prepare general journal entries to record the transactions for the year ended June 30, Year 9. Each journal entry should be numbered to correspond with the transaction described above. Omit explanations for the journal entries.

Your working paper should be organized as follows:

Transaction number	Accounts	Unrestricted Fund Dr(Cr)	Restricted Fund Dr(Cr)	Endowment Fund Dr(Cr)
(1)				

Use the following account titles in the journal entries:

Unrestricted Fund
  Accounts Payable
  Accounts Receivable for Student Tuition and Fees
  Allowance for Doubtful Accounts
  Cash
  Deferred Revenue
  Expenses
  Revenue
  State Appropriation Receivable

Restricted Fund
  Cash
  Expenditures
  Fund Balance
  Investments
  Revenue

Endowment Fund
  Cash
  Fund Balance
  Investments

13-4 Presented at the top of page 603 is the balance sheet of Resthaven Hospital on December 31, Year 6.

During Year 7 the following transactions were completed:

(1) Gross debits to Accounts Receivable for hospital services were as follows:

Room and board	$ 780,000
Other professional services	321,000
Total debits to Accounts Receivable	$1,101,000

(2) Deductions from gross revenue were as follows:

Provision for doubtful accounts	$30,000
Charity allowances	15,000
Total deductions from gross revenue	$45,000

(3) The Unrestricted Fund paid $18,000 to retire mortgage bonds payable with an equivalent face amount.

(4) During the year the Unrestricted Fund received unrestricted gifts of $50,000 and revenue from Endowment Fund investments of $6,500. The Unrestricted Fund has been designated to receive the revenue on Endowment Fund investments.

(5) New equipment costing $26,000 was acquired. An x-ray machine that originally cost $24,000 and had a carrying amount of $2,400 was sold for $500.

(6) Vouchers totaling $1,191,000 were issued for the following items:

Administrative services expense	$ 120,000
Interest expense	95,000
General services expense	225,000
Nursing services expense	520,000
Other professional services expense	165,000
Inventory of supplies	60,000
Accrued liabilities, Dec. 31, Year 6	6,000
Total vouchers issued	$1,191,000

RESTHAVEN HOSPITAL
Balance Sheet
December 31, Year 6

Unrestricted Fund

Assets		Liabilities & Fund Balance	
Current assets		Current liabilities	
Cash	$ 20,000	Accounts payable	$ 16,000
Accounts receivable. . .	37,000	Accrued liabilities	6,000
Less: Allowances and		Total current lia-	
doubtful ac-		bilities	$ 22,000
counts.	(7,000)	Mortgage bonds payable .	150,000
Inventory of supplies . .	14,000	Total liabilities	$ 172,000
Total current assets. .	$ 64,000	Fund balance:	
		Investment in plant . . .	$2,116,000
Plant assets		Undesignated.	12,000
Land	$ 370,000	Total fund balance . .	$2,128,000
Buildings	1,750,000		
Less: Accumulated			
depreciation . . .	(430,000)		
Equipment	680,000		
Less: Accumulated			
depreciation . . .	(134,000)		
Total plant assets . . .	$2,236,000	Total liabilities & fund	
Total assets.	$2,300,000	balance	$2,300,000

Restricted Funds

Plant Replacement and Expansion Fund

Assets		Fund Balance	
Cash	$ 53,800		
Investments.	71,200		
Total assets	$125,000	Fund balance	$125,000

Endowment Fund

Assets		Fund Balance	
Cash	$ 6,000		
Investments.	260,000		
Total assets	$266,000	Fund balance	$266,000

(7) Collections on accounts receivable totaled $985,000. Accounts receivable written off as uncollectible amounted to $11,000.

(8) Cash payments on accounts payable during the year were $825,000.

(9) Supplies of $37,000 were issued for nursing services.

(10) On December 31, Year 7, accrued interest earned on Plant Replacement and Expansion Fund investments was $800.

(11) Depreciation of buildings and equipment was as follows:

Buildings	$ 44,000
Equipment	73,000
Total depreciation	$117,000

(12) On December 31, Year 7, an accrual of $6,100 was made for interest on the mortgage bonds payable.

Instructions For the period January 1, Year 7, through December 31, Year 7, prepare journal entries (omit explanations) to record the transactions described above for the following funds of Resthaven Hospital:
Unrestricted Fund
Plant Replacement and Expansion Fund
Endowment Fund
Each journal entry should be numbered to correspond with the transactions described above.
Your working paper should be organized as follows:

Transaction number	Accounts	Unrestricted Fund Dr(Cr)	Plant Replacement and Expansion Fund Dr(Cr)	Endowment Fund Dr(Cr)
(1)				

In addition to the ledger accounts included in the December 31, Year 6, balance sheet of Resthaven Hospital, the following ledger accounts are pertinent:

Unrestricted Fund
Administrative Services Expense
Charity Allowances
Depreciation Expense
General Services Expense
Interest Expense
Loss on Disposal of Plant Assets
Nursing Services Expense
Other Professional Services Expense
Patient Service Revenue
Provision for Doubtful Accounts
Unrestricted Gift Support
Unrestricted Revenue from Endowment Fund

Plant Replacement and Expansion Fund
Interest Receivable

13-5 A newly elected board of directors of Hospital of Sun Valley, a nonprofit organization, decided that effective January 1, Year 98:

(a) The existing ledger account balances are to be adjusted and three separate funds (Unrestricted Fund, James Dupar Endowment Fund, and Plant Replacement Fund) are to be established.
(b) The fund balance of the James Dupar Endowment Fund and an amount equal to the Accumulated Depreciation account of the Unrestricted Fund are to be invested in securities.
(c) The accounting records are to be maintained in accordance with the AICPA's "Hospital Audit Guide."

The board of directors engaged you to determine the appropriate ledger account balances for each of the funds. The trial balance of the ledger on January 1, Year 98, follows:

HOSPITAL OF SUN VALLEY
Trial Balance
January 1, Year 98

	Debit	Credit
Cash	$ 50,000	
Investment in U.S. Treasury bills	105,000	
Investment in common stocks	417,000	
Interest receivable	4,000	
Accounts receivable	40,000	
Inventories	25,000	
Land	407,000	
Building	245,000	
Equipment	283,000	
Accumulated depreciation		$ 376,000
Accounts payable		70,000
Bank loan payable		150,000
James Dupar Endowment Fund		119,500
Surplus		860,500
Totals	$1,576,000	$1,576,000

Additional information

(1) Under the terms of the will of James Dupar, "the principal of the bequest is to be fully invested in trust forevermore in mortgages secured by productive real estate and/or in U.S. government securities . . . and the revenue therefrom is to be used to defray current expenses."

(2) The James Dupar Endowment Fund account balance consists of the following:

Cash received in Year 1 by bequest from James Dupar	$ 81,500
Net gains realized from Year 56 through Year 89 from the sale of real	
estate acquired in mortgage foreclosures	23,500
Revenue received from Year 90 through Year 97 from investment in	
U.S. Treasury bills	14,500
Balance, Jan. 1, Year 98	$119,500

(3) The Land account balance is composed of the following:

Year 20 appraisal of land at $10,000 and building at $5,000 received	
by donation at that time. (The building was demolished in Year 40)	$ 15,000
Appraisal increase based on insured value in land title policies is-	
sued in Year 57	380,000
Landscaping costs for trees planted	12,000
Balance, Jan. 1, Year 98	$407,000

(4) The Building account balance is composed of the following:

Cost of present hospital building completed in January, Year 57,
when the hospital began operations $300,000
Adjustment to record appraised value of building in Year 67 . . . . (100,000)
Cost of elevator installed in January, Year 83 45,000
Balance, Jan. 1, Year 98 . . . . $245,000

The economic lives of the hospital building and the elevator when new were 50 years and 20 years, respectively, with no residual value.
(5) The hospital's equipment was inventoried on January 1, Year 98. The total of the inventory agreed with the Equipment account balance in the ledger. The Accumulated Depreciation ledger account on January 1, Year 98, included $158,250 applicable to equipment, and that amount was approved by the board of directors as being accurate. All depreciation is computed on a straight-line basis, with no residual value.
(6) A bank loan was obtained to finance the cost of new operating room equipment acquired in Year 94. Interest on the loan was paid to December 31, Year 97.

Instructions Prepare a working paper for Hospital of Sun Valley to present the adjustments necessary to restate the ledger account balances and to distribute the adjusted balances to establish the required fund accounts. Formal journal entries are not required; however, explain each adjustment (including supporting computations) at the bottom of the working paper. The following column headings are suggested:
   Unadjusted trial balance
   Adjustments
   Adjusted trial balance
   Unrestricted Fund
   James Dupar Endowment Fund
   Plant Replacement Fund

13-6 The accountant for Freida's Vocational School, a nonprofit organization, resigned on March 1, Year 8, after having prepared the following trial balance and analysis of cash on February 28, Year 8:

FREIDA'S VOCATIONAL SCHOOL
Trial Balance
February 28, Year 8

Debits

Cash for general current operations	$258,000
Cash for restricted current uses	30,900
Common stock donated by L. M. Nash	91,000
Bonds donated by O. P. Quinn	150,000
Land	22,000
Building	33,000
General current operating expenses	38,000
Faculty recruitment expenses	4,100
Total debits	$627,000

(Continued)

FREIDA'S VOCATIONAL SCHOOL
Trial Balance (concluded)
February 28, Year 8

Credits

Mortgage note payable	$ 30,000
Support from gifts for general operations	210,000
Support from gifts for restricted uses	196,000
Student fees	31,000
Surplus	160,000
Total credits	$627,000

FREIDA'S VOCATIONAL SCHOOL
Analysis of Cash
For Six Months Ended February 28, Year 8

Cash for general current operations:			
Balance, Sept. 1, Year 7		$ 80,000	
Add: Student fees	$ 31,000		
Gift of H. I. Johnson	210,000	241,000	
Subtotal		$321,000	
Less: General current operating			
expenses	$ 38,000		
Payment for land and building	25,000	63,000	$258,000
Cash for restricted current uses:			
Gift of H. I. Johnson for faculty recruitment	$ 35,000		
Less: Faculty recruitment expenses	4,100	30,900	
Checking account balance, Feb. 28, Year 8		$288,900	

You were engaged to determine the appropriate ledger account balances for the school as of August 31, Year 8, the close of the school's first fiscal year. Your examination disclosed the following information:

(1) In September, Year 7, L. M. Nash donated 1,000 shares of Wilder, Inc., common stock with a current fair value of $91 a share on the date of donation. The terms of the gift provide that the stock and any dividend revenue are to be retained intact. On any date designated by the board of directors, the assets are to be liquidated and the proceeds used to assist the school's headmaster in acquiring a personal residence. The school will not retain any financial interest in the residence.

(2) O. P. Quinn donated 12% bonds in September, Year 7, with a face amount and current fair value of $150,000 on the date of donation. Annual payments of $12,500 are to be made to the donor during the donor's lifetime. On the donor's death the fund is to be used to construct a school cafeteria. The actuarial valuation of the O. P. Quinn annuity on August 31, Year 8, was $122,143.

(3) No transactions have been recorded in the school's accounting records since February 28, Year 8. An employee of the school prepared the following analysis of the checking account for the period March 1 through August 31, Year 8:

Balance, Mar. 1, Year 8			$288,900
Less: General current operating expenses .	$14,000		
Acquisition of equipment.	47,000	$61,000	
Less: Student fees.		8,000	
Net expenses		$53,000	
Payment for headmaster's residence	$91,200		
Less: Sale of 100 shares of Wilder, Inc.,			
common stock.	90,600	600	53,600
Subtotal			$235,300
Add: Interest on 12% bonds		$18,000	
Less: Payment to O. P. Quinn		12,500	5,500
Balance, Aug. 31, Year 8			$240,800

Instructions Prepare a working paper for Freida's Vocational School presenting the trial balance on February 28, Year 8, adjusting entries, transaction entries from March 1 through August 31, Year 8, and distributions to the proper funds. The following column headings are recommended:
    Unadjusted trial balance, Feb. 28, Year 8
    Adjustments and transactions—Debit
    Adjustments and transactions—Credit
    Adjusted trial balance, Aug. 31, Year 8
    Unrestricted Current Fund
    Restricted Current Fund
    O. P. Quinn Annuity Fund
    Plant Fund—Investment in Plant
Formal journal entries are not required; however, explain each adjustment and transaction (including supporting computations) at the bottom of the working paper. Disregard accrued interest on the mortgage note payable.

SPECIAL TOPICS IN FINANCIAL ACCOUNTING

14 INSTALLMENT SALES; CONSIGNMENTS

INSTALLMENT SALES

Although the concept of the installment sale first was developed in the field of real estate and for high-priced durable goods, it has spread through nearly every sector of the economy.[1] Almost all single-family residences are sold on the installment plan, with monthly payments extending as long as 25 to 30 years. Installment sales also are used by dealers in home furnishings, automobiles, appliances, and farm equipment. For these products the installment payments usually are made monthly for periods of from 6 to 36 months.

For many business enterprises, installment sales have been a key factor in achieving large-scale operations. The automobile industry, for example, could not have developed to its present size without the use of installment sales. The large volume of output achieved by the automobile industry has made possible economies in tooling, production, and distribution that could not have been achieved on a small scale of operations. Credit losses often increase when sales are made on the installment plan, but this disadvantage generally is more than offset by the expanded sales volume.

Installment sales pose some difficult problems for accountants. The most basic of these problems is the matching of costs and revenue. Should the gross profit from an installment sale be recorded as realized in the accounting period the sale is made, or should it be spread over the term of the installment contract? What should be done with costs that occur in periods subsequent to the sale? How should defaults, trade-ins, and repossessions be recorded?

Regardless of the accounting issues raised by installment sales, we may assume that installment sales will continue to be a major force in our economy. Accountants, therefore, must examine the issues and develop the most effective techniques possible for measuring, controlling, and reporting installment sales. As we progress through this chapter, it will be apparent that installment sales are one of the many thorny problems confronting accountants as they search for a consistent body of accounting principles within the conceptual framework of accounting.

---

[1] Early in 1982, the installment debt of consumers in the United States was in excess of $340 billion. In contrast, the total installment debt of consumers 35 years earlier was less than $9 billion.

Characteristics of installment sales

An installment sale of real or personal property or services provides for a series of payments over a period of months or years. A down payment generally is required. Because the seller must wait a considerable period of time to collect the selling price, it is customary to provide for interest and carrying charges on the unpaid balance.

The risk of noncollection to the seller is increased greatly when sales are made on the installment plan. Customers generally are in weaker financial condition than those who buy on open account; furthermore, the credit rating of the customers and their ability to pay may change significantly during the period covered by an installment contract. To protect themselves against this greater risk of noncollection, sellers of real or personal property generally select a form of contract called a **security agreement** that enables them to repossess the property if the purchaser fails to make payments.

The sellers' right to protect their **security interest** (uncollected balance of a sales contract) and to repossess the asset sold varies by type of industry, the form of the contract, and the statutes relating to repossessions. For the service-type enterprise, repossession obviously is not available as a safeguard against the failure to collect. For sales of certain types of merchandise, the sellers' right to repossess may be more of a threat than a real assurance against loss. The asset sold may have been damaged or may have depreciated to a point that it is worth less than the balance due on the installment contract. A basic rule designed to minimize losses from nonpayment of installment contracts is to require a sufficient down payment to cover the loss of value when an asset moves out of the "new" category. A corollary rule is that the cash payments by the purchaser should not be outstripped by the projected decline in value of the asset sold. For example, if a customer who purchases a used car on the installment plan finds after a year or so that the car is currently worth less than the balance owed on the contract, the customer's motivation to continue the payments may be reduced.

Competitive pressures in an industry often will not permit a business enterprise to adhere to rigid credit standards. Furthermore, repossession may be a difficult and expensive process. Reconditioning and repair may be necessary to make the repossessed merchandise salable, and the resale of such merchandise may be difficult. For these reasons, doubtful accounts expense is likely to be significantly higher on installment sales than on regular credit sales.

A related problem is the increased collection expense when payments are spread over an extended period. Accounting expenses also are increased when sales are made on the installment plan, and large amounts of working capital are tied up in installment contracts receivable. In recognition of these problems, many retailers sell installment contracts receivable to finance companies that specialize in credit and collection activities.

Realization of gross profit on installment sales

The determination of net income on installment sales is complicated by the fact that the amounts of revenue and related costs and expenses seldom are known in the accounting period when sales are made. Substantial expenses (as for collection, accounting, repairs, and repossession) may be incurred in subsequent accounting periods. In some situations, *the risk of noncollection may be so great as to raise doubt that any revenue or profit is realized at the time of sale.*

The first objective in the development of accounting policies for installment sales should be a reasonable matching of costs and revenue. However, in recognition of the diverse business conditions under which installment sales are made, accountants use the following three approaches for the recognition of gross profit on installment sales: (1) the accrual basis of accounting, (2) the cost recovery method, and (3) the installment method of accounting.

Accrual Basis of Accounting   To recognize the entire gross profit as realized at the time of an installment sale is to say in effect that installment sales are the same as regular sales on credit. The merchandise has been delivered to customers, and accounts receivable of definite amount have been acquired. The excess of the accounts receivable over the cost of merchandise sold is *realized gross profit* in the traditional meaning of the term. The journal entry consists of a debit to Installment Contracts Receivable and a credit to Installment Sales. If the perpetual inventory system is used, a second journal entry is needed to transfer the cost of the merchandise from the Inventories account to the Cost of Installment Sales account. No recognition is given to the seller's retention of title to the merchandise because the normal expectation is completion of the contract through collection of the receivable. Implicit in this recognition of gross profit at the time of sale is the assumption that most expenses relating to the sale will be recognized in the same accounting period.

The expenses relating to the sale include collection and doubtful accounts expenses. Recognition of these expenses in the period of the sale requires estimates of the customer's performance over the entire term of the installment contract. Such estimates may be considerably more difficult to make than the normal provision for doubtful accounts expense from regular sales. However, with careful analysis of experience in the industry and in the particular business enterprise, reasonably satisfactory estimates can be made in most situations. The journal entries to record such expenses consist of debits to expense accounts and credits to asset valuation accounts such as Allowance for Doubtful Installment Contracts and Allowance for Collection Costs. The allowance accounts are debited in later periods as uncollectible installment contracts become known and as collection costs are incurred.

Cost Recovery Method   In some cases, installment contracts receivable may be collectible over a long period of time. In addition, the terms of sale may not be definite, and the financial position of customers may be unpredictable, thus making it virtually impossible to find a reasonable basis for estimating the degree of collectibility of the receivables. In such cases, either the installment method or the cost recovery method of accounting may be used for installment sales. Under the **cost recovery method,** no profit is recognized until all costs of the merchandise sold have been recovered. After all costs have been recovered, additional collections on the installment contracts receivable are recorded as revenue, and only current collection costs are recognized as expenses. The cost recovery method of accounting rarely is used; therefore, it is not illustrated in this chapter.

Installment Method of Accounting   The third approach to the measurement of income from installment sales is to recognize gross profit in installments over the term of the contract as cash is collected. Emphasis is shifted from the acquisition of receivables to the collection of the receivables as the basis for realization of gross profit; in other words, *a modified cash basis of accounting is substituted for the accrual basis of accounting.* This modified cash basis is known as the **installment method of accounting.**

The installment method of accounting

Under the installment method of accounting, each cash collection on the contract is regarded as including both a return of cost and a realization of gross profit in the ratio that these two elements were included in the selling price.

   For example, assume that a farm equipment dealer sells for $10,000 a machine that cost $7,000. The $3,000 excess of the sales price over cost is regarded as **deferred gross profit.** Because cost and gross profit constituted 70% and 30%, respectively, of the sales price, this 70:30 ratio is used to divide each collection under the contract between the recovery of cost and the realization of gross profit. If $1,000 is received as a down payment, $300 of the deferred gross profit is considered realized in the current accounting period. At the end of each period, the Deferred Gross Profit account will equal 30% of the installment contract receivable remaining uncollected. The Realized Gross Profit on Installment Sales account will show for each period an amount equal to 30% of the collections during that period. In this example, the question of interest and carrying charges is omitted; it is considered later in the chapter.

   The method described is acceptable under current income tax laws. The installment method may be used for the computation of taxable income for "any disposition of property where at least one payment is to be received after the close of the taxable year in which the disposition occurs." The opportunity to postpone the recognition of taxable income has been responsible for the popularity of the installment method for income tax purposes. Although the income tax advantages are readily apparent, the theoretical support for the installment method of accounting is less impressive.

Many years ago a committee of the American Accounting Association (AAA) stated:[2]

> There is no sound accounting reason for the use of the installment method for financial statement purposes in the case of closed transactions in which collection is dependent upon lapse of time and the probabilities of realization are properly evaluated. In the opinion of the Committee, such income has accrued and should be recognized in the financial statements, . . .

Accounting Research Study No. 3 stated that revenue should be recognized in the accounting period in which the major economic activity necessary for the production and disposition of goods is performed, and rejected the use of the installment method of accounting.[3]

> Collectibility of receivables is not necessarily less predictable because collections are scheduled in installments. The postponement of recognition of revenues until they can be measured by actual cash receipt is not in accordance with the concept of an accrual accounting. Any uncertainty as to collectibility should be expressed by a separately calculated and separately disclosed estimate of uncollectibles rather than by a postponement of the recognition of revenue.

Subsequently, **APB Opinion No. 10** virtually removed the installment method of accounting from the body of generally accepted accounting principles because it reaffirmed the general concept that income is realized when a sale is made, unless the circumstances are such that the collection of the selling price is not reasonably assured. **APB Opinion No. 10** stated:[4]

> Revenues should ordinarily be accounted for at the time a transaction is completed, with appropriate provision for uncollectible accounts. Accordingly, . . . in the absence of the circumstances referred to above, the installment method of recognizing revenue is not acceptable.

The "circumstances" in which the use of installment method of accounting is permitted are: (1) Collection of installment receivables is not reasonably assured, (2) receivables are collectible over an extended period of time, and (3) there is no reasonable basis for estimating the degree of collectibility. In such situations, either the installment method or the cost recovery method of accounting may be used.

Because the installment method of accounting still may be used for financial accounting in some cases, and because **it is widely used for income tax purposes,** we shall illustrate its use in the following pages, first for a single sale of land and then for retail sales of merchandise.

---

[2] *Accounting and Reporting Standards for Corporate Financial Statements and Preceding Statements and Supplements,* AAA (Sarasota: 1957), p. 33.

[3] Robert T. Sprouse and Maurice Moonitz, *Accounting Research Study No. 3,* "A Tentative Set of Broad Accounting Principles for Business Enterprises," AICPA (New York: 1962), p. 48.

[4] *APB Opinion No. 10,* "Omnibus Opinion—1966," AICPA (New York: 1966), p. 149.

Single sale of land on the installment plan

The owner of land that has appreciated in value often is willing to sell only on the installment plan so that the gain can be spread over several years for income tax purposes. Federal income tax regulations permit the use of the installment method if the contract price will be collected in two or more installments spanning two or more years.

Let us assume that on December 31, Year 1, Clara Kane, who maintains accounting records on a calendar-year basis, sold for $100,000 a parcel of land acquired for $52,000. Commission and other expenses of sale in the amount of $8,000 were charged to Kane in the escrow statement. Because Kane was not a dealer in real estate, these expenses are considered as additional costs of the land rather than expenses of the year in which the sale took place. Thus, the gain on the sale of the land is $40,000 ($100,000 − $52,000 − $8,000 = $40,000), and all collections of cash from the purchaser are regarded as consisting of 60% cost recovery and 40% realization of gain (profit).

The contract of sale called for a down payment of $25,000 and promissory notes, with principal payments every six months for five years in the amount of $7,500 plus interest at the annual rate of 10% on the unpaid principal balance of the notes. A portion ($8,000) of the down payment was applied in the escrow statement to pay the commission and other expenses of sale. The journal entries presented on page 617 record the sale of the land on December 31, Year 1, the collections on the notes in Year 2, and the realization of a portion of the deferred gain in Years 1 and 2. Because this was a sale by a nondealer in real estate, there was no need to use an Installment Sales account, and the deferred gain on sale of land was recorded at the time of sale.

Journal entries for the remaining four years would follow the same pattern illustrated for Year 1 and Year 2, assuming that the purchaser makes all payments as required by contract.

This example brings out the contrast between the timing of gross profits on ordinary sales and on sales accounted for by the installment method of accounting. If the land sold by Clara Kane had been recorded as an ordinary sale, a gross profit of $40,000 would have been reported in Year 1; use of the installment method of accounting resulted in the recognition of only $10,000 gross profit in Year 1, and $6,000 ($15,000 × 0.40 = $6,000) in each of the next five years. If a sale on the installment plan results in a loss, *the entire loss must be recognized in the year of sale.*

Retail sale of merchandise on the installment plan

In the preceding example we dealt with a single sale of land on the installment plan by a nondealer. Now we shall consider a large volume of installment sales of merchandise by a retailing enterprise that uses the

CLARA KANE
Journal Entries to Record Sale of Land on Installment Plan
For Year 1 and Year 2

Year 1

Dec. 31 Cash (net of $8,000 paid for commission and other
      expenses of sale) 17,000
    Notes Receivable. 75,000
        Land 52,000
        Deferred Gain on Installment Sale of Land . . 40,000
    To record sale of land on installment plan; notes re-
    ceivable are due at the rate of $7,500 every six months,
    plus 10% annual interest on the unpaid principal
    balance of notes. Commission and other expenses of
    sale of $8,000 were deducted in computation of net
    cash received and deferred gain.

31 Deferred Gain on Installment Sale of Land 10,000
        Realized Gain on Installment Sale of Land. . . 10,000
    To record realized gain, computed at 40% of cash col-
    lected as down payment in Year 1 ($25,000 × 0.40 =
    $10,000).

Year 2

June 30 Cash 11,250
        Interest Revenue 3,750
        Notes Receivable 7,500
    To record collection of semiannual principal install-
    ment on note receivable ($7,500), plus interest for six
    months ($75,000 × 0.10 × $\frac{6}{12}$ = $3,750).

Year 2

Dec. 31 Cash 10,875
        Interest Revenue 3,375
        Notes Receivable 7,500
    To record collection of semiannual principal install-
    ment on notes receivable ($7,500), plus interest for six
    months on unpaid balance ($75,000 − $7,500) ×
    0.10 × $\frac{6}{12}$ = $3,375).

31 Deferred Gain on Installment Sale of Land 6,000
        Realized Gain on Installment Sale of Land. . . 6,000
    To record realized gain computed at 40% of amount
    collected on notes receivable in Year 2 ($15,000 ×
    0.40 = $6,000).

installment method of accounting because the collectibility of the installment contracts receivable cannot be reasonably estimated.

A first requirement is to keep separate all sales made on the installment plan as distinguished from regular sales. The accounting records for installment receivables usually are maintained by contract rather than by customer; if a customer makes several purchases on the installment plan, it is convenient to account for each contract separately. However, it is not necessary to compute the rate of gross profit on each sale or to apply a different profit rate to collections on each contract. The average rate of gross profit on all installment sales during a year generally is computed and applied to all cash collections (net of interest and carrying charges) on installment contracts receivable originating in that year.

Illustration of Accounting for Installment Sales of Merchandise   To illustrate the accounting for installment sales of merchandise, assume that Oak Desk Company sells merchandise on the installment plan, as well as on regular terms (cash or 30-day open accounts), and uses the perpetual inventory system. For an installment sale, the customer's account is debited for the full amount of the selling price, including interest and carrying charges, and is credited for the amount of the down payment. The Installment Contract Receivable account thus provides a complete record of the transaction. Uncollectible installment contracts expense is recognized at the time the accounts receivable are *known to be uncollectible.* Assume that on January 1, Year 5, Oak Desk's general ledger included the following ledger account balances:

Account balances, Jan. 1, Year 5

Installment contracts receivable—Year 3	$20,000 dr
Installment contracts receivable—Year 4	85,000 dr
Deferred interest and carrying charges on installment sales	17,500 cr
Deferred gross profit—Year 3 installment sales	4,500 cr
Deferred gross profit—Year 4 installment sales	19,460 cr

The gross profit rate on installment sales (excluding interest and carrying charges) was 25% in Year 3 and 28% in Year 4. During Year 5, the following transactions were completed by Oak Desk Company:

(1) Installment sales, cost of installment sales, and deferred gross profit for Year 5 are listed below:

Installment sales and cost of installment sales for Year 5

Installment sales (excluding $30,000 deferred interest and carrying charges)	$200,000
Cost of installment sales	138,000
Deferred gross profit—Year 5 installment sales ($200,000 − $138,000)	62,000
Rate of gross profit on installment sales ($62,000 ÷ $200,000)	31%

(2) Cash collections on installment contracts receivable during Year 5 are summarized below:

	Selling price	Interest and carrying charges	Total cash collected
Installment contracts receivable—Year 5 . .	$ 80,000	$10,000	$ 90,000
Installment contracts receivable—Year 4 . .	44,500	12,500	57,000
Installment contracts receivable—Year 3 . .	17,000	1,850	18,850
Totals	$141,500	$24,350	$165,850

(3) Customers who purchased merchandise in Year 3 were unable to pay the balance of their contracts, $1,150. The contracts consisted of $1,000 sales price and $150 of interest and carrying charges, and included $250 ($1,000 × 0.25 = $250) of deferred gross profit. The current fair (net realizable) value of the merchandise repossessed was $650.

Recording Transactions The journal entries to record the transactions for Oak Desk Company relating to installment sales for Year 5 are:

(1) Installment Contracts Receivable—Year 5 230,000
    Cost of Installment Sales. 138,000
        Installment Sales.   200,000
        Deferred Interest and Carrying Charges on Install-
        ment Sales.   30,000
        Inventories   138,000
    To record installment sales and cost of installment sales
    for Year 5.

(2) Cash 165,850
        Installment Contracts Receivable—Year 5   90,000
        Installment Contracts Receivable—Year 4   57,000
        Installment Contracts Receivable—Year 3   18,850
    To record collections on installment contracts during
    Year 5.

(3) Inventories (repossessed merchandise) 650
    Deferred Gross Profit—Year 3 Installment Sales 250
    Deferred Interest and Carrying Charges on Installment
    Sales 150
    Uncollectible Installment Contracts Expense. 100
        Installment Contracts Receivable—Year 3   1,150
    To record default on Year 3 installment contracts and re-
    possession of merchandise.

Adjusting Entries The adjusting journal entries for Oak Desk Company on December 31, Year 5, are as follows:

Adjusting entries at end of Year 5

Installment Sales	*200,000*	
Cost of Installment Sales		*138,000*
Deferred Gross Profit—Year 5 Installment Sales		*62,000*
To record deferred gross profit on Year 5 installment sales.		
Deferred Gross Profit—Year 5 Installment Sales	*24,800*	
Deferred Gross Profit—Year 4 Installment Sales	*12,460*	
Deferred Gross Profit—Year 3 Installment Sales	*4,250*	
Realized Gross Profit on Installment Sales		*41,510*
To record realized gross profit on installment sales,		
as computed below:		

Year 5: $80,000 × 0.31 . . . . $24,800
Year 4: $44,500 × 0.28 12,460
Year 3: $17,000 × 0.25 4,250
Total realized gross profit $41,510

Deferred Interest and Carrying Charges on Installment Sales .	*24,350*	
Revenue from Interest and Carrying Charges		*24,350*
To record revenue from interest and carrying charges for		
Year 5 (see page 619 for computations).		

The Realized Gross Profit on Installment Sales and the Revenue from Interest and Carrying Charges accounts are closed to the Income Summary account at the end of Year 5. The accounts relating to installment sales appear in Oak Desk Company's general ledger at the end of Year 5 as follows:

Account balances at end of Year 5

Ledger accounts	Balances
Installment contracts receivable—Year 4 ($85,000 − $57,000)	$ 28,000 dr
Installment contracts receivable—Year 5 ($230,000 − $90,000)	140,000 dr
Deferred interest and carrying charges on installment sales ($17,500 + $30,000 − $150 − $24,350)	23,000 cr
Deferred gross profit—Year 4 installment sales ($19,460 − $12,460) .	7,000 cr
Deferred gross profit—Year 5 installment sales ($62,000 − $24,800) .	37,200 cr

These amounts may be arranged as illustrated on page 621 to prove the accuracy of the deferred gross profit on installment contracts receivable at the end of Year 5.

OAK DESK COMPANY
Proof of Deferred Gross Profit
December 31, Year 5

	Installment contracts receivable	Deferred interest and carrying charges	Net installment contracts receivable	Gross profit percentage	Deferred gross profit
Year 4					
contracts . . .	$ 28,000	$ 3,000	$ 25,000	28%	$ 7,000
Year 5					
contracts . . .	140,000	20,000	120,000	31	37,200
Totals.	$168,000	$23,000	$145,000		$44,200

Alternative computation of gross profit percentage

Instead of segregating the collections applicable to the selling price and to the interest and carrying charges, a retailing enterprise may determine the gross profit percentage by inclusion of the interest and carrying charges in the selling price. The resulting **larger gross profit percentage** then is applied to the total amount of cash collected in each accounting period to determine the realized gross profit. Application of this method to the Year 5 installment sales of Oak Desk Company is illustrated below:

Gross profit percentage for Year 5

Sales, including interest and carrying charges of $30,000.	$230,000
Gross profit on installment sales ($230,000 − $138,000 cost of installment sales)	92,000
Gross profit percentage on installment sales ($92,000 ÷ $230,000) . . .	40%

The 40% gross profit percentage thus determined is applied to the total cash collections on installment contracts receivable in each year to compute the realized gross profit on installment sales. Under this approach, the realized gross profit on installment sales for Year 5 is $36,000 ($90,000 × 0.40 = $36,000).[5]

The use of the installment method of accounting requires installment contracts receivable and cash collections to be segregated by year of origin. In addition, the gross profit rate must be computed separately for each year. However, a single controlling account for installment contracts receivable may be used if the accounting records are computer-

---

[5] This procedure must be used for federal income tax purposes by dealers in personal property who compute taxable income on the installment basis.

ized or if the installment contracts receivable are analyzed at the end of each year to ascertain uncollected balances by year of origin.

The journal entry on page 619 to record the default on installment contracts originating in Year 3 and the repossession of merchandise by Oak Desk Company is explained in the following section.

Defaults and repossessions

If a customer defaults on an installment contract for services and no further collection can be made, we have an example of default without the possibility of repossession. A similar situation exists for certain merchandise that has no significant resale value. The journal entry required in such cases is to write off the uncollectible installment contract receivable, cancel the deferred gross profit related to the receivable, and debit Uncollectible Installment Contracts Expense for the difference. In other words, the uncollectible installment contracts expense is equal to the *unrecovered cost* included in the balance of the installment contract receivable.

However, in most cases a default by a customer leads to repossession of merchandise. The uncollectible installment contracts expense is reduced by the current fair value of the merchandise repossessed, and it is possible for the repossession to result in a gain.

The principal difficulty in accounting for defaults followed by repossession is the estimate of the *current fair value* of the merchandise at the time of repossession. In the determination of a current fair value of repossessed merchandise, the objective is to choose an amount that will allow for any reconditioning costs and provide a normal gross profit on resale. Any reconditioning costs incurred are added to the Inventories account, provided this does not become unreasonable in relation to the expected selling price. For financial accounting purposes, the carrying amount of the repossessed merchandise should not exceed its *net realizable value.*

The journal entry on page 619 to record the defaults and repossessions by Oak Desk Company accomplishes the following: (1) It eliminates the defaulted installment contracts receivable of $1,150, (2) it cancels the deferred gross profit of $250 ($1,000 × 0.25 = $250) and the deferred interest and carrying charges of $150 applicable to the defaulted installment contracts receivable, (3) it recognizes an asset equal to the $650 current fair value of the repossessed merchandise, and (4) it recognizes uncollectible installment contracts expense of $100, the difference between the unrecovered cost in the defaulted installment contracts receivable ($750) and the current fair value of the repossessed merchandise ($650). When the installment method of accounting is used, no loss or expense is recognized with respect to the deferred gross profit and interest and carrying charges contained in the defaulted installment contract receivable, because these amounts had not been recognized previously as realized revenue.

Other accounting issues relating to installment sales

Special accounting issues arise in connection with (1) the acceptance of used property as a trade-in, (2) the computation of interest on installment contracts receivable, (3) the use of the installment method of accounting solely for income tax purposes, and (4) retail land sales. These issues are discussed in the following sections.

Trade-ins A familiar example of the use of trade-ins is the acceptance by a dealer of a used car as partial payment for a new car. An accounting problem exists only if the dealer grants an **overallowance** on the used car taken in trade. An overallowance is the excess of the trade-in allowance over the current fair value of the used car in terms of the dealer's ability to resell it at a price that will recover all direct costs and result in a normal gross profit. A rough approximation of the current fair value of the used car to the dealer may be the currently quoted wholesale price for used cars of the particular make and model.

An overallowance on trade-ins is significant because it represents a reduction in the stated selling price of the new merchandise. ***The stated selling price must be reduced by the amount of the overallowance*** to compute the net selling price. The gross profit on the sale of the new merchandise is the difference between the net selling price and cost.

As an illustration, assume that merchandise with a cost of $2,400 is sold on the installment plan for $3,300. Used merchandise is accepted as a trade-in at a "value" of $1,100, but the dealer expects to spend $50 in reconditioning the used merchandise before reselling it for only $1,000. Assume that the customary gross profit percentage on used merchandise of this type is 15%, an amount that will cover the selling and overhead costs, and also provide a normal gross profit on the resale. The current fair value of the trade-in and the amount of the overallowance are computed as follows:

Computation of overallowance	Trade-in allowance given to customer		$1,100
	Deduct current fair value of trade-in:		
	Estimated resale value of merchandise traded in $1,000		
	Less: Reconditioning cost expected to be incurred . . . $ 50		
	Gross profit ($1,000 × 0.15). 150	200	
	Current fair value of merchandise traded in		800
	Overallowance on trade-in		$ 300

Assuming that a perpetual inventory system is used, the journal entry to record the installment sale and the trade-in appears on page 624.

Cost of the new article was $2,400; therefore, the deferred gross profit on the installment sale of $3,000 amounts to $600. The gross profit percentage is 20% ($600 ÷ $3,000 = 0.20). This percentage will be ap-

Inventories (trade-ins)	800	
Installment Contracts Receivable ($3,300 − $1,100)	2,200	
Cost of Installment Sales	2,400	
Installment Sales ($3,300 − $300)		3,000
Inventories (new)		2,400

To record sale of merchandise for $3,000, consisting of gross sales price of $3,300 minus a $300 overallowance on the trade-in.

plied in the computation of realized gross profit on the basis of cash collections. The current fair value of the merchandise accepted as a trade-in, $800, is considered equivalent to a cash collection for this purpose.

Interest on Installment Contracts Receivable   Installment contracts usually provide for interest and carrying charges to be paid concurrently with each installment payment. Such *deferred payment charges,* regardless of the label placed on them, represent a cost of borrowing to the purchaser and may be referred to collectively as "interest." Only the portion of the payment that is applied to reduce the principal of the contracts is considered in the measurement of realized gross profit under the installment method of accounting.

The arrangement for adding interest to installment contracts may follow one of the following plans:

1 Equal periodic payments, with a portion of each payment representing interest on the principal balance, and the remainder of the payment representing a reduction of principal

2 Interest computed on each individual installment payment of principal from the beginning date of the contract to the date each payment of principal is received

3 Interest computed each month on the outstanding principal balance during the month

4 Interest computed throughout the entire contract period on the original amount of the sale minus any down payment

The first plan probably is the most widely used. Contracts with customers generally state how payments are to be allocated between principal and interest. Regardless of the plan used by dealers to add interest to installment contracts, interest revenue for financial accounting is computed periodically by applying the *effective interest rate* to the outstanding principal balance of the installment contracts receivable.

Installment Method for Income Tax Purposes Only   The installment method of accounting is widely used for income tax purposes because it postpones the payment of income taxes. For example, assume that Markowski Company, a retailing enterprise, uses the accrual basis of accounting for financial accounting purposes. The pre-tax accounting income for Year 10 is $200,000, as indicated by the following condensed partial income statement (revenue from interest and carrying charges is ignored in this example):

MARKOWSKI COMPANY

Condensed Partial Income Statement (accrual basis of accounting)

For Year 10

Sales	$800,000
Cost of goods sold	500,000
Gross profit on sales	$300,000
Operating expenses	100,000
Income before income taxes	$200,000

Assume that the deferred gross profit on installment sales was $55,000 at the beginning of Year 10 and $105,000 at the end of Year 10, and that Markowski Company uses the installment method of accounting for income tax purposes. The taxable income for Year 10 is determined as follows:

Taxable income for Year 10

Pre-tax accounting income for Year 10 (accrual basis of accounting). .		$200,000
Less: Deferred gross profit on installment sales, end of Year 10.	$105,000	
Add: Deferred gross profit on installment sales, beginning of Year 10.	55,000	(50,000)
Taxable income for Year 10, (installment method of accounting)		$150,000

Income taxes for Year 10 would be recorded as follows, assuming that the income tax rate for Markowski Company is 45% of taxable income:

Journal entry to record income taxes for Year 10

Income Taxes Expense	90,000	
Income Taxes Payable		67,500
Deferred Income Tax Liability		22,500
To record income taxes for Year 10, determined as follows:		
Income taxes expense: $200,000 × 0.45 = $90,000.		
Income taxes payable: $150,000 × 0.45 = $67,500.		
Deferred income tax liability: $50,000 × 0.45 = $22,500.		

The deferred income tax liability is classified as a current liability in the balance sheet because the installment contracts receivable to which the deferred taxes relate are classified as current assets. For a complete discussion of the problem of income tax allocation, refer to the *Intermediate Accounting* text of this series.

Accounting for Retail Land Sales In 1973, the AICPA published an *Industry Accounting Guide,* "Accounting for Retail Land Sales," that called for the use of the accrual basis of accounting for land development projects in which collections on installment contracts receivable are reasonably assured and *all four* of the following conditions are present:[6]

1 The land clearly will be useful for residential or recreational purposes at the end of the normal payment period.

2 The project's improvements have progressed beyond preliminary stages, and there is evidence that the project will be completed according to plan.

3 The installment contracts receivable are not subject to subordination to new loans on the land (except for home construction purposes).

4 Collection experience for the project indicates that collectibility of the installment contracts receivable is reasonably predictable and the 90% of the contracts in force six months *after sales are recorded* will be collected in full.

Unless all four of these conditions for the use of the accrual basis of accounting are met for the entire project, the installment method of accounting should be used for all sales of land. If all four conditions subsequently are satisfied, a change to the accrual basis of accounting should be adopted for the entire project and accounted for as a *change in accounting estimate.*

The *Industry Accounting Guide* suggested that the procedures to be applied under the installment method of accounting for retail land sales should include the following:[7]

1 The entire contract price applicable to the installment sale, without reduction for cancellations or discounts, is reported as revenue in the income statement of the year the sale is recorded.

2 Cost of sales (including provision for future improvement costs) and nondeferable operating expenses (except to the extent deferred in *3* below) are charged to income of the current accounting period.

3 Gross profit, less selling costs directly associated with the project, is deferred and recognized in income as payments of principal are received on the installment contracts receivable.

4 Interest at the stated contract rate is recorded as revenue when received, and the unamortized deferred profit is *deducted from related installment contracts receivable* in the balance sheet.

5 Disclosure is made of the portion of sales and contracts receivable applicable to the installment method of accounting.

Presentation of installment sales data in financial statements

The presentation of accounts relating to installment sales in the financial statements raises some interesting theoretical issues, regardless of

---

[6] *An AICPA Industry Accounting Guide,* "Accounting for Retail Land Sales," AICPA (New York: 1973), pp. 7–8.

[7] Ibid., pp. 15–16.

whether the accrual basis of accounting or the installment method of accounting is used.

Income Statement A partial income statement for Year 5 for Oak Desk Company, which uses the installment method of accounting, is presented below. This statement is based on the installment sales information illustrated on pages 618 to 621, plus additional assumed data for regular sales.

	Installment sales	Regular sales	Combined
OAK DESK COMPANY			
Partial Income Statement			
For Year Ended December 31, Year 5			
Sales	$200,000	$300,000	$500,000
Cost of goods sold.	138,000	222,000	360,000
Gross profit on sales	$ 62,000	$ 78,000	$140,000
Less: Deferred gross profit on Year 5 install-			
ment sales	37,200		37,200
Realized gross profit on Year 5 sales	$ 24,800	$ 78,000	$102,800
Add: Realized gross profit on prior years' in-			
stallment sales (see page 620)			16,710
Total realized gross profit			$119,510

If the accrual basis of accounting were used for all sales, a gross profit of $140,000 would be reported in Year 5. The three-column form illustrated above, although useful for internal purposes, generally would not be used to report the results of operations to outsiders. In a multiple-step income statement, revenue from interest and carrying charges on installment contracts is reported as Other Revenue.

Balance Sheet Installment contracts receivable, net of deferred interest and carrying charges, are classified as current assets, although the collection period often extends more than a year beyond the balance sheet date. This rule is applicable whether the accrual basis of accounting or the installment method of accounting is used. The definition of current assets specifically includes installment contracts and notes receivable if they conform generally to normal trade practices and terms in the industry. This classification is supported by the concept that current assets include all resources expected to be realized in cash, sold, or consumed during the normal operating cycle of the business enterprise.

The listing of installment contracts receivable in the current asset section of the balance sheet is more informative when the amounts maturing each year are disclosed. Such disclosure by a large publicly owned corporation is illustrated on page 628.

Current assets:

Installment contracts receivable **(Note 1)**	$998,200,000
Less: Provision for doubtful contracts	(9,700,000)
Unearned interest and carrying charges	(20,100,000)
Net installment contracts receivable	$968,400,000

Note 1: Installment contracts receivable arise from sales of residential houses to customers for time payments over periods of 12 to 18 years. Of the gross amount of $998,200,000, an amount of $905,580,000 is due after one year. Installment contracts receivable are included in current assets because they are within the operating cycle of the residential home construction industry. Installment payments estimated to be receivable within each of the next five years are $92,620,000, $89,880,000, $93,100,000, $88,900,000, and $79,700,000, respectively, and $554,000,000 after five years.

The classification of deferred gross profit on installment sales in the balance sheet **when the installment method of accounting is used for financial accounting** has long troubled accountants. A common practice for many years was to classify the deferred gross profit in the liabilities section of the balance sheet. Critics of this treatment pointed out that no obligation to an outsider existed and that the liability classification was improper.

The existence of a deferred gross profit account indicates that the profit element in installment contracts receivable has not been realized. Acceptance of this view suggests that the installment contracts receivable will be overstated unless the deferred gross profit is deducted from installment contracts receivable. This classification as an asset valuation account is theoretically preferable and was recommended in the **AICPA Industry Accounting Guide,** "Accounting for Retail Land Sales."[8]

In view of these conflicting approaches, it has been suggested that the deferred gross profit be subdivided into three parts: (1) an allowance for collection costs and doubtful contracts that would be deducted from installment contracts receivable, (2) a liability representing future income taxes on the gross profit not yet realized, and (3) a residual income element. The residual income element would be classified by some accountants as a separate item in the stockholders' equity section and by others in an undefined section between liabilities and stockholders' equity. Such a detailed classification of deferred gross profit in the balance sheet seldom is encountered in the business world.

The lack of agreement as to the classification of deferred gross profit in the balance sheet is evidence of the inherent contradiction between the installment method of accounting and the accrual basis of account-

[8] Ibid., p. 16.

ing. Because the chief reason for the use of the installment method of accounting is the income tax advantage it affords, a satisfactory solution in most cases is to recognize gross profit on installment sales on the accrual basis of accounting for financial accounting purposes and to defer recognition of gross profit for income tax purposes until installment contracts receivable are collected.

CONSIGNMENTS

The meaning of consignments

The term **consignment** means a transfer of possession of merchandise from the owner to another person who acts as the sales agent of the owner. Title to the merchandise remains with the owner, who is called a **consignor;** the sales agent who has possession of the merchandise is called a **consignee.**

From a legal viewpoint, a consignment represents a **bailment.** [9] The relationship between the consignor and the consignee is that of **principal** and **agent,** and the law of agency controls the determination of the obligations and rights of the two parties.

Consignees are responsible to consignors for the merchandise placed in their custody until it is sold or returned. Because consignees do not acquire title to the merchandise, they neither include it in inventories nor record an account payable or other liability. The only obligation of consignees is to give reasonable care to the consigned merchandise and to account for it to consignors. When the merchandise is sold by a consignee, the resulting account receivable is the property of the consignor. At this point the consignor records a sale.

The shipment of merchandise on consignment may be referred to by the consignor as a **consignment out,** and by the consignee as a **consignment in.**

Distinguishing between a consignment and a sale

Although both a sale and a consignment involve the shipment of merchandise, a clear distinction between the two is necessary for the proper measurement of income. Because title does not pass when merchandise is shipped on consignment, the consignor continues to carry the consigned merchandise as part of inventories. No profit should be recognized at the time of the consignment shipment because there is no change in ownership of merchandise. If the consignee's business should fail, the consignor would not be in the position of a creditor; in-

---

[9] A *bailment* is a contract for the delivery or transfer of possession of money or personal property for a particular purpose, such as for safekeeping, repairs, or sale.

stead, the consignor is the rightful owner of any unsold consigned merchandise.

Why should a producer or wholesaler prefer to consign merchandise rather than to make outright sales? One possible reason is that the consignor may be able to persuade dealers to stock the items on a consignment basis, whereas they would not be willing to purchase the merchandise outright. Second, the consignor avoids the risk inherent in selling on credit to dealers of questionable financial strength.

From the viewpoint of a consignee, the acquisition of merchandise on consignment rather than by purchase requires less capital investment and avoids the risk of loss if the merchandise cannot be sold.

Rights and duties of the consignee

When merchandise is shipped on consignment, a formal written contract is needed on such points as credit terms to be granted to customers by the consignee, expenses of the consignee to be reimbursed by the consignor, commission allowed to the consignee, frequency of reporting and payment by the consignee, and handling and care of the consigned merchandise. In addition to any explicit contractual provisions, the general rights and duties of the consignee may be summarized as follows:

Rights of Consignee	*Duties of Consignee*
1 To receive **compensation** for merchandise sold for the account of consignor.	*1* To give **care and protection** reasonable in relation to the nature of the consigned merchandise.
2 To receive **reimbursement** for expenditures (such as freight and insurance) made in connection with the consignment.	*2* To keep the consigned merchandise **separate from owned inventories** or be able to identify the consigned merchandise. Similarly, the consignee must **identify** and **segregate the consignment receivables** from other receivables.
3 To sell consigned merchandise on **credit** if the consignor has not forbidden credit sales.	*3* To use care **in extending credit** on the sale of consigned merchandise and to be diligent in **setting prices** on consigned merchandise and in collecting consignment receivables.
4 To make the usual **warranties** as to the quality of the consigned merchandise and to bind the consignor to honor such warranties.	*4* To **render complete reports** of sales of consigned merchandise and to make appropriate and timely payments to the consignor.

In granting credit, as in caring for the consigned merchandise, the consignee is obliged to act prudently and to protect the property rights of the consignor. Because the receivables from the sale of consigned merchandise are the property of the consignor, the consignor bears any credit losses, providing the consignee has exercised due care in granting credit and making collections. However, the consignee may guarantee the collection of receivables; under this type of consignment contract, the consignee is said to be a ***del credere agent.***

The consignee also must follow any special instructions by the consignor as to care of the merchandise. If the consignee acts prudently in providing appropriate care and protection, the consignee is not liable for any damage to the merchandise that may occur.

The account sales

The report rendered by the consignee is called an ***account sales;*** it includes the quantity of merchandise received and sold, expenses incurred, advances made, and amounts owed or remitted. Payments may be made as portions of the shipment are sold or may not be required until the consigned merchandise either has been sold or has been returned to the consignor.

Assume that Sherri Company ships on consignment to Robert Thorell 10 television sets to be sold at $400 each. The consignee is to be reimbursed for freight costs of $135 and is to receive a commission of 20% of the stipulated selling price. After selling all the consigned merchandise, Thorell sends the consignor an account sales similar to the one below, accompanied by a check for the amount due:

Account sales

> ### ROBERT THORELL
> **Beverly Hills, California**
> **Account Sales**
>
> August 31 ,19____
>
> Sales for account and risk of:
>
> Sherri Company
>
> Denver, Colorado
>
> Sales: 10 TV sets @ $400 . . . . $4,000
>
> Charges:
>   Freight costs. $135
>   Commission ($4,000 × 0.20). 800   935
> Balance (remittance to consignor) $3,065
>
> Consigned TV sets on hand . . . . _none_

Accounting for consignees

The receipt of the consignment shipment of 10 television sets by Robert Thorell may be recorded in any of several ways. The objective is to create a memorandum record of the consigned merchandise; no purchase has been made and no liability exists. The receipt of the consignment could be recorded by a **memorandum notation** in the general journal, by an entry in a separate ledger of consignment shipments, or by a memorandum entry in a general ledger account entitled Consignment In—Sherri Company. In this illustration, the latter method is used, and the ledger account appears as follows:

Consignee receives
merchandise on
consignment

	Consignment In—Sherri Company			
Date	Explanation	Debit	Credit	Balance
	Received 10 TV sets to be sold for $400 each at a commission of 20% of selling price			

The journal entries for the consignee to record the payment of freight costs on the shipment and the sale of the television sets are as follows:

Consignee records freight costs and sale of consigned TV sets

```
Consignment in—Sherri Company. . . . . . . . . . . . . . . . . .    135
     Cash . . . . . . . . . . . . . . . . . . . . . . . . . . . . . .        135
To record payment of freight costs on shipment from consignor.


Cash . . . . . . . . . . . . . . . . . . . . . . . . . . . . . . .  4,000
     Consignment In—Sherri Company . . . . . . . . . . . . .      4,000
To record sale of 10 TV sets at $400 each.
```

The journal entry to record the 20% commission charged by the consignee consists of a debit to the Consignment In account and a credit to a revenue account, as follows:

Commission revenue recorded by consignee

```
Consignment In—Sherri Company. . . . . . . . . . . . . . . . .    800
     Commission Revenue—Consignment Sales . . . . . . . . . . .        800
To record commission of 20% earned on TV sets sold.
```

The payment by the consignee of the full amount owed is recorded by a debit to the Consignment In account and results in closing that account. The journal entry is at the top of page 633.

To record payment to consignor

Consignment In—Sherri Company 3,065
    Cash 3,065
To record payment in full to consignor.

After the posting of this journal entry, the ledger account for the consignment appears as follows in the consignee's accounting records:

Summary of Consignment In account

Consignment In—Sherri Company

Date	Explanation	Debit	Credit	Balance
	Received 10 TV sets to be sold for $400 each at a commission of 20% of selling price			
	Freight costs	135		135 dr
	Sales: 10 sets @ $400 each		4,000	3,865 cr
	Commission: $4,000 × 0.20	800		3,065 cr
	Payment to consignor	3,065		-0-

Several variations from the pattern of journal entries illustrated might be mentioned. If the policy of Robert Thorell is to debit inbound freight costs on both consignment shipments and purchases of merchandise to a Freight In account, the portion applicable to the Sherri Company consignment should be reclassified at a later date by a debit to Consignment In—Sherri Company and a credit to Freight In. If a cash advance is made by the consignee to the consignor, it is recorded as a debit to the Consignment In account, and the final payment is reduced by the amount of advance. If merchandise is received on consignment from several consignors, a Consignments In controlling account may be used, and a supporting account for each consignment set up in a subsidiary consignments ledger.

If the consignee, Robert Thorell, does not determine profits from consignment sales separately from regular sales, the sale of the consigned merchandise is credited to the regular Sales account. Concurrently, a journal entry is made debiting Cost of Goods Sold (or Purchases) and crediting the Consignment In account for the amount payable to the consignor for each unit sold (sales price minus the commission). Costs chargeable to the consignor are recorded by debits to the Consignment In account and credits to Cash or expense accounts, if the costs previously were recorded in expense accounts. No journal entry is made for commission revenue, because the profit element is measured by the difference between the amount credited to Sales and the amount debited to Cost of Goods Sold (or Purchases). The Consignment In account is closed by a debit for the payment made to the consignor in settlement. This method may be less desirable, because information relating to gross profits on consignment sales as compared with regular sales may be needed by the consignee as a basis for business decisions.

At the end of the accounting period when financial statements are prepared, some Consignment In accounts in the subsidiary consignments ledger may have debit balances and others credit balances. A debit balance will exist in a Consignment In account if the total of expenditures, commission, and advances to the consignor is larger than the proceeds of sales of that particular lot of consigned merchandise. A credit balance will exist if the proceeds of sales are in excess of the expenditures, commission, and advances to the consignor. The total of the Consignment In accounts with debit balances is included among the current assets in the balance sheet; the total of the Consignment In accounts with credit balances is classified as a current liability. Any commission earned but not recorded is entered in the accounting records before financial statements are prepared. The balance of the Consignments In controlling account represents the difference between the subsidiary accounts with debit balances and those with credit balances.

Accounting for consignors

When the consignor ships merchandise to consignees, it is essential to have a record of the location of this portion of inventories. Therefore, the consignor may establish in the general ledger a Consignment Out account for every consignee (or every shipment on consignment). If consignment shipments are numerous, the consignor may prefer to use a controlling account for subsidiary consignment-out accounts. If the inventory records are computerized, special coding may be used to identify inventories in the hands of consignees. The Consignment Out account should not be intermingled with accounts receivable, because it represents a special category of inventories rather than receivables.

Separate determination of gross profit

First, let us distinguish between a separate determination of **net income** on consignment sales and a separate determination of **gross profits** on consignment sales. Another possibility to consider is a separate determination of consignment sales revenue apart from regular sales revenue.

Although it may be useful to develop detailed information on the profitability of selling through consignees as compared with selling through regular channels, the accumulation of such information must be influenced by several practical considerations. First, the determination of a separate net income from consignment sales seldom is feasible, because this would require allocations of many operating expenses on a rather arbitrary basis. The work required would be extensive, and the resulting data would be no better than the arbitrary expense allocations. In general, the determination of **net income** from consignment sales cannot be justified.

The determination of gross profits from consignment sales as distinguished from gross profits on regular sales is much simpler, because it is based on the identification of **direct costs** associated with consignment sales. However, the compilation of these direct costs may be an expensive process, especially if the gross profit is computed by individual consignments or consignees. A separate determination of gross profits on consignments becomes more desirable if consignment transactions are substantial in relation to regular sales.

A separation of consignment sales revenue from regular sales revenue usually is a minimum step to develop information needed by management if consignment sales are an important part of total sales volume. However, no separation of consignment sales from regular sales may be justified if only an occasional sale is made through consignees.

Accounting for consignor illustrated

The choice of accounting methods by the consignor depends on whether (1) consignment gross profits are determined separately from gross profits on regular sales, or (2) sales on consignment are combined with regular sales without any effort to measure gross profits separately for the two categories of sales.

The journal entries required under these alternative methods of accounting for consignment shipments now will be illustrated, first under the assumption that gross profits on consignment sales are determined separately, and second under the assumption that consignment sales are combined with regular sales without a separate determination of gross profits. The assumed transactions for these illustrations already have been described from the consignee's viewpoint but now are restated to include the data relating to the consignor. In all remaining illustrations, we assume that the consignor uses the perpetual inventory system.

Sherri Company shipped on consignment to Robert Thorell 10 television sets that cost $250 each. The selling price was set at $400 each. The cost of packing was $30; all costs incurred in the packing department were debited by Sherri to the Packing Expense account. Freight costs of $135 by an independent truck line to deliver the shipment to Robert Thorell were paid by the consignee. All 10 sets were sold by the consignee for $400 each. After deducting the commission of 20% and the freight costs of $135, Robert Thorell sent Sherri Company a check for $3,065, along with the account sales illustrated on page 631.

SHERRI COMPANY (Consignor)

Journal Entries, Ledger Account, and Income Statement Presentation for a Completed Consignment

Explanations	Gross profits determined separately	Gross profits not determined separately

(1) Shipment of merchandise costing $2,500 on consignment; consigned merchandise is transferred to a separate inventories account. Consignor uses the perpetual inventory system.	Consignment Out—Robert
	Thorell 2,500
	   Inventories 2,500
		Consignment Out—Robert
		Thorell 2,500
		   Inventories 2,500

(2) Packing expense of $30 allocated to consigned merchandise; this expense previously was recorded in the Packing Expense account.	Consignment Out—Robert Thorell . . . . 30 Packing Expense . . . 30	No journal entry required; total packing expense is reported among operating expenses.

(3) Consignment sales of $4,000 reported by consignee and payment of $3,065 received. Charges by consignee: freight costs, $135; commission, $800.	Cash 3,065
	Consignment Out—Robert
	Thorell 135
	Commission Expense—
	   Consignment Sales 800
	   Consignment Sales . . 4,000
		Cash 3,065
		Freight Expense 135
		Commission Expense 800
		   Sales 4,000

(4) Cost of consignment sales recorded, $2,665 ($2,500 + $30 + $135 = $2,665).

Cost of Consignment Sales .	2,665	
Consignment Out—		
Robert Thorell		2,665

Cost of Goods Sold	2,500	
Consignment Out—		
Robert Thorell		2,500

(5) Summary of Consignment Out account:

Consignment Out—Robert Thorell	
2,500	2,665
30	
135	
2,665	

Consignment Out—Robert Thorell	
2,500	2,500
	2,665

(6) Presentation in the income statement:

Consignment sales		$4,000
Less: Cost of consignment		
sales	$2,665	
Commission	800	3,465
Gross profit on consignment		
sales		$ 535

Included in total sales	$4,000
Included in cost of all merchandise	
sold	2,500
Included in total packing expense . .	30
Included in total freight expense	135
Included in total commission	
expense	800

The journal entries for the consignor, assuming that gross profits on consignment sales are determined separately, and gross profits on consignment sales are not determined separately, are summarized on pages 636 and 637 for the completed consignment.

If the consigned merchandise is sold on credit, the consignee may send the consignor an account sales but no check. In this case the consignor's debit would be to Accounts Receivable rather than to the Cash account. When sales are reported by the consignee and gross profits are not determined separately by the consignor, the account credited is Sales rather than Consignment Sales, because there is no intent to separate regular sales from consignment sales. Similarly, the commission paid to consignees is combined with other commission expense, and freight costs applicable to sales on consignment are recorded in the Freight Expense account.

Accounting for partial sale of consigned merchandise

In the preceding example, we have assumed that the consignor received an account sales showing that all the merchandise shipped on consignment had been sold by the consignee. The account sales was accompanied by remittance in full, and the consignor's journal entries were designed to record the gross profit from the completed consignment.

Let us now change our conditions by assuming that only four of the ten TV sets consigned by Sherri Company to Robert Thorell had been sold by the end of the accounting period. To prepare financial statements, the consignor must determine the amount of gross profit realized on the four units sold and the inventory value of the six unsold units. The account sales received by Sherri Company at the end of the current period includes the following information:

ROBERT THORELL
Account Sales to Sherri Company

Sales: 4 TV sets at $400		$1,600
Charges: Freight costs	$135	
Commission ($1,600 × 0.20)	320	455
Total payable to consignor		$1,145
Check enclosed		500
Balance payable to consignor		$645
Consigned merchandise on hand		6 TV sets

The journal entries for the consignor to account for this uncompleted consignment are presented on pages 640 and 641.

In the illustration of a partial consignment sale, we have employed the familiar accounting principle of carrying forward as part of inventories a pro rata portion of the costs incurred to place the inventories in a location and condition necessary for sale. The commission charged by the consignee for the units sold is an operating expense of the current accounting period.

Return of unsold merchandise by consignee

We have stressed that the costs of packing and shipping merchandise to a consignee, whether paid directly by the consignor or by the consignee, properly are included in inventories. However, if the consignee for any reason returns merchandise to the consignor, the packing and freight costs incurred on the original outbound shipment should be recorded as an expense of the current accounting period. The *place utility* originally created by these costs is lost when the merchandise is returned. Any costs incurred by the consignor on the return shipment also should be recorded as an expense, along with any repair costs necessary to place the merchandise in salable condition.

Finally, a clear distinction should be made between freight costs on consignment shipments and outbound freight costs on regular sales. The freight costs on consignment shipments create an increment in value of the merchandise that is still the property of the consignor. This increment, together with the cost of purchasing or producing the merchandise, is to be offset against revenue in future accounting periods when the consigned merchandise is sold. Outbound freight costs on regular sales are recorded as expenses of the period that such sales are made.

Advances from consignees

Although cash advances from a consignee sometimes are credited to the Consignment Out account, a better practice is to credit a liability account, Advances from Consignees. The Consignment Out account then will continue to show the carrying amount of the merchandise on consignment, rather than being shown net of a liability to the consignee.

Nature of the Consignment Out account

When accounting students encounter for the first time a ledger account such as Consignment Out, they may gain a clear understanding of its function more quickly by considering where it belongs in the five basic types of accounts: assets, liabilities, owners' equity, revenue, and expenses. Classification of the Consignment Out account in this structure will depend on the methods employed by a business enterprise in accounting for consignments.

Whether or not an enterprise uses a system of determining gross profits on consignment sales separately from regular sales, the Con-

SHERRI COMPANY (Consignor)

Journal Entries, Ledger Account, and Balance Sheet Presentation for a Partial Sale of Consigned Merchandise

Explanations	Gross profits determined separately	Gross profits not determined separately

(1) Shipment of merchandise costing $2,500 on consignment; consigned merchandise is transferred to a separate Inventories account. Consignor uses the perpetual inventory system.	Consignment Out—Robert Thorell 2,500
	  Inventories 2,500
		Consignment Out—Robert Thorell 2,500
		  Inventories 2,500

(2) Packing expense of $30 allocated to consigned merchandise; this expense previously was recorded in the Packing Expense account.	Consignment Out—Robert Thorell . . . . 30 Packing Expense . . . 30	No journal entry required; total packing expense is reported among operating expenses.

(3) Consignment sales of $1,600 reported by consignee and payment of $500 received. Charges by consignee: freight costs, $135; commission, $320.	Cash 500
	Accounts Receivable . . 645
	Consignment Out—Robert Thorell 135
	Commission Expense—Consignment Sales 320
	  Consignment Sales . . 1,600
		Cash 500
		Accounts Receivable . . 645
		Freight Expense 135
		Commission Expense . . 320
		  Sales 1,600

(4) Cost of consignment sales recorded:
($250 + $3 + $13.50) × 4 = $1,066;
$250 × 4 = $1,000
	Cost of Consignment Sales . 1,066
	  Consignment Out—
	  Robert Thorell 1,066
		Cost of Goods Sold . . . 1,000
		  Consignment Out—Robert
		  Thorell 1,000

(5) Direct costs relating to unsold merchandise in hands of consignee deferred when profits are not determined separately:

Packing costs ($3 × 6)	$18
Freight costs ($13.50 × 6)	81
Total.	$99

No journal entry required.

Consignment Out—Robert Thorell

Thorell	99
Packing Expense	18
Freight Expense	81

(6) Summary of Consignment Out account:

Consignment Out—Robert Thorell

Debit		Credit	
2,500		1,066	
30		1,599	Balance
135			
2,665		2,665	
1,599	Balance		

Consignment Out—Robert Thorell

Debit		Credit	
2,500		1,000	
99		1,599	Balance
2,599		2,599	
1,599	Balance		

(7) Presentation in the balance sheet:

Current assets:

Inventories on consignment	$1,599

Current assets:

Inventories on consignment	$1,599

signment Out account belongs in the asset category. The account is debited for the cost of merchandise shipped to a consignee; when the consignee reports sale of all or a portion of the merchandise, the cost is transferred from Consignment Out to Cost of Consignment Sales. To be even more specific, Consignment Out is a current asset, one of the inventories group to be listed on the balance sheet as Inventories on Consignment, or perhaps combined with other inventories if the amount is not material. As stated earlier, the costs of packing and transporting consigned merchandise constitute costs of inventories, and these costs are recorded as debits to the Consignment Out account.

Another concept of the Consignment Out account is summarized briefly as follows: The Consignment Out account may be debited for the cost of merchandise shipped to the consignee and credited for the sales proceeds remitted by the consignee. This generally will result in a credit balance in the Consignment Out account when the entire shipment has been sold. This credit balance represents the profit earned by the consignor and is closed by a debit to Consignment Out and a credit to an account such as Profit on Consignment Sales. No separate accounts are used for Consignment Sales and Cost of Consignment Sales, and the income statement does not show the amount of sales made through consignees. Under this system, the Consignment Out account does not fit in any of the five basic classes of accounts. It is a mixture of asset elements and revenue and must be closed or reduced to its asset element (cost of unsold consigned merchandise) before financial statements are prepared at the end of an accounting period.

The methods we have illustrated in accounting for consignments are widely used, but many variations from these methods are possible.

REVIEW QUESTIONS

1 What are the most important characteristics that distinguish an installment sale from an ordinary sale on 30-day credit terms?

2 In a discussion of the theoretical support for the installment method of accounting, a student stated: "If a business enterprise is going to sell personal property over a period as long as 36 months, no one can predict how difficult or costly collections may be. To recognize the gross profit as realized at the time of sale would violate well-established accounting concepts such as **conservatism** and **reliability**." What opposing arguments can you offer?

3 What position did **APB Opinion No. 10** establish for the use of the installment method of accounting for financial accounting purposes?

4 On November 10, Year 3, Ann Haggard agreed to sell for $150,000 a tract of land acquired five years ago for $60,000. The purchaser offered to pay $44,000 down and the balance in 20 semiannual installments plus interest at 15% on the unpaid principal balance. Haggard agreed to these terms, and the sale was completed.

  Assuming that Haggard (who is not a dealer in real estate) computes net income on a calendar-year basis and elects to use the installment method of accounting for income tax purposes, how much gross profit did she realize in Year 3 for income tax purposes?

5 The following journal entry appears in the accounting records of a land developer who uses the installment method of accounting:

Inventories (repossessed land)	2,000	
Deferred Gross Profit on Installment Sales—Year 10	1,505	
Uncollectible Installment Contracts Expense	795	
Installment Contracts Receivable		4,300

Compute the rate of gross profit on the original sale. What was the probable source of the $2,000 debit to the Inventories account?

6 How should the **current fair value** of merchandise traded in be determined? What accounting treatment would you recommend for any **overallowance** granted to customers on merchandise accepted as a trade-in?

7 What conditions generally must be present before the accrual basis of accounting may be used to account for retail sales of land on the installment plan?

8 Discuss the balance sheet classification of deferred gross profit on the installment sales of land. Include former practice and theoretical considerations in your answer.

9 How does a **consignment** of merchandise differ from a **sale** of merchandise?

10 Majors Corporation sells merchandise for cash and on 30-day credit terms; it also makes sales through consignees. Explain how the two methods of marketing differ with respect to the time when profit is realized. What relationship, if any, exists between the realization of profit and the receipt of cash by Majors Corporation?

11 Give reasons why the use of consignments may be advantageous for the consignor and for the consignee.

12 On December 31, HP Motors received a report from one of its consignees that 40 motors of a consignment of 100 had been sold. No check was enclosed, but the report indicated that payment would be made later. HP Motors maintains its accounting records on a calendar-year basis and uses the perpetual inventory system. It determines profits on consignment sales separately from profits on regular sales. What accounting action, if any, should be taken by HP Motors on December 31 with respect to the consignee's report?

13 A manufacturer of outboard motors accumulates production costs on job cost sheets. On March 20, Lot No. K-37, consisting of 100 identical motors, was completed at a cost of $14,000. Twenty-five motors were shipped on consignment to a dealer in Florida, and another 25 were sent to a consignee in California. The remaining 50 motors were in the manufacturer's stockroom on March 31, the end of the fiscal year. Neither consignee submitted an account sales for March. Explain the quantity and valuation of motors in the manufacturer's balance sheet on March 31.

14 Identify each of the following ledger accounts by indicating whether it belongs in the general ledger of consignors or consignees; whether it normally

has a debit balance or a credit balance; and how the account would be classified in the financial statements.

a Cost of Consignment Sales

b Consignment Out

c Consignment Sales

d Consignment In

15 What difference, if any, do you see between outbound freight costs on regular sales and outbound freight costs on consignment shipments?

16 Cal Marine, Inc., makes a number of shipments on consignment, although
most of its merchandise is sold on 30-day credit terms. Consignment shipments are recorded on sales invoices that are posted as debits to Accounts
Receivable and credits to Sales. Cal Marine has not been audited by independent public accountants, but at the suggestion of the company's bank you
are retained to audit the financial statements for the current year.

    Would you take exception to Cal Marine's method of accounting for con-
signments? Explain. What adjusting journal entries, if any, are required at
year-end?

EXERCISES

Ex. 14-1 Select the best answer for each of the following multiple-choice questions:

1 Dalton Company sold machinery to Ford Company on January 1, Year 1. The
cash selling price would have been $379,100, but the sale was made on an in-
stallment contract that required annual payments of $100,000, including inter-
est at 10%, over five years. The first payment was due on December 31, Year 1.
What amount of interest revenue should be included in Dalton's income statement for the year ended December 31, Year 3 (the third year of the contract)?

  a $24,180   **b** $24,871   **c** $37,910   **d** $50,000   **e** Some other amount

2 An automobile dealer lists a new model costing $5,000 at $8,000. A customer
trades in an old model for an allowance of $2,000; the balance of $6,000 plus
interest is payable $310 a month for 24 months. The dealer expects to sell the
old model for $1,800 after reconditioning it at a cost of $300. Normal gross
profit on used automobiles is 10%. In the journal entry to record the sale of the
new model, the accountant for the dealer should:

  a Debit the Inventories (trade-ins) account for $2,000

  b Credit the Inventories (new) account for $4,320

  c Credit the Installment Sales account for $7,320

  d Debit the Loss on Trade-Ins account for $680

3 Which of the following is not a factor in the determination of current fair value
of merchandise repossessed under a defaulted installment sales contract?

  a Deferred gross profit on contract on date of default

  b Necessary reconditioning costs for the merchandise

  c Normal gross profit on resale of the merchandise

  d Expected selling price (after reconditioning) of the merchandise

4 Joanie Reberry received a consignment of 100 toys from Dan Company on October 7, Year 5. Dan instructed Reberry to sell the toys for $100 each, which
represented a gross profit rate of 20% to Dan. Reberry paid freight costs of
$240 on the shipment on October 7, Year 5. Reberry should debit the Consign-
ment In—Dan Company account on October 7, Year 5, in the amount of:

  a $240   **b** $10,000   **c** $8,000   **d** $8,240   **e** Some other amount

5 The inventories of Benson Company on September 30, Year 1, included the
following items:

	Amount
Merchandise on consignment (owned by Benson), at selling price (including markup of 40% on cost)	$7,000
Merchandise purchased, in transit (shipped by supplier FOB shipping point)	6,000
Merchandise held on consignment by Benson	4,000
Merchandise out on approval (selling price $2,500, cost $2,000) ...	2,500

Based on the above information, Benson's inventories on September 30, Year 1, should be reduced by:

a $6,500   **b** $7,300   **c** $8,500   **d** $13,500   **e** Some other amount

Ex. 14-2 On September 30, Year 1, Urban Land Company sold for $50,000 a tract of land that had a cost of $30,000. Urban Land received a down payment of $8,000, the balance to be received at the rate of $3,000 every three months, starting December 31, Year 1. In addition, the purchaser agreed to pay interest at the rate of 2% a quarter on the unpaid principal. Because collection of the installments was highly uncertain, Urban Land elected to report the gain under the installment method of accounting, both for financial accounting and for income tax purposes.

Prepare journal entries to record the (**a**) sale of the land, (**b**) receipt of the first installment on December 31, and (**c**) gain realized in Year 1 under the installment method of accounting. Ignore expenses of sale.

Ex. 14-3 Early in Year 1, Vargo Company sold a parcel of land with a carrying amount of $40,000 for $100,000. The purchaser paid $10,000 down and agreed to pay the balance plus interest in three equal annual installments starting on December 31, Year 1.

Assuming that collections are made as agreed, prepare a working paper showing the gross profit that Vargo would recognize each year under (**a**) the accrual basis of accounting, (**b**) the installment method of accounting, and (**c**) the cost recovery method of accounting. Ignore expenses of sale.

Ex. 14-4 Gross profits for Sunset Home Products, Inc., were 35%, 33%, and 30% of sales price for Year 1, Year 2, and Year 3, respectively. The following account balances are available at the end of Year 3:

Sales	Installment contracts receivable	Deferred gross profit (before adjustment)
Year 1	$ 6,000	$ 7,230
Year 2	61,500	60,750
Year 3	195,000	120,150

The installment contracts receivable and the deferred gross profit include interest and carrying charges.

Prepare a journal entry at the end of Year 3 to record the realized gross profit on installment sales.

Ex. 14-5 In Year 5, merchandise was sold on an installment contract by Fong for $1,600 at a gross profit of 25% on cost. In Year 5, a total of $600 was collected on this contract; in Year 6, no collections were made on this contract, and the merchandise was repossessed. The current fair value of the merchandise was $680; however, Fong's accountant recorded the repossession as follows:

Allowance for Doubtful Installment Contracts Receivable 1,000

     Installment Contracts Receivable—Year 5   1,000

To write off balance of defaulted installment contract receivable.

Prepare a journal entry to correct the accounting records, assuming that the ledger accounts are still open for Year 6 and that Fong uses an allowance for doubtful installment contracts receivable. Ignore interest and carrying charges, and assume that Fong records installment sales on the accrual basis of accounting.

Ex. 14-6 Chasen Motors sold a new car for a list price of $6,600. Cash of $300 was received on the sale, together with a used car accepted at a trade-in allowance of $1,500. The balance of $4,800 was due in 24 monthly installments. Cost of the new car was $5,100. Chasen Motors anticipated reconditioning cost on the trade-in of $200 and a resale price of $1,300. Used cars normally are sold at a gross profit of 25% of selling price.

Prepare journal entries to record (**a**) the sale of the new car, (**b**) reconditioning costs of $200 on the car acquired as a trade-in, and (**c**) the sale of the used car for cash at a "sacrifice" price of $1,250. Ignore interest and carrying charges.

Ex. 14-7 Coronado Corporation sells merchandise on three-year installment sales contracts. On February 28, Year 5, the end of Coronado's first fiscal year, the pre-tax results of operations are summarized below:

Sales	$1,000,000
Cost of goods sold	700,000
Operating expenses	80,000

The balance of the Installment Contracts Receivable account on February 28, Year 5, was $600,000. No allowance for doubtful contracts receivable was required.

Prepare a journal entry to record federal and state income taxes on February 28, Year 5, assuming that Coronado accounts for sales on the accrual basis of accounting for financial accounting and on the installment basis of accounting for income taxes. Assume a combined federal and state income tax rate of 45%.

Ex. 14-8 For financial accounting, Holland Company uses the accrual basis of accounting for installment sales; for income taxes, it uses the installment method of accounting. Holland has no other differences between pre-tax accounting income and taxable income. For the fiscal year ended November 30, Year 2, Holland's pre-tax accounting income was $500,000; its combined federal and state income tax rates totaled 60%. The income tax accounting records show total deferred gross profit on installment sales on November 30, Year 1, of $80,000 and on November 30, Year 2, of $120,000.

Prepare the journal entry or entries to record Holland's income taxes expense for the year ended November 30, Year 2.

Ex. 14-9 The Consignment Out account in the accounting records of Idaho Company for Year 1 appears below:

Consignment Out—Bend Sales Company

Date	Explanation	Debit	Credit	Balance
	Shipped 20 units	3,200		3,200 dr
	Freight costs paid by consignor	260		3,460 dr
	Unpacking costs incurred by consignee	100		3,560 dr
	Commission on sale of 12 units	360		3,920 dr
	Selling price of 12 units		3,600	320 dr

Idaho debited the Consignment Out account for all costs relating to the consignment and credited the account for the full selling price of units sold. Cash of $3,140 was received from the consignee.

a Prepare a journal entry in the accounting records of the consignor to correct the Consignments Out account at the end of Year 1, assuming that consignment profits are determined separately. (Show computations.)

b Prepare the journal entries that would appear in the accounting records of the consignee, assuming that consignment profits are determined separately. The consignee sold the units for cash and made remittance in full to the consignor at the end of Year 1.

Ex. 14-10 Dan Thomas consigns radios to retailers, debiting Accounts Receivable for the retail sales price of the radios consigned and crediting Sales. All costs relating to consigned radios are debited to expenses of the current accounting period. Net remittances from consignees are credited to Accounts Receivable.

In December, 500 radios costing $60 a unit and retailing for $100 a unit were consigned to Sunset Shop. Freight costs of $1,100 were debited to Freight Expense by the consignor. On December 31, Sunset Shop remitted $35,550 to Dan Thomas, in full settlement to date; Accounts Receivable was credited for this amount. The consignee deducted a commission of $10 on each radio sold and $450 for delivering the radios sold.

a Compute the number of radios sold by Sunset Shop, the consignee.

b Prepare a single correcting journal entry required in the accounting records of the consignor on December 31, assuming that the accounting records are still open, that the perpetual inventory system is used, and that profits on consignments are determined separately by use of separate revenue and expense accounts. Allocate costs between radios sold and radios on hand.

Ex. 14-11 Information relating to regular sales and consignment sales of Jewelry Products for the year ended June 30, Year 6, follows:

	Regular sales	Consignment sales	Total
Sales	$120,000	$30,000	$150,000
Cost of goods sold	84,000	26,000	110,000
Operating expenses	?	1,760	16,910

Income taxes expense is 20% of pre-tax accounting income.

You ascertain that merchandise costing $6,500 is in the possession of consignees and is included in cost of consignment merchandise sold. Operating expenses of $15,150 (more than half of which are fixed) are to be allocated to regular sales and to consignment sales on the basis of volume. The $1,760 of operating expenses relating to consignment sales includes a commission of 5% and $260 of costs incurred by consignees relating to the entire shipment costing $26,000.

Prepare an income statement showing the net income on regular sales, consignment sales, and total sales in separate columns. Advise management of Jewelry Products whether it should continue to sell on a consignment basis.

CASES

Case 14-1 Janice Denson and Tyrone Awan, certified public accountants, are attempting to develop the management advisory services segment of their practice. One of the firm's income tax clients, Zorro Corporation, affords an opportunity for work along this line. Zorro, a manufacturer of machinery, in the past has sold its products through wholesalers and also directly to some large retail outlets.

During a telephone conversation on income tax matters between the president of Zorro and Janice Denson, the president posed the following question: "We are considering making sales of our products on a consignment basis as well as through our present outlets; would it be feasible to establish an accounting system that would show separately the net income we earned on consignment sales? I don't have time to discuss it now, but write me a memo and let me have your reactions."

Instructions Prepare a memo that Janice Denson might write to the president of Zorro Corporation, making any assumptions you consider necessary and summarizing the issues involved and the alternatives available.

Case 14-2 Sound Delight sells stereo equipment and maintains its accounting records on a calendar-year basis. On October 1, Year 1, Sound Delight sold a stereo set to Hermine Pak. Cost of the set was $800, and the selling price was $1,200. A down payment of $300 was received along with a contract calling for the payment of $50 on the first day of each month for the next 18 months. No interest or carrying charge was added to the contract. Hermine Pak paid the monthly installments promptly on November 1 and December 1, Year 1. She also made seven payments in Year 2 but then defaulted on the contract. Sound Delight repossessed the set on November 1, Year 2.

Instructions
a State three different amounts that might be reported as realized income from this transaction for Year 1, and indicate the circumstances under which each of the three amounts might be acceptable.
b Without regard to income tax considerations, which of the three amounts do you believe has the strongest support from a theoretical standpoint? Which has the weakest support? Explain.
c If the stereo set repossessed on November 1, Year 2, has a wholesale value of $200 and a retail value of $300, prepare a journal entry to record the repossession under the installment method of accounting. Explain fully the reasoning applicable to the journal entry. Assume that an allowance for doubtful installment contracts is not used.

Case 14-3 Teakwood Sales Company sells furniture on the installment plan. For its income tax returns, it reports gross profit from sales under the installment method of accounting. For financial accounting, it considers the entire gross profit to be earned in the year of sale.

Instructions
a Discuss the relative merits of the two methods of reporting gross profit.
b Explain the installment method of accounting used for income tax purposes.
c Discuss the effects of the concurrent use of these two bases of accounting by Teakwood Sales Company on its annual net income. What recommendation would you make to the company to produce an income statement in accordance with generally accepted accounting principles?

Case 14-4 Hungry Bear sells franchises to independent operators. The contract with the franchisee includes the following provisions:

(1) The franchisee is charged an initial fee of $30,000. Of this amount $5,000 is payable when the contract is signed, and a $5,000 noninterest-bearing promissory note is payable at the end of each of the five subsequent years.
(2) All the initial franchise fee collected by the franchisor is to be refunded and the remaining obligation canceled if, for any reason, the franchisee fails to open the franchise.
(3) In return for the initial franchise fee, the franchisor agrees to (1) assist the franchisee in selecting the location for the business, (2) negotiate the lease for the land, (3) obtain financing and assist with building design, (4) super-

vise construction, (5) establish accounting and income tax records, and (6) provide advice over a five-year period relating to such matters as employee and management training, quality control, and product promotion.

(4) In addition to the initial franchise fee, the franchisee is required to pay to Hungry Bear a monthly fee of 2% of sales for menu planning, recipe innovations, and the privilege of purchasing ingredients from Hungry Bear at or below prevailing market prices.

Management of Hungry Bear estimates that the value of the services rendered to the franchisee at the time the contract is signed amounts to at least $5,000. All franchisees to date have opened their locations at the scheduled time, and none has defaulted on any of the notes receivable.

The credit ratings of all franchisees would entitle them to borrow at the current interest rate of 10%. The present value of an ordinary annuity of five annual rents of $5,000 each discounted at 10% is $18,954.

Instructions

a Discuss the alternative methods that Hungry Bear might use to account for the initial franchise fee; evaluate each method by applying generally accepted accounting principles to this situation; and prepare illustrative journal entries for each method. Assume that a Discount on Notes Receivable account is used.

b Given the nature of the contract with franchisees, when should revenue be recognized by Hungry Bear? Discuss the question of revenue realization for both the initial franchise fee and the additional monthly fee of 2% of sales, and prepare illustrative journal entries for both types of revenue.

c Assume that Hungry Bear sells some franchises for $40,000, which includes $10,000 for the rental of equipment for its economic life of ten years, that $15,000 of the fee is payable immediately and the balance on noninterest-bearing promissory notes at $5,000 a year; that no portion of the $10,000 rental payment is refundable in case the franchisee goes out of business; and that title to the equipment remains with the franchisor. What would be the preferable method of accounting for the rental portion of the initial franchise fee? Explain.

PROBLEMS

14-1 Houston Technologies, Inc., sells computers. On January 2, Year 5, Houston entered into an installment sale contract with Andersen Company for a seven-year period expiring December 31, Year 11. Equal annual payments under the installment contract are $1,000,000 and are due on January 2. The first payment was made on January 2, Year 5.

Additional information is as follows:
(1) The cash selling price of the computer was $5,355,000. ($1,000,000 × 5.355 present value of annuity due of 7 rents of 1 at 10% = $5,355,000.)
(2) The cost of the computer was $4,284,000.
(3) Interest relating to the installment period amounted to $1,645,000, based on a stated (and appropriate) interest rate of 10%. For income tax purposes, Houston uses the accrual basis of accounting for recording interest revenue.
(4) Circumstances are such that the collection of the installment contract receivable is reasonably assured.
(5) The installment sale qualified for the installment method of accounting for income tax purposes.
(6) The income tax rate for Houston is 45%.

Instructions

a Compute the pre-tax accounting income (loss) that Houston should record for financial accounting as a result of this transaction for the year ended December 31, Year 5. Compute interest revenue for a full year and show supporting computations.

b Compute the amount of deferred income taxes, if any, that Houston should record for financial accounting as a result of this transaction for the year ended December 31, Year 5. Show supporting computations.

c Prepare a journal entry to record income taxes expense on December 31, Year 5, as a result of this transaction. Ignore any expenses other than cost of goods sold.

14-2   Mojave Company accounts for its retail sales of recreational land under the installment method of accounting because the collection of contracts *is not reasonably assured.* The balances in the accounts for installment contracts receivable at the beginning and end of Year 10 were:

	January 1, Year 10	December 31, Year 10
Installment contracts receivable—Year 8 (sales and cost of goods sold for Year 8 were $600,000 and $480,000, respectively)	$420,000	$320,000
Installment contracts receivable—Year 9 (sales and cost of goods sold for Year 9 were $675,000 and $526,500, respectively)	595,000	470,000
Installment contracts receivable—Year 10 (sales and cost of goods sold for Year 10 were $920,000 and $690,000, respectively)		800,000

The company opened for business early in Year 8 and sells the land on 60-month contracts.

An allowance for doubtful contracts is not used. Interest and carrying charges are included in the selling price and in the computation of the yearly gross profit rates.

Upon default in payment by customers in Year 10, the company repossessed land that had a current fair value on the date of repossession of $3,800; in recording the repossession, the company debited Inventories and credited Installment Contracts Receivable—Year 8 for $3,800. The sale of the land had been made in Year 8 for $10,000, and $4,000 had been collected prior to the default.

Instructions

a Prepare a journal entry to record the total realized gross profit for the year ended December 31, Year 10.

b Prepare any correcting journal entries required as a result of the incorrect treatment of the repossession of land in Year 10.

14-3   Mod, Inc., a new department store, plans to use the installment method of recognizing gross profit on installment sales for income tax purposes. Under this method, the expected 40% gross profit on sales will be recognized only as cash payments are received; this serves to postpone until future accounting periods taxable income equal to 40% of the year-end balance in installment contracts receivable. Because collection of the full sales price *is reasonably assured,* for financial accounting Mod recognizes the entire gross profit at the time sales are made. The following information has been developed as a part of the company's income-planning activities:

	Year 1	Year 2	Year 3	Year 4	Year 5
Expected installment sales	$1,000,000	$1,500,000	$1,800,000	$2,000,000	$2,000,000
Expected installment contracts					
receivable balances at year-end . . .	200,000	400,000	500,000	550,000	525,000
Gross profit to be recognized:					
In accounting records	400,000	600,000	720,000	800,000	800,000
In income tax returns	320,000	520,000	680,000	?	?

Instructions

a Compute the two missing items in the summary above.

b Compute the balances that should appear in the Deferred Income Tax Liability account at the end of each of the five years, assuming an income tax rate of 45%. State how these balances should be classified in the balance sheet (remember the defined relationship between current assets and the operating cycle).

c Assume that Mod's projections show income before income taxes of $220,000 in Year 1 and $350,000 in Year 5. Prepare partial income statements for these two years (as if the projected events had actually occurred), showing in the statements or accompanying notes the provisions for current and deferred income taxes.

d Assume that, at the beginning of Year 6, Mod decided to stop selling on the installment plan, and that by the end of the year all installment contracts receivable had been collected. If income before income taxes for Year 6 is assumed to be $400,000, prepare a journal entry to record Mod's income taxes for Year 6.

14-4 Newport Sales Company started operations in Year 1. It sells merchandise on the installment plan and on regular 30-day open accounts. Activities for Year 1 are summarized below:

Regular sales	$360,000
Installment sales, including $90,000 deferred interest and carrying charges	690,000
Cost of regular sales	203,000
Cost of installment sales	360,000
Operating expenses	177,000
Collections on regular sales	310,000
Collections on installment sales, including $30,000 interest and carrying charges, all of which were earned in Year 1	255,000

Newport Sales uses the perpetual inventory system and does not include interest and carrying charges in the computation of gross profit on installment sales. Income taxes are levied at 45% of taxable income.

Instructions

a Prepare journal entries to record all transactions and adjustments for Year 1, using only the information given in the problem. Assume that the accrual basis of accounting is used for financial accounting and the installment method is used for income tax purposes. Accrued interest and carrying charges at the end of Year 1 may be ignored. Closing entries are not required.

b Prepare journal entries to record all transactions for Year 1 (including the establishment of deferred gross profit and adjusting entries), using only the information given in the problem. Assume that the installment method of accounting is used both for financial accounting and for income tax purposes. Closing entries are not required.

14-5   Art Company derives a major part of its revenue from sales made by consignees throughout the United States. The company determines profits on consignment sales by the use of separate sales, cost of goods sold, and expense accounts. Under the perpetual inventory system designed by the company's accountant, all costs relating to consigned merchandise initially are recorded in the Inventory on Consignment account. During the last quarter of Year 1, the following transactions were completed with Peter Jason, a new consignee in Memphis:

Oct. 2   Consigned 25 lathes costing $12,000, and paid $500 shipping costs.

Nov. 28   Sent a mechanic to Memphis to install safety devices on 10 lathes that had not yet been sold. The costs of this alteration were: parts from inventories, $60; cash expenditure, $40.

Dec. 31   Received an account sales as follows:

Sales: 20 lathes @ $950		$19,000
Charges: Commission (15% of $19,000)	$2,850	
Advertising	95	
Delivery and installation costs on 20		
lathes sold	140	3,085
Balance (check no. 1269 enclosed)		$15,915

Instructions

a Prepare a working paper for Art Company showing the allocation of costs and expenses to lathes sold by Jason and to the consignment inventories at the end of Year 1.

b Prepare journal entries for Art Company to record the transactions with Jason, including a journal entry to record the cost of consignment sales on December 31, Year 1.

14-6   Ken Cable sells tables for Rosewood, Inc., on a consignment basis. The ledger account below for Ken Cable summarizes consignment activities for the month of May:

Consignment In—Rosewood, Inc.

Date	Explanation	Debit	Credit	Balance
May 4	Memorandum entry: Received 10 tables			
4	Freight and insurance paid	370		370 dr
31	Delivery costs of 6 tables sold	240		610 dr
31	Sale of 6 tables		14,544	13,934 cr
31	Commission revenue realized	2,180		11,754 cr
31	Storage charges for 4 unsold tables	72		11,682 cr
31	Remittance to consignor	4,682		7,000 cr

The cost of the tables for Rosewood, Inc., was $1,440 each. The accounting policies of Rosewood provide for a separate determination of profits on consigned tables as distinguished from profits on direct sales. Rosewood uses the perpetual inventory system and also maintains a separate Consignment Out account for each consignee. All costs applicable to a consignment of tables are debited to the Consignment Out account. When sales are reported by a consignee, the gross sales price is credited to Consignment Sales. The Consignment

Out account then is credited for the cost of the units sold, and this amount is transferred (debited) to a Cost of Consignment Sales account.

Instructions

a Prepare all journal entries required in the accounting records of the consignor, Rosewood, Inc., during the month of May. The tables were shipped to Ken Cable on May 1.

b Construct the Consignment Out ledger account for Rosewood, Inc., relating to the transactions with Ken Cable, showing all journal entries during the month of May.

c How should the month-end balances in the Consignment Out and Consignment In accounts appear in the financial statements of the consignor (Rosewood, Inc.) and the consignee (Ken Cable), respectively, on May 31?

14-7 Valleyview Corporation sold a parcel of undeveloped land on December 31, Year 1, for "a consideration of $318,611." The land had a carrying amount of $179,997 in the accounting records of Valleyview. The consideration received consisted of the following:

Cash down payment, Dec. 31, Year 1	$ 51,310
Three promissory notes of $100,000 each with payments starting Dec.	
31, Year 2, including interest at an annual rate of 6% (present value of	
an ordinary annuity of three rents of 1 at 6% = 2.673012)	267,301
Total consideration received	$318,611

You conclude that 10% is a more reasonable rate of interest and that the current fair value of the three promissory notes should be computed as follows:

Annual payments due on three notes	$100,000
Present value of ordinary annuity of three rents of $1 discounted	
at 10%	2.486852
Current fair value of notes	$248,685

The notes were recorded by Valleyview Corporation at current fair value on a 10%-yield basis without the use of a Discount on Notes Receivable account. The gain realized each year on this transaction should be recorded net of a 25% income tax rate applicable to long-term capital gains.

Instructions

a Assuming that the installment method of accounting is used for this transaction, both for financial accounting and for income tax purposes, prepare journal entries to record all transactions through Year 4. Round all computations to nearest dollar.

b Assuming that the installment method of accounting is used to report the gain for income tax purposes and that the accrual basis is used for financial accounting, prepare journal entries to record all transactions from December 31, Year 1, through December 31, Year 4.

14-8 On January 2, Year 5, Homeowners, Inc., entered into a contract with a manufacturer to purchase air conditioners and to sell the units on the installment plan with collections over 30 months, with no separately identified interest or carrying charge.

For income tax purposes, Homeowners elected to report income from its sales of air conditioners under the installment method of accounting.

Purchases and sales of new units were as follows:

	Units purchased		Units sold	
	Quantity	Price (each)	Quantity	Price (each)
Year 5.	4,800	$100	4,000	$150
Year 6.	7,200	90	8,000	140
Year 7.	3,200	105	2,800	143

Cash receipts on installment contracts receivable were as follows:

	Cash receipts		
	Year 5	Year 6	Year 7
Year 5 sales	$120,000	$240,000	$240,000
Year 6 sales		280,000	460,000
Year 7 sales			100,000

In Year 7, 160 units from the Year 6 sales were repossessed and sold for $90 each on the installment plan. At the time of repossession, $4,800 had been collected from the original purchasers, and the units had a current fair value of $10,080.

Operating expenses for Year 7 were $200,000. No charge has been made against current revenue for the applicable insurance expense under a three-year policy expiring June 30, Year 8, costing $9,600, and for an advance payment of $40,000 on a new contract to purchase air conditioners beginning January 2, Year 8.

Instructions Assuming that the weighted-average method is used for determining the cost of inventories, including repossessed air conditioners, prepare working papers to compute the following:

a (1) The cost of goods sold on the installment plan for each year
   (2) The weighted-average unit cost of goods sold on the installment plan for each year
b The gross profit percentages for each year
c The gain or loss on repossessions in Year 7
d The taxable income from installment sales for Year 7

14-9 Lei Corporation sells a limited number of its products through consignees. In the spring of Year 1, Lei arranged to sell outboard motors through a consignee, Ernie's. The motors were to be sold by the consignee at a price of $300 each, and the consignee was allowed a 15% commission on gross selling price. The consignee agreed to guarantee the accounts receivable and to remit all collections less the commission on consignment accounts receivable collected. The consignee also was allowed to deduct certain reimbursable costs; these costs were chargeable to the consignor as incurred. Both the consignor and the consignee maintain perpetual inventory records.

Transactions relating to the consignment during the first six months of year 1 were as follows:

Consignor's (Lei Corporation's) transactions:

Apr. 10   Shipped 90 motors to consignee; cost of each motor, $180.
                 Total packing costs paid for shipment, $360.
June 30   Received account sales from consignee and check for $12,765.

Consignee's (Ernie's) transactions:

Apr. 15   Received 90 motors and paid freight charges, $450.
May 1–June 23   Sold 60 motors and collected $15,600.
June 2   Paid $45 for minor repairs on six motors sold.
June 30   Mailed account sales to consignor with a check for $12,765.

Instructions

a Prepare all journal entries in the accounting records of Lei Corporation and in the accounting records of Ernie's, assuming that both enterprises report profits on consignment sales separately. Closing journal entries are not required.

b Prepare all journal entries in the accounting records of Lei Corporation and in the accounting records of Ernie's, assuming that consignment sales are combined with regular sales. Closing journal entries are not required.

c Would the balance of the Consignment In account maintained by Ernie's be the same amount on June 30 under the differing assumptions in **a** and **b** above? What is the balance in the Consignment In account, and how is it reported in the balance sheet of Ernie's on June 30?

14-10 Hilo Sales Corporation began operations on January 2, Year 1. All sales of new merchandise are made on installment contracts. Because of the risks of noncollection, Hilo Sales recognizes profit from the sale of new merchandise under the installment method of accounting and employs the periodic inventory system. The following information was taken from the accounting records of Hilo Sales on December 31 for the years indicated:

	Year 2	Year 1
Installment contracts receivable:		
Year 1 sales	$ 17,300	$ 40,000
Year 2 sales	56,000	
Cash sales of trade-ins	20,500	
Installment sales	310,000	221,000
Purchases	176,700	170,180
Inventories of new merchandise, Jan. 1	42,000	
Operating expenses	59,296	53,700
Uncollectible installment contracts expense	9,900	

Your audit for the year ended December 31, Year 2, disclosed the following:

(1) The inventories of new and repossessed merchandise on hand on December 31, Year 2, were $35,882 and $4,650, respectively.

(2) When a customer defaults on a contract, the repossessed merchandise is recorded at its approximate wholesale market value in a separate inventory account. Differences between the unpaid balance on the contract and the wholesale value are debited to the Uncollectible Installment Contracts Expense account. Repossessed merchandise is sold on the installment plan.

(3) The wholesale value of repossessed merchandise is determined as follows:
   (a) Merchandise repossessed during year of sale is valued at 40% of original selling price.
   (b) Merchandise repossessed subsequent to the year of sale is valued at 20% of original selling price.

(4) There were no defaulted installment contracts during Year 1. An analysis of installment contracts defaulted and written off during Year 2 follows:

	Original selling price	Unpaid contract balance
Year 1 contracts	$19,500	$10,500
Year 2 contracts	11,000	8,200

(5) On January 1, Year 2, Hilo Sales began granting allowances on merchandise traded in as part payment on new sales. During Year 2, Hilo Sales granted trade-in allowances of $22,600. The wholesale market value of traded-in merchandise was $15,800. All merchandise traded in during the year was sold for cash.

(6) Hilo Sales uses the installment method of accounting for merchandise sold on the installment plan, both for financial accounting and for income tax purposes. The income tax rate is 20%.

Instructions

a Compute the amounts of deferred gross profit on installment sales on December 31, Year 1 and Year 2. Include a supporting computation of the gross profit percentage on installment sales for each year.

b Compute the adjustment (if any) that you would recommend for the Uncollectible Installment Contracts Expense account on December 31, Year 2.

c Prepare an income statement (showing cash sales, installment sales, and total sales) for the year ended December 31, Year 2. A total of 20,000 shares of a single class of capital stock is outstanding. The following supporting exhibits should be prepared:

(1) Unrealized gross profit on Year 2 installment sales

(2) Realized gross profit on Year 1 installment sales

(3) Realized gross profit on sales of traded-in merchandise

15 SEGMENTS; INTERIM REPORTS; ACCOUNTING AND REPORTING FOR THE SEC

In this chapter we deal with three topics that have received considerable attention from accountants in recent years. Reporting for segments of a business enterprise and interim reports have been the subject of pronouncements of the FASB, the AICPA, and the SEC. In addition, the specialized requirements of accounting and reporting for the SEC by enterprises subject to its jurisdiction have undergone substantial modifications in recent years. All three topics are of considerable significance for accountants who deal with publicly owned business enterprises.

SEGMENT REPORTING

An *industry segment* is "a component of an enterprise engaged in providing a product or service or a group of related products and services primarily to unaffiliated customers (i.e., customers outside the enterprise) for a profit."[1] Another term usually considered synonymous with "industry segment" is *line of business.*

The wave of *conglomerate* business combinations in recent years, involving companies in different industries or markets, led to consideration of appropriate methods for reporting financial data for industry segments. Financial analysts and others interested in comparing one highly diversified business enterprise with another found that consolidated financial statements did not supply enough information for meaningful comparative statistics regarding operations of the diversified enterprises in specific industries.

---

[1] *FASB Statement No. 14,* "Financial Reporting for Segments of a Business Enterprise," FASB (Stamford: 1976), p. 5.

Background of segment reporting

The FASB has traced the history of segment reporting from the start of hearings in 1964 before the U.S. Senate Judiciary Committee's Subcommittee on Antitrust and Monopoly. The Subcommittee was considering economic concentration in American industry, especially in the so-called conglomerate (diversified) business enterprises.

Out of these hearings came a great deal of discussion among academicians, members of Congress, SEC officials, financial analysts, business executives, and AICPA representatives regarding the propriety of financial reporting for segments of a business enterprise. The concept of segment reporting was controversial because it was opposed to the philosophy that consolidated financial statements, rather than separate financial statements, fairly present the financial position and operating results of an economic entity, regardless of the legal or industry-segment structure of the entity.

In 1976, the FASB issued **FASB Statement No. 14,** "Financial Reporting for Segments of a Business Enterprise." The principal provisions of this **Statement** were as follows:[2]

> When an enterprise issues a complete set of financial statements that present financial position at the end of the enterprise's fiscal year and results of operations and changes in financial position for that fiscal year in conformity with generally accepted accounting principles, those financial statements shall include certain information relating to:
>
> *1* The enterprise's operations in different industries . . .
> *2* Its foreign operations and export sales . . .
> *3* Its major customers . . .
>
> If such statements are presented for more than one fiscal year, the information required by this Statement shall be presented for each such year, . . .

Initially, the disclosure of segment information was required in interim financial reports. However, the FASB rescinded that requirement a year after **FASB Statement No. 14** was issued. Interim reports are discussed in another section of this chapter.

In 1978, **FASB Statement No. 21** suspended the applicability of **FASB Statement No. 14** to nonpublic enterprises, pending completion of a project to determine whether nonpublic enterprises should have financial statement presentation and disclosure requirements that are more limited than those for publicly owned enterprises.

Operations in different industries

To comply with the requirements of **FASB Statement No. 14** regarding a business enterprise, accountants must carry out the following:

1 Specify the industry segments of the enterprise.
2 Compute the following for the specified segments: revenue, operating profit or loss, and identifiable assets.

[2] Ibid., pp. 1–2.

3 Determine which of the specified segments are **significant,** and thus possibly **reportable.**

4 Comply with the maximum and minimum limitations for disclosure of segment information.

5 Develop the required data for disclosure other than those listed in *2* above.

Specification of Industry Segments In developing **FASB Statement No. 14,** the FASB considered whether organizational lines or areas of economic activity, or a combination of both, should be used for segmentation of a business enterprise. The FASB settled on areas of economic activity— industries and geographical areas—as the bases for segmentation. In addition, the FASB required disclosure of information regarding the major customers of a business enterprise.

The FASB established the following guidelines for reporting operations in different industries:[3]

> The reportable segments of an enterprise shall be determined by (a) identifying the individual products and services from which the enterprise derives its revenue, (b) grouping those products and services by industry lines into industry segments . . ., and (c) selecting those industry segments that are significant with respect to the enterprise as a whole. . . .

The FASB decided that none of the systems that had been developed for classifying business activities was satisfactory for determining the industry segments of all business enterprises. Accordingly, the FASB left to enterprise management the determination of an enterprise's industry segments. The Board recommended use of the enterprise's **profit centers,** the smallest units of activity for which revenue and expense information is accumulated for internal management purposes, as a starting point in the identification of the enterprise's industry segments.

Computation of Revenue for Specified Segments A controversial issue in the computation of revenue for industry segments was the inclusion or exclusion of **intersegment sales or transfers.** Proponents of inclusion stated that intersegment sales or transfers are a significant element of the revenue of some industry segments, and that exclusion of those items would seriously understate segment revenue. Opponents countered that intersegment sales or transfers do not result from arm's-length transactions between parties of opposing interests. The FASB essentially compromised between the two positions on intersegment sales or transfers, as indicated in the following:[4]

> *Revenue.* Sales to unaffiliated customers and sales or transfers to other industry segments of the enterprise shall be separately disclosed in presenting revenue of a reportable segment. . . . for purposes of this Statement sales or transfers to other industry segments shall be accounted for on the basis used by the enterprise to price the intersegment sales or transfers. The basis of accounting for intersegment sales or transfers shall be disclosed. If the basis is changed, disclosure shall be made of the nature of the change and its effect on the reportable segments' operating profit or loss in the period of change.

[3] Ibid., p. 8.
[4] Ibid., p. 13.

Computation of Operating Profit or Loss for Specified Segments Even more controversial than the status of intersegment sales or transfers was the question of what measurement of operating results was appropriate for industry segments that are not separate accounting entities. The two extreme positions on reporting operating results for segments were (a) *a net income* should be reported for each segment, and (b) *no income amount* should be reported for a segment. Proponents of a net income presentation for segments, while recognizing that a number of assumptions may underlie the computation of net income, maintained that difficulties of estimation and computation should not preclude the reporting of a segment net income amount that potentially would be useful to investors and creditors.

The opposing position was that the arbitrary nature of many allocations of common costs, interest, and income taxes to segments makes the resultant net income amounts misleading rather than informative. Opponents of reporting segment net income cited as one allocation problem the difficulty of allocating income taxes to segments. Income tax allocation is difficult because of the existence of various tax avoidance alternatives to a diversified corporation, the differences between income tax liabilities when a consolidated income tax return is filed as compared with separate tax returns, and the existence of net operating loss carrybacks and carryforwards.

Some accountants advocated a compromise position between the two extremes. These accountants supported a segment contribution approach for reporting a segment's operating results. *Segment contribution* is defined as segment sales less *traceable expenses,* those expenses directly identified with a particular segment.[5]

The FASB took the following position on disclosure of segment income:[6]

> *Profitability.* Operating profit or loss . . ., defined . . . (as a segment's revenue minus all operating expenses, including expenses not directly traceable to the segment,) . . . shall be presented for each reportable segment. As part of its segment information, an enterprise shall explain the nature and amount of any unusual or infrequently occurring items . . . reported in its consolidated income statement that have been added or deducted in computing the operating profit or loss of a reportable segment. . . . Methods used to allocate operating expenses among industry segments in computing operating profit or loss should be consistently applied from period to period (but, if changed, disclosure shall be made of the nature of the change and its effect on the reportable segments' operating profit or loss in the period of change).

The FASB required that expenses not directly traceable to a segment should be allocated to each benefited segment on a **reasonable basis.** However, the following should never be included in the computation of

---

[5] *FASB Discussion Memorandum,* "An Analysis of Issues Related to Financial Reporting for Segments of a Business Enterprise," FASB (Stamford: 1974), pp. 29—30.
[6] *FASB Statement No. 14,* pp. 6, 13.

the operating profit or loss of a reportable segment:[7]

Revenue earned at the corporate level and not derived from the operations of any industry segment

General corporate expenses (incurred at an enterprise's central administrative office)

Interest expense

Domestic and foreign income taxes

Equity in income or loss from unconsolidated subsidiaries and other unconsolidated investees

Gain or loss on discontinued operations

Extraordinary items

Minority interest in net income of subsidiaries

Cumulative effect of a change in accounting principles

A "reasonable basis" for the allocation of expenses not directly traceable to a segment might be found in a pronouncement of the Cost Accounting Standards Board (CASB). In **Cost Accounting Standard (CAS) 403,** "Allocation of Home Office Expenses to Segments," the CASB provided a three-factor formula for the allocation of residual home office expenses to segments. The percentage of residual home office expenses to be allocated to a segment was the **arithmetic average** of the following three percentages for a fiscal period:[8]

1 Segment payroll dollars divided by total payroll dollars of all segments

2 Segment operating revenue (including intersegment transfers out, and reduced by intersegment transfers in) divided by total operating revenue of all segments

3 Segment average plant assets and inventories, at carrying amounts, divided by total carrying amount of average plant assets and inventories of all segments

Illustration of Allocation of Nontraceable Expenses To illustrate the allocation of nontraceable expenses to industry segments under the provisions of **CAS 403,** assume the data at the top of page 662 for the home office and two industry segments of Multiproduct Corporation for the year ended April 30, Year 7 (there were no intersegment transfers for the year). The three-factor formula under **CAS 403** is computed for Multiproduct Corporation in the middle of page 662.

The $200,000 amount of nontraceable expenses of the home office of Multiproduct Corporation is allocated to the two segments as follows:

Allocation of nontraceable expenses

To Chemical Products segment: $200,000 × 0.42	*$ 84,000*
To Food Products segment: $200,000 × 0.58	*116,000*
Total nontraceable expenses	*$200,000*

[7] Ibid., pp. 6–7.
[8] *Cost Accounting Standard 403*, sec. 403.50(c)(1).

Data for home office and two industry segments

	Home office	Chemical products	Food products	Total
Net sales (operating revenue) .		$550,000	$ 450,000	$1,000,000
Traceable expenses		$300,000	$ 350,000	$ 650,000
Nontraceable expenses	$200,000			200,000
Total expenses	$200,000	$300,000	$ 350,000	$ 850,000
Income before income taxes . .				$ 150,000
Income taxes expense				90,000
Net income				$ 60,000
Payroll dollars	$ 60,000	$160,000	$ 240,000	$ 460,000
Average plant assets and inventories	$ 80,000	$620,000	$1,380,000	$2,080,000

Computation of three-factor formula

	Chemical products		Food products	
Ratio of segment payroll dollars	$ 160,000 / $ 400,000 =	40%	$ 240,000 / $ 400,000 =	60%
Ratio of segment operating revenue	$ 550,000 / $1,000,000 =	55%	$ 450,000 / $1,000,000 =	45%
Ratio of average plant assets and inventories	$ 620,000 / $2,000,000 =	31%	$1,380,000 / $2,000,000 =	69%
Totals		126%		174%
Arithmetic averages (divide by 3) . .		42%		58%

Operating profit (loss) for the two industry segments of Multiproduct Corporation is computed as follows:

Operating profit (loss) of two industry segments

	Chemical products	Food products	Total
Net sales	$550,000	$450,000	$1,000,000
Traceable expenses	$300,000	$350,000	$ 650,000
Nontraceable expenses	84,000	116,000	200,000
Total expenses	$384,000	$466,000	$ 850,000
Operating profit (loss)	$166,000	$ (16,000)	$ 150,000

The authors question the wisdom of applying such an arbitrary formula to the allocation of nontraceable expenses to segments for financial reporting purposes. The CASB allocation formula appears to be one of expediency rather than theoretical soundness. This is borne out in the preceding illustration by the operating loss attributed to the Food Products segment of Multiproduct Corporation. The Food Products segment had higher ratios of payroll dollars and average plant assets and inventories, and thus was charged with a larger amount of non-traceable expenses. It does not necessarily follow that a direct correlation exists between nontraceable expenses and the aggregate amount of payroll dollars, plant assets, and inventories.

Computation of Identifiable Assets for Specified Segments No significant controversy was generated by the FASB's guidelines for the computation of identifiable assets for an industry segment, which are summarized below:[9]

> *Identifiable assets.* The identifiable assets of an industry segment are those tangible and intangible enterprise assets that are used by the industry segment, including (i) assets that are used exclusively by that industry segment and (ii) an allocated portion of assets used jointly by two or more industry segments. Assets used jointly by two or more industry segments shall be allocated among the industry segments on a reasonable basis. Because the assets of an industry segment that transfers products or services to another industry segment are not used in the operations of the receiving segment, no amount of those assets shall be allocated to the receiving segment. Assets that represent part of an enterprise's investment in an industry segment, such as goodwill, shall be included in the industry segment's identifiable assets. Assets maintained for general corporate purposes (i.e., those not used in the operations of any industry segment) shall not be allocated to industry segments. The identifiable assets of an industry segment shall not include advances or loans to or investments in another industry segment, except that advances or loans to other industry segments shall be included in the identifiable assets of a financial segment because the income therefrom is included in computing the financial segment's operating profit or loss . . . . Asset valuation allowances such as the following shall be taken into account in computing the amount of an industry segment's identifiable assets: allowance for doubtful accounts, accumulated depreciation, and marketable equity securities valuation allowance.

Determination of Significant Segments After an enterprise has identified its industry segments, its *significant segments* must be determined. The FASB decided that an industry segment is *significant,* and thus potentially a *reportable segment,* if it meets *one or more* of the following tests:[10]

> *1* Its revenue (including both sales to unaffiliated customers and intersegment sales or transfers) is 10% or more of the combined revenue (sales to unaffiliated customers and intersegment sales or transfers) of all of the enterprise's industry segments.
>
> *2* The absolute amount of its operating profit or operating loss is 10% or more of the greater, in absolute amount, of:
>   (a) The combined operating profit of all industry segments that did not incur an operating loss, or

[9] Ibid., pp. 7–8.
[10] Ibid., p. 10.

(b) The combined operating loss of all industry segments that did incur an operating loss. . . .

3 Its identifiable assets are 10% or more of the combined identifiable assets of all industry segments.

To illustrate the determination of significant industry segments of a business enterprise, assume that the four industry segments of Diverso, Inc., had the following revenue, operating profit or losses, and identifiable assets for the year ended December 31, Year 5:

	\multicolumn{4}{c}{Segment}			
	A	**B**	**C**	**D**	**Total**
Revenue.	$ 60,000	$ 80,000	$ 20,000	$ 50,000	$ 210,000
Operating profit					
(loss)	(20,000)	30,000	(10,000)	30,000	30,000
Identifiable					
assets	500,000	400,000	100,000	300,000	1,300,000

Segments A, B, and D of Diverso, Inc., meet the revenue test for significance because their revenue exceeds $21,000, which is 10% of total revenue of all four segments ($210,000 × 0.10 = $21,000). Segment C does not meet the revenue test for significance; its revenue of $20,000 is less than the $21,000 minimum. However, Segment C does meet the operating profit or loss test for significance, because the absolute amount of its operating loss—$10,000—exceeds $6,000, which is 10% of total operating profit of Segment B and Segment D [($30,000 + $30,000) × 0.10 = $6,000]. The $60,000 total operating profit was used for the test because it exceeded the $30,000 absolute amount total of the combined operating losses of Segment A and Segment C ($20,000 + $10,000 = $30,000). Because all four industry segments meet either the revenue test or the operating profit or loss test for significance, the identifiable assets test is not used.

Limitations on Disclosure of Segment Information   Because of the three possible methods for a segment to be considered **significant,** as described in the preceding section, the FASB placed both minimum and maximum limits on the number of significant segments to be considered **reportable,** and thus included in the disclosures for industry segments in the annual report of the business enterprise. If such limits had not been provided, an inordinate number of segments might have been reported. The limitations established by the FASB were as follows:[11]

1 The combined revenue from sales to unaffiliated customers of **all reportable segments** must constitute at least 75% of the combined revenue from sales to unaffiliated customers of **all industry segments.** (Minimum)

[11] Ibid., pp. 11, 12.

2 The number of reportable segments generally *should not exceed ten.* Closely related industry segments might be combined into a single reportable segment to achieve the limit of ten. (Maximum)

3 Disclosures required for reportable segments do not apply to a *dominant segment,* defined as a segment whose revenue, operating profit or loss, and identifiable assets each constitute more than 90% of related combined totals for all industry segments, with no other industry segment meeting the 10% test. However, the financial statements of an enterprise having a dominant industry segment, or operating in a single industry, must identify the industry.

Required Data to Be Disclosed for Reportable Segments In addition to revenue, operating profit or loss, and identifiable assets, the following disclosures were required by the FASB for reportable segments:[12]

1 Depreciation, depletion, and amortization

2 Additions to plant assets

3 Equity in net income and net assets of unconsolidated subsidiaries and influenced investees whose operations are integrated vertically with those of the segment

4 Effect of a change in accounting principle on segment operating profit or loss.

Operations in foreign areas and export sales

In *FASB Statement No. 14,* the FASB required business enterprises that operate in foreign geographic areas (individual foreign countries or groups of countries) to report information for each *significant foreign geographic area,* and in the aggregate for all other foreign geographic areas that are not significant. A foreign geographic area is considered significant if its revenue from sales to unaffiliated customers or its identifiable assets are at least 10% of related total amounts in the enterprise's financial statements. Comparable information is required for the enterprise's domestic operations, unless the domestic operations do not meet the same 10% test for significance.[13] Further, the FASB required information regarding *export sales* in the financial statements of enterprises whose export sales exceed 10% of total sales to unaffiliated customers.[14]

Major customers

Disclosure also is required of the revenue from sales to any single *major customer,* or from sales to individual domestic or foreign governments, which represent 10% or more of total sales of the enterprise. Also, the industry segment making the sales must be identified.[15] This informa-

[12] Ibid., p. 14.
[13] Ibid., p. 17.
[14] Ibid., p. 18.
[15] Ibid., p. 19; also, *FASB Statement No. 30,* "Disclosure of Information about Major Customers," FASB (Stamford: 1979), pp. 2–3.

tion is of significance to users of financial statements because of the adverse effects that might arise when a business enterprise loses a major customer.

Presentation of segment information, operations in foreign areas, and related disclosures

The FASB approved the following alternative methods for disclosure of information about the reportable segments and foreign operations of a business enterprise:[16]

1 Within financial statements, with appropriate explanatory disclosures in the notes to the financial statements.

2 Entirely in the notes to the financial statements.

3 In a separate schedule that is included as an integral part of the financial statements. If, in a report to securityholders, that schedule is located on a page that is not clearly a part of the financial statements, the schedule shall be referenced in the financial statements as an integral part thereof.

The financial statements of Walt Disney Productions in Appendix 2 illustrate the first of the foregoing methods. The basic segment information is included in the income statement on page 711; Note 5 on page 717 and the summary of significant accounting policies on page 714 provide additional data on segments of Walt Disney Productions.

SEC requirements for segment information

The requirements of the SEC for reporting of segment information are in **Regulation S-K,** which outlines non-financial statement information that must be included in reports to the SEC. The **Form 10-K** of Walt Disney Productions in Appendix 1, under "Item 1. Business" on pages 686 to 690, illustrates the disclosure of segment information required by **Regulation S-K.** (Both **Regulation S-K** and **Form 10-K** are discussed in a subsequent section of this chapter.)

Reporting the disposal of a segment of a business enterprise

To this point, we have discussed accounting standards developed by the Financial Accounting Standards Board for financial reporting for segments of a business enterprise. We conclude our consideration of segment reporting with the reporting for effects of the disposal of a segment of a business enterprise.

In 1973, the Accounting Principles Board issued **APB Opinion No. 30,** "Reporting the Results of Operations . . ." The APB's conclusions included the following with respect to disposal of a segment of a business enterprise:[17]

---

[16] *FASB Statement No. 14,* p. 15.

[17] *APB Opinion No. 30,* "Reporting the Results of Operations— . . .," AICPA (New York: 1973), pp. 558–559.

For purposes of this Opinion, the term **discontinued operations** refers to the operations of a segment of a business . . . that has been sold, abandoned, spun off, or otherwise disposed of or, although still operating, is the subject of a formal plan for disposal. . . . The Board concludes that the results of continuing operations should be reported separately from discontinued operations and that any gain or loss from disposal of a segment of a business . . . should be reported in conjunction with the related results of discontinued operations and not as an extraordinary item. Accordingly, operations of a segment that has been or will be discontinued should be reported separately as a component of income before extraordinary items and the cumulative effect of accounting changes (if applicable) in the following manner:

Income from continuing operations before income taxes	$XXXX	
Provision for income taxes	XXX	
Income from continuing operations		$XXXX
Discontinued operations (Note __):		
Income (loss) from operations of discontinued Division X (less applicable income taxes of $____) . .	$XXXX	
Loss on disposal of Division X, including provision of $____ for operating losses during phase-out period (less applicable income taxes of $____) . . .	XXXX	XXXX
Net income		$XXXX

Amounts of income taxes applicable to the results of discontinued operations and the gain or loss from disposal of the segment should be disclosed on the face of the income statement or in related notes. Revenues applicable to the discontinued operations should be separately disclosed in the related notes.

The provisions of **APB Opinion No. 30** are discussed in the following sections.

Income from Continuing Operations   The purpose of the income from continuing operations amount is to provide a basis of comparison in the comparative income statements of a business enterprise that has discontinued a segment of its operations. In order for the income from continuing operations amounts to be comparable, the operating results of the discontinued segment of its operations **must be excluded from income from continuing operations for all accounting periods presented in comparative income statements.** For example, in comparative income statements for the three years ended December 31, Year 7, for Wexler Company, which disposed of one of its five divisions during Year 7, the income from continuing operations amounts for Years 5 and 6, as well as for Year 7, exclude the operating results of the discontinued division.

Income (Loss) from Discontinued Operations   The income or loss, net of applicable income taxes, of Wexler Company's discontinued operations (division) is included in its entirety in this section of Wexler's income statement for Years 5 and 6. For Year 7, the net-of-tax income or loss of the discontinued operations is for the period from January 1, Year 7, until the **measurement date,** defined as the date on which management of Wexler committed itself to a formal plan for disposal of the division. Assuming a measurement date of September 30, Year 7, Wexler's Year 7 income statement would include the income or loss of the discontinued operations, net of income taxes, for the nine months ended September 30, Year 7, under the caption "Income (loss) from operations of discontinued Division ___."

Gain (Loss) on Disposal of Discontinued Operations   Included in the gain or loss on discontinued operations are the following:

1 Income or loss from discontinued operations during phase-out period. The **phase-out period** is the period between the **measurement date** and the **disposal date**—the date of closing the sale of the discontinued operations or ceasing the operations of an abandoned segment.
2 The gain or loss on the sale or abandonment of the industry segment.
3 The income taxes applicable to *1* and *2* above.

If the measurement date and the disposal date are in the same accounting period, the income statement for that period reflects actual amounts for income from continuing operations, income (loss) from discontinued operations, and gain (loss) on disposal of discontinued operations. However, if the disposal date is in an accounting period subsequent to the period of the measurement date, management of the enterprise must estimate on the measurement date whether disposal of the discontinued operations, including operating results of the phase-out period, will result in a gain or a loss, net of income taxes. If a **gain** is anticipated, it is not recorded until the **disposal date;** if a **loss** is expected, it must be recorded on the **measurement date.**

Computation of the gain or loss on disposal of an industry segment may be a difficult process, especially if the disposal date is a considerable period of time after the measurement date. To assist in such a computation, the APB provided the following guidelines:[18]

> The determination of whether a gain or a loss results from the disposal of a segment of a business should be made at the measurement date based on estimates at that date of the net realizable value of the segment after giving consideration to any estimated costs and expenses directly associated with the disposal and, if a plan of disposal is to be carried out over a period of time and contemplates continuing operations during that period, to any estimated income or losses from operations. If it is expected that net losses from operations will be incurred between the measurement date and the expected disposal date, the computation of the gain or loss on disposal should also include an estimate of such amounts. If it is expected that income will be generated from operations during that period, the computation of the gain or loss should include the estimated income, limited however to the amount of any loss otherwise recognizable from the disposal; any remainder should be accounted for as income when realized. The Board believes that the estimated amounts of income or loss from operations of a segment between measurement date and disposal date included in the determination of loss on disposal should be limited to those amounts that can be projected with reasonable accuracy. In the usual circumstance, it would be expected that the plan of disposal would be carried out within a period of one year from the measurement date and that such projections of operating income or loss would not cover a period exceeding approximately one year.

[18] Ibid., pp. 562–563.

Gain or loss from the disposal of a segment of a business should not include adjustments, costs, and expenses associated with normal business activities that should have been recognized on a going-concern basis up to the measurement date, such as adjustments of accruals on long-term contracts or write-down or write-off of receivables, inventories, property, plant, and equipment used in the business, equipment leased to others, or intangible assets. However, such adjustments, costs, and expenses which (a) are clearly a *direct* result of the decision to dispose of the segment and (b) are clearly not the adjustments of carrying amounts or costs, or expenses that should have been recognized on a going-concern basis prior to the measurement date should be included in determining the gain or loss on disposal. Results of operations before the measurement date should not be included in the gain or loss on disposal.

Costs and expenses *directly* associated with the decision to dispose include items such as severance pay, additional pension costs, employee relocation expenses, and future rentals on long-term leases to the extent they are not offset by sub-lease rentals.

Disclosure of Disposal of a Segment Because of the significance of discontinued operations in the financial history of a business enterprise, the APB required the following disclosures:[19]

In addition to the amounts that should be disclosed in the financial statements . . ., the notes to financial statements for the period encompassing the measurement date should disclose:

1 The identity of the segment of business that has been or will be discontinued.

2 The expected disposal date, if known.

3 The expected manner of disposal.

4 A description of the remaining assets and liabilities of the segment at the balance sheet date.

5 The income or loss from operations and any proceeds from disposal of the segment during the period from the measurement date to the date of the balance sheet.

An example of disclosure of discontinued operations, taken from the annual report of a publicly owned company, follows:

	Year ended Sept. 30,	
	Year 10	Year 9
Income from continuing operations . . .	$ 94,024,000	$60,919,000
Discontinued operations **(Note X):**		
Income from operations (less applicable income taxes of $10,450,000 and $8,300,000, respectively)	12,294,000	9,526,000
Gain on sale (less applicable income taxes of $25,976,000)	46,424,000	
Net income	$152,742,000	$70,445,000
		(Continued)

[19] Ibid., pp. 563–564.

Note X: Discontinued Operations

On August 25, Year 10, the Company sold its Ogas Division, for $130,000,000 cash. The Ogas Division was engaged principally in the manufacture of equipment for drilling of oil and gas wells. As a result of this disposition, the Company recognized a gain on disposal of $46,424,000, net of related income taxes of $25,976,000.

The Year 10 results of operations of the discontinued Ogas Division have been segregated in the income statement to show separately the results of continuing operations. Similarly, Year 9 and prior income statements have been restated to show the same segregation. The Ogas Division results of operations are reported without allocation of general corporate expenses or interest expense. The net sales of the Ogas Division were $110,009,000 and $88,226,000 for the period ended August 24, Year 10 (the disposal date), and the year ended September 30, Year 9, respectively.

INTERIM FINANCIAL REPORTS

Generally, financial statements are issued for the fiscal year of a business enterprise. However, many enterprises issue complete financial statements for interim accounting periods during the course of a fiscal year. For example, a closely held company with outstanding bank loans may be required to provide monthly or quarterly financial statements to the lending bank. However, interim financial statements usually are associated with the *quarterly reports* issued by publicly owned companies to their shareholders, the SEC, and the stock exchanges that list their capital stock. The New York Stock Exchange's listing agreement requires listed companies to publish quarterly financial reports. Companies subject to the periodic reporting requirements of the SEC must file Form 10-Q with the Commission 45 days after the end of each of the first three quarters of their fiscal years. In addition, the SEC requires disclosure of operating results for each quarter of the two most recent fiscal years in a "supplementary financial information" section of the annual report.[20]

Problems in interim financial reports

Except for 10-Q quarterly reports filed with the SEC, the form, content, and accounting practices for interim financial reports were left to the discretion of business enterprises until 1973. In that year, the Accounting Principles Board issued *Opinion No. 28,* "Interim Financial Reporting." Prior to the issuance of *Opinion No. 28,* there were unresolved problems regarding interim financial reports, including the following:

1 Enterprises employed a wider variety of accounting practices and estimating techniques for interim financial reports than they used in the annual financial statements examined by independent auditors. The enterprises' implicit view was that any misstatements in interim financial reports would be corrected by auditors' adjustments for the annual financial statements.

---

[20] *Regulation S-K,* Item 302(a), Securities and Exchange Commission (Washington).

2 Seasonal fluctuations in revenue and irregular incurrence of costs and expenses during the course of a business enterprise's fiscal year limited the comparability of operating results for interim periods of the fiscal year. Furthermore, time constraints in the issuance of interim statements limited the available time to accumulate end-of-period data for inventories, payables, and related expenses.

3 Accountants held two divergent views on the theoretical issues underlying interim financial statements. These differing views are described below:[21]

a Under the **discrete theory,** each interim period is viewed as a **basic accounting period;** thus, the results of operations for each interim period are determined in essentially the same manner as if the interim period were an annual accounting period. Under this theory, deferrals, accruals, and estimations at the end of each interim period are determined by following essentially the same principles and estimates or judgments that apply to annual periods.

b Under the **integral theory,** each interim period is viewed primarily as being an **integral part of the annual period.** Under this theory, deferrals, accruals, and estimates at the end of each interim period are affected by judgments made at the interim date as to results of operations for the balance of the annual period. Thus, an expense item that might be considered as falling entirely within an annual period (no fiscal year-end accrual or deferral) could be allocated among interim periods based on estimated time, sales volume, production volume, or some other basis.

The problems discussed in the preceding section led to a number of examples of published interim income statements with substantial quarterly earnings, and the income statements for the year showing a net loss.

APB Opinion No. 28

In 1973, the Accounting Principles Board issued **APB Opinion No. 28,** "Interim Financial Reporting." The stated objectives for the Opinion were to provide guidance on accounting and disclosure issues peculiar to interim reporting and to set forth minimum disclosure requirements for interim financial reports of publicly owned enterprises.[22] One part of the Opinion dealt with standards for determining interim financial information and another covered disclosure of summarized interim financial data by publicly owned enterprises. In **APB Opinion No. 28,** the Accounting Principles Board adopted the **integral theory:** that interim periods should be considered as integral parts of the annual accounting period.

The Accounting Principles Board established guidelines for the following components of interim financial reports: revenue, costs associated with revenue, all other costs and expenses, and income tax provisions. These guidelines are discussed in the following sections.

Revenue According to **APB Opinion No. 28,** revenue from products sold or services rendered should be recognized as **earned during an interim period on the same basis as followed for the full year.** Further, enter-

---

[21] *APB Opinion No. 28,* "Interim Financial Reporting," AICPA (New York: 1973), p. 521.
[22] Ibid., p. 522.

prises having significant seasonal variations in revenue should disclose the seasonal nature of their activities.[23]

Costs Associated with Revenue   Costs and expenses associated directly with or allocated to products sold or services rendered include costs of material, direct labor, and factory overhead. *APB Opinion No. 28* required the same accounting for these costs and expenses in interim financial reports as in fiscal year financial statements.[24] However, the *Opinion* provided the following exceptions with respect to determination of cost of goods sold for interim financial reports:[25]

1 Enterprises that use the *gross profit* method at interim dates to estimate cost of goods sold should disclose this fact in interim financial reports. In addition, any material adjustments reconciling estimated interim inventories with annual physical inventories should be disclosed.

2 Enterprises that use the *lifo inventory method* and *temporarily* deplete base layer of inventories during an interim reporting period should include in cost of goods sold for the interim period the estimated *cost of replacing the depleted lifo base layer.*

To illustrate, assume that Megan Company, which uses the lifo inventory method, temporarily depleted its base layer of inventories with a cost of $80,000 during the second quarter of the year ending December 31, Year 6. Replacement cost of the depleted base layer was $100,000 on June 30, Year 6. In addition to the usual debit to Cost of Goods Sold and credit to Inventories for the quarter ended June 30, Year 6, which would include the $80,000 amount from the base layer, Megan prepares the following journal entry on June 30, Year 6:

Journal entry for temporary depletion of base layer of lifo inventories

Cost of Goods Sold ($100,000 − $80,000)	*20,000*	
Liability Arising from Depletion of Base Layer of Lifo Inventories		*20,000*
To record obligation to replenish temporarily depleted base layer of lifo inventories.		

Assuming merchandise with a total cost of $172,000 was purchased by Megan on July 6, Year 6, the following journal entry is required:

Journal entry for restoration of base layer

Inventories ($172,000 − $20,000)	*152,000*	
Liability Arising from Depletion of Base Layer of Lifo Inventories	*20,000*	
Accounts Payable		*172,000*
To record purchase of merchandise and restoration of depleted base layer of lifo inventories.		

[23] Ibid., pp. 523, 527.
[24] Ibid., p. 524.
[25] Ibid., pp. 524–525.

3 Lower-of-cost-or-market write-downs of inventories should be provided for interim periods as for complete fiscal years, unless the interim date market declines in inventory are considered **temporary,** and not applicable at the end of the fiscal year. If an inventory market write-down in one interim period is offset by an inventory market price **increase** in a subsequent interim period, **a gain is recognized in the subsequent period to the extent of the loss recognized in preceding interim periods of the fiscal year.**

For example, assume that Reynolds Company, which uses lower-of-cost-or-market fifo accounting for its single merchandise item, had 10,000 units of merchandise with fifo cost of $50,000, or $5 a unit, in inventory at the beginning of Year 3. Assume further for simplicity that Reynolds made no purchases during Year 3. Quarterly sales and end-of-quarter replacement costs for inventory were as follows during Year 3:

<table>
<tr><td style="text-align:right">Quarterly sales and
end-of-quarter
replacement costs for
inventory</td><td>

Quarter	Quarterly sales (units)	End-of-quarter inventory replacement cost (per unit)
1	2,000	$6
2	1,500	4
3	2,000	7
4	1,200	3

</td></tr>
</table>

If the market decline in the second quarter was not considered to be **temporary,** Reynolds Company's cost of goods sold for the four quarters of Year 3 would be computed as follows:

<table>
<tr><td style="text-align:right">Computation of
quarterly cost of goods
sold</td><td>

Quarter	Computation for quarter	Cost of goods sold For quarter	Cumulative
1	2,000 × $5	$10,000	$10,000
2	(1,500 × $5) + (6,500 + $1)*	14,000	24,000
3	(2,000 × $4) − (4,500 × $1)†	3,500	27,500
4	(1,200 × $5) + (3,300 × $2)‡	12,600	40,100

</td></tr>
</table>

* 6,500 units remaining in inventory multiplied by $1 write-down to lower replacement cost.
† 4,500 units remaining in inventory multiplied by $1 write-up to original cost.
‡ 3,300 units remaining in inventory multiplied by $2 write-down to lower replacement cost.

The $40,100 cumulative cost of goods sold for Reynolds Company for Year 3 may be verified as follows:

<table>
<tr><td style="text-align:right">Verification of
cumulative cost of
goods sold</td><td>

6,700 units sold during Year 3, at $5 fifo cost per unit.	$33,500
Write-down of Year 3 ending inventory to replacement cost (3,300 units × $2).	6,600
Cost of goods sold for Year 3	$40,100
Alternative verification:	
Cost of goods available for sale (10,000 × $5)	$50,000
Less: Ending inventory, at lower of cost or market (3,300 × $3).	9,900
Cost of goods sold for Year 3	$40,100

</td></tr>
</table>

4 Enterprises using standard costs for inventories and cost of goods sold generally should report standard cost variances for interim periods as they do for fiscal years. Planned materials price variances and volume or capacity variances should be deferred at the end of interim periods if the variances are expected to be absorbed by the end of the fiscal year.

All Other Costs and Expenses   The following guidelines for all costs and expenses other than those associated with revenue are set forth in *APB Opinion No. 28:* [26]

> Costs and expenses other than product costs should be charged to income in interim periods as incurred, or be allocated among interim periods based on an estimate of time expired, benefit received or activity associated with the periods. Procedures adopted for assigning specific cost and expense items to an interim period should be consistent with the bases followed by the company in reporting results of operations at annual reporting dates. However, when a specific cost or expense item charged to expense for annual reporting purposes benefits more than one interim period, the cost or expense item may be allocated to those interim periods.
>
> Some costs and expenses incurred in an interim period, however, cannot be readily identified with the activities or benefits of other interim periods and should be charged to the interim period in which incurred. Disclosure should be made as to the nature and amount of such costs unless items of a comparable nature are included in both the current interim period and in the corresponding interim period of the preceding year.
>
> Arbitrary assignment of the amount of such costs to an interim period should not be made.
>
> Gains and losses that arise in any interim period similar to those that would not be deferred at year-end should not be deferred to later interim periods within the same fiscal year. . . .
>
> The amounts of certain costs and expenses are frequently subjected to year-end adjustments even though they can be reasonably approximated at interim dates. To the extent possible such adjustments should be estimated and the estimated costs and expenses assigned to interim periods so that the interim periods bear a reasonable portion of the anticipated annual amount. Examples of such items include inventory shrinkage, allowance for uncollectible accounts, allowance for quantity discounts, and discretionary year-end bonuses.

APB Opinion No. 28 includes a number of specific applications of the foregoing guidelines.

Income Tax Provisions   The techniques for computing income tax provisions in interim financial reports were described as follows in *APB Opinion No. 28:* [27]

> At the end of each interim period the company should make its best estimate of the effective tax rate expected to be applicable for the full fiscal year. The rate so determined should be used in providing for income taxes on a current year-to-date basis. The effective tax rate should reflect anticipated investment tax credits, foreign tax rates, percentage depletion, capital gains rates, and other available tax planning alternatives. However, in arriving at this effective

[26] Ibid., pp. 525–527.
[27] Ibid., pp. 527–528.

tax rate no effect should be included for the tax related to significant unusual or extraordinary items that will be separately reported or reported net of their related tax effect in reports for the interim period or for the fiscal year.

To illustrate, assume that at the end of the first quarter of Year 7, Carter Company's actual first quarter and forecasted fiscal year operating results were as follows:

	First quarter (actual)	Fiscal year (estimated)
Revenue	$400,000	$1,800,000
Less: Costs and expenses other than income taxes	300,000	1,500,000
Income before income taxes	$100,000	$ 300,000

Actual first quarter and forecasted fiscal year pre-tax accounting income

Assume further that there were no *timing differences* between Carter's pre-tax accounting income and taxable income, but that Carter had the following estimated *permanent differences* between pre-tax accounting income and federal and state taxable income for the fiscal year:

Estimated permanent differences

Dividend received deduction	$17,000
Goodwill amortization	5,000

If Carter's *nominal* federal and state income tax rates total 60%, Carter estimates its *effective* combined income tax rate for Year 7 as follows:

Computation of estimated effective income tax rate

Estimated income before income taxes	$300,000
Add: Nondeductible goodwill amortization	5,000
Less: Dividend received deduction	(17,000)
Estimated taxable income	$288,000
Estimated combined federal and state income taxes ($288,000 × 0.60)	$172,800
Estimated effective combined federal and state income tax rate for Year 7 ($172,800 ÷ $300,000)	57.6%

Carter's journal entry for income taxes for the first quarter of Year 7 is as follows:

Journal entry for income taxes for first quarter of fiscal year

Income Taxes Expense	57,600	
Income Taxes Payable		57,600

To provide for estimated federal and state income taxes for the first quarter of Year 7 as follows: $100,000 × 0.576 = $57,600.

For the second quarter of Year 7, Carter again estimates an effective combined federal and state income tax rate based on more current projections for permanent differences between pre-tax accounting income and taxable income for the entire year. However, the new effective rate *is not applied retroactively* to restate the first quarter's tax expense. For example, assume that Carter's second quarter estimate of the effective combined federal and state income tax rate was 58.2% and that Carter's pre-tax income for the second quarter was $120,000 (or $220,000 for first two quarters). Carter prepares the following journal entry for income taxes expense for the second quarter of Year 7:

Journal entry for income taxes for second quarter of fiscal year

Income Taxes Expense	70,440	
Income Taxes Payable		70,440

To provide for estimated federal and state income taxes for the second quarter of Year 7 as follows:

Cumulative income taxes expense ($220,000 × 0.582)	$128,040
Less: Income taxes provided for first quarter . . .	57,600
Income taxes expense for second quarter	$ 70,440

This computation of income taxes expense for interim periods is a highly simplified example. Many complex aspects of income taxes, such as net operating loss carrybacks and carryforwards, complicate the computations of income taxes for interim periods. *FASB Interpretation No. 18,* "Accounting for Income Taxes in Interim Periods," provides guidance for complex interim period income tax computations.

Reporting accounting changes in interim periods

In 1974, the FASB issued *FASB Statement No. 3,* "Reporting Accounting Changes in Interim Financial Statements," as an amendment to *APB Opinion No. 28.* Following are the two principal provisions of *FASB Statement No. 3:*[28]

> If a cumulative effect type accounting change is made during the *first* interim period of an enterprise's fiscal year, the cumulative effect of the change on retained earnings at the *beginning of that fiscal year* shall be included in net income of the first interim period (and in last-twelve-months-to-date financial reports that include that first interim period).

> If a cumulative effect type accounting change is made in *other than the first* interim period of an enterprise's fiscal year, *no* cumulative effect of the change shall be included in net income of the period of the change. Instead, financial information for the pre-change interim periods of the fiscal year in which the change is made shall be restated by applying the newly adopted accounting principle to those pre-change interim periods. The cumulative effect of the change on retained earnings at the *beginning of that fiscal year* shall be included in restated net income of the first interim period of the fiscal

[28] *FASB Statement No. 3,* "Reporting Accounting Changes in Interim Financial Statements," FASB (Stamford: 1974), p. 4.

year in which the change is made (and in any year-to-date or last-twelve-months-to-date financial reports that include the first interim period). Whenever financial information that includes those pre-change interim periods is presented, it shall be presented on the restated basis.

Disclosure of Interim Financial Data As minimum disclosure, **APB Opinion No. 28** provided that the following data should be included in publicly owned enterprises' interim financial reports to shareholders. The data are to be reported for the most recent quarter and the year to date, or 12 months to date of the quarter's end.[29]

1 Sales or gross revenue, provision for income taxes, extraordinary items (including related income tax effects), cumulative effect of a change in accounting principles or practices, and net income.
2 Primary and fully diluted earnings per share data for each period presented. . . .
3 Seasonal revenue, costs or expenses.
4 Significant changes in estimates or provisions for income taxes.
5 Disposal of a segment of a business and extraordinary, unusual or infrequently occurring items.
6 Contingent items.
7 Changes in accounting principles or estimates.
8 Significant changes in financial position.

An example of the presentation of interim financial data is illustrated in the excerpt from the annual report of Walt Disney Productions, page 721 of Appendix 2.

Conclusions on interim financial reports

APB Opinion No. 28, FASB Statement No. 3, and **FASB Interpretation No. 18** represented a substantial effort to upgrade the quality of interim financial reports. However, controversy continues on the subject of interim financial reporting—especially concerning the APB's premise that an interim period should be accounted for as an integral part of the applicable annual period. In recognition of this controversy and other problems of interim financial reporting, the FASB undertook a comprehensive study of the topic, and issued a **Discussion Memorandum** entitled "Interim Financial Accounting and Reporting." However, because of more pressing matters on its agenda, the FASB abandoned the project a few years later.

ACCOUNTING AND REPORTING FOR THE SEC

The Securities and Exchange Commission (SEC) is an agency of the United States government created in 1934 to oversee the interstate issuances and trading of securities. Since its creation, the SEC's functions have expanded to include administration of the following statutes:

[29] *APB Opinion No. 28*, p. 532.

Securities Act of 1933, governing interstate issuances of securities to the public

Securities Exchange Act of 1934, governing trading of securities on national securities exchanges and over the counter

Public Utility Holding Company Act of 1935, governing interstate public utility holding company systems for electricity and gas

Trust Indenture Act of 1939, governing the issuance of bonds, debentures, and similar debt securities under an indenture meeting the requirements of the Act

Investment Company Act of 1940 and ***Investment Advisers Act of 1940,*** governing operations of investment companies and investment advisers

Here we focus on SEC administration of the Securities Act of 1933 (the 1933 Act) and the Securities Exchange Act of 1934 (the 1934 Act).

Nature of reporting to the SEC

Most publicly owned companies are subject to either or both the 1933 Act and the 1934 Act. Companies planning to issue securities interstate to the public generally must file a ***registration statement*** with the SEC. Companies whose securities are traded on national stock exchanges also must file a registration statement; in addition, periodic reports must be made to the SEC by such companies. Most large companies whose securities are traded over the counter also must report periodically to the SEC.

Registration of Securities The SEC has developed a series of ***forms*** for the registration of securities. ***Forms S-1, S-2,*** and ***S-3*** are used by large companies to register securities to be issued to the public; ***Form S-18*** is used by small companies that issue securities for $5,000,000 or less. The principal form for registering securities for trading on a national exchange or over the counter is ***Form 10.*** The various forms are not a series of blanks to be filled in; they are guides for the ***format of information included in the registration statements.***

Periodic Reporting The principal forms established by the SEC for reporting by companies whose stock is traded on national exchanges or over the counter are ***Form 10-K, Form 10-Q,*** and ***Form 8-K. Form 10-K*** is an annual report to the SEC, which must be filed within 90 days following the close of the company's fiscal year. As indicated by the ***Form 10-K*** of Walt Disney Productions shown in Appendix 1 (pages 685 to 703), much of the information required by ***Form 10-K*** is ***incorporated by reference*** to the annual report to shareholders, which also must be filed with the SEC. (Excerpts from the annual report of Walt Disney Productions are included in Appendix 2, pages 704 to 721.)

Form 10-Q is a quarterly report to the SEC that is due 45 days after the end of each of the first three quarters of the company's fiscal year; a quarterly report for the fourth quarter of the fiscal year is not required.

The condensed financial statements that must be included in **Form 10-Q** are more extensive than the minimum disclosure requirements of **APB Opinion No. 28,** "Interim Financial Reporting" (see page 677), but the **10-Q** financial statements need not be audited.

Form 8-K is a current report that must be filed with the SEC within 15 days of the occurrence of events such as the following:

1 Change in control of the reporting company

2 Acquisition or disposal of assets by the reporting company, including business combinations

3 Bankruptcy or receivership of the reporting company

4 Change of independent auditors for the reporting company

In addition, a company may choose to report to the SEC on **Form 8-K** any other event that it considers important to shareholders.

Another important periodic report to the SEC is a **proxy statement,** which must be filed by companies that solicit proxies for annual meetings of their shareholders. A **preliminary proxy statement** must be filed with the SEC for review and comment prior to distribution of the **definitive proxy statement** to shareholders. Essentially, the proxy statement includes disclosure of all matters to be voted on at the forthcoming meeting of shareholders whose proxies are solicited. If the shareholders are to vote on authorization or issuances of securities, modification or exchanges of securities, or business combinations, the proxy statement must include financial statements of the company and of any proposed combinee.

Organization and functions of the SEC

The SEC is administered by five commissioners appointed for five-year terms by the President and confirmed by the Senate of the United States. No more than three commissioners can be members of the same political party. The organization and scope of the SEC is presented in the organization chart on page 680. In the following sections, we discuss three segments of the SEC: Chief accountant, Division of Corporation Finance, and Division of Enforcement.

Chief Accountant The chief accountant of the SEC, as an expert in accounting, is responsible for issuing pronouncements that establish the SEC's position on matters affecting accounting and auditing. The chief accountant also supervises disciplinary proceedings against accountants charged with violating the SEC's Rules of Practice. The chief accountant cooperates with the FASB and other private organizations interested in research and standards-setting in accounting and auditing.

Division of Corporation Finance The SEC's Division of Corporation Finance is responsible for reviewing the **Forms** and proxy statements filed with the SEC under the 1933 Act and the 1934 Act. The extent of the re-

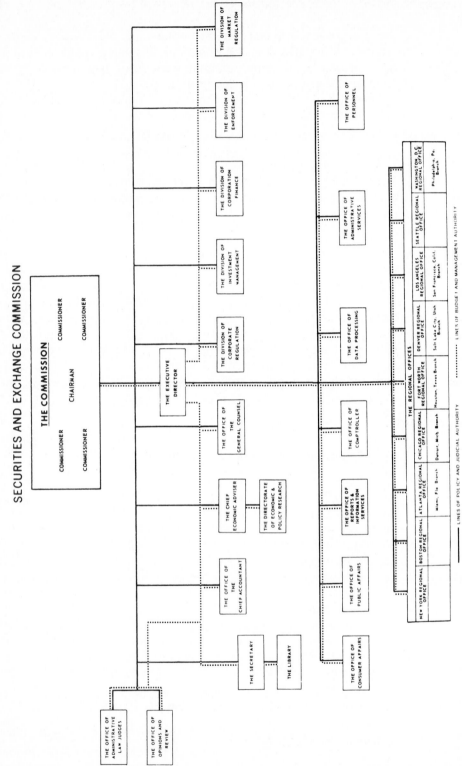

SECURITIES AND EXCHANGE COMMISSION

Source: 42d Annual Report of the SEC for the Fiscal Year Ended June 30, 1976 (Washington: 1977), p. iv, as modified.

views varies, depending on whether the filing company has a history of acceptable reporting to the SEC or is "unseasoned." The Division of Corporation Finance personnel consult with the chief accountant on the propriety of accounting presentations in filings with the SEC. Changes in the various **Forms** and in **Regulation S-X** and **Regulation S-K** are the responsibility of the Division of Corporation Finance.

Division of Enforcement The duties of the SEC's Division of Enforcement involve monitoring the compliance of companies subject to the SEC's jurisdiction with the 1933 Act and the 1934 Act. When noncompliance is ascertained, the Division of Enforcement often will obtain federal court injunctions prohibiting the company from further violations of the two Acts. Many of the notorious criminal indictments involving management fraud in recent years have been obtained through the efforts of the SEC's Division of Enforcement.

Interaction between SEC and FASB

Both the 1933 Act and the 1934 Act empower the SEC to establish rules for the accounting principles underlying financial statements and schedules included in reports filed with the SEC. The SEC rarely has used this authority directly. Instead, it usually has endorsed actions on accounting principles by organizations in the private sector (currently the Financial Accounting Standards Board), while reserving the right to issue its own pronouncements when necessary. This posture of the SEC has been described as follows:[30]

> In ASR 4 the Commission stated its policy that financial statements prepared in accordance with accounting practices for which there was no substantial authoritative support were presumed to be misleading and that footnote or other disclosure would not avoid this presumption. It also stated that, where there was a difference of opinion between the Commission and a registrant as to the proper accounting to be followed in a particular case, disclosure would be accepted in lieu of correction of the financial statements themselves only if substantial authoritative support existed for the accounting practices followed by the registrant and the position of the Commission had not been expressed in rules, regulations or other official releases. For purposes of this policy, principles, standards and practices promulgated by the FASB in its Statements and Interpretations will be considered by the Commission as having substantial authoritative support, and those contrary to such FASB promulgations will be considered to have no such support.
> . . . Information in addition to that included in financial statements conforming to generally accepted accounting principles is also necessary. Such additional disclosures are required to be made in various fashions, such as in financial statements and schedules reported on by independent public accountants or as textual statements required by items in the applicable forms and reports filed with the Commission. The Commission will continue to identify areas where investor information needs exist and will determine the appropriate methods of disclosure to meet these needs.

[30] *Codification of Financial Reporting Policies,* Securities and Exchange Commission (Washington: 1982), Sec. 101.

Thus, the SEC differentiated between **generally accepted accounting principles** and **disclosures** in financial statements and schedules, and expressed an intention to concentrate on pronouncements on disclosures. The principal devices used by the SEC to communicate its requirements for accounting principles and disclosures have been **Regulation S-X, Regulation S-K, Accounting Series Releases, Financial Reporting Releases,** and **Staff Accounting Bulletins.**

Regulation S-X   The SEC issued **Regulation S-X** to provide guidance for the form and content of financial statements and schedules required to be filed with the SEC under the laws that it administers. Since the adoption of **Regulation S-X** in 1940, the SEC has amended the document extensively, including a thorough overhaul in 1980 **(Accounting Series Release No. 280).**

Regulation S-X consists of numerous rules subdivided into 19 articles. Among the significant provisions of **Regulation S-X** are Rule 3-02, which requires audited income statements and statements of changes in financial position for three fiscal years, and Article 12, which illustrates the form and content of schedules to be filed in support of various financial statement items. Excerpts from the annual report of Walt Disney Productions in Appendix 2 (pages 711 and 713) illustrate the three-year comparative financial statements. Certain schedules illustrated in **Regulation S-X** are included in the **Form 10-K** of Walt Disney Productions in Appendix 1 (pages 698 to 702).

Regulation S-K   The SEC issued **Regulation S-K** in 1977 to provide guidance for the completion of non-financial statement disclosure requirements in the various **Forms** filed under the 1933 Act and the 1934 Act. As amended since its adoption, **Regulation S-K** contains 27 items of disclosure. Items 1 through 10 of the **Form 10-K** of Walt Disney Productions in Appendix 1 (pages 686 to 694) are in the format specified by **Regulation S-K.**

Accounting Series Release (ASRs)   In 1937 the SEC initiated a program of pronouncements by the chief accountant designed to contribute to the development of uniform standards and practice in major accounting questions. Through early 1982, 307 **ASRs** were issued, with more than half of them published after January, 1974. However, fewer than half of the **ASRs** dealt solely with accounting principles and disclosures; the remainder covered auditing standards, independence of auditors, and enforcement actions of the SEC involving accountants.

Two examples of **ASRs** dealing with accounting principles and disclosures are **ASR No. 142** and **ASR No. 149.** In **ASR No. 142,** "Reporting Cash Flow and Other Related Data," the SEC concluded that financial reports **should not** present **cash flow** (net income adjusted for noncash expenses and revenue) **per share** and other comparable per-share computations, other than those based on net income, dividends, or net assets. In **ASR No. 149,** ". . . Improved Disclosure of Income Tax Expense" (as amended by **ASR No. 280**), the SEC mandated several disclosures concerning income taxes. Note 3 of the annual report of Walt Disney Productions in Appendix 2 (page 715) illustrates the requirements of **ASR No. 149.**

Financial Reporting Releases In 1982, the SEC terminated the issuance of **Accounting Series Releases** and instituted **Financial Reporting Releases** for stating its views on financial reporting matters. (Enforcement actions of the SEC were to be publicized in **Accounting and Auditing Enforcement Releases.**)

Staff Accounting Bulletins (SABs) The following excerpt from **ASR No. 180** describes the **SAB**s issued by the SEC:

> The Securities and Exchange Commission today announced the institution of a series of Staff Accounting Bulletins intended to achieve a wider dissemination of the administrative interpretations and practices utilized by the Commission's staff in reviewing financial statements. The Division of Corporation Finance and the Office of the Chief Accountant began the series today with the publication of Bulletin No. 1. . . . The statements in the Bulletin are not rules or interpretations of the Commission nor are they published as bearing the Commission's official approval; they represent interpretations and practices followed by the Division and the Chief Accountant in administering the disclosure requirements of the federal securities laws.

The following example from **SAB No. 1** (subsequently superseded by **SAB No. 40**) illustrates the contents of a typical Bulletin:

> *Facts:* Company E proposes to include in its registration statement a balance sheet showing its subordinated debt as a portion of stockholders' equity.
>
> *Question:* Is this presentation appropriate?
>
> *Interpretive Response:* Subordinated debt may not be included in the stockholders' equity section of the balance sheet. Any presentation describing such debt as a component of stockholders' equity must be eliminated. Furthermore, any caption representing the combination of stockholders' equity and any subordinated debt must be deleted.

Integration project and other recent activities of SEC

The foregoing discussion indicates the complexity of the accounting and reporting requirements of the SEC. Compliance with these requirements often is a major undertaking for companies that report to the SEC.

In the early 1980s, the SEC completed the bulk of an integration project designed to provide, wherever possible, uniform reporting requirements in the various **Forms** filed with the SEC. The integration was focused on providing comparable requirements for the **transaction-oriented** Securities Act of 1933 and the **status-oriented** Securities Exchange Act of 1934.[31] In a number of **ASR**s, the SEC accomplished the following:

---

[31] *ASR No. 306,* Securities and Exchange Commission (Washington: 1982).

1 Through the **incorporation by reference** technique, enabled many companies to satisfy the reporting requirements of the 1933 Act by already-filed **Forms** provided to the SEC under the 1934 Act.

2 Permitted many of the requirements of **Form 10-K** to be met by reference to the annual report to shareholders. (For examples, see pages 686 to 694 of Appendix 1 and related pages 704 to 721 of Appendix 2.)

3 Conformed many of the accounting requirements of **Regulation S-X** to generally accepted accounting principles, thus permitting the form and content of financial statements included in annual reports to shareholders to suffice for reports to the SEC.

In addition to the integration project, the SEC has encouraged the voluntary filing of **projections of future economic performance** (also termed **financial forecasts**) in reports to it. In **Regulation S-K** the SEC provided guidelines for the preparation and disclosure of such projections. The SEC has long believed that users of financial reports would benefit from management's projections as a supplement to the historical data in the financial statements. However, the SEC has been reluctant to require projections in the various **Forms,** because there is widespread opposition to submission of financial forecasts to shareholders by accountants and business executives who fear the litigation consequences if forecasted results are not achieved.

(Study aids for Chapter 15 start on page 722.)

APPENDIX 1: FORM 10-K FOR WALT DISNEY PRODUCTIONS

SECURITIES AND EXCHANGE COMMISSION

Washington, D.C. 20549

FORM 10-K

ANNUAL REPORT PURSUANT TO SECTION 13 OR 15(d) OF
THE SECURITIES EXCHANGE ACT OF 1934

For the fiscal year ended September 30, 1981   Commission file number 1-4083

WALT DISNEY PRODUCTIONS

I.R.S. Employer
Identification No.
95-0684440

Incorporated in California

500 South Buena Vista Street, Burbank, California 91521

Area Code (213) 840-1000

Securities registered pursuant to Section 12(b) of the Act:

Title of each class	Name of each exchange on which registered
Walt Disney Productions Common Stock No par value	New York Stock Exchange, Inc. Pacific Stock Exchange, Inc.

Securities registered pursuant to Section 12(g) of the Act:
    None

Indicate by check mark whether the registrant (1) has filed all reports required to be filed with the Commission and (2) has been subject to such filing requirements for the past 90 days.
Yes..X.. No......

The aggregate market value of the voting stock held by non-affiliates amounted to a minimum of $1.6 billion on November 30, 1981.

There were 32,439,031 shares of Common Stock outstanding as of November 30, 1981.

Documents Incorporated by Reference

Portions of the Annual Report to Shareholders for the year ended September 30, 1981 are incorporated by reference into Parts I and II.

Portions of the Proxy Statement dated December 18, 1981 for the Annual Meeting of Shareholders to be held on January 28, 1982 are incorporated by reference into Parts I and III.

PART I

ITEM 1. Business

This report covers the activities of Walt Disney Productions and its subsidiary companies (hereinafter sometimes collectively referred to as the "Company") during the Company's fiscal year ended September 30, 1981 (hereinafter sometimes referred to as "1981"). The Company is a diversified international company engaged in family entertainment and operates in three business segments: Entertainment and Recreation, Motion Pictures and Consumer Products and Other. These business segments are described in the appropriate sections that follow. The information regarding revenues, operating income before corporate expenses and identifiable assets of the Company's business segments, together with foreign revenues by geographic area appearing in the Consolidated Statement of Income on page 37, in Note 5 of Notes to Consolidated Financial Statements on page 43 and under "Other Financial Data" on page 46 of the Walt Disney Productions Annual Report to Shareholders for the year ended September 30, 1981 ("1981 Annual Report to Shareholders") is hereby incorporated by reference. The Company employees approximately 25,000 people.

ENTERTAINMENT AND RECREATION

The Company operates an amusement theme park, "Disneyland," in California and wholly owned subsidiaries operate a destination resort, "Walt Disney World," in Florida. In addition to an amusement theme park, the Walt Disney World complex includes three hotels, camping, golfing and other recreational facilities, a shopping village, a conference center and other lodging accommodations.

Disneyland Park

The Company owns 310 acres and has under long-term lease an additional 42 acres of land in Anaheim, California, including the 230-acre site owned by the Company on which it operates an amusement theme park known as "Disneyland Park."

Disneyland Park consists of seven principal areas: Fantasyland, Adventureland, Frontierland, Tomorrowland, New Orleans Square, Main Street and Bear Country. In each area there are restaurants, refreshment stands and souvenir shops in keeping with the surrounding theme. A number of the Disneyland attractions and exhibits are sponsored by corporate participants. The Company periodically revitalizes the shows and presentations and adds new attractions to maintain the continuing appeal of Disneyland Park and to increase in-park capacity.

While Disneyland Park is operated on a year-round basis, historically the greater part of its business is in the Summer season with other peak periods during Spring vacation, Easter, Christmas and holiday periods. A summary of revenues from Disneyland Park for its various activities and total attendance for the five fiscal years ended with 1981 appearing on page 46 and management's financial analysis of operations appearing on pages 32 and 33 of the 1981 Annual Report to Shareholders are hereby incorporated by reference.

Walt Disney World Complex

Magic Kingdom and Resort Hotels

The Company owns approximately 28,000 acres of land located 15 miles southwest of Orlando, Florida, including the 2,500-acre site of the "Magic Kingdom" amusement theme park and a variety of other facilities designed to attract visitors for an extended stay by offering them a wide range of recreational activities for the entire family, including two 18-hole championship golf courses, tennis, sailing, water skiing, swimming, horseback riding and a number of noncompetitive sports and leisure time activities. Many of the recreational activities are centered about Bay Lake (a natural lake located wholly within the complex) and its beaches, and on a lagoon-style extension of Bay Lake located between the Park and the resort hotels. The Magic Kingdom park was opened to the public on October 1, 1971, and the related recreational facilities were opened at various times thereafter.

The Magic Kingdom park, which is similar in concept to Disneyland, consists of six principal areas designated as Main Street, Liberty Square, Frontierland, Tomorrowland, Fantasyland and Adventureland. Each of these areas features rides and attractions of the type that have been popular at Disneyland, together with restaurants, snack bars and shops comparable to such facilities at Disneyland. A number of the Walt Disney World attractions and exhibits are sponsored by corporate participants.

The Company owns and operates three resort hotels at Walt Disney World having a present capacity of 1,834 rooms, as well as the Fort Wilderness camping and recreational area. The occupancy rates for the three resort hotels for 1981 were: the Contemporary Resort—99%, the Polynesian Village Resort—97%, and the Golf Resort—94%. Such rates have not changed substantially over the past five years. Other recreational and service facilities available in the Walt Disney World complex include extensive parking facilities, an information service system, utility distribution systems, marinas, swimming pools, tennis courts, beach bathing facilities and the monorail transportation system.

Community of Lake Buena Vista

The Company has also developed approximately 1,200 acres known as the Community of Lake Buena Vista, including 260 units of townhouses, villas and homes, treehouses, a shopping facility known as Walt Disney World Village, an 18-hole golf course with a complete clubhouse facility and tennis courts and a conference center. The Walt Disney World Conference Center consists of conference rooms, banquet facilities and 140 villas for guests. The occupancy rates for the camping facilities, townhouses, pedestal-type homes, Fairway Villas and Club Villas were 84–92%. Such rates have not changed substantially over the past five years.

At Hotel Plaza, located in Lake Buena Vista, four major motor inns, having a present capacity of 1,653 guest rooms, are situated on property leased to them by the Company. The Company is continuing to negotiate with other hotel chains for possible additions to the Hotel Plaza and approximately 27 acres have been set aside for a new 825-room luxury hotel now under construction.

Epcot Center

On October 1, 1979, the Company's subsidiary, Walt Disney World Co., began construction of the Epcot Center at the Walt Disney World complex. Epcot is an acronym for Experimental Prototype Community of Tomorrow. Epcot Center will consist of two major themed areas: Future World and The World Showcase. The first of these will dramatize the history and future challenges of the critical problems facing the world today—providing a public window onto the worlds of energy, transportation, the land, the imagination and other subjects. At the entrance to the Epcot Center, Spaceship Earth will introduce the Epcot concept and invite guests to explore the many pavilions of Future World, including a "global marketplace of new ideas" which will be called Communicore. The World Showcase will be a "community of nations" focusing on the culture, traditions and accomplishments of people around the world and will include the American Adventure pavilion, which will present the history of the American people. A number of the attractions and exhibits at the Epcot Center will be sponsored by corporate participants, including General Motors (World of Motion), Exxon (Universe of Energy), Kraft (The Land), Bell System (Spaceship Earth), American Express and Coca-Cola (the American Adventure), General Electric (Future Probe), Kodak (Journey into Imagination), and Sperry Univac (Epcot Computer Central in the Communicore). This new project, which is expected to open in October 1982, will be linked to the existing Magic Kingdom park by monorail. Information regarding the cost and financing of the project appearing in Note 2 of Notes to the Consolidated Financial Statements on page 41 of the 1981 Annual Report to Shareholders is hereby incorporated by reference.

Other Information

The Company owns and operates a central energy plant for the generation of electrical power, facilities for the distribution of chilled and hot water, a system of water supply, a compressed air distribution system, a gas distribution system and fuel oil lines for service to the Company's Florida properties near Orlando.

The Company has a 51% interest in a partnership with a subsidiary of United Telecommunications, Inc., which operates Vista United Telecommunications that serves the Walt Disney World complex and the adjacent Community of Lake Buena Vista.

The Reedy Creek Improvement District, a governmental unit of the State of Florida within whose boundaries most of the Company's Florida land is located, owns and operates water control works servicing approximately 9,800 acres, including the Walt Disney World complex, and the Company's other inland Florida properties. The district also owns and operates facilities for solid waste disposal and a waste water treatment plant.

While Walt Disney World is operated on a year-round basis, historically the greater part of its business is in the Summer season with other peak periods during Spring vacation, Easter, Christmas and holiday periods. A summary of revenues received from Walt Disney World for its various activities and total attendance for the five fiscal years ended with 1981 appearing on page 46 and management's financial analysis of operations appearing on pages 32 and 33 of the 1981 Annual Report to Shareholders are hereby incorporated by reference.

2

Planning and Development

Employees of the Company provide planning, architectural, engineering, research and development services for Disneyland, Walt Disney World and the Epcot Center. Staff technicians developed the "Audio-Animatronics" system of three-dimensional animation and the WEDway "PeopleMover" transportation systems which have been installed in the Tomorrowland areas of Disneyland and Walt Disney World. In addition, the Walt Disney World version of the "PeopleMover," which uses linear induction motors, has been installed and is in operation as a mode of public transportation at the Houston International Airport.

Energy Shortage

In recent years the United States has experienced shortages of gasoline and other energy sources. Uncertainty as to the availability of gasoline had an adverse effect on tourism and, therefore, on attendance at Disneyland and Walt Disney World in the Winter of 1973-74 and the Spring and Summer of 1979. Neither the magnitude nor duration of any future shortages nor their effect on the Company's businesses can be reliably predicted.

Competitive Position

The theme park industry competes with all other forms of entertainment. Since the opening of Walt Disney World, the theme park industry has expanded significantly with the opening of several new theme parks in various sections of the country. In addition, some of the theme parks that existed prior to the Walt Disney World opening have been expanded and improved. However, during this time the profitability of the Company's two theme parks has continued to improve. The Company believes its theme parks benefit substantially from the Company's reputation in the entertainment business and from its other activities.

MOTION PICTURES

The Company produces motion pictures for theatrical and television distribution, including both network and independent television station broadcasting. The Company distributes its filmed product through its own distribution company in the United States and through foreign subsidiaries in certain countries and independent distribution companies throughout the rest of the world.

A summary of the Company's revenues from its motion picture business for the five fiscal years ended with 1981 appearing on page 46 and management's financial analysis of operations appearing on page 33 of the 1981 Annual Report to Shareholders are hereby incorporated by reference.

Theatrical Films

The Company produces and distributes for theatrical exhibition motion pictures using the animated cartoon technique and motion pictures using live actors, as well as motion pictures using both live actors and animated cartoons.

The Company currently produces several full-length live action motion pictures each year. One or two full-length animated motion pictures are in continual production, and a new full-length animated motion picture is released every three or four years. In addition, certain films from the Company's library are reissued on a regular basis. The Company's film library at September 30, 1981 consisted of 25 full-length animated features in color; 115 full-length live action features, most of which are in color; 8 "True-Life Adventure" feature films in color; and over 500 other films, principally short subjects. In July 1981, the Company released "The Fox and the Hound," a feature-length animated cartoon motion picture. During fiscal year 1981, the Company released the following live action features recently produced by it: "The Devil and Max Devlin," "Amy" and "Condorman." In addition, two co-production ventures with Paramount Pictures Corporation, "Popeye" and "Dragonslayer," were released. The Company is continuing to explore new opportunities for developing motion picture products through original story development, story acquisitions and co-production ventures.

All of the Company's theatrical feature motion pictures and theatrical short subjects are distributed in the United States by a wholly-owned subsidiary of Walt Disney Productions, Buena Vista Distribution Co., Inc.

The Company's pictures are also distributed in foreign countries. Most of the distribution outside the United States has been handled by other organizations, except that wholly-owned subsidiaries of Walt Disney Productions distribute the Company's films in the United Kingdom, France and Sweden.

3

The Company is responsible for the foreign distribution of ''Popeye'' and ''Dragonslayer,'' its co-production ventures with Paramount, while Paramount is responsible for domestic distribution.

The production and distribution of motion pictures is a highly competitive industry. The industry consists of a large number of companies, some of which produce and distribute films and others of which either produce films for distribution by others or distribute films produced by others. The Company produces and distributes films designed for family audiences and believes that it is one of the principal sources of such films.

The animated feature-length films of the Company have been preeminent, and in respect of these films the Company has had relatively little competition from other producers. The Company's competitive position in the motion picture industry may be affected by the quality of and public response to the motion pictures produced and distributed by it. Motion pictures compete with all other forms of entertainment.

Television Films

The Company began to produce television programs in 1954. Films produced by the Company for television presentation include both animated and live action films as well as films on nature and other subjects. Each year since 1961, the Company has made available approximately 48 television programs for the series ''Disney's Wonderful World'' pursuant to contracts with the National Broadcasting Company, Inc. The contract expired at the end of the 1980-81 season and was not renewed. The Company has reached agreement with CBS Television for the showing of 22 hours of television shows, 8 being new production, commencing in the 1981-82 season. These shows will include 8 new pilot films, 8 live action films and 6 animated films from the Disney film library. CBS has the option, but is not required, to rebroadcast up to 22 hours of these shows.

Following their domestic network presentation, certain of the Company's television programs have been syndicated by the Company abroad. At present, the Company's television programs are being telecast regularly in many countries including Australia, Brazil, Canada, France, Germany, Italy, Japan, Mexico, Spain, United Kingdom, Venezuela and others. Many programs telecast in countries outside the United States are dubbed in the local language. The Company has edited certain of its television programs into full-length features primarily for foreign theatrical exhibition.

The Company has made available a number of feature films to the pay television industry. The Company is continuing to evaluate this relatively new industry, as well as other evolving technologies, as a means of marketing its filmed product, and recently announced that it will operate a 16-hour-a-day pay cable programming service with Westinghouse Broadcasting (Group W) in a joint venture, debuting in late 1982 or early 1983. The Company has announced that, relative to pay cable, it will dedicate its filmed product (excluding most of the animated feature-length films as well as certain other films that will be produced in the future) to this joint venture after current licensing agreements expire.

The Company believes that its television programs complement the exploitation and marketing of its theatrical motion pictures and the exploitation of its ancillary businesses and of Disneyland and Walt Disney World.

CONSUMER PRODUCTS AND OTHER

The Company licenses the name Walt Disney, its characters, its literary properties and its songs and music to various manufacturers, retailers, printers and publishers. The Company also produces and distributes phonograph recordings, 8 millimeter prints of excerpts from its film library, video cassettes, 16 millimeter prints of product taken from the film library or developed on educational subjects, and a broad range of teaching aids. These activities are conducted through the character merchandising and publications, records and music publishing, and telecommunications and non-theatrical divisions and subsidiaries of the Company.

A summary of the Company's revenues from its consumer products and other business for the five fiscal years ended with 1981 appearing on page 46 and management's financial analysis of operations appearing on page 34 of the 1981 Annual Report to Shareholders are hereby incorporated by reference.

Telecommunications and Non-Theatrical

After motion pictures have been marketed in theatres or on television, the Company prepares and rents 16 millimeter prints of certain of them for limited usage by non-theatrical users, including businesses, religious and educational institutions and home viewers. The Company also sells a variety of audio-visual teaching materials and 8 millimeter prints of excerpts from its entertainment films.

In addition, the Company has entered the home video market. This new video technology permits the storage of both picture and sound on a cassette or disc for playback on a television set. In an authorized rental plan developed directly with retailers, the Company will share in proceeds from the sale and rental of selected Disney properties in both domestic and foreign markets.

Character Merchandising

The Company has licensed a large number of manufacturers and retailers of many products to use the Company's characters, including Mickey Mouse and Donald Duck, and the name Walt Disney in connection with their businesses. See ''Properties.'' The Company's licensing business has grown to be worldwide and produces royalties which are usually a fixed percentage of the selling price of the merchandise.

Publications

Extensive use has been made of the Company's literary properties and characters in multi-volume book sets, newspaper comic strips, magazines, comic books and other publications. The Company has for many years had contracts with leading printers and publishers providing for publication of these items in foreign countries and receives royalties based upon the selling prices and volume of sales of such publications.

Records and Music Publishing

Subsidiaries of the Company are engaged in the production and marketing of children's story and song record products relating to its theatrical and television productions as well as to other outside licensed products supporting the children's record market.

Competitive Position

The companies that are licensed by the Company must compete with many others in the manufacture and distribution of toys, novelties, games, clothing and book publishing. The Company competes with several other companies that produce and distribute records and albums for children. The Company believes that it is one of the principal sources of educational films and materials for school and personal use. Revenues are affected by the availability of funding to educational institutions, although the Company has introduced additional low-cost materials for the educational market in the United States.

TOKYO DISNEYLAND

The Company entered into a definitive agreement in April 1979 with Oriental Land Co., Ltd. governing the respective rights and obligations of the parties with regard to Tokyo Disneyland, a project similar in size and concept to Disneyland, located approximately 20 miles from downtown Tokyo. The Company's contribution, for which it is entitled to full reimbursement for all costs incurred on the project and royalties on certain revenues generated from the project, consists of theme park master planning, design, technology, operational experience, the Disneyland name and certain other values which have been established in connection with the Company's theme park complexes in the United States. Oriental Land Co., Ltd., a Japanese joint venture, will contribute the land and estimated funds in the amount of approximately $440 million required for the project. The Company has the right, but is not obligated, to contribute up to $2.5 million, or 10%, of the equity of a separate Japanese company which may be formed to own and operate Tokyo Disneyland. The master plan has been finalized and the preliminary facility design and actual site preparation are virtually complete. The official groundbreaking of Tokyo Disneyland took place on December 3, 1980 and construction is in progress. It is anticipated that Tokyo Disneyland will open to the public in 1983.

ITEM 2. Properties

The Company's studio facilities provide for the production of both live action motion pictures and animated cartoon motion pictures. The Company owns approximately 44 acres of land in Burbank, California on which are located its studios and executive offices. There are 61 buildings on the property in addition to smaller auxiliary structures and parking areas. The buildings include four soundproof Live Action Stages, a Dialogue-Sound Effects Stage, Orchestra Stage, Executive Office and Animation Building, Cutting Building, Camera Building, Warehouse Building, Central Heating Plant, Inkers and Painters Building, Process Laboratory, a Theatre with approximately 600 seats, a Restaurant Building and a Marketing Building. In addition, the

Company leases office and warehouse space for certain of its corporate activities, including the fabrication of rides and shows for Epcot and Tokyo Disneyland.

The Company also owns 691 acres of ranch property about 30 miles from Burbank. The property is used by the Company as a location site for the shooting of motion pictures and is available to other motion picture producers on a rental basis.

The Disneyland and Florida properties are described in Item 1 under "Entertainment and Recreation." In addition, the Company also owns approximately 88 acres in three non-contiguous parcels of property, with approximately 4,800 feet of ocean frontage, on the east coast of Florida, approximately 50 miles from Walt Disney World. No decision has yet been made by the Company as to the future use or development of this property. Since the acquisition by the Company of its various Florida properties, land prices in the area have risen substantially. However, the future value of such landholdings will depend on the progress and success of the development of the Walt Disney World complex and of the surrounding areas. Accordingly, no representation is made as to the current or future value of these landholdings.

It is the Company's practice to obtain United States and foreign legal protection for its theatrical and television motion pictures and its other original works, including the various names and designs of the cartoon characters and the publications and music which have been created in connection with the Company's motion pictures.

The Company uses and licenses others to use the name of Walter E. Disney pursuant to a Name Agreement with Retlaw Enterprises, Inc. Retlaw, a corporation organized by the late Walt Disney, is owned by members of his family, including Diane Disney Miller, the wife of Ronald W. Miller, President and Chief Operating Officer and a director of Walt Disney Productions. Pursuant to the Name Agreement, Retlaw granted the Company the right to use the Walt Disney name for certain commercial purposes on certain terms and conditions in return for certain royalties (including a 5% participation in profits, as defined, of the Walt Disney World operations, which would include the new Epcot Center). Under the provisions of the Name Agreement, the Company's rights and obligations will continue until at least April 1, 1983, as a result of the exercise by the Company in 1971 of its second ten-year option to renew such agreement. The Company has two additional ten-year options to further renew such agreement which, if both were to be exercised, would extend the term to the year 2003. Since the first such option is exercisable on or before April 1, 1982, the Company has been evaluating factors relevant to its possible exercise, including uncertainties regarding the creation and interpretation of the Name Agreement. As a result of such evaluation and in order to assure the Company of the perpetual right to use the Walt Disney name in connection with all of its business activities, the Company has entered into an agreement with the stockholders of Retlaw upon the consummation of which the Company would in effect acquire all of Retlaw's rights to the name, likeness and portrait of Walt Disney and certain other assets. The agreement provides for a purchase price to be paid by the Company to the stockholders of Retlaw of $46.2 million, payable in shares of common stock of the Company. Consummation of the agreement is subject to approval by the stockholders of the Company and certain other conditions.

ITEM 3. Legal Proceedings

The Company's subsidiary, Buena Vista Distribution Co., Inc., is a defendant with other motion picture distributors in a number of private treble damage actions asserting claims under the federal anti-trust laws as follows:

Balmoral Cinema, Inc. vs Allied Artists Pictures Corporation, et al. - Complaint filed 2/15/77 in U.S. District Court for the Western District of Tennessee; transferred to U.S. District Court, Southern District of Texas 4/3/79.

Bedford Century Plaza Cinema, Inc. vs Co-operative Theatres of Ohio, Inc., et al. - Complaint filed 6/18/80 in U.S. District Court, Northern District of Ohio, Western Division where presently pending.

Jim Bowie Corp. vs Co-operative Theatres of Ohio, Inc., et al. - Complaint filed 2/5/80 in U.S. District Court, Northern District of Ohio, Western Division where presently pending.

CNS Theatres, Inc. vs Warner Bros. Distributing Corp., et al. - Complaint filed 8/23/79 in U.S. District Court, District of Oregon where presently pending.

Jack Cruikshank vs Warner Bros. Distributing Corp., et al. - Complaint filed 9/20/79 in U.S. District Court, District of Oregon where presently pending.

Florida West Theatres, Inc. vs Warner Bros. Distributing Corp., et al. - Complaint filed 5/17/74 in U.S. District Court for the Middle District of Florida; transferred to U.S. District Court, Southern District of Texas 4/3/79.

General Cinema Corporation vs Buena Vista Distribution Co., Inc. - Complaint filed 8/23/78 in U.S. District Court, Central District of California and main action presently on appeal in U.S. Court of Appeals, 9th Circuit. Buena Vista's Counterclaim filed 9/20/78 and presently pending in U.S. District Court, Central District of California.

Harkins Amusement Enterprises, Inc. vs General Cinema Corporation, et al. - Complaint filed 9/21/77 in U.S. District Court for District of Arizona; transferred to U.S. District Court, Southern District of Texas 4/3/79.

Harkins Amusement Enterprises, Inc. vs General Cinema Corporation, et al. - Complaint filed 9/29/80 in U.S. District Court, District of Arizona where presently pending.

HBS Associates vs Buena Vista Distribution Co., Inc. - Complaint filed 4/15/81 in U.S. District Court, Northern District of Ohio, Eastern Division where presently pending.

Holiday Theatres, Inc. vs Wometco Enterprises, Inc. et al. - Complaint filed 6/15/78 in U.S. District Court for the Southern District of Florida - Miami Division where presently pending.

Moyer Theatres, Inc. vs Warner Bros. Distributing Corp., et al. - Complaint filed 8/16/79 in U.S. District Court, District of Oregon; Complaint dismissed September, 1981. Cross-claim filed on or about 8/31/79, and is still pending although stipulation of dismissal has been entered into.

Moyer Theatres, Inc. vs Warner Bros. Distributing Corp., et al. - Complaint filed 11/20/80 in U.S. District Court, District of Oregon; Complaint dismissed September, 1981. Cross-claim filed January, 1981, and is still pending although stipulation of dismissal has been entered into.

National Amusements, Inc. vs Buena Vista Distribution Co., Inc. - Complaint filed 2/2/81 in U.S. District Court for the District of Massachusetts where presently pending.

National Independent Theatre Exhibitors, Inc. vs Buena Vista Distribution Co., Inc. - Complaint filed 3/14/80 in U.S. District Court for the Northern District of Georgia, Atlanta Division where presently pending.

Patriot Cinemas, Inc. vs Universal Film Exchanges, Inc., et al. - Complaint filed 6/22/78 in U.S. District Court for the District of Massachusetts where presently pending.

Southway Theatres, Inc. vs Cinerama Releasing Corporation, et al. - Complaint filed 8/20/75 in U.S. District Court for the Northern District of Georgia, and presently on appeal in the U.S. Court of Appeals, 5th Circuit.

Southway Theatres vs American Multi Cinema, et al. - Complaint filed 1/30/81 in U.S. District Court for the Northern District of Georgia, Atlanta Division where presently pending.

Syufy Enterprises vs Columbia Pictures, et al. - Complaint filed 5/25/77 in U.S. District Court for the District of Utah; transferred to U.S. District Court, Southern District of Texas 4/3/79.

Tercar Theatre Company vs General Cinema Corporation, et al. - Complaint filed 8/15/77 in U.S. District Court for the Southern District of Texas, Houston Division where presently pending. A stipulation of discontinuance with regard to Buena Vista has been reached, upon which the Court has yet to act.

Universal Amusement Co., Inc. vs General Cinema Corporation, et al. - Complaint filed 1/26/78 in U.S. District Court for the Southern District of Texas, Houston Division where presently pending.

These actions, which seek damages aggregating hundreds of millions of dollars, are in various stages of pretrial proceedings. The Company has denied the material allegations of the complaints in these actions and in the opinion of management and counsel, the Company will not suffer any material liability by reason thereof.

ITEM 4(a). Security Ownership of Certain Beneficial Owners and Management

A discussion of the security ownership of certain beneficial owners and management appearing under "Election of Directors" on pages 1 and 2 of the Company's Proxy Statement dated December 18, 1981 for the Annual Meeting of Shareholders to be held on January 28, 1982 (the "1982 Proxy Statement") is hereby incorporated by reference.

ITEM 4 (b). Executive Officers of the Registrant

The executive officers of the registrant are elected each year at the annual meeting of the Board of Directors which follows the annual meeting of the shareholders. Each of the executive officers has been employed by the registrant for at least five years, except Mr. Ringquist, in the position or positions indicated below.

Name	Age	Title	Executive Officer Since
E. Cardon Walker	65	Chairman of the Board and Chief Executive Officer and Director[1]	1956
Donn B. Tatum	68	Chairman of the Executive Committee and Director[2]	1957
Ronald W. Miller	48	President and Chief Operating Officer and Director[3]	1968
Michael L. Bagnall	50	Senior Vice President—Finance[4]	1971
Ronald J. Cayo	48	Senior Vice President—Business and Legal Affairs[5]	1974
Vincent H. Jefferds	65	Senior Vice President—Walt Disney Marketing Division[6]	1969
Jack B. Lindquist	54	Senior Vice President—Advertising, Publicity, Promotion and Public Relations[7]	1978
Carl G. Bongirno	44	Vice President—Epcot[8]	1979
Barton K. Boyd	39	Vice President—Consumer Products and Merchandising[9]	1976
Jose M. Deetjen	44	Vice President—Tax Administration and Counsel[10]	1980
Robert W. Gibeaut	61	Vice President—Studio Operations	1975
Luther R. Marr	56	Vice President—Corporate and Stockholder Affairs[11]	1957
Richard T. Morrow	55	Vice President—General Counsel and Director	1964
Richard A. Nunis	49	Vice President—Walt Disney Outdoor Recreation Division[12]	1968
Lennart Ringquist	51	Vice President—Television[13]	1980
Howard M. Roland	46	Vice President—Construction Contract Administration and Purchasing	1976
Franklin Waldheim	85	Vice President and Eastern Counsel	1966
Thomas L. Wilhite	29	Vice President—Motion Picture and Television Production[14]	1981
Doris A. Smith	46	Secretary[15]	1978
Donald A. Escen	62	Treasurer[16]	1981
Bruce F. Johnson	48	Controller	1975

[1] Previously served as President until 1980.

[2] Previously served as Chairman of the Board until 1980.

[3] Previously served as Executive Vice President—Production and Creative Affairs until 1980; Vice President—Executive Producer until 1977.

[4] Previously served as Vice President—Finance until 1980; also served as Treasurer until 1979.

[5] Previously served as Vice President—Business Affairs until 1980.

[6] Previously served as Vice President—Marketing - Consumer Products Division until 1980.

[7] Previously served as Vice President—Marketing - Disneyland and Walt Disney World - Outdoor Recreation until 1980; Vice President—Marketing, Disneyland and Walt Disney World until 1978.

[8] Previously served as Vice President and Treasurer, Walt Disney World Co. until 1979.

[9] Previously served as Vice President—Retail Merchandising until 1980.

[10] Previously served as Manager of Tax Compliance until 1978; Director—Tax Administration until 1980.

[11] Previously served as Secretary—Legal until 1978.

[12] Previously served as Vice President—Operations - Disneyland and Walt Disney World - Outdoor Recreation until 1980.

[13] Mr. Ringquist has been in the television industry for more than 25 years, including 7 years with Metromedia Producers Corp. where he left the position of President and Chief Executive Officer to accept his current position with the Company.

[14] Previously served as Vice President—Creative Development, Motion Picture and Television Production Division until 1981; various staff capacities in Publicity and Creative Affairs until 1980.

[15] Previously served as Credit Manager and Assistant Secretary until 1978.

[16] Previously served as Assistant Treasurer and Assistant Controller until 1981.

PART II

ITEM 5: Market for the Registrant's Common Stock and Related Security Holder Matters

The information regarding the quarterly market price ranges, dividends and approximate number of shareholders appearing under "Market Price and Dividend Data" on page 47 and "Selected Financial Data" on page 45 of the Walt Disney Productions 1981 Annual Report to Shareholders is hereby incorporated by reference.

ITEM 6: Selected Financial Data

The summary of selected financial data appearing on page 45 of the Walt Disney Productions 1981 Annual Report to Shareholders is hereby incorporated by reference.

ITEM 7: Management's Discussion and Analysis of Financial Condition and Results of Operations

Information appearing under the caption "Financial Review" on pages 30 through 36 of the Walt Disney Productions 1981 Annual Report to Shareholders is hereby incorporated by reference.

ITEM 8: Financial Statements and Supplementary Data

The consolidated financial statements of the Company and its subsidiaries, together with the report thereon of Price Waterhouse, appearing on pages 37 through 44, the supplementary data under "Quarterly Financial Summary" appearing on page 47, and the supplementary information regarding inflation and changing prices appearing on page 35 and 36 of the Walt Disney Productions 1981 Annual Report to Shareholders are hereby incorporated by reference.

PART III

ITEM 9: Directors and Executive Officers of the Registrant

Information regarding directors appearing under "Election of Directors" on pages 1 through 3 of the 1982 Proxy Statement is hereby incorporated by reference.

Information regarding executive officers is set forth in Item 4(b) included in Part I of this Form 10-K as permitted by General Instruction G(3).

ITEM 10: Management Remuneration and Transactions

Information appearing under "Remuneration" on pages 4 through 9 of the 1982 Proxy Statement is hereby incorporated by reference.

PART IV

ITEM 11: Exhibits, Financial Statement Schedules, and Reports on Form 8-K

(a) 1. Financial Statements:

The following consolidated financial statements of Walt Disney Productions and subsidiaries which are incorporated by reference in Part II, Item 8 are included in Exhibit 13:
- Report of independent accountants
- Consolidated statement of income—for years ended September 30, 1981, 1980 and 1979
- Consolidated balance sheet—as of September 30, 1981 and 1980
- Consolidated statement of retained earnings—for years ended September 1981, 1980 and 1979
- Consolidated statement of changes in financial position—for years ended September 30, 1981, 1980 and 1979
- Notes to consolidated financial statements

Individual financial statements of the parent company have been omitted because 1) consolidated statements are being filed, 2) the company is primarily an operating company, and 3) the amount of minority interest and unguaranteed long-term debt of subsidiaries is not material. Financial statements of the joint venture in which the registrant has an equity interest have been omitted because it would not constitute a significant subsidiary.

9

2. Financial Statement Schedules:

Schedule I	—	Marketable securities - short term investments
Schedule II	—	Accounts receivable from officers and directors
Schedule V	—	Property, plant, and equipment
Schedule VI	—	Accumulated depreciation of property, plant and equipment
Schedule X	—	Supplementary income statement information

The schedules other than those listed above are omitted because of the absence of the conditions under which they are required, or because the information is set forth in the financial statements or notes thereto.

3. Exhibits:

Exhibit (3a) — Restated Articles of Incorporation filed as an exhibit to the report on Form 8-K for the month of February, 1977 is hereby incorporated by reference.

Exhibit (3b) — Amendment dated March 6, 1981 to the Restated Articles of Incorporation.

Exhibit (3c) — New Bylaws, as amended through September 9, 1981.

Exhibit (4a) — Loan Agreement dated October 29, 1979 with Bank of America National Trust and Savings Association.

Exhibit (4b) — Amendment Number 1 to Loan Agreement dated August 31, 1981.

Exhibit (4c) — A wholly owned subsidiary of the Company has issued $100 million of 15¾% Notes due 1986 which are guaranteed by the Company in a Eurodollar Offering. The Company has not filed copies of instruments defining the rights of holders of such Notes because such Notes do not exceed in the aggregate 10% of the consolidated assets of the Company. The Company undertakes to furnish copies of the instruments to the Commission upon request.

Exhibit (10a) — Retlaw Acquisition Agreement dated July 8, 1981 filed as Exhibit 1 to the 1982 Proxy Statement is hereby incorporated by reference.

Exhibit (10b) — Employment Agreement dated January 1, 1977 with Donn B. Tatum filed as Exhibit 4 to the Annual Report on Form 10-K for the year ended September 30, 1977 is hereby incorporated by reference.

Exhibit (10c) — Amendment dated June 7, 1977 to the Employment Agreement with Donn B. Tatum filed as Exhibit 5 to the Annual Report on Form 10-K for the year ended September 30, 1977 is hereby incorporated by reference.

Exhibit (10d) — Amendment dated August 8, 1980 to the Employment Agreement with Donn B. Tatum filed as Exhibit 6 to the Annual Report on Form 10-K for the year ended September 30, 1980 is hereby incorporated by reference.

Exhibit (10e) — Employment Agreement dated January 3, 1977 with E. Cardon Walker filed as Exhibit 6 to the Annual Report on Form 10-K for the year ended September 30, 1977 is hereby incorporated by reference.

Exhibit (10f) — Amendment dated August 8, 1980 to the Employment Agreement with E. Cardon Walker filed as Exhibit 5 to the Annual Report on Form 10-K for the year ended September 30, 1980 is hereby incorporated by reference.

Exhibit (10g) — Employment Agreement dated July 1, 1981, pursuant to which Ronald W. Miller, President and Chief Operating Officer, was employed by the Company for a period of five years commencing July 1, 1981.

Exhibit (10h) — Contract dated December 14, 1979, with E. Cardon Walker, to purchase a 2% interest in certain motion pictures to be produced by the registrant and to acquire an additional 2% profit participation filed as Exhibit 1 to the Annual Report on Form 10-K for the year ended September 30, 1980 is hereby incorporated by reference.

Exhibit (10i) — Amendment dated August 8, 1980 to said contract dated December 14, 1979 with E. Cardon Walker filed as Exhibit 3 to the Annual Report on Form 10-K for the year ended September 30, 1980 is hereby incorporated by reference.

Exhibit (10j) — Contract dated December 14, 1979, with Ronald W. Miller, to purchase 4% interest in certain motion pictures to be produced by the registrant and to acquire an additional 4% profit participation filed as Exhibit 2 to the Annual Report on Form 10-K for the year ended September 30, 1980 is hereby incorporated by reference.

10

Exhibit (10k) — Amendment dated June 27, 1980 to said contract dated December 14, 1979 with Ronald W. Miller filed as Exhibit 4 to the Annual Report on Form 10-K for the year ended September 30, 1980 is hereby incorporated by reference.

Exhibit (10l) — Amendment dated November 25, 1980 to said contract dated December 14, 1979 with Ronald W. Miller.

Exhibit (10m) — Contract dated December 15, 1977, as amended, with William H. Anderson, to purchase a 2% interest in certain motion pictures to be produced by the registrant filed as Exhibit 1 to the Annual Report on Form 10-K for the year ended September 30, 1978 is hereby incorporated by reference.

Exhibit (10n) — Walt Disney Productions Qualified Stock Option Plan, 1973 Stock Option Plan, and 1980 Stock Option Plan filed as Exhibits 1(a), 1(b), and 1(c) to the Registration Statement on Form S-8 dated January 30, 1981 are hereby incorporated by reference.

Exhibit (10o) — 1981 Incentive Plan filed as Exhibit 1 to the Proxy Statement dated January 12, 1981 for the Annual Meeting of Shareholders held on February 18, 1981 is hereby incorporated by reference.

Exhibit (10p) — Key Management Incentive Plan adopted pursuant to the 1981 Incentive Plan dated September 9, 1981.

Exhibit (13) — Annual Report to Shareholders for the year ended September 30, 1981.

Exhibit (22) — Subsidiaries of Walt Disney Productions (included on page 18 of this report)

The exhibits listed above are filed with the Securities and Exchange Commission but are not included in this booklet. Copies of these exhibits may be obtained by sending a request to the Secretary, Walt Disney Productions, 500 South Buena Vista Street, Burbank, California 91521.

(b) Reports on Form 8-K:
None

SIGNATURES

Pursuant to the requirements of Section 13 or 15(d) of the Securities Exchange Act of 1934, the registrant has duly caused this report to be signed on its behalf by the undersigned, thereunto duly authorized.

WALT DISNEY PRODUCTIONS
_____
(Registrant)

Date _December 18, 1981_   By_____E. Cardon Walker_____

(E. Cardon Walker, Chairman of the Board and Chief Executive Officer)

Pursuant to the requirements of the Securities Exchange Act of 1934, this report has been signed below by the following persons on behalf of the registrant and in the capacities and on the date indicated.

Signature	Title	Date
Principal Executive Officers		
E. Cardon Walker (E. Cardon Walker)	Chairman of the Board and Chief Executive Officer	December 18, 1981
Donn B. Tatum (Donn B. Tatum)	Chairman of the Executive Committee	December 18, 1981
Ronald W. Miller (Ronald W. Miller)	President and Chief Operating Officer	December 18, 1981
Principal Financial and Accounting Officers		
Michael L. Bagnall (Michael L. Bagnall)	Senior Vice President—Finance	December 18, 1981
Bruce F. Johnson (Bruce F. Johnson)	Controller	December 18, 1981
Directors		
Caroline Leonetti Ahmanson (Caroline Leonetti Ahmanson)	Director	December 18, 1981
William H. Anderson (William H. Anderson)	Director	December 18, 1981
Roy E. Disney (Roy E. Disney)	Director	December 18, 1981
Philip M. Hawley (Philip M. Hawley)	Director	December 18, 1981
Ignacio E. Lozano, Jr. (Ignacio E. Lozano, Jr.)	Director	December 18, 1981
Ronald W. Miller (Ronald W. Miller)	Director	December 18, 1981
Richard T. Morrow (Richard T. Morrow)	Director	December 18, 1981
Richard A. Nunis (Richard A. Nunis)	Director	December 18, 1981
Donn B. Tatum (Donn B. Tatum)	Director	December 18, 1981
E. Cardon Walker (E. Cardon Walker)	Director	December 18, 1981
Raymond L. Watson (Raymond L. Watson)	Director	December 18, 1981

REPORT OF INDEPENDENT ACCOUNTANTS ON
FINANCIAL STATEMENT SCHEDULES

Our examination of the consolidated financial statements referred to in our report dated November 23, 1981 appearing on page 44 of the 1981 Annual Report to Shareholders of Walt Disney Productions (which report and financial statements are incorporated by reference in this Annual Report on Form 10-K) also included an examination of the Financial Statement Schedules listed in Item 11(a)2 of this Form 10-K. In our opinion, these Financial Statement Schedules present fairly the information set forth therein when read in conjunction with the related consolidated financial statements.

PRICE WATERHOUSE

West Los Angeles, California
November 23, 1981

CONSENT OF INDEPENDENT ACCOUNTANTS

We hereby consent to the incorporation by reference in the Prospectus constituting part of the Registration Statement on Form S-8 (No. 2-70741) of Walt Disney Productions of our report dated November 23, 1981 appearing on page 44 of the Annual Report to Shareholders which is incorporated in this Annual Report on Form 10-K. We also consent to the incorporation by reference of our report on the Financial Statement Schedules which appears on page 13 of this Form 10-K.

PRICE WATERHOUSE

West Los Angeles, California
December 17, 1981

WALT DISNEY PRODUCTIONS AND SUBSIDIARIES
SCHEDULE I — MARKETABLE SECURITIES — SHORT TERM INVESTMENTS
SEPTEMBER 30, 1981

Name of Issuer and Title of Each Issue	Cost of Each Issue[1]
U.S. Government and Agencies	$ 23,896,000
Eurodollar Certificates of Deposit	
Bank of Tokyo, Ltd.	30,254,000
Sumitomo Bank, Ltd.	25,209,000
Fuji Bank, Ltd.	21,663,000
Dai Ichi Kangyo Bank, Ltd.	20,169,000
Barclays Bank, Ltd.	5,411,000
Bank of America	5,000,000
	107,706,000
Commercial Paper	
Citicorp	42,654,000
Manufacturers Hanover Trust Co.	14,358,000
Bankers Trust	9,597,000
BankAmericorp	4,861,000
	71,470,000
Bankers' Acceptances	
Bank of Tokyo, Ltd.	12,671,000
Deutsche Bank	5,254,000
Mitsui Bank of California	4,936,000
Long Term Credit Bank of Japan	4,634,000
Mitsubishi Trust and Banking Corp.	2,958,000
	30,453,000
Negotiable Certificates of Deposit	10,337,000
Other	4,546,000
	$248,408,000

[1]The principal amount and market value of each issue at balance sheet date
generally approximates the cost of each issue.

SCHEDULE II — ACCOUNTS RECEIVABLE FROM OFFICERS AND DIRECTORS
SEPTEMBER 30, 1981

Name of Debtor	Balance at End of Year Non-Current
Carl G. Bongirno, Vice President—Epcot	$211,000

The amount loaned was to facilitate moving from Florida to California in August of 1979 and is evidenced by a promissory note in the amount of $211,000 maturing in ten years or less, bearing annual interest at the rate of 3¾ % less than the Bank of America's rate current from time to time for home loans of more than $150,000, but not in excess of 8%, and secured by a first trust deed on the home.

14

WALT DISNEY PRODUCTIONS AND SUBSIDIARIES

SCHEDULE V — PROPERTY, PLANT AND EQUIPMENT

YEAR ENDED SEPTEMBER 30, 1979

Description	Balance at Beginning of Year	Additions At Cost	Retirements Or Sales	Transfers	Other[1]	Balance at End of Year
Rides and attractions	$ 277,695,000	$ 531,000	$ 582,000	$ 12,991,000		$ 290,635,000
Buildings	322,794,000	7,000	2,400,000	3,612,000		324,013,000
Equipment, furniture and fixtures	134,967,000	6,887,000	4,401,000	7,070,000		144,523,000
Land improvements	114,232,000	28,000	124,000	4,828,000		118,964,000
Leasehold improvements	3,693,000	33,000	193,000	469,000		4,002,000
	853,381,000	7,486,000	7,700,000	28,970,000		882,137,000
Construction and design projects in progress	39,374,000	52,020,000		(28,970,000)	$(1,628,000)	60,796,000
Land	16,888,000	90,000	714,000			16,264,000
	$ 909,643,000	$ 59,596,000	$8,414,000	$ -0-	$(1,628,000)	$ 959,197,000

YEAR ENDED SEPTEMBER 30, 1980

Description	Balance at Beginning of Year	Additions At Cost	Retirements Or Sales	Transfers	Other[1]	Balance at End of Year
Rides and attractions	$ 290,635,000	$ 1,000	$ 278,000	$ 48,533,000		$ 338,891,000
Buildings	324,013,000	22,000	446,000	(17,597,000)		305,992,000
Equipment, furniture and fixtures	144,523,000	2,438,000	1,841,000	14,698,000		159,818,000
Land improvements	118,964,000	19,000	130,000	5,173,000		124,026,000
Leasehold improvements	4,002,000	104,000	92,000	2,411,000		6,425,000
	882,137,000	2,584,000	2,787,000	53,218,000		935,152,000
Construction and design projects in progress	60,796,000	158,561,000		(53,218,000)	$(3,108,000)	163,031,000
Land	16,264,000	150,000				16,414,000
	$ 959,197,000	$161,295,000	$2,787,000	$ -0-	$(3,108,000)	$1,114,597,000

YEAR ENDED SEPTEMBER 30, 1981

Description	Balance at Beginning of Year	Additions At Cost	Retirements Or Sales	Transfers	Other[1]	Balance at End of Year
Rides and attractions	$ 338,891,000	$ 893,000	$5,323,000	$(31,886,000)		$ 302,575,000
Buildings	305,992,000	4,372,000	44,000	9,252,000		319,572,000
Equipment, furniture and fixtures	159,818,000	12,459,000	2,755,000	42,108,000		211,630,000
Land improvements	124,026,000	247,000	266,000	2,378,000		126,385,000
Leasehold improvements	6,425,000	210,000	273,000	1,699,000		8,061,000
	935,152,000	18,181,000	8,661,000	23,551,000		968,223,000
Construction and design projects in progress	163,031,000	332,861,000		(23,551,000)	$(3,079,000)	469,262,000
Land	16,414,000	160,000	155,000			16,419,000
	$1,114,597,000	$351,202,000	$8,816,000	$ -0-	$(3,079,000)	$1,453,904,000

[1]Prior year costs of design projects abandoned.

resort hotels at Walt Disney World, and increased food and merchandise sales at the Walt Disney World Village. Theme park per capita guest spending was influenced by admission media price increases averaging 6-8% in April-May 1979, March-April 1980 and June 1981 at the two parks, and 7% in November 1980 at Walt Disney World. In addition, selective increases continue to be made in food and merchandise prices and lodging accommodation rates.

Operating income for the segment has grown at an average annual rate of 14% over the last five years. However, the rate of growth has been less in 1980 and 1981 and operating margins have also declined. Costs and expenses of operations are increasing due primarily to higher labor rates and labor hours paid. The average labor rate, which includes employee benefits, increased in 1981, 1980 and 1979 by 10.6%, 6.3% and 7.9% at Disneyland and by 16.1%, 9.2% and 9.8% at Walt Disney World. In addition, significant increases have been experienced in other expenses, including operating materials, outside services and utilities. The gross profit margins for food and merchandise have remained substantially unchanged for all three years. Effective October 1, 1980, the Company extended the estimated useful lives of certain theme park ride and attraction assets based upon historical data and engineering studies. The effect of this change was to decrease depreciation by approximately $8 million (an increase in net income of approximately $.13 per share).

While attendance was down slightly in 1981, Disneyland enjoyed its second best attendance in history and Walt Disney World surpassed the 13 million mark for the sixth consecutive year.

Motion Pictures

	1981	Change	1980	Change	1979
Revenues	$174,575	+8%	$161,400	+20%	$134,785
Operating income	30,497	−37%	48,675	+21%	40,229
Operating margin	17%		30%		30%

Motion picture production and distribution is a highly competitive business, wherein the public's response to a given motion picture can have a major impact on the success of that product and, hence, a significant impact on the Company's motion picture business for any particular year. The new live action releases of "The Devil and Max Devlin", "Amy", "Dragonslayer" (a co-production with Paramount Pictures) and "Condorman" during 1981 resulted in very disappointing film rentals in the domestic theatrical market. In contrast, "The Fox and the Hound", the Company's twentieth fully animated feature film, performed very well domestically and is expected to do even better in the foreign market. Foreign theatrical film rentals in 1981, led by the original release of "The Black Hole" and reissues of "The Aristocats" and "101 Dalmatians", almost reached the record foreign revenues set in 1980. Television rentals contributed significantly to higher revenues with the licensing of several features to pay television and two features to commercial television, demonstrating the continuing value of the Disney film

library. Licensing agreements with pay television suppliers will expire in June 1982. The Company has recently announced that it will in the future dedicate its filmed product to a 16-hour-a-day pay cable programming service that the Company will operate with Westinghouse Broadcasting (Group W) in a joint venture, debuting in late 1982 or early 1983.

Operating income decreased significantly in 1981 due primarily to higher amortization of film negative costs and to write-downs, totaling $20.5 million, to their expected net realizable values of the four new live action releases referred to above. The higher amortization in 1981 is due to the higher film negative costs associated with "Popeye", "The Black Hole" and "The Fox and the Hound".

Operating margins have been adversely affected in 1981 due to the relatively low film rentals of the four new live action releases compared to the relatively high costs of production/amortization and distribution. Television rentals, in contrast, contributed a higher margin because of the relatively low cost of distribution and amortization associated with the films licensed to television during the year.

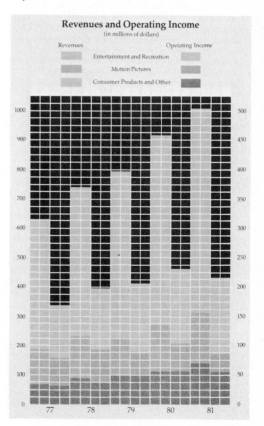

Revenues and Operating Income
(in millions of dollars)

Revenues — Operating Income

Entertainment and Recreation
Motion Pictures
Consumer Products and Other

FINANCIAL REVIEW Continued

Consumer Products and Other

	1981	Change	1980	Change	1979
Revenues	$138,654	+26%	$109,725	+21%	$90,909
Operating income	54,693	−1%	55,093	+23%	44,822
Operating margin	39%		50%		49%

The consumer products segment consists of the character merchandising and publications, the telecommunications and non-theatrical and the records and music publishing businesses. Also included in this segment in 1981 are the revenues of approximately $10 million and expenses related to the installation of the WEDway PeopleMover System at the Houston International Airport. There was a small profit on this project, which was accounted for on the completed contract method.

Revenues continue to increase in all businesses within the segment. Character merchandising and publication increases are predominately in the foreign territories as a result of an ongoing program of developing new product that is gradually introduced into new territories around the world. Home video disc and cassette domestic sales and rentals have contributed approximately $10.9 million in revenues to telecommunications and non-theatrical in the initial year of this growing market. Records and music publishing continues to develop new product to augment its popular standard line of records and music. The successful domestic release of the Mickey Mouse Disco record album in 1980 carried over into 1981 but at a considerably reduced volume.

Operating income and margins were adversely affected in 1981 by additional labor and other start-up costs associated with entering the home video cassette business in the domestic market in 1981 to be followed by expansion into the foreign market in 1982. During this period 8 millimeter filmed product is gradually being phased out in favor of home video product and educational media product sales have been impacted by government spending cutbacks.

General and Administrative Expense

	1981	Change	1980	Change	1979
Amount	$26,216	+24%	$21,130	+19%	$17,830
Percent of revenues	3%		2%		2%

In addition to normal increases in labor, materials and outside services, certain corporate functions and services are being expanded to meet the needs of the Company. The most significant increase is identified with the management information services division, which is adding new computer equipment and personnel in response to increased demands in the Company's existing businesses and in anticipation of the opening of the Epcot Center.

Design Projects Abandoned

	1981	Change	1980	Change	1979
Amount	$4,598	+7%	$4,294	+80%	$2,390

At the close of each fiscal quarter, management evaluates projects in the concept and design stages which have been in progress for varying periods of time. Those which are determined to have no future use are abandoned. A major portion of the design costs abandoned in 1981 and 1980 relate to the Epcot Center.

Interest Income—Net

	1981	Change	1980	Change	1979
Amount	$33,130	−21%	$42,110	+48%	$28,413

The Company has realized net interest income (after interest expense) from short term investments, such income being dependent upon fluctuations in interest rates and the amount of such investments. Interest income will continue to decrease as the funds currently invested are used to finance the Epcot Center project. (See discussion under Financial Position on page 32 and Note 2 of Notes to Consolidated Financial Statements.) Interest expense amounted to $1,749,000, $746,000 and $27,000 for fiscal years 1981, 1980 and 1979, respectively. Commencing with fiscal year 1982, the Company plans to capitalize interest expense as part of the cost of construction projects and motion picture films. The amount to be capitalized will be dependent upon the extent of borrowings and the associated rates of interest incurred.

Taxes on Income

	1981	Change	1980	Change	1979
Amount	$95,500	−15%	$112,800	+13%	$100,100
Percent of income before taxes on income	44.0%		45.5%		46.8%

An explanation of the provision for taxes on income for 1981, 1980 and 1979 is given in Note 3 of Notes to Consolidated Financial Statements.

SUPPLEMENTARY INFORMATION REGARDING INFLATION AND CHANGING PRICES

General Background

Inflation has become a subject of increasing significance in the U.S. economy during the past decade. During periods of continuing inflation the purchasing power of the dollar is eroded, meaning that it requires more dollars to purchase the same goods and services.

The primary financial statements traditionally reflect the historic cost rather than the current cost of assets required to maintain an enterprise's productive capability. Transactions are recorded in terms of the number of dollars actually received or expended without regard to changes in the purchasing power of the currency or changes in the cost of goods and services consumed.

There is no universally accepted method for measuring the effect of inflation in financial statements. In recognition of the need, however, to provide readers of financial statements with information to assist them in assessing that impact, the Financial Accounting Standards Board issued Statement of Financial Accounting Standards No. 33, "Financial Reporting and Changing Prices" (SFAS 33). The general objectives of reporting the effects of changing prices as expressed in SFAS 33 are to help users assess (a) future cash flows, (b) the maintenance of operating capability, (c) financial performance, and (d) the maintenance of general purchasing power.

The Statement prescribes two supplementary income computations. One deals with the effects of general inflation (constant dollars) and the other deals with the effects of changes in the specific prices of the resources actually used in the operations of the enterprise (current cost).

Under the "constant dollar" method, historical cost financial information is adjusted only for changes that have occurred in the general purchasing power of the dollar as measured by the Consumer Price Index for all Urban Consumers (CPI-U).

Under the "current cost" method, historical cost financial information is adjusted for changes in specific prices. Changes in specific prices may be due in part to changes in general purchasing power and in part to other market factors (such as technological improvements, variations in supply and demand for skills and commodities and shifts in consumer tastes). As a result, specific productive assets are measured at the current costs of replacement rather than at the historic costs originally incurred to acquire them. Current cost measurement techniques used by the Company include direct pricing, application of specific indexes, and functional and unit pricing.

Constant dollar and current cost adjustments for the current fiscal year are as follows:

SUPPLEMENTARY STATEMENT OF CONSOLIDATED INCOME ADJUSTED FOR CHANGING PRICES
For The Year Ended September 30, 1981
(In thousands of dollars, except per share data)

	As Included In Primary Financial Statements (Historical Cost)	As Adjusted For General Inflation (Constant Dollar)	As Adjusted For Changes In Specific Prices (Current Cost)
Revenues	$1,005,040	$1,005,040	$1,005,040
Costs and expenses:			
Cost of goods sold	163,215	168,000	167,000
Depreciation	38,886	67,900	70,800
Amortization	55,222	60,600	60,600
Other expenses	563,867	563,867	563,867
Interest income–net	(33,130)	(33,130)	(33,130)
Taxes on income	95,500	95,500	95,500
Total costs and expenses	883,560	922,737	924,637
Net income	$ 121,480	$ 82,303	$ 80,403
Earnings per share	$3.72	$2.52	$2.46
Gain from decline in purchasing power of net amounts owed		$ 4,000	$ 4,000
Increase in specific prices (current cost) of inventories; film production costs; and property, plant and equipment*			$ 106,000
Effects of increase in general inflation			161,000
Excess of increase in the general price level over increase in specific prices			$ 55,000

*At September 30, 1981 the current cost of inventories was $61,000, film production costs net of amortization was $132,000, and property plant and equipment net of accumulated depreciation was $1,640,000.

Net assets at year end are increased by $533 million when the cost of inventories, film production costs and the cost of property, plant and equipment are adjusted to average 1981 dollars (constant dollar) and by $583 million when adjusted to specific prices (current cost). This increase in the valuation of assets results in an increase in depreciation expense of $29 million (constant dollar) and $32 million (current cost). This adjustment of depreciation expense is the primary cause of the decrease in net income adjusted for the effects of inflation. In computing the above amounts, normal service lives and depreciation/amortization rates have been applied to the adjusted amounts. No adjustments are made to fully

Walt Disney Productions and Subsidiaries
FINANCIAL REVIEW Continued

adjusted amounts. No adjustments are made to fully depreciated assets currently utilized in the Company's business. Revenues and all other expenses are considered to reflect the average price levels for the year and accordingly have not been adjusted.

Net monetary assets represent cash or claims to cash less amounts owed. When prices are increasing, the holding of monetary assets results in a loss in general purchasing power. Similarly, amounts owed produce a gain in general purchasing power because the amount of money required to settle the liabilities represents dollars of diminishing purchasing power. At September 30, 1981, the excess of monetary liabilities over monetary assets resulted in a net gain in purchasing power. This gain is presented as supplementary information and has not been included in the Consolidated Statement of Income Adjusted For Changing Prices.

Construction costs generally rose at a rate less than the CPI-U during the year. Because the Company incurred significant construction costs during the year, increases in specific prices of property, plant and equipment and construction in progress were less than the increase in the general price level.

As required by SFAS 33, certain selected financial data are restated based on the average CPI-U for the year for each of the five years shown. Certain 1980 figures have been adjusted from amounts originally reported to reflect refinements in the development of inflation accounting data. The amounts as expressed in average 1981 dollars are as follows:

FIVE YEAR COMPARISON OF SELECTED SUPPLEMENTARY FINANCIAL DATA ADJUSTED FOR EFFECTS OF CHANGING PRICES
In Average 1981 Dollars
(In thousands of dollars, except for per share data)

		Year Ended September 30			
	1981	1980	1979	1978	1977
Revenues					
Constant dollars	$1,005,040	$1,016,000	$1,005,000	$994,000	$938,000
Net Income					
Constant dollars	$ 82,303	$ 108,000			
Current cost	80,403	103,000			
Earnings per share					
Constant dollars	$2.52	$3.32			
Current cost	2.46	3.18			
Net assets at year end					
Constant dollars	$1,700,000	$1,680,000			
Current cost	1,680,000	1,700,000			
Cash dividends per common share					
Constant dollars	$1.00	$ .80	$ .61	$ .45	$ .22
Market price per common share at year end					
Constant dollars	$46.75	$52.48	$50.78	$59.31	$58.84
Gain (loss) from decline in purchasing power of net amounts owed (monetary assets)	$ 4,000	$ (22,000)			
Average consumer price index	266	240	211	191	179

Management's Comments and Conclusions

Inflation accounting as required by SFAS 33 involves the use of numerous assumptions, approximations, and estimates, and should be viewed in that context and not as a precise indicator of the effects of inflation. The reader is cautioned not to attach too much significance to any one year's adjusted results. Even when several years are viewed consecutively, the information is considered to be of limited use until the reader completely understands the principles and concepts utilized in compiling the data.

The current cost of goods sold represents estimated costs at the time of sale rather than at the time of purchase. The relatively minor difference between cost of goods sold reported on an historical cost basis and that reported for current cost indicates that the Company's use of the moving average basis of accounting for the cost of its inventories results in cost of goods sold that generally approximates current cost.

As noted above, depreciation adjusted for inflation is significantly higher than the depreciation reported in the primary financial statements. However, this additional theoretical depreciation should not be interpreted as an indication of a decline in the Company's ability to maintain its productive capability. As a result of carefully planned and comprehensive refurbishing programs at its entertainment facilities, the productive capability is continuously renewed. The Company is not confronted with a problem of replacing very old and worn-out capital assets.

The cost of the Company's land, as included in net assets at year end under both the constant dollar and current cost measurement techniques, has been adjusted for changes in the CPI-U. The Company considers no other measure or index more appropriate to determine current cost of the service potential of its land.

In issuing SFAS 46, "Financial Reporting and Changing Prices: Motion Picture Films," the Financial Accounting Standards Board has recognized that current cost measures are not appropriate for motion picture films. As a result, amortization of film negative costs has been adjusted for changes in the CPI-U under both the constant dollar and current cost measures of inflation.

In accordance with SFAS 33, no adjustment has been made to the provision for income taxes included in the supplementary statement of income. The effective tax rate for 1981 rises from 44.0% on a historical cost basis to 53.7% on a constant dollar basis and 54.3% on the current cost basis. This information highlights the fact that inflation does erode real earnings growth and that effective tax burdens are often greater than the statutory rate, thus reducing funds available for increasing capacity and stimulating productivity.

Walt Disney Productions and Subsidiaries

CONSOLIDATED STATEMENT OF INCOME

(Dollar amounts in thousands, except per share data)	Year Ended September 30		
	1981	1980	1979
Revenues			
Entertainment and recreation	$ 691,811	$643,380	$571,079
Motion pictures	174,575	161,400	134,785
Consumer products and other	138,654	109,725	90,909
Total revenues	1,005,040	914,505	796,773
Costs and Expenses of Operations			
Entertainment and recreation	562,337	515,848	450,435
Motion pictures	144,078	112,725	94,556
Consumer products and other	83,961	54,632	46,087
Total costs and expenses of operations	790,376	683,205	591,078
Operating Income Before Corporate Expenses			
Entertainment and recreation	129,474	127,532	120,644
Motion pictures	30,497	48,675	40,229
Consumer products and other	54,693	55,093	44,822
Total operating income before corporate expenses	214,664	231,300	205,695
Corporate Expenses (Income)			
General and administrative	26,216	21,130	17,830
Design projects abandoned	4,598	4,294	2,390
Interest income—net	(33,130)	(42,110)	(28,413)
Total corporate expenses (income)	(2,316)	(16,686)	(8,193)
Income Before Taxes on Income	216,980	247,986	213,888
Taxes on income (note 3)	95,500	112,800	100,100
Net Income	$ 121,480	$135,186	$113,788
Earnings per Share	$3.72	$4.16	$3.51

CONSOLIDATED STATEMENT OF RETAINED EARNINGS

Balance at beginning of the year	$ 537,109	$425,203	$326,911
Net income for the year	121,480	135,186	113,788
Dividends—Cash ($1.00, $.72 and $.48 per share)	(32,406)	(23,280)	(15,496)
Balance at end of the year	$ 626,183	$537,109	$425,203

See notes to consolidated financial statements and summary of significant accounting policies.

Walt Disney Productions and Subsidiaries
CONSOLIDATED BALANCE SHEET

	September 30	
(Dollar amounts in thousands)	**1981**	1980
ASSETS		
Current Assets		
Cash	$ 5,869	$ 9,745
Short term investments, at cost which approximates market (note 2)	248,408	318,533
Accounts receivable, net of allowances	69,302	50,711
Inventories	59,773	54,648
Film production costs (note 1)	59,079	61,127
Prepaid expenses	15,398	11,438
Total current assets	457,829	506,202
Film Production Costs—Non-Current (note 1)	61,561	59,281
Property, Plant and Equipment, at cost		
Entertainment attractions, buildings and equipment	968,223	935,152
Less accumulated depreciation	(384,535)	(352,051)
	583,688	583,101
Construction and design projects in progress		
Epcot Center (note 2)	439,858	141,373
Other	29,404	21,658
Land	16,419	16,414
	1,069,369	762,546
Other Assets (note 4)	21,250	19,378
	$1,610,009	$1,347,407
LIABILITIES AND STOCKHOLDERS EQUITY		
Current Liabilities		
Accounts payable, payroll and other accrued liabilities (note 7)	$ 158,516	$ 109,047
Taxes on income (note 3)	33,057	36,244
Total current liabilities	191,573	145,291
Long Term Liabilities and Non-Current Advances (notes 2, 4 and 6)	161,886	30,429
Deferred Taxes on Income and Investment Credits (note 3)	89,432	96,889
Commitments and Contingencies (note 8)		
Stockholders Equity (note 4)		
Preferred shares, no par		
Authorized—5,000,000 shares, none issued		
Common shares, no par		
Authorized—75,000,000 shares		
Issued and outstanding—32,433,360 and 32,354,319 shares	540,935	537,689
Retained earnings	626,183	537,109
	1,167,118	1,074,798
	$1,610,009	$1,347,407

See notes to consolidated financial statements and summary of significant accounting policies.

Walt Disney Productions and Subsidiaries
CONSOLIDATED STATEMENT OF CHANGES IN FINANCIAL POSITION

(In thousands of dollars)	Year Ended September 30		
	1981	1980*	1979*
Cash provided by operations before taxes on income (see below)	**$316,949**	$326,504	$286,256
Taxes paid on income	**106,144**	121,822	103,399
Cash provided by operations	**210,805**	204,682	182,857
Cash dividends	**32,406**	23,280	15,496
	178,399	181,402	167,361
Investing activities			
Epcot Center, net of related payables	**285,651**	102,529	16,666
Other property, plant and equipment	**47,756**	47,145	39,963
Film production costs	**55,454**	68,409	44,436
Other	**5,930**	1,619	6,218
	394,791	219,702	107,283
	(216,392)	(38,300)	60,078
Financing activities			
Short and long term debt	**110,000**		
Participation fees	**24,745**	10,361	6,245
Other	**7,646**	1,327	968
	142,391	11,688	7,213
Increase (decrease) in cash and short term investments	**(74,001)**	(26,612)	67,291
Cash and short term investments, beginning of year	**328,278**	354,890	287,599
Cash and short term investments, end of year	**$254,277**	$328,278	$354,890

The difference between income before taxes on income as shown on the Consolidated Statement of Income and cash provided by operations before taxes on income is explained as follows:

Income before taxes on income	$216,980	$247,986	$213,888
Charges to income not requiring cash outlays:			
Depreciation	38,886	43,093	40,439
Amortization of film production costs	55,222	33,889	31,823
Other	9,449	6,530	4,151
Changes in:			
Accounts receivable, net of allowances	(18,591)	(13,589)	(10,414)
Inventories	(5,125)	(12,774)	(2,470)
Prepaid expenses	(3,960)	(2,461)	(693)
Accounts payable, payroll and other accrued liabilities	24,088	23,830	9,532
	99,969	78,518	72,368
Cash provided by operations before taxes on income	$316,949	$326,504	$286,256

*Restated to conform with 1981 format.

See notes to consolidated financial statements and summary of significant accounting policies.

DESCRIPTION OF THE BUSINESS AND SUMMARY OF SIGNIFICANT ACCOUNTING POLICIES

Walt Disney Productions and Subsidiaries

WALT DISNEY PRODUCTIONS is a diversified international company engaged in family entertainment and operates in three business segments:

Entertainment and Recreation

The Company operates an amusement theme park, "Disneyland", in California and wholly owned subsidiaries operate a destination resort, "Walt Disney World", in Florida. In addition to an amusement theme park, the Walt Disney World complex includes three hotels, camping, golfing and other recreational facilities, a shopping village, a conference center and other lodging accommodations.

Motion Pictures

The Company produces motion pictures for theatrical and television distribution. The Company distributes its filmed product through its own distribution company in the United States and through foreign subsidiaries in certain countries and independent distribution companies throughout the rest of the world.

Consumer Products and Other

The Company licenses the name Walt Disney, its characters, its literary properties and its songs and music to various manufacturers, retailers, printers and publishers. The Company also produces and distributes phonograph records, 8 millimeter prints of excerpts from its film library, video cassettes and 16 millimeter prints of product taken from the film library or developed on educational subjects, and a broad range of teaching aids. These activities are conducted through the character merchandising, publications, records and music publishing, and telecommunications and non-theatrical divisions and subsidiaries of the Company.

The following summary of the Company's significant accounting policies is presented as an integral part of the financial statements.

PRINCIPLES OF CONSOLIDATION

The consolidated financial statements include the accounts of the Company and its domestic and foreign subsidiaries, all wholly owned.

REVENUE RECOGNITION

Generally, revenue is recorded when the earning process is substantially complete and goods have been delivered or services performed. Revenue from entertainment and recreation activities is received principally in cash; revenue from participant/sponsors at the theme parks (which will include the Epcot Center) is recorded over the period of the applicable agreements commencing with the opening of the attraction. Revenue from the theatrical distribution of motion pictures is recognized when motion pictures are exhibited domestically and when revenues are reported from foreign distributors; revenue from television licensing agreements is generally recorded when the film is contractually available to the licensee and certain other conditions are met.

FILM PRODUCTION COSTS AND AMORTIZATION

Costs of completed theatrical and television film productions (negative costs), together with applicable capitalized exploitation costs, are amortized by charges to income in the proportion that gross revenue recognized by the Company during the year for each production bears to the estimated total gross revenue to be received. Estimates of total gross revenue are reviewed periodically and amortization is adjusted accordingly. If unamortized cost exceeds the estimated producers share of film rentals to be received, the carrying value of the film is adjusted to expected net realizable value.

INVENTORIES

Costs of merchandise, materials and supplies inventories are generally determined on the moving average basis and the retail method and are stated at the lower of cost or market.

PROPERTY, PLANT AND EQUIPMENT

The Company, at any one point in time, will have a number of projects in the concept, design, or construction phases related to entertainment attractions, buildings and equipment. All projects in progress are evaluated on a continuing basis and, upon completion, costs of major replacements and betterments are capitalized. If it is determined that a project in progress has no future use, the costs of such project are charged to income under the caption "Design Projects Abandoned".

Depreciation is provided principally on the straight line method using estimated service lives ranging from four to fifty years.

TAXES ON INCOME

Taxes are provided on all revenue and expense items included in the consolidated statement of income, regardless of the period in which such items are recognized for income tax purposes, except for items representing a permanent difference between pretax accounting income and taxable income. Investment tax credits, accounted for by the deferral method, are amortized as a reduction of the provision for taxes on income over the average service lives of the related assets.

STOCK OPTIONS

Proceeds from the sale of common stock issued under stock option plans are accounted for as capital transactions. If stock appreciation rights (SAR's) are granted in connection with options granted, income is charged or credited over the vesting period for the difference between the market price of the Company's stock and the option price of the appreciation rights outstanding.

EARNINGS PER SHARE

Earnings per common and common equivalent share are computed on the basis of the average number of shares outstanding during each year, retroactively adjusted to give effect to all stock splits and stock dividends. It is assumed that all dilutive stock options are exercised at the beginning of each year and that the proceeds are used to purchase shares of the Company's common stock at the average market price during the year.

Walt Disney Productions and Subsidiaries
NOTES TO CONSOLIDATED FINANCIAL STATEMENTS

1. Film Production Costs:

Theatrical and television film production costs consist of the following components (in thousands of dollars):

	1981	1980
Released, less amortization	$ 54,100	$ 46,337
Completed, not yet released	21,562	30,016
In process	44,978	44,055
	120,640	120,408
Less: Non-current film production costs	61,561	59,281
Current film production costs	$ 59,079	$ 61,127

Non-current film production costs include costs of theatrical and television films in process of production, portions of completed theatrical film costs allocated to television and portions of completed television film costs allocated to foreign markets.

2. Epcot Center Project:

On October 1, 1979, the Company began construction of the Epcot Center at Walt Disney World, a complex involving two major themed areas, Future World and World Showcase. The official opening will be on October 1, 1982 and the cost of those facilities that are planned to be completed and operational at that date is estimated to be approximately $800 million. Additional attractions and exhibits, estimated at $150 million, are planned for completion after the October 1982 opening. These amounts do not include certain interest expense which will be capitalized, or preopening costs estimated at $30 million which will be deferred and amortized over five years.

WED Enterprises, the Company's design division, is responsible for the engineering, master planning and imagineering for the Epcot Center. The Company has entered into agreements totaling approximately $500 million (of which approximately $270 million has been paid at September 30, 1981) for construction management services, construction contracts and architectural/engineering services.

It is contemplated that the proceeds from short term investments held by the Company, which include the funds obtained from a Eurodollar offering, will be used to fund the project, together with cash provided by future operations, payments from corporate participants in the project and, depending upon capital market conditions, other sources of debt financing and drawings under the Company's revolving line of credit. (See Note 6.) In accordance with the current corporate participation agreements, the Company expects to receive approximately $300 million in total participation fees and $70 million prior to opening day ($41.3 million has been received as of September 30, 1981 and is included in Long Term Liabilities and Non-Current Advances).

3. Taxes on Income (in thousands of dollars):

The income before provision and the provision for taxes on income is composed of the following:

	1981	1980	1979
Income before provision for taxes on income			
—United States	$212,885	$243,449	$209,531
—Foreign	4,095	4,537	4,357
Total income before provision for taxes on income	$216,980	$247,986	$213,888
Currently payable			
—Federal	$ 81,157	$ 97,352	$ 88,275
—State	10,058	11,668	10,280
—Foreign	6,717	5,454	4,935
Total currently payable	97,932	114,474	103,490
Deferred			
—Federal	2,526	4,194	790
—State	(458)	(668)	(280)
—Investment credits amortized	(4,500)	(5,200)	(3,900)
Total deferred	(2,432)	(1,674)	(3,390)
Total provision for taxes on income	$ 95,500	$112,800	$100,100

The significant components of deferred taxes on income included in the provision for taxes on income are as follows:

	1981	1980	1979
Excess of tax over book depreciation	$ 6,590	$ 2,230	$ 3,650
Epcot participation fees included in taxable income	(11,920)	(5,020)	(2,690)
Other	2,898	1,116	(4,350)
Total provision for deferred taxes on income	$(2,432)	$(1,674)	$(3,390)

The difference between the U.S. federal income tax rate and the Company's effective income tax rate is explained below:

	1981	1980	1979
Federal income tax rate	46.0%	46.0%	46.5%
State income taxes, net of federal income tax benefit	2.4	2.4	2.5
Reduction in taxes resulting from:			
Investment tax credits	(2.1)	(2.1)	(1.8)
Other	(2.3)	(.8)	(.4)
Effective income tax rate	44.0%	45.5%	46.8%

Net deferred taxes of $9,869 at September 30, 1981 ($4,845—1980) are included in taxes on income shown under current liabilities on the balance sheet.

Deferred investment tax credits amount to $19,370 at September 30, 1981 ($18,675—1980).

Walt Disney Productions and Subsidiaries
NOTES TO CONSOLIDATED FINANCIAL STATEMENTS Continued

4. Employee Benefits:
Pension and Deferred Compensation Plans
The Company contributes to various domestic trusteed pension plans under union and industry-wide agreements. Contributions are based on the hours worked by or gross wages paid to covered employees.

The Company has pension plans covering substantially all of its domestic employees not covered by union or industry pension plans. The plans are funded by Company and employee payments to a trust administered by a bank. In prior years, the Company prepaid the actuarially computed past service liability of the plans determined as of June 30, 1978, and the unamortized prepaid amount totaling $2,402,000 at September 30, 1981, is deferred and classified in other assets and is being amortized over periods ranging to 8 more years.

A comparison of accumulated plan benefits for the defined benefit plans with net assets available for benefits as of June 30, 1981, the date of the latest actuarial valuation, is as follows (in thousands of dollars):

Actuarial present value of accumulated plan benefits:	
Vested	$23,705
Nonvested	5,363
Total	$29,068
Net assets available for benefits	$41,569

The rate of return used in determining the actuarial present value of accumulated plan benefits is 8½%, based on Pension Benefit Guaranty Corporation (PBGC) interest assumptions as of June 30, 1981.

The Company also has a non-qualified and unfunded key employee retirement plan providing for Company and domestic employee contributions. The amount accrued as a long term liability under this plan was $13,999,000 at September 30, 1981 ($11,177,000—1980); the actuarially computed unrecorded past service liability at the date of the latest determination was approximately $7,500,000.

The aggregate amounts expensed for all of these plans was $7,598,000, $7,146,000 and $5,822,000 for fiscal years 1981, 1980 and 1979, respectively, including amortization of actuarially computed prior service costs, where applicable, over periods ranging to thirty-two more years.

Stock Option Plans
Stock options are granted to key executive, management and creative personnel at prices equal to market price at date of grant. The options and prices set forth below have been adjusted, where applicable, for all subsequent stock splits and stock dividends.

Transactions under the 1967, 1973 and 1980 Plans during fiscal year 1981 were as follows:

	Number of Shares	
	Options Granted	Available For Grant
Outstanding September 30, 1980		
($20.77 to $43.52 per share)	570,982	623,908
Options terminated	(21,190)	21,188
Options granted	575,000	(575,000)
Options exercised	(79,041)	
SAR's exercised	(20,458)	
Outstanding September 30, 1981		
($20.77 to $64.31 per share)	1,025,293*	70,096

*Includes 297,331 options with SAR's.

Options are exercisable beginning not less than one year after date of grant. Options which were originally granted as qualified options expire five years after date of grant and those granted as non-qualified options expire ten years after date of grant. At September 30, 1981, options on 3,659 shares granted under the 1967 Plan were exercisable at $43.52 per share; options on 372,270 shares granted under the 1973 Plan were exercisable at $20.77 to $40.81 per share; and none of the options granted under the 1980 Plan had become exercisable.

Under the Company's 1967 and 1973 Stock Option Plans, $2,268,000 was received in fiscal year 1981 ($1,240,000—1980) and credited to stockholders equity for 79,041 and 54,888 shares which were issued on the exercise of options in fiscal years 1981 and 1980, respectively. Income tax benefit from purchase of option shares by employees of $978,000 was credited to stockholders equity in fiscal year 1981 ($590,000—1980).

The 1980 Stock Option Plan permits the granting of stock appreciation rights in connection with any option granted under this plan or under the 1973 Stock Option Plan. In lieu of exercising a stock option, SAR holders are entitled, upon exercise of an SAR, to receive cash or common shares or a combination thereof in an amount equal to the excess of the fair market value of such shares on the date of exercise over the option price.

As of September 30, 1981, stock appreciation rights were outstanding with respect to 297,331 shares subject to options under the 1973 and 1980 Stock Option Plans. These stock appreciation rights were granted to a limited number of key employees. Income and overhead accounts were charged with $552,000 during fiscal year 1981 ($2,188,000—1980) in respect to SAR's.

In February 1981 the stockholders approved a new Incentive Plan to provide for incentives and awards to key employees under which 797,310 common shares remain reserved for issuance at September 30, 1981.

Employee Stock Ownership Plan for Salaried Employees
The Company also has an Employee Stock Ownership Plan (ESOP) for salaried employees. Under the Plan, the Company has claimed an additional 1% of the Company's qualified capital investments as an investment tax credit and paid such an amount to a trust which then purchases shares of the Company's stock in the open market for the employees' benefit. Relating to fiscal 1980 and 1979, respectively, $706,800 and $445,600 have been used to purchase 11,682 and 9,234 shares of stock. The Company may claim a tax credit equal to an additional ½% of the Company's qualified capital investments if this amount is used to match employee contributions. Commencing with fiscal 1980, the matching employer contribution used to purchase 10,994 shares of common stock was $334,300.

5. Business Segments (in thousands of dollars):

The Company operates in three business segments: Entertainment and Recreation, Motion Pictures and Consumer Products and Other. These business segments are described in the Summary of Significant Accounting Policies on page 40 of this report.

The Consolidated Statement of Income presents the revenue and operating income by business segment. Additional financial information relative to business segments follows.

Total revenues of $1,005,040 ($914,505—1980 and $796,773—1979) include foreign revenues (export sales) related to the following geographic areas:

	1981	1980	1979
Europe	$ 84,932	$ 95,749	$ 71,628
Western Hemisphere (excluding the United States)	26,014	24,413	19,947
Other	24,189	13,701	13,289
	$135,135	$133,863	$104,864

Capital expenditures by business segment were:

	1981	1980	1979
Entertainment and recreation	**$344,361**	$157,834	$ 54,804
Motion pictures	**4,040**	2,020	1,541
Consumer products and other	**277**	140	42
Corporate	**110**	306	242
	$348,788	$160,300	$ 56,629

Depreciation expense by business segment was:

	1981	1980	1979
Entertainment and recreation	**$ 37,338**	$ 41,780	$ 39,053
Motion pictures	**1,200**	921	805
Consumer products and other	**155**	199	411
Corporate	**193**	193	170
	$ 38,886	$ 43,093	$ 40,439

Effective October 1, 1980, the Company extended the estimated useful lives of certain theme park ride and attraction assets based upon historical data and engineering studies. The effect of this change was to decrease depreciation by approximately $8 million (an increase in net income of approximately $4.2 million, or $.13 per share).

Amortization expense of film production costs (classified under Motion Pictures) was $55,222, $33,889 and $31,823 for fiscal years 1981, 1980 and 1979, respectively. Included in 1981 are write-downs totaling $20.5 million of four new live action releases to their expected net realizable values ($9.5 million — 1980).

Identifiable assets by business segment were:

	1981	1980	1979
Entertainment and recreation	**$1,141,657**	$ 825,364	$ 684,856
Motion pictures	**157,106**	154,135	113,269
Consumer products and other	**39,239**	30,265	23,221
Corporate	**272,007**	337,643	375,078
	$1,610,009	$1,347,407	$1,196,424

Corporate assets are principally cash and short term investments.

6. Indebtedness:

Short Term

The Company issued commercial paper on September 24, 1981, totaling $10 million, which is included under current liabilities. The notes with interest at 14.85% to 15.05% are due on November 23, 1981.

Long Term

The Company issued 15¾% notes as of September 1, 1981, totaling $100 million as a result of a Eurodollar offering. The notes will mature on September 1, 1986, and are not redeemable before September 1, 1984. Interest on the notes is payable annually.

In addition, two unsecured notes were issued on August 5, 1981, totaling $5.1 million, as a result of the acquisition of a building at Lake Buena Vista, Florida. The notes with interest at 14.45% and 15.50% are due in five years but may be prepaid.

Line of Credit

The Company has available through September 1984 an unsecured revolving line of credit of $200 million generally at the prime rate for general corporate purposes. The revolving line can be increased to $300 million at the option of the Company. Under the line of credit, the Company is required to pay a fee on the unused portion of the commitment and to maintain certain compensating balances. There were no borrowings under the line of credit at September 30, 1981. Up to $150 million of the line of credit is available to support commercial paper, against which $10 million had been issued at September 30, 1981.

Walt Disney Productions and Subsidiaries
NOTES TO CONSOLIDATED FINANCIAL STATEMENTS Continued

7. Current Liabilities:

Accounts payable, payroll and other accrued liabilities at September 30 are as follows (in thousands of dollars):

	1981	1980
Commercial paper (note 6)	$ 10,000	
Accounts payable—trade	52,965	$ 40,011
Accounts payable—construction contracts	26,007	10,626
Payroll and employee benefits	34,597	30,338
Unearned deposits and advances	17,952	15,025
Cash dividends payable	8,108	5,824
Property, payroll and other taxes	8,887	7,223
	$158,516	$109,047

8. Commitments and Contingencies (in thousands of dollars):

Pursuant to an agreement for the use of the name of Walt Disney, Retlaw Enterprises, Inc. (a company owned by the family of the late Walter E. Disney) earned royalties of approximately $6,886, $7,107 and $6,557 from the Company for fiscal years 1981, 1980 and 1979, respectively; in accordance with such name agreement, the amount in 1981 included $3,800 ($3,550—1980 and $3,505—1979) as a participation by Retlaw of 5% in the profits, as defined in that agreement, of certain Walt Disney World operations.

The Company has entered into an agreement with the stockholders of Retlaw upon the consummation of which the Company would in effect acquire all of Retlaw's rights to the name, likeness and portrait of Walt Disney and the narrow-gauge steam railroad and monorail systems at Disneyland. The agreement provides for a purchase price to be paid by the Company to the stockholders of Retlaw of $46.2 million, payable in shares of common stock of the Company. Consummation of the agreement is subject to approval by the stockholders of the Company and certain other conditions.

The Company's subsidiary, Buena Vista Distribution Co., Inc., is a defendant with other motion picture distributors in a number of private treble damage actions asserting claims under the federal anti-trust laws. These actions, which seek damages aggregating hundreds of millions of dollars, are in various stages of pre-trial proceedings. The Company has denied the material allegations of the complaints in these actions, and in the opinion of management and counsel, the Company will not suffer any material liability by reason thereof.

Report of Independent Accountants

1880 CENTURY PARK EAST
WEST LOS ANGELES, CALIFORNIA 90067

November 23, 1981

To the Board of Directors and Stockholders
of Walt Disney Productions

In our opinion, the accompanying consolidated balance sheet and the related consolidated statements of income, retained earnings and changes in financial position present fairly the financial position of Walt Disney Productions and its subsidiaries at September 30, 1981 and 1980, and the results of their operations and the changes in their financial position for each of the three years in the period ended September 30, 1981, in conformity with generally accepted accounting principles consistently applied. Our examinations of these statements were made in accordance with generally accepted auditing standards and accordingly included such tests of the accounting records and such other auditing procedures as we considered necessary in the circumstances.

Price Waterhouse

Walt Disney Productions and Subsidiaries
SELECTED FINANCIAL DATA 1977–1981

(Dollar amounts and shares in thousands, except per share data)	**1981**	1980	1979	1978	1977
Statement of Income Data					
Revenues (Page 46)	**$1,005,040**	$ 914,505	$ 796,773	$ 741,143	$629,825
Operating income before corporate expenses	**214,664**	231,300	205,695	197,540	169,500
Corporate expenses	**30,814**	25,424	20,220	20,523	18,494
Interest income—net	**(33,130)**	(42,110)	(28,413)	(12,468)	(6,341)
Taxes on income	**95,500**	112,800	100,100	91,100	75,400
Net income	**121,480**	135,186	113,788	98,385	81,947
Balance Sheet Data					
Current assets	**$ 457,829**	$ 506,202	$ 484,141	$ 394,448	$289,894
Property, plant and equipment—net of depreciation	**1,069,369**	762,546	648,447	633,885	629,940
Total assets	**1,610,009**	1,347,407	1,196,424	1,083,141	964,475
Current liabilities	**191,573**	145,291	119,768	113,674	86,448
Long term obligations	**161,886**	30,429	18,616	11,393	10,781
Total liabilities and deferred credits	**442,891**	272,609	235,362	221,906	193,269
Total net assets (stockholders equity)	**1,167,118**	1,074,798	961,062	861,235	771,206
Statement of Changes in Financial Position Data					
Cash provided by operations	**$ 210,805**	$ 204,682	$ 182,857	$ 201,905	$153,116
Cash dividends	**32,406**	23,280	15,496	10,273	4,725
Investment in property, plant and equipment	**333,407**	149,674	56,629	45,367	44,517
Investment in film production	**55,454**	68,409	44,436	32,716	34,699
Per Share Data					
Net income (earnings)	**$ 3.72**	$ 4.16	$ 3.51	$ 3.04	$ 2.53
Cash dividends	**1.00**	.72	.48	.32	.15
Stockholders equity	**35.99**	33.22	29.76	26.71	23.97
Average number of common and common equivalent shares outstanding during the year	**32,629**	32,513	32,426	32,397	32,373
Other Data					
Stockholders at close of year	**60,000**	62,000	65,000	66,000	65,000
Employees at close of year	**25,000**	24,000	21,000	21,000	19,000

Walt Disney Productions and Subsidiaries
OTHER FINANCIAL DATA 1977–1981

(In thousands)	**1981**	1980	1979	1978	1977
Walt Disney World					
Admissions and rides	**$139,326**	$130,144	$121,276	$114,687	$100,792
Merchandise sales	**121,465**	116,187	101,856	86,860	72,906
Food sales	**114,951**	106,404	95,203	84,319	73,245
Lodging	**70,110**	61,731	54,043	44,972	39,902
Participant and other rentals	**8,148**	8,632	9,994	9,574	9,220
Other	**11,436**	10,279	7,251	5,226	4,453
Total revenues	**$465,436**	$433,377	$389,623	$345,638	$300,518
Theme park total attendance	**13,221**	13,783	13,792	14,071	13,057
Disneyland					
Admissions and rides	**$ 92,065**	$ 87,066	$ 75,758	$ 70,909	$ 65,913
Merchandise sales	**79,146**	72,140	60,235	49,312	39,485
Food sales	**44,920**	41,703	35,865	32,710	29,700
Participant and other rentals	**5,603**	5,432	5,266	4,676	4,784
Other	**657**	718	606	667	673
Total revenues	**$222,391**	$207,059	$177,730	$158,274	$140,555
Theme park total attendance	**11,343**	11,522	10,760	10,807	10,678
Walt Disney Travel Co.	**$ 3,984**	$ 2,944	$ 3,726*	$ 4,532*	$ 4,092*

*Includes Celebrity Sports Center which was sold in March, 1979.

	1981	1980	1979	1978	1977
Motion Pictures and Television					
Theatrical					
Domestic	**$ 54,624**	$ 63,350	$ 49,594	$ 69,010	$ 58,723
Foreign	**76,279**	78,314	57,288	57,912	36,585
Television					
Worldwide	**43,672**	19,736	27,903	25,213	22,750
Total revenues	**$174,575**	$161,400	$134,785	$152,135	$118,058
Consumer Products					
Telecommunications and non-theatrical	**$ 43,379**	$ 32,473	$ 29,240	$ 24,809	$ 20,714
Character merchandising	**30,555**	29,631	24,787	21,359	17,743
Publications	**24,658**	22,284	18,985	15,045	12,861
Records and music publishing	**27,358**	23,432	16,129	17,218	13,858
Other	**12,704**	1,905	1,768	2,133	1,426
Total revenues	**$138,654**	$109,725	$ 90,909	$ 80,564	$ 66,602

Walt Disney Productions and Subsidiaries
QUARTERLY FINANCIAL SUMMARY

(Dollar amounts in thousands, except per share data)	December 31	March 31	June 30	September 30
OPERATIONS BY QUARTER				
1981				
Revenues				
Entertainment and recreation	$135,832	$143,450	$198,079	$214,450
Motion pictures	34,174	56,623	31,227	52,551
Consumer products and other	33,504	34,993	28,721	41,436
Total revenues	$203,510	$235,066	$258,027	$308,437
Operating Income (Loss) Before Corporate Expenses				
Entertainment and recreation	$ 16,697	$ 18,765	$ 45,457	$ 48,555
Motion pictures	13,684	13,677	(1,985)	5,121
Consumer products and other	15,209	17,891	11,359	10,234
Total operating income before corporate expenses	$ 45,590	$ 50,333	$ 54,831	$ 63,910
Income Before Taxes on Income	$ 47,145	$ 50,231	$ 55,001	$ 64,603
Net Income	$ 25,945	$ 27,631	$ 30,201	$ 37,703
Earnings per Share	$.80	$.84	$.93	$1.15
1980				
Revenues				
Entertainment and recreation	$122,345	$138,863	$183,032	$199,140
Motion pictures	37,453	49,972	36,776	37,199
Consumer products and other	25,685	29,268	25,607	29,165
Total revenues	$185,483	$218,103	$245,415	$265,504
Operating Income Before Corporate Expenses				
Entertainment and recreation	$ 18,455	$ 24,425	$ 39,695	$ 44,957
Motion pictures	11,921	17,036	9,641	10,077
Consumer products and other	13,485	15,744	12,057	13,807
Total operating income before corporate expenses	$ 43,861	$ 57,205	$ 61,393	$ 68,841
Income Before Taxes on Income	$ 47,953	$ 61,613	$ 67,196	$ 71,224
Net Income	$ 25,653	$ 33,013	$ 35,896	$ 40,624
Earnings per Share	$.79	$1.02	$1.10	$1.25
MARKET PRICE AND DIVIDEND DATA				
1981				
Price per share:				
High	$52¼	$63¾	$67⅛	$63½
Low	$41¾	$49¼	$54¼	$43⅜
Dividend per share	$.25	$.25	$.25	$.25
1980				
Price per share:				
High	$45½	$48⅛	$52¾	$53⅞
Low	$35½	$40½	$41¼	$46¼
Dividend per share	$.18	$.18	$.18	$.18

The principal market for trading Walt Disney Productions common stock is the New York Stock Exchange.

REVIEW QUESTIONS

1 What is an *industry segment* of a business enterprise?

2 Is the concept of segment reporting consistent with the theory of consolidated financial statements? Explain.

3 Outline the segment reporting requirements of *FASB Statement No. 14,* "Financial Reporting for Segments of a Business Enterprise."

4 How is *operating profit or loss* computed for industry segments of a business enterprise?

5 Describe the *maximum* and *minimum* limitations on the extent of segment reporting by a business enterprise.

6 Describe the formula for the allocation of residual home office expenses set forth in *Cost Accounting Standard 403,* "Allocation of Home Office Expenses to Segments."

7 Differentiate between the *measurement date* and the *disposal date* for the discontinuance of a segment of a business enterprise. Define *phase-out period.*

8 Discuss the provisions of *APB Opinion No. 28,* "Interim Financial Reporting," dealing with the accounting for costs associated with revenue in interim financial reports.

9 Explain the technique included in *APB Opinion No. 28,* "Interim Financial Reporting," for the computation of income tax provisions in interim financial reports.

10 How is lower-of-cost-or-market accounting for inventories applied in interim financial reports?

11 Identify four of the six United States statutes administered by the SEC.

12 What position did the SEC take regarding its role in the establishment of accounting principles?

13 What are *Financial Reporting Releases?*

14 Does the SEC require the inclusion of *financial forecasts* in filings with the Commission?

15 How do accountants use *Regulation S-X* in filings with the SEC?

16 What is *Regulation S-K* of the SEC?

17 Differentiate between *Form 10-K* and *Form 8-K* filed with the SEC under the Securities Exchange Act of 1934.

18 Under what circumstances must financial statements of a business enterprise be included in a *proxy statement* issued to the enterprise's shareholders under the provisions of the Securities Exchange Act of 1934?

EXERCISES

Ex. 15-1 Select the best answer for each of the following multiple-choice questions:

1 Rawson Company is a diversified enterprise that discloses supplemental financial information for its industry segments. The following information is available for Year 6:

	Sales	Traceable expenses	Nontraceable expenses
Segment A	$400,000	$225,000	
Segment B	300,000	240,000	
Segment C	200,000	135,000	
Totals	$900,000	$600,000	$150,000

Nontraceable expenses are allocated based on the ratio of a segment's income before nontraceable expenses to total income before nontraceable expenses. This is an appropriate method of allocation. What is the operating profit for Segment B for Year 6?
a $0   **b** $10,000   **c** $30,000   **d** $50,000   **e** Some other amount

2 In January, Year 5, Horner Company paid $80,000 in property taxes on its plant for Year 5. Also in January, Year 5, Horner estimated that its year-end bonus to executives for Year 5 would be $320,000. What is the amount of the expenses related to these two items that should be reflected in Horner's quarterly income statement for the three months ended June 30, Year 5 (second quarter)?
a $0   **b** $20,000   **c** $80,000   **d** $100,000   **e** Some other amount

3 According to **APB Opinion No. 28,** "Interim Financial Reporting," income taxes expense in an income statement for the first interim period of an enterprise's fiscal year should be computed by:
a Applying the estimated income tax rate for the full fiscal year to the pre-tax accounting income for the interim period
b Applying the estimated income tax rate for the full fiscal year to the taxable income for the interim period
c Applying the statutory income tax rate to the pre-tax accounting income for the interim period
d Applying the statutory income tax rate to the taxable income for the interim period

4 The SEC's present position with respect to the inclusion of financial forecasts in filings with the Commission is that financial forecasts are:
a Permissible   **b** Mandatory   **c** Forbidden   **d** Unimportant

5 When a business enterprise discontinues an operation and disposes of the discontinued operation (segment), the transaction should be included in the income statement as a gain or loss on disposal and reported as:
a A prior period adjustment
b An extraordinary item
c An amount after income from continuing operations and before extraordinary items
d A bulk sale of plant assets included in income from continuing operations

6 **FASB Statement No. 14,** "Financial Reporting for Segments of a Business Enterprise," requires disclosure of information relating to all the following, except an enterprise's:
a Foreign operations and export sales
b Major suppliers
c Operations in different industries
d Major customers

7 Wade Company, which has a fiscal year ending February 28, had the following pre-tax accounting income and estimated effective annual income tax rates for the first three quarters of the year ended February 28, Year 8:

Quarter	Pre-tax accounting income	Estimated effective annual income tax rate at end of quarter
First	$60,000	40%
Second	70,000	40%
Third	40,000	45%

Wade's income taxes expense in its interim income statement for the third quarter is:
a $18,000   **b** $24,500   **c** $25,500   **d** $76,500   **e** Some other amount

Ex. 15-2   Rinker Company operates in three different industries, each of which is appropriately regarded as a reportable segment. Segment No. 1 contributed 60% of Rinker's total sales in Year 3. Sales for Segment No. 1 were $900,000 and traceable expenses were $400,000 in Year 3. Nontraceable expenses for Year 3 were $600,000. Rinker allocates nontraceable expenses based on the ratio of a segment's sales to total sales, an appropriate method of allocation.
Compute the operating profit or loss for Segment No. 1 for Year 3.

Ex. 15-3   Crossley Company had net income of $600,000 for the year ended December 31, Year 8, after inclusion of the following special events that occurred during the year:

(1) The decision was made on January 2 to discontinue the cinder block manufacturing segment.
(2) The cinder block manufacturing segment was sold on July 1.
(3) Operating income from January 2 to June 30 for the cinder block manufacturing segment amounted to $90,000 before income taxes.
(4) Cinder block manufacturing equipment with a carrying amount of $250,000 was sold for $100,000.

Crossley was subject to income taxes at the rate of 40%.

a Compute Crossley's income from continuing operations for Year 8.
b Compute Crossley's total income taxes (expenses and allocated) for Year 8.

Ex. 15-4   Marmon Corporation's statutory federal and state income tax rates total 30%. Marmon forecasts pre-tax accounting income of $100,000 for the year ending April 30, Year 7, with no timing differences between pre-tax accounting income and taxable income. Marmon forecasts the following permanent differences between pre-tax accounting income and taxable income for the year ending April 30, Year 7: Dividend received deduction, $20,000; goodwill amortization, $10,000. Marmon also anticipates investment tax credits of $5,000 for the year ending April 30, Year 7.
Compute Marmon Corporation's estimated effective combined federal and state income tax rate for the year ending April 30, Year 7.

Ex. 15-5   The nontraceable expenses of Coopers Company's corporate office for the year ended June 30, Year 2, total $310,000. The net sales, payroll, and average plant assets and inventories for the two industry segments of Coopers are as follows:

	Chemicals segment	Sporting goods segment
Net sales	$1,400,000	$600,000
Payroll	150,000	100,000
Average plant assets and inventories	710,000	290,000

Compute the amount of corporate office nontraceable expenses that should be allocated to the Chemicals Segment and the Sporting Goods Segment of Coopers Company, assuming that such expenses are allocated to the two segments on the basis of the arithmetic average of the percentage of net sales, payroll, and average plant assets and inventories applicable to each segment.

Ex. 15-6 Canton Company allocates nontraceable expenses to its three industry segments on the basis of net sales to unaffiliated customers. For the fiscal year ended April 30, Year 4, relevant segment data were as follows:

	Segment A	Segment B	Segment C
Revenue:			
Net sales to unaffiliated			
customers	$500,000	$300,000	$200,000
Intersegment transfers out	80,000	40,000	20,000
Costs and expenses:			
Traceable expenses	400,000	100,000	200,000
Intersegment transfers in	30,000	60,000	50,000

Nontraceable expenses of Canton Company for the year ended April 30, Year 4, totaled $100,000.

Compute for each industry segment of Canton Company the following amounts for the year ended April 30, Year 4: revenue, operating expenses, operating profit or loss. Use a column for each industry segment, as shown above.

Ex. 15-7 Basey Company has a fiscal year ending April 30. On July 31, Year 6, the end of the first quarter of Year 7, Basey estimated an effective combined federal and state income tax rate of 55% for Year 7. On October 31, Year 6, the end of the second quarter of Year 7, Basey estimated an effective combined federal and state income tax rate of 52% for Year 7. Pre-tax accounting income for Basey was as follows:

For three months ended July 31, Year 6 . . . . $200,000
For three months ended October 31, Year 6 250,000

Prepare journal entries for income taxes expense for Basey Company on July 31 and October 31, Year 6.

Ex. 15-8 The ledger accounts for plant assets of Bruno Company had the following balances at the beginning and end of Year 5:

	Jan. 1, Year 5	Dec. 31, Year 5
Land	$150,000	$200,000
Building	800,000	800,000
Machinery and equipment	325,000	400,000

During Year 5, Bruno acquired for $50,000 cash a parcel of real property adjoining its present land to provide space for constructing an addition to its building during Year 6. The net increase of $75,000 in the Machinery and Equipment account during Year 5 was composed of the following:

Additions at cost (none in excess of 2% of total assets) $125,000
Retirements at cost . . . . (20,000)
Write-down of idle machinery to net realizable value . . . . (30,000)
Net increase in Machinery and Equipment account during Year 5 . . $ 75,000

Prepare a Schedule V, entitled Plant Assets, for Bruno Company to include in its **Form 10-K** filed with the SEC for Year 5. Use the format on page 700.

Ex. 15-9   Data with respect to the foreign geographic area operations of Emmet Company for the year ended December 31, Year 3, follow:

Foreign Geographic Areas

	Latin America	Africa	Southeast Asia	Western Europe	Total
Net sales to out-siders	$40,000	$20,000	$25,000	$ 5,000	$90,000
Interarea transfers out	2,000	4,000	1,000	3,000	10,000
Interarea transfers in	4,000	3,000	2,000	1,000	10,000
Other traceable expenses	9,000	6,000	5,000	10,000	30,000
Nontraceable expenses					20,000

Emmet allocates nontraceable expenses to industry segments only.

Determine if each foreign geographic area of Emmet Company is significant for the year ended December 31, Year 3. Disregard identifiable assets of the foreign geographic areas.

Ex. 15-10   On January 2, Year 6, Luigi Company paid property taxes of $40,000 on its plant assets for Year 6. In March, Year 6, Luigi made customary annual major repairs to plant assets in the amount of $120,000. The repairs will benefit the entire Year 6. In April, Year 6, Luigi incurred a $420,000 loss from a market decline of inventories that was considered to be permanent.

Show how the above items are reported in Luigi's quarterly income statements for Year 6.

Ex. 15-11   Tovar Company's accounting records for the year ended August 31, Year 4, include the following data with respect to its Wallis Division. Sale of that division to Expansive Enterprises, Inc., for $300,000 was authorized by Tovar's board of directors on August 31, Year 4. Closing date of the sale was expected to be February 28, Year 5.

Wallis Division:

Net sales, year ended Aug. 31, Year 4	$200,000
Costs and expenses, year ended Aug. 31, Year 4	150,000
Estimated operating losses, six months ending Feb. 28, Year 5	40,000
Estimated carrying amount of net assets, Feb. 28, Year 5	330,000

Tovar's combined federal and state income tax rate is 60%. For the year ended August 31, Year 4, Tovar had $640,000 income from continuing operations before income taxes.

Prepare a partial income statement for Tovar Company for the year ended August 31, Year 4, to present the information given.

Ex. 15-12   Lundy Company sells a single product, which it purchases from three different vendors. On May 1, Year 8, Lundy's inventory of the product consisted of 1,000 units priced at fifo cost of $7,500. Lundy's merchandise transactions for the year ended April 30, Year 9, were as follows:

Quarter	Units purchased	Cost per unit purchased	Units sold	End-of-quarter replacement cost per unit
1	5,000	$8.00	4,500	$8.50
2	6,000	8.50	7,000	9.00
3	8,000	9.00	6,500	8.50*
4	6,000	8.50	5,500	9.50

* Decline not considered to be temporary.

Compute Lundy Company's cost of goods sold for each of the four quarters of the year ended April 30, Year 9. Show computations.

Ex. 15-13 Farber Company's journal entry for income taxes on September 30, Year 5, the end of its fiscal year, was as follows:

Income Taxes Expense ($37,312 + $12,100). 49,412

    Income Taxes Payable   49,412

To provide for income taxes for the year as follows:

	Federal	State
Pre-tax accounting income	$100,000	$100,000
Less: Nontaxable municipal bond interest	(10,000)	(10,000)
Add: Nondeductible goodwill amortization	4,000	4,000
Taxable income, state		$ 94,000
State income tax at 15%		$ 14,100
Less: Investment tax credits		(2,000)
State income tax	(12,100)	$ 12,100
Taxable income, federal	$ 81,900	
Federal income tax at 48%	$ 39,312	
Less: Investment tax credits	(2,000)	
Federal income tax	$ 37,312	

Prepare a reconciliation, in percentages rounded to the nearest tenth, between the statutory federal income tax rate, 48%, and Farber Company's effective income tax rate, 49.4% ($49,412 ÷ $100,000 = 49.4%), required by **ASR No. 149** for a note to Farber's September 30, Year 4, financial statements filed with the SEC in **Form 10-K.** Combine any reconciling items that individually are less than 5% of the statutory federal income tax rate. Use the format on page 715.

CASES

Case 15-1 Interim financial reporting is an important topic in financial accounting. There has been considerable discussion as to the proper method of reflecting results of operations at interim dates. **APB Opinion No. 28,** "Interim Financial Reporting," clarified some aspects of interim financial reporting.

Instructions

a Discuss generally how revenue should be recognized at interim dates and specifically how revenue should be recognized for industries subject to large seasonal fluctuations in revenue and for long-term construction contracts accounted for by the percentage-of-completion method at annual reporting dates.

b Discuss generally how product and period costs should be recognized at interim dates. Also discuss how inventory and cost of goods sold may be afforded special accounting treatment at interim dates.

c Discuss how income taxes expense is computed and reflected in interim reports of earnings.

Case 15-2 The Financial Accounting Standards Board requires the reporting of financial data for segments of a business enterprise.

Instructions

a What does financial reporting for segments of a business enterprise involve?

b Identify the reasons why financial data should be reported for segments of a business enterprise.

c Identify the possible disadvantages of reporting financial data for segments of a business enterprise.

d Identify the accounting difficulties inherent in segment reporting.

Case 15-3 Nanson Company, a publicly owned corporation listed on a major stock exchange, forecasted operations for the year ending December 31, Year 5, as follows:

NANSON COMPANY
Forecasted Income Statement
For Year Ending December 31, Year 5

Net sales (1,000,000 units)	$6,000,000
Cost of goods sold	3,600,000
Gross profit on sales	$2,400,000
Operating expenses	1,400,000
Operating income	$1,000,000
Nonoperating revenue and expenses	-0-
Income before income taxes	$1,000,000
Income taxes expense (current and deferred)	550,000
Net income	$ 450,000
Earnings per share of common stock	$4.50

Nanson has operated profitably for many years and has experienced a seasonal pattern of sales volume and production similar to the following ones forecasted for Year 5:

Sales volume is expected to follow a quarterly pattern of 10%, 20%, 35%, 35%, respectively, because of the seasonality of the industry. Also, due to production and storage capacity limitations it is expected that production will follow a pattern of 20%, 25%, 30%, 25%, per quarter, respectively.

At the conclusion of the first quarter of Year 5, the controller of Nanson prepared and issued the following interim income statement:

NANSON COMPANY
Income Statement
For Quarter Ended March 31, Year 5

Net sales (100,000 units)	$ 600,000
Cost of goods sold	360,000
Gross profit on sales	$ 240,000
Operating expenses	275,000
Operating loss	$ (35,000)
Loss from warehouse explosion	(175,000)
Loss before income taxes	$(210,000)
Income taxes expense	-0-
Net loss	$(210,000)
Loss per share of common stock	$(2.10)

The following additional information is available for the first quarter just completed, but was not included in the information released by Nanson:

(1) Nanson uses a standard cost system in which standards are set at currently attainable levels on an annual basis. At the end of the first quarter, underapplied fixed factory overhead (volume variance) of $50,000 was treated as an asset. Production during the first quarter was 200,000 units, of which 100,000 were sold.

(2) The operating expenses were forecasted on a basis of $900,000 fixed expenses for the year plus $0.50 variable expenses per unit sold.

(3) The warehouse explosion loss met the conditions of an extraordinary loss. The warehouse had a carrying amount of $320,000; $145,000 was recovered from insurance on the warehouse. No other gains or losses are anticipated this year from similar events or transactions, nor has Nanson had any similar losses in preceding years; thus, the full loss will be deductible as an ordinary loss for income tax purposes.

(4) The effective rate for federal and state income taxes combined is expected to average 55% of income before income taxes for Year 5. There are no permanent differences between pre-tax accounting income and taxable income.

(5) Earnings per share were computed on the basis of 100,000 shares of common stock outstanding. Nanson has only one class of capital stock issued, no long-term debt outstanding, no stock option plan, and no warrants to acquire common stock outstanding.

Instructions
a Without reference to the specific situation described, what are the standards of disclosure for interim financial data (published interim financial reports) for publicly owned corporations? Explain.

b Identify the weaknesses in form and content of Nanson Company's interim income statement, without reference to the additional information.

c For each of the five items of additional information, indicate the preferable treatment for interim reporting purposes and explain why that treatment is preferable.

Case 15-4 **a** In order to understand generally accepted accounting principles with respect to accounting for and reporting on segments of a business enterprise, as stated by the Financial Accounting Standards Board in **FASB Statement No. 14,** "Financial Reporting for Segments of a Business Enterprise," it is necessary to be familiar with certain unique terminology.

Instructions With respect to segments of a business enterprise, explain the following terms:

(1) *Industry segment*
(2) *Revenue*
(3) *Operating profit or loss*
(4) *Identifiable assets*

b A central issue in reporting on industry segments of a business enterprise is the determination of which segments are reportable.

Instructions

(1) What are the tests to determine whether or not an industry segment is reportable?
(2) What is the test to determine if enough industry segments have been separately reported on, and what is the guideline on the maximum number of industry segments to be reported?

PROBLEMS

15-1 Data with respect to the four industry segments of Wabash Company for the year ended November 30, Year 10, follow:

	Segment				Total
	Alpha	Beta	Gamma	Delta	
Net sales to outsiders	$40,000	$20,000	$25,000	$ 5,000	$90,000
Intersegment transfers out . . .	2,000	4,000	1,000	3,000	10,000
Intersegment transfers in	4,000	3,000	2,000	1,000	10,000
Other traceable expenses	9,000	6,000	5,000	10,000	30,000
Nontraceable expenses					20,000

Wabash allocated nontraceable expenses to industry segments by the following reasonable method: Alpha—40%; Beta—30%; Gamma—20%; Delta—10%.

Instructions

a Prepare a working paper to compute the operating profit or loss for Wabash Company's four industry segments for the year ended November 30, Year 10.

b Prepare a working paper to determine if each industry segment of Wabash Company is **significant** for the year ended November 30, Year 10. Disregard segment identifiable assets.

15-2 Cregar Company is "going public" early in Year 4, and is preparing to file a *Form S-1* with the SEC to register the common stock it plans to issue to the public. The accountant for Cregar prepared the following comparative income statements for inclusion in the *Form S-1:*

CREGAR COMPANY
Income Statements
For Years Ended December 31,

	Year 3	Year 2	Year 1
Net sales	$10,000,000	$9,600,000	$8,800,000
Cost of goods sold	6,200,000	6,000,000	5,400,000
Gross profit on sales	$ 3,800,000	$3,600,000	$3,400,000
Operating expenses	2,200,000	2,400,000	2,100,000
Income from operations	$ 1,600,000	$1,200,000	$1,300,000
Gain on disposal of segment	900,000		
Income before income taxes	$ 2,500,000	$1,200,000	$1,300,000
Income taxes expense	1,500,000	720,000	780,000
Net income	$ 1,000,000	$ 480,000	$ 520,000

During your audit of the foregoing income statements, you discover that Cregar contracted on January 1, Year 3, to sell for $3,200,000 the assets and product line of one of its industry segments. The sale was completed on December 31, Year 3, for a gain of $900,000 before income taxes. The discontinued operations' contribution to Cregar's income before income taxes for each year was as follows: Year 3, $640,000 loss; Year 2, $500,000 loss; Year 1, $200,000 income. Cregar's combined income tax rate is 60%.

Instructions Prepare corrected partial comparative income statements for Cregar Company for the three years ended December 31, Year 3, Year 2, and Year 1. Disregard notes to financial statements and earnings per share. Begin the income statements with income from continuing operations before income taxes. Show supporting computations.

15-3 For the year ending July 31, Year 6, Lang Corporation forecasted pre-tax accounting income of $800,000. Lang did not anticipate any timing differences between pre-tax accounting income and taxable income. However, the following permanent differences between accounting and taxable income for Year 6 were forecasted:

Dividend received deduction	$150,000
Goodwill amortization	20,000
Officers' life insurance premium expense	15,000

In addition, Lang anticipated investment tax credits of $50,000 for Year 6. Lang's combined federal and state income tax rate is 60%, and federal and state laws coincided with respect to determination of taxable income.

Lang's quarterly pre-tax accounting income for the year ended July 31, Year 6, is summarized below:

Quarter ended:

Oct. 31, Year 5	$180,000
Jan. 31, Year 6	230,000
Apr. 30, Year 6	195,000
July 31, Year 6	225,000

During Year 6, Lang did not alter its forecast of pre-tax accounting income for the year. However, effective January 31, Year 6, Lang revised its permanent difference estimate for the Year 6 dividend received deduction to $180,000 from $150,000, and its investment tax credits estimate for the year to $80,000 from

$50,000. The actual amounts for the permanent differences and investment tax credits computed by Lang on July 31, Year 6, were as follows:

Dividend received deduction	$175,000
Goodwill amortization	20,000
Officers' life insurance premium expense	16,000
Investment tax credits	90,000

Instructions
a Compute the effective combined federal and state income tax rates that Lang Corporation should use for its quarterly interim financial reports for the year ended July 31, Year 6. Round all percentage computations to the nearest tenth.

b Prepare Lang Corporation's journal entries for income taxes on October 31, Year 5, and January 31, April 30, and July 31, Year 6.

15-4 Bixler Company, a diversified manufacturing enterprise that does not report to the SEC, had four separate operating divisions engaged in the manufacture of products in each of the following industries: food products, health aids, textiles, and office equipment.

Financial data for the two years ended December 31, Year 8 and Year 7, are shown below:

	Net sales		Cost of goods sold		Operating expenses	
	Year 8	Year 7	Year 8	Year 7	Year 8	Year 7
Food products . . .	$3,500,000	$3,000,000	$2,400,000	$1,800,000	$ 550,000	$ 275,000
Health aids	2,000,000	1,270,000	1,100,000	700,000	300,000	125,000
Textiles	1,580,000	1,400,000	500,000	900,000	200,000	150,000
Office equipment .	920,000	1,330,000	800,000	1,000,000	650,000	750,000
Totals	$8,000,000	$7,000,000	$4,800,000	$4,400,000	$1,700,000	$1,300,000

On January 1, Year 8, Bixler adopted a plan to sell the assets and product line of the office equipment division at an anticipated gain. On September 1, Year 8, the division's assets and product line were sold for $2,100,000 cash, at a gain of $640,000 (exclusive of operations during the phase-out period).

Bixler's textiles division had six manufacturing plants that produced a variety of textile products. In April, Year 8, Bixler sold one of these plants and realized a gain of $130,000. After the sale, the operations at the plant that was sold were transferred to the remaining five textile plants that Bixler continued to operate.

In August, Year 8, the main warehouse of the food products division, located on the banks of the Colton River, was flooded when the river overflowed. The resulting uninsured damage of $420,000 is not included in the financial data given above. Historical records indicate that the Colton River normally overflows every four to five years, causing flood damage to adjacent property.

For the two years ended December 31, Year 8 and Year 7, Bixler earned interest revenue on investments of $70,000 and $40,000, respectively. For the two years ended December 31, Year 8 and Year 7, Bixler's net income was $960,000 and $670,000, respectively. Income taxes expense for each of the two years should be computed at a rate of 50%.

Instructions Prepare comparative income statements for Bixler Company for the two years ended December 31, Year 8 and Year 7. Footnotes and earnings per share disclosures are not required.

15-5 Cossage Company has three stores, each of which is an industry segment, in a state that recently enacted legislation permitting municipalities within the state to levy an income tax on corporations operating within their respective municipalities. The legislation established a uniform income tax rate that the municipalities may levy, and regulations that provided that the tax is to be computed on income derived within the taxing municipality after a reasonable and consistent allocation of nontraceable expenses. Nontraceable expenses, which have not been allocated to Cossage's individual stores previously, include warehouse, delivery, and corporate office expenses.

Each of the municipalities in which Cossage operates a store has levied the corporate income tax as provided by state legislation, and management is considering two plans for allocating nontraceable expenses to the stores. The Year 9 operating results for each store, before nontraceable expenses and income taxes, were as follows:

	Store			
	Hastings	Irving	Jamestown	Total
Net sales	$416,000	$353,600	$270,400	$1,040,000
Cost of goods sold	215,700	183,300	140,200	539,200
Gross profit on sales	$200,300	$170,300	$130,200	$ 500,800
Less: Local operating expenses:				
Fixed	$ 60,800	$ 48,750	$ 50,200	$ 159,750
Variable	54,700	64,220	27,448	146,368
Totals	$115,500	$112,970	$ 77,648	$ 306,118
Income before nontraceable expenses and income taxes	$ 84,800	$ 57,330	$ 52,552	$ 194,682

Nontraceable expenses in Year 9 were as follows:

Warehouse and delivery expenses:
Warehouse depreciation $20,000
Warehouse operations 30,000
Delivery expense . . . . 40,000 $ 90,000
Corporate office expenses:
Advertising $18,000
Corporate office salaries 37,000
Other corporate office expenses 28,000   83,000
Total nontraceable expenses $173,000

Additional information includes the following:

(1) One-fifth of the warehouse space is used to house the corporate office, and depreciation on this space is included in other corporate office expenses. Warehouse operating expenses vary with the quantity of merchandise sold.
(2) Delivery expense varies with distance and the number of deliveries. The distances from the warehouse to each store and the number of deliveries made in Year 9 were as follows:

Store	Miles	Number of deliveries
Hastings	120	140
Irving	200	64
Jamestown	100	104

(3) All advertising is arranged by the corporate office and is distributed in the areas in which stores are located.

Instructions

a For each of the following plans for allocating Cossage Company's nontraceable expenses, compute the income of each store that would be subject to the municipal income tax levy on corporation income:

Plan 1 Allocate all nontraceable expenses on the basis of sales volume.

Plan 2 First, allocate corporate office salaries and other corporate office expenses equally to warehouse operations and each store; second, allocate the resulting warehouse operations expenses, warehouse depreciation, and advertising to each store on the basis of sales volume; and third, allocate delivery expense to each store on the basis of delivery miles times number of deliveries.

b Which plan would you advise management to adopt? Explain.

15-6 The general ledger of Draco Company included the following amounts for the year ended December 31, Year 6:

Cost of goods sold—continuing operations	$ 8,000,000
Estimated loss on disposal of Southern Division, to be completed in	
first quarter of Year 7	50,000
Income taxes expense ($540,000 × 0.60)	324,000
Interest expense	100,000
Judgment paid in lawsuit of **Justin Company v. Draco Company,** initiated in Year 4	80,000
Loss from bankruptcy liquidation of major customer	150,000
Loss from operations of Southern Division, discontinued effective Dec. 31, Year 6 (measurement date)	120,000
Net sales—continuing operations	10,000,000
Operating expenses—continuing operations	800,000
Uninsured loss from earthquake at Northern Division	160,000

Draco's combined federal and state income tax rate is 60%. Draco had no timing or permanent differences between pre-tax accounting income and taxable income, and no investment tax credits for Year 6. Prior to Year 6, there had not been an earthquake in the Northern Division's locality for more than 50 years.

Instructions Prepare an income statement for Draco Company for the year ended December 31, Year 6, in accordance with the provisions of **APB Opinion No. 30,** "Reporting the Results of Operations." Disregard earnings per share data and notes to financial statements.

15-7 Principia Corporation was incorporated January 2, Year 4, with a public issuance of 3 million shares of $1 par common stock on that date for net proceeds of $5,750,000, net of out-of-pocket costs of the stock issuance. Immediately thereafter, Principia organized three wholly owned subsidiaries—Seattle Company and Boston Company in the United States, and London Company in the United Kingdom. Principia paid $1,500,000 cash for each subsidiary's 1,500,000 authorized shares of $1 par common stock.

The working paper for consolidated financial statements for Principia Corporation and subsidiaries is presented on pages 736 and 737. Other information is as follows:

(1) Each of the affiliated companies constitutes a different industry segment.
(2) Principia, Seattle, and Boston operate in the North America geographic area, and London operates in the Western Europe geographic area.
(3) None of the companies declared or paid dividends in Year 4.
(4) Each of the companies files separate income tax returns at an effective income tax rate of 60%.
(5) Intercompany receivables and payables represent loans or advances. (Receivables and payables arising from intercompany sales of merchandise were paid in full on December 31, Year 4.)
(6) $50,000 of Principia's operating expenses represents nontraceable expenses allocable to each industry segment in the ratio of the **average** of each segment's Year 4 sales to outsiders and December 31, Year 4, plant asset balances. The remainder of Principia's operating expenses represents general corporate expenses.
(7) Cash not required for each segment's current operations is forwarded to Principia for the acquisition of short-term investments.

Instructions Prepare the following for Principia Corporation and subsidiaries for Year 4 in accordance with the provisions of **FASB Statement No. 14,** "Financial Reporting for Segments of a Business Enterprise":

a Working paper to determine whether each industry segment constitutes a significant segment.

b Disclosures of information about the operations of Principia Corporation and subsidiaries in different industries. Use the following format:

PRINCIPIA CORPORATION AND SUBSIDIARIES
Information about the Companies' Operations in Different Industries
For Year Ended December 31, Year 4
(000 omitted)

	Principia industry	Seattle industry	Boston industry	London industry	Elimi-nations	Con-solidated
Sales to unaffiliated customers						
Intersegment sales						
Total revenue						
Operating profit (loss) . .						
Interest revenue						
General corporate expenses						
Interest expense.						
Income before income taxes						
Identifiable assets, Dec. 31, Year 4						
Corporate assets.						
Total assets, Dec. 31, Year 4						

(Continued on page 738)

PRINCIPIA CORPORATION AND SUBSIDIARIES
Working Paper for Consolidated Financial Statements
For Year Ended December 31, Year 4
(000 omitted)

Income Statement	Principia Corporation	Seattle Company	Boston Company	London Company*	Eliminations increase (decrease)		Consolidated
Revenue							
Net sales	500	400	300	200			1,400
Intercompany sales	40	30	20	10	(b)	(100)	
Intercompany investment income	32				(a)	(32)	
Interest revenue	20						20
Total revenue	592	430	320	210		(132)	1,420
Costs and expenses							
Cost of goods sold	375	320	210	130	(b)	(10)	1,025
Intercompany cost of goods sold	32	24	16	8	(b)	(80)	
Operating expenses	133	60	40	50			283
Interest expense		6	9	7			22
Income taxes expense	15	12	27	9	(b)	(6)	57
Total costs and expenses	555	422	302	204		(96)	1,387
Net income and retained earnings	37	8	18	6		(36)	33

Balance Sheet

Assets

					Eliminations	
Short-term investments	80					80
Inventories	500	600	700	800	(b) (10)	2,590
Other current assets	700	800	600	500		2,600
Prepaid income taxes					(b) 6	6
Intercompany receivables (payables)	80	(60)	50	(70)		
Investments in subsidiaries' common stock	4,532				(a) (4,532)	
Plant assets (net)	800	900	700	600		3,000
Intangible assets (net)	40	60	50	70		220
Total assets	6,732	2,300	2,100	1,900	(4,536)	8,496

Liabilities & Stockholders' Equity

					Eliminations	
Current liabilities	945	692	432	227		2,296
6% bonds payable		100	150	167		417
Common stock, $1 par	3,000	1,500	1,500	1,500	(a) (4,500)	3,000
Paid-in capital in excess of par	2,750					2,750
Retained earnings	37	8	18	6	(36)	33
Total liabilities & stockholders' equity	6,732	2,300	2,100	1,900	(4,536)	8,496

Explanation of eliminations:

(a) To eliminate intercompany investments and related equity accounts of subsidiaries.

(b) To eliminate intercompany sales, cost of goods sold, and unrealized profits in inventories, and to defer income taxes applicable to unrealized profits.

* Amounts remeasured to dollars from British pounds.

c Disclosures of information about the operations of Principia Corporation and subsidiaries in different geographic areas. Use the following format:

PRINCIPIA CORPORATION AND SUBSIDIARIES
Information about the Companies' Operations in Different Geographic Areas
For Year Ended December 31, Year 4
(000 omitted)

	North America	Western Europe	Eliminations	Consolidated
Sales to unaffiliated customers . . .				
Transfers among geographic areas .				
Total revenue.				
Operating profit (loss).				
Interest revenue				
General corporate expenses.				
Interest expense				
Income before income taxes.				
Identifiable assets, Dec. 31, Year 4 .				
Corporate assets				
Total assets, Dec. 31, Year 4				

Show supporting computations. Footnotes are not required. Disregard requirements for disclosure of export sales, major customers, depreciation and amortization, and additions to plant assets.

16 ACCOUNTING FOR MULTINATIONAL ENTERPRISES

A *multinational* (or *transnational*) *enterprise* is a business enterprise that carries on operations in more than one nation, through a network of branches, divisions, influenced investees, joint ventures, and subsidiaries. Multinational enterprises obtain raw material and capital in countries where such resources are plentiful. Multinational enterprises manufacture their products in nations where wages and other operating costs are lowest, and they sell their products in countries that provide the most profitable markets. Many of the largest multinational enterprises are headquartered in the United States (U.S.); one source has estimated the total number of such enterprises in the U.S. at 200. Among the largest of these companies are General Motors Corporation, Exxon Corporation, Ford Motor Company, General Electric Company, International Business Machines Corporation, International Telephone & Telegraph Corp., and Texaco, Inc.

In this chapter, we discuss the three principal accounting and reporting issues of multinational enterprises—uniformity in international accounting standards, accounting for transactions involving foreign currencies, and consolidated or combined financial statements for a U.S. enterprise and its foreign subsidiaries, investees, or branches.

UNIFORMITY IN INTERNATIONAL ACCOUNTING STANDARDS

The variety of accounting standards and practices among the nations of the world has been a substantial problem for multinational enterprises. Recently, however, significant efforts have been made to achieve uniformity in international accounting and auditing standards. The following summary describes these efforts:[1]

> The rapid growth in international activities by enterprises has led to a need and demand for international standards of financial accounting and reporting. A variety of private sector and governmental standard-setting organizations has developed to satisfy these needs and demands.

[1] Deloitte Haskins & Sells, *The Week in Review* (Feb. 20, 1981), pp. 3–4.

Five major international standard-setting organizations have emerged as leaders in this endeavor. The five organizations are as follows:

The *International Accounting Standards Committee* (*IASC*) IASC is a private voluntary organization formed in 1973 by leading accounting professional bodies from various countries. IASC concentrates on issuing financial accounting standards on specific problems which are similar in format to those issued by the Financial Accounting Standards Board. To date, IASC has issued thirteen Statements of International Accounting Standards and has issued six other Exposure Drafts. The Statements cover topics such as inventories, consolidated financial statements, depreciation accounting, research and development and income taxes. The Exposure Drafts include accounting for foreign currency translation, segments, pensions, changing prices, property, plant and equipment, and leases. IASC has no authority, but must rely on its member organizations (such as the AICPA in the U.S.) who have pledged to use their best efforts to have the international standards adopted by the respective national authoritative standard-setting bodies.

The *International Federation of Accountants* (*IFAC*) IFAC is a private voluntary organization comprised of 75 professional accounting organizations from 57 countries. IFAC concerns itself with auditing and other professional matters, such as ethics and education, that would lead to the development and enhancement of a coordinated worldwide accounting profession. IFAC has seven standing committees; the auditing practices committee has issued three International Audit Guidelines and four other Exposure Drafts. IFAC has no authority other than that which is self-imposed by the member organizations.

The *European Economic Community* (EEC) The EEC, also known as the Common Market, is a supra-government organization. Its authority is governmental, but is restricted to the ten member countries: France, West Germany, Italy, the United Kingdom, Belgium, Denmark, Greece, Ireland, Luxembourg and the Netherlands. EEC directives are addressed to and are binding on the Member States who must bring the Directives into national laws within specified periods. Eight Directives impinging on accounting reports and related matters have been issued to date. The most important of these is the Fourth Directive which deals with corporate powers, mergers, stock exchanges and listing requirements, and protection of employees in the event of employer insolvency. Six proposed Directives have also been issued, the most important of which is the amended proposed Seventh Directive dealing with consolidated statements. Other proposed Directives deal with corporate management, auditor qualifications, interim statements and employee information and consultation.

The *United Nations Commission on Transnational Corporations* This Commission is an arm of the United Nations (UN). As such, it is a quasi-governmental organization with worldwide participation. The Commission reports to the UN Economic and Social Council; its accounting standard setting work is assigned to a ''Working Group of Experts'' which has 34 members from UN countries. The Working Group of Experts has broad objectives for (a) the development of a comprehensive information system designed to determine the effects of transnational corporations on home and host countries, to contribute to national goals and worldwide economic growth, and to aid the negotiating capacity of host countries, and (b) development of a code of conduct for transnational corporations. Only two reports have been issued by the UN pertaining to accounting and related matters. One essentially presented extended lists of minimum requirements for the disclosure of accounting and financial information, the other dealt with minimum information to be made available by corporations designed to improve understanding of the structure, activities, and policies of the corporation as a whole. Six background papers have also been prepared. The work of the UN Commission is strongly influenced by a perceived desire (a) to aid Member countries, especially those from the developing countries, in coping with transnational corporations,

(b) to help the Member countries in their economic development, and (c) to assist and protect employees of transnational corporations.

The Organization for Economic Cooperation and Development (OECD) The OECD is an intergovernmental organization of 24 countries formed in 1960; it includes most of Western Europe and the Commonwealth countries, Japan, and the United States. The OECD is an outgrowth of the Organization for European Economic Cooperation established in 1948 under the Marshall Plan. In 1975, OECD formed a committee on International Investment and Multinational Enterprises; the Committee will offer Guidelines that establish standards for the activities of multinational enterprises including Guidelines on disclosure of information, competition, financing, taxation, and employment and industrial relations. Guidelines are voluntary and not legally enforceable, but the governments of the Member countries have agreed to recommend the observance of the Guidelines. Like the UN, the objectives of OECD are broader than financial reporting: they include economic growth and social progress objectives, regulation of entry of foreign enterprises and furtherance of world trade.

Of the five organizations described in the foregoing paragraphs, the IASC, with its membership of professional accounting organizations of more than 40 countries, is the most active in the setting of accounting standards. However, because it lacks authority to prescribe accounting standards, as the Financial Accounting Standards Board does in the United States, the accounting standards developed by the IASC are not certain of being used by all member countries of the IASC.

ACCOUNTING FOR TRANSACTIONS INVOLVING FOREIGN CURRENCIES

In most countries, a foreign country's currency is treated as though it were a **commodity,** or a **money-market instrument.** In the U.S., for example, foreign currencies are bought and sold by the international banking departments of commercial banks. These foreign currency transactions are entered into on behalf of the bank's multinational enterprise customers, and for the bank's own account.

The buying and selling of foreign currencies as though they were commodities result in variations in the **exchange rate** between the currencies of two countries. For example, a daily newspaper quoted the selected exchange rates shown on page 742.

The first rates quoted for each country's currency are **selling spot rates** charged by the bank for current sales of the foreign currency. The bank's **buying spot rate** for the currency typically is less than the selling spot rate; the **agio** (or **spread**) between the selling and buying spot rates represents gross profit to a trader in foreign currency.

The "30-day forward" and comparable exchange rates in the illustration on page 742 are **forward rates,** which apply to foreign currency transactions to be consummated at a future date. Forward rates apply to **forward exchange contracts,** which are discussed in a subsequent section of this chapter.

Foreign Exchange

Country	U.S. dollar equivalent	Currency per U.S. dollar
Argentina (Peso)	.000079	12700.00
Australia (Dollar)	1.0608	.9427
Austria (Schilling)	.0601	16.63
Belgium (Franc)	.0225	44.31
Brazil (Cruzeiro)	.0069	143.23
Britain (Pound)	1.8125	.5517
30-Day Forward	1.8150	.5510
90-Day Forward	1.8200	.5495
180-Day Forward	1.8273	.5473
Canada (Dollar)	.8231	1.2149
30-Day Forward	.8226	1.2156
90-Day Forward	.8214	1.2174
180-Day Forward	.8194	1.2204
China (Yuan)	.5454	1.8334
Colombia (Peso)	.0165	60.76
Denmark (Krone)	.1257	7.955
Ecuador (Sucre)	.0400	25.00
Finland (Markka)	.2198	4.549
France (Franc)	.1630	6.136
30-Day Forward	.1620	6.171
90-Day Forward	.1612	6.2035
180-Day Forward	.1598	6.2560
Greece (Drachma)	.0162	61.55
Hong Kong (Dollar)	.1728	5.7870
India (Rupee)	.1079	9.27
Indonesia (Rupiah)	.00154	648.00
Ireland (Pound)	1.4840	.6739
Israel (Shekel)	.0539	18.54
Italy (Lira)	.00077	1287.00
Japan (Yen)	.004147	241.15
30-Day Forward	.004178	239.35
90-Day Forward	.00423	236.15
180-Day Forward	.004317	231.65
Lebanon (Pound)	.2069	4.8325
Malaysia (Ringgit)	.4305	2.3230
Mexico (Peso)	.02234	44.76
Netherlands (Guilder)	.3840	2.6040
New Zealand (Dollar)	.7785	1.2845
Norway (Krone)	.1665	6.005
Pakistan (Rupee)	.0915	10.927
Peru (Sol)	.0018	556.99
Philippines (Peso)	.1201	8.325
Portugal (Escudo)	.0143	70.10
Saudi Arabia (Riyal)	.2924	3.4195
Singapore (Dollar)	.4718	2.1195
South Africa (Rand)	.9688	1.0322
South Korea (Won)	.0014	708.00
Spain (Peseta)	.0096	104.20
Sweden (Krona)	.1719	5.8185
Switzerland (Franc)	.5325	1.8780
30-Day Forward	.5368	1.8630
90-Day Forward	.5448	1.8357
180-Day Forward	.5548	1.8025
Taiwan (Dollar)	.0270	37.00
Thailand (Baht)	.0435	23.00
Uruguay (New Peso)	.0841	11.893
Venezuela (Bolivar)	.2329	4.2937
West Germany (Mark)	.4217	2.3715
30-Day Forward	.4238	2.3598
90-Day Forward	.4278	2.3375
180-Day Forward	.4335	2.3070

To illustrate the application of exchange rates, assume that a U.S. multinational enterprise required £10,000 (10,000 British pounds). At the selling exchange rate, the U.S. multinational enterprise would pay $18,125 (£10,000 × $1.8125 = $18,125) for the 10,000 British pounds.

Factors influencing fluctuations in exchange rates include a nation's balance of payments surplus or deficit, differing global rates of inflation, money-market variations (such as interest rates) in individual countries, capital investment levels, and monetary actions of central banks of various nations.

FASB Statement No. 52

In December 1981, the Financial Accounting Standards Board issued *FASB Statement No. 52,* "Foreign Currency Translation," in which it established uniform accounting standards for matters involving foreign currencies. In the following sections, we discuss the accounting standards established by the FASB for foreign currency transactions such as purchases and sales of merchandise and forward exchange contracts.

Transactions involving foreign currencies

A multinational enterprise headquartered in the U.S. engages in sales, purchases, and loans with independent foreign enterprises as well as with its branches, divisions, influenced investees, or subsidiaries in other countries. If the transactions with independent foreign enterprises are consummated in terms of the U.S. dollar, no accounting problems arise for the U.S. multinational enterprise. The sale, purchase, or loan transaction is recorded in dollars in the accounting records of the U.S. enterprise; the independent foreign enterprise must obtain the dollars necessary to complete the transaction through the foreign exchange department of its bank.

Often, however, the transactions described above are negotiated and settled in terms of the foreign enterprise's *local currency units* (LCU). In such circumstances, the U.S. enterprise must account for the transaction denominated in foreign currency in terms of U.S. dollars. This accounting, described as *foreign currency translation,* is accomplished by applying the appropriate exchange rate between the foreign currency and the U.S. dollar.

To illustrate, assume that on April 18, Year 6, Worldwide Corporation purchased merchandise from a West German supplier at a cost of 100,000 deutsche marks (DM). The April 18, Year 6, selling spot rate was DM1 = $0.45. Because Worldwide was a customer of good credit standing, the West German supplier made the sale on 30-day open account.

Assuming that Worldwide uses the perpetual inventory system, it records the April 18, Year 6, purchase as follows:

Journal entry for purchase of merchandise from West German supplier

Inventories.	45,000	
Accounts Payable.		45,000

To record purchase on 30-day open account from West German supplier for DM 100,000, translated at selling spot rate of DM1 = $0.45 (DM 100,000 × $0.45 = $45,000).

The **selling** spot rate was used in the journal entry, because it was the rate at which the liability to the West German supplier could have been settled on April 18, Year 6.

Transaction gains and losses

During the period that the account payable to the West German supplier remains unpaid, the **selling** spot rate for deutsche marks may change. If the selling spot rate **decreases,** Worldwide will realize a **transaction gain;** if the **selling** spot rate **increases,** Worldwide will incur a **transaction loss.** Transaction gains and losses are included in the determination of net income for the accounting period in which the spot rate changes.[2]

To illustrate, assume that on April 30, Year 6, the selling spot rate for deutsche marks was DM1 = $0.446, and Worldwide prepares financial statements monthly. The accountant for Worldwide records the following journal entry with respect to the account payable to the West German supplier:

Journal entry to record transaction gain on date financial statements are prepared

Accounts Payable	400	
Transaction Gains and Losses.		400

To record transaction gain applicable to April 18, Year 6, purchase from West German supplier, as follows:

Liability recorded on Apr. 18, Year 6.	$45,000
Less: Liability translated at Apr. 30, Year 6, selling spot	
rate DM1 = $0.446 (DM 100,000 × $0.446 = $44,600). .	44,600
Transaction gain.	$ 400

Assume further that the selling spot rate on May 18, Year 6, was DM1 = $0.44. The May 18, Year 6, journal entry for Worldwide's payment of the liability to the West German supplier is given at the top of page 745.

Two-Transaction Perspective and One-Transaction Perspective The journal entries above and on page 745 reflect the **two-transaction perspective**

[2] *FASB Statement No. 52,* "Foreign Currency Translation," FASB (Stamford: 1981), p. 6.

Journal entry for payment of liability to West German supplier

Accounts Payable.	44,600	
Transaction Gains and Losses		600
Cash.		44,000

To record payment for DM 100,000 draft to settle liability to West German supplier, and recognition of transaction gain (DM 100,000 × $0.44 = $44,000).

for viewing a foreign trade transaction. Under this concept, which was sanctioned by the FASB in **FASB Statement No. 52,** Worldwide's dealings with the West German supplier essentially were **two separate transactions.** One transaction was the purchase of the merchandise; the second transaction was the acquisition of the foreign currency required to pay the liability for the merchandise purchased. Supporters of the two-transaction perspective argue that an importer's or exporter's assumption of a risk of fluctuations in the exchange rate for a foreign currency is a financial decision, not a merchandising decision.

Advocates of an opposing viewpoint, the **one-transaction perspective,** maintain that Worldwide's total transaction gains of $1,000 ($400 + $600 = $1,000) on its purchase from the West German supplier should be applied to reduce the cost of the merchandise purchased. Under this approach, Worldwide would not prepare a journal entry on April 30, Year 6, but would prepare the following journal entry on May 18, Year 6 (assuming that all the merchandise purchased on April 18 had been sold by May 18):

Journal entry under one-transaction perspective

Accounts Payable.	45,000	
Cost of Goods Sold		1,000
Cash.		44,000

Payment for DM 100,000 (DM 100,000 × $0.44 = $44,000) to settle liability to West German supplier, and allocation of resultant transaction gain to cost of goods sold.

In effect, supporters of the one-transaction perspective for foreign trade activities consider the original amount recorded for a foreign merchandise purchase as an **estimate,** subject to adjustment when the exact cash outlay required for the purchase is known. Thus, the one-transaction proponents emphasize the **cash-payment** aspect of the transaction, rather than the **bargained-price** aspect of the transaction.

The authors concur with the FASB's support for the two-transaction perspective for foreign trade activities and for loans receivable and payable denominated in a foreign currency. The separability of the merchandising and financing aspects of a foreign trade transaction is an undeniable fact. In delaying payment of a foreign trade purchase transaction, an importer has made a decision to assume the risk of exchange rate fluctuations. This risk assumption is measured by the transaction gain or loss recorded at the time of payment for the purchase of merchandise (or on the dates of intervening financial statements).

Forward exchange contracts

Forward exchange contracts are another type of transaction involving foreign currencies. A **forward exchange contract** is an agreement to exchange currencies of different countries on a specified date at the forward rate in effect when the contract was made. As indicated by the exchange rates illustrated on page 742, forward rates may be larger or smaller than spot rates for a foreign currency, depending on the foreign currency dealer's expectations regarding fluctuations in exchange rates for the currency.

FASB Statement No. 52 established separate accounting standards for the following types of forward exchange contracts:

1 Contracts not intended to hedge a net investment in a foreign enterprise or an identifiable foreign currency commitment
2 Contracts intended to hedge an identifiable foreign currency commitment
3 Contracts for speculation in a foreign currency

In the following sections we discuss the three types of forward exchange contracts, including illustrative journal entries.

Forward Exchange Contract Not Intended to Hedge   Returning to the illustration of Worldwide Corporation, assume that on April 5, Year 6, in anticipation of initiating import transactions with various West German suppliers, Worldwide acquired a 60-day forward exchange contract for DM 500,000. Because Worldwide had no specific commitment to pay deutsche marks on April 5, Year 6, the forward exchange contract was not a hedge of an **identifiable** foreign currency commitment. Exchange rates for deutsche marks on April 5, Year 6, were as follows:

Exchange rates for deutsche marks	
Spot rates:	
Buying	*$0.443*
Selling	*0.452*
Forward rates:	
30-day contracts	*0.464*
60-day contracts	*0.478*
90-day contracts	*0.489*

Thus, the liability for the DM 500,000, 60-day forward exchange contract acquired by Worldwide on April 5, Year 6, was $239,000 (DM 500,000 × $0.478 = $239,000). The present value of the liability is equal to the $226,000 **selling spot rate** value of the contract (DM 500,000 × $0.452 = $226,000). The **discount** on the forward exchange contract, measured by the foreign currency amount of the contract multiplied by the difference between the forward rate and the spot rate on the date of the contract, is an **interest cost** that is apportioned to interest expense over the term of the contract.

Worldwide's April 5, Year 6, journal entry to record the acquisition of the forward exchange contract is as follows:

Journal entry for acquisition of forward exchange contract

Investment in Forward Exchange Contract (DM 500,000 ×
   $0.452 selling spot rate) *226,000*
Discount on Forward Exchange Contract Payable [DM
   500,000 × ($0.478 − $0.452)] *13,000*
      Forward Exchange Contract Payable (DM 500,000 ×
       $0.478 forward rate) *239,000*
To record acquisition of DM 500,000 forward exchange con-
tract for 60 days at forward rate of DM 1 = $0.478.

During the 60-day term of the DM 500,000 forward exchange contract, Worldwide realizes a transaction gain or loss whenever the spot rate for deutsche marks changes, because the present value of the investment in the contract likewise changes. For example, if the selling spot rate for deutsche marks on April 30, Year 6, was DM 1 = $0.446 and Worldwide prepares monthly financial statements, the following journal entry is required on April 30, Year 6:

Journal entry to record transaction loss on forward exchange contract

Transaction Gains and Losses [DM 500,000 × ($0.452 − $0.446)] .   *3,000*
Interest Expense ($13,000 × 25/60) *5,417*
      Investment in Forward Exchange Contract *3,000*
      Discount on Forward Exchange Contract Payable *5,417*
To recognize transaction loss on forward exchange contract re-
sulting from decrease of spot exchange rate for deutsche marks
to $0.446 from $0.452, and to amortize discount on contract to
Apr. 30, Year 6.

If the selling spot rate for deutsche marks was DM 1 = $0.449 on May 31, Year 6, the following journal entry is appropriate on that date:

Journal entry to record transaction gain on forward exchange contract

Investment in Forward Exchange Contract [DM 500,000 × ($0.449 − $0.446)]	1,500	
Interest Expense ($13,000 × 31/60)	6,717	
Transaction Gains and Losses.................		1,500
Discount on Forward Exchange Contract Payable.......		6,717
To recognize transaction gain on forward exchange contract resulting from increase of spot exchange rate for deutsche marks to $0.449 from $0.446, and to amortize discount on contract to May 31, Year 6.		

Assuming a selling spot rate of DM1 = $0.451 on June 4, Year 6, the maturity date of Worldwide's 60-day forward exchange contract, the following journal entries are required:

Journal entry to record transaction gain on forward exchange contract

Investment in Forward Exchange Contract [DM 500,000 × ($0.451 − $0.449)]	1,000	
Interest Expense ($13,000 × 4/60)	866	
Transaction Gains and Losses...............		1,000
Discount on Forward Exchange Contract Payable...		866
To recognize transaction gain on forward exchange contract resulting from increase of spot exchange rate for deutsche marks to $0.451 from $0.449, and to amortize discount on contract to June 4, Year 6.		

Journal entry to record payment of forward exchange contract

Investment in Deutsche Marks (DM 500,000 × $0.451)	225,500	
Forward Exchange Contract Payable (DM 500,000 × $0.478).	239,000	
Investment in Forward Exchange Contract		225,500
Cash		239,000
To record payment of DM 500,000 forward exchange contract, and receipt of deutsche marks.		

After these journal entries are posted, Worldwide's Investment in Forward Exchange Contract and Discount on Forward Exchange Contract Payable ledger accounts appear as shown on page 749.

Worldwide incurred interest expense of $13,000, and a net transaction loss of $500 ($3,000 − $1,500 − $1,000 = $500), during the 60-day term of its DM 500,000 forward exchange contract. In return, Worldwide benefited from knowing what its total outlay for deutsche marks would be on June 4, Year 6, the maturity date of the forward exchange contract. On receipt of the deutsche marks, Worldwide could pay for imports from West German suppliers at a known U.S. dollar amount as the suppliers' invoices came due.

The transaction gains and losses amounts are included in Worldwide's monthly income statements. The balance of the Investment in Forward Exchange Contract ledger account is a current asset, and the

Selected ledger accounts related to forward exchange contract

	Investment in Forward Exchange Contract			
Date	Explanation	Debit	Credit	Balance
4/5/6	Acquisition of 60-day, DM 500,000 contract	226,000		226,000 dr
4/30/6	Transaction loss		3,000	223,000 dr
5/31/6	Transaction gain	1,500		224,500 dr
6/4/6	Transaction gain	1,000		225,500 dr
6/4/6	Receipt of deutsche marks		225,500	-0-

	Discount on Forward Exchange Contract Payable			
Date	Explanation	Debit	Credit	Balance
4/5/6	Acquisition of forward exchange contract	13,000		13,000 dr
4/30/6	Amortization		5,417	7,583 dr
5/31/6	Amortization		6,717	866 dr
6/4/6	Amortization		866	-0-

balance of the Forward Exchange Contract Payable account, less the balance of the related discount account, is a current liability in the monthly balance sheets for Worldwide. Subsequent to June 4, Year 6, any balance in the Investment in Deutsche Marks ledger account is a current asset in Worldwide's balance sheets.

Forward Exchange Contract to Hedge an Identifiable Commitment *FASB Statement No. 52* established the following conditions for a forward exchange contract intended to hedge an identifiable foreign currency commitment:[3]

1 The foreign currency transaction is designated as, and is effective as, a hedge of a foreign currency commitment.

2 The foreign currency commitment is firm.

For a forward exchange contract meeting the above conditions, and in an amount not exceeding the related foreign currency commitment, the following are *deferred and included in the dollar amount of the related foreign currency transaction:*

1 The discount or premium on the forward exchange contract applicable to the period of the commitment (Alternatively, the discount or premium may be amortized, as illustrated on pages 747 and 748.[4])

2 Transaction gains during the term of the contract

3 Transaction losses during the term of the contract, unless deferral would cause the recognition of a loss, such as a write-down of inventories to net realizable value, in a subsequent accounting period

The amount of a forward exchange contract meeting the conditions for a hedge of an identifiable foreign currency commitment may exceed

[3] Ibid., p. 9.
[4] Ibid., p. 8.

the amount of the related commitment. If so, any transaction gain or loss applicable to the amount of the forward exchange contract in excess of the commitment is deferred only to the extent that the forward contract is intended to provide a hedge on an *after-income taxes basis.* Such a deferred gain or loss is offset against the related income taxes on the transaction gains or losses in the accounting period that the income taxes are reflected in the accounting records.[5] Transaction gains and losses that are not deferred are reflected in the income statement when the exchange rate changes.

To illustrate the accounting for a forward exchange contract that is a hedge of an identifiable foreign currency commitment, assume that Worldwide Corporation on May 1, Year 6, issued a purchase order to a West German supplier at a total price of DM 175,000. Delivery and payment were scheduled for June 30, Year 6.

To hedge against fluctuations in the exchange rate for deutsche marks, Worldwide acquired on May 1, Year 6, a firm forward exchange contract for the receipt of DM 175,000 on June 30, Year 6. Selected exchange rates for deutsche marks from May 1 to June 30, Year 6, were as follows:

Exchange rates for deutsche marks

	May 1	May 31	June 30
Spot rates:			
Buying	$0.454	$0.449	$0.455
Selling	0.462	0.458	0.466
Forward rates:			
30-day contracts	0.477	0.472	0.487
60-day contracts	0.493	0.488	0.495
90-day contracts	0.519	0.502	0.520

Worldwide's journal entries for acquisition of the forward exchange contract, receipt of the merchandise from the West German supplier, payment of the forward exchange contract, and payment of the supplier's invoice, are presented on page 751.

The result of the journal entries is that the merchandise purchased by Worldwide from the West German supplier is valued at the total cost, including financing costs, of the transaction with the supplier. These costs are summarized at the top of page 752.

The illustrated accounting is appropriate because the forward exchange contract was acquired to hedge an identifiable foreign currency commitment. Acquisition of such a contract enabled Worldwide to predetermine its total cost of the merchandise purchased from the West German supplier at $86,275, the total cash outlay for the forward exchange contract.

[5] The complicated accounting for after–income taxes hedges is illustrated on pages 9–13 of *FASB Statement No. 20,* "Accounting for Forward Exchange Contracts," FASB (Stamford: 1977), which was superseded by *FASB Statement No. 52,* "Foreign Currency Translations," FASB (Stamford: 1981).

WORLDWIDE CORPORATION
General Journal

Year 6

May 1 Investment in Forward Exchange Contract
   (DM 175,000 × $0.462 selling spot rate) 80,850
  Discount on Forward Exchange Contract Payable. . . 5,425
   Forward Exchange Contract Payable
    (DM 175,000 × $0.493 forward rate).   86,275
  To record acquisition of DM 175,000 forward exchange
  contract for 60 days, at forward rate of DM1 = $0.493.

  31 Deferred Transaction Gains and Losses
   [DM 175,000 × ($0.462 − $0.458)]. 700
    Investment in Forward Exchange Contract . . .   700
   To defer transaction loss resulting from decrease of
   spot exchange rate for deutsche marks to DM 1 =
   $0.458 from DM 1 = $0.462.

June 30 Investment in Forward Exchange Contract
   [DM 175,000 × ($0.466 − $0.458)]. 1,400
    Deferred Transaction Gains and Losses   1,400
   To defer transaction gain resulting from increase of
   spot exchange rate for deutsche marks to DM 1 =
   $0.466 from DM 1 = $0.458.

  30 Inventories ($81,550 − $700 + $5,425). 86,275
   Deferred Transaction Gains and Losses
    ($1,400 − $700). 700
    Discount on Forward Exchange Contract Pay-
     able.   5,425
    Accounts Payable (DM 175,000 × $0.466)   81,550
   To record purchase of merchandise from West German
   supplier for DM 175,000, translated at selling exchange
   rate of DM 1 = $0.466, and to increase cost of mer-
   chandise for discount on forward exchange contract,
   less deferred net transaction gain on contract.

  30 Forward Exchange Contract Payable. 86,275
   Investment in Deutsche Marks 81,550
    Investment in Forward Exchange Contract
     ($80,850 − $700 + $1,400)   81,550
    Cash   86,275
   To record payment of forward exchange contract, and
   receipt of deutsche marks.

  30 Accounts Payable 81,550
    Investment in Deutsche Marks.   81,550
   To record settlement of liability to West German
   supplier.

**Total cost
of merchandise
purchased from West
German supplier**

Invoice cost of merchandise (DM 175,000 × $0.466 selling spot rate on	
date received)	*$81,550*
Discount on forward exchange contract for deutsche marks	*5,425*
Net deferred transaction gain on forward exchange contract	*(700)*
Total cost of merchandise	*$86,275*

Forward Exchange Contract for Speculation There is no separate accounting treatment for the discount or premium on a forward exchange contract acquired for speculation in the foreign currency involved. The speculation forward exchange contract is similar to a short-term investment in a marketable bond that will not be held to maturity; thus, the accounting for discount or premium is similar for these two investments.

The transaction gain or loss on a speculation forward exchange contract is computed by multiplying the foreign currency amount of the contract by the difference between (1) the forward rate available for the remaining term of the contract, and (2) the contracted forward rate or the forward rate last used to compute a transaction gain or loss. Transaction gains and losses on speculation forward exchange contracts are included in the computation of net income for the period in which the forward rate changes.

To illustrate, assume the following exchange rates for deutsche marks from May 1 to June 30, Year 6:

**Exchange rates for
deutsche marks**

	May 1	**May 31**	**June 30**
Spot rates:			
Buying	*$0.454*	*$0.449*	*$0.455*
Selling	*0.462*	*0.458*	*0.466*
Forward rates:			
30-day contracts	*0.477*	*0.472*	*0.487*
60-day contracts	*0.493*	*0.488*	*0.495*
90-day contracts	*0.519*	*0.502*	*0.520*

On May 1, Year 6, Speco, Inc., acquired a 60-day forward exchange contract for DM 200,000, in anticipation of an increase in the spot rates for deutsche marks during the 60-day period.

The journal entries of Speco, Inc., for the forward exchange contract, assuming that Speco prepares monthly financial statements, are presented on page 753.

The increase in the spot rates for deutsche marks that Speco, Inc., had anticipated did not occur; thus, Speco incurred a total transaction loss of $7,600 ($4,200 + $3,400 = $7,600) on the forward exchange contract for speculation.

SPECO, INC.
General Journal

Year 6

May 1 Investment in Forward Exchange Contract
    (DM 200,000 × $0.493) 98,600
        Forward Exchange Contract Payable. 98,600
    To record acquisition of DM 200,000 forward exchange
    contract for 60 days, at forward rate of DM 1 = $0.493.

   31 Transaction Gains and Losses
    [DM 200,000 × ($0.493 − $0.472)]. 4,200
        Investment in Forward Exchange Contract . . . 4,200
    To recognize transaction loss on forward exchange
    contract resulting from difference between contracted
    forward rate (DM 1 = $0.493) and forward rate for re-
    maining 30-day term of contract (DM 1 = $0.472).

June 30 Investment in Deutsche Marks 94,400
    Forward Exchange Contract Payable. 98,600
        Investment in Forward Exchange Contract
        ($98,600 − $4,200) 94,400
        Cash 98,600
    To record payment of DM 200,000 forward exchange
    contract, and receipt of deutsche marks.

   30 Cash (DM 200,000 × $0.455). 91,000
    Transaction Gains and Losses [DM 200,000 ×
    ($0.472 − $0.455)] 3,400
        Investment in Deutsche Marks. 94,400
    To record sale of DM 200,000 at buying spot rate of
    DM 1 = $0.455, and resultant transaction loss.

Summary of Accounting for Forward Exchange Contracts The foregoing discussion of accounting for forward exchange contracts is summarized in the table on page 754.

CONSOLIDATED OR COMBINED FINANCIAL STATEMENTS FOR FOREIGN SUBSIDIARIES OR BRANCHES

When a U.S. multinational enterprise prepares consolidated or combined financial statements that include the assets, liabilities, and operations of foreign subsidiaries or branches, the U.S. enterprise must **translate** the amounts in the financial statements of the foreign entities from the entities' **functional currency** to U.S. dollars. Similar treatment must

Accounting for Forward Exchange Contracts

Purpose of contract	Discount or premium on contract		Transaction gains or losses on contract	
	Measurement	Accounting	Measurement	Accounting
Not intended to hedge a foreign currency commitment	Difference between forward rate and spot rate on date of contract	Apportioned to expense or revenue over term of contract	Difference between spot rates on date of measurement and date of contract (or date of most recent measurement)	Included in income statement for accounting period in which exchange rate changes
Hedge of identifiable foreign currency commitment	Difference between forward rate and spot rate on date of contract	Amount related to period of commitment deferred and included in dollar basis of related foreign currency transaction	Difference between spot rates on date of measurement and date of contract (or date of most recent measurement)	Gains deferred and included in dollar basis of related foreign currency transaction to extent amount of contract does not exceed amount of commitment. Gain on amount in excess of commitment deferred to extent amount provides a hedge on an after–income tax basis. Gain attributable to remainder of any excess included in income statement for accounting period in which exchange rate changes Losses comparably deferred unless deferral would lead to recognition of loss in subsequent accounting period
Speculation	Difference between forward rate and spot rate on date of contract	Not accounted for separately	Difference between forward rate for remaining term of contract and contract rate or rate last used to compute transaction gain or loss	Included in income statement for accounting period in which exchange rate changes

be given to the assets and income statement amounts associated with foreign subsidiaries that are not consolidated, and with other foreign investees for which the U.S. enterprise uses the equity method of accounting.

Functional currency

The FASB has defined the *functional currency* of a foreign entity as follows:[6]

> An entity's functional currency is the currency of the primary economic environment in which the entity operates; normally, that is the currency of the environment in which an entity primarily generates and expends cash. . . .
>
> For an entity with operations that are relatively self-contained and integrated within a particular country, the functional currency generally would be the currency of that country. However, a foreign entity's functional currency might not be the currency of the country in which the entity is located. For example, the parent's currency generally would be the functional currency for operations that are a direct and integral component or extension of the parent company's operations.

To assist in the determination of the functional currency of a foreign entity, the FASB provided the following guidelines:[7]

> The salient economic factors set forth below, and possibly others, should be considered both individually and collectively when determining the functional currency.
>
> *a* Cash flow indicators
>   (1) Foreign Currency—Cash flows related to the foreign entity's individual assets and liabilities are primarily in the foreign currency and do not directly impact the parent company's cash flows.
>   (2) Parent's Currency—Cash flows related to the foreign entity's individual assets and liabilities directly impact the parent's cash flows on a current basis and are readily available for remittance to the parent company.
> *b* Sales price indicators
>   (1) Foreign Currency—Sales prices for the foreign entity's products are not primarily responsive on a short-term basis to changes in exchange rates but are determined more by local competition or local government regulation.
>   (2) Parent's Currency—Sales prices for the foreign entity's products are primarily responsive on a short-term basis to changes in exchange rates; for example, sales prices are determined more by worldwide competition or by international prices.
> *c* Sales market indicators
>   (1) Foreign Currency—There is an active local sales market for the foreign entity's products, although there also might be significant amounts of exports.
>   (2) Parent's Currency—The sales market is mostly in the parent's country or sales contracts are denominated in the parent's currency.
> *d* Expense indicators
>   (1) Foreign Currency—Labor, materials, and other costs for the foreign entity's products or services are primarily local costs, even though there also might be imports from other countries.

[6] *FASB Statement No. 52,* pp. 3–4.
[7] Ibid., pp. 25–27.

   (2) Parent's Currency—Labor, materials, and other costs for the foreign
       entity's products or services, on a continuing basis, are primarily costs
       for components obtained from the country in which the parent com-
       pany is located.
 e Financing indicators
   (1) Foreign Currency—Financing is primarily denominated in foreign cur-
       rency, and funds generated by the foreign entity's operations are suffi-
       cient to service existing and normally expected debt obligations.
   (2) Parent's Currency—Financing is primarily from the parent or other
       dollar-denominated obligations, or funds generated by the foreign en-
       tity's operations are not sufficient to service existing and normally ex-
       pected debt obligations without the infusion of additional funds from
       the parent company. Infusion of additional funds from the parent com-
       pany for expansion is not a factor, provided funds generated by the
       foreign entity's expanded operations are expected to be sufficient to
       service that additional financing.
 f Intercompany transactions and arrangements indicators
   (1) Foreign Currency—There is a low volume of intercompany transac-
       tions and there is not an extensive interrelationship between the oper-
       ations of the foreign entity and the parent company. However, the for-
       eign entity's operations may rely on the parent's or affiliates'
       competitive advantages, such as patents and trademarks.
   (2) Parent's Currency—There is a high volume of intercompany transac-
       tions and there is an extensive interrelationship between the opera-
       tions of the foreign entity and the parent company. Additionally, the
       parent's currency generally would be the functional currency if the for-
       eign entity is a device or shell corporation for holding investments, ob-
       ligations, intangible assets, etc., that could readily be carried on the
       parent's or an affiliate's books.

The foregoing guidelines indicate the importance of determining the
appropriate functional currency for a foreign entity. The functional currency of the foreign entity underlies the application of the **monetary
principle** (discussed in **Intermediate Accounting** of this series) for the
entity.

Alternative methods for translating
foreign entities' financial statements

If the exchange rate for the functional currency of a foreign subsidiary
or branch remained constant instead of fluctuating, translation of the
foreign entity's financial statements to U.S. dollars would be simple. All
financial statement amounts would be translated to U.S. dollars at the
constant exchange rate. However, exchange rates fluctuate frequently.
Thus, accountants charged with translating amounts in a foreign entity's financial statements to U.S. dollars face a problem similar to that
involving inventory valuation during a period of price fluctuations.
Which exchange rate or rates should be used to translate the foreign
entity's financial statements? A number of answers were proposed for
this question prior to the issuance of **FASB Statement No. 52.** The several methods for foreign currency translation may be grouped into three
basic classes: **current/noncurrent, monetary/nonmonetary,** and **current rate.** (A fourth method, the **temporal method,** essentially is the

same as the monetary/nonmonetary method.) The three classes differ principally in translation techniques for balance sheet accounts.

Current/Noncurrent Method   In the *current/noncurrent method* of translation, current assets and current liabilities are translated at the exchange rate in effect on the balance sheet date of the foreign entity (the *current rate*). All other assets and liabilities, and the elements of owners' equity, are translated at the *historical rates* in effect at the time the assets, liabilities, and equities first were recorded in the foreign entity's accounting records. In the income statement, depreciation and amortization are translated at historical rates applicable to the related assets, while all other revenue and expenses are translated at an *average* exchange rate for the accounting period.

The current/noncurrent method of translating foreign investees' financial statements was sanctioned by the AICPA for many years. This method supposedly best reflected the *liquidity* aspects of the foreign entity's financial position by showing the current U.S. dollars equivalents of its working capital components. Today, the current/noncurrent method has few supporters. The principal theoretical objection to the current/noncurrent method is that, with respect to inventories, it represents a departure from historical cost. Inventories are translated at the *current rate,* rather than at *historical rates* in effect when the inventories were acquired, when the current/noncurrent method of translating foreign currency accounts is followed.

Monetary/Nonmonetary Method   The *monetary/nonmonetary method* of translating foreign currencies focuses on the characteristics of assets and liabilities of the foreign entity, rather than on their balance sheet classifications. This method is founded on the same monetary/nonmonetary aspects of assets and liabilities that are employed in historical-cost/constant-dollar accounting, described in *Intermediate Accounting* of this series. *Monetary assets and liabilities*—those representing claims or obligations expressed in a fixed monetary amount—are translated at the current exchange rate. All other assets, liabilities, and owners' equity accounts are translated at appropriate historical rates. In the income statement, average exchange rates are applied to all revenue and expenses except depreciation, amortization, and cost of goods sold, which are translated at appropriate historical rates.

Supporters of the monetary/nonmonetary method emphasized its retention of the historical-cost principle in the foreign entity's financial statements. Because the foreign entity's financial statements are consolidated or combined with those of the U.S. multinational enterprise, consistent accounting principles are applied in the consolidated or combined financial statements. The monetary/nonmonetary method essentially was sanctioned by the FASB prior to the issuance of *FASB Statement No. 52.*

Current Rate Method Critics of the monetary/nonmonetary method point out that this method emphasizes the *parent company* aspects of a foreign entity's financial position and operating results. By reflecting the foreign entity's changes in assets and liabilities, and operating results, as though they were made in the parent company's *reporting currency,* the monetary/nonmonetary method misstates the actual financial position and operating relationships of the foreign entity.

Critics of the monetary/nonmonetary method of foreign currency translation generally have supported the *current rate method.* Under the current rate method, all balance sheet accounts other than owners' equity accounts are translated at the current exchange rate. Owners' equity accounts are translated at historical rates.

To emphasize the *functional currency* aspects of the foreign entity's operations, all revenue and expenses may be translated at the current rate on the respective transaction dates, if practical. Otherwise, an average exchange rate is used for all revenue and expenses.

Standards for translation established by the FASB

FASB Statement No. 52 adopted the curent rate method, as described in the preceding section of this chapter, for *translating* a foreign entity's financial statements from the entity's functional currency to the *reporting currency* of the parent company, which for a United States enterprise is the U.S. dollar.[8] If a foreign entity's accounting records are maintained in a currency other than its functional currency, account balances must be *remeasured* to the functional currency before the foreign entity's financial statements may be translated.[9] *Remeasurement* essentially is accomplished by the monetary/nonmonetary method of translation described on page 757. If a foreign entity's functional currency is the U.S. dollar, *remeasurement* eliminates the need for *translation* of the entity's financial statements. Because remeasurement, if required, *must precede translation,* remeasurement techniques are illustrated in the next section.

Remeasurement of a foreign entity's accounting records

The FASB provided the following guidelines for remeasurement:[10]

> The remeasurement process should produce the same result as if the entity's books of record had been initially recorded in the functional currency. To accomplish that result, it is necessary to use historical exchange rates between the functional currency and another currency in the remeasurement process for certain accounts (the current rate will be used for all others), . . . it is also necessary to recognize currently in income all . . . gains and losses from remeasurement of monetary assets and liabilities that are not denominated in

---

[8] Ibid., p. 5.
[9] Ibid.
[10] Ibid., pp. 31–32.

the functional currency (for example, assets and liabilities that are not deno-minated in dollars if the dollar is the functional currency).

The list below includes the nonmonetary balance sheet items and related revenue and expense accounts that should be **remeasured using historical rates** to produce the same result in terms of the functional currency that would have occurred if those items had been recorded initially in the functional currency. (All other items are remeasured using the current rate.)

Marketable securities carried at cost:
  Equity securities
  Debt securities not intended to be held until maturity
Inventories carried at cost
Short-term prepayments such as insurance, advertising, and rent
Plant assets and accumulated depreciation of plant assets
Patents, trademarks, licenses, formulas, goodwill, and other intangible assets
Deferred charges and credits, except deferred income taxes
Deferred revenue
Common stock
Preferred stock carried at issuance price
Examples of revenue and expenses related to nonmonetary items:
  Cost of goods sold
  Depreciation of plant assets
  Amortization of intangible assets such as goodwill, patents, licenses, etc.
  Amortization of deferred charges or credits except deferred income taxes

The appropriate historical or current exchange rate generally is the rate applicable to conversion of the foreign currency for dividend remittances.[11] Accordingly, a U.S. multinational enterprise having foreign branches, investees, or subsidiaries typically uses the buying spot rate on the balance sheet date or applicable historical date to remeasure the foreign currency financial statements.

Illustration of remeasurement of a foreign entity's account balances

To illustrate the remeasurement of a foreign entity's account balances to the entity's functional currency from another currency, we return to the Smaldino Company illustration in Chapter 3, with merchandise shipments by the home office billed to the branch (Branch X) in excess of cost. We assume that both the home office and the branch use the perpetual inventory system, that the branch is located in France, and that the functional currency of the branch is the U.S. dollar, although the branch maintains its accounting records in French francs (F).

Year 1 transactions of Smaldino's home office and branch illustrated in Chapter 3 are repeated on page 760. Following each transaction is the exchange rate for French francs on the transaction date.

[11] Ibid., p. 11.

Transactions for Year 1

(1) Cash of $1,000 was sent by the home office to the French branch (F1 = $0.20).

(2) Merchandise with a cost of $60,000 was shipped by the home office to the French branch at a billed price of $90,000 (F1 = $0.20).

(3) Equipment was acquired by the French branch for F 2,500, to be carried in the home office accounting records (F1 = $0.20).

(4) Sales by the French branch on credit amounted to F 500,000 (F1 = $0.16). Cost of goods sold was F 337,500.

(5) Collections of accounts receivable by the branch amounted to F 248,000 (F1 = $0.25).

(6) Payments for operating expenses by the French branch totaled F 80,000 (F1 = $0.25).

(7) Cash of F 156,250 was remitted by the French branch to home office (F1 = $0.24).

(8) Operating expenses incurred by the home office charged to the French branch totaled $3,000 (F1 = $0.24).

The exchange rate at the end of Year 1 was F1 = $0.23.

The foregoing transactions are recorded by the home office and by the French branch with the journal entries (explanations omitted) on page 761.

In the home office accounting records, the Investment in Branch X (French branch) ledger account appears (in dollars before the accounts are closed), as follows:

Home office reciprocal account with branch (in dollars)

Investment in Branch X (French Branch)

Date	Explanation	Debit	Credit	Balance
	Cash sent to branch	$ 1,000		$ 1,000 dr
	Merchandise shipped to branch	90,000		91,000 dr
	Equipment acquired by branch, recorded in home office accounting records		$ 500	90,500 dr
	Cash received from branch		37,500	53,000 dr
	Operating expenses billed to branch	3,000		56,000 dr

In the branch accounting records, the Home Office ledger account appears (in francs before the accounts are closed), as shown at the top of page 762. The branch trial balance (in francs) at the end of Year 1 is in the middle of page 762.

Remeasurement of Branch Trial Balance　Remeasurement of the branch trial balance is illustrated at the top of page 763.

SMALDINO COMPANY
Home Office and Branch General Journals
For Year 1

Home Office Accounting Records (U.S. dollars)			French Branch (Branch X) Accounting Records (French francs)		
(1) Investment in			Cash	5,000	
Branch X	1,000		Home Office . .		5,000
Cash.		1,000			
(2) Investment in			Inventories	450,000	
Branch X	90,000		Home Office . .		450,000
Inventories . . .		60,000			
Allowance for					
Overvaluation					
of Inventories:					
Branch X . . .		30,000			
(3) Equipment: Branch X.	500		Home Office	2,500	
Investment in			Cash.		2,500
Branch X . . .		500			
(4) None			Accounts		
			Receivable	500,000	
			Cost of Goods Sold .	337,500	
			Sales		500,000
			Inventories . . .		337,500
(5) None					
			Cash	248,000	
			Accounts		
			Receivable . .		248,000
(6) None					
			Operating Expenses .	80,000	
			Cash.		80,000
(7) Cash	37,500				
Investment in			Home Office	156,250	
Branch X . . .		37,500	Cash.		156,250
(8) Investment in					
Branch X	3,000		Operating Expenses .	12,500	
Operating			Home Office . .		12,500
Expenses . . .		3,000			

Branch reciprocal account with home office (in francs)

Home Office				
Date	Explanation	Debit	Credit	Balance
	Cash received from home office		F 5,000	F 5,000 cr
	Merchandise received from home office		450,000	455,000 cr
	Equipment acquired by branch	F 2,500		452,500 cr
	Cash sent to home office	156,250		296,250 cr
	Operating expenses billed by home office		12,500	308,750 cr

SMALDINO COMPANY
Branch X (French Branch) Trial Balance
December 31, Year 1

	Debit	Credit
Cash.	F 14,250	
Accounts receivable	252,000	
Inventories.	112,500	
Home office		F 308,750
Sales		500,000
Cost of goods sold	337,500	
Operating expenses	92,500	
Totals.	F 808,750	F 808,750

In the review of the remeasurement of the French branch trial balance on page 763, the following should be noted:

1 Monetary assets are remeasured at the current rate; the single nonmonetary asset—inventories—is remeasured at the appropriate historical rate.

2 To achieve quickly the same result as remeasurement of the Home Office account transactions at appropriate historical rates, the balance of the home office's Investment in Branch X account (in dollars) is substituted for the branch's Home Office account (in francs). All equity accounts—regardless of legal form of the investee—are remeasured at historical rates.

3 A simple average of beginning-of-year and end-of-year exchange rates is used to remeasure revenue and expense accounts other than cost of goods sold, which is remeasured at the appropriate historical rates. In practice, a quarterly, monthly, or even daily weighted average might be computed.

4 A balancing amount labeled as a **transaction gain** is used to reconcile the total debits and total credits of the branch's remeasured trial balance. This transaction gain is included in the branch's net income for Year 1, because it results from the branch's transactions having been recorded in French **francs** rather than in **dollars,** the branch's functional currency.[12]

---

[12] Ibid., p. 31.

SMALDINO COMPANY

Remeasurement of Branch X (French Branch) Trial Balance to U.S. Dollars

December 31, Year 1

	Balance (French francs) dr (cr)	×	Exchange rates	=	Balance (U.S. dollars) dr (cr)
Cash	F 14,250		$0.23 (1)		$ 3,278
Accounts receivable	252,000		0.23 (1)		57,960
Inventories	112,500		0.20 (2)		22,500
Home office	(308,750)		(3)		(56,000)
Sales	(500,000)		0.215 (4)		(107,500)
Cost of goods sold	337,500		0.20 (2)		67,500
Operating expenses	92,500		0.215 (4)		19,887
Subtotals	F -0-				$ 7,625
Transaction gain	-0-				(7,625)
Totals	F -0-				$ -0-

(1) Current rate (on Dec. 31, Year 1)
(2) Historical rate (when goods were shipped to branch by home office)
(3) Balance of Investment in Branch X account in home office accounting records
(4) Average of beginning (F1 = $0.20) and ending (F1 = $0.23) exchange rates for Year 1

After the trial balance of the French branch has been remeasured from French francs to U.S. dollars, combined financial statements for home office and branch may be prepared as illustrated in Chapter 3.

Translation of a foreign entity's financial statements

To illustrate the translation of the financial statements of a foreign entity whose functional currency is not the U.S. dollar, assume that on May 31, Year 6, Colossus Company, a U.S. multinational company, acquired 30% of the outstanding common stock of a corporation in Venezuela, which we shall term Venezuela Investee. Although the investment of Colossus enabled it to exercise influence over the operations and financial policies of Venezuela Investee, that entity's functional currency was the bolivar (B). Colossus acquired its investment in Venezuela Investee for B600,000, which Colossus acquired at the selling spot rate of B1 = $0.25, for a total cost of $150,000. Out-of-pocket costs of the investment may be disregarded. Stockholders' equity accounts of Venezuela Investee on May 31, Year 6, were as follows:

Common stock	B	500,000
Paid-in capital in excess of par		600,000
Retained earnings		900,000
Total stockholders' equity	B	2,000,000

There was no difference between the cost of Colossus Company's investment and its equity in the net assets of Venezuela Investee (B2,000,000 × 0.30 = B600,000, the cost of the investment).

Translation of Venezuela Investee's financial statements for the year ended May 31, Year 7, is illustrated on page 765. The exchange rates for the bolivar are as follows:

May 31, Year 6	*$0.25*
May 31, Year 7	*0.27*
Average for year ended May 31, Year 7	*0.26*

In the review of the translation of the foreign investee's financial statements, the following features should be emphasized:

1 All assets and liabilities are translated at the current rate.

2 The paid-in capital accounts and the beginning retained earnings are translated at the historical rate on the date of Colossus Company's acquisition of its investment in Venezuela Investee.

3 The average rate for the year ended May 31, Year 7, is used to translate all revenue and expenses in the income statement.

4 A balancing amount labeled as **cumulative translation adjustments** is used to reconcile total liabilities and stockholders' equity with total assets in the translated balance sheet of Venezuela Investee. Cumulative translation adjustments are included in the stockholders' equity section of the translated balance sheet.[13]

Following the translation of Venezuela Investee's financial statements from bolivars (the **functional currency** of Venezuela Investee) to U.S. dollars (the **reporting currency** of Colossus Company), Colossus prepares the following journal entries in U.S. dollars under the equity method of accounting for an investment in common stock:

Journal entries under
equity method of
accounting

COLOSSUS COMPANY
General Journal
May 31, Year 7

Investment in Venezuela Investee Common Stock
  ($520,000 × 0.30) *156,000*
     Investment Income *156,000*
To record 30% of net income of Venezuela Investee.

Dividends Receivable ($162,000 × 0.30) *48,600*
     Investment in Venezuela Investee Common Stock ...   *48,600*
To record dividends receivable from Venezuela Investee.

---

[13] Ibid., p. 6.

VENEZUELA INVESTEE
Translation of Financial Statements to U.S. Dollars
For Year Ended May 31, Year 7

	Venezuelan bolivars	× Exchange rates	= U.S. dollars
Income Statement			
Net sales	B 6,000,000	$0.26 (1)	$1,560,000
Costs and expenses	4,000,000	0.26 (1)	1,040,000
Net income	B 2,000,000		$ 520,000
Statement of Retained Earnings			
Retained earnings, beginning of year .	B 900,000	0.25 (2)	$ 225,000
Add: Net income	2,000,000		520,000
Subtotal	B 2,900,000		$ 745,000
Less: Dividends*	600,000	0.27 (3)	162,000
Retained earnings, end of year.	B 2,300,000		$ 583,000
Balance Sheet			
Assets			
Current assets.	B 200,000	0.27 (3)	$ 54,000
Plant assets (net).	4,500,000	0.27 (3)	1,215,000
Other assets.	300,000	0.27 (3)	81,000
Total assets	B 5,000,000		$1,350,000
Liabilities & Stockholders' Equity			
Current liabilities	B 100,000	0.27 (3)	$ 27,000
Long-term debt	1,500,000	0.27 (3)	405,000
Common stock	500,000	0.25 (2)	125,000
Paid-in capital in excess of par	600,000	0.25 (2)	150,000
Retained earnings	2,300,000		583,000
Cumulative translation adjustments. .			60,000
Total liabilities & stockholders' equity.	B 5,000,000		$1,350,000

* Dividends were declared on May 31, Year 7.
(1) Average rate for year ended May 31, Year 7
(2) Historical rate (on May 31, Year 6, date of Colossus Company's investment)
(3) Current rate (on May 31, Year 7)

After the journal entries on page 764 are posted, the investment account of Colossus Company (in U.S. dollars) appears as follows:

	Investment in Venezuela Investee Common Stock			
Date	Explanation	Debit	Credit	Balance
5/31/6	Acquisition of 30% of common stock	150,000		150,000 dr
5/31/7	Share of net income	156,000		306,000 dr
5/31/7	Dividends		48,600	257,400 dr

The $257,400 balance of the investment account is equal to Colossus Company's share of the total stockholders' equity, *excluding cumulative translation adjustments,* in the translated balance sheet of Venezuela Investee [($125,000 + $150,000 + $583,000) × 0.30 = $257,400]. Cumulative translation adjustments do not enter into the computation of the translated net income or dividends of Venezuela Investee; therefore, no portion of cumulative translation adjustments is reflected in the investor's investment account. Cumulative translation adjustments are included in the stockholders' equity section of Venezuela Investee's translated balance sheet until sale or liquidation of Colossus Company's investment in Venezuela Investee. At that time, the amount of the cumulative translation adjustments is included in the computation of the gain or loss on sale or liquidation of the investment in Venezuela Investee.[14]

Other aspects of foreign currency translation

In addition to the topics we have discussed thus far, the four topics discussed in the following sections are included in *FASB Statement No. 52.*

Transaction Gains and Losses Excluded from Net Income   The FASB provided that gains and losses from the following foreign currency transactions should be accounted for in the same manner as translation adjustments:[15]

1 Foreign currency transactions that are designated as, and are effective as, economic hedges of a net investment in a foreign entity, commencing as of the designation date
2 Intercompany foreign currency transactions that are of a long-term investment nature (that is, settlement is not planned or anticipated in the foreseeable future), when the entities to the transaction are consolidated, combined, or accounted for by the equity method . . .

To illustrate an economic hedge of a net investment in a foreign entity, let us return to the Venezuela Investee illustration in the preceding section and assume that, to hedge its investment, Colossus Company borrowed B1,020,000 from a Venezuela bank on May 31, Year 7. B1,020,000 is equal to the carrying amount, in bolivars, of Colossus

[14] Ibid.
[15] Ibid., p. 8.

Company's investment on May 31, Year 7 [(B500,000 + B600,000 + B2,300,000) × 0.30 = B1,020,000]. If the exchange rate for bolivars was B1 = $0.28 on May 31, Year 8, Colossus had a transaction loss of $10,200 [B1,020,000 × $0.28 − $0.27) = $10,200] during the year ended May 31, Year 8, on the loan payable to the Venezuela bank. Disregarding income taxes, the $10,200 transaction loss on the Venezuela bank loan is included in the cumulative translation adjustments in the translated balance sheet of Venezuela Investee on May 31, Year 8, as an offset to Colossus Company's 30% share of any *increase* in the May 31, Year 7, cumulative translation adjustments that results from translation of Venezuela Investee's financial statements for Year 8. For example, if the May 31, Year 8, cumulative translation adjustments in Venezuela Investee's translated balance sheet on May 31, Year 8, was at least $70,200, which is a $10,200 increase ($70,200 − $60,000 = $10,200) over the May 31, Year 7, balance, Colossus would record the change in the exchange rate of bolivars on May 31, Year 8, in the following journal entry on that date:

Cumulative Translation Adjustments	10,200	
Loan Payable to Venezuela Bank		10,200

To record translation adjustment on loan obtained to hedge investment in Venezuela Investee as follows:

Liability recorded on May 31, Year 7 (B1,020,000 × $0.27)	$275,400
Liability translated at spot rate B1 = $0.28 (B1,020,000 × $0.28)	285,600
Translation adjustment	$ (10,200)

Any amount of the $10,200 that *exceeded* the net change in the cumulative translation adjustments in the May 31, Year 8, translated balance sheet of Venezuela Investee would be recorded by Colossus as a debit to the Transaction Gains and Losses ledger account, which is included in the income statement.

Functional Currency in Highly Inflationary Economies   The FASB required that the functional currency of a foreign entity in a highly inflationary economy be identified as the reporting currency (the U.S. dollar for a United States multinational enterprise). The FASB defined a *highly inflationary economy* as one having cumulative inflation of 100% or more over a three-year period.[16] Thus, financial statements of a foreign entity in a country experiencing severe inflation (*hyperinflation*) are remeasured to U.S. dollars, regardless of the criteria for determination of the functional currency described on pages 755 and 756.

[16] Ibid., p. 5.

Income Taxes Related to Foreign Currency Translation Conventional interperiod and intraperiod income tax allocation procedures were prescribed by the FASB for the income tax effects of foreign currency translation, as follows:[17]

1 Interperiod tax allocation for timing differences associated with transaction gains and losses that are reported in different accounting periods for financial accounting and income taxes [Interperiod tax allocation is discussed in *Intermediate Accounting* of this series.]
2 Interperiod tax allocation for timing differences associated with translation adjustments that do not meet the *indefinite reversal criteria* for undistributed earnings of subsidiaries [See Chapter 9, page 403.]
3 Intraperiod tax allocation for translation adjustments included in the stockholders' equity section of the balance sheet [Intraperiod tax allocation is discussed in *Intermediate Accounting* of this series.]

Disclosure of Foreign Currency Translation The FASB required disclosure, in the income statement or in notes to the financial statements, of the aggregate transaction gains or losses of an accounting period. Further, the FASB required disclosure of changes in cumulative translation adjustments during an accounting period, in a separate financial statement, in notes to financial statements, or in a statement of changes in equity. The minimum required disclosure is:[18]

1 Beginning and ending amounts of cumulative translation adjustments
2 Aggregate adjustments during the accounting period for translation adjustments, hedges of net investments, and long-term intercompany transactions
3 Income taxes allocated to translation adjustments during the period
4 Decreases due to sale or liquidation of an investment in a foreign entity

Appraisal of accounting standards for foreign currency translation

FASB Statement No. 52 was approved by the FASB by a bare four-to-three majority, which indicates the degree of dissatisfaction with the standards it established for foreign currency translation. Among the criticisms of **FASB Statement No. 52** are the following:

1 It established an indefensible distinction between *transaction gains and losses* arising from *remeasurement* and *translation adjustments* resulting from *translation.* Both *remeasurement* and *translation* involve comparable activities—the restatement of amounts in a foreign currency to another currency; thus, they should be accounted for in the same manner.
2 It provided for the inclusion of an item in stockholders' equity—cumulative translation adjustments—that does not meet the traditional definition of *owners' equity.*
3 It abandons the historical-cost principle by sanctioning use of the current rate method for translation of foreign currency financial statements.

It remains to be seen whether **FASB Statement No. 52** will be accepted by the business community. **FASB Statement No. 8,** ''Accounting

---

[17] Ibid., pp. 9–10.
[18] Ibid., pp. 12–13.

for the Translation of Foreign Currency Transactions and Foreign Currency Financial Statements," which was superseded by **FASB Statement No. 52,** was in effect for little more than six years, during which time it was the subject of continuous controversy. **FASB Statement No. 8** was criticized for its requirements that translation adjustments be included in net income and that the monetary/nonmonetary method be used to translate a foreign entity's financial statements. Critics of **FASB Statement No. 8** alleged that those requirements resulted in uncontrollable and misleading fluctuations in earnings of U.S. multinational enterprises. The FASB might undertake a revision of **FASB Statement No. 52** once the conceptual framework project (described in **Intermediate Accounting** of this series) is completed. Thus, the outlook for accounting for multinational enterprises appears to be one of continued study and possible significant changes in the future.

REVIEW QUESTIONS

1 What is a **multinational** enterprise?

2 Identify four of the organizations that support the development of international accounting standards.

3 Differentiate between the **International Federation of Accountants** and the **International Accounting Standards Committee.**

4 Define the following terms associated with foreign currencies:
  a Exchange rate
  b Forward rate
  c Selling rate
  d Spot rate

5 A newspaper listed quoted prices for the Japanese yen (¥) as follows:
  Buying rate: ¥1 = $0.0039
  Selling rate: ¥1 = $0.0043
How many U.S. dollars does a U.S. enterprise have to exchange for ¥50,000 at the above rates to settle an account payable in that amount to a Japanese supplier? Explain.

6 On March 27, Year 3, a U.S. multinational enterprise purchased merchandise on 30-day credit terms from a Philippines exporter at an invoice cost of ₱80,000. (₱ is the symbol for the Philippines peso.) What U.S. dollar amount does the U.S. enterprise credit to Accounts Payable if the March 27, Year 3, exchange rates for Philippine pesos are as follows:
  Buying rate: ₱1 = $0.11
  Selling rate: ₱1 = $0.12

7 How does a United States multinational enterprise **hedge** against the risk of fluctuations in exchange rates for foreign currencies? Explain.

8 Explain the **one-transaction perspective** regarding the nature of a transaction gain or loss.

9 What arguments are advanced in support of the **two-transaction perspective** for transaction gains and losses? Explain.

10 Should transaction gains or losses be recorded in the accounting records prior to collection of a receivable or payment of a liability in foreign currency? Explain.

11 Differentiate between *transaction gains and losses* and *translation adjustments.*

12 Differentiate between the *current/noncurrent method* and the *current rate method* of translating foreign currency financial statements.

13 What is a *forward exchange contract?*

14 What exchange rate is used to remeasure to U.S. dollars (the functional currency) the Intercompany Accounts Payable account of a foreign subsidiary of a U.S. parent company? Explain.

15 What disclosures relating to foreign currency matters are required in the financial statements or footnotes of U.S. multinational enterprises?

16 Differentiate *remeasurement to functional currency* from *foreign currency translation.*

17 What *transaction gains and losses* are excluded from net income?

18 What is the functional currency of a foreign investee in a highly inflationary economy?

19 List three criticisms of *FASB Statement No. 52,* "Foreign Currency Translation."

EXERCISES

Ex. 16-1   Select the best answer for each of the following multiple-choice questions:

1 U.S. Company purchased 5,000 toys from Central America Exporters, S.A., at 12.5 pesos each, when the selling exchange was $0.08 a peso. What amount should U.S. Company record as the total dollar cost for the merchandise purchased?
   a $400   *b* $625   *c* $5,000   *d* $6,250   *e* Some other amount

2 According to *FASB Statement No. 52,* "Foreign Currency Translation," all elements of financial statements of a foreign subsidiary of a U.S. parent company should be translated from a functional currency to U.S. dollars by the:
   a Monetary/nonmonetary method
   b Current rate method
   c Temporal method
   d Current/noncurrent method

3 The discount or premium on a forward contract that is not speculative and does not have a related gain or loss deferred is:
   a Included with the gain or loss on the contract
   b Accounted for separately from the gain or loss on the contract
   c Included with translation adjustments
   d Not accounted for separately

4 A gain that is a consequence of translation of foreign currency financial statements should be:
   a Included in net income of the accounting period in which it occurs
   b Deferred and amortized over a period not to exceed 40 years

       c Deferred until a subsequent accounting period when a loss occurs and off-set against that loss

       d Included as a separate item in the equity section of the balance sheet

5 Gains and losses resulting from remeasurement of foreign currency financial statements to functional currency should be included as:

       a A part of equity in the balance sheet

       b An extraordinary item in the income statement for the accounting period in which the rate changes

       c An ordinary item in the income statement for losses but deferred for gains

       d An ordinary item in the income statement for the accounting period in which the rate changes

6 According to **FASB Statement No. 52,** "Foreign Currency Translation," remeasurement of a foreign subsidiary's accounting records to the subsidiary's functional currency should be accomplished by the:

       a Monetary/nonmonetary method

       b Current rate method

       c Current/noncurrent method

       d Functional currency method

Ex. 16-2 On March 31, Year 5, Kingston Company acquired a 30-day forward exchange contract for 100,000 local currency units (LCU) of a foreign country. The contract was not acquired to hedge LCU foreign currency commitments. On April 30, Year 5, Kingston paid cash to settle the contract and obtain the LCU 100,000. Kingston prepares adjusting entries and financial statements only at the end of its fiscal year, April 30. Relevant exchange rates for one unit of the local currency were as follows:

	March 31, Year 5	*April 30, Year 5*
Spot rates:		
Buying	*$0.18*	*$0.19*
Selling	*0.20*	*0.22*
Forward rates:		
30-day contracts	*0.25*	*0.28*

    Prepare journal entries for Kingston Company on March 31, Year 5, and April 30, Year 5.

Ex. 16-3 On November 5, Year 9, Transnational Company sold merchandise costing $500 to an Indian customer for 10,000 rupees (Rs). On December 5, Year 9, Transnational received from the Indian customer a draft for Rs 10,000, which it exchanged for U.S. dollars. Transnational closes its accounting records monthly and uses the perpetual inventory system. Selected spot exchange rates for the rupee were as follows:

	Nov. 5	*Nov. 30*	*Dec. 5*
Buying spot rate	*$0.09*	*$0.10*	*$0.11*
Selling spot rate	*0.12*	*0.13*	*0.14*

    Prepare journal entries related to the transaction with the Indian customer in the accounting records of Transnational Company.

Ex. 16-4 A wholly owned foreign subsidiary of Multiverse Company had selected expense accounts stated in local currency units (LCUs) for the fiscal year ended November 30, Year 10, as follows:

Doubtful accounts expense	*LCU 60,000*
Patent amortization expense (patent acquired Dec. 1, Year 7)	*40,000*
Rent expense	*100,000*

The functional currency of the foreign subsidiary is the U.S. dollar. The exchange rates for LCUs for various dates or periods were as follows:

December 1, Year 7	*$0.25*
November 30, Year 10	*0.20*
Average for fiscal year ended Nov. 30, Year 10	*0.22*

Compute the total dollar amount to be included in the remeasured income statement of Multiverse Company's foreign subsidiary for the fiscal year ended November 30, Year 10, for the foregoing expense accounts.

Ex. 16-5 The accountant for Transglobal Company is a proponent of the one-transaction perspective of accounting for foreign trade transactions. On November 19, Year 1, Transglobal's accountant prepared the following journal entry:

Accounts Payable	*60,000*	
Cost of Goods Sold ($3,000 × 33⅓%)	*1,000*	
Inventories ($3,000 × 66⅔%)	*2,000*	
Cash		*63,000*

To record payment for F315,000 draft (F315,000 × $0.20 = $63,000) to settle liability to French supplier, and allocation of resultant transaction loss to cost of goods sold and to inventories.

Prepare a journal entry on November 19, Year 1, to correct the foregoing journal entry.

Ex. 16-6 The foreign subsidiary of Paloma Company, a U.S. multinational enterprise, has plant assets on December 31, Year 5, with a cost of 3,600,000 local currency units (LCU). Of this amount, plant assets with a cost of LCU 2,400,000 were acquired in Year 3, when the exchange rate was LCU 1 = $0.625; and plant assets with a cost of LCU 1,200,000 were acquired in Year 4, when the exchange rate was LCU 1 = $0.556. The exchange rate on December 31, Year 5, was LCU 1 = $0.500, and the weighted-average exchange rate for Year 5 was LCU 1 = $0.521. The foreign subsidiary depreciates plant assets by the straight-line method over a 10-year economic life with no residual value. The U.S. dollar is the functional currency of the foreign subsidiary.

Compute for Year 5 the depreciation expense for Paloma Company's foreign subsidiary, in U.S. dollars, for the remeasured income statement.

Ex. 16-7 On August 6, Year 7, Concordia Company, a U.S. multinational enterprise that uses the perpetual inventory system, purchased from a Belgium supplier on 30-day open account goods costing 80,000 Belgian francs. On that date, various exchange rates for Belgian francs (BF) were as follows:

Spot rates:
    Buying: BF1 = $0.025
    Selling: BF1 = $0.029
30-day forward rate: BF1 = $0.031

Also on August 6, Year 7, Concordia acquired a 30-day forward exchange contract for BF 80,000, to hedge the BF commitment.

Prepare journal entries to record the August 6, Year 7, transactions of Concordia Company, as well as the related transactions on September 5, Year 7, on which date the selling spot rate was BF 1 = $0.029. Concordia does not close its accounting records monthly or prepare monthly financial statements.

Ex. 16-8 On June 30, Year 6, Iberia Company, a U.S. multinational enterprise, sold merchandise costing $75,000 to a Portuguese customer, receiving in exchange a 60-day, 12% note for 7,500,000 escudos (Esc). The buying rate for escudos on June 30, Year 6, was Esc 1 = $0.014. On August 29, Year 6, Iberia received from the Portuguese customer a draft for Esc 7,650,000, which Iberia converted on that date to U.S. dollars at the buying rate for escudos of Esc 1 = $0.016.

Prepare journal entries for Iberia Company to record the June 30, Year 6, sale, under the perpetual inventory system, and the August 29, Year 6, conversion of the Portuguese customer's Esc 7,650,000 draft to U.S. dollars.

CASES

Case 16-1 Ostmark Company, a U.S. multinational enterprise, has a subsidiary in Austria. On April 1, Year 3, Ostmark acquired for $50,000 a draft for 500,000 Austrian schillings (S) and remitted it to the Austrian subsidiary as a long-term, noninterest-bearing advance. The advance was to be repaid ultimately in U.S. dollars. The Austrian schilling is the functional currency of the subsidiary.

You were engaged as independent auditor for the examination of the March 31, Year 4, consolidated financial statements of Ostmark Company and subsidiaries (including the Austrian subsidiary). On March 31, Year 4, the selling spot rate for schillings was S1 = $0.05. Ostmark's controller translated the Payable to Ostmark Company liability in the Austrian subsidiary's balance sheet from S500,000 to $25,000 (S500,000 × $0.05 = $25,000). Because the $25,000 translated balance of the subsidiary's Payable to Ostmark Company account did not offset the $50,000 balance of Ostmark's Receivable from Austrian Subsidiary account on March 31, Year 4, Ostmark's controller prepared the following working paper elimination on March 31, Year 4:

Cumulative Translation Adjustments—Austrian Subsidiary . . .   25,000

  Receivable from Austrian Subsidiary—Ostmark *25,000*

To record translation adjustment resulting from decline in exchange rate for schillings to S1 = $0.05 on March 31, Year 4,
from S1 = $0.10 on April 1, Year 3.

Instructions Evaluate the accounting treatment described above.

Case 16-2 During January, Year 12, Perisphere Corporation, a U.S. multinational enterprise, established a subsidiary, Sillah Company, in a foreign country. Perisphere owns 90% of Sillah's outstanding common stock; the remaining 10% is owned by citizens of the foreign country.

Instructions
a What criteria should Perisphere use to determine whether to prepare consolidated financial statements with Sillah for the year ended December 31, Year 12? Explain.
b What criteria should Perisphere use to determine the functional currency of Sillah? Explain.

Case 16-3 Pacific Basin Company, a U.S. multinational enterprise, has a branch in Hong Kong. The Hong Kong branch purchases locally all its merchandise acquired for resale. The branch sells to Hong Kong customers exclusively, and measures its cost of goods sold by the fifo method.

For many years, the exchange rate between the U.S. dollar and the Hong Kong dollar (HK$) has remained stable. However, there were substantial fluctuations in the exchange rate during Year 6, as evidenced by the following selling spot rates for Hong Kong dollars on the dates the Hong Kong branch purchased merchandise:

Jan. 2	*HK$1 = $0.20*
Apr. 1	*HK$1 = $0.16*
July 1	*HK$1 = $0.24*
Oct. 1	*HK$1 = $0.22*
Dec. 31	*HK$1 = $0.26*

Instructions Discuss the propriety of translating the Year 6 cost of goods sold of Pacific Basin Company's Hong Kong branch to U.S. dollars at the following alternative exchange rates:
a Historical fifo exchange rates
b Average exchange rate
c Current exchange rate (on December 31, Year 6)

PROBLEMS

16-1 On March 1, Year 2, Transcontinent Company, a U.S. multinational enterprise, established a branch in Mideastia, a foreign country. Transcontinent sent cash and merchandise (billed at cost) to the Mideastia Branch only on March 1, Year 2, and the branch made sales and incurred rent and other operating expenses in Mideastia during the month of March, Year 2. Transcontinent maintained accounts in its general ledger for the branch's plant assets. Because the Mideastia Branch's operations are an integral component of Transcontinent's operations, the U.S. dollar is the functional currency of the Mideastia Branch; however, the branch maintained its accounting records in local currency units (LCU).

The general ledger trial balance of the Mideastia Branch on March 31, Year 2, is as follows:

TRANSCONTINENT COMPANY
Mideastia Branch Trial Balance
March 31, Year 2

	Debit	**Credit**
Cash	LCU 2,000	
Accounts receivable	58,000	
Allowance for doubtful accounts		LCU 1,000
Inventories	126,000	
Home office		220,000
Sales		184,000
Cost of goods sold	160,000	
Operating expenses	59,000	
Totals	LCU 405,000	LCU 405,000

Appropriate exchange rates for Mideastia Branch's local currency units were as follows:

Mar. 1, Year 2	$0.60
Mar. 31, Year 2	0.64
Average for March, Year 2	0.62

Instructions Prepare a working paper to remeasure the trial balance of Mideastia Branch of Transcontinent Company to U.S. dollars, the branch's functional currency, from local currency units. The March 31, Year 2, balance (before closing entries) of the Investment in Mideastia Branch ledger account in Transcontinent's ledger was $132,000. Use the following headings for your working paper:

Account title	Balance (LCUs) dr (cr)	Exchange rates	Balance (U.S. dollars) dr (cr)

16-2 On August 1, Year 3, Caribbean Company, a U.S. multinational enterprise that prepares financial statements monthly, acquired a 60-day forward exchange contract for £50,000. Exchange rates for the British pound (£) on various dates in Year 3 were as follows:

	Aug. 1	Aug. 31	Sept. 30
Spot rates:			
Buying	$1.80	$1.82	$1.83
Selling	1.90	1.91	1.92
Forward rates:			
30-day contracts	1.92	1.94	1.94
60-day contracts	1.94	1.96	1.97
90-day contracts	1.97	1.99	1.98

Instructions Prepare journal entries (omit explanations) for Caribbean's forward exchange contract during its 60-day term under the following assumptions:
a The contract was acquired for speculation.
b The contract was not acquired as a hedge.
c The contract was firm and was designated as a hedge of a £50,000 purchase order issued by Caribbean on August 1, Year 3, to a British supplier to be delivered and paid for on September 30, Year 3.

16-3 The trial balance in local currency units (LCU) of the Foreign Branch of Sarasota Company on April 30, Year 7, the end of the branch's first month of operations, is shown at the top of page 776. The functional currency of Foreign Branch is the U.S. dollar.

SARASOTA COMPANY
Foreign Branch Trial Balance
April 30, Year 7

	Balance dr (cr)
Cash	LCU 10,000
Accounts receivable	50,000
Inventories (1,600 units at fifo cost)	124,375
Home office	(104,565)
Sales (2,100 units at LCU 133)	(279,300)
Cost of goods sold	152,289
Operating expenses	47,201
Total	LCU -0-

Additional information

(1) Foreign Branch sells a single product, which it acquires from the home office of Sarasota Company.

(2) The Investment in Foreign Branch ledger account in the accounting records of the home office of Sarasota Company (prior to end-of-period adjusting and closing entries) follows:

Investment in Foreign Branch ($)

Date	Explanation	Debit	Credit	Balance
4/1/7	Cash sent to branch	10,000		10,000 dr
4/1/7	1,000 units of merchandise shipped to branch @ $80 a unit	80,000		90,000 dr
4/3/7	Equipment acquired by branch (recorded in Home Office accounting records)		5,500	84,500 dr
4/10/7	1,200 units of merchandise shipped to branch @ $81 a unit	97,200		181,700 dr
4/20/7	1,500 units of merchandise shipped to branch @ $82 a unit	123,000		304,700 dr
4/29/7	Cash received from branch		210,000	94,700 dr
4/30/7	Operating expenses billed to branch	25,000		119,700 dr

(3) The Home Office ledger account in the accounting records of the Foreign Branch of Sarasota Company (prior to end-of-period closing entries) at the top of page 777.

(4) Exchange rates for the local currency units (LCU) of the country in which Foreign Branch operates were as follows during April, Year 7:

Apr. 1–Apr. 6	$1.10
Apr. 7–Apr. 18	1.12
Apr. 19–Apr. 30	1.05

Home Office (LCU)

Date	Explanation	Debit	Credit	Balance
4/2/7	Cash received from home office		9,091	9,091 cr
4/2/7	1,000 units of merchandise received from home office @ LCU 72.73		72,730	81,821 cr
4/2/7	Equipment acquired by branch	5,000		76,821 cr
4/11/7	1,200 units of merchandise received from home office @ LCU 72.32		86,784	163,605 cr
4/21/7	1,500 units of merchandise received from home office @ LCU 78.10		117,150	280,755 cr
4/28/7	Cash sent to home office	200,000		80,755 cr
4/30/7	Operating expenses billed by home office		23,810	104,565 cr

Instructions Remeasure the April 30, Year 7, trial balance of the Foreign Branch of Sarasota Company to U.S. dollars, its functional currency, from local currency units. Compute all exchange rates to the nearest cent.

16-4 On December 1, Year 5, Pan-Europe Corporation, a U.S. multinational enterprise, formed a foreign subsidiary, which issued all of its currently outstanding common stock on that date. Selected items from the subsidiary's trial balances, all of which are shown in local currency units (LCU), are as follows:

	Nov. 30, Year 7	Nov. 30, Year 6
Accounts receivable (net of allowance for doubtful accounts of LCU 2,200 on Nov. 30, Year 7, and LCU 2,000 on Nov. 30, Year 6)	LCU 40,000	LCU 35,000
Inventories, at cost	80,000	75,000
Plant assets (net of accumulated depreciation of LCU 31,000 on Nov. 30, Year 7, and LCU 14,000 on Nov. 30, Year 6)	163,000	150,000
Long-term debt	100,000	120,000
Common stock, authorized 10,000 shares, LCU 10 par, issued and outstanding 5,000 shares on Nov. 30, Year 7, and Nov. 30, Year 6	50,000	50,000

Additional information

(1) Exchange rates were as follows:

Dec. 1, Year 5–June 30, Year 6	2 LCU to $1
July 1, Year 6–Sept. 30, Year 6	1.8 LCU to $1
Oct. 1, Year 6–May 31, Year 7	1.7 LCU to $1
June 1, Year 7–Nov. 30, Year 7	1.5 LCU to $1
Average monthly rate for fiscal year ended Nov. 30, Year 6	1.9 LCU to $1
Average monthly rate for fiscal year ended Nov. 30, Year 7	1.6 LCU to $1

(2) An analysis of the accounts receivable (net) balance follows:

	Year ended November 30,	
	Year 7	Year 6
Accounts receivable:		
Balances, beginning of year	LCU 37,000	
Sales (LCU 36,000 a month in Year 7 and		
LCU 31,000 a month in Year 6)	432,000	LCU 372,000
Collections	(423,600)	(334,000)
Write-offs (April, Year 7, and November,		
Year 6)	(3,200)	(1,000)
Balances, end of year	LCU 42,200	LCU 37,000
Allowance for doubtful accounts:		
Balances, beginning of year	LCU 2,000	
Provision for doubtful accounts	3,400	LCU 3,000
Write-offs (April, Year 7, and November, Year 6)	(3,200)	(1,000)
Balances, end of year	LCU 2,200	LCU 2,000

(3) An analysis of inventories, for which the first-in, first out (fifo) inventory method is used, follows:

	Year ended November 30,	
	Year 7	Year 6
Inventories, beginning of year	LCU 75,000	
Purchases (May, Year 7, and May, Year 6) . . .	335,000	LCU 375,000
Goods available for sale	410,000	375,000
Inventories, end of year	80,000	75,000
Cost of goods sold	LCU 330,000	LCU 300,000

(4) On December 1, Year 5, Pan-Europe's foreign subsidiary acquired land for LCU 24,000 and depreciable plant assets for LCU 140,000. On June 4, Year 7, additional depreciable plant assets were acquired for LCU 30,000. Plant assets are being depreciated by the straight-line method over a 10-year economic life with no residual value. A full year's depreciation is taken in the year of acquisition of plant assets.

(5) On December 15, Year 5, 14% serial bonds with a face amount of LCU 120,000 were issued. These bonds mature serially each year through December 15, Year 11, and interest is paid semiannually on June 15 and December 15. The first principal payment was made on December 15, Year 6.

Instructions Prepare a working paper to remeasure the foregoing items to U.S. dollars, the functional currency of Pan-Europe Corporation's foreign subsidiary, on November 30, Year 7, and November 30, Year 6, respectively. Show supporting computations. Round all exchange rates to the nearest cent.

16-5 Imex Company, a United States multinational enterprise with an April 30 fiscal year, had the following transactions, among others, during March and April, Year 8:

| | | Exchange rates | | |
| | | Spot | | |
Date	Explanation of transactions	Buying	Selling	Forward
Year 8				
Mar. 6	Received merchandise purchased from Brazilian supplier on 30-day open account, cost 100,000 cruzeiros (Cr$). Acquired firm 30-day forward exchange contract for Cr$100,000 as effective hedge.	$0.006	$0.007	$0.008
18	Received merchandise purchased from Danish supplier on 30-day open account, cost 75,000 kroner (DKr).	0.12	0.13	0.14
25	Sold merchandise to Swiss customer on 30-day open account for 50,000 francs (Sfr). Cost of goods sold $15,000.	0.52	0.53	0.54
Apr. 4	Received merchandise purchased from Spanish supplier on 30-day open account for 150,000 pesetas (Ptas).	0.008	0.009	0.010
5	Liquidated Cr$100,000 forward exchange contract, and paid Brazilian supplier for Mar. 6 purchase.	0.006	0.007	0.009
17	Acquired draft for DKr75,000 for payment to Danish supplier for Mar. 18 purchase.	0.13	0.14	0.15
24	Received draft for Sfr50,000 from Swiss customer for sale of Mar. 25. Exchanged draft for U.S. dollar credit to bank checking account.	0.53	0.54	0.55
30	Obtained exchange rates quotation for Spanish pesetas.	0.009	0.01	0.011

Instructions

a Prepare journal entries for Imex Company to record the above transactions in U.S. dollars, under the perpetual inventory system.

b Prepare an adjusting journal entry for Imex Company on April 30, Year 8. Imex does not prepare monthly financial statements.

16-6 On August 1, Year 8, Westpac Corporation, a U.S. multinational enterprise, established a sales branch in Singapore. The transactions of Westpac's home office with the Singapore branch, and the branch's own transactions, during August, Year 8, are described below. Following each transaction is the appropriate spot exchange rate for Singapore dollars (S$).

(1) Cash of $50,000 sent to branch (S$1 = $0.45)
(2) Merchandise with a cost of $75,000 shipped to branch at a billed price of $100,000 (S$1 = $0.45)
(3) Rent of leased premises for August paid by branch, S$1,000 (S$1 = $0.45)
(4) Store and office equipment acquired by branch for S$5,000, to be carried in home office accounting records (S$1 = $0.45)
(5) Sales by branch on credit, S$25,000 (S$1 = $0.46). Cost of goods sold, S$15,000
(6) Collections of accounts receivable by branch, S$20,000 (S$1 = $0.455)
(7) Payment of operating expenses by branch, S$5,000 (S$1 = $0.47)
(8) Cash remitted to home office by branch, S$10,000 (S$1 = $0.44)
(9) Operating expenses incurred by home office charged to branch, $2,000 (S$1 = $0.445)
(10) Uncollectible account receivable written off by branch, S$1,000 (S$1 = $0.44)

Instructions   Prepare journal entries for the home office of Westpac Corporation in U.S. dollars, and for the Singapore branch in Singapore dollars, to record the foregoing transactions. Both home office and branch use the perpetual inventory system and the direct write-off method of accounting for uncollectible accounts. Round all amounts to the nearest dollar. Omit journal entry explanations.

16-7   Portero Corporation, a U.S. multinational enterprise, combined with Sudamerica Company on January 2, Year 3, by the acquisition at carrying amount of all of Sudamerica's outstanding common stock. Sudamerica is located in Nicaduras, whose monetary unit, the functional currency of Sudamerica, is the peso ($N). Sudamerica's accounting records were continued without change. A trial balance, in Nicaduran pesos, on January 2, Year 3, follows:

SUDAMERICA COMPANY
Trial Balance (Nicaduran pesos)
January 2, Year 3

	Debit	Credit
Cash	$N 3,000	
Accounts receivable	5,000	
Inventories	32,000	
Plant assets	204,000	
Accumulated depreciation		$N 42,000
Accounts payable		81,400
Common stock		50,000
Retained earnings		70,600
Totals	$N 244,000	$N 244,000

Sudamerica's trial balance, in Nicaduran pesos, on December 31, Year 4, follows:

SUDAMERICA COMPANY
Trial Balance (Nicaduran pesos)
December 31, Year 4

	Debit	Credit
Cash	$N 25,000	
Accounts receivable	20,000	
Allowance for doubtful accounts		$N 500
Receivable from Portero Corporation	33,000	
Inventories	110,000	
Plant assets	210,000	
Accumulated depreciation		79,900
Notes payable		60,000
Accounts payable		22,000
Income taxes payable		40,000
Common stock		50,000
Retained earnings		100,600
Sales—local		170,000
Sales—foreign		200,000
Cost of goods sold	207,600	
Depreciation expense	22,400	
Other operating expenses	60,000	
Income taxes expense	40,000	
Gain on sale of plant assets		5,000
Totals	$N 728,000	$N 728,000

Additional information

(1) All of Sudamerica's foreign sales are made to Portero and are accumulated in the Sales—Foreign ledger account. The balance in the Receivable from Portero Corporation account is the total of unpaid invoices. All foreign sales are billed in U.S. dollars. The reciprocal accounts in Portero's accounting records show total Year 4 purchases as $471,000 and the total of unpaid invoices as $70,500. Portero remits pesos to pay for the purchases.

(2) Depreciation is computed by the straight-line method over a 10-year economic life with no residual value for all depreciable assets. Machinery costing $N20,000 was acquired by Sudamerica on December 31, Year 3, and no depreciation was recorded for this machinery in Year 3. There have been no other depreciable assets acquired since January 2, Year 3, and no assets are fully depreciated.

(3) Certain assets that were in the Plant Assets account on January 2, Year 3, were sold on December 31, Year 4. For Year 4, a full year's depreciation was recorded before the assets were removed from the accounting records. Information regarding the sale follows:

Cost of assets	$N 14,000
Accumulated depreciation	4,900
Carrying amount	$N 9,100
Proceeds of sale	14,100
Gain on sale of plant assets	$N 5,000

(4) No journal entries have been made in the Retained Earnings account of Sudamerica since its acquisition other than the net income for Year 3. The Retained Earnings account balance on December 31, Year 3, was translated to $190,000.

(5) The exchange rates for the Nicaduran peso follow:

Jan. 2, Year 3	$2.00
Year 3 average	2.10
Dec. 31, Year 3	2.20
Year 4 average	2.30
Dec. 31, Year 4	2.40

(6) The accumulated translation adjustments totaled $22,000 (credit) on December 31, Year 3.

Instructions Prepare a working paper to translate the financial statements of Sudamerica Company for the year ended December 31, Year 4, from Nicaduran pesos to dollars. The working paper should show the financial statement amounts in pesos, the exchange rates, and the amounts in dollars.

16-8 Hightower Company, a U.S. multinational enterprise, established a branch in Brazentina in Year 2. The branch carried its accounting records in the Brazentina peso (BP), although its functional currency was the U.S. dollar.

You were engaged to examine Hightower's combined financial statements for the year ended December 31, Year 9. You engaged a licensed professional accounting firm in Brazentina to examine the branch accounts. The firm reported that the branch accounts were fairly stated in pesos, except that a Brazentina franchise fee and any possible adjustments required by home office accounting procedures were not recorded. Trial balances for the home office and the branch of Hightower Company on December 31, Year 9, are shown below and at the top of page 783.

HIGHTOWER COMPANY
Home Office and Branch
Trial Balances
December 31, Year 9

	Home office (U.S. dollars) dr (cr)	Branch (Brazentina pesos) dr (cr)
Cash	$ 90,000	BP 110,000
Accounts receivable (net)	160,000	150,000
Inventories, beginning of year	510,000	80,000
Short-term prepayments	18,000	
Investment in Brazentina branch	10,000	
Branch market research	12,000	
Plant assets	750,000	1,000,000
Accumulated depreciation	(350,000)	(650,000)
Current liabilities	(240,000)	(220,000)
Long-term debt	(200,000)	(230,000)
Home office		(30,000)
Common stock	(300,000)	
Retained earnings	(145,000)	

(Continued)

HIGHTOWER COMPANY
Home Office and Branch
Trial Balances (concluded)
December 31, Year 9

	Home office (U.S. dollars) dr (cr)	Branch (Brazentina pesos) dr (cr)
Sales	(4,035,000)	(1,680,000)
Intracompany sales	(160,000)	
Purchases	3,010,000	1,180,000
Intracompany purchases	140,000	
Depreciation expense	50,000	100,000
Other operating expenses	680,000	190,000
Totals	$ -0-	BP -0-

Additional information

(1) The Brazentina peso was devalued July 1, Year 9, from BP1 = $0.25 to BP1 = $0.20. The former exchange rate had been in effect since Year 1.

(2) Included in the balance of the home office's Investment in Brazentina Branch ledger account was a $4,000 billing for merchandise shipped during Year 9. The branch did not receive the shipment during Year 9. Home office sales to the branch are marked up $33\frac{1}{3}$% on cost and shipped FOB home office. Branch sales to home office are made at branch cost. There were no seasonal fluctuations in branch sales to outsiders during the year.

(3) The branch had beginning and ending inventories valued at fifo cost of BP80,000 [exclusive of the amount in (2), above], of which one-half on each date had been acquired from the home office. The home office had December 31, Year 9, inventories valued at fifo cost of $520,000.

(4) The Branch Market Research ledger account balance is the unamortized portion of a $15,000 fee paid by the home office in January, Year 8, to a U.S. firm for market research for the branch. Currency restrictions prevented the branch from paying the fee. The home office agreed to accept merchandise from the branch over a five-year period, during which the market research fee was to be amortized.

(5) There were no changes in the branch's plant assets during Year 9.

(6) The government of Brazentina imposes a franchise fee of 10 pesos per 100 pesos of net income before franchise fee of the branch, in exchange for certain exclusive trading rights granted to the branch. The fee is payable each May 1 for the preceding calendar year's trading rights; it had not been recorded by the branch on December 31, Year 9.

Instructions

a Prepare journal entries on December 31, Year 9, to correct the accounting records of:
  (1) The home office of Hightower Company
  (2) The Brazentina branch of Hightower Company

b Prepare a working paper to combine the financial statement of Hightower Company's home office and Brazentina branch, with all amounts stated in U.S. dollars. Formal combined financial statements are not required. Do not prepare formal combination eliminations; instead, explain the eliminations, including supporting computations, at the bottom of the working paper. Disregard income taxes. Assume that the branch purchases occurred evenly throughout Year 9.

The following columnar headings are suggested for the working paper:

Home office adjusted trial balance—dr (cr)
Branch adjusted trial balance:
  In Brazentina pesos—dr (cr)
  Exchange rates (remeasurement)
  In dollars—dr (cr)
Eliminations—dr (cr)
Home office and branch combined—dr (cr)

16-9   Separate financial statements of Panamer Corporation, a U.S. multinational enterprise, and its two subsidiaries for the year ended December 31, Year 6, are
shown on page 785. (IN is the symbol for the Itican peso.)

Additional information

(1) On December 31, Year 5, Panamer acquired 900 of the 1,000 outstanding
    shares of common stock of U.S. Subsidiary for $9,000, and all 1,000 shares of
    the outstanding common stock of Itican Subsidiary for $12,000. The identifi-
    able net assets of both combinees were fairly valued at their carrying
    amounts on December 31, Year 5. Panamer adopted the equity method of
    accounting for its investments in both subsidiaries.
(2) Both of Panamer's subsidiaries depreciate plant assets by the straight-line
    method over 10-year economic lives, with no residual values. None of the
    subsidiaries' plant assets was fully depreciated on December 31, Year 5, or
    on December 31, Year 6. There were no additions to or retirements of Itican
    Subsidiary's plant assets during Year 6.
(3) On December 31, Year 6, Panamer shipped merchandise billed at $4,000 to
    U.S. Subsidiary. There were no intercompany sales to Itican Subsidiary.
(4) On December 18, Year 6, U.S. Subsidiary declared a dividend of $1 a share,
    payable January 16, Year 7, to stockholders of record January 10, Year 7.
(5) Exchange rates for the Itican peso, which is the functional currency of Itican
    Subsidiary, were as follows:

    Dec. 31, Year 5, through Mar. 31, Year 6 .... *$0.12*

    Apr. 1, Year 6, through Dec. 31, Year 6 .... *$0.08*

Instructions
a Prepare a working paper to translate Itican Subsidiary's financial statements
from Itican pesos to U.S. dollars. Use weighted average exchange rates where
appropriate.
b Prepare correcting journal entries for Panamer Corporation and for U.S. Subsidiary on December 31, Year 6.
c Prepare a working paper for consolidated financial statements and working
paper eliminations for Panamer Corporation and subsidiaries on December
31, Year 6. The working papers should reflect the translated balances in **a**
and the adjustments in **b.** Disregard income taxes.

PANAMER CORPORATION AND SUBSIDIARIES
Separate Financial Statements
For Year Ended December 31, Year 6

	Panamer Corporation (dollars)	U.S. Subsidiary (dollars)	Itican Subsidiary (pesos)
Income Statements			
Revenue			
Sales	$400,000	$21,000	IN 381,000
Intercompany sales to U.S. Subsidiary	10,000		
Total revenue	$410,000	$21,000	IN 381,000
Costs and expenses			
Cost of goods sold	$300,000	$15,000	IN 300,000
Intercompany cost of goods sold	7,500		
Depreciation expense	3,000	550	17,500
Selling expenses	34,500	2,400	16,500
Other operating expenses.	35,000	1,650	18,000
Income taxes expense.	15,000	400	15,000
Total costs and expenses.	$395,000	$20,000	IN 367,000
Net income.	$ 15,000	$ 1,000	IN 14,000
Statements of Retained Earnings			
Retained earnings, beginning of year	$ 25,000	$ 2,000	IN 7,000
Net income.	15,000	1,000	14,000
Subtotal	$ 40,000	$ 3,000	IN 21,000
Dividends.		1,000	
Retained earnings, end of year	$ 40,000	$ 2,000	IN 21,000
Balance Sheets			
Assets			
Cash.	$ 10,000	$ 1,500	IN 10,000
Accounts receivable (net)	30,000	8,000	35,000
Intercompany receivables (payables)	4,000	(900)	
Inventories	20,000		83,000
Investment in U.S. Subsidiary common stock .	9,000		
Investment in Itican Subsidiary common stock	12,000		
Plant assets	45,000	5,500	175,000
Accumulated depreciation.	(15,000)	(2,000)	(75,000)
Total assets	$115,000	$12,100	IN 228,000
Liabilities & Stockholders' Equity			
Accounts payable.	$ 25,000		IN 7,000
Dividends payable		$ 100	
Long-term debt			100,000
Common stock, 1,000 shares	50,000	10,000	100,000
Retained earnings.	40,000	2,000	21,000
Total liabilities & stockholders' equity	$115,000	$12,100	IN 228,000

5

ACCOUNTING
FOR FIDUCIARIES

17 BANKRUPTCY: LIQUIDATION AND REORGANIZATION

Business failures are a common occurrence in the United States economy. According to the National Small Business Association, there were nearly 50,000 business failures in the year ended June 30, 1981.[1] As might be expected, poor management and inadequate accounting records are the most commonly cited causes of business failures.

The situation that precedes the typical business failure is inability to pay liabilities as they become due. Unsecured creditors often resort to lawsuits to satisfy their unpaid claims against a business enterprise. Secured creditors may force foreclosure proceedings for real property or may repossess personal property that collateralizes a **security agreement.** The Internal Revenue Service may seize the assets of a business enterprise that has failed to pay FICA and income taxes withheld from its employees.

A business enterprise may be unable to pay its liabilities as they become due even though the current fair values of its assets exceed its liabilities. For example, an enterprise may experience a severe cash shortage in times of price inflation because of the lag between the purchase or production of goods at inflated costs and the recovery of the inflated costs through increased selling prices.

More typical of the failing business enterprise than the conditions described in the foregoing paragraph is the state of insolvency. **Insolvent** is defined in the Bankrupty Code as follows:[2]

"insolvent" means—
(A) with reference to an entity other than a partnership, financial condition such that the sum of such entity's debts is greater than all of such entity's property, at a fair valuation, exclusive of—
 (i) property transferred, concealed, or removed with intent to hinder, delay, or defraud such entity's creditors; and
(ii) property that may be exempted from property of the estate under . . . this title; and
(B) with reference to a partnership, financial condition such that the sum of such partnership's debts is greater than the aggregate of, at a fair valuation—

---

[1] Deloitte Haskins & Sells, *The Week in Review,* Oct. 2, 1981, p. 5.
[2] *Bankruptcy Code,* sec. 101 (26).

789

(i) all of such partnership's property, exclusive of the kind specified in sub-paragraph (A) (i) of this paragraph; and

(ii) the sum of the excess of the value of each general partner's separate property, exclusive of property of the kind specified in subparagraph (A) (ii) of this paragraph, over such partner's separate debts;

The terms *insolvent* and *bankrupt* often are used as interchangeable adjectives. Such usage is technically incorrect; *insolvent* refers to the financial condition of a person or business enterprise, and *bankrupt* refers to a legal state. In this chapter we discuss various legal and accounting issues associated with bankruptcy.

THE BANKRUPTCY CODE

Article 1, Section 8 of the Constitution of the United States authorized Congress to establish uniform laws on the subject of bankruptcies throughout the United States. For the first 89 years under the Constitution, the United States had a national bankruptcy law for only a total of 16 years. During the periods in which national bankruptcy laws were not in effect, state laws on insolvency prevailed. In 1898 a Bankruptcy Act was enacted that, as amended, remained in effect for 80 years. Enactment of the Bankruptcy Act caused state laws on insolvency to be relatively dormant. In 1978 the Bankruptcy Reform Act established the present Bankruptcy Code, and in 1980 a Bankruptcy Tax Act established a uniform group of income tax rules for bankruptcy and insolvency.

Section 2075 of Title 28, Chapter 131 of the U.S. Code provides that the United States Supreme Court may prescribe by general rules the various legal practices and procedures under the Bankruptcy Code. Thus, the Bankruptcy Rules established by the Supreme Court constitute important interpretations of provisions of the Bankruptcy Code.

BANKRUPTCY LIQUIDATION

The process of *bankruptcy liquidation* involves the realization (sale) of the assets of an individual or a business enterprise and the distribution of the cash proceeds to the creditors of the individual or enterprise. Creditors having *security interests* collateralized by specific assets of the debtor are generally entitled to obtain satisfaction of their claims from the assets pledged as collateral. The Bankrupty Code provides for priority treatment for certain other unsecured creditors; their claims are satisfied in full, if possible, from proceeds of realization of the debtor's noncollateralized assets. Unsecured creditors without priority receive cash, in proportion to the amounts of their claims, from the remaining proceeds of realization of the debtor's assets.

Voluntary petition

The Bankruptcy Code provides that any "person," except a railroad, insurance company, bank, credit union, or savings and loan association, may file a petition in a federal bankruptcy court for *voluntary liquidation.* The official form for a *voluntary bankruptcy petition* must be accompanied by supporting exhibits of the petitioner's debts and property. The debts are classified as follows: (1) creditors having priority; (2) creditors holding security; and (3) creditors having unsecured claims without priority. The debtor's property is reported as follows: real property, personal property, property not otherwise scheduled, and property claimed as exempt. Valuations of property are at *market* or *current fair values.* Also accompanying the voluntary bankruptcy petition is a *statement of affairs* (not to be confused with the *accounting* statement of affairs illustrated in a subsequent section of this chapter), which contains a series of questions concerning all aspects of the debtor's financial condition and operations.

Involuntary petition

If a debtor other than a farmer, a nonprofit organization, or the types precluded from filing voluntary petitions owes unpaid amounts to 12 or more unsecured creditors who are not employees, relatives, stockholders, or other "insiders," three or more of the creditors having unsecured claims totaling $5,000 or more may file in a federal bankruptcy court a creditor's petition for bankruptcy, also known as an *involuntary petition.* If fewer than 12 creditors are involved, one or more creditors having unsecured claims of $5,000 or more may file the petition. The creditors' petition must claim either (1) the debtor is not paying debts as they come due, or (2) within 120 days prior to the date of the petition, a custodian was appointed for or had taken possession of the debtor's property.

Creditors having priority

The Bankruptcy Code provides that the following unsecured debts are to be paid in full, in the order specified if adequate cash is not available for all, out of a debtor's estate before any cash is paid to other unsecured creditors:

1 Administrative expenses.
2 Claims arising in the course of the debtor's business or financial affairs after the commencement of an involuntary bankruptcy proceeding but before appointment of a trustee or order for relief.
3 Claims for wages, salaries, and commissions, including vacation, severance, and sick leave pay not in excess of $2,000 per claimant, earned within 90 days before the date of filing the petition or cessation of the debtor's business.
4 Claims for contributions to employee benefit plans arising within 180 days before the date of filing the petition or cessation of the debtor's business. The

limit of such claims is $2,000 times the number of employees covered by the plans, less the aggregate amount paid to the covered employees under priority **3.**

5 Claims for cash deposited for goods or services for the personal, family, or household use of the depositor, not in excess of $900.

6 Claims of governmental units for various taxes or duties, subject to varying time limitations.

Property claimed as exempt

Certain property of a bankruptcy petitioner is not includable in the debtor's estate. The Bankruptcy Code excludes from coverage of the Act the various allowances provided in the laws of the United States or of the state of the debtor's residence, whichever is more beneficial to the debtor. Typical of these allowances are residential property exemptions provided by homestead laws and exemptions for life insurance policies payable on death to the spouse or a relative of the debtor.

Role of court in liquidation

The ***federal bankruptcy court*** in which a voluntary or involuntary petition for bankruptcy liquidation is filed oversees all aspects of the bankruptcy proceedings.

One of the first acts of the court is either to dismiss the voluntary or involuntary bankruptcy petition or to grant an order for relief under the Bankruptcy Code. The filing of a voluntary petition in bankruptcy is in effect an order for relief; in an involuntary petition, order for relief is made by the court after a hearing at which the debtor may attempt to refute the creditor's charges that the debtor was not paying debts as they came due. Any suits that are pending against a debtor for whom a voluntary or involuntary bankruptcy petition is filed generally are ***stayed*** until order for relief or dismissal of the petition; after order for relief such suits are further stayed until the question of the debtor's discharge is determined by the court. Further, the court appoints an interim trustee after the order for relief, to serve permanently or until a trustee is elected by the creditors.

Role of creditors

Within a period of 10 to 30 days after an order for relief, the bankruptcy court must call a meeting of the creditors. At the meeting, the "outsider" creditors appoint a trustee to manage the debtor's estate. A majority vote in number and amount of claims of all unsecured and nonpriority creditors present is required for actions by creditors.

Role of trustee

The trustee elected by the creditors or appointed by the court assumes custody of the debtor's nonexempt property. The principal duties of the trustee are to continue operating the debtor's business if directed by the court, liquidate the property of the debtor's estate, and pay cash to unsecured creditors. The trustee is responsible for keeping accounting records to enable the filing of a final report with the bankruptcy court.

The Bankruptcy Code empowers the trustee to invalidate a **preference,** defined as the transfer of cash or property to an "outsider" creditor for an existing debt, made while the debtor was insolvent and within 90 days of filing of the bankruptcy petition, provided the transfer caused the creditor to receive more cash or property than would be received in the bankruptcy liquidation. The trustee may recover from the creditor the cash or property constituting the preference and include it in the debtor's estate.

Discharge of debtor

Once the debtor's property has been liquidated, all secured and priority creditor claims have been paid, and all remaining cash has been paid to unsecured, nonpriority creditors, the debtor may receive a **discharge,** defined as the release of the debtor from all unliquidated debts, except the following:

1 Taxes payable by the debtor to the United States or to any state or subdivision, including taxes attributable to improper preparation of tax returns by the debtor

2 Debts resulting from the debtor's obtaining money or property under false pretenses or representations, or willful conversion of the property of others

3 Debts not scheduled by the debtor in support of the bankruptcy petition, such creditors not being informed of the bankruptcy proceedings

4 Debts arising from embezzlement or other fraudulent acts by the debtor acting in a fiduciary capacity

5 Amounts payable for alimony or child support

6 Debts for willful and malicious injuries to the persons or property of others

7 Debts for fines, penalties, or forfeitures payable to a governmental unit, other than for tax penalties

8 With certain exceptions, debts for educational loans made, insured, or guaranteed by a governmental unit or a nonprofit university or college

A debtor will not be discharged if any crimes, misstatements, or other malicious acts were committed by the debtor in connection with the court proceedings. In addition, a debtor will not be discharged if the current bankruptcy petition was filed within six years of a previous bankruptcy discharge to the same debtor.

Role of accountant in bankruptcy liquidation

The accountant's role in liquidation proceedings is concerned with proper reporting of the financial condition of the debtor and adequate accounting and reporting for the trustee for the debtor's estate.

Financial condition of debtor enterprise: Statement of affairs

A business enterprise that enters liquidation proceedings is a **quitting concern,** not a **going concern.** Consequently, a balance sheet, which reports the financial position of a going concern, is inappropriate for an enterprise in liquidation.

The financial statement designed for a business enterprise entering liquidation is the **statement of affairs** (not to be confused with the legal bankruptcy form with the same title described on page 791). The purpose of the statement of affairs is to present the assets and liabilities of the debtor enterprise from a **liquidation viewpoint,** because liquidation is the outcome of the bankruptcy proceedings. Thus, assets in the statement of affairs are valued at **current fair values;** carrying amounts of the assets are presented on a memorandum basis. In addition, assets and liabilities in the statement of affairs are classified according to the rankings and priorities set forth in the Bankruptcy Code; the current/non-current classification used in a balance sheet for a going concern is not appropriate for the statement of affairs.

Illustration of Statement of Affairs The balance sheet of Sanders Company on June 30, Year 4, the date the company filed a voluntary bankruptcy petition, is shown on page 795.

Other information available from notes to financial statements and from estimates of current fair values of assets follows:

1 Notes receivable with a face amount plus accrued interest totaling $15,800, and a current fair value of $13,300, collateralize the notes payable to Pacific National Bank.

2 Finished goods are expected to be sold at a markup of $33\frac{1}{3}\%$ over cost, with disposal costs estimated at 20% of selling prices. Estimated cost to complete goods in process is $15,400, of which $3,700 would be cost of material and factory supplies used. The estimated selling price of goods in process when completed is $40,000, with disposal costs estimated at 20% of selling prices. Estimated current fair values for material and factory supplies not required to complete goods in process are $8,000 and $1,000, respectively. All short-term prepayments are expected to be consumed in the course of liquidation.

3 Land and buildings, which collateralize the first mortgage bonds payable, have a current fair value of $95,000. Machinery with a carrying amount of $18,200 and current fair value of $10,000 collateralizes notes payable to suppliers in the amount of $12,000, including accrued interest. The current fair value of the remaining machinery is $9,000, net of disposal costs of $1,000, and the current fair value of tools after the amounts used in completing the goods in process inventory is $3,255.

4 Salaries and wages payable are debts having priority under the Bankruptcy Code.

SANDERS COMPANY
Balance Sheet
June 30, Year 4

Assets

Current assets:

Cash	$ 2,700
Notes receivable and accrued interest, less allowance for doubtful notes, $6,000.	13,300
Accounts receivable, less allowance for doubtful accounts, $23,240 .	16,110
Inventories, at fifo cost:	
Finished goods.	12,000
Goods in process	35,100
Material	19,600
Factory supplies	6,450
Short-term prepayments	950
Total current assets	$106,210

Plant assets, at cost:

Land	$20,000	
Buildings (net)	41,250	
Machinery (net).	48,800	
Tools (net)	14,700	
Total plant assets		124,750
Total assets.		$230,960

Liabilities & Stockholders' Equity

Current liabilities:

Notes payable:

Pacific National Bank, including accrued interest	$ 15,300
Suppliers, including accrued interest	51,250
Accounts payable	52,000
Salaries and wages payable	8,850
Property taxes payable	2,900
Accrued interest on first mortgage bonds payable	1,800
FICA and income taxes withheld and accrued	1,750
Total current liabilities	$133,850
First mortgage bonds payable	90,000
Total liabilities	$223,850

Stockholders' equity:

Common stock, $100 par, 750 shares authorized and issued	$75,000	
Deficit	(67,890)	7,110
Total liabilities & stockholders' equity		$230,960

SANDERS COMPANY
Statement of Affairs
June 30, Year 4

Carrying amount	Assets	Current fair value	Estimated amount available	Loss or (gain) on realization
	Assets pledged for fully secured liabilities:			
$ 20,000	Land	} $95,000		$(33,750)
41,250	Building			
	Less: Fully secured liabilities (contra).	91,800	$ 3,200	
	Assets pledged for partially secured liabilities:			
13,300	Notes and interest receivable (deducted contra).	$13,300		
18,200	Machinery (deducted contra). . . .	$10,000		8,200
	Free assets:			
2,700	Cash	$ 2,700	2,700	
16,110	Accounts receivable.	16,110	16,110	
	Inventories:			
12,000	Finished goods	12,800	12,800	(800)
35,100	Goods in process	20,300*	20,300*	14,800
19,600	Material	8,000	8,000	11,600
6,450	Factory supplies	1,000	1,000	5,450
950	Short-term prepayments	-0-	-0-	950
30,600	Machinery.	9,000	9,000	21,600
14,700	Tools	3,255	3,255	11,445
	Total estimated amount available		$76,365	$ 39,495
	Less; Unsecured liabilities with priority (contra).		13,500	
	Estimated amount available for unsecured, non-priority creditors (66¢ on the dollar)		$62,865	
	Estimated deficiency to unsecured, nonpriority creditors (34¢ on the dollar)		32,385	
$230,960			$95,250	

```
 * Estimated selling price . . . . . . . . . . . . . . . . . . . . . . . . . . . . . . . . . . .   $40,000
   Less: Estimated "out-of-pocket" completion costs ($15,400 − $3,700). . . . . . . . .   (11,700)
           Estimated disposal costs ($40,000 × 0.20) . . . . . . . . . . . . . . . . . . . . .    (8,000)
   Net realizable value . . . . . . . . . . . . . . . . . . . . . . . . . . . . . . . . . . . . . .   $20,300
```

The statement of affairs for Sanders Company on June 30, Year 4, is shown above and on page 797.

Carrying amount	SANDERS COMPANY Statement of Affairs (concluded) June 30, Year 4 Liabilities & stockholders' equity		Amount unsecured
	Unsecured liabilities with priority:		
$ 8,850	Salaries and wages payable.........	$ 8,850	
2,900	Property taxes payable...........	2,900	
1,750	FICA and income taxes withheld and ac-		
	crued.....................	1,750	
	Total (deducted contra)	$13,500	
	Fully secured liabilities:		
90,000	First mortgage bonds payable	$90,000	
1,800	Accrued interest on first mortgage bonds		
	payable....................	1,800	
	Total (deducted contra)	$91,800	
	Partially secured liabilities:		
15,300	Notes and accrued interest payable to		
	Pacific National Bank............	$15,300	
	Less: Net realizable value of notes receiv-		
	able pledged as collateral (contra)	13,300	$ 2,000
12,000	Notes and accrued interest payable to		
	suppliers..................	$12,000	
	Less: Estimated realizable value of ma-		
	chinery pledged as collateral (contra) . .	10,000	2,000
	Unsecured liabilities without priority:		
39,250	Notes payable to suppliers		39,250
52,000	Accounts payable................		52,000
7,110	Stockholders' equity		
$230,960			$95,250

The following points should be stressed in the review of the June 30, Year 4, statement of affairs for Sanders:

1 The "Carrying amount" columns in the statement of affairs serve as a tie-in to the balance sheet of Sanders on June 30, Year 4, as well as a basis for determination of expected losses or gains on realization of assets.

2 Assets are assigned to one of three groups: pledged for fully secured liabilities, pledged for partially secured liabilities, and free. This grouping of assets facilitates the computation of estimated amounts available for unsecured creditors—those with priority and those without priority.

3 Liabilities are grouped in the categories reported by a debtor in the exhibits supporting a voluntary bankruptcy petition (see page 791): unsecured with priority, fully secured, partially secured, and unsecured without priority.

4 A *contra,* or *offset,* technique is used where the *legal right of setoff* exists. For example, amounts due to fully secured creditors are deducted from the estimated current fair value of the assets serving as collateral; and unsecured liabilities with priority are deducted from estimated amounts available to unsecured creditors from the proceeds of asset realization.

5 An estimated settlement per dollar of unsecured liabilities without priority can be computed by dividing the estimated amount available for unsecured, nonpriority creditors by the total unsecured liabilities, thus:

$$\frac{\$62,865}{\$95,250} = 66 \text{ cents on the dollar}$$

The foregoing computation enables the bankruptcy court to estimate the aggregate cash that will be available to unsecured, nonpriority creditors in a liquidation proceeding.

Some accountants recommend the preparation of a **statement of estimated deficiency to unsecured creditors** as an adjunct to the statement of affairs. This supplementary financial statement appears unnecessary, because the information it contains is included entirely in the "Estimated amount available" column of the statement of affairs. If the balance sheet prepared on the same date as a statement of affairs includes adequate allowances for doubtful accounts and for estimated liabilities, the statement of affairs will be adequate for a comprehensive analysis of the financial condition of a "quitting concern."

Accounting and reporting for trustee

Traditionally, the accounting records and reports for trustees have been extremely detailed and elaborate. However, the provisions of the applicable Bankruptcy Rule are general; therefore, simple accounting records and reports should be adequate. The authors recommend the following with respect to the accounting records for a liquidating debtor:

1 The accounting records of the debtor should be used during the period that a trustee carries on the operations of the debtor's business.

2 An **accountability** technique should be used once the trustee begins realization of the debtor's assets. In the accountability method of accounting the assets and liabilities for which the trustee is responsible are recorded in the accounting records of the trustee at their statement of affairs valuations, with a balancing debit to a memorandum-type balancing account with a title such as Estate Deficit. The amount of the debit is equal to the estimated deficiency to unsecured creditors in the statement of affairs. Appropriate cash receipts and cash payments journal entries are made for the trustee's realization of assets and payment of liabilities. No "gain" or "loss" account is necessary because the business enterprise in liquidation does not require an income statement. Differences between cash amounts realized and carrying amounts of the related assets or liabilities are debited or credited directly to the Estate Deficit account.

3 The **interim** and **final reports** of the trustee to the bankruptcy court are a statement of cash receipts and cash payments, a statement of realization and liquidation, and, for interim reports, supporting exhibits of assets not yet realized and liabilities not yet liquidated.

Illustration of Accountability Technique   Assume that Arline Wells, the trustee in the voluntary bankruptcy proceedings for Sanders Company (see pages 794 and 795), took custody of the assets of Sanders on June 30, Year 4. The accountant for the trustee prepared the following journal entry on June 30, Year 4:

Journal entry for bankruptcy trustee

SANDERS COMPANY, IN BANKRUPTCY
Arline Wells, Trustee
General Journal
June 30, Year 4

Cash	2,700	
Notes and Interest Receivable	13,300	
Accounts Receivable	16,110	
Finished Goods Inventory	12,800	
Goods in Process Inventory	20,300	
Material Inventory	8,000	
Factory Supplies	1,000	
Land and Buildings	95,000	
Machinery ($10,000 + $9,000)	19,000	
Tools	3,255	
Estate Deficit	32,385 (1)	
Notes and Interest Payable		66,550
Accounts Payable		52,000
Salaries and Wages Payable		8,850
Property Taxes Payable		2,900
FICA and Income Taxes Withheld and Accrued		1,750
Accrued Interest on First Mortgage Bonds Payable		1,800
First Mortgage Bonds Payable		90,000

To record current fair values of assets and liabilities of Sanders Company, in voluntary bankruptcy proceedings.

(1) *Equal to estimated deficiency to unsecured, nonpriority creditors in statement of affairs on page 796.*

When the trustee realizes assets of Sanders, the required journal entry is a debit to Cash, a credit to the appropriate asset account, and a debit or credit to the Estate Deficit account for a loss or gain on realization, respectively. Expenses of administering the estate also are debited to the Estate Deficit account.

Statement of Realization and Liquidation The traditional statement of realization and liquidation was a complex and not too readable accounting presentation. A form of realization and liquidation statement that should be more useful to the bankruptcy court than the traditional statement is illustrated on page 800. This financial statement is based on the assumed activities of the trustee for the estate of Sanders Company during the month of July, Year 4, including operating the business long enough to complete the goods in process inventory.

SANDERS COMPANY, IN BANKRUPTCY
Arline Wells, Trustee
Statement of Realization and Liquidation
For Month Ended July 31, Year 4

Estate deficit, June 30, Year 4 . . . . $32,385

Assets realized:

	Current fair value, June 30, Year 4	Realization proceeds	Loss or (gain)	
Accounts receivable.	$14,620	$12,807	$ 1,813	
Finished goods inventory. .	12,800	11,772	1,028	
Goods in process				
inventory.	14,820	15,075	(255)	
Totals	$42,240	$39,654		2,586

Liabilities with priority liquidated at carrying amounts:

Salaries and wages payable.	$ 8,850	
Property taxes payable.	2,900	
FICA and income taxes withheld and accrued.	1,750	
Total liabilities with priority liquidated	$13,500	

Estate administration expenses paid 1,867

Estate deficit, July 31, Year 4. . . . . $36,838

An accompanying statement of cash receipts and cash payments for the month ended July 31, Year 4, would show the sources of the $39,654 total realization proceeds, and the dates, check numbers, payees, and amounts of the $13,500 paid for liabilities with priority and the $1,867 paid for estate administration expenses. Supporting exhibits would summarize assets not yet realized and liabilities not yet liquidated.

Liquidation involves realization of the assets of the debtor's estate. In many cases, an insolvent business enterprise may be restored to a sound financial footing if it can defer payment of its debts. A chapter of the Bankruptcy Code, dealing with reorganization, enables a business enterprise to continue operations under court protection from creditor lawsuits, while it formulates a plan to pay its debts.

BANKRUPTCY REORGANIZATION

Chapter 11 of the Bankruptcy Code provides for the court-supervised reorganization of a debtor business enterprise. Typically, a reorganization involves the reduction of amounts payable to some creditors, other creditors' acceptance of equity securities of the debtor for their claims, and a restructuring of the par or stated value of the common stock of the debtor.

A voluntary petition for reorganization may be filed by a railroad or by any "person" eligible to petition for liquidation (see page 791) except a stockbroker or a commodity broker. Requirements for a creditors' (involuntary) petition for reorganization are the same as the requirements for a liquidation petition (see page 791).

Appointment of trustee or examiner

During the process of reorganization, management or owners of the business enterprise may continue to operate the enterprise. Alternatively, the bankruptcy court may appoint a trustee to manage the enterprise. A trustee is appointed because of fraud, dishonesty, incompetence, or gross mismanagement by current owners or managers, or to protect the interests of creditors or shareholders of the enterprise. In some reorganization cases not involving a trustee, the court may appoint an examiner to investigate possible fraud or mismanagement by the current managers or owners of the enterprise; the appointment of an examiner is limited to enterprises having unsecured liabilities, other than payables for goods, services, or taxes, exceeding $5,000,000.

Among the powers and duties of the trustee are the following:

1 Prepare and file in court a list of creditors of each class and their claims and a list of stockholders of each class.

2 Investigate the acts, conduct, property, liabilities, and business operations of the enterprise, consider the desirability of continuing operations, and formulate a plan for such continuance for submission to the judge if management has not done so.

3 Report to the judge any facts ascertained as to fraud against or mismanagement of the enterprise.

Plan of reorganization

The plan of reorganization submitted by the management or the trustee to the bankruptcy court is given to the enterprise's creditors and stockholders, to the Secretary of the Treasury, and possibly to the Securities and Exchange Commission. The plan must include provisions altering or modifying the interests and rights of the creditors and stockholders of the enterprise, as well as a number of additional provisions. The SEC may review the plan and may be heard in the court's consideration of the plan. Before a plan of reorganization is confirmed by the bankruptcy court, the plan must be accepted by a majority of the creditors, whose claims must account for two-thirds of the total liabilities, and by shareholders owning at least two-thirds of the outstanding capital stock of each class. If one or more classes of shareholders or creditors has not accepted a plan, the court may confirm the plan if the plan is fair and equitable to the nonacceptors. Confirmation of the plan of reorganization by the court makes the plan binding on the enterprise, on all creditors and owners of the enterprise, and on any other enterprise issuing securities or acquiring property under the plan.

Accounting for a reorganization

The accounting for a reorganization typically requires journal entries for write-downs of assets; reductions of par or stated value of capital stock (with recognition of resultant paid-in capital in excess of par or stated value); extensions of due dates of notes payable; exchanges of debt securities for equity securities; and the elimination of a deficit. The journal entries for a bankruptcy reorganization thus resemble the entries to record a **quasi-reorganization,** as illustrated in **Intermediate Accounting** of this series. In essence, the only difference for accounting purposes between a bankruptcy reorganization and a quasi-reorganization is the authority for the journal entries. Bankruptcy reorganization journal entries result from a directive of the bankruptcy court; journal entries for a quasi-reorganization are authorized by action of stockholders.

It is important for an accountant to be thoroughly familiar with the plan of reorganization, in order to account properly for its implementation. The accountant must be careful to avoid charging post-reorganization operations with losses that arose before the reorganization.

To illustrate the accounting for a reorganization, assume that Sanders Company (see pages 794 and 795) filed a petition for reorganization, rather than for liquidation, on June 30, Year 4. The plan of reorganization, which was approved by stockholders and all unsecured creditors and confirmed by the court, included the following:

1 Deposit $25,000 with escrow agent, as soon as cash becomes available, to cover liabilities with priority and costs of reorganization proceedings.

2 Amend articles of incorporation to provide for 10,000 shares of authorized common stock of $1 par. The new common stock is to be exchanged on a share-for-share basis for the 750 shares of outstanding $100 par common stock.

3 Extend due date of unsecured notes payable to suppliers totaling $15,250 for four years, until May 31, Year 9. Increase the interest rate on the notes from 14% to 18%, the current fair rate of interest.

4 Exchange 1,600 shares of new $1 par common stock (at current fair value of $15 a share) for unsecured notes payable to suppliers totaling $24,000.

5 Pay vendors 70 cents per dollar of accounts payable owed.

The following journal entries, numbered to correspond with the provisions of the reorganization plan outlined above, were recorded by Sanders Company as cash became available from operations:

SANDERS COMPANY
General Journal

(1) Cash with Escrow Agent 25,000
    Cash 25,000
To record deposit of cash with escrow agent under terms of
bankruptcy reorganization.

    Salaries and Wages Payable 8,850
    Property Taxes Payable 2,900
    FICA and Income Taxes Withheld and Accrued 1,750
        Cash with Escrow Agent 13,500
To record escrow agent's payment of liabilities with priority.

    Costs of Bankruptcy Proceedings 11,000
        Cash with Escrow Agent 11,000
To record escrow agent's payment of costs of bankruptcy
proceedings.

(2) Common Stock, $100 par 75,000
        Common Stock, $1 par 750
        Paid-in Capital in Excess of Par 74,250
To record issuance of 750 shares of $1 par common stock in
exchange for 750 shares of $100 par common stock.

(3) 14% Notes Payable to Suppliers, due May 31, Year 5 15,250
        18% Notes Payable to Suppliers, due May 31, Year 9 15,250
To record extension of due dates of notes payable to suppliers and increase of interest rate from 14% to 18%.

(4) Notes Payable to Suppliers 24,000
        Common Stock, $1 par 1,600
        Paid-in Capital in Excess of Par 22,400
To record exchange of 1,600 shares of $1 par common stock
for $24,000 face amount of notes payable, at current fair
value of $15 a share.

(5) Accounts Payable 52,000
        Cash 36,400
        Gain from Discharge of Indebtedness in Bankruptcy . 15,600
To record payment of $0.70 per dollar of accounts payable
to vendors.

After the plan of reorganization has been carried out, the following journal entry is appropriate for eliminating the $67,890 accumulated deficit of Sanders Company on June 30, Year 4:

Journal entry to eliminate deficit

Paid-in Capital in Excess of Par	63,290	
Gain from Discharge of Indebtedness in Bankruptcy	15,600	
Costs of Bankruptcy Proceedings		11,000
Retained Earnings		67,890
To eliminate deficit on June 30, Year 4, and close bankruptcy gain and costs to Paid-in Capital in Excess of Par account.		

The effect of the foregoing journal entries is to show a "clean slate" for Sanders Company as a result of the approved bankruptcy reorganization and the write-off of the accumulated deficit existing on the date of the petition for reorganization. The extension of due dates of some liabilities, conversion of other liabilities to common stock, and liquidation of accounts payable at less than their face amount, should enable Sanders to resume operations as a going concern. For a reasonable number of years subsequent to the reorganization, Sanders should "date" the retained earnings in its balance sheets to disclose that the earnings were accumulated after the reorganization.

Footnote disclosure of reorganization

The elaborate and often complex issues involved in a reorganization must be disclosed in a note to the financial statements for the period in which the plan of reorganization was carried out. The following abridged note to financial statements appeared in an annual report of Anta Corporation, successor to two corporations that were victims of major management fraud:

> Anta Corporation was formed . . . by the reorganization . . . of Four Seasons Nursing Centers of America, Inc., and Four Seasons Equity Corporation and their subsidiaries (the reorganized companies). A Court-appointed Board of Directors assumed responsibility for the operations of the Company on September 15, 19_.
>
> The Plan of Reorganization provided for the issuance of common stock of the Company at the rate of one share of $1 par value stock for each $7 of unsecured indebtedness (over $200) of the reorganized companies, and for distribution to persons who suffered losses as a result of acquiring for value any stock, warrant or other security of the reorganized companies before July 22, 19_, and who filed a claim for such losses with the Trustee, on a pro rata basis (based on the dollar amount of loss) of one-half the number of shares of common stock issued to unsecured creditors. All previously issued common stock, warrants and options have been canceled under the Terms of the Plan. Creditors who had approved claims against the reorganized companies for work performed or material delivered (Class B-2) were paid in cash in full under the terms of the Plan of Reorganization. . . .

Evaluation of Bankruptcy Code

Since its enactment in 1978, the Bankruptcy Code has been criticized by credit grantors as being too liberal and thus popularizing bankruptcy as a means of avoiding payment of debts. Supporters of the Bankruptcy Code have alleged that lax credit-granting policies have caused the upsurge in bankruptcy petitions since the Code was enacted. Committees of Congress have reacted to these allegations by restudying provisions of the Bankruptcy Code for possible amendments.

In 1982 the Supreme Court declared unconstitutional the 1978 Bankruptcy Reform Act, because it created a new system of federal bankruptcy courts and judges. (Previously, federal district courts and judges and court-appointed *referees* had administered bankruptcy proceedings.) The Supreme Court's decision did not affect the accounting procedures for bankruptcy liquidations and reorganizations, because the Court stayed the effect of its decision to permit Congress to remedy the defects of the 1978 Act.

REVIEW QUESTIONS

1 Define *insolvency* as that term is used in the Bankruptcy Code for an entity other than a partnership.

2 What are *Bankruptcy Rules?*

3 Identify the various classes of creditors whose claims are dealt with in bankruptcy liquidations.

4 Describe the process of *liquidation* under the Bankruptcy Code.

5 Differentiate between a *voluntary* and an *involuntary bankruptcy petition.*

6 Can any business enterprise file a voluntary bankruptcy petition for liquidation? Explain.

7 What is a *statement of affairs* under the Bankruptcy Code?

8 List the unsecured debts having priority over other unsecured debts under the provisions of the Bankruptcy Code.

9 Who can file an *involuntary petition* for bankruptcy liquidation?

10 Describe the priority of claims for wages and salaries under the Bankruptcy Code.

11 Describe the authority of a bankruptcy trustee with respect to a *preference.*

12 What are the effects of a *discharge* in bankruptcy liquidation proceedings? Explain.

13 What use is made of the accounting financial statement known as a *statement of affairs?* Explain.

14 Describe the ***accountability*** method of accounting used by a trustee in a bankruptcy liquidation.

15 For what types of bankruptcy reorganizations might an ***examiner*** be appointed by the court?

16 What is the role of the SEC in a bankruptcy reorganization?

17 Must all classes of creditors accept a reorganization plan before the plan may be confirmed by the bankruptcy court? Explain.

EXERCISES

Ex. 17-1   Select the best answer for each of the following multiple-choice questions:

1 In the journal entry to open the accounting records of a trustee in a bankruptcy liquidation, the debit to the Estate Deficit ledger account is in the statement of affairs amount of the:
a Estimated deficiency to unsecured, nonpriority creditors
b Total estimated amount available
c Estimated amount available for unsecured, nonpriority creditors
d Stockholders' equity of the debtor corporation

2 In journal entries for a bankruptcy reorganization, the difference between the carrying amount of a liability of the debtor and the amount accepted by the creditor in full settlement of the liability is credited to:
a Retained earnings (deficit)
b Paid-in capital in excess of par
c Paid-in capital from reorganization
d Cash with escrow agent
e Some other ledger account

3 The bankruptcy trustee for Insolvent Company sold assets having a carrying amount of $10,000 for $8,500 cash. The journal entry (explanation omitted) to record the sale is:

a	Cash	8,500	
	Loss on Realization of Assets	1,500	
	Assets		10,000
b	Cash	8,500	
	Estate Administration Expenses	1,500	
	Assets		10,000
c	Cash	8,500	
	Cost of Goods Sold	10,000	
	Sales		8,500
	Assets		10,000
d	Cash	8,500	
	Estate Deficit	1,500	
	Assets		10,000

4 In the ***accounting*** statement of affairs, assets pledged for partially secured liabilities are:
a Deducted from the related liabilities in the liabilities and stockholders' equity section

    b Included in the "estimated amount available" column of the assets section

    c Reduced by the related liabilities in the assets section

    d Included only in the "carrying amount" column of the assets section

5 If a secured creditor's claim exceeds the current fair value of the collateral of a debtor in bankruptcy liquidation, the secured creditor will be paid the total amount realized from the sale of the collateral and will:

    a Not have any claim for the balance

    b Become an unsecured creditor for the balance

    c Retain a secured creditor status for the balance

    d Be paid the balance only after all unsecured creditors without priority are paid.

6 Insolvus Company is in serious financial difficulty and is unable to meet current unsecured obligations of $25,000 to some 15 creditors who are demanding immediate payment. Insolvus owes Payless Company $5,000, and Payless has decided to file an involuntary bankruptcy petition against Insolvus. Which of the following is necessary in order for Payless to file?

    a Payless must be joined by at least two other creditors

    b Insolvus must have committed an act of bankruptcy within six months of the filing

    c Payless must allege and subsequently establish that the liabilities of Insolvus exceed the current fair value of its assets

    d Payless must be a secured creditor

Ex. 17-2 Edward Ross, the trustee in bankruptcy for Winslow Company, set up accounting records based on the April 30, Year 5, statement of affairs for Winslow. The trustee completed the following transactions early in May, Year 5:

    May 2 Sold for $10,000 cash the finished goods inventory with a statement of affairs valuation of $10,500.

         3 Paid wages with a statement of affairs valuation of $8,000.

         4 Collected $6,000 on accounts receivable with a statement of affairs valuation of $6,200. The balance was considered to be uncollectible.

         7 Paid trustee fee for one week, $500.

    Prepare journal entries in the accounting records of Edward Ross, trustee in bankruptcy for Winslow Company, for the transactions described above. Omit explanations.

Ex. 17-3 Among the provisions of the reorganization of Hayward Company under the Bankruptcy Code were the following:

    (1) Issued 1,000 shares of $5 par common stock in exchange for 1,000 shares of $100 par common stock outstanding.

    (2) Issued 200 shares of $5 par common stock (current fair value $10 a share) for notes payable to suppliers with unpaid principal of $2,500 and accrued interest of $500.

    (3) Paid $8,000 to vendors in full settlement of claims of $10,000.

    Prepare journal entries (omit explanations) for the foregoing provisions, all of which were completed on January 20, Year 7.

Ex. 17-4 From the traditional statement of realization and liquidation on page 808, prepare a more concise statement of realization and liquidation similar to the one illustrated on page 800.

Ex. 17-5 In auditing the financial statements of Delbert Company for the six months ended December 31, Year 10, you find items *a* through *e* on page 808 had been debited or credited to the Retained Earnings account during the six months immediately following a bankruptcy reorganization, which was finalized and made effective July 1, Year 10.

REED COMPANY, IN BANKRUPTCY
Selma Ross, Trustee
Statement of Realization and Liquidation
For Month of January, Year 2

Assets to be realized:		Liabilities to be liquidated:	
Accounts receivable	$ 7,500	Notes payable	$ 5,000
Inventories	12,500	Accounts payable	30,000
Equipment	10,000	Accrued interest payable. .	150
Subtotal	$30,000	Subtotal	$35,150
Supplementary charges:		Liabilities assumed:	
Administration expenses. .	2,950	Accrued interest payable. .	50
Interest expense.	50	Assets realized:	
Liabilities liquidated:		Accounts receivable	6,500
Accounts payable	6,000	Inventories	14,500
Liabilities not liquidated:		Assets not realized:	
Notes payable	5,000	Equipment	10,000
Accounts payable	24,000	Net loss	2,000
Accrued interest payable. .	200		
Total	$68,200	Total	$68,200

a Debit of $25,000 arising from an additional income tax assessment applicable to Year 9.

b Credit of $48,000 resulting from gain on sale of equipment that was no longer used in the business. This equipment had been written down by a $50,000 increase in the Accumulated Depreciation account on July 1, Year 10.

c Debit of $15,000 resulting from the loss on plant assets destroyed in a fire on November 2, Year 10.

d Debit of $32,000 representing cash dividends declared on preferred stock.

e Credit of $60,400, the net income for the six-month period ended December 31, Year 10.

For each of these items, state whether you believe it to be correctly debited or credited to the Retained Earnings account. Give a brief reason for your conclusion.

Ex. 17-6 The statement of affairs for Wicks Corporation shows that approximately $0.78 on the dollar probably will be paid to unsecured creditors without priority. The corporation owes Stark Company $23,000 on a promissory note, plus accrued interest of $940. Inventories with a current fair value of $19,200 collateralize the note payable.

Compute the amount that Stark should receive from Wicks assuming that actual payments to unsecured creditors without priority consist of 78% of total claims. Round all amounts to the nearest dollar.

Ex. 17-7 Compute the amount that will be paid to each class of creditors, using the following data taken from the statement of affairs for Kent Corporation:

Assets pledged for fully secured liabilities (*current fair value, $75,000*)	$ 90,000
Assets pledged for partially secured liabilities (*current fair value, $52,000*)	74,000
Free assets (*current fair value, $40,000*)	70,000
Unsecured liabilities with priority	7,000
Fully secured liabilities	30,000
Partially secured liabilities	60,000
Unsecured liabilities without priority	112,000

Ex. 17-8 The following information for Progress Book Company was obtained by an accountant retained by the company's creditors:
   a Furniture and fixtures: Carrying amount, $70,000; current fair value, $60,500; pledged on a note payable of $42,000 on which unpaid interest of $800 has accrued.
   b Book manuscripts owned: Carrying amount, $15,000; current fair value, $7,200; pledged on a note payable of $9,000; interest on the note is paid to date.
   c Books in process of production: Accumulated cost (direct material, direct labor, and factory overhead), $37,500; estimated sales value on completion, $60,000; additional out-of-pocket costs of $14,200 will be required to complete the books in process.
   Prepare the headings for the asset side of a statement of affairs and illustrate how each of the three items described should be shown in the statement.

CASES

Case 17-1 You have been asked to conduct a training program explaining the preparation of a statement of affairs (financial statement) for the staff of Bixby & Canfield, CPAs.

   Instructions Explain how each of the following is presented in a statement of affairs (financial statement) for a corporation in bankruptcy liquidation proceedings:
   a Assets pledged for partially secured liabilities
   b Unsecured liabilities with priority
   c Stockholders' equity

Case 17-2 Paul Martin has been appointed trustee of Zeman Company, a corporation involved in liquidation under the Bankruptcy Code. He asks you for advice on what accounting records he should maintain and what financial statements he should prepare in his role of trustee.

   Instructions Give Paul Martin the advice he requested, in the form of a letter.

PROBLEMS

17-1 The following information is available on October 31, Year 5, for Dodge Company, which is having difficulty paying its liabilities as they become due:

	Carrying amount
Cash	$ 4,000
Accounts receivable (net): Current fair value equal to carrying amount	46,000
Inventories: Net realizable value, $18,000; pledged on $21,000 of notes payable	39,000
Plant assets: Current fair value, $67,400; pledged on mortgage note payable	134,000
Accumulated depreciation	27,000
Supplies: Current fair value, $1,500	2,000
Wages payable, all earned during October, Year 5	5,800
Property taxes payable	1,200
Accounts payable	60,000
Notes payable, $21,000 secured by inventories	40,000
Mortgage note payable, including accrued interest of $400	50,400
Common stock, $5 par	100,000
Deficit	59,400

Instructions

a Prepare a statement of affairs in the form illustrated on pages 796 and 797.

b Prepare a working paper to compute the estimated percentage of claims each group of creditors should expect to receive if Dodge Company petitions for liquidation in bankruptcy.

17-2 Robaire Corporation was in financial difficulty because of declining sales and poor cost controls. Its stockholders and principal creditors had asked for an estimate of the financial results of the sale of the assets, the payment of liabilities, and the liquidation of the corporation. Thus, the accountant for Robaire prepared the statement of affairs that appears on pages 812 and 813.

On January 2, Year 4, Robaire filed a voluntary petition for liquidation under the Bankruptcy Code. Charles Stern was appointed as trustee by the bankruptcy court to take custody of the assets, make payments to creditors, and implement an orderly liquidation. The trustee completed the following transactions:

Jan. 2   Recorded the assets and liabilities of Robaire Corporation in a separate set of accounting records. The assets were recorded at current fair value and all liabilities were recorded at the estimated amounts payable to the various groups of creditors.

Jan. 7   Sold the land and buildings at an auction for $52,000 cash and paid $42,550 to the mortgagee. The payment included interest of $50 that accrued in January.

Jan. 10   Made cash payments as follows:

Wages payable...	$1,500
FICA and income taxes withheld and accrued	800
Completion of inventories	400
Liquidation costs	600

(Continued)

Jan. 31   Cash receipts from Jan. 8 to Jan. 31 were as follows:

Collection of accounts receivable at carrying amount, including $10,000 of assigned accounts 17,500

Sale of inventories. 18,000

Sale of Public Service Company bonds 920

Jan. 31   Additional cash payments were:

Liquidation costs 1,250

Note payable to bank (from proceeds of collection of assigned accounts receivable) 10,000

Dividend of $0.50 on the dollar to unsecured creditors . . . 30,500

Instructions

a Prepare journal entries for the foregoing transactions in the accounting records of the trustee for Robaire Corporation.

b Prepare a statement of realization and liquidation for the month of January,
Year 4. Use the form illustrated on page 800.

c Prepare a trial balance for the trustee on January 31, Year 4.

17-3   Javits Corporation advises you that it is facing bankruptcy proceedings. As the
company's independent auditor, you are aware of its financial condition.

The unaudited balance sheet of Javits on July 10, Year 10, is presented below:

JAVITS CORPORATION

Balance Sheet

July 10, Year 10

Assets

Cash	$ 12,000
Short-term investments, at cost	20,000
Accounts receivable, less allowance for doubtful accounts	90,000
Finished goods inventory	60,000
Material inventory	40,000
Short-term prepayments	5,000
Land	13,000
Buildings (net)	90,000
Machinery (net)	120,000
Goodwill	20,000
Total assets	$470,000

Liabilities & Stockholders' Equity

Notes payable to banks	$135,000
Accounts payable	94,200
Wages payable	15,000
Mortgage notes payable	130,000
Common stock	100,000
Retained earnings (deficit)	(4,200)
Total liabilities & stockholders' equity	$470,000

ROBAIRE CORPORATION
Statement of Affairs
December 31, Year 3

Carrying amount	Assets	Current fair value	Estimated amount available	Loss or (gain) on realization
	Assets pledged for fully secured liabilities:			
$ 4,000	Land	$20,000		$(16,000)
25,000	Buildings	30,000		(5,000)
	Total	$50,000		
	Less: Fully secured liabilities (contra) . . .	42,500	$ 7,500	
	Assets pledged for partially secured liabilities:			
10,000	Accounts receivable (deducted contra) .	$10,000		
	Free assets:			
700	Cash	$ 700	700	
10,450	Accounts receivable	10,450	10,450	
40,000	Inventories $19,350			
	Less: Cost to complete 400	18,950	18,950	21,050
9,100	Factory supplies	-0-	-0-	9,100
5,750	Public Service Company bonds	900	900	4,850
38,000	Machinery and equipment	18,000	18,000	20,000
	Total estimated amount available		$56,500	$34,000
	Less: Unsecured liabilities with priority (contra) . . .		5,500	
	Estimated amount available for unsecured, nonpriority creditors.		$51,000	
	Estimated deficiency to unsecured, nonpriority creditors.		10,000	
$143,000			$61,000	

Additional information

(1) Cash includes a $500 travel advance that has been spent.

(2) Accounts receivable of $40,000 have been pledged as collateral for notes payable to banks in the amount of $30,000. Credit balances of $5,000 are netted in the accounts receivable total. All accounts are expected to be collected except those for which an allowance has been established.

(3) Short-term investments consist of U.S. government bonds costing $10,000 and 500 shares of Owens Company common stock. The current fair value of the bonds is $10,000; the current fair value of the stock is $18 a share. The bonds have accrued interest receivable of $200. The short-term investments are pledged as collateral for a $20,000 note payable to bank.

(4) Estimated realizable value of finished goods is $50,000 and of material is $30,000. For additional out-of-pocket costs of $10,000 the material would realize $59,900 as finished goods.

(5) Short-term prepayments will be consumed during the liquidation period.

(6) The current fair value of plant assets is as follows: Land, $25,000; buildings, $110,000; machinery, $65,000.

ROBAIRE CORPORATION
Statement of Affairs (concluded)
December 31, Year 3

Carrying amount	Liabilities & stockholders' equity		Amount unsecured
	Unsecured liabilities with priority:		
$ 1,500	Wages payable	$ 1,500	
800	FICA and income taxes withheld and		
	accrued	800	
	Estimated liquidation cost payable	3,200	
	Total (deducted contra)	$ 5,500	
	Fully secured liabilities:		
42,000	Mortgage note payable	$42,000	
500	Accrued interest payable	500	
	Total (deducted contra)	$42,500	
	Partially secured liabilities:		
25,000	Notes payable to bank	$25,000	
	Less: Assigned accounts receivable	10,000	$15,000
	Unsecured liabilities without priority:		
20,000	Notes payable to suppliers		20,000
26,000	Accounts payable		26,000
27,200	Stockholders' equity		
$143,000			$61,000

(7) Accounts payable include $15,000 withheld FICA and income taxes and $6,000 payable to creditors who had been reassured by the president of Javits that they would be paid. There are unrecorded employer's FICA taxes in the amount of $500.

(8) Wages payable are not subject to any limitations under the Bankruptcy Code.

(9) Mortgage notes payable consist of $100,000 secured by land and buildings, and a $30,000 installment contract secured by machinery. Total unrecorded accrued interest for these liabilities amounts to $2,400.

(10) Probable judgment on a pending damage suit is estimated at $50,000.

(11) Costs to be incurred in connection with the liquidation are estimated at $10,000.

(12) You have not submitted an invoice for $5,000 for the April 30, Year 10, annual audit of Javits, and you estimate a $1,000 fee for liquidation work.

Instructions
a Prepare correcting journal entries for Javits Corporation on July 10, Year 10.
b Prepare a statement of affairs for Javits Corporation on July 10, Year 10. Amounts in the statement should reflect the journal entries in *a.*

17-4   The trial balance of Laurel Company on June 30, Year 6, is shown below:

LAUREL COMPANY
Trial Balance
June 30, Year 6

	Debit	Credit
Cash	$ 14,135	
Notes receivable	29,000	
Accrued interest on notes receivable	615	
Accounts receivable	19,500	
Common stock subscriptions receivable	5,000	
Allowance for doubtful accounts		$ 800
Inventories..........................	48,000	
Land	10,000	
Building	50,000	
Accumulated depreciation of building		15,000
Machinery and equipment	33,000	
Accumulated depreciation of machinery and equipment .		19,000
Furniture and fixtures	21,000	
Accumulated depreciation of furniture and fixtures		9,500
Goodwill	8,000	
Organization costs	1,600	
Note payable to City Bank		18,000
Notes payable to Municipal Trust Company		6,000
Notes payable to vendors		24,000
Accrued interest on notes payable		1,280
Accounts payable		80,520
Wages payable		1,400
FICA and income taxes withheld and accrued		430
Mortgage bonds payable		32,000
Accrued interest payable on mortgage bonds		1,820
Common stock		65,000
Common stock subscribed		5,000
Retained earnings—deficit	39,900	
Totals	$279,750	$279,750

Additional information

(1) Notes receivable of $25,000 were pledged to collateralize the $18,000 note payable to City Bank. Interest of $500 was accrued on the pledged notes and $600 was accrued on the $18,000 note payable to the bank. All the pledged notes were collectible. Of the remaining notes receivable, a $1,000 noninterest-bearing note was uncollectible. The note had been received for an unconditional cash loan.

(2) Accounts receivable include $7,000 from Boren Company, which currently is being liquidated. Creditors expect to realize $0.40 on the dollar. The allowance for doubtful accounts is adequate to cover any other uncollectible accounts. A total of $3,200 of the remaining collectible accounts receivable was

pledged as collateral for the notes payable to Municipal Trust Company of $6,000 with accrued interest of $180 on June 30, Year 6.

(3) The subscriptions receivable from stockholders for no-par common stock are due July 31, Year 6, and are considered fully collectible.

(4) Inventories are valued at cost and are expected to realize 25% of cost on a forced liquidation sale after the write-off of $10,000 of obsolete stock.

(5) Land and buildings, which are appraised at 110% of their carrying amount, are mortgaged as collateral for the bonds. Interest of $1,820 was accrued on the bonds on June 30, Year 6. The company expects to realize 20% of the cost of its machinery and equipment, and 50% of the cost of its furniture and fixtures after incurring refinishing costs of $800.

(6) Estimated costs of liquidation are $4,500. Depreciation and accruals have been adjusted to June 30, Year 6.

(7) The company has net operating loss carryovers for income tax purposes of $22,000 for Year 4, and $28,000 for Year 5. Assume the income tax rate in effect for those years was 50%.

Instructions Prepare a statement of affairs for Laurel Company on June 30, Year 6.

17-5 Bilbo Corporation, which is in bankruptcy reorganization, had $105,000 of dividends in arrears on its 7% cumulative preferred stock on March 31, Year 20. While retained earnings were adequate to permit the payment of accumulated dividends, Bilbo's management did not wish to weaken its working capital position. They also realized that a portion of the plant assets was no longer used by Bilbo. Therefore, management proposed the following plan of reorganization, which was accepted by stockholders and confirmed by the bankruptcy court, to be effective on April 1, Year 20:

(1) The preferred stock was to be exchanged for $300,000 face amount and current fair value of 15%, 10-year bonds. Dividends in arrears were to be settled by the issuance of $120,000 of $10 par, 15%, noncumulative preferred stock having a current fair value equal to par.

(2) Common stock was to be assigned a par of $50 a share.

(3) Goodwill was to be written off; plant assets were to be written down, based on appraisal and estimates of current fair value, by a total of $103,200, consisting of $85,400 increase in the Accumulated Depreciation account and $17,800 decrease in plant assets; other current assets were to be written down by $10,460 to reduce accounts receivable and inventories to net realizable values.

The condensed balance sheet on March 31, Year 20, is presented below and on page 816.

BILBO CORPORATION

Balance Sheet

March 31, Year 20

Assets

Cash		$ 30,000
Other current assets		252,890
Plant assets	$1,458,250	
Less: Accumulated depreciation	512,000	946,250
Goodwill		50,000
Total assets		$1,279,140

(Continued)

BILBO CORPORATION
Balance Sheet (concluded)
March 31, Year 20

Liabilities & Stockholders' Equity

Current liabilities	$ 132,170
7% cumulative preferred stock, $100 par ($105,000 dividends in	
arrears)	300,000
Common stock, no-par, 9,000 shares issued and outstanding	648,430
Paid-in capital in excess of par: preferred stock	22,470
Retained earnings	176,070
Total liabilities & stockholders' equity	$1,279,140

Instructions

a Prepare journal entries to give effect to the plan of reorganization on April 1, Year 20.

b Prepare a balance sheet on April 30, Year 20, assuming that net income for April was $15,000. The operations resulted in $11,970 increase in cash, $18,700 increase in other current assets, $7,050 increase in current liabilities, and $8,620 increase in the Accumulated Depreciation account.

17-6   Tapp Corporation is in bankruptcy reorganization because one of the three stockholders, Adam Wright, cannot get along with the other two, Ben Yates and Carla Zorb. At the end of Year 7, Yates and Zorb agree to reorganize the corporation into a partnership.

The information relative to the reorganization plan, confirmed by the bankruptcy court, follows:

(1) The balance sheet of Tapp Corporation on December 31, Year 7, is shown below and on page 817.

TAPP CORPORATION
Balance Sheet
December 31, Year 7

Assets

Current assets:		
Cash		$105,000
Accounts receivable, net of $22,000 allowance for doubtful accounts		135,000
Inventories		225,000
Short-term prepayments		4,500
Total current assets		$469,500
Building, at current fair value	$125,000	
Less: Accumulated depreciation	27,500	97,500
Investment in land		20,000
Other assets		10,000
Total assets		$597,000

(Continued)

TAPP CORPORATION

Balance Sheet (concluded)

December 31, Year 7

Liabilities & Stockholders' Equity

Current liabilities:

Note payable to Adam Wright, a stockholder	$ 30,000	
Accounts payable	110,000	
Accrued liabilities	32,000	
Total current liabilities	$172,000	

Stockholders' equity:

Preferred stock, $100 par (liquidation value $110); author-		
ized, 1,000 shares; in treasury, 400 shares; outstanding,		
600 shares	$100,000	
Common stock, no par; stated value $1; authorized,		
200,000 shares; issued and outstanding, 100,000		
shares	100,000	
Paid-in capital in excess of stated value of common		
stock	150,000	
Total paid-in capital	$350,000	
Unrealized appreciation from revaluation of building . . .	50,000	
Retained earnings	72,250	
Subtotal	$472,250	
Less: Treasury stock, 400 shares of preferred stock, at		
cost	47,250	425,000
Total liabilities & stockholders' equity	$597,000	

(2) The capital stock records of Tapp on December 31, Year 7, indicate that the three stockholders have retained their respective interests since the corporation was organized five years ago as follows:

		Preferred		Common	
Stockholder	**Total invested**	**Shares**	**Amount**	**Shares**	**Amount**
Ben Yates	$115,000	300	$30,000	35,000	$ 85,000
Carla Zorb	105,000	100	10,000	40,000	95,000
Adam Wright.	90,000	200	20,000	25,000	70,000
Totals.	$310,000	600	$60,000	100,000	$250,000

(3) In accordance with the reorganization plan, Tapp will acquire Wright's preferred and common stock, and thereafter Tapp will be liquidated by an appropriate disposition of its net assets.

(4) In order to finance the acquisition of Wright's stock, the building was appraised as a basis for an $80,000 mortgage loan arranged by Tapp with an insurance company. The appraisal was made on December 31, Year 7, and was recorded as follows:

	Current fair value per appraisal	Cost	Unrealized appreciation
Building	$125,000	$70,000	$55,000
Less: Accumulated depreciation . . .	27,500	22,500	5,000
Totals	$ 97,500	$47,500	$50,000

(5) Wright's stock is to be acquired for cash of $110 a share for the preferred stock and $3 a share for the common stock. The stock acquired from Wright is to be retired.

(6) After the acquisition of Wright's stock, disposition of the net assets of Tapp in complete liquidation is to be made as follows:
  (a) The note payable to Wright is to be paid in cash.
  (b) The treasury stock is to be canceled, and the preferred stock owned by Yates and Zorb is to be retired at $110 a share.
  (c) The investment in land is to be transferred to Zorb at its current fair value of $36,000.
  (d) The remaining assets are to be acquired and the liabilities (including the $80,000 mortgage loan) are to be assumed by a partnership organized by Yates and Zorb. Yates is to withdraw cash from the partnership as necessary to equalize his capital account with that of Zorb.

Instructions Prepare a working paper giving effect to the reorganization of Tapp Corporation into a partnership on December 31, Year 7, in accordance with the agreement among the three stockholders. Use the following columnar headings in the working paper:

Accounts	Tapp Corporation balance sheet, Dec. 31, Year 7		Transactions to implement reorganization		Yates & Zorb Partnership balance sheet, Dec. 31, Year 7	

18 ACCOUNTING FOR ESTATES AND TRUSTS

Estates and trusts are accounting entities as well as taxable entities. The individuals or corporations that manage the assets of estates and trusts are *fiduciaries;* they exercise stewardship for those assets in accordance with the provisions of a will, a trust document, or state laws.

In this chapter we deal first with certain aspects of estates, including wills, and then discuss and illustrate the accounting for estates; the last section covers the legal and accounting aspects of trusts.

LEGAL AND ACCOUNTING ASPECTS OF ESTATES

State laws (generally termed *probate codes*) regulate the administration and distribution of estates of decedents, missing persons, and other individuals subject to protection of courts. The many variations among the probate codes of the 50 states led to the drafting of a *Uniform Probate Code,* developed by the National Conference of Commissioners on Uniform State Laws and approved by the American Bar Association. Although the Uniform Probate Code has not yet been adopted by all states, we shall use the Code to illustrate certain legal issues underlying accounting for estates.

Provisions of Uniform Probate Code governing estates

The Uniform Probate Code identifies an *estate* as all the property of a decedent, trust, or other person whose affairs are subject to the Code.[1] *Person* is defined as an individual, a corporation, an organization, or other legal entity.

The Uniform Probate Code also provides that the real and personal property of a decedent is to be awarded to the persons specified in the decedent's *will.* In the absence of a will—a condition known as *intestacy*—the decedent's property goes to heirs, as enumerated in the Code. Thus, as the Code points out, the intentions of a *testator* (a person creating a will) control the disposition of a decedent's property.[2]

[1] Uniform Probate Code, Sec. 1-201(11).
[2] Ibid., Sec. 2-603.

Wills The Uniform Probate Code provides that a will shall be in writing, signed by the testator, or in the testator's name by some other person in the testator's presence and by the testator's direction, and also signed by at least two witnesses. The chief exception to these requirements is a **holographic will**—a will having its essential provisions and signature in the handwriting of the testator.

Probate of Wills Probate of a will is action by the probate court (also known as **surrogate** or **orphan's** court) to validate the will. The Uniform Probate Code provides for two types of probate—**informal** and **formal.** Informal probate is initiated by the application of an interested party filed with a court official known as a **registrar.** After thorough review of the completeness and propriety of an application for informal probate, the registrar issues a written statement of informal probate, thus making the will effective.

Formal probate is litigation to determine whether a decedent left a valid will, and it is initiated by a petition filed by an interested party requesting the probate court to order probate of the will. The petition also may request a finding that the decedent died **intestate** (without a valid will). During the court hearings, any party to the formal probate proceedings may oppose the will; however, the burden of proof that the will is invalid is on the contestant of the will. After completion of the hearings, the court enters an order for formal probate of a will found to be valid, or an order that the decedent died intestate. Generally, no formal or informal probate proceedings may be undertaken more than three years after the decedent's death.

Appointment of Personal Representative In both informal and formal probate proceedings, the probate appoints a **personal representative** of the decedent to administer the decedent's estate. A personal representative named in the decedent's will is called an **executor.** If the decedent died intestate, the court-appointed personal representative is known as an **administrator.** The Uniform Probate Code requires the probate court to issue **letters testamentary** to the personal representative before administration of the estate may begin. Because personal representatives are fiduciaries, they must observe standards of care in administering estates that prudent persons would observe in dealing with the property of others. The personal representative is entitled to reasonable compensation for services.

Powers and Duties of Personal Representative The personal representative of a decedent is empowered to take possession and control of the decedent's property, and to have title to the property in trust for the benefit of creditors and beneficiaries of the estate. The personal representative has many additional powers, such as: (1) the right to continue any single proprietorship of the decedent for not more than four months following the date of the personal representative's appointment and (2) the authority to allocate items of revenue and expenses of the estate to either **estate principal** (corpus) or **estate income,** as provided by the will or by law. Such allocations comprise the chief accounting problem for an estate and are discussed in a subsequent section of this chapter.

Not later than 30 days after appointment, the personal representative must inform the decedent's **devisees** or heirs of the appointment. A **devisee** is any person or trust named in a will to receive real or personal property of the decedent in a transfer known as a **devise.** Within three months after appointment, the personal representative must prepare an inventory of assets owned by the decedent on date of death, together with a list of any liens against the assets. The assets in the inventory must be stated at current fair value on date of death. The personal representative may retain the services of an appraiser to obtain the current fair values of the assets. The inventory of decedent's assets is filed with the probate court, and copies are provided to parties who request them. If, after the filing of the original inventory, other assets of the decedent are discovered, the personal representative must file a supplementary inventory with the probate court.

Exempt Property and Allowances In a manner similar to the bankruptcy laws discussed in Chapter 17, the Uniform Probate Code provides for certain exemptions from claims against the estate assets, even by devisees. These exemptions are as follows:

1 *Homestead allowance.* The decedent's surviving spouse, or surviving minor and dependent children, are entitled to an aggregate **homestead allowance** of $5,000. This allowance is in addition to any share of the estate passing to the spouse or children pursuant to the provisions of the will.
2 *Exempt property.* The decedent's surviving spouse or children are entitled to an aggregate $3,500 value of automobiles, household furniture and furnishings, appliances, and personal effects.
3 *Family allowance.* The surviving spouse and children who were being supported by the decedent are entitled to a reasonable cash allowance, payable in a lump sum not exceeding $6,000, or in installments not exceeding $500 a month for one year, during the administration of the estate. The family allowance has priority over all claims against the estate, but does not have priority over the homestead allowance.

Claims of Creditors against the Estate The personal representative for an estate is required to publish a notice once a week for three successive weeks, in a newspaper of general circulation, requesting creditors of the estate to present their claims within four months after the date of the first publication, or be forever barred. If the estate assets not exempt under the Uniform Probate Code are insufficient to pay all creditors' claims in full, the personal representative pays the claims in the following order:

1 Expenses of administering the estate

2 Decedent's funeral expenses and medical and hospital expenses of the decedent's last illness

3 Debts and taxes with preference under federal or state laws

4 All other claims

Four months after publication of the first notice to estate creditors, the personal representative initiates payment of claims in the order outlined above, after first providing for homestead, family, and support allowances.

Distributions to Devisees   The personal representative also has the duty of distributing estate assets to the devisees named in the will. The assets are to be distributed in kind to the extent possible, rather than first being converted to cash and then distributed.

If estate assets that are not exempt are insufficient to cover creditors' claims as well as all devises, the devises *abate*—or are reduced—in the sequence provided for in the decedent's will. If the will is silent as to order of abatement, the Uniform Probate Code provides the following *abatement sequence:*

1 Property not specifically mentioned in the will

2 *Residuary devises,* which are devises of all estate property remaining after general and specific devises are satisfied

3 *General devises,* which are gifts of a sum of money or a number of countable monetary assets, such as 500 shares of Mercury Company common stock

4 *Specific devises,* which are gifts of identified objects, such as named paintings, automobiles, stock certificates, or real property

Devises may be granted to the devisees *in trust,* which requires the establishment of a *testamentary trust*–one provided for by a will. Trusts are discussed in a subsequent section of this chapter.

Estate and Inheritance Taxes   The federal estate tax assessed against the net assets of an estate, and inheritance taxes assessed by various states against devisees and heirs of a decedent, often called *death taxes,* must be apportioned to the various devisees in the manner outlined in the will. If the will is silent on apportionment, the Uniform Probate Code applies. The Code provides that the estate and inheritance taxes are to be apportioned to the various devisees in the ratio of each devisee's interest to the aggregate interests of all devisees.

Closing the Estate   No earlier than six months after the date of appointment, a personal representative may close an estate by filing a statement with the probate court. The written content of this statement is described in the Uniform Probate Code; this legal statement usually is accompanied by a financial statement known as a *charge and discharge statement.*

PAUL HASTING, EXECUTOR
Of the Will of Jessica Davis, Deceased
General Journal (continued)

Mar. 31   *Distributions to Income Beneficiaries*   55

            Income Cash   55

       To distribute income cash payable to residuary devisee Nancy Grimes, as required by the will.

Apr. 2   *Principal Cash*   2,050

       Loss on Disposal of Principal Assets   137

            Automobile   2,187

       To record sale of automobile at a loss.

    4   *Devises Distributed*   5,000

            Principal Cash   5,000

       To record distribution of general devise to Universal Charities.

   16   *Liabilities Paid*   3,922

            Principal Cash   3,922

       To record following liabilities paid:

	Funeral expenses (Watts Mortuary)	$ 810
	Hospital bills (Suburban Hospital)	1,928
	Doctor's fees (Charles Carson, M.D.) . . .	426
	Final federal income tax	457
	Morningside Department Store	214
	Various residence bills	87
	Total	$3,922

   19   *Principal Cash*   1,526

            Medical Insurance Claim Receivable   1,526

       To record collection of medical insurance claim.

   24   *Income Cash*   1,500

       Principal Cash   1,000

            Payable to Devisees   1,000

            Dividend Revenue   1,500

       To record receipt of quarterly cash dividends on common stock, as follows:

	Preston Company (payable to Nancy Grimes)	$1,000
	Arthur Corporation	300
	Campbell Company	1,200
	Total	$2,500

(Continued)

PAUL HASTING, EXECUTOR
Of the Will of Jessica Davis, Deceased
General Journal (continued)

Apr. 25 Receivable from Devisees	23,576	
Principal Cash		23,576

To record payment of federal estate tax and state
inheritance taxes on behalf of devisees, as follows:

Federal estate tax	$18,556
State inheritance taxes	5,020
Total	$23,576

26 Principal Cash	6,295	
Receivable from Devisees		6,295

To record receipt of cash from specific devisees for
their shares of federal estate tax and state inheritance taxes, as follows:

Frances Davis Grimes: ($23,576 × 0.102)*	$2,405
Wallace Davis: ($23,576 × 0.165)*	3,890
Total	$6,295

27 Devises Distributed	30,000	
Receivable from Devisees		4,173
Principal Cash		25,827

To record payment of cash to general devisees, less
amounts receivable for their shares of federal estate
tax and state inheritance taxes, as follows:

$10,000 devises payable to Alice Martin,	
Angelo Bari, Nolan Ames: $10,000 × 3 .	$30,000
Less: Share of death taxes:	
($23,576 × 0.059* × 3)	4,173
Net cash paid	$25,827

(Continued)

* See explanation on page 830.

PAUL HASTING, EXECUTOR
Of the Will of Jessica Davis, Deceased
General Journal (concluded)

Apr. 30	Mortgage Note Payable	15,500	
	Accrued Interest Payable.	78	
	Devises Distributed	52,886	
	Payable to Devisees.	1,000	
	Marketable Securities.		8,000
	Residence.		40,800
	Furniture and Furnishings		2,517
	Paintings and Other Art Objects		16,522
	Clothing, Jewelry, Personal Effects.		625
	Principal Cash		1,000

To transfer to devisee Nancy Grimes cash for dividend received on Preston Company common stock, and to record distribution of devises as follows:

General devise to Nancy Grimes:		
200 shares of Preston Company common stock	$ 8,000	
Specific devise to Frances Davis Grimes:		
Paintings, other art objects, clothing, jewelry, personal effects	17,147	
Specific devise to Wallace Davis:		
Residence, net of mortgage note payable, with furniture and furnishings	27,739	
Total	$52,886	

May 1	Administrative Expenses	2,500	
	Principal Cash		2,500
	To record payment of executor's fee.		
3	Devises Distributed	85,797	
	Distributions to Income Beneficiaries	1,500	
	Principal Cash (balance of account)		21,714
	Income Cash		1,500
	Certificate of Deposit		26,475
	Marketable Securities.		24,500
	Receivable from Devisees (balance of account)		13,108

To record distribution of residuary devise (principal and income) to First National Bank, trustee for Nancy Grimes, devisee.

Apr. 16 Journal Entry The Liabilities Paid account represents a reduction of the executor's accountability for estate assets; it is neither an asset account nor an expense account.

Apr. 24 Journal Entry Dividends received on marketable securities required segregation in the accounting records, because the securities are allocable to separate devises, as follows:

> Preston Company common stock, $1,000: Allocable to general devise to Nancy Grimes
>
> Arthur Corporation and Campbell Company common stocks, $1,500: Allocable to residuary devise to Nancy Grimes

Although Nancy Grimes is the recipient of both devises, the residuary devise ultimately will be placed in a testamentary trust for the devisee.

Apr. 25 Journal Entry The will of Jessica Davis was silent regarding allocation of estate and inheritance taxes. Consequently, in accordance with the provisions of the Uniform Probate Code, the federal estate tax and state inheritance taxes are allocated in the ratio of interests of devisees, other than the nontaxable nonprofit organization, in the estate. The following summary shows these ratios:

<table>
<tr><td>

Ratios of devisee
interests in estate of
Jessica Davis
</td><td>

PAUL HASTING, EXECUTOR

Of the Will of Jessica Davis, Deceased

Ratio of Devisee Interests

April 25, Year 3

Devisee	Current fair value of estate interest	Ratio to total of all estate interests
Alice Martin	$ 10,000	5.9%
Angelo Bari.	10,000	5.9
Nolan Ames	10,000	5.9
Nancy Grimes (general devise).	8,000	4.7
Frances Davis Grimes	17,147 (1)	10.2
Wallace Davis	27,739 (2)	16.5
Nancy Grimes (residuary devise). . . .	85,797	50.9
Totals	$168,683 (3)	100.0%

(1) $16,522 + $625 = $17,147
(2) ($40,800 + $2,517) − ($15,500 + $78) = $27,739
(3) $162,242 + $18,000 − $137 − $5,000 − $3,922 − $2,500 = $168,683
</td></tr>
</table>

Apr. 26 and Apr. 27 Journal Entries The executor requested the specific devisees to pay in cash their shares of the federal estate tax and state inheritance taxes. The executor withheld the general devisees' death taxes from the cash payable to them.

May 1 Journal Entry The entire fee of the executor was charged to estate principal because the time spent by Paul Hasting on income assets was nominal. The allocation of fees is more appropriate for a trust than for an estate of relatively short duration.

May 3 Journal Entry No adjusting entries are required for interest on the certificate of deposit or any declared but unpaid dividends on the marketable securities. An accrual-basis cutoff for an estate is appropriate only at the time the executor prepares the inventory of estate assets in order to facilitate the distinction between estate principal and estate income. If the will provides that the accrual basis of accounting must be used, the executor must comply.

In the preceding illustration, federal and state income taxes on the estate were disregarded. In addition, it was assumed that devisee Wallace Davis immediately occupied the decedent's residence, so that depreciation on the residence was not required as it would be if rent revenue were realized from a lease. A further assumption was that devisee Wallace Davis paid the March 31 and April 30, Year 3, installments on the mortgage note secured by the residence.

Trial Balance of Estate Accounts Following is a trial balance of the ledger accounts of the Estate of Jessica Davis on May 3, Year 3:

	Debit	Credit
PAUL HASTING, EXECUTOR _Of the Will of Jessica Davis, Deceased_ _Trial Balance_ _May 3, Year 3_		
Principal		
Estate principal balance.		$162,242
Assets discovered		18,000
Loss on disposal of principal assets	$ 137	
Liabilities paid	3,922	
Devises distributed.	173,683	
Administrative expenses	2,500	
Totals	$180,242	$180,242
Income		
Interest revenue		$ 55
Dividend revenue.		1,500
Distributions to income beneficiaries.	$ 1,555	
Totals	$ 1,555	$ 1,555

Charge and Discharge Statement The executor's charge and discharge statement and supporting exhibits for the Estate of Jessica Davis are presented below and on pages 833 and 834. The items in the statement were taken from the trial balance on page 831. Although the executor's activities essentially ended May 3, the Uniform Probate Code precludes closing an estate earlier than six months after the issuance of letters testamentary.

PAUL HASTING, EXECUTOR
Of the Will of Jessica Davis, Deceased
Charge and Discharge Statement
For Period March 18 through September 18, Year 3

First, as to Principal

I charge myself as follows:

Inventory of estate assets, Mar. 18, Year 3 (Exhibit 1).	$162,242	
Assets discovered (Exhibit 2)	18,000	$180,242

I credit myself as follows:

Loss on disposal of principal assets (Exhibit 3)	$ 137	
Liabilities paid (Exhibit 4)	3,922	
Devises distributed (Exhibit 5).	173,683	
Administrative expenses (Exhibit 6)	2,500	180,242
Balance, Sept. 18, Year 3		$ -0-

Second, as to Income

I charge myself as follows:

Interest revenue (bank savings account)	$ 55	
Dividend revenue (Exhibit 7).	1,500	$ 1,555

I credit myself as follows:

Distributions of income (Exhibit 8)		1,555
Balance, Sept. 18, Year 3		$ -0-

---

The charge and discharge statement shows the executor's **accountability,** not the financial position or cash transactions of the estate. The statement discloses the charges to the executor for estate principal and estate income assets for which the executor is accountable, and the credits to the executor for the dispositions made of estate assets.

Closing Entry for Estate   Once the executor's closing statement and charge and discharge statement have been accepted by the probate court, the accountant for the estate may prepare an appropriate closing entry. The closing entry for the Estate of Jessica Davis on September 18, Year 3, appears at the bottom of page 834.

The example of estate accounting in this chapter was simplified in terms of details and time required for the liquidation of the estate. In practice, many estates—especially those involved in formal probate proceedings—take many months and sometimes years to settle. For

PAUL HASTING, EXECUTOR
Of the Will of Jessica Davis, Deceased
Exhibits Supporting Charge and Discharge Statement
For Period March 18 through September 18, Year 3

Exhibit 1—Inventory of estate assets, Mar. 18, Year 3:

Bank checking account		$ 2,157
Bank savings account (including accrued interest)		30,477
Savings and loan association 2-year certificate of deposit maturing June 30, Year 3 (including accrued interest)		26,475
Accrued salary earned for period Mar. 1 to 8, Year 3		214
Claim against medical insurance carrier		1,526
Social security benefits receivable		14,820
Proceeds of life insurance policy (payable to estate)		25,000
Marketable securities:		
Common stock of Preston Company, 200 shares		8,000
Common stock of Arthur Corporation, 100 shares		6,500
Residence	$40,800	
Less: Balance of mortgage note payable, including accrued interest of $78	15,578	25,222
Furniture and furnishings		2,517
Paintings and other art objects		16,522
Clothing, jewelry, personal effects		625
Automobile		2,187
Total inventory of estate assets		$162,242

Exhibit 2—Assets discovered:

On Mar. 25, Year 3, a certificate for 600 shares of Campbell Company common stock was discovered among the decedent's personal effects. All other securities were located in the decedent's safe deposit box at First National Bank (valued at market value on date of Jessica Davis' death).	$ 18,000

Exhibit 3—Loss on disposal of principal assets:

Sale of automobile, Apr. 3, Year 3:

Carrying amount	$ 2,187
Less: Cash proceeds	2,050
Loss on disposal of principal assets	$ 137

Exhibit 4—Liabilities paid:

Watts Mortuary	$ 810
Surburban Hospital	1,928
Charles Carson, M.D.	426
Final federal income tax	457
Morningside Department Store	214
Various residence bills	87
Total liabilities paid	$ 3,922

(Continued)

PAUL HASTING, EXECUTOR
Of the Will of Jessica Davis, Deceased
Exhibits Supporting Charge and Discharge Statement (concluded)
For Period March 18 through September 18, Year 3

Exhibit 5—Devises distributed:

General devise to Universal Charities: Cash	$ 5,000
General devise to Alice Martin: Cash	10,000
General devise to Angelo Bari: Cash	10,000
General devise to Nolan Ames: Cash	10,000
General devise to Nancy Grimes: 200 shares of Preston Company common stock	8,000
Specific devise to Frances Davis Grimes: Paintings, other art objects, clothing, jewelry, personal effects	17,147
Specific devise to Wallace Davis: Residence, net of mortgage note payable, with furniture and furnishings	27,739
Residuary devise to Nancy Grimes: Cash, certificate of deposit, 100 shares of Arthur Corporation common stock, and 600 shares of Campbell Company common stock	85,797
Total devises distributed	$173,683

Exhibit 6—Administrative expenses:

Fee of executor (charged entirely to principal because income administration activities were nominal)	$ 2,500

Exhibit 7—Dividend revenue:

Arthur Corporation common stock	$ 300
Campbell Company common stock	1,200
Total dividend revenue	$ 1,500

Exhibit 8—Distributions of income:

Mar. 31, Year 3: To residuary devisee Nancy Grimes	$ 55
May 3, Year 3: To First National Bank, trustee for Nancy Grimes	1,500
Total distributions of income	$ 1,555

Journal entry to close estate of Jessica Davis

Estate Principal Balance	162,242	
Assets Discovered	18,000	
Interest Revenue	55	
Dividend Revenue	1,500	
Loss on Disposal of Principal Assets		137
Liabilities Paid		3,922
Devises Distributed		173,683
Administrative Expenses		2,500
Distributions to Income Beneficiaries		1,555

To close estate of Jessica Davis in accordance with probate court authorization.

many estates, preparation of the federal estate tax return is a complex task. Furthermore, the estate of an intestate decedent involves complicated legal issues. The accountant involved in accounting for an estate must be familiar with provisions of the decedent's will and with appropriate state probate laws and principal and income laws, and should work closely with the attorney and executor (or administrator) for the estate.

LEGAL AND ACCOUNTING ASPECTS OF TRUSTS

A trust created by a will, as illustrated in the preceding sections of this chapter, is termed a **testamentary trust.** A trust created by the act of a living person is known as an **inter vivos** or **living trust.** The parties to a trust are (1) the **settlor** (also known as the **donor** or **trustor**)—the individual creating the trust, (2) the **trustee**—the fiduciary individual or corporation holding legal title to the trust property and carrying out the provisions of the **trust document** for a fee, and (3) the **beneficiary**—the party for whose benefit the trust was established. As we have noted previously, the income from trust property may be distributed to an **income beneficiary,** but the principal of a trust ultimately goes to a **principal beneficiary** or **remainderman.**

Provisions of Uniform Probate Code governing trusts

The Uniform Probate Code contains detailed sections dealing with trust registration, jurisdiction of courts concerning trusts, duties and liabilities of trustees, and powers of trustees. The Code requires that a trustee of a trust must register the trust with the appropriate state probate court. Registration subjects the trust to the jurisdiction of the court. The court's jurisdiction may include appointing or removing a trustee, reviewing the trustee's fees, and reviewing or settling interim or final accountings of the trustee. The trustee is required by the Code to administer the trust expeditiously for the benefit of the beneficiaries, and to use standards of care appropriate for a prudent person in dealing with the property of others. The trustee must keep the trust beneficiaries reasonably informed as to the administration of the trust, and furnish the beneficiaries a statement of the trust accounts annually (or more frequently if necessary) and at the termination of the trust.

Provisions of Revised Uniform Principal and Income Act governing trusts

The provisions for allocations between principal and income included in the Revised Uniform Principal and Income Act (see page 823) are applicable to trusts as well as to estates.

Illustration of accounting for a trust

The journal entries in the accounting records of a trust usually differ from those of an estate because of the longer life of a trust. Whereas the personal representative for an estate attempts to complete the administration of the estate as expeditiously as possible, the trustee for a trust must comply with the provisions of the trust document during the stated term of the trust. Accordingly, the trustee's activities include investment of trust assets and maintenance of accounting records for both trust principal and trust income.

To illustrate the accounting issues for a trust, we shall return to the testamentary trust created by the will of Jessica Davis (see page 824). The trust was created by the residuary devise to Nancy Grimes, which required the trustee to pay income from the trust to Grimes at the end of each calendar quarter until her twenty-first birthday (October 1, Year 8), at which time the trust principal would be paid to Grimes. Thus, Grimes is both the income beneficiary and the principal beneficiary.

The journal entries on page 837 illustrate the activities of First National Bank, trustee for Nancy Grimes, during the calendar quarter ended June 30, Year 3. The journal entries for the Nancy Grimes Trust are **cash-basis** entries; there is no need to accrue interest or dividends on trust investments because financial position or income statements normally are not prepared for a trust.

The May 3, Year 3, opening journal entry for the trust is the counterpart of the journal entry for the Estate of Jessica Davis on the same date (see page 829), except that the amount receivable from the trust beneficiary for federal estate tax and state inheritance tax was offset against the gross amount of the devise, and the $72,689 difference ($85,797 − $13,108 = $72,689) was recorded as the trust principal balance.

Trial Balance of Trust Accounts The trial balance of the Nancy Grimes Trust on June 30, Year 3, appears on page 838.

Charge and Discharge Statement for Trust A charge and discharge statement for the trustee of the Nancy Grimes Trust would resemble the charge and discharge statement for an estate illustrated on pages 832 to 834. The major difference would be an exhibit for the details of the $72,439 ($72,689 − $250 = $72,439) trust principal balance on June 30, Year 3.

Periodic Closing Entry for Trust A closing entry should be made for a trust at the end of each period for which a charge and discharge statement is prepared to clear the nominal accounts for the next reporting period. The closing entry for the Nancy Grimes Trust on June 30, Year 3, is as illustrated in the middle of page 838.

At the time specified in the trust document for transfer of the trust principal to the principal beneficiary, a journal entry would be made to

NANCY GRIMES TRUST
First National Bank, Trustee
General Journal

Year 3

May 3	Principal Cash	21,714	
	Income Cash	1,500	
	Certificate of Deposit	26,475	
	Marketable Securities	24,500	
	Trust Principal Balance		72,689
	Trust Income Balance		1,500

To record receipt of principal and income assets in trust from Paul Hasting, executor of estate of Jessica Davis.

May 6	Marketable Securities	19,900	
	Accrued Interest Receivable	180	
	Principal Cash		20,080

To record acquisition of following securities:

$15,000 face amount of 12% bonds of Warren Company, due Mar. 31, Year 23	$15,000	
Accrued interest	180	
$5,000 face amount of commercial paper of Modern Finance Company, due July 5, Year 3, acquired at 12% discount	4,900	
Total cash paid	$20,080	

June 30	Principal Cash	26,475	
	Income Cash	612	
	Certificate of Deposit		26,475
	Interest Revenue		612

To record proceeds of matured certificate of deposit and interest since Mar. 18, Year 3.

30	Administrative Expenses	250	
	Expenses Chargeable to Income	250	
	Principal Cash		250
	Income Cash		250

To record payment of trustee fee for period May 3–June 30, Year 3, chargeable equally to principal and to income.

| 30 | Marketable Securities | 25,000 | |
| | Principal Cash | | 25,000 |

To record acquisition of 14% U.S. Treasury notes due June 30, Year 8, at face amount.

| 30 | Distributions to Income Beneficiary | 1,862 | |
| | Income Cash | | 1,862 |

To record regular quarterly distribution to income beneficiary Nancy Grimes.

NANCY GRIMES TRUST
First National Bank, Trustee
Trial Balance
June 30, Year 3

	Debit	Credit
Principal		
Principal cash	$ 2,859	
Marketable securities	69,400	
Accrued interest receivable	180	
Trust principal balance		$72,689
Administrative expenses	250	
Totals	$72,689	$72,689
Income		
Trust income balance		$ 1,500
Interest revenue		612
Expenses chargeable to income	$ 250	
Distributions to income beneficiary	1,862	
Totals	$ 2,112	$ 2,112

Periodic closing entry for a trust

Trust Principal Balance	250	
Trust Income Balance	1,500	
Interest Revenue	612	
Administrative Expenses		250
Expenses Chargeable to Income		250
Distributions to Income Beneficiary		1,862
To close nominal accounts of trust.		

debit the Distributions to Principal Beneficiary account and credit the various trust principal asset accounts. A closing entry for the termination of the trust would then be required, in the form of the comparable estate journal entry illustrated on page 834.

REVIEW QUESTIONS

1 Is the Uniform Probate Code in effect throughout the United States?

2 Define the following terms:
 a *Estate*
 b *Intestacy*
 c *Testator*
 d *Executor*
 e *Administrator*
 f *Letters testamentary*

> *g* **Devise**
> *h* **Remainderman**
> *i* **Inter vivos trust**
> *j* **Settlor**

3 Compare *informal probate* with *formal probate* of a will.

4 Compare the standards of care required of a *personal representative* with the standards of care required of a *trustee.*

5 Why must there be a sharp distinction between *principal* and *income* in the administration of an estate?

6 Describe the *exempt property and allowances* provisions of the Uniform Probate Code.

7 What type of *devise* is each of the following? Explain.
  a The beach house at 1411 Ocean Avenue, Long Beach, California
  b $25,000 cash
  c $60,000 face amount of U.S. Treasury bonds
  d 1,000 shares of Rogers Corporation common stock represented by certificate No. G-1472
  e All my remaining property

8 Is the accrual basis of accounting ever used for an estate or a trust? Explain.

9 Explain the requirements for depreciation accounting contained in the Revised Uniform Principal and Income Act.

10 Describe the use of the Assets Discovered ledger account in accounting for an estate.

11 Compare a personal representative's *charge and discharge statement* with the financial statements issued by a business enterprise.

12 Discuss the similarities and differences in the journal entries for estates and for trusts.

EXERCISES

Ex. 18-1 Select the best answer for each of the following multiple-choice questions:

1 Assets in the inventory of property of a decedent must be valued at:
  a Carrying amount to the decedent
  b Current fair value
  c Historical cost to the decedent
  d Amounts established by the probate court

2 If estate assets that are not exempt are insufficient to cover creditors' claims as well as all devises, and the will is silent as to abatement, the Uniform Probate Code provides the following abatement sequence:
  a Property not specifically mentioned in will, residuary devises, general devises, specific devises
  b Residuary devises, specific devises, property not specifically mentioned in the will, general devises
  c General devises, residuary devises, property not specifically mentioned in the will, specific devises
  d None of the foregoing

3 First Bank and Trust Company is the trustee of the Collins Trust. A significant portion of the trust principal has been invested in high-rated bonds. Some of the bonds have been acquired at face amount, some at a discount, and others at a premium. Which of the following is a proper allocation of the various items to income?

    a The income beneficiary is entitled to the entire interest without dilution for the premium paid, but is not entitled to the proceeds attributable to the discount on collection

    b The income beneficiary is entitled to the entire interest without dilution and to the proceeds attributable to the discount

    c The income beneficiary is entitled to only the interest less the amount of the premium amortized over the term of the bond

    d The income beneficiary is entitled to the full interest and to an allocable share of the gain resulting from the discount

4 Carl Raymond's will named Norman Reid as the executor of Raymond's estate. In respect to Reid's serving as executor, which of the following is correct?

    a He serves without compensation unless the will provides otherwise

    b He may acquire the estate's assets the same as any other person dealing at arm's length

    c Raymond must have obtained Reid's consent in writing to serve as executor of the estate

    d On appointment by the probate court, Reid serves as the personal representative of the estate.

5 Martha Mather's will created a trust, and designated her husband as the income beneficiary and her children as the remaindermen. She is dead. Which of the following does not apply to the trust?

    a It is a testamentary trust

    b The husband has the right to appoint the ultimate beneficiaries

    c The children have a vested interest in the trust

    d The trustee owes a fiduciary duty to both the husband and the children

Ex. 18-2 Marjorie Singer is trustee of a testamentary trust established in the will of Carla Cohen. The trust principal consists of stocks, bonds, and a building subject to a mortgage note. The will provides that trust income is to be paid to the surviving husband, Luka Cohen, during his lifetime, that the trust will terminate upon his death, and that the principal then is to be distributed to the Soledad School for Girls. Indicate whether each of the following statements is true or false:

    a A cash dividend received on one of the trust securities may not be used without compensating Luka Cohen.

    b A 5% stock dividend on Z Co. stock should be distributed to Luka Cohen.

    c The cost of insurance on the office building should be deducted from the income paid to Luka Cohen.

    d Monthly principal payments to amortize the mortgage note are deducted from income.

    e Proceeds from fire insurance on the office building would be a part of the trust principal.

    f The cost of exercising stock warrants is chargeable to trust income.

    g The Soledad School for Girls is the residuary beneficiary of the trust established under Carla Cohen's will.

    h If Luka Cohen and the Soledad School for Girls agree to terminate the trust and divide the trust assets, the trustee would have to comply with their wishes.

Ex. 18-3 Indicate whether each of the following items would be charged to trust principal or to trust income of a testamentary trust, assuming that the Revised Uniform Principal and Income Act is to be followed:

a Depreciation of building.
b Legal fees for managing trust assets
c Special assessment tax levied on real property for street improvements
d Interest on mortgage note payable
e Loss on disposal of trust investments
f Major repairs to property prior to disposal of the property

Ex. 18-4 Indicate how each of the following cash payments should be allocated or classified in the charge and discharge statement for an estate:
a Executor's fees
b Estate and inheritance taxes
c Fire insurance premiums
d Special assessments that add permanent value to real property
e Monthly family allowances to beneficiaries
f Expenses of probating the will of a decedent
g Legal fees for defending claims against the estate
h Funeral and terminal-illness expenses

Ex. 18-5 Selected transactions completed by the executor of the estate of Charles Fellner, who died on October 15, Year 10, are listed below:

Oct. 20 Inventory of estate assets (at current fair value) was filed with the court as follows:

Cash	*$ 56,700*
Real property	*148,000*
Jenson Company common stock	*60,000*
9% bonds of Guam Corporation ($40,000 face amount)	*40,000*
Accrued interest on bonds of Guam Corporation	*600*
Personal and household effects	*23,500*

Oct. 29 A certificate for 150 shares of IBM Corporation common stock valued at $9,000 was found in the coat pocket of an old suit belonging to the decedent.
Nov. 10 A dividend of $520 was received on the Jenson Company common stock. The stock was willed as a specific devise to Rollo Fellner, son of Charles Fellner.
Nov. 15 Liabilities of Charles Fellner in the amount of $30,000 were paid.
Nov. 22 Administrative expenses of $3,240 were paid. All expenses are chargeable to principal.
Nov. 29 The bonds of Guam Corporation were sold at 98, plus accrued interest of $1,050.
Nov. 30 The Jenson Company common stock and the cash dividend of $520 received on November 10 were transferred to Rollo Fellner.

Prepare journal entries to record the transaction listed above in the accounting records of the executor for the estate of Charles Fellner.

Ex. 18-6 Helen Long, executor for the estate of Harvey Hill, who died on August 10, Year 2, prepared the following trial balance on February 10, Year 3:

	Debit	Credit
Principal cash	$ 26,000	
Income cash	490	
Estate principal balance		$117,000
Assets discovered		1,800
Gain on disposal of principal assets		1,200
Administrative expenses	3,000	
Liabilities paid	24,500	
Devises distributed	66,500	
Interest revenue		3,590
Distributions to income beneficiaries	2,000	
Expenses chargeable to income	1,100	
Totals	$123,590	$123,590

Prepare a charge and discharge statement for the period August 10, Year 2, through February 10, Year 3. Do not prepare supporting exhibits.

Ex. 18-7   Pursuant to the will of Gabriela Bonita, the balance of her estate after probate is to be transferred to a testamentary trust. The following trial balance was prepared from the ledger accounts of the estate on June 30, Year 5:

	Debit	Credit
Principal cash	$115,000	
Income cash	6,750	
Marketable securities	105,000	
Estate principal balance		$265,000
Assets discovered		13,000
Gain on disposal of principal assets		12,000
Administrative expenses	5,400	
Liabilities paid	16,000	
Devises distributed	48,600	
Interest revenue		4,000
Dividend revenue		4,500
Expenses chargeable to income	1,750	
Totals	$298,500	$298,500

a Prepare a journal entry to close the accounting records of the estate.
b Prepare a journal entry to open the accounting records of the trust.

Ex. 18-8   The inexperienced accountant for Lillian Crane, executor of the will of Marion Wilson, deceased, prepared the following journal entries, among others:

Apr. 25 Marketable Securities	10,400	
Estate Principal Balance		10,400

    To record supplemental inventory for property discovered subsequent to filing of original inventory.

Apr. 30 Distribution Expense	800	
Income Cash		800

    To record distribution of income cash to residuary devisee, as required by the will.

(Continued)

May 27 *Accounts Payable*	7,400	
Principal Cash		7,400

To record following liabilities paid:

Funeral expenses	$2,500
Hospital bills	3,800
Doctor's fees	1,100
Total	$7,400

Prepare journal entries for Lillian Crane, executor of the will of Marion Wilson, deceased, on May 31, to correct the foregoing journal entries. Do not reverse the foregoing entries.

CASES

Case 18-1   The estate of Paul Easley included the following items on the date of death, April 16, Year 2 (all assets are a part of the residuary devise):

(1) Sunrise Company 12% bonds due June 16, Year 12; face amount $100,000, current fair value on April 16, Year 2 (excluding accrued interest), $103,500; interest payable June 16 and December 16 of each year.
(2) Polanco Corporation common stock, 5,000 shares, dividend of $1 a share declared April 1, payable May 1 to stockholders of record April 14.
(3) Polanco Corporation 8%, $100 par, cumulative preferred stock, 1,000 shares. (Dividends are paid semiannually January 1 and July 1, and there are no dividends in arrears.)

Instructions
a The executor of the estate asks you for advice as to which items constitute income and which constitute principal of the estate.
b Suppose that dividends were in arrears on the Polanco Corporation 8%, $100 par, cumulative preferred stock; would your answer to **a** be any different? If so, explain in what way.

Case 18-2   James Imahiro transferred a manufacturing enterprise and 10,000 shares of MP Company common stock to Fidelity Trust Company to be held in trust for the benefit of his son, Robert, for life, with the remainder to go to Robert's son, Edward. Fidelity Trust Company insured the enterprise with Boston Insurance Company under two policies. One policy was a standard fire insurance policy covering the buildings and equipment. The other policy covered any loss of income during periods when the enterprise was inoperable as a result of fire or other catastrophe. The buildings and equipment subsequently were destroyed by fire, and Boston Insurance Company paid claims under both policies to Fidelity Trust Company.

Shortly after the 10,000 shares of MP Company common stock had been transferred to Fidelity Trust Company, MP Company declared a dividend of 10 shares of Monte Oil Corporation common stock for each 100 shares of MP Company common stock held. The Monte Oil common stock had been acquired as an investment by MP Company.

During the same year, MP Company directors split the common stock two-for-one. After the distribution of the new shares, Fidelity Trust Company sold 10,000 shares of MP Company common stock.

Instructions   How should Fidelity Trust Company handle the events that have been described above as to distribution between the income beneficiary and the remainderman? State reasons for making the distribution in the manner that you recommend.

Case 18-3   In analyzing the accounting records of Stanley Koyanagi, executor of the estate of Edward Dunn, who died January 16, Year 7, you review the will and other documents, which reveal that (1) Dunn's son had been specifically bequeathed the decedent's only rental property and 12% bonds of Padre Corporation, $50,000 face amount due March 1, Year 21; (2) Dunn's daughter was the beneficiary of a life insurance policy (face amount $100,000) on which the decedent had paid the premiums; and (3) Dunn's widow had been left the remainder of the estate in trust.

Your examination also reveals the following transactions occurring from the time of Dunn's death to March 1, Year 7:

(1) Jan. 20 $3,105 was received from the redemption of $3,000 face amount of Camm Corporation 13% bonds that matured on January 15, Year 7.

(2) Jan. 20 $500 was received from Pittson Corporation as a cash dividend of $1 a share on common stock, declared December 1, Year 6, payable January 15, Year 7, to stockholders of record January 2, Year 7.

(3) Jan. 20 $5,040 was paid to Witter & Company, brokers, for the acquisition of five Seaboard, Inc., 14% bonds due June 30, Year 18.

(4) Jan. 21   30 shares of common stock were received from Ragusa Company, constituting a 2% stock dividend declared December 14, Year 6, distributable January 20, Year 7, to stockholders of record January 15, Year 7.

(5) Feb. 1 $200 quarterly interest was paid by the executor on a promissory note payable due January 31, Year 8.

(6) Feb. 1   Dunn's physician was paid $2,500 for services rendered during Dunn's last illness.

(7) Feb. 2 $600 was collected from East Corporation as a cash dividend of $0.25 a share on common stock, declared January 18, Year 7, payable January 30, Year 7, to stockholders of record January 27, Year 7.

(8) Feb. 3 $575 rent revenue for February was received and deposited in the bank.

(9) Feb. 10 $890 was paid for property taxes covering the period from February 1 to July 31, Year 7.

(10) Mar. 1 $1,802 was paid to the Internal Revenue Service as the remaining income tax owed by the decedent for Year 6 taxable income.

Instructions   Indicate whether each transaction should be:
Allocated between principal and income
Allocated between principal and beneficiaries (devisees)
Attributed solely to income
Attributed soley to principal
Attributed soley to beneficiaries (devisees)
Give reasons supporting your conclusions as to how each transaction should be handled.

Case 18-4   Thompson Logan died on September 1, Year 1. Logan's will established a trust providing that the income, after costs of administration, be paid to his widow Begonia during her lifetime.

During the first year of the trust, the trustee received the following:
(1) Dividend revenue:

Cash dividends declared on Aug. 5, Year 1, payable to stockholders of record Aug. 30 .... $ 9,200

Cash dividends declared at various times from Sept. 2, Year 1, to July 31, Year 2 27,500

(Continued)

Stock dividend declared on Dec. 1, Year 1, and received Dec. 28, Year 2, a total of 75 shares of Anatolia Company common stock. The market value of the stock on date of declaration of the dividend was $40 a share.

(2) Interest revenue:

Semiannual interest on municipal bonds paid on Dec. 1, Year 1 . . .	$ 4,000
Semiannual interest on municipal bonds paid on June 1, Year 2 (bonds were acquired by trustee)	5,500
Semiannual interest on corporate bonds paid on Feb. 28 and Aug. 31, Year 2 (for the two periods)	21,200

(3) Marketable securities with an inventory valuation of $45,000 were sold for $49,280.

The trustee's expenses and fees paid in accordance with the provisions of the trust document totaled $4,444.

Instructions

a Prepare an income statement for the year ended August 31, Year 2, to show the amount to which Begonia Logan is entitled in accordance with the terms of the trust document.

b For those items not considered income, explain why they are excluded.

PROBLEMS

18-1 Lisa Popov died on June 5, Year 10. Mike Flinn was named executor of the estate in the will prepared by Popov's attorney. On December 31, Year 10, the accountant for the executor prepared the following trial balance:

MIKE FLINN, EXECUTOR
Of the Will of Lisa Popov, Deceased
Trial Balance
December 31, Year 10

	Debit	Credit
Principal cash	$ 40,000	
Income cash	3,000	
Investments in bonds	168,300	
Investments in common stocks	124,300	
Household effects	9,500	
Gains on disposal of principal assets		$ 2,200
Assets discovered		16,800
Liabilities paid	26,200	
Administrative expenses	9,000	
Devises distributed	10,000	
Estate principal balance		368,300
Dividend revenue		4,200
Interest revenue		8,500
Expenses chargeable to income	720	
Distributions to income beneficiaries	8,980	
Totals	$400,000	$400,000

Instructions The amount in the Estate Principal Balance account represents the inventory of estate assets on June 5, Year 10. Prepare a charge and discharge statement for the estate of Lisa Popov. Supporting exhibits are not required for any items except the listing of assets comprising the estate principal balance on December 31, Year 10.

18-2 Angel Moreno died on March 1, Year 8, leaving a valid will in which he named Andrew Kallman as executor and trustee of his assets pending final distribution to Peter Kell, a nephew. The will instructed the executor to transfer Moreno's personal effects and automobile to the nephew, to pay estate taxes, outstanding liabilities, and administrative expenses of the estate, and to transfer the remaining estate assets to a trust for the benefit of the nephew. Income from the estate and the trust is to be paid to the nephew, who will receive the principal (corpus) upon graduation from business school.

The inventory of estate assets on March 1, Year 8, consisted of the following:

Cash	$ 24,440
Certificate of deposit at Chicago Federal Savings and Loan Association;	
includes accrued interest of $1,100	101,100
Personal effects	13,200
Automobile	2,800
Investments in common stocks	77,000

The following transactions were completed by the executor through December 10, Year 8:

(1) Discovered a savings account of $6,290 in the name of Angel Moreno. (Debit Principal Cash.)
(2) Paid administrative expenses for the estate, $5,200. All expenses are chargeable to principal.
(3) Sold common stock with a carrying amount of $20,000 for $26,020, net of commissions.
(4) Transferred personal effects and automobile to Peter Kell.
(5) Received income as follows (there were no expenses chargeable to income): Interest, $5,200 (includes accrued interest on certificate of deposit on March 1, Year 8); dividends, $1,400.
(6) Distributed the income of the estate to Peter Kell.
(7) Paid liabilities of decedent, $8,050.
(8) Paid estate taxes, $32,000. (Debit the account Estate Taxes Paid.)
(9) Closed the accounting records of the estate and transferred assets to the Peter Kell Trust.

Instructions
a Prepare journal entries to record the transactions and to close the accounting records of the estate. Disregard homestead allowance, exempt property, and family allowance.
b Prepare a charge and discharge statement immediately after the transfer of estate assets to the Peter Kell Trust. Do not prepare any supporting exhibits.
c Prepare a journal entry to establish the accounting records for the testamentary trust, the Peter Kell Trust.

18-3 John Lee died in Year 1, and under the terms of the will the devisees were listed as follows:

(1) Alice Lee, widow of John Lee, was left a general devise of $100,000 payable immediately, and in addition a life interest in 50% of the residuary estate.
(2) Betty Lee, daughter, was left 25% of the residuary estate. One-half of this was left outright, and the other half was to remain in trust.

(3) Carol Lee, daughter, was left a life interest in 15% of the residuary estate.

(4) David Lee, son, was left a 10% interest in the residuary estate, to be paid outright.

John Lee's will specified that the executor had the power to defer sale of any estate assets and to hold such assets in trust until, in the opinion of the executor, conditions were favorable, and to make intermediate distributions of principal from the funds so realized to the beneficiaries. The income from the estate (or trust) was to be distributed annually in the proportion of the beneficiaries' interests.

On December 31, Year 3, the following advances on principal were made:

Betty Lee	*$400,000*
David Lee	*250,000*

The general devise to Alice Lee had not been paid as of December 31, Year 3.

The trustee rendered the first accounting to the probate court on December 31, Year 3, on which date all income, after payment of all expenses applicable to income, was paid to the beneficiaries.

The probate court's decree on the accounting of December 31, Year 3, specified that (1) in considering the distribution of future income, all intermediate payments of principal should be treated as advances to the beneficiaries; and (2) in order to make a fair and equitable division of income, interest at 15% a year was to be charged or credited to the beneficiaries subsequent to Year 3.

The income for Year 4 amounted to $715,500 after all expenses applicable to income had been paid. No other distributions of principal were made.

Instructions Prepare a journal entry to record the payments to income beneficiaries on December 31, Year 4. Support the journal entry with an exhibit showing how the amounts payable to the beneficiaries were determined. Disregard homestead allowance, exempt property, and family allowance.

18-4   Duke Hester died December 31, Year 1, and left all property in trust to his daughter, Sally. Income was to be paid to her as she needed it, and at her death the trust principal was to go to Hester's nephew, Neal Hester. Any income (including accrued interest) not paid to Sally by the time of her death would be paid to her estate. Duke Hester appointed Donald Chu trustee at a fee of $3,100 a year. All expenses of settling the estate were paid and accounted for by the executor before the trustee assumed responsibility for the trust.

Sally Hester died on October 1, Year 5, and left all her property in trust to her cousin, Lori Miller. Donald Chu, who also was appointed executor and trustee of Sally Hester's estate, agreed not to charge additional fees for these services. All income subsequent to October 1, Year 5, was to be paid to Lori Miller as soon as the income was received by the trustee. The estate of Sally Hester consisted solely of her unexpended income from the Duke Hester Trust. Principal cash of the Duke Hester Trust was invested immediately at 8% interest, payable quarterly.

From October 1, Year 5, to December 31, Year 6, Neal Hester received "advances" from the income of his uncle's trust. On December 31, Year 6, the remainder of the trust was turned over to Neal Hester.

The property received by Donald Chu under the will of Duke Hester on January 1, Year 2, consisted of the following:

(1) 20,000 shares of Armco Corporation common stock with a current market value of $25 a share.

(2) $150,000 bonds of Armco Corporation, paying interest on June 30 and December 31 at 9% a year. The bonds had a current market value equal to their face amount.

In the five years ended December 31, Year 6, the trustee received the following dividends on the Armco Corporation common stock: February 1, Year 2, Year 3, and Year 4, $25,000 a year; February 1, Year 5, and Year 6, $30,000 a year. The trustee made the following payments:

Trustee's fees and expenses: $3,100 a year

To beneficiaries:

Sally Hester, income beneficiary of the Duke Hester Trust, from Dec. 31, Year 1, to Oct. 1, Year 5:

Year 2	$18,625
Year 3	17,500
Year 4	19,375
Year 5	28,500

Neal Hester, principal beneficiary of the Duke Hester Trust, from Oct. 1, Year 5, to Dec. 31, Year 6:

Year 5	$ 8,500
Year 6	23,000

Lori Miller, beneficiary of the Sally Hester Trust, from Oct. 1, Year 5, to Dec. 31, Year 6:

Year 5 and Year 6, all trust income as determined on cash basis of accounting.

The trustee of the Duke Hester Trust kept the remaining cash in a checking account, where it earned no interest for the beneficiaries.

Instructions

a Prepare a statement for the Duke Hester Trust from December 31, Year 1, to October 1, Year 5, showing the undistributed income comprising the Sally Hester Trust. Assume that interest on the Armco Corporation bonds was accrued by the trustee from July 1 to October 1, Year 5. Disregard homestead allowance, exempt property, and family allowance.

b Compute the amount to be distributed to Neal Hester on December 31, Year 6.

c Compute the income received by Lori Miller from the Sally Hester Trust in Year 5 and in Year 6.

18-5 Sarah Manfred died in an accident on May 31, Year 1. The will provided that all liabilities and expenses were to be paid and that the property was to be distributed as follows:

(1) Personal residence to George Manfred, widower of Sarah Manfred.

(2) U.S. Treasury 12% bonds and Permian Company common stock—to be placed in trust. All income to go to George Manfred during his lifetime.

(3) Sonar Corporation 9% bonds—bequeathed to Eleanor Manfred, daughter of Sarah Manfred.

(4) Cash—a bequest of $15,000 to Matthew Manfred, son of Sarah Manfred.

(5) Residue of estate—to be divided equally between the two children of Sarah Manfred, Eleanor and Matthew.

The will further provided that during the administration period George Manfred was to be paid $500 a month from estate income. Estate and inheritance taxes were to be borne by the residue of the estate. Matthew Manfred was named as executor and trustee.

The following inventory of the decedent's property was prepared:

Personal residence	$195,000
Jewelry—diamond ring	14,600
Portland National Bank—checking account; balance May 31, Year 1 .	143,000
$100,000 U.S. Treasury 12% bonds, due Year 20, interest payable Mar. 1 and Sept. 1 (includes accrued interest of $3,000)	103,000

$10,000 Sonar Corporation 9% bonds, due Year 10, interest payable May 31 and Nov. 30	9,900
Permian Company common stock, 800 shares	64,000
Dividends receivable on Permian Company common stock	800
XY Company common stock, 700 shares	70,000

The executor opened an estate checking account and transferred the decedent's checking account balance to it. Other deposits in the estate checking account through July 1, Year 2, were as follows:

Interest received on $100,000 U.S. Treasury 12% bonds:	
Sept. 1, Year 1	$ 6,000
Mar. 1, Year 2	6,000
Dividends received on Permian Company common stock:	
June 15, Year 1, declared May 7, Year 1, payable to holders of record	
May 27, Year 1	800
Sept. 15, Year 1	800
Dec. 15, Year 1	1,200
Mar. 15, Year 2	1,500
June 15, Year 2	1,500
Net proceeds of June 19, Year 1, sale of 700 shares of XY Company common stock	68,810

Payments were made from the estate's checking account through July 1, Year 2, for the following:

Liabilities of decedent paid (including funeral expenses)	$12,000
Additional prior years' federal and state income taxes, plus interest, to May 31, Year 1	1,810
Year 1 income taxes of Sarah Manfred for the period Jan. 1, Year 1, through May 31, Year 1, in excess of amounts paid by the decedent on declarations of estimated tax	9,100
Federal and state fiduciary income taxes, fiscal years ending June 30, Year 1, and June 30, Year 2	2,400
Estate and inheritance taxes	73,000
Monthly payments to George Manfred, 13 payments of $500	6,500
Attorney's and accountant's fees (allocated entirely to principal)	25,000

The executor, Matthew Manfred, waived his fee. However, he desired to receive his mother's diamond ring in lieu of the $15,000 cash devise. All parties agreed to this in writing, and the court's approval was secured. All devises other than the assets to be held in trust and the residue of the estate were delivered on July 1, Year 1.

Instructions

a Prepare a charge and discharge statement as to principal and income, with supporting exhibits, to accompany the attorney's formal court accounting on behalf of the executor of the Estate of Sarah Manfred for the period from May 31, Year 1, through July 1, Year 2. In accordance with the will, the executor accrued the interest and dividends on the estate investments to July 1, Year 2. Disregard homestead allowance, exempt property, and family allowance.

b Prepare a summary showing the allocation of principal and income assets on July 1, Year 2, between the trust for the benefit of George Manfred and the residual estate to be divided between Eleanor Manfred and Matthew Manfred.

18-6   The will of Nikola Toma directed that the executor, Scott Hodgkins, liquidate the entire estate within two years of the date of death and pay the net proceeds and income to United Way. Nikola Toma, a bachelor, died on February 1, Year 10, after a brief illness.

An inventory of the decedent's property was prepared, and the current fair value of all items was determined. The preliminary inventory, before the computation of any appropriate income accruals on inventory items, follows:

	Current fair value
United California Bank checking account	$ 8,500
$60,000 face amount Sun City bonds, interest rate 12%, payable Jan. 1 and July, maturity date July 1, Year 14	59,000
2,000 shares Rex Corporation common stock	220,000
Term life insurance: beneficiary, Estate of Nikola Toma	20,000
Residence ($86,500) and furniture ($8,000)	94,500

During Year 10, the following transactions occurred:

(1) The interest on the Sun City bonds was collected. The bonds were sold on July 1, for $59,000, and the proceeds and interest accrued on February 1, Year 10 ($600), were paid to United Way.

(2) Rex Corporation paid cash dividends of $1 a share on March 1 and December 1, and distributed a 10% stock dividend on July 1. All dividends were declared 45 days before each payment date and were payable to holders of record as of 40 days before each payment date. In September, 1,000 shares of Rex Corporation common stock were sold at $105 a share, and the proceeds were paid to United Way.

(3) Because of a depressed real estate market, the personal residence was rented furnished at $300 a month commencing April 1, Year 10. The rent was paid monthly, in advance. Property taxes of $1,200 for the calendar Year 10 were paid. The house and furnishings had estimated economic lives of 40 years and 8 years, respectively. The part-time gardener was paid four months' wages totaling $500 on April 30 for services performed, and then was released.

(4) The United California Bank checking account was closed, and the balance of $8,500 was transferred to a bank checking account for the estate.

(5) The proceeds of the term life insurance were received on March 1 and deposited in the bank checking account for the estate.

(6) The following cash payments were made:
   (a) Funeral expenses and expenses of last illness, $3,500.
   (b) Balance due on Year 9 income taxes of decedent, $700.
   (c) Attorney's and accountant's fees, $15,000, of which $1,000 was allocated to income.

(7) On December 31, the balance of the undistributed income, except for $250, was paid to United Way. The balance of the cash on hand derived from the principal of the estate also was paid to United Way on December 31. On December 31, the executor resigned and waived all fees.

Instructions   Prepare a charge and discharge statement, together with supporting exhibits, for the executor of the Estate of Nikola Toma for the period February 1–December 31, Year 10. Disregard depreciation.

APPENDIX

COMPOUND INTEREST TABLES

Table 1   Future Amount of 1 at Compound Interest Due in n Periods: $a_{\overline{n}|i} = (1 + i)^n$

n \ i	$\frac{1}{2}$%	1%	$1\frac{1}{2}$%	2%	$2\frac{1}{2}$%	3%
1	1.005000	1.010000	1.015000	1.020000	1.025000	1.030000
2	1.010025	1.020100	1.030225	1.040400	1.050625	1.060900
3	1.015075	1.030301	1.045678	1.061208	1.076891	1.092727
4	1.020151	1.040604	1.061364	1.082432	1.103813	1.125509
5	1.025251	1.051010	1.077284	1.104081	1.131408	1.159274
6	1.030378	1.061520	1.093443	1.126162	1.159693	1.194052
7	1.035529	1.072135	1.109845	1.148686	1.188686	1.229874
8	1.040707	1.082857	1.126493	1.171659	1.218403	1.266770
9	1.045911	1.093685	1.143390	1.195093	1.248863	1.304773
10	1.051140	1.104622	1.160541	1.218994	1.280085	1.343916
11	1.056396	1.115668	1.177949	1.243374	1.312087	1.384234
12	1.061678	1.126825	1.195618	1.268242	1.344889	1.425761
13	1.066986	1.138093	1.213552	1.293607	1.378511	1.468534
14	1.072321	1.149474	1.231756	1.319479	1.412974	1.512590
15	1.077683	1.160969	1.250232	1.345868	1.448298	1.557967
16	1.083071	1.172579	1.268986	1.372786	1.484506	1.604706
17	1.088487	1.184304	1.288020	1.400241	1.521618	1.652848
18	1.093929	1.196147	1.307341	1.428246	1.559659	1.702433
19	1.099399	1.208109	1.326951	1.456811	1.598650	1.753506
20	1.104896	1.220190	1.346855	1.485947	1.638616	1.806111
21	1.110420	1.232392	1.367058	1.515666	1.679582	1.860295
22	1.115972	1.244716	1.387564	1.545980	1.721571	1.916103
23	1.121552	1.257163	1.408377	1.576899	1.764611	1.973587
24	1.127160	1.269735	1.429503	1.608437	1.808726	2.032794
25	1.132796	1.282432	1.450945	1.640606	1.853944	2.093778
26	1.138460	1.295256	1.472710	1.673418	1.900293	2.156591
27	1.144152	1.308209	1.494800	1.706886	1.947800	2.221289
28	1.149873	1.321291	1.517222	1.741024	1.996495	2.287928
29	1.155622	1.334504	1.539981	1.775845	2.046407	2.356566
30	1.161400	1.347849	1.563080	1.811362	2.097568	2.427262
31	1.167207	1.361327	1.586526	1.847589	2.150007	2.500080
32	1.173043	1.374941	1.610324	1.884541	2.203757	2.575083
33	1.178908	1.388690	1.634479	1.922231	2.258851	2.652335
34	1.184803	1.402577	1.658996	1.960676	2.315322	2.731905
35	1.190727	1.416603	1.683881	1.999890	2.373205	2.813862
36	1.196681	1.430769	1.709140	2.039887	2.432535	2.898278
37	1.202664	1.445076	1.734777	2.080685	2.493349	2.985227
38	1.208677	1.459527	1.760798	2.122299	2.555682	3.074783
39	1.214721	1.474123	1.787210	2.164745	2.619574	3.167027
40	1.220794	1.488864	1.814018	2.208040	2.685064	3.262038
41	1.226898	1.503752	1.841229	2.252200	2.752190	3.359899
42	1.233033	1.518790	1.868847	2.297244	2.820995	3.460696
43	1.239198	1.533978	1.896880	2.343189	2.891520	3.564517
44	1.245394	1.549318	1.925333	2.390053	2.963808	3.671452
45	1.251621	1.564811	1.954213	2.437854	3.037903	3.781596
46	1.257879	1.580459	1.983526	2.486611	3.113851	3.895044
47	1.264168	1.596263	2.013279	2.536344	3.191697	4.011895
48	1.270489	1.612226	2.043478	2.587070	3.271490	4.132252
49	1.276842	1.628348	2.074130	2.638812	3.353277	4.256219
50	1.283226	1.644632	2.105242	2.691588	3.437109	4.383906

Table 1 Future Amount of 1 (*continued*)

n \ i	3½%	4%	4½%	5%	5½%	6%
1	1.035000	1.040000	1.045000	1.050000	1.055000	1.060000
2	1.071225	1.081600	1.092025	1.102500	1.113025	1.123600
3	1.108718	1.124864	1.141166	1.157625	1.174241	1.191016
4	1.147523	1.169859	1.192519	1.215506	1.238825	1.262477
5	1.187686	1.216653	1.246182	1.276282	1.306960	1.338226
6	1.229255	1.265319	1.302260	1.340096	1.378843	1.418519
7	1.272279	1.315932	1.360862	1.407100	1.454679	1.503630
8	1.316809	1.368569	1.422101	1.477455	1.534687	1.593848
9	1.362897	1.423312	1.486095	1.551328	1.619094	1.689479
10	1.410599	1.480244	1.552969	1.628895	1.708144	1.790848
11	1.459970	1.539454	1.622853	1.710339	1.802092	1.898299
12	1.511069	1.601032	1.695881	1.795856	1.901207	2.012196
13	1.563956	1.665074	1.772196	1.885649	2.005774	2.132928
14	1.618695	1.731676	1.851945	1.979932	2.116091	2.260904
15	1.675349	1.800944	1.935282	2.078928	2.232476	2.396558
16	1.733986	1.872981	2.022370	2.182875	2.355263	2.540352
17	1.794676	1.947901	2.113377	2.292018	2.484802	2.692773
18	1.857489	2.025817	2.208479	2.406619	2.621466	2.854339
19	1.922501	2.106849	2.307860	2.526950	2.765647	3.025600
20	1.989789	2.191123	2.411714	2.653298	2.917757	3.207135
21	2.059431	2.278768	2.520241	2.785963	3.078234	3.399564
22	2.131512	2.369919	2.633652	2.925261	3.247537	3.603537
23	2.206114	2.464716	2.752166	3.071524	3.426152	3.819750
24	2.283328	2.563304	2.876014	3.225100	3.614590	4.048935
25	2.363245	2.665836	3.005434	3.386355	3.813392	4.291871
26	2.445959	2.772470	3.140679	3.555673	4.023129	4.549383
27	2.531567	2.883369	3.282010	3.733456	4.244401	4.822346
28	2.620172	2.998703	3.429700	3.920129	4.477843	5.111687
29	2.711878	3.118651	3.584036	4.116136	4.724124	5.418388
30	2.806794	3.243398	3.745318	4.321942	4.983951	5.743491
31	2.905031	3.373133	3.913857	4.538039	5.258069	6.088101
32	3.006708	3.508059	4.089981	4.764941	5.547262	6.453387
33	3.111942	3.648381	4.274300	5.003189	5.852362	6.840590
34	3.220860	3.794316	4.466362	5.253348	6.174242	7.251025
35	3.333590	3.946089	4.667348	5.516015	6.513825	7.686087
36	3.450266	4.103933	4.877378	5.791816	6.872085	8.147252
37	3.571025	4.268090	5.096860	6.081407	7.250050	8.636087
38	3.696011	4.438813	5.326219	6.385477	7.648803	9.154252
39	3.825372	4.616366	5.565899	6.704751	8.069487	9.703507
40	3.959260	4.801021	5.816365	7.039989	8.513309	10.285718
41	4.097834	4.993061	6.078101	7.391988	8.981541	10.902861
42	4.241258	5.192784	6.351615	7.761588	9.475526	11.557033
43	4.389702	5.400495	6.637438	8.149667	9.996679	12.250455
44	4.543342	5.616515	6.936123	8.557150	10.546497	12.985482
45	4.702359	5.841176	7.248248	8.985008	11.126554	13.764611
46	4.866941	6.074823	7.574420	9.434258	11.738515	14.590487
47	5.037284	6.317816	7.915268	9.905971	12.384133	15.465917
48	5.213589	6.570528	8.271456	10.401270	13.065260	16.393872
49	5.396065	6.833349	8.643671	10.921333	13.783849	17.377504
50	5.584927	7.106683	9.032636	11.467400	14.541961	18.420154

Table 1 Future Amount of 1 (*continued*)

n \ i	7%	8%	9%	10%	12%	15%
1	1.070000	1.080000	1.090000	1.100000	1.120000	1.150000
2	1.144900	1.166400	1.188100	1.210000	1.254400	1.322500
3	1.225043	1.259712	1.295029	1.331000	1.404928	1.520875
4	1.310796	1.360489	1.411582	1.464100	1.573519	1.749006
5	1.402552	1.469328	1.538624	1.610510	1.762342	2.011357
6	1.500730	1.586874	1.677100	1.771561	1.973823	2.313061
7	1.605781	1.713824	1.828039	1.948717	2.210681	2.660020
8	1.718186	1.850930	1.992563	2.143589	2.475963	3.059023
9	1.838459	1.999005	2.171893	2.357948	2.773079	3.517876
10	1.967151	2.158925	2.367364	2.593742	3.105848	4.045558
11	2.104852	2.331639	2.580426	2.853117	3.478550	4.652391
12	2.252192	2.518170	2.812665	3.138428	3.895976	5.350250
13	2.409845	2.719624	3.065805	3.452271	4.363493	6.152788
14	2.578534	2.937194	3.341727	3.797498	4.887112	7.075706
15	2.759032	3.172169	3.642482	4.177248	5.473566	8.137062
16	2.952164	3.425943	3.970306	4.594973	6.130394	9.357621
17	3.158815	3.700018	4.327633	5.054470	6.866041	10.761264
18	3.379932	3.996019	4.717120	5.559917	7.689966	12.375454
19	3.616528	4.315701	5.141661	6.115909	8.612762	14.231772
20	3.869684	4.660957	5.604411	6.727500	9.646293	16.366537
21	4.140562	5.033834	6.108808	7.400250	10.803848	18.821518
22	4.430402	5.436540	6.658600	8.140275	12.100310	21.644746
23	4.740530	5.871464	7.257874	8.954302	13.552347	24.891458
24	5.072367	6.341181	7.911083	9.849733	15.178629	28.625176
25	5.427433	6.848475	8.623081	10.834706	17.000064	32.918953
26	5.807353	7.396353	9.399158	11.918177	19.040072	37.856796
27	6.213868	7.988061	10.245082	13.109994	21.324881	43.535315
28	6.648838	8.627106	11.167140	14.420994	23.883866	50.065612
29	7.114257	9.317275	12.172182	15.863093	26.749930	57.575454
30	7.612255	10.062657	13.267678	17.449402	29.959922	66.211772
31	8.145113	10.867669	14.461770	19.194342	33.555113	76.143538
32	8.715271	11.737083	15.763329	21.113777	37.581726	87.565068
33	9.325340	12.676050	17.182028	23.225154	42.091533	100.699829
34	9.978114	13.690134	18.728411	25.547670	47.142517	115.804803
35	10.676581	14.785344	20.413968	28.102437	52.799620	133.175523
36	11.423942	15.968172	22.251225	30.912681	59.135574	153.151852
37	12.223618	17.245626	24.253835	34.003949	66.231843	176.124630
38	13.079271	18.625276	26.436680	37.404343	74.179664	202.543324
39	13.994820	20.115298	28.815982	41.144778	83.081224	232.924823
40	14.974458	21.724521	31.409420	45.259256	93.050970	267.863546
41	16.022670	23.462483	34.236268	49.785181	104.217087	308.043078
42	17.144257	25.339482	37.317532	54.763699	116.723137	354.249540
43	18.344355	27.366640	40.676110	60.240069	130.729914	407.386971
44	19.628460	29.555972	44.336960	66.264076	146.417503	468.495017
45	21.002452	31.920449	48.327286	72.890484	163.987604	538.769269
46	22.472623	34.474085	52.676742	80.179532	183.666116	619.584659
47	24.045707	37.232012	57.417649	88.197485	205.706050	712.522358
48	25.728907	40.210573	62.585237	97.017234	230.390776	819.400712
49	27.529930	43.427419	68.217908	106.718957	258.037669	942.310819
50	29.457025	46.901613	74.357520	117.390853	289.002190	1083.657442

Table 2 Present Value of 1 at Compound Interest Due in *n* Periods: $p_{\overline{n}|i} = \dfrac{1}{(1 + i)^n}$

n	½%	1%	1½%	2%	2½%	3%
1	0.995025	0.990099	0.985222	0.980392	0.975610	0.970874
2	0.990075	0.980296	0.970662	0.961169	0.951814	0.942596
3	0.985149	0.970590	0.956317	0.942322	0.928599	0.915142
4	0.980248	0.960980	0.942184	0.923845	0.905951	0.888487
5	0.975371	0.951466	0.928260	0.905731	0.883854	0.862609
6	0.970518	0.942045	0.914542	0.887971	0.862297	0.837484
7	0.965690	0.932718	0.901027	0.870560	0.841265	0.813092
8	0.960885	0.923483	0.887711	0.853490	0.820747	0.789409
9	0.956105	0.914340	0.874592	0.836755	0.800728	0.766417
10	0.951348	0.905287	0.861667	0.820348	0.781198	0.744094
11	0.946615	0.896324	0.848933	0.804263	0.762145	0.722421
12	0.941905	0.887449	0.836387	0.788493	0.743556	0.701380
13	0.937219	0.878663	0.824027	0.773033	0.725420	0.680951
14	0.932556	0.869963	0.811849	0.757875	0.707727	0.661118
15	0.927917	0.861349	0.799852	0.743015	0.690466	0.641862
16	0.923300	0.852821	0.788031	0.728446	0.673625	0.623167
17	0.918707	0.844377	0.776385	0.714163	0.657195	0.605016
18	0.914136	0.836017	0.764912	0.700159	0.641166	0.587395
19	0.909588	0.827740	0.753607	0.686431	0.625528	0.570286
20	0.905063	0.819544	0.742470	0.672971	0.610271	0.553676
21	0.900560	0.811430	0.731498	0.659776	0.595386	0.537549
22	0.896080	0.803396	0.720688	0.646839	0.580865	0.521893
23	0.891622	0.795442	0.710037	0.634156	0.566697	0.506692
24	0.887186	0.787566	0.699544	0.621721	0.552875	0.491934
25	0.882772	0.779768	0.689206	0.609531	0.539391	0.477606
26	0.878380	0.772048	0.679021	0.597579	0.526235	0.463695
27	0.874010	0.764404	0.668986	0.585862	0.513400	0.450189
28	0.869662	0.756836	0.659099	0.574375	0.500878	0.437077
29	0.865335	0.749342	0.649359	0.563112	0.488661	0.424346
30	0.861030	0.741923	0.639762	0.552071	0.476743	0.411987
31	0.856746	0.734577	0.630308	0.541246	0.465115	0.399987
32	0.852484	0.727304	0.620993	0.530633	0.453771	0.388337
33	0.848242	0.720103	0.611816	0.520229	0.442703	0.377026
34	0.844022	0.712973	0.602774	0.510028	0.431905	0.366045
35	0.839823	0.705914	0.593866	0.500028	0.421371	0.355383
36	0.835645	0.698925	0.585090	0.490223	0.411094	0.345032
37	0.831487	0.692005	0.576443	0.480611	0.401067	0.334983
38	0.827351	0.685153	0.567924	0.471187	0.391285	0.325226
39	0.823235	0.678370	0.559531	0.461948	0.381741	0.315754
40	0.819139	0.671653	0.551262	0.452890	0.372431	0.306557
41	0.815064	0.665003	0.543116	0.444010	0.363347	0.297628
42	0.811009	0.658419	0.535089	0.435304	0.354485	0.288959
43	0.806974	0.651900	0.527182	0.426769	0.345839	0.280543
44	0.802959	0.645445	0.519391	0.418401	0.337404	0.272372
45	0.798964	0.639055	0.511715	0.410197	0.329174	0.264439
46	0.794989	0.632728	0.504153	0.402154	0.321146	0.256737
47	0.791034	0.626463	0.496702	0.394268	0.313313	0.249259
48	0.787098	0.620260	0.489362	0.386538	0.305671	0.241999
49	0.783183	0.614119	0.482130	0.378958	0.298216	0.234950
50	0.779286	0.608039	0.475005	0.371528	0.290942	0.228107

Table 2   Present Value of 1 (*continued*)

n \ i	3½%	4%	4½%	5%	5½%	6%
1	0.966184	0.961538	0.956938	0.952381	0.947867	0.943396
2	0.933511	0.924556	0.915730	0.907029	0.898452	0.889996
3	0.901943	0.888996	0.876297	0.863838	0.851614	0.839619
4	0.871442	0.854804	0.838561	0.822702	0.807217	0.792094
5	0.841973	0.821927	0.802451	0.783526	0.765134	0.747258
6	0.813501	0.790315	0.767896	0.746215	0.725246	0.704961
7	0.785991	0.759918	0.734828	0.710681	0.687437	0.665057
8	0.759412	0.730690	0.703185	0.676839	0.651599	0.627412
9	0.733731	0.702587	0.672904	0.644609	0.617629	0.591898
10	0.708919	0.675564	0.643928	0.613913	0.585431	0.558395
11	0.684946	0.649581	0.616199	0.584679	0.554911	0.526788
12	0.661783	0.624597	0.589664	0.556837	0.525982	0.496969
13	0.639404	0.600574	0.564272	0.530321	0.498561	0.468839
14	0.617782	0.577475	0.539973	0.505068	0.472569	0.442301
15	0.596891	0.555265	0.516720	0.481017	0.447933	0.417265
16	0.576706	0.533908	0.494469	0.458112	0.424581	0.393646
17	0.557204	0.513373	0.473176	0.436297	0.402447	0.371364
18	0.538361	0.493628	0.452800	0.415521	0.381466	0.350344
19	0.520156	0.474642	0.433302	0.395734	0.361579	0.330513
20	0.502566	0.456387	0.414643	0.376889	0.342729	0.311805
21	0.485571	0.438834	0.396787	0.358942	0.324862	0.294155
22	0.469151	0.421955	0.379701	0.341850	0.307926	0.277505
23	0.453286	0.405726	0.363350	0.325571	0.291873	0.261797
24	0.437957	0.390121	0.347703	0.310068	0.276657	0.246979
25	0.423147	0.375117	0.332731	0.295303	0.262234	0.232999
26	0.408838	0.360689	0.318402	0.281241	0.248563	0.219810
27	0.395012	0.346817	0.304691	0.267848	0.235605	0.207368
28	0.381654	0.333477	0.291571	0.255094	0.223322	0.195630
29	0.368748	0.320651	0.279015	0.242946	0.211679	0.184557
30	0.356278	0.308319	0.267000	0.231377	0.200644	0.174110
31	0.344230	0.296460	0.255502	0.220359	0.190184	0.164255
32	0.332590	0.285058	0.244500	0.209866	0.180269	0.154957
33	0.321343	0.274094	0.233971	0.199873	0.170871	0.146186
34	0.310476	0.263552	0.223896	0.190355	0.161963	0.137912
35	0.299977	0.253415	0.214254	0.181290	0.153520	0.130105
36	0.289833	0.243669	0.205028	0.172657	0.145516	0.122741
37	0.280032	0.234297	0.196199	0.164436	0.137930	0.115793
38	0.270562	0.225285	0.187750	0.156605	0.130739	0.109239
39	0.261413	0.216621	0.179665	0.149148	0.123924	0.103056
40	0.252572	0.208289	0.171929	0.142046	0.117463	0.097222
41	0.244031	0.200278	0.164525	0.135282	0.111339	0.091719
42	0.235779	0.192575	0.157440	0.128840	0.105535	0.086527
43	0.227806	0.185168	0.150661	0.122704	0.100033	0.081630
44	0.220102	0.178046	0.144173	0.116861	0.094818	0.077009
45	0.212659	0.171198	0.137964	0.111297	0.089875	0.072650
46	0.205468	0.164614	0.132023	0.105997	0.085190	0.068538
47	0.198520	0.158283	0.126338	0.100949	0.080748	0.064658
48	0.191806	0.152195	0.120898	0.096142	0.076539	0.060998
49	0.185320	0.146341	0.115692	0.091564	0.072549	0.057546
50	0.179053	0.140713	0.110710	0.087204	0.068767	0.054288

Table 2   Present Value of 1 (*continued*)

n \ i	7%	8%	9%	10%	12%	15%
1	0.934580	0.925926	0.917431	0.909091	0.892857	0.869565
2	0.873439	0.857339	0.841680	0.826446	0.797194	0.756144
3	0.816298	0.793832	0.772183	0.751315	0.711780	0.657516
4	0.762895	0.735030	0.708425	0.683013	0.635518	0.571753
5	0.712986	0.680583	0.649931	0.620921	0.567427	0.497177
6	0.666342	0.630170	0.596267	0.564474	0.506631	0.432328
7	0.622750	0.583490	0.547034	0.513158	0.452349	0.375937
8	0.582009	0.540269	0.501866	0.466507	0.403883	0.326902
9	0.543934	0.500249	0.460428	0.424098	0.360610	0.284262
10	0.508349	0.463193	0.422411	0.385543	0.321973	0.247185
11	0.475093	0.428883	0.387533	0.350494	0.287476	0.214943
12	0.444012	0.397114	0.355535	0.318631	0.256675	0.186907
13	0.414964	0.367698	0.326179	0.289664	0.229174	0.162528
14	0.387817	0.340461	0.299246	0.263331	0.204620	0.141329
15	0.362446	0.315242	0.274538	0.239392	0.182696	0.122894
16	0.338735	0.291890	0.251870	0.217629	0.163122	0.106865
17	0.316574	0.270269	0.231073	0.197845	0.145644	0.092926
18	0.295864	0.250249	0.211994	0.179859	0.130040	0.080805
19	0.276508	0.231712	0.194490	0.163508	0.116107	0.070265
20	0.258419	0.214548	0.178431	0.148644	0.103667	0.061100
21	0.241513	0.198656	0.163698	0.135131	0.092560	0.053131
22	0.225713	0.183941	0.150182	0.122846	0.082643	0.046201
23	0.210947	0.170315	0.137781	0.111678	0.073788	0.040174
24	0.197147	0.157699	0.126405	0.101526	0.065882	0.034934
25	0.184249	0.146018	0.115968	0.092296	0.058823	0.030378
26	0.172195	0.135202	0.106393	0.083905	0.052521	0.026415
27	0.160930	0.125187	0.097608	0.076278	0.046894	0.022970
28	0.150402	0.115914	0.089548	0.069343	0.041869	0.019974
29	0.140563	0.107328	0.082155	0.063039	0.037383	0.017369
30	0.131367	0.099377	0.075371	0.057309	0.033378	0.015103
31	0.122773	0.092016	0.069148	0.052099	0.029802	0.013133
32	0.114741	0.085200	0.063438	0.047362	0.026609	0.011420
33	0.107235	0.078889	0.058200	0.043057	0.023758	0.009931
34	0.100219	0.073045	0.053395	0.039143	0.021212	0.008635
35	0.093663	0.067635	0.048986	0.035584	0.018940	0.007509
36	0.087535	0.062625	0.044941	0.032349	0.016910	0.006529
37	0.081809	0.057986	0.041231	0.029408	0.015098	0.005678
38	0.076457	0.053690	0.037826	0.026735	0.013481	0.004937
39	0.071455	0.049713	0.034703	0.024304	0.012036	0.004293
40	0.066780	0.046031	0.031838	0.022095	0.010747	0.003733
41	0.062412	0.042621	0.029209	0.020086	0.009595	0.003246
42	0.058329	0.039464	0.026797	0.018260	0.008567	0.002823
43	0.054513	0.036541	0.024584	0.016600	0.007649	0.002455
44	0.050946	0.033834	0.022555	0.015091	0.006830	0.002134
45	0.047613	0.031328	0.020692	0.013719	0.006098	0.001856
46	0.044499	0.029007	0.018984	0.012472	0.005445	0.001614
47	0.041587	0.026859	0.017416	0.011338	0.004861	0.001403
48	0.038867	0.024869	0.015978	0.010307	0.004340	0.001220
49	0.036324	0.023027	0.014659	0.009370	0.003875	0.001061
50	0.033948	0.021321	0.013449	0.008519	0.003460	0.000923

Table 3   Future Amount of Ordinary Annuity of 1 per Period: $A_{\overline{n}|i} = \dfrac{(1 + i)^n - 1}{i}$

n	½%	1%	1½%	2%	2½%	3%
1	1.000000	1.000000	1.000000	1.000000	1.000000	1.000000
2	2.005000	2.010000	2.015000	2.020000	2.025000	2.030000
3	3.015025	3.030100	3.045225	3.060400	3.075625	3.090900
4	4.030100	4.060401	4.090903	4.121608	4.152516	4.183627
5	5.050251	5.101005	5.152267	5.204040	5.256329	5.309136
6	6.075502	6.152015	6.229551	6.308121	6.387737	6.468410
7	7.105879	7.213535	7.322994	7.434283	7.547430	7.662462
8	8.141409	8.285671	8.432839	8.582969	8.736116	8.892336
9	9.182116	9.368527	9.559332	9.754628	9.954519	10.159106
10	10.228026	10.462213	10.702722	10.949721	11.203382	11.463879
11	11.279167	11.566835	11.863262	12.168715	12.483466	12.807796
12	12.335562	12.682503	13.041211	13.412090	13.795553	14.192030
13	13.397240	13.809328	14.236830	14.680332	15.140442	15.617790
14	14.464226	14.947421	15.450382	15.973938	16.518953	17.086324
15	15.536548	16.096896	16.682138	17.293417	17.931927	18.598914
16	16.614230	17.257864	17.932370	18.639285	19.380225	20.156881
17	17.697301	18.430443	19.201355	20.012071	20.864730	21.761588
18	18.785788	19.614748	20.489376	21.412312	22.386349	23.414435
19	19.879717	20.810895	21.796716	22.840559	23.946007	25.116868
20	20.979115	22.019004	23.123667	24.297370	25.544658	26.870374
21	22.084011	23.239194	24.470522	25.783317	27.183274	28.676486
22	23.194431	24.471586	25.837580	27.298984	28.862856	30.536780
23	24.310403	25.716302	27.225144	28.844963	30.584427	32.452884
24	25.431955	26.973465	28.633521	30.421862	32.349038	34.426470
25	26.559115	28.243200	30.063024	32.030300	34.157764	36.459264
26	27.691911	29.525632	31.513969	33.670906	36.011708	38.553042
27	28.830370	30.820888	32.986679	35.344324	37.912001	40.709634
28	29.974522	32.129097	34.481479	37.051210	39.859801	42.930923
29	31.124395	33.450388	35.998701	38.792235	41.856296	45.218850
30	32.280017	34.784892	37.538681	40.568079	43.902703	47.575416
31	33.441417	36.132740	39.101762	42.379441	46.000271	50.002678
32	34.608624	37.494068	40.688288	44.227030	48.150278	52.502759
33	35.781667	38.869009	42.298612	46.111570	50.354034	55.077841
34	36.960575	40.257699	43.933092	48.033802	52.612885	57.730177
35	38.145378	41.660276	45.592088	49.994478	54.928207	60.462082
36	39.336105	43.076878	47.275969	51.994367	57.301413	63.275944
37	40.532785	44.507647	48.985109	54.034255	59.733948	66.174223
38	41.735449	45.952724	50.719885	56.114940	62.227297	69.159449
39	42.944127	47.412251	52.480684	58.237238	64.782979	72.234233
40	44.158847	48.886373	54.267894	60.401983	67.402554	75.401260
41	45.379642	50.375237	56.081912	62.610023	70.087617	78.663298
42	46.606540	51.878989	57.923141	64.862223	72.839808	82.023196
43	47.839572	53.397779	59.791988	67.159468	75.660803	85.483892
44	49.078770	54.931757	61.688868	69.502657	78.552323	89.048409
45	50.324164	56.481075	63.614201	71.892710	81.516131	92.719861
46	51.575785	58.045885	65.568414	74.330564	84.554034	96.501457
47	52.833664	59.626344	67.551940	76.817176	87.667885	100.396501
48	54.097832	61.222608	69.565219	79.353519	90.859582	104.408396
49	55.368321	62.834834	71.608698	81.940590	94.131072	108.540648
50	56.645163	64.463182	73.682828	84.579401	97.484349	112.796867

Table 3 Future Amount of Ordinary Annuity of 1 (*continued*)

n \ i	3½%	4%	4½%	5%	5½%	6%
1	1.000000	1.000000	1.000000	1.000000	1.000000	1.000000
2	2.035000	2.040000	2.045000	2.050000	2.055000	2.060000
3	3.106225	3.121600	3.137025	3.152500	3.168025	3.183600
4	4.214943	4.246464	4.278191	4.310125	4.342266	4.374616
5	5.362466	5.416323	5.470710	5.525631	5.581091	5.637093
6	6.550152	6.632975	6.716892	6.801913	6.888051	6.975319
7	7.779408	7.898294	8.019152	8.142008	8.266894	8.393838
8	9.051687	9.214226	9.380014	9.549109	9.721573	9.897468
9	10.368496	10.582795	10.802114	11.026564	11.256260	11.491316
10	11.731393	12.006107	12.288209	12.577893	12.875354	13.180795
11	13.141992	13.486351	13.841179	14.206787	14.583498	14.971643
12	14.601962	15.025805	15.464032	15.917127	16.385591	16.869941
13	16.113030	16.626838	17.159913	17.712983	18.286798	18.882138
14	17.676986	18.291911	18.932109	19.598632	20.292572	21.015066
15	19.295681	20.023588	20.784054	21.578564	22.408664	23.275970
16	20.971030	21.824531	22.719337	23.657492	24.641140	25.672528
17	22.705016	23.697512	24.741707	25.840366	26.996403	28.212880
18	24.499691	25.645413	26.855084	28.132385	29.481205	30.905653
19	26.357181	27.671229	29.063562	30.539004	32.102671	33.759992
20	28.279682	29.778079	31.371423	33.065954	34.868318	36.785591
21	30.269471	31.969202	33.783137	35.719252	37.786076	39.992727
22	32.328902	34.247970	36.303378	38.505214	40.864310	43.392290
23	34.460414	36.617889	38.937030	41.430475	44.111847	46.995828
24	36.666528	39.082604	41.689196	44.501999	47.537998	50.815577
25	38.949857	41.645908	44.565210	47.727099	51.152588	54.864512
26	41.313102	44.311745	47.570645	51.113454	54.965981	59.156383
27	43.759060	47.084214	50.711324	54.669126	58.989109	63.705766
28	46.290627	49.967583	53.993333	58.402583	63.233510	68.528112
29	48.910799	52.966286	57.423033	62.322712	67.711354	73.629798
30	51.622677	56.084938	61.007070	66.438848	72.435478	79.058186
31	54.429471	59.328335	64.752388	70.760790	77.419429	84.801677
32	57.334502	62.701469	68.666245	75.298829	82.677498	90.889778
33	60.341210	66.209527	72.756226	80.063771	88.224760	97.343165
34	63.453152	69.857909	77.030256	85.066959	94.077122	104.183755
35	66.674013	73.652225	81.496618	90.320307	100.251364	111.434780
36	70.007603	77.598314	86.163966	95.836323	106.765189	119.120867
37	73.457869	81.702246	91.041344	101.628139	113.637274	127.268119
38	77.028895	85.970336	96.138205	107.709546	120.887324	135.904206
39	80.724906	90.409150	101.464424	114.095023	128.536127	145.058458
40	84.550278	95.025516	107.030323	120.799774	136.605614	154.761966
41	88.509537	99.826536	112.846688	127.839763	145.118923	165.047684
42	92.607371	104.819598	118.924789	135.231751	154.100464	175.950545
43	96.848629	110.012382	125.276404	142.993339	163.575989	187.507577
44	101.238331	115.412877	131.913842	151.143006	173.572669	199.758032
45	105.781673	121.029392	138.849965	159.700156	184.119165	212.743514
46	110.484031	126.870568	146.098214	168.685164	195.245719	226.508125
47	115.350973	132.945390	153.672633	178.119422	206.984234	241.098612
48	120.388257	139.263206	161.587902	188.025393	219.368367	256.564529
49	125.601846	145.833734	169.859357	198.426663	232.433627	272.958401
50	130.997910	152.667084	178.503028	209.347996	246.217476	290.335905

Table 3   Future Amount of Ordinary Annuity of 1 (*continued*)

n \ i	7%	8%	9%	10%	12%	15%
1	1.000000	1.000000	1.000000	1.000000	1.000000	1.000000
2	2.070000	2.080000	2.090000	2.100000	2.120000	2.150000
3	3.214900	3.246400	3.278100	3.310000	3.374400	3.472500
4	4.439943	4.506112	4.573129	4.641000	4.779328	4.993375
5	5.750740	5.866601	5.984711	6.105100	6.352847	6.742381
6	7.153291	7.335929	7.523335	7.715610	8.115189	8.753738
7	8.654021	8.922803	9.200435	9.487171	10.089012	11.066799
8	10.259803	10.636628	11.028474	11.435888	12.299693	13.726819
9	11.977989	12.487558	13.021036	13.579477	14.775656	16.785842
10	13.816448	14.486562	15.192930	15.937425	17.548735	20.303718
11	15.783599	16.645487	17.560293	18.531167	20.654583	24.349276
12	17.888451	18.977126	20.140720	21.384284	24.133133	29.001667
13	20.140643	21.495297	22.953385	24.522712	28.029109	34.351917
14	22.550488	24.214920	26.019189	27.974983	32.392602	40.504705
15	25.129022	27.152114	29.360916	31.772482	37.279715	47.580411
16	27.888054	30.324283	33.003399	35.949730	42.753280	55.717472
17	30.840217	33.750226	36.973705	40.544703	48.883674	65.075093
18	33.999033	37.450244	41.301338	45.599173	55.749715	75.836357
19	37.378965	41.446263	46.018458	51.159090	63.439681	88.211811
20	40.995492	45.761964	51.160120	57.274999	72.052442	102.443583
21	44.865177	50.422921	56.764530	64.002499	81.698736	118.810120
22	49.005739	55.456755	62.873338	71.402749	92.502584	137.631638
23	53.436141	60.893296	69.531939	79.543024	104.602894	159.276384
24	58.176671	66.764759	76.789813	88.497327	118.155241	184.167841
25	63.249038	73.105940	84.700896	98.347059	133.333870	212.793017
26	68.676470	79.954415	93.323977	109.181765	150.333934	245.711970
27	74.483823	87.350768	102.723135	121.099942	169.374007	283.568766
28	80.697691	95.338830	112.968217	134.209936	190.698887	327.104080
29	87.346529	103.965936	124.135356	148.630930	214.582754	377.169693
30	94.460786	113.283211	136.307539	164.494023	241.332684	434.745146
31	102.073041	123.345868	149.575217	181.943425	271.292606	500.956918
32	110.218154	134.213537	164.036987	201.137767	304.847719	577.100456
33	118.933425	145.950620	179.800315	222.251544	342.429446	644.665525
34	128.258765	158.626670	196.982344	245.476699	384.520979	765.365353
35	138.236878	172.316804	215.710755	271.024368	431.663496	881.170156
36	148.913460	187.102148	236.124723	299.126805	484.463116	1014.345680
37	160.337402	203.070320	258.375948	330.039486	543.598690	1167.497532
38	172.561020	220.315945	282.629783	364.043434	609.830533	1343.622161
39	185.640292	238.941221	309.066463	401.447778	684.010197	1546.165485
40	199.635112	259.056519	337.882445	442.592556	767.091420	1779.090308
41	214.609570	280.781040	369.291865	487.851811	860.142391	2046.953854
42	230.632240	304.243523	403.528133	537.636992	964.359478	2354.996933
43	247.776497	329.583005	440.845665	592.400692	1081.082615	2709.246473
44	266.120851	356.949646	481.521775	652.640761	1211.812529	3116.633443
45	285.749311	386.505617	525.858734	718.904837	1358.230032	3585.128460
46	306.751763	418.426067	574.186021	791.795321	1522.217636	4123.897729
47	329.224386	452.900152	626.862762	871.974853	1705.883752	4743.482388
48	353.270093	490.132164	684.280411	960.172338	1911.589803	5466.004746
49	378.999000	530.342737	746.865648	1057.189572	2141.980579	6275.405458
50	406.528929	573.770156	815.083556	1163.908529	2400.018249	7217.716277

Table 4 Present Value of Ordinary Annuity of 1 per Period: $P_{\overline{n}|i} = \dfrac{1 - \dfrac{1}{(1 + i)^n}}{i}$

n	½%	1%	1½%	2%	2½%	3%
1	0.995025	0.990099	0.985222	0.980392	0.975610	0.970874
2	1.985099	1.970395	1.955883	1.941561	1.927424	1.913470
3	2.970248	2.940985	2.912200	2.883883	2.856024	2.828611
4	3.950496	3.901966	3.854385	3.807729	3.761974	3.717098
5	4.925866	4.853431	4.782645	4.713460	4.645829	4.579707
6	5.896384	5.795476	5.697187	5.601431	5.508125	5.417191
7	6.862074	6.728195	6.598214	6.471991	6.349391	6.230283
8	7.822959	7.651678	7.485925	7.325481	7.170137	7.019692
9	8.779064	8.566018	8.360517	8.162237	7.970866	7.786109
10	9.730412	9.471305	9.222185	8.982585	8.752064	8.530203
11	10.677027	10.367628	10.071118	9.786848	9.514209	9.252624
12	11.618932	11.255077	10.907505	10.575341	10.257765	9.954004
13	12.556151	12.133740	11.731532	11.348374	10.983185	10.634955
14	13.488708	13.003703	12.543382	12.106249	11.690912	11.296073
15	14.416625	13.865053	13.343233	12.849264	12.381378	11.937935
16	15.339925	14.717874	14.131264	13.577709	13.055003	12.561102
17	16.258632	15.562251	14.907649	14.291872	13.712198	13.166118
18	17.172768	16.398269	15.672561	14.992031	14.353364	13.753513
19	18.082356	17.226009	16.426168	15.678462	14.978891	14.323799
20	18.987419	18.045553	17.168639	16.351433	15.589162	14.877475
21	19.887979	18.856983	17.900137	17.011209	16.184549	15.415024
22	20.784059	19.660379	18.620824	17.658048	16.765413	15.936917
23	21.675681	20.455821	19.330861	18.292204	17.332110	16.443608
24	22.562866	21.243387	20.030405	18.913926	17.884986	16.935542
25	23.445638	22.023156	20.719611	19.523456	18.424376	17.413148
26	24.324018	22.795204	21.398632	20.121036	18.950611	17.876842
27	25.198028	23.559608	22.067617	20.706898	19.464011	18.327031
28	26.067689	24.316443	22.726717	21.281272	19.964889	18.764108
29	26.933024	25.065785	23.376076	21.844385	20.453550	19.188455
30	27.794054	25.807708	24.015838	22.396456	20.930293	19.600441
31	28.650800	26.542285	24.646146	22.937702	21.395407	20.000428
32	29.503284	27.269589	25.267139	23.468335	21.849178	20.388766
33	30.351526	27.989693	25.878954	23.988564	22.291881	20.765792
34	31.195548	28.702666	26.481728	24.498592	22.723786	21.131837
35	32.035371	29.408580	27.075595	24.998619	23.145157	21.487220
36	32.871016	30.107505	27.660684	25.488842	23.556251	21.832253
37	33.702504	30.799510	28.237127	25.969453	23.957318	22.167235
38	34.529854	31.484663	28.805052	26.440641	24.348603	22.492462
39	35.353089	32.163033	29.364583	26.902589	24.730344	22.808215
40	36.172228	32.834686	29.915845	27.355479	25.102775	23.114772
41	36.987291	33.499689	30.458961	27.799489	25.466122	23.412400
42	37.798300	34.158108	30.994050	28.234794	25.820607	23.701359
43	38.605274	34.810008	31.521232	28.661562	26.166446	23.981902
44	39.408232	35.455454	32.040622	29.079963	26.503849	24.254274
45	40.207196	36.094508	32.552337	29.490160	26.833024	24.518713
46	41.002185	36.727236	33.056490	29.892314	27.154170	24.775449
47	41.793219	37.353699	33.553192	30.286582	27.467483	25.024708
48	42.580318	37.973959	34.042554	30.673120	27.773154	25.266707
49	43.363500	38.588079	34.524683	31.052078	28.071369	25.501657
50	44.142786	39.196118	34.999688	31.423606	28.362312	25.729764

Table 4   **Present Value of Ordinary Annuity of 1** (*continued*)

n \ i	3½%	4%	4½%	5%	5½%	6%
1	0.966184	0.961538	0.956938	0.952381	0.947867	0.943396
2	1.899694	1.886095	1.872668	1.859410	1.846320	1.833393
3	2.801637	2.775091	2.748964	2.723248	2.697933	2.673012
4	3.673079	3.629895	3.587526	3.545951	3.505150	3.465106
5	4.515052	4.451822	4.389977	4.329477	4.270284	4.212364
6	5.328553	5.242137	5.157872	5.075692	4.995530	4.917324
7	6.114544	6.002055	5.892701	5.786373	5.682967	5.582381
8	6.873956	6.732745	6.595886	6.463213	6.334566	6.209794
9	7.607687	7.435332	7.268791	7.107822	6.952195	6.801692
10	8.316605	8.110896	7.912718	7.721735	7.537626	7.360087
11	9.001551	8.760477	8.528917	8.306414	8.092536	7.886875
12	9.663334	9.385074	9.118581	8.863252	8.618518	8.383844
13	10.302738	9.985648	9.682852	9.393573	9.117079	8.852683
14	10.920520	10.563123	10.222825	9.898641	9.589648	9.294984
15	11.517411	11.118387	10.739546	10.379658	10.037581	9.712249
16	12.094117	11.652296	11.234015	10.837770	10.462162	10.105895
17	12.651321	12.165669	11.707191	11.274066	10.864609	10.477260
18	13.189682	12.659297	12.159992	11.689587	11.246074	10.827603
19	13.709837	13.133939	12.593294	12.085321	11.607654	11.158116
20	14.212403	13.590326	13.007936	12.462210	11.950382	11.469921
21	14.697974	14.029160	13.404724	12.821153	12.275244	11.764077
22	15.167125	14.451115	13.784425	13.163003	12.583170	12.041582
23	15.620410	14.856842	14.147775	13.488574	12.875042	12.303379
24	16.058368	15.246963	14.495478	13.798642	13.151699	12.550358
25	16.481515	15.622080	14.828209	14.093945	13.413933	12.783356
26	16.890352	15.982769	15.146611	14.375185	13.662495	13.003166
27	17.285365	16.329586	15.451303	14.643034	13.898100	13.210534
28	17.667019	16.663063	15.742874	14.898127	14.121422	13.406164
29	18.035767	16.983715	16.021889	15.141074	14.333101	13.590721
30	18.392045	17.292033	16.288889	15.372451	14.533745	13.764831
31	18.736276	17.588494	16.544391	15.592811	14.723929	13.929086
32	19.068865	17.873552	16.788891	15.802677	14.904198	14.084043
33	19.390208	18.147646	17.022862	16.002549	15.075069	14.230230
34	19.700684	18.411198	17.246758	16.192904	15.237033	14.368141
35	20.000661	18.664613	17.461012	16.374194	15.390552	14.498246
36	20.290494	18.908282	17.666041	16.546852	15.536068	14.620987
37	20.570525	19.142579	17.862240	16.711287	15.673999	14.736780
38	20.841087	19.367864	18.049990	16.867893	15.804738	14.846019
39	21.102500	19.584485	18.229656	17.017041	15.928662	14.949075
40	21.355072	19.792774	18.401584	17.159086	16.046125	15.046297
41	21.599104	19.993052	18.566109	17.294368	16.157464	15.138016
42	21.834883	20.185627	18.723550	17.423208	16.262999	15.224543
43	22.062689	20.370795	18.874210	17.545912	16.363032	15.306173
44	22.282791	20.548841	19.018383	17.662773	16.457851	15.383182
45	22.495450	20.720040	19.156347	17.774070	16.547726	15.455832
46	22.700918	20.884654	19.288371	17.880067	16.632915	15.524370
47	22.899438	21.042936	19.414709	17.981016	16.713664	15.589028
48	23.091244	21.195131	19.535607	18.077158	16.790203	15.650027
49	23.276565	21.341472	19.651298	18.168722	16.862751	15.707572
50	23.455618	21.482185	19.762008	18.255925	16.931518	15.761861

Table 4   Present Value of Ordinary Annuity of 1 (*continued*)

n \ i	7%	8%	9%	10%	12%	15%
1	0.934579	0.925926	0.917431	0.909091	0.892857	0.869565
2	1.808018	1.783265	1.759111	1.735537	1.690051	1.625709
3	2.624316	2.577097	2.531295	2.486852	2.401831	2.283225
4	3.387211	3.312127	3.239720	3.169865	3.037349	2.854978
5	4.100197	3.992710	3.889651	3.790787	3.604776	3.352155
6	4.766540	4.622880	4.485919	4.355261	4.111407	3.784483
7	5.389289	5.206370	5.032953	4.868419	4.563757	4.160420
8	5.971299	5.746639	5.534819	5.334926	4.967640	4.487322
9	6.515232	6.246888	5.995247	5.759024	5.328250	4.771584
10	7.023582	6.710081	6.417658	6.144567	5.650223	5.018769
11	7.498674	7.138964	6.805191	6.495061	5.937699	5.233712
12	7.942686	7.536078	7.160725	6.813692	6.194374	5.420619
13	8.357651	7.903776	7.486904	7.103356	6.423548	5.583147
14	8.745468	8.244237	7.786150	7.366687	6.628168	5.724476
15	9.107914	8.559479	8.060688	7.606080	6.810864	5.847370
16	9.446649	8.851369	8.312558	7.823709	6.973986	5.954235
17	9.763223	9.121638	8.543631	8.021553	7.119630	6.047161
18	10.059087	9.371887	8.755625	8.201412	7.249670	6.127966
19	10.335595	9.603599	8.950115	8.364920	7.365777	6.198231
20	10.594014	9.818147	9.128546	8.513564	7.469444	6.259331
21	10.835527	10.016803	9.292244	8.648694	7.562003	6.312462
22	11.061241	10.200744	9.442425	8.771540	7.644646	6.358663
23	11.272187	10.371059	9.580207	8.883218	7.718434	6.398837
24	11.469334	10.528758	9.706612	8.984744	7.784316	6.433771
25	11.653583	10.674776	9.822580	9.077040	7.843139	6.464149
26	11.825779	10.809978	9.928972	9.160945	7.895660	6.490564
27	11.986709	10.935165	10.026580	9.237223	7.942554	6.513534
28	12.137111	11.051078	10.116128	9.306567	7.984423	6.533508
29	12.277674	11.158406	10.198283	9.369606	8.021806	6.550877
30	12.409041	11.257783	10.273654	9.426914	8.055184	6.565980
31	12.531814	11.349799	10.342802	9.479013	8.084986	6.579113
32	12.646555	11.434999	10.406240	9.526376	8.111594	6.590533
33	12.753790	11.513888	10.464441	9.569432	8.135352	6.600463
34	12.854009	11.586934	10.517835	9.608575	8.156564	6.609099
35	12.947672	11.654568	10.566821	9.644159	8.175504	6.616607
36	13.035208	11.717193	10.611763	9.676508	8.192414	6.623137
37	13.117017	11.775179	10.652993	9.705917	8.207513	6.628815
38	13.193473	11.828869	10.690820	9.732651	8.220993	6.633752
39	13.264928	11.878582	10.725523	9.756956	8.233030	6.638045
40	13.331709	11.924613	10.757360	9.779051	8.243777	6.641778
41	13.394120	11.967235	10.786569	9.799137	8.253372	6.645025
42	13.452449	12.006699	10.813366	9.817397	8.261939	6.647848
43	13.506962	12.043240	10.837950	9.833998	8.269589	6.650302
44	13.557908	12.077074	10.860505	9.849089	8.276418	6.652437
45	13.605522	12.108402	10.881197	9.862808	8.282516	6.654293
46	13.650020	12.137409	10.900181	9.875280	8.287961	6.655907
47	13.691608	12.164267	10.917597	9.886618	8.292822	6.657310
48	13.730474	12.189136	10.933575	9.896926	8.297163	6.658531
49	13.766799	12.212163	10.948234	9.906296	8.301038	6.659592
50	13.800746	12.233485	10.961683	9.914814	8.304498	6.660515

INDEX

consolidated retained earnings, $448,404; minority interest in net assets, $43,568

9-9 Consolidated net income, $51,940; consolidated retained earnings, $535,540; minority interest in net assets, $24,920

10-1 Debit goodwill, $52,650

10-2 *b* Debit retained earnings of subsidiary— Prime, $235,000

10-3 *a* Credit intercompany investment income, $34,363; *b* Debit minority interest in net income, $637

10-5 *a* Credit intercompany investment income, $11,600; *b* Consolidated net income, $110,960; consolidated retained earnings, $215,160; minority interest in net assets, $232,240

10-6 *c* Consolidated net income, $144,525; consolidated retained earnings, $292,336; minority interest in net assets, $40,000

10-7 Consolidated net income, $2,848,450; consolidated retained earnings, $15,531,950; goodwill, $1,347,500

10-8 *a* Credit realized gain on sale of subsidiary, $16,000; *b* Consolidated net income, $862,200; consolidated retained earnings, $2,762,600; minority interest in net assets, $285,200

10-9 *a* $533,500; *b* Consolidated total assets, $7,775,000; *c* Total financial resources provided, $1,485,000

10-10 *b* Consolidated total assets, $7,444,670; minority interest in net assets, $411,570

11-4 *a* (1) Favorable fund balance variance, $1,000; (2) Total fund balance, $78,850

11-5 *c* Trial balance totals, $870,000

11-6 Property tax levy required, $3,361,000

12-7 *b* Trial balance totals, $34,200

13-1 *a* Unrestricted fund equity percentages: (1) 22.00%; (2) 18.33%

13-5 Unrestricted fund: Undesignated fund balance, $90,000; designated fund balance— depreciation, $438,000

13-6 Fund balances: Unrestricted current fund, $135,000; restricted current fund, $30,900

14-1 *a* Pre-tax income, $1,506,500; *b* Deferred income taxes, $391,950

14-2 *a* Credit realized gross profit, $76,740; *b* Debit uncollectible installment contracts expense, $1,000

14-3 *a* Gross profit in Year 4 tax return, $780,000; *b* Deferred tax liability, end of Year 3, $90,000; *c* Net income for Year 5, $192,500; *d* Debit income taxes expense, $180,000

14-4 *a* Credit deferred income tax liability, $67,500; *b* Debit income taxes expense, $45,000

14-5 *a* Ending inventory, $2,550

14-6 *a* Debit cost of consignment sales, $9,102

14-7 *a* Dec. 31, Year 3: Debit deferred gain on sale, $33,058; *b* Dec. 31, Year 4: Debit deferred income tax liability, $9,091

14-8 *a* (1) Cost of goods sold, Year 7, $304,880; (2) Weighted-average unit cost, Year 6, $91; *b* Gross profit percentage, Year 5, $33\frac{1}{3}$%; *c* Loss on repossessions, $1,360; *d* Taxable income, $62,940

14-10 *a* Deferred gross profit, Year 1, $16,800; *c* Net income, $32,000

15-1 *a* Operating loss for Segment Delta, $5,000

15-2 Net income, Year 2, $480,000

15-3 Effective income tax rate, first quarter, 45.1%; *b* July 31: Debit income taxes expense, $88,045

15-4 Net income, Year 8, $960,000

15-5 *a* (1) Jamestown pre-tax income, $7,572; (2) Irving pre-tax loss, $365

15-6 Net income, $216,000

15-7 *b* Principia operating profit, $118,000; *c* North America operating profit, $172,000

16-1 Transaction loss, $140

16-3 Transaction loss, $9,479

16-4 Accumulated depreciation, Nov. 30, Year 7, $16,010

16-7 Cumulative transaction adjustments, $75,940 cr

16-8 *b* Transaction gain, $20,113

16-9 *a* Cumulative translation adjustments, $4,420 cr; *c* Consolidated net income, $16,406; consolidated retained earnings, $41,406; minority interest in net assets, $1,218

17-1 *a* Estimated deficiency, $20,500

17-2 *b* Estate deficit, Jan. 31, Year 4, $9,380; *c* Trial balance totals, $31,850

17-3 *b* Estimated deficiency, $22,500

17-4 Estimated deficiency, $32,400

17-5 Total assets, $1,137,530

17-6 Yates, capital, $135,000; Zorb, capital, $135,000

18-1 Estate principal balance, Dec. 31, Year 10, $342,100

18-2 *c* Credit trust principal balance, $169,600

18-3 Cash to Carol, $119,700

18-4 *a* Undistributed trust income, $60,000; *b* Amount to Neal Hester, $661,500; *c* Income for Year 6, $4,800

18-5 *a* Estate principal balance, July 1, Year 2, $258,700; *b* Benefit of George Manfred, $168,000

18-6 Estate principal balance, Dec. 31, Year 10, $214,500